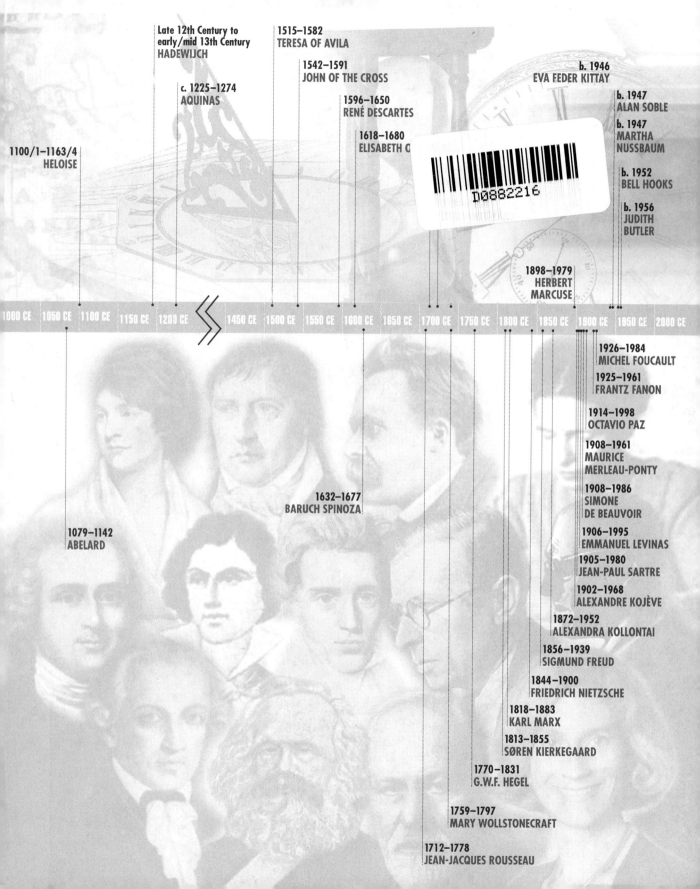

Late 12th Century to
early/mid 13th Century
HADEWIJCH

1515–1582
TERESA OF AVILA

1542–1591
JOHN OF THE CROSS

b. 1946
EVA FEDER KITTAY

c. 1225–1274
AQUINAS

1596–1650
RENÉ DESCARTES

b. 1947
ALAN SOBLE

b. 1947
MARTHA
NUSSBAUM

1618–1680
ELISABETH O

b. 1952
BELL HOOKS

1100/1–1163/4
HELOISE

b. 1956
JUDITH
BUTLER

1898–1979
HERBERT
MARCUSE

| 1000 CE | 1050 CE | 1100 CE | 1150 CE | 1200 CE | 1450 CE | 1500 CE | 1550 CE | 1600 CE | 1650 CE | 1700 CE | 1750 CE | 1800 CE | 1850 CE | 1900 CE | 1950 CE | 2000 CE |

1926–1984
MICHEL FOUCAULT

1925–1961
FRANTZ FANON

1914–1998
OCTAVIO PAZ

1908–1961
MAURICE
MERLEAU-PONTY

1632–1677
BARUCH SPINOZA

1908–1986
SIMONE
DE BEAUVOIR

1906–1995
EMMANUEL LEVINAS

1905–1980
JEAN-PAUL SARTRE

1079–1142
ABELARD

1902–1968
ALEXANDRE KOJÈVE

1872–1952
ALEXANDRA KOLLONTAI

1856–1939
SIGMUND FREUD

1844–1900
FRIEDRICH NIETZSCHE

1818–1883
KARL MARX

1813–1855
SØREN KIERKEGAARD

1770–1831
G.W.F. HEGEL

1759–1797
MARY WOLLSTONECRAFT

1712–1778
JEAN-JACQUES ROUSSEAU

A Passion for Wisdom

Readings in Western Philosophy on Love and Desire

EDITED BY

ELLEN K. FEDER

KARMEN MACKENDRICK

SYBOL S. COOK

PEARSON

Prentice
Hall

Upper Saddle River, New Jersey 07458

Library of Congress Cataloging-in-Publication Data

A passion for wisdom : readings in Western philosophy on love and desire
/ edited by Ellen K. Feder, Karmen MacKendrick, Sybol Cook.

    p.   cm.

Includes bibliographical references.

   ISBN 0-13-049455-0

  1. Love. 2. Desire (Philosophy) I. Feder, Ellen K. II. MacKendrick,
Karmen III. Cook, Sybol.

BD436.P38 2004
128'.46--dc22

2003026355

Editorial Director: Charlyce Jones-Owen
Senior Acquisitions Editor: Ross Miller
Editorial Assistant: Carla Worner
Assistant Editor: Wendy Yurash
Director of Marketing: Beth Mejia
Managing Editor: Joanne Riker
Production Liaison: Fran Russello
Manufacturing Buyer: Christina Helder
Cover Design: Bruce Kenselaar
Cover Illustration/Photo: Michael Wyetzner
Time Line Creation: Laura Gardner
Composition/Full-Service Project Management: Patty Donovan/Pine Tree Composition
Printer/Binder: Hamilton Printing Company
Cover Printer: Phoenix Color Corp.

Pearson Education, Ltd., London
Pearson Education Singapore, Pte. Ltd.
Pearson Education Canada, Ltd.
Pearson Education—Japan
Pearson Education Australia PTY, Limited
Pearson Education North Asia Ltd.

Pearson Educación de Mexico,
  S.A. de C.V.
Pearson Education Malaysia, Pte. Ltd.
Pearson Education, Upper Saddle River,
  New Jersey

10 9 8 7 6 5 4 3 2 1

ISBN 0-13-049455-0

Contents

VI Contemporary Philosophy

Preface

The introduction to philosophy is always a bit difficult. Not only is philosophy a subject that seems not to *have* an introductory level—faculty, graduate students, and first-year students alike read Plato's dialogues—but it is also a subject that tends to elude definition. We may know philosophy when we see it, but saying what constitutes philosophy is exceptionally difficult. And so, generally, philosophers resort to etymology, and explain the root of philosophy in the Greek *philo-sophia*, literally, the love of wisdom.

In the debates that then ensue about the nature and meaning of wisdom, however, the first half of this term often drops out of consideration, with wisdom alone coming under philosophical consideration. We have endeavored here to take wisdom seriously, but more, to take love seriously. Trusting that love, and, accordingly, questions of passion and of desire are central to philosophical inquiry, we have gathered a collection of readings bringing wisdom to bear on love itself. Philosophy about love covers the range of philosophical subdisciplines such as metaphysics (questions about what is ultimately real), epistemology (questions about the nature of knowing), and value theory (questions about what has value, such as moral value in ethics and artistic value in aesthetics). It also covers the broad historical range of Western philosophy from the pre-Socratics to the present day. We have tried as well to present readings in a range of philosophical styles, to provide some sense of the number of ways one might undertake philosophical inquiry.

This reader is structured as a series of short texts or substantial excerpts from longer texts. An introduction to each philosopher gives biographical information and situates the work in a historical and intellectual context. Study or discussion questions are designed to help you focus your reading or to suggest ways to pursue further the lines of inquiry that the reading opens. An important aspect of this collection of readings is the historical *connection* among ideas, the philosophical conversation as it unfolds over millennia of consideration of the same topics. A well-known French text from 1963 calls philosophy "The Infinite Conversation,"[1] and this is the sense that unfolds here.

The conversation begins with the poetry of Sappho, from the sixth century B.C.E. For Sappho, love, whether erotic or parental, is a path to truth—truth about persons, but also about the world as a whole, and it is inaccessible to more conventional ways of knowing. For the pre-Socratic philosopher Empedocles, love is as much cosmological as human—that is, it is a creative force forming the entire universe. However, for him issues of love and desire are approached chiefly as questions of ethics, with attention to their role in a good and well-balanced life. This emphasis recurs in the better-known readings from Plato and Aristotle. Plato considers several possible understandings of love. But the final consideration, attributed to his own teacher Socrates, has love as the path to the best possible life, drawing parallels between ordinary human love and a higher, abstract love of the Good itself. Plato's pupil Aristotle is more worldly and practical in his consideration of the ethics of *friendship*, central to human virtue and the possibility of human happiness. We cannot live rightly, he argues, if we love no one.

The later selections in ancient philosophy take up Epicurean and Stoic philosophy. The selection from Epicurus suggests a somewhat different approach to desire, one less focused on relations between persons and more on our desires understood as appetites. Still, he places the understanding of desire, and proper conduct in relation to it, at the heart of a life well lived. The last of the readings in ancient philosophy comes from Marcus Aurelius's *Meditations,* which recommends a Stoic approach, giving in neither to pleasure nor to pain. Aurelius, a Roman emperor writing some five centuries after Empedocles, nonetheless has the same issue—What is the role of love and desire in a life well lived?—at the heart of his philosophy, where he mentions Socrates by name as an important influence.

In ancient philosophy, then, the chief concern regarding love and desire is how wisdom might properly regulate them, so that they play the right role in the best possible life, a fundamentally ethical concern. When we move into medieval Western philosophy, love and desire (like other philosophical issues) are thought chiefly in a religious or theological context. In most of the philosophical work from this era, the understanding is that human desire is—or at any rate should be—ultimately for God; divine desire is, like the desire driving the cosmos for Empedocles, ultimately creative. Desire is still essential to living well, but for the medievals living well is seldom to be understood in secular terms.

The date dividing ancient from medieval philosophy is quite fuzzy. Although he is very early to be included among the medievals, Plotinus, in his extremely influential neo-Platonism, sets the tone for centuries of mysticism. Neo-Platonism takes up elements of both Platonic thought (especially the idea of the highest form, which emerges in Diotima's speech in the *Symposium*) with Aristotle's emphasis on flourishing and the fullness of life—an emphasis taken up by later ancient thinkers as well. There may also be an Eastern influence here. While there is no strong evidence that Plotinus visited Asia, the contemplation he recommends involves a withdrawal from external distraction much like that recommended in both Hindu and Buddhist meditative traditions. The path to happiness recommended by Plotinus is a meditative direction of desire toward what he calls The One—an idea derived from the Platonic form of the Good. Such ideas will be taken up in the Christian tradition most importantly by Augustine, whose *Confessions* vividly expresses the tension between carnal and religious desires. Augustine believes fervently that desire should be directed to God, but he finds himself constantly distracted by less lofty urges, drawn back into the world by them.

Plato is not the only ancient influence here. Thomas Aquinas later takes up Aristotelian logic in the service of that same tradition, seeking to show that Aristotle's careful rationality is fully compatible with Christian faith in the understanding of the love between human beings and either one another or their god. Aquinas's concerns are metaphysical but also, like Aristotle's, ethical—what is love, and how should it be directed?

Medieval philosophy sees important contributions by women as well, in both mysticism and theoretical and even practical philosophy. The latter is epitomized near the end of the selection of Medieval readings by St. Teresa of Avila's directions to young nuns in *The Way of Perfection*. Here, Teresa pragmatically suggests that young nuns take care that their friendships not become petty or competitive and that their highest love be directed toward God. Hadewijch writes poetically of the love between humans and God, her style in many ways typical of that of educated religious women of the time. Her metaphors, like those of many later mystics (women and men alike), make little distinction between human and divine love, using the former as an accessible image for the latter. In a way, this echoes Plato's strategy at the end of the *Symposium,* where we begin in human love and make our way to higher states.

While the chief line of thought on desire in this era runs between human and divine and emphasizes the joys of religious practice, the letters of Heloise and Abelard offer us a glimpse of the complexities of love and desire between humans, at the same time reminding us of the restrictive elements of Christianity, its frequent denial of the passions when they get too close to the flesh. This section ends at the Counterreformation—the Catholic response to the movements of the Protestant Reformation—with the advice of Teresa to the nuns of her order (Teresa was responsible for politically important reforms among the Carmelites), and, finally, with the overtly erotic religious poetry of her student, St. John of the Cross. John's poetry shows the influence not only of his teacher but also of the line of secular love imagery we noted earlier in Hadewijch.

Philosophy begins to move away from theological concerns (and from the condemnation of sin) with modernism, the onset of which is usually dated to the sixteenth-century work of René Descartes. (In fact, "modern" in philosophy refers to the period from the sixteenth to nineteenth centuries, which can be confusing when the term is so often used to denote what is currently present.) Largely abandoning faith in favor of reason, modern philosophy turns to questions of knowing and the nature of the human mind, as well as of right conduct. The prevailing arguments are between logical rationalism (represented here by Descartes) and experimental empiricism (represented here by David Hume, who is also importantly influential on Kantian philosophy later on). One might expect such thought, with its resolute rationality or focus on the senses, to be less concerned with the apparently irrational passions. But it is exactly in this context that passion and desire become *themselves* topics of investigation, rather than psychical or spiritual movements that may be taken for granted. That is, philosophers no longer assume *that* we are passionate, desirous, or loving and then try to figure out *how* we might best be those things; rather, they question what it means to love or to desire in the first place, and what place these acts have in the workings of the human mind.

Although much less well known than Descartes, Elisabeth of Bohemia was an important force in the formation of Cartesian thought; it is in discussion with her that Descartes forms the ideas in his theory of the passions of the soul—roughly equivalent, for him, to our concept of mind, but with the added element of immortality. David Hume, who takes the converse view that there is no *thing* we can call mind but only a set of mental acts, focuses in the reading here on ethical questions. Specifically, he looks at the "value" of chastity and modesty, and he comes to some surprising and deeply practical, very human, conclusions. While usually classified, like Descartes, as a rationalist, Baruch Spinoza is an unusual case. What reason demonstrates for him is almost neo-Platonic; in his *Ethics,* he provides us with an image of an ideal life in a world in which, in fact, everything is part of God. Returning to ancient concerns, with the added theological twist dating from medieval philosophy and the rationalism of modernity, Spinoza provides a unique understanding of the good life.

Later modern philosophy takes an even more rational turn. The movement called the Enlightenment, which will give philosophical weight to the French Revolution, emphasizes the harmony not between reason and faith but between reason and nature. Enlightenment philosophers, wary of the negative and repressive potential of culture, often emphasize the education of the young. In this reader the Enlightenment is represented in both its sunny and dark sides, by Jean-Jacques Rousseau and the Marquis de Sade, respectively. Each gives us a philosophy of the proper upbringing necessary to the creation of the good citizen—in each case desire has both an educational and a sociopolitical function, though they're conceived very differently by each thinker. Rousseau's student Emile is ideally educated to be the landowning married man who is a good citizen in what is roughly a representative democracy, while Sade's Eugenie is educated to seize every possible pleasure in working toward an ideal society of hedonistic libertarianism.

Mary Wollstonecraft's work takes a somewhat different turn. While the philosophers of the French Revolution declared the "rights of man," Wollstonecraft reminds us of the—often unobserved—rights of women. Responding to the deep sexism of Rousseau's ideals for both politics and education, Wollstonecraft emphasizes reason and virtue in their interconnectedness for women and men alike. This emphasis on the universality of reason will be most fully realized in Immanuel Kant's ethics. Likewise emphasizing the importance of reason for virtue, Kant is usually regarded as the important transitional figure between modern and nineteenth-century philosophy. Reason, central to the very possibility of ethics (a being that cannot reason, such as a plant or a rock, can be neither ethical nor unethical), is for Kant the very opposite of desire, which renders the will irrational. Kant's understanding of desire is almost Stoic in its strictness—our everyday appetites and desires for happiness ought always to be subordinated to ethical concerns, with reason reigning supreme in human existence.

It is in the modern era that philosophy begins to sort itself into the categories now familiar to us, with Descartes, Elisabeth, and Hume representing metaphysics and epistemology; Rousseau, Sade, and Wollstonecraft giving us political philosophy; and Spinoza and Kant working in ethics. But even here we see clear continuations of earlier concerns—especially of what, if anything, the proper regulation of desire might be.

Interest in questions of desire intensifies again in the philosophy of the nineteenth and early twentieth centuries. Here, as in modern philosophy, desire is understood across philosophical subdisciplines, with an increasing emphasis on the questions of human nature that Descartes and Hume began to explore. Georg Wilhelm Friedrich Hegel's influential work suggests that desire is formative in human consciousness—we need other people in order to be, or become, ourselves. Our interaction with those others is begun by desire, a point that will be emphasized in the twentieth century by Hegel's interpreter Alexandre Kojève. Hegel recognizes the fact that our initial desires are not entirely reciprocal; we want to get more than we give. Like Kant he emphasizes our desire to be recognized as fully free, self-governing human beings—unlike Kant, however, he sees that very recognition as depending upon desire. Karl Marx famously gives Hegel's philosophy a now-familiar economic spin, taking into account desires beyond, though including, those between persons. Marx points out the economic element of recognition: just compensation for labor.

In another line of nineteenth-century thought, Søren Kierkegaard insists upon the value of religious subjectivity—and vigorously opposes Hegel's sense of historical certainty, the idea that history invariably leads us toward a particular result. He also resists the abstract character of Hegelian dialectic, though not the dialectical movement itself, which clearly influences his own thought. For Kierkegaard, the emphasis is not on the logically determined conclusion but on the unsettled quality of thought always in motion. He also enables us to see love in quite divergent senses—not all of them, for this complicated thinker are straightforwardly religious or ethical; some are aesthetic as well.

Friedrich Nietzsche's philosophy puts desire at the heart not only of the scholar's undertaking but of human life itself. Nietzsche's famous "will to power" is in fact a force of desire, a relation that may move between humans and objects outside them, between human subjects, or indeed within a single person. Much of this desire is unconscious, and in fact Nietzsche's sense of strong unconscious mental forces is an important precedent to Sigmund Freud's analysis of the structure of the human mind.

Occurring at the onset of the twentieth century but clearly rooted in the nineteenth-century thought of Nietzsche, Freud's famous understanding of the libido is less overtly, but just as deeply, economic as is Marx's sense of desire. Freud is concerned with the investment and expenditure of the energy of the libido—the drive both to live and to reproduce, responsible for love of both self and others. The clinical twist he gives this idea also hints at an ethical foundation: What is the best or healthiest way to invest the force of this erotic drive? Freud follows and joins Nietzsche in theorizing the economy of desire, though Nietzsche's is a still more dynamic, fluctuating exchange. Together with Hegel, these theorists become increasingly influential in the twentieth century, setting the stage for theories of human existence beyond subjectivity.

Aware of Freudian psychoanalysis, Alexandra Kollontai reminds us not to lose the central life forces of love and desire to the political—even when the latter is central in our lives, as in times of revolution. Her work is in conversation with Marx as well as with Freud, as she picks up on his ideals for a working people's revolution. Later, of course, the erotic itself, and particularly the sexual, will become highly politicized territory, especially as later twentieth-century thinkers alter our understanding not just of eros but of politics as well.

Philosophy in the twentieth century sees a multiplication of philosophical methods through which desire is increasingly understood as an issue at once ethical and political. In twentieth-century and contemporary philosophy, love and desire have been more central issues in Continental philosophy, the school of thought influenced mainly by European philosophers, than in Analytic philosophy, chiefly influenced by Anglo-American theorists—though both traditions are represented here. In one of the century's most influential discussions of desire, Alexandre Kojève reinterprets Hegel to see desire as perhaps *the* central focus in Hegel's philosophy of human experience. Kojève's reading is particularly influential, in turn, on twentieth-century phenomenologists such as Maurice Merleau-Ponty. Twentieth-century and (contemporary) phenomenology is a philosophy focused on understanding the varieties of human experience, especially on questions about the relation between the experienced object and the experiencing subject. Merleau-Ponty concerns himself with the ways in which desire and pleasure structure our experiences, not only of other human subjects, but even of our worlds on a much larger scale—potentially, our relation to the entire world is tinged by desire. Emphasizing *touch* as well as sight (on which philosophers have more commonly focused), Merleau-Ponty notes that every surface we touch touches back. Touch suggests a very different sense of what he calls the "flesh of the world" than does sight. Sight is more easily analyzed as a relation between a capable, active subject and a wholly passive object, Touch, however, is always dual and reciprocal.

Jean-Paul Sartre shows the joint influence of both Freud and Hegel in considering the vagaries of "love" relationships, though he rejects Freud's notion that some part of the human mind is unconscious in the sense of being wholly inaccessible to direct awareness. His analysis of the "look" is explicitly visual, and in it the duality of subject and object, and the much more powerful position of subjectivity, are emphasized.

The concerns with desire's objects, along with its aims and variations, is Hegel's influence as well as Freud's, and the impact of psychoanalysis is evident throughout later philosophy. For Hegel, we recall, desire emerges in the play between difference and recognition—our desire to be recognized in our full humanity and our willingness or unwillingness to extend that recognition to those different from ourselves. This play comes to the fore in the selections from Simone de Beauvoir and Frantz Fanon, where considerations of difference, especially of race and gender, are fundamentally and explicitly important. Beauvoir famously asks what makes a person a woman, and what being a female means in a world where women are more commonly understood, even by themselves, as the *objects* of desire. Fanon likewise scrutinizes questions of who the subject and object of desire not only are, but are popularly understood to be—and the effects of this understanding on those perceived. Race as well as gender is a category not only of identity but of desire, and indeed these two elements may be inseparable.

Like Kollontai, Herbert Marcuse weds Freud's analysis of desire to Marxist political concerns though his concern with the negative effects of an emphasis on productivity made him critical of Marxism as practiced as well as of capitalism. Marcuse suggests that the repression of desire is historically specific rather than universally necessary, seeing desire—libidinal energy—not merely as a productive force but importantly in terms of creativity and pleasure.

Working in a context specifically influenced both by ancient traditions in Judaic philosophy and the specifically twentieth-century concerns raised by the Holocaust, Emmanuel Levinas, like Nietzsche, sees ethical philosophy as foundational to *all* philosophical concerns. For Levinas, ethics is fundamentally a relation to one different from myself, but he argues against Hegel's notion that we can fully understand another as like ourselves. Difference, according to Levinas, is infinite and inexhaustible, and in this we find not only the necessity of ethics but also the possibility of desire.

Finally, Michel Foucault takes up Nietzsche's understanding of power and desire, and his complex understanding of the multiple influences of history, to analyze questions in the history of ethics. Specifically, he takes up ethical concerns around questions of eroticism and well-being, questions of proper conduct in relation to pleasure and eroticism. Thus we are returned, late in the twentieth century, to the concerns of the ancient philosophers.

Just as modern philosophy began the new consideration of the very nature of desire itself, so contemporary philosophy has taken up a new kind of consideration by often explicitly theorizing the relation of desire to philosophy. In each of the readings in the final section, the sense of philosophy as a conversation, which continues both within and across historical periods, is evident. In her consideration of the ways in which some desire comes to be connected with illness or pathology, Judith Butler brings together the influences of twentieth-century readings of Hegel with both psychoanalysis and, most obviously, the influence of Foucault. She both builds upon and challenges his understanding of the ways in which the most basic Freudian categories—Eros and death—have functioned in social understandings of desire.

bell hooks notes the delicate role of Eros in education, rendering contemporary a tradition we can trace back to Socrates, who was most famous as a teacher—and was executed by an unsympathetic state for the corruption of his pupils. Learning too can be seductive, as Plato clearly realized. And philosophy, of all forms of study, is perhaps most about learning and teaching, about the very nature of knowledge itself and the pleasures inherent in its exchange.

Martha Nussbaum likewise takes up ancient philosophical discussions in her ethical consideration of love and desire. Her analysis is situated in the contemporary context of care ethics—ethical responses based upon care for others, associated chiefly with feminist philosophy. Care ethics arises in part out of the sense that we need to address Kant's version of ethics, with its insistence that desire, passion, and happiness must be quite excluded from ethics. Although part of this contemporary context, Nussbaum's discussion is also influenced by the concerns of Aristotelian ethics.

In papers developed from their 1995 debate (published in 1997), Alan Soble and Eva Feder Kittay continue consideration of ethical and social traditions. Taking up the Antioch College "Sexual Offense Prevention Policy," a code of conduct that sets rules regulating the sexual behaviors of its students, faculty, and staff, Soble and Kittay engage with one another in debating questions of how and whether desire may legitimately be regulated, even if we agree that desire is a political matter.

One might be tempted to conclude, from the closeness of these concerns to those of ancient philosophy, that philosophers never get anywhere in their arguments. This is not precisely the case, though one might argue that the philosophical point is as much a matter of the discussion itself as of its outcome. Rather, philosophical concerns are both timeless and contextual. Grounded very much in the time of their appearance, they may take up theological, interpersonal, legal, and other issues. But underlying those issues are concerns too important not to recur—of the nature of the human person, of relations between us and all the various elements of our worlds, and of the desire, passion, and affection we invest in those relations. The love of wisdom demands a constant search, a constant reopening of questions in new times and places. This is the conversation from which the passages here are excerpted, to which we now may turn.

ENDNOTE

1. Maurice Blanchot, *The Infinite Conversation*, trans. Susan Hanson (Minneapolis: University of Minnesota Press, 1993).

Acknowledgments

The editors express deepest gratitude to the contributors of introductory essays for this volume. Special thanks are due to David-Olivier Gougelet, University of Memphis; James H. Stam, George Washington University; Andrea Tschemplik, American University; and Roberto Toledo, SUNY Stony Brook, for their original translations of selections by Frantz Fanon, Empedocles, G.W.F. Hegel, Princess Elisabeth of Bohemia, and René Descartes. We are also grateful to Michael Wyetzner, who generously granted permission to reproduce his drawing for the cover of this volume.

Ross Miller and Carla Worner of Prentice Hall, and Patty Donovan of Pine Tree Composition, provided invaluable assistance and encouragement throughout the production of this volume. We are grateful to our reviewers: Barbara Andrew, William Paterson University of New Jersey; Alan Soble, University Research Professor, University of New Orleans; Sean P. O'Connell, Albertus Magnus College; Kerry Walters, William Bittinger Professor of Philosophy, Gettysburg College; and Gabriela R. Carone, University of Colorado, Boulder, who offered helpful suggestions for improving the manuscript. Shelley Harshe and Nicholas Webster provided superb assistance with the preparation of the manuscript. We also benefited from timely encouragement and advice from Barbara Andrew, Carolyn Betensky, Marcos Bisticas-Cocoves, and Elizabeth Falcon. We thank American University's College of Arts and Sciences for a Mellon Grant to assist in the final preparation of the volume. Finally, we thank our students, whose work in the courses from which this volume emerged has been inspirational.

Ellen K. Feder
Karmen MacKendrick
Sybol S. Cook

Contributors of Introductions

Sybol Cook (SC), Johns Hopkins University
William Dale Cowling (WDC), Oregon State University
David-Olivier Gougelet (DG), University of Memphis
Evan Haney (EH), University of Oregon
Brenda Hanzl (BH), American University
Erik Jacobson (EJ), Harvard University
Jena G. Jolissaint (JGJ), University of Oregon
Rory E. Kraft, Jr. (REK), Michigan State University
Stephen E. Lahey (SEL), LeMoyne College
Terrance MacMullan (TM), Eastern Washington University
Jen McWeeny (JM), University of Oregon
Melanie B. Mineo, (MBM)
Lura Munns (LM), American University
Sean O'Connell (SO), Albertus Magnus College
Amy A. Oliver (AAO), American University
Michael Schmidt (MS), American University
James H. Stam (JHS), George Washington University
Andrea Tschemplik (AT), American University

chapter one

Sappho

"Love is bittersweet." Sappho's sliver of verse that has survived for over two millennia can strike a modern ear as trite and clichéd. Is this because it is indeed trite, or is it because we have lost sight of its initial brilliance? A contemporary philosopher, Paul Ricoeur, argues that the poetic function of symbol, myth, metaphor, and poetry generally is to take us from the known to the unknown, opening to us new worlds, new possibilities for being in relation to ourselves and to others.[1] In good poetry, an event of meaning occurs. A poem tells us something that can be said in no other way, giving rise to a kind of thinking that takes us beyond ordinary judgments, opinions, and beliefs. Poetry can shatter the usual categories and conceptions that mediate our response to the other. It is a testament to the original power of Sappho's verse that we now live in a world so informed by its insight that it has become a commonplace. But if we can retrieve its initial freshness, if we can glimpse the profound way in which Sappho's body of poetry opened a new possibility for being human, we will at the same time discover a rich clue for addressing the question of the relation of passion and wisdom even as we become more self-conscious regarding our own horizons of meaning.

Sappho was a lyric poet living at the turn of the sixth century, B.C.E. Her society was informed by the epic poetry of Homer, which set up a world in which it would be impossible to experience love as bittersweet given its account of the human condition. Today, the common conception of the self in the West is of an individual who is a self-directed agent largely independent of social position. By contrast, Homer's people were not unified, free agents. They were composed of quasi-material parts, including a thinking part, an emotional part, and a life force, *nous*, *thymos*, and *psyche*, respectively. Given this quasi-material view, *thymos* as the seat of emotion could not be at odds with itself. It had to be in one state or another and therefore could not encompass an experience of love as bittersweet.[2] Just as it would make sense to many of us today to say, "The spirit is willing, but the flesh is weak," so it would make sense to a Homeric Greek to say that one is willing, but that one's *thymos* is not. But it would not make sense to say that one's *thymos* is at odds with itself. Moreover, this quasi-material conception of *thymos, nous,* and *psyche* precluded a developed sense of self-determination. One's actions stemmed from the influence of external forces. If one refused to act when action was warranted, it was because a god hardened one's heart.[3] Finally, the world of the Homeric Greek demanded that the self be understood and judged in terms of social position. One was born into a social role, and one violated the boundaries of that role to one's peril.[4] There was a cosmic order incorporating a social order keeping chaos at bay.

By suggesting that the individual could experience love simultaneously as bitter and sweet, Sappho breaks with the Homeric understanding of the human person, giving birth to a new conception of the self as having an internal life and as being capable of serving as a locus of deliberation and evaluation.[5] Consider the following verse:

> Some men say an army of horse and some men say an army on foot
> and some men say an army of ships is the most beautiful thing
> on the black earth. But I say it is
> what you love.[6]

Here, Sappho moves beyond the evaluations mandated by social convention to speak in her own voice, to deliver her own appraisal. Much like Plato's Socrates, she calls into question the authority of tradition, but unlike Socrates, she does not call one to transcend this fleeting world of appearance in order to gain insight into an eternal, enduring reality. Instead, she responds to the inimitable individual.

As becomes clear in the *Symposium*, Socrates sees love of the individual as a vehicle that enables one to move beyond "conventional wisdom," to gain insight into the universal truth, but along the way, one must recognize the individual as a mere appearance of the truth to be transcended on the path to enlightenment. Conversely, for Sappho, love of the individual awakens an awareness of the self as a locus of appreciation and valuation, providing a different sort of wisdom that enables one to stand independent of society's standards. This is marked through her use of lyric poetry. Unlike epic, lyric, often composed for singing at festivals and at pivotal celebrations in people's lives such as marriages,[7] gives voice to the inner lives and feelings of specific individuals. It bestows a kind of immortality on the individual by identifying the individual's experience as a manifestation of the ever recurring, rhythmic, cycle of life. Through one's love of another, one participates in love eternal and thereby has access to truth beyond the mediation of social convention.[8]

It is perhaps this access to truth through *eros* and not through convention that accounts for why Sappho, like Socrates who likewise challenged conventional wisdom in the name of truth, has been an object of hostility for supporters of the status quo. While Plato called Sappho the "tenth muse," her work has met with resistance. Some might argue that its source is the unmistakable same-sex erotic desire that many of her poems express. Clearly, the ways in which Sappho's "lesbianism" has been interpreted, glossed over, denied, dismissed, or heralded have said much about different sensibilities in different ages. Greek and Roman writers, for instance, "masculinized" Sappho, seeing her as a "man" in "woman's" clothing, in order to retain the classical view of dominant and subordinate positions in sexual relations as sacrosanct, and thereby preserve a patriarchal approach to sexuality. Conversely, Victorians either expressed indignation that Sappho would be interpreted as having or expressing such distasteful desires, or used her work to support a view of feminine expression as an indicator of female perversion. But more recently, Sappho's erotic interest in both men and women has gained greater acceptance, and many commentators have begun celebrating her work as an expression of erotic desire that has something compelling to say to us today.[9]

Yet, the antipathy that has greeted Sappho's work calls for a deeper explanation. Anacreon, another lyric poet who lived only a few generations after Sappho and who also expressed same-sex desire in his work, has not met with the same resistance as Sappho. The fact that he was a male is no doubt crucial here. But more crucial is that Anacreon's work does not challenge a patriarchal approach to understanding human relations.[10] Sappho's work, many would argue, does. Just as Sappho opens a new world with her neologism, "bittersweet," so she discloses new possibilities for human relations by suggesting that eros can establish a reciprocal relationship, that it can lead to a recognition by individuals of each other as subjects, as opposed to conceiving of love in terms of a lover's desire for an object.[11]

Later in this volume, Martha Nussbaum suggests that emotion cannot be separated from understanding. One might argue that Sappho's love clamors for a new understanding, a new wisdom, regarding what it means to be a human being and what it means to love. Her experience of *eros* engenders a view of the self that enables her to speak of love as bittersweet and to develop an awareness of the possibility for human relations to be intersubjective, such that love might be for another and not for an object of desire. But one might as convincingly argue that Sappho's wisdom, her understanding of the self and of human relations, makes possible a new path for love.

Of the estimated three hundred poems that Sappho wrote, collected in nine "books" by Greek scholars in ancient Alexandria, only one complete poem, fittingly, a hymn to Aphrodite, remains.[12] Similarly, the events of Sappho's life are largely shrouded in mystery. The earliest female writer from whom we have surviving texts, Sappho lived on the Island of Lesbos in the city of Mytilene; she may have been married and may have had a daughter; she was the center of a circle of women whose exact relation to her is unclear; Ovid provides an almost universally discredited report that she killed herself for love of a younger man, Phaon, who did not return her affections; she was exiled to Sicily for unknown reasons from approximately 604 to 595 B.C.E.[13] But it is testament to the power of her verse and to the extraordinary person with whom we have come to identify it that both compel attention today, giving truth to Sappho's prediction:

> Someone will remember us
> I say
> Even in another time.[14]

QUESTIONS

1. Are there consistent types of images or words that Sappho uses in relation to love? If so, what do these tell you about her understanding of it?

2. What state of mind does the experience of love cause? Does love make one wise? How are love and intellect related in Sappho's work?

3. Separation, loss, and jealousy are themes running through Sappho's poems. How does she understand these? What does her treatment of them suggest regarding her view of love, of what it means to be human, and of the appropriate relation between human beings who are in love?

4. Write your own poem about love or choose a contemporary poem that you like. Compare it with Sappho's poems. What are the differences and similarities between them? What do these differences and similarities have to tell us about the differences and similarities in worldview of the two poets?

5. Can Sappho's poetry still speak to us today, or has it become just an artifact?

ENDNOTES

1. See, for instance, Paul Ricoeur, *Interpretation Theory: Discourse and the Surplus of Meaning* (Fort Worth: Texas Christian University Press, 1976), pp. 37, 52–53; Paul Ricoeur, "Creativity in Language," *Philosophy Today* 17 (summer 1973): 110–11.

2. Bruno Snell, *The Discovery of the Mind in Greek Philosophy and Literature* (New York: Dover Publications, 1982), pp. 8–22, 43–70, particularly p. 60. See also Anne Carson, *Eros the Bittersweet* (Normal, Ill.: Dalkey Archive Press, 1998), pp. 3–9.

3. Snell, *The Discovery of the Mind*, p. 20.

4. Alasdair MacIntyre, *A Short History of Ethics* (Notre Dame: University of Notre Dame Press, 1998), pp. 2–13.

5. MacIntyre, *Short History of Ethics*, p. 48.

6. *If Not, Winter: Fragments of Sappho*, trans. Anne Carson (New York: Alfred A. Knopf, 2002), p. 27.

7. Lyric poetry was typically accompanied by the lyre, from which its name derives. It is interesting to note that Sappho's poetry was initially not written, but passed down orally, and that Sappho was, in fact, credited with three musical inventions, a particular type of lyre known as a *pektis,* an instrument for picking it known as a *plectron*, and an emotional mode known as the mixolydian mode, which was later used by Greek tragic poets. (See *If Not, Winter,* p. ix.)

8. *The Discovery of the Mind*, pp. 44–47.

9. For discussions of the role of ideology in Sappho scholarship, see Nancy Sorkin Rabinowitz, "Introduction," in *Among Women*, ed. Nancy Sorkin Rabinowitz and Lisa Auanger (Austin: University of Texas Press, 2002), pp. 1–33; Ellen Greene, "Subjects, Objects, and Erotic Symmetry in Sappho's Fragments," in *Among Women*, ed. Nancy

Sorkin Rabinowitz and Lisa Auanger (Austin: University of Texas Press, 2002), p. 82; Harriette Andreadis, "Sappho in Early Modern England: A Study in Sexual Reputation," in *Re-Reading Sappho,* ed. Ellen Greene (Berkeley: University of California Press, 1996), pp. 105–21.

10. For a discussion of the difference between Sappho and Anacreon in this regard, see Margaret Williamson, "Sappho and the Other Woman," in *Reading Sappho*, pp. 248–64.

11. Defenses of this interpretation include Williamson, "Sappho and the Other Woman," pp. 248–64; and Eva Stehle, "Romantic Sensuality, Poetic Sense: A Response to Hallett and Sappho," in *Reading Sappho*, pp. 143–49. There are, however, those who take issue with this interpretation. See, for instance, Page Dubois, *Sappho Is Burning* (Chicago: University of Chicago Press, 1988), p. 9. Also worth noting is Jack Winkler's discussion of the antipathy to Sappho's work springing from "the fact that it is a *woman* speaking about women and sexuality," in Jack Winkler, "Gardens of Nymphs: Public and Private in Sappho's Lyrics," in *Reading Sappho*, pp. 89–109.

12. Margaret Williamson provides an excellent account of the major sources for extant work from Sappho, references in texts by other ancient authors and papyri scrolls, many of which were uncovered as waste paper in a town dump in what was Roman Egypt. Williamson offers interesting insights into the difficulties of reconstructing the poems and a detailed discussion of possible reasons for their loss, such as their dependence on being continuously transcribed, loss of interest in the work of pagan writers with the rise of Christianity, possible hostility toward her work as Christianity spread, loss of interest due to the dialect in which her poems were written, and the durability of papyri. See Margaret Williamson, *Sappho's Immortal Daughters* (Cambridge, Mass.: Harvard University Press, 1995), pp. 34–59.

13. For a discussion of the various myths surrounding Sappho's life and the ideological impetus for them, see Williamson, "Sappho and the Other Woman," pp. 5–33 and Holt N. Parker, "Sappho Schoolmistress," in *Re-Reading Sappho,* pp. 146–83.

14. *If Not, Winter: Fragments of* Sappho, p. 297.

SELECTED BIBLIOGRAPHY

Carson, Anne. *Eros the Bittersweet.* Normal, Ill.: Dalkey Archive Press, 1998.

Dubois, Page. *Sappho Is Burning.* Chicago: University of Chicago Press, 1995.

Greene, Ellen, ed. *Reading Sappho.* Berkeley: University of California Press, 1996.

Greene, Ellen, ed. *Re-Reading Sappho.* Berkeley: University of California Press, 1996.

Rabinowitz, Nancy Sorkin, and Lisa Auanger, eds. *Among Women: From the Homosocial to the Homoerotic in the Ancient World.* Austin: University of Texas Press, 2002.

Snyder, Jane McIntosh. *Lesbian Desire in the Lyrics of Sappho.* New York: Columbia University Press, 1997.

Williamson, Margaret. *Sappho's Immortal Daughters.* Cambridge, Mass., Harvard University Press, 1995.

Selected Fragments

Sappho

1

Deathless Aphrodite of the spangled mind,
child of Zeus, who twists lures, I beg you
do not break with hard pains,
    O lady, my heart

but come here if ever before
you caught my voice far off
and listening left your father's
    golden house and came,

yoking your car. And fine birds brought you,
quick sparrows over the black earth
whipping their wings down the sky
    through midair—

they arrived. But you, O blessed one,
smiled in your deathless face
and asked what (now again) I have suffered and
  why
    (now again) I am calling out

and what I want to happen most of all
in my crazy heart. Whom should I persuade
  (now again)
to lead you back into her love? Who, O
    Sappho, is wronging you?

For if she flees, soon she will pursue.
If she refuses gifts, rather will she give them.
If she does not love, soon she will love
    even unwilling.

Come to me now: loose me from hard
care and all my heart longs
to accomplish, accomplish. You
    be my ally.

2

]
here to me from Krete to this holy temple
where is your graceful grove
of apple trees and altars smoking
    with frankincense.

And in it cold water makes a clear sound
  through
apple branches and with roses the whole place
is shadowed and down from radiant-shaking
  leaves
    sleep comes dropping.

And in it a horse meadow has come into bloom
with spring flowers and breezes
like honey are blowing
    [   ]

In this place you Kypris taking up
in gold cups delicately
nectar mingled with festivities:
    pour.

16

Some men say an army of horse and some men
  say an army on foot
and some men say an army of ships is the most
  beautiful thing
on the black earth. But I say it is
    what you love.

Easy to make this understood by all.
For she who overcame everyone
in beauty (Helen)
    left her fine husband

behind and went sailing to Troy.
Not for her children nor her dear parents
had she a thought, no—
　　　　]led her astray

　　　　　　]for
　　　　　　]lightly
　　　　]reminded me now of Anaktoria
　　　　who is gone.

I would rather see her lovely step
and the motion of light on her face
than chariots of Lydians or ranks
　　　　of footsoldiers in arms.

　　　　]not possible to happen
　　　　]to pray for a share
　　　　]
　　　　]
　　　　]
　　　　]
　　　　]

　　　　toward[

　　　　]
　　　　]
　　　　]

　　　　out of the unexpected.

17

Close to me now as I pray,
lady Hera, may your gracious form appear,
to which the sons of Atreus prayed,
　　　　glorious kings.

They won very many prizes
first at Troy then on the sea
and set out for here but
　　　　could not complete the road

until they called on you and Zeus of suppliants
and Thyone's lovely child.

Now be gentle and help me too
　　　　as of old[

Holy and beautiful
maiden
around[
　　　　]

]
]
to be
　　　　]to arrive.

22

　　　　]
　　　　]work
　　　　]face
　　　　]
　　　　]
　　　　if not, winter
　　　　]no pain
　　　　]
]I bid you sing
of Gongyla, Abanthis, taking up
your lyre as (now again) longing
　　　　floats around you,

you beauty. For her dress when you saw it
stirred you. And I rejoice.
In fact she herself once blamed me
　　　　Kyprogeneia

because I prayed
this word:
I want

23

　　　　]of desire
　　　　]
　　　　]for when I look at you

]such a Hermione
]and to yellowhaired Helen I liken you
]
]among mortal women, know this
]from every care
]you could release me
     ]
       ]dewy riverbanks
       ]to last all night long
               ] [

31

He seems to me equal to gods that man
whoever he is who opposite you
sits and listens close
      to your sweet speaking

and lovely laughing—oh it
puts the heart in my chest on wings
for when I look at you, even a moment, no
    speaking
        is left in me

no: tongue breaks and thin
fire is racing under skin
and in eyes no sight and drumming
      fills ears

and cold sweat holds me and shaking
grips me all, greener than grass
I am and dead—or almost
      I seem to me.

But all is to be dared, because even a person of
    poverty

38

you burn me

44

Kypros
herald came
Idaos   swift messenger
]
and of the rest of Asia   imperishable fame.
Hektor and his men are bringing a glancing girl
from holy Thebe and from onflowing Plakia—
delicate Andromache on ships over the salt
sea. And many gold bracelets and purple
perfumed clothes, painted toys,
and silver cups innumerable and ivory.
So he spoke. And at once the dear father rose
    up.
And news went through the wide town to
    friends.
Then sons of Ilos led mules beneath
fine-running carts and up climbed a whole
    crowd
of women and maidens with tapering ankles,
but separately the daughters of Priam   [
And young men led horses under chariots   [
]in great style
]charioteers
]
               ]like to gods
               ]holy all together
set out   for Ilios
and sweetflowing flute and kithara were
    mingled
with the clip of castanets and piercingly then
    the maidens
sang a holy song and straight up the air went.
amazing sound   [
and everywhere in the roads was [
bowls and cups   [
myrrh and cassia and frankincense were
    mingled.
And all the elder women shouted aloud
and all the men cried out a lovely song

calling on Paon farshooting god of the lyre,
and they were singing a hymn for Hektor and
    Andromache
      like to gods.

44Aa

]
for goldhaired Phoibos whom Koos' daughter
    bore
after she mingled with Kronos' highnamed son.
But Artemis swore the great oath of the gods:
By your head! forever virgin shall I be
]untamed on solitary mountains
]Come, nod yes to this for my sake!
So she spoke. Then the father of blessed gods
    nodded yes.
Virgin deershooter wild one the gods
call her as her name.
]Eros comes nowhere near her
]

44Ab

                [
                [
                [
                [
of the Muses   [
makes and of the Graces   [
with slender
                [
for mortals: there is a share [
]

47

                    Eros shook my
mind like a mountain wind falling on oak trees

51

I don't know what to do
              two states of mind in me

94

I simply want to be dead.
Weeping she left me

with many tears and said this:
Oh how badly things have turned out for us.
Sappho, I swear, against my will I leave you.

And I answered her:
Rejoice, go and
remember me. For you know how we cherished
    you.

But if not, I want
to remind you
            ]and beautiful times we had.

For many crowns of violets
and roses
      ]at my side you put on

and many woven garlands
made of flowers
around your soft throat.

And with sweet oil
costly
you anointed yourself

and on a soft bed
delicate
you would let loose your longing

and neither any[   ]nor any
holy place nor
was there from which we were absent

no grove[   ]no dance
        ]no sound
      [

130

Eros the melter of limbs (now again) stirs me—
sweetbitter unmanageable creature who steals in

132

I have a beautiful child who is like golden flowers
in form, darling Kleis
in exchange for whom I would not
                              all Lydia or lovely

147

someone will remember us
                    I say
                    even in another time

chapter two

Empedocles

Empedocles (c. 492–c. 432 B.C.E.) is a significant Greek philosopher from the Presocratic period. The central element of Empedocles' thought studied today is his cosmology, or world design. Empedocles presents a view of reality as being composed of four universal elements: earth, air, fire, and water. These elements are continually brought together by a unifying force (Love) and dissolved again into component parts by an unraveling force (Strife). This cycle of creation and destruction is never ending, and anything that exists is only a temporary alignment of the elements, as they are alternately mixed and separated by Love and Strife. There are four possible positions for the elements: completely mixed (fully unified by Love), completely separated (fully divided by Strife), partially unified by Love, and partially separated by Strife. Although it would be difficult to discern whether a cycle is currently progressing toward unification or separation, Empedocles believed the stages of partial unification and partial separation need to be understood separately.

We know Empedocles' writings, like those of all Presocratic philosophers, only through fragments that appear in secondary sources; no copy of any of his works exists. We have additional information from sources that cite his influence and paraphrase his works and ideas. His two major works, from which historians believe all of the existent fragments come, are the epic poems *On Nature* and *Purifications*. Empedocles' writings are important because they present elements of both of the dominant philosophic methods in Greece prior to the death of Socrates (c. 399 B.C.E.), the philosophies of the Pythagoreans and of Parmenides.

Best remembered for the Pythagorean theorem of right triangles ($a^2 + b^2 = c^2$) and his work in the mathematics of music, Pythagoras (c. 570–494 B.C.E.) and his followers saw the world not as something explainable through number but as something that at its very basis *was* number. Pythagoras believed in reincarnation and prescribed strict rules for his followers that ranged from vegetarianism to the proper manner of putting

---

on shoes. While some of these rules appear to be for social reasons, many of them stem from Pythagoras's belief that the soul is immortal, changing through the cycle of reincarnation into many different forms of life. Pythagoras also believed that events recur in cycles, with nothing ever being truly new.[1]

Although there is some evidence that Parmenides (c. 515 B.C.E.) began his philosophic life as a Pythagorean, his writings show that he turned away from them quite forcefully. The key element of Parmenides' philosophy is his belief that the One, or Being, is the unity of everything that exists and that change is illusion. This viewpoint depends on the understanding that for something to be created or destroyed, a movement between nonexistence and existence is implied. For Parmenides, reality exists and must always have existed. Otherwise, something comes from nothing, a notion that cannot be understood. Further, since something cannot turn into nothing, real objects cannot change or be destroyed. Any perceived change is illusion, or the result of a prior inferior understanding of the One.[2]

Empedocles borrowed elements from both of these traditions in putting forth his own cosmology. From the Pythagoreans he adopted the theory of cycles, and from Parmenides he adopted the insistence that no object can be understood to have come from nothing. The following assertions of Empedocles illustrate the importance of the Pythagoreans and Parmenides to his thought:

> There is a double coming into being of mortal things and a double passing away. One is brought about, and again destroyed, by the coming together of all things, the other grows up and is scattered as things are again divided. And these things never cease from continual shifting . . . but in so far as they never cease from continual interchange of places, thus far are they ever changeless in the cycle.[3] Fools—for they have no far-reaching thoughts— who fancy that that which formerly was not can come into being or that anything can perish and be utterly destroyed. For coming into being from that which in no way is inconceivable, and it is impossible and unheard-of that that which is should be destroyed. For it will ever be there wherever one may keep pushing it.[4]

In the first passage we can see most clearly how, for Empedocles, cycles of creation and destruction are predicated upon the Pythagorean belief that "events recur in certain cycles." The second statement displays the debt he owes to Parmenides. Empedocles' idea that "coming into being from that which in no way is inconceivable" clearly seems to be a restatement of Parmenides' question of how something that formerly was not could "come into being." By combining these philosophic traditions, Empedocles was able to propose his theory of elements. The elements, like the Parmenidian unity, cannot be destroyed and are present in all of reality. Yet they can be rearranged in a cyclical manner that the Pythagoreans would have understood. In order to explain the variations of reality, and its continuing change, Empedocles introduced the contrasting forces of Love and Strife. While this mixture of the two traditions is one that the Pythagoreans would accept more readily than Parmenides, it should be understood that only by combining both traditions could Empedocles' philosophy be written.

Although little is known of Empedocles' life, we do know that he was a physician as well as a philosopher and that he was truly a flamboyant character. He was born in Sicily and is known to have visited the mainland of southern Italy, where he no doubt encountered the local Pythagoreans. Empedocles claimed to be a god, and there are many stories of his fantastic achievements, such as diverting two streams in order to save the town of Selinus from a plague, or keeping a woman with no pulse and no respiration alive for a month. In addition to his philosophical work, he was a strong proponent of democracy and was reported to be an excellent public speaker. Aristotle, in his *Sophist* (a lost dialogue), called Empedocles the founder of rhetoric. There are conflicting stories of Empedocles' death. In one account, he leapt into the volcano at Mt. Etna to prove that he was a god. In another account, he simply left the city-state, never to be seen again.

REK

QUESTIONS

1. What arguments does Empedocles use or assume in asserting that the material world and its elements have lasted forever?
2. What are the implications of taking Love and Strife as the cosmological principles of unity and division?

ENDNOTES

1. From Porphyrius. *Life of Pythagoras*: "(Pythagoras) maintains that the soul is immortal; next, that it changes into other kinds of living things; also that events recur in certain cycles, and that nothing is ever absolutely new." Diels and Kranz (DK) fragment 14, 8a, trans. Kirk & Raven (K&R) fragment 271.
2. Simplicius explains Parmenides on this point: "One way only is left to be spoken of, and that it *is*; and on this way are full many signs that what *is* is uncreated and imperishable, for it is entire, immovable and without end. . . . Nor will the force of true belief allow that, besides what is, there could also arise anything from what is not. . . . How could what *is* thereafter perish? and how could it come into being? For if it came into being, it is not, nor if it is going to be in the future. So coming into being is extinguished and perishing unimaginable" (K&R, 347).
3. Simplicius, *Commentary on Aristotle's Physics* 158, 1, K&R, p. 423.
4. Aristotle, *On Melissus Xenophanes Gorgias*, 2.

SELECTED BIBLIOGRAPHY

Guthrie, W.K.C. *A History of Greek Philosophy*, vol. 2. Cambridge: Cambridge University Press, 1965.

Kirk, G. S., and J. E. Raven, eds. *The Presocratic Philosophers*. Cambridge: Cambridge University Press, 1966.

Schofield, Malcom. "Empedocles." In *Routledge Encyclopedia of Philosophy*, vol. 3, edited by Edward Craig, 293–98. London : Routledge, 1998.

Selected Fragments

Empedocles

[Empedocles] makes out the bodily elements to be four: fire and air and water and earth, these being eternal, but undergoing changes in magnitude—largeness and smallness—according to [a process of] compounding and dividing. More precisely expressed, however, his first principles are Love and Strife, by which these [elements] are moved. For it is necessary for the elements to continue moving alternately, at one time being compounded through Love and at the other time being divided by Strife. Consequently too, according to him, there are six first principles.

From: Aristotle, *Metaphysics I, iii. 984a8;* Simplicius, *Physics 25, 21*

And these things never stop exchanging places continually. Now they are all united into One by Love; and now in turn they each separate in the hatred of Strife.

From: Simplicius, *Physics 158, 6*

From these things indeed sprouted forth all things—as many as were and as many as are and will be: trees and men and women, beasts and birds and water-nursed fishes, and the age-long enduring gods too, foremost in distinctions. For these are the very things that are, running through one another, and they become different to the extent that they change through mixing.

From: Simplicius, *Physics 159, 21*

And [the elements] are successively predominant as the cycle turns round, and they decay into one another and, by Fate, in turn they grow [into one another]. For these are the very things that are; running through one another, they become human beings and the tribes of the other beasts, sometimes coming together into a single ordered whole (cosmos) by Love, and sometimes moving apart from each other by the hatred of Strife, until such time as they are subdued, growing together into a single whole.

From: Simplicius, *Physics 33, 18*

They are fools—for their concerns are not far-thinking—who hope that that which previously was not would come to be or that anything could completely perish and be destroyed. For it is hopeless to think that that which does not exist at all should come to be, and it is inconceivable and unheard of that that which exists should be destroyed; for wherever and whenever something may impel it, that is where it will be.

From: Plutarch, *Adversus Colotes 12;* Aristotle *De Melisso,* Xenophane, *Gorgia II 975b1*

Equal to itself from every direction, however, and wholly boundless, a rounded sphere, exulting in its circular changelessness.

From: Stobaeus, *Eclogae Physicae et Ethicae I 15, 2ab*

Let me tell you something else: There is no birth of any mortal thing, nor any end to deathly destruction; but there is only mixture and exchange of the things mixed, and among human beings that is named birth.

From: Plutarch, *Adversus Colotes 12*

Let me tell you a double [tale]: once it increased, so as to be One alone from out of many; and then they grew apart so as to be many from One. There is a double genesis of mortal things, and their decay is also double; for the coming together of all elements gives birth to the One and then destroys that; and the other in turn, having been made to grow together, is scattered apart when [the elements] separate. And these things never cease from their continual exchange; at one point everything comes together into One through Love; and at another point the individual [things] separate through the hatred of strife. <Thus to that extent that the One has learned to grow out of the many,> and a multitude in turn proceeds from the dissolution of the One, to that extent they come into being and they have no steady life; but to the extent that their continual exchange never ceases, to that extent they are always

motionless and unchanging according to the cycle.

From: Simplicius, *Physics 158, 6*

But listen to [my] words, for learning will increase your understanding. As I said before, when revealing the ends of my words, I will tell you a double tale: for at one time a single unity developed out of the many, and at another time the many came to be by division out of the One—fire and water and earth and air enormously high, and dreadful Strife, separated from them and balanced with them in every direction, and Love among them, equally present in length and breadth. Look upon her with your mind; and do not linger with your eyes, astonished; for even by mortals she is thought to be inborn in their limbs; and it is by means of her that they think kindly things and accomplish peaceful deeds, calling her with the eponym of Joy and Aphrodite. No mortal man has seen her, revolving to and fro among them. But listen to the unambiguous course of my account. For all of these [elements] are equal and are of an equally great an age, but each is in charge of a different task and each has a different character, and in turn they are dominant according to the changing times; and besides these nothing comes into existence or passes away; for if they were forever being destroyed, they would never be at all. After all, what could increase this All? Where would it come from? And how would these things come to be destroyed, since nothing is devoid of them? No, these things are just themselves, and running through one another they become different things in different places and yet are always continuously steadfast.

From: Simplicius, *Physics 157, 25*

I want to return, however, to the path of verses that I earlier blazed, drawing it out word by word, namely this: When Strife came to the lowest depth of the whirl and Love came to be in the middle of the whirl, therein all these things came together to be just One; not right away, but coming together at will, one from here and another from there. From this mixture, however, myriad tribes of mortal creatures poured forth, whereas, conversely, many stayed unmixed in this mixing process, as many as Strife still held back from aloft; for it had not completely retreated, blameless, to the outer limits of the circle, but in part some things remained inside the limbs, and others departed. And to the extent that [Strife] kept running out ahead, the immortal thrust of gentle-minded blameless Love always followed behind. Rapidly what had earlier been thought to be immortal grew to be mortal; and things that were formerly unmixed [came to be] mixed, through the exchanges of the paths. And from these mixed things poured forth myriad tribes of mortal creatures, furnished with all varieties of forms, a wonder to behold.

From: Simplicius, *On the Heavens 528, 30*

chapter three

Plato

Plato (c. 428–347 B.C.E.) was thirty years old when his friend and master, Socrates (c. 470–399 B.C.E.), was tried and sentenced to death for impiety and for "corrupting the youth of Athens." The event changed forever the direction of Plato's life and work: he promptly abandoned his political ambitions and took up the mantle of philosophy, both to vindicate Socrates and to determine the features of a truly just state. The result was his articulation of a philosophical system that has become a cornerstone of Western thought. More than two thousand years after his death, we still honor Plato as one of the most innovative and influential thinkers—even arguably as *the* preeminent philosopher—of the Western tradition.

Plato was born a member of the ruling class in Athens, so it is not at all surprising that he aspired to a political career. His father, Ariston, is said to have descended from the early kings of Athens, and his mother, Perictione, was distantly related to Solon, the legendary lawmaker. When Ariston died, Perictione married an associate of the statesman Pericles, a leader of Athens during its period of greatest political, economic, and intellectual flourishing, the Golden Age. We understand Plato's political aspirations all the more, however, when we consider the political and moral turbulence he witnessed firsthand as a young Athenian—internal divisions and confusion fueled largely by the Peloponnesian War with Sparta but partly by the skeptical and relativist teachings of the Sophists.

The Sophists were a class of educators who rose to prominence in Athens during the Golden Age in response to an increasing demand for higher education. Most were itinerant teachers who charged for the instruction they gave in a variety of subjects but especially in rhetoric, the art of persuasive speaking. They boasted of their ability to argue both sides of any issue and even of their skill in making "the weaker argument into the stronger."[1] It is easy to see that this assertion presupposes a skeptical attitude about the reality of objective truth or our claims to know things with certainty. The skeptics argued that we cannot really know anything with certainty, because every potential object

Symposium from *The Symposium and The Phaedo* by Plato, translated and edited by Raymond Larson. Crofts Classics Series. Copyright © 1980 by Harlan Davidson, Inc. Reprinted with permission.

of knowledge in the world is in a state of flux. The relativists took skepticism a step further, pointing out that because we can only grasp things by using our senses, not only is certain knowledge impossible, but the things we claim to know vary from one person to the next. That is, insofar as there is no objective truth, truth or rightness can only be judged by each individual according to the way circumstances appear to him or her.

The teachings of the Sophists ultimately served to undermine Athenian politics such that Plato, increasingly disillusioned, forsook politics and became a follower of Socrates. Unlike the Sophists, Socrates used the art of argumentation not to win arguments but to pursue *truth*. Plato embraced both the content of Socrates' philosophy and his intriguing dialectical method: a style of investigation that pursues truth by posing questions, offering answers, and challenging those answers by posing additional questions. The objective of dialectic is to "tease" the truth out of one's established beliefs by repeatedly questioning, correcting, and refining those beliefs. Socrates' method of questioning usually involved an interlocutor toward whom he often seemed antagonistic, so relentless was his pursuit of answers. However, it helps to remember that Socrates' aim was to get at the truth, not to outsmart his interlocutor. Indeed, one of his most memorable qualities is his frequent profession of his own ignorance.[2]

After Socrates' execution, Plato fled Athens and traveled to Italy, Sicily, and Egypt. In Italy and Sicily, he associated with the Pythagoreans, whose mathematical researches greatly influenced his developing ideas about knowledge and certainty. Upon returning to Athens in 387 B.C.E., Plato began to attract a community of followers with whom he advanced the teachings of Socrates, and he established a school in an olive grove called "Academus," located just outside of Athens. The Academy, as the school is now known, was completely devoted to research and teaching in a variety of subjects, including mathematics,[3] philosophy, political theory, astronomy, and biology; it is often described as the first European university. Plato's hope was to train a new generation of statesmen who would become enlightened rulers of Athens.

In addition to teaching and researching, Plato began to compose written dialogues that advanced his philosophical ideas through dramatized conversations and debates, usually featuring Socrates and other well-known Athenians. He wrote thirty-five dialogues in all as well as thirteen letters. The early period of Plato's writing represents his commitment to advancing Socrates' philosophy, which especially emphasized the distinction between knowledge and opinion. Socrates believed that inasmuch as knowledge is the human being's distinctive excellence, the relentless pursuit of truth is our highest aim. He was convinced, however, that although all of us possess the truth within our souls, we are not in touch with that truth; rather, what we openly express are really just beliefs and opinions. The aim of Socrates' dialectical questioning was to expose opinions as being just that and, having revealed their limitations, to pursue truth itself.

Accordingly, in the early dialogues Plato typically portrays Socrates as encountering someone who claims to be knowledgeable about a given subject—the nature of temperance, friendship, or piety, for example.[4] Socrates himself professes ignorance and seeks help from this "knowledgeable" person. As Socrates questions his interlocutor, it becomes evident that this person's knowledge is not as representative of truth as he claims. Moreover, because Socrates also is unable to reach a conclusion on the subject, the question is left unanswered. This open ending is a distinctive feature of Plato's early dialogues, the objective here being not to posit theories on the subjects in question so much as to emphasize the difference between knowledge and opinion. The ability to make this distinction was, for Socrates and Plato, the beginning of wisdom.

Increasingly convinced, nonetheless, of the ability of humans to achieve certainty, Plato began to probe his subjects more deeply. In his "middle period" dialogues, which include *Symposium,* the text presented here, Plato openly challenges the skepticism and relativism of the Sophists, aiming first to demonstrate that we do have knowledge of certain kinds of objects and, second, to describe the nature of those objects. To the skeptics' assertion that we cannot know anything with certainty, Plato answered that certainly we can. We know for certain that $2 + 2 = 4$. We also know that an equilateral quadrilateral with four right angles is a square. In fact, all of the truths of mathematics and geometry are certain. To the relativists Plato replied, moreover, that these truths do not vary according to how things appear to different individuals; the fact that an equilateral quadrilateral with four right angles is a square is true for *everyone.* Concepts such as these are accessible to all human beings, and so there *are* such things as universal truths. While it is true that in the world we see squares of many different sizes, colors, and so on, what we are perceiving here are merely *particular* squares—productions or specific instantiations of the concept of a square.

This brings us to Plato's theory of Forms, an important key to his philosophy. In distinguishing knowledge from opinion, Plato claimed that knowledge must have two essential characteristics. First, it must be certain and infallible. Second, it must therefore have as its objects only such things as are truly real—that is to say, objects that are permanent and unchanging. Because only pure concepts are permanent and unchanging, they are the only proper objects of knowledge. Plato called such pure concepts "Forms." Thus, there is a Form of a square—"an equilateral quadrilateral with four right angles"—and this, Plato would say, is the truly real square in contrast to the many particular squares we observe in the phenomenal world. Plato would add that the particular squares we see in the world are merely *copies* of the Form of Square, and whatever degree of reality we ascribe to these particular squares (for we do commonly think of them as "real") stems from their resemblance to, or "participation in," the Form of Square. We form *opinions* of particulars through sense perception, but we attain *knowledge* of the Forms through reason. The intellect, developed through dialectical reasoning, can attain intellectual insights that are certain, and the objects of these insights are the eternal Forms.

In *Symposium,* dialectical reasoning is used to derive the meaning of Love. The dialogue chronicles the events of a memorable banquet held in honor of the tragedian Agathon's first victory in a dramatic contest. In typical fashion, Agathon's symposium[5] is held in his home, and the guests dine while reclining on couches arranged in a circle. After dinner, the guests ordinarily would have continued their drinking while conversing or being entertained by musicians or dancers, but Phaedrus, a great lover of rhetoric, convinces the company instead to give speeches in praise of the "ancient and powerful" god of Love.

Eros—rendered as "Love" in the translation included here—governs a specific type of love; the Greek word *eros* means intense passion and attachment and usually refers to sexual love between two individuals. *Symposium,* however, emphasizes the intimacy shared between an adult male and a teenage boy in a particular Athenian tradition: a relationship in which the older partner was educator and mentor to the younger, who would sometimes become his lover. In response to Phaedrus's request, the guests offer speeches—six in all—in praise of Love. A seventh speech is delivered at the end of the evening by an inebriated gate crasher, the statesman and general Alcibiades, who in youth had aspired to become Socrates' lover.

In the penultimate address, Socrates recapitulates a discourse on love he claims to have had with a priestess named Diotima. Diotima begins by recounting the origin of Love—his having been born to a god, Poros (Plenty), and a mortal woman, Penia (Poverty)—proclaiming that Love is not a god at all but a spirit, "in between" the mortal and the immortal and between resourcefulness and lack.[6] The priestess explains that those who are in love are searching for something they do not understand; ultimately they seek immortality through a love that is "possessing the good forever" and "reproduction in the beautiful"—whether or not they are conscious of the fact (206A–207A). Sexual love enables one to achieve a kind of immortality through the perpetuation of one's genes, but Diotima is aware of the "final revelation" of love (210A). She describes a process whereby an individual, beginning with an attraction to the beauty of one person's body, gradually ascends through stages of deepening insight concerning what is beautiful until he comes to discover and to love the Form of Beauty itself. Thus, in *Symposium* Plato shows how dialectic can be employed to derive the meaning of Love as well as of Beauty, which he asserts is the true object of Love.

Other works by Plato include the *Apology* and *Crito,* which chronicle the trial and death of Socrates; *Phaedo,* which in addition to portraying the death of Socrates posits Plato's famous theory of Forms; and *Republic* and *Laws,* Plato's major political works. In his later years, Plato pursued one of his great dreams: a singular opportunity to apply philosophy to practical politics. In 367 B.C.E. he became tutor to the new ruler of Syracuse, Dionysius the Younger, teaching him the art of philosophical rule. Sadly, the experiment failed; opponents of Plato's plan threatened his life, forcing him to return to Athens. He devoted his final years to lecturing at the Academy and writing. When Plato died, at age eighty, the Academy was not closed but continued under the leadership of his student Speusippus. The Academy continued in existence until A.D. 529, making it the longest surviving university in the Western world.

SC

QUESTIONS

1. In *Symposium,* Plato has devoted an entire text to the analysis of love. What do you think are Plato's motivations for treating love as a philosophical subject?

2. Some commentators claim that the various myths that appear in Plato's works can be interpreted to reveal positive statements of Plato's own philosophical views on given subjects. Others think that the myths concern difficult questions that cannot be given the same kind of philosophical scrutiny as others and that this is why Plato treats them mythically. How do you interpret Aristophanes' myth? What do you think it says or suggests about the role of love in human life?

3. Examine Diotima's speech as recounted by Socrates (201E–212B) and explain Diotima's notions of love and beauty. How and why does Diotima relate the two?

ENDNOTES

1. Today, the term *sophist* has distinctly negative connotations; it now refers to someone who presents a clever argument, but is actually wrong. Similarly, a sophism is a misleading argument that appears sound but is not, and sophistry is the intentional use of such arguments.

2. See, for example, *Symposium* 206B and 207C.

3. The inscription over the entrance to the Academy read, "Let no one unversed in geometry enter here," attesting to Plato's conviction of the singular importance of mathematics for the development of thought.

4. Most of these dialogues pursue the nature of the traditional virtues: *Charmides* aims to define temperance, *Lysis* pursues the meaning of friendship, *Laches* addresses courage, *Euthyphro* explores the nature of piety, and Book I of the *Republic* seeks a definition of justice. *Protagoras,* another early dialogue, defends the thesis that knowledge is virtue (*aretê,* or human excellence) and can be taught.

5. The word *symposium* literally means "drinking together."

6. This accords with Plato's conviction that the Forms are not only objects of knowledge but also a source of inspiration.

SELECTED BIBLIOGRAPHY

Grube, G.M.A. *Plato's Thought.* Indianapolis, Ind.: Hackett, 1980.

Kirk, G.S., and J.E. Raven. *The Presocratic Philosophers.* Cambridge: Cambridge University Press, 1957.

Plato. *Plato: Complete Works,* edited by John M. Cooper and D.S. Hutchinson. Indianapolis, Ind.: Hackett, 1997.

Plato. *The Symposium and The Phaedo,* trans. and ed. Raymond Larson. Wheeling, IL: Harland Davidson, 1980.

Robinson, John Manley. *An Introduction to Early Greek Philosophy.* Boston, Mass.: Houghton-Mifflin, 1968.

Vlastos, Gregory. *Platonic Studies.* Princeton, N.J.: Princeton University Press, 1981.

The Symposium

Plato

APOLLODORUS: I should be able to tell you the story—I've practiced it enough. Why, just the day before yesterday I was going up to Athens from my home in Phalerum[1] when a man I know saw me and called after me playfully: "Hey, Apollodorus! Wait for me, you Phalerian!"

So I waited. He caught up with me and said: "Apollodorus, I've been looking all over for you. I want to hear about that party of Agathon's with Socrates and Alcibiades and all the rest—what were the love speeches like? Someone else told me about them, but his story wasn't very clear. He had heard it from Phoenix, Philip's son, and he said you knew about it too. So tell me the whole thing. As Socrates' friend you're the one to report what he says. But first, were you there?"

"The story couldn't have been very clear," I said, "if you think the party was so recent that I could have been there."

"That's the impression I got," he said.

"I don't see how, Glaucon," I said. "You know that Agathon moved out of Athens years ago,[2] and I've been with Socrates for less than three. Since then, I've been with him every day and made it my business to know everything he says and does. Before that, I just ran around in circles like you. I thought I was doing something important and philosophy was just a waste of time, but really I was a miserable fool—like you."

"Stop joking and answer my question," he said. "When was the party?"

"We were still children," I said. "Agathon had just won first prize with his first tragedy.[3] It was the day after he celebrated the victory with his players."

"That really was long ago," he said. "But who told you—Socrates?"

---

[1] A harbor about three miles southwest of Athens. One must walk "up" to reach the city.

[2] Agathon moved to Macedonia about 407 B.C. and died there about 401. The external dialogue therefore takes place about 402, "years" after 407, but before 401 (since Agathon is spoken of as being still alive).

[3] Greek dramatists competed in the theater for first, second, and third prize. Agathon presented his first tragedy in 416 B.C.; he therefore gave his party about fourteen years before this telling of it.

"No," I said, "the same one that told Phoenix: a fellow called Aristodemus of Cydathenaeum—a little man who always went barefoot. He had been there, and as far as I could tell, he was one of Socrates' most ardent lovers at the time. Of course I've checked some of the details with Socrates, and they agree with what Aristodemus said."

"Why not tell it to me then?" he said. "We may as well talk as we go into town."

So I told it and got some practice, as I said. I guess I can tell it again if you gentlemen really want to hear it. Philosophical talk ravishes me anyhow, besides being useful, and I love it as much when I'm talking as when I listen to somebody else. But your rich businessmen's talk makes me exasperated. I feel sorry for you as my friends because what you consider so important is really just waste of time.

Now maybe you think that I'm a miserable dog. Well, I think so too. But I don't think you fellows are miserable—I know damn well you are!

COMPANION: You're always the same, Apollodorus. You insult everyone, including yourself, and you seem to think that everyone but Socrates is absolutely wretched. I don't know where you got the nickname "Maniac" from, but every time you open your mouth you surely act like one: You snap and snarl at your friends, at yourself— at everyone but Socrates.

APOLLODORUS: So you think this attitude proves I'm mad and out of tune?

COMPANION: Let's not argue about it now, Apollodorus. Please, just do as we asked and tell us those speeches.

APOLLODORUS: All right, they were something like this. But wait, I'll try to tell it all from the beginning, the way Aristodemus told it to me.

Well, Aristodemus said he ran into Socrates, freshly bathed and wearing fancy shoes instead of being barefoot. So he asked him where he was going all dressed up like that.

"To dinner at Agathon's," Socrates answered (said Aristodemus). "I didn't go to the victory celebration yesterday because I was afraid of the crowd, so I promised I'd come today. That's why I'm all dressed up: 'beauty to beauty.' Say, how do you feel about going to dinner uninvited?"

"However you say," I said (said Aristodemus).

"Come along then," said Socrates. "We'll pervert the old proverb: 'birds of a feather flock together.' Homer, you know, had the insolence to corrupt it completely. He made Agamemnon a great warrior but his brother Menelaus 'a soft spearman.'[4] Then, when Agamemnon was giving a feast, Menelaus came uninvited. So the poorer man went to the better man's feast. The result of course was that 'birds of a kind were caught in a bind.'"

"If I go, Socrates, I'm afraid I'll be following Menelaus's example instead of yours—a nobody going to an intellectual's feast. So think up a good defense because I won't admit that I came uninvited. I'll say you invited me."

"We'll put our heads together[5] and figure something out on the way," said Socrates. "Let's go."

Their conversation was something like that, said Aristodemus, and then they left. But on the way Socrates somehow fell into thought and stopped. Aristodemus stopped too, but Socrates told him to go on ahead. So he did. But, he said, when he got to Agathon's place he found himself in an embarrassing situation: The door

---

[4]The phrase is from *Iliad* 17.588. Menelaus comes uninvited in *Iliad* 2.402–410.
[5]A quotation from *Iliad* 10.224.

was open and a slave rushed out and brought him in to the guests, who were just getting ready to eat. The moment Agathon saw him, he cried, "Aristodemus, hello! You're just in time for dinner. If you've come for anything else, you'll have to put it off. I was looking for you yesterday to give you an invitation, but I couldn't find you anywhere. But why didn't you bring Socrates?"

"I turned around," said Aristodemus, "and he wasn't following me. So I said that I *had* brought Socrates. In fact, he had brought me."

"Fine," said Agathon. "Where is he"

"He was right behind me. I wonder where he is."

He said Agathon turned to a slave: "Go look for him and bring him here, will you, boy? Aristodemus, please sit by Eryximachus."

Aristodemus said one of the boys brought water and helped him wash. Then the other boy returned and said, "That Socrates has gone into a neighbor's porch. He just stands there. When I called he wouldn't come."

"That's odd," Agathon replied (said Aristodemus). "Call him again and don't take no for an answer."

"Leave him alone," I demanded (said Aristodemus). "This is a habit of his—he goes off and stands wherever he happens to be. I'm sure he'll be along soon if you leave him alone. Don't bother him."

"Well, whatever you say," Agathon replied (said Aristodemus). "Now, boys, please serve us. Do it however you like—the way you do when no one's standing over you, which is something that *I* would never do. Pretend that we are your guests and you have to please us and earn our compliments."

Then they ate, he said, but still no Socrates. Agathon suggested they send after him again,

but Aristodemus said that he wouldn't let them. Socrates finally came in when they were half done with dinner. Considering his habits, he hadn't been away very long. "Come over here and sit by me," said Agathon—he was reclining alone on the right[6]—"I want to touch you and get some of that wisdom that came to you in the porch. I know you have it; you wouldn't have left till you did."

Aristodemus said Socrates sat down and said: "It would be nice if wisdom were as you say, Agathon, and it would flow from a full person to an emptier one when they touched, as water through wool from a full to an empty cup. If it did, I couldn't imagine anything more valuable than sitting by you because I know you'd fill me with beautiful wisdom. My wisdom's a poor, dubious thing—like a dream—but yours is brilliant and effusive. Why, just the day before yesterday you displayed your youthful brilliance

---

[6]Guests reclined in pairs on couches, with a small portable table for their food. The seating arrangement at Agathon's symposium was something like this:

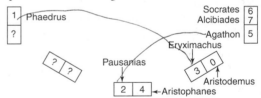

The far left, where Phaedrus is sitting, was the place of honor. The host usually took the lowest place, on the far right. Agathon occupies this position until Socrates arrives and reclines to his right. Alcibiades arrives late (212d) and sits between Agathon and Socrates. At the end (223b), Agathon moves to sit on Socrates' right. The speakers speak from left to right as indicated by the numbers. Aristophanes and Eryximachus exchange turns. Question marks indicate unnamed guests, whose speeches are not reported. Aristodemus, the narrator, apparently gives no speech.

and dazzled more than thirty thousand witnesses from all over Greece."[7]

"Don't be insolent, Socrates," Agathon replied (said Aristodemus). "In a little while you and I will settle this dispute over wisdom, and Dionysus will be the judge. But now eat your dinner."

He said Socrates reclined, and they finished their dinner. Then they poured the libations, chanted the hymn to the gods, and performed the other rituals.[8] Next they turned to the drinking. Pausanias, he said, opened the discussion something like this: "Well, gentlemen, what's the easiest way to handle the drinking? To tell the truth, I'm still in bad shape from yesterday and could use a little recuperation. I think you could too, since most of you were here. So how shall we go about it?"

Aristophanes, said Aristodemus, replied: "As you say, Pausanias—the easiest way. I was completely stupefied yesterday."

"I agree," said Eryximaches, son of Acumenus. "Now how about Agathon? Are you up to it today?"

"No, I'm not up to it either."

"We would consider it an absolute godsend," observed Eryximachus (said Aristodemus), "—particularly Aristodemus, Phaedrus, and I— if you heavy drinkers were temporarily incapacitated, because we never have any capacity. I exempt Socrates from my remarks; he doesn't care one way or the other—either way will suit him. Now, since none of the present company seems particularly inclined to overindulge, this may be an auspicious occasion for me to explain the true nature of drink. The findings of medical science have convinced me that intoxication is detrimental to the health. I would never intentionally drink to excess or advise one of my patients to do so, especially if he still had a hangover from the previous day."

"I always do whatever you say," interrupted Phaedrus the Myrrhinusian, "especially in medical matters. The others will too, if they have any sense."

So, said Aristodemus, everyone agreed to drink more for pleasure than to get drunk.

"I take it we are resolved then," continued Eryximachus, "to drink only as much as we wish and to compel no one to drink more. I now move that we dismiss this flute girl who has just come in. She can play to herself or to the women inside while we spend the time in conversation. If you're wondering what kind, I've a proposal to make."

Aristodemus said they told him to make it.

"The beginning of my speech," Eryximachus began (said Aristodemus), "is taken from Euripides' *Melanippe*:[9] Not mine the tale—but Phaedrus's here. More than once Phaedrus has accosted me and indignantly complained: 'Isn't it a scandal, Eryximachus, that of all the poets who have written hymns and odes to the gods, not one has ever seen fit to compose a poem in honor of the great and venerable god of Love? And if you look through the works of the great

---

[7] By presenting his prize-winning tragedy. "Youthful" contrasts Agathon's youth with Socrates' age (he was fifty-three in 416 B.C.). Dionysus, below, was the god of both wine and the drama.

[8] A dinner was distinct from a symposium, or drinking party, which now follows. The dinner was formally concluded by a hymn and libations to the gods. A symposium was governed by formal rules, which is why Pausanias asks about the drinking procedure. There was normally a "master of ceremonies," who prescribed the manner of drinking and the accompanying activities. Here Phaedrus serves as the leader until Alcibiades later (213e) appoints himself master of ceremonies.

[9] A lost tragedy. Prodicus, below, was a famous sophist whose specialty was the precise definition of words.

sophists, like Prodicus, you'll find plenty of prose eulogies to Heracles and other heroes, but not a single one to Love. That's outrageous enough, but recently I came across a book by some sophist who had composed a marvelous encomium on—the usefulness of salt! About drivel like that they make a terrible fuss, but not one soul has yet had the nerve to write a decent hymn to Love. A god is neglected while salt gets extolled to the skies!'

"I move Phaedrus's point as well taken. I would therefore like to favor him publicly by suggesting this as a fitting occasion to adorn the neglected god. If that seems congenial to you. I'm sure we'll find sufficient entertainment in speeches. Here is my proposal: Each of us will give a speech—as beautiful as he can make it—in praise of Love. We shall go from left to right, beginning with Phaedrus, who not only is sitting the first on the left, but is also the father of the speech."

"No one will vote against you, Eryximachus," said Socrates (according to Aristodemus). "I hardly could, because love is the only thing that I claim to know. Neither could Agathon and Pausanias, and certainly not Aristophanes, who devotes all his time to Dionysus[10] and Aphrodite. As far as I can see, we'll all second your proposal, even if it won't be a fair contest for us who speak last. But if the first speakers do a good job, we'll be satisfied. So go ahead, Phaedrus, and good luck."

Aristodemus said the others concurred and urged Phaedrus to begin.

Now Aristodemus couldn't remember every speech in detail, and I can't remember everything he told me. But I'll relate the main points of each speech I consider worth telling.

---

[10]As patron god of the theater. Aphrodite was the goddess of love.

SPEECH OF PHAEDRUS

Well, as I said, Phaedrus was the first speaker. Aristodemus said he opened with something about Love being a great god, amazing among gods and men. "The reasons are many," he said," but chief is his birth. Love is revered as the most ancient of gods. Here is my proof: Love has no parents. No one, layman or poet, has ever disputed that. Hesiod, in fact, confirms it when he says that first Chaos was born, and then 'Broad-bosomed Earth, sure, eternal foundation of all,/ and Love.'[11] Acusilaus agrees that after Chaos these two, Earth and Love, were born. And Parmenides says that Birth 'Planned Love as first of all the gods.' Thus from all sides it is agreed that Love is an ancient and venerable god.

"Being ancient and venerable, Love is the source of great blessings to man. And the greatest blessing I can name is for a young boy to find a good lover and a lover a good boy. To live a beautiful life a man must be guided by a principle which nothing—neither birth, nor wealth, nor office—can so beautifully inspire as Love. This principle is shame for the shameful and emulation of the beautiful. Without that, neither a city nor an individual can do anything beautiful or great. Suppose a man in love is caught doing something shameful or suffering it because he's too cowardly to resist: I say he'll be more distressed if seen by his loved one than if by a friend or even his father. The same for a loved one—he'll be terribly ashamed if his lover sees him do something ugly.

"If there were a way to give birth to a state or an army of nothing but lovers and loved ones who would shun shameful activity while vying with

---

[11]The quotation is from *Theogony* 117. Acusilaus was a poet whose works are lost. Parmenides was an early fifth-century philosopher who believed that "everything is one." Therefore there can be no change or plurality in the real world. The visible world of change is an illusion.

each other for honor, that would be the best possible organization, and in battle a few such men could defeat practically the whole world. A loving man would never throw away his sword or break ranks if he knew his loved one would see him; he'd rather die a thousand deaths. As for abandoning his loved one or not helping him in danger, no one is so base that Love cannot inspire him with courage, as though he were noble by nature. In short, the effect Homer describes of 'a god breathing might'[12] into heroes is Love's effect upon lovers, brought forth from himself.

"And only lovers—not only men, but women too—will die for the sake of another. Alcestis, daughter of Pelias, provides sufficient proof of that for us Greeks. She was the only one willing to die for her husband, and though his parents still lived, she so far excelled them in affection because of Love that she showed them to be strangers to their son and parents only in name. So beautiful was this act judged to be by both gods and men that the gods granted Alcestis a favor they've conferred upon only a tiny number of all those who have done beautiful deeds: Out of admiration for her they allowed her soul to return from the dead. Thus even gods award the highest honors to courage and diligence in Love.

"But Orpheus,[13] son of Oeagrus, was sent back from Hades undone. He had gone for his wife, but the gods gave him only a phantom because they considered him a weakling (he was merely a minstrel) who didn't dare to die for love, like Alcestis, but had sneaked into Hades alive. Therefore they justly made his death be delivered by women; they didn't honor him and send him to the Isles of the Blest, as they did Achilles, Thetis' son. Achilles had learned from his mother that he would die at Troy if he killed Hector; if not, he would die at home of old age. Nevertheless, he dared to avenge his lover Patroclus and chose not merely to die in his place but to follow him into death. Hence the gods' extreme admiration and honor for him: he had considered his lover to be so important.

"Aeschylus talks nonsense when he says Achilles was Patroclus's lover rather than his loved one.[14] Achilles was more beautiful than Patroclus or any hero, much younger and still beardless, as Homer says. Much as the gods honor excellence[15] in love, they are truly amazed, astounded, and happy at the affection of a loved one—more so than at the lover's affection for him. The lover is more divine than the loved one; he is possessed by a god. That's why the gods honored Achilles more than Alcestis and sent him to the Isles of the Blest.

---

[12]The reference is to *Iliad* 10.482, 15.60, etc. Alcestis, below, is the heroine of Euripides' *Alcestis*. She makes a bargain with Death to die in place of her husband Admetus so that he may go on living.

[13]A legendary musician. When his wife Eurydice died, Orpheus persuaded the lord of the underworld to allow him to bring her back, on condition that he not look back at her until they reached the upper world. He did look back and so lost her. Phaedrus changes the story for his own purposes. The scene below between Achilles and his mother Thetis is from *Iliad* 18.73–137. Achilles is placed on the Isles of the Blest by Pindar in *Olympian* 2.68–83.

[14]In the *Myrmidons,* a lost tragedy. As usual in Plato, love is presented primarily as pederastic: the love between a man and a youth. The distinction made here and throughout the dialogue between "lover" and "loved one" is common in Greek, though it may puzzle an English reader. We tend to emphasize the similarity and equality that exists between (as we say) "a pair of lovers." The Greeks, however, emphasized the difference and disparity between them. They thought of the relationship as resembling that between master and slave; the loved one has the power to control the one who loves him. There must always be a lover and a loved one; never two lovers (impossible by definition). The reference to Homer, which follows, is to *Iliad* 2.673 and 11.786.

[15]*Arete,* traditionally translated as "virtue." Its basic sense is excellence or ability at something—being good at it. Though strictly a limited term (excellence *at* something), Plato tends to make it absolute: the excellence or virtue that makes any thing distinctively that which it is, especially that which makes a man a man.

"Thus I maintain that Love is the most ancient and honored of gods, most effective in providing excellence and happiness for all men, living and dead."

Phaedrus's speech was something like that, said Aristodemus, and then came several speeches that he couldn't remember very well. So he skipped them and went on to the speech of Pausanias.

SPEECH OF PAUSANIAS

Pausanias (said Aristodemus) began like this: "Phaedrus, I think your proposal was bad, to eulogize Love in this simple way. If Love were one, it would be all right. But Love is not one. Since he is not one, the proper way to proceed is first to proclaim which Love to praise. I shall try to set this straight by telling first which Love to praise and then by praising him as he deserves.

"We all know: no Love, no Aphrodite.[16] If she were one, Love were one. But she is two, so Love is two. Of course there are two Aphrodites. The older is the motherless daughter of Uranus. We call her Uranian Aphrodite. The younger is the daughter of Zeus and Dione. We call her Common Aphrodite. We're thus compelled to call the Love who works with the first goddess Heavenly Love, the other Common Love. We must properly praise all the gods, but I must try to present this pair's prerogatives.

"Every act is neutral, neither beautiful nor ugly in itself. Take what we're doing—drinking, singing, or speaking: None in itself is beautiful. Beauty only comes from doing, the way an act is done. If done properly, it's beautiful, otherwise not. So for loving and Love: Not all are beautiful and worth our praise; only the one who turns us to beautiful loving.

"Common Love is truly common and doesn't care what he does. This is the Love that worthless people love. These love women as much as boys, their bodies more than their souls, and they even prefer their loved ones to be perfectly mindless because all they want is action, regardless of how it's done. Hence they do whatever they feel like, indifferent to good and bad. Their Love comes from the young goddess who shared at birth in both the male and the female. But Heavenly Love loves boys and comes from the Aphrodite who shared not in the female but only in the male and who is older and free from insolence. Hence men fired by that Love pursue males; they dote on the naturally strong and intelligent. Even in pederasty you can spot the lovers driven by pure Heavenly Love. They don't love young boys but wait till they start to have sense, which is when they begin to get their first beard.

"I think a lover who starts with a boy at that age shows his true intent: to spend his life with him. He doesn't deceive a senseless child, then laugh and flit off in contempt to some other young thing. There should be a law against loving young boys; it would save a lot of energy from being squandered on uncertain affairs. It's always uncertain how a young boy will turn out—sound in mind and body or not. Good men impose this law on themselves, but we should force the herd to obey it too, just as we keep them, as far as we can, from making love to free-born women. These are the lovers that give Love a bad name: People look at them and see their unfairness and lack of tact and dare to call it ugly to gratify[17] lovers. You'd hardly think anyone could criticize this or anything else that's done in a fair, orderly way.

---

[16] I.e., "no love, no sex." Aphrodite was the goddess of sexual love and so is often used as a synonym for sex. The dual mythology of Love and Aphrodite which follows is probably Plato's own invention. Uranus is Heaven (one of the Titans, or elder gods). "Uranian" is therefore synonymous with "Heavenly."

[17] To "gratify" or "favor" a lover is a polite euphemism for sexual intercourse.

[handwritten: acting like an idiot for love]

"The love customs in most states are easy to grasp; they're simple. But here they're complex. In Elis, Boeotia,[18] and wherever people are unskilled at speech, they simply call gratifying a lover beautiful. No one there would call it ugly, mainly so they won't have to use words to persuade the young men, which they couldn't do anyway. But in Ionia and other places controlled by the Persians they regard gratifying lovers as ugly. These barbarians even consider sports and philosophy shameful, owing to their despotic government. Absolute rulers could hardly tolerate big ideas, strong friendships, and tight associations among their subjects—precisely the things that sports and philosophy, but especially Love, tend to produce. The Athenian tyrants[19] learned that the hard way: Aristogiton and Harmodius had such a solid friendship that it brought down their government. So wherever custom calls it ugly to gratify lovers, it rests on the lawmakers' malice, the rulers' greed, and the subjects' cowardice. Where it proclaims it a simple good, the law stems from the mental indolence of its makers.

"But we have a beautiful custom and, as I said, one not easy to grasp. Reflect how we value open love above the furtive kind, especially the love of noble, aristocratic young men (even if they're homlier than the others); how much encouragement a lover gets from all sides (hardly as though loving were regarded as shameful!); how a conquest enhances his reputation while failure destroys it; how, in attempting a seduction, a lover receives permission to do things that would bring him the vilest disgrace if attempted for any other motive but love—if, say, a man wanted money or office or power from someone and stopped to do the things that lovers do to their sweethearts—making pleas and entreaties, swearing eternal vows, sleeping on their doorsteps, offering to be their slaves and to do things for them that no real slave would ever do—why, his friends and enemies alike would restrain him, his friends by rebuking him and feeling ashamed, his enemies by denouncing him as a servile, groveling flatterer, whereas a lover who does these very same things is not merely excused but set above criticism, as though seduction were considered a beautiful thing, while the strangest thing of all, according to public opinion, is that the gods forgive a lover—and no one else—for breaking an oath because 'a sex oath is no oath'; therefore, so our custom declares, both gods and men grant a lover complete license to do whatever he wants—reflect upon that, and you'll be forced to conclude that our custom creates a perfect climate for both loving and being friendly to lovers. But when fathers assign slaves to keep their sons from talking to lovers, and when a boy's friends criticize him if they see him talking to one, and when these boys' elders don't even try to control them or scold them for their vicious tongues—when you see things like that, you might well conclude that the custom here is the ugliest of all.

"The truth, I believe, is as I said at the start: gratifying a lover is not a simple act, beautiful or ugly in itself. It depends how it's done: It's beautiful if done beautifully, ugly if not. Ugly means gratifying a base lover basely; beautiful means gratifying a good lover well. A base lover is that common lover, who loves the body more than the soul; he's fickle because what he loves is unstable. When the bloom leaves the body he loves, he 'flutters away'[20] and puts all his oaths and promises to shame. But the lover of character is a lover for life, because he's welded to that which is stable.

---

[18]Elis and Boeotia were considered by the Athenians to be backwater areas, and the Boeotians were considered particularly stupid. Ionia, below, was the Greek Asia Minor seacoast. Being close to Persia, it was often under Persian domination.

[19]Athens was ruled by tyrants from 546 to 510 B.C. In 514, Harmodius and Aristogiton assassinated the tyrant's brother and so helped bring down the tyranny.

---

[20]These words are used of a dream in *Iliad* 2.71.

But beloved cannot do anything

"Our custom well tests these two types of lover and says, 'Gratify this type but shun the other.' It incites the lover to chase, the beloved to flee, that the race may test them and expose which class each belongs to. And it denounces as ugly a loved one's rapid submission. Time should pass, for time tests most things well. Nor must a loved one submit for money or political power, whether beaten into cringing submission by cruelty he cannot endure or lured by financial or political favors he fails to despise. We believe that nothing is certain or stable about money and power except their natural inability to engender noble friendship.

"Our custom leaves only one path open for loved ones to gratify lovers. Just as it permits lovers to be the willing slaves of their loved ones in anything without being denounced as servile flatterers, so it permits loved ones to perform only one kind of voluntary service that will keep them from being denounced. That is service for excellence. Our custom states that if one person desires to serve another erotically to become a better man through him, either in knowledge or in some other part of excellence, such voluntary slavery is neither servile nor ugly.

"These two customs—the first concerning boy love, the second concerning knowledge and other excellence—must both contribute to the same end if gratifying a lover is to turn out well. When lover and loved one, each observing his proper custom, come together for the same end—the lover rightly serving his loved one to gain his permission, the loved one rightly permitting what may be permitted to one that can make him knowing and good—and when the lover can provide the intelligence and excellence the loved one needs to get knowledge and education, it is then and only then—at the conjunction of those two customs contributing to a common end—that gratifying a lover turns out beautiful.

"In this situation even getting deceived brings no shame, whereas gratifying a lover for any other motive is ugly whether you're deceived or not. Suppose a boy gratifies a rich lover for money and then gets cheated out of it when the lover is exposed as poor. That's ugly even though the boy was deceived. He has betrayed his true nature—a willingness to do anything for money; and that's not beautiful. But the deception is beautiful if, for the sake of self-improvement, a boy favors a lover who seems good and then finds himself deceived when his lover is exposed as bad and lacking excellence. He too has revealed his true nature—eagerness to do anything for anyone for the sake of excellence and becoming a better man; and that's the most beautiful thing there is.

"Thus gratifying lovers for excellence is utterly beautiful. This is the Heavenly Love of the Uranian goddess, valuable to both states and individuals, because he forces the lover and loved one each to care for his own excellence. All other loves come from Common Aphrodite. That, Phaedrus," he said, "is my impromptu presentation in praise of Love."

Pausanias paused (I learned to speak jingles like that from the sophists), and Aristodemus said it was Aristophanes' turn. But he had the hiccups from "repletion" or something and couldn't give a speech, so he turned to Eryximachus the doctor, who was reclining beside him, and said: "Eryximachus, if you were a friend, you'd either stop my hiccups or speak in my place until they stop by themselves."

"I shall do both," Eryximachus said. "I'll take your turn and when your indisposition abates you may take mine. As I speak, refrain from breathing awhile and the agitation should cease. If not, gargle with water. If they remain violent, tickle your nose with something to induce sneezing. Do that once or twice and they'll relent, no matter how severe they may be."

"Speak," said Aristophanes. "I'll try it."

SPEECH OF ERYXIMACHUS

"Well now, Pausanias seems to have charged into his speech well enough but didn't really end it, so it's up to me to apply a proper ending. I think he made a useful distinction in distinguishing double Love. But I believe one may observe from my science, medicine, that Love operates not only in human souls upon beautiful young men, but in and upon everything—in all living bodies and plants and in practically all that exists: Love is a great and marvelous god whose influence extends to all things human and divine.

"I shall begin with medicine, so I may venerate my science as well as the god. Now the nature of the body displays double love. Physical illness and health are admittedly different and unlike, and unlikes desire and love different things. So one kind of love exists in a healthy body, another exists in a sick. As Pausanias just said about people—it is beautiful to gratify good men but ugly to gratify lechers—so also with bodies: it is beautiful, even necessary, to gratify the good in each body (such gratification is called medicine), but ugly to gratify the sick and the bad, which we must in fact frustrate to become good technicians. Now medicine, briefly defined, is the science of bodily loves as they pertain to repletion and evacuation, and a man who can diagnose the beautiful love and the ugly will be a good diagnostician, while one who can exchange the one for the other and apply love where it is needed and excise it from where it doesn't belong will be a good practitioner. He must also, of course, be able to reconcile the body's hostile elements and cause them to love one another. The most hostile are opposites like the hot and the cold, the wet and the dry, the bitter and the sweet. According to our poets here—[21] and I for one believe them—Asclepius, our patron, knew how to apply love and affinity to these opposites and so founded my science.

"This Love, I maintain, charts the whole course of medicine and also of athletics and agriculture. It will be obvious to even a casual observer that the same is true of music, as Heraclitus perhaps tried to say, though he didn't choose his words very well. 'The One,' he says, 'differs from itself and agrees, like the harmony of a lyre and bow.'[22] But it is quite absurd to say that harmony differs from itself or consists of elements which currently differ. Perhaps he was trying to say that a harmony comes from elements which previously differed—high and low notes—but which have been brought to agreement by the science of music. It could hardly come from notes that currently differ. A harmony is a concord and a concord an agreement, and you can never have agreement between parties as long as they differ. Nor can you harmonize elements that differ or disagree. So with rhythm: It comes from elements which previously differed—fast and slow beats—and which later are made to agree. Here it is music, as before it was medicine, that makes all these opposites agree by introducing love and affinity among them. So music is the science of love as it pertains to harmony and rhythm. In the theoretical constitution of harmony and rhythm the love elements are easy to diagnose and double love doesn't yet come in. But applying

---

[21] I.e., Agathon and Aristophanes. Asclepius was the god of medicine.

[22] Heraclitus was an early fifth-century philosopher who believed that everything is in flux and strife; the only thing permanent is change. The quotation is abridged by Plato. In full it reads: "It is at variance and yet agrees with itself; there is a back-stretched connection, as in the lyre and bow." This seems to mean that reality exists because of a constant internal tension and strife, just as a bow may be said to exist because of the tension between bow and string. Break the string and you no longer have a bow but only its constituents. Eryximachus gets confused because he takes the word *harmony* in its later musical sense rather than in its earlier sense of "connection," which Heraclitus intended.

rhythm and harmony for people's benefit, either by creating music—which is called composition—or by properly performing songs already composed—called education—[23] is difficult and calls for a skilled technician.

"So again the conclusion comes round: We must gratify orderly men and try to make orderly those who are not, preserving their love, which is the beautiful, Heavenly Love who comes from the Uranian Muse. Common Love comes from the Muse of popular music, and one must prescribe him cautiously in only small doses so people may enjoy him without catching lechery, just as in my profession one must be careful about diet, so that people may enjoy food without harming their health. Thus in music and medicine and all technical skills, human and divine, we must try to preserve, insofar as we can, both of these Loves. For both are in all.

"Even the arrangement of the seasons is filled with both of these Loves, and when the opposites I mentioned earlier encounter orderly Love and attain a temperate, harmonious blending, they come bearing health and good fellowship to men, animals, and crops, and there is justice. But when the insolent Love dominates the seasons, he destroys everything and injustice is unleashed. Such conditions are conducive to plagues and other discordant diseases that afflict both animals and crops. Frost, hail, and blight are bred from the disorder and greed of these love forces, the science of which we call astronomy, because it studies the movements of stars and the seasons of the year.

"Finally we come to sacrifice and prophecy—the communion of gods and men—which pertain solely to the preservation and cure of Love. All kinds of impiety, toward gods and one's parents, living or dead, tend to occur when people fail in all of their works to honor, gratify, and venerate the orderly Love over the other. So prophecy is the technique charged with the examination and cure of these Loves, as the science of friendship between gods and men, which studies those principles of human love that influence piety and righteousness.

"Thus total Love has wide and extensive or, more succinctly, total power, and the Love concerned for the good and consummated with temperance and justice among both us and the gods has the greatest power of all: He provides total happiness and makes us capable of friendship and social intercourse with one another and with those greater than us, the gods.

"Now perhaps in my eulogy I've overlooked much, but it wasn't intentional. And it's your task, Aristophanes, to fill in whatever I may have missed. Or if you intend to speak differently, do—your hiccups seem to have stopped."

"Yes," admitted Aristophanes (said Aristodemus), "but not till I gave them the sneeze treatment. I'm amazed that my body's 'orderly love' desires such disgusting noises and gurgles. But it must; they stopped as soon as I sneezed."

"Be careful, my friend," said Eryximahcus. "If you intend to make jokes, you'll force me to censor your speech to make sure you don't try to be funny. So it's up to you if you want to be left in peace."

Aristophanes laughed: "You're right, Eryximachus. I take back what I said. Don't watch me; I'm nervous about my speech. Not that I may say something funny—that would be profitable and native to my Muse—but something ridiculous."

"You can't take a cheap shot at me and get away with it, Aristophanes. Watch what you say—I'll hold you responsible for it. But if I like your speech, I may let you go."

---

[23]This is not arbitrary; in Greek "music" also means "education."

SPEECH OF ARISTOPHANES

"Yes, Eryximachus, I will speak differently from you and Pausanias. You see, I don't think men realize the power of Love. If they did, they'd make him the fine temples, altars, and sacrifices he deserves, not neglect him as they do. Of all the gods Love is the most concerned for our welfare; he is our ally who heals those wounds which, if once cured, would bring mankind perfect happiness. I shall therefore try to initiate you into his power, and you shall go out and teach others.

"First I must teach you about man's nature and its sufferings. Originally our nature was quite different than now. First of all, there were three sexes instead of just two. Besides the male and the female there was a third sex that shared in the traits of both of the others. This was once a real sex, but its form disappeared and only its name—hermaphrodite—now remains, as a term of reproach.

"Originally every man was whole, and shaped like a sphere. His chest and back formed a circle, he had four arms, four legs, and one head with two identical faces facing in opposite ways. As you can imagine, his ears numbered four, his genitals two, and so on for the rest. He walked upright like us and could go in either direction. But whenever he was in a hurry, he would throw his arms and his legs straight out from his body, turn cartwheels like an acrobat, and with eight limbs to support him, spin quickly to wherever he wanted to go.

"Here is the reason for the three sexes and the forms that they took: The male was descended from the Sun, the female from the Earth, and the sex that shared in both came from the Moon, who shares in both the Sun and the Earth. Original man was spherical and his gait circular like his divine parents. These men had terrible strength and mighty ambitions, so that what Homer says of the Giants Ephialtes and Otus[24] is said also of them: they attempted to scale heaven and make an attack on the gods.

"Zeus and the other gods held a conference to decide what to do. It ended in frustration. They couldn't blast men with lightning, as they had the Giants, and eliminate the race—that would also eliminate the honors and sacrifices that they got from them. But they couldn't tolerate this outrage either.

"Zeus thought long, then had an idea: 'I think I've found a scheme,' he said, 'to foil this nefarious plot and still let men live. We'll cut them in half and kill two birds with one stone: They'll be weaker and also more useful to us because there'll be twice as many of them. Let 'em walk on two legs. And if they still don't keep the peace,' he thundered, 'I'll sunder them again, by god, and they can hop around on one leg, like sack-racers!'[25]

"With that Zeus split men the way you cut crab apples for pickling or slice a hard-boiled egg with a hair. As he did, he told Apollo to twist their heads around toward the wound so that man would always have to face his cut side and behave in a more orderly way. Then he told him to heal the wounds. So Apollo turned the heads around and then pulled in the skin from all sides toward what we now call the belly, the way you pull in a purse with its drawstrings. He drew it up tight to make a little mouth in the middle and then tied it off. This is what we now call the navel. Then he propped up the chest with ribs and smoothed out the wrinkles, using a tool like shoemakers use to smooth out wrinkles in leather. But he left a few wrinkles

---

[24] The reference is to *Odyssey* 11.307–20.

[25] Literally: "hop on greased wine skins," a reference to a contest held at a country festival (the "Ascolia"). The contestants apparently had their legs tied together, and the contest was similar to a sack race.

around the belly-button as a remainder of our ancient wound.

"After man's nature had been split, each half longed for its other, and they would come together, throw their arms around each other and entwine because they craved to grow back together again. And since each refused to do anything apart from the other, they began to die of starvation and general indolence. Whenever one half would die, the survivor would seek out another half and entwine with it, whether it happened to be the half of a whole women—this half is what we now call a woman—or of a man. Thus man was becoming extinct.

"But Zeus pitied man and cooked up another scheme: He moved the genitals around to the front. Till then they'd been in the back because they'd been on the outside before, and men had conceived not on each other but on the earth, like grasshoppers. But Zeus put the genitals in front and made men conceive on each other, the male on the female, and again killed two birds with one stone: If a man had intercourse with a woman, she'd conceivè and perpetuate the race; if with a man, they'd at least be repleted, stop, and go back to work to take care of the other needs of life. It was then that man was endowed with mutual Love, the restorer of our original nature who attempts to make one out of two and heal our human condition.

"Thus we're each but the token of a man—cut in half the way parting friends break dice in half so they can recognize each other again by matching the pieces. Each of us is searching for his matching token. Men cut from the common sex—which was then called hermaphrodite—love women. Ladies' men and most seducers come from this sex, as do men-hungry women, the *femmes fatales.* Women who come from the original female are lesbians, more interested in women than in men. Men cut

from the original male pursue males. As boys they love men and enjoy entwining and sleeping with them because they themselves are slices of the male. These are the best young men, by nature the most masculine. Those who say they are shameless lie. They sleep with men not out of shamelessness but out of boldness, manliness, and courage, because they cherish what resembles themselves. Here is my proof: These are the only boys who grow up fit for politics. When such a man comes of age, he becomes a lover of boys, uninterested in marriage and raising a family, which he does only because custom demands it. As one completely devoted to boy love and male companionship, he'd prefer to stay single and live with boys, cherishing his own kind.

"Now when a person, boy lover or anyone else, finds his other half, an amazing love, kinship, and passion seizes them and makes them unwilling to part from each other for even a little while. These are the lovers who stay together for life, though even they couldn't say what it is that they want from each other. No one would think it was sex that bound them in such deep and serious joy. Clearly their soul desires something else, but it can't say what, though it hints at it darkly, in riddles.

"Suppose while two lovers were lying embraced, Hephaestus[26] should appear to them with his tools and ask: 'What is it, O mortals, you want from each other?' And if they were perplexed he would say: 'Is it this—to be joined so closely that you never shall part by night or by day? If so, I'm here to melt you and weld you together, and make you one out of two so you may live all your life together as one and die all your death together in Hades as one rather than two.—Well? Is that what you love? Will that satisfy you?'

---

[26]The blacksmith god.

"We all know that no lover would refuse such an offer. He'd believe he had heard just what he had always desired: to melt and merge with his loved one and become one out of two. This is because our original nature was one and we were whole. Our name for this desire and pursuit after wholeness is 'love.'

"Originally, I say, we were one, but because of our injustice the gods dispersed and resettled us, as the Spartans did the Arcadians. And if we don't behave in an orderly way, we must fear that the gods may cut us in half again and make us run around like relief figures carved on monuments—split down the middle through the nose, like fish fillets. Therefore every man must exhort every other to show reverence toward the gods; that we may avoid such a fate, and with Love as our leader and guide, attain what we truly desire. Let no man, therefore, act contrary to Love—he does so who angers the gods—but let us make up with him and be friends and so find our own proper loved ones, which is a thing that now happens to only a few.

"I hope Eryximachus doesn't make fun of my speech and accuse me of referring to Pausanias and Agathon. Perhaps they are slices of the male and naturally masculine. But I refer to all men and all women when I say that the whole human race will be happy if each of us consummates his love by finding his loved one and returning with him to our original condition. If this is the best condition, then whichever of us has come the closest to it—by finding the loved one who matches his nature—must be the best of us all. And if we would praise the god who is the cause of this boon, we will justly sing paeans to Love, who for the present performs a great service by bringing us together with our own and who holds out for the future the greatest hope that if we show reverence toward the gods, he will heal our ancient wounds, restore our pristine nature, and so make us blessed and happy again.

"That, Eryximachus, is my speech about Love—different from yours. Please don't make fun of it, so we can hear what the others will say. I guess I should say 'the other two,' because only Agathon and Socrates are left."

"Oh, I shan't," Eryximachus assured him (said Aristodemus). "I found it quite pleasant. If I weren't aware that Socrates and Agathon are experts on love, I'd be terribly anxious for them after hearing so many different speeches on the subject. But as it is, I'm quite optimistic."

"You competed very well yourself, Eryximachus," said Socrates (according to Aristodemus). "But if you were in my place, or rather in the place I'll undoubtedly be after Agathon has made his beautiful speech, you'd be as helpless and terrified as I am."

"Socrates," said Agathon, "you're trying to jinx me by making me think my audience has great expectations of me as a clever speaker."

"I saw your proud self-assurance the other day, Agathon, as you mounted the stage with your actors. You looked out over that huge crowd before you presented your play and didn't show the least sign of nervousness. After seeing that, I'd be pretty forgetful if I thought you'd be upset now in front of our little group."

"Do you think I'm so stage-struck that I don't even know a small audience of intellectuals is more frightening to a sensible man than a crowd of fools?"

"I'm sure I'd be making a mistake if I thought you at all unsophisticated, Agathon. I know if you found some people you thought clever, you'd care more about them than about the crowd. But that leaves us out, I'm afraid: we were there the other day and were part of the crowd. But if you found some others who were clever, you'd probably feel ashamed around them if you did something that you thought was shameful. Isn't that so?"

"Yes," replied Agathon (said Aristodemus).

"But you wouldn't be ashamed around the crowd if you did something that you thought was shameful?"

But Phaedrus, Aristodemus said, interrupted them: "Don't answer him, Agathon. If you do, he won't care about anything as long as he has someone to talk to—especially if that someone is handsome. I enjoy listening to Socrates' discussions, but I have to look after the Love speeches and make sure I get one from each of you. So each give a speech and then you can have a discussion."

"You're right, Phaedrus," said Agathon, "—nothing will stop me. There'll be plenty of opportunities later for discussions with Socrates."

SPEECH OF AGATHON

"First I shall seek to tell how to speak and then speak. Of the previous speakers none, it seems, celebrated the god but felicitated man for the goods of which the god is the cause. But what sort is the god who confers all those gifts no one has said. There's but one right way to make any eulogy on any subject: to expound in a speech what sort of cause of what sort of effects the subject of that eulogy is. So with Love: It's right to praise him first as he is, then his gifts.

"Of all the happy gods, I say—may divine Right and Wrath permit me to say!—the happiest is Love, being most beautiful and best. He is most beautiful thus: First, Phaedrus, he is youngest of all. Of this he himself provides fairest proof, by fleeing in fear from old age—a very fast thing, it is clear, since it comes upon us quicker than it ought. Love by nature hates old age and comes not within its reach. But with the young he consorts and ever resorts. And it was truly said of old: Like ever consorts with its like.

"Though agreeing with Phaedrus in much, here I do not. Love's not older than Cronus and Iapetus,[27] but youngest, say I, of the gods, and remains ever so. The old horrors told of the gods by Hesiod and Parmenides, if they speak true, occurred not under Love but Necessity. The gods would never have chained or castrated each other or done those other violent deeds, had Love been with them. Peace and friendship had reigned, as now, since Love has ruled as their king.

"Young then he is, and gentle. It would take a poet like Homer to reveal this god's gentleness. Homer calls Ruin a goddess and gentle—gentle at least in her feet: 'And gentle her feet; for not o'er the glebe/does she glide, but treads on the heads of men.'[28] A beautiful proof this would seem of Ruin's gentleness, who treads not on the rough but the soft. The same proof may suffice to show Love as gentle. For he treads not upon earth nor even on heads—which are not very soft—but in the softest of the soft he treads as well as dwells. In the dispositions and souls of gods and men he founds his abode, though not in all without discrimination; should he find a soul with a rough disposition he leaves; if soft, he settles. And clinging always in all ways to the softest of the soft, he must himself be the gentlest of the gentle.

"Youngest he is then and gentlest, and also flowing of form. He cannot be rigid or stiff, else he could never enwrap in all ways, slipping in and out through every soul unheeded. His flowing and well-proportioned form is evidenced by his gracefulness, a quality universally granted, since eternal strife persists between awkwardness and Love.

"His habit of inhabiting flowers signals the god's fair complexion. He lights not in a soul, a

---

[27]Both Titans or elder gods. Cronus castrated his father Uranus and seized control of the universe, and Zeus in turn deposed Cronus (his father) and chained him in Tartarus. These are the "horrors" mentioned below.
[28]The quotation is from *Iliad* 19. 92–93.

body, or anything bloomless or faded, but in a fragrant and flowering place he settles to stay.

"As for his beauty, that must suffice, though much has been left unsaid. I must now pass on to his virtues. Chiefest of these is justice: Love, in his dealings with gods and men, neither wrongs nor is wronged in return. Passive, he's not passive by force—force may never touch Love—and active, all actively serve Love by consent, and what consenting parties consentingly do—that, says our law, the 'state's sovereign,'[29] is just.

"Besides being just, Love is aboundingly temperate. Temperance admittedly means mastery of desires and pleasures, than which none is stronger than Love. If stronger, the others, weaker, are mastered by Love; if mastered, Love must master, perforce, all desires and pleasures and so be immoderately temperate.

"Love has such courage as 'not even Ares can withstand.'[30] For Ares possesses not Love, but Love Ares—love of Aphrodite, so the story goes—and the possessor is more powerful than the possessed. And he who overpowers the most courageous god must be most courageous of all.

"I've spoken of Love's justice, temperance, and courage; his wisdom remains. I shall repair this liability to the best of my ability. First, to honor my craft as Eryximachus did his, Love is so wise a poet as to make poets of others. Whoever Love touches turns poet, 'be he ever so museless before.'[31] This may pass as proof that Love is a great poet in all production pertaining to the Muse. For what one neither knows nor possesses can be neither given nor taught to another. Touching the creation of all living creatures, who would contest it's the wisdom of Love which causes the birth and the growth of all living things? In the practice of crafts we agree that the man who has this god for a teacher will turn out brilliant and famous, but who the god touches not shall be dark and obscure. Apollo under the guidance of Love invented archery, prophecy, therapy; thus even he must be a disciple of Love. So in music the Muses, Hephaestus in smithing, Athena in weaving, and Zeus in the 'steering of gods and men.' Hence the affairs of the gods were arranged after Love had been born—love of beauty, it's clear, since Love does not pair with the ugly. Before that, as I said at the start, many are the horrors said to have happened amongst them, under Necessity's rule. But since this god came to be, love of beauty has engendered all manner of good among gods and men.

"Thus, Phaedrus, I hold that Love is first fairest and best, then the cause of like effects in others. I'm moved to speak verse and proclaim it is he who makes

> Peace among mortals, the hushed calm on the deep, stillness of winds, and in sorrow sweet sleep.[32]

Love brings us to brotherhood, flings us from otherhood, all unions uniting like this, joining us one to the other, leading our sacrifices, dances, and feasts. All mildness providing, all wildness deriding, toward benevolence beneficent, toward malevolence maleficent, cheerful and good. To the wise he appears, all gods he endears. By the unfortunate he is pursued, the fortunate by him are imbued. Father of delicacy, luxury, effeminacy, the Graces, desire, longing, and need. For the good he's concerned, all evil he's spurned. In longing and pain, in speaking and strain, our pilot, companion, best savior, and friend; brightest adornment of gods and of men, our fairest leader and

[29]Quoted from Alcidamas, a pupil of Gorgias.
[30]From the *Thyestes,* a lost play by Sophocles. Ares is the god of war, in the *Odyssey* the lover of Aphrodite.
[31]An allusion to a line from the *Stheneboea,* a lost play of Euripides.

[32]An echo of *Odyssey* 5.391.

best, whom all ought to follow exalting in fair-sounding song, taking part in that hymn by which he bewitches the mind of gods and of men.

"That is my speech, Phaedrus, dedicated to the god and partaking, in so far as I could make it, equally of playfulness and restrained seriousness."

When Agathon had finished, Aristodemus said they all cheered wildly because the young man's speech had been so appropriate to both himself and the god.

Socrates looked at Eryximachus: "Son of Acumenus," he said, "do you still feel I felt a futile fear before, or was I a prophet when I said Agathon would give an amazing speech and I'd be at a loss for words?"

"I think you prophesied one thing truly: that Agathon would make a fine speech. As for your being at a loss—I doubt it," replied Eryximachus (said Aristodemus).

"My friend," said Socrates, "how could anyone not be at a loss if he had to follow such a fair and many-sided speech as that? Perhaps the earlier parts weren't so amazing, but that ending! Who could have listened to that gorgeous diction and phrasing without being smitten? When I reflected that I wouldn't be able to come anywhere near such gorgeousness, I was tempted to sneak away for shame, but there was no place to go. It reminded me so much of Gorgias[33] that I felt like the man in Homer: I was afraid at the end that Agathon would throw the Gorgon's head of Gorgias, gorged with garrulity, into my speech and turn me to stone with speechlessness. I realized that it had been idiotic of me to agree to take a turn at praising Love and to claim I was an expert when it turns out that I don't even know how to make a eulogy. In my stupidity, you see, I thought all you had to do was tell the truth about the subject and, once that had been established, select the most beautiful facts and arrange them as fittingly as possible. I was actually quite smug about my ability to make a good speech because I thought I knew the right way to do it.

"Now it turns out that isn't the right way at all. The right way, it seems, is to give your subject the most beautiful attributes you can think of, whether it has them or not. If they're false, that doesn't make any difference. It seems the proposal was not to eulogize Love, but to appear to. I assume that's why you exploited every conceivable argument to attribute to Love, saying he is so and so and the cause of such and such: to make him appear as good and as beautiful as possible to people who don't know him—hardly to people who do!—and to make your speeches beautiful and grand.

"But I don't understand that method of making a eulogy, and it was out of ignorance that I agreed to make one. 'My tongue, not my heart, made the promise,'[34] and so I must break it. I won't give a eulogy like that—I couldn't do it. But I am willing to tell the truth, if you'd like, in my own way—not in competition with your speeches, because that would make me look like a fool. So, Phaedrus, see if you can use a plain speech that tells the truth about Love, presented only with such diction and phrasing as occurs to me as I speak."

Phaedrus and the others, Aristodemus said, told Socrates to go ahead and speak in any way he thought proper.

"Now, Phaedrus," Socrates said, "please let me ask Agathon a few little questions so I can start speaking from a point we've agreed on."

---

[33]The most famous sophist and orator of the time. His style, characterized by short, balanced clauses, jingles, and other ear ticklers, is parodied in the ending of Agathon's speech. The pun on the Gorgon below refers to the monster whose look turned men to stone, *Odyssey* 11.634–35.

[34]Euripides, *Hippolytus* 612. This notorious line, parodied by Aristophanes in his comedies, seemed to sanction perjury as long as you had "your finger crossed."

"Go ahead," said Phaedrus. Then, said Aristodemus, Socrates began something like this:

"Agathon, my friend, I thought you opened your speech very well when you said we should show first what Love is like and then his functions. I really liked that opening. Now, since you did such a marvelous job of describing his other qualities, tell me about this one too: Is Love the love *of* something or not? By that I don't mean is he the love of a mother, for instance, or of a father—that would be a ridiculous question.[35] But if I asked, 'Is a father the father *of* someone or not?' I suppose if you wanted to give the right answer, you'd say he's the father of a son or a daughter. Isn't that true?"

"Of course," said Agathon.

"The same for a mother?"

Agathon agreed, said Aristodemus.

"All right," said Socrates, "answer a few more questions so you'll see what I'm after. Suppose I asked: 'What about brother? Does that in itself imply a brother *of* someone?' "

Agathon said it did, said Aristodemus.

"Of a brother or sister, right?"

Agathon agreed, he said.

"Now try to answer my original question: Is Love the love *of* something or not?"

"He certainly is."

"Remember that answer," said Socrates, "—and also what you said the object of Love is. Now tell me, does Love *desire* what he's the love of or not?"

"Certainly," he said.

"Does he *possess* what he desires and loves and still desire and love it, or not?"

"Probably not."

"Probably or necessarily? To me it seems astonishingly clear, Agathon, that desire necessarily lacks what it desires and that without lack there can be no desire. How about you?"

[35] *Eros* is passionate, sexual love; therefore the question is ridiculous when applied to a parent.

"It seems necessary to me too."

"Well said, Agathon. Would someone tall desire to be tall, or someone strong to be strong?"

"That's impossible from what we've agreed on."

"Because he wouldn't lack the qualities he has."

"Right," replied Agathon (said Aristodemus).

"If someone strong wished to be strong, or someone fast to be fast, or someone healthy to be healthy—I'm harping on this so we won't be misled, because a person might think that someone who had these qualities could also desire them. But if you think about it, Agathon, a person must already possess each quality he has whether he wants to or not. And who would desire something like that? So if a man were to say: 'I'm healthy and I also wish to be healthy, I'm rich and I want to be rich, and I desire precisely the things that I have,' we'd reply, 'My friend, you already have health, wealth, and strength, so what you must want is to continue to possess them in the future, since for the present you already have them whether you want them or not. So when you say you desire what you already have, don't you really mean, "I wish to possess in the future the things I have right now"?'—wouldn't he agree that this is so?"

"Yes," said Agathon.

"Then that means he loves what is not yet possessed or available: the preservation and continuance of present things into the future."

"Indeed."

"So our friend and everyone else who desires, desires what is not present or available; and the objects of love and desire are things lacking, not part of oneself, and not possessed."

"True."

"Let's sum up our conclusions then: Love is first the love *of* things, then of things he now lacks. Isn't that so?"

"Yes."

"Now recall what you said in your speech is the object of Love. If you like, I'll recall it for you. I believe you said something like this: The affairs of the gods were arranged through love of beauty; there can be no love of the ugly. Didn't you say something like that?"

"Yes," said Agathon.

"And a most suitable speech it was too. But if that's true, can Love be anything except the love of beauty?"

"No."

"Didn't we agree that he lacks what he loves and doesn't have it?"

"Yes."

"So Love must lack beauty and not have it."

"That follows."

"Very interesting. Do you really maintain that something which lacks beauty and never has it is beautiful?"

"No."

"Then do you still say that Love is beautiful?"

And Agathon said: "I'm afraid I didn't know what I was talking about when I said that."

"But your speech was so beautiful, Agathon. Now one more question: Do you think that whatever is beautiful is also good?"

"Yes, I do," Aristodemus said Agathon replied.

"Therefore if Love lacks beautiful things, and if beautiful things are good, then Love must also lack good things."

"Have it your way, Socrates. I can't contradict you."

"It must be the truth you can't contradict, beloved Agathon," said Socrates—"you could contradict Socrates easily."

SPEECH OF SOCRATES

"I'll leave you alone now, Agathon. The speech I'm about to give is one that I once heard from a Mantinean[36] lady named Diotima, who was very wise

---

[36]Mantinea was a town in the Peloponnese. Diotima is probably an invented character.

in many ways—once when the Athenians were sacrificing to avert the plague she postponed it for ten years—and she taught me all about Love. It is her speech, then, that I shall relate as well as I can all by myself, starting from the points Agathon and I agreed on.

"Agathon, you were right to say that we should expound first what Love is and is like, and then his functions. And the easiest way for me to do that, I think, is to go through the same questions and answers the lady once went through with me. In different words I said much the same thing to her as Agathon said to me just now: that Love is a great god whose object is beauty. And she refuted me with the arguments I just used, pointing out that by my own reasoning Love was neither beautiful nor good.

'Do you mean to say he's ugly and bad?' I said.

'Hush!' she said. 'Do you think whatever isn't beautiful must necessarily be ugly?'

'Absolutely,' I said.

'And whoever isn't wise is ignorant? Or do you see that there's something between wisdom and ignorance?'

'What could that be?'

'Holding right opinions without being able to give reasons for them. You surely don't think something unreasoned is knowledge, do you? And stumbling onto reality isn't ignorance either. So I suppose this thing between knowledge and ignorance ought to be called "right opinion." '

'True,' I said.

'Then don't go forcing something not beautiful to be ugly or something not good to be bad. Just because you admit that Love is neither good nor beautiful, don't think he has to be ugly and bad— he's really between them.'

'But everyone says he's a great god.'

'Everyone ignorant, you mean? Or also people who know?'

'I mean everyone.'

"She laughed and said: 'Socrates, how can everyone say he's a great god when there are people who say he's not even a god?'

'Who says that?' I asked.

'One,' she said, 'is you; another is me.'

'Diotima—how can you say that?'

'Easy. Look, do you call all gods beautiful and happy? Or would you dare to say there's one who isn't?'

'Heavens, no! I'd never say something like that.'

'By happy do you mean those who have good and beautiful things?'

'Certainly,' I said.

'But you just admitted that Love desires good and beautiful things precisely because he lacks them.'

'Yes, I did admit that.'

'Then how can he be a god if he lacks good and beautiful things?'

'He can't, I guess.'

'See? Even you don't believe that Love is a god.'

'Then what is he? A mortal?'

'No.'

'Well, what then?'

'Just as we said before: something between.'

'What can that be, Diotima?'

'A great spirit, Socrates. The whole spirit world, in fact, lies between the mortal and the divine.'

'What is its function?'

'To convey and interpret things from men to gods and from gods to men: requests and sacrifices from men, commands and returns for sacrifices from the gods. Being in the middle, the spirit world fills both worlds and binds the all to itself. Through the spirit world passes divination and the sacred sciences concerned with sacrifices, initiations, spells, all kinds of magic, and wizardry. Gods don't mingle with men; all communication and intercourse between us, sleeping or awake, takes place through the spirit world. A man versed in such things is a spiritual man; one versed in any-

thing else, whether a science or a trade, is merely a technician. There are a vast number and variety of spirits, Socrates, and one of them is Love.'

'Who are his mother and father?' I asked.

'That's a long story,' she said, 'but I'll tell it to you anyway. When Aphrodite was born, the gods held a feast. Among them was Resource, the son of Cunning. They had just finished a lavish meal when Poverty came begging at the door. Now, Resource had gotten drunk on the nectar—wine hadn't been invented yet—gone out into Zeus's garden, and fallen asleep in a stupor. Because of her resourcelessness, Poverty plotted to have a child by Resource, lay with him, and conceived Love. That's why Love became a servant and follower of Aphrodite: He was conceived at her birthday feast and is by nature a lover of beauty, and Aphrodite is very beautiful.

'As the son of Resource and Poverty, this is Love's plight: First, he's always a pauper, and far from being gentle and fair, as the crowd imagines, he's stiff and rough, shoeless and homeless, forever living in squalor and sleeping without a bed—outdoors on the ground, in streets, or on doorsteps. Having his mother's nature, he always cohabits with Need.

'Like his father, however, Love is a schemer after the beautiful and the good, an intrepid hunter full of courage, boldness, and endurance. He's forever hatching plots, and since he's resourceful and hungry for knowledge, he's a confirmed philosopher, a sorcerer and brewer of potions, and a skilled sophist. By nature he's neither mortal nor immortal, but when things go well for him, he'll come to life and flourish in a day, then die, then revive again. That's because of the resourcefulness he inherits from his father. But what his resourcefulness contrives always slips away from him, and he's never rich or poor for long because he's in the middle, between wisdom and ignorance.

'It's like this, you see. No god is a philosopher or desires to be wise. He *is* wise, and if there's anyone else who is wise, he's no philosopher either. So with ignorant people: They aren't philosophers and they don't desire wisdom. That's exactly why ignorance is so hard to deal with: An ignorant person is neither good nor intelligent, yet he's satisfied with himself because he can't desire what he doesn't think he lacks.'

'Then who are the philosophers,' I asked, 'if they're neither the wise nor the ignorant?'

'By now that should be obvious even to a child, Socrates. They're the ones in between, like Love. Wisdom, of course, is extremely beautiful, and since Love loves beauty, he must also love wisdom and be a philosopher, someone halfway between wisdom and ignorance. Love's heredity accounts for that also because his father was wise and resourceful, his mother unwise and resourceless.

'So much for the spirit's nature, dear Socrates. Your notion of Love was just a mistake, and not a very surprising one either. Judging by your statements, I'd say you mistook Love to be Love's object rather than its loving force. I suppose that's why Love appeared so beautiful to you—love's object really is beautiful and delicate, blessed and perfect. But its loving force has an entirely different form, as I've explained.'

'Well, dear lady, you surely are a fine speaker. But if that's what Love is like, what use is he to man?'

'That's the next thing I'll have to try to teach you, Socrates. You now know Love's nature and parentage, and his object is beauty, as you said. Now, what if someone asked us: "Why is Love of beauty, Socrates and Diotima?" or more clearly: "A lover loves beautiful things. Why?" '

'To get them,' I said.

'But that reply demands a further question: What does one gain by acquiring beautiful things?'

'I don't really seem to have an answer to that.'

'Well, suppose he exchanged goodness for beauty and said: "All right, Socrates, a lover loves good things. Why?" '

'To get them,' I said.

'And what does one gain by acquiring good things?'

'I do have an answer to that: happiness.'

'Because having good things is what makes happy people happy, and we don't have to ask, "Why does a person want to be happy?" The answer seems to be final.'

'That's true,' I said.

'Do you think this want and this love are common to all men and everyone always wants to have good things?'

'I think so.'

'Then why don't we call them all lovers? Why some and not others?'

'I'm surprised at that myself,' I said.

'It's not so surprising,' she said. 'You see, we abstract one form of love and give it the name of the whole. The other forms are called by different names.' "

'How do you mean?'

'Well, consider this: You know that creation is a broad thing. It's the sole cause of the emergence of anything from non-existence to existence, so that the production of things by any craft is creation, and all craftsmen are creators.'

'True.'

'And yet you also know they aren't called creators, but have different names. Out of all creativity one part has been abstracted—the creation of music and poetry—and given the name of the whole. These are the only things called creation, and people with that kind of creativity are the only ones called creators.'

'True.'

'Well, the same with Love. Briefly put, all desire for happiness and good things is the prodigious, crafty love in us all. But people given to any other kind of love—such as love of money, sports, or knowledge—aren't called lovers or in love. Only those eagerly bent on pursuing one particular form of love are called lovers from the name of the whole.'

'I'll bet you're right,' I said.

'There's a story going around that love means searching for your own half. But I contend that love is neither of one's half nor of one's whole—unless, of course, it happened to be good—since a man would be willing to cut off his own hand or foot if he thought it was no good. So, my friend, I don't think we each cherish our own, unless you define the good as your own and the bad as the alien. Because what a man loves is nothing other than the good. Or do you think differently?'

'No, by Zeus, I don't.'

'Well, can we simply say that men love the good?'

'Yes.'

'Wait a minute—shouldn't we add that they love to *possess* the good?'

'Yes, we should.'

'And not just to possess it, but to possess it forever?'

'Yes, we should add that too.'

'Love then, to define it succinctly, is the love of possessing the good forever.'

'That's perfectly true,' I said.

'Then what kind of pursuit of the good ought to be called love, and in what kind of activity is this eager intensity displayed? What is Love's function? Can you tell me?'

'If I could, Diotima, I wouldn't marvel at your wisdom and keep coming back to you to learn these very things.'

'Then I'll tell you: Love's function is reproduction in the beautiful, both in body and in soul.'

'Diotima, it would take prophecy to figure that out, and I don't have it.'

'But I have,' she said, 'a way to make this clear to you. You see, Socrates, all men are pregnant in both body and soul, and when we reach a certain age, our nature desires to give birth. But birth isn't possible in the ugly, only in the beautiful. The intercourse of man and woman is procreation. This is a divine thing, for pregnancy and birth are what is deathless in creatures that die. But pregnancy and birth cannot take place in discord, and ugliness is discordant with the divine, whereas beauty is concordant. Therefore Beauty is the goddess of birth. That's why when Pregnancy approaches beauty it feels cheerful and light-hearted; it relaxes and easily gives birth. Near ugliness, however, it frowns in pain, tenses and contracts in avoidance and revulsion, and doesn't give birth but painfully bears a withered, stillborn fetus. Hence the extreme excitement for beauty in someone who's pregnant: it's a release from the terrible pangs of labor. For Love, Socrates, is not the love of beauty, as you think.'

'What is it then?'

'Love of reproduction and procreation in the beautiful.'

'Oh.'

'Absolutely,' she said. 'And why of procreation? Because that's as close as a mortal can come to perpetuity and immortality. And if what we've said is true—that Love is the love of possessing the good *forever*—then we must desire immortality as well as the good. So Love is necessarily the love of immortality as well as of the good.'

"That's what Diotima used to teach me whenever she spoke about Love, and once she asked: 'Socrates, what do you suppose is the cause of all this love and desire? Or haven't you ever noticed the terrible state that birds and animals get into when they desire to reproduce? They fall sick with love, first in regard to mating, then in regard to rearing their young. The weakest creatures will fight the strongest and even die for the sake of the young; they go hungry to feed them, and they make any sacrifice they must. You might think men acted this way out of calculation, but what can be the cause of such behavior in animals? Can you tell me?'

"I said I didn't know.

"She replied: 'How on earth do you expect to become an expert on love if you can't even figure that out?'

'But Diotima, I just said that's exactly why I come to you, because I realize I need a teacher. So tell me the reason for this and for everything else about love.'

'Well, Socrates, if you really believe that the natural object of love is what we've so often said, don't be surprised at the conclusion, which is the same for animals as for men: It's the nature of mortality to strive to exist forever and be immortal. And it can do so only through reproduction, so that a new, different individual always replaces the old. Even the individual, though each creature is said to be the same throughout its life—as a man, for example, is called the same man from youth to old age—nevertheless, he never has the same attributes. He is constantly being renewed, and old attributes are being destroyed. So with hair, flesh, bones, blood, the whole body and even the soul: A man's personality, habits, opinions, desires, pleasures, pains, fears—none stay the same, but new ones come into being as the old die away.

'Knowledge is even stranger: We're never the same even in what we know, not only because new knowledge comes into being and old knowledge passes away, but also because each bit of knowledge suffers the same thing that we do. What we call "practice," or "reviewing," exists because knowledge departs. Forgetting is the departure of knowledge; reviewing preserves knowledge by implanting a fresh, seemingly identical memory to replace a departing one. All mortal creatures are preserved the same way: not by remaining exactly

the same forever like a god, but by each aging and departing individual always leaving behind a new, different one like himself. That's the device, Socrates, by which mortals partake of immortality, physically and otherwise. Immortals have their own way. So don't be surprised if every creature naturally respects its own offspring. It's for the sake of immortality that this love and eagerness accompanies them all.'

"I was amazed and said: 'Wise Diotima, is that really true?'

"Like an accomplished professor she replied: 'Irrefutably. Consider, if you will, human ambition as an illustration of my point. Unless you bear in mind what I've said, you'll be astounded at the irrationality of man's terrible erotic drive "to achieve fame and immortal renown for all future time." A man will risk greater dangers to win fame than to protect his children—he'll squander his wealth, endure hardships, even sacrifice his life. Do you think Alcestis would have died for Admetus, Achilles followed Patroclus into death, or your own king Codrus[37] willingly have died before his time to keep the throne for his family if they hadn't all believed that the memory we still have of their excellence would be immortal? Far from it, Socrates. I hold that all men do all things for the sake of immortal excellence and a glorious reputation like theirs, and the better the man, the more he does. For men love immortality.

'Men pregnant in body go to women to express their love, hoping in that way to provide an immortal memory for themselves and happiness for all future time. But those pregnant in soul—there are some,' she said, 'more pregnant in soul than in

---

[37]An early king of Athens. When Dorians were invading the city an oracle proclaimed that it would fall unless Codrus were killed. He therefore slipped out in disguise, quarreled with some Dorian soldiers and got himself killed, thus saving the city and the throne for his descendants.

body, who conceive and give birth to the things of the mind, such as knowledge and excellence of the type that poets and inventors beget. By far the highest, most beautiful knowledge is called temperance and justice, which concern the administration of states and of private affairs.

'Such a young man, divine and since childhood pregnant in soul, desires to give birth when he comes of age and so goes looking for beauty, since he cannot give birth in the ugly. Being pregnant, he cherishes beautiful bodies, and if he finds one whose soul is also beautiful, graceful, and noble, he rejoices in the combination and teems with resource in conversation about excellence and the qualities and activities appropriate to the good man, and tries to teach this one.

'By attaching himself to a beautiful person and associating with him, he brings forth what he has carried so long, and present and absent he thinks of his friend and brings up his progeny with him, so that such lovers have a far stronger intimacy than ordinary parents because the children they share are more beautiful and also immortal. Everyone would prefer such offspring to human children and, looking at Homer, Hesiod, and the other great poets, envy them the progeny they left behind, who have brought them an eternal memory and immortal fame. Or you may prefer children such as Lycurgus the lawgiver[38] left as saviors of Sparta and of practically all of Greece. At Athens, Solon is also honored for begetting the laws, as are countless other men elsewhere in Greece and in foreign countries, for causing beautiful works to appear by giving birth to every kind of excellence. Some of these men are honored like gods for their progeny, but no one has ever been so honored for human children.

---

[38]The traditional founder of the Spartan constitution and framer of her laws. Solon, below, was an early lawgiver of Athens and a founder of her democracy.

'So far, Socrates, the mysteries have been like a path which, if followed correctly, leads to the final revelations. Perhaps even you may be initiated this far. The rest, I'm afraid, will be completely beyond you. Still, I'll reveal it—I won't lack enthusiasm. So try to follow, if you can.

'A man who would approach love properly must begin as a child and go to beautiful bodies and first, if his guide directs him properly, love one beautiful body and in it bring forth beautiful words and ideas; next he must notice that the beauty of any one body is akin to that of all others, so that if one must pursue beauty of form, it is absurd not to regard the beauty of all bodies as one and the same. He has now become a lover of all beautiful bodies; his violent excitement for one abates, and he begins to despise it as petty. The next step is to honor spiritual beauty above physical beauty, so that if he finds a man good in soul without a blossoming body, he'll be satisfied, love and care for him, and, by giving birth to the kind of discussions that improve a young man, be forced to observe the beauty of laws and customs, to see once again that all beauty is kindred and so conclude that physical beauty is only a paltry thing.

'After customs he must be led to knowledge and see its beauty also, so that, having by now looked upon much beauty, he'll no longer admire a particular manifestation of it—fawning on an individual person, sweetheart, or custom like a worthless, small-minded slave—but rather, absorbed in the contemplation of a vast sea of beauty, give birth to sublime words and sentiments in the unstinting practice of philosophy until, having thus grown in power, he may glimpse a unique knowledge—of a beauty I shall now describe. So try to pay attention, as well as you possibly can.

'A man brought so far in love through the contemplation of beautiful things viewed in their proper sequence will, toward the end of his education, suddenly see something by nature astonishingly beautiful. This, Socrates, is the goal of all his previous struggles. First, it always *is,* and neither comes into being and passes away nor increases and declines; secondly, it is not beautiful in part, ugly in part, or now the one, now the other; not beautiful compared to this, ugly compared to that, nor yet beautiful here but ugly there, so as to appear beautiful to some but ugly to others. Its beauty does not give the illusion of being the beauty of a face, hands, or of anything the body partakes of, or of speech or a knowledge; nor is it *in* something else, as in an animal, the earth, the sky, or in any other thing. It is instead the beautiful itself as it always *is,* one of a kind, by itself with itself; and all other beautiful things partake of that beautiful itself in such a way that their own coming to be and passing away neither increases it, diminishes it, nor affects it in any way.

'When, by proper boy love, a man ascends from things here and begins to glimpse the beautiful over there, he has almost reached the final goal. This is the proper way to go or be led to Love: to begin from beautiful things and ever climb, as on a ladder, from one beautiful body to two and from two to all, from bodies to beautiful customs, from customs to beautiful knowledge, and from knowledge finally to reach that knowledge which is none other than the revelation of the beautiful itself, and so recognize at last what beauty really is.'

'That, dear Socrates,' said the Mantinean lady, 'is the time, if ever there is one, when life is worth living—spent in contemplating the beautiful itself. If you should ever see that, Socrates, it won't seem to you to compare with the beauty of gold or of clothing or of boys and young men, whose beauty now so smites you—and others too—that you'd abstain from food and drink if you could and spend all your time watching the boys and consorting only with them. What then do you think would happen if a man could see pure beauty itself, clean and undefiled; if he caught a glimpse of it as it is, not contaminated by human flesh or color or any other corruptible trash, but simple, divine beauty itself? Do you think life would be worthless then, when a man could look over there with the proper faculty[39] and contemplate and consort with the beautiful? Don't you realize that it's only then, when he sees the beautiful itself with the faculty able to see it, that a man will bear not phantoms of excellence—since it's no phantom he clings to—but true excellence, because he clings to the truth? That in bearing and rearing true excellence this man, if any, will become god-beloved and immortal?'

"That, Phaedrus and gentlemen, is what Diotima said, and I believe her. And because I believe her, I try to convince others that our human nature could not easily find a better partner than Love to help us attain that possession. Therefore I say that all men should honor Love, as I honor him and distinctively practice his ways, and I exhort others to do so, and now as always I glorify Love's power and courage with all the strength that I have.

"That is my speech, Phaedrus. Accept it, if you will, as a proper eulogy to Love. If not, then call it whatever you like."

When Socrates had finished, said Aristodemus, they all congratulated him except Aristophanes, who was trying to say something about the reference to his "story." Suddenly there was a terrific racket at the outside door. He said it sounded like revelers, and they could hear a flute girl playing. Agathon told the boys to go see who it was: "If it's some of our friends, let them in. If not, say the party is over and we're going to bed."

Moments later, said Aristodemus, they heard Alcibiades shouting drunkenly in the yard:

---

[39]I.e., reason or mind. Cf. *Phaedrus* 247c (in a similar context): "Visible only to the soul's pilot, mind."

"Where's Agathon? Take me to Agathon!" The flute girl and some others half-carried him in. There he stood in the doorway with a bushy wreath of violets and ivy on his head, and lots of ribbons. "Joy, gentlemen!" he cried. "Can I join the party roaring drunk, or should we just do what we came for—wreathe Agathon—and go? I couldn't come last night, you know, but I'm here now, with ribbons on my head to take from my head and put on the wisest and beautifullest head in town, if I may say so, like this. Will you laugh at me because I'm drunk? Well, I don't care—I know I'm telling the truth. So out with it: Can I join you on these terms? Will you drink with me or not?"

They all cheered, Aristodemus said, and told Alcibiades to come in and take a seat, and Agathon invited him in too. So in he came, led by his crew. He was undoing the ribbons as he entered and didn't notice Socrates because the ribbons were in front of his eyes. He sat down right next to Agathon, between him and Socrates, who had moved over when he saw him. He gave Agathon a hug and tied the ribbons on his head.

"Boys," said Agathon, "take off Alcibiades' shoes so he may recline as the third on this couch."

"Please do," said Alcibiades. "But who's the third?" As he spoke he turned around and saw Socrates. Up he leapt, exclaiming, "Heracles! What's this? Socrates! What are you doing here? You were lurking here to ambush me, popping up as usual where I least expected you. Why are *you* here? And why are you *here,* next to Agathon? You never sit by Aristophanes or some other clown, do you? Oh no, leave it to you to finagle a seat next to the handsomest man in the house!"

"Please protect me, Agathon," said Socrates. "This fellow's love's no trifling matter. From the moment I first fell in love with him I haven't been able to even look at a handsome man without him flying into a jealous rage. He makes a dreadful scene and insults me and can hardly keep his hands off me. So see that he doesn't do anything now; reconcile us, and if he starts to get violent, protect me—I'm terrified of his insane devotion."

"There's no reconciliation between you and me, Socrates," said Alcibiades. "I'll get even with you later. Now give me some of those ribbons, Agathon. I'm going to wreathe this amazing head too, so he can't say I wreathed you but not him, even though he beats everyone at words all the time, and not just the day before yesterday like you." With that he took some of the ribbons and wreathed Socrates, then leaned back again.

Aristodemus said Alcibiades settled down and said: "Gentlemen, you look sober to me. That's no way to be—you should drink! That was our agreement when you let me in. So as master of ceremonies I choose—myself, till you catch up. Agathon, have them bring me something big to drink out of—no, never mind. Boy, bring me that wine cooler over there!" (He saw that it held almost half a gallon.) He had it filled, drained it, then told the boy to fill it again for Socrates. As it was being filled, he said: "These tricks don't get me anywhere with Socrates, gentlemen. No matter how much you tell him to drink, he drinks it and doesn't even get drunk."

The cooler was refilled, and Socrates drained it. Then, said Aristodemus, Eryximachus spoke up: "Alcibiades, is this any way to carry on, simply drinking like parched travelers with no singing or talking over our cups?"

"Eryximachus, best son of the best and soberest father—joy!"

"Joy," said Eryximachus. "How shall we do it?"

"However you say. We have to listen to you because 'One doctor is worth a host of others.'[40] So give us your prescription."

---

[40]The quotation is from *Iliad* 11.514.

"All right, here it is. Before you came, we resolved that we each would give a speech from left to right—as beautiful as we could make them—in praise of Love. The rest of us have spoken. Now since you've taken a drink but given no speech, it's only fair for you to give one too. Then set Socrates any topic you choose; he may do the same for the man on his left, and so on."

"Oh, that's beautiful, Eryximachus—to make a drunk man compete with sober ones so he doesn't have a chance. You don't believe Socrates, do you? Everything's just the opposite of what he says—if I tried to praise anyone else, man or god, with him around he wouldn't keep his hands off me."

"Why don't you be quiet?" said Socrates.

"No, by Poseidon—not another word about it. I won't praise anyone else as long as you're here."

"Well, go ahead then and praise Socrates if you wish."

"Do you mean it, Eryximachus? Can I attack him right here and get even with him in front of you all?"

"Hold on!" cried Socrates. "What have you got up your sleeve? Are you planning to praise me to make me look ridiculous, or what?"

"I'm planning to tell the truth," said Alcibiades. "Is that all right with you?"

"Of course," Socrates replied (said Aristodemus). "I'll encourage you to do that."

"All right then," Alcibiades said. "Let's do it like this. If I say anything that isn't true, break right in and call me a liar. Because I won't tell a lie on purpose. But don't be surprised if I get my story mixed up. Someone in my condition can hardly be resourceful enough to list your peculiarities in logical order."

SPEECH OF ALCIBIADES

"Gentlemen, I shall try to praise Socrates in similes. He'll probably think I'm doing it to make him look ridiculous, but my purpose is truth, not ridicule. I claim that Socrates is just like those carved Silenuses[41] you see standing in wood carvers' shops holding flutes and shepherd's pipes. They're hollow, and when you open them, you find little statues of the gods inside. I also claim he's like the satyr Marsyas. Even you will hardly deny that you *look* like a satyr, Socrates. But you're like them in other ways too. You're insolent. Isn't that so?—if you try to deny it, I'll produce witnesses. But you don't play the flute, you say? Ah, you do something much more amazing. Marsyas used instruments to bewitch men with the magic of his mouth. Even today when his tunes are played—I call the tunes Olympus[42] played Marsyas's because he was his teacher—his tunes, whether played by an expert or some cheap flute girl, are the only ones that can make men possessed and show who's divine enough to be initiated into the sacred mysteries. But you beat Marsyas, Socrates; you do the same thing with the naked voice alone, unaided by instruments. The most eloquent speakers on the most interesting topics leave us young fellows cold. But when we hear your discussions—either in person or second-hand—even if the speaker's not worth a damn—all of us, men, women, and children, are stricken and possessed.

"Gentlemen, if I wasn't afraid of sounding drunk, I'd take an oath and confess what I've suffered, and still do suffer, whenever this one speaks.

---

[41]Bestial spirits of the woods who spent their lives in lechery and debauchery. They are portrayed on vases as bald, bearded old men with flat faces, pug noses, and enormous erections. They sometimes have horses' ears and often chase nymphs. But they also have great wisdom, and Silenus (singular) was the teacher of the god Dionysus, sort of a mythological Falstaff. Socrates is often likened to Silenus for both his ugliness and wisdom, and his portraits show a great similarity to pictures of Silenuses. Satyrs were similar to Silenuses. Marsyas was supposed to have invented the flute. He challenged Apollo to a flute-playing contest, lost, and for his insolence was skinned alive.

[42]A Phrygian musician.

Whenever I hear him, my heart jumps higher than a Corybant,[43] tears stream down my cheeks, and I see that hordes of others suffer the same thing. When I used to listen to Pericles or other great speakers, I'd say to myself, 'This is a great speaker.' But I never went through anything like this: My soul didn't riot and accuse me of being a slave. But old Marsyas here has often gotten me into such a state that I felt life wasn't worth living if I kept on as I am. You can't say that's a lie either, Socrates. Why, even now if I cared to lend him my ear I know I'd never hold out—I'd still suffer the same thing. He forces me to admit that even though I'm lacking myself, I still neglect my own self and try to run the government. So I have to hold my ears and run away from him like Odysseus from the Sirens[44]—else I'd sit right down by him and never get away until I'd grown old and gray.

"And this one's made me suffer what no one would ever think I could: shame. He's the only one who's ever made me feel ashamed. I know I can't contradict him and say I shouldn't do what he says, but when I leave him, I'm seduced by my popularity with the crowd. So I sneak away and avoid him, and when I do see him, I'm ashamed for ignoring the things we've agreed on. Sometimes I almost wish he were dead, but if that happened, I know I'd be more miserable than ever. I just don't know what to do about him.

"Those are the symptoms that I and many others have suffered from this satyr's piping. Now I'll show how else he's like a satyr and what amazing powers he has. Not one of you knows him, but I'll expose him now that I've begun. You see Socrates as lusting after beautiful young men and always hanging around with them, starry-eyed and dazzled, ignorant of everything and not knowing a

thing. Isn't that a regular satyr act? Damn right it is. But that's just an exterior he wraps around himself like a hollowed-out Silenus. Inside, gentlemen of the symposium, opened up, you can't imagine how full of temperance he is. He doesn't care if someone's handsome—it's inconceivable how he despises beauty—or rich, or has any of the honors the crowd adores. I swear he thinks that's all worthless and we're nothing, and so he spends his life acting ignorant and playing games with people. But when he's serious and opened up—I'll bet no one's ever seen the statues inside him. But I saw them once, and they seemed to me so golden and divine, so amazing and beautiful that—to put it bluntly—I had to do whatever Socrates said.

"I thought he was serious about my beauty, and I considered that a fantastic stroke of luck because all I'd have to do was favor him to learn everything he knew. You know how fantastically conceited I was about my beauty. So one day I sent my escort[45] home and managed to get alone with this one for the first time—I'd never been alone with him before. Now, gentlemen, I must tell you the whole truth, so pay attention—and if I tell a lie, Socrates, you denounce me. Well, I was *tête-à-tête* with him and thrilled, because I expected him to speak with me like a lover to his loved one. Nothing happened. He spent the day with me, talked with me the way he always did, and then went home.

"After that I invited him to train with me, to see if I could get anywhere that way. And he did train and even wrestle with me many times, with no one else around. What can I say? Nothing came of it.

"When that scheme failed, I decided to drop the subtle approach and make a direct attack and find out what was going on. So I invited him to dinner for two, like some lover plotting against his loved one. At first he turned me down, but finally

---

[43]Corybants were wild religious celebrants who, like dervishes, danced themselves into a state of mystical ecstasy and possession.

[44]The scene referred to is found in *Odyssey* 12.165–200.

[45]Greek boys normally did not go out unescorted; their escorts are the "slaves" that Pausanias referred to in 183c.

he gave in. The first time he came, he ate and wanted to go home. I was ashamed and let him go. But I tried the same scheme again, and this time I kept him talking after dinner until far into the night. Then when he wanted to leave, I said it was too late and insisted that he stay. So he slept in the couch next to mine—the one he'd reclined on at dinner—and there was no one in the room but us.

"So far this has been a nice story that you could tell to anyone. But you'd never hear the rest if it wasn't for two things: first, the old saying—'wine and children tell the truth'; second, I think it'd clearly be wrong for someone making a eulogy to obscure such a brilliant and arrogant deed as this. Besides, I'm like a man suffering from snakebite. They say a man in that condition will only talk about it to others who've been bitten, because they're the only ones who'll understand and forgive him if his pain makes him talk and act wild. But I've been bitten by something more painful than a snake in the most sensitive spot—in the heart or soul or whatever you want to call it—by the words of philosophy, which are sharper than a snake's tooth when they sink in the soul of a decent young man, and they make him talk and act wild. Now here I see Phaedruses, Agathons, Eryximachuses, Pausaniases, Aristophaneses, Aristodemuses, and Socrates himself; you've all been stung by the madness and frenzy of philosophy, so you can hear the rest. You'll forgive what happened then and what's said now. But you slaves and anyone else who's rude and uninitiated—block your ears with heavy gates.

"Well, gentlemen, when the lights were out and the boys had left I decided not to beat around the bush but tell him exactly what I thought. So I nudged him and said:

'Socrates, are you asleep?'

'Not yet,' he said.

'Do you know what?'

'No, what?'

'I think you're the only man worthy of being my lover, but you seem shy about bringing it up. Here's how I feel about it: I think I'd be silly not to favor you in this or in anything else you might need, like property of mine or my friends. Nothing is more valuable to me than to become as good a man as I can, and I'm sure I'll never find a better partner to help me than you. And I'd feel much more ashamed around intelligent people if I didn't favor a man like you than I would with the ignorant mob if I did.'

"He didn't exactly lose control. He played dumb and answered in his usual way: 'You *are* a clever rascal, Alcibiades, if what you say is true, and I have the power to make you a better man. You must see some tremendous beauty in me totally different from your own good looks. If you're trying to get some of it by trading beauty for beauty, then you're planning to cheat me royally by exchanging counterfeit beauty for genuine, like Diomedes, who traded bronze armor for armor of gold.[46] But sly as you are, you'd better examine me closer to make sure I don't deceive you. The eye of the mind, you know, only begins to see sharply when the eyes in the head start to dim. And you're still a long way from that.'

'Well, now you know how I feel about it, anyhow. But you decide what you think is best for us both.'

'Well said,' he said. 'In the future we'll deliberate and do whatever we think best both in this and in everything else.'

"I'd shot my sharpest arrows in this skirmish, and I thought I'd wounded him. So without permitting the defendant another word, I got up, threw my coat over him (it was winter), climbed under his old cloak, flung my arms around this ut-

---

[46]An allusion to *Iliad* 6.234–36.

terly divine and amazing man and slept with him the whole night long.[47] You can't say that's a lie either, Socrates. At that point the defendant treated me with such insolence, disdain, and contempt that he spurned my beauty—the thing I valued the most, gentlemen of the jury! (I call you that because you must be the judges of Socrates' arrogance.) By all the gods and goddesses, gentlemen, I swear that when I got up the next morning after having slept with Socrates, nothing more had happened than if I'd slept with my father or an older brother.

"Can you imagine my state of mind after that, torn between humiliation at being rejected and admiration for this one's nature, temperance, and courage? He knew more and had more backbone than anyone I'd ever met, so I couldn't get angry and risk losing him, but I couldn't figure out a way to bind him to me either. I knew he'd turn down money as easy as Ajax turned cold steel, and he'd dodged the one trap I thought could hold him. So I was baffled and ran around like a slave, enslaved to this one as no one's ever been enslaved before.

"All that happened before the Potidaean campaign,[48] where we were tentmates together. There Socrates showed he could endure hardships not only better than me but better than everyone in the whole army. When we'd be cut off somewhere and had to go hungry—which often happens on campaigns—no one came near him in endurance, and at feasts no one enjoyed himself as much as this one without even drinking wine. But when we made him drink, he'd drink us all under the table. The most amazing thing is that no one's ever seen him drunk. I bet we'll soon have proof of that tonight.

"As for enduring cold—winters in Potidaea are awful—Socrates was amazing. Once it was hideously cold; everything was frozen solid, and everyone either stayed inside, or if he had to go out, he bundled up fantastically and put on shoes and wrapped his feet in felt and sheepskin. But this one walked around in the same old cloak he always wore, and he waded barefoot through the ice easier than the others did with shoes on, and the soldiers began to suspect him of showing contempt for them.

"So much for that. But 'what a feat this mighty man dared and wrought'[49] on that campaign—and one worth hearing too. He fell into thought one morning trying to figure something out, and when it didn't come, he didn't give up but stood there searching for it. It got to be noon; people began to notice and shake their heads in amazement and say to each other: 'Socrates has been standing since

---

[47]Athenian legal language used a special pronoun to refer to one's adversary in court, which Alcibiades applies to Socrates. Here the reader expects Alcibiades to use a stock courtroom phrase: "this utterly vile and despicable scoundrel." Instead he says: "this utterly divine and amazing man," a contrary-to-expectation joke (like "once seen, never—remembered"). The legal metaphor is made explicit below.

Alcibiades' formal charge against Socrates is *hubris,* which had a wide range of meaning in Greek: presumption, arrogance, violence, etc. It has been translated throughout as "insolence." Its basic idea is that of encroaching upon the rights and privileges of another, whether of a man, a god, or even a natural force (so in 188a-b Eryximachus can say that "insolent Love" causes disorder in the seasons and in the natural world). *Hubris* is not necessarily moral; it is a mere mechanical force, like a law of nature. It throws the world out of balance, but balance will be restored, mechanically, by another law of nature, *dike* ("justice"). In a narrower sense, *hubris* was a legal term for "assault and battery" or for contempt for another's person.

[48]At the beginning of the Peloponnesian war, 432–430 B.C. Potidaea is in the Chalcidice. The battle mentioned below (in d), where Alcibiades distinguished himself, occurred during the siege of Potidaea.

[49]The quotation is from *Odyssey* 4.242.

morning, reflecting.'[50] Finally in the evening after supper some of the Ionians brought their beds outside, partly to sleep in the cool breeze—it was summer then—and partly to watch Socrates to see if he'd stand there all night. And he did, till dawn. Then he said a prayer to the rising sun and walked away.

"And in battle—you've got to give him his due there too. When we fought the one where the generals awarded me the medal for bravery, it was this one who saved me. I'd been wounded, but he didn't abandon me—he rescued both me and my armor. You know I told the generals to give the medal to you, Socrates—you can't criticize me there or say I lied. But they looked at my rank and wanted to give it to me, and you were even more enthusiastic than the generals and insisted that I get it instead of you.

"And you should have seen him the time the army was retreating from Delium.[51] He was in the infantry, but I had a horse. The rest of our troops had been scattered, and this one was retreating with Laches. I happened to be nearby and saw them, told them to buck up, and said I wouldn't desert them. This time I could watch Socrates better than at Potidaea—I was on a horse and less scared. The first thing I noticed was how much better Socrates kept his head than Laches did. Then I thought of your line from the *Clouds*, Aristophanes. He walked there just like he does here in Athens, 'strutting along like a peacock, rolling his eyes around.'[52] He gave both friend and foe the same level look, and you could see from a distance that here was a man who'd defend himself if someone tried to touch him. That's why they

both got away: the enemy almost never bother men like that; they go after the ones that run away in panic.

"There are many other amazing things you could say in praise of Socrates, but the most amazing is his absolute uniqueness: He's not like anyone, living or dead. To Achilles you could compare Brasidas[53] and other generals, Pericles to orators like Nestor and Antenor, and everyone to somebody else. But this one's so strange, both himself and his speech, that you could search and search and never find anyone like him, ancient or modern, unless of course you compared him to what I've compared him to—not to a man but to satyrs and Silenuses, both him and his discussions.

"Which brings up something I've completely overlooked: Socrates' discussions are also like those Silenuses that open up. The first time you hear them they sound completely ridiculous. He wraps them up in words and phrases that remind you of the hide of some insolent old satyr. He talks about mules and saddles and blacksmiths and shoemakers and tanners, and he always seems to say the same things in the same way, so that anyone thoughtless or inexperienced would laugh himself sick. But once you see them open and get inside them, you'll find that they are the only words that make any sense—they're divine and full of statues of excellence, and they concern everything a man ought to consider if he wants to become perfectly good.

"That, gentlemen, is my speech in praise of Socrates, mixed with my complaints about his insolence toward me. And I'm not the only one he's treated like that: He's also deceived Charmides, Glaucon's son, Euthydemus, the son of Diocles, and many others, by pretending to be their lover and then turning out to be their loved one instead.

---

[50]A funny-sounding word in Attic. In the *Clouds* Aristophanes named Socrates' school the "Reflectory."

[51]A fortification in Boeotia, captured by the Athenians in 424 B.C. The Thebians attacked and defeated them as they were withdrawing their main army.

[52]*Clouds* 362.

[53]A Spartan general. Nestor (a Greek) and Antenor (a Trojan) were old and respected advisors in the *Iliad*.

So I warn you, Agathon, don't let this one deceive you. Learn from our experiences and beware, so you don't learn like the fool in the proverb—by suffering."

When Alcibiades had finished, Aristodemus said they all laughed at his frankness because he still seemed to be devoted to Socrates.

Socrates, he said, responded: "You seem sober to me, Alcibiades. Otherwise you'd never have been able to turn your speech back on itself so deftly and hide your real motive for saying everything you did, tucking it in like an afterthought at the very end as though your whole speech did not exist for the sole purpose of breaking up Agathon and me, because you think I should love only you and Agathon should be loved by only you. But you didn't fool us—we saw through your little satyr play.[54] Agathon, my dear, let's not let him have his way; let's fix it so no one can ever break us up."

"I think you're right, Socrates," Agathon replied (said Aristodemus). "I infer from where he's sitting that he's trying to come between us. But he won't get away with it; I'm coming over to sit by you."

"Right," said Socrates. "Come over here and sit on the other side of me."

"O Zeus!" cried Alcibiades. "Witness what this one makes me suffer. He thinks he has to beat me in everything. But if I can't get my way in this, you old fox, at least let Agathon sit between us."

"Impossible," said Socrates. "You praised me, and now I have to praise the man on my right. If Agathon were to sit on your right, he'd have to praise me before I could praise him. No, let him go, you rascal, and don't be jealous if I praise the young man. The truth is that I want to very much."

"Oh!" said Agathon. "You can't keep me here, Alcibiades. I'm moving. There's nothing I'd like better than have Socrates praise me."

"It's the same old story," said Alcibiades. "With Socrates around no one else has a chance at the handsome young men. See how easily he found an excuse to get Agathon to sit by him."

Agathon got up to move. Suddenly a mob of revelers came to the door, found it left open by someone in leaving, and came in and sat down with the rest. The place was filled with uproar and confusion and everyone was forced to guzzle wine without order or restraint.

Aristodemus said that Eryximachus and Phaedrus and some others got up and left, and he fell asleep and slept a long time because the nights were long at that time of year. He woke up toward morning when the roosters were already crowing, and he saw that the others were either asleep or had left and that only Agathon, Aristophanes, and Socrates were awake and drinking wine from a large cup that they passed from left to right. Socrates was having a discussion with them. Aristodemus said he couldn't remember much of it—he had missed the beginning and kept dozing off through the rest—but the main point Socrates was trying to force them to accept was that the writing of both tragedy and comedy is the job of the same man, and a skilled tragedian also knows how to write comedies. They were being forced to agree, though they weren't following very well and kept nodding off, and first Aristophanes fell asleep and then, when it was fully light, Agathon fell asleep too.

Socrates, having put the two poets to sleep, got up and left, and Aristodemus said he followed him, as was his habit. He said Socrates went to the Lyceum and took a bath, spent the day as he spent every other, and towards evening, he said, went home to bed.

---

[54]A coarse burlesque presented as the fourth play after a tragic trilogy.

chapter four

Aristotle

"It is from a feeling of wonder that men start now, and did start in the earliest times, to practice philosophy," wrote Aristotle (384–322 B.C.E), Greek philosopher, scientist, and most famous student of Plato. However, in contrast to his teacher, who stood in awe of transcendent Forms as constituting ultimate reality and as being the only entities that can be known,[1] Aristotle was riveted by the intricate order and harmony of the natural world, which for him was every bit as real as Plato's Forms, if not more so. In fact, Aristotle was so convinced of the genuine reality of this world and of our ability to *know* it that he devoted himself to the enormous task of demonstrating that very fact. The result was a corpus of philosophical and scientific writings of unprecedented breadth that systematically investigated every branch of human knowledge developed in his time.

Aristotle was born north of Greece at Stagira, in Macedonia, the son of a physician to the king. At age seventeen he went to Athens to study at Plato's Academy. He remained there, first as a student and later as a teacher, for about twenty years, until Plato's death in 347 B.C.E. Aristotle's exalted status in the Academy might have designated him to succeed Plato, but the increasing divergence of his philosophical convictions from Plato's teaching rendered that unfeasible. Instead, Aristotle traveled to Assos, in Asia Minor, and later to Lesbos, where with a new associate, Theophrastus,[2] he launched extensive investigations in natural science. In 345 B.C.E., Aristotle returned to Macedonia and became tutor to the king's son, Alexander, later known as Alexander the Great. When Alexander became king in 335 B.C.E., Aristotle returned to Athens, where Platonism flourished as the dominant teaching. He therefore established his own school, the Lyceum.[3]

Although Aristotle rejected Plato's core teaching concerning the Forms, he nevertheless shared Plato's conviction that we can only acquire knowledge of that which is certain and unchanging. Interestingly, Aristotle also acknowledged with Plato that the world of phenomena is a realm of constant change; however, Aristotle considered it most significant that these changes happen "invariably or for the most part . . . in a

Aristotle. *Nicomachaean Ethics.* From *The Complete Works of Aristotle: The Revised Oxford Translation*, edited by Jonathan Barnes. Copyright © 1984 by Princeton University Press. Reprinted by permission of Princeton University Press.

given way."[4] Changes in the natural world, in other words, are ordered and patterned, and these patterns appear to be regular and enduring. Aristotle concluded that there are therefore forms[5] immanent in nature and that these forms are the proper objects of knowledge.

The study of nature therefore remained Aristotle's primary philosophical concern. He established early that to pursue knowledge of natural forms he needed first a proper logical method for apprehending them. Aristotle deemed the dialectical method of Socrates and Plato inappropriate for this purpose, for dialectic ultimately only tests the internal consistency of sets of opinions. He therefore devised an *analytical* logic to test specifically the validity of claims about the world, not only on the basis of their logical consistency but also, more importantly, on the basis of their correspondence to experience and observation. The four works that comprise Aristotle's *Organon* ("instrument")[6] analyze language and its structure in order to reveal the precise meaning, functions, and relations of the words we use and of the statements we form with words. For instance, the categories are ten ways to classify words; according to Aristotle, individual words signify substance, quantity, quality, relation, place, time, situation, condition, action, or passion.[7] Words, however, do not in and of themselves make claims about the world or express truth or falsehood; only when we combine words to form statements or *propositions* about the world do we make claims that may be true or false. Demonstrative propositions can be tested for their validity on the basis of their agreement or disagreement with observed phenomena and so are the proper subjects of Aristotle's analytic. In *Prior Analytics*, Aristotle presents the syllogistic form of argument as the preeminent analytic method, for it never leads from true premises to false conclusions—the ultimate criterion of validity.[8]

Although Aristotle conceived of analytical logic as a means of achieving a higher degree of certainty in philosophical and scientific inquiry, inasmuch as it both constructs and tests claims about the actual world and experience, he nevertheless believed that there are domains of human experience in which we are likely to achieve a lesser degree of certainty than in others—in ethics, for instance. He writes in Book 1 of *Nicomachean Ethics* (the text presented here), "Our treatment will be adequate if it has as much clearness as the subject matter admits of; for precision is not to be sought for alike in all discussions. . . . Now fine and just actions, which political science investigates, exhibit much variety and fluctuation."[9] Accordingly, Aristotle adds, the educated person seeks "precision in each class of things just so far as the nature of the subject admits."[10]

Aristotle observed that human actions vary and fluctuate, but he also believed that, as with other phenomena of nature, these variations occur for the most part according to patterns. Ethics, the study of "fine and just actions," therefore can be pursued to some degree as a science, but Aristotle stresses that it is by no means an entirely theoretical discipline. On the contrary, ethics is a distinctively practical science. That is, Aristotle conceived of ethics as a discipline in which generalizations can be made, but in which these generalizations themselves only hold for the most part; this is because he believed that every single human action, though partly explicable in terms of general patterns of human behavior, must also always be explained in terms of the particular motivations of the agent in his or her particular circumstance. But Aristotle also emphasized that ethics is a practical science inasmuch as its objective is not knowledge for its own sake but, rather, knowledge for the sake of improving our lives. Accordingly, for Aristotle, ethics does not prescribe a set of general, universal rules of "fine and just" moral action. Rather, it provides guidance as to how we develop skills in applying general knowledge of virtue to particular, concrete cases of moral action.

Ethics, specifically, is concerned with the practical *good* for human beings. Aristotle begins in *Nicomachean Ethics* by acknowledging that people have many different opinions about what counts as good, but he believes that we can nevertheless gain insight into what human beings generally, perhaps even universally, agree upon as good. Aristotle is not concerned here with compiling an inventory of things people generally consider to be good—for he thinks it is rather easy to see that nearly everyone agrees that it is good to experience pleasure, health, wealth, honor, and friendship, for instance. Rather, Aristotle wants to know which, if any, of these goods is more desirable than all the others—ethics, for Aristotle, is the search for the *highest* good. In other words, Aristotle recognizes that even the goods we may universally count as good are not pursued purely for their own sake, but rather as a means to achieving other goods. For example, most of us desire health not just for the sake of being healthy but so that we can freely pursue activities that we enjoy.

What Aristotle is after is a good that can be said to be pursued, not as a means to some further good, but as an end in itself. He concludes that this highest end is *eudaimonia*, which is sometimes translated as "happiness," but which is perhaps better rendered as "flourishing." Aristotle believes that everyone would agree that no one pursues happiness or flourishing as a means to some further end, but that we pursue all other goods as a means of flourishing. Flourishing, then, is the highest good toward which all human actions ultimately aim. Moreover, Aristotle conceives of flourishing itself as an *activity*, not as a state or condition in which one finds oneself nor as a theoretical ideal, such as Plato's Form of the Good. Aristotle's highest good is a way of conducting one's life.

But what *is* flourishing? What kind of activity is it? Aristotle reasons that if flourishing is the highest end and aim of all human activity, then it must be indexed to whatever is the distinctive human excellence (*aretê*); that is, flourishing must involve the activity of human beings that distinguishes human beings from other animals—that which is the activity proper to human beings—for only then can we really speak of *human* flourishing.

Recall that Aristotle believes that the forms immanent in nature are the proper objects of knowledge. That is, although he recognizes that natural objects are composed of both matter (which he conceives of as potential, or material to be developed) and form (the defining essence of an entity that determines its mature shape), Aristotle believes that we understand things best when we understand their forms. On his view, the form of all living things is *soul*, which he conceives of as the very *functioning* of a body through which organisms achieve their mature shapes and *flourish*. All organisms possess souls but of different types. Plants have nutritive souls that facilitate growth and reproduction. Animals possess nutritive, but also appetitive souls that permit responses (such as desire) to sense stimuli and (therefore) locomotion. Human beings have both nutritive and appetitive souls but are distinguished by their further possession of *rational* souls responsible for their faculties of reason and volition. These activities associated with the rational soul—reasoning and willing—therefore constitute the human being's distinctive excellence and are the activities indexed to human flourishing.

Accordingly, Aristotle distinguishes two general categories of human virtue—intellectual and moral virtue; *Nicomachean Ethics* is an analysis of the relation of both of these categories of virtue to human flourishing. He concludes that human beings achieve the highest degree of flourishing when engaged in a life of contemplation, but the next highest degree comes with practicing moral virtue.

Aristotle conceives of moral virtue as an expression of character; that is, as the habit of choosing actions well. Specifically, it is the ability to regulate our desires (the functioning of our appetitive souls) through rational choice (volition, or willing). Aristotle maintains that our ability to regulate our desires is not instinctive, so we must *learn* to regulate them *properly*—that is, we must acquire skill in avoiding extremes of desire, for both too much and too little of any given desire usually leads to practical problems. For example, the desire for food is a perfectly rational and necessary desire, but when excessive is gluttony and when deficient can lead to starvation, both extremes can compromise one's health and flourishing.

Thus, the central doctrine of Aristotle's account of moral virtue is the doctrine of the mean, according to which the desire-regulating virtues are understood as being means between extreme desires, or vices. Liberality (generosity), for example, is a mean between prodigality (the vice of wanting to give too much) and meanness (the vice of not wanting to give enough). The ten other moral virtues Aristotle addresses in the text are courage, temperance, magnificence, pride, right ambition, good temper, friendliness, truthfulness, tact, and justice. He identifies practical wisdom as the intellectual virtue that enables us to determine the appropriate moral virtue (mean desire) to be chosen in a given circumstance. Aristotle defines moral virtue, then, as "a state concerned with choice, lying in a mean relative to us, being determined by reason and in the way in which the man of practical wisdom would determine it."[11] For Aristotle, moreover, virtue is not simply a specific character trait or action, but the habit of acting well through rational choice.

Friendliness indeed ranks as one of the moral virtues for Aristotle, for he thinks friendship "is an excellence or implies excellence, and is besides most necessary with a view to living."[12] He believes friendship is essential to happiness because human beings are naturally social animals. Aristotle is quick to point out, however, that friendships come in different kinds, "equal in number to the number of things that are lovable,"[13] and so he is concerned to determine which type is genuinely conducive to human flourishing.

In addition to the works in ethics, Aristotle composed numerous treatises on psychology, politics, rhetoric, aesthetics, biology, natural science, metaphysics, and logic. Of these, perhaps his most famous are the *Politics, The Constitution of Athens, Poetics, Physics*, and *Metaphysics*. When Alexander died, in 323 B.C.E., the pro-Macedonian government in Athens was overthrown, and Aristotle, like Socrates before him, was charged with impiety. Aristotle fled to Chalcis in Euboea, lest Athens "should sin twice against philosophy." He died in Chalcis the following year.

SC

QUESTIONS

1. Evaluate Aristotle's claim that "without friends no one would choose to live, though he had all other goods"? How does he support this claim?

2. Explain Aristotle's classification of friendships. Is his analysis comprehensive, or are there kinds of friendship that fall outside these classifications?

3. Describe in your own words the key features of the kind of friendship Aristotle thinks is most conducive to human flourishing. Evaluate Aristotle's account and reasoning.

4. How can unequal and dissimilar people be friends, according to Aristotle? What are the characteristics of such friendships?

5. Why does Aristotle compare love to honor?

6. Evaluate Aristotle's account of self love. Do you agree with his claim that "the attributes by which a friend is defined" are "the attributes found most of all in the man's attitude of himself"? Why or why not? Can you provide examples from your own experience that confirm or challenge this account?

ENDNOTES

1. See chapter 3, pages 19.

2. Theophrastus would become Aristotle's primary successor and first custodian of his writings.

3. The Lyceum also came to be known as the peripatetic ("walking" or "strolling") school because its students and teachers typically held their discussions while walking about the grounds together.

4. Aristotle, *Physics*, 198b5.

5. Aristotle's forms are not Plato's Forms, however, as we shall see.

6. These four works are *Categories, On Interpretation, Prior Analytics*, and *Posterior Analytics*.

7. Aristotle considered substance to be the most important category, for we speak of the other nine terms only in relation to a thing that *is*. Thus, for Aristotle, substances are the ultimately real. He acknowledged two kinds: first substances are *individuals*, such as

the individual human being, "Socrates," or the individual dog, "Rin Tin Tin"; second substances are the *species* to which first substances belong, for example, "human" or "dog."

8. A syllogism is a pair of propositions (called *premisses*) that, when considered together, yield a new logical conclusion. The classic example is,

Premise 1: All men are mortal.

Premise 2: Socrates is a man.

Conclusion: Therefore, Socrates is mortal.

9. Aristotle, *Nicomachean Ethics*, 1.3.

10. Ibid.

11. Ibid., 2.6.

12. Ibid., 8.1.

13. Ibid., 8.3.

SELECTED BIBLIOGRAPHY

Aristotle. *Nicomachean Ethics. The Collected Works of Aristotle: The Revised Oxford Translation*, ed. Jonathan Barnes. Princeton, N.J.: Princeton University Press, 1984.

Aristotle. *On the Soul. The Collected Works of Aristotle: The Revised Oxford Translation*, ed. Jonathan Barnes. Princeton, N.J.: Princeton University Press, 1984.

Aristotle. *Physics. The Collected Works of Aristotle: The Revised Oxford Translation*, ed. Jonathan Barnes. Princeton, N.J.: Princeton University Press, 1984.

from *Nichomachean Ethics*

Aristotle

BOOK VIII

1. After what we have said, a discussion of friendship would naturally follow, since it is an excellence or implies excellence, and is besides most necessary with a view to living. For without friends no one would choose to live, though he had all other goods; even rich men and those in possession of office and of dominating power are thought to need friends most of all; for what is the use of such prosperity without the opportunity of beneficence, which is exercised chiefly and in its most laudable form towards friends? Or how can prosperity be guarded and preserved without friends? The greater it is, the more exposed is it to risk. And in poverty and in other misfortunes men think friends are the only refuge. It helps the young, too, to keep from error; it aids older people by ministering to their needs and supplementing the activities that are failing from weakness; those in the prime of life it stimulates to noble actions—'two going together'—for with friends men are more able both to think and to act. Again, parent seems by nature to feel it for offspring and offspring for parent, not only among men but among birds and among most animals; it is felt mutually by members of the same race, and especially by men, whence we praise lovers of their fellow men. We may see even in our travels how near and dear every man is to every other. Friendship seems too to hold states together, and lawgivers to care more for it than for justice; for unanimity seems to be something like friendship, and this they aim at most of all, and expel faction as their worst enemy; and when men are friends they have no need of justice, while when they are just they need friendship as well, and the truest form of justice is thought to be a friendly quality.

But it is not only necessary but also noble; for we praise those who love their friends, and it is thought to be a fine thing to have many friends; and again we think it is the same people that are good men and are friends.

Not a few things about friendship are matters of debate. Some define it as a kind of likeness and say like people are friends, whence come the sayings 'like to like', 'birds of a feather flock together', and so on; others on the contrary say 'two of a trade never agree'. On this very question they inquire more deeply and in a more scientific fashion, Euripides saying that 'parched earth loves the rain, and stately heaven when filled with rain loves to fall to earth', and Heraclitus that 'it is what opposes that helps' and 'from different tones comes the fairest tune' and 'all things are produced through strife'; while Empedocles, as well as others, expresses the opposite view that like aims at like. The scientific problems we may leave alone (for they do not belong to the present inquiry); let us examine those which are human and involve character and feeling, e.g. whether friendship can arise between any two people or people cannot be friends if they are wicked, and whether there is one species of friendship or more than one. Those who think there is only one because it admits of degrees have relied on an inadequate indication; for even things different in species admit of degree. We have discussed this matter previously.

2. The kinds of friendship may perhaps be cleared up if we first come to know the object of love. For not everything seems to be loved but only the lovable, and this is good, pleasant, or useful; but it would seem to be that by which some good or pleasure is produced that is useful, so that it is the good and the pleasant that are lovable as ends. Do men love, then, *the* good, or what is good for *them*? These sometimes clash. So too with regard to the pleasant. Now it is thought that each loves what is good for himself, and that the good is without qualification lovable, and what is good for each man is lovable for him; but each man loves not what is good for him but what seems good. This however will make no difference; we shall just have to say that this is that which seems lovable. Now there are three grounds on which people love; of the love of lifeless objects we do not use the word 'friendship'; for it is not mutual love, nor is there a wishing of good to the other (for it would surely be ridiculous to wish wine well; if one wishes anything for it, it is that it may keep, so that one may have it oneself); but to a friend we say we ought to wish what is good for his sake. But to those who thus wish good we ascribe only goodwill, if the wish is not reciprocated; goodwill when it *is* reciprocal being friendship. Or must we add 'when it is recognized'? For many people have goodwill to those whom they have not seen but judge to be good or useful; and one of these might return this feeling. These people seem to bear goodwill to each other; but how could one call them friends when they do not know their mutual feelings? To be friends, then, they must be mutually recognized as bearing goodwill and wishing well to each other for one of the aforesaid reasons.

3. Now these reasons differ from each other in kind; so therefore, do the corresponding forms of love and friendship. There are therefore three kinds of friendship, equal in number to the things that are lovable; for with respect to each there is a mutual and recognized love, and those who love each other wish well to each other in that respect in which they love one another. Now those who love each other for their utility do not love each other for themselves but in virtue of some good which they get from each other. So too with those who love for the sake of pleasure; it is not for their character that men love ready-witted people, but because they find them pleasant. Therefore those who love for the sake of utility love for the sake of what is good for *themselves*, and those who love for the sake of pleasure do so for the sake of what is pleasant to *themselves*, and not in so far as the other is the person loved but in so far as he is useful or pleasant. And thus these friendships are only incidental; for it is not as being the man he is that the loved person is loved, but as providing some good or pleasure. Such friendships, then, are easily dissolved, if the parties do not remain like themselves; for if the one party is no longer pleasant or useful the other ceases to love him.

Now the useful is not permanent but is always changing. Thus when the motive of the friendship is done away, the friendship is dissolved, inasmuch as it existed only for the ends in question. This kind of friendship seems to exist chiefly between old people (for at that age people pursue not the pleasant but the useful) and, of those who are in their prime or young, between those who pursue utility. And such people do not live much with each other either; for sometimes they do not even find each other pleasant; therefore they do not need such companionship unless they are useful to each other; for they are pleasant to each other only in so far as they rouse in each other hopes of something good to come. Among such friendships people also class the friendship of host and guest. On the other hand the friendship of young people

seems to aim at pleasure; for they live under the guidance of emotion, and pursue above all what is pleasant to themselves and what is immediately before them; but with increasing age their pleasures become different. This is why they quickly become friends and quickly cease to be so; their friendship changes with the object that is found pleasant, and such pleasure alters quickly. Young people are amorous too; for the greater part of the friendship of love depends on emotion and aims at pleasure; this is why they fall in love and quickly fall out of love, changing often within a single day. But these people do wish to spend their days and lives together; for it is thus that they attain the purpose of their friendship.

Perfect friendship is the friendship of men who are good, and alike in excellence; for these wish well alike to each other *qua* good, and they are good in themselves. Now those who wish well to their friends for their sake are most truly friends; for they do this by reason of their own nature and not incidentally; therefore their friendship lasts as long as they are good—and excellence is an enduring thing. And each is good without qualification and to his friend, for the good are both good without qualification and useful to each other. So too they are pleasant; for the good are pleasant both without qualification and to each other, since to each his own activities and others like them are pleasurable, and the actions of the good *are* the same or like. And such a friendship is as might be expected lasting since there meet in it all the qualities that friends should have. For all friendship is for the sake of good or of pleasure—good or pleasure either in the abstract or such as will be enjoyed by him who has the friendly feeling—and is based on a certain resemblance; and to a friendship of good men all the qualities we have named belong in virtue of the nature of the friends themselves; for in the case of this kind of friendship the other qualities also are alike in both friends, and that which is good without qualification is also without qualification pleasant, and these are the most lovable qualities. Love and friendship therefore are found most and in their best form between such men.

But it is natural that such friendships should be infrequent; for such men are rare. Further, such friendship requires time and familiarity; as the proverb says, men cannot know each other till they have 'eaten salt together'; nor can they admit each other to friendship or be friends till each has been found lovable and been trusted by each. Those who quickly show the marks of friendship to each other wish to be friends, but are not friends unless they both are lovable and know the fact; for a wish for friendship may arise quickly, but friendship does not.

4. This kind of friendship, then is complete both in respect of duration and in all other respects, and in it each gets from each in all respects the same as, or something like what, he gives; which is what ought to happen between friends. Friendship for the sake of pleasure bears a resemblance to this kind; for good people too are pleasant to each other. So too does friendship for the sake of utility; for the good are also useful to each other. Among men of these sorts too, friendships are most permanent when the friends get the same thing from each other (e.g. pleasure), and not only that but also from the same source, as happens between ready-witted people, not as happens between lover and beloved. For these do not take pleasure in the same things, but the one in seeing the beloved and the other in receiving attentions from his lover; and when the bloom of youth is passing the friendship sometimes passes too (for the one finds no pleasure in the sight of the other, and the other gets no attentions from the first); but many lovers on the other hand are constant, if familiarity has led them to love each other's characters, these being alike. But those who exchange not

pleasure but utility in their love are both less truly friends and less constant. Those who are friends for the sake of utility part when the advantage is at an end; for they were lovers not of each other but of profit.

For the sake of pleasure or utility, then, even bad men may be friends of each other, or good men of bad, or one who is neither good nor bad may be a friend to any sort of person, but for their own sake clearly only good men can be friends; for bad men do not delight in each other unless some advantage come of the relation.

The friendship of the good too alone is proof against slander; for it is not easy to trust any one's talk about a man who has long been tested by oneself; and it is among good men that trust and the feeling that he would never wrong me and all the other things that are demanded in true friendship are found. In the other kinds of friendship, however, there is nothing to prevent these evils arising.

For men apply the name of friends even to those whose motive is utility, in which sense states are said to be friendly (for the alliances of states seem to aim at advantage), and to those who love each other for the sake of pleasure, in which sense children are called friends. Therefore we too ought perhaps to call such people friends, and say that there are several kinds of friendship—firstly and in the proper sense that of good men *qua* good, and by similarity the other kinds; for it is in virtue of something good and something similar that they are friends, since even the pleasant is good for the lovers of pleasure. But these two kinds of friendship are not often united, nor do the same people become friends for the sake of utility and of pleasure; for things that are only incidentally connected are not often coupled together.

Friendship being divided into these kinds; bad men will be friends for the sake of pleasure or of utility, being in this respect like each other, but good men will be friends for their own sake, i.e. in virtue of their goodness. These, then, are friends without qualification; the others are friends incidentally and through a resemblance to these.

5. As in regard to the excellences some men are called good in respect of a state, others in respect of an activity, so too in the case of friendship; for those who live together delight in each other and confer benefits on each other, but those who are asleep or locally separated are not performing, but are disposed to perform, the activities of friendship; distance does not break off the friendship absolutely, but only the activity of it. But if the absence is lasting, it seems actually to make men forget their friendship; hence the saying 'out of sight, out of mind'. Neither old people nor sour people seem to make friends easily; for there is little that is pleasant in them, and no one can spend his days with one whose company is painful, or not pleasant, since nature seems above all to avoid the painful and to aim at the pleasant. Those, however, who approve of each other but do not live together seem to be well-disposed rather than actual friends. For there is nothing so characteristic of friends as living together (since while it is people who are in need that desire benefits, even those who are blessed desire to spend their days together; for solitude suits such people least of all); but people cannot live together if they are not pleasant and do not enjoy the same things, as friends who are companions seem to do.

The truest friendship, then, is that of the good, as we have frequently said; for that which is without qualification good or pleasant seems to be lovable and desirable, and for each person that which is good or pleasant to him; and the good man is lovable and desirable to the good man for both these reasons. Now it looks as if love were a passion, friendship a state; for love may be felt just as much towards lifeless things, but mutual love involves choice and choice springs from a state; and men wish well to those whom they love, for their

sake, not as a result of passion but as a result of a state. And in loving a friend men love what is good for themselves; for the good man in becoming a friend becomes a good to his friend. Each, then, both loves what is good for himself, and makes an equal return in goodwill and in pleasantness; for friendship is said to be equality, and both of these are found most in the friendship of the good.

6. Between sour and elderly people friendship arises less readily, inasmuch as they are less good-tempered and enjoy companionship less; for these are thought to be the greatest marks of friendship and most productive of it. This is why, while young men become friends quickly, old men do not; it is because men do not become friends with those in whom they do not delight; and similarly sour people do not quickly make friends either. But such men may bear goodwill to each other; for they wish one another well and aid one another in need; but they are hardly *friends* because they do not spend their days together nor delight in each other, and these are thought the greatest marks of friendship.

One cannot be a friend to many people in the sense of having friendship of the complete type with them, just as one cannot be in love with many people at once (for love is a sort of excess, and it is the nature of such only to be felt towards one person); and it is not easy for many people at the same time to please the same person very greatly, or perhaps even to be good for him. One must, too, acquire some experience of the other person and become familiar with him, and that is very hard. But with a view to utility or pleasure it is possible that many people should please one; for many people are useful or pleasant, and these services take little time.

Of these two kinds that which is for the sake of pleasure is the more like friendship, when both parties get the same things from each other and delight in each other or in the same things, as in the friendships of the young; for generosity is more found in such friendships. Friendship based on utility is for the commercially minded. People who are blessed, too, have no need of useful friends, but do need pleasant friends; for they wish to live with others, and, though they can endure for a short time what is painful, no one could put up with it continuously, nor even with the Good itself if it were painful to him; this is why they look out for friends who are pleasant. Perhaps they should look out for friends who, being pleasant, are also good, and good for them too; for so they will have all the characteristics that friends should have.

People in positions of authority seem to have friends who fall into distinct classes; some people are useful to them and others are pleasant, but the same people are rarely both; for they seek neither those whose pleasantness is accompanied by excellence nor those whose utility is with a view to noble objects, but in their desire for pleasure they seek for ready-witted people, and their other friends they choose as being clever at doing what they are told, and these characteristics are rarely combined. Now we have said that the good man is at the same time pleasant and useful; but such a man does not become the friend of one who surpasses him, unless he is surpassed also in excellence; if this is not so, he does not establish equality by being proportionally exceeded. But such men are not so easy to find.

However that may be, the aforesaid friendships involve equality; for the friends get the same things from one another and wish the same things for one another, or exchange one thing for another, e.g. pleasure for utility; we have said, however, that they are both less truly friendships and less permanent. But it is from their likeness and their unlikeness to the same thing that they are thought both to be and not to be friendships. It is by their likeness to the friendship of excellence that they seem to be friendships (for one of them involves pleasure and the other utility, and these characteristics belong to the friendship of excellence as well); while it is because the friendship of excellence is proof against slander and lasting, while these quickly change (besides differing from the former in many other respects), that they appear *not* to be friendships; i.e. it is because of their unlikeness to the friendship of excellence.

7. But there is another kind of friendship, viz. that which involves an inequality, e.g. that of father to son and in general of elder to younger, that of man to wife and in general that of ruler to subject. And these friendships differ also from each other; for it is not the same that exists between parents and children and between rulers and subjects, nor is even that of father to son the same as that of son to father, nor that of husband to wife the same as that of wife to husband. For the excellence and the function of each of these is different, and so are the reasons for which they love; the love and the friendship are therefore different also. Each party, then, neither gets the same from the other, nor ought to seek it; but when children render to parents what they ought to render to those who brought them into the world, and parents render what they should to their children, the friendship of such persons will be lasting and excellent. In all friendships implying inequality the love also should be proportional, i.e. the better should be more loved than he loves, and so should the more useful, and similarly in each of the other cases; for when the love is in proportion to the merit of the parties, then in a sense arises equality, which is held to be characteristic of friendship.

But equality does not seem to take the same form in acts of justice and in friendship; for in acts of justice what is equal in the primary sense is that which is in proportion to merit, while quantitative equality is secondary, but in friendship quantitative equality is primary and proportion to merit secondary. This becomes clear if there is a great interval in respect of excellence or vice or wealth or anything else between the parties; for then they are no longer friends, and do not even expect to be so. And this is most manifest in the case of the gods; for they surpass us most decisively in all good things. But it is clear also in the case of kings; for with them, too, men who are much their inferiors do not expect to be friends; nor do men of no account expect to be friends with the best or wisest men. In such cases it is not possible to define exactly up to what point friends can remain friends; for much can be taken away and friendship remain, but when one party is removed to a great distance, as God is, the possibility of friendship ceases. This is in fact the origin of the question whether friends really wish for their friends the greatest goods, e.g. that of being gods; since in that case their friends will no longer be friends to them, and therefore will not be good things for them (for friends *are* good things). Now if we were right in saying that friend wishes good to friend for his sake, his friend must remain the sort of being he is, whatever that may be; therefore it is for him only so long as he remains a man that he will wish the greatest goods. But perhaps not *all* the greatest goods; for it is for himself most of all that each man wishes what is good.

8. Most people seem, owing to ambition, to wish to be loved rather than to love; which is why most men love flattery; for the flatterer is a friend in an inferior position, or pretends to be such and to love more than he is loved; and being loved seems to be akin to being honoured, and this is what most people aim at. But it seems to be not for its own sake that people choose honour, but incidentally. For most people enjoy being honoured by those in positions of authority because of their hopes (for they think that if they want anything they will get it from them; and therefore they delight in honour as a token of favour to come); while those who desire honour from good men, and men who know, are aiming at confirming their own opinion of themselves; they delight in honour, therefore, because they believe in their own goodness on the strength of the judgement of those who speak about them. In being loved, on the other hand, people delight for its own sake; whence it would seem to be better than being honoured, and friendship to be desirable in itself. But it seems to lie in loving rather than in being loved, as is indicated by the delight mothers take in loving; for some mothers hand over their children to be brought up, and so long as they know their fate they love them and do not seek to be loved in return (if they cannot have both), but seem to be satisfied if they see them prospering; and they themselves love their children even if these owing to their ignorance give them nothing of a mother's due. Now since friendship depends more on loving, and it is those who love their friends that are praised, loving seems to be the characteristic excellence of friends, so that it is only those in whom this is found in due measure that are lasting friends, and only their friendship that endures.

It is in this way more than any other that even unequals can be friends; they can be equalized. Now equality and likeness are friendship, and especially the likeness of those who are like in excellence; for being steadfast in themselves they hold fast to each other, and neither ask nor give base services, but (one may say) even prevent them; for it is characteristic of good men neither to go wrong themselves nor to let their friends do so. But wicked men have no steadfastness (for they do not even stay similar to themselves), but become friends for a short time because they delight in each other's wickedness. Friends who are useful or pleasant last longer; i.e. as long as they provide each other with enjoyments or advantages. Friendship for utility's sake seems to be that which most easily exists between contraries, e.g. between poor and rich, between ignorant and learned; for what a man actually lacks he aims at, and he gives something else in return. Under this head, too, one might bring lover and beloved, beautiful and ugly. This is why lovers sometimes seem ridiculous, when they demand to be loved as they love; if they are equally lovable their claim can perhaps be justified, but when they have nothing lovable about them it is ridiculous. Perhaps, however, contrary does not even aim at contrary in its own nature, but only incidentally, the desire being for what is intermediate; for that is what is good, e.g. it is good for the dry not to become wet but to come to the intermediate state, and similarly with the hot and in all other cases. These subjects we may dismiss; for they are indeed somewhat foreign to our inquiry.

9. . . .

The friendship of children to parents, and of men to gods, is a relation to them as to something good and superior; for they have conferred the greatest benefits, since they are the causes of their being and of their nourishment, and of their education from their birth; and this kind of friendship possesses pleasantness and utility also, more than that of strangers, inasmuch as their life is lived more in common. The friendship of brothers has the characteristics found in that of comrades (and especially when these are good), and in general between people who are like each other, inasmuch as they belong more to each other and start with a love for each other from their very birth, and inasmuch as those born of the same parents and brought up together and similarly educated are more akin in character; and the test of time has been applied most fully and convincingly in their case.

Between other kinsmen friendly relations are found in due proportion. Between man and wife friendship seems to exist by nature; for man is naturally inclined to form couples—even more than to form cities, inasmuch as the household is earlier and more necessary than the city, and reproduction is more common to man than with the animals. With the other animals the union extends only to this point, but human beings live together not only for the sake of reproduction but also for the various purposes of life; for from the start the functions are divided, and those of man and woman are different; so they help each other by throwing their peculiar gifts into the common stock. It is for these reasons that both utility and pleasure seem to be found in this kind of friendship. But this friendship may be based also on excellence, if the parties are good; for each has its own excellence and they will delight in the fact. And children seem to be a bond of union (which is the reason why childless people part more easily); for children are a good common to both and what is common holds them together.

How man and wife and in general friend and friend ought mutually to behave seems to be the same question as how it is just for them to behave; for a man does not seem to have the same duties to a friend, a stranger, a comrade, and a schoolfellow.

. . . **13.** There are three kinds of friendship, as we said at the outset of our inquiry, and in respect of each some are friends on an equality and others by virtue of a superiority (for not only can equally good men become friends but a better man can make friends with a worse, and similarly in friendships of pleasure or utility the friends may be equal or unequal in the benefits they confer). This being so, equals must effect the required equalization on a basis of equality in love and in all other respects, while unequals must render what is in proportion to their superiority or inferiority.

Complaints and reproaches arise either only or chiefly in the friendship of utility, and this is only to be expected. For those who are friends on the ground of excellence are anxious to do well by each other (since that is a mark of excellence and of friendship), and between men who are emulating each other in this there cannot be complaints or quarrels; no one is offended by a man who loves him and does well by him—if he is a person of nice feeling he takes his revenge by doing well by the other. And the man who excels will not complain of his friend, since he gets what he aims at; for each man desires what is good. Nor do complaints arise much even in friendships of pleasure; for both get at the same time what they desire, if they enjoy spending their time together; and even a man who complained of another for *not* affording him pleasure would seem ridiculous, since it is in his power not to spend his days with him.

But the friendship of utility is full of complaints; for as they use each other for their own interests they always want to get the better of the bargain, and think they have got less than they should, and blame their partners because they do not get all they want and deserve; and those who do well by others cannot help them as much as those whom they benefit want.

Now it seems that, as justice is of two kinds, one unwritten and the other legal, one kind of friendship of utility is moral and the other legal. And so complaints arise most of all when men do not dissolve the relation in the spirit of the same type of friendship in which they contracted it. The *legal* type is that which is on fixed terms; its purely commercial variety is on the basis of immediate payment, while the more liberal variety allows time but stipulates for a definite *quid pro quo*. In this variety the debt is clear and not ambiguous, but in the postponement it contains an element of friendliness; and so some states do not allow suits arising out of such agreements, but think men who have bargained on a basis of credit ought to be content. The *moral* type is not on fixed terms; it makes a gift, or does whatever it does, as to a friend; but one expects to receive as much or more, as having not given but lent; and if a man is worse off when the relation is dissolved than he was when it was

contracted he will complain. This happens because all or most men, while they wish for what is noble, choose what is advantageous; now it is noble to do well by another without a view to repayment, but it is the receiving of benefits that is advantageous.

Therefore if we can we should return the equivalent of what we have received (for we must not make a man our friend against his will; we must recognize that we were mistaken at the first and took a benefit from a person we should not have taken it from—since it was not from a friend, nor from one who did it just for the sake of acting so—and we must settle up just as if we had been benefited on fixed terms). Indeed, one would agree to repay if one could (if one could not, even the giver would not have expected one to do so); therefore if it is possible we must repay. But at the outset we must consider the man by whom we are being benefited and on what terms he is acting, in order that we may accept the benefit on these terms, or else decline it.

It is disputable whether we ought to measure a service by its utility to the receiver and make the return with a view to that, or by the beneficence of the giver. For those who have received say they have received from their benefactors what meant little to the latter and what they might have got from others—minimizing the service; while the givers, on the contrary, say it was the biggest thing they had, and what could not have been got from others, and that it was given in times of danger or similar need. Now if the friendship is one that aims at *utility*, surely the advantage to the receiver is the measure. For it is he that asks for the service, and the other man helps him on the assumption that he will receive the equivalent; so the assistance has been precisely as great as the advantage to the receiver, and therefore he must return as much as he has received, or even more (for that would be nobler). In friendships based on *excellence* on the other hand, complaints do not arise, but the choice of the doer is a sort of measure; for in choice lies the essential element of excellence and character.

14. Differences arise also in friendship based on superiority for each expects to get more out of them, but when this happens the friendship is dissolved. Not only does the better man think he ought to get more, since more should be assigned to a good man, but the more useful similarly expects this; they say a useless man should not get as much as they should, since it becomes an act of public service and not a friendship if the proceeds of the friendship do not answer to the worth of the benefits conferred. For they think that, as in a commercial partnership those who put more in get more out, so it should be in friendship. But the man who is in a state of need and inferiority makes the opposite claim; they think it is the part of a good friend to help those who are in need; what, they say, is the use of being the friend of a good man or a powerful man, if one is to get nothing out of it?

At all events it seems that each party is justified in his claim, and that each should get more out of the friendship than the other—not more of the same thing, however, but the superior more honour and the inferior more gain; for honour is the prize of excellence and of beneficence, while gain is the assistance required by inferiority. . . .

BOOK IX

1. In all friendships between dissimilars it is, as we have said, proportion that equalizes the parties and preserves the friendship; e.g. in the political form of friendship the shoemaker gets a return for his shoes in proportion to his worth, and the weaver and the rest do the same. Now here a common measure has been provided in the form of money, and therefore everything is referred to this and measured by this; but in the friendship of lovers sometimes the lover complains that his excess of love is not met by love in return (though perhaps there is nothing lovable about him), while often the beloved complains that the lover who formerly promised everything now performs nothing. Such incidents happen when the lover loves the beloved for the sake of pleasure while the beloved loves the lover for the sake of utility, and they do not both possess the qualities expected of them. If these be the objects of the friendship it is dissolved when they do not get the things that formed the motives of their love; for each did not love the other person himself but the qualities he had, and these were not enduring; that is why the friendships also are transient. But the love of characters, as has been said, endures because it is self-dependent. Differences arise when what they get is something different and not what they desire; for it is like getting nothing at all when we do not get what we aim at; compare the story of the person who made promises to a lyre-player, promising him the more, the better he sang, but in the morning, when the other demanded the fulfilment of his promises, said that he had given pleasure for pleasure. Now if this had been what each wanted, all would have been well; but if the one wanted enjoyment but the other gain, and the one has what he wants while the other has not, the terms of the association will not have been properly fulfilled; for what each in fact wants is what he attends to, and it is for the sake of that that he will give what he has.

But who is to fix the worth of the service; he who makes the offer or he who has got the advantage? At any rate the one who offers seems to leave it to him. This is what they say Protagoras used to do; whenever he taught anything whatsoever, he bade the learner assess the value of the knowledge, and accepted the amount so fixed. But in such matters some men approve of the saying 'let a man have his fixed reward'.[1]...

3. Another question that arises is whether friendships should or should not be broken off when the other party does not remain the same. Perhaps we may say that there is nothing strange in breaking off a friendship based on utility or pleasure, when our friends no longer have these attributes. For it was of these attributes that we were the friends; and when these have failed it is reasonable to love no longer. But one might complain of another if, when he loved us for our usefulness or pleasantness, he pretended to love us for our character. For, as we said at the outset, most differences arise between friends when they are not friends in the spirit in which they think they are. So when a man has made a mistake and has thought he was being loved for his character, when the other person was doing nothing of the kind, he must blame himself; but when he has been deceived by the pretences of the other person, it is just that he should complain against his deceiver—and with more justice than one does against people who counterfeit the currency, inasmuch as the wrongdoing is concerned with something more valuable.

But if one accepts another man as good, and he becomes bad and is seen to do so, must one still love him? Surely it is impossible, since not everything can be loved, but only what is good. What is evil neither can nor should be loved; for one should not be a lover of evil, nor become like what is bad; and we have said that like is dear to like. Must the friendship, then, be forthwith broken off? Or is this not so in all cases, but only when one's friends are incurable in their wickedness? If they are capable of being reformed one should rather come to the assistance of their character or

their property, inasmuch as this is better and more characteristic of friendship. But a man who breaks off such a friendship would seem to be doing nothing strange; for it was not to a man of this sort that he was a friend; when his friend has changed, therefore, and he is unable to save him, he gives him up.

But if one friend remained the same while the other became better and far outstripped him in excellence, should the latter treat the former as a friend? Surely he cannot. When the interval is great this becomes most plain, e.g. in the case of childish friendships; if one friend remained a child in intellect while the other became a fully developed man, how could they be friends when they neither approved of the same things nor delighted in and were pained by the same things? For not even with regard to each other will their tastes agree, and without this (as we saw) they cannot be friends; for they cannot live together. But we have discussed these matters.

Should he, then, behave no otherwise towards him than he would if he had never been his friend? Surely he should keep a remembrance of their former intimacy, and as we think we ought to oblige friends rather than strangers, so to those who have been our friends we ought to make some allowance for our former friendship, when the breach has not been due to excess of wickedness.

4. Friendly relations with one's neighbours, and the marks by which friendships are defined, seem to have proceeded from a man's relations to himself. For men think a friend is one who wishes and does what is good, or seems so, for the sake of his friend, or one who wishes his friend to exist and live, for his sake; which mothers do to their children, and friends do who have come into conflict. And others think a friend is one who lives with and has the same tastes as another, or one who grieves and rejoices with his friend; and this too is

---

[1]Hesiod, *Works and Days* 370.

found in mothers most of all. It is by some one of these characteristics that friendship too is defined.

Now each of these is true of the good man's relation to himself (and of all other men in so far as they think themselves good; excellence and the good man seem, as has been said, to be the measure of every class of things). For his opinions are harmonious, and he desires the same things with all his soul; and therefore he wishes for himself what is good and what seems so, and does it (for it is characteristic of the good man to exert himself for the good), and does so for his own sake (for he does it for the sake of the intellectual element in him, which is thought to be the man himself); and he wishes himself to live and be preserved, and especially the element by virtue of which he thinks. For existence is good to the good man, and each man wishes himself what is good, while no one chooses to possess the whole world if he has first to become some one else (for that matter, even now God possesses the good); he wishes for this only on condition of being whatever he is; and the element that thinks would seem to be the individual man, or to be so more than any other element in him. And such a man wishes to live with himself; for he does so with pleasure, since the memories of his past acts are delightful and his hopes for the future are good, and therefore pleasant. His mind is well stored too with subjects of contemplation. And he grieves and rejoices, more than any other, with himself; for the same thing is always painful, and the same thing always pleasant, and not one thing at one time and another at another; he has, so to speak, nothing to regret.

Therefore, since each of these characteristics belongs to the good man in relation to himself, and he is related to his friend as to himself (for his friend is another self), friendship too is thought to be one of these attributes, and those who have these attributes to be friends.

Whether there is or is not friendship between a man and himself is a question we may dismiss for the present; there would seem to be friendship in so far as he is two or more, to judge from what has been said, and from the fact that the extreme of friendship is likened to one's love for oneself.

But the attributes named seem to belong even to the majority of men, poor creatures though they may be. Are we to say then that in so far as they are satisfied with themselves and think they are good, they share in these attributes? Certainly no one who is thoroughly bad and impious has these attributes, or even seems to do so. They hardly belong even to inferior people; for they are at variance with themselves, and have appetites for some things and wishes for others. This is true, for instance, of incontinent people; for they choose, instead of the things they themselves think good, things that are pleasant but hurtful; while others again, through cowardice and laziness, shrink from doing what they think best for themselves. And those who have done many terrible deeds and are hated for their wickedness even shrink from life and destroy themselves. And wicked men seek for people with whom to spend their days, and shun themselves; for they remember many a grievous deed, and anticipate others like them, when they are by themselves, but when they are with others they forget. And having nothing lovable in them they have no feeling of love to themselves. Therefore also such men do not rejoice or grieve with themselves; for their soul is rent by faction, and one element in it by reason of its wickedness grieves when it abstains from certain acts, while the other part is pleased, and one draws them this way and the other that, as if they were pulling them in pieces. If a man cannot at the same time be pained and pleased, at all events after a short time he is pained *because* he was pleased, and he could have wished that these things had not been pleasant to him; for bad men are laden with regrets.

Therefore the bad man does not seem to be amicably disposed even to himself, because there is nothing in him to love; so that if to be thus is the height of wretchedness, we should strain every nerve to avoid wickedness and should endeavour to be good; for so one may be both friendly to oneself and a friend to another.

5. Goodwill is a friendly sort of relation, but is not *identical* with friendship; for one may have goodwill both towards people whom one does not know, and without their knowing it, but not friendship. This has indeed been said already. But goodwill is not even friendly feeling. For it does not involve intensity or desire, whereas these accompany friendly feeling; and friendly feeling implies intimacy while goodwill may arise of a sudden, as it does towards competitors in a contest; we come to feel goodwill for them and to share in their wishes, but we would not *do* anything with them; for, as we said, we feel goodwill suddenly and love them only superficially.

Goodwill seems, then, to be a beginning of friendship, as the pleasure of the eye is the beginning of love. For no one loves if he has not first been delighted by the form of the beloved, but he who delights in the form of another does not, for all that, love him, but only does so when he also longs for him when absent and craves for his presence; so too it is not possible for people to be friends if they have not come to feel goodwill for each other, but those who feel goodwill are not for all that friends; for they only *wish* well to those for whom they feel goodwill, and would not do anything with them nor take trouble for them. And so one might by an extension of the term say that goodwill is inactive friendship, though when it is prolonged and reaches the point of intimacy it becomes friendship—not the friendship based on utility nor that based on pleasure; for goodwill too does not arise on those terms. The man who has received a benefit bestows goodwill in return for what has been done to him, and in doing so is doing what is just; while he who wishes some one to prosper because the hopes for enrichment through him seems to have goodwill not to him but rather to himself, just as a man is not a friend to another if he cherishes him for the sake of some use to be made of him. In general, goodwill arises on account of some excellence and worth, when one man seems to another beautiful or brave or something of the sort, as we pointed out in the case of competitors in a contest. . . .

8. The question is also debated, whether a man should love himself most, or some one else. People criticize those who love themselves most, and call them self-lovers, using this as an epithet of disgrace, and a bad man seems to do everything for his own sake, and the more so the more wicked he is—and so men reproach him, for instance, with doing nothing of his own accord—while the good man acts for honour's sake, and the more so the better he is, and acts for his friend's sake, and sacrifices his own interest.

But the facts clash with these arguments, and this is not surprising. For men say that one ought to love best one's best friend, and a man's best friend is one who wishes well to the object of his wish for his sake, even if no one is to know of it; and these attributes are found most of all in a man's attitude towards himself, and so are all the other attributes by which a friend is defined; for, as we have said, it is from this relation that all the characteristics of friendship have extended to others. All the proverbs, too, agree with this, e.g. 'a single soul', and 'what friends have is common property', and 'friendship is equality', and 'charity begins at home'; for all these marks will be found most in a man's relation to himself; he is his own best friend and therefore ought to love himself best. It is therefore a reasonable question, which of the two views we should follow; for both are plausible.

Perhaps we ought to mark off such arguments from each other and determine how far and in what respects each view is right. Now if we grasp the sense in which each party uses the phrase 'lover of self', the truth may become evident. Those who use the term as one of reproach ascribe self-love to people who assign to themselves the greater share of wealth, honours, and bodily pleasures; for these are what most people desire, and busy themselves about as though they were the best of all things, which is the reason, too, why they become objects of competition. So those who are grasping with regard to these things gratify their appetites and in general their feelings and the irrational element of the soul; and most men are of this nature thus the epithet has taken its meaning from the prevailing type of self-love, which is a bad one); it is just, therefore, that men who are lovers of self in this way are reproached for being so. That it is those who give themselves the preference in regard to objects of this sort that most people usually call lovers of self is plain; for if a man were always anxious that he himself, above all things, should act justly, temperately, or in accordance with any other of the excellences, and in general were always to try to secure for himself the honourable course, no one will call such a man a lover of self or blame him.

But such a man would seem more than the other a lover of self; at all events he assigns to himself the things that are noblest and best, and gratifies the most authoritative element in himself and in all things obeys this; and just as a city or any other systematic whole is most properly identified with the most authoritative element in it, so is a man; and therefore the man who loves this and gratifies it is most of all a lover of self. Besides, a man is said to have or not to have self-control according as his intellect has or has not the control, on the assumption that this is the man himself; and the things men have done from reason are thought most properly their own acts and voluntary acts. That this is the man himself, then, or is so more than anything else, is plain, and also that the good man loves most this part of him. Whence it follows that he is most truly a lover of self, of another type than that which is a matter of reproach, and as different from that as living according to reason is from living as passion dictates, and desiring what is noble from desiring what seems advantageous. Those, then, who busy themselves in an exceptional degree with noble actions all men approve and praise; and if *all* were to strive towards what is noble and strain every nerve to do the noblest deeds, everything would be as it should be for the common good, and every one would secure for himself the goods that are greatest, since excellence is the greatest of goods.

Therefore the good man should be a lover of self (for he will both himself profit by doing noble acts, and will benefit his fellows), but the wicked man should not; for he will hurt both himself and his neighbours, following as he does evil passions. For the wicked man, what he does clashes with what he ought to do, but what the good man ought to do he does; for the intellect always chooses what is best for itself, and the good man obeys his intellect. It is true of the good man too that he does many acts for the sake of his friends and his country, and if necessary dies for them; for he will throw away both wealth and honours and in general the goods that are objects of competition, gaining for himself nobility; since he would prefer a short period of intense pleasure to a long one of mild enjoyment, a twelvemonth of noble life to many years of humdrum existence, and one great and noble action to many trivial ones. Now those who die for others doubtless attain this result; it is therefore a great prize that they choose for themselves. They will throw away wealth too on condition that their friends will gain more; for while a man's friend gains wealth he himself achieves nobility; he is therefore assigning the greater good to himself. The same too is true of honour and office; all these things he will sacrifice to his friend; for this is noble and laudable for himself. Rightly then is he thought to be good, since he chooses nobility before all else. But he may even give up actions to his friend; it may be nobler to become the cause of his friend's acting than to act himself. In all the actions, therefore, that men are praised for, the good man is seen to assign to himself the greater share in what is noble. In this sense, then, as has been said, a man should be a lover of self; but in the sense in which most men are so, he ought not.

9. It is also disputed whether the happy man will need friends or not. It is said that those who are blessed and self-sufficient have no need of friends; for they have the things that are good, and therefore being self-sufficient they need nothing further while a friend, being another self, furnishes what a man cannot provide by his own effort; whence the saying 'when fortune is kind, what need of friends?'[2] But it seems strange, when one assigns all good things to the happy man, not to assign friends, who are thought the greatest of external goods. And if it is more characteristic of a friend to do well by another than to be well done by, and to confer benefits is characteristic of the good man and of excellence, and it is nobler to do well by friends than by strangers, the good man will need people to do well by. This is why the question is asked whether we need friends more in prosperity or in adversity, on the assumption that not only does a man in adversity need people to

confer benefits on him, but also those who are prospering need people to do well by. Surely it is strange, too, to make the blessed man a solitary; for no one would choose to possess all good things on condition of being alone, since man is a political creature and one whose nature is to live with others. Therefore even the happy man lives with others; for he has the things that are by nature good. And plainly it is better to spend his days with friends and good men than with strangers or any chance persons. Therefore the happy man needs friends.

What then is it that the first party means, and in what respect is it right? Is it that most men identify friends with useful people? Of such friends indeed the blessed man will have no need, since he already has the things that are good; nor will he need those whom one makes one's friends because of their pleasantness, or he will need them only to a small extent (for his life, being pleasant, has no need of adventitious pleasure); and because he does not need *such* friends he is thought not to need friends.

But that is surely not true. For we have said at the outset that happiness is an activity; and activity plainly comes into being and is not present at the start like a piece of property. If happiness lies in living and being active, and the good man's activity is virtuous and pleasant in itself, as we have said at the outset, and if a thing's being one's own is one of the attributes that make it pleasant, and if we can contemplate our neighbours better than ourselves and their actions better than our own, and if the actions of virtuous men who are their friends are pleasant to good men (since these have both the attributes that are naturally pleasant)—if this be so, the blessed man will need friends of this sort, since he chooses to contemplate worthy actions and actions that are his own, and the actions of a good man who is his friend have both these qualities.

[2]Euripides, *Orestes* 667.

Further, men think that the happy man ought to live pleasantly. Now if he were a solitary, life would be hard for him; for by oneself it is not easy to be continuously active; but with others and towards others it is easier. With others therefore his activity will be more continuous, being in itself pleasant, as it ought to be for the man who is blessed; for a good man *qua* good delights in excellent actions and is vexed at vicious ones, as a musical man enjoys beautiful tunes but is pained at bad ones. A certain training in excellence arises also from the company of the good, as Theognis remarks.

If we look deeper into the nature of things, a virtuous friend seems to be naturally desirable for a virtuous man. For that which is good by nature, we have said, is for the virtuous man good and pleasant in itself. Now life is defined in the case of animals by the power of perception, in that of man by the power of perception or thought; and a power is referred to the corresponding activity, which is the essential thing; therefore life seems to be essentially perceiving or thinking. And life is among the things that are good and pleasant in themselves, since it is determinate and the determinate is of the nature of the good; and that which is good by nature is also good for the virtuous man (which is the reason why life seems pleasant to all men); but we must not apply this to a wicked and corrupt life nor to a life spent in pain; for such a life is indeterminate, as are its attributes. The nature of pain will become plainer in what follows. But if life itself is good and pleasant (which it seems to be, from the very fact that all men desire it, and particularly those who are good and blessed; for to such men life is most desirable, and their existence is the most blessed; and if he who sees perceives that he sees, and he who hears, that he hears, and he who walks, that he walks, and in the case of all other activities similarly there is something which perceives that we are active, so that if we perceive, we perceive that we perceive, and if we think, that we think; and if to perceive that we perceive or think is to perceive that we exist (for existence was defined as perceiving or thinking); and if perceiving that one lives is one of the things that are pleasant in themselves (for life is by nature good, and to perceive what is good present in oneself is pleasant); and if life is desirable, and particularly so for good men, because to them existence is good and pleasant (for they are pleased at the consciousness of what is in itself good); and if as the virtuous man is to himself, he is to his friend also (for his friend is another self):—then as his own existence is desirable for each man, so, or almost so, is that of his friend. Now his existence was seen to be desirable because he perceived his own goodness, and such perception is pleasant in itself. He needs, therefore, to be conscious of the existence of his friend as well, and this will be realized in their living together and sharing in discussion and thought; for this is what living together would seem to mean in the case of man, and not, as in the case of cattle, feeding in the same place.

If, then, existence is in itself desirable for the blessed man (since it is by its nature good and pleasant), and that of his friend is very much the same, a friend will be one of the things that are desirable. Now that which is desirable for him he must have, or he will be deficient in this respect. The man who is to be happy will therefore need virtuous friends.

10. Should we, then, make as many friends as possible, or—as in the case of hospitality it is thought to be suitable advice, that one should be 'neither a man of many guests nor a man with none[3]—will that apply to friendship as well; should a man neither be friendless nor have an excessive number of friends?

---

[3]Hesiod, *Works and Days* 715.

To friends made with a view to *utility* this saying would seem thoroughly applicable; for to do services to many people in return is a laborious task and life is not long enough for its performance. Therefore friends in excess of those who are sufficient for our own life are superfluous, and hindrances to the noble life; so that we have no need of them. Of friends made with a view to *pleasure*, also, few are enough, as a little seasoning in food is enough.

But as regards *good* friends, should we have as many as possible, or is there a limit to the number of one's friends, as there is to the size of a city? You cannot make a city of ten men, and if there are a hundred thousand it is a city no longer. But the proper number is presumably not a single number, but anything that falls between certain fixed points. So for friends too there is a fixed number—perhaps the largest number with whom one can live together (for that, we found, is thought to be most characteristic of friendship); and that one cannot live with many people and divide oneself up among them is plain. Further, they too must be friends of one another, if they are all to spend their days together; and it is a hard business for this condition to be fulfilled with a large number. It is found difficult, too, to rejoice and to grieve in an intimate way with many people, for it may likely happen that one has at once to be merry with one friend and to mourn with another. Presumably, then, it is well not to seek to have as many friends as possible, but as many as are enough for the purpose of living together; for it would seem actually impossible to be a great friend to many people. This is why one cannot love several people; love tends to be a sort of excess friendship, and that can only be felt towards one person; therefore great friendship too can only be felt towards a few people. This seems to be confirmed in practice; for we do not find many people who are friends in the comradely way of friendship, and the famous friendships of this sort are always between two people. Those who have many friends and mix intimately with them all are thought to be no one's friend, except in the way proper to fellow-citizens, and such people are also called obsequious. In the way proper to fellow-citizens, indeed, it is possible to be the friend of many and yet not be obsequious but a genuinely good man; but one cannot have with many people the friendship based on excellence and on the character of our friends themselves, and we must be content if we find even a few such.

11. Do we need friends more in good fortune or in bad? They are sought after in both; for while men in adversity need help, in prosperity they need people to live with and to make the objects of their beneficence; for they wish to do well by others. Friendship, then, is more necessary in bad fortune, and so it is useful friends that one wants in this case; but it is more noble in good fortune, and so we also seek for good men as our friends, since it is more desirable to confer benefits on these and to live with these. For the very presence of friends is pleasant both in good fortune and also in bad, since grief is lightened when friends sorrow with us. Hence one might ask whether they share as it were our burden, or—without that happening—their presence by its pleasantness, and the thought of their grieving with us, make our pain less. Whether it is for these reasons or for some other that our grief is lightened, is a question that may be dismissed; at all events what we have described appears to take place.

But their presence seems to contain a mixture of various factors. The very seeing of one's friends is pleasant, especially if one is in adversity, and becomes a safeguard against grief (for a friend tends to comfort us both by the sight of him and by his words, if he is tactful, since he knows our character and the things that please or pain us); but to see him pained at our misfortunes is painful; for every one shuns being a cause of pain to his friends. For this reason people of a manly nature guard against making their friends grieve with them, and, unless he be exceptionally insensible to pain, such a man cannot stand the pain that ensues for his friends, and in general does not admit fellow-mourners because he is not himself given to mourning; but women and womanly men enjoy sympathisers in their grief, and love them as friends and companions in sorrow. But in all things one obviously ought to imitate the better type of person.

On the other hand, the presence of friends in our *prosperity* implies both a pleasant passing of our time and the thought of their pleasure at our own good fortune. For this cause it would seem that we ought to summon our friends readily to share our good fortunes (for the beneficent character is a noble one), but summon them to our bad fortunes with hesitation; for we ought to give them as little a share as possible in our evils—whence the saying 'enough is *my* misfortune'. We should summon friends to us most of all when they are likely by suffering a few inconveniences to do us a great service.

Conversely, it is fitting to go unasked and readily to the aid of those in adversity (for it is characteristic of a friend to render services, and especially to those who are in need and have not demanded them; such action is nobler and pleasanter for both persons); but when our friends are prosperous we should join readily in their activities (for they need friends for these too), but be tardy in coming forward to be the objects of their kindness; for it is not noble to be keen to receive benefits. Still, we must no doubt avoid getting the reputation of kill-joys by repulsing them; for that sometimes happens.

The presence of friends, then, seems desirable in all circumstances.

12. Does it not follow, then, that, as for lovers the sight of the beloved is the thing they love most, and they prefer this sense to the others because on it love depends most for its being and for its origin, so for friends the most desirable thing is living together? For friendship is a partnership, and as a man is to himself, so is he to his friend; now in his own case the perception of his existence is desirable, and so therefore is that of his friend's, and the activity of this perception is produced when they live together, so that it is natural that they aim at this. And whatever existence means for each class of men, whatever it is for whose sake they value life, in *that* they wish to occupy themselves with their friends; and so some drink together, others dice together, others join in athletic exercises and hunting, or in the study of philosophy, each class spending their days together in whatever they love most in life; for since they wish to live with their friends, they do and share in those things as far as they can.[4] Thus the friendship of bad men turns out an evil thing (for because of their instability they unite in bad pursuits, and besides they become evil by becoming like each other), while the friendship of good men is good, being augmented by their companionship; and they are thought to become better too by their activities and by improving each other; for from each other they take the mould of the characteristics they approve—whence the saying 'noble deeds from noble men[5]—So much, then, for friendship; our next task must be to discuss pleasure.

---

[4]Reading ώς οἶόν τε for οἷς οἰ ονται συζῆν.
[5]Theognis, 35.

chapter five

Epicurus

Epicurus (341–270 B.C.E.) endures as a singularly audacious figure in the history of philosophy, and his voice is just as vibrant today as it was twenty-three centuries ago. Twenty-three centuries after he lived, the question to which he devoted his work—"How can we be happy?"—persists. His conclusion, that the noblest life is a simple one, built upon friendship, the highest of human goods, resonates still. Epicurus's quest for happiness led him to break radically with many of the customs of his society, gaining him an unearned reputation as a rebel, heretic, and hedonist.

Epicurus was born in Samos, a town near Athens, in the year 341 B.C.E. In late fourth-century Greece, philosophers commanded considerable political and social influence. Epicurus achieved a degree of notoriety that was uncommon even in his day. However, his novel philosophy also aroused scorn and anger from many of his fellow citizens and made him a political refugee at times. Perhaps his creativity stemmed from the fact that, unlike other major thinkers of his time, he was largely self-taught. Undoubtedly his most infamous act of social rebellion was to invite women to participate as equal members of his philosophical community outside of Athens, the Garden.[1] The gossiping and criticism that coeducation provoked echoed through philosophical commentaries for centuries.[2]

Epicurus was calm in the face of this ridicule. In fact, his philosophy was grounded in the belief that achieving a calm and contented existence is our most important task. We get a sense of his amiability from his simple declaration that "[o]ne must philosophize and at the same time laugh."[3] Ironically, he discouraged his followers from trying to find personal happiness through the sexual promiscuity his detractors imagined taking place in the Garden. Indeed, he taught that sex "never helped anyone, and one must be satisfied if it has not harmed."[4] True happiness instead is found in the serene life that has conquered anxiety and fear, not in one crammed full of revelry and indulgence. As Epicurus wrote to his student Menoeceus, "[W]hen I say that pleasure is the goal of living I do not mean the pleasures of libertines or the pleasures inherent in positive enjoy-

Epicurus. From "Letter to Menoceus." *The Philosophy of Epicurus*; letters, doctrines, and parallel passages from *Lucretius*. Translated, with commentary and introduction, by George K. Strodach. Copyright © 1963 by Northwestern University Press. Reprinted with permission.

ment. . . . I mean, on the contrary, the pleasure that consists in freedom from bodily pain and mental agitation."[5] It is remarkable that Epicurus was the person to champion this view, because he was so plagued by chronic and incessant illness that it was harder for him than almost anyone else to follow his teaching. However, in spite of the fact that he suffered from agonizing illnesses, he counseled his followers that "pain does not linger continuously in the flesh."[6] Epicurus was faithful to his philosophy even as he died in searing pain in 270 B.C.E. Showing his characteristic love of life and friendship, his last letter read:

> I write to you while experiencing a blessedly happy day, and at the same time the last day of my life . . . discomforts afflict me which could not be surpassed for their intensity. But against all these things are ranged the joy in my soul produced by the recollection of the discussions we have had.[7]

Epicurus lived through a time of dramatic upheaval for the Greeks.[8] He was a toddler when Athens and other Greek city-states lost the battle of Chaeronea to King Philip II of Macedonia in 338 B.C.E. This defeat to a foreign monarch was more than just a military humiliation; it signaled the total collapse of the Greek social order. For centuries, the Greeks, and Athenians in particular, defined themselves according to their political autonomy. Their idea of a person was inseparable from that of a politically active citizen. In a world where a distant king, and not the local citizens, held political power, the ancient Greeks had to reimagine not only the individual's role within society, but also the very purpose of life. Epicurus therefore came of age at a time when the ancient Greeks were experimenting with new philosophies that focused on individual needs and desires, instead of the needs of the state. To this extent, he was a product of his era. However, Epicurus's path to personal happiness was different from those of other schools for three reasons. First, he denied that the gods had any impact on the lives of human beings. While he accepted that the gods existed, he argued that the gods were supremely happy and thus never bothered with human affairs. Second, Epicurus's philosophy was not intended for the educated few, but for all people, regardless of their social class or gender. He therefore expressed his views in simple, straightforward terms. He even condensed the core of his work to what was called the "Four-Part Cure" for human suffering: "Don't fear god, don't worry about death, what is good is easy to get, and what is terrible is easy to endure."[9] Finally, in an era when people were turning away from communal forms of life in order to find personal happiness, Epicurus argued that true personal happiness is impossible without a community of friends. Earlier philosophers like Socrates and Plato placed a similar emphasis on friendship, but it played a paramount role for Epicurus. Where other philosophers believed that friendship was a means for achieving the ultimate goal of wisdom, Epicurus held that friendship itself was the highest goal.

Much of what we know of Epicurus and his philosophy comes from excerpts and summaries made by later philosophers and historians. Although none of his major works has survived, we fortunately have several letters that offer us a glance into his character. The *Letter to Menoeceus*, presented here, is the most significant of these surviving texts because it offers us a synopsis of his philosophy that is unparalleled in its elegance and clarity. His words to his friend and student Menoeceus read like an elaboration and defense of his famous "Four-Part Cure." He first gives an impassioned argument for the importance of studying philosophy as part of achieving happiness. The next section details the reasons why we should not fear the gods, and offers advice regarding the danger of believing those who would ascribe human prejudices and desires to the gods. He goes on to make the case that worrying about death is a waste of time. The remainder of the essay focuses on the heart of Epicureanism, namely, the idea that the goal of life is to be happy. Again, Epicurus shows us an idea of happiness that is simple and even brave. It depends on our use of philosophy and friendship to calm our worries and wisely distinguish between quick pleasures that are followed by pain and anxiety (like excessive drinking or casual sex) and those that are easy to achieve and bring us peace (like enjoying a glass of water or conversing with intimate friends). He ends by encouraging us, his readers, with the thought that nothing in the universe—neither gods, nor foreign kings, nor even calamity and disease—can block our road to happiness.

TM

QUESTIONS

1. Epicurus claims that all people can be happy, regardless of their situation, so long as they follow his teaching. Do you agree? What, if anything, does he fail to account for?

2. In his *Letter to Menoeceus*, Epicurus argues that death is nothing. Do his arguments cause you to think differently about death? If so, how? If not, why not?

3. Do you think that happiness should be the ultimate goal of human life? What advantages are there to a life guided by happiness? What are some of its disadvantages?

4. Imagine Epicurus followed you around for a week. Imagine that you periodically told him about your mental state: when you are happy, bored, anxious, or afraid. How do you think he would assess the way you live your life? Is it too preoccupied with things you cannot help (like the future, or what people think of you)? What might Epicurus suggest that you change about your life?

5. Do you agree with Epicurus that true friendship is necessary for happiness?

ENDNOTES

1. Frischer, pp. 61–62.

2. For a concise biography (as well as excellent treatment of his philosophy), see A.J. Festugiere, O.P., *Epicurus and His Gods*.

3. *The Vatican Collection of Epicurean Sayings,* #41 from Inwood and Gerson, p. 38.

4. *Report of Epicurus's Ethical Views*: Diogones Laertius 10.118, from Inwood and Gerson, p. 43.

5. Epicurus, *Letter to Menoeceus*.

6. *The Principle Doctrines*: Diogenes Laertius 10.121–135, from Inwood and Gerson, p. 32.

7. *Letter to Idomeneus*: Diogenes Laertius 10.22, as quoted in Inwood and Gerson, p. 79.

8. For a wonderful overview of this time in Greek history, see H. D. Kitto *The Greeks*. Baltimore, Md: Penguin, 1954.

9. Philodemus. *Herculaneum Papyrus 1005*, 4.9–14, from Inwood and Gerson, p. vi.

SELECTED BIBLIOGRAPHY

Farrington, Benjamin. *The Faith of Epicurus.* New York: Basic Books, 1967.

Festugiere, A. J., O.P. *Epicurus and His Gods,* trans. C.W. Chilton. Oxford: Blackwell, 1955.

Frischer, Bernard. *The Sculpted Word: Epicureanism and Philosophical Recruitment in Ancient Greece.* Berkley: University of California Press, 1982.

Inwood, B., and L.P. Gerson, ed. and trans. *The Epicurus Reader: Selected Writings and Testimonia.* Indianapolis, Ind.: Hackett Publishing, 1994.

from *Letter to Menoeceus*

Epicurus

No one should postpone the study of philosophy when he is young, nor should he weary of it when he becomes mature, because the search for mental health is never untimely or out of season.[1] To say that the time to study philosophy has not yet arrived or that it is past is like saying that the time for happiness is not yet at hand or is no longer present. Thus both the young and the mature should pursue philosophy, the latter in order to be rejuvenated as they age by the blessings that accrue from pleasurable past experience, and the youthful in order to become mature immediately through having no fear of the future. Hence we should make a practice of the things that make for happiness, for assuredly when we have this we have everything, and we do everything we can to get it when we don't have it.

THE PRECONDITIONS OF HAPPINESS

I. You should do and practice all the things I constantly recommended to you, with the knowledge that they are the fundamentals of the good life. (1) First of all, you should think of deity as imperishable and blessed being (as delineated in the universal conception of it common to all men), and you should not attribute to it anything foreign to its immortality or inconsistent with its blessedness.

[1]This letter, together with the important collection of individual sayings and teachings known as *Leading Doctrines*, is the chief source of our knowledge about Epicurus' ethics and his theory of the good life. In it he sets forth, in a flowing and untechnical style, the following salient points: the right attitude toward the gods (123–24) and toward death (124–27), the limitation of desires to those that are necessary and natural (127–29), the doctrine of pleasure and pain (hedonism, 129–32) and of *ataraxia* (freedom from pain in body and mind, 131), the role of reason or "good judgment" (132–33), and the role of determinism, chance, and freedom in the moral life (133–35).

On the contrary, you should hold every doctrine that is capable of safeguarding its blessedness in common with its imperishability. (L23) The gods do indeed exist, since our knowledge of them is a matter of clear and distinct perception; but they are not like what the masses suppose them to be, because most people do not maintain the pure conception of the gods. The irreligious man is not the person who destroys the gods of the masses but the person who imposes the ideas of the masses on the gods. (L24) The opinions held by most people about the gods are not true conceptions of them but fallacious notions, according to which awful penalties are meted out to the evil and the greatest of blessings to the good. (L25) The masses, by assimilating the gods in every respect to their own moral qualities, accept deities similar to themselves and regard anything not of this sort as alien.[2]

(2) Second, you should accustom yourself to believing that death means nothing to us, since every good and every evil lies in sensation; but death is the privation of sensation. Hence a correct comprehension of the fact that death means nothing to us makes the mortal aspect of life pleasurable, not by conferring on us a boundless period of time but by removing the yearning for deathlessness. There is nothing fearful in living for the person who has really laid hold of the fact that there is nothing fearful in not living. So it is silly for a person to say

that he dreads death—not because it will be painful when it arrives but because it pains him now as a future certainty; for that which makes no trouble for us when it arrives is a meaningless pain when we await it. This, the most horrifying of evils, means nothing to us, then, because so long as we are existent death is not present and whenever it is present we are nonexistent. Thus it is of no concern either to the living or to those who have completed their lives. For the former it is nonexistent, and the latter are themselves nonexistent. (L26)

Most people, however, recoil from death as though it were the greatest of evils; at other times they welcome it as the end-all of life's ills. The sophisticated person, on the other hand, neither begs off from living nor dreads not living. Life is not a stumbling block to him, nor does he regard not being alive as any sort of evil. As in the case of food he prefers the most savory dish to merely the larger portion, so in the case of time he garners to himself the most agreeable moments rather than the longest span.

Anyone who urges the youth to lead a good life but counsels the older man to end his life in good style is silly, not merely because of the welcome character of life but because of the fact that living well and dying well are one and the same discipline.[3] Much worse off, however, is the person who says it were well not to have been born "but once born to pass Hades' portals as swiftly as may be." Now if he says such a thing from inner persuasion why does he not withdraw from life? Everything is in readiness for him once he has firmly resolved on this course. But if he speaks facetiously he is a trifler standing in the midst of men who do not welcome him.

---

[2] I.e., the Greek gods were made in the image of man. They were popularly represented as having human passions, vices, and virtues and as engaging in activities such as quarreling, lovemaking, creating, rewarding, and punishing—all of which Epicurus regarded as contradictory to their perfection, serenity, and self-contemplation. The "true conception" of the gods was no doubt set forth in detail by Epicurus in his treatise *On the Gods*, which is now lost, but there are plenty of hints to be found in the *Letter to Herodotus*, the *Letter to Pythocles*, and in Lucretius and Cicero. The gods were wholly concerned with their own perfection and bliss and had no interest whatever in human beings or in the physical universe that they had no part in creating.

---

[3] I.e., a good life in the Epicurean sense is a preparation for dying well, without fear or repining. One who has lived the pleasant life of *ataraxia* can die with the serenity and composure that have become habitual.

It should be borne in mind, then, that the time to come is neither ours nor altogether not ours. In this way we shall neither expect the future outright as something destined to be nor despair of it as something absolutely not destined to be.[4]

THE GOOD LIFE

II. It should be recognized that within the category of desire certain desires are natural, certain others unnecessary and trivial; that in the case of the natural desires certain ones are necessary, certain others merely natural; and that in the case of necessary desires certain ones are necessary for happiness, others to promote freedom from bodily discomfort, others for the maintenance of life itself.[5] A steady view of these matters shows us how to refer all moral choice and aversion to bodily health and imperturbability of mind, these being the twin goals of happy living. It is on this account that we do everything we do—to achieve freedom from pain and freedom from fear. When once we come

by this, the tumult in the soul is calmed and the human being does not have to go about looking for something that is lacking or to search for something additional with which to supplement the welfare of soul and body. Accordingly we have need of pleasure only when we feel pain because of the absence of pleasure, but whenever we do not feel pain we no longer stand in need of pleasure.[6] And so we speak of pleasure as the starting point and the goal of the happy life because we realize that it is our primary native good, because every act of choice and aversion originates with it, and because we come back to it when we judge every good by using the pleasure feeling as our criterion. (L27)

Because of the very fact that pleasure is our primary and congenital good we do not select every pleasure; there are times when we forgo certain pleasures, particularly when they are followed by too much unpleasantness.[7] Furthermore, we regard certain states of pain as preferable to pleasures, particularly when greater satisfaction results from our having submitted to discomforts for a long period of time.[8] Thus every pleasure is a good by reason of its having a nature akin to our own, but not every pleasure is desirable. In like manner every state of pain is an evil, but not all pains are uniformly to be

---

[4]The relaxed and self-sufficient Epicurean did not eagerly reach out for the future, nor did he write it off altogether. His habitual composure made him ready to extend a calm present into an equally calm future. By contrast, the Cyrenaic, who lived much more intensely, never banked on the future at all but lived by the motto "Only the present is ours." See Diogenes Laertius, *Life of Epicurus*, note 44.

[5]In addition to the right attitude toward death and the gods, the curtailing of desires to the bare minimum was essential for the good life as Epicurus understood it. . . . For the strict Epicurean the only legitimate desires are those whose fulfillment will produce freedom from pain in body and mind, which is what Epicurus meant by "pleasure" (simple diet and clothing, shelter, and companionship together with the right attitude toward death and the gods). All other desires that aim at positive satisfactions or intense pleasure (such as a rich diet, sex, esthetic pursuits) may add diversity to life but are in reality unnecessary and superfluous, or they may actually be harmful in their consequences (such as the pursuit of wealth, fame, power, excitement, etc.). These are characteristic of the worldly sophisticate or the crass Cyrenaic but must be forgone by the strict sectarian in his own self-interest.

[6]Cf. *L.D.* 3: "The quantitative limit of pleasure is the elimination of all feelings of pain. Wherever the pleasurable state exists there is neither bodily pain nor mental pain nor both together, so long as the state continues." Pleasure is the "starting point," i.e., the natural psychological basis, of the happy life. Thus because of the ambiguity of "pleasure" Epicurus is able to say that "we speak of pleasure as the starting point and the goal of the happy life" and to make the claim that the good life is one lived in accordance with nature. But the ethical goal of *ataraxia* is a philosophical refinement of "our primary native good" and a far cry from the active pleasure that untutored nature craves. For this reason some have classified Epicurus as a neutral hedonist (or simply a "neutralist") rather than as a genuine hedonist.

[7]E.g., the sexual act, which Epicurus regarded as natural but unnecessary except for reproductive purposes.

[8]E.g., necessary surgery, if it is followed by physical comfort after convalescence.

rejected. At any rate, it is our duty to judge all such cases by measuring pleasures against pains, with a view to their respective assets and liabilities, inasmuch as we do experience the good as being bad at times and, contrariwise, the bad as being good.

In addition, we consider limitation of the appetites a major good, and we recommend this practice not for the purpose of enjoying just a few things and no more but rather for the purpose of enjoying those few in case we do not have much.[9] We are firmly convinced that those who need expensive fare least are the ones who relish it most keenly and that a natural way of life is easily procured, while trivialities are hard to come by.[10] Plain foods afford pleasure equivalent to that of a sumptuous diet, provided that the pains of penury are wholly eliminated. Barley bread and water yield the peak of pleasure whenever a person who needs them sets them in front of himself. Hence becoming habituated to a simple rather than a lavish way of life provides us with the full complement of health; it makes a person ready for the necessary business of life; it puts us in a position of advantage when we happen upon sumptuous fare at intervals and prepares us to be fearless in facing fortune.[11]

Thus when I say that pleasure is the goal of living I do not mean the pleasures of libertines or the pleasures inherent in positive enjoyment, as is supposed by certain persons who are ignorant of our doctrine or who are not in agreement with it or who interpret it perversely.[12] I mean, on the contrary, the pleasure that consists in freedom from bodily pain and mental agitation. The pleasant life is not the product of one drinking party after another or of sexual intercourse with women and boys or of the sea food and other delicacies afforded by a luxurious table. (L28) On the contrary, it is the result of sober thinking—namely, investigation of the reasons for every act of choice and aversion and elimination of those false ideas about the gods and death which are the chief source of mental disturbances.[13]

The starting point of this whole scheme and the most important of its values is good judgment, which consequently is more highly esteemed even than philosophy.[14] All the other virtues stem from sound judgment, which shows us that it is impossible to live the pleasant Epicurean life without also living sensibly, nobly, and justly and, vice versa, that it is impossible to live sensibly, nobly,

---

[9]Like the Stoics, the Epicureans made much of self-sufficiency (independence of what life gives or takes away) and maintained that the basic material requirements for the happy life are easily met.

[10]Epicurus would have considered a good American steak dinner as falling under the rubric of "trivialities," not to mention the disgustingly opulent fare that Trimalchio set before his Roman guests in Petronius' *Satyricon*. Epicurus practiced what he preached. Cf. Diogenes Laertius, *Life of Epicurus*, sect. 11: "Epicurus himself remarked in his letters that he was satisfied with just water and plain bread. 'Send me a small pot of cheese,' he wrote, 'so that I can have a costly meal whenever I like.' "

[11]I.e., it makes for self-sufficiency.

[12]Any way of life based on pleasure is liable to be caricatured by malicious rivals (here Cyrenaics and Stoics) as sensual and "libertine." The "high liver" is the least sophisticated of men; he is the creature of uncontrolled drives and ignorant fears.

[13]Far from being sensual, the pleasant life of the garden is synonymous with the philosophical life.

[14]"Good judgment" (often translated as "prudence") is here contrasted with, and given higher rank than, "philosophy," or the theoretical grasp of first principles. The same contrast between "intellectual virtue" and "practical wisdom" is found in Plato and Aristotle, but these two philosophers, being rationalists, rank theoretical knowledge higher. The theory of the good life takes precedence over the practical wisdom that is derived from experience. The empirically minded Epicurus shows his independence of the rationalist tradition by reversing the order of importance. The practical good sense that stems directly from nature is more to be esteemed than the body of theory which is the product of philosophical reason. It is this sound common sense that shows us how to discriminate among pleasures in concrete situations and limit our pleasures so as to avoid pain and prompts us to pursue the conventional virtues such as justice. Despite this new emphasis, Epicurus could hardly deny that a theoretical grasp of the atomic theory and its implications must precede the practice of the good life of *ataraxia*.

and justly without living pleasantly. The traditional virtues grow up together with the pleasant life; they are indivisible.[15] Can you think of anyone more moral than the person who has devout beliefs about the gods, who is consistently without fears about death, and who has pondered man's natural end? Or who realizes that the goal of the good life is easily gained and achieved and that the term of evil is brief, both in extent of time and duration of pain?[16] Or the man who laughs at the "decrees of Fate," a deity whom some people have set up as sovereign of all?

The good Epicurean believes that certain events occur deterministically, that others are chance events, and that still others are in our own hands. He sees also that necessity cannot be held morally responsible and that chance is an unpredictable thing, but that what is in our own hands, since it has no master, is naturally associated with blameworthiness and the opposite.[17] (Actually it would be better to subscribe to the popular mythology than to become a slave by accepting the determinism of the natural philosophers, because popular religion underwrites the hope of supplicating the gods by offerings but determinism contains an element of necessity, which is inexorable.) As for chance, the Epicurean does not assume that it is a deity (as in popular belief)[18] because a god does nothing irregular; nor does he regard it as an unpredictable cause of all events. It is his belief that good and evil are not the chance contributions of a deity, donated to mankind for the happy life, but rather that the initial circumstances for great good and evil are sometimes provided by chance. He thinks it preferable to have bad luck rationally than good luck irrationally. In other words, in human action it is better for a rational choice to be unsuccessful than for an irrational choice to succeed through the agency of chance.

Think about these and related matters day and night, by yourself and in company with someone like yourself. If you do, you will never experience anxiety, waking or sleeping, but you will live like a god among men. For a human being who lives in the midst of immortal blessings is in no way like a mortal man!

---

[15]Because of the stigma attached to pleasure in the minds of the ignorant or the perverse, Epicurus emphasizes that the pleasant life of *ataraxia*, though unconventional and divorced from the everyday life of the community, actually supports and fosters all the conventional virtues—in fact that justice and nobility of character are impossible unless one adopts the Epicurean way of life. This whole section is a final answer to his critics. Far from being immoral or a radical departure from the past, Epicureanism continues to maintain the best elements of the Greek moral and religious tradition.

[16]The therapeutic power of his philosophy to reduce or neutralize all forms of pain, both physical and mental, is often stressed by Epicurus as one of its most attractive features.

[17]Epicurus held that: (1) Physical events, such as the movements of the heavenly bodies, are governed by necessity or, as we should say, by natural determinism but that necessity is essentially amoral, and to regard human life as determined, as Democritus did, would be equivalent to reducing man to moral slavery.

[18]After the decay of the religion of the Olympian gods and of belief in their moral government of the world, control of human affairs (e.g., war and peace, famine, pestilence, etc.) was popularly assigned to a single new power, variously called Chance or Fortune. The worship of this deity was extremely widespread in the Hellenistic period among both Greeks and Romans and is often regarded as an evolutionary stage in the development of monotheism.

Epicurus takes a naturalistic view of chance. It is not a deity, "as in popular belief," but apparently a type of causation, metaphysical in nature but not orderly and predictable like the mechanical necessity that governs the regular processes of nature. It is chance that causes certain atoms to swerve and collide with other atoms, thereby producing entire systems called worlds, and it is the chance swerving of soul atoms that makes possible free will. Paradoxically our moral freedom depends on chance, but the impact of chance events on our lives is minimized by Epicurus.

chapter six

Marcus Aurelius

The value of philosophy—particularly for the Stoics and for Marcus Aurelius—did not lie in the academic pursuit of truths for the sake of argument or idle chatter. It was a penetrating study: a self-scrutinizing, practical way of life whose value lay in the application of insights not only to living the good life frankly, simply, and well, but to the search for, service to, and union with God. Its overarching purpose was served by psychagogy,[1] an introspective self-discipline of soul and body by means of ascetic spiritual exercises designed to get down to the business of both plain living, and, paradoxically, becoming like a god.

For Philosopher-Emperor Marcus Antoninus Aurelius (121–180 C.E.), the mature commitment to philosophy came through the discourses of the Stoic slave Epictetus. With Epictetus (c. 55–c. 135 C.E.), a "new phase" passed over Stoicism; philosophical doctrine was transformed into religious devotion, with the Epictetan version of Stoicism being seen as a neo-Cynicism.[2]

Unquestionably, Aurelius borrows from Epictetus many of his main philosophical points, such as community based on equality and freedom for all; the uselessness of textbooks and rules of logic; acceptance and resignation, rather than blame and defiance, for the impartial works of Nature and men; the indifference toward death and a physical interpretation of it; the brotherhood of all humanity; and the life of compassionate detachment, with all relationships based on kindness, justice, and mutual accord—to name but a few. Not unexpectedly, then, the ascetic sensibility of the Cynics resonates in the words of Aurelius: "Wilt thou one day, O my soul, be good, simple, single, stript naked, brighter than this mortal envelope?" (*Med.* X.1).

Aside from a handful of letters discovered among the papers of his mentor and teacher of rhetoric, Fronto, the *Meditations*—a sort of private diary, or manual of devotion, of his inner life—is the only surviving work of Marcus Aurelius. It was on his return to the Danube region, while at war "among the misty swamps and reedy islands of that melancholy region,"[3] that the lonely, besieged Aurelius kept the accounts of his

---

hours: twelve short books of pithy personal thoughts, remarks, and philosophical say-ings—the fruit of a diligent, habitual, and critical self-examination. Whenever "practice falls short of precept" (*Med.* V.9), the elixir for the wayward soul is words, and, written "To Himself,"[4] Aurelius's words and the Stoic philosophy they reflected were the tools of healing. Always close at hand, they were "not a matter for public display, but for pri-vate consolation" (*Med.* V.9), penned as a "pep-talk," props to get him back on the straight and narrow. "Principles," he writes, "can only lose their vitality when the first impressions from which they derive have sunk into extinction; and it is for you to keep fanning these continually into a fresh flame" (*Med.* VII.2).

One of the most important things for the Stoic philosopher to acquire was clarity of vision; he or she was to see things as they really are. For the Stoics, the psychological barriers that stood in the way of the rational clarity of perception so desirous to them were what they called *pathôn*, the passions.[5] The passions are described by Zeno as over-reactive responses, that is, irrational emotions or excessive impulses that distort and fal-sify perception. He outlined four main types of irrational emotion: grief, desire, fear, and pleasure, each with its own subtypes. It should be understood that, for the Stoics, it was not that a person should not feel emotion, but that the emotions felt should be ra-tional rather than irrational. Accordingly, there were classes of emotion that the Stoics held to be rational; these were caution, wishing, and joy, each with its own set of sub-types. Unlike earlier Stoics, such as Zeno, Aurelius was of the view that sins of passion were not of equal worth. It was a "philosophic truth" for Aurelius that sins committed through the passion of desire or lust were more blameworthy than sins committed through the passion of anger, since the former were intentional and bent on gratifica-tion of pleasure, whereas the latter were unintentional and painful, the guilty party "driven to an involuntary loss of control by some injustice" (*Med.* II.10).

An antidote to the passions was philosophical devotion to the ideal of *apatheia*, im-partiality or dispassion, which culminated in thoughts and actions freed from the chains and claims of the passions. *Apatheia* was gained through the psychological faculty of *diakrisis*, or discrimination: a vigilant capacity to scrutinize the thoughts and actions of the human heart, distinguishing legitimate as opposed to illegitimate, rational as op-posed to irrational, expressions of emotion and instinctual needs. It was the Stoic view that the chasing after, the desiring and acquiring, of worldly goods and pleasures made people unhappy; thus philosophic self-scrutiny helped discern what the essentials of the good life were. Speculations were to go to the bottom of things, penetrate into them and expose their real natures, assessing whether what was desired applied itself to the good life and the good of the soul. This therapy of *epithumia,* or desire, would enable the Stoic philosopher to maintain the esteemed clarity and impartiality of vision associ-ated with *apatheia*, and keep him or her free of illusion. Like God, who "views the inner minds of men, stripped of every material sheath and husk and dross," the Stoic philoso-pher was compelled, as well, to school himself or herself to do likewise (*Med.* XII.2).

The difficulty of this method, however, lay in the certainty that this path to freedom was full of deprivation and suffering, one that could easily degenerate into a world-negating, body-hating philosophy—which Aurelius has been accused of. Moderation was healthy; excess unhealthy—even an excess of moderation. Thus, impulses should always be rational, "subject to modification, free from self-interest, and duly proportioned to the merits of the case" (*Med.* XI.37). Emotions "of the flesh, be they of pleasure or pain," should never affect the "supreme and sovereign portion of the soul," namely, reason; feelings were meant to be limited, and "confined to their proper sphere" (*Med.* V.26). Thus, possessing strength enough to refrain from indulging feelings, or to consent to them at will, through rationality, was the hallmark of Stoic self-mastery (*Med.* I.16; IV.3).

When all was said and done, philosophy was a daily "struggle against passion's mastery" (*Med.* III.4)—all about learning how to live rationally and happily with less—and equally, how to die a good death, for it was far better to die (even take your own life, for the Stoics) than to live badly. According to Epictetus, death was not considered an evil; there was nothing dishonorable in it. In fact, philosophy was the art of "dying" while still alive—to desire, to the passions, to worldly pursuits, to the fear of death itself. However, unlike Epictetus, who referred to the subject of death less frequently and far more casually, it would appear that Aurelius, far from being indifferent to death, was enamored of it, morbidly absorbed with it, devoting an estimated sixty-two chapters of the *Meditations* to the theme of his own death and that of others!

Philosophy and virtue, for Aurelius, lay not in the "purple's dye" of imperial station, but in the rectifying of one's own character. Virtue was the only nobility. Not proud to be a Caesar, he had rather a "contempt for the purple" (*Med.* VI.13; IX.36) and focused in his writings on the transience of ambition and achievement. Rather than finding fulfillment in his public and professional life, he found tedium and weariness. Preferring the simplicity of Cynic practices of behavior and dress, he resisted wearing the clothing appropriate to his station as an imperial, dressing as a private citizen. A resolute ascetic, his extreme distaste for life in the body—"his duties of the flesh"—was mitigated and made bearable by seeing them as a service to God.

As Aurelius grew older, his public and private lives were strewn—inordinately so—with the rues and distractions of mortality. Enduring the loss of all but one of his sons, and plagued with ill health, but especially grieving the rebellion and deaths of beloved friend Cassius and wife Faustina (implicated in the betrayal)—the warmth, humanity, and easy camaraderie of happier days vanished into bitterness and alienation. No longer sure whom he could trust, Aurelius became more and more withdrawn from the bonds of common human affection and felt little desire to commingle with his fellow humanity. To love others became a duty, the feeling of brotherly love no longer coming either easily or naturally.

There was a character of idealism and a vision of perfection in Aurelius, sown from the seeds of his youth, that he strives for heroically, which, in the end, proves neither humane nor realistic. Although his imperial rule was a continual attempt to emulate the philosopher-king of the Platonic *Republic*—and he is seen by posterity as being the only emperor aside from Julian to attempt such an ideal—Aurelius does not presume

achievement of the "ideal commonwealth" (*Med.* IX.29). Moreover, his solitary demeanor and disillusionment with his public role as emperor were partially the repercus-
sion of the rigor of that ideal.

While Aurelius contemplated suicide as a means to end life in the face of approaching senility, he also mused over the wisdom of nerving oneself up to wait quietly for the
end of life. Doubt as to the exact cause of his death remains. What *is* known is that
while Aurelius and his only surviving son—and successor—Commodus were fighting
the good fight to the north of those same marshy swamps where the *Meditations* were
composed, Aurelius fell ill with an unnamed disease. It is written that, for several days
thereafter, Aurelius took no food or drink, wishing only to die. It is further suspected
that, rather than dying of that unnamed disease (the consensus being smallpox), the
royal physicians, as a favor to Commodus, ended his father's life—perhaps an assisted
suicide.

Marcus Antoninus Philosophus, or "Marcus Antoninus the Philosopher" as the
Historia Augusta distinguishes him, died on March 17, 180, and when his ashes were returned to Rome, they were interred in the vault of Hadrian.

MBM

QUESTIONS

1. What is psychagogy? Why is it such an important element of philosophy? How does the
   imperative to "know thyself" figure into this enterprise? (*Med.* II.2; II.9; II.12; II.13;
   II.17)

2. Why is philosophy thought of as the "art of dying"? What was Aurelius's view on death?
   (*Med.* II.11; II.12; II.17)

3. Discuss why, for Aurelius, "the longest life and the shortest amount to the same thing."
   (*Med.* II.14)

4. What are the passions? Why, according to Theophrastus, are "sins of desire" more serious
   than "sins of anger"? (*Med.* II.10)

5. Discuss the Cynic Monimus's view that "things are determined by the view taken of
   them." What truth might Aurelius refer to here? (*Med.* II.15)

6. According to Aurelius, what, for the human soul, are some of the greatest of self-inflicted
   wrongs? Related to this, what is the philosopher's purpose in life? (*Med.* II.16; II.17)

ENDNOTES

1. Rutherford, p. 15. Psychagogy (psook'a go jee), or *"philosophic* self-scrutiny" as a psy-
   chotherapeutic technique was well established in Greco-Roman culture. "The fundamental principle of Greek morality, [to know thyself], originally an acknowledgement of

human limitation and of divine power, gradually acquired a more cognitive and intro-spective sense. This new significance found a more detailed expression and interpretation in the insistence of several philosophic schools on habitual self-examination," namely, the Pythagorean, the Platonic, the Peripatetic, the Epicurean, the Cynic, and the Stoic.

2. Bussell, p. 76. The Cynic school was founded by Antisthenes (c. 445–365 B.C.E.), a stu-dent of Socrates. A minor Socratic sect, their central belief was that a virtuous life lived according to the will of nature was the way to happiness, as opposed to the living of a conventional life comprised of the pursuit of values such as formal education, wealth, or social status. The Cynic Crates was the teacher of Zeno, the founder of the Stoic school. Cynic following was sparse due to its extremist views, but Stoicism integrated central Cynic ethics, tempering its anti-intellectualism and unconventionality into a more so-phisticated and mainstream system. Cynicism may have been a "shortcut" to virtue (Dio-genes Laertius, VII.121), but it was via Stoicism that Cynic thought had its greatest historical impact. Aurelius makes several references to the Cynics in his *Meditations* (II.15; IV.30; VI.13; VI.47; VII.36; VIII.3; XI.6).

3. Aurelius, *Meditations*, p. 20.

4. Aurelius, *Marcus Aurelius: Meditations*, p. 31. "The Greek title at the head of Marcus's book does not mean 'Meditations' at all; the meaning of its two words is simply 'To Him-self.'"

5. Zeno, VII.110–120. Diogenes Laertius, Vol. II, pp. 215–25.

SELECTED BIBLIOGRAPHY

Aurelius, Marcus. *Marcus Aurelius: Meditations*, trans. Robin Hard and intro. Christopher Gill. Ware, U.K.: Wordsworth Editions, 1997.

Aurelius, Marcus. *Meditations*, trans. Maxwell Staniforth. Harmondsworth, U.K.: Penguin Books, Penguin Classics, 1980.

Bussell, F.W. *Marcus Aurelius and the Later Stoics*. The World's Epoch-Makers, ed. Oliphant Smeaton. Edinburgh: T. & T. Clarke, 1910.

Cassius Dio Cocceianus. *The Roman History: The Reign of Augustus/Cassius Dio*, trans. Ian Scott-Kilvert and intro. John Carter. New York: Penguin Books, 1987.

Diogenes Laertius. *Lives of Eminent Philosophers*, trans. R.D. Hicks. New York: G.P. Putnam's Sons, 1925.

Farquharson, A.S.L. *Marcus Aurelius*. 2d ed., ed. D.A. Rees. Oxford, U.K.: Basil Blackwell, 1952.

Hadot, Pierre. *Philosophy as a Way of Life: Spiritual Exercises from Socrates to Foucault*, ed. Arnold I. Davidson and trans. Michael Chase. Oxford, U.K.: Blackwell, 1995.

Hadot, Pierre. *The Inner Citadel: The Meditations of Marcus Aurelius*, trans. Michael Chase. Cambridge, Mass.: Harvard University Press, 1998.

Nussbaum, Martha. *The Therapy of Desire: Theory and Practice in Hellenistic Ethics*. Princeton, N.J.: Princeton University Press, 1994.

Rutherford, R.B. *The Meditations of Marcus Aurelius: A Study.* Oxford Classical Monographs. New York: Clarendon Press, 1989.

Zeno. *Letters of Zeno.* Edinburgh, U.K.: Committee of Citizens, 1783.

from *Meditations*

Marcus Aurelius

5.   Hour by hour resolve firmly, like a Roman and a man, to do what comes to hand with correct and natural dignity, and with humanity, independence, and justice. Allow your mind freedom from all other considerations. This you can do, if you will approach each action as though it were your last, dismissing the wayward thought, the emotional recoil from the commands of reason, the desire to create an impression, the admiration of self, the discontent with your lot. See how little a man needs to master, for his days to flow on in quietness and piety: he has but to observe these few counsels, and the gods will ask nothing more.

6.   Wrong, wrong thou art doing to thyself, O my soul; and all too soon thou shalt have no more time to do thyself right. Man has but one life; already thine is nearing its close, yet still hast thou no eye to thine own honour, but art staking thy happiness on the souls of other men.[1]

7.   Are you distracted by outward cares? Then allow yourself a space of quiet, wherein you can add to your knowledge of the Good and learn to curb your restlessness. Guard also against another kind of error: the folly of those who weary their days in much business, but lack any aim on which their whole effort, nay, their whole thought, is focussed.

8.   You will not easily find a man coming to grief through indifference to the workings of another's soul; but for those who pay no heed to the motions of their own, unhappiness is their sure reward.

9.   Remembering always what the World-Nature is, and what my own nature is, and how the one stands in respect to the other—so small a fraction of so vast a Whole—bear in mind that no man can hinder you from conforming each word and deed to that Nature of which you are a part.

10.   When Theophrastus is comparing sins—so far as they are commonly acknowledged to be comparable—he affirms the philosophic truth that sins of desire are more culpable than sins of passion. For passion's revulsion from reason at least seems to bring with it a certain discomfort, and a half-felt sense of constraint; whereas sins of desire, in which pleasure predominates, indicate a more self-indulgent and womanish disposition. Both experience and philosophy, then, support the contention that a sin which is pleasurable deserves graver censure than one which is painful. In the one case the offender is like a man stung into an involuntary loss

---

[1]That is, on whether others decide to approve or censure your actions.

of control by some injustice; in the other, eagerness to gratify his desire moves him to do wrong of his own volition.

11.   In all you do or say or think, recollect that at any time the power of withdrawal from life is in your own hands. If gods exist, you have nothing to fear in taking leave of mankind, for they will not let you come to harm. But if there are no gods, or if they have no concern with mortal affairs, what is life to me, in a world devoid of gods or devoid of Providence? Gods, however, do exist, and do concern themselves with the world of men. They have given us full power not to fall into any of the absolute evils; and if there were real evil in life's other experiences, they would have provided for that too, so that avoidance of it could lie within every man's ability. But when a thing does not worsen the man himself, how can it worsen the life he lives? The World-Nature cannot have been so ignorant as to overlook a hazard of this kind, nor, if aware of it, have been unable to devise a safeguard or a remedy. Neither want of power nor want of skill could have led Nature into the error of allowing good and evil to be visited indiscriminately on the virtuous and the sinful alike. Yet living and dying, honour and dishonour, pain and pleasure, riches and poverty, and so forth are equally the lot of good men and bad. Things like these neither elevate nor degrade; and therefore they are no more good than they are evil.

12.   Our mental powers should enable us to perceive the swiftness with which all things vanish away: their bodies in the world of space, and their remembrance in the world of time. We should also observe the nature of all objects of sense—particularly such as allure us with pleasure, or affright us with pain, or are clamorously urged upon us by the voice of self-conceit—the cheapness and contemptibility of them, how sordid they are, and

how quickly fading and dead. We should discern the true worth of those whose word and opinion confer reputations. We should apprehend, too, the nature of death; and that if only it be steadily contemplated, and the fancies we associate with it be mentally dissected, it will soon come to be thought of as no more than a process of nature (and only children are scared by a natural process)—or rather, something more than a mere process, a positive contribution to nature's well-being. Also we can learn how man has contact with God, and with which part of himself this is maintained, and how that part fares after its removal hence.

13.   Nothing is more melancholy than to compass the whole creation, 'probing into the deeps of earth', as the poet says, and peering curiously into the secrets of others' souls, without once understanding that to hold fast to the divine spirit within, and serve it loyally, is all that is needful. Such service involves keeping it pure from passion, and from aimlessness, and from discontent with the works of gods or men; for the former of these works deserve our reverence, for their excellence; the latter our goodwill, for fraternity's sake, and at times perhaps our pity too, because of men's ignorance of good and evil—an infirmity as crippling as the inability to distinguish black from white.

14.   Were you to live three thousand years, or even thirty thousand, remember that the sole life which a man can lose is that which he is living at the moment; and furthermore, that he can have no other life except the one he loses. This means that the longest life and the shortest amount to the same thing. For the passing minute is every man's equal possession, but what has once gone by is not ours. Our loss, therefore, is limited to that one fleeting instant, since no one can lose what is already past, nor yet what is still to come—for how can he be deprived of what he does not possess? So two things should be borne in mind. First, that all the cycles of creation since the beginning of time exhibit the same recurring pattern, so that it can make no difference whether you watch the identical spectacle for a hundred years, or for two hundred, or for ever. Secondly, that when the longest- and the shortest-lived of us come to die, their loss is precisely equal. For the sole thing of which any man can be deprived is the present; since this is all he owns, and nobody can lose what is not his.

15.   There are obvious objections to the Cynic Monimus's statement that 'things are determined by the view taken of them'; but the value of his aphorism is equally obvious, if we admit the substance of it so far as it contains a truth.

16.   For a human soul, the greatest of self-inflicted wrongs is to make itself (so far as it is able to do so) a kind of tumour or abscess on the universe; for to quarrel with circumstances is always a rebellion against Nature—and Nature includes the nature of each individual part. Another wrong, again, is to reject a fellow-creature or oppose him with malicious intent, as men do when they are angry. A third, to surrender to pleasure or pain. A fourth, to dissemble and show insincerity or falsity in word or deed. A fifth, for the soul to direct its acts and endeavours to no particular object, and waste its energies purposelessly and without due

thought; for even the least of our activities ought to have some end in view—and for creatures with reason, that end is conformity with the reason and law of the primordial City and Commonwealth.

17.   In the life of a man, his time is but a moment, his being an incessant flux, his senses a dim rushlight, his body a prey of worms, his soul an unquiet eddy, his fortune dark, and his fame doubtful. In short, all that is of the body is as coursing waters, all that is of the soul as dreams and vapours; life a warfare, a brief sojourning in an alien land; and after repute, oblivion. Where, then, can man find the power to guide and guard his steps? In one thing and one alone: Philosophy. To be a philosopher is to keep unsullied and unscathed the divine spirit within him, so that it may transcend all pleasure and all pain, take nothing in hand without purpose and nothing falsely or with dissimulation, depend not on another's actions or inactions, accept each and every dispensation as coming from the same Source as itself—and last and chief, wait with a good grace for death, as no more than a simple dissolving of the elements whereof each living thing is composed. If those elements themselves take no harm from their ceaseless forming and re-forming, why look with mistrust upon the change and dissolution of the whole? It is but Nature's way; and in the ways of Nature there is no evil to be found.

chapter seven

Plotinus

Plotinus, who renewed and reinterpreted Platonic philosophy, was the most influential philosopher in the period between Aristotle and Augustine. He was born in Egypt in 205 and died in Rome in 270. We know little of his early life, but we do know that he spent time searching Alexandria for a philosopher who could be his teacher and that his search was finally answered when he found Ammonius Saccas, who was also the teacher of the Christian theologian Origen. Ammonius himself never wrote down his philosophical views, and we can judge his greatness only from the reports of his students. After staying with Ammonius for eleven years, Plotinus joined the army of Emperor Gordian, which was set to march against Persians, with the intent of studying Persian and Indian philosophy first hand. His goal was thwarted when Gordian was killed. Plotinus eventually moved to Rome and opened his own school, which quickly became famous. He taught for many years, and his student Porphyry characterized his teaching style as conversational. It was only after he was prodded by his students that Plotinus, at the age of forty-nine, began writing. Each of his treatises—intended as teaching tools for use in discussion with his students—reflects the entire scope of Plotinus's thought. Plotinus left Porphyry in charge of editing and publishing these writings, and Porphyry did his best to impose an apparent order on the fifty-four treatises left behind. He arranged them by subject matter and, since he was partial to the numbers six and nine, used the arbitrary principle of grouping the work into six books with nine treatises each. The title *Enneads* is derived from the nine divisions. The extant texts could be characterized as unsystematic writings reflecting systematic thought.

Plotinus refers to himself as an interpreter of Plato's thought[1]—not just a commentator on the text but someone who is trying to fathom and clarify Plato's intentions in his writings. Plotinus sees in the Platonic dialogues the basis for a systematic unity. Many earlier thinkers had continued a Platonic tradition, either by advancing Plato's thought in the Academy itself, which continued in various forms for many centuries, or in criticisms of Platonic positions, such as those of Aristotle and the Stoics. Plotinus mentions

From *The Enneads* by Plotinus, translated by Stephen MacKenna, abridged by John Dillon (Penguin Classics, 1991). This abridgement copyright © 1991 John Dillon.

many of these, referring to most of the famous ancient and Hellenistic thinkers, but it is only Plato whom he calls "divine" and "godlike."[2] In contrast with other thinkers who have been called "Platonists," Plotinus both interpreted Plato and answered the objections of his critics. Plotinus was branded "the father of Neo-Platonism" in the eighteenth century, a term coined by German intellectual historians, who initially introduced the phrase "New Platonism" as a pejorative term, referring to works that appeared to be inspired by Plato, but which, in their view, distorted and falsified Plato's work. Later, neo-Platonism came into its own: Hegel considered Neo-Platonism "a recovery of the spirit of man, indeed, of the spirit of the world."[3]

The fact that Plotinus defined his own task as exegetical needs to be understood in the proper context. For nearly two-thousand years, philosophy was above all the discipline of interpreting texts. Thus, for example, in the thirteenth century, Thomas Aquinas commented on numerous Aristotelian texts, following the long tradition begun in ancient times and preserved and continued by Muslim and Jewish scholars. As is clear from the works of all these thinkers, the task of interpretation brings with it opportunities for developing one's own thoughts, and many of the exegetes become important innovators as well. Plotinus is a great example of the latter, because in addressing the long-standing difficulties involved in explaining the relationship between the One and the many, he develops his own ingenious account of reality, a system of emanations and contemplation.

Plotinus's starting point is the One, or the Good. In this he is starting from the passage in Plato's *Republic*, Book VI (509b), where Socrates asserts that the Good is both the cause of being and knowing and itself beyond being and knowing—commenting on passages in which Socrates speaks indirectly and in images, referring to the sun as "the offspring of the Good." The One is perfect in itself and by itself, and for Plotinus perfection is a state of dynamic activity rather than anything static. The creative activity of the One leads to an overflowing, and this ultimately results in multiplicity: The One emanates or overflows into the many. We must note, however, that the One remains the same, one in itself, and is not diminished in any way. The first product of this activity is Intellect (*Nous*), which represents intelligible reality and includes the world of Platonic forms. It gives rise to rational principles as well, which are marked by their need for discursive reasoning, in contrast to the intuitive comprehension of the intelligible. To the extent that Intellect is an emanation of the One, it is completely dependent on its source and it connects with this source through contemplation. By contemplating the One, Intellect in its turn experiences creative activity and brings forth Soul (*psyche*). Plotinus refers to these different levels as "The Three Primary Hypostases," or the three primary substantial realities.

"Hypostasis" is an interesting term, because it can mean both "sediment" and "substance." Given that all is the result of an initial creative overflowing, "sediment" might be an appropriate term when speaking from the perspective of the One, whereas "real substance" would be the appropriate way of speaking from our perspective. This twofold characterization is appropriate throughout the discussion of the unfolding of reality and our corresponding relation to that. On the one hand, we have emanation, on the other contemplation—downward emanation, upward contemplation. It would be a mistake to consider the lower levels to be some kind of degradation, because everything is a necessary expression of the One and thus related to the primary One. To better understand the human situation, we need to take a closer look at the soul and its descent into the body. Plotinus set up the Soul as an outgrowth from Intellect in the following way: Intellect (*Nous*) represents a level of Being that is both One and many; it is itself One, but in its contemplation of the One it gives birth to all rational principles—what in Plato is the intelligible world, the world of forms. The multiplicity of beings demands further differentiation and thus Soul is born, whose task it is to inform matter and thus give rise to nature. In this creative activity, Soul looks to Intellect and its principles, and as a result of this creative contemplation, there arises a multiplicity of individual souls who embody matter. As long as the individual soul remains focused on the "World-Soul"—and its intellectual activity of governing matter and at the same time nourishing itself—Soul is unproblematic. It is when the individual soul attempts to break away from the World-Soul that potential problems develop:

> But there comes a stage at which they descend from the universal to become partial and self-centered; in a weary desire of standing apart they find their way, each to a place of its very own. This state long maintained, the Soul is a deserter from the totality; its differentiation has severed it; its vision is no longer set in the Intellectual; it is a partial thing, isolated, weakened, full of care, intent upon the fragment; severed from the whole, it nestles in one form of being. . . . With this comes what is known as the casting of the wings, the enchaining in body.[4]

The difficulty that the soul now faces is to work through the senses before it can reach the intelligible reality, to reach toward the contemplation of the One. The awareness of the loss of the whole, the experience of being incomplete, is most clearly expressed in *eros*. Plotinus views *eros* as a desire to become whole again. His interpretation of *eros* is fueled by Diotima's account in Plato's *Symposium*. He acknowledges his source numerous times and informs the reader of his principle of interpreting Diotima's myth concerning the birth of *Eros:* "[D]oes not philosophy itself relate the births of the unbegotten and discriminate where all is one substance? The truth is conveyed in the only manner possible, it is left to our good sense to bring all together again."[5] In this manner reading and interpreting also repeat the movement from the One to multiplicity and back to the One.

The educational goal of the *Enneads* is to bring about an *epistrophe,* a return to the One. The passage presented here charts the steps toward such a return: the account of the birth of Eros points to different levels of love, from the passive affection of the soul at the lowest level to the active godlike level, directed toward the intelligible reality, the first emanation from the One.

AT

QUESTIONS

1. How does Plotinus differentiate pure love of beauty from love for beauty mixed with desire? What role do the senses, particularly vision, play in Plotinus's account of love?
2. How is "perverse love" like "false thoughts"?
3. How does Plotinus differentiate between god-love and spirit-love?
4. What do Zeus and Aphrodite signify?

ENDNOTES

1. Cf. Plotinus, *Enneads V,* 1, 8.
2. Cf. in the current selection at III, 5, 1 1st paragraph.
3. Cf. Hegel, pp. 12–14.
4. Plotinus, *Enneads IV,* 8th Tractate, pp. 338–339.
5. Plotinus, *Enneads III,* 5th Tractate, p. 186 see below p. 105.

SELECTED BIBLIOGRAPHY

Gerson, Lloyd P., ed. *The Cambridge Companion to Plotinus.* Cambridge, England: Cambridge University Press, 1996.

Hegel, G.W.F. *Vorlesungen über die Geschichte der Philosophie,* vol. 3, Jubiläumsausgabe, ed. Hermann Glockner. Stuttgart: Fr. Frommanns Verlag, 1959, vol. 19.

Plotinus, *The Enneads,* trans. Stephen MacKenna, abridged by John Dillon. London, England: Penguin Classics, 1991.

Rist, J.M. *Eros and Psyche: Studies in Plato, Plotinus and Origen.* Toronto, Canada: University of Toronto Press, 1964.

FIFTH TRACTATE
LOVE [50]

from *Enneads*

Plotinus

Summary

This late treatise is the nearest thing we have in Plotinus' work to the connected exegesis of a myth—though even this is not very systematic, and the myth is a Platonic one, that of the birth of Eros in the Symposium (203 Bff.). It constitutes an important statement of Plotinus' doctrine on Love, both the affection in the soul and the metaphysical reality (ch. 2–5), as well as on daemons in general (ch. 6–7), and on the interpretation of myths (ch. 9).

1. What is Love? A God, a Celestial Spirit, a state of mind? Or is it, perhaps, sometimes to be thought of as a God or Spirit and sometimes merely as an experience? And what is it essentially in each of these respects?

These important questions make it desirable to review prevailing opinions on the matter, the philosophical treatment it has received and, especially, the theories of the great Plato who has many passages dealing with Love, from a point of view entirely his own.

Plato does not treat of it as simply a state observed in souls; he also makes it a Spirit-being; so that we read of the birth of Eros,[1] under definite circumstances and by a certain parentage.

Now everyone recognizes that the emotional state for which we make this 'Love' responsible rises in souls aspiring to be knit in the closest union with some beautiful object, and that this aspiration takes two forms, that of the good whose devotion is for beauty itself, and that other which seeks its consummation in some vile act. But this generally admitted distinction opens a new question: we need a philosophical investigation into the origin of the two phases.

It is sound, I think, to find the primal source of Love in a tendency of the Soul towards pure beauty, in a recognition, in a kinship, in an unreasoned consciousness of friendly relation. The vile and ugly is in clash, at once, with Nature and with God: Nature produces by looking to the Good, for it looks towards Order—which has its being in the consistent total[2] of the good, while the unordered is ugly, a member of the system of evil—and besides, Nature itself, clearly, springs from the divine realm, from Good and Beauty; and when anything brings delight and the sense of kinship, its very image attracts.

Reject this explanation, and no one can tell how the mental state rises and what are its causes: it is the explanation of even copulative love, which is the will to beget in beauty;[3] Nature seeks to produce the beautiful and therefore by all reason cannot desire to procreate in the ugly.

Those that desire earthly procreation are satisfied with the beauty found on earth, the beauty of

---

[1]This refers to the myth of the birth of Eros from Poverty (*Penia*) and Resourcefulness (*Poros*) in the *Symp.* 203 Bff. The tractate is in fact largely an exegesis of this myth (especially from ch. 5 onwards) to an extent unusual with Plotinus.

[2]Actually a reference to the Pythagorean Table of Opposites. What is ordered or limited is in the *systoichia* (column) of the Good. The impulse to beauty is an impulse towards cosmic order.

[3]A quotation of *Symp.* 206c 4–5.

image and of body; it is because they are strangers to the Archetype, the source of even the attraction they feel towards what is lovely here. There are souls to whom earthly beauty is a leading to the memory of that in the higher realm and these love the earthly as an image; those that have not attained to this memory do not understand what is happening within them, and take the image for the reality. Once there is perfect self-control, it is no fault to enjoy the beauty of earth; where appreciation degenerates into carnality, there is sin.

Pure Love seeks the beauty alone, whether there is Reminiscence or not; but there are those that feel, also, a desire of such immortality as lies within mortal reach; and these are seeking Beauty in their demand for perpetuity, the desire of the eternal; Nature teaches them to sow the seed and to beget in beauty, to sow towards eternity, but in beauty through their own kinship with the beautiful. And indeed the eternal is of the one stock with the beautiful, the Eternal-Nature is the first shaping of beauty and makes beautiful all that rises from it.

The less the desire for procreation, the greater is the contentment with beauty alone, yet procreation aims at the engendering of beauty; it is the expression of a lack; the subject is conscious of insufficiency and, wishing to produce beauty, feels that the way is to beget in a beautiful form. Where the procreative desire is lawless or against the purposes of nature, the first inspiration has been natural, but they have diverged from the way, they have slipped and fallen, and they grovel; they neither understand whither Love sought to lead them nor have they any instinct to production; they have not mastered the right use of the images of beauty; they do not know what the Authentic Beauty is.

Those that love beauty of person without carnal desire love for beauty's sake; those that have—for women, of course—the copulative love, have the further purpose of self-perpetuation: as long as they are led by these motives, both are on the right path, though the first have taken the nobler way. But, even in the right, there is the difference that the one set, worshipping the beauty of earth, look no further, while the others, those of recollection, venerate also the beauty of the other world while they, still, have no contempt for this in which they recognize, as it were, a last outgrowth, an attention of the higher. These, in sum, are innocent frequenters of beauty, not to be confused with the class to whom it becomes an occasion of fall into the ugly—for the aspiration towards a good degenerates into an evil often.

So much for love, the state.
Now we have to consider Love, the God.

2.   The existence of such a being is no demand of the ordinary man, merely; it is supported by Theologians (Orphic teachers) and, over and over again, by Plato to whom Eros is child of Aphrodite,[4] minister of beautiful children, inciter of human souls towards the supernal beauty or quickener of an already existing impulse thither. All this requires philosophical examination. A cardinal passage is that in The Banquet[5] where we are told Eros was not a child of Aphrodite but born on the day of Aphrodite's birth, Penia, Poverty, being the mother, and Poros, Possession, the father.

The matter seems to demand some discussion of Aphrodite since in any case Eros is described as being either her son or in some association with her. Who then is Aphrodite, and in what sense is Love either her child or born with her or in some way both her child and her birth-fellow?

---

[4]This and the following phrase are taken from the *Phaedr.* 242d9 and 265c 2–3, Plotinus also has the *Phaedr.* myth in mind in his exegesis.
[5]*Symp.* 203 BC.

To us Aphrodite is twofold;[6] there is the heavenly Aphrodite, daughter of Ouranos or Heaven: and there is the other the daughter of Zeus and Dione, this is the Aphrodite who presides over earthly unions; the higher was not born of a mother and has no part in marriages, for in Heaven there is no marrying.

The Heavenly Aphrodite, daughter of Kronos (Saturn)—who is no other than the Intellectual Principle—must be the Soul at its divinest: unmingled as the immediate emanation of the unmingled; remaining ever Above, as neither desirous nor capable of descending to this sphere, never having developed the downward tendency, a divine Hypostasis essentially aloof, so unreservedly an Authentic Being as to have no part with Matter—and therefore mythically 'the unmothered'—justly called not Celestial Spirit but God, as knowing no admixture, gathered cleanly within itself.

Any nature springing directly from the Intellectual Principle must be itself also a clean thing: it will derive a resistance of its own from its nearness to the Highest, for all its tendency, no less than its fixity, centres upon its author whose power is certainly sufficient to maintain it Above.

Soul then could never fall from its sphere; it is closer held to the divine Mind than the very sun could hold the light it gives forth to radiate about it, an outpouring from itself held firmly to it, still.

But following upon Kronos—or, if you will, upon Heaven (Ouranos),[7] the father of Kronos—the Soul directs its Act towards him and holds closely to him and in that love brings forth the Eros through whom it continues to look towards him. This Act of the Soul has produced an Hypostasis, a Real-Being; and the mother and this Hypostasis—her offspring, noble Love—gaze together upon Divine Mind. Love, thus, is ever intent upon that other loveliness, and exists to be the medium between desire and that object of desire. It is the eye of the desirer; by its power what loves is enabled to see the loved thing. But it is first; before it becomes the vehicle of vision, it is itself filled with the sight; it is first, therefore, and not even in the same order—for desire attains to vision only through the efficacy of Love, while Love, in its own Act, harvests the spectacle of beauty playing immediately above it.

3.   That Love is a Hypostasis (a 'Person'),[8] a Real-Being sprung from a Real-Being—lower than the parent but authentically existent—is beyond doubt.

For the parent-Soul was a Real-Being sprung directly from the Act of the Hypostasis that ranks before it: it had life; it was a constituent in the Real-Being of all that authentically is—in the Real-Being which looks, rapt, towards the very Highest. That was the first object of its vision; it looked towards it as towards its good, and it rejoiced in the looking; and the quality of what it saw was such that the contemplation could not be void of effect; in virtue of that rapture, of its position in regard to its object, of the intensity of its gaze, the Soul conceived and brought forth an offspring worthy of itself and of the vision. Thus; there is a strenuous activity of contemplation in the Soul; there is an emanation towards it from the object contemplated; and Eros is born, the Love which is an eye filled with its vision, a seeing that bears its image

---

[6]As expounded by Pausanias, earlier in the *Symposium* (180D). Plotinus makes use of this distinction to ground his distinction between a higher Soul, which remains transcendent, and a lower one, which enters into the physical world.

[7]A concession to traditional mythology. In Hesiod, *Theog.* 188ff., Aphrodite is born from the foam generated when Ouranos' genitals are cast into the sea by Kronos, when he castrates him.

[8]This seems almost a breach of Plotinus' system of three hypostases, but in fact Eros is just an aspect of soul. The second soul, or nature (also with its Eros) is more nearly another hypostasis.

with it; Eros taking its name, probably, from the fact that its essential being is due to this ὄρασις,[9] this seeing. Of course Love, as an emotion, will take its name from Love, the Person, since a Real-Being cannot but be prior to what lacks this reality. The mental state will be designated as Love, like the Hypostasis, though it is no more than a particular act directed towards a particular object; but it must not be confused with the Absolute Love, the Divine Being. The Eros that belongs to the supernal Soul must be of one temper with it; it must itself look aloft as being of the household of that Soul, dependent upon that Soul, its very offspring; and therefore caring for nothing but the contemplation of the Gods.

Once that Soul which is the primal source of light to the heavens is recognized as an Hypostasis standing distinct and aloof, it must be admitted that Love too is distinct and aloof. To describe the Soul as 'celestial' is not to question its separateness (or immateriality); our own best we conceive as inside ourselves and yet something apart. So, we must think of this Love—as essentially resident where the unmingling Soul inhabits.

But besides this purest Soul, there must be also a Soul of the All: at once there is another Love—the eye with which this second Soul looks upwards—like the supernal Eros engendered by force of desire. This Aphrodite, the secondary Soul, is of this Universe—not Soul unmingled alone, not Soul the Absolute—giving birth, therefore, to the Love concerned with the universal life; no, this is the Love presiding over marriages; but it, also, has its touch of the upward desire; and, in the degree of that striving, it stirs and leads upwards the souls of the young and every soul with which it is incorporated in so far as there is a natural tendency to

remembrance of the divine. For every soul is striving towards The Good, even the mingling Soul and that of particular beings, for each holds directly from the divine Soul, and is its offspring.

4. Does each individual Soul, then, contain within itself such a Love in essence and substantial reality?

Since not only the pure All-Soul but also that of the Universe contains such a Love, it would be difficult to explain why our personal Soul should not. It must be so, even, with all that has life.

This indwelling love is no other than the Spirit which, as we are told, walks with every being,[10] the affection dominant in each several nature. It implants the characteristic desire; the particular Soul, strained towards its own natural objects, brings forth its own Eros, the guiding spirit realizing its worth and the quality of its Being.

As the All-Soul contains the Universal Love, so must the single Soul be allowed its own single Love: and as closely as the single Soul holds to the All-Soul,[11] never cut off but embraced within it, the two together constituting one principle of life, so the single separate Love holds to the All-Love. Similarly, the individual Love keeps with the individual Soul as that other, the great Love, goes with the All-Soul; and the Love within the All permeates it throughout so that the one Love becomes many, showing itself where it chooses at any moment of the Universe, taking definite shape in these its partial phases and revealing itself at its will.

In the same way we must conceive many Aphrodites in the All, Spirits entering it together with Love, all emanating from an Aphrodite of the All, a train of particular Aphrodites dependent

---

[9]A characteristically wild Greek etymology—*eros* from (*h*) *orasis* (Plotinus would not have pronounced the *h*).

[10]The personal *eros* seems here to be identified with the guardian daemon, cf. III. 4.

[11]A reference to the unity of individual souls in the All-Soul, which yet maintains them all distinct, cf. IV. 3, 8; VI. 4, 14.

upon the first, and each with the particular Love in attendance: this multiplicity cannot be denied, if Soul be the mother of Love, and Aphrodite mean Soul, and Love be an act of a Soul seeking good.

This Love, then, leader of particular souls to The Good, is twofold: the Love in the loftier Soul would be a god ever linking the Soul to the divine; the Love in the mingling Soul will be a celestial spirit.

5.   But what is the nature of this Spirit—of the Celestials (Daimones) in general?

The Spirit-Kind is treated in the Symposium where, with much about the others, we learn of Eros—Love—born to Penia—Poverty—and Poros—Possession—who is son of Metis—Resource—at Aphrodite's birth feast.

But (the passage has been misunderstood[12] for) to take Plato as meaning, by Eros, this Universe— and not simply the Love native within it—involves much that is self-contradictory.

For one thing, the universe is described as a blissful god[13] and as self-sufficing, while this 'Love' is confessedly neither divine nor self-sufficing but in ceaseless need.

Again, this Cosmos is a compound of body and soul; but Aphrodite to Plato is the Soul itself, therefore Aphrodite would necessarily be a constituent part of Eros, (not mother but) dominant member! A man is the man's Soul; if the world is, similarly, the world's Soul, then Aphrodite, the Soul, is identical with Love, the Cosmos! And why should this one spirit, Love, be the Universe to the exclusion of all the others, which certainly are sprung from the same Essential-Being? Our only escape would be to make the Cosmos a complex of Celestials.

Love, again, is called the Dispenser of beautiful children:[14] does this apply to the Universe? Love is represented as homeless, bedless, and bare-footed:[15] would not that be a shabby description of the Cosmos and quite out of the truth?

6.   What then, in sum, is to be thought of Love and of his 'birth' as we are told of it?

Clearly we have to establish the significance, here, of Poverty and Possession, and show in what way the parentage is appropriate: we have also to bring these two into line with the other Celestials,[16] since one spirit nature, one spirit essence, must characterize all unless they are to have merely a name in common.

We must, therefore, lay down the grounds on which we distinguish the Gods from the Celestials—that is, when we emphasize the separate nature of the two orders and are not, as often in practice, including these Spirits under the common name of Gods.

It is our teaching and conviction that the Gods are immune to all passion, while we attribute experience and emotion to the Celestials which, though eternal Beings and directly next to the Gods, are already a step towards ourselves and stand between the divine and the human.

But by what process (of degeneration) was the immunity lost? What in their nature led them downwards to the inferior?

And other questions present themselves.

Does the Intellectual Realm include no member of this spirit order, not even one? And does the

---

[12]A criticism of such an interpretation as is found in Plutarch's *On Isis and Osiris* (374DE), where Eros is identified with the physical universe, as product of Form (*Poros*) and Matter (*Penia*).

[13]*Tim.* 3468.

[14]*Phaedr.* 265c2.

[15]*Symp.* 203d 1–2.

[16]That is, daemons. The distinction between Gods and daemons is an old subject of discussion in Platonism, going back to Xenocrates.

Cosmos contain only these spirits, God being confined to the Intellectual? Or are there Gods in the sub-celestial too, the Cosmos itself being a God, the third, as is commonly said,[17] and the Powers down to the Moon being all Gods as well?

It is best not to use the word 'Celestial' of any Being of that Realm; the word 'God' may be applied to the Essential-Celestial—the auto-daimon, if he exists—and even to the Visible Powers of the Universe of Sense down to the Moon; Gods, these too, visible, secondary, sequent upon the Gods of the Intellectual Realm, consonant with Them, held about Them, as the radiance about the star.

What, then, are these spirits?

A Celestial is the representative generated by each Soul when it enters the Cosmos.

And why, by a Soul entering the Cosmos?

Because Soul pure of the Cosmos generates not a Celestial Spirit but a God; hence it is that we have spoken of Love, offspring of Aphrodite the Pure Soul, as a God.

But, first, what prevents every one of the Celestials from being an Eros, a Love? And why are they not untouched by Matter like the Gods?

On the first question: every Celestial born in the striving of the Soul towards the good and beautiful is an Eros; and all the souls within the Cosmos do engender this Celestial; but other Spirit-Beings, equally born from the Soul of the All, but by other faculties of that Soul, have other functions: they are for the direct service of the All, and administer particular things to the purpose of the Universe entire. The Soul of the All must be adequate to all that is and therefore must bring into being spirit powers serviceable not merely in one function but to its entire charge.

But what participation can the Celestial have in Matter, and in what Matter?

Certainly none in bodily Matter; that would make them simply living things of the order of sense. And if, even, they are to invest themselves in bodies of air or of fire, their nature must have already been altered before they could have any contact with the corporeal. The Pure does not mix, unmediated, with body—though many think that the Celestial-Kind, of its very essence, comports a body aerial or of fire.

But (since this is not so) why should one order of Celestial descend to body and another not? The difference implies the existence of some cause or medium working upon such as thus descend. What would constitute such a medium?

We are forced to assume that there is a Matter of the Intellectual Order,[18] and that Beings partaking of it are thereby enabled to enter into the lower Matter, the corporeal.

7.   This is the significance of Plato's account of the birth of Love.

The drunkenness of the father Poros or Possession is caused by Nectar, 'wine yet not existing'; Love is born before the realm of sense has come into being: Penia (Poverty) had participation in the Intellectual before the lower image of that divine Realm had appeared; she dwelt in that Sphere, but as a mingled being consisting partly of Form but partly also of that indetermination which belongs to the Soul before she attains the Good and when all her knowledge of Reality is a fore-intimation veiled by the indeterminate and unordered: in this state (of fore-feeling and desiring The Good) Poverty brings forth the Hypostasis, Love.

This, then, is a union of Reason with something that is not Reason but a mere indeterminate striv-

---

[17]This term is used by Numenius to describe the cosmos (Frs 11; 21 Des Places).

[18]Plotinus makes use of the concept of intelligible matter elsewhere, in II. 4, but in a quite different sense. Here it is postulated as a kind of prefiguration of matter at the intelligible level, as a cause of declination of some entities, and is identified with Poverty at its archetypal level.

ing in a being not yet illuminated: the offspring Love, therefore, is not perfect, not self-sufficient, but unfinished, bearing the signs of its parentage, the undirected striving and the self-sufficient Reason. This offspring is a Reason-Principle but not purely so; for it includes within itself an aspiration ill-defined, unreasoned, unlimited—it can never be sated as long as it contains within itself that element of the Indeterminate. Love, then, clings to the Soul, from which it sprang as from the principle of its Being, but it is lessened by including an element of the Reason-Principle which did not remain self-concentrated but blended with the indeterminate, not, it is true, by immediate contact but through its emanation. Love, therefore, is like a goad;[19] it is without resource in itself; even winning its end, it is poor again.

It cannot be satisfied because a thing of mixture never can be so: true satisfaction is only for what has its plenitude in its own being; where craving is due to an inborn deficiency, there may be satisfaction at some given moment but it does not last. Love, then, has on the one side the powerlessness of its native inadequacy, on the other the resource inherited from the Reason-Kind.

Such must be the nature and such the origin of the entire Spirit Order: each—like its fellow, Love—has its appointed sphere, is powerful there, and wholly devoted to it, and, like Love, none is ever complete of itself but always straining towards some good which it sees in things of the partial sphere.

We understand, now, why good men have no other Love—no other Eros of life—than that for the Absolute and Authentic Good, and never follow the random attractions known to those ranged under the lower Spirit Kind.

Each human being is set under his own Spirit-Guides, but this is mere blank possession when they ignore their own and live by some other spirit adopted by them as more closely attuned to the operative part of the Soul in them. Those that go after evil are natures that have merged all the Love-Principles within them in the evil desires springing in their hearts and allowed the right reason, which belongs to our kind, to fall under the spell of false ideas from another source.

All the natural Loves, all that serve the ends of Nature, are good; in a lesser Soul, inferior in rank and in scope; in the greater Soul, superior; but all belong to the order of Being. Those forms of Love that do not serve the purposes of Nature are merely accidents attending on perversion: in no sense are they Real-Beings or even manifestations of any Reality; for they are no true issue of Soul; they are merely accompaniments of a spiritual flaw which the Soul automatically exhibits in the total of disposition and conduct.

In a word; all that is truly good in a Soul acting to the purposes of nature and within its appointed order, all this is Real-Being: anything else is alien, no act of the Soul, but merely something that happens to it: a parallel may be found in false mentation, notions behind which there is no reality as there is in the case of authentic ideas, the eternal, the strictly defined, in which there is at once an act of true knowing, a truly knowable object and authentic existence—and this not merely in the Absolute, but also in the particular being that is occupied by the authentically knowable and by the Intellectual-Principle manifest in every several form. In each particular human being we must admit the existence of the authentic Intellective Act and of the authentically knowable object—though not as wholly merged into our being, since we are not these in the absolute and not exclusively these.

It follows that Love, like our intellectual activities, is concerned with absolute things: if we sometimes are for the partial, that affection is not direct

---

[19]A reference to *Phaedr.* 240 dI.

but accidental, like our knowledge that a given triangular figure is made up of two right angles because the absolute triangle is so.[20]

8. But what are we to understand by this Zeus with the garden into which, we are told, Poros or Wealth entered?[21] And what is the garden?

We have seen that the Aphrodite of the Myth is the Soul and that Poros, Wealth, is the Reason-Principle of the Universe: we have still to explain Zeus and his garden.

We cannot take Zeus to be the Soul, which we have agreed is represented by Aphrodite.

Plato, who must be our guide in this question, speaks in the Phaedrus[22] of this God, Zeus, as the Great Leader—though elsewhere[23] he seems to rank him as one of three—but in the Philebus[24] he speaks more plainly when he says that there is in Zeus not only a royal Soul, but also a royal Intellect.

As a mighty Intellect and Soul, he must be a principle of Cause; he must be the highest for several reasons but especially because to be King and Leader is to be the chief cause: Zeus then is the Intellectual Principle. Aphrodite, his daughter, issue of him, dwelling with him, will be Soul, her very name Aphrodite (= the $\dot{\alpha}\beta\rho\dot{\alpha}$, delicate) indicating the beauty and gleam and innocence and delicate grace of the Soul.

And if we take the male gods to represent the Intellectual Powers and the female gods to be their souls—to every Intellectual Principle its companion Soul—we are forced, thus also, to make Aphrodite the Soul of Zeus; and the identification is confirmed by Priests and Theologians who consider Aphrodite and Hera one and the same and call Aphrodite's star ('Venus') the star of Hera.[25]

9. This Poros, Possession, then, is the Reason-Principle of all that exists in the Intellectual Realm and in the supreme Intellect; but being more diffused, kneaded out as it were, it must touch Soul, be in Soul (as the next lower principle).

For, all that lies gathered in the Intellect is native to it: nothing enters from without; but 'Poros intoxicated' is some Power deriving satisfaction outside itself: what, then, can we understand by this member of the Supreme filled with Nectar but a Reason-Principle falling from a loftier essence to a lower? This means that the Reason-Principle upon 'the birth of Aphrodite' left the Intellectual for the Soul, breaking into the garden of Zeus.

A garden is a place of beauty and a glory of wealth: all the loveliness that Zeus maintains takes its splendour from the Reason-Principle within him; for all this beauty is the radiation of the Divine Intellect upon the Divine Soul, which it has penetrated. What could the Garden of Zeus indicate but the images of his Being and the splendours of his glory? And what could these divine splendours and beauties be but the Reason-Principles streaming from him?

These Reason-Principles—this Poros who is the lavishness, the abundance of Beauty—are at one and are made manifest; this is the Nectar-drunkenness. For the Nectar of the gods can be no other than what the god-nature receives from outside itself, and that whose place is after the divine Mind (namely, Soul) receives a Reason-Principle.

The Intellectual Principle possesses itself to satiety, but there is no 'drunken' abandonment in this

---

[20]An example borrowed from Aristotle, e.g. Met. V 30, 1025 a 32.

[21]*Symp.* 203b 5–6.

[22]246 e 4.

[23]A reference to *Epistle* II 312 E, a key passage for Neoplatonists.

[24]30 d 1–2. This conjunction of proof-texts is a good example of Plotinus's (and later Platonist) exegetical methods.

---

[25]The priests and theologians cannot be identified, but the giving of the name 'Hera' to the planet Venus is attested in the pseudo-Aristotelian *De Mundo* (first century A.D.?), 392 a 26, and 'Timaeus Locrus' 96E (also probably first century A.D.).

possession which brings nothing alien to it. But the Reason-Principle—as its offspring, a later hypostasis—is already a separate Being and established in another Realm, and so is said to lie in the garden of this Zeus who is divine Mind; and this lying in the garden takes place at the moment when, in our way of speaking, Aphrodite enters the realm of Being.

'Our way of speaking'[26]—for myths, if they are to serve their purpose, must necessarily import time-distinctions into their subject and will often present as separate, Powers which exist in unity but differ in rank and faculty; and does not philosophy itself relate the births of the unbegotten and discriminate where all is one substance? The truth is conveyed in the only manner possible; it is left to our good sense to bring all together again.

On this principle we have, here, Soul (successively) dwelling with the divine Intelligence, breaking away from it, and yet again being filled to satiety with Reason-Principles—the beautiful abounding in all plenty, so that every splendour become manifest in it with the images of whatever is lovely—Soul which, taken as one all, is Aphrodite, while in it may be distinguished the Reason-Principles summed under the names of Plenty and Possession, produced by the downflow of the Nectar of the over realm. The splendours contained in Soul are thought of as the garden of Zeus with reference to their existing within Life; and Poros sleeps in this garden in the sense of being sated and heavy with its produce. Life is eternally manifest, an eternal existent among the existences, and the banqueting of the gods means no more than that they have their Being in that vital blessedness. And Love—'born at the banquet of the gods'—has of necessity been eternally in existence, for it springs from the intention of the Soul towards its Best, towards the Good; as long as Soul has been, Love has been.

Still this Love is of mixed quality. On the one hand there is in it the lack which keeps it craving: on the other, it is not entirely destitute; the deficient seeks more of what it has, and certainly nothing absolutely void of good would ever go seeking the Good.

It is said then to spring from Poverty and Possession in the sense that Lack and Aspiration and the Memory of the Reason-Principles, all present together in the Soul, produce that Act towards The Good which is Love. Its Mother is Poverty, since striving is for the needy; and this Poverty is Matter, for Matter is the wholly poor: the very ambition towards the Good is a sign of existing indetermination; there is a lack of shape and of Reason in that which must aspire towards the Good, and the greater degree of indetermination implies the lower depth of materiality. To the thing aspiring the Good is an Ideal-Principle distinct and unchanging, and aspiration prepares that which would receive the Good to offer itself as Matter to the incoming power.

Thus Love is, at once, in some degree a thing[27] of Matter and at the same time a Celestial sprung of the Soul's unsatisfied longing for The Good.

---

[26]Plotinus now embarks on an important theoretical analysis of myth, illustrating it by reference to the present one.

[27]This is a very obscure passage, but probably means: 'what is turned towards itself (reading *hauto,* not *auto,* as does Ficino) is Form, remaining alone in itself, when it also desires to receive (something other than itself), this causes it to be Matter to what comes upon it.' The contrast here is between the self-related and other-related aspects of Soul.

chapter eight

Saint Augustine

St. Augustine (354–430), Christian philosopher and Doctor of the Western Church, was the most successful and influential of the early Christian thinkers committed to synthesizing two traditions of wisdom: classical Greek philosophy and Christianity. Specifically, Augustine interpreted several challenging themes of Christian doctrine—such as the nature of God and his relationship to human souls—by invoking what he considered to be the most relevant and more intelligible ideas in Greek thought, especially the philosophy of Plato. Accordingly, Augustine is the primary bridge between classical antiquity and medieval Scholastic philosophy,[1] making him one of the chief architects of Western thought.

Augustine was born Aurelius Augustinus in the Roman community of Tagaste, North Africa, just thirty-one years after Emperor Constantine converted to Christianity and granted religious toleration to Christians. He thus grew up in a culture that shared distinctively pagan and Christian features, a fact that had a profound effect upon his life and thought. There were tensions between Christian doctrine and pagan philosophies that stimulated turbulent debates in which Augustine himself came to occupy a central place. On the other hand, many fourth-century Christians fully embraced their Greco-Roman heritage instead of rejecting it upon their conversion, seeking only to give their classical heritage new spiritual direction in light of the teachings of Christ. The son of a Christian mother[2] and a pagan father, Augustine became, like his mother, the latter type of Christian in adulthood. His father shaped his youth, however, and stressed education and career as the key ingredients of a successful life.

Augustine's *Confessions* (397), his first major work and the first known autobiography in the Western tradition, recounts his long journey from an adolescence devoted to the pursuit of an education, reputation, and sensual pleasure, to his conversion at age thirty-three and subsequent commitment to an ascetic life of spiritual introspection. The text reveals that even in youth Augustine possessed a penchant for reflection, as well as a brilliant mind. His passion for wisdom was set ablaze at age nineteen when he read Cicero's *Hortensius,* which urges the pursuit of wisdom through the study of phi-

---

losophy. Augustine's Latin education in rhetoric and literature supplied him with little knowledge of Greek philosophy, so he turned to the Bible to study the teachings of Jesus who was, it was said, the very wisdom of God.

Augustine found the Bible disappointing, both because he considered its literary style unsophisticated and because many of its concepts seemed unintelligible. He was particularly dissatisfied with the biblical account of evil: If God is the author of all creation, does it not follow that he is the source of evil? If so, then how can God be perfectly good? Augustine found the tenets of another religion, Manicheanism, more satisfying on this score, as it conceived of the universe as the battleground of *equal* and *opposite* forces of good and evil residing in soul and matter respectively. In Manicheanism, there is no such thing as an omnipotent creator god who can be said to be responsible for the presence of evil. Augustine appreciated, moreover, the Manichean view of the human being as a soul "caught" in a material body, suggesting that he himself was essentially good and not responsible for the sins of his body. He grew dissatisfied, however, when he recognized that this presumption of his essential goodness, like many other Manichean concepts, lacked any real imperative—it had no power actually to produce good moral behavior.

At the same time that Augustine drifted away from Manicheanism, he began serious study of Greek philosophy, especially the Skeptics. He went to Rome and later accepted the prestigious imperial position of professor of rhetoric of Milan. His mother joined him, and so he escorted her regularly to hear the sermons of Ambrose, bishop of Milan. Ambrose's rhetorical style greatly pleased Augustine, but he also grew increasingly intrigued by the content of the sermons, which reflected Ambrose's superior understanding of classical philosophy. Ambrose's thought especially appealed to Augustine because it succeeded in making obscure Christian concepts intelligible. The bishop appropriated Greek philosophy and the Neo-Platonism of Plotinus and others who rendered splendid intellectual interpretations of the fall and rise of the human soul. Ambrose derived from Plato's theory of the Forms, for instance, that God is an immaterial reality; Plato's highest Form, the Good, is comparable to the Supreme Being of Christianity. Augustine grasped from this Neo-Platonist interpretation of Scripture that Christian doctrine could be understood allegorically rather than literally—an intelligible interpretation of Christianity is possible after all.[3]

Augustine was thus inspired to undertake a serious study of the Bible and Neo-Platonism. In time he felt compelled to convert to Christianity, but he hesitated—he was not certain that he could relinquish his preoccupation with career, reputation, and sex.[4] He later wrote in *Confessions*, "I was held fast, not in fetters clamped upon me by another, but by my own will, which had the strength of iron chains. . . . Two wills within me, one old, one new, one the servant of the flesh, the other of the spirit, were in conflict and between them they tore my soul apart" (*Confessions,* 8.5).

Augustine reported in *Confessions* that a mystical experience ended his torment. In a garden in Milan a traveler told him about Christians who had renounced the world and given themselves wholly to God. This discussion, he wrote, "precipitated a vast storm bearing a massive downpour of tears":

> I felt that I was still the captive of my sins, and in my misery I kept crying, "How long shall I go on saying 'tomorrow, tomorrow'? Why not now? Why not make an end of my ugly sins at this moment?"
>
> I was asking myself these questions, weeping all the while with the most bitter sorrow in my heart, when all at once I heard the sing-song voice of a child in a nearby house. Whether it was the voice of a boy or a girl I cannot say, but again and again it repeated the refrain "Take it and read, take it and read." At this I looked up, thinking hard whether there was any kind of game in which children used to chant words like those, but I could not remember ever hearing them before. I stemmed my flood of tears and stood up, telling myself that this could only be a divine command to open my book of Scripture and read the first passage on which my eyes should fall. . . .
>
> So I hurried back to the place where Alypius was sitting, for when I stood up to move away I had put down the book containing Paul's Epistles. I seized it and opened it, and in silence I read the first passage on which my eyes fell: Not in reveling and drunkenness, not in lust and wantonness, not in quarrels and rivalries. Rather arm yourselves with the Lord Jesus Christ; spend no more thought on nature and nature's appetites (Romans 13:13, 14). I had no wish to read more and no need to do so. For in an instant, as I came to the end of the sentence, it was as thought the light of confidence flooded into my heart and all the darkness of doubt was dispelled. (*Confessions,* 8.12)

Confident that he had received, by the grace of God, the power to renounce the world, Augustine spent a winter in retreat and then presented himself to Ambrose on Easter Day 387 for public baptism.

Within a decade of his conversion, Augustine was made priest and ordained bishop of Hippo. In that same decade, he also completed *Confessions.* The text is comprised of thirteen books, of which the first nine constitute Augustine's memorable autobiographical narrative. The remaining books, which include a polemical discussion of the book of Genesis, mainly express Augustine's conviction that even the persistent study of Scripture and pursuit of divine wisdom are inadequate for attaining perfection. He reveals how, even as a bishop, he must acknowledge his imperfections. "I do not know to what temptation I will surrender next," he writes, and he recognizes in that uncertainty the need to rely perpetually upon the grace of God to achieve salvation and happiness.

Augustine understood *Confessions* to be more than simply an autobiographical account of sin and conversion. The autobiographical form of the text is completely incidental to his purpose of conducting a rigorous self-examination, a process that he considered a necessary step in the pursuit of happiness. As its title suggests, *Confessions* is, for Augustine, *consciously* a specific form of authorized religious speech: one that acknowledges one's imperfections, praises God, and professes one's faith.

The necessity, from Augustine's perspective, for *Confessions* becomes evident when one examines the broader context of his thought. The full scope of Augustine's philosophy is too vast to be contained in this brief introduction, but several of his core themes emerge clearly in his discussion of an issue of fundamental concern: the necessary conditions for human happiness. Beginning with the premise that all human beings desire to be happy, Augustine's lengthy deductive argument concludes by asserting that the attainment of happiness requires an appropriate ordering of one's loves, beginning first and foremost with the love of God, who is the only proper object of desire. According to Augustine one of the things the wisdom of God reveals is that the universe is comprised of a great chain of being, a hierarchy of entities organized according to the degree of being they possess. To be happy, one must learn to order one's many loves—for God, people, and things—according to their position in the chain. To be happy, one must love God, the highest being and source of all being, above everyone and everything. Similarly one should love human beings more than animals, plants, and inanimate objects. Accordingly, one runs into trouble when one loves money more than people or God. Similarly, the extent to which it is acceptable to use people or things as means rather than ends is inversely proportional to their degree of being. One must *enjoy* God solely as an end in himself and never as a means to achieving other ends. People should be treated as ends as well, although it may be acceptable to regard them as means to loving God. One should never use a person as a means of acquiring *things* that one loves; it may be acceptable, however, to treat things as means of expressing one's love for people.

Augustine's exposition of *Confessions*—again, primarily a process of self-examination—served to bring these ideas to clearer light for him, but in publishing the text, he clearly also intended it for the edification of others. Ultimately he believed it succeeded in demonstrating that the intellect alone is inadequate to achieve happiness. The will must also be brought into proper alignment if the pursuit is to be successful. Accordingly, Augustine asserted that philosophy is inadequate to guide human beings to truth. Religion must be joined to philosophy in order to manage the will, and the chief concern of religion should be the relationship between God and the individual soul. Augustine thus concluded that wisdom is ultimately a *unity:* the conjoining of the will and the intellect, belief and understanding, religion and philosophy.

In the year 410, the city of Rome was captured by the Visigoths, and many Romans blamed the event on Christians' rejection of the pagan gods. To answer the "blasphemies and errors" of the accusations, Augustine contributed his second major work, *The City of God* (413–26). He posited the idea that all humanity inhabits spiritually "two cities," one heavenly and the other earthly. Individuals *choose* (in accordance with God's will and grace) where they "dwell"—either in the heavenly realm of peace in God or in the earthly world of disorder, death, and disappointment.

Other works by Augustine include *Christian Doctrine* (396–97, 426), *On the Trinity* (399–412, 420), *On Genesis According to the Letter* (401–15), and *Reconsiderations* (426–27).

QUESTIONS

1. What is Augustine's conception of love?
2. In what ways is Augustine's love of God also the love of wisdom (*philosophia*)?
3. What characteristics distinguish good from evil desire for Augustine?
4. Consider for a moment the people and things that you love and rank them, if you can, according to the degree that you love them. How closely does your ranking conform to Augustine's idea of the proper ordering of one's loves? Does this prompt you to agree or disagree with Augustine?
5. For Augustine, in what sense can we choose what we desire?
6. What similarities can you discern between the conception of love rendered in Augustine's account and that described by Diotima in Plato's *Symposium?* Support your answer with examples and textual support.

ENDNOTES

1. The Scholastic philosophers of the middle ages and Renaissance were completely devoted to reconciling classical Greek philosophy to Scripture, although they looked more to Aristotle than to Plato.
2. Augustine's mother was Monica, now venerated in Catholicism as St. Monica.
3. In Book 12 of *Confessions,* Augustine goes even further to acknowledge the possibility of multiple interpretations: "As long as each interpreter is endeavouring to find in the holy scriptures the meaning of the author who wrote it, what evil is it if an exegesis he gives is one shown to be true by you, light of all sincere souls, even if the author whom he is reading did not have that idea and, though he grasped a truth, had not discerned that seen by the interpreter?" (12.18)
4. One of Augustine's more significant relationships was with an unnamed mistress with whom he had a son, Adeodatus. Adeodatus died in adolescence.

SELECTED BIBLIOGRAPHY

Augustine. *The City of God,* trans. Henry Bettenson. Middlesex, England: Penguin Books, 1972.

Augustine. *Confessions,* trans. R.S. Pine-Coffin. New York: Penguin, 1997.

Augustine. *On Free Choice of the Will,* trans. Benjamin G. Hackstaff. New York: Macmillan Company, 1964.

Augustine. *The Teacher.* In *Ancient Christian Writers,* ed. Johannes Quasten and Joseph C. Plumpe. Westminster, Md.: Newman Press, 1964.

Kirwan, Christopher. *Augustine.* New York: Routledge, 1989.

Miles, Margaret R. *Desire and Delight: A New Reading of Augustine's Confessions.* New York: Crossroad Publishing Company, 1992.

O'Donnell, James J. *Augustine.* Twayne's World Authors Series: Latin Literature, ed. Philip Levine. Boston: Twayne Publishers, 1985.

from *Confessions*

St. Augustine

BOOK II

1

I MUST now carry my thoughts back to the abominable things I did in those days, the sins of the flesh which defiled my soul. I do this, my God, not because I love those sins, but so that I may love you. For love of your love I shall retrace my wicked ways. The memory is bitter, but it will help me to savour your sweetness, the sweetness that does not deceive but brings real joy and never fails. For love of your love I shall retrieve myself from the havoc of disruption which tore me to pieces when I turned away from you, whom alone I should have sought, and lost myself instead on many a different quest. For as I grew to manhood I was inflamed with desire for a surfeit of hell's pleasures. Foolhardy as I was, I ran wild with lust that was manifold and rank. In your eyes my beauty vanished and I was foul to the core, yet I was pleased with my own condition and anxious to be pleasing in the eyes of men.

2

I cared for nothing but to love and be loved. But my love went beyond the affection of one mind for another, beyond the arc of the bright beam of friendship. Bodily desire, like a morass, and adolescent sex welling up within me exuded mists which clouded over and obscured my heart, so that I could not distinguish the clear light of true love from the murk of lust. Love and lust together seethed within me. In my tender youth they swept me away over the precipice of my body's appetites and plunged me in the whirlpool of sin. More and more I angered you, unawares. For I had been deafened by the clank of my chains, the fetters of

the death which was my due to punish the pride in my soul. I strayed still farther from you and you did not restrain me. I was tossed and spilled, floundering in the broiling sea of my fornication, and you said no word. How long it was before I learned that you were my true joy! You were silent then, and I went on my way, farther and farther from you, proud in my distress and restless in fatigue, sowing more and more seeds whose only crop was grief.

Was there no one to lull my distress, to turn the fleeting beauty of these new-found attractions to good purpose and set up a goal for their charms, so that the high tide of my youth might have rolled in upon the shore of marriage? The surge might have been calmed and contented by the procreation of children, which is the purpose of marriage, as your law prescribes, O Lord. By this means you form the offspring of our fallen nature, and with a gentle hand you prune back the thorns that have no place in your paradise. For your almighty power is not far from us, even when we are far from you. Or, again, I might have listened more attentively to your voice from the clouds, saying of those who marry that they will *meet with outward distress, but I leave you your freedom;*[1] that *a man does well to abstain from all commerce with women,*[2] and that *he who is unmarried is concerned with God's claim, asking how he is to please God; whereas the married man is concerned with the world's claim, asking how he is to please his wife.*[3] These were the words to which I should have listened with more care, and if I had made myself a *eunuch for love of the kingdom*

---

[1] 1 Cor. 7: 28.
[2] 1 Cor. 7: 1.
[3] 1 Cor. 7: 32, 33.

of heaven,[4] I should have awaited your embrace with all the greater joy.

But, instead, I was in a ferment of wickedness. I deserted you and allowed myself to be carried away by the sweep of the tide. I broke all your lawful bounds and did not escape your lash. For what man can escape it? You were always present, angry and merciful at once, strewing the pangs of bitterness over all my lawless pleasures to lead me on to look for others unallied with pain. You meant me to find them nowhere but in yourself, O Lord, for you teach us by inflicting pain,[5] you smite so that you may heal,[6] and you kill us so that we may not die away from you. Where was I then and how far was I banished from the bliss of your house in that sixteenth year of my life? This was the age at which the frenzy gripped me and I surrendered myself entirely to lust, which your law forbids but human hearts are not ashamed to sanction. My family made no effort to save me from my fall by marriage. Their only concern was that I should learn how to make a good speech and how to persuade others by my words.

3

In the same year my studies were interrupted. I had already begun to go to the near-by town of Madaura to study literature and the art of public speaking, but I was brought back home while my father, a modest citizen of Thagaste whose determination was greater than his means, saved up the money to send me farther afield to Carthage. I need not tell all this to you, my God, but in your presence I tell it to my own kind, to those other men, however few, who may perhaps pick up this book. And I tell it so that I and all who read my words may realize the depths from which we are to

cry to you. Your ears will surely listen to the cry of a penitent heart which lives the life of faith.

No one had anything but praise for my father who, despite his slender resources, was ready to provide his son with all that was needed to enable him to travel so far for the purpose of study. Many of our townsmen, far richer than my father, went to no such trouble for their children's sake. Yet this same father of mine took no trouble at all to see how I was growing in your sight or whether I was chaste or not. He cared only that I should have a fertile tongue, leaving my heart to bear none of your fruits, my God, though you are the only Master, true and good, of its husbandry.

In the meanwhile, during my sixteenth year, the narrow means of my family obliged me to leave school and live idly at home with my parents. The brambles of lust grew high above my head and there was no one to root them out, certainly not my father. One day at the public baths he saw the signs of active virility coming to life in me and this was enough to make him relish the thought of having grandchildren. He was happy to tell my mother about it, for his happiness was due to the intoxication which causes the world to forget you, its Creator, and to love the things you have created instead of loving you, because the world is drunk with the invisible wine of its own perverted, earth-bound will. But in my mother's heart you had already begun to build your temple and laid the foundations of your holy dwelling, while my father was still a catechumen and a new one at that. So, in her piety, she became alarmed and apprehensive, and although I had not yet been baptized, she began to dread that I might follow in the crooked path of those who do not keep their eyes on you but turn their backs instead.

How presumptuous it was of me to say that you were silent, my God, when I drifted farther and farther away from you! Can it be true that you said nothing to me at that time? Surely the words

---

[4]Matt. 19: 12.
[5]See Ps. 93: 20 (94: 20).
[6]See Deut. 32: 39.

which rang in my ears, spoken by your faithful servant, my mother, could have come from none but you? Yet none of them sank into my heart to make me do as you said. I well remember what her wishes were and how she most earnestly warned me not to commit fornication and above all not to seduce any man's wife. It all seemed womanish advice to me and I should have blushed to accept it. Yet the words were yours, though I did not know it. I thought that you were silent and that she was speaking, but all the while you were speaking to me through her, and when I disregarded her, your handmaid, I was disregarding you, though I was both her son and your servant. But I did this unawares and continued headlong on my way. I was so blind to the truth that among my companions I was ashamed to be less dissolute than they were. For I heard them bragging of their depravity, and the greater the sin the more they gloried in it, so that I took pleasure in the same vices not only for the enjoyment of what I did, but also for the applause I won.

Nothing deserves to be despised more than vice; yet I gave in more and more to vice simply in order not to be despised. If I had not sinned enough to rival other sinners, I used to pretend that I had done things I had not done at all, because I was afraid that innocence would be taken for cowardice and chastity for weakness. These were the companions with whom I walked the streets of Babylon. I wallowed in its mire as if it were made of spices and precious ointments, and to fix me all the faster in the very depths of sin the unseen enemy trod me underfoot and enticed me to himself, because I was an easy prey for his seductions. For even my mother, who by now had escaped from the centre of Babylon, though she still loitered in its outskirts, did not act upon what she had heard about me from her husband with the same earnestness as she had advised me about chastity. She saw that I was already infected with a disease that would become dangerous later on, but if the growth of my passions could not be cut back to the quick, she did not think it right to restrict them to the bounds of married love. This was because she was afraid that the bonds of marriage might be a hindrance to my hopes for the future— not of course the hope of the life to come, which she reposed in you, but my hopes of success at my studies. Both my parents were unduly eager for me to learn, my father because he gave next to no thought to you and only shallow thought to me, and my mother because she thought that the usual course of study would certainly not hinder me, but would even help me, in my approach to you. To the best of my memory this is how I construe the characters of my parents. Furthermore, I was given a free rein to amuse myself beyond the strict limits of discipline, so that I lost myself in many kinds of evil ways, in all of which a pall of darkness hung between me and the bright light of your truth, my God. What malice proceeded from my pampered heart![7]

4

It is certain, O Lord, that theft is punished by your law, the law that is written in men's hearts and cannot be erased however sinful they are. For no thief can bear that another thief should steal from him, even if he is rich and the other is driven to it by want. Yet I was willing to steal, and steal I did, although I was not compelled by any lack, unless it were the lack of a sense of justice or a distaste for what was right and a greedy love of doing wrong. For of what I stole I already had plenty, and much better at that, and I had no wish to enjoy the things I coveted by stealing, but only to enjoy the theft itself and the sin. There was a pear-tree near our vineyard, loaded with fruit that was attractive neither to look at nor to taste. Late one night a

[7]See Ps. 72: 7 (73: 7).

band of ruffians, myself included, went off to shake down the fruit and carry it away, for we had continued our games out of doors until well after dark, as was our pernicious habit. We took away an enormous quantity of pears, not to eat them ourselves, but simply to throw them to the pigs. Perhaps we ate some of them, but our real pleasure consisted in doing something that was forbidden.

Look into my heart, O God, the same heart on which you took pity when it was in the depths of the abyss. Let my heart now tell you what prompted me to do wrong for no purpose, and why it was only my own love of mischief that made me do it. The evil in me was foul, but I loved it. I loved my own perdition and my own faults, not the things for which I committed wrong, but the wrong itself. My soul was vicious and broke away from your safe keeping to seek its own destruction, looking for no profit in disgrace but only for disgrace itself.

5

The eye is attracted by beautiful objects, by gold and silver and all such things. There is great pleasure, too, in feeling something agreeable to the touch, and material things have various qualities to please each of the other senses. Again, it is gratifying to be held in esteem by other men and to have the power of giving them orders and gaining the mastery over them. This is also the reason why revenge is sweet. But our ambition to obtain all these things must not lead us astray from you, O Lord, nor must we depart from what your law allows. The life we live on earth has its own attractions as well, because it has a certain beauty of its own in harmony with all the rest of this world's beauty. Friendship among men, too, is a delightful bond, uniting many souls in one. All these things and their like can be occasions of sin because, good though they are, they are of the lowest order of

good, and if we are too much tempted by them we abandon those higher and better things, your truth, your law, and you yourself, O Lord our God. For these earthly things, too, can give joy, though not such joy as my God, who made them all, can give, because *honest men will rejoice in the Lord; upright hearts will not boast in vain.*[8]

When there is an inquiry to discover why a crime has been committed, normally no one is satisfied until it has been shown that the motive might have been either the desire of gaining, or the fear of losing, one of those good things which I said were of the lowest order. For such things are attractive and have beauty, although they are paltry trifles in comparison with the worth of God's blessed treasures. A man commits murder and we ask the reason. He did it because he wanted his victim's wife or estates for himself, or so that he might live on the proceeds of robbery, or because he was afraid that the other might defraud him of something, or because he had been wronged and was burning for revenge. Surely no one would believe that he would commit murder for no reason but the sheer delight of killing? Sallust tells us that Catiline was a man of insane ferocity, 'who chose to be cruel and vicious without apparent reason',[9] but we are also told that his purpose was 'not to allow his men to lose heart or waste their skill through lack of practice'.[10] If we ask the reason for this, it is obvious that he meant that once he had made himself master of the government by means of this continual violence, he would obtain honour, power, and wealth and would no longer go in fear of the law because of his crimes or have to face difficulties through lack of funds. So even Catiline did not love crime for crime's sake. He loved some-

---

[8]Ps. 63: 11 (64: 10).
[9]Sallust, *Catilina* XVI.
[10]Sallust, *Catilina* XVI.

thing quite different, for the sake of which he committed his crimes.

6

If the crime of theft which I committed that night as a boy of sixteen were a living thing, I could speak to it and ask what it was that, to my shame, I loved in it. I had no beauty because it was a robbery. It is true that the pears which we stole had beauty, because they were created by you, the good God, who are the most beautiful of all beings and the Creator of all things, the supreme Good and my own true Good. But it was not the pears that my unhappy soul desired. I had plenty of my own, better than those, and I only picked them so that I might steal. For no sooner had I picked them than I threw them away, and tasted nothing in them but my own sin, which I relished and enjoyed. If any part of one of those pears passed my lips, it was the sin that gave it flavour.

And now, O Lord my God, now that I ask what pleasure I had in that theft, I find that it had no beauty to attract me. I do not mean beauty of the sort that justice and prudence possess, nor the beauty that is in man's mind and in his memory and in the life that animates him, nor the beauty of the stars in their allotted places or of the earth and sea, teeming with new life born to replace the old as it passes away. It did not even have the shadowy, deceptive beauty which makes vice attractive—pride, for instance, which is a pretence of superiority, imitating yours, for you alone are God, supreme over all; or ambition, which is only a craving for honour and glory, when you alone are to be honoured before all and you alone are glorious for ever. Cruelty is the weapon of the powerful, used to make others fear them: yet no one is to be feared but God alone, from whose power nothing can be snatched away or stolen by any man at any time or place or by any means. The lustful use

caresses to win the love they crave for, yet no caress is sweeter than your charity and no love is more rewarding than the love of your truth, which shines in beauty above all else. Inquisitiveness has all the appearance of a thirst for knowledge, yet you have supreme knowledge of all things. Ignorance, too, and stupidity choose to go under the mask of simplicity and innocence, because you are simplicity itself and no innocence is greater than yours. You are innocent even of the harm which overtakes the wicked, for it is the result of their own actions. Sloth poses as the love of peace: yet what certain peace is there besides the Lord? Extravagance masquerades as fullness and abundance: but you are the full, unfailing store of never-dying sweetness. The spendthrift makes a pretence of liberality: but you are the most generous dispenser of all good. The covetous want many possessions for themselves: you possess all. The envious struggle for preferment: but what is to be preferred before you? Anger demands revenge: but what vengeance is as just as yours? Fear shrinks from any sudden, unwonted danger which threatens the things that it loves, for its only care is safety: but to you nothing is strange, nothing unforeseen. No one can part you from the things that you love, and safety is assured nowhere but in you. Grief eats away its heart for the loss of things which it took pleasure in desiring, because it wants to be like you, from whom nothing can be taken away.

So the soul defiles itself with unchaste love when it turns away from you and looks elsewhere for things which it cannot find pure and unsullied except by returning to you. All who desert you and set themselves up against you merely copy you in a perverse way; but by this very act of imitation they only show that you are the Creator of all nature and, consequently, that there is no place whatever where man may hide away from you.

What was it, then, that pleased me in that act of theft? Which of my Lord's powers did I imitate in a perverse and wicked way? Since I had no real power to break his law, was it that I enjoyed at least the pretence of doing so, like a prisoner who creates for himself the illusion of liberty by doing something wrong, when he has no fear of punishment, under a feeble hallucination of power? Here was the slave who ran away from his master and chased a shadow instead! What an abomination! What a parody of life! What abysmal death! Could I enjoy doing wrong for no other reason than that it was wrong?

7

What return shall I make to the Lord[11] for my ability to recall these things with no fear in my soul? I will love you, Lord, and thank you, and praise your name, because you have forgiven me such great sins and such wicked deeds. I acknowledge that it was by your grace and mercy that you melted away my sins like ice. I acknowledge, too, that by your grace I was preserved from whatever sins I did not commit, for there was no knowing what I might have done, since I loved evil even if it served no purpose. I avow that you have forgiven me all, both the sins which I committed of my own accord and those which by your guidance I was spared from committing.

What man who reflects upon his own weakness can dare to claim that his own efforts have made him chaste and free from sin, as though this entitled him to love you the less, on the ground that he had less need of the mercy by which you forgive the sins of the penitent? There are some who have been called by you and because they have listened to your voice they have avoided the sins which I here record and confess for them to read. But let them not deride me for having been cured by the same Doctor who preserved them from sickness, or at least from such grave sickness as mine. Let them

love you just as much, or even more, than I do, for they can see that the same healing hand which rid me of the great fever of my sins protects them from falling sick of the same disease.

8

It brought me no happiness, for *what harvest did I reap from acts which now make me blush,*[12] particularly from that act of theft? I loved nothing in it except the thieving, though I cannot truly speak of that as a 'thing' that I could love, and I was only the more miserable because of it. And yet, as I recall my feelings at the time, I am quite sure that I would not have done it on my own. Was it then that I also enjoyed the company of those with whom I committed the crime? If this is so, there was something else I loved besides the act of theft; but I cannot call it 'something else', because companionship, like theft, is not a thing at all.

No one can tell me the truth of it except my God, who enlightens my mind and dispels its shadows. What conclusion am I trying to reach from these questions and this discussion? It is true that if the pears which I stole had been to my taste, and if I had wanted to get them for myself, I might have committed the crime on my own if I had needed to do no more than that to win myself the pleasure. I should have had no need to kindle my glowing desire by rubbing shoulders with a gang of accomplices. But as it was not the fruit that gave me pleasure, I must have got it from the crime itself, from the thrill of having partners in sin.

9

How can I explain my mood? It was certainly a very vile frame of mind and one for which I suffered; but how can I account for it? *Who knows his own frailties?*[13]

---

[11]Ps. 115: 12 (116: 12).

[12]Rom. 6: 21.
[13]Ps. 18: 13 (19: 12).

We were tickled to laughter by the prank we had played, because no one suspected us of it although the owners were furious. Why was it, then, that I thought it fun not to have been the only culprit? Perhaps it was because we do not easily laugh when we are alone. True enough: but even when a man is all by himself and quite alone, sometimes he cannot help laughing if he thinks or hears or sees something especially funny. All the same, I am quite sure that I would never have done this thing on my own.

My God, I lay all this before you, for it is still alive in my memory. By myself I would not have committed that robbery. It was not the takings that attracted me but the raid itself, and yet to do it by myself would have been no fun and I should not have done it. This was friendship of a most unfriendly sort, bewitching my mind in an inexplicable way. For the sake of a laugh, a little sport, I was glad to do harm and anxious to damage another; and that without thought of profit for myself or retaliation for injuries received! And all because we are ashamed to hold back when others say 'Come on! Let's do it!'

10

Can anyone unravel this twisted tangle of knots? I shudder to look at it or think of such abomination. I long instead for innocence and justice, graceful and splendid in eyes whose sight is undefiled. My longing fills me and yet it cannot cloy. With them is certain peace and life that cannot be disturbed. The man who enters their domain goes to *share the joy of his Lord.*[14] He shall know no fear and shall lack no good. In him that is goodness itself he shall find his own best way of life. But I deserted you, my God. In my youth I wandered away, too far

---

[14]Matt. 25: 21.

from your sustaining hand, and created of myself a barren waste.

BOOK III

1

I WENT to Carthage, where I found myself in the midst of a hissing cauldron of lust. I had not yet fallen in love, but I was in love with the idea of it, and this feeling that something was missing made me despise myself for not being more anxious to satisfy the need. I began to look around for some object for my love, since I badly wanted to love something. I had no liking for the safe path without pitfalls, for although my real need was for you, my God, who are the food of the soul, I was not aware of this hunger. I felt no need for the food that does not perish, not because I had had my fill of it, but because the more I was starved of it the less palatable it seemed. Because of this my soul fell sick. It broke out in ulcers and looked about desperately for some material, worldly means of relieving the itch which they caused. But material things, which have no soul, could not be true objects for my love. To love and to have my love returned was my heart's desire, and it would be all the sweeter if I could also enjoy the body of the one who loved me.

So I muddied the stream of friendship with the filth of lewdness and clouded its clear waters with hell's black river of lust. And yet, in spite of this rank depravity, I was vain enough to have ambitions of cutting a fine figure in the world. I also fell in love, which was a snare of my own choosing. My God, my God of mercy, how good you were to me, for you mixed much bitterness in that cup of pleasure! My love was returned and finally shackled me in the bonds of its consummation. In the midst of my joy I was caught up in the coils of trouble, for I was lashed with the cruel, fiery rods of jealousy and suspicion, fear, anger, and quarrels.

3

Yet all the while, far above, your mercy hovered faithfully about me. I exhausted myself in depravity, in the pursuit of an unholy curiosity. I deserted you and sank to the bottom-most depths of scepticism and the mockery of devil-worship. My sins were a sacrifice to the devil, and for all of them you chastised me. I defied you even so far as to relish the thought of lust, and gratify it too, within the walls of your church during the celebration of your mysteries. For such a deed I deserved to pluck the fruit of death, and you punished me for it with a heavy lash. But, compared with my guilt, the penalty was nothing. How infinite is your mercy, my God! You are my Refuge from the terrible dangers amongst which I wandered, head on high, intent upon withdrawing still further from you. I loved my own way, not yours, but it was a truant's freedom that I loved.

Besides these pursuits I was also studying for the law. Such ambition was held to be honourable and I determined to succeed in it. The more unscrupulous I was, the greater my reputation was likely to be, for men are so blind that they even take pride in their blindness. By now I was at the top of the school of rhetoric. I was pleased with my superior status and swollen with conceit. All the same, as you well know, Lord, I behaved far more quietly than the 'Wreckers', a title of ferocious devilry which the fashionable set chose for themselves. I had nothing whatever to do with their outbursts of violence, but I lived amongst them, feeling a perverse sense of shame because I was not like them. I kept company with them and there were times when I found their friendship a pleasure, but I always had a horror of what they did when they

lived up to their name. Without provocation they would set upon some timid newcomer, gratuitously affronting his sense of decency for their own amusement and using it as fodder for their spiteful jests. This was the devil's own behaviour or not far different. 'Wreckers' was a fit name for them, for they were already adrift and total wrecks themselves. The mockery and trickery which they loved to practise on others was a secret snare of the devil, by which they were mocked and tricked themselves.

4

These were the companions with whom I studied the art of eloquence at that impressionable age. It was my ambition to be a good speaker, for the unhallowed and inane purpose of gratifying human vanity. The prescribed course of study brought me to a work by an author named Cicero, whose writing nearly everyone admires, if not the spirit of it. The title of the book is *Hortensius* and it recommends the reader to study philosophy. It altered my outlook on life. It changed my prayers to you, O Lord, and provided me with new hopes and aspirations. All my empty dreams suddenly lost their charm and my heart began to throb with a bewildering passion for the wisdom of eternal truth. I began to climb out of the depths to which I had sunk, in order to return to you. For I did not use the book as a whetstone to sharpen my tongue. It was not the style of it but the contents which won me over, and yet the allowance which my mother paid me was supposed to be spent on putting an edge on my tongue. I was now in my nineteenth year and she supported me, because my father had died two years before.

My God, how I burned with longing to have wings to carry me back to you, away from all earthly things, although I had no idea what you would do with me! For *yours is the wisdom.*[15] In Greek the word 'philosophy' means 'love of wisdom', and it was with this love that the *Hortensius* inflamed me. There are people for whom philosophy is a means of misleading others, for they misuse its great name, its attractions, and its integrity to give colour and gloss to their own errors. Most of these so-called philosophers who lived in Cicero's time and before are noted in the book. He shows them up in their true colours and makes quite clear how wholesome is the admonition which the Holy Spirit gives in the words of your good and true servant, Paul: *Take care not to let anyone cheat you with his philosophizings, with empty fantasies drawn from human tradition, from worldly principles; they were never Christ's teaching. In Christ the whole plenitude of Deity is embodied and dwells in him.*[16]

But, O Light of my heart, you know that at that time, although Paul's words were not known to me, the only thing that pleased me in Cicero's book was his advice not simply to admire one or another of the schools of philosophy, but to love wisdom itself, whatever it might be, and to search for it, pursue it, hold it, and embrace it firmly. These were the words which excited me and set me burning with fire, and the only check to this blaze of enthusiasm was that they made no mention of the name of Christ. For by your mercy, Lord, from the time when my mother fed me at the breast my infant heart had been suckled dutifully on his name, the name of your Son, my Saviour. Deep inside my heart his name remained, and nothing could entirely captivate me, however learned, however neatly expressed, however true it might be, unless his name were in it.

---

[15]Job 12: 13.
[16]Col. 2: 8, 9.

5

So I made up my mind to examine the holy Scriptures and see what kind of books they were. I discovered something that was at once beyond the understanding of the proud and hidden from the eyes of children. Its gait was humble, but the heights it reached were sublime. It was enfolded in mysteries, and I was not the kind of man to enter into it or bow my head to follow where it led. But these were not the feelings I had when I first read the Scriptures. To me they seemed quite unworthy of comparison with the stately prose of Cicero, because I had too much conceit to accept their simplicity and not enough insight to penetrate their depths. It is surely true that as the child grows these books grow with him. But I was too proud to call myself a child. I was inflated with self-esteem, which made me think myself a great man.

6

I fell in with a set of sensualists, men with glib tongues who ranted and raved and had the snares of the devil in their mouths. They baited the traps by confusing the syllables of the names of God the Father, God the Son Our Lord Jesus Christ, and God the Holy Ghost, the Paraclete, who comforts us. These names were always on the tips of their tongues, but only as sounds which they mouthed aloud, for in their hearts they had no inkling of the truth. Yet 'Truth and truth alone' was the motto which they repeated to me again and again, although the truth was nowhere to be found in them. All that they said was false, both what they said about you, who truly are the Truth, and what they said about this world and its first principles, which were your creation. But I ought not to have been content with what the philosophers said about such things, even when they spoke the truth. I should have passed beyond them for love of you, my supreme Father, my good Father, in whom all beauty has its source.

Truth! Truth! How the very marrow of my soul within me yearned for it as they dinned it in my ears over and over again! To them it was no more than a name to be voiced or a word to be read in their libraries of huge books. But while my hunger was for you, for Truth itself, these were the dishes on which they served me up the sun and the moon, beautiful works of yours but still only your works, not you yourself nor even the greatest of your created things.[17] For your spiritual works are greater than these material things, however brightly they may shine in the sky.

But my hunger and thirst were not even for the greatest of your works, but for you, my God, because you are Truth itself *with whom there can be no change, no swerving from your course.*[18] Yet the dishes they set before me were still loaded with dazzling fantasies, illusions with which the eye deceives the mind. It would have been better to love the sun itself, which at least is real as far as we can see. But I gulped down this food, because I thought that it was you. I had no relish for it, because the taste it left in my mouth was not the taste of truth—it could not be, for it was not you but an empty sham. And it did not nourish me, but starved me all the more. The food we dream of is very like the food we eat when we are awake, but it does not nourish because it is only a dream. Yet the things they gave me to eat were not in the least like you, as now I know since you have spoken to me. They were dream-substances, mock realities, far less true than the real things which we see with the sight of our eyes in the sky or on the earth. These things are seen by bird and beast as well as by ourselves, and they are far more certain than

any image we conceive of them. And in turn we can picture them to ourselves with greater certainty than the vaster, infinite things which we surmise from them. Such things have no existence at all, but they were the visionary foods on which I was then fed but not sustained.

But you, O God whom I love and on whom I lean in weakness so that I may be strong, you are not the sun and the moon and the stars, even though we see these bodies in the heavens; nor are you those other bodies which we do not see in the sky, for you created them and, in your reckoning, they are not even among the greatest of your works. How far, then, must you really be from those fantasies of mine, those imaginary material things which do not exist at all! The images we form in our mind's eye, when we picture things that really do exist, are far better founded than these inventions; and the things themselves are still more certain than the images we form of them. But you are not these things. Neither are you the soul, which is the life of bodies and, since it gives them life, must be better and more certain than they are themselves. But you are the life of souls, the life of lives. You live, O Life of my soul, because you are life itself, immutable.

Where were you in those days? How far away from me? I was wandering far from you and I was not even allowed to eat the husks on which I fed the swine. For surely the fables of the poets and the penmen are better than the traps which those impostors set! There is certainly more to be gained from verses and poems and tales like the flight of Medea than from their stories of the five elements disguised in various ways because of the five dens of darkness. These things simply do not exist and they are death to those who believe in them. Verses and poems can provide real food for thought, but although I used to recite verses about Medea's flight through the air, I never maintained that they were true; and I never believed the poems which I

---

[17]Saint Augustine is here speaking of the Manichees, for whom astronomy was a part of theology.
[18]James 1: 17.

heard others recite. But I did believe the tales which these men told.

These were the stages of my pitiful fall into the depths of hell, as I struggled and strained for lack of the truth. My God, you had mercy on me even before I had confessed to you; but I now confess that all this was because I tried to find you, not through the understanding of the mind, by which you meant us to be superior to the beasts, but through the senses of the flesh. Yet you were deeper than my inmost understanding and higher than the topmost height that I could reach. I had blundered upon that woman in Solomon's parable who, ignorant and unabashed, sat at her door and said *Stolen waters are sweetest, and bread is better eating when there is none to see.*[19] She inveigled me because she found me living in the outer world that lay before my eyes, the eyes of the flesh, and dwelling upon the food which they provided for my mind.

BOOK X

6

My love of you, O Lord, is not some vague feeling: it is positive and certain. Your word struck into my heart and from that moment I loved you. Besides this, all about me, heaven and earth and all that they contain proclaim that I should love you, and their message never ceases to sound in the ears of all mankind, so that there is no excuse for any not to love you. But, more than all this, *you will show pity on those whom you pity; you will show mercy where you are merciful;*[20] for if it were not for your mercy, heaven and earth would cry your praises to deaf ears.

But what do I love when I love my God? Not material beauty or beauty of a temporal order; not

the brilliance of earthly light, so welcome to our eyes; not the sweet melody of harmony and song; not the fragrance of flowers, perfumes, and spices; not manna or honey; not limbs such as the body delights to embrace. It is not these that I love when I love my God. And yet, when I love him, it is true that I love a light of a certain kind, a voice, a perfume, a food, an embrace; but they are of the kind that I love in my inner self, when my soul is bathed in light that is not bound by space; when it listens to sound that never dies away; when it breathes fragrance that is not borne away on the wind; when it tastes food that is never consumed by the eating; when it clings to an embrace from which it is not severed by fulfilment of desire. This is what I love when I love my God.

But what is my God? I put my question to the earth. It answered, 'I am not God', and all things on earth declared the same. I asked the sea and the chasms of the deep and the living things that creep in them, but they answered, 'We are not your God. Seek what is above us.' I spoke to the winds that blow, and the whole air and all that lives in it replied, 'Anaximenes[21] is wrong. I am not God.' I asked the sky, the sun, the moon, and the stars, but they told me, 'Neither are we the God whom you seek.' I spoke to all the things that are about me, all that can be admitted by the door of the senses, and I said, 'Since you are not my God, tell me about him. Tell me something of my God.' Clear and loud they answered, 'God is he who made us.' I asked these questions simply by gazing at these things, and their beauty was all the answer they gave.

Then I turned to myself and asked, 'Who are you?' 'A man,' I replied. But it is clear that I have both body and soul, the one the outer, the other

---

[19]Prov. 9: 17.
[20]Rom. 9: 15.

[21]Anaximenes of Miletus, the philosopher, who lived in the sixth century B.C. His teaching was that air is the first cause of all things.

the inner part of me. Which of these two ought I to have asked to help me find my God? With my bodily powers I had already tried to find him in earth and sky, as far as the sight of my eyes could reach, like an envoy sent upon a search. But my inner self is the better of the two, for it was to the inner part of me that my bodily senses brought their messages. They delivered to their arbiter and judge the replies which they carried back from the sky and the earth and all that they contain, those replies which stated 'We are not God' and 'God is he who made us'. The inner part of man knows these things through the agency of the outer part. I, the inner man, know these things; I, the soul, know them through the senses of my body. I asked the whole mass of the universe about my God, and it replied, 'I am not God. God is he who made me.'

Surely everyone whose senses are not impaired is aware of the universe around him? Why, then, does it not give the same message to us all? The animals, both great and small, are aware of it, but they cannot inquire into its meaning because they are not guided by reason, which can sift the evidence relayed to them by their senses. Man, on the other hand, can question nature. He is able to *catch sight of God's invisible nature through his creatures,*[22] but his love of these material things is too great. He becomes their slave, and slaves cannot be judges. Nor will the world supply an answer to those who question it, unless they also have the faculty to judge it. It does not answer in different language—that is, it does not change its aspect—according to whether a man merely looks at it or subjects it to inquiry while he looks. If it did, its appearance would be different in each case. Its aspect is the same in both cases, but to the man who merely looks it says nothing, while to the other it gives an answer. It would be nearer the truth to say

that it gives an answer to all, but it is only understood by those who compare the message it gives them through their senses with the truth that is in themselves. For truth says to me, 'Your God is not heaven or earth or any kind of bodily thing.' We can tell this from the very nature of such things, for those who have eyes to see know that their bulk is less in the part than in the whole. And I know that my soul is the better part of me, because it animates the whole of my body. It gives it life, and this is something that no body can give to another body. But God is even more. He is the Life of the life of my soul.

26

Where, then, did I find you so that I could learn of you? For you were not in my memory before I learned of you. Where else, then, did I find you, to learn of you, unless it was in yourself, above me? Whether we approach you or depart from you, you are not confined in any place. You are Truth, and you are everywhere present where all seek counsel of you. You reply to all at once, though the counsel each seeks is different. The answer you give is clear, but not all hear it clearly. All ask you whatever they wish to ask, but the answer they receive is not always what they want to hear. The man who serves you best is the one who is less intent on hearing from you what he wills to hear than on shaping his will according to what he hears from you.

27

I have learnt to love you late, Beauty at once so ancient and so new! I have learnt to love you late! You were within me, and I was in the world outside myself. I searched for you outside myself and, disfigured as I was, I fell upon the lovely things of your creation. You were with me, but I was not with you. The beautiful things of this world kept me far from you and yet, if they had not been in

---

[22]Rom. 1: 20.

you, they would have had no being at all. You called me; you cried aloud to me; you broke my barrier of deafness. You shone upon me; your radiance enveloped me; you put my blindness to flight. You shed your fragrance about me; I drew breath and now I gasp for your sweet odour. I tasted you, and now I hunger and thirst for you. You touched me, and I am inflamed with love of your peace.

28

When at last I cling to you with all my being, for me there will be no more sorrow, no more toil. Then at last I shall be alive with true life, for my life will be wholly filled by you. You raise up and sustain all whose lives you fill, but my life is not yet filled by you and I am a burden to myself. The pleasures I find in the world, which should be cause for tears, are at strife with its sorrows, in which I should rejoice, and I cannot tell to which the victory will fall. Have pity on me, O Lord, in my misery! My sorrows are evil and they are at strife with joys that are good, and I cannot tell which will gain the victory. Have pity on me, O Lord, in my misery! I do not hide my wounds from you. I am sick, and you are the physician. You are merciful: I have need of your mercy. Is not our life on earth a period of trial? For who would wish for hardship and difficulty? You command us to endure these troubles, not to love them. No one loves what he endures, even though he may be glad to endure it. For though he may rejoice in his power of endurance, he would prefer that there should be nothing for him to endure. When I am in trouble I long for good fortune, but when I have good fortune I fear to lose it. Is there any middle state between prosperity and adversity, some state in which human life is not a trial? In prosperity as the world knows it there is twofold cause for grief, for there is grief in the fear of adversity and grief in joy that does not last. And in what the world

knows as adversity the causes of grief are threefold, for not only is it hard to bear, but it also causes us to long for prosperous times and to fear that our powers of endurance may break. Is not man's life on earth a long, unbroken period of trial?

29

There can be no hope for me except in your great mercy. Give me the grace to do as you command, and command me to do what you will! You command us to control our bodily desires. And, as we are told, when I knew that no man can *be master of himself, except of God's bounty, I was wise enough already to know whence the gift came.*[23] Truly it is by continence that we are made as one and regain that unity of self which we lost by falling apart in the search for a variety of pleasures. For a man loves you so much the less if, besides you, he also loves something else which he does not love for your sake. O Love ever burning, never quenched! O Charity, my God, set me on fire with your love! You command me to be continent. Give me the grace to do as you command, and command me to do what you will!

30

It is truly your command that I should be continent and restrain myself from *gratification of corrupt nature, gratification of the eye, the empty pomp of living.*[24] You commanded me not to commit fornication, and though you did not forbid me to marry, you counselled me to take a better course. You gave me the grace and I did your bidding, even before I became a minister of your sacrament. But in my memory, of which I have said much, the images of things imprinted upon it by my former habits still linger on. When I am awake they obtrude themselves upon me, though with little

---

[23]Wisdom 8: 21.
[24]John 2: 16.

strength. But when I dream, they not only give me pleasure but are very much like acquiescence in the act. The power which these illusory images have over my soul and my body is so great that what is no more than a vision can influence me in sleep in a way that the reality cannot do when I am awake. Surely it cannot be that when I am asleep I am not myself, O Lord my God? And yet the moment when I pass from wakefulness to sleep, or return again from sleep to wakefulness, marks a great difference in me. During sleep where is my reason which, when I am awake, resists such suggestions and remains firm and undismayed even in face of the realities themselves? Is it sealed off when I close my eyes? Does it fall asleep with the senses of the body? And why is it that even in sleep I often resist the attractions of these images, for I remember my chaste resolutions and abide by them and give no consent to temptations of this sort? Yet the difference between waking and sleeping is so great that even when, during sleep, it happens otherwise, I return to a clear conscience when I wake and realize that, because of this difference, I was not responsible for the act, although I am sorry that by some means or other it happened to me.

The power of your hand, O God Almighty, is indeed great enough to cure all the diseases of my soul. By granting me more abundant grace you can even quench the fire of sensuality which provokes me in my sleep. More and more, O Lord, you will increase your gifts in me, so that my soul may follow me to you, freed from the concupiscence which binds it, and rebel no more against itself. By your grace it will no longer commit in sleep these shameful, unclean acts inspired by sensual images, which lead to the pollution of the body: it will not so much as consent to them. For to you, the Almighty, who are *powerful enough to carry out your purpose beyond all our hopes and dreams,*[25] it is

no great task to prescribe that no temptations of this kind, even such slight temptations as can be checked by the least act of will, should arouse pleasure in me, even in sleep, provided that my dispositions are chaste. This you can do for me at any time of life, even in the prime of manhood. But now I make this confession to my good Lord, declaring how I am still troubled by this kind of evil. *With awe in my heart I rejoice*[26] in your gifts, yet I grieve for my deficiencies, trusting that you will perfect your mercies in me until I reach the fullness of peace, which I shall enjoy with you in soul and body, when *death is swallowed up in victory.*[27]

31

There is another evil which we meet with day by day. If only it were the only one! For we repair the daily wastage of our bodies by eating and drinking, until the time comes when you *will bring both food and our animal nature to an end.*[28] When that time comes, your wonderful fullness will spell the end of our need, and you will *clothe this corruptible nature of ours with incorruptible life.*[29] But for the present I find pleasure in this need, though I fight against it, for fear of becoming its captive. Every day I wage war upon it by fasting. Time and again I force my body to obey me, but the pain which this causes me is cancelled by the pleasure of eating and drinking. For of course hunger and thirst are painful. Like a fever they parch and kill unless they are relieved by the remedies of food and drink. And since, to console us, we have your gifts—for you have given us earth and water and sky to serve us in our weakness—the remedies are there for us to find and we think of this hardship as a source of delight.

---

[25]Eph. 3: 20.

[26]Ps. 2: 11.
[27]1 Cor. 15: 54.
[28]1 Cor. 6: 13.
[29]1 Cor. 15: 53.

Because you have taught me to understand this, I look upon food as a medicine. But the snare of concupiscence awaits me in the very process of passing from the discomfort of hunger to the contentment which comes when it is satisfied. For the process itself is a pleasure and there is no other means of satisfying hunger except the one which we are obliged to take. And although the purpose of eating and drinking is to preserve health, in its train there follows an ominous kind of enjoyment, which often tries to outstrip it, so that it is really for the sake of pleasure that I do what I claim to do and mean to do for the sake of my health. Moreover, health and enjoyment have not the same requirements, for what is sufficient for health is not enough for enjoyment, and it is often hard to tell whether the body, which must be cared for, requires further nourishment, or whether we are being deceived by the allurements of greed demanding to be gratified. My unhappy soul welcomes this uncertainty, using it to vindicate and excuse itself. It is glad that the proper requirements of health are in doubt, so that under the pretence of caring for health it may disguise the pursuit of pleasure.

Every day I try my hardest to resist these temptations. I call for your helping hand and tell you of my difficulties, because this is a problem which I have not yet resolved. I hear the voice of my God who commands us: *Do not let your hearts grow dull with revelry and drunkenness.*[30] Drunkenness is far from me. By your grace may you prevent it from coming near! But there have been times when overeating has stolen upon your servant. By your mercy may you keep it far from me! For no man *can be master of himself, except of God's bounty.*[31]

You grant us many gifts when we pray for them. And even before we pray for them, all the good things that we have ever received have come from you. That we should later recognize that they came from you is also your gift. I have never been a drunkard myself, but I have known drunkards made sober by you. Therefore, just as it is by your doing that men who were once drunkards are not so for ever, it is also by your doing that those who were never drunkards are not drunkards now. And in the same way it is also by your doing that men of both sorts know that it was you who did this for them.

I have also heard these other words of yours: *Do not follow the counsel of appetite. Turn your back on your own liking.*[32] By your gift I have also heard and found great comfort in the words: *We gain nothing by eating, lose nothing by abstaining.*[33] This means that eating will not bring me plenty nor abstinence reduce me to misery. I have heard these words too: *I have learned to be content with my circumstances as they are. I know what it is to have abundant means and what it is to live in want. Nothing is beyond my powers, thanks to the strength God gives me.*[34] Here speaks a true soldier of the heavenly army, not mere dust like the rest of us! But remember, O Lord, that we are dust. Remember that you made man from dust, and that he was lost and found again. My heart goes out to Paul for the words that he wrote by your inspiration: *Nothing is beyond my powers, thanks to the strength God gives me.*[35] But he too was dust and could not do all things by his own power. Give me strength, O Lord, so that I may do all things. Give me the grace to do as you command, and command me to do what you will! Paul acknowledges your gifts and the boast that he makes is made in the Lord.[35] I have also heard another of your servants begging for your gifts in these words: *Let the itch of gluttony pass me by.*[36] All this makes it clear, O holy God,

---

[30]Luke 21: 34.
[31]Wisdom 8: 21.

[32]Ecclus. 18: 30.
[33]1 Cor. 8: 8.
[34]Philipp. 4: 11–13.
[35]See 11 Cor. 10: 17.
[36]Ecclus. 23: 6.

that when your commands are obeyed, it is from you that we receive the power to obey them.

Good Father, you have taught me that nothing can be *unclean for those who have clean hearts,*[37] *yet it goes ill with the man who eats to the hurt of his own conscience.*[38] You have taught me that *all is good that God has made, nothing is to be rejected; only we must be thankful to him when we partake of it;*[39] that *it is not what we eat that gives us our standing in God's sight;*[40] that *no one must be allowed to take us to task over what we eat or drink;*[41] and that no man, *over his meat,* should *mock at him who does not eat it,* nor, *while he abstains, pass judgement on him who eats it.*[42] For these lessons which I have learnt all praise and all thanks be to you, my God, my Master, to you who knock at the door of my ears and shed your light over my heart! Deliver me from all temptation. It is the uncleanness of gluttony that I fear, not unclean meat. For I know that Noe was allowed to eat all kinds of meat that were suitable as food; that Elias was fed on meat; and that John the Baptist, remarkable ascetic though he was, was not polluted by the flesh of living creatures, the locusts which were granted him as food. On the other hand I know that Esau was defrauded by his greed for a dish of lentils; that David reproached himself for longing for a drink of water; and that Christ our King was tempted not by meat but by bread. And the Israelites in the desert deserved rebuke, not because they wanted meat, but because in their greed for food they sulked and grumbled against the Lord.

In the midst of these temptations I struggle daily against greed for food and drink. This is not an evil which I can decide once and for all to repudiate and never to embrace again, as I was able to do in the case of fornication. I must therefore hold back my appetite with neither too firm nor too slack a rein. But is there anyone, O Lord, who is never enticed a little beyond the strict limit of need? If there is such a one, he is a great man. Let him praise your name. But I am not such a man: I am a poor sinner. Yet I too praise your name, and Christ, who conquered the world, pleads with you for my sins. He numbers me among the weak members of his Body, for *your eyes looked upon me, when I was yet unformed; all human lives are already written in your record.*[43]

32

The sense of smell does not trouble me greatly with its attractions. I do not miss sweet scents when they are absent, but neither do I refuse them where I find them. I am even ready to do without them altogether. This, at least, is my own opinion of myself, but I may be wrong. For the powers of my inner self are veiled in darkness which I must deplore. When my mind speculates upon its own capabilities, it realizes that it cannot safely trust its own judgement, because its inner workings are generally so obscure that they are only revealed in the light of experience; and, besides this, during this life, which may be called a perpetual trial, no one should be confident that although he has been able to pass from a worse state to a better, he may not also pass from a better state to a worse. Our only hope, our only confidence, the only firm promise that we have is your mercy.

33

I used to be much more fascinated by the pleasures of sound than the pleasures of smell. I was enthralled by them, but you broke my bonds and set

[37]Tit. 1: 15.
[38]Rom. 14: 20.
[39]1 Tim. 4: 4.
[40]1 Cor. 8: 8.
[41]Col. 2: 16.
[42]Rom. 14: 3.

[43]Ps. 138: 16 (139: 16).

me free. I admit that I still find some enjoyment in the music of hymns, which are alive with your praises, when I hear them sung by well-trained, melodious voices. But I do not enjoy it so much that I cannot tear myself away. I can leave it when I wish. But if I am not to turn a deaf ear to music, which is the setting for the words which give it life, I must allow it a position of some honour in my heart, and I find it difficult to assign it to its proper place. For sometimes I feel that I treat it with more honour than it deserves. I realize that when they are sung these sacred words stir my mind to greater religious fervour and kindle in me a more ardent flame of piety than they would if they were not sung; and I also know that there are particular modes in song and in the voice, corresponding to my various emotions and able to stimulate them because of some mysterious relationship between the two. But I ought not to allow my mind to be paralysed by the gratification of my senses, which often leads it astray. For the senses are not content to take second place. Simply because I allow them their due, as adjuncts to reason, they attempt to take precedence and forge ahead of it, with the result that I sometimes sin in this way but am not aware of it until later.

Sometimes, too, from over-anxiety to avoid this particular trap I make the mistake of being too strict. When this happens, I have no wish but to exclude from my ears, and from the ears of the Church as well, all the melody of those lovely chants to which the Psalms of David are habitually sung; and it seems safer to me to follow the precepts which I remember often having heard ascribed to Athanasius, bishop of Alexandria, who used to oblige the lectors to recite the psalms with such slight modulation of the voice that they seemed to be speaking rather than chanting. But when I remember the tears that I shed on hearing the songs of the Church in the early days, soon after I had recovered my faith, and when I realize

that nowadays it is not the singing that moves me but the meaning of the words when they are sung in a clear voice to the most appropriate tune, I again acknowledge the great value of this practice. So I waver between the danger that lies in gratifying the senses and the benefits which, as I know from experience, can accrue from singing. Without committing myself to an irrevocable opinion, I am inclined to approve of the custom of singing in church, in order that by indulging the ears weaker spirits may be inspired with feelings of devotion. Yet when I find the singing itself more moving than the truth which it conveys, I confess that this is a grievous sin, and at those times I would prefer not to hear the singer.

This, then, is my present state. Let those of my readers whose hearts are filled with charity, from which good actions spring, weep with me and weep for me. Those who feel no charity in themselves will not be moved by my words. But I beg you, O Lord my God, to look upon me and listen to me. Have pity on me and heal me, for you see that I have become a problem to myself, and this is the ailment from which I suffer.

34

Finally I must confess how I am tempted through the eye. Let the ears of your Church, the ears of my devout brothers in Christ, listen to my words, so that I may bring to an end my discussion of the body's temptations to pleasure, which still provoke me as *I sigh, longing for the shelter of that home which heaven will give me.*[44]

The eyes delight in beautiful shapes of different sorts and bright and attractive colours. I would not have these things take possession of my soul. Let God possess it, he who made them all. He made them all *very good,*[45] but it is he who is my Good,

---

[44] II Cor. 5: 2.
[45] Gen. 1: 31.

not they. All day and every day, while I am awake, they are there before my eyes. They allow me no respite such as I am granted in moments of silence when there is no singing and sometimes no sound at all to be heard. For light, the queen of colours, pervades all that I see, wherever I am throughout the day, and by the ever-changing pattern of its rays it entices me even when I am occupied with something else and take no special note of it. It wins so firm a hold on me that, if I am suddenly deprived of it, I long to have it back, and if I am left for long without it, I grow dispirited.

But the true Light is the Light which Tobias saw when, though his eyes were blind, he taught his son the path he should follow in life, and himself led the way, charity guiding his steps so that he did not stray. It is the Light which Isaac saw when the sight of his eyes was dimmed and clouded by old age and it was granted to him, not to bless his sons in full knowledge as to which was which, but to know them by blessing them. It is the Light which Jacob saw when, though his eyes were blinded by old age, a Light shone in his heart and cast its beams over the tribes of Israel yet to come, as he foresaw them in the persons of his sons. It is the Light which he saw when he laid his hands on his grandchildren, the sons of Joseph, not in the way that their father, who saw only the outward act, tried to make him do it, but mystically crossed, in the way that he discerned by the Light that shone within him. This is the true Light. It is one alone and all who see and love it are one.

But in our life in the world this earthly light, of which I was speaking, is a seasoning, sweet and tempting, but dangerous for those whose love for it is blind. Yet those who have learnt to praise you for this as well as for your other gifts, *O God, Maker of all things,*[46] sing you a hymn of praise for

it: they are not beguiled by it in their dreams. For myself, I wish to be as they are. I resist the allurements of the eye for fear that as I walk upon your path, my feet may be caught in a trap. Instead, I raise the eyes of my spirit to you, so that you may *save my feet from the snare.*[47] Time and again you save them, for I fail to escape the trap. You never cease to free me, although again and again I find myself caught in the snares that are laid all about me. For you are *the guardian of Israel, one who is never weary, never sleeps.*[48]

By every kind of art and the skill of their hands men make innumerable things—clothes, shoes, pottery, and other useful objects, besides pictures and various works which are the fruit of their imagination. They make them on a far more lavish scale than is required to satisfy their own modest needs or to express their devotion, and all these things are additional temptations to the eye, made by men who love the worldly things they make themselves but forget their own Maker and destroy what he made in them. But, O my God, my Glory, for these things too I offer you a hymn of thanksgiving. I make a sacrifice of praise to him who sanctifies me, for the beauty which flows through men's minds into their skilful hands comes from that Beauty which is above their souls and for which my soul sighs all day and night. And it is from this same supreme Beauty that men who make things of beauty and love it in its outward forms derive the principle by which they judge it: but they do not accept the same principle to guide them in the use they make of it. Yet it is there, and they do not see it. If only they could see it, they would not depart from it. They would preserve their strength for you,[49] not squander it on luxuries that make them weary.

---

46 Saint Ambrose's 'Evening Hymn'; see Book IX, chapter 12.

47 Ps. 24: 15 (25: 15).
48 Ps. 120: 4 (121: 4).
49 See Ps. 58: 10 (59: 9).

Though I say this and see that it is true, my feet are still caught in the toils of this world's beauty. But you will free me, O Lord; I know that you will free me. For *ever I keep your mercies in mind.*[50] I am caught and need your mercy, and by your mercy you will save me from the snare. Sometimes, if I have not fallen deep into the trap, I shall feel nothing when you rescue me; but at other times, when I am fast ensnared, I shall suffer the pain of it.

35

I must now speak of a different kind of temptation, more dangerous than these because it is more complicated. For in addition to our bodily appetites, which make us long to gratify all our senses and our pleasures and lead to our ruin if we stay away from you by becoming their slaves, the mind is also subject to a certain propensity to use the sense of the body, not for self-indulgence of a physical kind, but for the satisfaction of its own inquisitiveness. This futile curiosity masquerades under the name of science and learning, and since it derives from our thirst for knowledge and sight is the principal sense by which knowledge is acquired, in the Scriptures it is called *gratification of the eye.*[51] For although, correctly speaking, to see is the proper function of the eyes, we use the word of the other senses too, when we employ them to acquire knowledge. We do not say 'Hear how it glows', 'Smell how bright it is', 'Taste how it shines', or 'Feel how it glitters', because these are all things which we say that we see. Yet we not only say 'See how it shines' when we are speaking of something which only the eyes can perceive, but we also say 'See how loud it is', 'See how it smells', 'See how it tastes', and 'See how hard it is'. So, as I

said, sense-experience in general is called the lust of the eyes because, although the function of sight belongs primarily to the eyes, we apply it to the other organs of sense as well, by analogy, when they are used to discover any item of knowledge.

We can easily distinguish between the motives of pleasure and curiosity. When the senses demand pleasure, they look for objects of visual beauty, harmonious sounds, fragrant perfumes, and things that are pleasant to the taste or soft to the touch. But when their motive is curiosity, they may look for just the reverse of these things, simply to put it to the proof, not for the sake of an unpleasant experience, but from a relish for investigation and discovery. What pleasure can there be in the sight of a mangled corpse, which can only horrify? Yet people will flock to see one lying on the ground, simply for the sensation of sorrow and horror that it gives them. They are even afraid that it may bring them nightmares, as though it were something that they had been forced to look at while they were awake or something to which they had been attracted by rumours of its beauty. The same is true of the other senses, although it would be tedious to give further examples. It is to satisfy this unhealthy curiosity that freaks and prodigies are put on show in the theatre, and for the same reason men are led to investigate the secrets of nature, which are irrelevant to our lives, although such knowledge is of no value to them and they wish to gain it merely for the sake of knowing. It is curiosity, too, which causes men to turn to sorcery in the effort to obtain knowledge for the same perverted purpose. And it even invades our religion, for we put God to the test when we demand signs and wonders from him, not in the hope of salvation, but simply for the love of the experience.

In this immense forest, so full of snares and dangers, I have pared away many sins and thrust them from my heart, for you have given me the grace to do this, O God, my Saviour. But as long

---

[50] Ps. 25: 3 (26: 3).
[51] 1 John 2: 16.

as my daily life is passed in the midst of the clamour raised by so many temptations of this sort, when can I presume to say that nothing of this kind can hold my attention or tempt me into idle speculation? It is true that the theatres no longer attract me; the study of astrology does not interest me; I have never dealt in necromancy; and I detest all sacrilegious rites. But how often has not the enemy used his wiles upon me to suggest that I should ask for some sign from you, O Lord my God, to whom I owe my humble, undivided service? I beseech you, by Christ our King and by Jerusalem the chaste, our only homeland, that just as I now withhold my consent from these suggestions, I may always continue to ward them off and keep them still farther from me. But when I pray to you for the salvation of another, the purpose and intention of my prayer is far different. For you do what you will and you grant me, as you always will, the grace to follow you gladly.

Yet who can tell how many times each day our curiosity is tempted by the most trivial and insignificant matters? Who can tell how often we give way? So often it happens that, when others tell foolish tales, at first we bear with them for fear of offending the weak, and then little by little we begin to listen willingly. I no longer go to watch a dog chasing a hare at the games in the circus. But if I should happen to see the same thing in the country as I pass by, the chase might easily hold my attention and distract me from whatever serious thoughts occupied my mind. It might not actually compel me to turn my horse from the path, but such would be the inclination of my heart; and unless you made me realize my weakness and quickly reminded me, either to turn my eyes from the sight and raise my thoughts to you in contemplation, or to despise it utterly and continue on my way, I should simply stop and gloat. What excuse can I make for myself when often, as I sit at home, I cannot turn my eyes from the sight of a lizard catching flies or a spider entangling them as they fly into her web? Does it make any difference that these are only small animals? It is true that the sight of them inspires me to praise you for the wonders of your creation and the order in which you have disposed all things, but I am not intent upon your praises when I first begin to watch. It is one thing to rise quickly from a fall, another not to fall at all.

My life is full of such faults, and my only hope is in your boundless mercy. For when our hearts become repositories piled high with such worthless stock as this, it is the cause of interruption and distraction from our prayers. And although, in your presence, the voices of our hearts are raised to your ear, all kinds of trivial thoughts break in and cut us off from the great act of prayer.

36

Must I not consider this too as one of the faults which I ought to despise? Can anything restore me to hope except your mercy? That you are merciful I know, for you have begun to change me. You know how great a change you have worked in me, for first of all you have cured me of the desire to assert my claim to liberty, so that you may also pardon me all my other sins, *heal all my mortal ills, rescue my life from deadly peril, crown me with the blessings of your mercy, content all my desire for good.*[52] You know how great a change you have worked in me, for you have curbed my pride by teaching me to fear you and you have tamed my neck to your yoke. And now that I bear your yoke, I find its burden light, for this was your promise and you have kept your word. In truth, though I did not know it, it was light even in the days when I was afraid to bend my neck to it.

---

[52]Ps. 102: 3–5 (103: 3–5).

But, O Lord, you who alone rule without pride since you are the only true Lord and no other lord rules over you, there is a third kind of temptation which, I fear, has not passed from me. Can it ever pass from me in all this life? It is the desire to be feared or loved by other men, simply for the pleasure that it gives me, though in such pleasure there is no true joy. It means only a life of misery and despicable vainglory. It is for this reason more than any other that men neither love you nor fear you in purity of heart. It is for this reason that *you thwart the proud and keep your grace for the humble.*[53] This is why, with a voice of thunder, you condemn the ambitions of this world, so that *the very foundations of the hills quail and quake.*[54] This is why the enemy of our true happiness persists in his attacks upon me, for he knows that when men hold certain offices in human society, it is necessary that they should be loved and feared by other men. He sets his traps about me, baiting them with tributes of applause, in the hope that in my eagerness to listen I may be caught off my guard. He wants me to divorce my joy from the truth and place it in man's duplicity. He wants me to enjoy being loved and feared by others, not for your sake, but in your place, so that in this way he may make me like himself and keep me to share with him, not the true fellowship of charity, but the bonds of common punishment. For he determined to set his throne in the north,[55] where, chilled and benighted, men might serve him as he imitates you in his perverse, distorted way.

But we, O Lord, are your *little flock.*[56] Keep us as your own. Spread your wings and let us shelter beneath them. Let us glory in you alone. If we are loved or feared by others, let it be for your sake.

No man who seeks the praise of other men can be defended by men when you call him to account. Men cannot save him when you condemn. But it happens too, not that praise is given to the man who is *proud of his wicked end achieved*[57] or that the evildoer wins applause, but that a man is praised for some gift which you have given him. And if he takes greater joy in the praise which he receives than in the possession of the gift for which men praise him, then the price he pays for their applause is the loss of your favour and he, the receiver of praise, is worse off than the giver. For the one finds pleasure in God's gift in man, while the other finds less pleasure in God's gift than in the gift of men.

37

Day after day without ceasing these temptations put us to the test, O Lord. The human tongue is a furnace in which the temper of our souls is daily tried. And in this matter too you command us to be continent. Give me the grace to do as you command, and command me to do what you will! You know how I have cried to you from the depths of my heart, and how I have wept floods of tears because of this difficulty. For I cannot easily deduce how far I am cured of this disease, and I have great fear of offending you unawares by sins to which I am blind, though to your eyes they are manifest. In other kinds of temptation I have some means of examining myself, but in this I have almost none. For I can see what progress I have made in the ability to restrain my mind from giving in to sensual pleasures or idle curiosity. It becomes plain when I do without these things, either voluntarily or for lack of the occasion, because I then ask myself how

---

[53] 1 Pet. 5: 5.
[54] Ps. 17: 8 (18: 7).
[55] The allusion is to Is. 14: 13, 14.
[56] Luke 12: 32.

---

[57] Ps. 9: 24 (10: 3).

much, or how little, it troubles me to be without them. The same is true of wealth, which men grasp because they want the means of satisfying one or another of these three kinds of temptation, or perhaps two or even all three of them. If the soul, when it has riches, cannot tell whether it despises them, it can put itself to the proof by discarding them. But if we are to do without praise in order to test our powers, are we to live such outrageously wicked and abandoned lives that all who know us will detest us? Is it possible to imagine a more insane proposal than this? If praise is normally associated with a good life and good works, and rightly so, we ought neither to cease living good lives nor to abandon the rightful consequence. But I cannot tell whether or not I have the forbearance to do without anything, unless it is taken away from me.

What, then, is my attitude to temptation of this kind? What am I to confess to you, O Lord? I can only say that I am gratified by praise, but less by praise than by the truth. For if I were asked whether I would prefer to be commended by all my fellow men for wild delusions and errors on all counts, or to be stigmatized by them for constancy and assurance in the truth, it is clear which I would choose. But I wish that words of praise from other men did not increase the joy I feel for any good qualities that I may have. Yet I confess that it does increase my joy. What is more, their censure detracts from it. And when I am worried by this wretched failing, an excuse occurs to me, though how good an excuse it is only you know, O God: it leaves me in doubt. For you have commanded us not only to be continent, but also to be just; that is, to withhold our love from certain things and to bestow it on others. You want us not only to love you, but also to love our neighbour. For this reason I tell myself that when I am gratified by the praise of a man who well understands what it is that he praises, the true reason for my pleasure is that my neighbour has made good progress and shows promise for the future. Similarly, when I hear him cast a slur upon something which he does not understand or something which in fact is good, I am sorry that he should have this failing. I am sometimes sorry, too, to hear my own praises, either when others commend me for qualities which I am not glad to possess, or when they value in me, more highly than their due, qualities which may be good, but are of little importance. But here again I cannot tell whether this feeling comes from reluctance to allow the man who praises me to disagree with me about my own qualities, not because I am concerned for his welfare, but because the good qualities which please me in myself please me still more when they please others as well. For in a certain sense it is no compliment to me when my own opinion of myself is not upheld, in other words either when qualities which displease me are commended, or when those which please me least are most applauded.

Am I not right, then, to say that I am in doubt about this problem? My God, in the light of your truth I see that if my feelings are stirred by the praise which I receive, it should not be for my own sake but for the good of my neighbour. But whether this is so with me I do not know, for in this matter I know less about myself than I know of you. I beg you, my God, to reveal me to my own eyes, so that I may confess to my brothers in Christ what wounds I find in myself, for they will pray for me. Let me examine myself again, more closely. If it is the good of my neighbour that touches my heart when I hear my own praises, why am I less aggrieved when blame is unjustly laid at another's door than when it is laid at mine? Why do insults sting me more when they are offered to me than when I hear them offered to others with equal injustice? Can I plead ignorance in this case too? Or is the truth of the matter that I deceive myself and that in heart and tongue alike I am guilty of falsehood in your presence? O Lord, keep such folly far from me, for fear that my lips should sin, *sleeking my head with the oil of their flattery.*[58]

38

I am poor and needy and I am better only when in sorrow of heart I detest myself and seek your mercy, until what is faulty in me is repaired and made whole and finally I come to that state of peace which the eye of the proud cannot see. Yet in what others say about us and in what they know of our deeds there is grave danger of temptation. For our love of praise leads us to court the good opinion of others and hoard it for our personal glorification. And even when I reproach myself for it, the love of praise tempts me. There is temptation in the very process of self-reproach, for often, by priding himself on his contempt for vainglory, a man is guilty of even emptier pride; and for this reason his contempt of vainglory is an empty boast, because he cannot really hold it in contempt as long as he prides himself on doing so.

39

Deep in our inner selves there is another evil, the outcome of the same kind of temptation. This is self-complacency, the vanity of those who are pleased with themselves, although they either fail to please others or have no wish to do so and even actively displease them. But though they are pleasing to themselves, they are gravely displeasing to you, because they congratulate themselves not only upon qualities which are not good, as though they were good, but also upon good qualities received from you, as though they were their own gifts to themselves; or else they recognize them as yours,

[58]Ps. 140: 5 (141: 5).

but claim them for their own merits; or, again, they know that they have received them by your grace alone, but still they grudge your grace to others and will not rejoice in it with them.

You see how my heart trembles and strains in the midst of all these perils and others of a like kind. It is not as though I do not suffer wounds, but I feel rather that you heal them over and over again.

40

You have walked everywhere at my side, O Truth, teaching me what to seek and what to avoid, whenever I laid before you the things that I was able to see in this world below and asked you to counsel me. As far as my senses enabled me to do so, I surveyed the world about me and explored both the life which my body has from me and the senses themselves. Next I probed the depths of my memory, so vast in its ramifications and filled in so wonderful a way with riches beyond number. I scrutinized all these things and stood back in awe, for without you I could see none of them, and I found that none of them was you. Nor was I myself the truth, I who found them, I who explored them all and tried to distinguish and appraise each according to its worth. Some of them were conveyed to me by means of my physical senses, and I subjected them to question. Others, which closely concerned my own self, I encountered in my feelings. I enumerated the various means by which their messages were brought to me and distinguished between them. And in the great treasury of my memory there were yet other things that I examined. Some of them I returned to the keeping of my memory, others I picked out for study. But when I was doing all this, I was not myself the truth; that is, the power by which I did it was not the truth; for you, the Truth, are the unfailing Light from which I sought counsel upon all these things, asking whether they were, what they were, and how they were to be valued. But I heard you teaching me and I heard the commands you gave.

Often I do this. I find pleasure in it, and whenever I can relax from my necessary duties, I take refuge in this pleasure. But in all the regions where I thread my way, seeking your guidance, only in you do I find a safe haven for my mind, a gathering-place for my scattered parts, where no portion of me can depart from you. And sometimes you allow me to experience a feeling quite unlike my normal state, an inward sense of delight which, if it were to reach perfection in me, would be something not encountered in this life, though what it is I cannot tell. But my heavy burden of distress drags me down again to earth. Again I become a prey to my habits, which hold me fast. My tears flow, but still I am held fast. Such is the price we pay for the burden of custom! In this state I am fit to stay, unwilling though I am; in that other state, where I wish to stay, I am not fit to be. I have double cause for sorrow.

41

I have now considered the sorry state to which my sins have brought me, according to the three different forms which temptation may take, and I have invoked your helping hand to save me. For in my wounded heart I saw your splendour and it dazzled me. I asked: Who can come close to such glory? *Your watchful care has lost sight of me.*[59] You are the Truth which presides over all things. But in my selfish longing I did not wish to lose you. Together with you I wanted to possess a lie, much as a man will not utter so glaring a falsehood that it blinds his own eyes to the truth. And in this way I

lost you, because you do not deign to be possessed together with a lie.

42

Whom could I find to reconcile me to you? Ought I to have sought the help of the angels? But if I had sought their help, what prayers should I have uttered? What rites should I have used? Many men, so I have heard, for lack of strength to return to you by themselves, have tried to do so by this means, but they ended by craving for strange visions, and their only reward was delusion. For they tried to find you in all the conceit and arrogance of their learning. They thrust out their chests in pride, when they should have beaten their breasts in mourning. And because they resembled them at heart, they attracted to their side the fallen angels, *the princes of the lower air,*[60] their companions and associates in pride. But these allies tricked them, using magic craft, for while they sought a mediator who would cleanse them of their impurities, it was no mediator that they found. It was the devil, *passing for an angel of light,*[61] and it was a potent lure for their proud flesh that he was not a creature of flesh and blood. For they were mortal men and sinners; but you, O Lord, to whom they wanted to be reconciled, are immortal and without sin. But a mediator between God and man must have something in common with God and something in common with man. For if in both these points he were like men, he would be far from God; and if in both of them he were like God, he would be far from men. In neither case could he be a mediator. But since, by the hidden pronouncements of your justice, you have given the devil licence to make a mockery of pride, he poses as a mediator. For in

---

[59]Ps. 30: 23 (31: 22).

[60]Eph 2: 2.
[61]11 Cor. 11: 14.

one point he is like man: he is sinful. And in the other he pretends to be like God: because he is not clothed with a mortal body of flesh and blood, he tries to represent himself as immortal. But since *sin offers death for wages,*[62] in common with men he has this reason to be condemned to die.

---

[62]Rom. 6: 23.

chapter nine

Saint Thomas Aquinas

St. Thomas Aquinas (c. 1225–1274) was born into a period of dramatic change for Christian Europe. The rediscovery of Greek philosophical texts that accompanied the European encounter with the Muslim world challenged the Western Christian worldview, and Aquinas harmonized Augustinian theology with Aristotle to define philosophical discourse well into Modernity. But his synthesis is of more than historical interest. Roman Catholicism is in many ways defined by the "perennial philosophy" of Thomism, so that understanding Aquinas is essential for comprehending Catholicism in the twenty-first century. Finally, Aquinas's belief in the value of reason in biblical Christianity continues to inspire philosophers and theologians, even after Aristotelianism has been succeeded by a more complex scientific theoretical framework.

Thirteenth-century Europe enjoyed a renaissance comparable to the better known Renaissance of the sixteenth century. Universities nurtured the cultural identity of society by reexamining Roman legal processes to establish a just social order, giving rise to a professional class of lawyers, physicians, and clergy that could employ practices of Roman antiquity under the authority of a universal Catholic Church. When the Crusades introduced the riches of Muslim civilization to European culture, this balance was threatened. The universities had been defined by their Scholastic approach of "faith seeking understanding," in which Augustinian theology was the rock on which social theories were built. The Muslims had treasured writings of Aristotle lost to the West, and had incorporated the rational approach of Aristotle's science into an Islamic scholasticism called *kalam*. When Europeans rediscovered Aristotle, the possibility that infidels—non-Christians—had tapped into novel truths unavailable to the faithful was terrifying.

Aristotle had argued that reason can uncover the truth by applying logic to evidence available to our senses. That there is a God Aristotle felt obvious, but that God created the universe by no means followed. That we have souls in addition to physical bodies Aristotle also recognized, but that souls might find happiness beyond death he dismissed as improbable. Happiness, he argued, is the virtuous activity of our souls in this

From Saint Thomas Aquinas, *The Summa Theologica of Saint Thomas Aquinas*, translated by the Fathers of the English Dominican Province. Revised by Daniel J. Sullivan. Chicago: Encyclopedia Britannica, 1952.

life, which virtue is explicable in concepts grounded in our experiences. Muslims had interpreted Aristotle according to an approach in which the lines between the mundane and the divine are complexly intertwined. When Europeans discovered these teachings, they felt their choice to involve either adopting Muslim Aristotelianism or allowing Aristotle's thought to subvert their Augustinian worldview. Attempts at banning Aristotle's works at major universities such as Paris were useless; the appeal of the forbidden only whetted many scholars' appetites for this new science.

Into this intellectual maelstrom came Aquinas. Born of Italian nobility, Thomas was earmarked at an early age for life as a churchman, likely an important bishop. Rather than move naturally to ecclesiastical authority, Thomas joined the Order of the Dominican Friars, priests and monks who had taken a vow of poverty to evangelize, abstaining from the privileges of ecclesiastical life. One story has his brothers kidnapping Thomas and imprisoning him in a tower. Here they introduced a girl into his room, hoping to tempt him with the physical pleasures. Thomas is said to have chased the girl from his room with sticks snatched from the fireplace and held in the form of a burning cross, leaving his brothers no alternative but to allow him to rejoin his Order. This vignette has led many to suppose that Aquinas's view of the pleasures of ordinary human life—married love, family, and the home—was dim, and is still used to bolster the idea that he could only appreciate love on a purely intellectual plane.

The outline of Aquinas's biography appears to bear this out. After studying at the University of Naples, and learning from the eminent Aristotelian scholar Albertus Magnus in Paris and Cologne, Aquinas was ordained a priest in 1251, and by 1256 he had acquired a reputation as a formidable intellect. He was named regent master at the University of Paris from 1256–1259, at the Dominican House of Studies in Rome from 1265–1268, and again at Paris from 1268–1272. He was constantly in demand as a professor and theologian of the church until his untimely death on March 7, 1274. He began his writing career at Paris in the early 1250s, and produced a monumental body of writings over the next twenty years, including Commentaries on the *Sentences* of Peter Lombard, on works of great theologians, on the Gospels, and on most of the newly discovered works of Aristotle. The fruits of his academic disputations lie in his *Disputed Questions*, which variously address the nature of Truth, Evil, and Divine Power, as well as in *Quodlibetal Questions* on assorted theological topics. His theological acumen is evident in *The Golden Chain*, a compendium of Patristic commentary on the Gospels still used by many preachers and theologians. But these pale in the face of his two major works. The first, which has come to be called *Summa Contra Gentiles*, is a series of arguments addressing questions that had divided Christians among themselves, and had been raised against Christianity by Jews and Muslims. The first three books of the *Contra Gentiles* defend Christianity using arguments that do not rely on Scriptural revelation, while the last book has Thomas using revealed truth to explicate Christian theology. The second major work, the *Summa Theologica*, is a massive collection of interrelated treatises of philosophical and dogmatic theology, and is the source of the selections included here.

To understand *Summa Theologica*, one must be aware of its structure. The *Summa* appears to be an endless concatenation of questions on every theological topic imaginable, from God's existence to the nature of sin to how grace operates and what penance involves. In fact, there is an underlying theological structure to the *Summa* that itself expresses a theological truth. The *Summa* is divided into three extended treatises, or parts. The first part, consisting of 119 separate questions, is about the divine nature and how God relates to creation. How we can rationally understand the divine nature, and how our faith instructs this understanding of God into recognition of a trinity leads to thinking about how God differs from creation, and about how angels serve God. Indeed, Aquinas's angelology has earned him the nickname "The Angelic Doctor," and much of Western Christianity's conception of what angels are lies in this section of the *Summa*. How God created, and how the divine will governs creation lead to Thomas's views on the relation of man to creation and to God.

The second part is itself divided into two sections, known as *Prima Secundae* (the first part of the second part, 114 questions) and *Secunda Secundae* (the second part of the second part, 189 questions). Here Aquinas considers the purpose of life, the relation of earthly happiness to happiness after death, and the behavior defining these species of happiness. What motivates us to act, how our passions affect us, and how habits develop and are defined by the terms "virtue" and "vice" lead to his assessment of how God's law develops in our understanding as natural law, human law, and the law of Scripture. While Aristotelian metaphysics underlies his discussion of the divine nature in the first part, Aristotle's ethical and political thought, and his conception of how we operate, very much defines the *Prima Secundae*. Only toward the end of Aquinas's discussion of how we ought live does our dependence on divine assistance, or grace, arise. This serves as a bridge to the *Secunda Secundae*, in which Aquinas explains faith, hope, and love and their place in human and divine justice. The need for grace in a Christian life, demanding prudence, fortitude, and temperance, provides Thomas an opportunity to explore virtues in markedly theological terms. The truth of Scripture requires that Aristotle's rationally grounded system recognize humans to be more than simply rational, social animals. The promise of eternal salvation and our reliance on God's goodwill suggest that Aristotle's approach is valid only insofar as his system leads one to think about a spiritual life in addition to the virtuous life envisioned by the classical thinkers.

The third part, consisting of ninety questions and an additional supplement of ninety-nine questions, is explicitly concerned with Christian doctrine. Who Jesus Christ is, what the Incarnation involves, how Mary figures in things, what the Holy Ghost is, and what the sacraments are figure prominently, and his Aristotelian philosophical approach affords readers a lucid expression of the fundamental aspects of Catholic teaching. The final questions of the third part concern the general resurrection promised in Scripture and the final judgment to follow.

One might wonder why so much emphasis is placed on the overall structure of the *Summa* when it seems to start out as a generally philosophical work but gradually meanders into specifically theological issues. Certainly, many contemporary readers of

Aquinas are familiar only with the philosophical elements of the first two parts, leaving the last parts of the *Summa* to seminarians and fanatics. The logic of the structure is easy to miss, but once clear, demonstrates Aquinas's genius. He believed, as do all monotheists, that creation is a loving self-expression of the creator. God creates from nothing, giving creation a structure that exists perfectly in the divine mind, and shaping it to move toward its final good, which is, ultimately, God. As such, the *Summa* begins with the perfection of the divine being, explores God's threefold nature and attributes, and launches out into the act of creation from there. Our place in creation is the beginning of creation's ultimate realization of its end: a conscious, created appreciation of the absolute good toward which it moves. Aquinas believed that humanity, alone in creation, has a capacity to self-control and self-awareness that permits consciousness. Reason's recognition that the purpose of our consciousness is union with God's consciousness depends for its realization on the premise that all things exist to realize the purposes for which they are created. Human reason is easily led astray into selfish concerns and mistakes about nature, thanks to the incident in the Garden narrated in Genesis. The result is that human reason can assume that its purpose is itself; hence, Aquinas's structure shows the need for the revealed truth of Scripture. With this assistance, created human consciousness is capable of becoming what it was created for, the act in which creation recognizes its purpose and end in reunion with God.

SEL

QUESTIONS

1. How do differences in the one who loves, such as having will instead of mere appetite or the capacity for knowledge instead of mere life, change the nature of love in Thomas's understanding?
2. How can love both begin and end in the loved object?
3. What qualities distinguish *true* friendship?
4. In what sense must we know an object in order to love it? In what sense is knowledge unnecessary?
5. Aquinas claims we can and even should love our enemies. How can love and enmity be compatible? The added difficulty of loving an enemy is a source of merit, he claims, but not the only one—what are others?

SELECTED BIBLIOGRAPHY

Aquinas, Thomas. *Aquinas' Shorter Summa*. Manchester, N.H.: Sophia Institute Press, 2002.
Clark, Mary T. *An Aquinas Reader*. New York: Fordham University Press, 2000.
Davies, Brian. *Aquinas*. London: Continuum, 2002.
Davies, Brian. *The Thought of Thomas Aquinas*. Oxford: Clarendon Press, 1992.

Kerr, Fergus. *After Aquinas*. Oxford: Blackwell Publishers, 2002.

Kretzman, Norman, and Elenore Stump. *The Cambridge Companion to Aquinas*. New York: Cambridge University Press, 1993.

McDermott, Timothy. *St. Thomas Aquinas: Summa Theologiae: A Concise Translation*. Westminister, Md: Christian Classics, 1989.

McInerny, Ralph. *Thomas Aquinas, Selected Writings*. London: Penguin Books, 1998.

O'Meara, Thomas F. *Thomas Aquinas Theologian*. Notre Dame, Ind.: University of Notre Dame, 1997.

Torrell, Jean-Pierre. *Saint Thomas Aquinas: The Person and His Work*. Washington, D.C.: Catholic University Press, 1996.

Wippel, John F. *The Metaphysical Thought of Thomas Aquinas*. Washington, D.C.: Catholic University Press, 2000.

from *Summa Theologica*

Saint Thomas Aquinas

QUESTION XX

God's Love

(In Four Articles)

WE next consider those things that pertain absolutely to the will of God. In the appetitive part of the soul there are found in ourselves both the passions of the soul, as joy, love, and the like; and the habits of the moral virtues, as justice, fortitude, and the like. Hence we shall first consider the love of God, and secondly His justice and mercy (Q. XXI). About the first there are four points of inquiry: (1) Whether love exists in God? (2) Whether He loves all things? (3) Whether He loves one thing more than another? (4) Whether He loves more the better things?

ARTICLE 1. *Whether Love Exists in God?*

We proceed thus to the First Article: It seems that love does not exist in God.

Objection 1. For in God there are no passions. Now love is a passion. Therefore love is not in God.

Obj. 2. Further, love, anger, sorrow, and the like, are divided against one another. But sorrow and anger are not attributed to God, unless by metaphor. Therefore neither is love attributed to Him.

Obj. 3. Further, Dionysius says (*Div. Nom.* iv):[1] "Love is a uniting and binding force." But this cannot take place in God, since He is simple. Therefore love does not exist in God.

On the contrary, It is written: *God is love* (I John 4. 16).

I answer that, We must assert that in God there is love, because love is the first movement of the will and of every appetitive power. For since the acts of the will and of every appetitive power tend towards good and evil as to their proper objects, and since good is essentially and especially the object of the will and the appetite, while evil is only the object secondarily and indirectly, as opposed to good, it follows that the acts of the will and appetite that look towards good must naturally be

[1]Sect. 15 (PG 3, 713).

prior to those that look towards evil; thus, for instance, joy is prior to sorrow, love to hate, because what exists of itself is always prior to that which exists through another.

Again, the more universal is naturally prior to what is less so. Hence the intellect is first ordered to universal truth, and in the second place to particular and special truths. Now there are certain acts of the will and appetite that regard good under some special condition, as joy and delight regard good present and possessed, whereas desire and hope regard good not as yet possessed. Love, however, regards good in general, whether possessed or not. Hence love is naturally the first act of the will and appetite, for which reason all the other appetitive movements presuppose love as their first root. For nobody desires anything nor rejoices in anything except as a good that is loved; nor is there hate except of something as opposed to the thing loved. Similarly, it is clear that sorrow, and other things like it, must be referred to love as to their first principle. Hence, in whomsoever there is will and appetite, there must also be love, since if the first is wanting, all that follows is also wanting. Now it has been shown that will is in God (Q. XIX, A. 1), and hence we must attribute love to Him.

Reply Obj. 1. The knowing power does not move except through the medium of the appetitive; and just as in ourselves the universal reason moves through the medium of the particular reason, as stated in the book on the *Soul*,[2] so in ourselves the intellectual appetite, which is called the will, moves through the medium of the sensitive appetite. Hence, in us the sensitive appetite is the proximate moving force of our bodies. Some bodily change therefore always accompanies an act of the sensitive appetite, and this change affects especially the heart, which is the first principle of movement in animals. Therefore acts of the sensitive appetite, since they have joined to them some bodily change, are called passions, but acts of the will are not so called. Love, therefore, and joy and delight are passions, in so far as they denote acts of the sensitive appetite; but in so far as they denote acts of the intellective appetite, they are not passions. It is in this latter sense that they are in God. Hence the Philosopher says:[3] "God rejoices by an operation that is one and simple," and for the same reason He loves without passion.

Reply Obj. 2. In the passions of the sensitive appetite there may be distinguished a certain material element—namely, the bodily change—and a certain formal element, which is on the part of the appetite. Thus in anger, as the Philosopher says,[4] the material element is the rising of the blood about the heart or something of this kind, but the formal, the appetite for vengeance. Again, as regards the formal element of certain passions a certain imperfection is implied, as in desire, which is of the good we have not, and in sorrow, which is about the evil we have. This applies also to anger, which supposes sorrow. Certain other passions, however, as love and joy, imply no imperfection. Since therefore none of these can be attributed to God on their material side, as has been said (*ad* I), neither can those that even on their formal side imply imperfection be attributed to Him, except metaphorically, from likeness of effects, as already shown (QQ. III, A. 2, Ans. 2 and XIX, A. II). However, those that do not imply imperfection, such as love and joy, can be properly predicated of God, though without attributing passion to Him, as said before (Ans. I).

Reply Obj. 3. An act of love always tends towards two things: to the good that one wills, and to the person for whom one wills it, since to love a

---

[2] Aristotle, III, 11 (434ª20).

[3] *Ethics*, VII, 14 (1154ᵇ26).
[4] *Soul*, I, 1 (403ª30).

person is to wish that person good. Hence, in so far as we love ourselves, we wish ourselves good, and, so far as possible, union with that good. So love is called the unitive force, even in God, yet without implying composition; for the good that He wills for Himself is no other than Himself, Who is good by His essence, as above shown (Q. VI, A. 3). And by the fact that anyone loves another, he wills good to that other. Thus he puts the other, as it were, in the place of himself, and regards the good done to him as done to himself. And for this reason love is called a binding force, since it attaches another to ourselves, and refers his good to our own. And in this way also the divine love is a binding force, since God wills good to others; yet it implies no composition in God.

ARTICLE 2. *Whether God Loves All Things?*

We proceed thus to the Second Article: It seems that God does not love all things.

Objection 1. For according to Dionysius (*Div. Nom.* iv, 1),[5] love places the lover outside himself, and carries him over in a certain way into the object of his love. But it is not admissible to say that God is placed outside of Himself, and passes into other things. Therefore it is inadmissible to say that God loves things other than Himself.

Obj. 2. Further, the love of God is eternal. But things apart from God are not from eternity, except in God. Therefore God does not love anything except as it exists in Himself. But as existing in Him, it is no other than Himself. Therefore God does not love things other than Himself.

Obj. 3. Further, love is twofold—the love, namely, of desire, and the love of friendship. Now God does not love irrational creatures with the love of desire, since He needs no creature outside Himself. Nor with the love of friendship, since there

can be no friendship with irrational creatures, as the Philosopher shows.[6] Therefore God does not love all things.

Obj. 4. Further, it is written (Ps. 5. 7): *Thou hatest all the workers of iniquity.* Now nothing is at the same time hated and loved. Therefore God does not love all things.

On the contrary, It is said (Wisd. II. 25): *Thou lovest all things that are, and hatest none of the things which Thou hast made.*

I answer that, God loves all existing things. For all existing things, in so far as they exist, are good, since the being of a thing is itself a good, and likewise, whatever perfection it possesses. Now it has been shown above (Q. XIX, A. 4) that God's will is the cause of all things. It must be, therefore, that a thing has being, or any kind of good, only in so far as it is willed by God. To every existing thing, then, God wills some good. Hence, since to love anything is nothing else than to will good to that thing, it is manifest that God loves everything that exists. Yet not as we love. Because since our will is not the cause of the goodness of things, but is moved by it as by its object, our love, whereby we will good to anything, is not the cause of its goodness; but conversely its goodness, whether real or imaginary, calls forth our love, by which we will that it should preserve the good it has, and receive besides the good it has not, and to this end we direct our actions. But the love of God infuses and creates goodness.

Reply Obj. 1. A lover is placed outside himself and made to pass into the object of his love in so far as he wills good to the beloved, and works for that good by his forethought even as he works for his own. Hence Dionysius says (*loc. cit.*): "On behalf of the truth we must make bold to say even this, that He Himself, the cause of all things, by the abundance of His loving goodness, is placed

---

[5]Sect. 13 (PG 3, 712).

[6]*Ethics*, VIII, 2 (1155[b]27).

outside Himself by His providence for all existing things."

Reply Obj. 2. Although creatures have not existed from eternity, except in God, yet because they have been in Him from eternity, God has known them eternally in their proper natures, and for that reason has loved them, even as we, by the likenesses of things within us, know things existing in themselves.

Reply Obj. 3. Friendship cannot exist except towards rational creatures, who are capable of returning love, and communicating one with another in the various works of life, and who may fare well or ill, according to the changes of fortune and happiness, even as to them is benevolence properly speaking exercised. But irrational creatures cannot attain to loving God, nor to any share in the intellectual and blessed life that He lives. Properly speaking, therefore, God does not love irrational creatures with the love of friendship, but as it were with the love of desire, in so far as He orders them to rational creatures, and even to Himself. Yet this is not because He stands in need of them, but only on account of His goodness, and of the services they render to us. For we can desire a thing for others as well as for ourselves.

Reply Obj. 4. Nothing prevents one and the same thing being loved under one aspect, while it is hated under another. God loves sinners in so far as they are natures; for they both are, and are from Him. In so far as they are sinners, they are not, but fall away from being; and this in them is not from God. Hence under this aspect, they are hated by Him.

ARTICLE 3. *Whether God Loves All Things Equally?*

We proceed thus to the Third Article: It seems that God loves all things equally.

Objection 1. For it is said: *He hath equally care of all* (Wisd. 6. 8). But God's providence over things comes from the love with which He loves them. Therefore He loves all things equally.

Obj. 2. Further, the love of God is His essence. But God's essence does not admit of more and less; neither therefore does His love. He does not therefore love some things more than others.

Obj. 3. Further, as God's love extends to created things, so do His knowledge and will extend. But God is not said to know some things more than others, nor to will one thing more than another. Neither therefore does He love some things more than others.

On the contrary, Augustine says (*Tract. in Joan.* CX).[7] "God loves all things that He has made, and amongst them rational creatures more, and of these especially those who are members of His only-begotten Son; and much more than all, His only-begotten Son Himself."

I answer that, Since to love a thing is to will it good, anything may be loved more, or less, in a twofold way. In one way on the part of the act of the will itself, which is more or less intense. In this way God does not love some things more than others, because He loves all things by an act of the will that is one, simple, and always the same. In another way on the part of the good itself that a person wills for the beloved. In this way we are said to love that one more than another for whom we will a greater good, though our will is not more intense. In this way we must say that God loves some things more than others. For since God's love is the cause of goodness in things, as has been said (A. 2), no one thing would be better than an other if God did not will greater good for one than for another.

Reply Obj. 1. God is said to have equally care of all not because by His care He deals out equal good to all, but because He administers all things with a like wisdom and goodness.

Reply. Obj. 2. This argument is based on the intensity of love on the part of the act of the will, which is the divine essence. But the good that God

---

[7]PL 35, 1924.

wills for His creatures, is not the divine essence. Therefore nothing prevents its increase or decrease.

Reply Obj. 3. To understand and to will denote the act alone, and do not include in their meaning objects from the diversity of which God may be said to know or will more or less as has been said with respect to God's love.

ARTICLE 4. *Whether God Always Loves More the Better Things?*

We proceed thus to the Fourth Article: It seems that God does not always love more the better things.

Objection 1. For it is manifest that Christ is better than the whole human race, being God and man. But God loved the human race more than He loved Christ, for it is said: *He spared not His own Son, but delivered Him up for us all* (Rom. 8. 32). Therefore God does not always love more the better things.

Obj. 2. Further, an angel is better than a man. Hence it is said of man: *Thou hast made him a little less than the angels* (Ps. 8. 6). But God loved men more than He loved the angels, for it is said: *Nowhere doth He take hold of the angels, but of the seed of Abraham He taketh hold* (Heb. 2. 16). Therefore God does not always love more the better things.

Obj. 3. Further, Peter was better than John, since he loved Christ more. Hence the Lord knowing this to be true, asked Peter, saying: "*Simon, son of John, lovest thou Me more than these?*" Yet Christ loved John more than He loved Peter. For as Augustine says,[8] commenting on the words, *Simon, son of John, lovest thou Me?* "By this very mark is John distinguished from the other disciples, not that He loved him only, but that He loved him more than the rest." Therefore God does not always love more the better things.

Obj. 4. Further, the innocent man is better than the repentant, since repentance is, as Jerome says,[9] "a second plank after shipwreck." But God loves the penitent more than the innocent, since He rejoices over him the more. For it is said; *I say to you that there shall be joy in heaven upon one sinner that doth penance, more than upon ninety-nine just who need not penance* (Luke 15. 7). Therefore God does not always love more the better things.

Obj. 5. Further, the just man who is foreknown is better than the predestined sinner. Now God loves more the predestined sinner, since He wills for him a greater good, life eternal. Therefore God does not always love more the better things.

On the contrary, Everything loves what is like it, as appears from (Ecclus. 13. 19): *Every beast loveth its like.* Now the better a thing is, the more like is it to God. Therefore the better things are more loved by God.

I answer that, We must say from what has been said before, that God loves more the better things. For it has been shown (A. 3), that God's loving one thing more than another is nothing else than His willing for that thing a greater good; for God's will is the cause of goodness in things, and the reason why some things are better than others, is that God wills for them a greater good. Hence it follows that He loves more the better things.

Reply Obj. 1. God loves Christ not only more than He loves the whole human race, but more than He loves the entire created universe, because He willed for Him the greater good in giving Him *a name that is above all names,* (Philipp. 2. 9) in so far as He was true God. Nor did anything of His excellence diminish when God delivered Him up to death for the salvation of the human race; rather did He become thereby a glorious victor: *The government was placed upon His shoulder,* according to Isa. 9. 6.

---

[8] *In Joann., tract.* CXXIV (PL 35, 1971).

[9] *In Isa.,* 11, 3 (PL 24, 66).

Reply Obj. 2. God loves the human nature assumed by the Word of God in the person of Christ more than He loves all the angels, for that nature is better, especially by reason of the union with the Godhead. But speaking of human nature in general, and comparing it with the angelic, the two are found equal, in the order of grace and of glory, since according to Apoc. 21. 17, *the measure of a man and of an angel* is the same. Yet so that, in this respect, some angels are found more to be preferred than some men, and some men more to be preferred than some angels. But as to natural condition an angel is better than a man. God therefore did not assume human nature because He loved man, absolutely speaking, more, but because the needs of man were greater; just as the master of a house may give some costly delicacy to a sick servant that he does not give to his own son in sound health.

Reply Obj. 3. This doubt concerning Peter and John has been solved in various ways. Augustine (*loc. cit.*) interprets it mystically, and says that the active life, signified by Peter, loves God more than the contemplative signified by John, because the former is more conscious of the miseries of this present life, and therefore the more ardently desires to be freed from them, and depart to God. God, he says, loves more the contemplative life, since He preserves it longer. For it does not end, as the active life does, with the life of the body.

Some say[10] that Peter loved Christ more in His members, and therefore was loved more by Christ also, for which reason He gave him the care of the Church; but that John loved Christ more in Himself, and so was loved more by Him, on which account Christ commended His mother to his care. Others say[11] that it is uncertain which of them

loved Christ more with the love of charity, and uncertain also which of them God loved more and ordained to a greater degree of glory in eternal life. Peter is said to have loved more, in regard to a certain promptness and fervour, but John to have been more loved, with respect to certain marks of familiarity which Christ showed to him rather than to others, on account of his youth and purity. But others say[12] that Christ loved Peter more, from his more excellent gift of charity, but John more, from his gifts of intellect. Hence, absolutely speaking, Peter was the better and the more beloved, but, in a certain sense, John was the better, and was loved the more. However, it may seem presumptuous to pass judgment on these matters, since *the Lord* and no other *is the weigher of spirits* (Prov. 16. 2).

Reply Obj. 4. The penitent and the innocent are related as exceeding and exceeded. For whether innocent or penitent, those are the better and the better loved who have most grace.

Other things being equal, innocence is the nobler thing and the more beloved. God is said to rejoice more over the penitent than over the innocent because often penitents rise from sin more cautious, humble, and fervent. Hence Gregory commenting on these words (*Hom.* xxxiv *in Ev.*)[13] says that, "In battle the general loves the soldier who after flight returns and bravely pursues the enemy more than him who has never fled, but has never done a brave deed."

Or it may be answered that gifts of grace, equal in themselves, are more as conferred on the penitent, who deserved punishment, than as conferred on the innocent, to whom no punishment was due; just as a hundred marks are a greater gift to a poor man than to a king.

Reply Obj. 5. Since God's will is the cause of goodness in things, the goodness of one who is

---

[10]Albert the Great, *In Sent.*, III, d. 31, A. 12 (BO XXVIII, 593). Cf. Bonaventure, *In Sent.*, III, d. 32, Q. 6 (QR III, 707).
[11]Albert and Bonaventure (cf. preceding note) attribute this position to Bernard. Cf. Bernard, *Serm.* XXIX (PL 183, 622).

[12]Cf. Albert the Great, *Enarr. in Joann.*, (BO XXIV, 13).
[13]Bk. II (PL 76, 1248).

loved by God is to be weighed according to the time when some good is to be given to him by the divine goodness. According therefore to the time when there is to be given by the divine will to the predestined sinner a greater good, the sinner is the better, although according to some other time he is the worse; because even according to some time he is neither good nor bad.

QUESTION XXVI

Of the passions of the soul in particular, and first, of love

(In Four Articles)

WE have now to consider the soul's passions in particular, and (1) The passions of the concupiscible part; (2) The passions of the irascible part (Q. XL).

The first of these considerations will be threefold, since we shall consider (1) Love and hatred; (2) Desire and aversion (Q. XXX); (3) Pleasure and sadness (Q. XXXI).

Concerning love, three points must be considered: (1) Love itself; (2) The cause of love (Q. XXVII); (3) The effects of love (Q. XXVIII). Under the first head there are four points of inquiry: (1) Whether love is in the concupiscible power? (2) Whether love is a passion? (3) Whether love is the same as dilection? (4) Whether love is properly divided into love of friendship, and love of concupiscence?

ARTICLE I. *Whether Love Is in the Concupiscible Power?*

We proceed thus to the First Article: It seems that love is not in the concupiscible power.

Objection I. For it is written (Wis. 8. 2): *Her*, namely, wisdom, *have I loved, and have sought her out from my youth*. But the concupiscible power, being a part of the sensitive appetite, cannot tend to wisdom, which is not apprehended by the senses. Therefore love is not in the concupiscible power.

Obj. 2. Further, love seems to be identified with every passion, for Augustine says:[14] "Love, yearning for the object beloved, is desire; having and enjoying it, is joy; fleeing what is contrary to it, is fear; and feeling what is contrary to it, is sadness." But not every passion is in the concupiscible power; indeed, fear, which is mentioned in this passage, is in the irascible power. Therefore we must not say absolutely that love is in the concupiscible power.

Obj. 3. Further, Dionysius (*Div. Nom* iv)[15] mentions a "natural love." But natural love seems to pertain rather to the natural powers, which belong to the vegetal soul. Therefore love is not absolutely in the concupiscible power.

On the contrary, The Philosopher says that "love is in the concupiscible power."[16]

I answer that, Love is something pertaining to the appetite, since good is the object of both. Therefore love differs according to the difference of appetites. For there is an appetite which arises from an apprehension existing, not in the subject of the appetite, but in some other, and this is called the natural appetite. Because natural things seek what is suitable to them according to their nature, by reason of an apprehension which is not in them, but in the Author of their nature, as stated in the First Part (Q. VI, A. I. Reply 2; Q. CIII, A. I. Reply I, 3). And there is another appetite arising from an apprehension in the subject of the appetite, but from necessity and not from free choice. Such is, in irrational animals, the sensitive appetite, which, however, in man, has a certain share of liberty, in so far as it obeys reason. Again, there is another appetite following from an apprehension in the subject of the appetite according to

---

[14] *City of God*, XIV, 7 (PL 41, 410).
[15] Sect. 15 (PG 3, 713).
[16] *Topics*, II, 7 (113ᵇ2).

free choice. And this is the rational or intellectual appetite, which is called the will.

Now in each of these appetites, the name love is given to the principle of movement towards the end loved. In the natural appetite the principle of this movement is the appetitive subject's connaturalness with the thing to which it tends, and may be called natural love; thus the connaturalness of a heavy body for the centre is by reason of its weight and may be called natural love. In like manner the aptitude of the sensitive appetite or of the will to some good, that is to say, its very satisfaction in good, is called sensitive love, or intellectual or rational love. So that sensitive love is in the sensitive appetite, just as intellectual love is in the intellectual appetite. And it belongs to the concupiscible power, because it has to do with good absolutely, and not under the aspect of difficulty, which is the object of the irascible faculty.

Reply Obj. 1. The words quoted refer to intellectual or rational love.

Reply Obj. 2. Love is spoken of as being fear, joy, desire and sadness, not essentially but causally.

Reply Obj. 3. Natural love is not only in the powers of the vegetal soul, but in all the soul's powers, and also in all the parts of the body, and universally in all things, because, as Dionysius says (*Div. Nom.* iv),[17] "Beauty and goodness are beloved by all things," since each single thing has a connaturalness with that which is naturally suitable to it.

ARTICLE 2. *Whether Love Is a Passion?*

We proceed thus to the Second Article: It would seem that love is not a passion. For no power is a passion.

Objection 1. But every love is a power, as Dionysius says (*Div. Nom.* iv)[18] Therefore love is not a passion.

Obj. 2. Further, love is a kind of union or bond, as Augustine says (*De Trin.* vii, 10).[19] But a union or bond is not a passion, but rather a relation. Therefore love is not a passion.

Obj. 3. Further, Damascene says (*De Fide Orthod.* ii, 22)[20] that "passion is a movement." But love does not imply the movement of the appetite; for this is desire, of which movement love is the principle. Therefore love is not a passion.

On the contrary, The Philosopher says that "love is a passion."[21]

I answer that, Passion is the effect of the agent on the patient. Now a natural agent produces a twofold effect on the patient: for in the first place it gives it the form, and secondly it gives it the movement that results from the form. Thus the generator gives the generated body both weight and the movement resulting from weight, so that weight, from being the principle of movement to the place which is connatural to that body by reason of its weight, can, in a way, be called natural love. In the same way the appetible thing gives the appetite, first, a certain adaptation to itself, which consists in satisfaction in that thing; and from this follows movement towards the appetible thing. For the appetitive movement is circular, as stated in the book on the *Soul*,[22] because the appetible thing moves the appetite, introducing itself, as it were, to its intention, while the appetite moves towards the realization of the appetible thing, so that the movement ends where it began. Accordingly, the first change wrought in the appetite by the appetible thing is called love, and is nothing else than satisfaction in that thing; and from this satisfaction results a movement towards that same thing, and this movement is desire; and lastly, there is rest which is joy. Since, therefore, love consists in a

[17]Sect. 10 (PG 3, 708).
[18]Sect. 15 (PG 3, 713).

[19]PL 42, 960.
[20]PG 94, 940.
[21]*Ethics*, VIII, 5 (1157[b]28).
[22]Aristotle, III, 10 (433[b]22).

change wrought in the appetite by the appetible thing, it is evident that love is a passion: properly so called, according as it is in the concupiscible part; in a wider and extended sense, according as it is in the will.

Reply Obj. 1. Since power denotes a principle of movement or action, Dionysius calls love a power in so far as it is a principle of movement in the appetite.

Reply Obj. 2. Union belongs to love in so far as by reason of the satisfaction of the appetite, the lover stands in relation to that which he loves as though it were himself or part of himself. Hence it is clear that love is not the very relation of union, but that union is a result of love. Hence, too, Dionysius says that "love is a unitive force" (*Div. Nom.* iv)[23] and the Philosopher says that "union is the work of love."[24]

Reply Obj. 3. Although love does not denote the movement of the appetite in tending towards the appetible object, yet it denotes that movement by which the appetite is changed by the appetible thing, so as to have satisfaction in it.

ARTICLE 4. *Whether Love Is Properly Divided into Love of Friendship and Love of Concupiscence?*

We proceed thus to the Fourth Article: It would seem that love is not properly divided into love of friendship and love of concupiscence.[25]

Objection 1. For "love is a passion, while friendship is a habit," according to the Philosopher.[26] But habit cannot be a part of a division of passions. Therefore love is not properly divided into love of concupiscence and love of friendship.

Obj. 2. Further, a thing cannot be divided by another member of the same division; for man is not a member of the same division as animal. But concupiscence is a member of the same division as love, as a passion distinct from love. Therefore concupiscence is not a division of love.

Obj. 3. Further, according to the Philosopher[27] friendship is threefold, that which is founded on usefulness, that which is founded on pleasure, and that which is founded on goodness. But useful and pleasant friendship are not without concupiscence. Therefore concupiscence should not be divided against friendship.

On the contrary, We are said to love certain things, because we desire them; thus "a man is said to love wine, on account of its sweetness which he desires," as stated in the *Topics*.[28] But we have no friendship for wine and the like things, as stated in the *Ethics*.[29] Therefore love of concupiscence is distinct from love of friendship.

I answer that, As the Philosopher says,[30] "to love is to wish good to someone." Hence the movement of love has a twofold tendency: towards the good which a man wishes to someone, whether for himself or for another; and towards that to which he wishes some good. Accordingly, man has love of concupiscence towards the good that he wishes to another, and love of friendship towards him to whom he wishes good.

Now the members of this division are related as primary and secondary, since that which is loved with the love of friendship is loved absolutely and for itself; but that which is loved with the love of concupiscence is loved not absolutely and for itself, but for something else. For just as being *per se* is absolutely that which has being, while that which exists in another has relative being, so, because good is convertible with being, the good which itself has goodness is good absolutely; but that

[23]Sect. 12 (PG 3, 709).

[24]*Politics*, II, 4 (1262[b]10).

[25]Cf. Albert, *Summa Theol.*, II, 4, Q. XIV, n. 4, A. 2 (BO XXXII, 200); *In Sent.*, III, d. 28, A. 2 (BO XXVIII, 537); Bonaventure, *In Sent.*, II, d. 3, Pt. II, A. 3, Q. 1 (QR II, 125).

[26]*Ethics*, VIII, 5 (1157[b]28).

[27]*Ibid.*, VIII, 3 (1156[a]7).

[28]Aristotle, II, 3 (111[a]3).

[29]Aristotle, VIII, 2 (1155[b]29).

[30]*Rhetoric*, II, 4 (1380[b]35).

which is another's good is a relative good. Consequently the love with which a thing is loved in order that it may have some good, is love absolutely, while the love with which a thing is loved that it may be another's good is relative love.

Reply Obj. 1. Love is not divided into friendship and concupiscence, but into love of friendship, and love of concupiscence. For a friend is, properly speaking, one to whom we wish good, while we are said to desire what we wish for ourselves.

Hence the *Reply to the Second Objection* is evident.

Reply Obj. 3. When friendship is based on usefulness or pleasure, a man does indeed wish his friend some good, and in this respect the character of friendship is preserved. But since he refers this good further to his own pleasure or use, the result is that friendship of the useful or pleasant, in so far as it is drawn to the love of concupiscence, loses the character of true friendship.

QUESTION XXVII

Of the Principal Act of Charity, Which is Love

(In Eight Articles)

WE must now consider the act of charity, and (1) the principal act of charity, which is love, (2) the other acts or effects which follow from that act (Q. XXVIII).

Under the first head there are eight points of inquiry: (1) Which is the more proper to charity, to love or to be loved? (2) Whether to love considered as an act of charity is the same as goodwill? (3) Whether God should be loved for His own sake? (4) Whether God can be loved immediately in this life? (5) Whether God can be loved wholly? (6) Whether the love of God is according to measure? (7) Which is the better, to love one's friend, or one's enemy? (8) Which is the better, to love God, or one's neighbour?

ARTICLE 1. *Whether To Be Loved Is More Proper to Charity Than To Love*

We proceed thus to the First Article: It would seem that it is more proper to charity to be loved than to love.

Objection 1. For the better charity is to be found in those who are themselves better. But those who are better should be more loved. Therefore to be loved is more proper to charity.

Obj. 2. Further, That which is to be found in more subjects seems to be more in keeping with nature, and, for that reason, better. Now, as the Philosopher says,[31] "many would rather be loved than love, and lovers of flattery always abound." Therefore it is better to be loved than to love, and consequently it is more in keeping with charity.

Obj. 3. Further, The cause of anything being such is yet more so. Now men love because they are loved, for Augustine says (*De Catech. Rud.* iv)[32] that "nothing incites another more to love you than that you love him first." Therefore charity consists in being loved rather than in loving.

On the contrary, The Philosopher says[33] that "friendship consists in loving rather than in being loved." Now charity is a kind of friendship. Therefore it consists in loving rather than in being loved.

I answer that, To love belongs to charity as charity. For, since charity is a virtue, by its very essence it has an inclination to its proper act. Now to be loved is not the act of the charity of the person loved; for this act is to love, but to be loved belongs to him as coming under the common notion of good, in so far as another is moved towards the good of the person loved by an act of charity. Hence it is clear that to love is more proper to

---

[31]*Ethics*, VIII, 8 (1159a12).
[32]PL 40, 314.
[33]*Ethics*, VIII, 8 (1159a27).

charity than to be loved, for that which befits a thing substantially and by reason of itself pertains to it more than that which is befitting to it by reason of something else. This can be exemplified in two ways. First, in the fact that friends are more commended for loving than for being loved; indeed, if they be loved and yet love not, they are blamed. Secondly, because a mother, whose love is the greatest, seeks rather to love than to be loved; "for some women," as the Philosopher observes,[34] "entrust their children to a nurse; they do love them indeed, yet seek not to be loved in return, if they happen not to be loved."

Reply Obj. 1. A better man, through being better, is more lovable, but through having more perfect charity, loves more. He loves more, however, in proportion to the person he loves. For a better man does not love that which is beneath him less than it can be loved, while he who is less good fails to love one who is better as much as he can be loved.

Reply Obj. 2. As the Philosopher says,[35] men wish to be loved in so far as they wish to be honoured. For just as honour is bestowed on a man in order to bear witness to the good which is in him, so by being loved a man is shown to have some good, since good alone is lovable. Accordingly men seek to be loved and to be honoured, for the sake of something else, namely to make known the good which is in the person loved. On the other hand, those who have charity seek to love for the sake of loving, as though this were itself the good of charity, even as the act of any virtue is that virtue's good. Hence it is more proper to charity to wish to love than to wish to be loved.

Reply Obj. 3. Some love on account of being loved, not so that to be loved is the end of their loving, but because it is a kind of way leading a man to love.

[34]*Ibid.*
[35]*Ibid.* (1159[a]16).

ARTICLE 2. *Whether To Love Considered As an Act of Charity Is the Same As Goodwill?*

We proceed thus to the Second Article: It would seem that to love, considered as an act of charity, is nothing else than goodwill.

Objection 1. For the Philosopher says[36] that "to love is to wish a person well." But this is goodwill. Therefore the act of charity is nothing but goodwill.

Obj. 2. Further, The act belongs to the same subject as the habit. Now the habit of charity is in the power of the will, as stated above (Q. XXIV, A. I). Therefore the act of charity is also an act of the will. But it tends to good only, and this is goodwill. Therefore the act of charity is nothing else than goodwill.

Obj. 3. Further, The Philosopher reckons five things pertaining to friendship,[37] the first of which is that a man should wish his friend well; the second, that he should wish him to be and to live; the third, that he should take pleasure in his company; the fourth, that he should make choice of the same things; the fifth, that he should grieve and rejoice with him. Now the first two pertain to goodwill. Therefore goodwill is the first act of charity.

On the contrary, The Philosopher says in the same book[38] that "goodwill is neither friendship nor love, but the beginning of friendship." Now charity is friendship, as stated above (Q. XXIII, A. 1). Therefore goodwill is not the same as to love considered as an act of charity.

I answer that, Goodwill properly speaking is that act of the will by which we wish well to another. Now this act of the will differs from actual love, considered not only as being in the sensitive appetite but also as being in the intellective appetite or will. For the love which is in the sensitive

[36]*Rhetoric*, II, 4 (1380[b]35; 1381[a]19).
[37]*Ethics*, IX, 4 (1166[a]3).
[38]*Ibid.*, 5 (1166[b]30; 1167[a]3).

appetite is a passion. Now every passion seeks its object with a certain eagerness. And the passion of love is not aroused suddenly, but is born of an earnest consideration of the object loved; hence the Philosopher, showing the difference between goodwill and the love which is a passion, says[39] that "goodwill does not imply impetuosity or desire," that is to say, does not have an eager inclination, because it is by the sole judgment of his reason that one man wishes another well. Again love of this kind arises from familiarity, but goodwill sometimes arises suddenly, as happens to us if we look at men fighting, and we wish one of the fighters to win. But the love, which is in the intellective appetite also differs from goodwill, because it denotes a certain union of affections between the lover and the beloved, in so far as the lover thinks of the beloved as in some way united to him, or belonging to him, and so tends towards him. On the other hand, goodwill is a simple act of the will by which we wish a person well, even without presupposing the above mentioned union of the affections with him. Accordingly, to love, considered as an act of charity, includes goodwill, but such dilection or love adds union of affections, and so the Philosopher says[40] that "goodwill is a beginning of friendship."

Reply Obj. 1. The Philosopher, by thus defining "to love," does not describe it fully, but mentions only that part of its definition in which the act of love is chiefly manifested.

Reply Obj. 2. To love is indeed an act of the will tending to the good, but it adds a certain union with the beloved, which union is not denoted by goodwill.

Reply Obj. 3. These things mentioned by the Philosopher belong to friendship because they arise from a man's love for himself, as he says in the same passage, in so far as a man does all these things in respect of his friend, even as he does them to himself; and this belongs to the aforesaid union of the affections.

ARTICLE 3. *Whether out of Charity God Ought To Be Loved for Himself?*

We proceed thus to the Third Article: It seems that God is loved out of charity, not for Himself but for the sake of something else.

Objection 1. For Gregory says in a homily (*In Evang.* xi).[41] "The soul learns from the things it knows to love those it knows not," where by things unknown he means the intelligible and the Divine, and by things known he indicates the objects of the senses. Therefore God is to be loved for the sake of something else.

Obj. 2. Further, Love follows knowledge. But God is known through something else, according to Rom. 1. 20: *The invisible things of God are clearly seen, being understood by the things that are made.* Therefore He is also loved on account of something else and not for Himself.

Obj. 3. Further, Hope begets charity as a gloss says[42] on Matt. 1. 1, and "fear leads to charity," according to Augustine in his commentary on the First Canonical Epistle of John (*Tract.* ix).[43] Now hope looks forward to obtain something from God, while fear shuns something which can be inflicted by God? Therefore it seems that God is to be loved on account of some good we hope for, or some evil to be feared. Therefore He is not to be loved for Himself.

On the contrary, According to Augustine,[44] "to enjoy is to cleave to something for its own sake." Now God is to be enjoyed as he says in the same book.[45] Therefore God is to be loved for Himself.

---

[39]*Ibid.*, IX, 5 (1166^{b}33).
[40]*Ibid.* (1167^{a}3).

[41]PL 76, 1114.
[42]*Glossa interl.* (v, 5r).
[43]PL 35, 2048.
[44]*Christian Doctrine*, 1, 5 (PL 34, 21).
[45]*Ibid.*, 1, 4 (PL 34, 20).

I answer that, The preposition "for" denotes a relation of causality. Now there are four kinds of cause, namely final, formal, efficient, and material, to which a material disposition also is to be reduced, though it is not a cause absolutely but relatively. According to these four kinds of causes one thing is said to be loved for another. In respect of the final cause, we love medicine, for instance, for health; in respect of the formal cause, we love a man for his virtue, because, that is, by his virtue he is formally good and therefore lovable; in respect of the efficient cause, we love certain men because, for instance, they are the sons of such and such a father; and in respect of the disposition which is reducible to the genus of a material cause, we speak of loving something for that which disposed us to love it, for example we love a man for the favours received from him, although after we have begun to love our friend, we no longer love him for his favours, but for his virtue.

Accordingly, as regards the first three ways, we love God, not for anything else, but for Himself. For He is not ordered to anything else as to an end, but is Himself the last end of all things; nor does He require to receive any form in order to be good, for His very substance is His goodness, which is itself the exemplar of all other good things; nor again does goodness accrue to Him from anything else, but from Him to all other things.

In the fourth way, however, He can be loved for something else, because we are disposed by certain things to advance in His love, for instance, by favours bestowed by Him, by the rewards we hope to receive from Him, or even by the punishments which we are minded to avoid through Him.

Reply Obj. 1. "From the things it knows the soul learns to love what it knows not," not as though the things it knows were the reason for its loving things it knows not, through being the formal, final, or efficient cause of this love, but because this knowledge disposes man to love the unknown.

Reply Obj. 2. Knowledge of God is indeed acquired through other things, but after He is known, He is no longer known through them, but through Himself, according to John 4. 42: *We now believe, not for thy saying: for we ourselves have heard Him, and know that this is indeed the Saviour of the world.*

Reply Obj. 3. Hope and fear lead to charity by way of a certain disposition, as was shown above (Q. XVII, A. 8; Q. XIX, AA. 4, 7, 10; also above, Ans.).

ARTICLE 4. *Whether God Can Be Loved Immediately in This Life?*

We proceed thus to the Fourth Article: It seems that God cannot be loved immediately in this life.

Objection 1. For "the unknown cannot be loved" as Augustine says (*De Trin.* x, 1, 2).[46] Now we do not know God immediately in this life, since *we see now through a glass, in a dark manner* (I Cor. 13. 12). Neither, therefore, do we love Him immediately.

Obj. 2. Further, He who cannot do what is less, cannot do what is more. Now it is more to love God than to know Him, since *he who is joined* to God by love, *is one spirit* with Him (I Cor. 6. 17). But man cannot know God immediately. Therefore much less can he love Him immediately.

Obj. 3. Further, Man is severed from God by sin, according to Isa. 59. 2: *Your iniquities have divided between you and your God.* Now sin is in the will rather than in the intellect. Therefore man is less able to love God immediately than to know Him immediately.

On the contrary, Knowledge of God, because it is mediate, is said to be *enigmatic,* and *falls away* in heaven, as stated in I Cor. 13. 12. But charity *does*

---

[46]PL 42, 974, 975.

not fall away as stated in the same passage (*verse* 8). Therefore the charity of the way adheres to God immediately.

I answer that, As stated above (Q. XXVI, A. 1, Reply 2), the act of a cognitive power is completed by the thing known being in the knower, while the act of an appetitive power consists in the appetite being inclined towards the thing in itself. Hence it follows that the movement of the appetitive power is towards things in respect of their own condition, while the act of a cognitive power follows the mode of the knower.

Now in itself the very order of things is such that God is knowable and lovable for Himself, since He is essentially truth and goodness itself, by which other things are known and loved. But with regard to us, since our knowledge is derived through the senses, those things are knowable first, which are nearer to our senses, and the last term of knowledge is that which is most remote from our senses.

Accordingly, we must assert that to love, which is an act of the appetitive power, tends, even in this state of life, to God first, and flows on from Him to other things, and in this sense charity loves God immediately, and other things through God. On the other hand, with regard to knowledge, it is the reverse, since we know God through other things, either as a cause through its effects, or by way of pre-eminence or negation as Dionysius states (*Div. Nom.* i).[47]

Reply Obj. 1. Although the unknown cannot be loved, it does not follow that the order of knowledge is the same as the order of love, since love is the term of knowledge, and consequently, love can begin at once where knowledge ends, namely in the thing itself which is known through another thing.

Reply Obj. 2. Since to love God is something greater than to know Him, especially in this state of life, it follows that love of God presupposes knowledge of God. And because this knowledge does not rest in creatures, but, through them, tends to something else, love begins there, and thence goes on to other things by a kind of circular movement; for knowledge begins from creatures, tends to God, and love begins with God as the last end, and passes on to creatures.

Reply Obj. 3. Turning away from God, which is brought about by sin, is removed by charity, but not by knowledge alone; hence charity, by loving God, unites the soul immediately to Him with a chain of spiritual union.

ARTICLE 5. *Whether God Can Be Loved Wholly?*

We proceed thus to the Fifth Article: It seems that God cannot be loved wholly.

Objection 1. For love follows knowledge. Now God cannot be wholly known by us, since this would imply comprehension of Him. Therefore He cannot be wholly loved by us.

Obj. 2. Further, Love is a kind of union, as Dionysius shows (*Div. Nom.* iv).[48] But the heart of man cannot be wholly united to God, because *God is greater than our heart* (I John 3. 20). Therefore God cannot be loved wholly.

Obj. 3. Further, God loves Himself wholly. If therefore He be loved wholly by another, this one will love Him as much as God loves Himself. But this is unreasonable. Therefore God cannot be wholly loved by a creature.

On the contrary, It is written (Deut. 6. 5): *Thou shalt love the Lord thy God with thy whole heart.*

I answer that, Since love may be understood as something between lover and beloved, when we ask whether God can be wholly loved the question

---

[47]Sect. 5 (PG 3, 593).

[48]Sect. 12 (PG 3, 709).

may be understood in three ways. First so that the mode "wholly" be referred to the thing loved, and thus God is to be loved wholly, since man should love all that pertains to God. Secondly, it may be understood as though "wholly" referred to the lover and thus again God ought to be loved wholly, since man ought to love God with all his might, and to order all he has to the love of God, according to Deut. 6. 5: *Thou shalt love the Lord thy God with thy whole heart.* Thirdly, it may be understood by way of comparison of the lover to the thing loved, so that the mode of the lover equal the mode of the thing loved. This is impossible: for, since a thing is lovable in proportion to its goodness, God is infinitely lovable, since His goodness is infinite. Now no creature can love God infinitely, because all power of creatures, whether it be natural or infused, is finite.

This suffices for the *Replies to the Objections*, because the first three objections consider the question in this third sense, while the last takes it in the second sense.

ARTICLE 6. *Whether in Loving God We Ought To Observe Any Mode?*

We proceed thus to the Sixth Article: It would seem that we ought to observe some mode in loving God.

Objection 1. For the notion of good consists in "mode, species and order," as Augustine states (*De Nat. Boni*, iii)[49] Now the love of God is the best thing in man, according to Coloss. 3. 14: *Above all . . . things, have charity.* Therefore there ought to be a mode of the love of God.

Obj. 2. Further, Augustine says (*De Morib. Eccl.* viii).[50] "Prithee, tell me which is the mode of love. For I fear lest I burn with the desire and love of my Lord, more or less than I ought." But it would be

useless to seek the mode of the Divine love unless there were one. Therefore there is a mode of the love of God.

Obj. 3. Further, As Augustine says (*Gen. ad. lit.* iv, 3),[51] "the measure which is appointed to each thing, is its mode." Now the measure of the human will, as also of external action, is the reason. Therefore just as it is necessary for the reason to appoint a mode to the exterior effect of charity, according to Rom. 12. 1: *Your reasonable service*, so also the interior love of God requires a mode.

On the contrary, Bernard says (*De Dilig. Deum*, 1)[52] that "God is the cause of our loving God; the measure is to love Him without measure."

I answer that, As appears from the words of Augustine quoted above (obj. 3) mode signifies a determination of measure, which determination is to be found both in the measure and in the thing measured, but not in the same way. For it is found in the measure essentially, because a measure is of itself the determining and modifying rule of other things; but in the things measured, it is found relatively, that is in so far as they attain to the measure. Hence there can be nothing unmodified in the measure; but the thing measured is unmodified if it fails to attain to the measure, whether by deficiency or by excess.

Now in all matters of appetite and action the measure is the end, because the proper reason for all that we desire or do should be taken from the end, as the Philosopher proves.[53] Therefore the end has a mode by itself, while the means take their mode from being proportionate to the end. Hence, according to the Philosopher,[54] in every art, the desire for the end is endless and unlimited, while there is a limit to the means. Thus the physician

---

[49]PL 42, 553.
[50]PL 32, 1316.

[51]PL 34, 299.
[52]PL 182, 974.
[53]*Physics*, 11, 9 (200ª32).
[54]*Politics*, 1, 9 (1257ᵇ26).

does not put limits to health, but makes it as perfect as he possibly can; but he puts a limit to medicine, for he does not give as much medicine as he can, but according as health demands, so that if he give too much or too little, the medicine would be immoderate.

Again, the end of all human actions and affections is the love of God, by which we attain principally to our last end, as stated above (Q. XXIII, A. 6), and therefore the mode in the love of God must not be taken as in a thing measured where we find too much or too little, but as in the measure itself, where there cannot be excess, and where the more the rule is attained the better it is, so that the more we love God the better our love is.

Reply Obj. 1. That which is so by its essence takes precedence of that which is so through another, and therefore the goodness of the measure which has the mode essentially, takes precedence of the goodness of the thing measured, which has its mode through something else; and so too, charity, which has a mode as a measure has, is above the other virtues, which have a mode through being measured.

Reply Obj. 2. As Augustine adds in the same passage, the measure of our love for God, is to love Him with our whole heart, that is, to love Him as much as He can be loved, and this pertains to the mode which is proper to the measure.

Reply Obj. 3. An affection whose object is subject to reason's judgment, should be measured by reason. But the object of the Divine love which is God surpasses the judgment of reason, and therefore it is not measured by reason but exceeds it. Nor is there parity between the interior act and external acts of charity. For the interior act of charity has the character of an end, since man's ultimate good consists in his soul cleaving to God, according to Ps. 72. 28: *It is good for me to adhere to my God;* but the exterior acts are as means to the end,

and so have to be measured both according to charity and according to reason.

ARTICLE 7. *Whether It Is More Meritorious To Love an Enemy Than To Love a Friend?*

We proceed thus to the Seventh Article: It seems more meritorious to love an enemy than to love a friend.

Objection 1. For it is written (Matt. 5. 46): *If you love them that love you, what reward shall you have?* Therefore it is not deserving of reward to love one's friend. But, as the same passage proves, to love one's enemy is deserving of a reward. Therefore it is more meritorious to love one's enemy than to love one's friend.

Obj. 2. Further, An act is the more meritorious through proceeding from a greater charity. But it belongs "to the perfect children of God" to love their enemies as Augustine says[55] while those also who have imperfect charity love their friends. Therefore it is more meritorious to love one's enemy than to love one's friend.

Obj. 3. Further, Where there is more effort for good, there seems to be more merit, since *every man shall receive his own reward according to his own labour* (I Cor. 3. 8). Now a man has to make a greater effort to love his enemy than to love his friend, because it is more difficult. Therefore it seems more meritorious to love one's enemy than to love one's friend.

Obj. 4. *On the contrary,* The better an action is, the more meritorious it is. Now it is better to love one's friend, since it is better to love a better man, and the friend who loves you is better than the enemy who hates you. Therefore it is more meritorious to love one's friend than to love one's enemy.

I answer that, God is the reason for our loving our neighbour out of charity, as stated above

---

[55] *Enchiridion*, LXXIII (PL 40, 266).

(Q. XXV, A. 1). When therefore it is asked which is better or more meritorious, to love one's friend or one's enemy, these two loves may be compared in two ways: first, on the part of our neighbour whom we love, secondly, on the part of the reason for which we love him.

In the first way, love of one's friend surpasses love of one's enemy, because a friend is both better and more closely united to us, so that he is a more suitable matter of love, and consequently the act of love pervading this matter is better, and therefore its opposite is worse, for it is worse to hate a friend than an enemy.

In the second way, however, it is better to love one's enemy than one's friend, and this for two reasons. First, because it is possible to love one's friend for another reason than God, whereas God is the only reason for loving one's enemy. Secondly, because if we suppose that both are loved for God, our love for God is proved to be all the stronger through carrying a man's affections to things which are furthest from him, that is, even to the love of his enemies, just as the power of a fire is proved to be the stronger according as it throws its heat to more distant objects. Hence our love for God is proved to be so much the stronger, as the things we accomplish for its sake are the more difficult, just as the power of fire is so much the stronger, as it is able to set fire to a less inflammable matter.

Yet just as the same fire acts with greater force on what is near than on what is distant, so too, charity loves with greater fervour those who are united to us than those who are far removed; and in this respect the love of friends, considered in itself, is more ardent and better than the love of one's enemy.

Reply Obj. 1. The words of Our Lord must be taken in their strict sense, because the love of one's friends is not meritorious in God's sight when we love them merely because they are our friends; and this would seem to be the case when we love our friends in such a way that we love not our enemies. On the other hand the love of our friends is meritorious if we love them for God's sake, and not merely because they are our friends.

The *Reply to the other objections* is evident from what has been said in the article, because the two arguments that follow consider the reason for loving, while the last considers the question on the part of those who are loved.

ARTICLE 8. *Whether It Is More Meritorious To Love One's Neighbour Than to Love God?*

We proceed thus to the Eighth Article: It would seem that it is more meritorious to love one's neighbour than to love God.

Objection 1. For the more meritorious thing would seem to be what the Apostle preferred. Now the Apostle preferred the love of our neighbour to the love of God, according to Rom. 9. 3; *I wished myself to be an anathema from Christ, for my brethren.* Therefore it is more meritorious to love one's neighbour than to love God.

Obj. 2. Further, In a certain sense it seems to be less meritorious to love one's friend, as stated above (A. 7). Now God is our chief friend, since *He hath first loved us* (I John 4. 10). Therefore it seems less meritorious to love God.

Obj. 3. Further, Whatever is more difficult seems to be more virtuous and meritorious, since virtue is about that which is difficult and good.[56] Now it is easier to love God than to love one's neighbour, both because all things love God naturally, and because there is nothing unlovable in God, and this cannot be said of one's neighbour. Therefore it is more meritorious to love one's neighbour than to love God.

On the contrary, That on account of which a thing is such, is yet more so. Now the love of one's

---

[56]*Ethics*, 11, 3 (1105ᵃ9).

neighbour is not meritorious except by reason of his being loved for God's sake. Therefore the love of God is more meritorious than the love of our neighbour.

I answer that, This comparison may be taken in two ways. First, by considering both loves separately; and then, without doubt, the love of God is the more meritorious, because a reward is due to it for its own sake, since the ultimate reward is the enjoyment of God, to Whom the movement of the love of God tends. Hence a reward is promised to him that loves God (John 14. 21): *He that loveth Me, shall be loved of My Father, and I will . . . manifest Myself to him.* Secondly, the comparison may be understood to be between the love of God alone on the one side, and the love of one's neighbour for God's sake, on the other. In this way love of our neighbour includes love of God, while love of God does not include love of our neighbour. Hence the comparison will be between perfect love of God, extending also to our neighbour, and inadequate and imperfect love of God, for *this commandment we have from God, that he, who loveth God, love also his brother* (I John 4. 21).

Reply Obj. 1. According to one gloss,[57] the Apostle did not desire this, that is, to be severed from Christ for his brethren, when he was in a state of grace, but had formerly desired it when he was in a state of unbelief, so that we should not imitate him in this respect.

We may also reply, with Chrysostom (*De Compunct.* 1)[58] that this does not prove the Apostle to have loved his neighbour more than God, but that he loved God more than himself. For he wished to be deprived for a time of the Divine enjoyment which pertains to love of oneself in order that God might be honoured in his neighbour, which pertains to the love of God.

Reply Obj. 2. A man's love for his friends is sometimes less meritorious in so far as he loves them for their sake, so as to fall short of the true reason for the friendship of charity, which is God. Hence that God be loved for His own sake does not diminish the merit, but is the entire reason for merit.

Reply Obj. 3. The "good" has, more than the "difficult," to do with the reason of merit and virtue. Therefore it does not follow that whatever is more difficult is more meritorious, but only what is more difficult and at the same time better.

---

[57] *Glossa ordin.* (VI, 20E); *Glossa* Lombardi (PL 191, 1454).

[58] PG 47, 406; *In Rom.*, hom., XVI (PG 60, 599).

chapter ten

Hadewijch

Hadewijch of Antwerp, one of the most important mystics of the late Middle Ages, used a profoundly emotional "love mysticism" to describe her relationship with the Divine. Typically, Hadewijch described a contemplative state in which her soul felt the embrace of God and she remained united to him though the soul. Through her poetry, she announces an "erotic" union of soul and flesh that is reminiscent of the imagery found in the Song of Songs. Although some scholars argue that the mystical union she describes is not corporeal but, rather, a unity of emotion and desire, this remains a matter of interpretation.

Hadewijch lived during the thirteenth century and was probably the leader of a secular order known as the Beguines, a group of women who chose to adopt a lifestyle of devotion to God but not to enter convents.[1] There is no extant record of the details of Hadewijch's life, and we must extract what little information we can about her world from the prose and poetry she produced. It seems likely, given the manner in which she used her knowledge of chivalry and courtly life, that she was born in the late twelfth century to a wealthy, perhaps aristocratic, family. Not surprisingly, she made extensive use of the biblical sources widely available during this period. However, she must have been widely and systematically educated as there are also numerous references in her writings to topics ranging from astronomy to rhetoric.

In an age when both women's spirituality and sexuality were seen as dangerous by the patriarchal church authorities, the Beguines gathered as a community of women who were not bound by the rules of the cloister, nor sequestered in the homes of their wealthy husbands, relegated to a life of subservience and anonymity. Although the Beguine order would eventually be suppressed by the church, the intensity and depth of their devotion continues to represent one of the most powerful moments of Western mystical spirituality.

Hadewijch's emergence as a spiritual leader was owing to her mystical connection to God through the very real and embodied nature of sensual Love. This put her at great

---

Excerpts from Hadewijch, *The Complete Works*. Translated with an introduction by Mother Columba Hart, O.S.B. Copyright © 1980. Used with permission of Paulist Press. www.paulistpress.com.

risk of persecution from the church. According to established dogma, the body, especially the female body, was seen as the site of corruption.[2] Both her written work and the very fact of her mystical experiences would have garnered the attention of church officials since they held that the purity of the female body—the virgin body—was constantly in danger of becoming corrupted by an erotic gaze or by merely appearing in public.

Hadewijch's mystical visions offered women of the Beguine order the opportunity to transform the cultural images of their bodies by suggesting that the soul (which was taken to be female) could be linked without mediation to God. The female body, for Hadewijch, was capable of a love so intense that union with God could be realized. This love that brought one closer to God was not, however, a transcendent experience, since the female body in its relation to the Divine arose first from a somatic consciousness. This union of the soul with the Divine through Love was at the core of Hadewijch's spiritual quest. She expressed her particular notion of Love as *Minne,* an ambiguous term that marks both the Divine and the manner in which human beings answer to the Divine.

Minne can refer simultaneously to the Divine as "beloved," to the erotic energy that allows us to experience the full range of mature love and relationships in this world, or it can mark the very provocative and potentially threatening "taste" for the sensual. However, whenever this possibility arises, it must fall to Reason to quench the tendency to allow embodied, sensual desire to prevail. Hadewijch knew that, without Reason's guidance, the journey toward the Divine cannot even begin, much less succeed. However, even as Reason is the corrective to the potential excesses of embodied desire that allows us to seek our own path to the Divine, so Love as desire, as sensual longing, is the reason we set out on the journey in the first place.[3] This richly ambiguous collection of ideas all find their expression in Hadewijch's use of *Minne.*

Hadewijch's written work includes fourteen "Visions" and forty-five "Poems in Stanza." As a poet, she was credited with creating the genre of "mystical love lyrics" which clearly express the fact that she was a person for whom there could be no lived experience independent of her relationship to the Divine. The poems, expressed thematically in the manner of the poetry of courtly love,[4] also included elements of the Catholic liturgy and mystical numerology. There are also numerous letters in which she explains in great detail to her sisters in the Beguine order her concerns for their souls and connections between Love and the Divine. In the letters she also expresses some of her fears for her own future in the order.

These fears apparently were realized when she was exiled from the sisters. As far as scholars have been able to determine, she was never allowed to return. Although we have no record of her life after the exile, she may have been charged by the Inquisition with the heresy of the "Free Spirit"[5] and possibly executed, this being the fate of many medieval women who could not deny their soul's deepest longings. It is tempting, however, to speculate that when she disappeared from the Beguine order she found a place and time of repose where she was able to spend her remaining days engaged in contemplation of her profoundly timeless vision of Love's relation to the Divine.

WDC

QUESTIONS

1. In Letter 20, paragraph 56, Hadewijch says that reason and love are incompatible. However, in Letter 29 she seems to be saying that there is a connection between reason and Love. Consider ways to reconcile these apparently contradictory ideas.

2. What might Hadewijch be saying when she claims (in Letter 13) that "we must do without the satisfaction of Love to satisfy Love"?

3. Provide an account of Hadewijch's notion of "Love."

ENDNOTES

1. The Beguine order was composed of women from the upper classes who did not want to take vows and enter a convent but who, nonetheless, desired to live a contemplative life of devotion to God. Their order originated in what is now Holland and Northern Belgium and quickly spread into Germany. These women apparently were seeking an alternative to the narrowly defined life of a wealthy woman confined, for the most part, to the duties of a nobleman's wife.

2. It is important to note, though, that such erotic/somatic experiences of the Divine were not at all uncommon during this period and were indulged, to an extent, by the church authorities. See, for example, *The Life of St. Teresa* (Chapter 12 in this volume).

3. Compare Hadewijch's ideas of Love as "erotic energy" with those of Diotima in Plato's *Symposium.*

4. This would not be surprising if, as has been speculated, Hadewijch was from an aristocratic family. She would have understood the roots of courtly love in the fundamental relationship between a knight and his liege lord. The service owed by the knight to his lord would also apply to the lady of the castle. The knight was inspired to do great deeds for the lady whose favor he hoped to win. This "love" between knight and lady was, in most of the important romances, expressed as an idealized romance that was never consummated. The courtly romances that were part of the literature of Hadewijch's time were not taken literally; they were seen as models of behavior. Excellent examples of this genre can be found in such works as *Sir Gawain and the Green Knight,* Chretien de Troyes's *The Knight of the Cart* (where Lancelot first announces his love for Guenevere), and, of course, the many King Arthur variations. Part of the genius of Hadewijch was her ability to convey in her own work this model of service based on love.

5. Originally associated with a woman named Marguerite Porete who was burned at the Place de Grieve in the late eleventh century, the essence of the Heresy of the Free Spirit derived from Porete's statement that "a soul annihilated in the love of the Creator could, and should, grant to nature all that it desires." There are two heresies suggested by these remarks: pantheism and antinomianism; that is, not only can a soul become one with God, but in consequence of such a state it can ignore the moral law. These two heresies

constituted the Heresy of the Free Spirit. Clearly, Church Fathers in Hadewijch's day, even though they were willing to indulge certain practices, would have been alert to and suspicious of lifestyles or writings that would have even hinted at such possibilities.

SELECTED BIBLIOGRAPHY

Gordon, Rudy. *The Mystical Language of Sensation in the Later Middle Ages.* New York: Routledge, 2002.

Hadewijch. *The Complete Works.* Trans. and intro. Mother Columba Hart, O.S.B. New York: Paulist Press, 1980.

McGinn, Bernard. *Meister Eckhart and the Beguine Mystics: Hadewijch of Brabant, Mechthild of Magdeburg, and Marguerite of Porete.* New York: Continuum, 1994.

Milhaven, John Giles. *Hadewijch and Her Sisters: Other Ways of Loving and Knowing.* Albany: State University of New York Press, 1993.

Wilson, Katharina M. *Medieval Women Writers.* Atlanta: University of Georgia Press, 1984.

LETTERS
from *Her Letters, Poetry, and Visions*

Hadewijch

LETTER 4
ROLE OF REASON

This I entreat you, that you consider all the points in which you have erred, and that you reform yourself in them with all your power.[1] For we err in very many things that men judge good, and that really are good; but reason errs in these things when men do not understand them properly or practice them; this is where reason fails. Then when reason is obscured, the will grows weak and powerless and feels an aversion to effort, because reason does not enlighten it. Consequently the memory loses its deep notions, and the joyous confidence, and the repeated zealous intentions by which its confidence taught it to endure more easily the misery of waiting for its Beloved. All this depresses the noble soul; but when it reaches this state, hope in God's goodness consoles it once more. But one must err and suffer before being thus freed.

Now consider all the things I shall say to you about where reason errs, and reform yourself in these things with all your ardor. And do not let it grieve you then that you fall short in some things. For the knight who is humble will not be concerned about his gashes if he looks at the wounds of his holy Lord. When God judges the time has come, everything will be quickly restored to order,

---

[1] The repeated command "Reform yourself!" explains Hadewijch's emphasis on the errors of reason. Some special difficulty made this instruction necessary. From many other passages in her works we know how highly she prized the faculty of reason as bestowed on us by God to enable us to walk securely in his paths.

so suffer with patience. To the reason, God will give light, constancy, and truth; the reason will gain over the will, and thus new strength will remain with it. And the memory will find itself courageous when God with his omnipotence drives away every sort of anguish and fear.

To put it briefly, reason errs in fear, in hope, in charity, in a rule of life one wishes to keep, in tears, in the desire of devotion, in the bent for sweetness, in terror of God's threats, in distinction between beings, in receiving, in giving—and in many things we judge good, reason may err.

Reason well knows that God must be feared, and that God is great and man is small. But if reason fears God's greatness because of its littleness, and fails to stand up to his greatness, and begins to doubt that it can ever become God's dearest child, and thinks that such a great Being is out of its reach—the result is that many people fail to stand up to the great Being. Reason errs in this and in many other things.

In hope many people err by hoping God has forgiven them all their sins. But if in truth their sins were fully forgiven, they would love God and perform works of love. Hope leads them to count on things that never eventuate, for they are too lazy and do not pay their debt either to love or to God, to whom they owe pains to the death. In hope reason errs, and they who are of this mind also err in many things. But on this point I need say much less to you than on the other points.

In charity men err through injudicious service, for instance when they give out of mere liking where there is no need, or render superfluous service, or weary themselves when there is no need. Often emotional attraction motivates what is called charity.

In keeping a rule of life, people encumber themselves with many things from which they could be free; and that causes reason to err. A spirit of good will assures greater interior beauty than any rule of life could devise.

In tears, people err a great deal. Although reason remonstrates with us, that we should weep because we lack what is ours, yet it is often self-will; in this we err extremely.

In desires for devotion, all souls err who are seeking anything other than God. For we must seek God and nothing else. And anything he gives in addition, we must gladly take.

In seeking spiritual sweetness, people err greatly; for there is very much emotional attraction in it, whether toward God or toward men.

God's threats or all sorts of torment that we fear cause reason to err, if we are often more influenced by fear than love in what we do or omit.

Making distinctions in a multiplicity of occupations to be undertaken or rejected greatly curtails the liberty of love.

In accepting what could be dispensed with, outwardly or inwardly, reason errs.

In possession of any sort, in repose without cares, and in imperturbable peace with God and men, reason errs.

As for the gift of oneself, one errs greatly if he wishes to make it before its time, or lend himself to many alien things for which he is not destined or chosen by Love.

In grief, in pain, in repose, in quarreling, in reconciliation, in sweetness or bitterness—to spend too much time in all these things, reason errs.

In yielding obedience to various and sundry claims, reason errs extremely: All the other points are included in this one. To be obedient to fear according to our whims, and to the other points without control; to be obedient in fear, hope, emotional attraction, and all the other things we obey that do not belong to perfect love: Reason errs in all this.

My motive for telling you that reason errs in all these points, which people try to present in a favorable light, is that they are important points, and reason by its nature throws light on each of these points according to their value.

LETTER 11
INCIDENTALLY ABOUT HADEWIJCH

O dear child! May God give you what my heart desires for you—that God may be loved by you worthily.

Yet I have never been able, dear child, to bear the thought that anyone prior to me should have loved him more than I. I do believe, however, that there were many who loved him as much and as ardently, and yet I cannot endure it that anyone should know or love him so intensely as I have done.

Since I was ten years old I have been so overwhelmed by intense love that I should have died, during the first two years when I began this, if God had not given me other forms of strength than people ordinarily receive, and if he had not renewed my nature with his own Being. For in this way he soon gave me reason, which was enlightened to some extent by many a beautiful disclosure; and I had from him many beautiful gifts, through which he let me feel his presence and revealed himself. And through all these tokens with which I met in the intimate exchange of love between him and me—for as it is the custom of friends between themselves to hide little and reveal much, what is most experienced is the close feeling of one another, when they relish, devour, drink, and swallow up each other—by these tokens that God, my Love, imparted to me in so many ways at the beginning of my life, he gave me such confidence in him that ever since that time it has usually been in my mind

that no one loved him so intensely as I. But reason in the meantime made me understand that I was not the closest to him; nevertheless the chains of love that I felt never allowed me to feel or believe this. So that is how it is with me: I do not, finally, believe that he can be loved the most intensely by me, but I also do not believe there is any man living by whom God is loved so much. Sometimes Love so enlightens me that I know what is wanting in me—that I do not content my Beloved according to his sublimity; and sometimes the sweet nature of Love blinds me to such a degree that when I can taste and feel her it is enough for me; and sometimes I feel so rich in her presence that I myself acknowledge she contents me.

LETTER 13
LOVE UNAPPEASABLE

Man must so keep himself pure from sin among all vicissitudes that he will seek his growth in all things and work, according to the manner prescribed by reason, above all things. And so God will work all things for him and with him, and he with God will *fulfill all justice* (Matt. 3:15) and will desire that, in himself and in all of us, God may accomplish the just works of his Nature.

To choose and will this above all is the law of the loving heart, whether condemnations or blessings follow. And this is always its desire and prayer, to be in exclusive union with Love, as we read in the Song of Songs: *Dilectus meus mibi et ego illi* (Song 2:16).[2] Thus shall there be a single meeting in the one will of unitive love.

He who wishes all things to be subject to him must himself be subject to his reason, above whatever he wills or whatever anyone else wills of him.

---

[2]My Beloved to me, and I to him.

For no one can become perfect in Love unless he is subject to his reason. For reason loves God on account of his sublimity, noble men because they are loved by God, and ignoble men because they are in want of Love. Therefore one must exert his uttermost power in all things according to the perfection of Love, who is ever unappeasable no matter how much trouble one takes for her. For even should it happen that a man in all men's eyes seems to satisfy God by his behavior, nevertheless he falls so short when it comes to perfect satisfaction of Love that he must live more and more in accord with Love's demands, and his longings must far surpass what he has.

What satisfies Love best of all is that we be wholly destitute of all repose, whether in aliens, or in friends, or even in Love herself. And this is a frightening life Love wants, that we must do without the satisfaction of Love in order to satisfy Love. They who are thus drawn and accepted by Love, and fettered by her, are the most indebted to Love, and consequently they must continually stand subject to the great power of her strong nature, to content her. And that life is miserable beyond all that the human heart can bear.

For nothing in their life satisfies them—either their gifts, or their service, or consolations, or all they can accomplish. For interiorly Love draws them so strongly to her, and they feel Love so vast and so incomprehensible; and they find themselves too small for this, and too inadequate to satisfy that Essence which is Love. And they are aware that they themselves owe such a heavy debt, which they must pay by contenting Love in all manners, that with relation to everything else they can experience neither pleasure nor pain, either in themselves or in other people, except where Love herself is concerned. Only in this case could they experience pleasure or pain: pleasure in proportion as Love was advanced or grew in themselves and in others; pain, in proportion as Love was hindered or harmed in those who love—in themselves and in others—whom aliens gladly hinder and harm insofar as they can.

Take the trouble to labor for the progress of Love and of sublime charity; for charity understands all God's commandments without error and fulfills them without labor. For he who loves does not labor, because he does not feel his labor. And he who loves ardently runs faster and attains more quickly to God's holiness, which is God himself, and to God's totality, which is God himself. In view of his totality may all your service be perfect, like the zeal befitting perfection, which contents him in his whole Nature wherein he is all-loving. May God grant you to realize the whole debt you owe him: pains that are merited, but principally the single love with which, as he himself has commanded, men should love God above all.

LETTER 20
TWELVE NAMELESS HOURS

That nature from which veritable Love arises has twelve hours, which fling Love forth from herself and carry her back again into herself. And as Love then returns into herself, she gathers in everything for the sake of which the nameless hours had driven her outside: a seeking mind, a desiring heart, and a loving soul.[3] And when Love brings these in, she casts them into the abyss of the strong nature from which Love is born and on which she is nourished. Then the nameless hours come into the unknown nature. Then Love has returned to herself and has fruition of her nature, beneath, above,

---

[3]From this sentence it is inferred that the Twelve Hours fall into three groups of four, corresponding respectively to the seeking mind, desiring heart, and loving soul.

and all round her. And all they who then remain beneath this experience shudder for those who have passed into it, and who must work, live, and die in it, as Love and her nature bid.

The first nameless hour of the twelve that draw the mind into the nature of Love is that in which Love reveals herself and makes herself felt, unawares and unlonged for when, in view of Love's dignity, this is least expected; and the strong nature that Love is in herself remains to the soul incomprehensible. And therefore this is rightly called a nameless hour.

The second nameless hour is that in which Love makes the heart taste a violent death and causes it to die without being able to die. And yet the soul has only recently learned to know Love and has scarcely passed from the first hour into the second.

The third nameless hour is that in which Love teaches by what means one can die and live in Love, and reveals that there can be no loving without great pain.

The fourth nameless hour is that in which Love permits the soul to taste her secret judgments, which are deeper and darker than the abysses (Ps. 35:7). Then she makes known to it the misery of being without love. And nevertheless the soul does not experience the essence of Love. This is rightly called a nameless hour when, before the soul knows Love by experience, it accepts her judgments.

The fifth nameless hour is that in which Love allures the soul and heart and makes the soul ascend out of itself and out of the nature of Love, into the nature of Love. And then the soul loses its amazement at the power of Love and the darkness of her judgments, and forgets the pain of Love. And then it experiences Love in no other way but in Love herself. This seems to be a lower state, yet it is not. Therefore it may well be called a nameless hour when, although nearest to knowing, one is poorest in knowledge.

The sixth nameless hour is that in which Love disdains reason and all that is in, above, or below reason. What belongs to reason is altogether at variance with what suits the true nature of Love, for reason can neither take anything away from Love nor give anything to Love. For the true law of Love is an ever-increasing flood without stay or respite.

The seventh nameless hour is that nothing can dwell in Love, and nothing can touch her except desire. The most secret name of Love is this touch, and that is a mode of operation that takes its rise from Love herself. For Love is continually desiring, touching, and feeding on herself; yet Love is utterly perfect in herself. Love can dwell in all things. Love can dwell in charity for others, but charity for others cannot dwell in Love. No mercy can dwell in Love, no graciousness, humility, reason, fear; no parsimony, no measure, nothing. But Love dwells in all these, and they are all nourished on Love. Yet Love herself receives no nourishment except from her own integrity.

The eighth nameless hour is that the nature of Love in her countenance is most mysterious to know. What one is, is usually best revealed by one's countenance. In Love, however, this is what is most secret; for this is Love herself in herself. Her other parts and her works are easier to know and understand.

The ninth nameless hour is, that where Love is in her fiercest storm, sharpest assault, and deepest inroad, her countenance shines the sweetest, most peaceful, and loveliest, and she shows herself the most lovable. And the more deeply she wounds him at whom she rushes, the more gently, with the dignity of her countenance, she engulfs this loved one within herself.

The tenth nameless hour is that Love stands on trial before none, but all things stand on trial before her (cf. 1 Cor. 2:15). Love borrows from God the power of decision over those she loves. Love will not yield to saints, men here below, Angels, heaven, or earth. She has vanquished the Divinity by her nature. She cries with a loud voice, without stay or respite, in all the hearts of those who love: "Love ye Love!" This voice makes a noise so great and so unheard-of that it sounds more fearful than thunder (cf. Apoc. 6:1). This command is the chain with which Love fetters her prisoners, the sword with which she wounds those she has touched, the rod with which she chastises her children, and the mastership by which she teaches her disciples.

The eleventh nameless hour is that in which Love powerfully possesses him whom she loves, so that his mind cannot wander for an instant, his heart desire, or his soul love, outside of Love. Love renders his memory so unified that he can no longer think of saints, men here below, heaven or earth, Angels or himself, or God, but only of Love, who has taken possession of him in an ever-new presence.

The twelfth nameless hour is like Love in her highest nature. Now Love first breaks out of herself; and she works by herself and always sinks back into herself, for she finds all satisfaction in her own nature. So she is self-sufficient: Were no one to love Love, Love's name would give her enough lovableness in her own splendid nature. Her name is her being within herself; her name is her works outside herself; her name is her crown above herself; and her name is her depths beneath herself.

These are the twelve nameless hours of Love. For in none of these twelve hours can anyone understand the love of Love, except, as I have said, those who are cast into the abyss of Love's strong nature, or those who are fitted to be cast into it. These last rather believe in Love than understand her.

LETTER 29
HADEWIJCH EVICTED

God be with you! and may he give you consolation with the veritable consolation of himself, with which he suffices to himself and to all creatures according to their being and their deserts. O sweet child, your sadness, dejection, and grief give me pain! And this I entreat you urgently, and exhort you, and counsel you, and command you as a mother commands her dear child, whom she loves for the supreme honor and sweetest dignity of Love, to cast away from you all alien grief, and to grieve for my sake as little as you can. What happens to me, whether I am wandering in the country or put in prison—however it turns out, it is the work of Love.

I know well, also, that I am not the cause of such grief to you; and I am close to you in heart, and trusted; and for me, you—after Sara—are the dearest person alive. Therefore I well understand that you cannot easily leave off grieving over my disgrace. But be aware, dear child, that this is an alien grief. Think about it yourself; if you believe with all your heart that I am loved by God, and he is doing his work in me, secretly or openly, and that he renews his old wonders in me (cf. Ecclus. 36:6), you must also be aware that these are doings of Love, and that this must lead aliens to wonder at me and abhor me. For they cannot work in the domain of Love, because they know neither her coming nor her going. And with these persons I have little shared their customs in their eating, drinking, or sleeping; I have not dressed up in their clothes, or colors, or outward magnificence. And from all the things that can gladden the human heart, from what it can obtain or receive, I never derived joy except for brief moments from the experience of the Love that conquers all.

But from its first awakening and upward turning, my enlightened reason (which, ever since God revealed himself in it, has enlightened me as to whatever in myself and in others was lacking in perfection) showed me and led me to the place where I am to have fruition of my Beloved in unity according to the worthiness of my ascent.

This place of Love which enlightened reason showed me, was so far above human thought that I was obliged to understand I might no longer have joy or grief in anything, great or small, except in this, that I was a human being, and that I experienced Love with a loving heart; but that, since God is so great, I with my humanity may touch the Godhead without attaining fruition.

This desire of unattainable fruition, which Love has always given me for the sake of fruition of Love, has injured me and wounded me in the breast and in the heart: *in armariolo et in antisma. Amariolo*—that is, the innermost of the arteries of the heart, with which we love; and *antisma*—that is, the innermost of the spirits by which we live, and the one sensitive to the greatest preoccupation.

I have lived with these persons nevertheless with all the works I could perform in their service. And they found me prepared with ready virtue for all their needs. This was no doubt unjustifiably. I have also been with them in all things; since God first touched me with the totality of love, I have felt everyone's need according to what he was. With God's charity I have felt and given favor to each one according to that person's needs. With his wisdom I have felt his mercy, and why one must forgive people so much, and how they fall and get up again; and how God gives and takes away (Job 1:21); and how he strikes and heals (Job 5:18); and how he gives himself gratuitously. With his sublimity I have felt the sins of all those whom in this life I have heard named and have seen. And this is why ever since, with God, I have passed just judgments according to the depths of his truth, on us all as we also were. With his unity in love I have felt constantly, since then, the experience of being lost in the fruition of Love, or the suffering of being deprived of this fruition, and the ways of veritable Love in all things, and its mode of operation in God and in all men.

In love I have experienced all these attributes, and I have acted with justice toward these persons, however much they have failed me. But if I possess this in love with my eternal being, I do not possess it yet in fruition of Love in my own being. And I remain a human being, who must suffer to the death with Christ in Love; for whoever lives in veritable Love will suffer opprobrium from all aliens, until Love comes to herself, and until she is full-grown within us in virtues, whereby Love becomes one with men.

POETRY

7 The New Path

1

At the new year[4]
We hope for the new season
That will bring new flowers
And new joys manifold.
5 He who for Love's sake suffers fears
May well live joyful:
She shall not escape him;
For Love's rich power
Is new and indeed friendly
10 And sweet of demeanor,
And sweetens with a recompense
Every new sadness.

2

Oh, how new in my eyes was anyone
Who served new Love
15 With new veritable fidelity—
As the tyro should rightly do

When Love first reveals herself to him.
So even if he had few friends,
That could have saddened him little
20 Had he kept close to Love;
For Love gives the new good
That makes the new mind,
That renews itself in all
Wherein Love newly touched it.

3

25 Oh, Love is ever new,
And she revives every day!
Those who renew themselves she causes to be
     born again
To continual new acts of goodness.
How, alas, can anyone
30 Remain old, fainthearted at Love's presence?
Such a person lives truly old in sadness,
Always with little profit;
For he has lost sight of the new path,
And he is denied the newness
35 That lies in new service of Love,
In the nature of the love of new lovers.

4

Alas, where is new Love now
With her new good things?
For my distress brings me
40 Into many a new woe;
My soul melts away

---

[4]Renewal is one of the principal motifs of Hadewijch's writings; cf. Spaapen, "Le Mouvement des 'Frères du libre esprit' et les mystiques flamandes du xiiie siècle," *Revue d'ascétique et de mystique* 42 (1966): 435–436. Stressed especially in Stanzaic Poems 1 and 33, it is most explicitly set forth in Stanzaic Poem 7. By way of the renewal of plant life in springtime, Hadewijch arrives at the renewal of the mind by Love, playing on three antitheses—old versus new, old versus young, and old-and-young. Age combined with youth is a literary theme; Boethius's Philosophy is a woman "of undiminished strength yet of extreme old age," *De consolatione philosophiae* 1, *prosa* 1 (CCSL 94:2); and Martianus Capella's Grammar is "an old woman indeed but of great charm," *Martianus Capella and the Seven Liberal Arts,* vol. 2, *The Marriage of Philology and Mercury,* trans. W. Stahl and R. Johnson (New York: Columbia University Press, 1977), p. 64. Of course Hadewijch is thinking not of many or few years, but of mature experience and youthful ardor.

In the madness of Love;[5]
The abyss into which she hurls me
Is deeper than the sea;
45 For Love's new deep abyss
Renews my wound:
I look for no more health
Until I experience Love as all new to me.

5

But old souls, they of new wisdom,
50 Who newly give themselves away to Love
And spare themselves no new trouble—

These I call renewed and old.
They live high-mindedly;
For they become attached to Love
55 And constantly gaze on her with ardor.
This is why their power in love grows,
For they must exercise themselves as tyros
And, as old, lean upon Love
To go where their Beloved will lead them,
60 With mind renewed by new violent longing.

VISIONS

VISION 12
THE PERFECT BRIDE

Once on Epiphany, during Mass, I was taken up out of myself in the spirit; there I saw a city, large, and wide, and high, and adorned with perfections. And in the midst of it there sat Someone upon a round disk, which continually opened and closed itself again upon hidden mysteries. And he who sat there above the disk was sitting in constant stillness; but in the disk his Being circled about in unspeakable swiftness without stopping. And the abyss in which the disk ran as it circled about was of such unheard-of depth and so dark that no horror can be compared to it. And the disk, seen from above, was set with all kinds of precious stones and in the color of pure gold; but on the darkest side, where it ran so fearfully, it was like fearful flames, which devoured heaven and earth and in which all things perished and were swallowed up.

And he who sat upon the disk was One whose Countenance none could perceive without belonging to the terrible flames of this disk and being thrown into the deep abyss which lay underneath. And that Countenance drew all the dead to it living; and everything that was withered blossomed because of it; and all the poor who saw it received great riches; and all the sick became strong; and all who were in multiplicity and division became one in that Countenance.

And he who sat in this high place was clothed with a robe whiter than white (cf. Mark 9:2), on the breast of which was written: "The Most Loved of all beloveds" (cf. Apoc. 19:16). That was his name.

---

[5]The term used here by Hadewijch, *orewoet,* denotes a state of intense longing for God. The translation "madness of love" suggests itself because *orewoet* is considered to be the equivalent of *insania amoris,* employed by William of Saint Thierry, cf. *NDA* 3.2 (ML 184:383–384).

Then I fell down before that Countenance in order to adore the truth of that terrifying Being whom I there saw revealed.

Then came a flying eagle, crying with a loud voice, and said: "The loved one does not yet know all she shall become!"

And a second eagle said: "The loved one does not yet know what her highest way is!"

And a third said: "The loved one does not yet know what the great kingdom is that she as bride shall receive from her Bridegroom!"

And the fourth said to me: "Have patience, and watch, and do not fall down before that Countenance! They who fall down before the Countenance and adore receive grace; they who contemplate the Countenance standing receive justice and are enabled to fathom the deep abysses that for those unacquainted with them are so terrifying to know."

At that moment I was taken up, through the voice of this eagle who spoke to me. And then there came into the city a great crowd in festive apparel, and each one rich in her own works. They were all virtues; and they were conducting a bride to her Beloved. They had served her nobly and had looked after her so proudly that they could present her as worthy to be received by the mighty great God as his bride.

And she was clad in a robe made of her undivided and perfect will, always devoid of sorrow, and prepared with all virtue, and fitted out with everything that pertains thereto. And that robe was adorned with all the virtues, and each virtue had its symbol on the robe and its name written, that it might be known.

The first of the virtues was Faith: She had lifted her up from her lowness.

The second, Hope, had raised her above herself to great confidence of attaining eternal joy.

The third, veritable Fidelity, bore witness that she was noble; for she never departed from fidelity because of any distress, however great it was.

The fourth, Charity, bore witness that she was rich, for she never gave up her works outward or inward, and she never lacked rich gifts by which she honored Charity; for she practiced rich liberality because of lofty abandonment.

The fifth, Desire, bore witness how vast she was in her territory, and how beautiful and splendid in her full wealth, so that she might well entertain all the greatness of heaven.

The sixth, Humility, bore witness that she was so deep and so unfathomable that she could truly receive greatness to the full in her unfathomableness.

The seventh, Discernment, bore witness that she was so clear-sighted that she set every being in its place: heaven in its height, hell in its depth, or purgatory in its manner of being; the Angels in their orders; or men, each according to what befits him, when he falls, and when he gets up again. Thus to let God act accorded well with the robe of the undivided will.

The eighth, her veracious mighty Works, bore witness that she was so strong that nothing could hold her back, so that she alone would not have conquered all opposition and made all lowness lofty and all loftiness low.

The ninth, Reason, showed that she was well ordered and that Reason was her rule, by which she always performed works of justice, and which enlightened her with regard to all the dearest will of her Beloved, so that like him she gave blessing and condemnation in all that he loved and all that he hated; and she gave all that he gave, and she took all that he took.

The tenth, Wisdom, showed her to be familiar with all the power of every perfect virtue that must be encountered in order to content the Beloved perfectly. Wisdom showed that she also had profound knowledge of each Person of the Trinity, in the Unity that was the very deep abyss beneath the wonderful, terrifying disk on which sat the One who was to receive the Bride.

The eleventh, Peacefulness, showed and bore witness to her, as pleasing in appearance and beautiful, and as possessing knowledge of the total embrace and of a perfect kiss (cf. Ps. 84:11), and of all the honor and all the encounter the loved one must offer to the Beloved in love; and that she had been announced and born with him; and that her body was born from the other; and that she grew up with him and lived together with him as man in all like pains, in poverty, in ignominy, and in compassion for all those with whom justice was angry; and that her body was nourished interiorly and exteriorly from the other, and never received alien consolation; and that she died with him, and freed all the prisoners with him, and bound what he bound; and with him rose again, and one with him ascended to his Father; and there with him acknowledged his Father as Father, and him as Son with him; and with him she acknowledged the Holy Spirit as Holy Spirit; and with him, like him, she knew all as One, and the Essence in which they are One. To all this her Peacefulness bore witness for her, that she has thus lived and that, later on, she will live perfectly as his, truly with love in love.

The twelfth was Patience, who had protected her from all evil, without any sorrow in all sorrow, and was as it were an instrument of good works, through which she was as if in a new embrace. And Patience showed her as conformed to God, in one Being and in one work.

Thus is the robe of undivided will wholly adorned through the divine Nature. Thus festively attired comes the bride, with all this beautiful company represented in symbols. She wore on her breast an ornament with the divine seal (cf. Apoc. 7:2, 9:4), by which she had knowledge of the undivided divine Unity. This was a symbol that she had understood the *bidden word* (Job 4:12) of God himself out of the abyss. So in this company she came into the city, led between Fruition of Love and Command of the Virtues; Command accompanied her there, but Fruition met her there.

And when she was led thus to the high seat I have already described, the eagle, who had previously spoken to me, said: "Now see through the Countenance, and become the veritable bride of the great Bridegroom, and behold yourself in this state!" And in that very instant I saw myself received in union by the One who sat there in the abyss upon the circling disk, and there I became one with him in the certainty of unity. Then the eagle said, when I was received: "Now behold, allpowerful one, whom I previously called the loved one, that you did not know all you should become, and what your highest way was, and what the great kingdom was that you as bride should receive from your Bridegroom. When previously you fell down before the Countenance, you, like an ordinary soul, confessed it as frightening. When you stood up and contemplated it, you saw yourself perfect, together with us, a veritable bride, sealed with love. You, all-powerful one, have received most profoundly that *bidden word* which Job understood, in the text beginning: *Porro dictum est*" (Job 4:12).

In that abyss I saw myself swallowed up. Then I received the certainty of being received, in this form, in my Beloved, and my Beloved also in me.

chapter eleven

Heloise and Abelard

The letters between Heloise (c. 1100–c. 1164) and Abelard (1079–1142) record a human tragedy; they describe a situation in which two competing goods conflict and cannot be peaceably resolved. To one side stood their love for each other: passionate, innocent, physical, and, in Heloise's case, undying. To the other stood their devotion to God and the Christian doctrine they both cherished as God's commandment. By pursuing their love for each other, they ran afoul of this doctrine and offended many powerful people. The tension between these two kinds of love—ascetic love of God and erotic love of a worldly lover—is palpable in the letters they exchanged years after their last amorous encounter. In his letters, Abelard repents and denounces their relationship as sinful. He still loves Heloise, but only as a child of Christ and not as a lover. Heloise does not repent for what they did. She does not see herself as choosing a flawed love for Abelard over the sacred love of God. Instead, she argues that her love for Abelard *was* holy and good, even if it did violate the law. As a consequence, she never condemns their love and even chastises Abelard for calling their love base.

Heloise and Abelard's story is famous largely because each lover was individually remarkable. Abelard, whose Christian name was Pierre, was born in 1079 to a minor noble family in the French city of Nantes. As the eldest son, he was particularly well cared for by his family. As a member of a noble family, Pierre was supposed to be a warrior. In his *Historia calamitatum* (The History of My Misfortunes) Abelard declares that a knight's life offered him no allure: "I was so carried away by my love of learning that I renounced the glory of a soldier's life, made over my inheritance and rights of the eldest son to my brothers. . . . I preferred the weapons of dialectic to all the other teachings of philosophy, and armed with these I chose the conflicts of disputation instead of the trophies of war."[1]

We will never know how Abelard would have fared as a knight, though we do know he could not have been any fiercer as a philosophical combatant. The language of warfare is particularly apt to describe his style of philosophizing. Abelard mastered an innovative pedagogical technique that was becoming popular in the theological schools during his lifetime. This method, called *disputatio* (roughly meaning "disputing") replaced the older method of teaching called *lectio*, or lecture. Whereas teachers previously

---

taught by summarizing and expanding on an accepted textual authority, such as the Bible, the new method used tools drawn from ancient Greek texts to engage in open debates on important ideas. As Andrea Nye points out, the result was "a lively dialectical contest, something like an academic cockfight, often ill-tempered, pugilistic, and with little regard for the truth."[2] Abelard used this new method to publicly humiliate respected teachers—most notably William of Champeaux and Anselm of Laon—and steal away their pupils. While at the height of his fame as a teacher in the Cathedral school of Notre-Dame, he took note of a particularly attentive female student, and sought her out. It was a decision that irrevocably changed both lives.

Heloise was already famous when Abelard met her as a girl of fourteen. Her childhood, however, was fairly unremarkable. She, like many young girls of her day, called a convent her home. Orphaned at a young age, Heloise was raised by the nuns of Saint Marie in the small riverside hamlet of Argenteuil. In Medieval Europe, convents were one of the very few places that a woman could receive an education and Heloise relished the opportunity. She took full advantage of the sisters' tutelage and their library to cultivate her extraordinary intellectual potential. In addition to her mother tongue, Heloise could read and write in Latin, Greek, and Hebrew. Marjorie Worthington tells us that "her knowledge of Latin was so thorough that she was able to express her deepest emotions in that tongue."[3] When Heloise was sent to her uncle and only living relative, Fulbert, an influential official at the Cathedral of Notre Dame, for a brief visit, he was so taken by his young niece's intelligence that he decided to raise her himself. Indeed, he was so proud of her that he didn't hesitate when France's most renowned philosopher offered to be her private tutor.

A brief but fiery secret affair soon followed. Although Heloise was more than twenty years younger than Abelard, their difference in age was not considered unusual at the time and was not the reason they kept their relationship hidden. According to the rules of the church, teachers such as Abelard were required to remain celibate. Inheriting a long-standing prejudice against women, the church forbade men of learning to have any intimate relationships with women. Furthermore, Fulbert himself had hired Abelard under the assumption that he was giving his niece the best possible moral as well as intellectual education.

Abelard and Heloise found it increasingly difficult to hide their relationship from her uncle and his superiors. Love poems Abelard composed for Heloise became wildly popular. When she became pregnant with their son, whom they named Astralabe, Heloise fled Paris. The rumors flying all over Paris eventually pierced Fulbert's naïve credulity, and he started to plot against Abelard. He pretended to be appeased when Abelard offered to marry his niece in secret, so that God could bless their relationship and Abelard could go on teaching. Interestingly, Abelard recounts in his *Historia calamitatum* that Heloise "absolutely rejected this marriage" because she thought it would detract from his philosophy.[4] The secret marriage did not appease her uncle, for once Abelard's guard was down, Fulbert exacted his revenge. He bribed Abelard's servants, snuck into his room with some accomplices while he was asleep, and castrated him.

The news of Fulbert's brutality traveled quickly, and it was not long before throngs of sympathetic Parisians mourning his calamity surrounded Abelard's home. Burning from the shame of his fall, Abelard turned his back on the world and entered a monastery. Before he did so, he forced Heloise to take up the habit of a nun. At the age of twenty, after only six years outside the convent's walls, she reluctantly renounced worldly pleasures, relinquished her son, and returned to Saint Marie. After they took religious vows, their relationship was primarily conducted through their letters. The lovers met again at least once, years later when Abelard helped Heloise and her sisters find a new dwelling for their community.

When Heloise read a copy of Abelard's *Historia calamitatum*, she was struck by his characterization of their relationship as the cause of his downfall. She replied with letters that revealed the passion still burning in her. She refused to be ashamed of their love. In her first letter she declares, "God knows I never sought anything in you except yourself. . . . The name of wife may seem more sacred or more binding, but sweeter for me will always be the word mistress, or . . . concubine or whore."[5] The four letters they exchanged describing their divergent perspectives on their affair are not only important historical windows into two fascinating lives, but are insightful meditations on the nature of love itself.

The two letters collected here, which are the third and fourth letters in their exchange, reveal a love triangle. Abelard laments their relationship as a distraction that pulled them both from God. He writes, "To him, I beseech you, not to me, should be directed all your devotion, all your compassion, all your remorse."[6] Where Abelard is ashamed of his past love of Heloise and is committed to loving only God, Heloise cleaves to her love for Abelard, going as far as accusing God of "the greatest cruelty in regard to this outrage," namely, the events that tore her from Abelard.[7]

While Abelard remained a notable figure in philosophy, making powerful enemies with his brash style and dangerous questions, he never regained his previous stature. Heloise became the abbess of her convent and proved to be an effective administrator and protector for her sisters, though we are left with the sense that all of her good works for God and the church grew from her passionate love for Abelard. When Heloise learned of Abelard's death in 1142, she petitioned Peter the Venerable to exhume her lover's body and rebury it on the grounds of her community, the Paraclete.[8] When she died on May 16, 1164, she was buried there with him.

TM

QUESTIONS

1. Compare the tone of Heloise's letter to that of Abelard's. How would you characterize each letter? How does the tone of each letter correspond to the letter's argument?

2. What do you make of the fact that Heloise still cares for Abelard so passionately, even after she agreed to become a nun?

3. How do you assess Abelard's attitude toward Heloise in his letter? Is he being cruel to her for calling their affair sinful, or is he being kind by helping her learn from their mutual mistake?

4. Do you think that the sort of disagreement we see between Abelard and Heloise would be possible today?

ENDNOTES

1. Abelard. *Historia calamitatum,* as quoted in *The Letters of Abelard and Heloise,* p. 58.
2. Nye, *Words of Power*, p. 87.
3. Worthington, *Immortal Lovers,* p. 11.
4. Abelard, *Historia calamitatum,* p. 70.
5. Heloise, *Letter I,* as quoted in *The Letters of Abelard and Heloise,* ed. Betty Radice, p. 113.
6. Abelard, *Letter IV,* p. 153.
7. Heloise, *Letter III,* p. 132.
8. Gilson, *Heloise and Abelard*, p. 122.

SELECTED BIBLIOGRAPHY

Gilson, Etinne. *Heloise and Abelard.* Chicago: Henry Regnery, 1951.

Nye, Andrea. *Words of Power: A Feminist Reading of the History of Logic.* New York: Routledge, 1990.

Radice, Betty, ed. *The Letters of Abelard and Heloise.* Middlesex, England: Penguin Books, 1974.

Southern, R.W. *The Making of the Middle Ages.* London: Hutchinson Publishers, 1967.

Worthington, Marjorie. *The Immortal Lovers: Heloise and Abelard.* London: Robert Hale Limited, 1962.

from *The Letters of Heloise and Abelard*

Heloise and Abelard

LETTER 3. HELOISE TO ABELARD

To her only one after Christ, she who is his alone in Christ.

I am surprised, my only love, that contrary to custom in letter-writing and, indeed, to the natural order, you have thought fit to put my name before yours in the greeting which heads your letter, so that we have woman before man, wife before husband, handmaid before master, nun before monk, deaconess[1] before priest and abbess before abbot.

---

[1] It is not clear what Heloise means here by 'deaconess', though subservience is implied from its use in the early Church.

Surely the right and proper order is for those who write to their superiors or equals to put their names before their own, but in letters to inferiors, precedence in order of address follows precedence in rank.[2]

We were also greatly surprised when instead of bringing us the healing balm of comfort you increased our desolation and made the tears to flow which you should have dried. For which of us could remain dry-eyed on hearing the words you wrote towards the end of your letter: 'But if the Lord shall deliver me into the hands of my enemies so that they overcome and kill me . . .'? My dearest, how could you think such a thought? How could you give voice to it? Never may God be so forgetful of his humble handmaids as to let them outlive you; never may he grant us a life which would be harder to bear than any form of death. The proper course would be for you to perform our funeral rites, for you to commend our souls to God, and to send ahead of you those whom you assembled for God's service—so that you need no longer be troubled by worries for us, and follow after us the more gladly because freed from concern for our salvation. Spare us, I implore you, master, spare us words such as these which can only intensify our existing unhappiness; do not deny us, before death, the one thing by which we live. 'Each day has trouble enough of its own,'[3] and that day, shrouded in bitterness, will bring with it distress enough to all it comes upon. 'Why is it necessary,' says Seneca, 'to summon evil'[4] and to destroy life before death comes?

You ask us, my love, if you chance to die when absent from us, to have your body brought to our burial-ground so that you may reap a fuller harvest from the prayers we shall offer in constant memory of you. But how could you suppose that our memory of you could ever fade? Besides, what time will there be then which will be fitting for prayer, when extreme distress will allow us no peace, when the soul will lose its power of reason and the tongue its use of speech? Or when the frantic mind, far from being resigned, may even (if I may say so) rage against God himself, and provoke him with complaints instead of placating him with prayers? In our misery then we shall have time only for tears and no power to pray; we shall be hurrying to follow, not to bury you, so that we may share your grave instead of laying you in it. If we lose our life in you, we shall not be able to go on living when you leave us. I would not even have us live to see that day, for if the mere mention of your death is death for us, what will the reality be if it finds us still alive? God grant we may never live on to perform this duty, to render you the service which we look for from you alone; in this may we go before, not after you!

And so, I beg you, spare us—spare her at least, who is yours alone, by refraining from words like these. They pierce our hearts with swords of death, so that what comes before is more painful than death itself. A heart which is exhausted with grief cannot find peace, nor can a mind preoccupied with anxieties genuinely devote itself to God. I beseech you not to hinder God's service to which you specially committed us. Whatever has to come to us bringing with it total grief we must hope will come suddenly, without torturing us far in advance

---

[2]Heloise shows her knowledge of the rules for composing formal letters (*Dictamen* or *Ars dictandi*) which are found in several treatises from the eleventh century onwards, notably in that by Alberic (later Cardinal), theologian and monk of Monte Cassino, born in 1008. The rule of precedence is generally observed; it is a tribute to Heloise's status and reputation when Peter the Venerable, abbot of Cluny, in writing to her as abbess of the Paraclete, puts her name before his own.
[3]Matthew vi, 34.

[4]Seneca, *Epistulae ad Lucilium*, 24. 1.

with useless apprehension which no foresight can relieve. This is what the poet has in mind when he prays to God:

> May it be sudden, whatever you plan for us; may man's mind Be blind to the future. Let him hope on in his fears.[5]

But if I lose you, what is left for me to hope for? What reason for continuing on life's pilgrimage, for which I have no support but you, and none in you save the knowledge that you are alive, now that I am forbidden all other pleasures in you and denied even the joy of your presence which from time to time could restore me to myself? O God—if I dare say it—cruel to me in everything! O merciless mercy! O Fortune who is only ill-fortune, who has already spent on me so many of the shafts she uses in her battle against mankind that she has none left with which to vent her anger on others. She has emptied a full quiver on me, so that henceforth no one else need fear her onslaughts, and if she still had a single arrow she could find no place in me to take a wound. Her only dread is that through my many wounds death may end my sufferings; and though she does not cease to destroy me, she still fears the destruction which she hurries on.

Of all wretched women I am the most wretched, and amongst the unhappy I am unhappiest. The higher I was exalted when you preferred me to all other women, the greater my suffering over my own fall and yours, when I was flung down; for the higher the ascent, the heavier the fall. Has Fortune ever set any great or noble woman above me or made her my equal, only to be similarly cast down and crushed with grief? What glory she gave me in you, what ruin she brought upon me through you! Violent in either

extreme, she showed no moderation in good or evil. To make me the saddest of all women she first made me blessed above all, so that when I thought how much I had lost, my consuming grief would match my crushing loss, and my sorrow for what was taken from me would be the greater for the fuller joy of possession which had gone before; and so that the happiness of supreme ecstasy would end in the supreme bitterness of sorrow.

Moreover, to add to my indignation at the outrage you suffered, all the laws of equity in our case were reversed. For while we enjoyed the pleasures of an uneasy love and abandoned ourselves to fornication (if I may use an ugly but expressive word) we were spared God's severity. But when we amended our unlawful conduct by what was lawful, and atoned for the shame of fornication by an honourable marriage, then the Lord in his anger laid his hand heavily upon us, and would not permit a chaste union though he had long tolerated one which was unchaste. The punishment you suffered would have been proper vengeance for men caught in open adultery. But what others deserve for adultery came upon you through a marriage which you believed had made amends for all previous wrong doing; what adulterous women have brought upon their lovers, your own wife brought on you. Nor was this at the time when we abandoned ourselves to our former delights, but when we had already parted and were leading chaste lives, you presiding over the school in Paris and I at your command living with the nuns at Argenteuil. Thus we were separated, to give you more time to devote yourself to your pupils, and me more freedom for prayer and meditation on the Scriptures, both of us leading a life which was holy as well as chaste. It was then that you alone paid the penalty in your body for a sin we had both committed. You alone were punished though we were both to blame, and you paid all, though you had deserved

---

[5]Lucan, *Pharsalia* 2, 14–15.

less, for you had made more than necessary reparation by humbling yourself on my account and had raised me and all my kind to your own level—so much less then, in the eyes of God and of your betrayers, should you have been thought deserving of such punishment.

What misery for me—born as I was to be the cause of such a crime! Is it the general lot of women to bring total ruin on great men? Hence the warning about women in Proverbs:[6] 'But now, my son, listen to me, attend to what I say: do not let your heart entice you into her ways, do not stray down her paths; she has wounded and laid low so many, and the strongest have all been her victims. Her house is the way to hell, and leads down to the halls of death.' And in Ecclesiastes.[7] I put all to the test . . . I find woman more bitter than death; she is a snare, her heart a net, her arms are chains. He who is pleasing to God eludes her, but the sinner is her captive.'

It was the first woman in the beginning who lured man from Paradise, and she who had been created by the Lord as his helpmate became the instrument of his total downfall. And that mighty man of God, the Nazarite whose conception was announced by an angel,[8] Delilah alone overcame; betrayed to his enemies and robbed of his sight, he was driven by his suffering to destroy himself along with his enemies. Only the woman he had slept with could reduce to folly Solomon, wisest of all men; she drove him to such a pitch of madness that although he was the man whom the Lord had chosen to build the temple in preference to his father David, who was a righteous man, she plunged him into idolatry until the end of his life, so that he abandoned the worship of God which he had preached and taught in word and writing.[9] Job, holiest of men, fought his last and hardest battle against his wife, who urged him to curse God.[10] The cunning arch-tempter well knew from repeated experience that men are most easily brought to ruin through their wives, and so he directed his usual malice against us too, and attacked you by means of marriage when he could not destroy you through fornication. Denied the power to do evil through evil, he effected evil through good.

At least I can thank God for this: the tempter did not prevail on me to do wrong of my own consent, like the women I have mentioned, though in the outcome he made me the instrument of his malice. But even if my conscience is clear through innocence, and no consent of mine makes me guilty of this crime, too many earlier sins were committed to allow me to be wholly free from guilt. I yielded long before to the pleasures of carnal desires, and merited then what I weep for now. The sequel is a fitting punishment for my former sins, and an evil beginning must be expected to come to a bad end. For this offence, above all, may I have strength to do proper penance, so that at least by long contrition I can make some amends for your pain from the wound inflicted on you; and what you suffered in the body for a time, I may suffer, as is right, throughout my life in contrition of mind, and thus make reparation to you at least, if not to God.

For if I truthfully admit to the weakness of my unhappy soul, I can find no penitence whereby to appease God, whom I always accuse of the greatest cruelty in regard to this outrage. By rebelling against his ordinance, I offend him more by my indignation than I placate him by making amends

---

[6]Proverbs vii, 24–7.
[7]Ecclesiastes vii, 26.
[8]Samson, in Judges xiii, 3.

[9]1 Kings xi, 1–8.
[10]Job ii, 9–10.

through penitence. How can it be called repentance for sins, however great the mortification of the flesh, if the mind still retains the will to sin and is on fire with its old desires?[11] It is easy enough for anyone to confess his sins, to accuse himself, or even to mortify his body in outward show of penance, but it is very difficult to tear the heart away from hankering after its dearest pleasures. Quite rightly then, when the saintly Job said 'I will speak out against myself,' that is, 'I will loose my tongue and open my mouth in confession to accuse myself of my sins,' he added at once 'I will speak out in bitterness of soul.'[12] St Gregory comments on this: 'There are some who confess their faults aloud but in doing so do not know how to groan over them—they speak cheerfully of what should be lamented. And so whoever hates his faults and confesses them must still confess them in bitterness of spirit, so that this bitterness may punish him for what his tongue, at his mind's bidding, accuses him.'[13] But this bitterness of true repentance is very rare, as St Ambrose observes, when he says: 'I have more easily found men who have preserved their innocence than men who have known repentance.'[14]

In my case, the pleasures of lovers which we shared have been too sweet—they can never displease me, and can scarcely be banished from my thoughts. Wherever I turn they are always there before my eyes, bringing with them awakened longings and fantasies which will not even let me sleep. Even during the celebration of the Mass, when our prayers should be purer, lewd visions of those pleasures take such a hold upon my unhappy soul that my thoughts are on their wantonness instead of on prayers. I should be groaning over the sins I have committed, but I can only sigh for what I have lost. Everything we did and also the times and places are stamped on my heart along with your image, so that I live through it all again with you. Even in sleep I know no respite. Sometimes my thoughts are betrayed in a movement of my body, or they break out in an unguarded word. In my utter wretchedness, that cry from a suffering soul could well be mine: 'Miserable creature that I am, who is there to rescue me out of the body doomed to this death?'[15] Would that in truth I could go on: 'The grace of God through Jesus Christ our Lord.' This grace, my dearest, came upon you unsought—a single wound of the body by freeing you from these torments has healed many wounds in your soul. Where God may seem to you an adversary he has in fact proved himself kind: like an honest doctor who does not shrink from giving pain if it will bring about a cure. But for me, youth and passion and experience of pleasures which were so delightful intensify the torments of the flesh and longings of desire, and the assault is the more overwhelming as the nature they attack is the weaker.

Men call me chaste; they do not know the hypocrite I am. They consider purity of the flesh a virtue, though virtue belongs not to the body but to the soul. I can win praise in the eyes of men but deserve none before God, who searches our hearts and loins[16] and sees in our darkness. I am judged religious at a time when there is little in religion which is not hypocrisy, when whoever does not offend the opinions of men receives the highest

---

[11]Heloise's concern for true repentance is closely linked with her belief in the ethic of intention. See Letter I, note 2, p. 115. Inner contrition for sin is all-important.
[12]Cf. Job x, I.
[13]*Moralia*, 9. 43.
[14]*De paenitentia*, 2.10.

[15]Romans vii, 24.
[16]Psalm viii, 10.

praise. And yet perhaps there is some merit and it is somehow acceptable to God, if a person whatever his intention gives no offence to the Church in his outward behaviour, does not blaspheme the name of the Lord in the hearing of unbelievers nor disgrace the Order of his profession amongst the worldly. And this too is a gift of God's grace and comes through his bounty—not only to do good but to abstain from evil—though the latter is vain if the former does not follow from it, as it is written: 'Turn from evil and do good.'[17] Both are vain if not done for love of God.

At every stage of my life up to now, as God knows, I have feared to offend you rather than God, and tried to please you more than him. It was your command, not love of God which made me take the veil. Look at the unhappy life I lead, pitiable beyond any other, if in this world I must endure so much in vain, with no hope of future reward. For a long time my pretence deceived you, as it did many, so that you mistook hypocrisy for piety; and therefore you commend yourself to my prayers and ask me for what I expect from you. I beg you, do not feel so sure of me that you cease to help me by your own prayers. Do not suppose me healthy and so withdraw the grace of your healing. Do not believe I want for nothing and delay helping me in my hour of need. Do not think me strong, lest I fall before you can sustain me. False praise has harmed many and taken from them the support they needed. The Lord cries out through Isaiah: 'O my people! Those who call you happy lead you astray and confuse the path you should take.'[18] And through Ezekiel he says: 'Woe upon you women who hunt men's lives by sewing magic bands upon the wrists and putting veils over the heads of persons of every age.'[19] On the other hand, through Solomon it is said that 'The sayings of the wise are sharp as goads, like nails driven home.'[20] That is to say, nails which cannot touch wounds gently, but only pierce through them.

Cease praising me, I beg you, lest you acquire the base stigma of being a flatterer or the charge of telling lies, or the breath of my vanity blows away any merit you saw in me to praise. No one with medical knowledge diagnoses an internal ailment by examining only outward appearance. What is common to the damned and the elect can win no favour in the eyes of God: of such a kind are the outward actions which are performed more eagerly by hypocrites than by saints. 'The heart of man is deceitful and inscrutable; who can fathom it?'[21] And: 'A road may seem straightforward to a man, yet may end as the way to death.'[22] It is rash for man to pass judgement on what is reserved for God's scrutiny, and so it is also written: 'Do not praise a man in his lifetime.'[23] By this is meant, do not praise a man while in doing so you can make him no longer praiseworthy.

To me your praise is the more dangerous because I welcome it. The more anxious I am to please you in everything, the more I am won over

---

[17]Psalm xxxvii, 27.
[18]Isaiah iii, 12 (Vulgate version).

[19]Ezekiel xiii, 18, a much disputed verse. This is the N.E.B. translation; the Knox translation of the Vulgate says 'stitching an elbow cushion for every comer, making a soft pillow for the heads of young and old' and suggests that these are stuffed with magical herbs. Heloise appears to understand it as an attack on those who raise false hopes by superstitious practices.
[20]Ecclesiastes xii, II.
[21]Jeremiah xvii, 9.
[22]Proverbs xiv, 12; xvi, 25.
[23]Ecclesiasticus xi, 28: the Vulgate (verse 30) reads *Ante mortem ne laudes bominem quemquam*, which cannot bear the explanation Heloise gives it. The N.E.B. translates the Hebrew 'Call no man happy before his death'. It continues 'for it is by his end that a man is known for what he is.' The similar classical tag means of course that death is the only guarantee against a reversal of fortune.

and delighted by it. I beg you, be fearful for me always, instead of feeling confidence in me, so that I may always find help in your solicitude. Now particularly you should fear, now when I no longer have in you an outlet for my incontinence. I do not want you to exhort me to virtue and summon me to the fight, saying 'Power comes to its full strength in weakness'[24] and 'He cannot win a crown unless he has kept the rules.'[25] I do not seek a crown of victory; it is sufficient for me to avoid danger, and this is safer than engaging in war. In whatever corner of heaven God shall place me, I shall be satisfied. No one will envy another there, and what each one has will suffice. Let the weight of authority reinforce what I say—let us hear St Jerome: 'I confess my weakness, I do not wish to fight in hope of victory, lest the day comes when I lose the battle. What need is there to forsake what is certain and pursue uncertainty?'[26]

LETTER 4. ABELARD TO HELOISE

To the bride of Christ, Christ's servant.

The whole of your last letter is given up to a recital of your misery over the wrongs you suffer, and these, I note, are on four counts. First you complain that contrary to custom in letter-writing, or indeed against the natural order of the world, my letter to you put your name before mine in its greeting. Secondly, that when I ought to have offered you some remedy for your comfort I actually increased your sense of desolation and made the tears flow which I should have checked. This I did by writing 'But if the Lord shall deliver me into the hands of my enemies, so that they overcome

and kill me . . .' Thirdly you went on to your old perpetual complaint against God concerning the manner of our entry into religious life and the cruelty of the act of treachery performed on me. Lastly, you set your self-accusations against my praise of you, and implored me with some urgency not to praise you again.

I have decided to answer you on each point in turn, not so much in self-justification as for your own enlightenment and encouragement, so that you will more willingly grant my own requests when you understand that they have a basis of reason, listen to me more attentively on the subject of your own pleas as you find me less to blame in my own, and be less ready to refuse me when you see me less deserving of reproach.

What you call the unnatural order of my greeting, if you consider it carefully, was in accordance with your own view as well as mine. For it is common knowledge, as you yourself have shown, that in writing to superiors one puts their name first, and you must realize that you became my superior from the day when you began to be my lady on becoming the bride of my Lord; witness St Jerome, who writes to Eustochium 'This is my reason for writing "my lady Eustochium". Surely I must address as "my lady" her who is the bride of my Lord.'[27] It was a happy transfer of your married state, for you were previously the wife of a poor mortal and now are raised to the bed of the King of kings. By the privilege of your position you are set not only over your former husband but over every servant of that King. So you should not be surprised if I commend myself in life as in death to the prayers of your community, seeing that in common law it is accepted that wives are better able than their households to intercede with their husbands, being ladies rather than servants. As an

---

[24] 2 Corinthians xii, 9.
[25] 2 Timothy ii, 5.
[26] *Adversus Vigilantium*, 16.

[27] *Epistulae*, 22.2

illustration of this, the Psalmist says of the queen and bride of the King of kings: 'On your right stands the queen,'[28] as if it were clearly stated that she is nearest to her husband and close to his side, and moves forward with him, while all the rest stand apart or follow behind. . . .

[A]s St Augustine reminds us,[29] the Lord said 'I am truth'[30] not 'I am custom.' Anyone who cares to may entrust himself to the prayers of these men, which are offered with doors open, but you who have been led by the King of heaven himself into his chamber and rest in his embrace, and with the door always shut are wholly given up to him, are more intimately joined to him, in the Apostle's words, 'But anyone who is joined to the Lord is one spirit with him.'[31] So much the more confidence, then, have I in the purity and effectiveness of your prayers, and the more urgently I demand your help. And I believe these prayers are offered more devoutly on my behalf because we are bound together in such great mutual love.

But if I have distressed you by mentioning the dangers which beset me or the death I fear, it was done in accordance with your own request, or rather, entreaty. For the first letter you wrote me has a passage which says: 'And so in the name of Christ, who is still giving you some protection for his service, we beseech you to write as often as you think fit to us who are his handmaids and yours, with news of the perils in which you are still storm-tossed. We are all that are left you, so at least you should let us share your sorrow or your joy. It is always some consolation in sorrow to feel that it is shared, and any burden laid on several is carried more lightly or removed.'[32] Why then do you accuse me of making you share my anxiety when I

was forced to do so at your own behest? When I am suffering in despair of my life, would it be fitting for you to be joyous? Would you want to be partners only in joy, not grief, to join in rejoicing without weeping with those who weep?[33] There is no wider distinction between true friends and false than the fact that the former share adversity, the latter only prosperity.

Say no more, I beg you, and cease from complaints like these which are so far removed from the true depths of love! Yet even if you are still offended by this, I am so critically placed in danger and daily despair of life that it is proper for me to take thought for the welfare of my soul, and to provide for it while I may. Nor will you, if you truly love me, take exception to my forethought. Indeed, had you any hope of divine mercy being shown me, you would be all the more anxious for me to be freed from the troubles of this life as you see them to be intolerable. At least you must know that whoever frees me from life will deliver me from the greatest suffering. What I may afterwards incur is uncertain, but from what I shall be set free is not in question. Every unhappy life is happy in its ending, and those who feel true sympathy and pain for the anxieties of others want to see these ended, even to their own loss, if they really love those they see suffer and think more of their friends' advantage than of their own. So when a son has long been ill a mother wants his illness to end even in death, for she finds it unbearable, and can more easily face bereavement than have him share her misery. And anyone who takes special pleasure in the presence of a friend would rather have him happy in absence than present and unhappy, for he finds suffering intolerable if he cannot relieve it. In your case, you are not even permitted to enjoy my presence, unhappy though it is, and so, when any provision you are able to

---

[28]Psalm xiv, 9.
[29]*De baptismo, 3.6.9.*
[30]Cf. John xiv, 16.
[31]I Corinthians vi, 17.
[32]Letter I, p. 110.

[33]Cf. Romans xii, 15.

make for me is to your own advantage, I cannot see why you should prefer me to live on in great misery rather than be happier in death. If you see your advantage in prolonging my miseries, you are proved an enemy, not a friend. But if you hesitate to appear in such a guise, I beg you, as I said before, to cease your complaints.

However, I approve of your rejection of praise, for in this very thing you show yourself more praiseworthy. It is written that 'He who is first in accusing himself is just'[34] and 'Whoever humbles himself will be exalted.'[35] May your written words be reflected in your heart! If they are, yours is true humility and will not vanish with anything I say. But be careful, I beg you, not to seek praise when you appear to shun it, and not to reject with your lips what you desire in your heart. St Jerome writes to the virgin Eustochium on this point, amongst others: 'We are led on by our natural evil. We give willing ear to our flatterers, and though we may answer that we are unworthy and an artful blush suffuses our cheeks, the soul inwardly delights in its own praise.'[36] Such artfulness Virgil describes in wanton Galatea, who sought what she wanted by flight, and by feigning rejection led on her lover more surely towards her:

She flees to the willows and wishes first to be seen.[37]

Before she hides she wants to be seen fleeing, so that the very flight whereby she appears to reject the youth's company ensures that she obtains it. Similarly, when we seem to shun men's praise we are directing it towards ourselves, and when we pretend that we wish to hide lest anyone discovers what to praise in us, we are leading the unwary[38] on to give us praise because in this way we appear to deserve it. I mention this because it is a common occurrence, not because I suspect such things of you; I have no doubts about your humility. But I want you to refrain from speaking like this, so that you do not appear to those who do not know you so well to be seeking fame by shunning it, as Jerome says. My praise will never make you proud, but will summon you to higher things, and the more eager you are to please me, the more anxious you will be to embrace what I praise. My praise is not a tribute to your piety which is intended to bolster up your pride, and we ought not in fact to believe in our friends' approval any more than in our enemies' abuse.

I come at last to what I have called your old perpetual complaint, in which you presume to blame God for the manner of our entry into religion instead of wishing to glorify him as you justly should.[39] I had thought that this bitterness of heart at what was so clear an act of divine mercy had long since disappeared. The more dangerous such bitterness is to you in wearing out body and soul alike, the more pitiful it is and distressing to me. If you are anxious to please me in everything, as you claim, and in this at least would end my torment, or even give me the greatest pleasure, you must rid yourself of it. If it persists you can neither please me nor attain bliss with me. Can you bear me to come to this without you—I whom you declare yourself ready to follow to the very fires of hell? Seek piety in this at least, lest you cut yourself off from me who am hastening, you believe, towards God; be the readier to do so because the goal we

---

[34]Proverbs xviii, 17. The N.E.B. translates the whole verse: 'In a lawsuit the first speaker seems right, until another steps forward and cross-questions him.' The Knox translation of the Vulgate has a note on the obscurity of the Hebrew, and translates the Latin as 'An innocent man is the first to lay bare the truth.' Neither seems to suit the interpretation given by Abelard.

[35]Luke xviii, 14.

[36]*Epistulae* xxii, 24.

[37]*Eclogues*, 3. 65.

[38]Latin *imprudentes*. The alternative reading is *impudentes* (wanton).

[39]Cf. Letter 1, note 1, p. 116.

must come to will be blessed, and our companionship the more welcome for being happier. Remember what you have said, recall what you have written, namely that in the manner of our conversion, when God seems to have been more my adversary, he has clearly shown himself kinder.[40] For this reason at least you must accept his will, that it is most salutary for me, and for you too, if your transports of grief will see reason. You should not grieve because you are the cause of so great a good, for which you must not doubt you were specially created by God. Nor should you weep because I have to bear this, except when our blessings through the martyrs in their sufferings and the Lord's death sadden you. If it had befallen me justly, would you find it easier to bear? Would it distress you less? In fact if it had been so, the result would have been greater disgrace for me and more credit to my enemies, since justice would have won them approval while my guilt would have brought me into contempt. And no one would be stirred by pity for me to condemn what was done.

However, it may relieve the bitterness of your grief if I prove that this came upon us justly, as well as to our advantage, and that God's punishment was more properly directed against us when we were married than when we were living in sin. After our marriage, when you were living in the cloister with the nuns at Argenteuil and I came one day to visit you privately, you know what my uncontrollable desire did with you there, actually in a corner of the refectory, since we had nowhere else to go. I repeat, you know how shamelessly we behaved on that occasion in so hallowed a place, dedicated to the most holy Virgin. Even if our other shameful behaviour was ended, this alone would deserve far heavier punishment. Need I recall our previous fornication and the wanton impurities which preceded our marriage, or my supreme act of betrayal, when I deceived your uncle about you so disgracefully, at a time when I was continuously living with him in his own house? Who would not judge me justly betrayed by the man whom I had first shamelessly betrayed? Do you think that the momentary pain of that wound is sufficient punishment for such crimes? Or rather, that so great an advantage was fitting for such great wickedness? What wound do you suppose would satisfy God's justice for the profanation such as I described of a place so sacred to his own Mother? Surely, unless I am much mistaken, not that wound which was wholly beneficial was intended as a punishment for this, but rather the daily unending torment I now endure.

You know too how when you were pregnant and I took you to my own country you disguised yourself in the sacred habit of a nun, a pretence which was an irreverent mockery of the religion you now profess. Consider, then, how fittingly divine justice, or rather, divine grace brought you against your will to the religion which you did not hesitate to mock, so that you should willingly expiate your profanation in the same habit, and the truth of reality should remedy the lie of your pretence and correct your falsity. And if you would allow consideration of our advantage to be an element in divine justice, you would be able to call what God did to us then an act not of justice, but of grace.

See then, my beloved, see how with the dragnets of his mercy the Lord has fished us up from the depth of this dangerous sea, and from the abyss of what a Charybdis he has saved our shipwrecked selves, although we were unwilling, so that each of us may justly break out in that cry: 'The Lord takes thought for me'.[41] Think and think again of the great perils in which we were and from which the Lord rescued us; tell always with the deepest

---

[40]Cf. Letter 3, p. 133.

[41]Vulgate only, the last verse of Psalm xxxix (xl).

gratitude how much the Lord has done for our souls. Comfort by our example any unrighteous who despair of God's goodness, so that all may know what may be done for those who ask with prayer, when such benefits are granted sinners even against their will. Consider the magnanimous design of God's mercy for us, the compassion with which the Lord directed his judgement towards our chastisement, the wisdom whereby he made use of evil itself and mercifully set aside our impiety, so that by a wholly justified wound in a single part of my body he might heal two souls. Compare our danger and manner of deliverance, compare the sickness and the medicine. Examine the cause, our deserts, and marvel at the effect, his pity.

You know the depths of shame to which my unbridled lust had consigned our bodies, until no reverence for decency or for God even during the days of Our Lord's Passion, or of the greater sacraments could keep me from wallowing in this mire.[42] Even when you were unwilling, resisted to the utmost of your power and tried to dissuade me, as yours was the weaker nature I often forced you to consent with threats and blows. So intense were the fires of lust which bound me to you that I set those wretched, obscene pleasures, which we blush even to name, above God as above myself; nor would it seem that divine mercy could have taken action except by forbidding me these pleasures altogether, without future hope. And so it was wholly just and merciful, although by means of the supreme treachery of your uncle, for me to be reduced in that part of my body which was the seat of lust and sole reason for those desires, so that I could increase in many ways; in order that this member should justly be punished for all its wrongdoing in us, expiate in suffering the sins

committed for its amusement, and cut me off from the slough of filth in which I had been wholly immersed in mind as in body. Only thus could I become more fit to approach the holy altars, now that no contagion of carnal impurity would ever again call me from them. How mercifully did he want me to suffer so much only in that member, the privation of which would also further the salvation of my soul without defiling my body nor preventing any performance of my duties! Indeed, it would make me readier to perform whatever can be honourably done by setting me wholly free from the heavy yoke of carnal desire.

So when divine grace cleansed rather than deprived me of those vile members which from their practice of utmost indecency are called 'the parts of shame' and have no proper name of their own, what else did it do but remove a foul imperfection in order to preserve perfect purity? Such purity, as we have heard, certain sages have desired so eagerly that they have mutilated themselves, so as to remove entirely the shame of desire. The Apostle too is recorded as having besought the Lord to rid him of this thorn in the flesh, but was not heard.[43] The great Christian philosopher Origen provides an example,[44] for he was not afraid to mutilate himself in order to quench completely this fire within him, as if he understood literally the words that those men were truly blessed who castrated themselves for the Kingdom of Heaven's sake,[45] and believed them to be truthfully carrying out the bidding of the Lord about offending members, that we should cut them off and throw them away;[46] and as if he interpreted as historic fact, not as a hidden symbol, that prophecy of Isaiah in which the Lord prefers eunuchs to the rest of the faithful: 'The eunuchs

---

[42]Intercourse even between married couples was forbidden by the Church during Lent, the Passion, and on the vigils of the major feasts.

[43]2 Corinthians xii, 7–8.
[44]Cf. Eusebius, *Historia Ecclesiae*, 6. 8.
[45]Matthew xix, 12.
[46]Matthew xviii, 8.

who keep my sabbaths, and choose to do my will I will give a place in my own house and within my walls and a name better than sons and daughters. I will give them an everlasting name which shall not perish . . .'[47]

Come too, my inseparable companion, and join me in thanksgiving, you who were made my partner both in guilt and in grace. For the Lord is not unmindful also of your own salvation, indeed, he has you much in mind, for by a kind of holy presage of his name he marked you out to be especially his when he named you Heloise, after his own name, Elohim. In his mercy, I say, he intended to provide for two people in one, the two whom the devil sought to destroy in one; since a short while before this happening he had bound us together by the indissoluble bond of the marriage sacrament. At the time I desired to keep you whom I loved beyond measure for myself alone, but he was already planning to use this opportunity for our joint conversion to himself. Had you not been previously joined to me in wedlock, you might easily have clung to the world when I withdrew from it, either at the suggestion of your relatives or in enjoyment of carnal delights. See then, how greatly the Lord was concerned for us, as if he were reserving us for some great ends, and was indignant or grieved because our knowledge of letters, the talents which he had entrusted to us, were not being used to glorify his name; or as if he feared for his humble and incontinent servant, because it is written 'Women make even the wise forsake their faith.[48] Indeed, this is proved in the case of the wisest of men, Solomon.[49]

How great an interest the talent of your own wisdom pays daily to the Lord in the many spiritual daughters you have borne for him, while I remain totally barren and labour in vain amongst the sons of perdition! What a hateful loss and grievous misfortune if you had abandoned yourself to the defilement of carnal pleasures only to bear in suffering a few children for the world, when now you are delivered in exultation of numerous progeny for heaven! Nor would you have been more than a woman, whereas now you rise even above men, and have turned the curse of Eve into the blessing of Mary. How unseemly for those holy hands which now turn the pages of sacred books to have to perform degrading services in women's concerns! God himself has thought fit to raise us up from the contamination of this filth and the pleasures of this mire and draw us to him by force— the same force whereby he chose to strike and convert Paul[50]—and by our example perhaps to deter from our audacity others who are also trained in letters. . . .

See, sister, what great mourning there is amongst those who love their king over the death of his only and first begotten son. Behold the lamentation and grief with which the whole household and court are consumed; and when you come to the bride of the only son who is dead, you will find her wailing intolerable and more than you can bear. This mourning, sister, should be yours and also the wailing, for you were joined to this bridegroom in blessed matrimony. He bought you not with his wealth, but with himself. He bought and redeemed you with his own blood. See what right he has over you, and know how precious you are. This is the price which the Apostle has in mind when he considers how little he is worth for whom the price was paid, and what return he should make for such a gift: 'God forbid that I should boast of anything but the Cross of our Lord Jesus Christ, through whom the world is crucified to me and I to the world!'[51] You are greater than heaven,

---

[47]Isaiah lvi, 4–5.
[48]Ecclesiasticus xix, 2.
[49]1 Kings xi, 1 ff.

[50]Cf. Acts xxvi, 12 ff.
[51]Galatians vi, 14.

greater than the world, for the Creator of the world himself became the price for you. What has he seen in you, I ask you, when he lacks nothing, to make him seek even the agonies of a fearful and inglorious death in order to purchase you? What, I repeat, does he seek in you except yourself? He is the true friend who desires yourself and nothing that is yours, the true friend who said when he was about to die for you: 'There is no greater love than this, that a man should lay down his life for his friends.'[52]

It was he who truly loved you, not I. My love, which brought us both to sin, should be called lust, not love. I took my fill of my wretched pleasures in you, and this was the sum total of my love. You say I suffered for you, and perhaps that is true, but it was really through you, and even this, unwillingly; not for love of you but under compulsion, and to bring you not salvation but sorrow. But he suffered truly for your salvation, on your behalf of his own free will, and by his suffering he cures all sickness and removes all suffering. To him, I beseech you, not to me, should be directed all your devotion, all your compassion, all your remorse. Weep for the injustice of the great cruelty inflicted on him, not for the just and righteous payment demanded of me, or rather, as I said, the supreme grace granted us both. For you are unrighteous if you do not love righteousness, and most unrighteous if you consciously oppose the will, or more truly, the boundless grace of God. Mourn for your Saviour and Redeemer, not for the seducer who defiled you, for the Master who died for you, not for the servant who lives and, indeed, for the first time is truly freed from death.

---

[52]John xv, 13.

chapter twelve

Saint Teresa of Avila

Saint Teresa of Avila (1515–1582) was a Spanish nun and mystic of the Order of Carmelites. Named for Mount Carmel, where the Hebrew prophet Elijah held contest with the priests of Baal, the Carmelites had their roots in the Crusades and were fully established in Europe by the early thirteenth century, living according to a conspicuously simple "Rule." St. Teresa led a movement of renewal among the Carmelites, returning to the life of discalced (shoeless) poverty.

She was born Teresa de Cepeda y Ahumada to a father who had two children by his first wife and ten by his second, of whom Teresa was the third. Her grandfather was a *converso*—a Jew who converted to Christianity rather than face expulsion from Spain as ordered by Ferdinand and Isabella in 1492—who managed to marry his children to aristocrats and successful merchants. At seven Teresa and a brother decided to leave home for Moorish lands with the intent of becoming Christian martyrs, but they were intercepted en route by an uncle. After her mother died, fourteen-year-old Teresa turned to an image of the Virgin Mary, asking to be taken as her daughter. She was given over to an Augustinian convent in her teens and entered a Carmelite monastery at twenty. There she suffered a near fatal illness, involving coma and paralysis. She attributed her recovery to a miracle by St. Joseph. For some twenty years afterward, she had visions and intense mystical experiences, which were generally doubted or downplayed by her superiors and confessors. Over those years she became leader of a movement to return to an older tradition of Carmelites who were hermits, barefoot, and who observed strict vows of poverty. Over the objections of many church officials and of townspeople, she established the first convent of discalced (barefoot) Carmelites in Spain and then a series of others and gained a following among priests and lay people as well. St. John of the Cross (1542–1591) became one of her most devoted followers.

Saint Teresa's *Life* remains to this day one of the most popular works written in Spanish, partly because of its very direct and lucid prose, and especially since that straightforward exposition contrasts with the highly unusual happenings and inexplicable experiences recorded. Her prose makes the transcendent and divine seem near at hand. Events of her life both major and minor become steps on the path to spiritual discipline and mystical vision, The Road to Perfection. Although she describes this as a ladder of love, the visions she has are not only of blissful divine union, but of devils and hellfire and torture as well.

Teresa's career and spirituality were defined in important ways by the Catholic "Counter-Reformation" reaction to Protestant expansion—the founding of the Jesuits and revitalization of other monastic orders. The Carmelite reform movement was part of this broad sweep. While *The Life* sets forth her mystical visions, Teresa's practical side is evident in her text, *The Way of Perfection*, which details her contributions to this reform.

The famous Bernini sculpture of Saint Teresa is part of a full altar assembly with strips of brilliant gold streaming down and with members of the Cornaro family included as sideline observers. It is based on chapter 29 of the autobiography, where Saint Teresa describes a particular vision of a very beautiful angel:

> In his hands I saw a great golden spear, and at the iron tip there appeared to be a point of fire. This he plunged into my heart several times so that it penetrated to my entrails. When he pulled it out, I felt that he took them with it, and left me utterly consumed by the great love of God. The pain was so severe that it made me utter several moans. The sweetness caused by this intense pain is so extreme that one cannot possibly wish it to cease.

The erotic overtones of this passage are accentuated in Bernini's statue. The eroticism is not only in Teresa's facial expression of enraptured swoon—suggesting orgasm—and protruding bare foot—mark of the discalced nun and hinting at fetishism. In art history the winged boy with arrow is more commonly identified as Eros, the Greek God of (sexual) Love—Cupid in his Latin guise. In Plato's *Symposium*, the theme of Eros is unfolded from the "lower level" of an inspection of physical and sexual desire into the "higher" understanding of desire as a force in all of nature, and on to a fully universal interpretation of Love.[1] In Saint Teresa, erotic and divine love, sharply distinguished in traditional Christian theology, seem almost fused.[2]

The transport of the vision of divine love is for Saint Teresa an intensity of life and a death to the world. Mystical union with God is a kind of "love-death":

> I now live outside myself
> After dying for love;
> Since I live in the Lord,
> Who sought me for himself.
> When I gave my heart to him
> I placed on him this legend:
> I am dying because I'm not dying![3]

The poem illustrates the play of paradoxes, as well as fascination with death. We know of Teresa's childhood desire for martyrdom, and of the sometime connection of her visions with morbidity. But death is also symbol of that union with God in which a human being becomes deaf to extraneous noise and dead to the mundane—and thus most genuinely alive. Contradictions fall together in the vision of union with God.

Mystics claim direct access to God—an immediate knowledge of God different from the routes that logic and sense experience take toward lesser realms and matters—indeed absorption into and identity with God, often in ecstatic experience or through a disciplined process of purgation, the emptying out of the self. God may be understood as personal (in Judaic, Christian, and Islamic mysticism) or as nonpersonal (in Buddhism and Taoism) or as the "everything" of some pantheists. Because of their "nonlinear," logic-defying, seemingly self-contradictory expressions, mystics were often at odds with religious orthodoxy and dogma. Because of its claims to divine immediacy, mysticism was a threat to religious hierarchy, or so it was often seen in the Christian Church.

And so it was with Saint Teresa. After all the by-ways of a varied life, she was vilified by many; she was accused before the Inquisition of engaging in orgies with her father confessor—when she was sixty and he half that! And she was excommunicated and exiled by her enemies, the calced Carmelites. But she died revered by many, amid reports that her body did not decay but rather smelled for months like roses. She was canonized by Pope Gregory XV in 1622. In addition, Saint Teresa is one of only three women ever to be officially designated "Doctor of the Church."[4]

JHS

QUESTIONS

1. In what way(s) do Teresa's visions demonstrate to Teresa God's love for her?
2. What are the promises and perils of the love of another in friendship?
3. What are the promises and perils of love for one's confessor?

ENDNOTES

1. Cf. Chapter 3 of this volume.
2. In contrast with *erôs* (desire), St. Paul's word for divine love is *agápê*; *philía* is the term for friendship and fraternal love.
3. Saint Teresa, "Vivo ya fuera de mí," trans. J. Stam. There are several versions of this and a very similar poem by St. John of the Cross.
4. The title "Doctor of the Church" is given to eminent theologians. Pope Paul VI named Saint Teresa and Saint Catherine of Siena in 1970 and Pope John Paul II added St. Thérése of Lisieux in 1997.

SELECTED BIBLIOGRAPHY

Hatzfeld, Helmut Anthony. *Saint Teresa of Avila*. New York: Twayne, 1969.

Medwick, Cathleen. *Teresa of Avila: The Progress of a Soul*. New York: Alfred Knopf, 1999.

Nevin, Winifred. *Teresa of Avila: The Woman*. Milwaukee; Wisc.: Bruce Publishers, 1956.

Underhill, Evelyn. *Mysticism: A Study in the Nature and Development of Man's Spiritual Consciousness*. New York: Noonday Press, 1955 (1910).

from *The Life of Saint Teresa of Avila by Herself*

Saint Teresa of Avila

CHAPTER 29

She continues, and describes some great favours which the Lord showed her, relating also what the Lord said to her, to reassure her and enable her to answer those who argued against her

I have wandered far from my subject. I was trying to explain the reasons why this kind of vision cannot be the work of the imagination. For, how could we picture Christ's Humanity merely through having dwelt on it, or compose His great beauty out of our own heads? If such a conception were to be anything like the original, it would take quite a long time to build up. One can indeed construct such a picture from the imagination, and can spend quite a while regarding it, and reflecting on the form and brightness of it. One can gradually perfect this picture and commit it to the memory. What is there to prevent this, since it is the work of the intelligence? But when it comes to the visions I am speaking of, there is no way of building them up. We have to look at them when the Lord is pleased to show them to us—to look as He wishes and at what He wishes. We can neither add nor subtract anything, nor can we obtain a vision by any actions of our own. We cannot look at it when we like or refrain from looking at it; if we try to look at any particular feature of it, we immediately lose Christ.

For two and a half years, God granted me this favour at frequent intervals. But more than three years ago He took it from me, in this form of a continual experience, and gave me something of a higher kind, of which I shall perhaps speak later. During all that time, though I saw that He was speaking to me, though I gazed on His very great beauty, and felt the sweetness with which those words of His, which were sometimes stern, issued from His fair and divine mouth, and though, at the same time, I greatly longed to see the colour of His eyes, or His stature, so as to be able to describe them later, I was never worthy enough to see them, nor was it any good my trying to do so. On the contrary, these efforts lost me the vision altogether. Though I sometimes see Him looking at me with compassion, His gaze is so powerful that my soul cannot endure it. It is caught in so sublime a rapture that it loses this lovely vision in order to increase its enjoyment of the whole. So here there is no question of willingness or unwillingness. It is clear that all the Lord wants of us is humility and shame, and that we shall accept what is given us, with praise for the Giver.

This is true of all visions without exception. There is nothing that we can do about them; no effort of ours makes us see more or less, or calls up or dispels a vision. The Lord desires us to see very clearly that this work is not ours but His Majesty's. We are the less able, therefore, to take pride in it; on the contrary it makes us humble and afraid, when we see that just as the Lord takes away our power of seeing what we will, so He can also remove these favours and His grace, with the result that we are utterly lost. Let us always walk in fear therefore, so long as we are living in this exile.

Almost always Our Lord appeared to me as He rose from the dead, and it was the same when I saw Him in the Host. Only occasionally, to hearten me if I was in tribulation, He would show me His wounds, and then He would appear sometimes on the Cross and sometimes as He was in the Garden. Sometimes too, but rarely, I saw Him wearing the crown of thorns, and sometimes carrying His Cross as well, because of my deeds, let me say, and those of others. But always His body was glorified. Many were the reproaches and trials that I suffered when I spoke of this, and many were my fears and persecutions. They felt so certain of my being possessed by a devil that some of them wanted to exorcize me. This did not worry me much, but I was distressed when I found my confessors unwilling to hear my confession, or when I heard that people were talking to them about me. Nevertheless, I could not be sorry that I had seen these celestial visions. I would not have exchanged a single one of them for all the blessings and delights in the world. I always regarded them as a grand mercy from the Lord, and I think they were a very great treasure. Often the Lord Himself would reassure me, and I found my love for Him growing exceedingly. I would go and complain to Him about all my trials, and I always emerged from prayer comforted and with new strength. But I did not dare to contradict my critics, for I saw that this made things worse, since they attributed my arguments to lack of humility. I discussed things with my confessor, however, and he never failed to give me great comfort if he saw that I was worried.

When the visions became more frequent, one of those who had helped me before, and who had taken my confession sometimes when the minister could not, began to say that clearly I was being deceived by the devil. He ordered me, since I had no power of resistance, always to make the sign of the Cross when I had a vision, and to snap my fingers at it, in the firm conviction that this was the devil's work. Then it would not come again. He told me to have no fear, for God would protect me and take the vision away. This command greatly distressed me, for I could not think that the vision came from anything but God. It was a terrible thing for me to do; and, as I have said, I could not possibly wish my vision to be taken from me. However, in the end I obeyed him. I prayed God frequently to free me from deception; indeed, I did so continually, with many tears, and I also invoked St Peter and St Paul. For the Lord had told me, when He first appeared to me on their festival, that they would preserve me from being deceived. I used often to see them very clearly, on my left, and that was no imaginary vision. These glorious saints were my very true lords.

The duty of snapping my fingers when I had this vision of the Lord deeply distressed me. For when I saw Him before me, I would willingly have been hacked to death rather than believe that this was of the devil. It was a heavy kind of penance for me, and so that I need not be so continually crossing myself, I used to go about with a crucifix in my hand. I carried it almost continually, but I did not snap my fingers very often, because that hurt me too much. It reminded me of the insults He had suffered from the Jews, and I begged Him to pardon me, since I was only acting out of obedience to one who was in His place, and not to blame me, seeing that he was one of the ministers whom He had Himself placed in His Church. He told me not to worry, since I was quite right to obey, and that He would Himself show them the truth. When they forbade me to pray, He seemed to me to be angry. He told me to say to them that this was tyranny. He showed me ways of making sure that these visions were not of the devil, and I will give some of them later.

Once when I was holding the cross of a rosary in my hand, He took it from me into His own; and when He returned it to me, it consisted of four large stones much more precious than diamonds—incomparably so for it is, of course, impossible to make comparisons between things seen supernaturally and the precious stones of this world; diamonds seem imperfect counterfeits beside the precious stones of a vision. On these were exquisitely incised the five wounds of Christ. He told me that henceforth this cross would appear so to me always, and so it has. I have never been able to see the wood of which it was made but only these stones. However, they have been seen by no one but myself. Once they started telling me to test my visions and resist them, these favours became much more frequent. In my efforts to divert my attention, I never ceased praying, and I seemed to be in a state of prayer even when asleep. For now my love was growing, and I would complain to the Lord, saying that I could not bear it. But desire and strive though I might to cease thinking of Him, it was beyond my power; I was as obedient as possible in every way, but I could do little or nothing about it. The Lord never released me from my obedience. But though He told me to do as I was told, He reassured me in another way by telling me how to answer my critics; and this He

still does. The arguments He gave me were so strong that I felt perfectly secure.

Shortly afterwards, His Majesty began, as He had promised, to make it even plainer that it was He. There grew so great a love of God within me that I did not know who had planted it there. It was entirely supernatural; I had made no efforts to obtain it. I found myself dying of the desire to see God, and I knew no way of seeking that other life except through death. This love came to me in mighty impulses which, although less unbearable and less valuable than those that I have described before, robbed me of all power of action. Nothing gave me satisfaction, and I could not contain myself; I really felt as if my soul were being torn from me. O supreme cunning of the Lord, with what delicate skill did You work on Your miserable slave! You hid Yourself from me, and out of Your love You afflicted me with so delectable a death that my soul desired it never to cease.

No one who has not experienced these mighty impulses can possibly understand that this is no emotional unrest, nor one of those fits of uncontrollable devotion that frequently occur and seem to overwhelm the spirit. These are very low forms of prayer. Indeed, such quickenings should be checked by a gentle endeavour to become recollected, and to calm the soul. Such prayer is like the violent sobbing of children. They seem to be going to choke, but their rush of emotion is immediately checked if they are given something to drink. In the same way here, reason must step in and take command, for this may merely be a display of temperament. With reflection there comes a fear that there is some imperfection here, which may be largely physical. So the child must be quieted with a loving caress, which will draw out its love in a gentle way and not, as they say, bludgeon it. This love must flow into interior reflection, not boil over like a cooking-pot that has been put on too fierce a fire, and so spills its contents. The source of the fire must be controlled. An endeavour must be made to quench its flames with gentle tears, and not with that painful weeping that springs from the feelings I have described, and does so much damage. I used at first to shed tears of this kind which left my mind so confused and my spirit so weary that I was not fit to resume my prayers for a day or more. Great discretion is needed at first, therefore, so that everything may go on smoothly, and so that spiritual transformations may take place within. All exterior demonstrations should be carefully prevented.

The true impulses are very different. We do not pile the wood beneath the fire ourselves; it is rather as if it were already burning and we were suddenly thrown in to be consumed. The soul makes no effort to feel the pain caused it by the Lord's presence, but is pierced to the depths of its entrails, or sometimes to the heart, by an arrow, so that it does not know what is wrong or what it desires. It knows quite well that it desires God, and that the arrow seems to have been tipped with some poison which makes it so hate itself out of love of the Lord that it is willing to give up its life for Him. It is impossible to describe or explain the way in which God wounds the soul, or the very great pain He inflicts on it, so that it hardly knows what it is doing. But this is so sweet a pain that no delight in the whole world can be more pleasing. The soul, as I have said, would be glad always to be dying of this ill.

This combination of joy and sorrow so bewildered me that I could not understand how such a thing could be. O what it is to see a soul wounded! I mean one that sufficiently understands its condition as to be able to call itself wounded, and for so excellent a cause. It clearly sees that this love has come to it through no action of its own, but that out of the very great love that the Lord has for it a spark seems suddenly to have fallen on it and set it all on fire. O how often, when I am in this state,

do I remember that verse of David, *As the heart panteth after the water brooks,*[1] which I seem to see literally fulfilled in myself.

When these impulses are not very strong, things appear to calm down a little, or at least the soul seeks some respite, for it does not know what to do. It performs certain penances, but hardly feels them; even if it draws blood it is no more conscious of pain than if the body were dead. It seeks ways and means to express some of its feelings for the love of God, but its initial pain is so great that I know of no physical torture that could drown it. Such medicines can bring no relief; they are on too low a level for so high a disease. But there is some alleviation and a little of the pain passes if the soul prays God to give it some remedy for its suffering, though it can see no way except death by which it can expect to enjoy its blessing complete. But there are other times when the impulses are so strong that it can do absolutely nothing. The entire body contracts; neither foot nor arm can be moved. If one is standing at the time, one falls into a sitting position as though transported, and cannot even take a breath. One only utters a few slight moans, not aloud, for that is impossible, but inwardly, out of pain.

Our Lord was pleased that I should sometimes see a vision of this kind. Beside me, on the left hand, appeared an angel in bodily form, such as I am not in the habit of seeing except very rarely. Though I often have visions of angels, I do not see them. They come to me only after the manner of the first type of vision that I described. But it was our Lord's will that I should see this angel in the following way. He was not tall but short, and very beautiful; and his face was so aflame that he appeared to be one of the highest rank of angels, who seem to be all on fire. They must be of the kind

---

[1]Psalm xlii [Vulg. xli].

called cherubim, but they do not tell me their names. I know very well that there is a great difference between some angels and others, and between these and others still, but I could not possibly explain it. In his hands I saw a great golden spear, and at the iron tip there appeared to be a point of fire. This he plunged into my heart several times so that it penetrated to my entrails. When he pulled it out, I felt that he took them with it, and left me utterly consumed by the great love of God. The pain was so severe that it made me utter several moans. The sweetness caused by this intense pain is so extreme that one cannot possibly wish it to cease, nor is one's soul then content with anything but God. This is not a physical, but a spiritual pain, though the body has some share in it—even a considerable share. So gentle is this wooing which takes place between God and the soul that if anyone thinks I am lying, I pray God, in His goodness, to grant him some experience of it.

Throughout the days that this lasted I went about in a kind of stupor. I had no wish to look or to speak, only to embrace my pain, which was a greater bliss than all created things could give me. On several occasions when I was in this state the Lord was pleased that I should experience raptures so deep that I could not resist them even though I was not alone. Greatly to my distress, therefore, my raptures began to be talked about. Since I have had them, I have ceased to feel this pain so much, though I still feel the pain that I spoke of in a previous chapter—I do not remember which.[2] The latter is very different in many respects, and much more valuable. But when this pain of which I am now speaking begins, the Lord seems to transport the soul and throw it into an ecstasy. So there is no opportunity for it to feel its pain or suffering, for the enjoyment comes immediately. May He be blessed for ever, who has granted so many favours to one who has so ill repaid these great benefits.

from *The Way of Perfection*

CHAPTER IV[3]

An exhortation to obey the Rule. Three very important matters in the spiritual life. One must strive after sublime perfection in order to accomplish so great an enterprise. How to practise prayer.

1. *The greatness of the work we have undertaken.* 2. *Prayer.* 3. *The three principal aids to prayer.* 4. *The evils of particular friendships.* 5. *Special danger of these in a small community.* 6. *Precautions against them.* 7. *Mutual charity.* 8. *Natural and supernatural love.* 9. *How to regard our confessors.* 10. *Discretion in our intercourse with them.* 11. *When a second confessor is*

needed. 12. *Precautions against worldly confessors.* 13. *Evils caused by unsuitable confessors.*

1. You see upon how great an enterprise you have embarked for the sake of the Father Provincial, the Bishop of the diocese, and of your Order, in which all else is included, all being for the good of the Church, for which we are bound to pray as a matter of obligation. As I said, what lives are not those bound to live who have had the courage to engage in this design, if they would not be confounded, before God and man, for their audacity? Clearly we must work hard; it is a great help to have high aspirations: by their means we may cause

---

[3]Valladolid edition, ch. iv.; Escorial, ch. v.

[2]Chapter 20.

our actions to become great also, although there are different ways of doing so. If we endeavour to observe our Rule and Constitutions very faithfully, I hope that God will grant our petitions. I ask of you nothing new, my daughters, but only that we should keep what we have professed, as we are bound to do, although there are very diverse ways of observing it.

2. The very first chapter of our Rule bids us "Pray without ceasing"[4]. we must obey this with the greatest perfection possible, for it is our most important duty: then we shall not neglect the fasts, penances, and silence enjoined by the Rule. As you know, these are necessary if the prayer is to be genuine; prayer and self-indulgence do not go together. Prayer is the subject you have asked me to speak of: I beg of you, in return, to practise and to read, again and again, what I have already told you. Before speaking of spiritual matters, that is, of prayer. I will mention some things that must be done by those who intend to lead a life of prayer. These are so necessary that, with their help, a person who can hardly be called a contemplative may make great progress in serving God, but without them none can be a thorough contemplative: any one who imagined that she was so, would be much mistaken. May our Lord give me His grace for this task and teach me what to say that may be for His glory.[5]

3. Do not fancy, my friends and my sisters, that I am going to lay many charges on you: please God we may fulfil those that our holy Fathers enjoined and practised in our Rules and Constitutions, which include all the virtues and by performing

which our predecessors earned the name of Saints. It would be an error to seek another road or to try to learn some other way. I will explain three matters only, which are in our Constitutions : it is essential for us to understand how much they help us to preserve that peace, both interior and exterior, which our Lord so strongly enjoined. The first of these is love for one another: the second, detachment from all created things: the other is true humility, which, though I mention it last, is chief of all and includes the rest.[6] The first matter, that is, mutual charity, is most important, for there is no annoyance that cannot easily be borne by those who love one another: anything must be very out of the way to cause irritation. If this commandment were observed in this world as it ought to be, I believe it would be a great help towards obeying the others, but whether we err by excess or by defect, we only succeed in keeping it imperfectly.

4. You may think there can be no harm in excessive love for one another, but no one would believe what evil and imperfections spring from this source unless they had seen it for themselves. The devil sets many snares here which are hardly detected by those who are content to serve God in a superficial way—indeed, they take such conduct for virtue—those, however, who are bent on perfection understand the evil clearly, for, little by little it deprives the will of strength to devote itself entirely to the love of God. I think this injures women even more than men, and does serious damage to the community. It prevents a nun from loving all the others equally, makes her resent any injury done to her friend, causes her to wish she had something to give her favourite and to seek for opportunities to talk to her often, and tell her how

---

[4]*Rule* 5: "Meditating on the law of the Lord day and night, and watching in prayer."
[5]Escorial edition. I.H.S. Ch. vi. Urges the nuns to practise three things. Speaks of the first, that is, the love of our neighbour and of the evil of particular friendships.

[6]Valladolid edition, ch. v. Speaks of the first of these three subjects, namely, the love of our own neighbour, and of the evils of particular friendships.

much she loves her, and other nonsense of the sort, rather than of how much she loves God. These close friendships rarely serve to forward the love of God; in fact, I believe the devil originates them so as to make factions among the religious. When a friendship has the service of God for its object, it is at once manifest that the will is not only uninfluenced by passion but it rather helps to subdue the other passions.

5. In a large convent I permit such friendships, but in St. Joseph's, where there are, and can be, no more than thirteen nuns, all must love and help one another. Keep free of partialities, for the love of God, however holy they may be, for even among brothers they are like poison. I can see no advantage in them, and matters are far worse when they exist between relatives, for then they are a perfect pest. Believe me, sisters, though I may seem to you severe in excluding these attachments, yet this promotes high perfection and quiet peace, and weak souls are spared dangerous occasions. If we are inclined to care for one person more than another (which cannot be helped, for it is but human, and we often prefer the most faulty if they have more natural charm) let us control our likings firmly, and not allow ourselves to be overmastered by our affections.

6. Let us love virtue and holiness and always try to prevent ourselves from being attracted by externals, O my sisters, let us not permit our will to become the slave of any save of Him Who purchased it with His Blood, or, without knowing how, we shall find ourselves caught in a trap from which we cannot escape! Lord have mercy upon us! the childish nonsense that comes from this is untold, and is so petty that no one could credit it who had not witnessed the thing. It is best not to speak of it here, lest women's foibles should be learnt by those who know nothing about them, so I will give no

details, although they astonish even me at times. By the mercy of God, I have never been entangled in such things myself, but perhaps this may be because I have fallen into far graver faults. However, as I have said, I have often seen it, but as I told you, in a Superior it would be ruinous. In order to guard against these partialities, great care must be taken from the very first, and this more by watchfulness and kindness than by severity. A most useful precaution is for the nuns, according to our present habit, never to be with one another nor talk together except at the appointed times, but as the Rule enjoins, for the sisters not to be together but each one alone in her cell.[7] Let there be no common work-room in St. Joseph's, for although this is a praiseworthy custom, silence is better kept when one is alone. Solitude is very helpful to persons who practise prayer, and since prayer is the mortar which keeps this house together, we must learn to like what promotes it.[8]

7. To return to speak of our charity for one another. It seems superfluous to insist on this, for who would be so boorish as not to love those with whom they associate and live, cut off as they are from all conversation, intercourse and recreation with any one outside the house, whilst believing that they bear a mutual love for God, as He has for all of them, since for His sake they have left everything? More especially as goodness always attracts love, and, by the blessing of God, I trust that the runs of this convent will always be good. Therefore, I do not think there is much need for me to persuade you to love each other. But as regards the nature of this love and of the virtuous love that I wish you all to feel, and the means of knowing whether we possess this greatest of virtues—for it must be a very great virtue since our Lord so often enjoins it on us,

---

[7] *Rule* 5.
[8] *Rule* 14. *Const.* 5.

as He did most stringently upon His apostles—of this I will speak to you for a short time as well as my inaptitude will allow. If you find the matter explained in any other books, you need not read mine, for I very frequently do not understand what I am talking about, unless our Lord enlightens me.[9]

8.   I intend treating of two kinds of love: one which is entirely spiritual, free from any sort of affection or natural tenderness which could tarnish its purity, and another which is spiritual but mingled with the frailty and weakness of human nature. The latter is good and seems lawful, being such as is felt between relatives and friends, and is that which I have mentioned before. The first of these two ways of loving, and the one that I will discuss, is unmixed with any kind of passion that would disturb its harmony. This love, exercised with moderation and discretion, is profitable in every way, particularly when borne towards holy people or confessors, for that which seems only natural is then changed into virtue.[10] At times, however, these two kinds of love seem so combined that it is difficult to distinguish them from one another, especially as regards a confessor.

When persons who practise prayer discover that their confessor is a holy man who understands their spiritual state, they feel a strong affection for him; the devil then opens a perfect battery of scruples on the soul, which, as he intends, greatly disturb it, especially if the priest is leading his penitent to higher perfection. Then the evil one torments his victim to such a pitch that she leaves her director, so that the temptation gives her no peace either in one way or the other.

9.   In such a case it is best not to think about whether you like you confessor or not, or whether you wish to like him. If we feel friendship for those who benefit our bodies, why should we not feel as great a friendship for those who strive and labour to benefit our souls? On the contrary, I think a liking for my confessor is a great help to my progress if he is holy and spiritual, and if I see that he endeavours to profit my soul. Human nature is so weak that this feeling is often a help to our undertaking great things in God's service.

10.   If, however, the confessor be a man of indifferent character, we must not let him know of our liking for him. Great prudence and caution are necessary on account of the difficulty of knowing his disposition: it is best, on this account, to conceal our feelings from him. You should believe that your friendship for him is harmless and think no more about it. You may follow this advice when you see that all your confessor says tends to profit your soul and when you discover no levity in him, but are conscious that he lives in the fear of God: any one can detect this at once unless she wilfully blinds herself. If this be so, do not allow any temptation to trouble you about your liking for him—despise it, think no more about it, and the devil will grow tired and leave you alone. If, however, the confessor appears worldly-minded, be most guarded in every way; do not talk with him even when he converses on religious subjects, but make your confession briefly and say no more. It would be best to tell the Prioress that he does not suit your soul and to ask for some one else; this is the wisest course to take if it is possible, and can be done without injuring his reputation. I trust in God that it may be feasible for you.

11.   In these and other difficulties by which the devil may seek to ensnare us, it would be best, when you are doubtful as to what course to pursue,

---

[9]*Castle*, M. v. ch. iii. 12. Escorial edition, ch. vii. Speaks of two kinds of love and the importance of understanding what constitutes spiritual affection.
[10]*Life*, ch. xxxvii. 6; ch. xl. 24. *Rel.* ii. 8.

for you to consult some learned person, as the nuns are permitted to do,[11] to make your confession to him, and to follow his advice in the case, lest some great mistake should be made in remedying the evil. How many people go astray in the world for want of seeking guidance, especially in what affects their neighbours' interests! Some redress must be sought, for when the devil starts such works, unless he is stopped at once, the matter will become serious, therefore my advice about changing confessors is the best, and I trust in God that you will be able to do so.

12. Be convinced of the importance of this: the thing is dangerous, a hell in itself, and injurious to every one. Do not wait until much harm has come of it, but stop the matter at once in every feasible way: this may be done with a clear conscience. I trust, however, that God will prevent those vowed to a life of prayer from becoming attached to any one who does not serve God fervently, as He certainly will, unless they omit to practise prayer and to strive after perfection, as we profess to do in this house. If the nuns see that the confessor does not understand their language nor cares to speak of God, they cannot like him, for he differs from

---

[11] *Castle*, M. vi. ch. viii. 10, 11. *Found.* ch. xix. 1.

them. If he is of such a character, he will have extremely few chances of doing any harm here, and unless he is very foolish he will neither trouble himself about the servants of God, nor disturb those who have few pleasures and little or no opportunity of following their own way.

13. Since I have begun speaking on this subject, I may say that this is the only harm, or at any rate the greatest harm, that the devil can do within enclosed convents. It takes long to discover, so that great damage may have been wrought to perfection without any one knowing how, for if the confessor is worldly himself, he will treat the defect lightly in others. Deliver us, O Lord, for Thine own sake, from such misfortunes!

It is enough to unsettle all the nuns if their conscience tells them one thing and their confessor another. Where they are allowed no other director I do not know what to do, nor how to quiet their minds, for he who ought to bring them peace and counsel is the very author of the evil. There must be a great deal of trouble, resulting in much harm, in some places from these misplaced partialities, as I have seen in certain convents to my great sorrow, therefore you need not be surprised at the pains I have taken to make you understand the danger.

chapter thirteen

Saint John of the Cross

Juan de Yepes y Alvarez, Saint John of the Cross (1542–1591), was born in Fontiveros, near Ávila, and, after his father's death, grew up in straitened circumstances. After a Jesuit education, he entered a Carmelite monastery in his early twenties, received university training at Salamanca, and was ordained a priest. He met Teresa of Ávila the year that he completed his studies at Salamanca, shortly after she received permission to establish a house for the reformed Carmelites. His association with her was the decisive turning point of his life, and together they underwent the fluctuations of official approval and subsequent disapproval of the reform movement. He was vicar at a number of monasteries of the discalced Carmelites, the reform movement that Teresa initiated—barefoot monks and nuns, living for the most part in solitary contemplation, serious about their vows of poverty. He became involved in internal disputes and was even imprisoned for a time by "unreformed" shod Carmelites.

Some of his most famous poems date from these prison years, and several of his prose works start out as exegetical elaborations of the poems. Many poems center on images that are contradictory in their metaphoric weight: the "night of the soul" which is both the time of personal despair and the locus of spiritual union and bliss, where all petty distinctions are obliterated; the "flame of love" which consumes and creates at the same time. The poems give lucid body to the threefold path of mystical enlightenment that John of the Cross also elaborated in prose: the *via negativa* or way of purgation, the way of illumination, and the *unio mystica* or road of mystical union.

The pendular paradox of love is captured in his poem "Love is an I know not what":[1]

> Love is an I know not what,
> Which comes from I know not where,
> Which enters I know not how,
> And kills with I know not what.
> It is a delicate touch,
> Which touches noiselessly

And sometimes robs you of your senses,
Without your sensing how it touched,
Without knowing how it was,
It moves toward I know not where
And kills with I know not what.
It always remains still,
But, at once, should it so desire,
It moves just like the fire
To the depths of the sky above,
But even when it's still,
Even then I know not where;
And it moves I know not where
And it kills with I know not what.
It inflicts a divine wound
Which brings on a glorious death;
I know not what fortune this
For him who dies and stays with life.
God is seen and he is not,
He hides I know not how,
And enters I know not where
and kills with I know not what.[2]

Traditional theological distinctions, controversial in themselves, between love as friendship (*philía*), love as passionate desire (*eros*) and divine, unconditional love (*agápe*) are blurred in St. John's version of love and death.

John of the Cross in another poem plays the dual pull of death:

I live in myself without living
And in such a way that I hope
That I am dying because I am not dying.[3]

Death and love transform in radical ways. Symbolic death in a union with God obliterates boundaries. The social conventions of both heterosexual and homosexual love—most notably in the Greek "pederastic" practice of an adult lover and teenage beloved—draw sharp lines between the active and the passive, the pursuing male and evading female, the lover and the beloved.[4] But in the "dark night of the soul," all this petty social-human is transcended:

Oh, night that guided me, Oh night more lovely than the dawn,
Oh, night that joined Beloved with lover, Lover transformed in the Beloved![5]

Death and the dark night do not simply represent the "morbid underworld," but the vitality of transcendence.

Mysticism is, in a sense, more a tendency than a doctrine or a movement, a tendency found in most of the world's religions and sometimes outside them. The word comes from Greek meaning "shut the eyes," and was used for initiations in "mystery religions" of antiquity. The term is difficult to define because mystics themselves so frequently use indirect and metaphorical language to describe their experience. Not only is the language of the mystics poetical, but its terms will often merge logical and apparent opposites. Thus light and night, desert and oasis, winter and spring, abyss and mountaintop may be introduced as contrasts and then absorbed into a unity of meaning. In this vein Cardinal Nicholas of Cusa (1401–1464)—and, following him, Blaise Pascal (1623–1662)—spoke of God as a "coincidence of opposites," or, more precisely, in Cusanus's phrase, God is "the being beyond the wall of the coincidence of opposites."[6] Since Cusanus and Pascal were among the most eminent mathematicians of their times—Cusanus a prominent fifteenth-century Platonist and Pascal an important seventeenth-century physicist and inventor of probability theory—it is clear that they were not simply dismissive of all linear logic, science, and rational procedure. Rather they laid out boundaries for the respective domains of discursive and intuitive thinking and feeling. According to Pascal, the "spirit of geometry" is appropriate and successful in the mathematical and physical realms, but the "spirit of finesse" is required in approaching the mysterious contradictions of God and man.[7]

The theme of the ascent—the "path to perfection," the "ladder of love," the "road to union"—is the common property of philosophical theory and religious experience. The image of the philosophic visionary drawn up into a higher realm appears in Greek philosophy as early as Parmenides. Plato's *Symposium* and *Phaedrus* provide related, but quite different versions of philosophical ascent.[8] The theme is carried forward in explications of Christian conversion, neo-Platonic versions of philosophical initiation, and the whirling dance of Sufi dervishes in Persia. In both the *Symposium* and the *Phaedrus*, the soul rises in the context of love and through the impetus of love. Eros (Cupid) is regularly depicted with wings, because love "flies" and makes us "fly." The boundaries separating philosophical ascent, erotic ecstasy, and spiritual transport seem to dissolve in the mystic poetry and thought of both Saints Teresa and John of the Cross.

JHS

QUESTIONS

1. In what sense is the soul in a "dark night"?
2. What is John abandoning in his love for the Beloved?
3. What are the reasons that mystics and others claim that there are two fundamentally different ways of knowing, of which mystical experience represents one way? What is the other way? Do you think that both ways can be valid?

ENDNOTES

1. The motif of the "Je ne sais quoi" ("Yo no sé qué" or "I don't know what") was a commonplace of the era, sometimes used casually—as in titles of musical movements that did not fit standard dance repertoire—and sometimes with a metaphysical profundity betokening the mysterious secrets of the divinity.

2. San Juan de la Cruz, "Definición del amor," from *Poesías completas*, pp. 113–14 (attributed to St. John).

3. "Coplas del alma que pena por ver a Dios" and "Definición del amor" from *Poesías completas*, p. 67. The first phrase is ambiguous, also meaning "I live without living in myself"—the apparent contrary. Note how close this is to the poem by Saint Teresa quoted on p. 189.

4. In classical Athens, at least for the upper classes, males were dominant and expected to be "aggressive" in heterosexual and marital relations. However there was also a typical pattern of pederasty among the same "heterosexual" males, in which an adult married male pursued a teenage boy. The proprieties of these latter relationships involved a strict differentiation of the roles of the lover and the beloved. Permanent and equal "homosexual" relations between males or females were typically scorned.

5. St. John of the Cross, "Dark Night (Canciones del alma, que se goza de haber leegado al alto estado de la perfección, que es la unión con Dios, por el camino de la negación espiritual)," from *Dark Night of the Soul*, p. 33.

6. Cf. Nicholas of Cusa, *The Vision of God*, ch. 9; cf. Nicolas Cusanus, *Of Learned Ignorance*, Book I, ch. 22.

7. Cf. Pascal, I, 1–3; III, 234; 277, etc. (Brunschvicg numbering).

8. Cf. chapter 3 of this text.

SELECTED BIBLIOGRAPHY

Nicholas of Cusa. *The Vision of God*, trans. Emma Gurney Salter, intro. Evelyn Underhill. New York: Frederick Ungar Publishing Co., 1960 (1928).

Nicolas Cusanus, *Of Learned Ignorance*, intro. D.J.B. Hawkins, trans. Germain Heron. London: Routledge & Kegan Paul, 1954.

Otto, Rudolf. *Mysticism East and West: A Comparative Analysis of the Nature of Mysticism*, trans. Bertha L. Bracy and Richenda C. Payne. New York: Meridian Books, 1957 (1932).

Pascal, Blaise. *Pensées*, trans. W. F. Trotter. New York: Random House (Modern Library), 1941.

Peers, E. Allison. *Handbook to the Life and Times of St. Teresa and St. John of the Cross*. London: Burns, Oates, 1954.

St. John of the Cross. *Dark Night of the Soul*, trans. E. Allison Peers. Garden City, N.Y.: Doubleday & Co., 1959.

San Juan de la Cruz. "Definición del amor," from *Poesías completas*, trans. James H. Stam, ed. Luis Guarner. Barcelona, Spain: Editorial Fama, 1955.

Wojtyla, Karol (Pope John Paul II). *Faith According to St. John of the Cross*, trans. Jordan Aumann. San Francisco, Calif.: Ignatius Press, 1981.

from *Dark Night of the Soul*

Saint John of the Cross

DARK NIGHT

Exposition of the stanzas describing the method followed by the soul in its journey upon the spiritual road to the attainment of the perfect union of love with God, to the extent that is possible in this life. Likewise are described the properties belonging to the soul that has attained to the said perfection, according as they are contained in the same stanzas.

PROLOGUE

In this book are first set down all the stanzas which are to be expounded; afterwards, each of the stanzas is expounded separately, being set down before its exposition; and then each line is expounded separately and in turn, the line itself also being set down before the exposition. In the first two stanzas are expounded the effects of the two spiritual purgations: of the sensual part of man and of the spiritual part. In the other six are expounded various and wondrous effects of the spiritual illumination and union of love with God.

Stanzas of the Soul

1. On a dark night, Kindled in love with yearnings—oh, happy chance!—
   I went forth without being observed, My house being now at rest.
2. In darkness and secure, By the secret ladder, disguised—oh, happy chance!—
   In darkness and in concealment, My house being now at rest.
3. In the happy night, In secret, when none saw me,

Nor I beheld aught, Without light or guide, save that which burned in my heart.
4. This light guided me More surely than the light of noonday
   To the place where he (well I knew who!) was awaiting me—
   A place where none appeared.
5. Oh, night that guided me, Oh, night more lovely than the dawn,
   Oh, night that joined Beloved with lover, Lover transformed in the Beloved!
6. Upon my flowery breast, Kept wholly for himself alone,
   There he stayed sleeping, and I caressed him, And the fanning of the cedars made a breeze.
7. The breeze blew from the turret As I parted his locks;
   With his gentle hand he wounded my neck And caused all my senses to be suspended.
8. I remained, lost in oblivion; My face I reclined on the Beloved.
   All ceased and I abandoned myself, Leaving my cares forgotten among the lilies.

Begins the exposition of the stanzas which treat of the way and manner which the soul follows upon the road of the union of love with God.

Before we enter upon the exposition of these stanzas, it is well to understand here that the soul that utters them is now in the state of perfection, which is the union of love with God, having already passed through severe trials and straits, by means of spiritual exercise in the narrow way of eternal life whereof Our Saviour speaks in the Gospel, along which way the soul ordinarily passes in order to reach this high and happy union with God. Since this road (as the Lord Himself says likewise) is so strait, and since there are so few that enter by it,[1] the soul considers it a great happiness and good chance to have passed along it to the said perfection of love, as it sings in this first stanza, calling this strait road with full propriety 'dark night,' as will be explained hereafter in the lines of the said stanza. The soul, then, rejoicing at having passed along this narrow road whence so many blessings have come to it, speaks after this manner.

CHAPTER XIX

Begins to explain the ten steps[2] of the mystic ladder of Divine love, according to Saint Bernard and Saint Thomas. The first five are here treated.

We observe, then, that the steps of this ladder of love by which the soul mounts, one by one, to God, are ten. The first step of love causes the soul to languish, and this to its advantage. The Bride is speaking from this step of love when she says: 'I adjure you, daughters of Jerusalem, that, if ye find my Beloved, ye tell Him that I am sick with love.'[3] This sickness, however, is not unto death, but for the glory of God, for in this sickness the soul swoons as to sin and as to all things that are not God, for the sake of God Himself, even as David testifies, saying: 'My soul hath swooned away'[4]— that is, with respect to all things, for Thy salvation. For just as a sick man first of all loses his appetite and taste for all food, and his colour changes, so likewise in this degree of love the soul loses its taste and desire for all things and changes its colour and the other accidentals of its past life, like one in

love. The soul falls not into this sickness if excess of heat be not communicated to it from above, even as is expressed in that verse of David which says: *Pluviam voluntariam segregabis, Deus, hæreditati tuæ, et infirmata est,*[5] etc. This sickness and swooning to all things, which is the beginning and the first step on the road to God, we clearly described above, when we were speaking of the annihilation wherein the soul finds itself when it begins to climb[6] this ladder of contemplative purgation, when it can find no pleasure, support, consolation or abiding-place in anything soever. Wherefore from this step it begins at once to climb to the second.

2. The second step causes the soul to seek God without ceasing. Wherefore, when the Bride says that she sought Him by night upon her bed (when she had swooned away according to the first step of love) and found Him not, she said: 'I will arise and will seek Him Whom my soul loveth.'[7] This, as we say, the soul does without ceasing, as David counsels it, saying: 'Seek ye ever the face of God, and seek ye Him in all things, tarrying not until ye find Him;'[8] like the Bride, who, having enquired for Him of the watchmen, passed on at once and left them. Mary Magdalene did not even notice the angels at the sepulchre. On this step the soul now walks so anxiously that it seeks the Beloved in all things. In whatsoever it thinks, it thinks at once of the Beloved. Of whatsoever it speaks, in whatsoever matters present themselves, it is speaking and communing at once with the Beloved. When it eats, when it sleeps, when it watches, when it does aught soever, all its care is about the Beloved, as is said above with respect to the yearnings of love. And now, as love begins to recover its health and

---

[1]St. Matthew vii, 14.

[2][The word translated 'step' may also (and often more elegantly) be rendered 'degree.' The same word is kept, however, throughout the translation of this chapter except where noted below.]

[3]Canticles v, 8.

[4]Psalm cxlii, 7 [A.V., cxliii, 7].

---

[5]Psalm lxvii, 10 [A.V., lxviii, 9].

[6][*Lit.*, 'to enter (upon).']

[7]Canticles iii, 2.

[8]Psalm civ, 4 [A.V., cv, 4].

find new strength in the love of this second step, it begins at once to mount to the third, by means of a certain degree[9] of new purgation in the night, as we shall afterwards describe, which produces in the soul the following effects.

3. The third step of the ladder of love is that which causes the soul to work and gives it fervour so that it fails not. Concerning this the royal Prophet says: 'Blessed is the man that feareth the Lord, for in His commandments he is eager to labour greatly.'[10] Wherefore if fear, being the son of love, causes within him this eagerness to labour, what will be done by love itself? On this step the soul considers great works undertaken for the Beloved as small; many things as few; and the long time for which it serves Him as short, by reason of the fire of love wherein it is now burning. Even so to Jacob, though after seven years he had been made to serve seven more, they seemed few because of the greatness of his love.[11] Now if the love of a mere creature could accomplish so much in Jacob, what will love of the Creator be able to do when on this third step it takes possession of the soul? Here, for the great love which the soul bears to God, it suffers great pains and afflictions because of the little that it does for God; and if it were lawful for it to be destroyed a thousand times for Him it would be comforted. Wherefore it considers itself useless in all that it does and thinks itself to be living in vain. Another wondrous effect produced here in the soul is that it considers itself as being, most certainly, worse than all other souls: first, because love is continually teaching it how much is due to God; and second, because, as the works which it here does for God are many and it knows them all to be faulty and imperfect, they all bring it confusion and affliction, for it realizes in

how lowly a manner it is working for God, Who is so high. On this third step, the soul is very far from vainglory or presumption, and from condemning others. These anxious effects, with many others like them, are produced in the soul by this third step, wherefore it gains courage and strength from them in order to mount to the fourth step, which is that that follows.

4. The fourth step of this ladder of love is that whereby there is caused in the soul an habitual suffering because of the Beloved, yet without weariness. For, as Saint Augustine says, love makes all things that are great, grievous and burdensome to be almost naught. From this step the Bride was speaking when, desiring to attain to the last step, she said to the Spouse: 'Set me as a seal upon thy heart, as a seal upon thine arm; for love—that is, the act and work of love—is strong as death, and emulation and importunity last as long as hell.'[12] The spirit here has so much strength that it has subjected the flesh and takes as little account of it as does the tree of one of its leaves. In no way does the soul here seek its own consolation or pleasure, either in God, or in aught else, nor does it desire or seek to pray to God for favours, for it sees clearly that it has already received enough of these, and all its anxiety is set upon the manner wherein it will be able to do something that it pleasing to God and to render Him some service such as He merits and in return for what it has received from Him, although it be greatly to its cost. The soul says in its heart and spirit: Ah, my God and Lord! How many are there that go to seek in Thee their own consolation and pleasure, and desire Thee to grant them favours and gifts; but those who long to do Thee pleasure and to give Thee something at their cost, setting their own interests last, are very few. The failure, my God, is not in Thy unwillingness to grant us new favours, but in our neglect to use

---

[9][The word in the Spanish is that elsewhere translated 'step.']
[10]Psalm cxi, 1 [A.V., cxii, 1].
[11]Genesis xxix, 20.

[12]Canticles viii, 5.

those that we have received in Thy service alone, in order to constrain Thee to grant them to us continually. Exceeding lofty is this step of love; for, as the soul goes ever after God with love so true, imbued with the spirit of suffering for His sake, His Majesty oftentimes and quite habitually grants it joy, and visits it sweetly and delectably in the spirit; for the boundless love of Christ, the Word, cannot suffer the afflictions of His lover without succouring him. This He affirmed through Jeremias, saying: 'I have remembered thee, pitying thy youth and tenderness, when thou wentest after Me in the wilderness.'[13] Speaking spiritually, this denotes the detachment which the soul now has interiorly from every creature, so that it rests not and nowhere finds quietness. This fourth step enkindles the soul and makes it to burn in such desire for God that it causes it to mount to the fifth, which is that which follows.

5. The fifth step of this ladder of love makes the soul to desire and long for God impatiently. On this step the vehemence of the lover to comprehend the Beloved and be united with Him is such that every delay, however brief, becomes very long, wearisome and oppressive to it, and it continually believes itself to be finding the Beloved. And when it sees its desire frustrated (which is at almost every moment), it swoons away with its yearning, as says the Psalmist, speaking from this step, in these words: 'My soul longs and faints for the dwellings of the Lord.'[14] On this step the lover must needs see that which he loves, or die; at this step was Rachel, when, for the great longing that she had for children, she said to Jacob, her spouse: 'Give me children, else shall I die.'[15] Here men suffer hunger like dogs and go about and surround the city of God. On this step, which is one of hunger,

the soul is nourished upon love; for, even as is its hunger, so is its abundance; so that it rises hence to the sixth step, producing the effects which follow.

CHAPTER XX

Wherein are treated the other five steps of love.

On the sixth step the soul runs swiftly to God and touches Him again and again; and it runs without fainting by reason of its hope. For here the love that has made it strong makes it to fly swiftly. Of this step the prophet Isaias speaks thus: 'The saints that hope in God shall renew their strength; they shall take wings as the eagle; they shall fly and shall not faint,'[16] as they did at the fifth step. To this step likewise alludes that verse of the Psalm: 'As the hart desires the waters, my soul desires Thee, O God.[17] For the hart, in its thirst, runs to the waters with great swiftness. The cause of this swiftness in love which the soul has on this step is that its charity is greatly enlarged within it, since the soul is here almost wholly purified, as is said likewise in the Psalm, namely: *Sine iniquitate cucurri*.[18] And in another Psalm: 'I ran the way of Thy commandments when Thou didst enlarge my heart',[19] and thus from this sixth step the soul at once mounts to the seventh, which is that which follows.

2. The seventh step of this ladder makes the soul to become vehement in its boldness. Here love employs not its judgment in order to hope, nor does it take counsel so that it may draw back, neither can any shame restrain it; for the favour which God here grants to the soul causes it to become vehement in its boldness. Hence follows that

---

[13]Jeremias ii, 2.
[14]Psalm lxxxiii, 2 [A. V., lxxxiv, 2].
[15]Genesis xxx, 1.

[16]Isaias xl, 31.
[17]Psalm xli, 2 [A. V., xlii, 1].
[18]Psalm lviii, 5 [A. V., lix, 4].
[19]Psalm cxviii, 32 [A. V., cxix, 32].

which the Apostle says, namely: That charity believeth all things, hopeth all things and is capable of all things.[20] Of this step spake Moses, when he entreated God to pardon the people, and if not, to blot out his name from the book of life wherein He had written it.[21] Men like these obtain from God that which they beg of Him with desire. Wherefore David says: 'Delight thou in God and He will give thee the petitions of thy heart.'[22] On this step the Bride grew bold, and said: *Osculetur me osculo oris sui.*[23] To this step it is not lawful for the soul to aspire boldly, unless it feel the interior favour of the King's sceptre extended to it, lest perchance it fall from the other steps which it has mounted up to this point, and wherein it must ever possess itself in humility. From this daring and power which God grants to the soul on this seventh step, so that it may be bold with God in the vehemence of love, follows the eighth, which is that wherein it takes the Beloved captive and is united with Him, as follows.

3. The eighth step of love causes the soul to seize Him and hold Him fast without letting Him go, even as the Bride says, after this manner: 'I found Him Whom my heart and soul love; I held Him and I will not let Him go.'[24] On this step of union the soul satisfies her desire, but not continuously. Certain souls climb some way, and then lose their hold; for, if this state were to continue, it would be glory itself in this life; and thus the soul remains therein for very short periods of time. To the prophet Daniel, because he was a man of desires, was sent a command from God to remain on this step, when it was said to him: 'Daniel, stay upon thy step, because thou art a man of desires.'[25]

After this step follows the ninth, which is that of souls now perfect, as we shall afterwards say, which is that that follows.

4. The ninth step of love makes the soul to burn with sweetness. This step is that of the perfect, who now burn sweetly in God. For this sweet and delectable ardour is caused in them by the Holy Spirit by reason of the union which they have with God. For this cause Saint Gregory says, concerning the Apostles, that when the Holy Spirit came upon them visibly they burned inwardly and sweetly through love. Of the good things and riches of God which the soul enjoys on this step, we cannot speak; for if many books were to be written concerning it the greater part would still remain untold. For this cause, and because we shall say something of it hereafter, I say no more here than that after this follows the tenth and last step of this ladder of love, which belongs not to this life.

5. The tenth and last step of this secret ladder of love causes the soul to become wholly assimilated to God, by reason of the clear and immediate vision of God which it then possesses; when, having ascended in this life to the ninth step, it goes forth from the flesh. These souls, who are few, enter not into purgatory, since they have already been wholly purged by love. Of these Saint Matthew says: *Beati mundo corde: quoniam ipsi Deum videbunt.*[26] And, as we say, this vision is the cause of the perfect likeness of the soul to God, for, as Saint John says, we know that we shall be like Him.[27] Not because the soul will come to have the capacity of God, for that is impossible; but because all that it is will become like to God, for which cause it will be called, and will be, God by participation.

6. This is the secret ladder whereof the soul here speaks, although upon these higher steps it is no

---

[20]Corinthians xiii, 7.
[21]Exodus xxxii, 31–2.
[22]Psalm xxxvi, 4.
[23]Canticles i, 1.
[24]Canticles iii, 4.
[25]Daniel x, 11.

[26]St. Matthew v, 8.
[27]1 St. John iii, 2.

longer very secret to the soul, since much is revealed to it by love, through the great effects which love produces in it. But, on this last step of clear vision, which is the last step of the ladder whereon God leans, as we have said already, there is naught that is hidden from the soul, by reason of its complete assimilation. Wherefore Our Saviour says: 'In that day ye shall ask Me nothing,' etc.[28] But, until that day, however high a point the soul may reach, there remains something hidden from it—namely, all that it lacks for total assimilation in the Divine Essence. After this manner, by this mystical theology and secret love, the soul continues to rise above all things and above itself, and to mount upward to God. For love is like fire, which ever rises upward with the desire to be absorbed in the centre of its sphere.

---

[28]St. John, xvi, 23.

chapter fourteen

René Descartes

René Descartes (1596–1650), French mathematician, philosopher, and physiologist, was foremost among the distinguished group of "new philosophers" (including Johannes Kepler, Galileo Galilei, and Sir Francis Bacon) credited with revolutionizing scientific thinking in the seventeenth century. Descartes is, in fact, called the father of modern philosophy, for it was he who laid the philosophical foundations for our "modern" scientific method—grounded in reason and the observation of a completely material and mechanical universe—that finally undermined the dogmatism of the medieval and Renaissance scholastic tradition. Descartes bequeathed to Modernity more than a new and more reliable approach to science, however. On the way to establishing the new science, he confronted a surprising "truth" that transformed the metaphysical foundations of his system: *Cogito ergo sum*, or I am thinking, therefore I exist. Initially a strict materialist, Descartes was now compelled to posit the existence of *two* kinds of entities: minds (or souls) as well as material bodies. Explaining intelligibly the mysterious nature of mind and its interactions with the body became a lifelong endeavor for Descartes without completely satisfying results; in fact, the problem of mind-body interaction has persisted into the twenty-first century. *The Passions of the Soul* (1649), included in this volume, is Descartes' noteworthy and admirable attempt to explain this most mysterious facet of human existence.

Descartes was born the son of a French nobleman in Touraine, in the small town of La Haye (now called La Haye–Descartes). Sent at age ten to the prestigious Jesuit college of La Flèche in Anjou, he received a classical scholastic training in a tradition devoted exclusively to reconciling ancient classical philosophy (particularly the teachings of Aristotle) to Christian doctrine. Descartes early discovered in this system many inadequacies (such as Aristotle's explanation that stones fall to the ground because they have a "propensity to fall to the ground"). He later wrote, "Of philosophy I shall only say that, aware that philosophy has been cultivated over several centuries by the most excellent minds who have ever lived . . . there is nothing about which there is not some dispute—and thus nothing that is not doubtful."[1]

Despite his dissatisfaction with scholastic teaching, Descartes studied voraciously, for he was unswervingly committed to apprehending truth. Being often in poor health, he was allowed to remain in bed every morning until eleven o'clock (a habit he sustained for most of his life). There he engaged in systematic meditation, mostly contemplating the stark contrast between the arbitrary scholastic sciences and the rigorous certainty of mathematics. Of the latter, he wrote, "Those long chains of reasoning, each of them simple and easy, that geometricians commonly use to attain their most difficult demonstrations, have given me occasion for imagining that all the things that can fall within human knowledge follow one another in the same way."[2] Descartes' conviction that the logical principles of mathematics could be applied to all sciences to yield equally certain results in all disciplines became the impetus for his revolutionary philosophy.

Descartes not only envisioned a universal logical method for solving all scientific problems, but he was certain that this method would facilitate the explanation of all natural phenomena in mathematical terms. He began with a conception of a completely material, mechanical universe; if all natural phenomena are bodies of matter, then they are *res extensa* (extended things) fully describable in terms of their measurable extended attributes: size, shape, and motion. Descartes ultimately conceived of the whole body of knowledge as a unified system that he compared to a tree: metaphysics forms the roots, physics is the trunk, and all of the specific sciences (falling ultimately under the general categories of mechanics, medicine, and morals) comprise the branches. All the disciplines can therefore be understood as connected by a common systematic scientific procedure.

Although these ideas were forming in Descartes' thinking before he left La Flèche in 1612, seven years would pass before he would pursue his theories seriously as a vocation. Instead, immediately upon graduating he "left the study of letters completely . . . resolving to search for no other knowledge than what I could find within myself, or in the great book of the world."[3] He would acquire knowledge by traveling, observing nature and the behaviors and customs of humanity, rather than rely upon the dubious body of "knowledge" recorded in books by men of letters. After earning a law degree in 1616, Descartes enlisted as a gentleman volunteer in the Dutch army. On November 10, 1619, while waiting out a snowstorm in Southern Germany in his now-famous "stove-heated room," he had a series of perplexing visions that sealed his decision to take up his vast project. Convinced that the visions were a sign that he must indeed begin to establish his scientific system, but still unclear about how *exactly* to proceed, Descartes began quite simply by deriving axioms upon which to develop the system correctly. He arrived at four: (1) never accept as true anything that can be doubted; (2) solve complex problems by dividing them into as many simple problems as needed to "solve them best;" (3) follow an orderly analytical procedure, always beginning with simple objects and concepts and progressing "by degrees" to the more complex; and (4) record each and every step so that one may always check one's work for accuracy.

Equipped with these axioms, but believing that at age twenty-three he lacked sufficient knowledge to found a new philosophy, Descartes resolved to continue his apprenticeship in the world in order to expand his knowledge while "exercising" his ability to adhere to the axioms. Nine years later he finally felt ready, and in 1628 he emigrated to Holland to compose, in seclusion, the series of works that would set a new agenda for all subsequent philosophy and science. There he both refined his scientific method and applied it to various disciplines, most notably algebra and geometry (establishing, for example, the Cartesian coordinate system for measuring distances in geometry).

By 1633 Descartes completed two major treatises. *De Homine* (*Of Man*) was Descartes' first description of the mechanisms he believed accounted for automatic bodily responses to external stimuli; for this he has generally been credited with the founding of reflex theory. The second treatise, *Le Monde* (The World) was concerned with cosmology and physics and rendered a comprehensive, explanatory account of the universe, which he conceived as being completely mechanical. Preparing to submit both manuscripts for publication, Descartes quickly suppressed them upon hearing of Galileo's condemnation by the Roman Inquisition. Galileo was sentenced to house arrest for his controversial rejection of the geocentric theory of the universe—a notion that Descartes also advanced in *Le Monde*.

Descartes finally published in 1637 a sample of his work—anonymously. The main body of the work consisted of three essays on *Geometry*, *Optics*, and *Meteorology*, which demonstrated the application of his new scientific method. The essays were prefaced by Descartes' philosophical classic, *Discourse on the Method of Rightly Conducting One's Reason and Reaching the Truth in the Sciences*, which outlines both the derivation and content of his method. Perhaps the most controversial section of the *Discourse on Method* is Part Four, in which Descartes discusses how, in the process of rejecting from his thought all things that can be doubted (according to his first axiom), he remained distinctly aware of only one certainty: *I am thinking, therefore I exist*. Descartes had aimed to show that we can describe the universe accurately without having to depend on our sense perceptions, which are often misleading. He systematically rejected from his system all sense-dependent propositions that can be doubted—even that his body existed, for he might only be dreaming, or an evil demon may deceive him into thinking he possesses a body. The only certainty that remained clearly and distinctly for Descartes was that he was thinking. The essence of his existence therefore lay exclusively in his possession of a thinking mind, independent of the evident presence of his body.

This discovery forced Descartes to reject his conception of the universe as strictly material and revisit the metaphysical foundations of knowledge. He now had to address the nature of purely mental entities that, being nonspatial, are not describable in mathematical terms. He also had to provide an intelligible account of how a viable scientific method can be built upon this single certainty: the existence of thought. Descartes was thus compelled to prove the existence of God, who alone could guarantee the integrity of clear and distinct ideas (i.e., those that cannot reasonably be doubted). He reasoned that we can be assured success in solving problems if we adhere strictly to the dictates of God-given reason, which He has stamped onto our human minds like a trademark. At the same time, we avoid error simply by refusing to make rash or unclear judgments based upon unclear ideas.

These latter arguments of the *Discourse* were widely criticized, and Descartes responded in 1641 by publishing an extended discussion of his metaphysics, *Meditations on First Philosophy*. In *Meditations* he provided an even more thorough account of his progression from universal doubt to the certainty of his own existence, proofs for the existence of God, and descriptions of the relation between mind and body. Despite his effort to make his ideas more accessible, *Meditations* did not escape criticism. Contemporaries who read his manuscript presented six sets of objections; these were included in the first edition of the published volume. Descartes followed *Meditations* with his most thorough articulation of "mathematicized" science, *Principles of Philosophy* (1644), which he hoped would become a university textbook supplanting those based on Aristotelian science. In the later 1640s, he turned his attention to ethics and psychology and a more comprehensive "trialistic" account of mind-body interaction. Contrary to wide-ranging criticism that Cartesian dualism presented human souls as merely residing in bodies without any apparent interaction, Descartes had already clearly stated in *Meditations*, "By means of these sensations of pain, hunger, thirst and so on, nature also teaches not merely that I am present to my body in the way a sailor is present in a ship, but that I am most tightly joined and, so to speak, commingled with it, so much so that I and the body constitute one single thing."[4] Descartes had already added to his conception of the existence of minds and bodies, the notion of the *human being* as the intimate union of both; our experience of emotions and sensations was evidence of their union. His commitment to clarifying this conception was both fueled and facilitated by a lengthy correspondence with Princess Elisabeth of Bohemia, who raised compelling and provocative questions about the interaction; she wished him to explain how any such interaction can be possible between two supposedly utterly independent entities.

Descartes' correspondence with Princess Elisabeth culminated in the 1649 publication of his last great work, *The Passions of the Soul*. *Passions* attempts to explain human emotions and sensations physiologically by describing in detail the various mechanisms by which mind and body interact. In addition, Descartes maintains in the text that if we can understand these mechanisms, we can learn to manage and control our passions "so that the evils they cause become bearable and even a source of joy."[5] Thus had Descartes demonstrated, or so he believed, the successful application of his scientific method to morals.

The day after he submitted *Passions of the Soul* for publication, Descartes departed for Stockholm, having been summoned to serve as the private tutor of Queen Christina of Sweden. Traveling each day in the bitter cold for the five o'clock A.M. sessions which the queen demanded, Descartes contracted pneumonia and died shortly after his arrival. His parting words expressed that very philosophy of mind that continues to perplex modern thinking: "Now my soul, 'tis time to depart."

SC

QUESTIONS

1. Explain how Descartes distinguishes the body from the soul in *The Passions of the Soul*.
2. How, according to Descartes, can we properly distinguish "passions" from other kinds of experience?
3. How would you describe, briefly, Descartes' understanding of "passions of the soul" to someone who has not read the text?
4. How might Descartes explain physiologically the emotions and behaviors experienced and expressed by two people who are attracted to each other?
5. By what means may one judge the strength or weakness of a soul?

ENDNOTES

1. Descartes, *Discourse on Method,* in *Discourse on Method and Meditations on First Philosophy*, I.8.
2. Ibid., II.19.
3. Ibid., I.9.
4. Descartes, *Meditations on First Philosophy,* in *Discourse on Method and Meditations on First Philosophy*, VI.81.
5. Descartes, *The Passions of the Soul*, sect 212.

SELECTED BIBLIOGRAPHY

Cottingham, John. *Descartes.* The Great Philosophers Series, ed. Ray Monk and Frederic Raphael. New York: Routledge, 1999.

Descartes, René. *A Discourse on Method, Meditations on the First Philosophy, Principles of Philosophy*, trans. John Veitch. New York: Dutton, 1978.

Descartes, René. *Discourse on Method and Meditations on First Philosophy*, 3d ed., trans. Donald A. Cress. Indianapolis: Hackett Publishing, 1993.

Descartes, René. *The Passions of the Soul*, trans. Stephen Voss. Indianapolis, Ind.: Hackett Publishing Co., 1989.

Descartes, René. *The Philosophical Writings of Descartes*. 3 vols., trans. John Cottingham, Robert Stoothoff, and Dugold Murdoch. Cambridge, England: Cambridge University Press, 1985.

Gaukroger, Stephen. *Descartes: An Intellectual Biography*. New York: Oxford University Press, 1995.

Sorrell, Tom. *Descartes*. Past Masters Series, ed. Keith Thomas. New York: Oxford University Press, 1987.

Williams, Bernard. *Descartes: The Project of Pure Inquiry*. New York: Penguin Books, 1978.

from *The Passions of the Soul*

René Descartes

PART ONE

The passions in general and incidentally the whole nature of man

1. What is a passion with regard to one subject is always an action in some other regard

The defects of the sciences we have from the ancients are nowhere more apparent than in their writings on the passions. This topic, about which knowledge has always been keenly sought, does not seem to be one of the more difficult to investigate since everyone feels passions in himself and so has no need to look elsewhere for observations to establish their nature. And yet the teachings of the ancients about the passions are so meagre and for the most part so implausible that I cannot hope to approach the truth except by departing from the paths they have followed. That is why I shall be obliged to write just as if I were considering a topic that no one had dealt with before me. In the first place, I note that whatever takes place or occurs is generally called by philosophers a 'passion' with regard to the subject to which it happens and an 'action' with regard to that which makes it happen. Thus, although an agent and patient are often quite different, an action and passion must always be a single thing which has these two names on account of the two different subjects to which it may be related.

2. To understand the passions of the soul we must distinguish its functions from those of the body

Next I note that we are not aware of any subject which acts more directly upon our soul than the body to which it is joined. Consequently we should recognize that what is a passion in the soul is usually an action in the body. Hence there is no better way of coming to know about our passions than by examining the difference between the soul and the body, in order to learn to which of the two we should attribute each of the functions present in us.

3. The rule we must follow in order to do this

We shall not find this very difficult if we bear in mind that anything we experience as being in us, and which we see can also exist in wholly inanimate bodies, must be attributed only to our body. On the other hand, anything in us which we cannot conceive in any way as capable of belonging to a body must be attributed to our soul.

4. The heat and the movement of the limbs proceed from the body, and thoughts from the soul

Thus, because we have no conception of the body as thinking in any way at all, we have reason to believe that every kind of thought present in us belongs to the soul. And since we do not doubt that there are inanimate bodies which can move in as many different ways as our bodies, if not more, and which have as much heat or more (as experience shows in the case of a flame, which has in itself much more heat and movement than any of our limbs), we must believe that all the heat and all the movements present in us, in so far as they do not depend on thought, belong solely to the body.

5. It is an error to believe that the soul gives movement and heat to the body

In this way we shall avoid a very serious error which many have fallen into, and which I regard as the primary cause of our failure up to now to give a satisfactory explanation of the passions and of everything else belonging to the soul. The error consists in supposing that since dead bodies are devoid of heat and movement, it is the absence of the soul which causes this cessation of movement and heat. Thus it has been believed, without justification, that our natural heat and all the movements of our bodies depend on the soul; whereas we ought to hold, on the contrary, that the soul takes its leave when we die only because this heat ceases and the organs which bring about bodily movement decay.

6. The difference between a living body and a dead body

So as to avoid this error, let us note that death never occurs through the absence of the soul, but only because one of the principal parts of the body decays. And let us recognize that the difference between the body of a living man and that of a dead man is just like the difference between, on the one hand, a watch or other automaton (that is, a self-moving machine) when it is wound up and contains in itself the corporeal principle of the movements for which it is designed, together with everything else required for its operation; and, on the other hand, the same watch or machine when it is broken and the principle of its movement ceases to be active.

7. A brief account of the parts of the body and of some of their functions

To make this more intelligible I shall explain in a few words the way in which the mechanism of our body is composed. Everyone knows that within us there is a heart, brain, stomach, muscles, nerves, arteries, veins, and similar things. We know too that the food we eat goes down to the stomach and bowels, and that its juice then flows into the liver and all the veins, where it mixes with the blood they contain, thus increasing its quantity. Those who have heard anything at all about medicine know in addition how the heart is constructed and how the blood in the veins can flow easily from the vena cava into its right-hand side, pass from there into the lungs through the vessel called the arterial vein, then return from the lungs into the left-hand side of the heart through the vessel called the venous artery, and finally pass from there into the great artery, whose branches spread through the whole body. Likewise all those not completely blinded by the authority of the ancients, and willing to open their eyes to examine the opinion of Harvey regarding the circulation of the blood, do not doubt that the veins and arteries of the body are like streams through which the blood flows constantly and with great rapidity. It makes its way from the right-hand cavity of the heart through the arterial vein, whose branches are spread throughout the lungs and connected with those of the venous artery; and via this artery it passes from the lungs into the left-hand side of the heart. From there it goes into the great artery, whose branches are spread through the rest of the body and connected with the branches of the vena cava, which carries the same blood once again into the right-hand cavity of the heart. These two cavities are thus like sluices through which all the blood passes upon each complete circuit it makes through the body. It is known, moreover, that every movement of the limbs depends on the muscles, which are opposed to each other in such a way that when one of them becomes shorter it draws towards itself the part of the body to which it is attached, which simultaneously causes the muscle opposed to it to lengthen. Then, if the latter happens to shorten at some other time, it makes the former lengthen again, and draws towards itself the part to which they are attached. Finally, it is known that all these movements of the muscles, and likewise all sensations, depend on the nerves, which are like little threads or tubes coming from the brain and containing, like the brain itself, a certain very fine air or wind which is called the 'animal spirits'.

8. The principle underlying all these functions

But it is not commonly known how these animal spirits and nerves help to produce movements and sensations, or what corporeal principle makes them act. That is why, although I have already touched upon this question in other writings, I intend to speak briefly about it here. While we are alive there is a continual heat in our hearts, which is a kind of fire that the blood of the veins maintains there. This fire is the corporeal principle underlying all the movements of our limbs.

9. How the movement of the heart takes place

Its first effect is that it makes the blood which fills the cavities of the heart expand. This causes the blood, now needing to occupy a larger space, to rush from the right-hand cavity into the arterial vein and from the left-hand cavity into the great artery. Then, when this expansion ceases, fresh blood immediately enters the right-hand cavity of the heart from the vena cava, and the left-hand cavity from the venous artery. For there are tiny membranes at the entrances to these four vessels which are so arranged that the blood can enter the heart only through the latter two and leave it only through the former two. When the new blood has entered the heart it is immediately rarefied in the same way as before. This and this alone is what the pulse or beating of the heart and arteries consists in, and it explains why the beating is repeated each time new blood enters the heart. It is also the sole cause of the movement of the blood, making it flow constantly and very rapidly in all the arteries and veins, so that it carries the heat it acquires in the heart to all the other parts of the body, and provides them with nourishment.

10. How the animal spirits are produced in the brain

What is, however, more worthy of consideration here is that all the most lively and finest parts of the blood, which have been rarefied by the heat in the heart, constantly enter the cavities of the brain in large numbers. What makes them go there rather than elsewhere is that all the blood leaving the heart through the great artery follows a direct route towards this place, and since not all this blood can enter there because the passages are too narrow, only the most active and finest parts pass into it while the rest spread out into the other regions of the body. Now these very fine parts of the blood make up the animal spirits. For them to do this the only change they need to undergo in the brain is to be separated from the other less fine parts of the blood. For what I am calling 'spirits' here are merely bodies: they have no property other than that of being extremely small bodies which move very quickly, like the jets of flame that come from a torch. They never stop in any place, and as some of them enter the brain's cavities, others leave it through the pores in its substance. These pores conduct them into the nerves, and then to the muscles. In this way the animal spirits move the body in all the various ways it can be moved.

11. How the movements of the muscles take place

For, as already mentioned, the sole cause of all the movements of the limbs is the shortening of certain muscles and the lengthening of the opposed muscles. What causes one muscle to become shorter rather than its opposite is simply that fractionally more spirits from the brain come to it than to the other. Not that the spirits which come directly from the brain are sufficient by themselves to move the muscles; but they cause the other spirits already in the two muscles to leave one of them very suddenly and pass into the other. In this way the one they leave becomes longer and more relaxed, and the one they enter, being suddenly swollen by them, becomes shorter and pulls the limb to which it is attached. This is easy to understand, provided one knows that very few animal spirits come continually from the brain to each muscle, and that any muscle always contains a quantity of its own spirits. These move very quickly, sometimes merely eddying in the place where they are located (that is, when they find no passages open for them to leave from), and sometimes flowing into the opposed muscle. In each of the muscles there are small openings through which the spirits may flow from one into the other, and which are so arranged that when the spirits coming from the brain to one of the muscles are slightly more forceful than those going to the other, they open all the passages through which the spirits in the latter can pass into the former, and at the same time they close all the passages through which the spirits in the former can pass into the latter. In this way all the spirits previously contained in the two muscles are gathered very rapidly in one of them, thus making it swell and become shorter, while the other lengthens and relaxes.

12. How external objects act upon the sense organs

We still have to know what causes the spirits not to flow always in the same way from the brain to the muscles, but to come sometimes more to some muscles than to others. In our case, indeed, one of these causes is the activity of the soul (as I shall explain further on). But in addition we must note two other causes, which depend solely on the body. The first consists in differences in the movements produced in the sense organs by their objects. I have already explained this quite fully in the *Optics*.But in order that readers of this work should not need to consult any other, I shall say once again that there are three things to consider in the nerves. First, there is the marrow, or internal substance, which extends in the form of tiny fibres from the brain, where they originate, to the extremities of the parts of the body to which they are attached. Next, there are the membranes surrounding the fibres, which are continuous with those surrounding the brain and form little tubes in which the fibres are enclosed. Finally, there are the animal spirits which, being carried by these tubes from the brain to the muscles, cause the fibres to remain so completely free and extended that if anything causes the slightest motion in the part of the body where one of the fibres terminates, it thereby causes a movement in the part of the brain where the fibre originates, just as we make one end of a cord move by pulling the other end.

13. This action of external objects may direct the spirits into the muscles in various different ways

I explained in the *Optics* how the objects of sight make themselves known to us simply by producing, through the medium of the intervening transparent bodies, local motions in the optic nerve-fibres at the back of our eyes, and then in the regions of the brain where these nerves originate. I explained too that the objects produce as much variety in these motions as they cause us to see in the things, and that it is not the motions occurring in the eye, but those occurring in the brain, which directly represent these objects to the soul. By this example, it is easy to conceive how sounds, smells, tastes, heat, pain, hunger, thirst and, in general, all the objects both of our external senses and of our internal appetites, also produce some movement in our nerves, which passes through them into the brain. Besides causing our soul to have various different sensations, these various movements in the brain can also act without the soul, causing the spirits to make their way to certain muscles rather than others, and so causing them to move our limbs. I shall prove this here by one example only. If someone suddenly thrusts his hand in front of our eyes as if to strike us, then even if we know that he is our friend, that he is doing this only in fun, and that he will take care not to harm us, we still find it difficult to prevent ourselves from closing our eyes. This shows that it is not through the mediation of our soul that they close, since this action is contrary to our volition, which is the only, or at least the principal, activity of the soul. They close rather because the mechanism of our body is so composed that the movement of the hand towards our eyes produces another movement in our brain, which directs the animal spirits into the muscles that make our eyelids drop.

14. Differences among the spirits may also cause them to take various different courses

The other cause which serves to direct the animal spirits to the muscles in various different ways is the unequal agitation of the spirits and differences in their parts. For when some of their parts are coarser and more agitated than others, they penetrate more deeply in a straight line into the cavities and pores of the brain, and in this way they are directed to muscles other than those to which they would go if they had less force.

15. The causes of these differences

And this inequality may arise from the different materials of which the spirits are composed. One sees this in the case of those who have drunk a lot of wine: the vapours of the wine enter the blood rapidly and rise from the heart to the brain, where they turn into spirits which, being stronger and more abundant than those normally present there, are capable of moving the body in many strange ways. Such an inequality of the spirits may also arise from various conditions of the heart, liver, stomach, spleen and all the other organs that help to produce them. In this connection we must first note certain small nerves embedded in the base of the heart, which serve to enlarge and contract the openings to its cavities, thus causing the blood, according to the strength of its expansion, to produce spirits having various different dispositions. It must also be observed that even though the blood entering the heart comes there from every other place in the body, it often happens nevertheless that it is driven there more from some parts than from others, because the nerves and muscles responsible for these parts exert more pressure on it or make it more agitated. And differences in these parts are matched by corresponding differences in the expansion of the blood in the heart, which results in the production of spirits having different qualities. Thus, for example, the blood coming from the lower part of the liver, where the gall is located, expands in the heart in a different manner from the blood coming from the spleen; the latter expands differently from the blood coming from the veins of the arms or legs; and this expands differently again from the alimentary juices when, just after leaving the stomach and bowels, they pass rapidly to the heart through the liver.

16. How all the limbs can be moved by the objects of the senses and by the spirits without the help of the soul

Finally it must be observed that the mechanism of our body is so composed that all the changes occurring in the movement of the spirits may cause them to open some pores in the brain more than others. Conversely, when one of the pores is opened somewhat more or less than usual by an action of the sensory nerves, this brings about a change in the movement of the spirits and directs them to the muscles which serve to move the body in the way it is usually moved on the occasion of such an action. Thus every movement we make without any contribution from our will—as often happens when we breathe, walk, eat and, indeed, when we perform any action which is common to us and the beasts–depends solely on the arrangement of our limbs and on the route which the spirits, produced by the heat of the heart, follow naturally in the brain, nerves and muscles. This occurs in the same way that the movement of a watch is produced merely by the strength of its spring and the configuration of its wheels.

17. The functions of the soul

Having thus considered all the functions belonging solely to the body, it is easy to recognize that there is nothing in us which we must attribute to our soul except our thoughts. These are of two principal kinds, some being actions of the soul and others its passions. Those I call its actions are all our volitions, for we experience them as proceeding directly from our soul and as seeming to depend on it alone. On the other hand, the various perceptions or modes of knowledge present in us may be called its passions, in a general sense, for it is often not our soul which makes them such as they are, and the soul always receives them from the things that are represented by them.

18. The will

Our volitions, in turn, are of two sorts. One consists of the actions of the soul which terminate in the soul itself, as when we will to love God or, generally speaking, to apply our mind to some object which is not material. The other consists of actions which terminate in our body, as when our merely willing to walk has the consequence that our legs move and we walk.

19. Perception

Our perceptions are likewise of two sorts: some have the soul as their cause, others the body. Those having the soul as their cause are the perceptions of our volitions and of all the imaginings or other thoughts which depend on them. For it is certain that we cannot will anything without thereby perceiving that we are willing it. And although willing something is an action with respect to our soul, the perception of such willing may be said to be a passion in the soul. But because this perception is really one and the same thing as the volition, and names are always determined by whatever is most noble, we do not normally call it a 'passion', but solely an 'action'.

20. Imaginings and other thoughts formed by the soul

When our soul applies itself to imagine something non-existent—as in thinking about an enchanted palace or a chimera—and also when it applies itself to consider something that is purely intelligible and not imaginable—for example, in considering its own nature—the perceptions it has of these things depend chiefly on the volition which makes it aware of them. That is why we usually regard these perceptions as actions rather than passions.

21. Imaginings which are caused solely by the body

Among the perceptions caused by the body, most of them depend on the nerves. But there are some which do not and which, like those I have just described, are called 'imaginings'. These differ from the others, however, in that our will is not used in forming them. Accordingly they cannot be numbered among the actions of the soul, for they arise simply from the fact that the spirits, being agitated in various different ways and coming upon the traces of various impressions which have preceded them in the brain, make their way by chance through certain pores rather than others. Such are the illusions of our dreams and also the day-dreams we often have when we are awake and our mind wanders idly without applying itself to anything of its own accord. Now some of these imaginings are passions of the soul, taking the word 'passion' in its proper and more exact sense, and all may be regarded as such if the word is understood in a more general sense. Nonetheless, their cause is not so conspicuous and determinate as that of the perceptions which the soul receives by means of the nerves, and they seem to be mere shadows and pictures of these perceptions. So before we can characterize them satisfactorily we must consider how these other perceptions differ from one another.

22. *How these other perceptions differ from one another*

All the perceptions which I have not yet explained come to the soul by means of the nerves. They differ from one another in so far as we refer some to external objects which strike our senses, others to our body or to certain of its parts, and still others to our soul.

23. *The perceptions we refer to objects outside us*

The perceptions we refer to things outside us, namely to the objects of our senses, are caused by these objects, at least when our judgements are not false. For in that case the objects produce certain movements in the organs of the external senses and, by means of the nerves, produce other movements in the brain, which cause the soul to have sensory awareness of the objects. Thus, when we see the light of a torch and hear the sound of a bell, the sound and the light are two different actions which, simply by producing two different movements in some of our nerves, and through them in our brain, give to the soul two different sensations. And we refer these sensations to the subjects we suppose to be their causes in such a way that we think that we see the torch itself and hear the bell, and not that we have sensory awareness merely of movements that come from these objects.

24. *The perceptions we refer to our body*

The perceptions we refer to our body or to certain of its parts are those of hunger, thirst and other natural appetites. To these we may add pain, heat and the other states we feel as being in our limbs, and not as being in objects outside us.

Thus, at the same time and by means of the same nerves we can feel the cold of our hand and the heat of a nearby flame or, on the other hand, the heat of our hand and the cold of the air to which it is exposed. This happens without there being any difference between the actions which make us feel the heat or cold in our hand and those which make us feel the heat or cold outside us, except that since one of these actions succeeds the other, we judge that the first is already in us, and that its successor is not yet there but in the object which causes it.

25. *The perceptions we refer to our soul*

The perceptions we refer only to the soul are those whose effects we feel as being in the soul itself, and for which we do not normally know any proximate cause to which we can refer them. Such are the feelings of joy, anger and the like, which are aroused in us sometimes by the objects which stimulate our nerves and sometimes also by other causes. Now all our perceptions, both those we refer to objects outside us and those we refer to the various states of our body, are indeed passions with respect to our soul, so long as we use the term 'passion' in its most general sense; nevertheless we usually restrict the term to signify only perceptions which refer to the soul itself. And it is only the latter that I have undertaken to explain here under the title 'passions of the soul'.[1]

---

[1]The classification given in articles 17–25 may be represented schematically as follows:

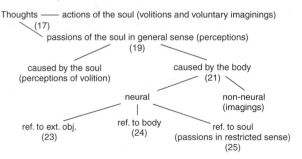

26. The imaginings which depend solely on the fortuitous movement of the spirits may be passions just as truly as the perceptions which depend on the nerves

It remains to be noted that everything the soul perceives by means of the nerves may also be represented to it through the fortuitous course of the spirits. The sole difference is that the impressions which come into the brain through the nerves are normally more lively and more definite than those produced there by the spirits—a fact that led me to say in article 21 that the latter are, as it were, a shadow or picture of the former. We must also note that this picture is sometimes so similar to the thing it represents that it may mislead us regarding the perceptions which refer to objects outside us, or even regarding those which refer to certain parts of our body. But we cannot be misled in the same way regarding the passions, in that they are so close and so internal to our soul that it cannot possibly feel them unless they are truly as it feels them to be. Thus often when we sleep, and sometimes even when we are awake, we imagine certain things so vividly that we think we see them before us, or feel them in our body, although they are not there at all. But even if we are asleep and dreaming, we cannot feel sad, or moved by any other passion, unless the soul truly has this passion within it.

27. Definition of the passions of the soul

After having considered in what respects the passions of the soul differ from all its other thoughts, it seems to me that we may define them generally as those perceptions, sensations or emotions of the soul which we refer particularly to it, and which are caused, maintained and strengthened by some movement of the spirits.

28. Explanation of the first part of this definition

We may call them 'perceptions' if we use this term generally to signify all the thoughts which are not actions of the soul or volitions, but not if we use it to signify only evident knowledge. For experience shows that those who are the most strongly agitated by their passions are not those who know them best, and that the passions are to be numbered among the perceptions which the close alliance between the soul and the body renders confused and obscure. We may also call them 'sensations', because they are received into the soul in the same way as the objects of the external senses, and they are not known by the soul any differently. But it is even better to call them 'emotions' of the soul, not only because this term may be applied to all the changes which occur in the soul—that is, to all the various thoughts which come to it—but more particularly because, of all the kinds of thought which the soul may have, there are none that agitate and disturb it so strongly as the passions.

29. Explanation of the other part of the definition

I add that they refer particularly to the soul, in order to distinguish them from other sensations, some referred to external objects (e.g. smells, sounds and colours) and others to our body (e.g. hunger, thirst and pain). I also add that they are caused, maintained and strengthened by some movement of the spirits, both in order to distinguish them from our volitions (for these too may be called 'emotions of the soul which refer to it', but they are caused by the soul itself), and also in order to explain their ultimate and most proximate cause, which distinguishes them once again from other sensations.

30. The soul is united to all the parts of the body conjointly

But in order to understand all these things more perfectly, we need to recognize that the soul is really joined to the whole body, and that we cannot properly say that it exists in any one part of the body to the exclusion of the others. For the body is a unity which is in a sense indivisible because of the arrangement of its organs, these being so related to one another that the removal of any one of them renders the whole body defective. And the soul is of such a nature that it has no relation to extension, or to the dimensions or other properties of the matter of which the body is composed: it is related solely to the whole assemblage of the body's organs. This is obvious from our inability to conceive of a half or a third of a soul, or of the extension which a soul occupies. Nor does the soul become any smaller if we cut off some part of the body, but it becomes completely separate from the body when we break up the assemblage of the body's organs.

31. There is a little gland² in the brain where the soul exercises its functions more particularly than in the other parts of the body

We need to recognize also that although the soul is joined to the whole body, nevertheless there is a certain part of the body where it exercises its functions more particularly than in all the others. It is commonly held that this part is the brain, or perhaps the heart—the brain because the sense organs are related to it, and the heart because we feel the passions as if they were in it. But on carefully examining the matter I think I have clearly established that the part of the body in which the soul directly exercises its functions is not the heart at all, or the whole of the brain. It is rather the innermost part of the brain, which is a certain very small gland situated in the middle of the brain's substance and suspended above the passage through which the spirits in the brain's anterior cavities communicate with those in its posterior

cavities. The slightest movements on the part of this gland may alter very greatly the course of these spirits, and conversely any change, however slight, taking place in the course of the spirits may do much to change the movements of the gland.

32. How we know that this gland is the principal seat of the soul

Apart from this gland, there cannot be any other place in the whole body where the soul directly exercises its functions. I am convinced of this by the observation that all the other parts of our brain are double, as also are all the organs of our external senses—eyes, hands, ears and so on. But in so far as we have only one simple thought about a given object at any one time, there must necessarily be some place where the two images coming through the two eyes, or the two impressions coming from a single object through the double organs of any other sense, can come together in a single image or impression before reaching the soul, so that they do not present to it two objects instead of one. We can easily understand that these images or other impressions are unified in this gland by means of the spirits which fill the cavities of the brain. But they cannot exist united in this way in any other place in the body except as a result of their being united in this gland.

33. The seat of the passions is not in the heart

As for the opinion of those who think that the soul receives its passions in the heart, this is not worth serious consideration, since it is based solely on the fact that the passions make us feel some change in the heart. It is easy to see that the only reason why this change is felt as occurring in the heart is that there is a small nerve which descends to it from the brain—just as pain is felt as in the foot by means of the nerves in the foot, and the stars are perceived as in the sky by means of their

---

²The pineal gland, which Descartes had identified as the seat of the imagination and the 'common' sense in the *Treatise on Man* (CSM 1 106).

light and the optic nerves. Thus it is no more necessary that our soul should exercise its functions directly in the heart in order to feel its passions there, than that it should be in the sky in order to see the stars there.

34. How the soul and the body act on each other

Let us therefore take it that the soul has its principal seat in the small gland located in the middle of the brain. From there it radiates through the rest of the body by means of the animal spirits, the nerves, and even the blood, which can take on the impressions of the spirits and carry them through the arteries to all the limbs. Let us recall what we said previously about the mechanism of our body. The nerve-fibres are so distributed in all the parts of the body that when the objects of the senses produce various different movements in these parts, the fibres are occasioned to open the pores of the brain in various different ways. This, in turn, causes the animal spirits contained in these cavities to enter the muscles in various different ways. In this manner the spirits can move the limbs in all the different ways they are capable of being moved. And all the other causes that can move the spirits in different ways are sufficient to direct them into different muscles. To this we may now add that the small gland which is the principal seat of the soul is suspended within the cavities containing these spirits, so that it can be moved by them in as many different ways as there are perceptible differences in the objects. But it can also be moved in various different ways by the soul, whose nature is such that it receives as many different impressions—that is, it has as many different perceptions as there occur different movements in this gland. And conversely, the mechanism of our body is so constructed that simply by this gland's being moved in any way by the soul or by any other cause, it drives the surrounding spirits towards the pores of the brain, which direct them through the nerves to the muscles; and in this way the gland makes the spirits move the limbs.

35. Example of the way in which the impressions of objects are united in the gland in the middle of the brain

Thus, for example, if we see some animal approaching us, the light reflected from its body forms two images, one in each of our eyes; and these images form two others, by means of the optic nerves, on the internal surface of the brain facing its cavities. Then, by means of the spirits that fill these cavities, the images radiate towards the little gland which the spirits surround: the movement forming each point of one of the images tends towards the same point on the gland as the movement forming the corresponding point of the other image, which represents the same part of the animal. In this way, the two images in the brain form only one image on the gland, which acts directly upon the soul and makes it see the shape of the animal.

36. Example of the way in which the passions are aroused in the soul

If, in addition, this shape is very strange and terrifying—that is, if it has a close relation to things which have previously been harmful to the body—this arouses the passion of anxiety in the soul, and then that of courage or perhaps fear and terror, depending upon the particular temperament of the body or the strength of the soul, and upon whether we have protected ourselves previously by defence or by flight against the harmful things to which the present impression is related. Thus in certain persons these factors dispose their brain in such a way that some of the spirits reflected from the image formed on the gland proceed from there to the nerves which serve to turn the back and move the legs in order to flee. The rest of the spirits go to nerves which expand or constrict the orifices of the heart, or else to nerves which agitate other parts of the body from which blood is sent to the heart, so that the blood is rarefied in a different manner from usual and spirits are sent to the brain which are adapted for maintaining and strengthening the passion of fear—that is, for holding open or re-opening the pores of the brain which direct the spirits into these same nerves. For merely by entering into these pores they produce in the gland a particular movement which is ordained by nature to make the soul feel this passion. And since these pores are related mainly to the little nerves which serve to contract or expand the orifices of the heart, this makes the soul feel the passion chiefly as if it were in the heart.

37. How all the passions appear to be caused by some movement of the spirits

Something similar happens with all the other passions. That is, they are caused chiefly by the spirits contained in the cavities of the brain making their way to nerves which serve to expand or constrict the orifices of the heart, or to drive blood towards the heart in a distinctive way from other parts of the body, or to maintain the passion in some other way. This makes it clear why I included in my definition of the passions that they are caused by some particular movement of the spirits.

38. Example of movements of the body which accompany the passions and do not depend on the soul

Moreover, just as the course which the spirits take to the nerves of the heart suffices to induce a movement in the gland through which fear enters the soul, so too the mere fact that some spirits at the same time proceed to the nerves which serve to move the legs in flight causes another movement in the gland through which the soul feels and per-

ceives this action. In this way, then, the body may be moved to take flight by the mere disposition of the organs, without any contribution from the soul.

39. How one and the same cause may excite different passions in different people

The same impression which the presence of a terrifying object forms on the gland, and which causes fear in some people, may excite courage and boldness in others. The reason for this is that brains are not all constituted in the same way. Thus the very same movement of the gland which in some excites fear, in others causes the spirits to enter the pores of the brain which direct them partly into nerves which serve to move the hands in self-defence and partly into those which agitate the blood and drive it towards the heart in the manner required to produce spirits appropriate for continuing this defence and for maintaining the will to do so.

40. The principal effect of the passions

For it must be observed that the principal effect of all the human passions is that they move and dispose the soul to want the things for which they prepare the body. Thus the feeling of fear moves the soul to want to flee, that of courage to want to fight, and similarly with the others.

41. The power of the soul with respect to the body

But the will is by its nature so free that it can never be constrained. Of the two kinds of thought I have distinguished in the soul—the first its actions, i.e. its volitions, and the second its passions, taking this word in its most general sense to include every kind of perception—the former are absolutely within its power and can be changed only indirectly by the body, whereas the latter are absolutely dependent on the actions which produce them, and can be changed by the soul only indirectly, except when it is itself their cause. And the activity of the soul consists entirely in the fact that simply by willing something it brings it about that the little gland to which it is closely joined moves in the manner required to produce the effect corresponding to this volition.

42. How we find in our memory the things we want to remember

Thus, when the soul wants to remember something, this volition makes the gland lean first to one side and then to another, thus driving the spirits towards different regions of the brain until they come upon the one containing traces left by the object we want to remember. These traces consist simply in the fact that the pores of the brain through which the spirits previously made their way owing to the presence of this object have thereby become more apt than the others to be opened in the same way when the spirits again flow towards them. And so the spirits enter into these pores more easily when they come upon them, thereby producing in the gland that special movement which represents the same object to the soul, and makes it recognize the object as the one it wanted to remember.

43. How the soul can imagine, be attentive, and move the body

When we want to imagine something we have never seen, this volition has the power to make the gland move in the way required for driving the spirits towards the pores of the brain whose opening enables the thing to be represented. Again, when we want to fix our attention for some time on some particular object, this volition keeps the gland leaning in one particular direction during that time. And finally, when we want to walk or move our body in some other way, this volition makes the gland drive the spirits to the muscles which serve to bring about this effect.

44. Each volition is naturally joined to some movement of the gland, but through effort or habit we may join it to others

Yet our volition to produce some particular movement or other effect does not always result in our producing it; for that depends on the various ways in which nature or habit has joined certain movements of the gland to certain thoughts. For example, if we want to adjust our eyes to look at a far-distant object, this volition causes the pupils to grow larger; and if we want to adjust them to look at a very near object, this volition makes the pupils contract. But if we think only of enlarging the pupils, we may indeed have such a volition, but we do not thereby enlarge them. For the movement of the gland, whereby the spirits are driven to the optic nerve in the way required for enlarging or contracting the pupils, has been joined by nature with the volition to look at distant or nearby objects, rather than with the volition to enlarge or contract the pupils. Again, when we speak, we think only of the meaning of what we want to say, and this makes us move our tongue and lips much more readily and effectively than if we thought of moving them in all the ways required for uttering the same words. For the habits acquired in learning to speak have made us join the action of the soul (which, by means of the gland, can move the tongue and lips) with the meaning of the words which follow upon these movements, rather than with the movements themselves.

45. The power of the soul with respect to its passions

Our passions, too, cannot be directly aroused or suppressed by the action of our will, but only indirectly through the representation of things which are usually joined with the passions we wish to have and opposed to the passions we wish to reject. For example, in order to arouse boldness and suppress fear in ourselves, it is not sufficient to have the volition to do so. We must apply ourselves to consider the reasons, objects, or precedents which persuade us that the danger is not great; that there is always more security in defence than in flight; that we shall gain glory and joy if we conquer, whereas we can expect nothing but regret and shame if we flee; and so on.

46. What prevents the soul from having full control over its passions

There is one special reason why the soul cannot readily change or suspend its passions, which is what led me to say in my definition that the passions are not only caused but also maintained and strengthened by some particular movement of the spirits. The reason is that they are nearly all accompanied by some disturbance which takes place in the heart and consequently also throughout the blood and the animal spirits. Until this disturbance ceases they remain present to our mind in the same way as the objects of the senses are present to it while they are acting upon our sense organs. The soul can prevent itself from hearing a slight noise or feeling a slight pain by attending very closely to some other thing, but it cannot in the same way prevent itself from hearing thunder or feeling a fire that burns the hand. Likewise it can easily overcome the lesser passions, but not the stronger and more violent ones, except after the disturbance of the blood and spirits has died down. The most the will can do while this disturbance is at its full strength is not to yield to its effects and to inhibit many of the movements to which it disposes the body. For example, if anger causes the hand to rise to strike a blow, the will can usually restrain it; if fear moves the legs in flight, the will can stop them; and similarly in other cases.

47. The conflicts that are usually supposed to occur between the lower part and the higher part of the soul

All the conflicts usually supposed to occur between the lower part of the soul, which we call 'sensitive', and the higher or 'rational' part of the soul—or between the natural appetites and the will—consist simply in the opposition between the movements which the body (by means of its spirits) and the soul (by means of its will) tend to produce at the same time in the gland. For there is within us but one soul, and this soul has within it no diversity of parts: it is at once sensitive and rational too, and all its appetites are volitions. It is an error to identify the different functions of the soul with persons who play different, usually mutually opposed roles—an error which arises simply from our failure to distinguish properly the functions of the soul from those of the body. It is to the body alone that we should attribute everything that can be observed in us to oppose our reason. So there is no conflict here except in so far as the little gland in the middle of the brain can be pushed to one side by the soul and to the other side by the animal spirits (which, as I said above, are nothing but bodies), and these two impulses often happen to be opposed, the stronger cancelling the effect of the weaker. Now we may distinguish two kinds of movement produced in the gland by the spirits. Movements of the first kind represent to the soul the objects which stimulate the senses, or the impressions occurring in the brain; and these have no influence on the will. Movements of the second kind, which do have an influence on the will, cause the passions or the bodily movements which accompany the passions. As to the first, although they often hinder the actions of the soul, or are hindered by them, yet since they are not directly opposed to these actions, we observe no conflict between them. We observe conflict only between movements of the second kind and the volitions which oppose them—for example, between the force with which the spirits push the gland so as to cause the soul to desire something, and the force with which the soul, by its volition to avoid this thing, pushes the gland in a contrary direction. Such a conflict is revealed chiefly through the fact that the will, lacking the power to produce the passions directly (as I have already said), is compelled to make an effort to consider a series of different things, and if one of them happens to have the power to change for a moment the course of the spirits, the next one may happen to lack this power, whereupon the spirits will immediately revert to the same course because no change has occurred in the state of the nerves, heart and blood. This makes the soul feel itself impelled, almost at one and the same time, to desire and not to desire one and the same thing; and that is why it has been thought that the soul has within it two conflicting powers. We may, however, acknowledge a kind of conflict, in so far as the same cause that produces a certain passion in the soul often also produces certain movements in the body, to which the soul makes no contribution and which the soul stops or tries to stop as soon as it perceives them. We experience this when an object that excites fear also causes the spirits to enter the muscles which serve to move our legs in flight, while the will to be bold stops them from moving.

48. How we recognize the strength or weakness of souls, and what is wrong with the weakest souls

It is by success in these conflicts that each person can recognize the strength or weakness of his soul. For undoubtedly the strongest souls belong to those in whom the will by nature can most easily conquer the passions and stop the bodily movements which accompany them. But there are some who can never test the strength of their will because they never equip it to fight with its proper weapons, giving it instead only the weapons which some passions provide for resisting other passions. What I call its 'proper' weapons are firm and determinate judgements bearing upon the knowledge of good and evil, which the soul has resolved to fol-

low in guiding its conduct. The weakest souls of all are those whose will is not determined in this way to follow such judgements, but constantly allows itself to be carried away by present passions. The latter, being often opposed to one another, pull the will first to one side and then to the other, thus making it battle against itself and so putting the soul in the most deplorable state possible. Thus, when fear represents death as an extreme evil which can be avoided only by flight, while ambition on the other hand depicts the dishonour of flight as an evil worse than death, these two passions jostle the will in opposite ways; and since the will obeys first the one and then the other, it is continually opposed to itself, and so it renders the soul enslaved and miserable.

49. The strength of the soul is inadequate without knowledge of the truth

It is true that very few people are so weak and irresolute that they choose only what their passion dictates. Most have some determinate judgements which they follow in regulating some of their actions. Often these judgements are false and based on passions by which the will has previously allowed itself to be conquered or led astray; but because the will continues to follow them when the passion which caused them is absent, they may be considered its proper weapons, and we may judge souls to be stronger or weaker according to their ability to follow these judgements more or less closely and resist the present passions which are opposed to them. There is, however, a great difference between the resolutions which proceed from some false opinion and those which are based solely on knowledge of the truth. For, anyone who follows the latter is assured of never regretting or repenting, whereas we always regret having followed the former when we discover our error.

50. There is no soul so weak that it cannot, if well-directed, acquire an absolute power its passions

It is useful to note here, as already mentioned above,[3] that although nature seems to have joined every movement of the gland to certain of our thoughts from the beginning of our life, yet we may join them to others through habit. Experience shows this in the case of language. Words produce in the gland movements which are ordained by nature to represent to the soul only their sounds when they are spoken or the shape of their letters when they are written; but nevertheless, through the habit we have acquired of thinking of what they mean when we hear the sounds or see the letters, these movements usually make us conceive this meaning rather than the shape of the letters or the sound of the syllables. It is also useful to note that although the movements (both of the gland and of the spirits and the brain) which represent certain objects to the soul are naturally joined to the movements which produce certain passions in it, yet through habit the former can be separated from the latter and joined to others which are very different. Indeed this habit can be acquired by a single action and does not require long practice. Thus, when we unexpectedly come upon something very foul in a dish we are eating with relish, our surprise may so change the disposition of our brain that we cannot afterwards look upon any such food without repulsion, whereas previously we ate it with pleasure. And the same may be observed in animals. For although they lack reason, and perhaps even thought, all the movements of the spirits and of the gland which produce passions in us are nevertheless present in them too, though in them they serve to maintain and strengthen only the movements of the nerves and the muscles which usually accompany the passions and not, as in us, the passions themselves. So when a dog sees a partridge, it is naturally disposed to run towards it; and when it hears a gun fired, the noise naturally impels it to run away. Nevertheless, setters are commonly trained so that the sight of a partridge makes them stop, and the noise they hear afterwards, when someone fires at the bird, makes them run towards it. These things are worth noting in order to encourage each of us to make a point of controlling our passions. For since we are able, with a little effort, to change the movements of the brain in animals devoid of reason, it is clear that we can do so still more effectively in the case of men. Even those who have the weakest souls could acquire absolute mastery over all their passions if we employed sufficient ingenuity in training and guiding them.

---

[3]Art. 44, p. 234 above.

chapter fifteen

Elisabeth of Bohemia

Recent Descartes scholarship has focused increasing attention upon a "minor figure," Princess Elisabeth of Bohemia (1618–1680), who exerted considerable influence upon the "father of modern philosophy." Elisabeth and Descartes conducted a seven-year correspondence to which many scholars partly attribute the development of Descartes' mature thought on mind-body interaction and on moral and political philosophy.[1] Despite the fact that Elisabeth very frequently was opposed to his views, Descartes nonetheless declared her to be the *only* thinker who "understood so generally and so well . . . all that is contained in [his] writings."[2] He expressed his esteem for her in his dedication of *Principles of Philosophy* (1644):

> I remark, in all those who are versant in metaphysics, that they are wholly disinclined from geometry; and on the other hand, that the cultivators of geometry have no ability for the investigations of first philosophy: insomuch that I can say with truth I know but one mind, and that is your own, to which both studies are congenial, and which I therefore, with propriety, designate incomparable. But what most of all enhances my admiration is, that so accurate and varied an acquaintance with the whole circle of the sciences is not found in some aged doctor who has employed many years in contemplation, but in a princess still young.[3]

Because of the depth and profundity of her philosophical understanding as well as her incisive method of questioning, many contemporary scholars acknowledge Elisabeth as a philosopher in her own right. This is the case even though her ideas come to us only through her correspondence with Descartes and not through any systematic treatises that expound her philosophical position.[4]

Elisabeth was born at Heidelberg to Elizabeth Stuart, daughter of James I of England, and Elector Palatine Frederick V. In 1619, Frederick became king of Bohemia, but in November 1620, before Elisabeth turned two, he was deposed and he lost his Palatine lands. Forced into exile, Frederick and his wife fled to Germany and left young Elisabeth with her grandmother and aunt in Silesia. Seven years later, Elisabeth was reunited with her parents and their growing family (there were now eleven children) in

Selected correspondence between Princess Elisabeth of Bohemia and René Descartes, Roberto Toledo, translator. © 2003 Used with permission.

Holland. There she received an excellent education in mathematics, the sciences, history, and jurisprudence, as well as in Scripture and court etiquette. She also studied French, English, German, Dutch, Greek, and Latin and earned the nickname "LaGreque" for her mastery of the classical languages. Enamored of the life of mind, Elisabeth was by no means troubled when at age eighteen it became clear that her family's poverty and her own staunch Protestantism would hinder her from marrying. She promptly relinquished the thought, being anyway "more interested in the life of study than marriage."[5]

Elisabeth read Descartes' *Meditations on First Philosophy* in 1642. A family friend informed Descartes, who had already heard about Elisabeth's exceptional intellectual ability, and arrangements were made, at Descartes' request, for the two to meet. According to Elisabeth's letter of May 16, 1643, that meeting never took place; however, in that letter Elisabeth seized the opportunity to question Descartes about his theory of mind and body interaction. Thus began one of the most famous and influential correspondences in the history of Western philosophy.

In the early correspondence, conducted during the spring and summer of 1643, Elisabeth poses incisive questions that target the most basic assumptions of Descartes' theory that mind, which he declared to be immaterial substance, is able to cause movements in the body, a material substance.[6] She challenges Descartes to clarify his claims about the *nature* of mind and of body, a "clear and distinct" idea of these substances being the bedrock of any viable theory of their interaction. Elisabeth quite frankly objects to Descartes' conception of the mind as purely unextended substance. Close examination of her letters reveals, moreover, not only that she finds Descartes' theory of mind and its capacities to be incompatible with his physics, but also that *she* has a theory of mind that perhaps offers a more viable solution to the problem of mind-body interaction.

Elisabeth was not the first to question Descartes about the interaction of mind and body, but where other critics were concerned largely with the *site* of mind-body interaction and the problem such location raises for Descartes' claim that the mind is unextended,[7] Elisabeth emphasized quite a different difficulty: Descartes' earlier account of motion in his *Optics* (1637) suggests it is *impossible* for an immaterial soul to move material substance. Accordingly, Elisabeth writes,

Might I implore you to tell me how the human soul (considering it is only a thinking substance) can determine the spirits of the body in order to produce voluntary actions? It seems that any determination of movement that occurs from the impulsion of the moved thing depends on the manner in which it is pushed by the thing that moves it, or else according to the quality and shape of the surface of the thing that moves it. Contact is required for the first two conditions, and extension for the third. You entirely exclude extension from your notion of the soul, and it appears to me that contact is incompatible with an immaterial thing.[8]

Perhaps to ensure that Descartes understands precisely what she considers to be the source of the difficulty, Elisabeth adds, "I ask for a more particular definition of the soul than the one in your metaphysics, that is to say, for a definition of the substance separated from its action, namely thought."[9] Elisabeth is prompting Descartes to reconsider his conception of the soul in order to render his account of mind-body interaction compatible with his general theory of motion. As their correspondence continues, Descartes offers a series of replies that Elisabeth rightly finds dissatisfying, for they repeatedly fail to *explain how* an immaterial substance can move matter. In the absence of a tenable explanation, Elisabeth finally confesses, "I admit that I could more easily concede extension and matter to the soul than the capacity to move a body, or to be moved by a body, to an immaterial thing."[10] In fact, it becomes increasingly clear that Elisabeth thinks the soul does have attributes other than its principal attribute of thought. Perhaps it is a *different* attribute of the soul that accounts for mind-body interaction.

Throughout the correspondence Elisabeth expresses concern, not only over the discrepancies between Descartes' physics and his metaphysical account of mind and body, but also over the implications of his metaphysics for moral philosophy. Her concern is implicit in her first letter, in which she asks, "how the human soul . . . can determine the spirits of the body in order to produce voluntary actions," such actions being, among others, those for which human beings are morally responsible. The issue of the mind's ability to exercise dominion over the body and emotions becomes more central in the correspondence from the summer of 1645. Descartes learns that Elisabeth has suffered from a prolonged illness, and he attributes her poor health to her mental state. His advice: "I fear that you will not be delivered from all of this if you do not, through the power of your virtue, render your soul content, despite the disappointments of bad fortune."[11] Descartes' "psychosomatic solution" is for Elisabeth to restore her bodily health by thinking positive thoughts.[12] Elisabeth objects, noting that a person's physical constitution frequently impedes his or her ability to exercise mental control over the body. She observes, "There is something that overtakes one in the passions, and even though it is foreseen, I am mistress of it only after a certain time, and in the meanwhile my body becomes so greatly disordered that I require several months to restore it."[13] She reasserts her conviction in a subsequent letter: "for there are maladies that completely deprive one of the power of reasoning, and consequently of enjoying a reasonable satisfaction; others diminish the force of reasoning and prevent one from following the maxims that good sense would institute."[14]

Elisabeth thus expresses again the difficulties in conceiving of the mind as capable of moving or controlling the body. She challenges Descartes to explain, moreover, how the body has such power as to produce passions in the soul. Finally, in a letter of September 13, 1645, she asks Descartes to give a detailed account of the passions, whereby he can explain the mutual interaction of mind and body in producing them: "I would . . . wish you to define the passions, so that they be well known; for those who name them perturbations of the soul would persuade me that the force of the passions consists only in overwhelming and subjecting reason, had not experience shown me there are passions that carry us to reasonable actions." Descartes responds to Elisabeth's request by writing *The Passions of the Soul* (1649).

Elisabeth's correspondence with Descartes continued until his death in 1650. During a stay in Germany, in 1646,[15] Elisabeth introduced Descartes' work to German professors. In 1667, she entered a Protestant convent at Herford in Westphalia, where she served first as coadjutrix[16] and later as abbess. As abbess she spent her final years as overseer of the principality of the abby, a population of about seven thousand with attendant farms, mills, factories, and vineyards. Under Elisabeth's leadership the abby offered refuge to persons with somewhat unorthodox religious beliefs, most notably Jean Labadie and his followers, and the Quakers William Penn and Robert Barclay.

SC

QUESTIONS

1. State, in your own words, Princess Elisabeth's objections to Descartes' theory of mind-body interaction.
2. Descartes claims we must understand three "primitive notions" if we are to explain mind, body, and their interaction. Explain these three notions and how Descartes thinks they are properly to be understood in the case of mind-body interaction.
3. In her letter of June 10/20, 1643, Elisabeth tells Descartes that she is "unable to comprehend, from what [he] had previously said concerning weight, the idea by which we should judge how the soul . . . can move the body." Recap Descartes' analogy of weight and its relation to bodily motion. Do you think the analogy succeeds in explaining how the mind-body interaction should be understood? Explain your answer.
4. What do you think is Elisabeth's theory of mind-body interaction?
5. Evaluate Descartes' diagnosis of Elisabeth's subsequent illness and his advice to her to "think positive thoughts." What sort of challenge does Elisabeth's response pose to Descartes?

ENDNOTES

1. See, for instance, John J. Blom, *Descartes: His Moral Philosophy and Psychology;* Stephen Gaukroger, *Descartes: An Intellectual Biography;* Lisa Shapiro, "Princess Elisabeth and Descartes: The Union of Soul and Body and the Practice of Philosophy" and Deborah Tollefsen, "Princess Elisabeth and the Problem of Mind-Body Interaction."
2. Descartes, *A Discourse on Method, Meditations on the First Philosophy, Principles of Philosophy,* p. 164.
3. Ibid.
4. See Lisa Shapiro; see also Deborah Tollefsen.

5. From Zedler, Beatrice H. "The Three Princesses." *Hypatia* 4 no. 1 (spring 1989): 30.

6. Cf. the discussion of Descartes in chapter 14.

7. For example, in the *Fifth Objections* to Descartes's *Meditations,* Pierre Gassendi challenged Descartes to explain the *union* of soul and body. Gassendi argued that if the two interact, then the soul must either be diffused throughout the body or located entirely in the brain. In either case, the soul must occupy space, but this is impossible if the soul is unextended, as Descartes claims.

8. Elisabeth to Descartes, May 6, 1643.

9. Ibid.

10. Elisabeth to Descartes, June 10, 1645.

11. Descartes to Elisabeth, May 18, 1645.

12. Tollefson, p. 66.

13. Elisabeth to Descartes, June 22, 1645; quoted in Blom, p. 127.

14. Elisabeth to Descartes, August 16, 1645; quoted in Blom, p. 135.

15. Elisabeth was sent by her mother to stay with an aunt in Germany when Elisabeth defended her brother Philip's *intentions* in stabbing a man to death in public. That man, a Monsieur L'Espinay, had offended the family by bragging of flirting with Elisabeth's mother and sister.

16. Assistant to the abbess.

SELECTED BIBLIOGRAPHY

Atherton, Margaret, ed.*Women Philosophers of the Early Modern Period.* Indianapolis: Hackett Publishing, 1994.

Blom, John. *Descartes: His Moral Philosophy and Psychology.* New York: New York University Press, 1978.

Descartes, René. *A Discourse on Method, Meditations on the First Philosophy, Principles of Philosophy,* trans. John Veitch. New York: Dutton, 1978.

Descartes, René. *The Philosophical Writings of Descartes.* 3 vols, trans. John Cottingham, Robert Stoothoff, and Dugold Murdoch. Cambridge: Cambridge University Press, 1985.

Gaukroger, Stephen. *Descartes: An Intellectual Biography.* New York: Oxford University Press, 1995.

Nye, Andrea. "Polity and Prudence," from *Hypatia's Daughters: Fifteen Hundred Years of Women Philosophers,* ed. Linda Lopez McAlister. Indianapolis: Indiana University Press, 1996.

Shapiro, Lisa. "Princess Elisabeth and Descartes: The Union of Soul and Body and the Practice of Philosophy," from *Feminism and History of Philosophy,* ed. Genevieve Lloyd. New York: Oxford University Press, 2002.

Tollefsen, Deborah. "Princess Elisabeth and the Problem of Mind-Body Interaction." *Hypatia* 14, no. 3 (summer 1999).

Correspondence Between Princess Elisabeth of Bohemia and René Descartes

Elisabeth of Bohemia

Elisabeth to Descartes
The Hague, 6 May 1643

Monsieur Descartes,

I learned with much joy and regret of your intention to see me a few days ago. I was just as moved by your generosity in being willing to relate your ideas to such an ignorant and untrained person as myself, as by the misfortune that kept me from the profitable conversation we might have had. Monsieur Pallot made me even more aware of how passionately interesting this would have been when he repeated the solutions you gave him for the obscurities found in the physics of Monsieur Regius, of which I would have been better instructed if I had heard them from your own mouth. I would also have been more knowledgeable about a question that I asked this same professor when he was in the city, and regarding which he referred me back to you for a satisfactory response. My shame in showing you so unruly a writing style as mine has prevented me until now from asking this favor of you by letter.

But today, Monsieur Pallot so assured me of your good will toward everyone, and particularly toward me, that I have expelled every other consideration from my mind, except that of availing myself of that good will. Might I implore you to tell me how the human soul (considering it is only a thinking substance) can determine the spirits of the body in order to produce voluntary actions? It seems that any determination of movement that occurs from the impulsion of the moved thing depends on the manner in which it is pushed by the thing that moves it, or else according to the quality and shape of the surface of the thing that moves it. Contact is required for the first two conditions, and extension for the third. You entirely exclude extension from your notion of the soul, and it appears to me that contact is incompatible with an immaterial thing. That is why I ask for a more particular definition of the soul than the one in your metaphysics, that is to say, for a definition of the substance separated from its action, namely thought. Because although we suppose that they are inseparable (which is nevertheless difficult to prove in the case of the mother's womb or in the case of fainting), in considering them apart, like the attributes of God, we can achieve a more perfect idea of them. Since you know the best medicine for my mind, I freely disclose the weaknesses in its speculations to you, and I hope that, in observing the oath of Hippocrates, you will bring it remedies without publicizing them. This I ask of you in addition to enduring these importunities from

Your truly devoted friend at your service,

Elisabeth.

Descartes to Elisabeth
Egmond du Hoef, 21 May 1643

Madame,

. . . I can say in all honesty that I believe the question your Highness proposes is the one that could be most reasonably asked of me in light of the writings I have published. There are two aspects of the human soul on which all the knowledge we can have of its nature depends; the first is that it thinks, and the second is that, being united with the body, it can act and suffer with it. I have said nearly nothing in regard to the latter, and I have only endeavored to understand the first well because my principal aim has been to prove the distinction between the soul and the body. To this end only the first could be of use, while the other would have been harmful. But seeing that your Highness is so discerning that one cannot conceal anything from her, I will attempt here to explain the manner in which I conceive the union of the soul and the body, and how the soul has the force to move the body.

First, I contend that there are certain primitive notions within us, which are like originals on whose model we form all our other knowledge. And there are but very few such notions. We have the most general one—being, number, duration, etc.—which apply to everything that we can conceive. Then, as regards the body specifically, we have only the notion of extension, from which follows the notions of shape and motion. Then, as regards the soul alone, we have the notion of thought, which comprises the perceptions of the understanding and the inclinations of the will. Finally, for the soul and body together, we have only that of their union, on which depends the notion of the force of the soul to move the body, and of the body to act on the soul by causing its feelings and passions.

I also contend that all human scientific knowledge consists precisely in distinguishing these notions, and in attributing each of them to the things to which they apply. For, when we want to explain some difficulty by means of a notion that does not apply to it, we cannot avoid falling into error. We will err also when we attempt to explain one of these notions by another since, being primitive notions, each of them can only be understood by itself. And inasmuch as the use of our senses has made the notions of extension, shape, and move-

ment much more familiar to us than the others, the principle cause of our errors is that we ordinarily want to make use of these notions in order to explain things to which they do not apply. For example, we try to use the imagination to conceive the nature of the soul, or else try to conceive the way in which the soul moves the body after the manner in which one body is moved by another body.

That is why, in the *Meditations,* which your Highness deigned to read, I tried to elucidate the notions which belong to the soul alone, distinguishing them from those that apply to the body alone. The next thing I must explain is how to conceive those that belong to the union of the soul with the body, without resorting to those that apply to the body alone or to the soul alone. In so doing, it seems to me that what I wrote at the end of my Response to the 6th Objection could be of use, for we cannot search for these simple notions anywhere except in our soul, which contains all of them according to its very nature. Yet our soul does not always adequately distinguish them from each other, nor does it attribute them to the objects to which they should be attributed.

Thus I believe we have hitherto confused the notion of the force by which the soul acts upon the body with that by which a body acts upon another body. We have attributed these forces not to the soul because we had as yet no understanding of it. We have attributed them instead to the diverse qualities of bodies, such as weight, heat, and the others, which we imagine to be real, that is to say, to exist independently of the body, and hence to be substances, even though we called them qualities. And in order to conceive of them, we have sometimes used the notions in us for understanding the soul and sometimes we have used those in us for understanding the body, depending on whether that which we attributed to them was material or immaterial. For example, in supposing that weight is a real quality, of which we have no other knowledge except that it has the force to move the body in which it exists towards the center of the earth, we have no difficulty in conceiving how it moves the body, nor how it is joined to it; and we do not think that this happens through the actual contact of one surface with another. For, in our inner experience, we find that we have a particular notion for conceiving this phenomenon, and I believe we use this notion incorrectly if we apply it to weight, which is in no way truly distinct from the body, as I hope to demonstrate in my *Physics.* Yet this notion has been given us in order to conceive the manner in which the soul moves the body.

I would be attesting to my ignorance in respect to the outstanding mind of your Highness if I were to employ any more words to explain myself, and yet I would be too presumptuous if I dared to think that my response should be entirely satisfactory to her. I hope to avoid committing either fault by adding nothing further here, except that if I am capable of writing or saying anything that can be agreeable to her, I will always deem it the utmost honor to take up my pen or to go to the Hague on that account; and that there is nothing in the world so dear to me as to be able to obey her commands. However, I can find no reason to observe the Hippocratic Oath here as your Highness requests since she has not communicated anything to me that does not deserve to be seen and admired be everyone. On this subject, I can only say that, infinitely esteeming your letter, I shall do as misers do with their treasures, hoarding them all the more zealously the more they esteem them. They are vexed when the rest of the world sees their treasures, and they derive their greatest contentment from looking upon them. Thus, I shall easily rejoice in being the only one with the good fortune to see it, and my greatest ambition is to be able to say, & to be truly, etc. .

Elisabeth to Descartes
The Hague, 10 June 1643

Monsieur Descartes,

Your good will is apparent not only in your identification and correction of the errors in my reasoning, as I had anticipated it would be, but is apparent also in the way that you try to console me for your assessment of my weaknesses by heaping false praise upon me. This praise might have been necessary to encourage me to continue working if I had not been raised in a place where the ordinary manner of conversation had accustomed me to hearing praises from people incapable of speaking the truth. If I had not learned to assume people meant the opposite of what they said, I would not have been so familiar with the idea of my own imperfection. This upbringing has made me not sensitive to criticism so much as eager to have the chance to improve myself.

I confess without shame, therefore, that I have encountered in myself all the causes of error which you note in your letter, and I confess also that I am as yet unable to banish them entirely since the life which I am constrained to lead does not grant me enough free time to acquire a habit of meditation according to your rules. Sometimes the matters of the household to which I must attend, and sometimes social obligations and civilities that I cannot avoid, so greatly wear on this weak mind with irritations and boredom, that they render it useless for anything else for a long while afterwards. This I hope will serve to excuse my stupidity in being unable to comprehend, by means of your previous notion of weight, how we should conceive the manner in which the soul (nonextended and immaterial) can move the body. Nor do I comprehend how this force that you had then understood, falsely attributing to it the name of a quality, as pulling the body toward the center of the earth, should be more persuasive in convincing us that a body can be pushed by an immaterial thing than the demonstration of a truth to the contrary (which you promised in your physics) confirms us in the opinion of its impossibility. It is possible that this idea (being unable to claim the same perfection and objective reality as that of God) is feigned from ignorance of what truly moves these bodies toward the center. Since no material cause presents itself to the senses, one would have attributed it to its contrary, the immaterial, which I have nevertheless only been able to conceive as the negation of matter, and as such, have no communication with it. I admit that I could more easily concede extension and matter to the soul than the capacity to move a body, or to be moved by a body, to an immaterial thing. If the first only occurs through information, the spirits that produce the motion would have to be intelligent, which you do not ascribe to anything corporeal. Although you show the possibility of the second in your metaphysical meditations, it is nevertheless very difficult to comprehend how a soul, as you have described it, after having had the faculty and habit of good reasoning, can just vanish like that; or how the soul, being able to subsist without a body and having nothing in common with it, can be so thoroughly ruled by it. But since you have undertaken to instruct me, I only entertain these considerations in the manner of friends I do not intend to keep; resting assured that, as with everything else you have desired that I know, you will provide a good explanation for the nature of an immaterial thing and the manner of its actions and passions in the body. I also beseech you to believe that there is no one as aware of her indebtedness to your charity as

Your truly devoted friend,

Elisabeth

Descartes to Elisabeth
Egmond du Hoef, 28 June 1643

Madame,

I am much obliged to your Highness in that, after seeing how poorly I explained myself in my last letter in regards to the question that she had the pleasure to put to me, she still deigns to have the patience to listen to me continue on the same subject and to allow me the opportunity to remark on the things that I had omitted. First, I distinguished three kinds of ideas or primitive notions which are each comprehended in a particular fashion and not through comparison with one another, namely the notion of the soul, the notion of the body, and the notion of the union between the soul and the body. I should have explained the difference that exists between these three types of notions, and between the operations of the soul by which we possess them, and I should have described the means of rendering each of them familiar and easily comprehensible to us. Second, having said why I had adopted the comparison with weight, I should have clarified that, although one wishes to conceive of the soul as material (which is to properly conceive of its union with the body), this conception does not preclude understanding the soul as separable from the body. This, I believe, addresses all the matters that your Highness has put before me here.

I take there to be a great difference between these three types of notions, in that the soul can only be conceived by pure intellect. The body, that is to say extension, shapes, and movements, can also be known solely by pure intellect, but much better by the intellect aided by the imagination; and finally, the things that apply to the union of the soul and the body are known only obscurely by the intellect alone, or even by the intellect aided by the imagination; but these things are known very clearly by the senses. This explains why those who never philosophize, and who rely only on their senses, do not doubt that the soul moves the body, and that the body acts on the soul, but they consider the one and the other as one single thing; that is to say, they conceive their union, because to conceive the union between two things is to conceive them as a single thing. Metaphysical thoughts, which exercise the pure intellect, serve to render the notion of the soul familiar to us; the study of mathematics, which principally exercises the imagination through the consideration of shapes and movements, accustoms us to form distinct notions of the body. It is from everyday living and ordinary conversation, and abstention from the study and meditation on things that exercise the imagination, that one learns to conceive the union of the soul and the body.

I almost fear that your Highness may think that I am not speaking seriously here; but that would be contrary to the respect that I owe her, and which I will never fail to render her. And I can say, in all honesty, that the principle rule that I have always followed in my studies, and which I believe has been the most conducive to acquiring some knowledge, has been to dedicate only very few hours a day to the thoughts which occupy the imagination, and very few hours a year to those which occupy the understanding alone, and to dedicate the rest of my time to the relaxation of the senses and the repose of the mind. Among the exercises of the imagination, I even count all serious conversations, and everything that requires attention. That is what has led me to retire to the country; although, in the busiest city in the world, I could have as many hours to myself as I devote now to my studies, I could not, however, employ them so usefully when my mind is fatigued from the attention that the bustle of life demands of me. I take the liberty to write this to your Highness to attest to my great admiration for the fact that, not only does she involve herself in the affairs and undertake the duties that are unavoidable for anyone of both great mind and noble birth, she also dedicates herself to the meditations that are required to clearly understand the distinction between the soul and the body.

But I believe that it has been these meditations, rather than thoughts that require less attention, which has led her to find obscurity in the notion that we have of their union; the human mind, it seems to me, is incapable of precisely conceiving, at the same time, the distinction between the soul and the body, and their union. For, that would require conceiving them as one thing only, and at the same time as two separate things, which is a contradiction. And for the subject of their union (supposing that your Highness still had the reasons which prove the distinction between the soul and the body strongly impressed in her mind, and not wishing to ask her to rid herself of them in order to conceive the notion of the union which everyone always senses inside himself without philosophizing; that is, the notion that he is one single person, who has both a mind and a body, with such a nature that the mind can move the body and experience the accidents that befall it), I have hitherto used the comparison with weight and other qualities that we commonly imagine as being united to some kind of body, as the mind is united to ours; and I did not worry that this comparison failed on account of these qualities not being real, as one imagines them to be. For, I believed your Highness had already been thoroughly persuaded that the soul is a distinct substance from the body.

Your Highness believes that it is easier to attribute matter and extension to the soul than to attribute to the soul the capacity of moving a body, and be moved by it, without having matter; I entreat her to freely attribute this matter and extension to the soul, for, that is nothing other than conceiving the soul as united to the body. And after having conceived that well, and having felt it in herself, it will be easy for her to consider how the matter that she had attributed to thought is not thought itself, and that the extension of matter is of a different nature than the extension of thought, in that the first is determined at a certain location, from which it excludes all other bodily extension, while this is not the case for the second. In this way, your Highness will not cease to return with ease to the knowledge of the distinction between the soul and the body, despite having conceived their union.

Finally, as I believe it is very necessary to have well understood, once in one's life, the principles of metaphysics, since they are the ones which provide our knowledge of God and of our soul, I also believe it would be very detrimental to occupy one's understanding with frequent meditation on them, since that would preclude it from dedicating itself as effectively to the functions of the imagination and of the senses. It is best to content oneself with retaining in one's memory and one's beliefs, the conclusions that one has derived from these principles, and then to employ the rest of one's studies to thoughts that involve the understanding acting in conjunction with the imagination and the senses. . . .

I am, etc.

Elisabeth to Descartes
The Hague, 1 July 1643

Monsieur Descartes,

I worry that you may be as inconvenienced by my esteem of your instructions, and my desire to avail myself of them, as you are by the ingratitude of those who deprive themselves, and would wish to deprive humankind, of them. I would not have sent you another testimony to my ignorance before you had the opportunity to dispel these latter of their obstinacy, if Sir Van Bergen had not obliged me—primarily through his civility—to wish to remain in this city until I had presented him with a response to your letter of June 28, in which you have clearly explained to me the three kinds of notions we have, their objects, and how one should employ them. I also observe that the senses show me that the soul moves body, but that, on the other hand, they do not teach me anything regarding the manner in which this occurs. Nor does the intellect or the imagination so instruct me. Therefore, I think there are properties of the soul which are unknown to us, and that could, perhaps, run counter to your conclusions regarding the nonextension of the soul, of which you persuaded me in your metaphysical meditations. And this doubt has its source in the rule that you provided in the *Meditations,* where you discuss the nature of the true and the false; specifically, you maintain that the source of all our errors lies in forming judgments in respect to things that we do not perceive clearly and distinctly. Even though extension is neither necessary nor opposed to thought, it can hinder some other function of the soul, which is no less essential to it. At a minimum, extension undermines the contradiction maintained by the scholastics that the soul is in the whole body, and yet also exists in its entirety in each of the body's parts. I do not excuse myself for confounding the notion of the soul with that of the body in the manner of common people, but that does not remove my original doubt. I will despair of finding certitude in anything in the world if you do not provide it to me since you are the only one who has saved me from the skepticism to which my first reasoning had driven me. Although I owe you this confession as a token of my gratitude, I would deem it most imprudent if I knew not, through my previous experience as much as through your reputation, that your good will and generosity were equal to your other merits. You could not attest to it in more obliging a manner than by the clarifications and advice that you share with me and that I esteem above the greatest treasures that could be possessed.

Your truly devoted friend at your service,

Elisabeth

Descartes to Elisabeth
Egmond du Hoef, 18 May 1645

Madame,

I have been extremely surprised to learn, in my correspondence with Monsieur Pollot, that your Highness has been ill for a long while, and I curse my solitude, for it is responsible for my not having known of it sooner[. . . .] These [Monsieur Pollot's] last letters informed me that your Highness had, for three or four weeks, a slow fever, accompanied by a dry cough, and that, after having recovered for five or six days, the illness returned. However, I also learned that, by the time that he sent me his letter (which took nearly fifteen days en route), your Highness was once again feeling better. The symptoms I observe here indicate to me an illness so severe, but which I nevertheless think your Highness can certainly remedy, that I cannot abstain from writing her with my impression of it. The honor that your Highness conferred to me the past summer, in wishing to know my opinion in regards to another indisposition that she had then, makes me hope that the liberty I am taking here will not be disagreeable to her.

The most common cause for a slow fever is sadness; and the relentlessness with which fortune persecutes your household continually upsets you with affairs so public and shocking that it does not require a great deal of conjecture, nor considerable experience in these matters, to determine that herein lies the principle cause of your indisposition. And I fear that you will not be delivered from all of this if you do not, through the power of your virtue, render your soul content, despite the disappointments of bad fortune. I know very well that it would be imprudent to wish to raise the spirits of someone to whom fortune imparts new subjects of displeasure every day. I am not the cruel sort of philosopher who believes a wise man should be heartless. I also know that your Highness is not as affected by that which regards her personally as by that which involves the matters of her household and the people she holds dear. This I esteem to be the most amiable of all her virtues.

It seems to me that the difference that exists between the greatest souls and the most base and common ones consists, principally, in that the common souls surrender themselves to their passions, and are only happy or unhappy depending on whether or not the things that affect them are pleasing or displeasing. In contrast, other souls are endowed with reasoning so strong and powerful that, although they also have passions, which are often even more violent than those of ordinary people, their reason always remains the master nonetheless. In this way, even their afflictions serve them and contribute to the perfect happiness that they are able to enjoy in this life. These individuals realize that, on the one hand, they are immortals capable of receiving the greatest contentment, and that, on the other hand, they are joined to fragile and mortal bodies that are subject to many infirmities and will inevitably perish in but few years. Consequently, they do everything in their power to be blessed with favorable fortune in this life, but nevertheless esteem it so little, in regard to eternity, that they consider events almost as if they were merely participants in a play. And in the same way that sad and lamentable stories, which we see represented in the theater, are often as entertaining as cheerful ones, despite the fact that they bring tears to our eyes, so do these greatest souls of whom I speak receive satisfaction, inside themselves, from everything that happens to them, even from the most irritating and intolerable of occurrences. Thus, when they experience pain in their bodies, they exert themselves to endure it patiently, and this proof of their fortitude is pleasing to them. For the same reason, if they see their friends suffering some great affliction, they sympathize with their hardship and do anything in their means to deliver them from it. These souls do not even fear placing their lives at risk, if necessary, on their friends' behalf. In so doing, the testimony of their conscience that they are thus fulfilling their duty and performing a virtuous and laudable action, makes them so content that any sadness, as a result of their compassion, does not afflict them. Finally, just as the greatest prosperity from fortune never overcomes them nor renders them more insolent, the greatest adversity cannot conquer them nor make them so sad that the body, to which they are joined, becomes ill.

I would fear that the way I write might be ridiculous if I employed it in writing to someone else; but, since I consider your Highness to have the most noble and elevated soul of anyone I know, I believe that she should also be the most content of them all. She will truly be so, in my opinion, provided it pleases her to direct her attention to the value of the goods which she possesses, and which could never be removed from her, and compares these with those of which fortune has stripped her, and with the disappointments with which fortune persecutes her through the person of her relatives. She will then discover reason to celebrate and be content with the goods that truly reside within her. The extreme devotion that I have to her is responsible for my having allowed myself such liberty in this discourse, which I very humbly ask her to excuse as coming from a person who is . . . etc.

Elisabeth to Descartes
The Hague, 24 May 1645

Monsieur Descartes,

I see that the charms of solitary life have not stripped you of the virtues required for society. Witnessing the generous kindness that you show to your friends and in your concern for my health, I would have been upset if this had led you to undertake a journey here, since Monsieur Pallot told me that you decided that rest was necessary for your conservation. And I assure you that none of the doctors who visited me daily, and examined all the symptoms of my illness, were able to discover the cause or to provide as helpful remedies as you have from afar. If they had been discerning enough to question the possible role of my mind in my bodily disorder, I would not have the boldness to admit it to them. However, to you Monsieur, I do so without any misgivings, assuring myself that so innocent an account of my defects will not deprive me of the place I hold in your heart; rather, it will confirm me of my place even more since you will see how necessary it is to me.

You should know that my body is thoroughly vulnerable to many of the weaknesses of my sex, which makes it easily prone to the afflictions of the soul and thus lacks the strength to manage them. It has a temperament that is subject to obstructions and which remains in a state strongly conducive to them, as is common in people who are unable to exercise frequently. Consequently, the heart does not need to be oppressed by sadness for a long time in order to obstruct the spleen and infect the rest of the body with its vapors. I imagine that this is the cause of my slow fever and dry cough that still persists, though the warm weather and the walks I have been taking have restored my strength a little. That is why I consented to the doctors' advice to drink water from the Spa (which is brought all the way here without it spoiling) when it arrives in a month, having discovered from experience that it clears the obstructions. However, I will not consume it until I know your opinion since you have the good will to wish to cure my body with the soul.

I will also continue to confess to you that, although I do not place my happiness in anything that depends on fortune or the will of men, and although I will not consider myself absolutely unhappy if I never see my household restored or my relatives free from misery, I would still not know how to consider the harmful accidents that happen to them except as instances of evil. Nor would I know how to consider the vain efforts I make on their behalf without some sort of worry, which is no sooner calmed by reasoning than another disaster produces a new anxiety. And I think that if you were entirely familiar with my life, you would not be so surprised by the causes of my present illness, as you would be by that fact that a sensitive mind like my own has managed to conserve itself so long after so much abuse in so weak a body, without any other advice except that from her own reasoning and without consolation except that from her own conscience.

I spent the entire past winter involved in affairs so frustrating that they prevented me from taking advantage of the liberty you granted me to present you with the difficulties I would find in my studies. Instead, these affairs only presented me with the sort of difficulties that required even more stupidity than I would have to be capable of if I had a hope of unburdening myself of them. Only a short while before my indisposition did I manage to take the leisure to read the philosophy of the Knight Digby that he wrote in English. I hoped to extract arguments from it to refute yours since the summary of the chapters indicated two places where he claimed to have done so. However, after referring to them, I was completely astonished to discover that he had understood nothing less well than that

which he approved of in your views on reflection and, consequently, he rejected those you hold in regards to refraction. He made no distinction between the movement of a ball and its direction, and he did not consider why a soft body that is malleable slows down movement, nor why a hard body only resists the other. Part of what he says concerning the heart is more excusable, if he has not read what you wrote to the doctor from Louvain. Dr. Jonsson told me that he is going to translate these two chapters, and I do not think you will be very interested in the rest of the book because it is of the caliber and adopts the method of that English priest who calls himself Albanus.[1] There are, however, some very beautiful meditations in the book, and it is difficult to expect more from a man who spent most of his life pursuing interests of love or ambition. I have no stronger and more constant desire than to be all my life

Your very devoted friend at your service,

Elisabeth

[postscript]

Monsieur Descartes,

In rereading what I am about to send you in regards to myself, I realize that I am neglecting one of your maxims, which is to never put anything in writing that can be badly interpreted by unforgiving readers. However, I have great faith in the care of Monsieur Pallot to properly deliver my letter to you, and in your discretion to cast it into the fire in the event that it may fall into the wrong hands.

---

[1]Thomas White.

chapter sixteen

Baruch Spinoza

"You ask me," wrote Baruch (Benedictus de) Spinoza (1632–1677) to a friend, "'how I know that my philosophy is the best of all those that have ever been taught in this world, are now being taught, or will ever be taught in the future.'. . . I do not presume that I have discovered the best philosophy, but I know that what I understand is the true one."[1] Spinoza contended that the true philosophy both reveals the intelligibility of the universe and explains the human being's place in it, and he devoted his entire life to demonstrating that fact. Believing, moreover, that the only tool required by the true philosophy was logical reasoning, he shared with his favorite philosophical antagonist, René Descartes, two important traits. First, insofar as he claimed that reason, and not experience, is our guide to ultimate reality, Spinoza was a rationalist. Second, in rejecting appeals to authority and insisting that propositions be accepted as true only if they are self-evident or derived from self-evident truths through deduction, Spinoza joins Descartes as one of the fathers of modern philosophy.

Spinoza lived his whole life in Holland, which during most of the seventeenth century celebrated intellectual and religious freedom and was a center of European intellectual life. He was born in Amsterdam, the son of a Jewish merchant who had fled there with his family from Portugal during the Inquisition. In Portugal, Spinoza's family had been "crypto-Jews," forced to convert to Christianity but secretly remaining true to their faith. In Amsterdam, they were prominent members of the Jewish community; there, Spinoza received a traditional Jewish education and became a Hebrew scholar. When he came of age, however, his own theological speculations, influenced partly by his study of Cartesian philosophy, brought him into conflict with community leaders. Spinoza openly contested several doctrines, such as that God has a body and that angels exist, and, refusing to be silenced, he was excommunicated from the Jewish community of Amsterdam in 1656.

Spinoza accepted a teaching position in a school for children run by a former Jesuit and used the opportunity to further his own education. Resolving always to be financially independent, he also learned the trade of grinding lenses for glasses and telescopes. During this time, Spinoza formed a discussion group on philosophical—especially Cartesian—and theological issues, through which he continued to develop his own ideas. In 1660 he retreated to the quiet village of Rijnsburg to formulate his ideas in writing.

Spinoza theorized during a time when modern science was beginning to flourish and seriously challenge theological speculation. He was himself a scientific thinker, who saw the "new science" not as opposed to philosophy but, to the contrary, wholly compatible with it. Like Descartes, Spinoza believed that scientific explanation rests upon metaphysics; he was convinced that a scientist must be able to give some sort of answer to such fundamental questions as "Why does anything exist?" in order really to explain the objects of scientific investigation. Furthermore, he thought it crucial to recognize that these fundamental questions cannot be answered by experiment but only by logical reasoning. It is this conviction, that reason alone grants us access to ultimate reality and renders the universe in principle fully intelligible, that makes Spinoza, like Descartes, a rationalist. Spinoza set out to prescribe precisely how the universe could be made intelligible by devising a system—a rational method—that would *demonstrate* that such a perfect scientific knowledge of every feature of nature is possible, that is, without resorting to leaps of faith or appeals to divine revelation.

To Spinoza's mind, the paradigm of clear, methodical reasoning was mathematics, for the truth of mathematical propositions can infallibly be discovered and confirmed, and the sole instrument of mathematical inquiry is reason. Mathematical proofs are founded upon self-evident truths, from which conclusions are deduced through chains of logical reasoning. These conclusions, moreover, are forever and everywhere indubitable. Spinoza resolved to apply the mathematical method of reasoning to all areas of inquiry—metaphysical, moral, and scientific—believing that in any subject it should be possible to begin with distinctly defined and self-evident ideas and to proceed logically to indubitable conclusions. He resolved, furthermore, to write in a learned Latin that was increasingly being used in the seventeenth century for technical rather than literary and conversational forms of writing, since terms could be given a precise, and therefore a clear and distinct, meaning. Spinoza thus positioned himself as "the mouthpiece of pure Reason,"[2] eliminating from his arguments appeals to the imagination and other means of persuasion. The true philosophy, he believed, was to be presented as purely objective and evident to all who are capable of sound reasoning.

In Rijnsburg, Spinoza composed his first works, *A Short Treatise on God, Man, and His Well-Being; Treatise on the Emendation of the Intellect;* and an adaptation in geometric form of Descartes' *Principles of Philosophy*. He also began writing his master work, the *Ethics*, from which selections are included here. In 1663 Spinoza left Rijnsburg for

The Hague and published his version of Descartes' *Principles*, the only work published under his name in his lifetime.

Spinoza devoted the next few years to developing his own system to be presented in the *Ethics*. The text is divided into five parts, each of which is composed in the geometrical form, beginning with definitions and axioms and proceeding through a succession of deduced propositions with supporting proofs and commentaries. In Part I, "Concerning God," Spinoza lays the metaphysical foundation for his systematic treatment of ethics. The most important of his opening list of definitions, for our purposes, are those involving the notions of substance, attribute, mode, and God:

> Def. 3: By substance I mean that which is in itself and is conceived through itself; that is, that the conception of which does not require the conception of another thing from which it has to be formed.
>
> Def. 4: By attribute I mean that which the intellect perceives of substance as constituting its essence.
>
> Def. 5: By mode, I mean the affections of substance; that is, that which is in something else and is conceived through something else.
>
> Def. 6: By God I mean an absolutely infinite being; that is, substance consisting of infinite attributes, each of which expresses eternal and infinite essence.

Substance, for Spinoza, is in fact the totality of the universe. This becomes clear in Proposition 14, which proclaims, "Besides God, no substance can be granted or conceived." This proposition expresses simultaneously Spinoza's pantheism[3]—his conviction that God is the universe as a whole—and his substance monism, the idea that there exists only one substance in the universe, not a multitude of substances as most of us commonly believe. Spinoza claims that what we commonly think of as many distinct substances—for example, that rock, this person—are actually modes, or particular and finite modifications, of the one substance, which he calls "God, or Nature" (*Deus, sive Natura*).[4]

An attribute is a property of the universe, that in the words of a famous Spinoza scholar, "sprawls across everything."[5] Spinoza defines God as "substance consisting of infinite attributes," but he only identifies two: thought (mind) and extension (body). Spinoza claims that, as attributes, thought and extension are properties of everything in the universe; everything that exists has some degree of mind and extension, however great or infinitesimal. Moreover, Spinoza's definition of an attribute as "that which the intellect perceives of substance as constituting its essence," expresses his conviction that substance, and modes of substance, can be understood through the analysis of their attributes. Spinoza adds, however, "Each attribute of one substance must be conceived through itself" (I, Pr.10), expressing his conviction that mind and body are entirely distinct and must be explained independently of each other; thus, the mental cannot be reduced to the physical and vice versa. What *is* true, according to Spinoza, is that any mode can in principle be understood and explained in terms of the attribute of thought as a *thinking* mode[6] (as a mental being or activity), and, *alternatively*, the same mode can be given a completely different description strictly in physical terms, that is, in terms of the attribute of extension as an *extended* mode.

Considering himself to have derived the true metaphysical picture of the universe—namely, that it is a unitary substance with infinitely many modes (e.g., human beings, rocks, trees) and attributes—Spinoza proceeds in Parts II and III of the *Ethics* to deduce the truths of human nature. Already he thinks he has cleared away significant metaphysical misconceptions having potentially negative ethical consequences, such as the traditional notion that human beings are superior to the rest of nature. Similarly, in claiming that thought and extension are distinct attributes of the one substance, Spinoza has also set the stage for challenging the doctrine of the supremacy of the mind (thought) over the body (extension), a theme that can be traced as far back as Plato. Spinoza's immediate target on this latter point, however, is Descartes, to whom he explicitly refers in the preface to Part III.[7] For Spinoza, because mind and body are entirely distinct and causally independent attributes of the one substance, Descartes' treatment of them as *substances* that, though distinct, are somehow mysteriously united and causally related in human beings is just plain wrong.

On Spinoza's view, human beings are indeed both thinking and extended. However, they are not, as Descartes claimed, composite substances composed of the unified elements of mind and body, for these attributes of mind and body are entirely distinct. Rather, we must conceive of the human mode as capable of being interpreted *either* in terms of the attribute of thought—as a mental being manifesting psychical functions—*or* in terms of extension, as an embodied being performing physical functions. One might well ask why it nevertheless *appears* to be the case that mind and body are causally connected and thus somehow united; after all, it seems clear that one can cause a bodily movement by mentally willing it. Spinoza explains, simply, "The order and connection of ideas is the same as the order and connection of things" (II, Pr. 7), by which he means that there is in reality only one series of events in the one substance, and each event can be described either in terms of thought or in terms of extension as different attributes of the same event. Thus, when describing the activity of raising one's hand, one should not conceive of it as two *successive* events, as if one first wills to raise one's hand and then, as a consequence of thinking, actually raises it. Rather, one should understand it as a single event that can be described *either* in terms of the mental activity of willing the raising of a hand *or* the physical activity of actually raising it. In general, Spinoza thinks that if we commit ourselves to deriving complete descriptions of human beings in terms of each attribute separately, that is, without confusing the two and trying to explain one in terms of the other, we avail ourselves of a method of analysis capable of yielding clear and distinct knowledge of the nature of human beings. Each separate account is legitimate, and taken together as a set of two complementary explanations, they can explain the full richness of human nature.

Spinoza devotes Part III of the *Ethics*, in fact, to demystifying the human experience of emotion. One question may spring immediately to mind, given the value Spinoza ascribes to reason: If mind is not a substance superior to body, and if it does not have as one of its functions the governing of bodily passions, how are we to understand and deal with our emotions, which do seem at times to interfere with our ability to reason clearly? Spinoza admits that human beings are creatures of passion and that we can be enslaved by our emotions; he also believes that we can manage and direct those passions and achieve genuine freedom and happiness in doing so.

Like Descartes, Spinoza draws a distinction between human actions and passions, but his account differs from Descartes' in that Spinoza does not conceive of activity and passivity strictly and simply in terms of, respectively, causing or suffering events. Rather, for Spinoza, activity and passivity are matters of the degree to which a person's mind comprehends, and thus has a kind of intellectual command over, factors in given events. On Spinoza's view, one and the same event, such as a particular emotion, can be understood as being either active or passive, depending on the individual's understanding of the experience. "In so far as [the mind] has adequate ideas," Spinoza writes, "it is necessarily active; and in so far as it has inadequate ideas, it is necessarily passive" (III, Pr. 1). An adequate idea is one that "in so far as it is considered in itself without relation to its object, has all the properties of a true idea" (II, Def. 4)—that is, a *self*-evident, clear and distinct idea, perfectly understood by the mind without reference to any other idea. An inadequate idea Spinoza calls "fragmented and confused" (III, Pr. 1, Proof), meaning simply that it cannot be understood in and of itself, without reference to other ideas. Predictably, Spinoza sees the human being's freedom and happiness as being bound up with his or her activity in this sense; the more clearly and distinctly one understands events in one's experience—that is, the more active one is in the course of events—the more freedom and happiness one experiences. When one does not have clear and distinct understanding of events—that is, when the mind is passive—one can be unduly manipulated and controlled by them; one is in a condition of bondage.

Accordingly, an emotion that is not adequately understood is a passion, but human beings can be active with respect to emotions by understanding them. This requires self-knowledge, an understanding that one is a finite mode of an infinitely various but unitary substance. A human being is therefore always affected by numerous external factors; one cannot avoid being affected by these factors, but one can come to understand them and thus master rather than be mastered by them. Spinoza therefore devotes Part III of the *Ethics,* "Of the Nature and Origin of the Emotions," to *explaining* such features of human experience as pleasure, pain, desire, love, and hatred. In Part IV he discusses how and why humans are enslaved by their emotions, and in Part V he explains how the intellect can set us free.

In 1670, hoping to publish the *Ethics* but anticipating controversy given the rise of Calvinism and the demise of the tolerance in the Dutch Republic, Spinoza wrote and published anonymously a *Theologico-Political Treatise* defending secular government and freedom of thought. The *Treatise* was banned. Spinoza abandoned hope of publishing the *Ethics* in his lifetime but stipulated in his will that it should be published posthumously. The *Ethics* appeared in 1677, the year of Spinoza's death from consumption, which presumably was complicated by breathing the dust of lens grinding.

The *Ethics*, too, was immediately banned upon publication, and for about a century after Spinoza's death, the term "Spinozism" carried a derogatory meaning. However, in the nineteenth century two German literary heroes, G.E. Lessing and Johann Wolfgang von Goethe, awakened widespread interest in Spinoza's thought. Since then, Spinoza's philosophy has had an interesting dual reception: idealist philosophers, such as G.W.F. Hegel, and Romantic thinkers have tended to emphasize Spinoza's pantheism, seeing in him a philosopher who interprets all of nature as a manifestation of God, or the one substance; Marxists and other proponents of materialism, by contrast, have stressed Spinoza's determinism and its implications for a strictly mechanical view of the universe.

In all events, since the nineteenth century Spinoza has been celebrated as the philosopher who demonstrates the power of human reason, as well as the rationality of both love and the pursuit of wisdom. These, he believed, contribute to our greatest happiness: the *amor intellectualis Dei*, the intellectual love of God.

SC

QUESTIONS

1. Explain in your own words why Spinoza used the geometrical method to present his treatise, which is not about mathematics but *ethics*.
2. Do you find Spinoza's "geometrical" arguments concerning love and desire compelling— or even "necessarily true"? What do you consider to be the strengths and weaknesses of the arguments?
3. Imagine and construct a debate between Spinoza and Descartes concerning mind and body interaction and the emotions, incorporating their respective conceptions of activity and passivity. Who do you believe wins the debate? Why?
4. Construct a similar dialogue between Spinoza and Princess Elisabeth of Bohemia. What is the outcome of the dialogue? Explain.

ENDNOTES

1. Spinoza, "Letter 76 to Alfred Burgh" in *The Letters*, p. 342.
2. Hampshire, *Spinoza*, p. 25.
3. Literally, "all-God." Spinoza was not the first Western philosopher to endorse pantheism; the presocratic philosopher, Parmenides, for instance, was a pantheist.

4. Spinoza thus challenged the traditional conception of God as a transcendent being, distinct from nature.

5. Jonathan Bennett, *A Study of Spinoza's Ethics*, Indianapolis, Ind: Hackett Publishing, 1984, p. 61.

6. Note that for Spinoza, a human mind is not a thinking *substance*, as Descartes proclaimed. Descartes speaks of two substances, mind and body; for Spinoza, there is only one substance with infinitely many attributes, two of which are mind and body. We shall see that this distinction has implications for Spinoza's treatment of the problem of mind-body interaction.

7. Cf. page 251 below.

SELECTED BIBLIOGRAPHY

Garrett, Don, ed. *The Cambridge Companion to Spinoza*. New York: Cambridge University Press, 1996.

Hampshire, Stuart. *Spinoza*. Baltimore, Md.: Penguin Books, 1962.

Lloyd, Genevieve. *Part of Nature: Self-Knowledge in Spinoza's Ethics*. Ithaca: Cornell University Press, 1994.

Scruton, Roger. *Spinoza*. New York: Routledge, 1999.

Spinoza, Baruch (Benedictus de). *The Collected Works of Spinoza*, trans. and ed. Edwin Curley. Princeton, N.J.: Princeton University Press, 1985.

Spinoza, Baruch (Benedictus de). *Ethics, Treatise on the Emendation of the Intellect, and Selected Letters*, trans. Samuel Shirley, ed. Seymour Feldman. Indianapolis, Ind.: Hackett Publishing, 1991.

Spinoza, Baruch (Benedictus de). *The Letters*, trans. Samuel Shirley. Indianapolis, Ind.: Hackett Publishing, 1995.

Yovel, Yirmiyahu. *Spinoza and Other Heretics*. 2 vols. Princeton, N.J.: Princeton University Press, 1989.

from the *Ethics*

Baruch Spinoza

PART III: CONCERNING THE ORIGIN AND NATURE OF THE EMOTIONS

Preface

Most of those who have written about the emotions (affectibus) and human conduct seem to be dealing not with natural phenomena that follow the common laws of Nature but with phenomena outside Nature. They appear to go so far as to conceive man in Nature as a kingdom within a kingdom. They believe that he disturbs rather than follows Nature's order, and has absolute power over his actions, and is determined by no other source than himself. Again, they assign the cause of human weakness and frailty not to the power of Nature in general, but to some defect in human nature, which they therefore bemoan, ridicule, despise, or, as is most frequently the case, abuse. He who can criticise the weakness of the human mind more eloquently or more shrilly is regarded as almost divinely inspired. Yet there have not been lacking outstanding figures who have written much that is excellent regarding the right conduct of life and have given to mankind very sage counsel; and we confess we owe much to their toil and industry. However, as far as I know, no one has defined the nature and strength of the emotions, and the power of the mind in controlling them. I know, indeed, that the renowned Descartes, though he too believed that the mind has absolute power over its actions, does explain human emotions through their first causes, and has also zealously striven to show how the mind can have absolute control over the emotions. But in my opinion he has shown nothing else but the brilliance of his own genius, as I shall demonstrate in due course; for I want now to return to those who prefer to abuse or deride the emotions and actions of men rather than to understand them. They will doubtless find it surprising that I should attempt to treat of the faults and follies of mankind in the geometric manner, and that I should propose to bring logical reasoning to bear on what they proclaim is opposed to reason, and is vain, absurd and horrifying. But my argument is this: in Nature nothing happens which can be attributed to its defectiveness, for Nature is always the same, and its force and power of acting is everywhere one and the same; that is, the laws and rules of Nature according to which all things happen and change from one form to another are everywhere and always the same. So our approach to the understanding of the nature of things of every kind should likewise be one and the same; namely, through the universal laws and rules of Nature. Therefore the emotions of hatred, anger, envy, etc., considered in themselves, follow from the same necessity and force of Nature as all other particular things. So these emotions are assignable to definite causes through which they can be understood, and have definite properties, equally deserving of our investigation as the properties of any other thing, whose mere contemplation affords us pleasure. I shall, then, treat of the nature and strength of the emotions, and the mind's power over them, by the same method as I have used in treating of God and the mind, and I shall consider human actions and appetites just as if it were an investigation into lines, planes, or bodies.

Definitions

1. I call that an adequate cause whose effect can be clearly and distinctly perceived through the said cause. I call that an inadequate or partial cause whose effect cannot be understood through the said cause alone.

2. I say that we are active when something takes place, in us or externally to us, of which we are the adequate cause; that is, (by preceding Def.), when from our nature there follows in us or externally to us something which can be clearly and distinctly understood through our nature alone. On the other hand, I say that we are passive when something takes place in us, or follows from our nature, of which we are only the partial cause.

3. By emotion (affectus) I understand the affections of the body by which the body's power of activity is increased or diminished, assisted or checked, together with the ideas of these affections.

Thus, if we can be the adequate cause of one of these affections, then by emotion I understand activity, otherwise passivity.

Postulates

1. The human body can be affected in many ways by which its power of activity is increased or diminished; and also in many other ways which neither increase nor diminish its power of activity.

This postulate or axiom rests on Postulate 1 and Lemmata 5 and 7, following Pr.13,II.

2. The human body can undergo many changes and nevertheless retain impressions or traces of objects (see Post.5,II) and consequently the same images of things;—for the definition of which see Sch.Pr.17,II.

Proposition 1

Our mind is in some instances active and in other instances passive. In so far as it has adequate ideas, it is necessarily active; and in so far as it has inadequate ideas, it is necessarily passive.

Proof

In every human mind, some of its ideas are adequate, others are fragmentary and confused (Sch.Pr.40,II). Now ideas that are adequate in someone's mind are adequate in God in so far as he constitutes the essence of that mind (Cor.Pr.11,II); and furthermore those ideas that are inadequate in the mind are also adequate in God (same Cor.), not in so far as he contains in himself the essence of that mind only, but in so far as he contains the minds of other things as well. Again, from any given idea some effect must necessarily follow (Pr.36,I), of which God is the adequate cause (Def.1,III) not in so far as he is infinite but in so far as he is considered as affected by the given idea (Pr.9,II). But in the case of an effect of which God is the cause in so far as he is affected by an idea which is adequate in someone's mind, that same mind is its adequate cause (Cor.Pr.11,II). Therefore our mind (Def.2,III), in so far as it has adequate ideas, is necessarily active—which is the first

point. Again, whatever necessarily follows from an idea that is adequate in God not in so far as he has in himself the mind of one man only, but in so far as he has the minds of other things simultaneously with the mind of the said man, the mind of that man is not the adequate cause of it, but the partial cause (Cor.Pr.11,II), and therefore (Def.2,III) in so far as the mind has inadequate ideas, it is necessarily passive—which was the second point. Therefore our mind etc.

Corollary

Hence it follows that the more the mind has inadequate ideas, the more it is subject to passive states (passionibus); and, on the other hand, it is the more active in proportion as it has a greater number of adequate ideas.

Proposition 2

The body cannot determine the mind to think, nor can the mind determine the body to motion or rest, or to anything else (if there is anything else).

Proof

All modes of thinking have God for their cause in so far as he is a thinking thing, and not in so far as he is explicated by any other attribute (Pr.6,II). So that which determines the mind to think is a mode of Thinking, and not of Extension; that is (Def.1,II), it is not the body. That was our first point. Now the motion-and-rest of a body must arise from another body, which again has been determined to motion or rest by another body, and without exception whatever arises in a body must have arisen from God in so far as he is considered as affected by a mode of Extension, and not in so far as he is considered as affected by a mode of

Thinking (Pr.6,II); that is, it cannot arise from mind, which (Pr.11,II) is a mode of Thinking. That was our second point. Therefore the body cannot . . . etc.

Scholium

This is more clearly understood from Sch.Pr.7,II, which tells us that mind and body are one and the same thing, conceived now under the attribute of Thought, now under the attribute of Extension. Hence it comes about that the order or linking of things is one, whether Nature be conceived under this or that attribute, and consequently the order of the active and passive states of our body is simultaneous in Nature with the order of active and passive states of the mind. This is also evident from the manner of our proof of Pr.12,II.

Yet, although the matter admits of no shadow of doubt, I can scarcely believe, without the confirmation of experience, that men can be induced to examine this view without prejudice, so strongly are they convinced that at the mere bidding of the mind the body can now be set in motion, now be brought to rest, and can perform any number of actions which depend solely on the will of the mind and the exercise of thought. However, nobody as yet has determined the limits of the body's capabilities: that is, nobody as yet has learned from experience what the body can and cannot do, without being determined by mind, solely from the laws of its nature in so far as it is considered as corporeal. For nobody as yet knows the structure of the body so accurately as to explain all its functions, not to mention that in the animal world we find much that far surpasses human sagacity, and that sleepwalkers do many things in their sleep that they would not dare when awake;—clear evidence that the body, solely from the laws of its own nature, can do many things at which its mind is amazed.

Again, no one knows in what way and by what means mind can move body, or how many degrees of motion it can impart to body and with what speed it can cause it to move. Hence it follows that when men say that this or that action of the body arises from the mind which has command over the body, they do not know what they are saying, and are merely admitting, under a plausible cover of words, that they are ignorant of the true cause of that action and are not concerned to discover it.

"But," they will say, "whether or not we know by what means the mind moves the body, experience tells us that unless the mind is in a fit state to exercise thought, the body remains inert. And again, experience tells us that it is solely within the power of the mind both to speak and to keep silent, and to do many other things which we therefore believe to depend on mental decision." Now as to the first point, I ask, does not experience also tell them that if, on the other hand, the body is inert, the mind likewise is not capable of thinking? When the body is at rest in sleep, the mind remains asleep with it and does not have that power of entertaining thoughts which it has when awake. Again, I think that all have experienced the fact that the mind is not always equally apt for concentrating on the same object; the mind is more apt to regard this or that object according as the body is more apt to have arising in it the image of this or that object.

"But," they will say, "it is impossible that the causes of buildings, pictures, and other things of this kind, which are made by human skill alone, should be deduced solely from the laws of Nature considered only as corporeal, nor is the human body capable of building a temple unless it be determined and guided by mind." However, I have already pointed out that they do not know what the body can do, or what can be deduced solely from a consideration of its nature, and that experience abundantly shows that solely from the laws of

its nature many things occur which they would
never have believed possible except from the direction of mind:—for instance, the actions of sleepwalkers, which they wonder at when they are
awake. A further consideration is the very structure
of the human body, which far surpasses in ingenuity all the constructions of human skill; not to
mention the point I made earlier, that from Nature, considered under any attribute whatsoever,
infinite things follow.

As to the second point, the human condition
would indeed be far happier if it were equally in
the power of men to keep silent as to talk. But experience teaches us with abundant examples that
nothing is less within men's power than to hold
their tongues or control their appetites. From this
derives the commonly held view that we act freely
only in cases where our desires are moderate, because our appetites can then be easily held in check
by the remembrance of another thing that frequently comes to mind; but when we seek something with a strong emotion that cannot be allayed
by the remembrance of some other thing, we cannot check our desires. But indeed, had they not
found by experience that we do many things of
which we later repent, and that frequently, when
we are at the mercy of conflicting emotions, we
'see the better and do the worse,' there would be
nothing to prevent them from believing that all
our actions are free. A baby thinks that it freely
seeks milk, an angry child that it freely seeks revenge, and a timid man that he freely seeks flight.
Again, the drunken man believes that it is from the
free decision of the mind that he says what he later,
when sober, wishes he had not said. So, too, the
delirious man, the gossiping woman, the child,
and many more of this sort think that they speak
from free mental decision, when in fact they are
unable to restrain their torrent of words. So experience tells us no less clearly than reason that it is on
this account only that men believe themselves to

be free, that they are conscious of their actions and
ignorant of the causes by which they are determined; and it tells us too that mental decisions are
nothing more than the appetites themselves, varying therefore according to the varying disposition
of the body. For each man's actions are shaped by
his emotion; and those who furthermore are a prey
to conflicting emotions know not what they want,
while those who are free from emotion are driven
on to this or that course by a slight impulse.

Now surely all these considerations go to show
clearly that mental decision on the one hand, and
the appetite and physical state of the body on the
other hand, are simultaneous in nature; or rather,
they are one and the same thing which, when considered under the attribute of Thought and explicated through Thought, we call decision, and
when considered under the attribute of Extension
and deduced from the laws of motion-and-rest, we
call a physical state. This will become clearer from
later discussion, for there is now another point
which I should like you to note as very important.
We can take no action from mental decision unless
the memory comes into play; for example, we cannot utter a word unless we call the word to mind.
Now it is not within the free power of the mind to
remember or to forget any thing. Hence comes the
belief that the power of the mind whereby we can
keep silent or speak solely from mental decision is
restricted to the case of a remembered thing. However, when we dream that we are speaking, we
think that we do so from free mental decision; yet
we are not speaking, or if we are, it is the result of
spontaneous movement of the body. Again, we
dream that we are keeping something secret, and
that we are doing so by the same mental decision
that comes into play in our waking hours when we
keep silent about what we know. Finally, we dream
that from a mental decision we act as we dare not
act when awake. So I would very much like to
know whether in the mind there are two sorts of

decisions, dreamland decisions and free decisions. If we don't want to carry madness so far, we must necessarily grant that the mental decision that is believed to be free is not distinct from imagination and memory, and is nothing but the affirmation which an idea, in so far as it is an idea, necessarily involves (Pr.49,II). So these mental decisions arise in the mind from the same necessity as the ideas of things existing in actuality, and those who believe that they speak, or keep silent, or do anything from free mental decision are dreaming with their eyes open.

Proposition 3

The active states (actiones) of the mind arise only from adequate ideas; its passive states depend solely on inadequate ideas.

Proof

The first thing that constitutes the essence of the mind is nothing else but the idea of a body actually existing (Prs.11 and 13,II), which idea is composed of many other ideas (Pr.15,II), of which some are adequate (Cor.Pr.38,II) while others are inadequate (Cor.Pr.29,II). Therefore whatever follows from the nature of the mind and must be understood through the mind as its proximate cause must necessarily follow from an adequate idea or an inadequate idea. But in so far as the mind has inadequate ideas, it is necessarily passive (Prop.1,III). Therefore the active states of mind follow solely from adequate ideas, and thus the mind is passive only by reason of having inadequate ideas.

Scholium

We therefore see that passive states are related to the mind only in so far as the mind has something involving negation: that is, in so far as the mind is considered as part of Nature, which cannot be clearly and distinctly perceived through itself independently of other parts. By the same reasoning I could demonstrate that passive states are a characteristic of particular things just as they are of the mind, and cannot be perceived in any other way; but my purpose is to deal only with the human mind.

Proposition 4

No thing can be destroyed except by an external cause.

Proof

This proposition is self-evident, for the definition of anything affirms, and does not negate, the thing's essence: that is, it posits, and does not annul, the thing's essence. So as long as we are attending only to the thing itself, and not to external causes, we can find nothing in it which can destroy it.

Proposition 5

Things are of a contrary nature, that is, unable to subsist in the same subject, to the extent that one can destroy the other.

Proof

If they were able to be in agreement with one other, or to co-exist in the same subject, there could be something in the said subject which could destroy it, which is absurd (preceding Pr.). Therefore . . . etc.

Proposition 6

Each thing, in so far as it is in itself, endeavors to persist in its own being.

Proof

Particular things are modes whereby the attributes of God are expressed in a definite and determinate way (Cor.Pr.25,I), that is (Pr.34,I), they are things which express in a definite and determinate way the power of God whereby he is and acts, and no thing can have in itself anything by which it can be destroyed, that is, which can annul its existence (Pr.4,III). On the contrary, it opposes everything that can annul its existence (preceding Pr.); and thus, as far as it can and as far as it is in itself, it endeavors to persist in its own being.

Proposition 7

The conatus[1] with which each thing endeavors to persist in its own being is nothing but the actual essence of the thing itself.

Proof

From the given essence of a thing certain things necessarily follow (Pr.36,I), nor do things effect anything other than that which necessarily follows from their determinate nature (Pr.29,I). Therefore, the power of any thing, or the conatus with which it acts or endeavors to act, alone or in conjunction with other things, that is (Pr.6,III), the power or conatus by which it endeavors to persist in its own being, is nothing but the given, or actual, essence of the thing.

Proposition 8

The conatus with which each single thing endeavors to persist in its own being does not involve finite time, but indefinite time.

---

[1]The term 'conatus' plays an important role in Spinoza's psychology. It expresses Spinoza's view that each thing exemplifies an inherent tendency towards self-preservation and activity. This term has a long history, going back to Cicero, who used it to express Aristotle's and the Stoics' notion of impulse (horme). It was later used by medieval and early modern philosophers, such as Hobbes, to connote the natural tendency of an organism to preserve itself. For a history of this term consult H. Wolfson, *The Philosophy of Spinoza* (New York 1969), volume 2, pp. 195–99.)

Proof

If it involved a limited period of time which would determine the duration of the thing, then solely from the power by which the thing exists it would follow that it could not exist after that limited period of time, but is bound to be destroyed. But (Pr.4,III), this is absurd. Therefore the conatus with which a thing exists does not involve any definite period of time. On the contrary (by the same Pr.4,III), if it is not destroyed by an external cause, it will always continue to exist by that same power by which it now exists. Therefore this conatus involves an indefinite time.

Proposition 9

The mind, both in so far as it has clear and distinct ideas and in so far as it has confused ideas, endeavors to persist in its own being over an indefinite period of time, and is conscious of this conatus.

Proof

The essence of the mind is constituted by adequate and inadequate ideas (as we showed in Pr.3,III), and so (Pr.7,III) it endeavors to persist in its own being in so far as it has both these kinds of ideas, and does so (Pr.8,III) over an indefinite period of time. Now since the mind (Pr.23,II) is necessarily conscious of itself through the ideas of the affections of the body, therefore the mind is conscious of its conatus (Pr.7,III).

Scholium

When this conatus is related to the mind alone, it is called Will (voluntas); when it is related to mind and body together, it is called Appetite (appetitus), which is therefore nothing else but man's essence, from the nature of which there necessarily follow those things that tend to his preservation, and which man is thus determined to perform. Further, there is no difference between appetite and Desire (cupiditas) except that desire is usually related to men in so far as they are conscious of their appetite. Therefore it can be defined as follows: desire is 'appetite accompanied by the consciousness thereof.'

It is clear from the above considerations that we do not endeavor, will, seek after or desire because we judge a thing to be good. On the contrary, we judge a thing to be good because we endeavor, will, seek after and desire it.

Proposition 10

An idea that excludes the existence of our body cannot be in our mind, but is contrary to it.

Proof

Whatsoever can destroy our body cannot be therein (Pr.5,III), and so neither can its idea be in God in so far as he has the idea of our body (Cor.Pr.9,II); that is (Prs.11 and 13,II), the idea of such a thing cannot be in our mind. On the contrary, since (Prs.11 and 13,II) the first thing that constitutes the essence of the mind is the idea of an actually existing body, the basic and most important element of our mind is the conatus (Pr.7,III) to affirm the existence of our body. Therefore the idea that negates the existence of our body is contrary to our mind.

Proposition 11

Whatsoever increases or diminishes, assists or checks, the power of activity of our body, the idea of the said thing increases or diminishes, assists or checks the power of thought of our mind.

Proof

This proposition is evident from Pr.7,II, or again from Pr.14,II.

Scholium

We see then that the mind can undergo considerable changes, and can pass now to a state of greater perfection, now to one of less perfection, and it is these passive transitions (passiones) that explicate for us the emotions of Pleasure (laetitia) and Pain (tristitia). So in what follows I shall understand by pleasure 'the passive transition of the mind to a state of greater perfection,' and by pain 'the passive transition of the mind to state of less perfection.' The emotion of pleasure when it is simultaneously related to mind and body I call Titillation (titillatio) or Cheerfulness (hilaritas); the emotion of pain when it is similarly related I call Anguish (dolor) or Melancholy (melancholia). But be it noted that titillation and anguish are related to man when one part of him is affected more than others, cheerfulness and melancholy when all parts are equally affected. As to Desire (cupiditas), I have explained what it is in Sch.Pr.9,III, and I acknowledge no primary emotion other than these three [i.e. pleasure, pain and desire]; for I shall subsequently show that the others arise from these three. But before going further, I should like to explain Pr.10,III at greater length, so that there may be a clearer understanding of the way in which an idea may be contrary to an idea.

In Sch.Pr.17,II we demonstrated that the idea which constitutes the essence of the mind involves the existence of the body for as long as the body exists. Then from what we proved in Cor.Pr.8,II and its Sch., it follows that the present existence of our mind depends solely on this, that the mind involves the actual existence of the body. Finally we proved that the power of the mind whereby it imagines (imaginatur) and remembers things depends also on this (Prs.17 and 18,II, and Sch.), that it involves the actual existence of the body. From this it follows that the present existence of the mind and its capacity to perceive through the senses are annulled as soon as the mind ceases to affirm the present existence of the body. But the cause of the mind's ceasing to affirm this existence of the body cannot be the mind itself (Pr.4,III), nor again that the body ceases to be. For (Pr.6,II) the cause of the mind's affirming the existence of the body is not that the body began to exist; therefore, by the same reasoning, it does not cease to affirm the existence of the body on account of the body's ceasing to be. This results from another idea, which excludes the present existence of our body and consequently that of our mind, and which is therefore contrary to the idea that constitutes the essence of our mind (Pr.8,II).

Proposition 12

The mind, as far as it can, endeavors to think of those things that increase or assist the body's power of activity.

Proof

As long as the human body is affected in a manner that involves the nature of an external body, so long will the human mind regard that latter body as present (Pr.17,II). Consequently, (Pr.7,II) as long as the human mind regards some external body as present, that is (Sch.Pr.17,II), thinks of it, so long is the human body affected in a manner that involves the nature of that external body. Accordingly, as long as the mind thinks of those things that increase or assist our body's power of activity, so long is the body affected in ways that increase or assist its power of activity (Post.1,III); and, consequently, so long is the mind's power of thinking increased or assisted (Pr.11,III). Therefore, (Pr.6 or 9,III) the mind, as far as it can, endeavors to think of those things.

Proposition 13

When the mind thinks of those things that diminish or check the body's power of activity, it endeavors, as far as it can, to call to mind those things that exclude the existence of the former.

Proof

As long as the mind thinks of something of this kind, so long is the power of mind and body diminished or checked (as we have proved in the preceding proposition). Nevertheless the mind will continue to think of it until it thinks of another thing that excludes the present existence of the former (Pr.17,II); that is, (as we have just demonstrated), the power of mind and body is diminished or checked until the mind thinks of something else that excludes the thing's existence, something which the mind therefore (Pr.9,III) endeavors, as far as it can, to think of or call to mind.

Corollary

Hence it follows that the mind is averse to thinking of things that diminish or check its power and the body's power.

Scholium

From what has been said we clearly understand what are Love, (amor) and Hatred (odium). Love is merely 'pleasure accompanied by the idea of an external cause,' and hatred is merely 'pain accompanied by the idea of an external cause.' Again, we see that he who loves necessarily endeavors to have present and to preserve the thing that he loves; on the other hand, he who hates endeavors to remove and destroy the thing that he hates. But we shall deal with these matters more fully in due course.

Proposition 14

If the mind has once been affected by two emotions at the same time, when it is later affected by the one it will also be affected by the other.

Proof

If the human body has once been affected by two bodies at the same time, when the mind later thinks of the one it will straightway recall the other too (Pr.18,II). Now the images formed by the mind reflect the affective states of our body more than the nature of external bodies (Cor.2,Pr.16,II). Therefore if the body, and consequently the mind (Def.3,III), has once been affected by two emotions, when it is later affected by the one, it will also be affected by the other.

Proposition 15

Anything can indirectly (per accidens) be the cause of Pleasure, Pain, or Desire:

Proof

Let it be supposed that the mind is affected by two emotions simultaneously, of which one neither increases nor diminishes its power of activity, and the other either increases it or diminishes it (Post.1,III). From the preceding proposition it is clear that when the mind is later affected by the former as its true cause—which, by hypothesis, of itself neither increases nor diminishes the mind's power of thinking—it will straightway be affected by the other, which does increase or diminish its power of thinking; that is (Sch.Pr.11,III), it will be affected by pleasure or pain. So the former will be the cause of pleasure or pain, not through itself, but indirectly. In this same way it can readily be demonstrated that the former thing can indirectly be the cause of desire.

Corollary

From the mere fact that we have regarded a thing with the emotion of pleasure or pain of which it is not itself the efficient cause, we may love or hate that thing.

Proof

From this mere fact it comes about (Pr.14,III) that the mind, when later thinking of this thing, is affected by the emotion of pleasure or pain; that is (Sch.Pr.11,III), the power of the mind and body is increased or diminished, etc. Consequently, (Pr.12,III), the mind desires to think of the said thing, or is averse to it (Cor.Pr.13,III); that is (Sch.Pr.13,III), it loves or hates the said thing.

Scholium

Hence we understand how it can come about that we love or hate some things without any cause known to us, but merely from Sympathy and Antipathy, as they are called. We should also classify in this category those objects that affect us with pleasure or pain from the mere fact that they have some resemblance to objects that are wont to affect us with the same emotions, as I shall demonstrate in the next Proposition.

I realise that the writers who first introduced the terms 'sympathy' and 'antipathy' intended them to mean certain occult qualities. Nevertheless, I think it is permissible for us to denote by them qualities that are also familiar or manifest.

Proposition 16

From the mere fact that we imagine a thing to have something similar to an object that is wont to affect the mind with pleasure or pain, we shall love it or hate it, although the point of similarity is not the efficient cause of these emotions.

Proof

By hypothesis, the point of similarity has been regarded by us in the object with the emotion of pleasure or pain; and so (Pr.14,III) when the mind is affected by its image, it will also straightway be affected by the one or other emotion. Consequently the thing which we perceive to have this said point of similarity will indirectly be the cause of pleasure or pain (Pr.15,III); and thus (preceding Corollary), we shall love or hate the thing even though the point of similarity is not the efficient cause of these emotions.

Proposition 17

If we imagine that a thing which is wont to affect us with an emotion of pain, has something similar to another thing which is wont to affect us with an equally great emotion of pleasure, we shall hate it and love it at the same time.

Proof

By hypothesis, this thing is in itself a cause of pain, and (Sch.Pr.13,III) in so far as we imagine it with this emotion, we hate it. But, in addition, in so far as we imagine it to have something similar to another thing which is wont to affect us with an equally great emotion of pleasure, we shall love it with an equally strong emotion of pleasure (preceding Pr.). So we shall hate it and love it at the same time.

Scholium

This condition of the mind arising from two conflicting emotions is called 'vacillation,' which is therefore related to emotion as doubt is related to imagination (Sch.Pr.44,II), and there is no difference between vacillation and doubt except in respect of intensity. But it should be observed that in the preceding Proposition I deduced these vacillations from causes which are, in the case of one emotion, a direct cause, and in the case of the other an indirect cause. This I did because they could in this way be more readily deduced from what had preceded, and not because I deny that vacillations generally arise from an object which is the efficient cause of both emotions. For the human body is composed (Post.1,II) of very many individual bodies of different nature, and so (Ax.1 after Lemma 3, q.v. after Pr.13,II) it can be affected by one and the same body in many different ways; on the other hand, since one and the same thing can be affected in many ways, it can likewise affect one and the same part of the body in different ways. From this we can readily conceive that

one and the same object can be the cause of many conflicting emotions.

Proposition 18

From the image of a thing past or future man is affected by the same emotion of pleasure or pain as from the image of a thing present.

Proof

As long as a man is affected by the image of a thing, he will regard the thing as present even though it may not exist (Pr.17,II and Cor.), and he does not think of it as past or future except in so far as its image is joined to the image of past or future time (Sch.Pr.44,II). Therefore the image of a thing, considered solely in itself, is the same whether it be related to future, past or present; that is (Cor.2,Pr.16,II), the state of the body, or the emotion, is the same whether the image be of a thing past or future or present. So the emotion of pleasure, and of pain, is the same whether the image be of a thing past or future or present.

Scholium 1

Here I call a thing past or future in so far as we have been, or shall be, affected by it; for example, in so far as we have seen or shall see it, it has refreshed or will refresh us, it has injured or will injure us, etc. For in so far as we imagine it in this way, to that extent we affirm its existence; that is, the body is not affected by any emotion that excludes the existence of the thing, and so (Pr.17,II) the body is affected by the image of the thing in the same way as if the thing itself were present. However, since it is generally the case that those who have had much experience vacillate when they are regarding a thing as future or past and are generally in doubt as to its outcome (Sch.Pr.44,II), the result is that emotions that arise from similar images of things are not so constant, but are generally disturbed by images of other things until men become more assured of the outcome.

Scholium 2

From what has just been said we understand what is Hope (spes), Fear (metus), Confidence (securitas), Despair (desperatio), Joy (gaudium) and Disappointment (conscientiae morsus). Hope is 'inconstant pleasure, arising from the image of a thing future or past, of whose outcome we are in doubt.' Fear is 'inconstant pain, likewise arising from the image of a thing in doubt.' Now if the element of doubt be removed from these emotions, hope becomes confidence and fear becomes despair, that is 'pleasure or pain arising from a thing which we have feared or have hoped.' Joy is 'pleasure arising from the image of a past thing of whose outcome we have been in doubt.' Finally, disappointment is 'the pain opposite to joy.'

Proposition 19

He who imagines that what he loves is being destroyed will feel pain. If, however, he imagines that it is being preserved, he will feel pleasure.

Proof

The mind, as far as it can, endeavors to imagine whatever increases or assists the body's power of activity (Pr.12,III), that is (Sch.Pr.13,III), those things it loves. But the imagination is assisted by whatever posits the existence of the thing, and, on the other hand, is checked by whatever excludes the existence of the thing (Pr.17,II). Therefore, the images of things that posit the existence of the loved object assist the mind's conatus wherewith it endeavors to imagine the loved object, that is (Sch.Pr.11,III), they affect the mind with pleasure. On the other hand, those things that exclude the existence of the loved object check that same conatus of the mind, that is (by the same Scholium), they affect the mind with pain. Therefore, he who

imagines that what he loves is being destroyed will feel pain, . . . etc.

Proposition 20

He who imagines that a thing that he hates is being destroyed will feel pleasure.

Proof

The mind (Pr.13,III) endeavors to imagine whatever excludes the existence of things whereby the body's power of activity is diminished or checked; that is (Sch.Pr.13,III), it endeavors to imagine whatever excludes the existence of things that it hates. So the image of a thing that excludes the existence of what the mind hates assists this conatus of the mind; that is (Sch.Pr.11,III), it affects the mind with pleasure. Therefore he who thinks that that which he hates is being destroyed will feel pleasure.

Proposition 21

He who imagines that what he loves is affected with pleasure or pain will likewise be affected with pleasure or pain, the intensity of which will vary with the intensity of the emotion in the object loved.

Proof

As we have shown in Proposition 19,III, the images of things which posit the existence of the object loved assist the mind's conatus whereby it endeavors to think of the object loved. But pleasure posits the existence of that which feels pleasure, and the more so as the emotion of pleasure is stronger; for pleasure (Sch.Pr.11,III) is a transition to a state of greater perfection. Therefore the image, which is in the lover, of the pleasure of the object loved, assists his mind's conatus; that is (Sch.Pr.11,III), it affects the lover with pleasure, and all the more to the extent that this emotion is in the object loved. That was the first point. Again, in so far as a thing is affected with some pain, to that extent it is being destroyed, and the more so according to the extent to which it is affected with pain (same Sch.Pr.11,III). Thus (Pr.19,III), he who imagines that what he loves is affected with pain will likewise be affected with pain, the intensity of which will vary with the intensity of this emotion in the object loved.

Proposition 22

If we imagine that someone is affecting with pleasure the object of our love, we shall be affected with love towards him. If on the other hand we think that he is affecting with pain the object of our love, we shall likewise be affected with hatred towards him.

Proof

He who affects with pleasure or pain the object of our love affects us also with pleasure or pain, assuming that we think of the object of our love as affected with that pleasure or pain (preceding Pr.). But it is supposed that this pleasure or pain is in us accompanied by the idea of an external cause. Therefore (Sch.Pr.13,III) if we think that someone is affecting with pleasure or pain the object of our love, we shall be affected with love or hatred towards him.

Scholium

Proposition 21 explains to us what is Pity (commiseratio), which we may define as 'pain arising from another's hurt.' As for pleasure arising from another's good, I know not what to call it. Furthermore, love towards one who has benefited another we shall call Approval (favor), and on the other hand hatred towards one who has injured another we shall call Indignation (indignatio). Finally, it should be observed that we pity not only the thing which we have loved (as we have demonstrated in

Pr.21), but also a thing for which we have previously felt no emotion, provided that we judge it similar to ourselves (as I shall show in due course). Likewise, we approve of one who has benefited someone like ourselves; and on the other hand, we are indignant with one who has injured someone like ourselves.

Proposition 23

He who imagines that what he hates is affected with pain will feel pleasure; if, on the other hand, he thinks of it as affected with pleasure, he will feel pain. Both of these emotions will vary in intensity inversely with the variation of the contrary emotion in that which he hates.

Proof

In so far as the thing hated is affected with pain, it is being destroyed, and the more so according to the degree of pain (Sch.Pr.11,III). So (Pr.20,III) he who imagines the object hated to be affected with pain will, on the contrary, be affected with pleasure, and the more so as he imagines the object hated to be affected with more pain. That was the first point. Again, pleasure posits the existence of that which feels pleasure (same Sch.Pr.11,III), and the more so as the pleasure is conceived to be greater. If anyone imagines him whom he hates to be affected with pleasure, this thought will check his conatus (Pr.13,III): that is, (Sch.Pr.11,III), he who hates will be affected with pain, etc.

Scholium

This pleasure can scarcely be unalloyed and devoid of conflict of feeling. For (as I shall forthwith demonstrate in Proposition 27) in so far as he imagines a thing similar to himself to be affected with an emotion of pain, to that extent he is bound to feel pain, and contrariwise if he imagines it to be affected with pleasure. But here it is only his hate that we are considering.

Proposition 24

If we imagine someone to be affecting with pleasure a thing that we hate, we shall be affected with hate towards him too. If on the other hand we think of him as affecting with pain the said thing, we shall be affected with love towards him.

Proof

The proof follows the same lines as Pr.22,III.

Scholium

These and similar emotions of hatred are related to Envy (invidia), which can therefore be defined as 'hatred in so far as it is considered to dispose a man to rejoice in another's hurt and to feel pain at another's good.'

Proposition 25

We endeavor to affirm of ourselves and of an object loved whatever we imagine affects us or the loved object with pleasure, and, on the other hand, to negate whatever we imagine affects us or the loved object with pain.

Proof

What we imagine affects the object loved with pleasure or pain affects us with pleasure or pain (Pr.21,III). Now the mind (Pr.12,III) endeavors, as far as it can, to think of things that affect us with pleasure; that is (Pr.17,II and Cor.), to regard them as present; and, on the other hand, (Pr.13,III) to exclude the existence of things that affect us with pain. Therefore we endeavor to affirm of ourselves and the loved object whatever we imagine affects us or the object loved with pleasure, and vice versa.

Proposition 26

We endeavor to affirm of that which we hate whatever we imagine affects it with pain, and on the other hand to deny what we imagine affects it with pleasure.

Proof

This proposition follows from Proposition 23,III, as does the preceding proposition from Proposition 21,III.

Scholium

Thus we see that it easily happens that a man may have too high an opinion of himself and of the object loved, and on the other hand too mean an opinion of the object of his hatred. This way of thinking, when it concerns the man who has too high an opinion of himself, is called Pride (superbia), and is a kind of madness, in that a man dreams with his eyes open that he can do all those things that his imagination encompasses, which he therefore regards as real, exulting in them, as long as he is incapable of thinking of those things that exclude their existence and limit his power of activity. Therefore pride is 'pleasure arising from the fact that a man has too high an opinion of himself.' Again, 'pleasure that arises from the fact that a man has too high an opinion of another' is called Over-esteem (existimatio). Finally, 'pleasure arising from the fact that a man has too mean an opinion of another' is called Disparagement (despectus).

Proposition 27

From the fact that we imagine a thing like ourselves, towards which we have felt no emotion, to be affected by an emotion, we are thereby affected by a similar emotion.

Proof

Images of things are affections of the human body, the ideas of which set before us external bodies as present (Sch.Pr.17,II); that is (Pr.16,II), the ideas of these affections involve the nature of our own body and simultaneously the nature of the external body as present. If therefore the nature of the external body is similar to the nature of our own body, then the idea of the external body in our thinking will involve an affection of our own body similar to the affection of the external body. Consequently, if we imagine someone like ourselves to be affected by an emotion, this thought will express an affection of our own body similar to that emotion. So from the fact that we imagine a thing like ourselves to be affected by an emotion, we are affected by a similar emotion along with it. But if we hate a thing similar to ourselves, to that extent (Pr.23,III) we shall be affected by a contrary, not similar, emotion along with it.

Scholium

This imitation of emotions, when it is related to pain, is called Pity (see Sch.Pr.22,III), but when it is related to desire it is called Emulation (aemulatio), which is therefore 'nothing else but the desire of some thing which has been engendered in us from the belief that others similar to ourselves have this same desire.'

Corollary 1

If we believe that someone, for whom we have felt no emotion, affects with pleasure a thing similar to ourselves, we shall be affected by love towards him. If, on the other hand, we believe that he affects the said object with pain, we shall be affected with hatred towards him.

Proof

This is proved from the preceding Proposition in the same way as Proposition 22 from Proposition 21,III.

Corollary 2

The fact that its distress affects us with pain cannot cause us to hate a thing that we pity.

Proof

If we could hate it on that account, then (Pr.23,III) we should be pleased at its pain, which is contrary to our hypothesis.

Corollary 3

As far as we can, we endeavor to free from distress the thing that we pity.

Proof

That which affects with pain a thing that we pity affects us too with similar pain (preceding Pr.), and so we shall endeavor to devise whatever annuls the existence of the former or destroys it (Pr.13,III): that is (Sch.Pr.9,III), we shall seek to destroy it; i.e. we shall be determined to destroy it. So we shall endeavor to free from its distress the thing we pity.

Scholium

This will or appetite to do good which arises from our pitying the thing to which we wish to do good is called Benevolence (benevolentia), which is therefore 'nothing else but desire arising from pity.' As to love and hatred towards one who has done good or ill to a thing that we think to be like ourselves, see Sch.Pr.22,III.

Proposition 28

We endeavor to bring about whatever we imagine to be conducive to pleasure; but we endeavor to remove or destroy whatever we imagine to be opposed to pleasure and conducive to pain.

Proof

As far as we can, we endeavor to imagine whatever we think to be conducive to pleasure (Pr.12,III): that is (Pr.17,II), we endeavor, as far as we can, to regard it as present, that is, existing in actuality. But the conatus of the mind, that is, its power to think, is equal to and simultaneous in nature with the conatus of the body, that is, its power to act (as clearly follows from Cor.Pr.7 and Cor.Pr.11,II). Therefore in an absolute sense we endeavor, that is, we seek and purpose (which is the same thing by Sch.Pr.9,III), to bring about its existence. That was our first point. Further, if we imagine that which we believe to be the cause of pain, that is (Sch.Pr.13,III), that which we hate, as being destroyed, we shall feel pleasure (Pr.20,III), and so (by the first part of this proposition) we shall endeavor to destroy it, or (Pr.13,III) to remove it from us so as not to regard it as present. That was our second point. Therefore we endeavor to bring about . . . etc.

Proposition 29

We also endeavor to do whatever we imagine men[2] to regard with pleasure, and on the other hand we shun doing whatever we imagine men to regard with aversion.

Proof

From the fact that we imagine men love or hate something, we shall love or hate the same thing (Pr.27,III); that is (Sch.Pr.13,III) from that very fact we shall feel pleasure or pain at the presence of the thing. So (preceding Pr.) we shall endeavor to do whatever we imagine men love or regard with pleasure . . . etc.

Scholium

This conatus to do, and also to avoid doing, something simply in order to please men is called Ambition (ambitio), especially when we endeavor so earnestly to please the multitude that we do, or avoid doing, things to our own hurt or another's hurt; otherwise, it is called Kindliness (humanitas). Again, the pleasure with which we think of another's action whereby he has endeavored to please us I call Praise (laus), and the pain with which, on the other hand, we dislike his action I call Blame (vituperium).

---

[2]Here, and in what follows, by 'men' I understand men for whom we have felt no emotion. [Spinoza]

Proposition 30

If anyone has done something which he imagines affects others with pleasure, he will be affected with pleasure accompanied by the idea of himself as cause; that is, he will regard himself with pleasure. If, on the other hand, he imagines he has done something which affects others with pain, he will regard himself with pain.

Proof

He who imagines he affects others with pleasure or pain will by that very fact be affected with pleasure or pain (Pr.27,III). Now since man (Prs.19 and 23,II) is conscious of himself through the affections by which he is determined to act, he who has done something which he thinks affects others with pleasure will be affected with pleasure along with the consciousness of himself as cause; that is, he will regard himself with pleasure. The contrary likewise follows.

Scholium

Since love (Sch.Pr.13,III) is pleasure accompanied by the idea of an external cause, and hate is pain also accompanied by the idea of an external cause, this pleasure and this pain are species of love and hatred. But as love and hatred have reference to external objects, we shall assign different names to these emotions. The pleasure that is accompanied by an external cause we shall call Honour (gloria), and the pain that is its opposite we shall call Shame (pudor); but be it understood that this is when the pleasure or pain arises from a man's belief that he is praised or blamed. Otherwise, the pleasure that is accompanied by the idea of an internal cause I shall call Self-contentment (Acquiescentia in se ipso), and the pain that is its opposite I shall call Repentance (paenitentia). Again, since it is possible (Cor.Pr.17,II) that the pleasure with which a man imagines he affects others is only imaginary, and (Pr.25,III) everyone endeavors to imagine of himself whatever he thinks affects himself with pleasure, it can easily happen that a vain man may be proud and imagine that he is popular with everybody, when he in fact is obnoxious.

Proposition 31

If we think that someone loves, desires, or hates something that we love, desire, or hate, that very fact will cause us to love, desire or hate the thing more steadfastly. But if we think he dislikes what we love, or vice versa, then our feelings will fluctuate.

Proof

From the mere fact that we imagine someone loves something, we shall love that same thing (Pr.27,III). But even apart from this consideration we are supposing that we love that same thing. Therefore to the existing love there is added a further cause whereby it is nurtured, and by that very fact we shall love more steadfastly the object of our love. Again, from the fact that we think someone dislikes something, we shall dislike the same thing (by the same proposition). But if we suppose that at the same time we love the thing, we shall therefore at the same time love and dislike that thing; that is, (see Sch.Pr.17,III) our feelings will fluctuate.

Corollary

From this and from Pr. 28,III it follows that everyone endeavors, as far as he can, that what he loves should be loved by everyone, and what he hates should be hated by everyone. Hence that saying of the poet:

"As lovers, let our hopes and fears be alike,
Insensitive is he who loves what another leaves."[3]

---

[3]Ovid, *Amores*, II, 19.

Scholium

This conatus to bring it about that everyone should approve of one's loves and hates is in reality ambition (see Sch.Pr.29,III). So we see that it is in everyone's nature to strive to bring it about that others should adopt his attitude to life; and while all strive equally to this end they equally hinder one another, and in all seeking the praise or love of all, they provoke mutual dislike.

Proposition 32

If we think that someone enjoys something that only one person can possess, we shall endeavor to bring it about that he should not possess that thing.

Proof

From the mere fact that we imagine somebody to enjoy something (Pr.27,III and Cor.1) we shall love that thing and desire to enjoy it. But by hypothesis we think that this pleasure is impeded by the fact that that person is enjoying the thing in question. Therefore (Pr.28,III) we shall endeavor to bring it about that he should not possess it.

Scholium

We therefore see that human nature is in general so constituted that men pity the unfortunate and envy the fortunate, in the latter case with a hatred proportionate to their love of what they think another possesses (by the preceding Proposition). Furthermore, we see that from the same property of human nature from which it follows that men are compassionate, it likewise follows that they are prone to envy and ambition. Finally, we shall find that common experience confirms all these points, especially if we turn our attention to childhood. For we find that children, their bodies being, as it were, continually in a state of equilibrium, laugh or weep merely from seeing others laugh or weep, and whatever else they see others do they immediately want to imitate. In short, they want for themselves whatever they see others take pleasure in because, as we have said, the images of things are the very affections of the human body, that is, the ways in which the human body is affected by external causes and disposed to this or that action.

Proposition 33

If we love something similar to ourselves, we endeavor, as far as we can, to bring it about that it should love us in return.

Proof

We endeavor, as far as we can, to think of something we love in preference to other things (Pr.12,III). So if the thing be like ourselves, we shall endeavor to affect it with pleasure in preference to other things (Pr.29,III); that is, we shall endeavor, as far as we can, to bring it about that the object of our love should be affected with pleasure accompanied by the idea of ourselves, that is (Sch.Pr.13,III), that it should love us in return.

Proposition 34

The greater the emotion with which we imagine the object of our love is affected towards us, the greater will be our vanity.

Proof

By the preceding proposition, we endeavor to bring it about, as far as we can, that the object of our love should love us in return; that is (Sch.Pr.13,III), that the object of our love should be affected with pleasure accompanied by the idea of ourselves. So the greater the pleasure with which we think that the object of our love is affected because of us, the more is this endeavor assisted; that is (Pr.11,III and Sch.), the greater the pleasure with which we are affected. Now since our pleasure is due to our having affected with pleasure another person like ourselves, we regard ourselves with

pleasure (Pr.30,III). Therefore, the greater the emotion with which we think the object loved is affected towards us, with that much greater pleasure shall we regard ourselves; that is (Sch. Pr.30,III), the greater will be our vanity.

Proposition 35

If anyone thinks that there is between the object of his love and another person the same or a more intimate bond of friendship than there was between them when he alone used to possess the object loved, he will be affected with hatred towards the object loved and will envy his rival.

Proof

The greater the love wherewith one thinks the object of his love is affected towards him, the greater will be his vanity (by the preceding proposition); that is (Sch.Pr.30,III), the more he will be pleased. So (Pr.28,III) he will endeavor, as far as he can, to imagine the object loved as bound to him as intimately as possible, and this conatus, or appetite, is fostered if he imagines someone else desires the same thing for himself (Pr.31,III). But we are supposing that this conatus, or appetite, is checked by the image of the object loved accompanied by the image of him with whom the object loved is associating. Therefore (Sch.Pr.11,III) this will cause him to be affected with pain accompanied by the idea of the object loved as cause and simultaneously by the image of his rival; that is (Sch.Pr.13,III), he will be affected with hatred towards the object loved and at the same time towards his rival (Cor.Pr.15,III), whom he will envy because (Pr.23,III) he enjoys the object loved.

Scholium

This hatred towards the object of one's love, joined with envy, is called Jealousy (zelotypia), which is therefore nothing else but 'vacillation arising from simultaneous love and hatred accompanied by the idea of a rival who is envied.'

Furthermore, this hatred towards the object of his love will be greater in proportion to the pleasure wherewith the jealous man was wont to be affected as a result of the returning of his love by the object of his love, and also in proportion to the emotion wherewith he was affected towards him whom he thinks of as being intimately associated with the object of his love. For if he used to hate him, that very fact will make him hate the object of his love (Pr.24,III) because he thinks of it as affecting with pleasure that which he hates, and also (Cor.Pr.15,III) because he is compelled to associate the image of the object of his love with the image of one whom he hates. This is generally the case with love towards a woman; for he who thinks of a woman whom he loves as giving herself to another will not only feel pain by reason of his own appetite being checked but also, being compelled to associate the image of the object of his love with the sexual parts of his rival, he feels disgust for her. Then there is in addition the fact that the jealous man will not receive the same warm welcome as he was wont to receive from the object of his love, and this is a further reason for the lover's pain, as I shall now demonstrate.

Proposition 36

He who recalls a thing which once afforded him pleasure desires to possess the same thing in the same circumstances as when he first took pleasure therein.

Proof

Whatever a man has seen together with the object that has afforded him pleasure will be indirectly a cause of pleasure (Pr.15,III), and so (Pr.28,III) he will desire to possess all this together with the object that afforded him pleasure, that is, he will desire to possess the object along with all the same attendant circumstances as when he first took pleasure in the object.

Corollary

If therefore he finds one of those attendant circumstances missing, the lover will feel pain.

Proof

In so far as he finds some attendant circumstance missing, to that extent he imagines something that excludes its existence. Now since he desires that thing or circumstance (preceding proposition) by reason of his love, then (Pr.19,III) in so far as he thinks it to be lacking he will feel pain.

Scholium

This pain, in so far as it regards the absence of that which we love, is called Longing (desiderium).

Proposition 37

The desire arising from pain or pleasure, hatred or love, is proportionately greater as the emotion is greater.

Proof

Pain diminishes or checks man's power of activity (Sch.Pr.11,III), that is, (Pr.7,III) it diminishes or checks the conatus wherewith a man endeavors to persist in his own being; and therefore it is contrary to this conatus (Pr.5,III), and the conatus of a man affected by pain is entirely directed to removing the pain. But, by the definition of pain, the greater the pain, the greater the extent to which it must be opposed to man's power of activity. Therefore the greater the pain, with that much greater power of activity will a man endeavor to remove the pain; that is (Sch.Pr.9,III), with that much greater desire, or appetite, will he endeavor to remove the pain. Again, since pleasure (Sch.Pr.11,III) increases or assists man's power of activity, it can readily be demonstrated in the same way that a man affected with pleasure desires nothing other than to preserve it, and with all the greater desire as the pleasure is greater. Finally, since hatred and love are emotions of pain or pleasure, it follows in the same way that the conatus, appetite or desire arising through hatred or love is greater in proportion to the hatred and love.

Proposition 38

If anyone has begun to hate the object of his love to the extent that his love is completely extinguished, he will, other things being equal, bear greater hatred towards it than if he had never loved it, and his hatred will be proportionate to the strength of his former love.

Proof

If anyone begins to hate the object of his love, more of his appetites are checked than if he had never loved it. For love is pleasure (Sch.Pr.13,III), which a man endeavors to preserve as far as he can (Pr.28,III), and this he does (same Sch.) by regarding the object loved as present and affecting it with pleasure (Pr.21,III), as far as he can. This conatus (preceding Pr.) is the greater as the love is greater, as also is the conatus that the object loved should return his love (Pr.33,III). But these conatus are checked by hatred towards the object loved (Cor.Pr.13 and Pr.23,III). Therefore for this reason, too, the lover will be affected with pain (Sch.Pr.11,III) which will be proportionate to his previous love; that is, in addition to the pain that was the cause of his hatred, a further pain arises from the fact that he has loved the object. Consequently, he will regard the loved object with a greater emotion of pain, that is (Sch.Pr.13,III), he will bear greater hatred towards it than if he had not loved it, and his hatred will be proportionate to the strength of his former love.

Proposition 39

He who hates someone will endeavor to injure him unless he fears that he will suffer a greater injury in return. On the other hand, he who loves someone will by that same law endeavor to benefit him.

Proof

To hate someone is (Sch.Pr.13,III) to imagine someone to be the cause of one's pain. So (Pr.28,III) he who hates someone will endeavor to remove or destroy him. But if he fears from him something more painful, or (which is the same thing), a greater injury, which he thinks he can avoid by not inflicting the harm he was intending on him whom he hates, he will desire to refrain from so doing (same Pr.28,III), and this conatus (Pr.37,III) will be greater than that which was directed toward inflicting harm. This latter conatus will therefore prevail, as we have said. The second part of this proof proceeds on the same lines. Therefore he who hates someone . . . etc.

Scholium

By 'good' I understand here every kind of pleasure and furthermore whatever is conducive thereto, and especially whatever satisfies a longing of any sort. By 'bad' I understand every kind of pain, and especially that which frustrates a longing. For I have demonstrated above (Sch.Pr.9,III) that we do not desire a thing because we judge it to be good; on the contrary, we call the object of our desire good, and consequently the object of our aversion bad. Therefore it is according to his emotion that everyone judges or deems what is good, bad, better, worse, best or worst. Thus the miser judges wealth the best thing, and its lack the worst thing. The ambitious man desires nothing so much as public acclaim, and dreads nothing so much as disgrace. To the envious man nothing is more pleasant than another's unhappiness, and nothing more obnoxious than another's happiness. Thus every man judges a thing good or bad, advantageous or disadvantageous, according to his own emotion.

Now the emotion whereby a man is so disposed as to refrain from what he wants to do or to choose to do what he does not want is called Timidity (timor), which is merely fear in so far as a man is thereby disposed to avoid by a lesser evil what he judges to be a future evil (see Pr.28,III). But if the evil that he fears is disgrace, then timidity is called Bashfulness (verecundia). Finally, if the desire to avoid a future evil is checked by the apprehension of another evil, so that he does not know what preference to make, then fear is called Consternation (consternatio), especially if both the feared evils are of the greatest.

Proposition 40

He who imagines he is hated by someone to whom he believes he has given no cause for hatred will hate him in return.

Proof

He who imagines someone to be affected with hatred will by that very fact himself be affected with hatred (Pr.27,III), that is (Sch.Pr.13, III), pain accompanied by the idea of an external cause. But, by hypothesis, he himself thinks that there is no other cause of this pain than he who hates him. Therefore from the fact that he imagines that he is hated by someone, he will be affected by pain accompanied by the idea of him who hates him; that is (by the same Sch.), he will hate that person.

Scholium

But if he thinks that he has provided just cause for hatred, then (Pr.30,III and Sch.) he will be affected with shame. But this (Pr.25,III) is rarely the case. Furthermore, this reciprocation of hatred can also arise from the fact that hatred is followed by a conatus to injure him who is hated (Pr.39,III). So he who imagines he is hated by someone will imagine him to be the cause of some evil or pain, and so he will be affected with pain, or fear, accompanied by the idea of him who hates him as being the cause; that is, he will be affected with hatred in return, as we said above.

Corollary 1

He who imagines that one he loves is affected with hatred towards him, will suffer the conflicting emotions of hatred and love. For in so far as he imagines he is hated by him, he is determined to hate him in return (preceding Pr.). But, by hypothesis, he nevertheless loves him. Therefore he will suffer the conflicting emotions of hatred and love.

Corollary 2

If anyone imagines that he has suffered some injury through hatred at the hands of one towards whom he has previously felt no emotion, he will immediately endeavor to return the said injury.

Proof

He who imagines that someone is affected with hatred towards him will hate him in return (preceding Pr.), and he will endeavor to devise anything that can affect that person with pain (Pr.26,III), and will seek to inflict it on him (Pr.39,III). But, by hypothesis, the first thing of that kind that comes to his mind is the injury that has been inflicted on himself. Therefore he will immediately endeavor to inflict that same injury on that person.

Scholium

The conatus to inflict injury on one whom we hate is called Anger (ira). The conatus to return an injury which we have suffered is called Revenge (vindicta).

Proposition 41

If anyone thinks that he is loved by someone and believes that he has given no cause for this (which is possible through Cor.Pr.15 and Pr.16,III), he will love him in return.

Proof

This is proved in the same way as the preceding proposition. See also its Scholium.

Scholium

If he believes that he has given just cause for this love, he will exult in it (Pr.30,III and Sch.), which is more often the case (Pr.25,III); and we have said that the contrary occurs when someone thinks that he is hated by someone (see Sch. preceding Pr.). Now this reciprocal love, and consequently (Pr.39,III) the conatus to benefit one who loves us and who (same Pr.39,III) endeavors to benefit us, is called Gratitude (gratia seu gratitudo). So it is evident that men are far more inclined to revenge than to repay a benefit.

Corollary

He who imagines that he is loved by one whom he hates will feel conflicting emotions of hate and love. This is proved in the same way as the first corollary of the preceding proposition.

Scholium

If hatred prevails, he will endeavor to injure him by whom he is loved, and this emotion is called Cruelty (crudelitas), especially if it is believed that he who loves has not given any cause for hatred between them.

Proposition 42

He who, moved by love or hope of honour, has conferred a benefit on someone, will feel pain if he sees that the benefit is ungratefully received.

Proof

He who loves a thing similar to himself endeavors, as far as he can, to bring it about that he is loved in return (Pr.33,III). So he who through love confers a benefit upon someone does so through his longing to be loved in return; that is (Pr.34,III), through hope of honour, or (Sch.Pr.30,III) pleasure. Thus (Pr.12,III) he will endeavor as far as he can to imagine this cause of honour, i.e. to regard it as actually existing. But, by hypothesis, he thinks of something else that excludes the existence of the said cause. Therefore (Pr.19,III) by that very fact he will feel pain.

Proposition 43

Hatred is increased by reciprocal hatred, and may on the other hand be destroyed by love.

Proof

If someone thinks that one whom he hates is affected with hatred towards him, a new source of hatred thereby arises (Pr.40,III), while the old hatred, by hypothesis, still continues. But if, on the other hand, he thinks that the said person is affected with love towards him, in so far as he thinks this, he regards himself with pleasure (Pr.30,III), and to that extent (Pr.29,III) he will endeavor to please him; that is (Pr.41,III) to that extent he endeavors not to hate him nor affect him with any pain. This conatus (Pr.37,III) will vary proportionately to the strength of the emotion from which it arises, and so if it should be greater than the emotion which arises from hatred whereby he endeavors to affect the object of his hatred with pain (Pr.26,III), it will prevail over it and will eradicate the feeling of hatred.

Proposition 44

Hatred that is fully overcome by love passes into love, and the love will therefore be greater than if it had not been preceded by hatred.

Proof

The proof proceeds along the same lines as that of Pr.38,III. For he who begins to love the object that he hated, that is, used to regard with pain, will feel pleasure by the very fact that he loves, and to this pleasure which love involves (see its Def. in Sch.Pr.13,III) is added the further pleasure arising from the fact that the conatus to remove the pain which hatred involves (as we demonstrated in Pr.37,III) is very much assisted, accompanied by the idea of the one whom he hated as being the cause.

Scholium

Although this is so, nobody will endeavor to hate an object or be affected with pain in order to enjoy this greater feeling of pleasure; that is, nobody will desire to suffer hurt in the hope of recovering from the hurt, or will want to be ill in the hope of recovering his health. For everyone will endeavor always to preserve his own being and to remove pain, as far as he can. If it were possible to conceive the contrary, that a man should want to hate someone so that he might later feel greater love for him, he will always want to be hating him. For the greater was the hatred, the greater will be the love; so he will always want his hatred to go on growing. And for the same reason a man will endeavor to be more and more ill so as later to enjoy greater pleasure from the restoration of health. So he will always endeavor to be ill, which is absurd (Pr.6,III).

Proposition 45

If anyone imagines that someone similar to himself is affected with hatred towards a thing similar to himself, which he loves, he will hate him.

Proof

The object loved returns the hatred of him who hates it (Pr.40,III), and so the lover who thinks that someone hates the object loved is thereby made to think of the object of his love as affected by hatred, that is (Sch.Pr.13,III), as affected by pain. Consequently he feels pain (Pr.21,III), a pain that is accompanied by the idea of him who hates the object of his love as being the cause; that is, (Sch.Pr.13,III), he will hate him.

Proposition 46

If anyone is affected with pleasure or pain by someone of a class or nation different from his own and the pleasure or pain is accompanied by the idea of that person as its cause, under the general category of that class or nation, he will love or hate not only him but all of that same class or nation.

Proof

This is evident from Pr.16,III.

Proposition 47

The pleasure that arises from our imagining that the object of our hatred is being destroyed or is suffering some other harm is not devoid of some feeling of pain.

Proof

This is evident from Pr.27,III. For in so far as we imagine a thing similar to ourselves to be affected with pain, to that extent we feel pain.

Scholium

This Proposition can also be proved from Cor.Pr.17,II. For whenever we call a thing to mind, although it may not actually exist, we regard it as present, and the body is affected in the same way. Therefore in so far as his remembrance of the thing is strong, to that extent the man is determined to regard it with pain. And whereas this determination, the image of the thing still persisting, is checked by the remembrance of those things that exclude its existence, it is not completely annulled, and so the man feels pleasure only in so far as this determination is checked. Hence it comes about that the pleasure that arises from the harm suffered by the object of our hatred is revived whenever we call to mind the said thing. For, as we have said, when the image of the said thing is activated, since it involves the existence of the thing it determines one to regard the thing with the same pain as when one was wont to regard it when it did exist. But since one has associated with the image of the said thing other images which exclude its existence, this determination to pain is immediately checked, and one feels a renewed pleasure, and this is so whenever the series of events is repeated.

It is this same cause that makes men feel pleasure whenever they recall some past ill and makes them enjoy talking about perils from which they have been saved. For when they imagine some peril they regard it as though it were still to come and are determined to fear it, a determination which is again checked by the idea of their escape which they associated with the idea of this peril when they did in fact escape it. This idea makes them feel safe once more, and so their pleasure is renewed.

chapter seventeen

David Hume

David Hume (1711–1776), Scottish philosopher and historian, is one of the most memorable and influential minds of the Enlightenment. He was, in that Age of Reason, one of the first critics of Enlightenment rationalism and arguably the most severe and uncompromising among them. Hume was convinced that the confidence placed in reason by rationalists, from Descartes to his own Enlightenment contemporaries, was actually *misplaced* upon a "weak foundation" and consequently the source of considerable philosophical confusion. "Principles taken upon trust, consequences lamely deduced from them, want of coherence in the parts, and evidence of the whole, these are everywhere to be met with in the systems of the most eminent philosophers, and seem to have drawn disgrace upon philosophy itself," he wrote. "There is nothing which is not the subject of debate, and in which men of learning are not of contrary opinions."[1] Hume's skepticism concerning the scope and power of reason was so forceful, in fact, that the nineteenth-century philosopher Immanuel Kant, originally a strict rationalist, credited Hume with having awakened him from his "dogmatic slumber."[2] Nineteenth-century utilitarians also drew inspiration from Hume, and in the twentieth century the founder of modern logic, Bertrand Russell, conceived of his own system as grounded in Humean thought.[3]

As a critic of rationalism, Hume belongs to the empiricist tradition in philosophy, in which he was preceded by the English philosophers John Locke (1632–1704) and Bishop George Berkeley (1685–1753). The empiricists rejected the claim of the rationalists that reason—the clear and distinct ideas of the mind from which human beings deduce all truths through logic—is the source of all knowledge, arguing to the contrary that all knowledge begins in *experience*, with the careful observation of phenomena perceived by the senses. Locke insisted against Descartes, for instance, that we have no basis for asserting that innate ideas have been placed in the mind by God; rather, he argued that the mind is originally a tabula rasa, a blank slate, upon which the data of experience are written to form knowledge. One of the problems early empiricists faced,

David Hume, "Of Chastity and Modesty," from *A Treatise of Human Nature*, ed. L.A. Selby-Bigge. 2d ed., rev. P.H. Nidditch. Copyright © 1978 by Oxford University Press. Reprinted by permission of Oxford University Press.

however, was the age-old problem of how to speak about things-in-themselves—how we can know the true nature of entities, independently of our individual sensory experiences of them. Both Locke and Berkeley compromised on this point in ways that positioned them dangerously close to the rationalists.[4] Hume, on the other hand, entirely consistent in his empiricist convictions, ran into none of the problems of his predecessors. He concluded that insofar as we have no direct experience of substances, we must remain skeptical of their existence. Furthermore, given that we cannot guarantee the reliability of human perception, we must remain skeptical of our ability to know the world. In fact, we would do well to distinguish more clearly what we can profess to know from what are actually the products of belief. Not only philosophy but the sciences as well, he argued, largely express our *beliefs* about the world, not our knowledge of it.

Hume reports in his autobiography that he had his breakthrough into this "new Scene of Thought" in his third year as a law student, when he was eighteen years old. While in school he spent substantially more time reading philosophy than law, and, in addition to reading Locke and Berkeley, he became acquainted with the work of the moral philosopher Francis Hutcheson, who claimed that our moral beliefs are not grounded fundamentally in doctrines, such as Christianity, or in reason; rather, they rest ultimately upon our *feelings*, and especially upon our feelings of approval and disapproval. Hume was convinced that this principle might be true not only of our moral beliefs but of all our claims about the world—that even what we call scientific knowledge might ultimately depend on our *feeling* that certain perceptions we have of the world are *true*. Five years passed before he had the confidence and presence of mind to develop his philosophical system.[5] In 1734 he traveled to La Flèche in France, took up residence in a tiny apartment near the library of the old Jesuit college, and after three years of intensive research and writing, produced his first book, *A Treatise of Human Nature* (1739–1740), from which "Of Chastity and Modesty" is taken.

The task that Hume undertook in writing the *Treatise* was to evaluate critically the faculty of human understanding, the seat of all presumed knowledge. After all, to defend his claim that what we call knowledge is actually belief based upon feelings, he would have to give an account of how and why this is the case. In the introduction to the *Treatise*, however, he states his objective rather less controversially, making the case that since all the sciences are the products of human understanding, an investigation into the nature and operations of the understanding must precede the other sciences if we are to secure them. Hume endeavored, furthermore, to conduct his investigation into the "science of Man" with the same rigor exemplified by Sir Isaac Newton in the physical sciences. He in fact subtitled the *Treatise*, "[a]n attempt to introduce the experimental method of reasoning into moral subjects," aiming to demonstrate how the complex faculties of the understanding can be reduced to primary elements operating according to laws of association in much the same way that Newton proved that the entire physical universe could be explained in terms of laws of motion founded upon basic mathematical principles. Accordingly, the three books of the Treatise are organized systematically, addressing first the elements, operations, and limitations of the understanding; second, the nature and functions of the passions and their relationship to the understanding; and finally, the nature and structure of morals and their relationship to the understanding and the passions.

Book I, "Of the Understanding," identifies the primary elements of human thought—impressions and ideas—and analyzes how human beings associate and relate those elements. Impressions are the "raw materials of thought,"[6] the immediate sense data of experience, which are, in turn, of two kinds: impressions of sensation (original impressions), such as colors, shapes, and sounds, and impressions of reflection (secondary impressions), which are feelings we experience—emotions and desires. Impressions of reflection are secondary because they are dependent on ideas, which are "the faint images of [impressions] in thinking and reasoning" produced by the mind.[7] Insofar as ideas are "the faint images" of impressions, Hume understood them to be *copies* of impressions and argued that there can be no ideas for which there are no corresponding impressions. To one who might object, saying we have ideas of many things for which it is impossible to have impressions—for example, we have an idea of unicorns although we have never received an impression of one—Hume responds by distinguishing between simple and complex impressions and ideas. Simple impressions and ideas are our most basic sensations and the thoughts that correspond to them—they cannot be broken down into simpler perceptions. We form complex ideas from combinations of simple ideas and impressions, such that while all simple ideas are copies of simple impressions, complex ideas are not necessarily direct copies of complex impressions. Thus, we can form the complex idea of a unicorn from the simple ideas of "horse" and "horn," of which we have received impressions.

The very fact that the mind is capable of forming complex ideas from simple ones (and even ideas from impressions) is an indication that it possesses certain faculties by which it *associates* ideas and impressions. There are two such faculties, memory and imagination, and Hume assures us that it is our powerful faculty of imagination that has led us to believe, for instance, in substances. In imagination, the mind "is not restrain'd to the same order and form with the original impressions" and is thus extremely facile and fluid in associating and organizing impressions and ideas.[8] Our belief in such "fictions" as substances is purely the product of the imagination's fluid manner of associating perceptions; we believe that colors, tastes, and so forth, inhere in "something" because our minds "run easily" to such an idea. The imaginative faculty of mind—and Hume adds that "the memory, senses, and understanding are . . . all of them founded on the imagination"—gives us the *feeling* that such things as substances exist.

Upon establishing the nature and functions of the understanding, Hume proceeds to develop Book II, "Of the Passions," which reveals how the same primary elements of the understanding operate to produce secondary impressions: the *passions*, such as desire, pride, shame, love, hatred, and the will. According to Hume, secondary impressions (of reflection) are feelings that arise spontaneously in response to ideas formed in the mind. For example, the idea, "ice cream", is likely to stimulate a feeling (an impression) of desire in most people. Some impressions of reflection are more complex. Hume says, for instance, that shame (the passion that figures most prominently in "Of Chastity and Modesty") is a feeling of displeasure that stems from a double relation of impressions and ideas: the impression of displeasure one feels when one perceives an object or behavior of which one disapproves, combined with the idea of that object's relation to oneself. That is to say that while the object of disapproval would generally stimulate a sensation of displeasure, such that one would likely disapprove of anyone who possessed it, this feeling of displeasure becomes *shame*, and not merely disapproval, when the object is related to *oneself*.

Only when Hume has clarified the nature and functions of both the understanding and the passions, does he proceed to Book III, "Of Morals," in which he presents arguments refuting the idea that morals can ever be founded entirely upon reason, arguing instead that they are shaped almost exclusively by our passions. He proclaimed, in fact, "Reason is, and ought only to be the slave of the passions."[9] First, Hume argues that reason's only power is to judge the truth or falsity of relations of ideas (such as "2 + 2 = 4") and matters of fact (such as "The temperature is currently 88°F."); as such, it can never by itself motivate one to action. Reasoning may *influence* one's *feelings* about a course of action but will never be the direct cause of action. Given that moral distinctions *do* motivate us to action, they cannot be based on reason alone. Hume argues secondly that if moral distinctions were based entirely on reason, then moral values would have to be exclusively relations of ideas or matters of fact. However, we can never locate goodness or badness, virtue or vice, in relations of ideas or matters of fact themselves—only in our *feelings* about them; therefore moral distinctions are based on sentiments.

Readers may find it interesting that the selection "Of Chastity and Modesty" appears as the final section of Book III, Part II: "Of Justice and Injustice." After all, we do not typically think of chastity and modesty as modes of conduct having to do with justice—except perhaps in issues concerning marriage and divorce. Here, Hume actually cites the conventional feminine "duties" of modesty and chastity as familiar examples of how systems of justice emerge from the practical needs of communities. That is, having only speculated that the concept of justice originated with the foundation of civil society, when early communities recognized the need to establish rules for assigning, stabilizing, and transferring property through promise keeping (fidelity),[10] Hume aims to convince his reader of the viability of that account by describing the more familiar case of "another set of duties, *viz.* the modesty and chastity which belong to the fair sex."[11] Hume saw marriage as a kind of community in which its members, a husband and wife, safeguard their property—and here Hume emphasized "the maintenance and education of their children"—through fidelity to each other, which they generally are able to recognize as in their best interest.[12] However, husbands and wives, like members of any community, do not always keep their promises to each other; it is not always easy to see how observing the rules ultimately serves one's interests, and some impetus other than self-interest is often needed to motivate one to fidelity. Civil society therefore promotes the adoption of the general point of view—that is, the ability to sympathize with *everyone's* desire always to have his or her interests protected and never to have them infringed. Through sympathy, the members of society come to approve of justice and disapprove of injustice; they establish *by convention* that justice is virtuous and injustice is vicious. Still, despite our cognitive understanding and moral conviction that upholding the public interest is also in our own best interest, Hume observes that we are, nevertheless, "naturally carried to commit acts of injustice." That is because human passions "are mightily govern'd by the imagination," such that our immediate interests, being contiguous and thus more vivid to the imagination, have a substantially greater impact upon our passions than our remote interests do.[13] Civil societies therefore find it prudent to entrust magistrates with the execution of justice, to represent the public interest, and thus to compensate for individuals' propensity to sacrifice their own remote interests for more immediate ones. In a marriage, however, there is no third person to mediate between a husband and wife; a different kind of third party is needed to prevent "injustice": the avoidance of shame.

Hume expected his *Treatise* to be hailed a philosophical masterpiece; to his surprise and dismay, reviews of it were highly unfavorable, so much so that Hume remarked that it "fell dead-born from the press."[14] He spent the next few decades reworking its content, and in 1748 published a more concise and accessible version entitled *An Enquiry Concerning Human Understanding*. Other works include *Essays, Moral and Political* (1741–1742), *Political Discourses* (1752), and the highly acclaimed six-volume *History of England* (1754–1762). Hume's *Dialogues Concerning Natural Religion* (1779) was published posthumously.

SC

QUESTIONS

1. Hume's explicit reason for including chastity and modesty in his discussion of justice is to render more convincing his earlier account of how systems of justice emerge from the practical needs of communities. Recap briefly Hume's account of how and why chastity and modesty have become feminine "duties."

2. Consider again the basis of Hume's claim, "Reason is, and ought only to be the slave of the passions." Do you agree with this claim? Explain.

3. Discuss the respective roles of reason and the passions in the "institution" of chastity/modesty.

ENDNOTES

1. Hume, *Treatise*, p. xiii.

2. Immanuel Kant, *Prolegomena to Any Future Metaphysics*, trans. Paul Carus, rev. James W. Ellington. Indianapolis, Ind.: Hackett Publishing, 1977, p. 5.

3. Quinton, *Hume,* p. 59.

4. Locke claimed that we actually *infer* the existence of things-in-themselves because, although we perceive only properties of things, we find it impossible to imagine these properties as somehow existing independently of some things of which they are the properties. The difficulty with this answer is that such inferences are actually *assumptions*—like the innate ideas of the rationalists—and not the direct data of experience. Berkeley avoided this difficulty but, to do so, ran headlong into another. He maintained that we indeed have no experience of physical substances underlying properties; all we can claim to know are properties, such that the world is not a collection of substances but a collection of perceptions and ideas of mind, a view that came to be known as idealism. "To be is to be perceived," he proclaimed. The question nevertheless remained of how we can claim to know anything with certainty given the fallibility of human perception. Berkeley argued, against Plato and Descartes, that our perceptions, in general, are reliable and orderly and that this reliability of perception is guaranteed by God, who is also a perceiver. The obvious problem, of course, is that Berkeley *assumed* the existence of God.

5. After his "breakthrough" Hume gave up the study of law (and its promise of financial security) in order to develop his "new Scene of Thought." Six months later he suffered a nervous breakdown; notwithstanding that and its attendant bouts of depression and anxiety, Hume spent five more years struggling to develop his system, to no avail. He resolved to abandon philosophy but soon changed his mind and opted for a change of scenery instead.

6. Quinton, *Hume,* p. 11.

7. Hume, *Treatise,* p. 1.

8. Ibid., p. 9.

9. Ibid., p. 415.

10. Ibid., p. 491–516.

11. Ibid., p. 570.

12. Ibid., p. 571.

13. Ibid., p. 535.

14. David Hume, *The Life of David Hume, Esq: Philosopher and Historian, Written by Himself.* Philadelphia: Robert Bell, 1778, p. 4.

SELECTED BIBLIOGRAPHY

Aiken, Henry D., ed. *Hume's Moral and Political Philosophy.* New York: Hafner Publishing, 1948.

Hume, David. *An Enquiry Concerning Human Nature,* ed. Eric Steinberg. Indianapolis, Ind.: Hackett Publishing Company, 1993.

Hume, David. *A Treatise of Human Nature.* 2d ed., ed. L.A. Selby-Bigge, rev. P.H. Nidditch. New York: Oxford University Press, 1978.

Jacobson Anne Jaap, ed. *Feminist Interpretations of David Hume.* University Park: Pennsylvania State University Press, 2000.

Quinton, Anthony. *Hume.* New York: Routledge, 1999.

from *A Treatise of Human Nature*

David Hume

SECTION XII

Of chastity and modesty

If any difficulty attend this system concerning the laws of nature and nations, 'twill be with regard to the universal approbation or blame, which follows their observance or transgression, and which some may not think sufficiently explain'd from the general interests of society. To remove, as far as possible, all scruples of this kind, I shall here consider another set of duties, *viz.* the *modesty* and *chastity* which belong to the fair sex: And I doubt not but these virtues will be found to be still more conspicuous instances of the operation of those principles, which I have insisted on.

There are some philosophers, who attack the female virtues with great vehemence, and fancy they have gone very far in detecting popular errors, when they can show, that there is no foundation in nature for all that exterior modesty, which we require in the expressions, and dress, and behaviour of the fair sex. I believe I may spare myself the trouble of insisting on so obvious a subject, and may proceed, without farther preparation, to examine after what manner such notions arise from education, from the voluntary conventions of men, and from the interest of society.

Whoever considers the length and feebleness of human infancy, with the concern which both sexes naturally have for their offspring, will easily perceive, that there must be an union of male and female for the education of the young, and that this union must be of considerable duration. But in order to induce the men to impose on themselves this restraint, and undergo chearfully all the fatigues and expences, to which it subjects them, they must believe, that the children are their own, and that their natural instinct is not directed to a wrong object, when they give a loose to love and tenderness. Now if we examine the structure of the human body, we shall find, that this security is very difficult to be attain'd on our part; and that since, in the copulation of the sexes, the principle of generation goes from the man to the woman, an error may easily take place on the side of the former, tho' it be utterly impossible with regard to the latter. From this trivial and anatomical observation is deriv'd that vast difference betwixt the education and duties of the two sexes.

Were a philosopher to examine the matter *a priori*, he wou'd reason after the following manner. Men are induc'd to labour for the maintenance and education of their children, by the persuasion that they are really their own; and therefore 'tis reasonable, and even necessary, to give them some security in this particular. This security cannot consist entirely in the imposing of severe punishments on any transgressions of conjugal fidelity on the part of the wife; since these public punishments cannot be inflicted without legal proof, which 'tis difficult to meet with in this subject. What restraint, therefore, shall we impose on women, in order to counter-balance so strong a temptation as they have to infidelity? There seems to be no restraint possible, but in the punishment of bad fame or reputation; a punishment, which has a mighty influence on the human mind, and at the same time is inflicted by the world upon surmizes, and conjectures, and proofs, that wou'd never be receiv'd in any court of judicature. In order, therefore, to impose a due restraint on the female sex, we must attach a peculiar degree of shame to their infidelity, above what arises merely from its injustice, and must bestow proportionable praises on their chastity.

But tho' this be a very strong motive to fidelity, our philosopher wou'd quickly discover, that it wou'd not alone be sufficient to that purpose. All human creatures, especially of the female sex, are apt to over-look remote motives in favour of any present temptation: The temptation is here the strongest imaginable: Its approaches are insensible and seducing: And a woman easily finds, or flatters herself she shall find, certain means of securing her reputation, and preventing all the pernicious consequences of her pleasures. 'Tis necessary, therefore, that, beside the infamy attending such licences, there shou'd be some preceding backwardness or dread, which may prevent their first approaches, and may give the female sex a repugnance to all expressions, and postures, and liberties, that have an immediate relation to that enjoyment.

Such wou'd be the reasonings of our speculative philosopher: But I am persuaded, that if he had not a perfect knowledge of human nature, he wou'd be apt to regard them as mere chimerical speculations, and wou'd consider the infamy attending infidelity, and backwardness to all its approaches, as principles that were rather to be wish'd than hop'd for in the world. For what means, wou'd he say, of persuading mankind, that the transgressions of conjugal duty are more infamous than any other kind of injustice, when 'tis evident they are more excusable, upon account of the greatness of the temptation? And what possibility of giving a backwardness to the approaches of a pleasure, to which nature has inspir'd so strong a propensity; and a propensity that 'tis absolutely necessary in the end to comply with, for the support of the species?

But speculative reasonings, which cost so much pains to philosophers, are often form'd by the world naturally, and without reflection: As difficul-ties, which seem unsurmountable in theory, are easily got over in practice. Those, who have an interest in the fidelity of women, naturally disapprove of their infidelity, and all the approaches to it. Those, who have no interest, are carried along with the stream. Education takes possession of the ductile minds of the fair sex in their infancy. And when a general rule of this kind is once establish'd, men are apt to extend it beyond those principles, from which it first arose. Thus batchelors, however debauch'd, cannot chuse but be shock'd with any instance of lewdness or impudence in women. And tho' all these maxims have a plain reference to generation, yet women past child-bearing have no more privilege in this respect, than those who are in the flower of their youth and beauty. Men have undoubtedly an implicit notion, that all those ideas of modesty and decency have a regard to generation; since they impose not the same laws, *with the same force*, on the male sex, where that reason takes not place. The exception is there obvious and extensive, and founded on a remarkable difference, which produces a clear separation and disjunction of ideas. But as the case is not the same with regard to the different ages of women, for this reason, tho' men know, that these notions are founded on the public interest, yet the general rule carries us beyond the original principle, and makes us extend the notions of modesty over the whole sex, from their earliest infancy to their extremest old-age and infirmity.

Courage, which is the point of honour among men, derives its merit, in a great measure, from artifice, as well as the chastity of women; tho' it has also some foundation in nature, as we shall see afterwards.

As to the obligations which the male sex lie under, with regard to chastity, we may observe, that according to the general notions of the world, they bear nearly the same proportion to the obligations of women, as the obligations of the law of nations do to those of the law of nature. 'Tis contrary to the interest of civil society, that men shou'd have an *entire* liberty of indulging their appetites in venereal enjoyment: But as this interest is weaker than in the case of the female sex, the moral obligation, arising from it, must be proportionably weaker. And to prove this we need only appeal to the practice and sentiments of all nations and ages.

chapter eighteen
Jean-Jacques Rousseau

In the midst of the rising bourgeois liberalism of "enlightened" eighteenth-century France, Jean-Jacques Rousseau (1712–1778), French philosopher and social and political theorist, emerged as an important, highly controversial social critic. Rousseau certainly expressed Enlightenment confidence in progress and in the infinite perfectibility of human beings, but he condemned civil society as it had evolved as unnatural and corrupt. "Man is born free, but everywhere he is in chains," he lamented.[1] Humankind's naturally good and happy—albeit brutish—original state had devolved through history into rampant moral corruption and abhorrent systems of social inequality. Rousseau therefore became a great advocate for the common people, especially for the cultivation of their natural virtues (such as freedom) through education. Because his ideas supplied much of the fuel for the French Revolution, Rousseau has been called "the prophet of modern democracy and nationalism."[2] He is further celebrated as one of the intellectual sources of ninteenth-century Romanticism, as well as of the development of twentieth-century psychological literature, psychoanalytic theory, and existentialist philosophy.

Rousseau was born in Geneva into a Swiss Protestant family but was raised by his aunt and uncle when his mother died shortly after his birth. At age thirteen, he was apprenticed to an engraver; when he turned sixteen, however, he ran away and fortunately found his way to Madame Louise de Warens, a wealthy and benevolent woman to whom he became secretary and companion and who profoundly influenced his life and thought. He remained with Madame Warens for fourteen years; in 1742, at age thirty, he moved to Paris and earned a living as a music teacher, music copyist, and political secretary.

Within a few years, Rousseau began to earn distinction for his published works, winning the Academy of Dijon Award in 1750 for his *Discours sur les sciences et les arts (Discourse on the Sciences and the Arts,* 1750). In 1752 his opera *Le devin du village* (*The Village Sage*) was performed for the first time. Despite these public successes, Rousseau was a determined social "outsider," a rebellious spirit who viewed contemporary French society with great contempt. In *Discourse on the Sciences and the Arts,* he had already

From *Emile, or On Education* by Jean-Jacques Rousseau, Allan Bloom, translator. Copyright © 1979 by Basic Books, Inc. Reprinted by permission of Basic Books, a member of Perseus Books, L.L.C.

begun to expound his view of science and art as products of a corrupt and corrupting civilization and of humankind's original natural, "primitive," state as morally superior to its civilized one. He devoted the next few years to considering what might have been the sources of humanity's corruption—of its pervasive greed and social inequality.

In 1755, he published *Discourse on the Origin and Foundation of Inequality among Mankind*, in which he speculated that throughout the stages of humankind's development—its progression beyond its original, naturally good, primitive state—there were crucial moments in which human beings considered it in their best interest to veer onto a different, albeit unnatural (and ultimately pernicious) course. Rousseau was convinced that the earliest primitive humans were, in the state of nature, *happy*.[3] He envisioned them as concerned exclusively with self-preservation, each one "wandering in the forests, without industry, without speech, without domicile, without war and without liaisons, with no need of his fellows, likewise with no desire to harm them."[4] These beings lived alone, subsisting on whatever nature supplied them. Males and females came together to gratify their sexual desires but then separated to enjoy their independence. Moreover, Rousseau believed that these early humans were, in their natural state, essentially good and lived harmoniously, any temptation to harm another being checked by their natural compassion—or fear of retaliation.

Of course, when men and women come together, children frequently emerge from their union. Rousseau believed the establishment of the family brought with it the condition of the possibility for the end to the primitive humans' original happy state: the desire for private property. The formation of the family was itself a positive development for humanity. The skills and amenities needed to sustain family life, such as a common language, common shelter, and hunting and gathering "technologies" greatly enhanced human existence. At the same time, however, many of these features of family life became sources of conflict and unhappiness as families, forming units within an emerging society, marked off resources for their sustenance. Says Rousseau, "The first person who, having fenced off a plot of ground, took it into his head to say *this is mine* and found people simple enough to believe him, was the true founder of civil society."[5] Thus was established the system of social inequality and injustice that Rousseau believed characterized civilization.

Thrust into its next stage of development, the establishment of civil society, in which individuals could claim rights to private property and rest assured that all would respect the privilege of ownership, humankind lost natural equality. Rousseau claimed, however, that although human beings lost their natural freedom and equality, they gained civil liberty and equality. This development also brought certain benefits, according to Rousseau, for he believed that civil society ideally enables human beings to cultivate the virtues, such as the capacity to *exercise* freedom, that distinguish humans from the other animals.[6] The state of nature surely was happy, but it did not facilitate the cultivation and full exercise of human excellences. Civil society, however, *might*. Of course, in Rousseau's view, humankind failed miserably in its civilization project.

According to Rousseau, then, the world was designed for human happiness, but human beings have ruined it. Moreover, while he argued that our social ills are the result of our own greed and tolerance of civil inequality, he emphasized that they are reinforced by, and perpetuated through, an improper education. Rousseau elaborated this view in *Emile, or On Education* (1762), stressing his belief in the inherent goodness of human beings and his ideal conception of society as one in which we do not band together merely to secure our property but rather to exercise our virtues fully. A proper education is essential to that full exercise of virtue and thus to the success of civil society. However, to truly succeed, children's education must follow a natural course. Each child must be taught to cultivate his virtues according to a plan and pace that matches the unique unfolding of his nature. The aim of education certainly is *not* to pour endless facts and pernicious social mores into children's minds but rather "to form [the] rare man"[7] of nature according to nature. In *Emile,* then, Rousseau expounds a revolutionary theory of education emphasizing the cultivation of expressive, free citizens.

The education of Emile requires twenty-five years and progresses through five stages in accordance with what Rousseau identifies as natural stages of human development. The five books of *Emile* correspond to each of these stages. In the first three stages of Emile's youth, he is given what Rousseau believes is a truly "natural" experience: he is raised apart from society under the guidance of his tutor, "Jean-Jacques." Stages 1 and 2 cover the boy's physical development through age twelve; his education equips him to grapple with the obstacles, challenges, and adversities of the natural world. Stage 3, occurring at ages twelve to fifteen, addresses the cultivation of Emile's reason and intellect. His teacher nurtures, guides, and focuses his natural curiosity instead of subjecting him to a rigid, standardized curriculum. In stage 4, the stage of socialization Emile experiences at ages fifteen to twenty, he is introduced to society for the first time. His education emphasizes those social "institutions" that nurture compassionate relationships among people—mainly friendship, religion, and sex. Finally, stage 5, covering ages twenty to twenty-five, addresses the character and education of Sophie, the woman who is to be a suitable life mate for Emile, who at age twenty-five takes his place in the world as a truly self-sufficient and free citizen. Sophie's education is essential to Emile's full cultivation, for Sophie plays a crucial role in Emile's transition from boyhood to manhood. Thus Book V expounds Rousseau's view of the passions; he describes how Emile confronts his complex emotions and desires both when he falls in love with Sophie and when he is compelled to leave her to explore the world. In this chapter, Rousseau also expresses his conviction that woman's distinctive feminine qualities, assigned to her by nature, have designated a different place for her in nature and in society: a woman's essential function is to please her husband.

The unconventional ideas Rousseau expressed in *Emile* not only provoked France's highest court, the archbishop of Paris, and the authorities in Geneva to condemn the book, but also antagonized several of his friends. In 1762 Rousseau fled first to Prussia and then to England where he enjoyed a brief friendship with David Hume.[8] Despite the book's being condemned, many parents nevertheless opted to raise their children according to Rousseau's plan.[9] Several notable educators and education theorists also embraced his views, among them Heinrich Pestalozzi (1746–1827), Friedrich Froebel (1782–1852), and Maria Montessori (1870–1952).

While Rousseau was in England, he wrote a treatise on botany, *La botanique* (published posthumously in 1802). He returned to France in 1768 under the assumed name Renou and in 1770 completed another of his most famous works, the autobiographical *Confessions* (also published posthumously, in 1782). Earlier works by Rousseau include the romance, *The New Heloise* (1761), and his famous political treatise, *The Social Contract* (1762). Rousseau died July 2, 1778, in Ermenonville, France.

SC

QUESTIONS

1. Discuss the conception of nature Rousseau advances in the first part of Book I of *Emile.*

2. What, according to Rousseau, are the relationships obtaining among the human being, nature, civilization, and education?

3. List, throughout the reading, as many characterizing traits as you can find that Rousseau ascribes to men and women, respectively. What do you take to be Rousseau's conceptions of men and of women?

4. What sort of education suits women, according to Rousseau? What do you find defensible, and what do you consider to be indefensible, in Rousseau's argument?

5. What are the mechanisms that constrain "immoderate passions" for men and women?

6. What does Rousseau say is the relationship between the family and the state? What are women's and men's roles in each?

ENDNOTES

1. Rousseau, *On the Social Contract,* p. 131.

2. For example, by Edgar Knoebel in *Classics of Western Thought,* Vol. III, New York: Harcourt Brace Jovanovich 1988, p. 131.

3. Depictions of the "state of nature," the human being's condition prior to civilization, are a common element of seventeenth- and eighteenth-century political theorizing. Thomas Hobbes and John Locke, for instance, also had conceptions of an original "state of nature" that inform their conceptions of the state of "civil society."

4. Rousseau, *Discourse on the Origin and Foundation of Inequality among Mankind,* p. 40.

5. Ibid., p. 43.

6. Aristotle held a similar conviction. He believed that humankind's possession of language was evidence that we were meant for social organization; accordingly, he saw the state as the highest expression of human potential—humanity's *telos,* if you will.

7. Rousseau, *Emile,* p. 41.

8. They soon quarreled when Rousseau, suddenly plagued by paranoia, accused Hume of plotting against him. They eventually denounced each other publicly.

9. Oddly enough, Rousseau had denied his own children this education—to the contrary, he had confined them to an orphanage! Later, in his *Confessions,* he reproached himself severely for this act.

SELECTED BIBLIOGRAPHY

Mahowald, Mary Briody. *Philosophy of Woman: An Anthology of Classic to Current Concepts.* Indianapolis, Ind.: Hackett Publishing Company, 1978.

Rousseau, Jean-Jacques. *Discourse on the Origin and Foundations of Inequality (Second Discourse),* from *The Collected Writings of Rousseau,* Vol. 3, ed. Roger D. Masters and Christopher Kelly, trans. Judith R. Bush, Roger D. Masters, and Christopher Kelly. Hanover, N.H.: University Press of New England, 1992.

Rousseau, Jean-Jacques. *Discourse on the Sciences and Arts: (First Discourse)* and *Polemics in The Collected Writings of Rousseau,* Vol. 2, ed. Roger D. Masters and Christopher Kelly, trans. Judith R. Bush, Roger D. Masters, and Christopher Kelly. Hanover, NH: University Press of New England, 1992.

Rousseau, Jean-Jacques. *Emile, or On Education,* trans. Allan Bloom. New York: Basic Books, 1979.

Rousseau, Jean-Jacques. *On the Social Contract* in *The Collected Writings of Rousseau,* Vol. 4, ed. Roger D. Masters and Christopher Kelly, trans. Judith R. Bush, Roger D. Masters, and Christopher Kelly. Hanover, NH: University Press of New England, 1992.

from *Emile, or on Education*

Jean-Jacques Rousseau

BOOK I

Everything is good as it leaves the hands of the Author of things; everything degenerates in the hands of man. He forces one soil to nourish the products of another, one tree to bear the fruit of another. He mixes and confuses the climates, the elements, the seasons. He mutilates his dog, his horse, his slave. He turns everything upside down; he disfigures everything; he loves deformity, monsters. He wants nothing as nature made it, not even man; for him, man must be trained like a school horse; man must be fashioned in keeping with his fancy like a tree in his garden.

Were he not to do this, however, everything would go even worse, and our species does not admit of being formed halfway. In the present state of things a man abandoned to himself in the midst of other men from birth would be the most disfigured of all. Prejudices, authority, necessity, example, all the social institutions in which we find ourselves submerged would stifle nature in him and put nothing in its place. Nature there would be like a shrub that chance had caused to be born in the middle of a path and that the passers-by soon cause to perish by bumping into it from all sides and bending it in every direction.

It is to you that I address myself, tender and foresighted mother,[1] who are capable of keeping the nascent shrub away from the highway and securing it from the impact of human opinions! Cultivate and water the young plant before it dies. Its fruits will one day be your delights. Form an enclosure around your child's soul at an early date. Someone else can draw its circumference, but you alone must build the fence.

Plants are shaped by cultivation, and men by education. If man were born big and strong, his size and strength would be useless to him until he had learned to make use of them. They would be detrimental to him in that they would keep others from thinking of aiding him.[2] And, abandoned to himself, he would die of want before knowing his needs. And childhood is taken to be a pitiable state! It is not seen that the human race would have perished if man had not begun as a child.

We are born weak, we need strength; we are born totally unprovided, we need aid; we are born stupid, we need judgment. Everything we do not have at our birth and which we need when we are grown is given us by education.

This education comes to us from nature or from men or from things. The internal development of our faculties and our organs is the education of nature. The use that we are taught to make of this development is the education of men. And what we acquire from our own experience about the objects which affect us is the education of things.

Each of us is thus formed by three kinds of masters. The disciple in whom their various lessons are at odds with one another is badly raised and will never be in agreement with himself. He alone in whom they all coincide at the same points and tend to the same ends reaches his goal and lives consistently. He alone is well raised.

Now, of these three different educations, the one coming from nature is in no way in our control; that coming from things is in our control only

---

[1] The first education is the most important, and this first education belongs incontestably to women; if the Author of nature had wanted it to belong to men, He would have given them milk with which to nurse the children. Always speak, then, preferably to women in your treatises on education; for, beyond the fact that they are in a position to watch over it more closely than are men and always have greater influence on it, they also have much more interest in its success, since most widows find themselves almost at the mercy of their children; then their children make mothers keenly aware, for good or ill, of the effect of the way they raised their children. The laws—always so occupied with property and so little with persons, because their object is peace not virtue—do not give enough authority to mothers. However, their status is more certain than that of fathers; their duties are more painful; their cares are more important for the good order of the family; generally they are more attached to the children. There are occasions on which a son who lacks respect for his father can in some way be excused. But if on any occasion whatsoever a child were unnatural enough to lack respect for his mother—for her who carried him in her womb, who nursed him with her milk, who for years forgot herself in favor of caring for him alone—one should hasten to strangle this wretch as a monster unworthy of seeing the light of day. Mothers, it is said, spoil their children. In that they are doubtless wrong—but less wrong than you perhaps who deprave them. The mother wants her child to be happy, happy now. In that she is right. When she is mistaken about the means, she must be enlightened. Fathers' ambition, avarice, tyranny, and false foresight, their negligence, their harsh insensitivity are a hundred times more disastrous for children than is the blind tenderness of mothers. Moreover, the sense I give to the name *mother* must be explained; and that is what will be done hereafter.

[2] Similar to them on the outside and deprived of speech as well as of the ideas it expresses, he would not be in a condition to make them understand the need he had of their help, and nothing in him would manifest this need to them.

in certain respects; that coming from men is the only one of which we are truly the masters. Even of it we are the masters only by hypothesis. For who can hope entirely to direct the speeches and the deeds of all those surrounding a child?

Therefore, when education becomes an art, it is almost impossible for it to succeed, since the conjunction of the elements necessary to its success is in no one's control. All that one can do by dint of care is to come more or less close to the goal, but to reach it requires luck.

What is that goal? It is the very same as that of nature. This has just been proved. Since the conjunction of the three educations is necessary to their perfection, the two others must be directed toward the one over which we have no power. But perhaps this word *nature* has too vague a sense. An attempt must be made here to settle on its meaning.

Nature, we are told, is only habit. What does that mean? Are there not habits contracted only by force which never do stifle nature? Such, for example, is the habit of the plants whose vertical direction is interfered with. The plant, set free, keeps the inclination it was forced to take. But the sap has not as a result changed its original direction; and if the plant continues to grow, its new growth resumes the vertical direction. The case is the same for men's inclinations. So long as one remains in the same condition, the inclinations which result from habit and are the least natural to us can be kept; but as soon as the situation changes, habit ceases and the natural returns. Education is certainly only habit. Now are there not people who forget and lose their education? Others who keep it? Where does this difference come from? If the name *nature* were limited to habits conformable to nature, we would spare ourselves this garble.

We are born with the use of our senses, and from our birth we are affected in various ways by the objects surrounding us. As soon as we have, so

to speak, consciousness of our sensations, we are disposed to seek or avoid the objects which produce them, at first according to whether they are pleasant or unpleasant to us, then according to the conformity or lack of it that we find between us and these objects, and finally according to the judgments we make about them on the basis of the idea of happiness or of perfection given us by reason. These dispositions are extended and strengthened as we become more capable of using our senses and more enlightened; but constrained by our habits, they are more or less corrupted by our opinions. Before this corruption they are what I call in us *nature*.

It is, then, to these original dispositions that everything must be related; and that could be done if our three educations were only different from one another. But what is to be done when they are opposed? When, instead of raising a man for himself, one wants to raise him for others? Then their harmony is impossible. Forced to combat nature or the social institutions, one must choose between making a man or a citizen, for one cannot make both at the same time.

Natural man is entirely for himself. He is numerical unity, the absolute whole which is relative only to itself or its kind. Civil man is only a fractional unity dependent on the denominator; his value is determined by his relation to the whole, which is the social body. Good social institutions are those that best know how to denature man, to take his absolute existence from him in order to give him a relative one and transport the *I* into the common unity, with the result that each individual believes himself no longer one but a part of the unity and no longer feels except within the whole. A citizen of Rome was neither Caius nor Lucius; he was a Roman. He even loved the country exclusive of himself. Regulus claimed he was Carthaginian on the grounds that he had become the property of his masters. In his status of foreigner he refused to sit in the Roman senate; a Carthaginian had to order him to do so. He was indignant that they wanted to save his life. He conquered and returned triumphant to die by torture. This has little relation, it seems to me, to the men we know.

The Lacedaemonian Pedaretus runs for the council of three hundred. He is defeated. He goes home delighted that there were three hundred men worthier than he to be found in Sparta. I take this display to be sincere, and there is reason to believe that it was. This is the citizen.

A Spartan woman had five sons in the army and was awaiting news of the battle. A Helot arrives; trembling, she asks him for news. "Your five sons were killed." "Base slave, did I ask you that?" "We won the victory." The mother runs to the temple and gives thanks to the gods. This is the female citizen.

He who in the civil order wants to preserve the primacy of the sentiments of nature does not know what he wants. Always in contradiction with himself, always floating between his inclinations and his duties, he will never be either man or citizen. He will be good neither for himself nor for others. He will be one of these men of our days: a Frenchman, an Englishman, a bourgeois. He will be nothing. . . .

Swept along in contrary routes by nature and by men, forced to divide ourselves between these different impulses, we follow a composite impulse which leads us to neither one goal nor the other. Thus, in conflict and floating during the whole course of our life, we end it without having been able to put ourselves in harmony with ourselves. . . .

But what will a man raised uniquely for himself become for others? If perchance the double object we set for ourselves could be joined in a single one by removing the contradictions of man, a great obstacle to his happiness would be removed. In order to judge of this, he would have to be seen wholly formed: his inclinations would have to have been observed, his progress seen, his development followed. In a word, the natural man would have to be known. I believe that one will have made a few steps in these researches when one has read this writing.

To form this rare man, what do we have to do? Very much, doubtless. What must be done is to prevent anything from being done. When it is only a question of going against the wind, one tacks. But if the sea is heavy and one wants to stand still, one must cast anchor. Take care, young pilot, for fear that your cable run or your anchor drag and that the vessel drift without your noticing.

In the social order where all positions are determined, each man ought to be raised for his. If an individual formed for his position leaves it, he is no longer fit for anything. Education is useful only insofar as fortune is in agreement with the parents' vocation. In any other case it is harmful to the student, if only by virtue of the prejudices it gives him. . . .

In the natural order, since men are all equal, their common calling is man's estate and whoever is well raised for that calling cannot fail to fulfill those callings related to it. Let my student be destined for the sword, the church, the bar. I do not care. Prior to the calling of his parents is nature's call to human life. Living is the job I want to teach him. On leaving my hands, he will, I admit, be neither magistrate nor soldier nor priest. He will, in the first place, be a man. All that a man should be, he will in case of need know how to be as well as anyone; and fortune may try as it may to make him change place, he will always be in his own place. *Occupavi te fortuna atque cepi omnesque aditus tuos interclusi, ut ad me aspirare non posses.*[3]

---

[3] *Tuscul.* V.[10]

Our true study is that of the human condition. He among us who best knows how to bear the goods and the ills of this life is to my taste the best raised: from which it follows that the true education consists less in precept than in practice. We begin to instruct ourselves when we begin to live. . . .

Thus education, instruction, and teaching are three things as different in their object as are the governess, the preceptor, and the master. But these distinctions are ill drawn; and, to be well led, the child should follow only a single guide.

We must, then, generalize our views and consider in our pupil abstract man, man exposed to all the accidents of human life. If men were born attached to a country's soil, if the same season lasted the whole year, if each man were fixed in his fortune in such a way as never to be able to change it—the established practice would be good in certain respects. The child raised for his station, never leaving it, could not be exposed to the disadvantages of another. But given the mobility of human things, given the unsettled and restless spirit of this age which upsets everything in each generation, can one conceive of a method more senseless than raising a child as though he never had to leave his room, as though he were going to be constantly surrounded by his servants? If the unfortunate makes a single step on the earth, if he goes down a single degree, he is lost. This is not teaching him to bear suffering; it is training him to feel it.

One thinks only of preserving one's child. That is not enough. One ought to teach him to preserve himself as a man, to bear the blows of fate, to brave opulence and poverty, to live, if he has to, in freezing Iceland or on Malta's burning rocks. You may very well take precautions against his dying. He will nevertheless have to die. And though his death were not the product of your efforts, still these efforts would be ill conceived. It is less a question of keeping him from dying than of mak-

ing him live. To live is not to breathe; it is to act; it is to make use of our organs, our senses, our faculties, of all the parts of ourselves which give us the sentiment of our existence. The man who has lived the most is not he who has counted the most years but he who has most felt life. Men have been buried at one hundred who died at their birth. They would have gained from dying young; at least they would have lived up to that time.

All our wisdom consists in servile prejudices. All our practices are only subjection, impediment, and constraint. Civil man is born, lives, and dies in slavery. At his birth he is sewed in swaddling clothes; at his death he is nailed in a coffin. So long as he keeps his human shape, he is enchained by our institutions.

It is said that many midwives claim that by kneading newborn babies' heads, they give them a more suitable shape. And this is tolerated! Our heads are ill fashioned by the Author of our being! We need to have them fashioned on the outside by midwives and on the inside by philosophers. The Caribs are twice as lucky as we are.

Hardly has the baby emerged from the mother's womb, and hardly has he enjoyed the freedom to move and stretch his limbs before he is given new bonds. He is swaddled, laid out with the head secured and the legs stretched out, the arms hanging beside the body. He is surrounded with linens and trusses of every kind which do not permit him to change position, and he is lucky if he has not been squeezed to the point of being prevented from breathing and if care was taken to lay him on his side in order that the waters that should come out of his mouth can fall by themselves, for he would not have the freedom of turning his head to the side to facilitate the flow.[4]

The newborn baby needs to stretch and move its limbs in order to arouse them from the torpor

---

[4]Buffon, *Histoire Naturelle,* vol. IV, p. 190.

in which, drawn up in a little ball, they have for so long remained. They are stretched out, it is true, but they are prevented from moving. Even the head is subjected to caps. It seems that we are afraid lest he appear to be alive. . . .

The inaction, the constraint in which a baby's limbs are kept can only hinder the circulation of the blood, of the humors, prevent the baby from fortifying himself, from growing, and cause his constitution to degenerate. In the places where these extravagant precautions are not taken, men are all tall, strong, and well proportioned. The countries where children are swaddled teem with hunchbacks, cripples, men with stunted or withered limbs, men suffering from rickets, men misshapen in every way. For fear that bodies be deformed by free movements, we hurry to deform the children by putting them into a press. We would gladly cripple them to keep them from laming themselves.

Could not so cruel a constraint have an influence on their disposition as well as on their constitution? Their first sentiment is a sentiment of pain and suffering. They find only obstacles to all the movements which they need. Unhappier than a criminal in irons, they make vain efforts, they get irritable, they cry. Their first voices, you say, are tears. I can well believe it. You thwart them from their birth. The first gifts they receive from you are chains. The first treatment they experience is torment. Having nothing free but the voice, how would they not make use of it to complain? They cry because you are hurting them. Thus garroted, you would cry harder than they do.

Where does this unreasonable practice come from? From a denatured practice. Since mothers, despising their first duty, have no longer wanted to feed their children, it has been necessary to confide them to mercenary women who, thus finding themselves mothers of alien children on whose behalf nature tells them nothing, have sought only to save themselves effort. It would be necessary to be constantly watchful over a child in freedom. But when it is well bound, one throws it in a corner without being troubled by its cries. . . .

Not satisfied with having given up nursing their children, women give up wanting to have them. The result is natural. As soon as the condition of motherhood becomes burdensome, the means to deliver oneself from it completely is soon found. They want to perform a useless act so as always to be able to start over again, and they turn to the prejudice of the species the attraction given for the sake of multiplying it. This practice, added to the other causes of depopulation, presages the impending fate of Europe. The sciences, the arts, the philosophy, and the morals that this practice engenders will not be long in making a desert of it. It will be peopled with ferocious beasts. The change of inhabitants will not be great. . . .

But let mothers deign to nurse their children, morals will reform themselves, nature's sentiments will be awakened in every heart, the state will be repeopled. This first point, this point alone, will bring everything back together. The attraction of domestic life is the best counterpoison for bad morals. The bother of children, which is believed to be an importunity, becomes pleasant. It makes the father and mother more necessary, dearer to one another; it tightens the conjugal bond between them. When the family is lively and animated, the domestic cares constitute the dearest occupation of the wife and the sweetest enjoyment of the husband. Thus, from the correction of this single abuse would soon result a general reform; nature would soon have reclaimed all its rights. Let women once again become mothers, men will soon become fathers and husbands again. . . .

Observe nature and follow the path it maps out for you. It exercises children constantly; it hardens their temperament by tests of all sorts; it teaches them early what effort and pain are. Teething puts them in a fever; sharp colics give them convulsions; long coughs suffocate them; worms torment them; plethora corrupts their blood; various leavens ferment in it and cause perilous eruptions. Almost all the first age is sickness and danger. Half the children born perish before the eighth year. The tests passed, the child has gained strength; and as soon as he can make use of life, its principle becomes sounder.

That is nature's rule. Why do you oppose it? Do you not see that in thinking you correct it, you destroy its product, you impede the effect of its care? To do on the outside what nature does on the inside redoubles the danger, according to you; and, on the contrary, this diverts the danger and weakens it. Experience teaches that even more children raised delicately die than do others. Provided the limit of their strength is not exceeded, less is risked in employing that strength than in sparing it. Exercise them, then, against the attacks they will one day have to bear. Harden their bodies against the intemperance of season, climates, elements; against hunger, thirst, fatigue. Steep them in the water of the Styx. Before the body's habit is acquired, one can give it the habit one wants to give it without danger. But when it has once gained its consistency, every alteration becomes perilous for it. A child will bear changes that a man would not bear; the fibers of the former, soft and flexible, take without effort the turn that they are given; those of the man, more hardened, change only with violence the turn they have received. A child, then, can be made robust without exposing its life and its health; and if there were some risk, still one must not hesitate. Since these are risks inseparable from human life, can one do better than shift them to that part of its span when they are least disadvantageous?

A child becomes more precious as he advances in age. To the value of his person is joined that of the effort he has cost; to the loss of his life is joined in him the sentiment of death. It is, then, especially of the future that one must think in looking after his preservation. It is against the ills of youth that he must be armed before he reaches them; for if the value of life increases up to the age of making use of it, what folly is it not to spare childhood some ills while multiplying them for the age of reason? Are those the lessons of the master? . . .

A governor! O what a sublime soul . . . in truth, to make a man, one must be either a father or more than a man oneself. . . .

Not in a condition to fulfill the most useful task, I will dare at least to attempt the easier one; following the example of so many others, I shall put my hand not to the work but to the pen; and instead of doing what is necessary, I shall endeavor to say it.

I know that in undertakings like this one, an author—always comfortable with systems that he is not responsible for putting into practice—may insouciantly offer many fine precepts which are impossible to follow. And in the absence of details and examples, even the feasible things he says, if he has not shown their application, remain ineffectual.

I have hence chosen to give myself an imaginary pupil, to hypothesize that I have the age, health, kinds of knowledge, and all the talent suitable for working at his education, for conducting him from the moment of his birth up to the one when, become a grown man, he will no longer have need of any guide other than himself. This method appears to me useful to prevent an author who distrusts himself from getting lost in visions; for when he deviates from ordinary practice, he has only to make a test of his own practice on his pupil. He will soon sense, or the reader will sense for him, whether he follows the progress of childhood and the movement natural to the human heart.

This is what I have tried to do in all the difficulties which have arisen. In order not to fatten the book uselessly, I have been content with setting down the principles whose truth everyone should sense. But as for the rules which might need proofs, I have applied them all to my Emile or to other examples; and I have shown in very extensive detail how what I have established could be put into practice. . . .

BOOK V

Now we have come to the last act in the drama of youth, but we are not yet at the dénouement. It is not good for man to be alone. Emile is a man. We have promised him a companion. She has to be given to him. That companion is Sophie. In what place is her abode? Where shall we find her? To find her, it is necessary to know her. Let us first learn what she is; then we shall better judge what places she inhabits. And even when we have found her, everything will still not have been done. "Since our young gentleman," says Locke, "is ready to marry, it is time to leave him to his beloved." And with that he finishes his work.

Sophie

Or The Woman

Sophie ought to be a woman as Emile is a man—that is to say, she ought to have everything which suits the constitution of her species and her sex in order to fill her place in the physical and moral order. Let us begin, then, by examining the similarities and the differences of her sex and ours.

In everything not connected with sex, woman is man. She has the same organs, the same needs, the same faculties. The machine is constructed in the same way; its parts are the same; the one functions as does the other; the form is similar; and in whatever respect one considers them, the difference between them is only one of more or less.

In everything connected with sex, woman and man are in every respect related and in every respect different. The difficulty of comparing them comes from the difficulty of determining what in their constitutions is due to sex and what is not. On the basis of comparative anatomy and even just by inspection, one finds general differences between them that do not appear connected with sex. They are, nevertheless, connected with sex, but by relations which we are not in a position to perceive. We do not know the extent of these relations. The only thing we know with certainty is that everything man and woman have in common belongs to the species, and that everything which distinguishes them belongs to the sex. From this double perspective, we find them related in so many ways and opposed in so many other ways that it is perhaps one of the marvels of nature to have been able to construct two such similar beings who are constituted so differently.

These relations and these differences must have a moral influence. This conclusion is evident to the senses; it is in agreement with our experience; and it shows how vain are the disputes as to whether one of the two sexes is superior or whether they are equal—as though each, in fulfilling nature's ends according to its own particular purpose, were thereby less perfect than if it resembled the other more! In what they have in common, they are equal. Where they differ, they are not comparable. A perfect woman and a perfect man ought not to resemble each other in mind any more than in looks, and perfection is not susceptible of more or less.

In the union of the sexes each contributes equally to the common aim, but not in the same way. From this diversity arises the first assignable difference in the moral relations of the two sexes. One ought to be active and strong, the other passive and weak. One must necessarily will and be able; it suffices that the other put up little resistance.

Once this principle is established, it follows that woman is made specially to please man. If man ought to please her in turn, it is due to a less direct necessity. His merit is in his power; he pleases by the sole fact of his strength. This is not the law of love, I agree. But it is that of nature, prior to love itself.

If woman is made to please and to be subjugated, she ought to make herself agreeable to man instead of arousing him. Her own violence is in her charms. It is by these that she ought to constrain him to find his strength and make use of it. The surest art for animating that strength is to make it necessary by resistance. Then *amour-propre* unites with desire, and the one triumphs in the victory that the other has made him win. From this there arises attack and defense, the audacity of one sex and the timidity of the other, and finally the modesty and the shame with which nature armed the weak in order to enslave the strong.

Who could think that nature has indiscriminately prescribed the same advances to both men and women, and that the first to form desires should also be the first to show them? What a strange depravity of judgment! Since the undertaking has such different consequences for the two sexes, is it natural that they should have the same audacity in abandoning themselves to it? With so great an inequality in what each risks in the union, how can one fail to see that if reserve did not impose on one sex the moderation which nature imposes on the other, the result would soon be the ruin of both, and mankind would perish by the means established for preserving it? If there were some unfortunate region on earth where philosophy had introduced this practice—especially in hot countries, where more women are born than men—men would be tyrannized by women. For,

given the ease with which women arouse men's senses and reawaken in the depths of their hearts the remains of ardors which are almost extinguished, men would finally be their victims and would see themselves dragged to death without ever being able to defend themselves. . . .

The Supreme Being wanted to do honor to the human species in everything. While giving man inclinations without limit, He gives him at the same time the law which regulates them, in order that he may be free and in command of himself. While abandoning man to immoderate passions, He joins reason to these passions in order to govern them. While abandoning woman to unlimited desires, He joins modesty to these desires in order to constrain them. In addition, He adds yet another real recompense for the good use of one's faculties—the taste we acquire for decent things when we make them the rule of our actions. All this, it seems to me, is worth more than the instinct of beasts.

Whether the human female shares man's desires or not and wants to satisfy them or not, she repulses him and always defends herself—but not always with the same force or, consequently, with the same success. For the attacker to be victorious, the one who is attacked must permit or arrange it; for does she not have adroit means to force the aggressor to use force? The freest and sweetest of all acts does not admit of real violence. Nature and reason oppose it: nature, in that it has provided the weaker with as much strength as is needed to resist when it pleases her; reason, in that real rape is not only the most brutal of all acts but the one most contrary to its end—either because the man thus declares war on his companion and authorizes her to defend her person and her liberty even at the expense of the agressor's life, or because the woman alone is the judge of the condition she is in, and a child would have no father if every man could usurp the father's rights.

Here, then, is a third conclusion drawn from the constitution of the sexes—that the stronger appears to be master but actually depends on the weaker. This is due not to a frivolous practice of gallantry or to the proud generosity of a protector, but to an invariable law of nature which gives woman more facility to excite the desires than man to satisfy them. This causes the latter, whether he likes it or not, to depend on the former's wish and constrains him to seek to please her in turn, so that she will consent to let him be the stronger. Then what is sweetest for man in his victory is the doubt whether it is weakness which yields to strength or the will which surrenders. And the woman's usual ruse is always to leave this doubt between her and him. In this the spirit of women corresponds perfectly to their constitution. Far from blushing at their weakness, they make it their glory. Their tender muscles are without resistance. They pretend to be unable to lift the lightest burdens. They would be ashamed to be strong. Why is that? It is not only to appear delicate; it is due to a shrewder precaution. They prepare in advance excuses and the right to be weak in case of need.

The progress of the enlightenment acquired as a result of our vices has greatly changed the old opinions on this point among us. Rapes are hardly ever spoken of anymore, since they are so little necessary and men no longer believe in them.[5] By contrast, they are very common in early Greek and Jewish antiquity, because those old opinions belong to the simplicity of nature, and only the experience of libertinism has been able to uproot them. If fewer acts of rape are cited in our day, this is surely not because men are more temperate but because they are less credulous, and such a complaint, which previously would have persuaded simple peoples, in our days would succeed only in attracting the laughter of mockers. It is more advantageous to keep quiet. In Deuteronomy there is a law by which a girl who had been abused was punished along with her seducer if the offense had been committed in the city. But if it had been committed in the country or in an isolated place, the man alone was punished: "For," the law says, "the girl cried out and was not heard." This benign interpretation taught the girls not to let themselves be surprised in well-frequented places.

The effect of these differences of opinion about morals is evident. Modern gallantry is their work. Finding that their pleasures depended more on the will of the fair sex than they had believed, men have captivated that will by attentions for which the fair sex has amply compensated them.

Observe how the physical leads us unawares to the moral, and how the sweetest laws of love are born little by little from the coarse union of the sexes. Women possess their empire not because men wanted it that way, but because nature wants it that way. It belonged to women before they appeared to have it. The same Hercules who believed he raped the fifty daughters of Thespitius was nevertheless constrained to weave while he was with Omphale; and the strong Samson was not so strong as Delilah. This empire belongs to women and cannot be taken from them, even when they abuse it. If they could ever lose it, they would have done so long ago.

There is no parity between the two sexes in regard to the consequences of sex. The male is male only at certain moments. The female is female her whole life or at least during her whole youth. Everything constantly recalls her sex to her; and, to fulfill its functions well, she needs a constitution which corresponds to it. She needs care during her pregnancy; she needs rest at the time of childbirth; she needs a soft and sedentary life to suckle her

---

[5]There can be such a disproportion of age and strength that real rape takes place; but treating here the relation between the sexes according to the order of nature. I take them both as they ordinarily are in that relation.

children; she needs patience and gentleness, a zeal and an affection that nothing can rebuff in order to raise her children. She serves as the link between them and their father; she alone makes him love them and gives him the confidence to call them his own. How much tenderness and care is required to maintain the union of the whole family! And, finally, all this must come not from virtues but from tastes, or else the human species would soon be extinguished.

The strictness of the relative duties of the two sexes is not and cannot be the same. When woman complains on this score about unjust man-made inequality, she is wrong. This inequality is not a human institution—or, at least, it is the work not of prejudice but of reason. It is up to the sex that nature has charged with the bearing of children to be responsible for them to the other sex. Doubtless it is not permitted to anyone to violate his faith, and every unfaithful husband who deprives his wife of the only reward of the austere duties of her sex is an unjust and barbarous man. But the unfaithful woman does more; she dissolves the family and breaks all the bonds of nature. In giving the man children which are not his, she betrays both. She joins perfidy to infidelity. I have difficulty seeing what disorders and what crimes do not flow from this one. If there is a frightful condition in the world, it is that of an unhappy father who, lacking confidence in his wife, does not dare to yield to the sweetest sentiments of his heart, who wonders, in embracing his child, whether he is embracing another's, the token of his dishonor, the plunderer of his own children's property. What does the family become in such a situation if not a society of secret enemies whom a guilty woman arms against one another in forcing them to feign mutual love?

It is important, then, not only that a woman be faithful, but that she be judged to be faithful by her husband, by those near her, by everyone. It is important that she be modest, attentive, reserved, and that she give evidence of her virtue to the eyes of others as well as to her own conscience. If it is important that a father love his children, it is important that he esteem their mother. These are the reasons which put even appearances among the duties of women, and make honor and reputation no less indispensable to them than chastity. There follows from these principles, along with the moral difference of the sexes, a new motive of duty and propriety which prescribes especially to women the most scrupulous attention to their conduct, their manners, and their bearing. To maintain vaguely that the two sexes are equal and that their duties are the same, is to lose oneself in vain declaiming; it is to say nothing so long as one does not respond to these considerations. . . .

Once it is demonstrated that man and woman are not and ought not to be constituted in the same way in either character or temperament, it follows that they ought not to have the same education. In following nature's directions, man and woman ought to act in concert, but they ought not to do the same things. The goal of their labors is common, but their labors themselves are different, and consequently so are the tastes directing them. After having tried to form the natural man, let us also see how the woman who suits this man ought to be formed so that our work will not be left imperfect.

Do you wish always to be well guided? Then always follow nature's indications. Everything that characterizes the fair sex ought to be respected as established by nature. You constantly say, "Women have this or that failing which we do not have." Your pride deceives you. They would be failings for you; they are their good qualities. Everything would go less well if they did not have these qualities. Prevent these alleged failings from degenerating, but take care not to destroy them.

For their part, women do not cease to proclaim that we raise them to be vain and coquettish, that we constantly entertain them with puerilities in order to remain more easily their masters. They blame on us the failings for which we reproach them. What folly! And since when is it that men get involved in the education of girls? Who prevents their mothers from raising them as they please? They have no colleges. What a great misfortune! Would God that there were none for boys; they would be more sensibly and decently raised! Are your daughters forced to waste their time in silliness? Are they made in spite of themselves to spend half their lives getting dressed up, following the example you set them? Are you prevented from instructing them and having them instructed as you please? Is it our fault that they please us when they are pretty, that their mincing ways seduce us, that the art which they learn from you attracts us and pleases us, that we like to see them tastefully dressed, that we let them sharpen at their leisure the weapons with which they subjugate us? So, decide to raise them like men. The men will gladly consent to it! The more women want to resemble them, the less women will govern them, and then men will truly be the masters.

All the faculties common to the two sexes are not equally distributed between them; but taken together, they balance out. Woman is worth more as woman and less as man. Wherever she makes use of her rights, she has the advantage. Wherever she wants to usurp ours, she remains beneath us. One can respond to this general truth only with exceptions, the constant mode of argument of the gallant partisans of the fair sex.

To cultivate man's qualities in women and to neglect those which are proper to them is obviously to work to their detriment. Crafty women see this too well to be duped by it. In trying to usurp our advantages, they do not abandon theirs. But it turns out that they are unable to manage both well—because the two are incompatible— and they remain beneath their own level without getting up to ours, thus losing half their value. Believe me, judicious mother, do not make a decent man of your daughter, as though you would give nature the lie. Make a decent woman of her, and be sure that as a result she will be worth more for herself and for us.

Does it follow that she ought to be raised in ignorance of everything and limited to the housekeeping functions alone? Will man turn his companion into his servant? Will he deprive himself of the greatest charm of society with her? In order to make her more subject, will he prevent her from feeling anything, from knowing anything? Will he make her into a veritable automaton? Surely not. It is not thus that nature has spoken in giving women such agreeable and nimble minds. On the contrary, nature wants them to think, to judge, to love, to know, to cultivate their minds as well as their looks. These are the weapons nature gives them to take the place of the strength they lack and to direct ours. They ought to learn many things but only those that are suitable for them to know.

Whether I consider the particular purpose of the fair sex, whether I observe its inclinations, whether I consider its duties, all join equally in indicating to me the form of education that suits it. Woman and man are made for one another, but their mutual dependence is not equal. Men depend on women because of their desires; women depend on men because of both their desires and their needs. We would survive more easily without them than they would without us. For them to have what is necessary to their station, they depend on us to give it to them, to want to give it to them, to esteem them worthy of it. They depend on our sentiments, on the value we set on their merit, on the importance we attach to their charms and their virtues. By the very law of nature women are at the mercy of men's judgments, as much for their own sake as for that of their children. It is not enough that they be estimable; they must be esteemed. It is not enough for them to be pretty; they must please. It is not enough for them to be temperate; they must be recognized as such. Their honor is not only in their conduct but in their reputation; and it is not possible that a woman who consents to be regarded as disreputable can ever be decent. When a man acts well, he depends only on himself and can brave public judgment; but when a woman acts well, she has accomplished only half of her task, and what is thought of her is no less important to her than what she actually is. From this it follows that the system of woman's education ought to be contrary in this respect to the system of our education. Opinion is the grave of virtue among men and its throne among women.

The good constitution of children initially depends on that of their mothers. The first education of men depends on the care of women. Men's morals, their passions, their tastes, their pleasures, their very happiness also depend on women. Thus the whole education of women ought to relate to men. To please men, to be useful to them, to make herself loved and honored by them, to raise them when young, to care for them when grown, to counsel them, to console them, to make their lives agreeable and sweet—these are the duties of women at all times, and they ought to be taught from childhood. So long as one does not return to this principle, one will deviate from the goal, and all the precepts taught to women will be of no use for their happiness or for ours. . . .

We are told that women are false. They become so. Their particular gift is skill and not falseness. According to the true inclinations of their sex, even when they are lying they are not false. Why do you consult their mouth when it is not the mouth which ought to speak? Consult their eyes, their color, their breathing, their fearful manner, their soft resistance. This is the language nature gives them for answering you. The mouth always says no and ought to say so. But the accent it adds to this answer is not always the same, and this accent does not know how to lie. Does not woman have the same needs as man without having the same right to express them? Her fate would be too cruel if, even in the case of legitimate desires, she did not have a language equivalent to the one she dare not use. Must her modesty make her unhappy? Must she not have an art of communicating her inclinations without laying them bare? What skill she needs to get stolen from her what she is burning to give! How important it is for her to learn to touch the heart of man without appearing to think of him! . . . Yes, I maintain that in keeping coquetry within its limits, one makes it modest and true; one makes it a law of decency.

Virtue is one, as one of my adversaries has very well said. One cannot split virtue up to accept one part and reject another. When someone loves it, he loves it in all its wholeness; and he closes his heart when he can—and always closes his mouth—to sentiments he ought not to have. Moral truth is not what is, but what is good. What is bad ought not to be and ought not to be admitted, especially when this admission gives it an effect it would not otherwise have had. If I were tempted to steal and by saying so I tempted another to be my accomplice, would not declaring my temptation to him be to succumb to it? Why do you say that modesty makes women false? Are those who lose it most completely also truer than the others? Far from it. They are a thousand times more false. One gets to that point of depravity only by dint of vices all of which one keeps and which reign only under the cover of intrigues and lies.[6] On the contrary, those who still have shame, who do not take pride in their faults, who know how to hide their desires from the very persons who inspire them, and whose avowals are the hardest to extract are also the truest, the most sincere, and the most constant in all their engagements and those on whose faith one can generally most rely.

I know of no one other than Mademoiselle de l'Enclos who can be cited as a known exception to these remarks. And Mademoiselle de l'Enclos passed for a marvel. In her contempt for the virtues of her sex, she had, it is said, preserved those of ours. People praise her frankness, her rectitude, the security one had in associating with her, her fidelity in friendship. Finally, to complete the picture of her glory, it is said that she had made herself a man. Wonderful. But with all her great reputation, I would have no more wanted that man for my friend than for my mistress. . . .

On the basis of these considerations I believe that one can determine in general what kind of cultivation suits the minds of women and toward what objects their reflections ought to be turned from their youth.

I have already said that the duties of their sex are easier to see than to fulfill. The first thing that they ought to learn is to love their duties out of regard for their advantages. This is the only way to make their duties easy for them. Each station and each age has its duties. We soon know our own, provided we love them. Honor woman's station, and in whatever rank heaven puts you, you will always be a good woman. The essential thing is to be what nature made us. A woman is always only too much what men want her to be.

The quest for abstract and speculative truths, principles, and axioms in the sciences, for everything that tends to generalize ideas, is not within the competence of women. All their studies ought to be related to practice. It is for them to apply the principles man has found, and to make the observations which lead man to the establishment of principles. Regarding what is not immediately connected with their duties, all the reflections of women ought to be directed to the study of men or to the pleasing kinds of knowledge that have only taste as their aim; for, as regards works of genius, they are out of the reach of women. Nor do women have sufficient precision and attention to succeed at the exact sciences. And as for the physical sciences, they are for the sex which is more active, gets around more, and sees more objects, the sex which has more strength and uses it more to judge the relations of sensible beings and the laws of nature. Woman, who is weak and who sees nothing outside the house, estimates and judges the forces she can put to work to make up for her weakness, and those forces are men's passions. Her science of mechanics is more powerful than ours; all her levers unsettle the human heart. She must have the art to make us want to do everything which her sex cannot do by itself and which is necessary or agreeable to it. She must, therefore, make a profound study of the mind of man—not an abstraction of the mind of man in general, but the minds of the men around her, the minds of the men to whom she is subjected by either law or opinion. She must learn to penetrate their sentiments by their words, their actions, their looks, their gestures. She must know how to communicate to them—by her words, her actions, her looks,

---

[6]I know that women who have openly taken a position on a certain question claim that they make the most of this frankness, and swear that, with only this exception, there is nothing estimable which is not to be found in them. But I do know that they never persuaded anyone but a fool of that. With the greatest curb on their sex removed, what remains to restrain them, and what part of honor will they take seriously when they have renounced that which belongs to them? Once having put their passions at ease, they no longer have any interest in resisting: *nec femina amissa pudicitia alia abnuerit.* Did an author ever know the human heart in the two sexes better than the one who said that?

her gestures—the sentiments that she wishes to communicate without appearing even to dream of it. Men will philosophize about the human heart better than she does; but she will read in men's hearts better than they do. It is for women to discover experimental morality, so to speak, and for us to reduce it to a system. Woman has more wit, man more genius; woman observes, and man reasons. From this conjunction results the clearest insight and the most complete science regarding itself that the human mind can acquire—in a word, the surest knowledge of oneself and others available to our species. And this is how art can constantly tend to the perfection of the instrument given by nature.

The world is the book of women. When they do a bad job of reading it, it is their fault, or else some passion blinds them. Nevertheless, the true mother of a family is hardly less of a recluse in her home than a nun is in her cloister. Thus it is necessary to do for young persons who are about to be married what is done or ought to be done for those who are put in convents—to show them the pleasures they abandon before letting them renounce them, lest the false image of those pleasures which are unknown to them come one day to lead their hearts astray and disturb the happiness of their retreat. In France girls live in convents and women frequent society. With the ancients it was exactly the opposite. Girls, as I have said, had many games and public festivals. Women led retired lives. This practice was more reasonable and maintained morals better. A sort of coquetry is permitted to marriageable girls; enjoying themselves is their chief business. Women have other concerns at home and no longer have husbands to seek; but they would not find this reform to their advantage, and unfortunately they set the tone. Mothers, at least make your daughters your companions. Give them good sense and a decent soul; then hide nothing from them which a chaste eye can look at.

Balls, feasts, games, even the theater—everything which seen in the wrong way, constitutes the charm of an imprudent youth—can be offered without risk to healthy eyes. The better they see these boisterous pleasures, the sooner they will be disgusted by them. . . .

Do you want, then, to inspire young girls with the love of good morals? Without constantly saying to them "Be pure," give them a great interest in being pure. Make them feel all the value of purity, and you will make them love it. It does not suffice to place this interest in the distant future. Show it to them in the present moment, in the relationships of their own age, in the character of their lovers. Depict for them the good man, the man of merit; teach them to recognize him, to love him, and to love him for themselves; prove to them that this man alone can make the women to whom he is attached—wives or beloveds—happy. Lead them to virtue by means of reason. Make them feel that the empire of their sex and all its advantages depend not only on the good conduct and the morals of women but also on those of men, that they have little hold over vile and base souls, and that a man will serve his mistress no better than he serves virtue. You can then be sure that in depicting to them the morals of our own days, you will inspire in them a sincere disgust. In showing them fashionable people, you will make them despise them; you will only be keeping them at a distance from their maxims and giving them an aversion for their sentiments and a disdain for their vain gallantry. You will cause a nobler ambition to be born in them—that of reigning over great and strong souls, the ambition of the women of Sparta, which was to command men. A bold, brazen, scheming woman who knows how to attract her lovers only by coquetry and to keep them only by favors makes them obey her like valets in servile and common things; however, in important and weighty things she is without authority over them.

But the woman who is at once decent, lovable, and self-controlled, who forces those about her to respect her, who has reserve and modesty, who, in a word, sustains love by means of esteem, sends her lovers with a nod to the end of the world, to combat, to glory, to death, to anything she pleases. This seems to me to be a noble empire, and one well worth the price of its purchase.[7]

This is the spirit in which Sophie has been raised—with more care than effort, and more by following her taste than by hindering it. Let us now say a word about her person in accordance with the portrait I made of her for Emile, on the basis of which he himself imagines the wife who can make him happy.

I shall never repeat often enough that I am leaving prodigies aside. Emile is no prodigy, and Sophie is not one either. Emile is a man and Sophie is a woman; therein consists all their glory. In the confounding of the sexes that reigns among us, someone is almost a prodigy for belonging to his own sex.

Sophie is well born; she has a good nature; she has a very sensitive heart, and this extreme sensitivity sometimes makes her imagination so active that it is difficult to moderate. Her mind is less exact than penetrating; her disposition is easy but nevertheless uneven; her face is ordinary but agreeable; her expression gives promise of a soul and does not lie. One can approach her with indifference but not leave her without emotion. Some have good qualities that are lacking to her; others have a greater measure of those good qualities she does possess; but none has a better combination of qualities for making a favorable character. She knows how to take advantage even of her defects, and if she were more perfect, she would be much less pleasing.

Sophie is not beautiful, but in her company men forget beautiful women, and beautiful women are dissatisfied with themselves. She is hardly pretty at first sight, but the more one sees her, the better she looks; she gains where so many others lose, and what she gains, she never loses again. Someone else may have more beautiful eyes, a more beautiful mouth, a more impressive face; but no one could have a better figure, a more beautiful complexion, a whiter hand, a daintier foot, a gentler glance, or a more touching expression. Without dazzling, she inspires interest, she charms, and one cannot say why.

Sophie loves adornment and is an expert at it. She is her mother's only lady's maid. She has considerable taste in dressing herself up to advantage, but she hates rich apparel; in her clothes one always sees simplicity joined with elegance. She likes not like what is brilliant but what is suitable. She is ignorant of what colors are fashionable, but she knows marvelously which look well on her. There is no young girl who appears to be dressed with less study and whose outfit is more studied; not a single piece of her clothing is chosen at random, and yet art is apparent nowhere. Her adornment is very modest in appearance and very coquettish in fact. She does not display her charms; she covers them, but, in covering them, she knows how to make them imagined. When someone sees her, he says, "Here is a modest, temperate girl." But so long as he stays near her, his eyes and his heart roam over her whole person without his being able

---

[7]Brantôme says that in the time of François I a young girl who had a talkative lover imposed an absolute and unlimited silence on him, which he kept so faithfully for two whole years that it was believed he had become mute as a result of illness. One day in the midst of company, his beloved—who, in those times when love was practiced with mystery, was not known to be such—boasted that she would cure him on the spot and did so with the single word "Speak." Is there not something grand and heroic in that love? What more could the philosophy of Pythagoras—for all its ostentation—have accomplished? What woman today could count on a similar silence for one day, even if she were to reward it with the greatest prize she can offer?

to take them away; and one would say that all this very simple attire was put on only to be taken off piece by piece by the imagination.

Sophie has natural talents. She is aware of them and has not neglected them. But not having been in a position to devote much art to their cultivation, she was content to train her pretty voice to sing tunefully and tastefully, her little feet to walk lightly, easily, and gracefully and to curtsey in all sorts of situations without difficulty and without awkwardness. Furthermore, she has had no singing master other than her father and no dancing master other than her mother. An organist in the neighborhood gave her some lessons in accompaniment on the harpsichord which she has since cultivated alone. At first, she thought only of making her hands appear to advantage on its black keys. Then she found that the harsh, dry sound of the harpsichord made the sound of her voice sweeter. Little by little she became sensitive to harmony. Finally, as she was growing up, she began to feel the charms of expression and to love music for itself. But it is a taste rather than a talent. She does not know how to read the notes of a tune.

What Sophie knows best and has been most carefully made to learn are the labors of her own sex, even those that are not usually considered, like cutting and sewing her dresses. There is no needlework which she does not know how to do and which she does not do with pleasure. But the work she prefers to every other is lacework, because there is none which results in a more agreeable pose and in which the fingers are put to use more gracefully and lightly. She has also devoted herself to all the details of the household. She understands the kitchen and the pantry. She knows the price of foodstuffs and their qualities; she knows very well how to keep the accounts; she serves her mother as butler. Destined to be mother of a family herself one day, she learns to govern her own household by governing her parents'. She can substitute for the domestics in the performance of their functions, and she always does so gladly. One can never command well except when one knows how to do the job oneself. That is her mother's reason for keeping her busy in this way. Sophie herself does not think so far ahead. Her first duty is that of a girl, and it is now the only one she thinks of fulfilling. The only thing she has in view is serving her mother and relieving her of a part of her cares. It is nevertheless true that she does not undertake them all with equal pleasure. For example, although she is a glutton, she does not like the kitchen. There is something that disgusts her in its details; she never finds it clean enough. In this regard she has an extreme delicacy, and its excessiveness has become one of her failings. She would rather let her whole dinner be thrown into the fire than get a spot on her cuff. She has never wanted to oversee the garden for the same reason. The earth seems unclean to her. As soon as she sees manure, she believes she smells its odor.

She owes this defect to her mother's lessons. According to the latter, cleanliness is one of the first duties of women—a special duty, indispensable, imposed by nature. Nothing in the world is more disgusting than an unclean woman, and the husband who is disgusted by her is never wrong. Sophie's mother has so often preached this duty to her daughter since childhood, has so often demanded cleanliness in Sophie's person, her things, her room, her work, her grooming, that all these attentions, which have turned into a habit, take a rather large part of her time and also preside over the rest of it. The result is that to do what she does well is only the second of her cares. The first is always to do it cleanly.

However, all this has not degenerated into vain affectation or softness. The refinements of luxury play no part in it. In her rooms there was never anything but simple water. She knows no perfume other than that of flowers; and her husband will never smell anything sweeter than her breath. Finally, the attention she gives to her exterior does not make her forget that she owes her life and her time to nobler cares. She is ignorant of or disdains that excessive cleanliness of body which soils the soul. Sophie is much more than clean. She is pure.

I said that Sophie was a glutton. She was naturally so. But she became moderate through habit, and now she is so through virtue. The case is not the same for girls as for boys, whom one can govern by gluttony up to a certain point. This inclination is not inconsequential for the fair sex. It is too dangerous to be left unchecked. When little Sophie went into her mother's cupboard as a child, she did not always come back empty-handed, and her fidelity was not above every temptation so far as sugarplums and bonbons were concerned. Her mother surprised her, scolded her, punished her, and compelled her to fast. She finally succeeded in persuading Sophie that bonbons spoil the teeth and that eating too much fattens the figure. Thus Sophie mended her ways. In growing up, she acquired other tastes which diverted her from this base sensuality. In women as in men, as soon as the heart becomes animated, gluttony is no longer a dominant vice. Sophie has preserved the taste proper to her sex. She loves dairy products and sugared things. She loves pastry and sweets but has very little taste for meat. She has never tasted either wine or hard liquor. Moreover, she eats very moderate amounts of everything. Her sex, which is less laborious than ours, has less need of restoratives. In all things she loves what is good and knows how to appreciate it. She also knows how to accommodate herself to what is not good without this privation being painful to her.

Sophie has a mind that is agreeable without being brilliant, and solid without being profound—a mind about which people do not say anything, because they never find in it either more or less than what they find in their own minds.

She has a mind which always pleases people who speak with her, although it is not ornamented according to the idea we have of the cultivation of women's minds; for hers is formed not by reading but only by the conversations of her father and mother, by her own reflections, and by the observations she has made in the little bit of the world she has seen. Gaiety is natural to Sophie; she was even frolicsome in her childhood, but her mother took care to repress her dizzy moods little by little, lest too sudden a change would give her instruction in the circumstance which made the repression necessary. She has therefore become modest and reserved even before the time to be so; and now that this time has come, it is easier for her to maintain the tone she has acquired than it would be for her to adopt it without an indication of the reason for this change. It is amusing to see her, due to a remnant of habit, abandon herself sometimes to childhood vivacities, and then suddenly come back to herself, become silent, lower her eyes, and blush. The intermediate stage between the two ages has to partake a bit of both.

Sophie's sensitivity is too great for her to preserve a perfect stability of disposition, but she is too gentle for that sensitivity to importune others very much; she harms only herself. Let one word which wounds her be spoken—she does not pout, but her heart swells. She tries to get away to cry. In the midst of her tears, let her father or her mother recall her and say one word, and she comes immediately to play and laugh while adroitly drying her tears and trying to stifle her sobs.

Nor is she entirely exempt from caprice. Her disposition, which is a bit too intense, degenerates into refractoriness, and then she is likely to forget herself. But leave her time to come back to herself, and her way of blotting out her wrong will almost make a merit of it. If she is punished, she is docile and submissive, and one sees that her shame comes not so much from the punishment as from the offense. If nothing is ever said to her, she will not fail to make amends for her offense herself, and so frankly and with such good grace that it is impossible to bear a grudge against her. She would kiss the ground before the lowliest domestic without this abasement causing her the least discomfort; and as soon as she is pardoned, her joy and her caresses show what a weight has been removed from her good heart. In a word, she suffers the wrongs of others with patience and makes amends for her own with pleasure. Such is the lovable nature of her sex before we have spoiled it. Woman is made to yield to man and to endure even his injustice. You will never reduce young boys to the same point. The inner sentiment in them rises and revolts against injustice. Nature did not constitute them to tolerate it. . . .

Sophie is religious, but her religion is reasonable and simple, with little dogma and less in the way of devout practices—or, rather, she knows no essential practice other than morality, and she devotes her entire life to serving God by doing good. In all the instructions her parents have given her on this subject, they have accustomed her to a respectful submission by always saying to her, "My daughter, this knowledge is not for your age. Your husband will instruct you in it when the time comes." For the rest, instead of long speeches about piety, they are content to preach piety to her by their example, and that example is engraved on her heart.

Sophie loves virtue. This love has become her dominant passion. She loves it because there is nothing so fine as virtue. She loves it because virtue constitutes woman's glory and because to her a virtuous woman appears almost equal to the angels. She loves it as the only route of true happiness and because she sees only misery, abandonment, unhappiness, and ignominy in the life of a shameless woman. She loves it, finally, as a thing that is dear to her respectable father and to her tender and worthy mother. They are not content with being happy because of their own virtue; they also want to be happy because of hers, and her chief happiness for herself is the hope of causing theirs. All these sentiments inspire in her an enthusiasm which lifts her soul and keeps all her petty inclinations subjected to so noble a passion. Sophie will be chaste and decent until her last breath. She has sworn it in the depth of her soul, and she has sworn it at a time when she already senses all that it costs to keep such an oath. She has sworn it at a time when she would have had to revoke the commitment if her senses were made to reign over her. . . .

Sophie is knowledgeable about the duties and rights of her sex and of ours. She knows the failings of men and the vices of women. She also knows the corresponding good qualities and virtues and has engraved them all in the depths of her heart. No one could have a higher idea of the decent woman than the idea she has conceived. And this idea does not dismay her; rather, she thinks with more satisfaction of the decent man, the man of merit; she feels that she is made for that man, that she is worthy of him, that she can return to him the happiness she will receive from him. She feels that she will surely know how to recognize him. The only problem is finding him.

Women are the natural judges of men's merit as men are of women's merit. That is their reciprocal right, and neither men nor women are ignorant of it. Sophie knows she has this right and makes use of it, but with the modesty suitable to her youth, her inexperience, and her position. She judges only things within her reach, and she judges only when it serves to develop some useful maxim. She speaks of those who are absent only with the greatest circumspection, especially if they are women. She thinks that what makes women slanderous and satirical is to speak of their own sex. So long as they limit themselves to speaking of ours, they are only equitable. Sophie, therefore, limits herself to that. As for women, she never speaks about them except to say the good things about them which she knows. It is an honor she believes she owes to her own sex. And as for those about whom she knows nothing good to say, she says nothing at all—and what that means is clear. . . .

She is quiet and respectful not only with women, but even with men married or men much older than she is. She will never accept a place above them except out of obedience, and she will resume her own below them as soon as she can. For she knows that the rights of age go before those of sex, since they have in their favor the prejudice of wisdom, which ought to be honored before everything else.

With young people of her own age, it is another matter. She needs a different tone to command respect from them, and she knows how to adopt it without abandoning the modest manner suitable to her. If they are modest and reserved themselves, she will gladly maintain with them the amiable familiarity of youth. Their conversations, full of innocence, will be bantering but decent. If they become serious, she wants them to be useful. If they degenerate into insipidity, she will soon make them stop, for she especially despises the petty jargon of gallantry, which she regards as very offensive to her sex. She knows that the man she seeks does not use that jargon, and she never willingly tolerates from another man anything that does not suit the one whose character is imprinted in the depth of her heart. The high opinion she has of the rights of her sex, the pride of soul which the purity of her sentiments gives her, that energy of virtue which she feels in herself and which makes her respectable in her own eyes—all cause her to hear with indignation the sugary remarks intended for her entertainment. She receives them not with an evident anger but with a disconcerting, ironical approval or an unexpectedly cold tone. Let a fair Phoebus retail his kindnesses to her, cleverly praise her for her cleverness, for her beauty, for her graces, for the reward of happiness that comes from pleasing her; she is the girl to interrupt him politely and say, "Monsieur, I am very much afraid I know all those things better than you do. If we have nothing less banal to say, I believe we can terminate the conversation here." To accompany these words with a full curtsey and then be twenty steps from him is the matter of only an instant. Ask your pleasing little fellows if it is easy to display their chit-chat to a mind as prickly as this one. . . .

Possessing so great a maturity of judgment and full-grown in all respects like a girl of twenty, Sophie at fifteen will not be treated as a child by her parents. As soon as they perceive the first restlessness of youth in her, they will hasten to provide against it before it develops any further. They will make tender and sensible speeches to her. Tender and sensible speeches are suitable to her age and her character. If that character is such as I imagine it, why would her father not speak to her pretty much as follows:

"Sophie, you are a big girl now, and it is not for the purpose of remaining a big girl forever that you have become one. We want you to be happy. It is for our sake that we want it, because our happiness depends on yours. The happiness of a decent girl lies in causing the happiness of a decent man. You must therefore think about getting married. You must think about it early, for the destiny of life depends on marriage, and there is never too much time to think about it.

"Nothing is more difficult than the choice of a good husband, unless it is perhaps the choice of a good wife. Sophie, you will be that rare woman, you will be the glory of our life and the happiness of our old age. But no matter how much merit you possess, the earth is not lacking in men who have still greater merit than you do. There is no man who ought not to be honored to get you; there are many who would honor you even more. The issue is to find among this number one who suits you, to know him, and to make yourself known to him. . . .

"It is up to the spouses to match themselves. Mutual inclination ought to be their first bond. Their eyes and their hearts ought to be their first guides. Their first duty once they are united is to love each other; and since loving or not loving is not within our control, this duty necessarily involves another, which is to begin by loving each other before being united. This is the right of nature, which nothing can abrogate. Those who have hindered it by so many civil laws have paid more attention to the appearance of order than to the happiness of marriage and the morals of citizens. You see, my Sophie, that we are not preaching a difficult morality to you. It leads only to making you your own mistress and having us rely on you for the choice of your husband.

"After having told you our reasons for leaving you entirely at liberty, it is just that we also speak to you about the reasons why you should use this liberty wisely. My daughter, you are good and reasonable, you have rectitude and piety, you have talents which suit decent women, and you are not unendowed with attractions. But you are poor. You have the most estimable goods, and you lack only those which are most esteemed. Therefore, aspire only to what you can get, and guide your ambition not by your judgments nor by ours, but by the opinion of men. If it were only a question of an equality of merit, I do not know any limit that I ought to put on your hopes. But do not raise them above your fortune, and do not forget that it is of the lowest rank. Although a man worthy of you would not count this inequality as an obstacle, you ought to do what he will not do. Sophie ought to imitate her mother, and enter only into a family which considers itself honored by her. You did not

see our opulence; you were born during our poverty. You make that poverty sweet for us, and you share it without difficulty. Believe me, Sophie, do not seek goods that we bless heaven for having delivered us from. We have tasted happiness only after having lost our riches.

"You are too lovable to please no one, and your poverty is not so great that a decent man would be embarrassed by you. You will be sought after, possibly by people who are not worthy of you. If they revealed themselves to you as they are, you would esteem them for what they are worth; all their pomp would not impress you for long. But although you have good judgment and you know what merit is, you lack experience and you are ignorant of the extent to which men can counterfeit themselves. A skillful faker can study your tastes in order to seduce you and feign virtues in your presence which he does not have. He would ruin you before you were aware of it, Sophie, and when you recognized your error, you would only be able to weep for it. The most dangerous of all traps, and the only one reason cannot avoid, is that of the senses. If you ever have the misfortune of falling into this trap, you will no longer see anything but illusions and chimeras; your eyes will be fascinated, your judgment clouded, your will corrupted. Your very error will be dear to you, and even if you were in a condition to recognize it, you would not want to recover from it. My daughter, it is to Sophie's reason that I entrust you; I do not entrust you to the inclination of her heart. So long as your blood is cool, remain your own judge. But as soon as you are in love, return yourself to your mother's care.

"I propose an agreement which is a mark of our esteem for you and re-establishes the natural order among us. Parents choose the husband of their daughter and consult her only for the sake of form. Such is the usual practice. We shall do exactly the opposite. You will choose, and we will be consulted. Use your right, Sophie; use it freely and wisely. The husband who suits you ought to be of your choice and not of ours. But it is for us to judge whether you are mistaken concerning this suitability and whether, without knowing it, you do something other than what you want. Birth, wealth, rank, and opinion will in no way enter in our decision. Take a decent man whose person pleases you and whose character suits you; whatever else he is, we will accept him as our son-in-law. His wealth will always be great enough if he can use his arms to work and if he has morals and loves his family. His rank will always be illustrious enough if he ennobles it by virtue. If the whole world should blame us, what difference does it make? We do not seek public approval. Your happiness is enough for us."

Readers, I do not know what effect a similar speech would have on girls raised in your way. As for Sophie, it is possible she will not respond with words. Shame and tenderness would not easily let her express herself. But I am quite sure that such a speech will remain engraved on her heart for the rest of her life, and that if one can count on any human resolution, it is on her heartfelt resolution to be worthy of her parents' esteem. . . .

After the conversation I have reported, her father and her mother, judging that eligible men would not come to offer themselves in the hamlet where they lived, sent her to spend a winter in the city at the home of an aunt, who was secretly informed of the purpose of this trip. For the haughty Sophie carried in the depth of her heart a noble pride in knowing how to triumph over herself; and whatever need she had of a husband, she would die a maiden rather than resolve to look for one.

To fulfill the intentions of Sophie's parents, her aunt presented her in homes, took her out to groups and parties, and made her see society—or rather made society see her, for Sophie cared little for all this bustle. It was noted, however, that she did not flee young people with agreeable appearances who appeared decent and modest. In her very reserve, she had a certain art of attracting them which rather resembled coquetry. But after having conversed with them two or three times, she gave up. She soon substituted for that air of authority which seems to accept homages a more humble bearing and a more forbidding politeness. Always attentive to herself, she no longer gave them the occasion to do her the least service. This was an adequate way of saying she did not want to be their beloved.

Sensitive hearts never like boisterous pleasures, the vain and sterile happiness of people who feel nothing and who believe that to numb one's life is to enjoy it. Sophie had not found what she was seeking and, despairing of finding it in this way, she became bored by the city. She loved her parents tenderly; nothing compensated her for their absence, nothing was able to make her forget them. She went back to join them long before the date fixed for her return.

She had hardly resumed her functions in her parents' household before it was observed that, although she maintained the same conduct, her disposition had changed. She had moments of distraction and impatience; she was sad and dreamy; she hid herself in order to cry. At first they believed she was in love and was ashamed of it. They spoke to her about it; she denied it. She protested that she had seen no one who could touch her heart, and Sophie did not lie.

However, her languor constantly increased, and her health began to deteriorate. Her mother, upset by this change, finally resolved to find out its cause. She took Sophie aside and set to work on her with that winning language and those invincible caresses that only maternal tenderness knows how to employ. "My daughter, you whom I carried in my womb and whom I unceasingly carry in my heart, pour out the secrets of your heart on your mother's bosom. What are these secrets that a mother cannot know? Who pities your troubles? Who shares them? Who wants to relieve them, if not your father and mother? Ah, my child, do you want me to die of your pain without knowing what it is?"

Far from hiding her chagrins from her mother, the young girl asked for nothing better than to have her as a consoler and confidant. But shame prevented Sophie from speaking, and her modesty found no language to describe a condition so little worthy of her as the emotion which was disturbing her senses in spite of herself. Finally, her very shame served her mother as an indication, and she drew out these humiliating admissions from her daughter. Far from afflicting Sophie with unjust reprimands, her mother consoled her, pitied her, cried for her. She was too wise to make a crime out of an ill that Sophie's virtue alone made so cruel. But why endure without necessity an ill for which the remedy was so easy and so legitimate? Why did she not make use of the freedom she had been given? Why did she not accept a husband, why did she not choose one? Did she not know that her fate depended on herself alone, and that, whomever she chose, he would be approved, since she could not choose a man who was not decent? She had been sent to the city. She had not wanted to remain. Several eligible men had presented themselves; she had rebuffed them all. What was she waiting for, then? What did she want? What an inexplicable contradiction!

The answer was simple. If she had only to find someone to help satisfy youthful needs, the choice would soon be made. But a master for the whole of life is not so easy to choose. And since these two choices cannot be separated, a girl must simply wait, and often lose her youth before finding the man with whom she wants to spend all the days of her life. Such was Sophie's case. She needed a lover, but that lover had to be a husband; and given the heart needed to match hers, the former was almost as difficult to find as the latter. All these glamorous young people were suitable to her only from the point of view of age; they always failed to suit her in all other ways. Their superficial minds, their vanity, their jargon, their unruly morals, and their frivolous imitations disgusted her. She sought a man and found only monkeys; she sought a soul and found none.

"How unhappy I am!" she said to her mother. "I need to love, and I see nothing pleasing to me. My heart rejects all those who attract my senses. I see not one who does not excite my desires, and not one who does not repel my desires. An attraction that is not accompanied by esteem cannot endure. Ah, that is not the man for your Sophie! The charming model of the man for her is imprinted too deeply on her soul. She can love only him; she can make only him happy; she can be happy with him alone. She prefers to pine away and do constant battle; she prefers to die unhappy and free rather than in despair with a man she does not love and whom she would make unhappy. It is better no longer to exist than to exist only to suffer."

Struck by this singular discourse, her mother found it too bizarre not to suspect some mystery. Sophie was neither affected nor silly. How had this extravagant delicacy been able to take root in her—she who had been taught from her childhood nothing so much as to adjust herself to the people with whom she had to live and to make a virtue of necessity? This model of the lovable man with which she was so enchanted and which returned so often in all her conversations caused her mother to conjecture that this caprice had some other foundation of which she was still ignorant, and that Sophie had not told all. The unfortunate girl, oppressed by her secret pain, sought only to unburden herself. Her mother pressed. Sophie hesitated; she finally yielded, and, going out without saying anything, returned a moment later with a book in her hand. "Pity your unhappy daughter. Her sadness is without remedy. Her tears will never dry up. You want to know the cause. Well, here it is," she said, throwing the book on the table. The mother took the book and opened it. It was *The Adventures of Telemachus*. At first she understood nothing of this enigma. But by dint of questions and obscure answers, she finally saw, with a surprise that is easy to conceive, that her daughter was the rival of Eucharis.

Sophie loved Telemachus and loved him with a passion of which nothing could cure her. As soon as her father and her mother knew of her mania, they laughed about it and believed they would bring her around by reason. They were mistaken. Reason was not entirely on their side. Sophie also had her own reason and knew how to turn it to account. How many times she reduced them to silence by using their own reasoning again them, by showing them that they had done all the harm themselves: that they had not formed her for a man of her times; that she would necessarily have to adopt her husband's ways of thinking or convert him to her own; that they had made the first means impossible by the way they had raised her, and that the other was precisely what she was seeking. "Give me," she said, "a man imbued with my maxims or one whom I can bring around to them, and I shall marry him. But until then, why do you scold me? Pity me. I am unhappy, not mad. Does the heart depend on the will? Didn't my father say so himself? Is it my fault if I love what does not exist? I am not a visionary. I do not want a prince. I do not seek Telemachus. I know that he is only a fiction. I seek someone who resembles him. And why cannot this someone exist, since I exist—I who feel within myself a heart so similar to his? No, let us not thus dishonor humanity. Let us not think that a lovable and virtuous man is only a chimera. He exists; he lives; perhaps he is seeking me. He seeks a soul that knows how to love him. But what sort of man is he? Where is he? I do not know. He is none of those I have seen. Doubtless he is none of those I shall see. O my mother, why have you made virtue too lovable for me? If I can love nothing but virtue, the fault is less mine than yours."

Shall I bring this sad narrative to its catastrophic end? Shall I tell of the long disputes which preceded the catastrophe? Shall I portray an exasperated mother exchanging her earlier caresses for harshness? Shall I show an irritated father forgetting his earlier agreements and treating the most virtuous of daughters like a madwoman? Shall I, finally, depict the unfortunate girl—even more attached to her chimera as a result of the persecution she has suffered for it—going with slow steps toward death and descending into the grave at the moment when they believe they are leading her to the altar? No, I put aside these dreadful objects. I need not go so far to show by what seems to me a sufficiently striking example that, in spite of the prejudices born of the morals of our age, enthusiasm for the decent and the fine is no more foreign to women than to men, and that there is nothing that cannot be obtained under nature's direction from women as well as from men.

Here someone will stop me and ask whether it is nature which prescribes our expending so much effort for the repression of immoderate desires? My answer is no, but it also is not nature which gives us so many immoderate desires. Now, everything that is not nature is against nature. I have proved that countless times.

Let us render his Sophie to our Emile. Let us resuscitate this lovable girl to give her a less lively imagination and a happier destiny. I wanted to depict an ordinary woman, and by dint of elevating her soul I have disturbed her reason. I went astray myself. Let us retrace our steps. Sophie has only a good nature in a common soul. Every advantage she has over other women is the effect of her education.

I proposed to say in this book all that can be done and to leave to the reader the choice—among the good things I may have said—of those that are within his reach. I had thought at the beginning that I would form Emile's companion at the outset and raise them for and with each other. But on reflection I found that all these arrangements were too premature and ill conceived, and that it was absurd to destine two children to be united before being able to know whether this union was in the order of nature and whether they had between them the compatibilities suitable for forming it. One must not confound what is natural in the savage state with what is natural in the civil state. In the former state all women are suitable for all men because both still have only the primitive and common form. In the latter, since each character is developed by social institutions and each mind has received its peculiar and determinate form not from education alone but from the well-ordered or ill-ordered conjunction of nature and education, men and women can no longer be matched except by presenting them to one another in order to see whether they suit one another in all respects—or at least in order to determine the choice resulting in the greatest degree of suitability. . . .

Such are the reflections which have determined me on the choice of Sophie. She is a pupil of nature just as Emile is, and she, more than any other, is made for him. She will be the woman of the man. She is his equal in birth and merit, his inferior in fortune. She does not enchant at first glance, but she pleases more each day. Her greatest charm acts only by degrees. It unfolds only in the intimacy of association, and her husband will sense it more than anyone in the world. Her education is neither brilliant nor neglected. She has taste without study, talents without art, judgment without knowledge. Her mind does not know, but it is cultivated for learning; it is a well-prepared soil that only awaits seed in order to bear fruit. . . . Happy

is he who is destined to instruct her. She will be not her husband's teacher but his pupil. Far from wanting to subject him to her tastes, she will adopt his. She is better for him as she is than if she were learned: he will have the pleasure of teaching her everything. It is finally time that they see each other. Let us work to bring them together.

Here we are in the country like true knights-errant, although not seeking adventures as they do; on the contrary, we flee adventures in leaving Paris. But we imitate the pace of those knights in our wandering, sometimes proceeding at full tilt and sometimes meandering. By dint of following my practice, one will have finally grasped its spirit, and I cannot imagine a reader still so prejudiced by custom as to suppose us both asleep in a good, well-closed post-chaise, progressing without seeing or observing anything, making worthless for ourselves the interval between departure and arrival, and by the speed of our progress wasting time in order to save it. . . .

One day, after having strayed more than usual in valleys and mountains where no path can be perceived, we can no longer find our way again. It makes little difference to us. All paths are good, provided one arrives. But, still, one has to arrive somewhere when one is hungry. Happily we find a peasant who takes us to his cottage. We eat his meager dinner with great appetite. On seeing us so tired and famished, he says to us, "If the good Lord had led you to the other side of the hill, you would have been better received . . . you would have found a house of peace . . . such charitable people . . . such good people . . . They are not better-hearted than I am, but they are richer, although it is said that they were previously much more so . . . they are not suffering, thank God, and the whole countryside feels the effects of what remains to them."

At this mention of good people, the good Emile's heart gladdens. "My friend," he says, looking at me, "let us go to that house whose masters are blessed in the neighborhood. I would be glad to see them. Perhaps they will be glad to receive us, too. I am sure they will receive us well. If they are of our kind, we shall be of theirs."

Having received good directions to the house, we leave and wander through the woods. On the way heavy rain surprises us. It slows us up without stopping us. Finally we find our way, and in the evening we arrive at the designated house. In the hamlet which surrounds it, this house alone, although simple, stands out. We present ourselves. We ask for hospitality. We are taken to speak to the master. He questions us, but politely. Without telling him the subject of our trip, we tell him the reason for our detour. From his former opulence he has retained a facility for recognizing the station of people by their manners. Whoever has lived in high society is rarely mistaken about that. On the basis of this passport we are admitted.

We are shown to a very little, but clean and comfortable apartment. A fire is made. We find linen, garments, everything we need. "What!" says Emile. "It is as though we were expected! Oh how right the peasant was! What attention, what goodness, what foresight! And for unknowns! I believe I am living in Homer's time." "Be sensitive to all this," I say to him, "but don't be surprised. Wherever strangers are rare, they are welcome. Nothing makes one more hospitable than seldom needing to be. It is the abundance of guests which destroys hospitality. In the time of Homer people hardly traveled, and travelers were well received everywhere. We are perhaps the only transients who have been seen here during the whole year." "It makes no difference," he replies. "That itself is praise—to know how to get along without guests and always to receive them well."

After we have dried ourselves and straightened up, we go to rejoin the master of the house. He presents his wife to us. She receives us not only politely but with kindness. The honor of her glances belongs to Emile. A mother in her situation rarely sees a man of that age enter her home without uneasiness or at least curiosity.

For our sake they have supper served early. On entering the dining room, we see five settings. We are seated, but an empty place remains. A girl enters, curtseys deeply, and sits down modestly without speaking. Emile, busy with his hunger or his answers, greets her and continues to speak and eat. The principle object of his trip is as distant from his thoughts as he believes himself to be still distant from its goal. The discussion turns to the travelers' losing their way. "Sir," the master of the house says to him, "you appear to me to be a likable and wise young man, and that makes me think that you and your governor have arrived here tired and wet like Telemachus and Mentor on Calypso's island." "It is true," Emile answers, "that we find here the hospitality of Calypso." His Mentor adds, "And the charms of Eucharis." But although Emile knows the *Odyssey*, he has not read *Telemachus*. He does not know who Eucharis is. As for the girl, I see her blush up to her eyes, lower them toward her plate, and not dare to murmur. Her mother, who notices her embarrassment, gives a sign to her father, and he changes the subject. In speaking of his solitude, he gradually gets involved in the story of the events which confined him to it: the misfortunes of his life, the constancy of his wife, the consolations they have found in their union, the sweet and peaceful life they lead in their retreat—and still without saying a word about the girl. All this forms an agreeable and touching story which cannot be heard without interest. Emile, moved and filled with tenderness, stops eating in order to listen. Finally, at the part where the most decent of men enlarges with great pleasure on the attachment of the worthiest of women, the young traveler is beside himself; with one hand he grips the husband's hand, and with the other he takes the wife's hand and leans toward it rapturously, sprinkling it with tears. The young man's naïve vivacity enchants everyone, but the girl, more sensitive than anyone to this mark of his good heart, believes she sees Telemachus affected by Philoctetes' misfortunes. She furtively turns her eyes toward him in order to examine his face better. She finds nothing there which denies the comparison. His easy bearing is free without being arrogant. His manners are lively without being giddy. His sensitivity makes his glance gentler, his expression more touching. The girl, seeing him cry, is ready to mingle her tears with his. But even with so fair a pretext, a secret shame restrains her. She already reproaches herself for the tears about to escape her eyes, as though it were bad to shed them for her family.

Her mother, who from the beginning of the supper has not stopped watching her, sees her constraint and delivers her from it by sending her on an errand. A minute later the young girl returns, but she is so little recovered that her disorder is visible to all eyes. Her mother gently says to her, "Sophie, pull yourself together. Will you never stop crying over the misfortunes of your parents? You, who console them for their misfortunes, must not be more sensitive to them than they are themselves."

At the name Sophie, you would have seen Emile shiver. Struck by so dear a name, he is wakened with a start and casts an avid glance at the girl who dares to bear it. "Sophie, O Sophie! Is it you whom my heart seeks? Is it you whom my heart loves?" He observes her and contemplates her with a sort of fear and distrust. He does not see exactly the face that he had depicted to himself. He does not know whether the one he sees is better or worse. He studies each feature; he spies on each movement, each gesture. In all he finds countless confused interpretations. He would give half his life for her to be willing to speak a single word. Uneasy

and troubled, he looks at me. His eyes put a hundred questions to me and make a hundred reproaches all at once. He seems to say to me with each look, "Guide me while there is time. If my heart yields and is mistaken, I shall never recover in all my days."

Emile is worse at disguising his feelings than any man in the world. How would he disguise them in the greatest disturbance of his life, in the presence of four spectators who examine him and of whom the most distracted in appearance is actually the most attentive? His disorder does not escape Sophie's penetrating eyes. Moreover, his eyes teach her that she is the cause of his disorder. She sees that this apprehensiveness is not yet love. But what difference does it make? He is involved with her, and that is enough. She will be most unlucky if he becomes involved with her with impunity.

Mothers have eyes just as their daughters do, and they have experience to boot. Sophie's mother smiles at the success of our projects. She reads the hearts of the two young people. She sees that it is time to captivate the heart of the new Telemachus. She gets her daughter to speak. Her daughter responds with her natural gentleness in a timid voice which makes its effect all the better. At the first sound of this voice Emile surrenders. It is Sophie. He no longer doubts it. If it were not she, it would be too late for him to turn back.

It is then that the charms of this enchanting girl flow in torrents into his heart, and he begins to swallow with deep draughts the poison with which she intoxicates him. He no longer speaks, he no longer responds; he sees only Sophie, he hears only Sophie. If she says a word, he opens his mouth; if she lowers her eyes, he lowers his; if he sees her breathe, he sighs. It is Sophie's soul which appears to animate him. How his own soul has changed in a few instants! It is no longer Sophie's turn to tremble; it is Emile's. Farewell freedom, naïveté, frankness! Confused, embarrassed, fearful, he no longer dares to look around him for fear of seeing that he is being looked at. Ashamed to let the others see through him, he would like to make himself invisible to everyone in order to sate himself with contemplating her without being observed. Sophie, on the contrary, is reassured by Emile's fear. She sees her triumph. She enjoys it:

Nol mostra già, ben che in suo cor ne rida.

Her countenance has not changed. But in spite of this modest air and these lowered eyes, her tender heart palpitates with joy and tells her that Telemachus has been found.

If I enter here into the perhaps too naïve and too simple history of their innocent love, people will regard these details as a frivolous game, but they will be wrong. They do not sufficiently consider the influence which a man's first liaison with a woman ought to have on the course of both their lives. They do not see that a first impression as lively as that of love, or the inclination which takes its place, has distant effects whose links are not perceived in the progress of the years but do not cease to act until death. We are given treatises on education consisting of useless, pedantic, bloated verbiage about the chimerical duties of children, and we are not told a word about the most important and most difficult part of the whole of education—the crisis that serves as a passage from childhood to man's estate. If I have been able to make these essays useful in some respect, it is especially by having expanded at great length on this essential part, omitted by all others, and by not letting myself be rebuffed in this enterprise by false delicacies or frightened by difficulties of language. If I have said what must be done, I have said what I ought to have said. It makes very little difference to me if I have written a romance. A fair romance it is indeed, the romance of human nature. If it is to be found only in this writing, is that my fault? This ought to be the history of my species. You

who deprave it, it is you who make a romance of my book.

Another consideration which strengthens the first is that I am dealing here not with a young man given over from childhood to fear, covetousness, envy, pride, and all the passions that serve as instruments for common educations, but with a young man for whom this is not only his first love but his first passion of any kind. On this passion, perhaps the only one he will feel intensely in his whole life, depends the final form his character is going to take. Once fixed by a durable passion, his way of thinking, his sentiments, and his tastes are going to acquire a consistency which will no longer permit them to deteriorate. . . .

We are permitted to return without being invited to stay over. This conduct is suitable. Board is given to passers-by who are at a loss for lodging, but it is not seemly for a lover to sleep in his beloved's home.

We hardly are out of this dear house before Emile thinks of establishing ourselves in the neighborhood. Even the nearest cottage seems too distant. He would like to sleep in the ditches of the manor. "Giddy young man!" I say to him in a tone of pity. "What, does passion already blind you? Do you already no longer see either propriety or reason? Unfortunate one! You believe you are in love, and you want to dishonor your beloved! What will be said when it is known that a young man who leaves her home sleeps in the vicinity? You love her, you say! Will you then ruin her reputation? Is that the payment for the hospitality her parents have granted you? Will you cause the disgrace of the girl from whom you expect your happiness?" "Well," he answers, "what difference do the vain talk of men and their unjust suspicions make? Haven't you yourself taught me to take no notice of it? Who knows better than I how much I honor Sophie, how much I want to respect her? My attachment will not cause her shame; it will cause her glory; it will be worthy of her. If my heart and my attentions everywhere render her the homage she deserves, how can I insult her?" "Dear Emile," I respond, embracing him, "you reason for yourself. Learn to reason for her. Do not compare the honor of one sex to that of the other. They have entirely different principles. These principles are equally solid and reasonable because they derive equally from nature; and the same virtue which makes you despise men's talk for yourself obliges you to respect it for your beloved. Your honor is in you alone, and hers depends on others. To neglect it would be to wound your own honor; and you do not render yourself what you owe yourself if you are the cause of her not being rendered what is owed her."

Then I explain the reasons for these differences to him, making him sense what an injustice it would be to take no account of these differences. Who has told him that he will be the husband of Sophie, whose sentiments he is ignorant of, whose heart (or whose parents) has perhaps made prior commitments, whom he does not know, and who perhaps suits him in none of the ways which can make for a happy marriage? Does he not know that for a girl every scandal is an indelible stain, which even her marriage to the man who caused it does not remove? What sensitive man wants to ruin the girl he loves? What decent man wants to make an unfortunate girl weep forever for the misfortune of having pleased him?

The young man, who is always extreme in his ideas, is frightened by the consequences I make him envisage, and he now believes he is never far enough away from Sophie's dwelling. He doubles his pace to flee more quickly. He looks around to see whether we are overheard. He would sacrifice his happiness a thousand times for the honor of the one he loves. He would rather not see her again in his life than cause her any displeasure. This is the first fruit of the cares I took in his youth to form in him a heart that knows how to love.

We have to find, then, an abode that is distant but within range. We seek, and we make inquiries; we learn that two leagues away there is a town. We go to find lodging there rather than in nearer villages, where our stay would become suspect. The new lover finally arrives there full of love, hope, joy, and, especially, good sentiments. And this is how, by directing his nascent passion little by little toward what is good and decent, without his being aware of it I dispose all of his inclinations to take the same bent.

I approach the end of my career. I already see it in the distance. All the great difficulties are overcome. All the great obstacles are surmounted. Nothing difficult is left for me to do, except not to spoil my work by hurrying to consummate it. In the uncertainty of human life, let us avoid above all the false prudence of sacrificing the present for the future; this is often to sacrifice what is for what will not be. Let us make man happy at all ages lest, after many cares, he die before having been happy. Now, if there is a time to enjoy life, it is surely the end of adolescence when the faculties of body and soul have acquired their greatest vigor. Man is then in the middle of his course, and he sees from the greatest distance the two end points which make him feel its brevity. If imprudent youth makes mistakes, it is not because it wants enjoyment; it is because it seeks enjoyment where it is not, and because, while preparing a miserable future for itself, it does not even know how to use the present moment.

Consider my Emile—now past twenty, well formed, well constituted in mind and body, strong, healthy, fit, skillful, robust, full of sense, reason, goodness, and humanity, a man with morals and taste, loving the beautiful, doing the good, free from the empire of cruel passions, exempt from the yoke of opinion, but subject to the law of wisdom and submissive to the voice of friendship, possessing all the useful talents and some of the agreeable ones, caring little for riches, with his means of support in his arms, and not afraid of lacking bread whatever happens. Now he is intoxicated by a nascent passion. His heart opens itself to the first fires of love. Its sweet illusions make him a new universe of delight and enjoyment. He loves a lovable object who is even more lovable for her character than for her person. He hopes for, he expects a return that he feels is his due. It is from the similarity of their hearts, from the conjunction of decent sentiments that their first inclination was formed. This inclination ought to be durable. He yields confidently, even reasonably, to the most charming delirium, without fear, without regret, without remorse, without any other worry than that which is inseparable from the sentiment of happiness. What is lacking to his happiness? Look, consider, imagine what he still needs that can accord with what he has. He enjoys together all the goods that can be obtained at once. None can be added except at the expense of another. He is as happy as a man can be. Shall I at this moment shorten so sweet a destiny? Shall I trouble so pure a delight? Ah, the whole value of life is in the felicity he tastes! What could I give him which was worth what I had taken away from him? Even in putting the crown on his happiness, I would destroy its greatest charm. This supreme happiness is a hundred times sweeter to hope for than to obtain. One enjoys it better when one looks forward to it than when one tastes it. O good Emile, love and be loved! Enjoy a long time before possessing. Enjoy love and innocence at the same time. Make your paradise on earth while awaiting the other one. I shall not shorten this happy time of your life. I shall spin out its enchantment for you. I shall prolong it as much as possible. Alas, it has to end, and end soon. But I shall at least make it last forever in your memory and make you never repent having tasted it.

Emile does not forget that we have things to return. As soon as they are ready, we take horses and set out at full speed; this one time, Emile would like to have arrived as soon as we leave. When the heart is opened to the passions, it is opened to life's boredom. If I have not wasted my time, his whole life will not pass in this way. . . .

Finally we arrive. The reception given us is far more simple and more obliging than the first time. We are already old acquaintances. Emile and Sophie greet each other with a bit of embarrassment and still do not speak to each other. What would they say to each other in our presence? The conversation they require has no need of witnesses. We take a walk in the garden. It has as its parterre a very well-arranged kitchen garden; as its park it has an orchard covered with large, beautiful fruit trees of every kind, interspersed with pretty streams and beds full of flowers. "What a beautiful place," cries out Emile, full of his Homer and always enthusiastic. "I believe I see the garden of Alcinous." The daughter would like to know who Alcinous is, and the mother asks. "Alcinous," I tell them, "was a king of Corcyra whose garden, described by Homer, is criticized by people of taste for being too simple and without enough adornment.[8] This

---

[8]On leaving the palace one finds a vast garden of four acres, hedged in all around, planted with great flowering trees, producing pears, pomegranates, and others of the fairest species, fig trees with sweet fruit and verdant olive trees. Never during the whole year are these beautiful trees without fruit; winter and summer the west wind's gentle breeze both fecundates some and ripens others. One sees the pear and the apple grow old and dry on their trees, the fig on the fig tree and the clusters of grapes on the vine stock. The inexhaustible vine does not stop bearing new grapes; some are cooked and preserved in the sun on a threshing floor, while others are used to make wine, leaving on the plant those still blossoming, fermenting, or beginning to turn dark. At one of its ends two well-cultivated patches covered with flowers are each adorned by a fountain, of which one waters the whole garden, and the other, after having passed through the house, is piped to a tall building in the city to provide water for the citizens.

Such is the description of Alcinous' royal garden in the seventh book of the *Odyssey*, where, to the shame of that old dreamer Homer and the princes of his time, one sees neither trellises nor statues nor waterfalls nor bowling greens.

Alcinous had a lovable daughter who dreamed, on the eve of a stranger's receiving hospitality from her father, that she would soon have a husband." Sophie is taken aback and blushes, lowers her eyes, bites her tongue. One cannot imagine such embarrassment. Her father, who takes pleasure in increasing it, joins in and says that the young princess herself went to wash the linen in the river. "Do you believe," he continues, "that she would have disdained to touch the dirty napkins, saying that they smelled of burnt fat?" Sophie, against whom the blow is directed, forgets her natural timidity and excuses herself with vivacity: her papa knows very well that all the small linen would have no other laundress than her if she had been allowed to do it,[9] and that she would have done more of it with pleasure if she had been so directed. While speaking these words, she looks at me on the sly with an apprehensiveness which I cannot help laughing at, reading in her ingenuous heart the alarm which makes her speak. Her father is cruel enough to pick up this bit of giddiness by asking her in a mocking tone what occasion she has for speaking on her own behalf here, and what she has in common with Alcinous' daughter? Ashamed and trembling, she no longer dares to breathe a word or look at anyone. Charming girl, the time for feigning is past. You have now made your declaration in spite of yourself. . . .

The visits are repeated. The conversations between our young people become more frequent. Intoxicated by love, Emile believes he has already attained his happiness. However, he does not get Sophie's formal consent. She listens to him and says nothing to him. Emile knows the extent of her modesty. He is not very surprised by so much restraint. He senses that he does not stand badly with her. He knows that it is fathers who marry off

children. He supposes that Sophie is waiting for an order from her parents. He asks her permission to solicit it. She does not oppose his doing so. He speaks to me about it; I speak for him in his own presence. What a surprise for him to learn that it is up to Sophie alone, and that to make him happy she has only to want to do so. He begins no longer to understand anything about her conduct. His confidence diminishes. He is alarmed; he sees that he has not gotten as far as he thought he had. And it is then that his tenderest love employs its most touching language to sway her.

Emile is not the kind of man who can guess what is hindering him. If he is not told, he will never find out, and Sophie is too proud to tell him. The difficulties which are holding her back would only make another girl more eager. She has not forgotten her parents' lessons. She is poor, and Emile is rich; she knows it. He has a great deal to do in order to gain her esteem! What merit must he possess in order to wipe away this inequality? But how could he dream of these obstacles? Does Emile know he is rich? Does he even deign to inquire about it? Thank heaven he has no need to be rich. He knows how to be beneficent without riches. The good he does is drawn from his heart and not from his purse. He gives his time, his care, his affections, and his person to the unhappy; and in estimating his benefactions, he hardly dares to count the money he scatters among the indigent.

Not knowing what to blame for his disgrace, he attributes it to his own fault; for who would dare to accuse the object of his adoration of caprice? The humiliation of his *amour-propre* increases his regret that his love has been spurned. He no longer approaches Sophie with that lovable confidence of a heart which feels it is worthy of hers. He is fearful and trembling before her. He no longer hopes to touch her by tenderness. He seeks to sway her by pity. Sometimes his patience wearies, and vexation is ready to take its place. Sophie seems to foresee these storms, and glances at him. This glance

---

[9]I admit that I am rather grateful to Sophie's mother for not having let her spoil with soap hands as soft as hers, hands which Emile will so often kiss.

alone disarms and intimidates him. He is more thoroughly subjected than before.

Troubled by this obstinate resistance and this invincible silence, he opens his heart to his friend. He confides to him the pain of a heart broken by sadness. He implores his assistance and his counsel. "What an impenetrable mystery! She is interested in my fate; I cannot doubt it. Far from avoiding me, she enjoys being with me. When I arrive, she gives signs of joy, and when I leave, of regret. She receives my attentions kindly. My services appear to please her. She deigns to give me advice, sometimes even orders. Nevertheless, she rejects my entreaties and my prayers. When I dare to speak of union, she imperiously imposes silence on me; and if I add another word, she leaves me on the spot. For what strange reason does she want me to be hers without wanting to hear a word about her being mine? You whom she honors, you whom she loves and whom she will not dare to silence, speak, make her speak. Serve your friend. Crown your work. Do not make all your care fatal to your pupil. Ah, what he has gotten from you will cause his misery if you do not complete his happiness!"

I speak to Sophie, and with little effort I extract from her a secret I knew before she told it to me. I have more difficulty in obtaining permission to inform Emile. Finally, I do obtain it and make use of it. This explanation sends him into a state of astonishment from which he cannot recover. He understands nothing of this delicacy. He cannot imagine what effect a few *écus* more or less have on character and merit. When I make him understand what they do to prejudices, he starts laughing, and, transported with joy, he wants to leave on the spot to go and tear up everything, throw out everything, renounce everything in order to have the honor of being as poor as Sophie and to return worthy of being her husband.

"What!" I say, stopping him and laughing in turn at his impetuosity. "Will this young mind never become mature; and after having philosophized your whole life, will you never learn to reason? How can you not see that, in following your insane project, you are going to make your situation worse and Sophie more intractable? It is a small advantage to have a bit more property than she does, but it would be a very big advantage to have sacrificed it all for her; and if her pride cannot resolve to accept the former obligation to you, how will it resolve to accept the latter? If she cannot endure that a husband be able to reproach her for having enriched her, will she endure that he be able to reproach her with having impoverished himself for her? O unhappy fellow, tremble lest she suspect you of having had this project! Instead, become economical and careful for love of her, lest she accuse you of wanting to win her by trickery and of voluntarily sacrificing to her what you lose by neglect.

"Do you believe that at bottom great property frightens her and that it is precisely wealth that is the source of her opposition? No, dear Emile, it has a more solid and weightier cause—namely, the effect that wealth has on the soul of the possessor. She knows that fortune's goods are always preferred over everything else by those who have them. The rich all count gold before merit. In regard to the family resources constituted by the contribution of money and services, they always find that the latter never compensate for the former; they think that someone is still in their debt when he has spent his life serving them while eating their bread. What is there for you to do, Emile, to reassure her about her fears? Make yourself well known to her. That is not the business of a day. Show her treasures in your noble soul that are sufficient to redeem those with which you have the misfortune to be endowed. By dint of constancy and time surmount her resistance. By dint of great and generous sentiments force her to forget your riches. Love her, serve her, serve her respectable parents. Prove to her that these efforts are the effect not of a mad and fleeting passion but of ineffaceable principles engraved in the depths of your heart. Give proper honor to merit that has been insulted by fortune. This is the only means of reconciling her to merit favored by fortune."

One may conceive what transports of joy this speech gives to the young man, how much confidence and hope it gives him. His decent heart is delighted that in order to please Sophie he has to do exactly what he would do on his own if Sophie did not exist or if he were not in love with her. However little one has understood his character, who will not be able to imagine his conduct on this occasion?

Now I am the confidant of my two good young people and the mediator of their loves! A fine employment for a governor! So fine that never in my life have I done anything which raised me so much in my own eyes and made me so satisfied with myself. Moreover, this employment does not fail to have its agreeable aspects. I am not unwelcome in the house. I am entrusted with the care of keeping the lovers in order. Emile, who is constantly trembling for fear of displeasing me, was never so docile. The little girl overwhelms me with friendliness by which I am not deceived, and I take for myself only what is intended for me. It is thus that she compensates herself indirectly for the respect she imposes on Emile. Through me she gives him countless tender caresses which she would rather die than give to him directly. And Emile, who knows that I do not want to harm his interests, is charmed that I am on good terms with her. When she refuses his arm in walking, he consoles himself with the fact that it is to prefer mine to his. He leaves without complaint, grasping my hand, and

saying softly to me with his eyes as well as his voice, "Friend, speak for me." His eyes follow us with interest. He tries to read our sentiments in our faces and to interpret our speeches by our gestures. He knows that nothing of what is said between us is inconsequential for him. Good Sophie, how your sincere heart is at ease when, without being heard by Telemachus, you can converse with his Mentor! With what lovable frankness you let him read everything going on in your tender heart! With what pleasure you show him all your esteem for his pupil! With what touching ingenuousness you let him discern even sweeter sentiments! With what feigned anger you send the importunate Emile away when impatience forces him to interrupt you! With what charming vexation you reproach him for his tactlessness when he comes and prevents you from speaking well of him, from hearing good things about him, and from always drawing some new reason for loving him from my responses!

Having thus gotten himself tolerated as a suitor, Emile takes advantage of all the rights of that position. He speaks, he urges, he entreats, he importunes. If he is spoken to harshly or if he is mistreated, it makes little difference to him provided that he make himself heard. Finally, though not without effort, he induces Sophie to be kind enough to assume openly a beloved's authority over him—to prescribe to him what he must do, to order instead of to ask, to accept instead of to thank, to regulate the number and the time of his visits, to forbid him to come until this day or to stay past that hour. All this is not done as a game but very seriously. Although it was an effort to get her to accept these rights, she makes use of them with a rigor that often reduces poor Emile to regret that he has given them to her. But whatever she commands, he does not reply, and often, when leaving to obey her, he looks at me with eyes full of joy telling me: "You see that she has taken possession of me." Meanwhile, the proud girl observes him stealthily and smiles secretly at her slave's pride. . . .

As the idolator enriches the object of his worship with treasures that he esteems and adorns on the altar the God he adores, so the lover—although he may very well see his mistress as perfect—constantly wants to add new ornaments to her. She does not need them in order to please him, but he needs to adorn her. It is a new homage he believes he is doing her and a new interest he adds to the pleasure of contemplating her. It seems to him that nothing beautiful is in its place when it is not ornamenting the supreme beauty. It is both a touching and a laughable spectacle to see Emile eager to teach Sophie all he knows, without considering whether what he wants to teach her is to her taste or is suitable for her. He tells her about everything, he explains everything to her with a puerile eagerness. He believes he has only to speak and she will understand on the spot. He fancies beforehand the pleasure he will have in reasoning and in philosophizing with her. He regards as useless all the attainments he cannot display to her eyes. He almost blushes at knowing something she does not know.

Therefore, he gives her lessons in philosophy, physics, mathematics, history—in a word, in everything. Sophie lends herself with pleasure to his zeal and tries to profit from it. When he can obtain permission to give his lessons on his knees before her, how content Emile is! He believes he sees the heavens opened. However this position, more constricting for the student than for the master, is not the most favorable for instruction. On such occasions she does not know exactly what to do with her eyes to avoid those that are pursuing them; and when they meet, the lesson does not gain by it.

The art of thinking is not foreign to women, but they ought only to skim the sciences of reasoning. Sophie gets a conception of everything and does not remember very much. Her greatest progress is in ethics and in matters of taste. As for physics, she remembers only some idea of its general laws and of the cosmic system. Sometimes on their walks, as they contemplate nature's marvels, their innocent and pure hearts dare to lift themselves up to its Author. They do not fear His presence. They open their hearts jointly before Him.

"What, two lovers in the flower of age use their tête-à-tête to speak of religion? They spend their time saying their catechism?" Why must you debase something sublime? Yes, no doubt they do say it, under the influence of the illusion which charms them. They see each other as perfect; they love one another; they converse with each other enthusiastically about what gives virtue its reward. The sacrifices they make to virtue render it dear to them. In the midst of transports that they must vanquish, they sometimes shed tears together purer than heaven's dew, and these sweet tears constitute the enchantment of their life. They are in the most charming delirium that human souls have ever experienced. Their very privations add to their happiness and do them honor in their own eyes for their sacrifices. Sensual men, bodies without souls, one day they will know your pleasures, and for their whole lives they will regret the happy time during which they denied them to themselves.

Despite their being on such good terms, they do not fail to have some disagreements, even some quarrels. The mistress is not without caprice nor the lover without anger. But these little storms pass rapidly and only have the effect of strengthening their union. Experience even teaches Emile not to fear them so much; the reconciliations are always more advantageous to him than the spats are harmful. The fruit of their first spat made him hope for as much from the others. He was wrong. But, in the end, if he does not always take away so palpable a profit, he always gains from these spats by seeing Sophie confirm her sincere interest in his heart. People will want to know what this profit is. I will gladly consent to tell them, for this example gives me the occasion to expound a most useful maxim and to combat a most baneful one.

Emile loves. Therefore, he is not bold. And it can even more readily be conceived that the imperious Sophie is not the girl to overlook his familiarities. Since moderation has its limits in all things, she could be charged with too much harshness rather than too much indulgence; and her father himself sometimes fears that her extreme pride will degenerate into haughtiness. In their most secret tête-à-têtes Emile would not dare to solicit the least favor nor even to appear to aspire to one. When she is so kind as to take his arm during a walk—a favor she does not allow to be turned into a right—he hardly dares occasionally to sigh and press this arm against his breast. Nevertheless, after long constraint he furtively ventures to kiss her dress, and several times he is lucky enough for Sophie to be so kind as not to notice it. One day when he wants to take the same liberty a bit more openly, she decides to take it amiss. He persists. She gets irritated. Vexation dictates a few stinging words. Emile does not endure them without reply. The rest of the day is passed in pouting, and they separate very discontented.

Sophie is ill at ease. Her mother is her confidant. How could she hide her chagrin from her? It is her first spat, and a spat that lasts an hour is so great a business! She repents her mistake. Her mother permits her to make amends. Her father orders her to do so.

The next day Emile is apprehensive and returns earlier than usual. Sophie is in her mother's dressing room. Her father is also there. Emile enters respectfully but with a sad air. Sophie's father and mother have hardly greeted him when Sophie turns around and, extending her hand, asks him in a caressing tone how he is. It is clear that this pretty hand has been extended only in order to be kissed. He takes it and does not kiss it. Sophie is a bit ashamed, and she withdraws her hand with as good grace as is possible for her. Emile, who is not experienced in women's ways and does not know the purpose of their caprices, does not forget easily and is not so quickly appeased. Sophie's father, seeing her embarrassment, succeeds in disconcerting her by mockery. The poor girl is confused and humiliated; she no longer knows what she is doing and would give anything in the world to dare to cry. The more she constrains herself, the more her heart swells. A tear finally escapes her in spite of her efforts. Emile sees this tear, rushes to her knees, takes her hand, and kisses it several times, entranced. "Really, you are too good," says her father, bursting out laughing. "I would have less indulgence for all these mad girls, and I would punish the mouth that offended me." Emboldened by this speech, Emile turns a suppliant eye toward Sophie's mother and, believing he sees a sign of consent, tremblingly approaches Sophie's face. She turns her head away and, in order to save her mouth, exposes a rosy cheek. The tactless boy is not satisfied. She resists feebly. What a kiss, if it were not stolen under a mother's eyes! Severe Sophie, take care. He will often ask you for permission to kiss your dress, provided that you sometimes refuse it.

After this exemplary punishment Sophie's father leaves to attend to some business; her mother sends Sophie away under some pretext, and then she addresses Emile and says to him in quite a serious tone: "Monsieur, I believe that a young man as well born and as well raised as you, who has sentiments and morals, would not want to repay the friendship a family has showed him by dishonoring it. I am neither unsociable nor a prude. I know what must be overlooked in the wildness of youth, and what I have tolerated under my eyes sufficiently proves it to you. Consult your friend about your duties. He will tell you what a difference there is between the games authorized by the presence of a father and mother and the liberties taken far away from them, liberties which abuse their confidence and turn into traps the same favors which are innocent under their eyes. He will tell you, sir, that my daughter has done you no other wrong than that of not noticing at the outset a practice she ought never to have tolerated. He will tell you that everything taken to be a favor becomes one, and that it is unworthy of a man of honor to abuse a young girl's simplicity to usurp in secret the same liberties that she can permit before everyone. One knows what propriety can permit in public; but no one knows where the man who sets himself up as the sole judge of his whims will stop himself in the shadows of secrecy."

After this just reprimand, addressed much more to me than to my pupil, this wise mother departs and leaves me admiring her rare prudence, which takes little account of one's kissing her daughter's mouth in front of her but is frightened of someone's daring to kiss her daughter's dress in private. Reflecting on the folly of our maxims, which always sacrifice true decency to propriety, I understand why language is more chaste as hearts become more corrupted and why rules of conduct are more exact as those subject to them become more dishonest.

In using this occasion to fill. Emile's heart with the duties I ought to have dictated to him earlier, I am struck by a new reflection which perhaps honors Sophie the most and which I am nevertheless very careful not to communicate to her lover. It is clear that this pretended pride for which others reproach her is only a very wise precaution to protect her from herself. Since she has the misfortune to sense a combustible temperament within herself, she dreads the first spark and keeps it at a distance with all her power. It is not from pride that she is severe; it is from humility. She assumes an empire over Emile

which she fears she does not have over Sophie. She uses the one to fight the other. If she were more confident, she would be much less proud. Apart from this one point, what girl in the world is more yielding and sweeter? Who endures an offense more patiently? Who is more fearful of committing one against others? Who makes fewer claims of every kind, except for the claim of virtue? Furthermore, it is not her virtue of which she is proud; she is proud only in order to preserve it. And when she can yield to the inclination of her heart without risk, she caresses even her lover. But her discreet mother does not relate all these details even to her father. Men ought not to know everything.

Far from seeming to have become proud as a result of her conquest, Sophie has become still more affable and less demanding with everyone—except perhaps with him who is the cause of this change. The sentiment of independence no longer swells her noble heart. She triumphs with modesty, winning a victory which costs her her freedom. Her bearing is less free and her speech is more timid now that she no longer hears the word *lover* without blushing. But contentment pierces through her embarrassment, and this very shame is not a disagreeable sentiment. It is especially with other young men that the difference in her conduct is most easily sensed. Since she no longer fears them, the extreme reserve that she used to have with them has been much relaxed. Now that she has made her choice, she has no qualms about acting graciously toward those to whom she is indifferent. Since she no longer takes any interest in them, she is less demanding about their merits, and she finds them always likable enough for people who will never mean anything to her.

If true love could make use of coquetry, I would even believe that I see some traces of it in the way Sophie behaves with these young men in the presence of her lover. One would say that, not content with the ardent passion which she kindles in him by means of an exquisite mixture of reserve and endearment, she is not sorry if she excites this passion still more by means of a bit of anxiety. One would say that by purposely making her young guests merry, she intends to torment Emile with the charms of a playfulness she does not dare to indulge in with him. But Sophie is too attentive, too good, and too judicious actually to torment him. Love and decency take the place of prudence for her in tempering this dangerous stimulant. She knows how to alarm him and to reassure him precisely when it is necessary. And if she sometimes makes him anxious, she never makes him sad. Let us pardon the concern she causes the man she loves by attributing it to her fear that he is never bound to her closely enough.

But what effect will this little trick have on Emile? Will he or won't he be jealous? This is what must be examined, for such digressions also enter into the aim of my book and stray very little from my subject.

I have previously showed how this passion is introduced into man's heart in regard to things which depend only on opinion. But in regard to love the case is different. Jealousy then appears to depend so closely on nature that it is hard to believe that it does not come from it. And the example of the animals, several of whom are jealous to the point of fury, seems unanswerably to establish that it does come from nature. Is it men's opinion which teaches cocks to tear one another apart and bulls to fight to the death?

The aversion against everything which disturbs and combats our pleasures is a natural emotion; that is incontestable. Up to a certain point the case is still the same with the desire for exclusive possession of what pleases us. But when this desire becomes a passion and transforms itself into a fury or a suspicious and gloomy whim called jealousy, then the case is different. This passion may or may not be natural. A distinction must be made.

The example drawn from the animals has been heretofore examined in the *Discourse on Inequality;* and now that I reflect on it anew, this examination appears to me solid enough to dare to refer readers to it. I shall add to the distinctions I have made in that writing only that the jealousy coming from nature depends very much on sexual potency. When this potency is or appears to be unlimited, this jealousy is at its peak; for then the male measures his rights according to his needs and can never see another male as anything but an intrusive competitor. In these same species the females, who always obey the first male that arrives, belong to the males only by right of conquest and cause eternal fights among them.

By contrast, in species in which one male is united with one female, in which mating produces a sort of moral bond—a sort of marriage—the female belongs by her own choice to the male to whom she has given herself, and commonly resists all others. And the male, who has this affection founded on preference as a guarantee of her fidelity, is thus less anxious at the sight of other males and lives more peacefully with them. In these species the male shares the care of the little ones, and by one of those laws of nature that one does not observe without being touched, it seems that the female repays the father for the attachment he has for his children.

Now, if we consider the human species in its primitive simplicity, it is easy to see from the male's limited potency and the moderation of his desires that he is destined by nature to be content with one female. This is confirmed by the numerical equality of the individuals of the two sexes, at least in our climates—an equality which by no means exists in species in which the greater strength of males causes several females to be united with a single male. And although it is the case that a man does not sit on the eggs like a pigeon, nor does he have breasts for giving milk and therefore in that respect belongs to the class of the quadrupeds, nevertheless the children crawl and are weak for so long that they and the mother would have difficulty doing without the attachment of the father and the care which results from it.

All these observations concur to prove that the jealous fury of the males in some species of animals is not at all conclusive for man, and the very exception of the southern climates where polygamy is established only confirms the principle. For the husbands' tyrannical precautions come from the plurality of women, and the sentiment of his own weakness leads the man to have recourse to coercion in order to elude the laws of nature.

Among us, where these same laws are less eluded in this way, but are eluded in an opposite and more odious manner, jealousy has its motive in the social passions more than in primitive instinct. In most liaisons of gallantry the lover hates his rivals far more than he loves his mistress. If he fears that he is not the only object of her attentions, it is the effect of that *amour-propre* whose origin I have showed, and he suffers far more out of vanity than out of love. Moreover, our maladroit institutions have made women so dissembling[10] and have so strongly inflamed their appetites that one can hardly count on their most proved attachment and that they can no longer demonstrate preferences which reassure a man against the fear of competitors.

As regards true love, the case is different. I have showed in the writing already cited that this sentiment is not as natural as is thought. There is a great difference between the sweet habit which makes a man affectionate toward his companion

and that unbridled ardor which intoxicates him with the chimerical attractions of an object which he no longer sees as it really is. This passion longs only for exclusions and preferences, and it differs from vanity only in that the latter, which demands everything and grants nothing, is always iniquitous, whereas love, which gives as much as it demands, is in itself a sentiment filled with equity. Moreover, the more love is demanding, the more it is credulous. The same illusion which causes it makes it easy to persuade. If love is anxious, esteem is confident; and love without esteem never existed in a decent heart because it is only the qualities he values that anyone loves in his beloved.

With all of this well clarified, one can specify with certainty the sort of jealousy Emile will be capable of; since this passion hardly has any seeds in the human heart, its form is determined exclusively by education. When he is in love and jealous, Emile will be not quick to anger, suspicious, and distrustful but delicate, sensitive, and timid. He will be more alarmed than irritated; he will pay far more attention to winning his mistress than to threatening his rival. If he can, he will get rid of him as an obstacle, without hating him as an enemy. If he hates his rival, it will not be for the audacity of contending with him for a heart to which he has laid a claim, but for making him run the real danger of losing her. His unjust pride will not be stupidly offended by someone's daring to enter into competition with him. Understanding that the right of preference is founded solely on merit and that honor is to be found in sucess, he will redouble his efforts to make himself lovable, and he will probably succeed. The generous Sophie, in exciting his love by giving him some moments of alarm, will know how to regulate them well and to compensate him for them; and it will not be long before the competitors, who were tolerated only to put Emile to the test, will be dismissed. . . .

---

[10]The species of dissimulation I mean here is the opposite of that which suits them and which they get from nature. The one consists in disguising the sentiments they have, and the other in feigning those they do not have. All society women spend their lives priding themselves on their pretended sensitivity and never love anything but themselves.

I do not imagine that anyone reading this book with some attention could believe that all the circumstances of the situation in which Emile finds himself have been gathered around him by chance. Is it by chance that, although the cities furnish so many lovable girls, the one who pleases him is to be found only in the depths of a distant retreat? Is it by chance that he meets her? Is it by chance that they suit one another? Is it by chance that they cannot lodge in the same place? Is it by chance that he finds a dwelling so far from her? Is it by chance that he sees her so rarely and that he is forced to purchase the pleasure of seeing her once in a while with so much exertion? He is becoming effeminated, you say? On the contrary, he is hardening himself. He has to be as robust as I have made him to withstand the exertion Sophie makes him endure. . . .

One morning, when they have not seen each other for two days, I enter Emile's room with a letter in my hand; staring fixedly at him, I say, "What would you do if you were informed that Sophie is dead?" He lets out a great cry, gets up, striking his hands together, and looks wild-eyed at me without saying a single word. "Respond then," I continue with the same tranquility. Then, irritated by my coolness, Emile approaches, his eyes inflamed with anger, and stops in an almost threatening posture: "What would I do . . . I don't know. But what I do know is that I would never again in my life see the man who had informed me." "Reassure yourself," I respond, smiling. "She is alive. She is well. She thinks of you, and we are expected this evening. But let us go and take a stroll, and we will chat."

The passion with which he is preoccupied no longer permits him to give himself to purely reasoned conversations as he had before. I have to interest him by this very passion to make him attentive to my lessons. This is what I have done by this terrible preamble. I am now quite sure that he will listen to me.

"You must be happy, dear Emile. That is the goal of every being which senses. That is the first desire which nature has impressed on us, and the only one which never leaves us. But where is happiness? Who knows it? All seek it, and none finds it. One man uses up life in pursuing it, and another dies without having attained it. My young friend, when I took you in my arms at your birth and, calling the Supreme Being to be witness of the commitment I dared to contract, dedicated my days to the happiness of yours, did I myself know what I was committing myself to? No, I only knew that in making you happy, I was sure to be. In making this useful quest for you, I was making it for both of us in common.

"So long as we do not know what we ought to do, wisdom consists in remaining inactive. Of all the maxims, this is the one of which man has the greatest need, and the one which he least knows how to follow. To seek happiness without knowing where it is, is to expose oneself to the danger of fleeing it and to run as many risks of finding the opposite of happiness as there are roads on which to go astray. But it is not everyone who knows how to refrain from acting. In the anxiety in which the ardor for well-being keeps us, we would rather make a mistake in pursuing it than do nothing to seek it; and once we have left the place where we can know it, we no longer know how to get back to it.

"Although afflicted with the same ignorance, I have tried to avoid the same mistake. In taking care of you, I resolved not to take a useless step and to prevent you from taking one. I kept to the road of nature while waiting for it to show me the road of happiness. It turned out that they were the same and that, by not thinking about it, I had followed the road of happiness.

"Be my witness and my judge. I shall never impugn you. Your first years were not sacrificed to those which were to follow. You have enjoyed all the goods nature gave you. Of the ills to which it subjects you and from which I could protect you, you have felt only those which could harden you against other ills. You have never suffered any of them except to avoid greater ones. You have known neither hatred nor slavery. Free and contented, you have stayed just and good; for pain and vice are inseparable, and man never becomes wicked except when he is unhappy. May the memory of your childhood be prolonged until your old age. I am not afraid that your good heart will ever recall your childhood without giving some thanks to the hand which governed it.

"When you entered the age of reason, I protected you from men's opinions. When your heart became sensitive, I preserved you from the empire of the passions. If I had been able to prolong this inner calm to the end of your life, I would have secured my work, and you would always be as happy as man can be. But, dear Emile, it is in vain that I have dipped your soul in the Styx; I was not able to make it everywhere invulnerable. A new enemy is arising which you have not learned to conquer and from which I can no longer save you. This enemy is yourself. Nature and fortune had left you free. You could endure poverty; you could tolerate the pains of the body; those of the soul were unknown to you. You were bound to nothing other than the human condition, and now your are bound to all the attachments you have given to yourself. In learning to desire, you have made yourself the slave of your desires. Without anything changing in you, without anything offending you, without anything touching your being, how many pains can now attack your soul! How many ills you can feel without being sick! How many deaths you can suffer without dying! A lie, a mistake, or a doubt can put you in despair. . . .

"You know how to suffer and die. You know how to endure the law of necessity in physical ills, but you have not yet imposed laws on the appetites of your heart, and the disorder of our lives arises from our affections far more than from our needs. Our desires are extended; our strength is almost nil. By his wishes man depends on countless things, and by himself he depends on nothing, not even his own life. The more he increases his attachments, the more he multiplies his pains. Everything on earth is only transitory. All that we love will escape us sooner or later, and we hold on to it as if it were going to last eternally. What a fright you had at the mere suspicion of Sophie's death! Did you, then, count on her living forever? Does no one die at her age? She is going to die, my child, and perhaps before you. Who knows if she is living at this very instant? Nature had enslaved you only to a single death. You are enslaving yourself to a second. Now you are in the position of dying twice.

"How pitiable you are going to be, thus subjected to your unruly passions! There will always be privations, losses, and alarms. You will not even enjoy what is left to you. The fear of losing everything will prevent you from possessing anything. As a result of having wanted to follow only your passions, you will never be able to satisfy them. You will always seek repose, but it will always flee before you. You will be miserable, and you will become wicked. How could you not be, since you have only your unbridled desires as a law? If you cannot tolerate involuntary privations, how will you impose any on yourself voluntarily? How will you know how to sacrifice inclination to duty and to hold out against your heart in order to listen to your reason? You who already wish never again to see the man who will inform you of your mistress's death, how would you see the man who would want to take her from you while she is still living—the one who would dare to say to you, 'She is dead to you. Virtue separates you from her'? If you have to live with her no matter what, it makes no difference whether Sophie is married or not, whether you are free or not, whether she loves you or hates you, whether she is given you or refused you; you want her, and you have to possess her whatever the price. Inform me, then, at what crime a man stops when he has only the wishes of his heart for laws and knows how to resist nothing that he desires?

"My child, there is no happiness without courage nor virtue without struggle. The word *virtue* comes from *strength.* Strength is the foundation of all virtue. Virtue belongs only to a being that is weak by nature and strong by will. It is in this that the merit of the just man consists; and although we call God good, we do not call Him virtuous, because it requires no effort for Him to do good. I have waited for you to be in a position to understand me before explaining this much profaned word to you. So long as virtue costs nothing to practice, there is little need to know it. This need comes when the passions are awakened. It has already come for you. Raising you in all the simplicity of nature, I have not preached painful duties to you but instead have protected you from the vices that make these duties painful. I have made lying more useless than odious to you; I have taught you not so much to give unto each what belongs to him as to care only for what is yours. I have made you good rather than virtuous. But he who is only good remains so only as long as he takes pleasure in being so. Goodness is broken and perishes under the impact of the human passions. The man who is only good is good only for himself.

"Who, then, is the virtuous man? It is he who knows how to conquer his affections; for then he follows his reason and his conscience; he does his duty; he keeps himself in order, and nothing can make him deviate from it. Up to now you were only apparently free. You had only the precarious freedom of a slave to whom nothing has been commanded. Now be really free. Learn to become

your own master. Command your heart, Emile, and you will be virtuous.

"Here, then, is another apprenticeship, and this apprenticeship is more painful than the first; for nature delivers us from the ills it imposes on us, or it teaches us to bear them. But nature says nothing to us about those which come from ourselves. It abandons us to ourselves. It lets us, as victims of our own passions, succumb to our vain sorrows and then glorify ourselves for the tears at which we should have blushed.

"You now have your first passion. It is perhaps the only one worthy of you. If you know how to rule it like a man, it will be the last. You will subject all the others, and you will obey only the passion for virtue.

"This passion is not criminal, as I well know. It is as pure as the souls which feel it. Decency formed it, and innocence nourished it. Happy lovers! For you the charms of virtue only add to those of love, and the gentle bond that awaits you is as much the reward of your moderation as it is of your attachment. But, tell me, sincere man, has this passion, which is so pure, any the less subjected you? Did you any the less make yourself its slave; and if tomorrow Sophie ceased being innocent, would you stifle it beginning tomorrow? Now is the moment to try your strength. There is no longer time to do so when that strength has to be employed. These dangerous trials ought to be made far from peril. A man does not exercise for battle in the face of the enemy but prepares himself for it before the war. He presents himself at the battle already fully prepared.

"It is an error to distinguish permitted passions from forbidden ones in order to yield to the former and deny oneself the latter. All passions are good when one remains their master; all are bad when one lets oneself be subjected to them. What is forbidden to us by nature is to extend our attachments further than our strength; what is forbidden to us by reason is to want what we cannot obtain; what is forbidden to us by conscience is not temptations but rather letting ourselves be conquered by temptations. It is not within our control to have or not to have passions. But it is within our control to reign over them. All the sentiments we dominate are legitimate; all those which dominate us are criminal. A man is not guilty for loving another's wife if he keep this unhappy passion enslaved to the law of duty. He is guilty for loving his own wife to the point of sacrificing everything to that love.

"Do not expect lengthy precepts of morality from me. I have only one precept to give you, and it comprehends all the others. Be a man. Restrain your heart within the limits of your condition. Study and know these limits. However narrow they may be, a man is not unhappy as long as he closes himself up within them. He is unhappy only when he wants to go out beyond them. He is unhappy only when, in his senseless desires, he puts in the rank of the possible what is not possible. He is unhappy when he forgets his human estate in order to forge for himself imaginary estates from which he always falls back into his own. The only goods that it is costly to be deprived of are those one believes one has a right to. The evident impossibility of obtaining them detaches one from them. Wishes without hope do not torment us. A beggar is not tormented by the desire to be a king. A king wants to be God only when he believes he is no longer a man. . . .

"Do you want, then, to live happily and wisely? Attach your heart only to imperishable beauty. Let your condition limit your desires; let your duties come before your inclinations; extend the law of necessity to moral things. Learn to lose what can be taken from you; learn to abandon everything when virtue decrees it, to put yourself above events and to detach your heart lest it be lacerated by them; to be courageous in adversity, so as never to be miserable; to be firm in your duty, so as never to be criminal. Then you will be happy in spite of fortune and wise in spite of the passions. Then you will find in the possession even of fragile goods a voluptuousness that nothing will be able to disturb. You will possess them without their possessing you; and you will feel that man, who can keep nothing, enjoys only what he knows how to lose. You will not, it is true, have the illusion of imaginary pleasures, but you will also not have the pains which are their fruit. You will gain much in this exchange, for these pains are frequent and real, and these pleasures are rare and vain. As the conqueror of so many deceptive opinions, you will also be the conqueror of the opinion that places so great a value on life. You will pass your life without disturbance and terminate it without fright. You will detach yourself from it as from all things. How many others are horror-stricken because they think that, in departing from life, they cease to be? Since you are informed about life's nothingness, you will believe that it is then that you begin to be. Death is the end of the wicked man's life and the beginning of the just man's."

Emile hears me with an attention that is mixed with anxiety. He fears some sinister conclusion to this preamble. He has a presentiment that, in showing him the necessity for exercising strength of soul, I want to subject him to this hard exercise. Like a wounded man who shudders on seeing the surgeon approach, he believes that he already feels on his wound the painful but salutary hand which prevents it from becoming infected.

Uncertain, troubled, and eager to know what I am getting at, Emile fearfully questions me instead of answering. "What must be done?" he asks me, almost trembling and without daring to raise his eyes. "That which must be done!" I answer in a firm tone: "You must leave Sophie." "What are you saying?" he shouts with anger. "Leave Sophie! Leave her, deceive her, be a traitor, a cheat, a perjuror. . . !" "What!" I respond, interrupting him. "Is it from me that Emile is afraid of learning to merit such names?" "No," he continues with the same impetuosity. "Not from you nor from another. In spite of you, I shall know how to preserve your work. I shall know how not to merit those names."

I had expected this initial fury. I let it pass without getting upset. A fine preacher of moderation I would make if I did not possess what I am preaching to him! Emile knows me too well to believe me capable of demanding from him anything which is bad, and he knows that it would be bad to leave Sophie in the sense he is giving to that word. Therefore, he waits for me finally to explain myself. Then I return to my discourse.

"Do you believe, dear Emile, that a man, in whatever situation he finds himself, can be happier than you have been for these past three months? If you believe it, disabuse yourself. Before tasting the pleasures of life, you have exhausted its happiness. There is nothing beyond what you have felt. The felicity of the senses is fleeting. It always loses its flavor when it is the heart's habitual state. You have enjoyed more from hope than you will ever enjoy in reality. Imagination adorns what one desires but abandons it when it is in one's possession. Except for the single. Being existing by itself, there is nothing beautiful except that which is not. If your present state could have lasted forever, you would have found supreme happiness. But everything connected with man feels the effects of his transitoriness. Everything is finite and everything is fleeting in human life; and if the state which makes us happy lasted endlessly, the habit of enjoying it would take away our taste for it. If nothing changes from without, the heart changes. Happiness leaves us, or we leave it.

"Time, which you did not measure, was flowing during your delirium. The summer is ending; winter approaches. Even if we could continue our visits during so hard a season, they would never tolerate it. In spite of ourselves, we must change our way of life; this one can no longer last. I see in your impatient eyes that this difficulty does not bother you. Sophie's confession and your own desires suggest to you an easy means for avoiding the snow and no longer having to make a trip in order to go and see her. The expedient is doubtless convenient. But when spring has come, the snow melts, and the marriage remains. You must think about a marriage for all seasons.

"You want to marry Sophie, and yet you have known her for less than five months! You want to marry her not because she suits you but because she pleases you—as though love were never mistaken about what is suitable, and as though those who begin by loving each other never end by hating each other. She is virtuous, I know. But is that enough? Is being decent sufficient for people to be suitable for each other? It is not her virtue I am putting in doubt; it is her character. Does a woman's character reveal itself in a day? Do you know in how many situations you must have seen her in order to get a deep knowledge of her disposition? Do four months of attachment give you assurance for a whole life? Perhaps two months of absence will make her forget you. Perhaps someone else is only waiting for your withdrawal in order to efface you from her heart. Perhaps on your return you will find her as indifferent as up to now you have found her responsive. The sentiments do not depend on principles. She may remain very decent and yet cease to love you. She will be constant and faithful. I tend to believe it. But who is answerable to you for her, and who is answerable to her for you so long as you have not put one another to the test? Will you wait to make this test until it becomes useless for you? Will you wait to know each other until you can no longer separate? . . .

"Let us speak about you. In aspiring to the status of husband and father, have you meditated enough upon its duties? When you become the head of a family, you are going to become a member of the state, and do you know what it is to be a member of the state? Do you know what government, laws, and fatherland are? Do you know what the price is of your being permitted to live and for whom you ought to die? You believe you have learned everything, and you still know nothing. Before taking a place in the civil order, learn to know it and to know what rank in it suits you.

"Emile, you must leave Sophie. I do not say abandon her. If you were capable of it, she would be only too fortunate not to have married you. You must leave in order to return worthy of her. Do not be so vain as to believe that you already merit her. Oh, how much there remains for you to do! Come and fulfill this noble task. Come and learn to bear her absence. Come and win the prize of fidelity, so that on your return you can lay claim to some honor from her and ask for her hand not as an act of grace but as a recompense."

Not yet practiced at struggling against himself and not yet accustomed to desire one thing and to will another, the young man does not give in. He resists; he argues. Why should he deny himself the happiness awaiting him? Would delaying to accept the hand which is offered him not be to disdain it? What need is there to go away from her in order to inform himself about what he ought to know? And even if that were necessary, why should he not leave her the assured pledge of his return in the form of indissoluble bonds? Let him be her husband, and he will be ready to follow me. Let them be united, and he will leave her without fear . . . "To be united in order to be separated. Dear Emile, what a contradiction! It is a fine thing for a lover to be able to live without his beloved, but a husband ought never to leave his wife except in case of necessity. To cure your scruples, I see that your delay ought to be involuntary. You must be able to tell Sophie that you are leaving her in spite of yourself. Very well, be content; and since you do

not obey reason, recognize another master. You have not forgotten the promise you made to me. Emile, you have to leave Sophie. I wish it."

After this statement he lowers his head, keeps quiet, and dreams for a moment; then, looking at me with assurance, he asks, "When do we leave?" "In a week," I answer. "Sophie must be prepared for this departure. Women are weaker. One owes them special consideration; and since this absence is not a duty for her as it is for you, it is permissible for her to bear it less courageously."

I am only too tempted to prolong the journal of my two young people's love up to their separation, but I have for a long time abused the indulgence of my readers. Let us be brief in order to finish once and for all.

Will Emile dare to act at his beloved's feet with the same assurance he has just shown to his friend? As for me, I believe he will. He ought to draw this assurance from the very truth of his love. He would be more uncomfortable before her if it cost him less to leave her. He would leave as the guilty party, and this role is always embarrassing for a decent heart. But the more the sacrifice costs him, the more he can lay a claim to honor in the eyes of her who makes it so difficult for him. He is not afraid that she will be misled about the motive which determines him. He seems to say to her with each glance, "O Sophie, read my heart and be faithful! You do not have a lover without virtue."

The proud Sophie, for her part, tries to bear with dignity the unforeseen blow which strikes her. She makes an effort to appear insensitive to it. But since she, unlike Emile, does not have the honor of combat and victory, her firmness holds up less well. She cries and groans in spite of herself, and the fear of being forgotten embitters the pain of separation. She does not cry before her lover; it is not to him that she shows her fears. She would choke rather than let a sigh escape her in his presence. It is I who receive her complaints, who see her tears, whom she affects to take as her confidant. Women are skillful and know how to disguise themselves. The more she grumbles in secret against my tyranny, the more attentive she is in flattering me. She senses that her fate is in my hands.

I console her. I reassure her. I make myself answerable for her lover, or rather her husband. Let her be as faithful to him as he will be to her, and I swear that in two years he will be her husband. She esteems me enough to believe that I do not want to deceive her. I am the guarantor of each for the other. Their hearts, their virtue, my probity, their parents' confidence—everything reassures them. But what good does reason do against weakness? They separate as if they were never to see each other again. . . .

On Travel

It is asked whether it is good for young people to travel, and there is much dispute about it. If the question were put differently and it were asked whether it is good that men have traveled, perhaps there would not be so much dispute. . . .

To become informed, it is not sufficient to roam through various countries. It is necessary to know how to travel. To observe, it is necessary to have eyes and to turn them toward the object one wants to know. There are many persons who are informed still less by travel than by books, because they are ignorant of the art of thinking; because when they read, their minds are at least guided by the author; and because when they travel, they do not know how to see anything on their own. Others do not become informed because they do not want to be informed. Their aim in traveling is so different that this one hardly occurs to them. It is very much an accident if one sees with exactitude what one does not care to look at. . . .

Now that Emile has considered himself in his physical relations with other beings and in his moral relations with other men, it remains for him to consider himself in his civil relations with his fellow citizens. To do that, he must begin by studying the nature of government in general, the diverse forms of government, and finally the particular government under which he was born, so that he may find out whether it suits him to live there. For by a right nothing can abrogate, when each man attains his majority and becomes his own master, he also becomes master of renouncing the contract that connects him with the community by leaving the country in which that community is established. It is only by staying there after attaining the age of reason that he is considered to have tacitly confirmed the commitment his ancestors made. He acquires the right of renouncing his fatherland just as he acquires the right of renouncing his father's estate. Furthermore, since place of birth is a gift of nature, one yields one's own place of birth in making this renunciation. According to rigorous standards of right, each man remains free at his own risk in whatever place he is born unless he voluntarily subjects himself to the laws in order to acquire the right to be protected by them.

Therefore, I might say to him: "Up to now you have lived under my direction. You were not in a condition to govern yourself. But now you are approaching the age when the laws put your property at your disposition and thus make you the master of your own person. You are going to find yourself alone in society, dependent on everything, even on your patrimony. You plan to settle down. This plan is laudable; it is one of man's duties. But, before marrying, you must know what kind of man you want to be, what you want to spend your life doing, and what measures you want to take to assure yourself and your family of bread. . . . Do you want to commit yourself to dependence on men whom you despise? Do you want to establish your fortune and determine your status by means of civil relations which will put you constantly at the discretion of others and force you to become a rascal yourself in order to escape from the clutches of other rascals?" . . .

I have a proposition to make to you. Let us consecrate the two years until your return to choosing an abode in Europe where you can live happily with your family, sheltered from all the dangers of which I have just spoken to you. If we succeed, you will have found the true happiness vainly sought by so many others, and you will not regret the time you have spent. If we do not succeed, you will be cured of a chimera. You will console yourself for an inevitable unhappiness, and you will submit yourself to the law of necessity."

I do not know whether all my readers will perceive where this proposed research is going to lead us. But I do know that if Emile, at the conclusion of his travels begun and continued with this intention, does not come back versed in all matter of government, in public morals, and in maxims of state of every kind, either he or I must be quite poorly endowed—he with intelligence and I with judgment. . . .

Our elements are clear, simple, and taken immediately from the nature of things. They will be formed from questions discussed between us, and we shall convert them into principles only when they are sufficiently resolved.

For example, by first going back to the state of nature, we shall examine whether men are born enslaved or free, associated with one another or independent. Whether they join together voluntarily or by force. Whether the force which joins them can form a permanent right by which this prior force remains obligatory, even when it is surmounted by another. . . . Or whether, once this force has expired, the force which succeeds it becomes obligatory in turn and destroys the obligation of the other, in such a way that one is only obliged to obey as long as one is forced to do so and is dispensed from it as soon as one can offer resistance—a right which, it seems, would not add very much to force and would hardly be anything but a play on words. . . .

We shall further examine whether conscience obliges one to give one's purse to a bandit who demands it on the highway, even if one could hide it from him. For, after all, the pistol he holds is also a power.

Whether the word *power* on this occasion means anything other than a legitimate power, one that consequently is subject to the laws from which it gets its being.

Assuming that one rejects this right of force and accepts the right of nature, or paternal authority, as the principle of societies, we shall investigate the extent of that authority, how it is founded in nature, and whether it has any other ground than the utility of the child, his weakness, and the natural love the father has for him. Whether when the child's weaknesses comes to an end and his reason matures, he does not therefore become the sole natural judge of what is suitable for his preservation, and consequently his own master, as well as become independent of every other man, even of his father. For it is even more certain that the son loves himself than it is that the father loves his son.

Whether when the father dies, the children are obliged to obey the eldest among them or someone else who will not have a father's natural attachment for them; and whether there will always be a single chief in each clan whom the whole family is obliged to obey. In which case we would investigate how the authority could ever be divided, and by what right there would be more than one chief on the whole earth governing mankind.

Assuming that peoples were formed by choice, we shall then distinguish right from fact; since men have thus subjected themselves to their brothers, uncles, or parents not because they were obliged to but because they wanted to, we shall ask whether this sort of society is not always simply a case of free and voluntary association.

Moving next to the right of slavery, we shall examine whether a man can legitimately alienate himself to another without restriction, without reserve, without any kind of condition: that is to say, whether he can renounce his person, his life, his reason, his *I,* and all morality in his actions—in a word, whether he can cease to exist before his death in spite of nature, which gives him immediate responsibility for his own preservation, and in spite of his conscience and his reason, which prescribe to him what he ought to do and what he ought to abstain from doing.

And if there is some reserve or restriction in the transaction of enslavement, we shall discuss whether this transaction does not then become a true contract in which each of the parties, having no common superior in this capacity,[11] remains his own judge as to the conditions of the contract; and whether each consequently remains free in this respect and master of breaking the contract as soon as he considers himself injured.

If a slave, then, cannot alienate himself without reserve to his master, how can a people alienate itself without reserve to its chief? And if the slave remains judge of whether his master observes their contract, will the people not remain judge of whether their chiefs observe their contract?

Forced to retrace our steps in this way, and examining the sense of the collective word *people,* we shall investigate whether the establishment of a people does not require at least a tacit contract prior to the one we are supposing.

Since the people is a people before electing a king, what made it such if not the social contract? Therefore the social contract is the basis of every civil society, and the nature of the society it forms must be sought in the nature of this transaction.

---

[11]If they had one, this common superior would be none other than the sovereign; and then the right of slavery would be founded on the right of sovereignty and would not be its source.

We shall investigate what the tenor of this contract is and whether it can be summed up in this formula: *Each of us puts his goods, his person, his life, and all his power in common under the supreme direction of the general will, and we as a body accept each member as a part indivisible from the whole.*

Assuming this, we shall note, in order to define the terms we need, that this act of association produces—in place of the particular person of each contracting party—a moral and collective body composed of as many members as the assembly has voices. This public person, understood generally, takes the name *body politic;* its members call it *state* when it is passive, *sovereign* when it is active, and *power* when it is compared with other bodies politic. Speaking of the members collectively they take the name *people;* individually they are called both *citizens,* as members of the city or participants in the sovereign authority, and *subjects,* as subject to the same authority.

We shall note that this act of association contains a reciprocal commitment of the public and the individuals, and that each individual, who is, so to speak, contracting with himself, is committed in two respects—as a member of the sovereign, to the individuals; as a member of the state, to the sovereign.

We shall further note that since no one is held to commitments made only with himself, public deliberation—which can obligate all the subjects with respect to the sovereign because of the two different relations in which each of them is envisaged—cannot obligate the state to itself. From which one can see that there neither is nor can be any other fundamental law properly speaking than the social pact alone. This does not mean that the body politic cannot in certain respects commit itself to another; for with respect to foreigners, it becomes a simple being, an individual.

Since the two contracting parties—that is, each individual and the public—have no common superior who can judge their differences, we shall examine whether each party remains the master of breaking the contract when it pleases him—that is to say, of renouncing it as soon as he believes himself injured.

In order to clarify this question, we shall observe that according to the social pact the sovereign is able to act only by common and general wills and that therefore its acts ought similarly to have only general and common objects. From this it follows that an individual could not be directly injured by the sovereign without everyone's being injured; but this cannot be, since it would be to want to harm oneself. Thus the social contract never has need of any guarantee other than the public force, because the injury can come only from individuals; and in that case they are not thereby free from their commitment but are punished for having violated it.

In order to decide all such questions, we shall be careful always to remind ourselves that the social pact is of a particular and unique nature, in that the people contracts only with itself—that is to say, the people as sovereign body contracts with the individuals as subjects. This condition constitutes the whole artifice of the political machine and sets it in motion. It alone renders legitimate, reasonable, and free from danger commitments that otherwise would be absurd, tyrannical, and subject to the most enormous abuses.

Inasmuch as the individuals have subjected themselves only to the sovereign, and the sovereign authority is nothing other than the general will, we shall see how each man who obeys the sovereign obeys only himself, and how one is more free under the social pact than in the state of nature.

After having compared natural liberty to civil liberty with respect to persons, we shall, with respect to possessions, compare the right of property with the right of sovereignty, individual domain with eminent domain. If the sovereign authority is founded on the right of property, this right is the one it ought to respect most. The right of property is inviolable and sacred for the sovereign authority as long as it remains a particular and individual right. But as soon as it is considered as common to all the citizens, it is subject to the general will, and this will can suppress it. Thus the sovereign has no right to touch the possessions of one or more individuals. But it can legitimately seize the possessions of all, as was done at Sparta in the time of Lycurgus; the abolition of debts by Solon, on the other hand, was an illegitimate act.

Since nothing obligates the subjects except the general will, we shall investigate how this will is manifested, by what signs one is sure of recognizing it, what a law is, and what the true characteristics of law are. This subject is entirely new: the definition of law remains to be made.

The moment the people considers one or more of its members individually, the people is divided. A relation is formed between the whole and its part which makes them into two separate beings: the part is one, and the whole, less this part, is the other. But the whole less a part is not the whole. Therefore, as long as this relation subsists, there is no longer a whole but two unequal parts.

By contrast, when the whole people makes a statute applying to the whole people, it considers only itself; and if a relation is formed, it is between the whole object seen from one point of view and the whole object seen from another point of view, without any division of the whole. Then the object applying to which the statute is made is general, and the will which makes the statute is also general. We shall examine whether there is any other kind of act that can bear the name of law.

If the sovereign can speak only by laws, and if the law can never have anything but a general object—one that relates equally to all the members of the state—it follows that the sovereign never has the power to make any statute applying to a particular object. But since it is important for the preservation of the state that particular things also be decided, we shall investigate how that can be done.

The acts of the sovereign can only be acts of general will—that is, laws. There must next be determining acts—acts of force or of government—for the execution of these same laws, and these acts can have only particular objects. Thus the act by which the sovereign decrees that a chief will be elected is a law, and the act by which that chief is elected in execution of the law is only an act of government.

Here, then, is a third relation in which the assembled people can be considered—as magistrate or executor of the law that it has declared in its capacity as sovereign.[12]

We shall examine whether it is possible for the people to divest itself of its right of sovereignty in order to vest that right in one or more men. For, since the act of election is not a law, and in this act the people itself is not sovereign, it is hard to see how it can transfer a right it does not have.

Inasmuch as the essence of sovereignty consists in the general will, it is also hard to see how one can be certain that a particular will always will agree with this general will. One ought rather to presume that the particular will will often be contrary to the general will, for private interest always tends to preferences, and the public interest always tends to equality. And even if such agreement were possible but not necessary and indestructible, that would suffice for making it impossible for sovereign right to result from it.

We shall investigate whether the chiefs of the people, under whatever name they may be elected, can ever, without violating the social pact, be anything but officers of the people whom the people direct to execute the laws; and whether these chiefs owe the people an account of their administration and are themselves subject to the laws whose observance they are charged with ensuring.

If the people cannot alienate its supreme right, can it entrust that right to others for a time? If it cannot give itself a master, can it give itself representatives? This question is important and merits discussion.

If the people can have neither a sovereign nor representatives, we shall examine how it can declare its laws by itself; whether it ought to have many laws, whether it ought to change them often, and whether it is easy for a large populace to be its own legislator.

Whether the Roman populace was not a large populace.

Whether it is good to have large populaces.

It follows from the preceding considerations that within the state there is an intermediate body between the subjects and the sovereign. This intermediate body, which is formed of one or more members, is in charge of public administration, the execution of the laws, and the maintenance of civil and political liberty.

The members of this body are called *magistrates* or *kings*—that is, governors. The whole body is called *prince* when considered with regard to the men who compose it, and *government* when considered with regard to its action.

If we consider the action of the whole body acting upon itself—that is, the relation of the whole to the whole or of the sovereign to the state—we can compare this relation to that of the extremes of a continuous proportion which has the government as its middle term. The magistrate receives from the sovereign the orders he gives to the people; and when everything is calculated, his product or power is of the same magnitude as the product

---

[12]Most of these questions and propositions are extracts from the treatise. *The Social Contract,* itself an extract from a larger work that was undertaken without consulting my strength and has long since been abandoned. The little treatise I have detached from it—of which this is the summary—will be published separately.

or power of the citizens, who are on the one hand subjects and on the other sovereigns. None of the three terms could be altered without immediately breaking the proportion. If the sovereign wants to govern, or if the prince wants to give laws, or if the subject refuses to obey, disorder replaces order, and the state is dissolved, falling into despotism or anarchy.

Let us suppose the state to be composed of ten thousand citizens. The sovereign can be considered only collectively and as a body. But each individual, as a subject, has a personal and independent existence. Thus the sovereign is to the subject as ten thousand is to one. That is, each member of the state has only a ten-thousandth part of the sovereign authority as his share, although he is totally subjected to that authority. If the people is composed of one hundred thousand men, the condition of the subjects does not change, and each always endures the whole empire of the laws, but his suffrage, which is reduced to a one-hundred-thousandth share, has ten times less influence in drawing up the laws. Thus, while the subject always remains one, the ratio of the sovereign to the subject increases in proportion to the number of citizens. From this it follows that the more the state expands, the more liberty diminishes.

Now, the less the particular wills correspond to the general will—that is, the less morals correspond to laws—the more the repressing force ought to increase. From another point of view, a larger state gives the depositories of public authority greater temptations and more means for abusing them; therefore the more force the government has in order to contain the people, the more force the sovereign ought to have in order to contain the government.

It follows from this double relation that the continuous proportion among the sovereign, the prince, and the people is not an arbitrary idea but a consequence of the nature of the state. Further, it

follows that since one of the extremes—that is, the people—is fixed, every time the doubled ratio increases or decreases, the simple ratio increases or decreases in turn, which cannot happen without the mean term changing the same number of times. From this we can draw the conclusion that there is not a single and absolute constitution of government, but that there ought to be as many governments differing in nature as there are states differing in size.

If it is the case that the more numerous the people are, the less morals correspond to the laws, we shall examine whether, by an evident enough analogy, it can also be said that the more numerous the magistrates are, the weaker the government is.

In order to clarify this maxim, we shall distinguish three essentially different wills in the person of each magistrate. First, there is the personal will of the individual, which is directed only to his own particular advantage. Second, there is the common will of the magistrates, which relates solely to the profit of the prince; this will can be called the "will *de corps*," which is general in relation to the government and particular in relation to the state of which the government is a part. In the third place, there is the will of the people or the sovereign will, which is general both in relation to the state considered as the whole and in relation to the government considered as part of the whole. Where there is perfect legislation, the particular and individual will ought to be almost nonexistent, and the will *de corps* belonging to the government ought to be very subordinate; consequently the general and sovereign will is the standard for all the others. However, according to the natural order, these different wills become more active to the extent that they are concentrated. The general will is always the weakest, the will *de corps* has the second rank, and the particular will is preferred over all others. The result is that each man is first of all himself, and then a magistrate, and then a citizen—a gradation directly opposed to that which the social order demands. . . .

I would not be surprised if my young man, who has good sense, were to interrupt me in the middle of all our reasoning and say, "Someone might say that we are building our edifice with wood and not with men, so exactly do we align each piece with the ruler!" "It is true, my friend, but keep in mind that right is not bent by men's passions, and that our first concern was to establish the true principles of political right. Now that our foundations are laid, come and examine what men have built on them; and you will see some fine things!" . . .

I have said why travel is not fruitful for everyone. What makes it still more unfruitful for young people is the way they are made to do it. Governors, who are more interested in their own entertainment than in their pupils' instruction, lead them from city to city, from palace to palace, from social circle to social circle; or, if the governors are learned and men of letters, they make their pupils spend their time roaming libraries, visiting antique shops, going through old monuments, and transcribing old inscriptions. In each country the pupils are involved with another century. It is as if they were involved with another country. The result is that, after having roamed Europe at great expense, abandoned to frivolities or boredom, they return without having seen anything which can interest them or learned anything which can be useful to them.

All capitals resemble one another. All peoples are mixed together in them, and all morals are confounded. It is not to capitals that one must go to study nations. Paris and London are but the same city in my eyes. Their inhabitants have some different prejudices, but an equal share of them, and all their practical maxims are the same. One knows what kinds of men must gather in courts and what morals must everywhere be produced by the crowding together of the people and the inequality of fortunes. As soon as I am told of a city of two hundred thousand souls, I know beforehand how people live there. Whatever else I would find out on the spot is not worth the effort of going to learn.

One must go to the remote provinces—where there is less movement and commerce, where foreigners travel less, where the inhabitants move around less and change fortune and status less—in order to study the genius and the morals of a nation. See the capital in passing, but go far away from it to observe the country. The French are not in Paris, they are in Touraine. The English are more English in Mercia than in London, and the Spanish are more Spanish in Galicia than in Madrid. It is at these great distances from the capital that a people reveals its character and shows itself as it is without admixture. There the good and bad effects of the government are more strongly felt, just as the measurement of arcs is more exact at the end of a longer radius. . . .

This study of diverse peoples in their remote provinces and in the simplicity of their original genius results in a general observation quite favorable to my epigraph and quite consoling to the human heart. It is that all nations appear much better when they are observed in this way. The closer they are to nature, the more their character is dominated by goodness. It is only by closing themselves up in cities and corrupting themselves by means of culture that they become depraved and exchange a few defects that are more coarse than harmful for appealing and pernicious vices.

From this observation there results a new advantage for the way of traveling I propose. By sojourning less in big cities where a horrible corruption reigns, young people are less exposed to being corrupted themselves. Among simpler men and in smaller societies they preserve a surer judgment, a healthier taste, and more decent morals. But in any event, this contagion is hardly to be feared for my Emile. He has all that is needed to guarantee him against it. Among all the precautions I have taken in this respect I give great weight to the attachment he bears in his heart.

People no longer know what true love is capable of doing to the inclinations of young people because those who govern them, understanding true love no better than their pupils do, turn them away from it. Nevertheless, a young man must either love or be debauched. It is easy to deceive by appearances. Countless young people will be cited who are said to live very chastely without love. But let someone name to me a grown man who is truly a man and who says in good faith that he has spent his youth this way. In regard to all the virtues and all our duties only the appearance is sought. I seek the reality, and I am mistaken if there are other means of getting at it than those I give.

The idea of getting Emile to fall in love before making him travel is not my invention. Here is the incident which suggested it to me.

I was in Venice visiting the governor of a young Englishman. It was winter, and we were sitting around the fire. The governor received his letters from the post. He read them and then reread one letter aloud to his pupil. It was in English, and I understood none of it. But during the reading I saw the young man tear off the very fine lace cuffs he was wearing and throw them one after the other into the fire. He did this as gently as he could so as not to be noticed. Surprised by this caprice, I looked him in the face and believed I saw some emotion there. But the external signs of the passions, which are quite similar in all men, nonetheless have national differences about which it is easy to be mistaken. Peoples have diverse languages on their faces as well as in their mouths. I awaited the end of the reading; then I showed the governor his pupil's naked wrists—which the young man nevertheless did his best to hide—and I said, "Is it possible for me to know what this means?"

The governor, seeing what had happened, started laughing and embraced his pupil with an air of satisfaction. After having obtained the latter's consent, he gave me the explanation I wished.

"The cuffs which Monsieur John has just torn off," he said to me, "are a present given to him by a lady of this city not long ago. Now you should know that Monsieur John is promised to a young lady in his country whom he loves very much and who deserves his love even more. This letter is from his beloved's mother, and I am going to translate for you the passage which caused the damage you witnessed.

"'Lucy does not cease working on Lord John's cuffs. Miss Betty Roldham came yesterday to spend the afternoon with her and insisted on joining in her work. Knowing that Lucy had risen earlier today than usual, I wanted to see what she was doing, and I found her busy undoing all that Miss Betty had done yesterday. She does not want a single stitch in her gift to be done by a hand other than her own.'"

Monsieur John went out a moment later to put on other cuffs, and I said to his governor, "You have a pupil with an excellent nature. But tell me the truth, wasn't the letter from Miss Lucy's mother arranged? Is it not an expedient you devised against the lady of the cuffs?" "No," he answered, "the thing is real. I have not put so much art in my efforts. I have made them with simplicity and zeal, and God has blessed my work."

The incident involving this young man did not leave my memory. It was not apt to produce nothing in the head of a dreamer like me.

It is time to finish. Let us take Lord John back to Miss Lucy—that is to say, Emile back to Sophie. With a heart no less tender than it was before his departure, Emile brings back to her a more enlightened mind, and he brings back to his country the advantage of having known governments by all their vices and peoples by all their virtues.

After having employed almost two years in roaming some of the great states of Europe and more of the small ones, after having learned Europe's two or three principal languages, and after having seen what is truly worthy of curiosity—whether in natural history, or in government, or in arts, or in men—Emile is devoured by impatience and warns me that the end is approaching. Then I say to him, "Well, my friend, you remember the principal object of our travels. You have seen and observed. What is the final result of your observations? What course have you chosen?" Either I am mistaken in my method, or he will answer me pretty nearly as follows:

"What course have I chosen! To remain what you have made me and voluntarily to add no other chain to the one with which nature and the laws burden me. The more I examine the work of men in their institutions, the more I see that they make themselves slaves by dint of wanting to be independent and that they use up their freedom in vain efforts to ensure it. In order not to yield to the torrent of things, they involve themselves in countless attachments. Then as soon as they want to take a step, they cannot and are surprised at depending on everything. It seems to me that in order to make oneself free, one has to do nothing. It suffices that one not want to stop being free. It is you, my master, who have made me free in teaching me to yield to necessity. Let it come when it pleases. I let myself be carried along without constraint, and since I do not wish to fight it, I do not attach myself to anything to hold me back. In our travels I have sought to find some piece of land where I could be absolutely on my own. But in what place among men does one not depend on their passions? All things considered, I have found that my very wish was contradictory; for, were I dependent on nothing else, I would at least depend on the land where I had settled. My life would be attached to this land like that of dryads was to their

trees. I have found that dominion and liberty are two incompatible words; therefore, I could be master of a cottage only in ceasing to be master of myself. . . .

"I remember that my property was the cause of our investigations. You proved very solidly that I could not keep my wealth and my freedom at the same time. But when you wanted me to be free and without needs at the same time, you wanted two incompatible things, for I could withdraw myself from dependence on man only by returning to dependence on nature. What will I do then with the fortune my parents left me? I shall begin by not depending on it. I shall loosen all the bonds which attach me to it. If it is left with me, it will stay with with me. If it is taken from me, I shall not be carried along with it. I shall not worry about holding on to it, but I shall remain firmly in my place. Rich or poor, I shall be free. I shall not be free in this or that land, in this or that region; I shall be free everywhere on earth. All the chains of opinion are broken for me; I know only those of necessity. I learned to bear these chains from my birth, and I shall bear them until my death, for I am a man. And why would I not know how to bear them as a free man since, if I were a slave, I would still have to bear them and those of slavery to boot?

"What difference does it make to me what my position on earth is? What difference does it make to me where I am? Wherever there are men, I am at the home of my brothers; wherever there are no men, I am in my own home. As long as I can remain independent and rich, I have property to live on, and I shall live. When my property subjects me, I shall abandon it without effort. I have arms for working, and I shall live. When my arms fail me, I shall live if I am fed, and I shall die if I am abandoned. I shall also die even if I am not abandoned. For death is not a punishment for poverty but a law of nature. At whatever time death comes,

I defy it. It will never surprise me while I am making preparations to live. It will never prevent me from having lived.

"This, my father, is my chosen course. If I were without passions, I would, in my condition as a man, be independent like God himself; for I would want only what is and therefore would never have to struggle against destiny. At least I have no more than one chain. It is the only one I shall ever bear, and I can glory in it. Come, then, give me Sophie, and I am free."

"Dear Emile, I am very glad to hear a man's speeches come from your mouth and to see a man's sentiments in your heart. This extravagant disinterestedness does not displease me at your age. It will decrease when you have children, and you will then be precisely what a good father of a family and a wise man ought to be. Before your travels I knew what their effect would be. I knew that when you looked at our institutions from close up, you would hardly gain a confidence in them which they do not merit. One aspires in vain to liberty under the safeguard of the laws. Laws! Where are there laws, and where are they respected? Everywhere you have seen only individual interest and men's passions reigning under this name. But the eternal laws of nature and order do exist. For the wise man, they take the place of positive law. They are written in the depth of his heart by conscience and reason. It is to these that he ought to enslave himself in order to be free. The only slave is the man who does evil, for he always does it in spite of himself. Freedom is found in no form of government; it is in the heart of the free man. He takes it with him everywhere. The vile man takes his servitude everywhere. The latter would be a slave in Geneva, the former a free man in Paris.

"If I were speaking to you of the duties of the citizen, you would perhaps ask me where the fatherland is, and you would believe you had confounded me. But you would be mistaken, dear Emile, for he who does not have a fatherland at least has a country. In any event, he has lived tranquilly under a government and the simulacra of laws. What difference does it make that the social contract has not been observed, if individual interest protected him as the general will would have done, if public violence guaranteed him against individual violence, if the evil he saw done made him love what is good, and if our institutions themselves have made him know and hate their own iniquities? O Emile, where is the good man who owes nothing to his country? Whatever country it is, he owes it what is most precious to man—the morality of his actions and the love of virtue. If he had been born in the heart of the woods, he would have lived happier and freer. But he would have had nothing to combat in order to follow his inclinations, and thus he would have been good without merit; he would not have been virtuous; and now he knows how to be so in spite of his passions. The mere appearance of order brings him to know order and to love it. The public good, which serves others only as a pretext, is a real motive for him alone. He learns to struggle with himself, to conquer himself, to sacrifice his interest to the common interest. It is not true that he draws no profit from the laws. They give him the courage to be just even among wicked men. It is not true that they have not made him free. They have taught him to reign over himself.

"Do not ask then, 'What difference does it make to me where I am?' It makes a difference to you that you are where you can fulfill all your duties, and one of those duties is an attachment to the place of your birth. Your compatriots protected you as a child; you ought to love them as a man. You ought to live amidst them, or at least in a place where you can be useful to them insofar as you can, and where they know where to get you if they ever have need of you. There are circumstances in which a man can be more useful to his fellow citizens outside of his fatherland than if he were living in its bosom. Then he ought to listen only to his zeal and to endure his exile without grumbling. This exile itself is one of his duties. But you, good Emile, on whom nothing imposes these painful sacrifices, you who have not taken on the sad job of telling the truth to men, go and live in their midst, cultivate their friendship in sweet association, be their benefactor and their model. Your example will serve them better than all our books, and the good they see you do will touch them more than all our vain speeches.

"I do not exhort you to go to live in the big cities for this purpose. On the contrary, one of the examples good men ought to give others is that of the patriarchal and rustic life, man's first life, which is the most peaceful, the most natural, and the sweetest life for anyone who does not have a corrupt heart. Happy is the country, my young friend, where one does not need to seek peace in a desert! But where is this country? A beneficent man can hardly satisfy his inclination in the midst of cities. There he finds he can exercise his zeal almost only on behalf of schemers or rascals. The greeting that cities give to the idlers who come there to hunt their fortunes succeeds only in completing the devastation of the country which instead ought to be repopulated at the expense of the cities. All men who withdraw from the hub of society are useful precisely because they withdraw from it, since all its vices come from its being overpopulated. They are even more useful when they can bring life, cultivation, and the love of their first state to forsaken places. I am moved by contemplating how many benefactions Emile and Sophie can spread around them from their simple retreat, and how much they can vivify the country and reanimate the extinguished zeal of the unfortunate village folk. I believe I see the people multiplying, the fields being fertilized, the earth taking on a new adornment. The crowd and the abundance

transform work into festivals, and cries of joy and benedictions arise from the midst of the games which center on the lovable couple who brought them back to life. The golden age is treated as a chimera, and it will always be one for anyone whose heart and taste have been spoiled. It is not even true that people regret the golden age, since those regrets are always hollow. What, then, would be required to give it a new birth? One single but impossible thing: to love it.

"It seems to be already reborn around Sophie's dwelling. You will do no more than complete together what her worthy parents have begun. But, dear Emile, do not let so sweet a life make you regard painful duties with disgust, if such duties are ever imposed on you. Remember that the Romans went from the plow to the consulate. If the prince or the state calls you to the service of the fatherland, leave everything to go to fulfill the honorable function of citizen in the post assigned to you. If this function is onerous to you, there is a decent and sure means to free yourself from it—to fulfill it with enough integrity so that it will not be left to you for long. Besides, you need have little fear of being burdened with such a responsibility. As long as there are men who belong to the present age, you are not the man who will be sought out to serve the state."

Why am I not permitted to paint Emile's return to Sophie and the conclusion of their love or rather the beginning of the conjugal love which unites them—love founded on esteem which lasts as long as life, on virtues which do not fade with beauty, on suitability of character which makes association pleasant and prolongs the charm of the first union into old age? But all these details might be pleasing without being useful, and up to now I have permitted myself only those agreeable details which I believed were of some utility. Shall I abandon this rule at the end of my task? No; I also feel that my pen is weary. I am too weak for works requiring so much endurance and would abandon this one if it were less advanced. In order not to leave it imperfect, it is time for me to finish.

Finally I see dawning the most charming of Emile's days and the happiest of mine. I see my attentions consummated, and I begin to taste their fruit. An indissoluble chain unites the worthy couple. Their mouths pronounce and their hearts confirm vows which will not be vain. They are wed. In returning from the temple, they let themselves be led. They do not know where they are, where they are going, or what is done around them. They do not hear; they respond only with confused words; their clouded eyes no longer see anything. O delirium! O human weakness! The sentiment of happiness crushes man. He is not strong enough to bear it. . . .

chapter nineteen

Mary Wollstonecraft

Mary Wollstonecraft (1759–1797) ignored the conventions of her time and pursued the then "unfeminine" work of a philosopher and scholar, making her at one point "the most famous woman in England."[1] Her writings provided a unique analysis and critique of the philosophy of the time. Wollstonecraft's works both challenged thinkers of her time such as Edmund Burke and Jean-Jacques Rousseau and laid a foundation for thinkers such as Simone de Beauvoir.

Early on in her life, Wollstonecraft found dissatisfaction with her place as a woman in society. She was born in Spitalfields, outside of London. Her father was a tradesman, which situated her family in the lower middle class. Although her father was able to attempt farming after her grandfather left the family a substantial inheritance, he proved unsuccessful, and the family's social position slowly deteriorated. With her father struggling in a lifestyle for which he was unfit, and a mother who doted upon her brothers, Wollstonecraft was often neglected as a child, and by the time she was sixteen, she often left the house in search of places to read and study. Family friends who had a love of books provided her with the chance to read and expand her mind far beyond what the local school would have offered her. As a young woman, she turned away from the idea of marriage, though whether this was a principled stance or a form of self-protection—because she believed it would never be offered to her—is unclear. Braced by her conviction, she survived in the usual roles of the spinster: as a hired companion, needleworker, and teacher. Wollstonecraft was known for being an exceptionally strong, emotional woman, and her experience of rejection by men in her early years was repeated throughout her lifetime.

In 1783, Wollstonecraft helped her sister Eliza escape from an abusive marriage, and they, along with childhood friend Fanny Blood, moved to Newington Green to open a small shop. Soon they opened a school, where Wollstonecraft taught. What she learned from observing her young pupils provided her the impetus to write her work *On the Education of Daughters* in 1786,[2] a collection of essays regarding her experiences as a teacher. In Newington Green, Wollstonecraft also met the people who would shape her

from Mary Wollstonecraft, *A Vindication of the Rights of Woman*, with an introduction by Elizabeth Robins Pennell. London: Walter Scott, 1891.

future as a philosopher: Dr. Richard Price and Dr. Samuel Johnson, two prominent liberal thinkers. Both these men belonged to a school of thought known as *rational dissenters*. They rejected the idea of original sin and believed that rationality should be used as the basis for making moral decisions. From this connection to the Dissenters, Wollstonecraft began to form her idea of the relationship between rationality and virtue, which she would detail in *A Vindication of the Rights of Woman*. She also met Joseph Johnson, a publisher who was known to support liberal causes and would publish all of her work, including her first work, *Thoughts on the Education of Daughters* (1786). At this point in her writing, Wollstonecraft seemed torn between the thoughts of equality promoted by the Dissenters and the blatantly sexist school of Rousseau (whom she originally idolized). From 1786–1788 she traveled throughout Ireland as a governess but was later dismissed from service. Unsure of what to do, she returned to her friend Joseph Johnson, who published her first work of fiction, *Mary*, which some believe to be an autobiographical account of her life. Johnson, despite customs of the time, allowed Wollstonecraft to live with him rent free and set her up as a translator and reviewer.

In the late 1780s, Edmund Burke published *Reflections on the Revolution in France*, which contains direct criticism of Dr. Price and the views of the Dissenters as a whole. Angered by this attack, Wollstonecraft wrote *A Vindication of the Rights of Men*, which was published anonymously in 1790 and reissued with her name in 1791. Although the scholars of the time did not acknowledge the work, it was a huge public success, earning her the nickname "The Amazon."[3] When Thomas Paine's *Rights of Man* was published, Wollstonecraft's name was linked with his as a revolutionary. Fueled by her success, and goaded by works such as Rousseau's *Emile*, she published *A Vindication of the Rights of Woman*, her most important work.

Following this success Wollstonecraft engaged in an ultimately unsuccessful affair with American soldier Gilbert Imlay and had a daughter, leaving her in the uncomfortable position of unwed mother. The failure of the affair took a toll on her, and she suffered through a rough period in her life, twice attempting suicide. In 1796 she called upon an old acquaintance, William Godwin.[4] Wollstonecraft first met Godwin in London in 1791, though initially neither liked the other. This time, however, both met with mutual respect for the other's work and developed a friendship that eventually deepened. They became lovers and for a brief while engaged in a publicly known affair. For the first time, someone presented Wollstonecraft with the ideal relationship of which she had written—he was her friend and intellectual partner, respecting her as an equal. Early in the relationship, she became pregnant. Although Godwin had been well known for his writings against marriage, both he and Wollstonecraft set aside their views and wed. Tragically, in 1797, Mary Wollstonecraft died from complications of birth five days after delivering a daughter, Mary.[5]

A Vindication of the Rights of Woman is a philosophical treatise grounded in Wollstonecraft's personal experiences. It is unique in that it is the result purely of her independent thought; though some feminist writings were circulating throughout Europe, there is no evidence that she was aware of them before she wrote. While generally seen as a critique of Rousseau's *Emile*, Wollstonecraft understood the work as a kind of corrective to it. She states, "Women, I allow, might have different duties to fulfill, but they are *human* duties, and the principles that should regulate the discharge of them, I sturdily maintain, must be the same."[6] She does not seek to disprove the philosophies of Rousseau and his followers (such as Dr. Gregory), but rather to extend the masculine conception of virtue to all of humanity by showing where and how their inconsistencies in the treatment of the sexes weaken the argument as a whole. Her goal is to see education in terms of *human* education, and in order to do this one must look at the virtues education strives to impart as *human* virtues. In this respect Wollstonecraft's work can be seen the foundation for thinkers such as Beauvoir.

Although Wollstonecraft had little formal education and her writing was at times unpolished, it left a deep mark on both the philosophical and the social world. Wollstonecraft challenged the structure of society not only through her writing, but through the way she lived her life. Although she found considerable recognition in the largely masculine world of ideas, she was always haunted by her failure to satisfy the conventional ideals of womanhood—the societal beliefs with which she had been raised. This internal struggle nearly destroyed her, but through courage and strength, she was able to turn that struggle outward and analyze it from a previously unseen angle. Her work not only looks at economic and political inequalities, but creates cracks in the social institutions used to create a sense of value and self-worth in all of humanity.

BH

QUESTIONS

1. How does Wollstonecraft's analysis of military men highlight her conceptions of virtue?
2. What is Wollstonecraft's critique of Rousseau?
3. What societal changes does Wollstonecraft propose?

ENDNOTES

1. Attributed to Godwin, her longtime friend and eventual husband.
2. See Eleanor Flexner, *Mary Wollstonecraft, a Biography*.
3. See Claire Tomalin, *The Life and Death of Mary Wollstonecraft*.
4. William Godwin was himself a philosopher. In *Political Justice*, the work that made him famous, he examines humans as developmental beings, influenced mainly by education and the state. He notes the problems of economic inequality, citing private property as the most glaring manifestation of this, and believed that individual liberty must be the cornerstone for society, to the point of supporting anarchy. In Eleanor Flexner, *Mary Wollstonecraft, a Biography*.

5. Mary Godwin would eventually marry the poet, Percy Bysshe Shelley, and author the classic tale, *Frankenstein's Monster* (1818).

6. See Ulrich Hardt, *A Critical Edition of Mary Wollstonecraft's A Vindication of the Right of Woman: With Strictures on Political and Moral Subjects*.

SELECTED BIBLIOGRAPHY

Flexner, Eleanor. *Mary Wollstonecraft, a Biography*. New York, N.Y.: Coward, McCann, and Geoghegan, 1972.

Hardt, Ulrich. *A Critical Edition of Mary Wollstonecraft's A Vindication of the Rights of Woman: With Strictures on Political and Moral Subjects*. Troy, N.Y.: Whitston Publishing, 1982.

Tomalin, Claire. *The Life and Death of Mary Wollstonecraft*. New York, N.Y.: Penguin, 1992.

Wollstonecraft, Mary. *A Vindication of the Rights of Woman*, with an introduction by Elizabeth Robins Pennell. London: Walter Scott, 1891.

from *A Vindication of the Rights of Woman*

Mary Wollstonecraft

AUTHOR'S INTRODUCTION

After considering the historic page, and viewing the living world with anxious solicitude, the most melancholy emotions of sorrowful indignation have depressed my spirits, and I have sighed when obliged to confess that either Nature has made a great difference between man and man, or that the civilization which has hitherto taken place in the world has been very partial. I have turned over various books written on the subject of education, and patiently observed the conduct of parents and the management of schools; but what has been the result?—a profound conviction that the neglected education of my fellow-creatures is the grand source of the misery I deplore, and that women, in particular, are rendered weak and wretched by a variety of concurring causes, originating from one hasty conclusion. The conduct and manners of women, in fact, evidently prove that their minds are not in a healthy state; for, like the flowers which are planted in too rich a soil, strength and usefulness are sacrificed to beauty; and the flaunting leaves, after having pleased a fastidious eye, fade, disregarded on the stalk, long before the season when they ought to have arrived at maturity. One cause of this barren blooming I attribute to a false system of education, gathered from the books written on this subject by men who, considering females rather as women than human creatures, have been more anxious to make them alluring mistresses than affectionate wives and rational mothers; and the understanding of the sex has been so bubbled by this specious homage, that the civilized women of the present century, with a few exceptions, are only anxious to inspire love, when they ought to cherish a nobler ambition, and by their abilities and virtues exact respect. . . .

I am aware of an obvious inference. From every quarter have I heard exclamations against masculine women, but where are they to be found? If by this appellation men mean to inveigh against their ardour in hunting, shooting, and gaming, I shall most cordially join in the cry; but if it be against the imitation of manly virtues, or, more properly speaking, the attainment of those talents and virtues, the exercise of which ennobles the human character, and which raises females in the scale of animal being, when they are comprehensively termed mankind, all those who view them with a philosophic eye must, I should think, wish with me, that they may every day grow more and more masculine.

This discussion naturally divides the subject. I shall first consider women in the grand light of human creatures, who, in common with men, are placed on this earth to unfold their faculties; and afterwards I shall more particularly point out their peculiar designation. . . .

My own sex, I hope, will excuse me, if I treat them like rational creatures, instead of flattering their *fascinating* graces, and viewing them as if they were in a state of perpetual childhood, unable to stand alone. I earnestly wish to point out in what true dignity and human happiness consists. I wish to persuade women to endeavour to acquire strength, both of mind and body, and to convince them that the soft phrases, susceptibility of heart, delicacy of sentiment, and refinement of taste, are almost synonymous with epithets of weakness, and that those beings who are only the objects of pity, and that kind of love which has been termed its sister, will soon become objects of contempt. . . .

Women are, in fact, so much degraded by mistaken notions of female excellence, that I do not mean to add a paradox when I assert that this artificial weakness produces a propensity to tyrannize, and gives birth to cunning, the natural opponent of strength, which leads them to play off those contemptible infantine airs that undermine esteem even whilst they excite desire. Let men become more chaste and modest, and if women do not grow wiser in the same ratio it will be clear that they have weaker understandings. It seems scarcely necessary to say that I now speak of the sex in general. Many individuals have more sense than their male relatives; and, as nothing preponderates where there is a constant struggle for an equilibrium without it has naturally more gravity, some women govern their husbands without degrading themselves, because intellect will always govern.

In the present state of society it appears necessary to go back to first principles in search of the most simple truths, and to dispute with some prevailing prejudice every inch of ground. To clear my way, I must be allowed to ask some plain questions, and the answers will probably appear as unequivocal as the axioms on which reasoning is built; though, when entangled with various motives of action, they are formally contradicted, either by the words or conduct of men.

In what does man's pre-eminence over the brute creation consist? The answer is as clear as that a half is less than the whole, in Reason.

What acquirement exalts one being above another? Virtue, we spontaneously reply.

For what purpose were the passions implanted? That man by struggling with them might attain a degree of knowledge denied to the brutes, whispers Experience.

Consequently the perfection of our nature and capability of happiness must be estimated by the degree of reason, virtue, and knowledge, that distinguish the individual, and direct the laws which bind society: and that from the exercise of reason, knowledge and virtue naturally flow, is equally undeniable, if mankind be viewed collectively. . . .

The most perfect education, in my opinion, is such an exercise of the understanding as is best calculated to strengthen the body and form the heart. Or, in other words, to enable the individual to attain such habits of virtue as will render it independent. In fact, it is a farce to call any being virtuous whose virtues do not result from the exercise of its own reason. This was Rousseau's opinion respecting men; I extend it to women, and confidently assert that they have been drawn out of their sphere by false refinement, and not by an endeavour to acquire masculine qualities. Still the regal homage which they receive is so intoxicating, that until the manners of the times are changed, and formed on more reasonable principles, it may be impossible to convince them that the illegitimate power which they obtain by degrading themselves is a curse, and that they must return to nature and equality if they wish to secure the placid satisfaction that unsophisticated affections impart. But for this epoch we must wait—wait perhaps till kings and nobles, enlightened by reason, and, preferring the real dignity of man to childish state, throw off their gaudy hereditary trappings; and if then women do not resign the arbitrary power of beauty—they will prove that they have *less* mind than man.

I may be accused of arrogance; still I must declare what I firmly believe, that all the writers who have written on the subject of female education and manners, from Rousseau to Dr Gregory,* have contributed to render women more artificial, weak characters, than they would otherwise have been; and consequently, more useless members of society. I might have expressed this conviction in a lower key, but I am afraid it would have been the whine of affectation, and not the faithful expression of my feelings of the clear result which experience and reflection have led me to draw. When I come to that division of the subject, I shall advert to the passages that I more particularly disapprove of, in the works of the authors I have just alluded to; but it is first necessary to observe that my objection extends to the whole purport of those

books, which tend, in my opinion, to degrade one-half of the human species, and render women pleasing at the expense of every solid virtue.

Though, to reason on Rousseau's ground, if man did attain a degree of perfection of mind when his body arrived at maturity, it might be proper, in order to make a man and his wife *one*, that she should rely entirely on his understanding; and the graceful ivy, clasping the oak that supported it, would form a whole in which strength and beauty would be equally conspicuous. But, alas! husbands, as well as their helpmates, are often only overgrown children,—nay, thanks to early debauchery, scarcely men in their outward form,—and if the blind lead the blind, one need not come from heaven to tell us the consequence.

Many are the causes that, in the present corrupt state of society, contribute to enslave women by cramping their understandings and sharpening their senses. One, perhaps, that silently does more mischief than all the rest, is their disregard of order.

To do everything in an orderly manner is a most important precept, which women, who, generally speaking, receive only a disorderly kind of education, seldom attend to with that degree of exactness that men, who from their infancy are broken into method, observe. This negligent kind of guess-work—for what other epithet can be used to point out the random exertions of a sort of instinctive common sense never brought to the test of reason?—prevents their generalizing matters of fact; so they do today what they did yesterday, merely because they did it yesterday.

This contempt of the understanding in early life has more baneful consequences than is commonly supposed; for the little knowledge which women of strong minds attain is, from various circumstances, of a more desultory kind than the knowledge of men, and it is acquired more by sheer observations on real life than from comparing

---

*John Gregory (1724–1773), physician and author of *A Father's Legacy to his Daughters* (1774), one of the most popular treatises on female education.

what has been individually observed with the results of experience generalized by speculation. Led by their dependent situation and domestic employments more into society, what they learn is rather by snatches; and as learning is with them in general only a secondary thing, they do not pursue any one branch with that persevering ardour necessary to give vigour to the faculties and clearness to the judgement. In the present state of society a little learning is required to support the character of a gentleman, and boys are obliged to submit to a few years of discipline. But in the education of women, the cultivation of the understanding is always subordinate to the acquirement of some corporeal accomplishment. Even when enervated by confinement and false notions of modesty, the body is prevented from attaining that grace and beauty which relaxed half-formed limbs never exhibit. Besides, in youth, their faculties are not brought forward by emulation; and having no serious scientific study, if they have natural sagacity, it is turned too soon on life and manners. They dwell on effects and modifications, without tracing them back to causes; and complicated rules to adjust behaviour are a weak substitute for simple principles.

As a proof that education gives this appearance of weakness to females, we may instance the example of military men, who are, like them, sent into the world before their minds have been stored with knowledge, or fortified by principles. The consequences are similar; soldiers acquire a little superficial knowledge, snatched from the muddy current of conversation, and from continually mixing with society, they gain what is termed a knowledge of the world; and this acquaintance with manners and customs has frequently been confounded with a knowledge of the human heart. But can the crude fruit of casual observation, never brought to the test of judgement, formed by comparing speculation and experience, deserve such a distinction? Soldiers, as well as women, practise the minor

virtues with punctilious politeness. Where is then the sexual difference, when the education has been the same? All the difference that I can discern arises from the superior advantage of liberty which enables the former to see more of life.

It is wandering from my present subject, perhaps, to make a political remark; but as it was produced naturally by the train of my reflections, I shall not pass it silently over.

Standing armies can never consist of resolute robust men; they may be well-disciplined machines, but they will seldom contain men under the influence of strong passions, or with very vigorous faculties; and as for any depth of understanding, I will venture to affirm that it is as rarely to be found in the army as amongst women. And the cause, I maintain, is the same. It may be further observed that officers are also particularly attentive to their persons, fond of dancing, crowded rooms, adventures, and ridicule.[1] Like the *fair* sex, the business of their lives is gallantry; they were taught to please, and they only live to please. Yet they do not lose their rank in the distinction of sexes, for they are still reckoned superior to women, though in what their superiority consists, beyond what I have just mentioned, it is difficult to discover.

The great misfortune is this, that they both acquire manners before morals, and a knowledge of life before they have from reflection any acquaintance with the grand ideal outline of human nature. The consequence is natural. Satisfied with common nature, they become a prey to prejudices, and taking all their opinions on credit, they blindly submit to authority. So that if they have any sense, it is a kind of instinctive glance that catches proportions, and decides with respect to

---

[1]Why should women be censured with petulant acrimony because they seem to have a passion for a scarlet coat? Has not education placed them more on a level with soldiers than any other class of men?

manners, but fails when arguments are to be pursued below the surface, or opinions analysed.

May not the same remark be applied to women? Nay, the argument may be carried still further, for they are both thrown out of a useful station by the unnatural distinctions established in civilized life. Riches and hereditary honours have made cyphers of women to give consequence to the numerical figure; and idleness has produced a mixture of gallantry and despotism into society, which leads the very men who are the slaves of their mistresses to tyrannize over their sisters, wives, and daughters. This is only keeping them in rank and file, it is true. Strengthen the female mind by enlarging it, and there will be an end to blind obedience; but as blind obedience is ever sought for by power, tyrants and sensualists are in the right when they endeavour to keep woman in the dark, because the former only want slaves, and the latter a plaything. The sensualist, indeed, has been the most dangerous of tyrants, and women have been duped by their lovers, as princes by their ministers, whilst dreaming that they reigned over them.

I now principally allude to Rousseau, for his character of Sophia is undoubtedly a captivating one, though it appears to me grossly unnatural. However, it is not the superstructure, but the foundation of her character, the principles on which her education was built, that I mean to attack; nay, warmly as I admire the genius of that able writer, whose opinions I shall often have occasion to cite, indignation always takes place of admiration, and the rigid frown of insulted virtue effaces the smile of complacency which his eloquent periods are wont to raise when I read his voluptuous reveries. Is this the man who, in his ardour for virtue, would banish all the soft arts of peace, and almost carry us back to Spartan discipline? Is this the man who delights to paint the useful struggles of passion, the triumphs of good dispositions, and the heroic flights which carry the glowing soul out of itself? How are these mighty sentiments lowered when he describes the pretty foot and enticing airs of his little favourite! But for the present I waive the subject, and instead of severely reprehending the transient effusions of overweening sensibility, I shall only observe that whoever has cast a benevolent eye on society must often have been gratified by the sight of humble mutual love not dignified by sentiment, or strengthened by a union in intellectual pursuits. The domestic trifles of the day have afforded matters for cheerful converse, and innocent caresses have softened toils which did not require great exercise of mind or stretch of thought; yet has not the sight of this moderate felicity excited more tenderness than respect?—an emotion similar to what we feel when children are playing or animals sporting[2]; whilst the contemplation of the noble struggles of suffering merit has raised admiration, and carried our thoughts to that world where sensation will give place to reason.

Women are therefore to be considered either as moral beings, or so weak that they must be entirely subjected to the superior faculties of men.

Let us examine this question. Rousseau declares that a woman should never for a moment feel herself independent, that she should be governed by fear to exercise her *natural* cunning, and made a coquettish slave in order to render her a more alluring object of desire, a *sweeter* companion to man, whenever he chose to relax himself. He carries the arguments, which he pretends to draw

---

[2]Similar feelings has Milton's pleasing picture of paradisiacal happiness ever raised in my mind; yet, instead of envying the lovely pair, I have with conscious dignity or satanic pride turned to hell for sublimer objects. In the same style, when viewing some noble monument of human art, I have traced the emanation of the Deity in the order I admired, till, descending from that giddy height, I have caught myself contemplating the grandest of all human sights; for fancy quickly placed in some solitary recess an outcast of fortune, rising superior to passion and discontent.

from the indications of nature, still further, and insinuates that truth and fortitude, the corner-stones of all human virtue, should be cultivated with certain restrictions, because, with respect to the female character, obedience is the grand lesson which ought to be impressed with unrelenting rigour.

What nonsense! When will a great man arise with sufficient strength of mind to puff away the fumes which pride and sensuality have thus spread over the subject? If women are by nature inferior to men, their virtues must be the same in quality, if not in degree, or virtue is a relative idea; consequently their conduct should be founded on the same principles, and have the same aim.

Connected with man as daughters, wives, and mothers, their moral character may be estimated by their manner of fulfilling those simple duties; but the end, the grand end, of their exertions should be to unfold their own faculties, and acquire the dignity of conscious virtue. They may try to render their road pleasant; but ought never to forget, in common with man, that life yields not the felicity which can satisfy an immortal soul. I do not mean to insinuate that either sex should be so lost in abstract reflections or distant views as to forget the affections and duties that lie before them, and are, in truth, the means appointed to produce the fruit of life; on the contrary, I would warmly recommend them, even while I assert that they afford most satisfaction when they are considered in their true sober light.

Probably the prevailing opinion that woman was created for man, may have taken its rise from Moses' poetical story; yet as very few, it is presumed, who have bestowed any serious thought on the subject ever supposed that Eve was, literally speaking, one of Adam's ribs, the deduction must be allowed to fall to the ground, or only be so far admitted as it proves that man, from the remotest antiquity, found it convenient to exert his strength to subjugate his companion, and his invention to show that she ought to have her neck bent under the yoke, because the whole creation was only created for his convenience or pleasure.

Let it not be concluded that I wish to invert the order of things. I have already granted that, from the constitution of their bodies, men seemed to be designed by Providence to attain a greater degree of virtue. I speak collectively of the whole sex; but I see not the shadow of a reason to conclude that their virtues should differ in respect to their nature. In fact, how can they, if virtue has only one eternal standard? I must therefore, if I reason consequentially, as strenuously maintain that they have the same simple direction as that there is a God.

It follows then that cunning should not be opposed to wisdom, little cares to great exertions, or insipid softness, varnished over with the name of gentleness, to that fortitude which grand views alone can inspire.

I shall be told that woman would then lose many of her peculiar graces, and the opinion of a well-known poet might be quoted to refute my unqualified assertion. For Pope has said, in the name of the whole male sex:

Yet ne'er so sure our passion to create,
As when she touch'd the brink of all we hate.

In what light this sally places men and women I shall leave to the judicious to determine. Meanwhile, I shall content myself with observing, that I cannot discover why, unless they are mortal, females should always be degraded by being made subservient to love or lust.

To speak disrespectfully of love is, I know, high treason against sentiment and fine feelings; but I wish to speak the simple language of truth, and rather to address the head than the heart. To endeavour to reason love out of the world would be to out-Quixote Cervantes, and equally offend against common sense; but an endeavour to restrain this tumultuous passion, and to prove that it should not be allowed to dethrone superior powers, or to usurp the sceptre which the understanding should ever coolly wield, appears less wild.

Youth is the season for love in both sexes; but in those days of thoughtless enjoyment provision should be made for the more important years of life, when reflection takes place of sensation. But Rousseau, and most of the male writers who have followed his steps, have warmly indicated that the whole tendency of female education ought to be directed to one point—to render them pleasing.

Let me reason with the supporters of this opinion who have any knowledge of human nature. Do they imagine that marriage can eradicate the habitude of life? The woman who has only been taught to please will soon find that her charms are oblique sunbeams, and that they cannot have much effect on her husband's heart when they are seen every day, when the summer is passed and gone. Will she then have sufficient native energy to look into herself for comfort, and cultivate her dormant faculties? or is it not more rational to expect that she will try to please other men, and, in the emotions raised by the experience of new conquests, endeavour to forget the mortification her love or pride has received? When the husband ceases to be a lover, and the time will inevitably come, her desire of pleasing will then grow languid, or become a spring of bitterness; and love, perhaps, the most evanescent of all passions, gives place to jealousy or vanity.

I now speak of women who are restrained by principle or prejudice. Such women, though they would shrink from an intrigue with real abhorrence, yet, nevertheless, wish to be convinced by the homage of gallantry that they are cruelly neglected by their husbands; or, days and weeks are spent in dreaming of the happiness enjoyed by congenial souls, till their health is undermined and their spirits broken by discontent. How then can the great art of pleasing be such a necessary study? it is only useful to a mistress. The chaste wife and serious mother should only consider her power to please as the polish of her virtues, and the affection of her husband as one of the comforts that render her task less difficult, and her life happier. But, whether she be loved or neglected, her first wish should be to make herself respectable, and not to rely for all her happiness on a being subject to like infirmities with herself.

The worthy Dr Gregory fell into a similar error. I respect his heart, but entirely disapprove of his celebrated *Legacy to his Daughters*.

He advises them to cultivate a fondness for dress, because a fondness for dress, he asserts, is natural to them. I am unable to comprehend what either he or Rousseau mean when they frequently use this indefinite term. If they told us that in a pre-existent state the soul was fond of dress, and brought this inclination with it into a new body, I should listen to them with a half-smile, as I often do when I hear a rant about innate elegance. But if he only meant to say that the exercise of the faculties will produce this fondness, I deny it. It is not natural; but arises, like false ambition in men, from a love of power.

Dr Gregory goes much further; he actually recommends dissimulation, and advises an innocent girl to give the lie to her feelings, and not dance with spirit, when gaiety of heart would make her feet eloquent without making her gestures immodest. In the name of truth and common sense, why should not one woman acknowledge that she can take more exercise than another? or, in other words, that she has a sound constitution; and why, to damp innocent vivacity, is she darkly to be told that men will draw conclusions which she little thinks of? Let the libertine draw what inference he pleases; but, I hope, that no sensible mother will restrain the natural frankness of youth by instilling such indecent cautions. Out of the abundance of the heart the mouth speaketh; and a wiser than Solomon hath said that the heart should be made clean, and not trivial ceremonies observed, which it is not very difficult to fulfil with scrupulous exactness when vice reigns in the heart.

Women ought to endeavour to purify their hearts; but can they do so when their uncultivated understandings make them entirely dependent on their senses for employment and amusement, when no noble pursuits set them above the little vanities of the day, or enable them to curb the wild emotions that agitate a reed, over which every passing breeze has power? To gain the affections of a virtuous man, is affectation necessary? Nature has given woman a weaker frame than man; but, to ensure her husband's affections, must a wife, who, by the exercise of her mind and body whilst she was discharging the duties of a daughter, wife, and mother, has allowed her constitution to retain its natural strength, and her nerves a healthy tone,—is she, I say, to condescend to use art, and feign a sickly delicacy, in order to secure her husband's affection? Weakness may excite tenderness, and gratify the arrogant pride of man; but the lordly caresses of a protector will not gratify a noble mind that pants for and deserves to be respected. Fondness is a poor substitute for friendship!

In a seraglio, I grant, that all these arts are necessary; the epicure must have his palate tickled, or he will sink into apathy; but have women so little ambition as to be satisfied with such a condition? Can they supinely dream life away in the lap of pleasure, or the languor of weariness, rather than assert their claim to pursue reasonable pleasures, and render themselves conspicuous by practising the virtues which dignify mankind? Surely she has not an immortal soul who can loiter life away merely employed to adorn her person, that she may amuse the languid hours, and soften the cares of a fellow-creature who is willing to be enlivened by her smiles and tricks, when the serious business of life is over.

Besides, the woman who strengthens her body and exercises her mind will, by managing her family and practising various virtues, become the friend, and not the humble dependent of her husband; and if she, by possessing such substantial qualities, merit his regard, she will not find it necessary to conceal her affection, nor to pretend to an unnatural coldness of constitution to excite her husband's passions. In fact, if we revert to history, we shall find that the women who have distinguished themselves have neither been the most beautiful nor the most gentle of their sex.

Nature, or, to speak with strict propriety, God, has made all things right; but man has sought him out many inventions to mar the work. I now allude to that part of Dr Gregory's treatise, where he advises a wife never to let her husband know the extent of her sensibility or affection. Voluptuous precaution, and as ineffectual as absurd. Love, from its very nature, must be transitory. To seek for a secret that would render it constant, would be as wild a search as for the philosopher's stone, or the grand panacea; and the discovery would be equally useless, or rather pernicious, to mankind. The most holy band of society is friendship. It has been well said, by a shrewd satirist, 'that rare as true love is, true friendship is still rarer.'

This is an obvious truth, and, the cause not lying deep, will not elude a slight glance of inquiry.

Love, the common passion, in which chance and sensation take place of choice and reason, is, in some degree, felt by the mass of mankind; for it is not necessary to speak, at present, of the emotions that rise above or sink below love. This passion, naturally increased by suspense and difficulties, draws the mind out of its accustomed state, and exalts the affections; but the security of marriage, allowing the fever of love to subside, a healthy temperature is thought insipid only by those who have not sufficient intellect to substitute the calm tenderness of friendship, the confidence of respect, instead of blind admiration, and the sensual emotions of fondness.

This is, must be, the course of nature. Friendship or indifference inevitably succeeds love. And this constitution seems perfectly to harmonize with the system of government which prevails in the moral world. Passions are spurs to action, and open the mind; but they sink into mere appetites, become a personal and momentary gratification when the object is gained, and the satisfied mind rests in enjoyment. . . .

Noble morality! and consistent with the cautious prudence of a little soul that cannot extend its views beyond the present minute division of existence. If all the faculties of woman's mind are only to be cultivated as they respect her dependence on man; if, when a husband be obtained, she have arrived at her goal, and meanly proud, rests satisfied with such a paltry crown, let her grovel contentedly, scarcely raised by her employments above the animal kingdom; but, if struggling for the prize of her high calling, she look beyond the present scene, let her cultivate her understanding without stopping to consider what character the husband may have whom she is destined to marry. Let her only determine, without being too anxious about present happiness, to acquire the qualities that ennoble a rational being, and a rough inelegant husband may shock her taste without destroying her peace of mind. She will not model her soul to suit the frailties of her companion, but to bear with them; his character may be a trial, but not an impediment to virtue. . . .

I own it frequently happens, that women who have fostered a romantic unnatural delicacy of feeling, waste their lives in *imagining* how happy they should have been with a husband who could love them with a fervid increasing affection every day,

and all day. But they might as well pine married as single, and would not be a jot more unhappy with a bad husband than longing for a good one. That a proper education, or, to speak with more precision, a well-stored mind, would enable a woman to support a single life with dignity, I grant; but that she should avoid cultivating her taste, lest her husband should occasionally shock it, is quitting a substance for a shadow. To say the truth, I do not know of what use is an improved taste, if the individual be not rendered more independent of the casualties of life; if new sources of enjoyment, only dependent on the solitary operations of the mind, are not opened. People of taste, married or single, without distinction, will ever be disgusted by various things that touch not less observing minds. On this conclusion the argument must not be allowed to hinge; but in the whole sum of enjoyment is taste to be denominated a blessing?

The question is, whether it procures most pain or pleasure? The answer will decide the propriety of Dr Gregory's advice, and show how absurd and tyrannic it is thus to lay down a system of slavery, or to attempt to educate moral beings by any other rules than those deduced from pure reason, which apply to the whole species.

Gentleness of manners, forbearance and long suffering, are such amiable Godlike qualities, that in sublime poetic strains the Deity has been invested with them; and, perhaps, no representation of His goodness so strongly fastens on the human affections as those that represent Him abundant in mercy and willing to pardon. Gentleness, considered in this point of view, bears on its front all the characteristics of grandeur, combined with the winning graces of condescension; but what a different aspect it assumes when it is the submissive demeanour of dependence, the support of weakness that loves, because it wants protection; and is forbearing, because it must silently endure injuries; smiling under the lash at which it dare not snarl.

Abject as this picture appears, it is the portrait of an accomplished woman, according to the received opinion of female excellence, separated by specious reasoners from human excellence. Or, they[3] kindly restore the rib, and make one moral being of a man and woman; not forgetting to give her all the 'submissive charms'.

How women are to exist in that state where there is neither to be marrying nor giving in marriage, we are not told. For though moralists have agreed that the tenor of life seems to prove that *man* is prepared by various circumstances for a future state, they constantly concur in advising *woman* only to provide for the present. Gentleness, docility, and a spaniel-like affection are, on this ground, consistently recommended as the cardinal virtues of the sex; and, disregarding the arbitrary economy of nature, one writer has declared that it is masculine for a woman to be melancholy. She was created to be the toy of man, his rattle, and it must jingle in his ears whenever, dismissing reason, he chooses to be amused.

To recommend gentleness, indeed, on a broad basis is strictly philosophical. A frail being should labour to be gentle. But when forbearance confounds right and wrong, it ceases to be a virtue; and, however convenient it may be found in a companion—that companion will ever be considered as an inferior, and only inspire a vapid tenderness, which easily degenerates into contempt. Still, if advice could really make a being gentle, whose natural disposition admitted not of such a fine polish, something towards the advancement of order would be attained; but if, as might quickly be demonstrated, only affection be produced by this indiscriminate counsel, which throws a stumbling-block in the way of gradual improvement, and true melioration of temper, the sex is not much benefited by sacrificing solid virtues to the attainment

---

[3]*Vide* Rousseau and Swedenborg.

of superficial graces, though for a few years they may procure the individuals regal sway.

As a philosopher, I read with indignation the plausible epithets which men use to soften their insults; and, as a moralist, I ask what is meant by such heterogeneous associations, as fair defects, amiable weaknesses, etc.? If there be but one criterion of morals, but one architype for man, women appear to be suspended by destiny, according to the vulgar tale of Mahomet's coffin; they have neither the unerring instinct of brutes, nor are allowed to fix the eye of reason on a perfect model. They were made to be loved, and must not aim at respect, lest they should be hunted out of society as masculine. . . .

But avoiding, as I have hitherto done, any direct comparison of the two sexes collectively, or frankly acknowledging the inferiority of woman, according to the present appearance of things, I shall only insist that men have increased that inferiority till women are almost sunk below the standard of rational creatures. Let their faculties have room to unfold, and their virtues to gain strength, and then determine where the whole sex must stand in the intellectual scale. Yet let it be remembered that for a small number of distinguished women I do not ask a place. . . .

If, I say, for I would not impress by declamation when Reason offers her sober light, if they be really capable of acting like rational creatures, let them not be treated like slaves; or, like the brutes who are dependent on the reason of man, when they associate with him; but cultivate their minds, give them the salutary sublime curb of principle, and let them attain conscious dignity by feeling themselves only dependent on God. Teach them, in common with man, to submit to necessity, instead of giving, to render them more pleasing, a sex to morals.

Further, should experience prove that they cannot attain the same degree of strength of mind, perseverance, and fortitude, let their virtues be the same in kind, though they may vainly struggle for the same degree; and the superiority of man will be equally clear, if not clearer; and truth, as it is a simple principle, which admits of no modification, would be common to both. Nay the order of society, as it is at present regulated, would not be inverted, for woman would then only have the rank that reason assigned her, and arts could not be practised to bring the balance even, much less to turn it.

These may be termed Utopian dreams. Thanks to that Being who impressed them on my soul, and gave me sufficient strength of mind to dare to exert my own reason, till, becoming dependent only on Him for the support of my virtue, I view, with indignation, the mistaken notions that enslave my sex.

I love man as my fellow; but his sceptre, real or usurped, extends not to me, unless the reason of an individual demands my homage; and even then the submission is to reason, and not to man. In fact, the conduct of an accountable being must be regulated by the operations of its own reason; or on what foundation rests the throne of God?

It appears to me necessary to dwell on these obvious truths, because females have been insulated, as it were; and while they have been stripped of the virtues that should clothe humanity, they have been decked with artificial graces that enable them to exercise a short-lived tyranny. Love, in their bosoms, taking place of every nobler passion, their sole ambition is to be fair, to raise emotion instead of inspiring respect; and this ignoble desire, like the servility in absolute monarchies, destroys all strength of character. Liberty is the mother of virtue, and if women be, by their very constitution, slaves, and not allowed to breathe the sharp invigorating air of freedom, they must ever languish like exotics, and be reckoned beautiful flaws

in nature. Let it also be remembered, that they are the only flaw.

As to the argument respecting the subjection in which the sex has ever been held, it retorts on man. The many have always been enthralled by the few; and monsters, who scarcely have shown any discernment of human excellence, have tyrannized over thousands of their fellow-creatures. Why have men of superior endowments submitted to such degradation? For, is it not universally acknowledged that kings, viewed collectively, have ever been inferior, in abilities and virtue, to the same number of men taken from the common mass of mankind—yet have they not, and are they not still treated with a degree of reverence that is an insult to reason? China is not the only country where a living man has been made a God. *Men* have submitted to superior strength to enjoy with impunity the pleasure of the moment; *women* have only done the same, and therefore till it is proved that the courtier, who servilely resigns the birthright of a man, is not a moral agent, it cannot be demonstrated that woman is essentially inferior to man because she has always been subjugated. . . .

Bodily strength from being the distinction of heroes is now sunk into such unmerited contempt that men, as well as women, seem to think it unnecessary; the latter, as it takes from their feminine graces, and from that lovely weakness, the source of their undue power; and the former, because it appears inimical to the character of a gentleman. . . .

I will allow that bodily strength seems to give man a natural superiority over woman; and this is the only solid basis on which the superiority of the sex can be built. But I still insist that not only the virtue but the *knowledge* of the two sexes should be the same in nature, if not in degree, and that women, considered not only as moral but rational creatures, ought to endeavour to acquire human virtues (or perfections) by the *same* means as men, instead of being educated like a fanciful kind of *half* being—one of Rousseau's wild chimeras.[4] . . .

But if strength of body be with some show of reason the boast of men, why are women so infatu-ated as to be proud of a defect? Rousseau has fur-nished them with a plausible excuse, which could only have occurred to a man whose imagination had been allowed to run wild, and refine on the impressions made by exquisite senses; that they might forsooth have a pretext for yielding to a nat-ural appetite without violating a romantic species of modesty, which gratifies the pride and libertin-ism of man.

Women, deluded by these sentiments, some-times boast of their weakness, cunningly obtaining power by playing on the *weakness* of men; and they may well glory in their illicit sway, for, like Turkish bashaws, they have more real power than their masters; but virtue is sacrificed to temporary grati-fications, and the respectability of life to the tri-umph of an hour.

But should it be proved that woman is naturally weaker than man, whence does it follow that it is natural for her to labour to become still weaker than nature intended her to be? Arguments of this cast are an insult to common sense, and savour of passion. The *divine right* of husbands, like the di-vine right of kings, may, it is to be hoped, in this enlightened age, be contested without danger; and though conviction may not silence many boister-ous disputants, yet, when any prevailing prejudice is attacked, the wise will consider, and leave the narrow-minded to rail with thoughtless vehemence at innovation. . . .

I have, probably, had an opportunity of observ-ing more girls in their infancy than J. J. Rousseau. I can recollect my own feelings, and I have looked

---

[4] Researches into abstract and speculative truths, the principles and axioms of sciences—in short, everything which tends to generalize our ideas—is not the proper province of women; their studies should be relative to points of practice; it belongs to them to apply those principles which men have discovered; and it is their part to make observations which direct men to the establishment of general principles. All the ideas of women, which have not the immediate tendency to points of duty, should be directed to the study of men, and to the at-tainment of those agreeable accomplishments which have taste for their object; for as to works of genius, they are beyond their capacity; neither have they sufficient precision or power of attention to succeed in sciences which require accuracy; and as to physical knowledge, it belongs to those only who are most active, most inquisitive, who comprehend the greatest variety of objects; in short, it belongs to those who have the strongest powers, and who exercise them most, to judge of the relations between sensible beings and the laws of nature. A woman who is naturally weak, and does not carry her ideas to any great extent, knows how to judge and make a proper esti-mate of those movements which she sets to work, in order to aid her weakness; and these movements are the passions of men. The mechanism she employs is much more powerful than ours, for all her levers move the human heart. She must have the skill to incline us to do everything which her sex will not enable her to do herself, and which is necessary or agree-able to her; therefore she ought to study the mind of man thoroughly, not the mind of man in general, abstractedly, but the dispositions of those men to whom she is subject either by the laws of her country or by the force of opinion. She should learn to penetrate into the real sentiments from their conver-sation, their actions, their looks and gestures. She should also have the art, by her own conversation, actions, looks, and ges-tures, to communicate those sentiments which are agreeable to them, without seeming to intend it. Men will argue more philosophically about the human heart; but women will read the heart of men better than they. It belongs to women—if I may be allowed the expression—to form an experimental morality, and to reduce the study of man to a system. Women have most wit, men have most genius; women observe, men reason. From the concurrence of both we derive the clearest light and the most perfect knowledge which the human mind is of itself capable of attaining. In one word, from hence we acquire the most intimate acquaintance, both with ourselves and others, of which our nature is capable; and it is thus that art has a constant tendency to perfect those endowments which nature has bestowed. The world is the book of women.'—ROUSSEAU's *Emilius*.

I hope my readers still remember the comparison which I have brought forward between women and officers.

steadily around me; yet, so far from coinciding with him in opinion respecting the first dawn of the female character, I will venture to affirm, that a girl, whose spirits have not been damped by inactivity, or innocence tainted by false shame, will always be a romp, and the doll will never excite attention unless confinement allows her no alternative. Girls and boys, in short, would play harmlessly together, if the distinction of sex was not inculcated long before nature makes any difference. I will go further, and affirm, as an indisputable fact, that most of the women, in the circle of my observation, who have acted like rational creatures, or shown any vigour of intellect, have accidentally been allowed to run wild, as some of the elegant formers of the fair sex would insinuate. . . .

Women are everywhere in this deplorable state; for, in order to preserve their innocence, as ignorance is courteously termed, truth is hidden from them, and they are made to assume an artificial character before their faculties have acquired any strength. Taught from their infancy that beauty is woman's sceptre, the mind shapes itself to the body, and roaming round its gilt cage, only seeks to adore its prison. Men have various employments and pursuits which engage their attention, and give a character to the opening mind; but women, confined to one, and having their thoughts constantly directed to the most insignificant part of themselves, seldom extend their views beyond the triumph of the hour. But were their understanding once emancipated from the slavery to which the pride and sensuality of man and their short-sighted desire, like that of dominion in tyrants, of present sway, has subjected them, we should probably read of their weaknesses with surprise. I must be allowed to pursue the argument a little further. . . .

It is time to effect a revolution in female manners—time to restore to them their lost dignity—and make them, as a part of the human species, labour by reforming themselves to reform the world. It is time to separate unchangeable morals from local manners. If men be demi-gods, why let us serve them! And if the dignity of the female soul be as disputable as that of animals—if their reason does not afford sufficient light to direct their conduct whilst unerring instinct is denied—they are surely of all creatures the most miserable! and, bent beneath the iron hand of destiny, must submit to be a *fair defect* in creation. But to justify the ways of Providence respecting them, by pointing out some irrefragable reason for thus making such a large portion of mankind accountable and not accountable, would puzzle the subtilest casuist. . . .

Why do men halt between two opinions, and expect impossibilities? Why do they expect virtue from a slave, from a being whom the constitution of civil society has rendered weak, if not vicious? . . .

Besides, if women be educated for dependence, that is, to act according to the will of another fallible being, and submit, right or wrong, to power, where are we to stop? Are they to be considered as vicegerents allowed to reign over a small domain, and answerable for their conduct to a higher tribunal, liable to error? . . .

I wish to sum up what I have said in a few words, for I here throw down my gauntlet, and deny the existence of sexual virtues, not excepting modesty. For man and woman, truth, if I understand the meaning of the word, must be the same; yet the fanciful female character, so prettily drawn by poets and novelists, demanding the sacrifice of truth and sincerity, virtue becomes a relative idea, having no other foundation than utility, and of that utility men pretend arbitrarily to judge, shaping it to their own convenience.

Women, I allow, may have different duties to fulfil; but they are *human* duties, and the principles that should regulate the discharge of them, I sturdily maintain, must be the same.

To become respectable, the exercise of their understanding is necessary, there is no other foundation for independence of character; I mean explicitly to say that they must only bow to the authority of reason, instead of being the *modest* slaves of opinion.

In the superior ranks of life how seldom do we meet with a man of superior abilities, or even common acquirements? The reason appears to me clear, the state they are born in was an unnatural one. The human character has ever been formed by the employments the individual, or class, pursues; and if the faculties are not sharpened by necessity, they must remain obtuse. The argument may fairly be extended to women; for, seldom occupied by serious business, the pursuit of pleasure gives that insignificancy to their character which renders the society of the *great* so insipid. The same want of firmness, produced by a similar cause, forces them both to fly from themselves to noisy pleasures, and artificial passions, till vanity takes place of every social affection, and the characteristics of humanity can scarcely be discerned. Such are the blessings of civil governments, as they are at present organized, that wealth and female softness equally tend to debase mankind, and are produced by the same cause; but allowing women to be rational creatures, they should be incited to acquire virtues which they may call their own, for how can a rational being be ennobled by anything that is not obtained by its *own* exertions?

chapter twenty

Immanuel Kant

Immanuel Kant (1724–1804), German Idealist philosopher, combined the work of previous thinkers with innovative ideas, providing both the culmination of modern thought and the impetus for much of nineteenth-century philosophy. He was born in the university city of Königsberg in East Prussia (now Kaliningrad, Russia) to a pietistic Lutheran family. He studied at the University of Königsberg, where he was schooled both in rationalists such as Leibniz and Wolf and empiricists such as Newton and Rousseau. Here he experienced the tension between the rationalists and the empiricists, to the resolution of which he would devote much of his own philosophy. In 1755 he began lecturing unsalaried at Königsberg, making his livelihood from student fees. In 1770 he became the Chair of Logic and Metaphysics at Königsberg and spent the next ten years creating and defining his groundbreaking philosophy. Despite numerous offers throughout his life to travel, lecture, and teach elsewhere, he spent his entire life in the city, claiming, "knowledge of men and the world can be acquired even without travel."[1] Kant lived a regimented and ordered life; as the poet Heinrich Heine once noted:

> I do not believe that the great clock of the cathedral there did its daily work more dispassionately and regularly than its compatriot Immanuel Kant. Rising, drinking coffee, writing, reading college lectures, eating, walking, all had their fixed time, and the neighbors knew that it was exactly half past three when Immanuel Kant in his grey coat, with his bamboo cane in hand, left his house door and went to the Lime tree avenue, which is still called, in memory of him, the Philosopher's Walk."[2]

Kant was well known and well liked in his community, and his political opinions were known to spark debate. He was a great proponent of the rights of man, equality, and civil liberty and believed that a republic or a constitutional monarchy was the best form of government. This made him a passionate supporter of revolutions (such as the American Revolution).[3] Despite his theoretical commitment to revolutionary ideas, he also believed in his duties as a citizen. Over the course of the Russian occupation during the Seven Years War, he continued to lecture and teach as usual, now teaching educated

---

Russians as well, and although he himself suffered from censorship,[4] his loyalties never faltered.

Kant's philosophical system is based on the authority of reason combined with the idea that epistemology (the study of the origin, nature, and extent of human knowledge) must function as "first philosophy," or the starting point for all philosophical thought. He began predominantly as a rationalist studying Descartes, but it was Hume who provided the intellectual starting point for Kant's remarkable synthesis of rational and empirical philosophies.[5] Kant argues that Hume erred in assuming that because knowledge *begins* with experience, it follows that all knowledge *arises from* experience. Kant's own philosophy, called transcendental idealism, holds that knowledge of objects is not based solely on experience, but on subjective existence, or things true to human beings *as such*, outside of individual experiences. He strives to clarify the difference between mere practical experience and pure or a priori principles (i.e., principles whose existence is independent of experience) which constitute knowledge. Kant's major work, *The Critique of Pure Reason* (1781), puts forth this idea that while human reason can discover a priori principles, it must take on the responsibility of determining the sources, extent, and bounds of these principles. In other words, Kant believes we do not merely experience the world (as empiricists believe), but also interpret it through reason. For knowledge, both experience (as the empiricists claimed) *and* reason (as the rationalists claimed) are necessary. This blending of empiricism and rationalism is called Kant's "Copernican Revolution."[6]

Through subsequent works (including the remaining two in his "critique trilogy"— *Critique of Practical Reason* [1788] and *Critique of Judgment* [1790])—Kant applied this belief to aesthetics and science, but he is best known for his work on ethics. Kant's theories allowed for important new ways of understanding and thinking about human freedom. During this time period, Newton had just achieved incredible success in the field of physics, causing a rise in the popularity of empirical philosophy. Kant, however, believed that if humans were merely subject to the spatial and temporal laws of physics, then there was no room for freedom. Since moral laws are valid only in the presence of free will, he strove to show that human reality was not fully encompassed by the empirical world. In other words, if right and wrong were determined only through experience, they would be subject to the same physical laws bodies are and would not be a result of free choice. Ethics, therefore, must be based in something outside the realm of experience, or in a priori laws.

This conclusion is both the motivating force behind and the underlying structure of *The Groundwork of the Metaphysics of Morals*, the text presented here. At the outset, Kant rails against "popular philosophy," which he defines as a mixture of empirical and a priori knowledge designed to please the reader. In other words, he accused other philosophers of ignoring the complex structure of knowledge in order to produce a philosophy that would be read and understood by the masses. Although he acknowledged that a philosophy need not be unpopular to be sound, he believed it must be grounded in what he called "a critique of pure practical reason." Therefore, before a philosophy could be simplified to be comprehended easily even by those untrained in the field, the complex foundation had to be laid. He explains that, "Since a metaphysic of morals, despite its horrifying title, can be in a high degree popular and suited to the ordinary intelligence, I think it useful to issue separately this preparatory work on its foundations so that later I need not insert the subtleties inevitable in these matters into doctrines more easy to understand."[7] Although the *Groundwork* is a short work designed to preface another, it provides a clear view of the crucial concepts in Kant's thought and stands alone as a complete work of moral philosophy.

Kant's moral philosophy is primarily concerned with obligation, or duty. Because morality is not grounded in experience, inclination—the will to do something or not do something based on feelings of pleasure or pain one has derived or believes one could derive from an action—can play no part in a moral decision. Actions that are "good," but are done out of a sense of personal gain, are not done *out of* duty, but *only in accordance with* duty. This does not make any act based on inclination immoral, simply *amoral*—or without moral worth. Take, for example, giving a large sum of money to charity. If the gift is made purely out of a sense of duty, it is moral. If it is made merely to get a tax break and to gain the respect of others, it is not immoral, that is, counter to duty, but amoral, or without moral worth. This need for purity of intent has led to the criticism that under Kant's philosophy it is difficult, if not impossible, to determine whether one is acting truly morally. Kant, however, acknowledges this difficulty. Although he believes that the system of morality may never be fully attainable, he believes that it should be known and understood as a model. He states, "In practical philosophy we are not concerned with accepting reasons for what *happens,* but with accepting laws for what *ought to happen,* even if it never does happen—that is, objective practical laws."[8]

It may appear counterintuitive that the reliance on a priori law constitutes freedom for individuals.[9] In clarifying this connection, Kant explains the difference between heteronymous and autonomous law. Heteronymous law is based on fear of punishment or hope of reward. This includes systems of religion and politics. These laws are imposed on man through some outside force (e.g., fines or jail as punishment or heaven as an eternal reward). Man finds himself following them not out of a sense of duty, but out of inclination—the desire to receive reward or avoid punishment. A system of morality based on laws set forth by a God or political ruler, then, cannot be a truly moral system, because the laws are based on man's inclinations, or his experience. For Kant, God is the example created from the a priori law, not the source of it. A priori laws, however, are different from heteronymous laws. They exist outside the realm of experience, and any rational mind will discover them for itself. Therefore, when a human being follows his own rationality to the creation of a law and then willingly imposes it upon himself, he is operating autonomously; he is self-legislating, or literally self-lawing (auto-nomos). Consequently, only under Kant's moral system is man following laws that he himself has discovered. Therefore, only under Kant's system is humankind truly afforded inherent dignity—and only then are human beings truly free.

Taken as a whole, Kant's system of morality is actually a reconciliation of a number of different ethical systems. He believes that a priori laws are necessary to morality, yet he also sees the importance of experience in knowledge itself. He recognizes the usefulness of a God, but argues that he is only an example of the embodiment of a priori laws, not the creator of them. Finally, he shows how it is only by acknowledging a priori laws and choosing to follow them that humans can exercise their reason, and in doing so, their freedom.

BH

QUESTIONS

1. What difference does Kant claim between a "pure moral philosophy" and an "anthropology of morals"? Why does he think a "pure moral philosophy" is necessary?

2. Kant writes in chapter 1 that "the very coolness of a scoundrel makes him, not merely more dangerous, but also immediately more abominable in our eyes than we should have taken him to be without it [coolness]" (AK 395). How does this passage illustrate the one difference Kant asserts between a goodwill and all other qualities, such as moderation in emotions, self-control, intelligence, wit, courage, resolution, and so on?

3. Why does Kant think that nothing in the world can be regarded as "good without qualification" except a *good will?*

4. Why does Kant think that only actions done from duty and not actions done from inclination have moral worth? In your answer, explain and give examples of what he means by "actions done from duty" and, on the other hand, "actions done from inclination."

5. At AK 415–17, Kant distinguishes categorical from hypothetical imperatives. In your own words, describe the difference between them. Give two examples of each.

6. How does Kant define happiness?

ENDNOTES

1. Körner, p. 219.
2. Heine, pp. 136–37, from Aiken, pp. 27–28.
3. Körner, p. 221.
4. In 1793, Kant published *Religion within the Boundaries of Mere Reason* through the philosophy department, avoiding the state censorship over religious publications. This infuriated the king who exacted from Kant a promise not to write on religious subjects.
5. Cf. Kant, *Prolegomena to Any Future Metaphysics*, p. 5.
6. The assumption at the time was that knowledge must conform to object, or that we create theories of knowledge based on what we observe to be true. Kant suggested a paradigm shift in which the assumption changed to the object conforming to knowledge.

Kant likened this move to that of Copernicus, who, when unable to explain the heavenly movements through the belief that the earth was the center of the universe, made the revolutionary discovery that the sun was in fact the center of the universe. In addition, Copernicus's ability to form his conclusion on a law existing outside of experience and transcending an idea of God helped structure Kant's formulation of a priori moral laws.

7. Kant, *Groundwork of the Metaphysics of Morals*, AK 391.

8. Ibid., AK 426–27.

9. Kant's treatment of this apparent contradiction is reminiscent of Rousseau's political system laid out in *The Social Contract* and in *Emile* and reflects Kant's own political views.

SELECTED BIBLIOGRAPHY

Heine, Heinrich. *Germany*, from *Works*, Vol. 5, pp. 136–37, from *The Age of Ideology: The Nineteenth Century Philosophers*, ed. Henry D. Aiken. New York: New American Library, 1956.

Kant, Immanuel. *Groundwork of the Metaphysics of Morals*, trans. H.J. Patton. New York: Harper Torchbooks, 1956.

Kant, Immanuel. *Prolegomena to Any Future Metaphysics*, trans. Paul Carus, rev. James W. Ellington. Indianapolis, Ind.: Hackett Publishing, 1977.

Körner, S. *Kant*. London: Penguin Books. 1955.

from the *Groundwork of the Metaphysics of Morals*

Immanuel Kant

PREFACE

[The different branches of philosophy.]

Ancient Greek philosophy was divided into three sciences: *physics, ethics*, and *logic*. This division fits the nature of the subject perfectly, and there is no need to improve on it—except perhaps by adding the principle on which it is based. By so doing we may be able on the one hand to guarantee its completeness and on the other to determine correctly its necessary subdivisions.

All rational knowledge is either *material* and concerned with some object, or *formal* and concerned solely with the form of understanding and reason themselves—with the universal rules of thinking as such without regard to differences in its objects. Formal philosophy is called *logic*; while material philosophy, which has to do with determinate objects and with the laws to which they are subject, is in turn divided into two, since the laws in question are laws either of *nature* or of *freedom*. The science of the first is called *physics*, that of the second *ethics*. The former is also called natural philosophy, the latter moral philosophy.

Logic can have no empirical part—that is, no part in which the universal and necessary laws of thinking are based on grounds taken from experience. Otherwise it would not be logic—that is, it would not be a canon for understanding and reason, valid for all thinking and capable of demonstration. As against this, both natural and moral philosophy can each have an empirical part, since the former has to formulate its laws for nature as an object of experience, and the latter for the will of man so far as affected by nature—the first set of laws being those in accordance with which everything happens, the second being those in accordance with which everything ought to happen, although they also take into account the conditions under which what ought to happen very often does not happen.

All philosophy so far as it rests on the basis of experience can be called *empirical* philosophy. If it sets forth its doctrines as depending entirely on *a priori* principles, it can be called *pure* philosophy. The latter when wholly formal is called *logic*; but if it is confined to determinate objects of the understanding, it is then called *metaphysics*.

In this way there arises the Idea of a two-fold metaphysic—*a metaphysic of nature and a metaphysic of morals*. Thus physics will have its empirical part, but it will also have a rational one; and likewise ethics—although here the empirical part might be called specifically *practical anthropology*, while the rational part might properly be called *morals*.

[The need for pure ethics.]

All industries, arts, and crafts have gained by the division of labour—that is to say, one man no longer does everything, but each confines himself to a particular task, differing markedly from others in its technique, so that he may be able to perform it with the highest perfection and with greater ease.... Here ... I confine myself to asking whether the nature of science does not always require that the empirical part should be scrupulously separated from the rational one, and that (empirical) physics proper should be prefaced by a metaphysic of nature, while practical anthropology should be prefaced by a metaphysic of morals—each metaphysic having to be scrupulously cleansed of everything empirical if we are to know how much pure reason can accomplish in both cases and from what sources it can by itself draw its own *a priori* teaching....

Since my aim here is directed strictly to moral philosophy, I limit my proposed question to this point only—Do we not think it a matter of the utmost necessity to work out for once a pure moral philosophy completely cleansed of everything that can only be empirical and appropriate to anthropology? That there must be such a philosophy is already obvious from the common Idea of duty and from the laws of morality. Every one must admit that a law has to carry with it absolute necessity if it is to be valid morally—valid, that is, as a ground of obligation; that the command 'Thou shalt not lie' could not hold merely for men, other rational beings having no obligation to abide by it—and similarly with all other genuine moral laws; that here consequently the ground of obligation must be looked for, not in the nature of man nor in the circumstances of the world in which he is placed, but solely *a priori* in the concepts of pure reason; and that every other precept based on principles of mere experience—and even a precept that may in a certain sense be considered universal, so far as it rests in its slightest part, perhaps only in its motive, on empirical grounds—can indeed be called a practical rule, but never a moral law.

Thus in practical knowledge as a whole, not only are moral laws, together with their principles, essentially different from all the rest in which there is some empirical element, but the whole of moral philosophy is based entirely on the part of it that is pure. When applied to man it does not borrow in the slightest from acquaintance with him (in anthropology), but gives him laws *a priori* as a rational being. These laws admittedly require in addition a power of judgement sharpened by experience, partly in order to distinguish the cases to which they apply, partly to procure for them admittance to the will of man and influence over practice; for man, affected as he is by so many inclinations, is capable of the Idea of a pure practical reason, but he has not so easily the power to realize the Idea *in concreto* in his conduct of life.

A metaphysic of morals is thus indispensably necessary, not merely in order to investigate, from motives of speculation, the source of practical principles which are present *a priori* in our reason, but because morals themselves remain exposed to corruption of all sorts as long as this guiding thread is lacking, this ultimate norm for correct moral judgement. For if any action is to be morally good, it is not enough that it should *conform* to the moral law—it must also be done *for the sake of the moral law*: where this is not so, the conformity is only too contingent and precarious, since the non-moral ground at work will now and then produce actions which accord with the law, but very often actions which transgress it. Now the moral law in its purity and genuineness (and in the field of action it is precisely this that matters most) is to be looked for nowhere else than in a pure philosophy. Hence pure philosophy (that is, metaphysics) must come first, and without it there can be no moral philosophy at all. Indeed a philosophy which mixes up these pure principles with empirical ones does not deserve the name of philosophy (since philosophy is distinguished from ordinary rational knowledge precisely because it sets forth in a separate science what the latter apprehends only as

confused with other things). Still less does it deserve the name of moral philosophy, since by this very confusion it undermines even the purity of morals themselves and acts against its own proper purpose.

CHAPTER 1 PASSAGE FROM ORDINARY RATIONAL KNOWLEDGE OF MORALITY TO PHILOSOPHICAL

[The Good Will.]

It is impossible to conceive anything at all in the world, or even out of it, which can be taken as good without qualification, except a *good will*. Intelligence, wit, judgement, and any other *talents* of the mind we may care to name, or courage, resolution, and constancy of purpose, as qualities of *temperament*, are without doubt good and desirable in many respects; but they can also be extremely bad and hurtful when the will is not good which has to make use of these gifts of nature. . . . It is exactly the same with *gifts of fortune*. Power, wealth, honour, even health and that complete well-being and contentment with one's state which goes by the name of 'happiness', produce boldness, and as a consequence often over-boldness as well, unless a good will is present by which their influence on the mind—and so too the whole principle of action—may be corrected and adjusted to universal ends; not to mention that a rational and impartial spectator can never feel approval in contemplating the uninterrupted prosperity of a being graced by no touch of a pure and good will, and that consequently a good will seems to constitute the indispensable condition of our very worthiness to be happy.

Some qualities are even helpful to this good will itself and can make its task very much easier. They have none the less no inner unconditioned worth, but rather presuppose a good will which sets a limit to the esteem in which they are rightly held and does not permit us to regard them as absolutely good. Moderation in affections and passions, self-control, and sober reflexion are not only good in many respects: they may even seem to constitute part of the *inner* worth of a person. Yet they are far from being properly described as good without qualification (however unconditionally they have been commended by the ancients). For without the principles of a good will they may become exceedingly bad; and the very coolness of a scoundrel makes him, not merely more dangerous, but also immediately more abominable in our eyes than we should have taken him to be without it.

[The Good Will and Its Results.]

A good will is not good because of what it effects or accomplishes—because of its fitness for attaining some proposed end: it is good through its willing alone—that is, good in itself. Considered in itself it is to be esteemed beyond comparison as far higher than anything it could ever bring about merely in order to favour some inclination or, if you like, the sum total of inclinations. Even if, by some special disfavour of destiny . . . this will is entirely lacking in power to carry out its intentions; if by its utmost effort it still accomplishes nothing, and only good will is left (not, admittedly, as a mere wish, but as the straining of every means so far as they are in our control); even then it would still shine like a jewel for its own sake as something which has its full value in itself. Its usefulness or fruitlessness can neither add to, nor subtract from, this value. . . .

[The Function of Reason.]

Yet in this Idea of the absolute value of a mere will, all useful results being left out of account in its assessment, there is something so strange that, in spite of all the agreement it receives even from ordinary reason, there must arise the suspicion that perhaps its secret basis is merely some high-flown fantasticality, and that we may have misunderstood the purpose of nature in attaching reason to our will as its governor. We will therefore submit our Idea to an examination from this point of view.

In the natural constitution of an organic being. . . . let us take it as a principle that in it no organ is to be found for any end unless it is also the most appropriate to that end and the best fitted for it. Suppose now that for a being possessed of reason and a will the real purpose of nature were his *preservation*, his *welfare*, or in a word his *happiness*. In that case nature would have hit on a very bad arrangement by choosing reason in the creature to carry out this purpose. For all the actions he has to perform with this end in view, and the whole rule of his behaviour, would have been mapped out for him far more accurately by instinct; and the end in question could have been maintained far more surely by instinct than it ever can be by reason. If reason should have been imparted to this favoured creature as well, it would have had to serve him only for contemplating the happy disposition of his nature, for admiring it, for enjoying it, and for being grateful to its beneficent Cause. . . . In a word, nature would have prevented reason from striking out into a *practical use* and from presuming, with its feeble vision, to think out for itself a plan for happiness and for the means to its attainment. Nature would herself have taken over the choice, not only of ends, but also of means, and would with wise precaution have entrusted both to instinct alone.

In actual fact too we find that the more a cultivated reason concerns itself with the aim of enjoying life and happiness, the farther does man get away from true contentment. This is why there arises in many . . . a certain degree of *misology*—that is, a hatred of reason; for when they balance all the advantage they draw . . . they discover that they have in fact only brought more trouble on their heads than they have gained in the way of happiness. . . .

These judgements have as their hidden ground the Idea of another and much more worthy purpose of existence, for which, and not for happiness, reason is quite properly designed, and to which, therefore, as a supreme condition the private purposes of man must for the most part be subordinated.

For since reason is not sufficiently serviceable for guiding the will safely as regards its objects and the satisfaction of all our needs (which it in part even multiplies)—a purpose for which an implanted natural instinct would have led us much more surely; and since none the less reason has been imparted to us as a practical power—that is, as one which is to have influence on the *will*; its true function must be to produce a *will* which is *good*, not as a *means* to some further end, but *in itself*; and for this function reason was absolutely necessary in a world where nature, in distributing her aptitudes, has everywhere else gone to work in a purposive manner. Such a will need not on this account be the sole and complete good, but it must be the highest good and the condition of all the rest, even of all our demands for happiness. In that case we can easily reconcile. . . . Our observation that the cultivation of reason which is required for the first and unconditioned purpose may in many ways, at least in this life, restrict the attainment of the second purpose—namely, happiness—which is always conditioned; and indeed that it can even reduce happiness to less than zero without nature proceeding contrary to its purpose; for reason, which recognizes as its highest practical function the establishment of a good will, in attaining this end is capable only of its own peculiar kind of contentment—contentment in fulfilling a purpose which in turn is determined by reason alone, even if this fulfilment should often involve interference with the purposes of inclination.

[The Good Will and Duty.]

We have now to elucidate the concept of a will estimable in itself and good apart from any further end. . . . We will therefore take up the concept of *duty*, which includes that of a good will, exposed, however, to certain subjective limitations and obstacles. These, so far from hiding a good will or disguising it, rather bring it out by contrast and make it shine forth more brightly.

[The Motive of Duty.]

I will here pass over all actions already recognized as contrary to duty, however useful they may be with a view to this or that end; for about these the question does not even arise whether they could have been done *for the sake of duty* inasmuch as they are directly opposed to it. I will also set aside actions which in fact accord with duty, yet for which men have *no immediate inclination*, but perform them because impelled to do so by some other inclination. For there it is easy to decide whether the action which accords with duty has been done *from duty* or from some purpose of self-interest. This distinction is far more difficult to perceive when the action accords with duty and the subject has in addition an *immediate* inclination to the action. For example, it certainly accords with duty that a grocer should not overcharge his inexperienced customer; and where there is much competition a sensible shopkeeper refrains from so doing and keeps to a fixed and general price for everybody so that a child can buy from him just as well as anyone else. Thus people are served *honestly*; but this is not nearly enough to justify us in believing that the shopkeeper has acted in this way from duty or from principles of fair dealing; his interests required him to do so. We cannot assume him to have in addition an immediate inclination towards his customers, leading him, as it were out of love, to give no man preference over another in the matter of price. Thus the action was done neither from duty nor from immediate inclination, but solely from purposes of self-interest.

On the other hand, to preserve one's life is a duty, and besides this every one has also an immediate inclination to do so. But on account of this the often anxious precautions taken by the greater part of mankind for this purpose have no inner worth, and the maxim of their action is without moral content. They do protect their lives *in conformity with duty*, but not *from the motive of duty*. When on the contrary, disappointments and hopeless misery have quite taken away the taste for life; when a wretched man, strong in soul and more angered at his fate than faint-hearted or cast down, longs for death and still preserves his life without loving it—not from inclination or fear but from duty; then indeed his maxim has a moral content.

To help others where one can is a duty, and besides this there are many spirits of so sympathetic a temper that, without any further motive of vanity or self-interest, they find an inner pleasure in spreading happiness around them and can take delight in the contentment of others as their own work. Yet I maintain that in such a case an action of this kind, however right and however amiable it may be, has still no genuinely moral worth. It stands on the same footing as other inclinations—for example, the inclination for honour, which if fortunate enough to hit on something beneficial and right and consequently honourable, deserves praise and encouragement, but not esteem; for its maxim lacks moral content, namely, the performance of such actions, not from inclination, but *from duty*. Suppose then that the mind of this friend of man were overclouded by sorrows of his own which extinguished all sympathy with the fate of others, but that he still had power to help those in distress, though no longer stirred by the need of others because sufficiently occupied with his own; and suppose that, when no longer moved by any inclination, he tears himself out of this deadly insensibility and does the action without any inclination for the sake of duty alone; then for the first time his action has its genuine moral worth. Still further: if nature had implanted little sympathy in this or that man's heart; if (being in other respects an honest fellow) he were cold in temperament and indifferent to the sufferings of others—perhaps because, being endowed with the special gift of patience and robust endurance in his own sufferings, he assumed the like in others or even demanded it; if such a man (who would in truth not be the worst product of nature) were not exactly fashioned by her to be a philanthropist, would he not still find in himself a source from which he might draw a worth far higher than any that a good-natured temperament can have? Assuredly he would. It is precisely in this that the worth of character begins to show—a moral worth and beyond all comparison the highest—namely, that he does good, not from inclination, but from duty.

To assure one's own happiness is a duty (at least indirectly); for discontent with one's state, in a press of cares and amidst unsatisfied wants, might easily become a great *temptation to the transgression of duty*. But here also, apart from regard to duty, all men have already of themselves the strongest and deepest inclination towards happiness, because precisely in this Idea of happiness all inclinations are combined into a sum total. The prescription for happiness is, however, often so constituted as greatly to interfere with some inclinations, and yet men cannot form under the name of 'happiness' any determinate and assured conception of the satisfaction of all inclinations as a sum. Hence it is not to be wondered at that a single inclination which is determinate as to what it promises and as to the time of its satisfaction may outweigh a wavering Idea; and that a man, for example, a sufferer from gout, may choose to enjoy what he fancies and put up with what he can—on the ground that on balance he has here at least not killed the enjoyment of the present moment because of some possibly groundless expectations of the good fortune supposed to attach to soundness of health. But in this case also, when the universal inclination towards happiness has failed to determine his will, when good health, at least for him, has not entered into his calculations as so necessary, what remains over, here as in other cases, is a law—the law of furthering his happiness, not from inclination, but from duty; and in this for the first time his conduct has a real moral worth.

It is doubtless in this sense that we should understand too the passages from Scripture in which we are commanded to love our neighbour and even our enemy. For love out of inclination cannot be commanded; but kindness done from duty—although no inclination impels us, and even although natural and unconquerable disinclination stands in our way—is *practical*, and not *pathological*, love, residing in the will and not in the propensions of feeling, in principles of action and not of melting compassion; and it is this practical love alone which can be an object of command.

[The Formal Principle of Duty.]

Our second proposition is this: An action done from duty has its moral worth, *not in the purpose* to be attained by it, but in the maxim in accordance with which it is decided upon; it depends therefore, not on the realization of the object of the action, but solely on the *principle* of *volition* in accordance with which, irrespective of all objects of the faculty of desire, the action has been performed. That the purposes we may have in our actions, and also their effects considered as ends and motives of the will, can give to actions no unconditioned and moral worth is clear from what has gone before. Where then can this worth be found if we are not to find it in the will's relation to the effect hoped for from the action? It can be found nowhere but *in the principle of the will*, irrespective of the ends which can be brought about by such an action; for between its *a priori* principle, which is formal, and its *a posteriori* motive, which is material, the will stands, so to speak, at a parting of the ways; and since it must be determined by some principle, it will have to be determined by the formal principle of volition when an action is done from duty, where, as we have seen, every material principle is taken away from it.

[Reverence for the Law.]

Our third proposition, as an inference from the two preceding, I would express thus: *Duty is the necessity to act out of reverence for the law*. For an object as the effect of my proposed action I can have an *inclination*, but *never reverence*, precisely because it is merely the effect, and not the activity, of a will. Similarly for inclination as such, whether my own or that of another, I cannot have reverence: I can at most in the first case approve, and in the second case sometimes even love—that is, regard it as favourable to my own advantage. Only something which is conjoined with my will solely as a ground and never as an effect—something which does not serve my inclination, but outweighs it or at least leaves it entirely out of account in my choice—and therefore only bare law for its own sake, can be an object of reverence and therewith a command. Now an action done from duty has to set aside altogether the influence of inclination, and along with inclination every object of the will; so there is nothing left able to determine the will except objectively the *law* and subjectively *pure reverence* for this practical law, and therefore the maxim* of obeying this law even to the detriment of all my inclinations.

Thus the moral worth of an action does not depend on the result expected from it, and so too does not depend on any principle of action that needs to borrow its motive from this expected result. For all these results (agreeable states and even the promotion of happiness in others) could have been brought about by other causes as well, and consequently their production did not require the will of a rational being, in which, however, the highest and unconditioned good can alone be found. Therefore nothing but the *idea of the law* in itself, *which admittedly is present only in a rational being*—so far as it, and not an expected result, is the ground determining the will—can constitute that pre-eminent good which we call moral, a good which is already present in the person acting on this idea and has not to be awaited merely from the result.**

---

*A *maxim* is the subjective principle of a volition: an objective principle (that is, one which would also serve subjectively as a practical principle for all rational beings if reason had full control over the faculty of desire) is a practical *law*.

**It might be urged against me that I have merely tried, under cover of the word '*reverence*', to take refuge in an obscure feeling instead of giving a clearly articulated answer to the question by means of a concept of reason. Yet although reverence is a feeling, it is not a feeling *received* through outside influence, but one *self-produced* by a rational concept, and therefore specifically distinct from feelings of the first kind, all of which can be reduced to inclination or fear. What I recognize immediately as law for me, I recognize with reverence, which means merely consciousness of the *subordination* of my will to a law without the mediation of external influences on my senses. Immediate determination of the will by the law and consciousness of this determination is called '*reverence*', so that reverence is regarded as the *effect* of the law on the subject and not as the *cause* of the law. Reverence is properly awareness of a value which demolishes my self-love. Hence there is something which is regarded neither as an object of inclination nor as an object of fear, though it has at the same time some analogy with both. The *object* of reverence is the *law* alone—that law which we impose *on ourselves* but yet as necessary in itself.

[The Categorical Imperative.]

But what kind of law can this be the thought of which, even without regard to the results expected from it, has to determine the will if this is to be called good absolutely and without qualification? Since I have robbed the will of every inducement that might arise for it as a consequence of obeying any particular law, nothing is left but the conformity of actions to universal law as such, and this alone must serve the will as its principle. That is to say, I ought never to act except in such a way *that I can also will that my maxim should become a universal law*. Here bare conformity to universal law as such (without having as its base any law prescribing particular actions) is what serves the will as its principle, and must so serve it if duty is not to be everywhere an empty delusion and a chimerical concept. The ordinary reason of mankind also agrees with this completely in its practical judgements and always has the aforesaid principle before its eyes.

Take this question, for example. May I not, when I am hard pressed, make a promise with the intention of not keeping it? Here I readily distinguish the two senses which the question can have—Is it prudent, or is it right, to make a false promise? The first no doubt can often be the case. I do indeed see that it is not enough for me to extricate myself from present embarrassment by this

---

Considered as a law, we are subject to it without any consultation of self-love; considered as self-imposed it is a consequence of our will. In the first respect it is analogous to fear, in the second to inclination. All reverence for a person is properly only reverence for the law (of honesty and so on) of which that person gives us an example. Because we regard the development of our talents as a duty, we see too in a man of talent a sort of *example of the law* (the law of becoming like him by practice), and this is what constitutes our reverence for him. All moral *interest*, so-called, consists solely in *reverence* for the law.

subterfuge: I have to consider whether from this lie there may not subsequently accrue to me much greater inconvenience than that from which I now escape, and also—since, with all my supposed *astuteness*, to foresee the consequences is not so easy that I can be sure there is no chance, once confidence in me is lost, of this proving far more disadvantageous than all the ills I now think to avoid—whether it may not be a *more prudent* action to proceed here on a general maxim and make it my habit not to give a promise except with the intention of keeping it. Yet it becomes clear to me at once that such a maxim is always founded solely on fear of consequences. To tell the truth for the sake of duty is something entirely different from doing so out of concern for inconvenient results; for in the first case the concept of the action already contains in itself a law for me, while in the second case I have first of all to look around elsewhere in order to see what effects may be bound up with it for me. When I deviate from the principle of duty, this is quite certainly bad; but if I desert my prudential maxim, this can often be greatly to my advantage, though it is admittedly safer to stick to it. Suppose I seek, however, to learn in the quickest way and yet unerringly how to solve the problem 'Does a lying promise accord with duty?' I have then to ask myself 'Should I really be content that my maxim (the maxim of getting out of a difficulty by a false promise) should hold as a universal law (one valid both for myself and others)? And could I really say to myself that every one may make a false promise if he finds himself in a difficulty from which he can extricate himself in no other way?' I then become aware at once that I can indeed will to lie, but I can by no means will a universal law of lying; for by such a law there could properly be no promises at all, since it would be futile to profess a will for future action to others who would not believe my profession or who, if they did so over-hastily, would pay me back in like coin; and consequently my maxim, as soon as it was made a universal law, would be bound to annul itself.

Thus I need no far-reaching ingenuity to find out what I have to do in order to possess a good will. . . . I ask myself only 'Can you also will that your maxim should become a universal law?' Where you cannot, it is to be rejected, and that not because of a prospective loss to you or even to others, but because it cannot fit as a principle into a possible enactment of universal law. For such an enactment reason compels my immediate reverence, into whose grounds (which the philosopher may investigate) I have as yet no *insight*, although I do at least understand this much: reverence is the assessment of a worth which far outweighs all the worth of what is commended by inclination, and the necessity for me to act out of *pure* reverence for the practical law is what constitutes duty, to which every other motive must give way because it is the condition of a will good *in itself*, whose value is above all else.

CHAPTER II PASSAGE FROM POPULAR MORAL PHILOSOPHY TO A METAPHYSIC OF MORALS

[The Use of Examples.]

If so far we have drawn our concept of duty from the ordinary use of our practical reason, it must by no means be inferred that we have treated it as a concept of experience. On the contrary, when we pay attention to our experience of human conduct, we meet frequent and—as we ourselves admit— justified complaints that we can adduce no certain examples of the spirit which acts out of pure duty, and that, although much may be done *in accordance with* the commands of *duty*, it remains doubtful whether it really is done *for the sake of duty* and so has a moral value. Hence at all times there have been philosophers who have absolutely denied the presence of this spirit in human actions and have ascribed everything to a more or less refined self-love. Yet they have not cast doubt on the rightness of the concept of morality. They have spoken rather with deep regret of the frailty and impurity of human nature, which is on their view noble enough to take as its rule an Idea so worthy of reverence, but at the same time too weak to follow it: the reason which should serve it for making laws it uses only to look after the interest of inclinations, whether singly or—at the best—in their greatest mutual compatibility.

In actual fact it is absolutely impossible for experience to establish with complete certainty a single case in which the maxim of an action in other respects right has rested solely on moral grounds and on the thought of one's duty. It is indeed at times the case that after the keenest self-examination we find nothing that without the moral motive of duty could have been strong enough to move us to this or that good action and to so great a sacrifice; but we cannot infer from this with certainty that it is not some secret impulse of self-love which has actually, under the mere show of the Idea of duty, been the cause genuinely determining our will. We are pleased to flatter ourselves with the false claim to a nobler motive, but in fact we can never, even by the most strenuous self-examination, get to the bottom of our secret impulses; for when moral value is in question, we are concerned, not with the actions which we see, but with their inner principles, which we cannot see.

Furthermore, to those who deride all morality as the mere phantom of a human imagination which gets above itself out of vanity we can do no service more pleasing than to admit that the concepts of duty must be drawn solely from experience . . . for by so doing we prepare for them an assured triumph. Out of love for humanity I am willing to allow that most of our actions may accord with duty; but if we look more closely at our scheming and striving, we everywhere come across the dear self, which is always turning up; and it is on this that the purpose of our actions is based—not on the strict command of duty, which would often require self-denial. . . . Nothing can protect us against a complete falling away from our Ideas of duty, or can preserve in the soul a grounded reverence for its law, except the clear conviction that even if there never have been actions springing from such pure sources, the question at issue here is not whether this or that has happened; that, on the contrary, reason by itself and independently of all appearances commands what ought to happen; that consequently actions of which the world has perhaps hitherto given no example—actions whose practicability might well be doubted by those who rest everything on experience—are nevertheless commanded unrelentingly by reason; and that, for instance, although up to now there may have existed no loyal friend, pure loyalty in friendship can be no less required from every man, inasmuch as this duty, prior to all experience, is contained as duty in general in the Idea of a reason which determines the will by *a priori* grounds.

It may be added that unless we wish to deny to the concept of morality all truth and all relation to a possible object, we cannot dispute that its law is of such widespread significance as to hold, not merely for men, but for all *rational beings as such*—not merely subject to contingent conditions and exceptions, but *with absolute necessity*. It is therefore clear that no experience can give us occasion to infer even the possibility of such apodeictic laws. For by what right can we make what is perhaps valid only under the contingent conditions of humanity into an object of unlimited reverence as a universal precept for every rational nature? And how could laws for determining *our* will be taken as laws for determining the will of a rational being as such—and only because of this for determining ours—if these laws were merely empirical and did not have their source completely *a priori* in pure, but practical, reason?

What is more, we cannot do morality a worse service than by seeking to derive it from examples. Every example of it presented to me must first itself be judged by moral principles in order to decide if it is fit to serve as an original example—that is, as a model: it can in no way supply the prime source for the concept of morality. Even the Holy One of the gospel must first be compared with our ideal of moral perfection before we can recognize him to be such. . . . Where do we get the concept of God as the highest good? Solely from the *Idea* of moral perfection, which reason traces *a priori* and conjoins inseparably with the concept of a free will. Imitation has no place in morality, and examples serve us only for encouragement—that is, they set beyond doubt the practicability of what the law commands; they make perceptible what the practical law expresses more generally; but they can never entitle us to set aside their true original, which resides in reason, and to model ourselves upon examples.

[Popular Philosophy.]

If there can be no genuine supreme principle of morality which is not grounded on pure reason alone independently of all experience, it should be unnecessary, I think, even to raise the question whether it is a good thing to set forth in general (*in abstracto*) these concepts which hold *a priori*, together with their corresponding principles, so far as our knowledge is to be distinguished from ordinary knowledge and described as philosophical. Yet in our days it may well be necessary to do so. For if we took a vote on which is to be preferred, pure rational knowledge detached from everything empirical—that is to say, a metaphysic of morals—or

popular practical philosophy, we can guess at once on which side the preponderance would fall.

It is certainly most praiseworthy to come down to the level of popular thought when we have previously risen to the principles of pure reason and are fully satisfied of our success. This could be described as first *grounding* moral philosophy on metaphysics and subsequently winning *acceptance* for it by giving it a popular character after it has been established. But it is utterly senseless to aim at popularity in our first enquiry, upon which the whole correctness of our principles depends. . . .

[Review of Conclusions.]

From these considerations the following conclusions emerge. All moral concepts have their seat and origin in reason completely *a priori*, and indeed in the most ordinary human reason just as much as in the most highly speculative: they cannot be abstracted from any empirical, and therefore merely contingent, knowledge. In this purity of their origin is to be found their very worthiness to serve as supreme practical principles, and everything empirical added to them is just so much taken away from their genuine influence and from the absolute value of the corresponding actions. It is not only a requirement of the utmost necessity in respect of theory, where our concern is solely with speculation, but is also of the utmost practical importance, to draw these concepts and laws from pure reason, to set them forth pure and unmixed, and indeed to determine the extent of this whole practical, but pure, rational knowledge—that is, to determine the whole power of pure practical reason. We ought never . . . to make principles depend on the special nature of human reason. Since moral laws have to hold for every rational being as such, we ought rather to derive our principles from the general concept of a rational being as such, and on this basis to expound the whole of ethics—which requires anthropology for its *application* to man—at first independently as pure philosophy, that is, entirely as metaphysics (which we can very well do in this wholly abstract kind of knowledge). We know well that without possessing such a metaphysics it is a futile endeavour, I will not say to determine accurately for speculative judgement the moral element of duty in all that accords with duty—but that it is impossible, even in ordinary and practical usage, particularly in that of moral instruction, to base morals on their genuine principles and so to bring about pure moral dispositions and engraft them on men's minds for the highest good of the world.

In this task of ours we have to progress by natural stages, not merely from ordinary moral judgement (which is here worthy of great respect) to philosophical judgement, as we have already done, but from popular philosophy, which goes no further than it can get by fumbling about with the aid of examples, to metaphysics. (This no longer lets itself be held back by anything empirical, and indeed—since it must survey the complete totality of this kind of knowledge—goes right to Ideas, where examples themselves fail.) For this purpose we must follow—and must portray in detail—the power of practical reason from the general rules determining it right up to the point where there springs from it the concept of duty.

[Imperatives in general.]

Everything in nature works in accordance with laws. Only a rational being has the power to act *in accordance with his idea* of laws—that is, in accordance with principles—and only so has he a *will*. Since *reason* is required in order to derive actions from laws, the will is nothing but practical reason. If reason infallibly determines the will, then in a

being of this kind the actions which are recognized to be objectively necessary are also subjectively necessary—that is to say, the will is then a power to choose *only that* which reason independently of inclination recognizes to be practically necessary, that is, to be good. But if reason solely by itself is not sufficient to determine the will; if the will is exposed also to subjective conditions (certain impulsions) which do not always harmonize with the objective ones; if, in a word, the will is not *in itself* completely in accord with reason (as actually happens in the case of men); then actions which are recognized to be objectively necessary are subjectively contingent, and the determining of such a will in accordance with objective laws is *necessitation*. That is to say, the relation of objective laws to a will not good through and through is conceived as one in which the will of a rational being, although it is determined by principles of reason, does not necessarily follow these principles in virtue of its own nature.

The conception of an objective principle so far as this principle is necessitating for a will is called a command (of reason), and the formula of this command is called an *Imperative*.

All imperatives are expressed by an '*ought*' (*Sollen*). By this they mark the relation of an objective law of reason to a will which is not necessarily determined by this law in virtue of its subjective constitution (the relation of necessitation). They say that something would be good to do or to leave undone; only they say it to a will which does not always do a thing because it has been informed that this is a good thing to do. The practically *good* is that which determines the will by concepts of reason, and therefore not by subjective causes, but objectively—that is, on grounds valid for every rational being as such. It is distinguished from the *pleasant* as that which influences the will, not as a principle of reason valid for every one, but solely through the medium of sensation by purely subjective causes valid only for the senses of this person or that.*

A perfectly good will would thus stand quite as much under objective laws (laws of the good), but it could not on this account be conceived as *necessitated* to act in conformity with law, since of itself, in accordance with its subjective constitution, it can be determined only by the concept of the good. Hence for the *divine* will, and in general for a *holy* will, there are no imperatives: '*I ought*' is here out of place, because '*I will*' is already of itself necessarily in harmony with the law. Imperatives are in consequence only formulae for expressing the relation of objective laws of willing to the subjective imperfection of the will of this or that rational being—for example, of the human will.

[Classification of Imperatives.]

All *imperatives* command either *hypothetically* or *categorically*. Hypothetical imperatives declare a possible action to be practically necessary as a means to the attainment of something else that one wills (or that one may will). A categorical imperative would be one which represented an action as objectively necessary in itself apart from its relation to a further end.

---

*The dependence of the power of appetition on sensations is called an inclination, and thus an inclination always indicates a *need*. The dependence of a contingently determinable will on principles of reason is called an *interest*. Hence an interest is found only where there is a dependent will which in itself is not always in accord with reason: to a divine will we cannot ascribe any interest. But even the human will can *take an interest* in something without therefore *acting from interest*. The first expression signifies *practical* interest in the action; the second *pathological* interest in the object of the action. The first indicates only dependence of the will on principles of reason by itself; the second its dependence on principles of reason at the service of inclination—that is to say, where reason merely supplies a practical rule for meeting the need of inclination. In the first case what interests me is the action; in the second case what interests me is the object of the action (so far as this object is pleasant to me). We have seen in Chapter I that in an action done for the sake of duty we must have regard, not to interest in the object, but to interest in the action itself and in its rational principle (namely, the law).

Every practical law represents a possible action as good and therefore as necessary for a subject whose actions are determined by reason. Hence all imperatives are formulae for determining an action which is necessary in accordance with the principle of a will in some sense good. If the action would be good solely as a means *to something else*, the imperative is *hypothetical*; if the action is represented as good *in itself* and therefore as necessary, in virtue of its principle, for a will which of itself accords with reason, then the imperative is *categorical*.

An imperative therefore tells me which of my possible actions would be good; and it formulates a practical rule for a will that does not perform an action straight away because the action is good—whether because the subject does not always know that it is good or because, even if he did know this, he might still act on maxims contrary to the objective principles of practical reason.

A hypothetical imperative thus says only that an action is good for some purpose or other, either *possible* or *actual*. In the first case it is a *problematic* practical principle; in the second case an *assertoric* practical principle. A categorical imperative, which declares an action to be objectively necessary in itself without reference to some purpose—that is, even without any further end—ranks as an *apodeictic* practical principle.

Everything that is possible only through the efforts of some rational being can be conceived as a possible purpose of some will; and consequently there are in fact innumerable principles of action so far as action is thought necessary in order to achieve some possible purpose which can be effected by it. All sciences have a practical part consisting of problems which suppose that some end is possible for us and of imperatives which tell us how it is to be attained. Hence the latter can in general be called imperatives of *skill*. Here there is absolutely no question about the rationality or goodness of the end, but only about what must be done to attain it. A prescription required by a doctor in order to cure his man completely and one required by a poisoner in order to make sure of killing him are of equal value so far as each serves to effect its purpose perfectly. Since in early youth we do not know what ends may present themselves to us in the course of life, parents seek above all to make their children learn things *of many kinds*; they provide carefully for *skill* in the use of means to all sorts of *arbitrary* ends, of none of which can they be certain that it could not in the future become an actual purpose of their ward, while it is always *possible* that he might adopt it. Their care in this matter is so great that they commonly neglect on this account to form and correct the judgement of their children about the worth of the things which they might possibly adopt as ends.

There is, however, *one* end that can be presupposed as actual in all rational beings (so far as they are dependent beings to whom imperatives apply); and thus there is one purpose which they not only *can* have, but which we can assume with certainty that they all *do* have by a natural necessity—the purpose, namely, of *happiness*. A hypothetical imperative which affirms the practical necessity of an action as a means to the furtherance of happiness is *assertoric*. We may represent it, not simply as necessary to an uncertain, merely possible purpose, but as necessary to a purpose which we can presuppose *a priori* and with certainty to be present in every man because it belongs to his very being. Now skill in the choice of means to one's own greatest well-being can be called *prudence** in the narrowest sense. Thus an imperative concerned with the choice of means to one's own

happiness—that is, a precept of prudence—still remains *hypothetical*: an action is commanded, not absolutely, but only as a means to a further purpose.

Finally, there is an imperative which, without being based on, and conditioned by, any further purpose to be attained by a certain line of conduct, enjoins this conduct immediately. This imperative is *categorical*. It is concerned, not with the matter of the action and its presumed results, but with its form and with the principle from which it follows; and what is essentially good in the action consists in the mental disposition, let the consequences be what they may. This imperative may be called the imperative of *morality*.

Willing in accordance with these three kinds of principle is also sharply distinguished by a *dissimilarity* in the necessitation of the will. To make this dissimilarity obvious we should, I think, name these kinds of principle most appropriately in their order if we said they were either *rules* of skill or *counsels* of prudence or *commands (laws)* of morality. For only *law* carries with it the concept of an *unconditioned*, and yet objective and so universally valid, *necessity*; and commands are laws which must be obeyed—that is, must be followed even against inclination. *Counsel* does indeed involve necessity, but necessity valid only under a subjective and contingent condition—namely, if this or that man counts this or that as belonging to his happiness. As against this, a categorical imperative is limited by no condition and can quite precisely be called a command, as being absolutely, although practically, necessary. We could also call imperatives of the first kind *technical* (concerned with art); of the second kind *pragmatic**

---

*The word 'prudence' (*Klugheit*) is used in a double sense: in one sense it can have the name of 'worldly wisdom' (*Weltklugheit*); in a second sense that of 'personal wisdom' (*Privatklugheit*). The first is the skill of a man in influencing others in order to use them for his own ends. The second is sagacity in combining all these ends to his own lasting advantage.[1] The latter is properly that to which the value of the former can itself be traced; and of him who is prudent in the first sense, but not in the second, we might better say that he is clever and astute, but on the whole imprudent.

---

*It seems to me that the proper meaning of the word '*pragmatic*' can be defined most accurately in this way. For those *Sanctions* are called Pragmatic which, properly speaking, do not spring as necessary laws from the Natural Right of States, but from *forethought* in regard to the general welfare. A *history* is written pragmatically when it teaches *prudence*—that is, when it instructs the world of to-day how to provide for its own advantage better than, or at least as well as, the world of other times.

(concerned with well-being); of the third kind *moral* (concerned with free conduct as such—that is, with morals).

[How are Imperatives Possible?]

The question now arises 'How are all these imperatives possible?' This question does not ask how we can conceive the execution of an action commanded by the imperative, but merely how we can conceive the necessitation of the will expressed by the imperative in setting us a task. How an imperative of skill is possible requires no special discussion. Who wills the end, wills (so far as reason has decisive influence on his actions) also the means which are indispensably necessary and in his power. So far as willing is concerned, this proposition is analytic: for in my willing of an object as an effect there is already conceived the causality of myself as an acting cause—that is, the use of means; and from the concept of willing an end the imperative merely extracts the concept of actions necessary to this end. (Synthetic propositions are required in order to determine the means to a proposed end, but these are concerned, not with the reason for performing the act of will, but with the cause which produces the object.) That in order to divide a line into two equal parts on a sure principle I must from its ends describe two intersecting arcs—this is admittedly taught by mathematics only in synthetic propositions; but when I know that the aforesaid effect can be produced only by such an action, the proposition 'If I fully will the effect, I also will the action required for it' is analytic; for it is one and the same thing to conceive something as an effect possible in a certain way through me and to conceive myself as acting in the same way with respect to it.

If it were only as easy to find a determinate concept of happiness, the imperatives of prudence would agree entirely with those of skill and would be equally analytic. For here as there it could alike be said 'Who wills the end, wills also (necessarily, if he accords with reason) the sole means which are in his power'. Unfortunately, however, the concept of happiness is so indeterminate a concept that although every man wants to attain happiness, he can never say definitely and in unison with himself what it really is that he wants and wills. The reason for this is that all the elements which belong to the concept of happiness are without exception empirical—that is, they must be borrowed from experience; but that none the less there is required for the Idea of happiness an absolute whole, a maximum of well-being in my present, and in every future, state. Now it is impossible for the most intelligent, and at the same time most powerful, but nevertheless finite, being to form here a determinate concept of what he really wills. Is it riches that he wants? How much anxiety, envy, and pestering might he not bring in this way on his own head! Is it knowledge and insight? This might perhaps merely give him an eye so sharp that it would make evils at present hidden from him and yet unavoidable seem all the more frightful, or would add a load of still further needs to the desires which already give him trouble enough. Is it long life? Who will guarantee that it would not be a long misery? Is it at least health? How often has infirmity of body kept a man from excesses into which perfect health would have let him fall!—and so on. In short, he has no principle by which he is able to decide with complete certainty what will make him truly happy, since for this he would require omniscience. Thus we cannot act on determinate principles in order to be happy, but only on empirical counsels, for example, of diet, frugality, politeness, reserve, and so on—things which experience shows contribute most to well-being on the average. From this it follows that imperatives of prudence, speaking strictly, do not command at all—that is, cannot exhibit actions objectively as practically *necessary*; that they are rather to be taken as recommendations (*consilia*), than as commands (*praecepta*), of reason; that the problem of determining certainly and universally what action will promote the happiness of a rational being is completely insoluble; and consequently that in regard to this there is no imperative possible which in the strictest sense could command us to do what will make us happy, since happiness is an Ideal, not of reason, but of imagination—an Ideal resting merely on empirical grounds, of which it is vain to except that they should determine an action by which we could attain the totality of a series of consequences which is in fact infinite. Nevertheless, if we assume that the means to happiness could be discovered with certainty, this imperative of prudence would be an analytic practical proposition; for it differs from the imperative of skill only in this—that in the latter the end is merely possible, while in the former the end is given. In spite of this difference, since both command solely the means to something assumed to be willed as an end, the imperative which commands him who wills the end to will the means is in both cases analytic. Thus there is likewise no difficulty in regard to the possibility of an imperative of prudence.

Beyond all doubt, the question 'How is the imperative of *morality* possible?' is the only one in need of a solution; for it is in no way hypothetical, and consequently we cannot base the objective necessity which it affirms on any presupposition, as we can with hypothetical imperatives. Only we must never forget here that it is impossible to settle *by an example*, and so empirically, whether there is any imperative of this kind at all: we must rather suspect that all imperatives which seem to be categorical may none the less be covertly hypothetical. Take, for example, the saying 'Thou shalt make no false promises'. Let us assume that the necessity for

this abstention is no mere advice for the avoidance of some further evil—as it might be said 'You ought not to make a lying promise lest, when this comes to light, you destroy your credit'. Let us hold, on the contrary, that an action of this kind must be considered as bad in itself, and that the imperative of prohibition is therefore categorical. Even so, we cannot with any certainty show by an example that the will is determined here solely by the law without any further motive, although it may appear to be so; for it is always possible that fear of disgrace, perhaps also hidden dread of other risks, may unconsciously influence the will. Who can prove by experience that a cause is not present? Experience shows only that it is not perceived. In such a case, however, the so-called moral imperative, which as such appears to be categorical and unconditioned, would in fact be only a pragmatic prescription calling attention to our advantage and merely bidding us take this into account.

We shall thus have to investigate the possibility of a *categorical* imperative entirely *a priori*, since here we do not enjoy the advantage of having its reality given in experience and so of being obliged merely to explain, and not to establish, its possibility. So much, however, can be seen provisionally—that the categorical imperative alone purports to be a practical *law*, while all the rest may be called *principles* of the will but not laws; for an action necessary merely in order to achieve an arbitrary purpose can be considered as in itself contingent, and we can always escape from the precept if we abandon the purpose; whereas an unconditioned command does not leave it open to the will to do the opposite at its discretion and therefore alone carries with it that necessity which we demand from a law.

In the second place, with this categorical imperative or law of morality the reason for our difficulty (in comprehending its possibility) is a very serious one. We have here a synthetic *a priori* practical proposition;* and since in theoretical knowledge there is so much difficulty in comprehending the possibility of propositions of this kind, it may readily be gathered that in practical knowledge the difficulty will be no less.

[The Formula of Universal Law.]

In this task we wish first to enquire whether perhaps the mere concept of a categorical imperative may not also provide us with the formula containing the only proposition that can be a categorical imperative; for even when we know the purport of such an absolute command, the question of its possibility will still require a special and troublesome effort, which we postpone to the final chapter.

When I conceive a *hypothetical* imperative in general, I do not know beforehand what it will contain—until its condition is given. But if I conceive a *categorical* imperative, I know at once what it contains. For since besides the law this imperative contains only the necessity that our maxim** should conform to this law, while the law, as we have seen, contains no condition to limit it, there remains nothing over to which the maxim has to conform except the universality of a law as such; and it is this conformity alone that the imperative properly asserts to be necessary.

There is therefore only a single categorical imperative and it is this: '*Act only on that maxim through which you can at the same time will that it should become a universal law*'.

Now if all imperatives of duty can be derived from this one imperative as their principle, then even although we leave it unsettled whether what we call duty may not be an empty concept, we shall still be able to show at least what we understand by it and what the concept means.

[The Formula of the Law of Nature.]

Since the universality of the law governing the production of effects constitutes what is properly called *nature* in its most general sense (nature as regards its form)—that is, the existence of things so far as determined by universal laws—the universal imperative of duty may also run as follows: '*Act as if the maxim of your action were to become through your will a universal law of nature*.'

[Illustrations.]

We will now enumerate a few duties, following their customary division into duties towards self and duties towards others and into perfect and imperfect duties.*

1. A man feels sick of life as the result of a series of misfortunes that has mounted to the point of

---

*Without presupposing a condition taken from some inclination I connect an action with the will *a priori* and therefore necessarily (although only objectively so—that is, only subject to the Idea of a reason having full power over all subjective impulses to action). Here we have a practical proposition in which the willing of an action is not derived analytically from some other willing already presupposed (for we do not possess any such perfect will), but is on the contrary connected immediately with the concept of the will of a rational being as something which is not contained in this concept.

**A *maxim* is a subjective principle of action and must be distinguished from an *objective principle*—namely, a practical law. The former contains a practical rule determined by reason in accordance with the conditions of the subject (often his ignorance or again his inclinations): it is thus a principle on which the subject *acts*. A law, on the other hand, is an objective principle valid for every rational being; and it is a principle on which he *ought to act*—that is, an imperative.

---

*It should be noted that I reserve my division of duties entirely for a future *Metaphysic of Morals* and that my present division is therefore put forward as arbitrary (merely for the purpose of arranging my examples). Further, I understand here by a perfect duty one which allows no exception in the interests of inclination, and so I recognize among *perfect duties*, not only outer ones, but also inner. This is contrary to the accepted usage of the schools, but I do not intend to justify it here, since for my purpose it is all one whether this point is conceded or not.

despair, but he is still so far in possession of his reason as to ask himself whether taking his own life may not be contrary to his duty to himself. He now applies the test 'Can the maxim of my action really become a universal law of nature?' His maxim is 'From self-love I make it my principle to shorten my life if its continuance threatens more evil than it promises pleasure'. The only further question to ask is whether this principle of self-love can become a universal law of nature. It is then seen at once that a system of nature by whose law the very same feeling whose function (*Bestimmung*) is to stimulate the furtherance of life should actually destroy life would contradict itself and consequently could not subsist as a system of nature. Hence this maxim cannot possibly hold as a universal law of nature and is therefore entirely opposed to the supreme principle of all duty.

2. Another finds himself driven to borrowing money because of need. He well knows that he will not be able to pay it back; but he sees too that he will get no loan unless he gives a firm promise to pay it back within a fixed time. He is inclined to make such a promise; but he has still enough conscience to ask 'Is it not unlawful and contrary to duty to get out of difficulties in this way?' Supposing, however, he did resolve to do so, the maxim of his action would run thus: 'Whenever I believe myself short of money, I will borrow money and promise to pay it back, though I know that this will never be done'. Now this principle of self-love or personal advantage is perhaps quite compatible with my own entire future welfare; only there remains the question 'Is it right?' I therefore transform the demand of self-love into a universal law and frame my question thus: 'How would things stand if my maxim became a universal law?' I then see straight away that this maxim can never rank as a universal law of nature and be self-consistent, but must necessarily contradict itself. For the univer-

sality of a law that every one believing himself to be in need can make any promise he pleases with the intention not to keep it would make promising, and the very purpose of promising, itself impossible, since no one would believe he was being promised anything, but would laugh at utterances of this kind as empty shams.

3. A third finds in himself a talent whose cultivation would make him a useful man for all sorts of purposes. But he sees himself in comfortable circumstances, and he prefers to give himself up to pleasure rather than to bother about increasing and improving his fortunate natural aptitudes. Yet he asks himself further 'Does my maxim of neglecting my natural gifts, besides agreeing in itself with my tendency to indulgence, agree also with what is called duty?' He then sees that a system of nature could indeed always subsist under such a universal law, although (like the South Sea Islanders) every man should let his talents rust and should be bent on devoting his life solely to idleness, indulgence, procreation, and, in a word, to enjoyment. Only he cannot possibly *will* that this should become a universal law of nature or should be implanted in us as such a law by a natural instinct. For as a rational being he necessarily wills that all his powers should be developed, since they serve him, and are given him, for all sorts of possible ends.

4. Yet a *fourth* is himself flourishing, but he sees others who have to struggle with great hardships (and whom he could easily help); and he thinks 'What does it matter to me? Let every one be as happy as Heaven wills or as he can make himself; I won't deprive him of anything; I won't even envy him; only I have no wish to contribute anything to his well-being or to his support in distress!' Now admittedly if such an attitude were a universal law of nature, mankind could get on perfectly well—better no doubt than if everybody prates about sympathy and goodwill, and even takes pains, on occasion, to practise them, but on the other hand cheats where he can, traffics in human rights, or violates them in other ways. But although it is possible that a universal law of nature could subsist in harmony with this maxim, yet it is impossible to *will* that such a principle should hold everywhere as a law of nature. For a will which decided in this way would be in conflict with itself, since many a situation might arise in which the man needed love and sympathy from others.[1] and in which, by such a law of nature sprung from his own will, he would rob himself of all hope of the help he wants for himself.

[The Canon of Moral Judgement.]

These are some of the many actual duties—or at least of what we take to be such—whose derivation from the single principle cited above leaps to the eye. We must *be able to will* that a maxim of our action should become a universal law—this is the general canon for all moral judgement of action. Some actions are so constituted that their maxim cannot even be *conceived* as a universal law of nature without contradiction, let alone be *willed* as what *ought* to become one. In the case of others we do not find this inner impossibility, but it is still impossible to *will* that their maxim should be raised to the universality of a law of nature, because such a will would contradict itself. It is easily seen that the first kind of action is opposed to strict or narrow (rigorous) duty, the second only to wider (meritorious) duty, and thus that by these examples all duties—so far as the type of obligation is concerned (not the object of dutiful action)—are fully set out in their dependence on our single principle.

If we now attend to ourselves whenever we transgress a duty, we find that we in fact do not will that our maxim should become a universal law—since this is impossible for us—but rather that its opposite should remain a law universally: we only take the liberty of making an *exception* to it for ourselves (or even just for this once) to the advantage of our inclination. Consequently if we weighed it all up from one and the same point of view—that of reason—we should find a contradiction in our own will, the contradiction that a certain principle should be objectively necessary as a universal law and yet subjectively should not hold universally but should admit of exceptions. Since, however, we first consider our action from the point of view of a will wholly in accord with reason, and then consider precisely the same action from the point of view of a will affected by inclination, there is here actually no contradiction, but rather an opposition of inclination to the precept of reason (*antagonismus*), whereby the universality of the principle (*universalitas*) is turned into a mere generality (*generalitas*) so that the practical principle of reason may meet our maxim half-way. This procedure, though in our own impartial judgement it cannot be justified, proves none the less that we in fact recognize the validity of the categorical imperative and (with all respect for it) merely permit ourselves a few exceptions which are, as we pretend, inconsiderable and apparently forced upon us.

We have thus at least shown this much—that if duty is a concept which is to have meaning and real legislative authority for our actions, this can be expressed only in categorical imperatives and by no means in hypothetical ones. At the same time—and this is already a great deal—we have set forth distinctly, and determinately for every type of application, the content of the categorical imperative, which must contain the principle of all duty (if there is to be such a thing at all). But we are still not so far advanced as to prove *a priori* that there actually is an imperative of this kind—that there is a practical law which by itself commands absolutely and without any further motives, and that the following of this law is duty.

[The Need for Pure Ethics.]

For the purpose of achieving this proof it is of the utmost importance to take warning that we should not dream for a moment of trying to derive the reality of this principle from *the special characteristics of human nature*. For duty has to be a practical, unconditioned necessity of action; it must therefore hold for all rational beings (to whom alone an imperative can apply at all), and *only because of this* can it also be a law for all human wills. Whatever, on the other hand, is derived from the special predisposition of humanity, from certain feelings and propensities, and even, if this were possible, from some special bent peculiar to human reason and not holding necessarily for the will of every rational being—all this can indeed supply a personal maxim, but not a law: it can give us a subjective principle—one on which we have a propensity and inclination to act—but not an objective one on which we should be *directed* to act although our every propensity, inclination, and natural bent were opposed to it; so much so that the sublimity and inner worth of the command is the more manifest in a duty, the fewer are the subjective causes for obeying it and the more those against—without, however, on this account weakening in the slightest the necessitation exercised by the law or detracting anything from its validity.

It is here that philosophy is seen in actual fact to be placed in a precarious position, which is supposed to be firm although neither in heaven nor on earth is there anything from which it depends or on which it is based. It is here that she has to show her purity as the authoress of her own laws—not as the mouthpiece of laws whispered to her by some implanted sense or by who knows what tutelary nature, all of which laws together, though they may always be better than nothing, can never furnish us with principles dictated by reason. These principles must have an origin entirely and completely *a priori* and must at the same time derive from this their sovereign authority—that they expect nothing from the inclinations of man, but everything from the supremacy of the law and from the reverence due to it, or in default of this condemn man to self-contempt and inward abhorrence.

Hence everything that is empirical is, as a contribution to the principle of morality, not only wholly unsuitable for the purpose, but is even highly injurious to the purity of morals; for in morals the proper worth of an absolutely good will, a worth elevated above all price, lies precisely in this—that the principle of action is free from all influence by contingent grounds, the only kind that experience can supply. Against the slack, or indeed ignoble, attitude which seeks for the moral principle among empirical motives and laws we cannot give a warning too strongly or too often; for human reason in its weariness is fain to rest upon this pillow and in a dream of sweet illusions (which lead it to embrace a cloud in mistake for Juno) to foist into the place of morality some misbegotten mongrel patched up from limbs of very varied ancestry and looking like anything you please, only not like virtue to him who has once beheld her in her true shape.* . . .

[The Formula of the End in Itself.]

The will is conceived as a power of determining oneself to action *in accordance with the idea of certain laws*. And such a power can be found only in

---

*To behold virtue in her proper shape is nothing other than to show morality stripped of all admixture with the sensuous and of all the spurious adornments of reward or self-love. How much she then casts into the shade all else that appears attractive to the inclinations can be readily perceived by every man if he will exert his reason in the slightest—provided he has not entirely ruined it for all abstractions.

rational beings. Now what serves the will as a subjective ground of its self-determination is an *end*; and this, if it is given by reason alone, must be equally valid for all rational beings. What, on the other hand, contains merely the ground of the possibility of an action whose effect is an end is called a *means*. The subjective ground of a desire is an *impulsion* (*Triebfeder*); the objective ground of a volition is a *motive* (*Bewegungsgrund*). Hence the difference between subjective ends, which are based on impulsions, and objective ends, which depend on motives valid for every rational being. Practical principles are *formal* if they abstract from all subjective ends; they are *material*, on the other hand, if they are based on such ends and consequently on certain impulsions. Ends that a rational being adopts arbitrarily as *effects* of his action (material ends) are in every case only relative; for it is solely their relation to special characteristics in the subject's power of appetition which gives them their value. Hence this value can provide no universal principles, no principles valid and necessary for all rational beings and also for every volition—that is, no practical laws. Consequently all these relative ends can be the ground only of hypothetical imperatives.

Suppose, however, there were something *whose existence* has *in itself* an absolute value, something which as *an end in itself* could be a ground of determinate laws; then in it, and in it alone, would there be the ground of a possible categorical imperative—that is, of a practical law.

Now I say that man, and in general every rational being, *exists* as an end in himself, *not merely as a means* for arbitrary use by this or that will: he must in all his actions, whether they are directed to himself or to other rational beings, always be viewed *at the same time as an end*. All the objects of inclination have only a conditioned value; for if there were not these inclinations and the needs

grounded on them, their object would be valueless. Inclinations themselves, as sources of needs, are so far from having an absolute value to make them desirable for their own sake that it must rather be the universal wish of every rational being to be wholly free from them. Thus the value of all objects that can *be produced* by our action is always conditioned. Beings whose existence depends, not on our will, but on nature, have none the less, if they are non-rational beings, only a relative value as means and are consequently called *things*. Rational beings, on the other hand, are called *persons* because their nature already marks them out as ends in themselves—that is, as something which ought not to be used merely as a means—and consequently imposes to that extent a limit on all arbitrary treatment of them (and is an object of reverence). Persons, therefore, are not merely subjective ends whose existence as an object of our actions has a value *for us*: they are *objective ends*—that is, things whose existence is in itself an end, and indeed an end such that in its place we can put no other end to which they should serve *simply* as means; for unless this is so, nothing at all of *absolute* value would be found anywhere. But if all value were conditioned—that is, contingent—then no supreme principle could be found for reason at all.

If then there is to be a supreme practical principle and—so far as the human will is concerned—a categorical imperative, it must be such that from the idea of something which is necessarily an end for every one because it is an *end in itself* it forms an *objective* principle of the will and consequently can serve as a practical law. The ground of this principle is: *Rational nature exists as an end in itself*. This is the way in which a man necessarily conceives his own existence: it is therefore so far a *subjective* principle of human actions. But it is also the way in which every other rational being conceives his existence on the same rational ground which is valid also for me;* hence it is at the same time an *objective* principle, from which, as a supreme practical ground, it must be possible to derive all laws for the will. The practical imperative will therefore be as follows: *Act in such a way that you always treat humanity, whether in your own person or in the person of any other, never simply as a means, but always at the same time as an end.* We will now consider whether this can be carried out in practice.

[Illustrations.]

Let us keep to our previous examples.

First, as regards the concept of necessary duty to oneself, the man who contemplates suicide will ask 'Can my action be compatible with the Idea of humanity *as an end in itself?*' If he does away with himself in order to escape from a painful situation, he is making use of a person merely as *a means* to maintain a tolerable state of affairs till the end of his life. But man is not a thing—not something to be used *merely* as a means: he must always in all his actions be regarded as an end in himself. Hence I cannot dispose of man in my person by maiming, spoiling, or killing. (A more precise determination of this principle in order to avoid all misunderstanding—for example, about having limbs amputated to save myself or about exposing my life to danger in order to preserve it, and so on—I must here forego: this question belongs to morals proper.)

Secondly, so far as necessary or strict duty to others is concerned, the man who has a mind to make a false promise to others will see at once that he is intending to make use of another man *merely as a means* to an end he does not share. For the man whom I seek to use for my own purposes by such a promise cannot possibly agree with my way of behaving to him, and so cannot himself share the end of the action. This incompatibility with the principle of duty to others leaps to the eye more obviously when we bring in examples of attempts on the freedom and property of others. For then it is manifest that a violator of the rights of man intends to use the person of others merely as a means without taking into consideration that, as rational beings, they ought always at the same time to be rated as ends—that is, only as beings who must themselves be able to share in the end of the very same action.*

Thirdly, in regard to contingent (meritorious) duty to oneself, it is not enough that an action should refrain from conflicting with humanity in our own person as an end in itself: it must also *harmonize with this end.* Now there are in humanity capacities for greater perfection which form part of nature's purpose for humanity in our person. To neglect these can admittedly be compatible with the *maintenance* of humanity as an end in itself, but not with the *promotion* of this end.

Fourthly, as regards meritorious duties to others, the natural end which all men seek is their own happiness. Now humanity could no doubt subsist if everybody contributed nothing to the happiness of others but at the same time refrained from deliberately impairing their happiness. This is, however, merely to agree negatively and not positively

---

*This proposition I put forward here as a postulate. The grounds for it will be found in the final chapter [not reproduced here].

*Let no one think that here the trivial '*quod tibi non vis fieri, etc.*' can serve as a standard or principle. For it is merely derivative from our principle, although subject to various qualifications: it cannot be a universal law since it contains the ground neither of duties to oneself nor of duties of kindness to others (for many a man would readily agree that others should not help him if only he could be dispensed from affording help to them), nor finally of strict duties towards others; for on this basis the criminal would be able to dispute with the judges who punish him, and so on.

with *humanity as an end in itself* unless every one endeavours also, so far as in him lies, to further the ends of others. For the ends of a subject who is an end in himself must, if this conception is to have its *full* effect in me, be also, as far as possible, *my* ends.

[The Formula of Autonomy.]

This principle of humanity, and in general of every rational agent, *as an end in itself* (a principle which is the supreme limiting condition of every man's freedom of action) is not borrowed from experience; firstly, because it is universal, applying as it does to all rational beings as such, and no experience is adequate to determine universality; secondly, because in it humanity is conceived, not as an end of man (subjectively)—that is, as an object which, as a matter of fact, happens to be made an end—but as an objective end—one which, be our ends what they may, must, as a law, constitute the supreme limiting condition of all subjective ends and so must spring from pure reason. That is to say, the ground for every enactment of practical law lies *objectively in the rule* and in the form of universality which (according to our first principle) makes the rule capable of being a law (and indeed a law of nature); *subjectively*, however, it lies in the *end*; but (according to our second principle) the subject of all ends is to be found in every rational being as an end in himself. From this there now follows our third practical principle for the will—as the supreme condition of the will's conformity with universal practical reason—namely, the Idea *of the will of every rational being as a will which makes universal law.*

By this principle all maxims are repudiated which cannot accord with the will's own enactment of universal law. The will is therefore not merely subject to the law, but is so subject that it must be considered as also *making the law* for itself and precisely on this account as first of all subject to the law (of which it can regard itself as the author).

[The Exclusion of Interest.]

Imperatives as formulated above—namely, the imperative enjoining conformity of actions to universal law on the analogy of *a natural order* and that enjoining the universal *supremacy* of rational beings in themselves *as ends*—did, by the mere fact that they were represented as categorical, exclude from their sovereign authority every admixture of interest as a motive. They were, however, merely *assumed* to be categorical because we were bound to make this assumption if we wished to explain the concept of duty. That there were practical propositions which commanded categorically could not itself be proved, any more than it can be proved in this chapter generally; but one thing could have been done—namely, to show that in willing for the sake of duty renunciation of all interest, as the specific mark distinguishing a categorical from a hypothetical imperative, was expressed in the very imperative itself by means of some determination inherent in it. This is what is done in the present third formulation of the principle—namely, in the Idea of the will of every rational being as *a will which makes universal law.*

Once we conceive a will of this kind, it becomes clear that while a will *which is subject to law* may be bound to this law by some interest, nevertheless a will which is itself a supreme lawgiver cannot possibly as such depend on any interest; for a will which is dependent in this way would itself require yet a further law in order to restrict the interest of self-love to the condition that this interest should itself be valid as a universal law.

Thus the *principle* that every human will is *a will which by all its maxims enacts universal law**—provided only that it were right in other ways—would be *well suited* to be a categorical imperative in this respect: that precisely because of the Idea of making universal law it is *based on no interest* and consequently can alone among all possible imperatives be *unconditioned*. Or better still—to convert the proposition—if there is a categorical imperative (that is, a law for the will of every rational being), it can command us only to act always on the maxim of such a will in us as can at the same time look upon itself as making universal law; for only then is the practical principle and the imperative which we obey unconditioned, since it is wholly impossible for it to be based on any interest.

We need not now wonder, when we look back upon all the previous efforts that have been made to discover the principle of morality, why they have one and all been bound to fail. Their authors saw man as tied to laws by his duty, but it never occurred to them that he is subject only to *laws which are made by himself* and yet are *universal*, and that he is bound only to act in conformity with a will which is his own but has as nature's purpose for it the function of making universal law. For when they thought of man merely as subject to a law (whatever it might be), the law had to carry with it some interest in order to attract or compel, because it did not spring as a law from *his own* will: in order to conform with the law his will had to be necessitated by *something else* to act in a certain way. This absolutely inevitable conclusion meant that all the labour spent in trying to find a

supreme principle of duty was lost beyond recall; for what they discovered was never duty, but only the necessity of acting from a certain interest. This interest might be one's own or another's; but on such a view the imperative was bound to be always a conditioned one and could not possibly serve as a moral law. I will therefore call my principle the principle of the *Autonomy* of the will in contrast with all others, which I consequently class under *Heteronomy*.

[The Formula of the Kingdom of Ends.]

The concept of every rational being as one who must regard himself as making universal law by all the maxims of his will, and must seek to judge himself and his actions from this point of view, leads to a closely connected and very fruitful concept—namely, that of *a kingdom of ends*.

I understand by a '*kingdom*' a systematic union of different rational beings under common laws. Now since laws determine ends as regards their universal validity, we shall be able—if we abstract from the personal differences between rational beings, and also from all the content of their private ends—to conceive a whole of all ends in systematic conjunction (a whole both of rational beings as ends in themselves and also of the personal ends which each may set before himself); that is, we shall be able to conceive a kingdom of ends which is possible in accordance with the above principles.

For rational beings all stand under the *law* that each of them should treat himself and all others, *never merely as a means*, but always *at the same time as an end in himself*. But by so doing there arises a systematic union of rational beings under common objective laws—that is, a kingdom. Since these laws are directed precisely to the relation of such beings to one another as ends and means, this kingdom can be called a kingdom of ends (which is admittedly only an Ideal).

---

*I may be excused from bringing forward examples to illustrate this principle, since those which were first used as illustrations of the categorical imperative and its formula can all serve this purpose here.

A rational being belongs to the kingdom of ends as a *member*, when, although he makes its universal laws, he is also himself subject to these laws. He belongs to it as its *head*, when as the maker of laws he is himself subject to the will of no other.

A rational being must always regard himself as making laws in a kingdom of ends which is possible through freedom of the will—whether it be as member or as head. The position of the latter he can maintain, not in virtue of the maxim of his will alone, but only if he is a completely independent being, without needs and with an unlimited power adequate to his will.

Thus morality consists in the relation of all action to the making of laws whereby alone a kingdom of ends is possible. This making of laws must be found in every rational being himself and must be able to spring from his will. The principle of his will is therefore never to perform an action except on a maxim such as can also be a universal law, and consequently such *that the will can regard itself as at the same time making universal law by means of its maxim*. Where maxims are not already by their very nature in harmony with this objective principle of rational beings as makers of universal law, the necessity of acting on this principle is practical necessitation—that is, *duty*. Duty does not apply to the head in a kingdom of ends, but it does apply to every member and to all members in equal measure.

The practical necessity of acting on this principle—that is, duty—is in no way based on feelings, impulses, and inclinations, but only on the relation of rational beings to one another, a relation in which the will of a rational being must always be regarded as *making universal law*, because otherwise he could not be conceived as *an end in himself*. Reason thus relates every maxim of the will, considered as making universal law, to every other will and also to every action towards oneself: it

does so, not because of any further motive or future advantage, but from the Idea of the *dignity* of a rational being who obeys no law other than that which he at the same time enacts himself.

[The Dignity of Virtue.]

In the kingdom of ends everything has either a *price* or a *dignity*. If it has a price, something else can be put in its place as an *equivalent*; if it is exalted above all price and so admits of no equivalent, then it has a dignity.

What is relative to universal human inclinations and needs has a *market price*; what, even without presupposing a need, accords with a certain taste—that is, with satisfaction in the mere purposeless play of our mental powers—has a *fancy price* (*Affektionspreis*); but that which constitutes the sole condition under which anything can be an end in itself has not merely a relative value—that is, a price—but has an intrinsic value—that is, *dignity*.

Now morality is the only condition under which a rational being can be an end in himself; for only through this is it possible to be a law-making member in a kingdom of ends. Therefore morality, and humanity so far as it is capable of morality, is the only thing which has dignity. Skill and diligence in work have a market price; wit, lively imagination, and humour have a fancy price; but fidelity to promises and kindness based on principle (not on instinct) have an intrinsic worth. In default of these, nature and art alike contain nothing to put in their place; for their worth consists, not in the effects which result from them, not in the advantage or profit they produce, but in the attitudes of mind—that is, in the maxims of the will—which are ready in this way to manifest themselves in action even if they are not favoured by success. Such actions too need no recommendation from any subjective disposition or taste in order to meet with immediate favour and approval; they need no immediate propensity or feeling for themselves; they exhibit the will which performs them as an object of immediate reverence; nor is anything other than reason required to *impose* them upon the will, not to *coax* them from the will—which last would anyhow be a contradiction in the case of duties. This assessment reveals as dignity the value of such a mental attitude and puts it infinitely above all price, with which it cannot be brought into reckoning or comparison without, as it were, a profanation of its sanctity.

What is it then that entitles a morally good attitude of mind—or virtue—to make claims so high? It is nothing less than the *share* which it affords to a rational being *in the making of universal law*, and which therefore fits him to be a member in a possible kingdom of ends. For this he was already marked out in virtue of his own proper nature as an end in himself and consequently as a maker of laws in the kingdom of ends—as free in respect of all laws of nature, obeying only those laws which he makes himself and in virtue of which his maxims can have their part in the making of universal law (to which he at the same time subjects himself). For nothing can have a value other than that determined for it by the law. But the law-making which determines all value must for this reason have a dignity—that is, an unconditioned and incomparable worth—for the appreciation of which, as necessarily given by a rational being, the word 'reverence' is the only becoming expression. *Autonomy* is therefore the ground of the dignity of human nature and of every rational nature.

[Review of the Formulae.]

The aforesaid three ways of representing the principle of morality are at bottom merely so many formulations of precisely the same law, one of them by itself containing a combination of the other two. There is nevertheless a difference between them, which, however, is subjectively rather than objectively practical: that is to say, its purpose is to bring an Idea of reason nearer to intuition (in accordance with a certain analogy) and so nearer to feeling. All maxims have, in short,

1. a *form*, which consists in their universality; and in this respect the formula of the moral imperative is expressed thus: 'Maxims must be chosen as if they had to hold as universal laws of nature';

2. a *matter*—that is, an end; and in this respect the formula says: 'A rational being, as by his very nature an end and consequently an end in himself, must serve for every maxim as a condition limiting all merely relative and arbitrary ends';

3. a *complete determination* of all maxims by the following formula, namely: 'All maxims as proceeding from our own making of law ought to harmonize with a possible kingdom of ends as a kingdom of nature'.* This progression may be said to take place through the categories of the *unity* of the form of will (its universality); of the *multiplicity* of its matter (its objects—that is, its ends); and of the *totality* or completeness of its system of ends. It is, however, better if in moral *judgement* we proceed always in accordance with the strict method and take as our basis the universal formula of the categorical imperative: '*Act on the maxim which can at the same time be made a universal law*'. If, however, we wish also to secure acceptance for the moral law, it is very useful to bring one and the same action under the above-mentioned three

---

*Teleology views nature as a kingdom of ends; ethics views a possible kingdom of ends as a kingdom of nature. In the first case the kingdom of ends is a theoretical Idea used to explain what exists. In the second case it is a practical Idea used to bring into existence what does not exist but can be made actual by our conduct—and indeed to bring it into existence in conformity with this Idea.

concepts and so, as far as we can, to bring the universal formula nearer to intuition.

[Review of the Whole Argument.]

We can now end at the point from which we started out at the beginning—namely, the concept of an unconditionally good will. The *will* is *absolutely good* if it cannot be evil—that is, if its maxim, when made into a universal law, can never be in conflict with itself. This principle is therefore also its supreme law: 'Act always on that maxim whose universality as a law you can at the same time will'. This is the one principle on which a will can never be in conflict with itself, and such an imperative is categorical. Because the validity of the will as a universal law for possible actions is analogous to the universal interconnexion of existent things in accordance with universal laws—which constitutes the formal aspect of nature as such—we can also express the categorical imperative as follows: '*Act on that maxim which can at the same time have for its object itself as a universal law of nature*'. In this way we provide the formula for an absolutely good will.

Rational nature separates itself out from all other things by the fact that it sets itself an end. An end would thus be the matter of every good will. But in the Idea of a will which is absolutely good—good without any qualifying condition (namely, that it should attain this or that end)—there must be complete abstraction from every end that has to be *produced* (as something which would make every will only relatively good). Hence the end must here be conceived, not as an end to be produced, *but as a self-existent* end. It must therefore be conceived only negatively—that is, as an end against which we should never act, and consequently as one which in all our willing we must never rate *merely* as a means, but always at the

same time as an end. Now this end can be nothing other than the subject of all possible ends himself, because this subject is also the subject of a will that may be absolutely good; for such a will cannot without contradiction be subordinated to any other object. The principle 'So act in relation to every rational being (both to yourself and to others) that he may at the same time count in your maxim as an end in himself' is thus at bottom the same as the principle 'Act on a maxim which at the same time contains in itself its own universal validity for every rational being'. For to say that in using means to every end I ought to restrict my maxim by the condition that it should also be universally valid as a law for every subject is just the same as to say this—that a subject of ends, namely, a rational being himself, must be made the ground for all maxims of action, never *merely* as a means, but as a supreme condition restricting the use of every means—that is, always also as an end.

Now from this it unquestionably follows that every rational being, as an end in himself, must be able to regard himself as also the maker of universal law in respect of any law whatever to which he may be subjected; for it is precisely the fitness of his maxims to make universal law that marks him out as an end in himself. It follows equally that this dignity (or prerogative) of his above all the mere things of nature carries with it the necessity of always choosing his maxims from the point of view of himself—and also of every other rational being—as a maker of law (and this is why they are called persons). It is in this way that a world of rational beings (*mundus intelligibilis*) is possible as a kingdom of ends—possible, that is, through the making of their own laws by all persons as its members. Accordingly every rational being must so act as if he were through his maxims always a law-making member in the universal kingdom of ends. The formal principle of such maxims is 'So act as if your maxims had to serve at the same time as a universal law (for all rational beings)'. Thus a kingdom of ends is possible only on the analogy of a kingdom of nature; yet the kingdom of ends is possible only through maxims—that is, self-imposed rules—while nature is possible only through laws concerned with causes whose action is necessitated from without. In spite of this difference, we give to nature as a whole, even although it is regarded as a machine, the name of a 'kingdom of nature' so far as—and for the reason that—it stands in a relation to rational beings as its ends. Now a kingdom of ends would actually come into existence through maxims which the categorical imperative prescribes as a rule for all rational beings, *if these maxims were universally followed.* Yet even if a rational being were himself to follow such a maxim strictly, he cannot count on everybody else being faithful to it on this ground, nor can he be confident that the kingdom of nature and its purposive order will work in harmony with him, as a fitting member, towards a kingdom of ends made possible by himself—or, in other words, that it will favour his expectation of happiness. But in spite of this the law 'Act on the maxims of a member who makes universal laws for a merely possible kingdom of ends' remains in full force, since its command is categorical. And precisely here we encounter the paradox that without any further end or advantage to be attained the mere dignity of humanity, that is, of rational nature in man—and consequently that reverence for a mere Idea—should function as an inflexible precept for the will; and that it is just this freedom from dependence on interested motives which constitutes the sublimity of a maxim and the worthiness of every rational subject to be a law-making member in the kingdom of ends; for otherwise he would have to be regarded as subject only to the law of nature—the law of his own needs. Even if it were thought

that both the kingdom of nature and the kingdom of ends were united under one head and that thus the latter kingdom ceased to be a mere Idea and achieved genuine reality, the Idea would indeed gain by this the addition of a strong motive, but never any increase in its intrinsic worth; for, even if this were so, it would still be necessary to conceive the unique and absolute lawgiver himself as judging the worth of rational beings solely by the disinterested behaviour they prescribed to themselves in virtue of this Idea alone. The essence of things does not vary with their external relations; and where there is something which, without regard to such relations, constitutes by itself the absolute worth of man, it is by this that man must also be judged by everyone whatsoever—even by the Supreme Being. Thus *morality* lies in the relation of actions to the autonomy of the will—that is, to a possible making of universal law by means of its maxims. An action which is compatible with the autonomy of the will is *permitted*; one which does not harmonize with it is *forbidden*. A will whose maxims necessarily accord with the laws of autonomy is a *holy*, or absolutely good, will. The dependence of a will not absolutely good on the principle of autonomy (that is, moral necessitation) is *obligation*. Obligation can thus have no reference to a holy being. The objective necessity to act from obligation is called *duty*.

From what was said a little time ago we can now easily explain how it comes about that, although in the concept of duty we think of subjection to the law, yet we also at the same time attribute to the person who fulfils all his duties a certain sublimity and *dignity*. For it is not in so far as he is *subject* to the law that he has sublimity, but rather in so far as, in regard to this very same law, he is at the same time its *author* and is subordinated to it only on this ground. We have also shown above how neither fear nor inclination, but solely reverence for the law, is the motive which can give an action moral worth. Our own will, provided it were to act only under the condition of being able to make universal law by means of its maxims—this ideal will which can be ours is the proper object of rev- erence; and the dignity of man consists precisely in his capacity to make universal law, although only on condition of being himself also subject to the law he makes.

chapter twenty-one

Marquis De Sade

Donatien-Alphonse-François, comte de Sade (1740–1814), known to us simply as the Marquis de Sade, is famous primarily for his sexual debauchery and the violent and sexually explicit nature of his novels. However, his works are also compelling as philosophical texts, providing a powerful critique of the Enlightenment. Sade's life work was aimed at the liberation of the passions from the repressive constraints imposed upon them by religion and the customs of his time. He was born in Paris to Jean-Baptiste-Joseph-François, comte de Sade, and Marie-Eléonore de Maillé de Carman, lady-in-waiting to the Princess de Condé. His education was supervised by his uncle, Jacques-François-Paul-Aldonse, until he enrolled in Louis le Grand Collège, a Jesuit school, in 1750, where he was given a personal tutor, Abbé Jacques-François Amblet. In what is generally accepted to be an autobiographical passage in *Aline et Valcour*, Sade describes his teacher as "both severe and intelligent," and notes that the Abbé "would probably have exerted a good influence on my youth, but unfortunately I did not keep him long enough."[1]

In 1763, against his wishes, Sade married Mademoiselle Renée-Pélagie de Montreuil in an arranged marriage of alliance between his family and the wealthy Montreuils. Shortly after his wedding, Sade was arrested for the first of many "sexual excesses," the most well-known of which involved Rose Keller, a poor widow he found begging in the streets and then abused. Keller dropped her charges against Sade after being paid off by his wife, but he was eventually incarcerated for his crimes against Keller in 1768, though he remained in custody for only a few months. A few years later, he was condemned to the guillotine for practicing sodomy and for the poisoning of several young prostitutes. While Sade was never actually decapitated, he was incarcerated in 1772, first in Vincennes and later in the Bastille, where he remained until July 4, 1789, when he was transferred to Charenton Asylum after being accused of provoking the crowd below with shouts out of his cell window (including cries that the prisoners were being slaughtered). He was no longer residing in the Bastille when it was stormed on July 14,

Excerpts from D.A.F. Sade, *Philosophy in the Bedroom*. From *Justine, Philosophy in the Bedroom, and Other Writings,* translated and edited by Richard Seaver and Austryn Wainhouse. Copyright © 1965 by Richard Seaver and Austryn Wainhouse. Used by permission of Grove/Atlantic, Inc.

though he was freed from Charenton shortly thereafter. Although arrested several times between 1791 and 1803, including an arrest for the publication of obscene material in 1801, Sade was in and out of prisons until he was definitively placed in Charenton in 1803, where he remained until his death in 1814. In his will he requested that he not receive any burial rites but be placed in a grave which would then be strewn with acorns, "in order that the spot become green again, and the copse grown back thick over it, the traces of my grave may disappear from the face of the earth as I trust the memory of me shall fade out of the minds of all men."[2] Against his final wishes, Sade was buried in Charenton cemetery, and despite significant efforts, some of which extended into the twentieth century, to censor and even destroy his writings, he left behind a massive body of work, including his novels *Justine, The 120 Days of Sodom, Juliette*, and *Philosophy in the Bedroom*.

Sade's novels present a wide variety of characters, some thoroughly wicked, some merely libertine, some atheist, others devout. Given such a myriad of mouthpieces, nothing could be further from Sade's intentions than to take any of these creatures literally; as Georges Bataille notes, "of the various philosophies [Sade] attributes to his characters we cannot retain a single one."[3] The characters he conjures up in *Philosophy in the Bedroom* are shocking not only because they perform horrific acts, but also because they justify and explain such acts in a rational manner. As Madame de Saint Ange asserts, "[M]easure is required even in the depths of infamy and delirium." Sade himself appears to be in possession of the most horrific of imaginations, being able to comprehend rationally the mind of the libertine monster, as well as that of the most pious citizen. Yet even given the spectrum of theories his characters expound, it is clear that Sade's philosophy is centered around dispelling what he took to be certain myths about the nature of the erotic and the violent, namely, the commonly held doctrine of "natural" prohibitions against sexual and criminal transgressions. This required him to dismantle the dominant values of the Enlightenment one by one, beginning with certain residual vestiges of Christian morality and the ideal that reason was necessary to control "unnatural" and "excessive" passions in order to realize a more perfect human society. Enlightenment thinkers—most notably Kant—held that humans are free insofar as they rationally deliberate about their actions. Education—such as that offered to the young Emile[4]—could provide individuals the tools necessary to cultivate reason. The Enlightenment thus set forth the thesis that human liberation and the good life were the necessary and happy outcomes of rationality. Against this view, Sade posited reflection and calculation toward the end of fulfilling one's most passionate and even violent desires.

The marquis's novels also make a case for the notion that sexual freedom is necessary for women as well as for men, a position somewhat inconsistent with his jealousy over his wife and mistresses yet explicitly maintained by and in reference to his female characters. *Philosophy in the Bedroom* in particular deals with this issue in terms of questioning the firmly held equation of a woman's sexual pleasure with her reproductive function. As Sade proclaims in the dedication of *Philosophy in the Bedroom*, "young maidens, too long constrained by a fanciful Virtue's absurd and dangerous bonds and by those of a disgusting religion" should imitate the novel's young heroine Eugénie by spurning "all those ridiculous precepts" in which they have been inculcated. Such indoctrination is for Sade not only irrational (as shown by how reasonably his characters dispel it) but also against human nature, for according to Sade there is no sexual desire so perverse as to be against nature; in short, if one can imagine it, one is justified by nature to act upon it. Far from maintaining the goodness of virtue and reason above and against the irrationality of the passions, Sade was concerned throughout his life with reflecting upon and rationally justifying the pursuit of pleasure, in all its violence and splendor.

Sade's critiques of the Enlightenment, as well as his explorations into the nature of human desire, have exerted great influence on a variety of twentieth-century French thinkers, including Georges Bataille and Michel Foucault. According to Bataille, in his life and work the marquis was the first person to give a rational voice to the violence inherent in human desire, and as such he dealt a decisive blow to the Enlightenment picture of subjectivity as inherently rational and good. According to Foucault, Sade maintained that it is not natural tendencies but rather external power structures that shape our desires; hence all desires are "natural," in the sense of being physically possible, though not all are permissible within a given value system.[5]

German critical theorists Max Horkheimer and Theodor Adorno agree with Bataille and Foucault that Sade chipped away at the façade that was the Enlightenment, but argue that his characters are still very much grounded in and indebted to Enlightenment myths. For Horkheimer and Adorno, Sade's Juliette attempts to transcend the repressive model of sexuality (female sexuality in particular) posited by Enlightenment ideals; in her brute rationality and calculation, however, she fails to fully transcend these ideals.[6] Despite the attempts by both his family and countrymen to silence him and repress his work, the Marquis de Sade has emerged as a significant figure in contemporary discussions about the nature of human desire.

JGJ

QUESTIONS

1. Explain Dolmancé's critique of the current value system. How might his libertinage manifest itself as part of that critique? What is the relationship between theory and practice advanced in this text?

2. Explain the political theory outlined in the treatise "Yet Another Effort, Frenchmen, If You Would Become Republicans." How are the ideas presented thus like or unlike those set forth by Dolmancé himself? What is being suggested here about the relationship between morality and politics (particularly in terms of sexual practices and their social and political meaning)?

3. Madame de Saint-Ange and Dolmancé, as Eugénie's self-proclaimed teachers in the ways of libertinage, maintain that she must not only be shown how to be a libertine, but also must be instructed in the philosophy behind such actions as well. How might this text be seen as a critique of the Enlightenment?

ENDNOTES

1. Sade, p. 74.
2. *Ibid.*, p. 157.
3. Bataille, p. 110.
4. See chapter 18.
5. See Foucault.
6. See Adorno and Horkheimer.

SELECTED BIBLIOGRAPHY

Adorno, Theodor, and Max Horkheimer. *The Dialectic of Enlightenment*, trans. John Cumming. New York: Continuum, 2000.

Bataille, Georges. "Sade," from *Literature and Evil*, trans. Alastair Hamilton. New York: Marion Boyers, 1997.

Foucault, Michel. *The History of Sexuality*, Vol. I, trans. Robert Hurley. New York: Vantage Books, 1990.

Sade, D.A.F. *The Marquis de Sade: Justine. Philosophy in the Bedroom, and Other Writings*, trans. and ed. Richard Seaver and Austryn Wainhouse. New York: Grove Press, 1965.

Sawhney, Deepak Narang, ed. *Must We Burn Sade*? New York: Humanity Books, 1999.

Seaver, Richard and Austryn Wainhouse, trans and eds. *Justine, Philosophy in the Bedroom, and Other Writings*. New York: Grove Press. 1965.

from *Philosophy in the Bedroom*

Marquis De Sade

TO LIBERTINES

Voluptuaries of all ages, of every sex, it is to you only that I offer this work; nourish yourselves upon its principles: they favor your passions, and these passions, whereof coldly insipid moralists put you in fear, are naught but the means Nature employs to bring man to the ends she prescribes to him; harken only to these delicious promptings, for no voice save that of the passions can conduct you to happiness.

Lewd women, let the voluptuous Saint-Ange be your model; after her example, be heedless of all that contradicts pleasure's divine laws, by which all her life she was enchained.

You young maidens, too long constrained by a fanciful Virtue's absurd and dangerous bonds and by those of a disgusting religion, imitate the fiery Eugènie; be as quick as she to destroy, to spurn all those ridiculous precepts inculcated in you by imbecile parents.

And you, amiable debauchees, you who since youth have known no limits but those of your desires and who have been governed by your caprices alone, study the cynical Dolmancé, proceed like him and go as far as he if you too would travel the length of those flowered ways your lechery prepares for you; in Dolmancé's academy be at last convinced it is only by exploring and enlarging the sphere of his tastes and whims, it is only by sacrificing everything to the senses' pleasure that this individual, who never asked to be cast into this universe of woe, that this poor creature who goes under the name of Man, may be able to sow a smattering of roses atop the thorny path of life.

DIALOGUE THE FIRST

Madame De Saint-Ange, Le Chevalier De Mirvel

MADAME DE SAINT-ANGE—Good day, my friend. And what of Monsieur Dolmancé?

LE CHEVALIER—He'll be here promptly at four; we do not dine until seven—and will have, as you see, ample time to chat.

MADAME DE SAINT-ANGE—You know, my dear brother, I do begin to have a few misgivings about my curiosity and all the obscene plans scheduled for today. Chevalier, you overindulge me, truly you do. The more sensible I should be, the more excited and libertine this accursed mind of mine becomes—and all that you have given me but serves to spoil me. . . . At twenty-six, I should be sober and staid, and I'm still nothing but the most licentious of women. . . . Oh, I've a busy brain, my friend; you'd scarce believe the ideas I have, the things I'd like to do. I supposed that by confining myself to women I would become better behaved . . . ; that were my desires concentrated upon my own sex I would no longer pant after yours: pure fantasy, my friend; my imagination has only been pricked the more by the pleasures I thought to deprive myself of. I have discovered that when it is a question of someone like me, born for libertinage, it is useless to think of imposing limits or restraints upon oneself—impetuous desires immediately sweep them away. In a word, my dear, I am an amphibious creature: I love everything, everyone, whatever it is, it amuses me; I should like to combine every species—but you must admit, Chevalier, is it not the height of extravagance for me to wish to know this unusual Dolmancé who in all his life, you tell me, has been unable to see a woman according to the prescriptions of common usage, this Dolmancé who, a sodomite out of principle, not only worships his own sex but never yields to ours save when we consent to put at his disposal those so well beloved charms of which he habitually makes use when consorting with men? . . . I trust he does not believe in God!

LE CHEVALIER—His is the most complete and thoroughgoing corruption, and he the most evil individual, the greatest scoundrel in the world.

MADAME DE SAINT-ANGE—Ah, how that warms me! Me-thinks that I'll be wild about this man. And what of his fancies, brother?

LE CHEVALIER—You know them full well; Sodom's delights are as dear to him in their active as in their passive form. For his pleasures, he cares for none but men; if however he sometimes deigns to employ women, it is only upon condition they be obliging enough to exchange sex with him. I've spoken of you to him; I advised him of your intentions, he agrees, and in his turn reminds you of the rules of the game. I warn you, my dear, he will refuse you altogether if you attempt to engage him to undertake anything else. "What I consent to do with your sister is," he declares, "an extravagance, an indiscretion with which one soils oneself but rarely and only by taking ample precautions." . . .

MADAME DE SAINT-ANGE—Well, my chivalrous friend, as reward for your touching consideration, today I am going to hand over to your passions a young virgin, a girl, more beautiful than Love itself.

LE CHEVALIER—What! With Dolmancé . . . you're bringing a woman here?

MADAME DE SAINT-ANGE—It is a matter of an education; that of a little thing I knew last autumn at the convent, while my husband was at the baths. We could accomplish nothing there, we dared try nothing, too many eyes were fixed upon us, but we made a promise to meet again, to get together as soon as possible. Occupied with nothing but this desire, I have, in order to satisfy it, become acquainted with her family. Her father is a libertine—I've enthralled him. At any rate, the lovely one is coming, I am waiting for her; we'll spend two days together . . . two delicious days; I shall employ the better part of the time educating the young lady. Dolmancé and I will put into this pretty little head every principle of the most unbridled libertinage, we will set her ablaze with our own fire, we will feed her upon our philosophy, inspire her with our desires, and as I wish to join a little practice to theory, as I like the demonstrations to keep abreast of the dissertations, I have destined to you, dear brother, the harvest of Cythera's myrtle, and to Dolmancé shall go the roses of Sodom. I'll have two pleasures at once: that of enjoying these criminal lecheries myself, and that of giving the lessons, of inspiring fancies in the sweet innocent I am luring into our nets. . . .

Be certain I'll spare nothing to pervert her, degrade her, demolish in her all the false ethical notions with which they may already have been able to dizzy her; in two lessons, I want to render her as criminal as am I . . . as impious . . . as debauched, as depraved. . . .

LE CHEVALIER—And tell me, please, who is this youngster?

MADAME DE SAINT-ANGE—Her name is Eugénie, daughter of a certain Mistival, one of the wealthiest commercial figures in the capital, aged about thirty-six; her mother is thirty-two at the very most, and the little girl fifteen. Mistival is as libertine as his wife is pious. As for Eugénie, dear one, I should in vain undertake to figure her to you; she is quite beyond my descriptive powers . . . satisfy yourself with the knowledge that assuredly neither you nor I have ever set eyes on anything so delicious, anywhere. . . .

LE CHEVALIER—The portrait you have just made for me assures my promptness. . . . Ah, heaven! to go out . . . to leave you, in the state I am in . . . Adieu! . . . a kiss . . . a kiss, my dear sister, to satisfy me at least till then. (*She kisses him, touches the prick straining in his breeches, and the young man leaves in haste.*)

DIALOGUE THE FIFTH

Dolmancé, Le Chevalier, Augustin, Eugenié, Madame De Saint-Ange

MADAME DE SAINT-ANGE, *presenting Augustin*—Let's on with it, friends, let's to our frolics; what would life be without its little amusements? . . .

EUGENIE, *blushing*—Heavens! I am so ashamed!

DOLMANCE—Rid yourself of that weak-hearted sentiment; all actions, and above all those of libertinage, being inspired in us by Nature, there is not one, of whatever kind, that warrants shame. Be smart there, Eugénie, act the whore with this young man; consider that every provocation sensed by a boy and originating from a girl is a natural offertory, and that your sex never serves Nature better than when it prostitutes itself to ours; that 'tis, in a word, to be fucked that you were born, and that she who refuses her obedience to this intention Nature has for her does not deserve to see the light longer. . . .

LE CHEVALIER—Approach, sister; to comply with Dolmancé's strictures and with yours, I am

going to stretch out on this bed; you will lie in my arms, and expose your gorgeous buttocks to him, and very wide indeed you shall spread them. . . . Yes, just so: we're ready to begin.

DOLMANCE—No, not quite; wait for me; I must first of all enter your sister's ass, since Augustin whispers me to do it; next, I'll marry you: remember, let's not fall short of any of our principles and remember also that a student is observing us, and we owe her precise demonstrations. Eugénie, come frig me while I determine this low fellow's enormous engine; lend a hand with my own erection, pollute my prick, very lightly, roll it upon your buttocks. . . . (*She does so.*) . . .

Now ready yourself, Madame; open that sublime ass to my impure ardor; Eugénie, guide the dart, it must be your hand that conducts it to the vent, your hand must make it penetrate; immediately it is in, get a grip on good Augustin here, and fill my entrails up with him; those are an apprentice's chores and thence there is much instruction to be had; that, my dear, is why I put you to this trouble. . . .

MADAME DE SAINT-ANGE—Why, my dears, there I am fucked from either side! By Jesus! What a divine pleasure! No, there's none like it in all the world. Ah, fuck! how I pity the woman who has not tasted it! Rattle me, Dolmancé, smite away . . . let the violence of your movements impale me upon my brother's blade and you, Eugénie, do you contemplate me; come, regard me in vice; come, learn, from my example, to savor it, to be transported, to taste it with delectation. . . . Behold, my love, behold all that I simultaneously do: scandal, seduction, bad example, incest, adultery, sodomy! Oh, Satan! one and unique god of my soul, inspire thou in me something yet more, present further perversions to my smoking heart, and then shalt thou see how I shall plunge myself into them all! . . .

I am slain! . . . Eugénie, let me kiss thee, let me eat thee! let me consume, batten upon thy fuck as I loose my own! . . . (*Augustin, Dolmancé and the Chevalier act in chorus; the fear of appearing monotonous prevents us from recording expressions which, upon such occasions, are all very apt to resemble one another.*) . . .

From now on we must occupy ourselves exclusively with her; consider her, brother, she's the prey; examine that charming maidenhead; 'twill soon belong to thee.

EUGENIE—Oh, no! not by the fore-end! 'twould hurt me overmuch; from behind as much as you please, as Dolmancé dealt with me a short while ago.

MADAME DE SAINT-ANGE—Naive and delicious girl! She demands of you precisely what one has so much difficulty obtaining from others.

EUGENIE—Oh, 'tis not without a little remorse; for you have not entirely reassured me upon the criminal enormity I have always heard ascribed to this, especially when it is done between man and man, as has just occurred with Dolmancé and Augustin; tell me, Monsieur, tell me how your philosophy explains this species of misdemeanor. 'Tis frightful, is it not?

DOLMANCE—Start from one fundamental point, Eugénie: in libertinage, nothing is frightful, because everything libertinage suggests is also a natural inspiration. . . .

EUGENIE—Oh, 'tis natural?

DOLMANCE—Yes, natural, so I affirm it to be: Nature has not got two voices, you know, one of them condemning all day what the other commands, and it is very certain that it is nowhere but from her organ that those men who are infatuated with this mania receive the impressions that drive them to it. They who wish to denigrate the taste or proscribe its practice declare it is harmful to population; how dull-witted they are, these imbeciles who think of nothing but the multiplication of their kind, and who detect nothing but the crime in anything that conduces to a different end. Is it really so firmly established that Nature has so great a need for this overcrowding as they would like to have us believe? is it very certain that one is guilty of an outrage whenever one abstains from this stupid propagation? To convince ourselves, let us for an instant scrutinize both her operations and her laws. Were it that Nature did naught but create, and never destroy, I might be able to believe, with those tedious sophists, that the sublimest of all actions would be incessantly to labor at production, and following that, I should grant, with them, that the refusal to reproduce would be, would perforce have to be, a crime; however, does not the most fleeting glance at natural operations reveal that destructions are just as necessary to her plan as are creations? that the one and the other of these functions are interconnected and enmeshed so intimately that for either to operate without the other would be impossible? that nothing would be born, nothing would be regenerated without destructions? Destruction, hence, like creation, is one of Nature's mandates. . . .

But, the fools and the populators continue to object—and they are naught but one—this procreative sperm cannot have been placed in your loins for any purpose other than reproduction: to misuse it is an offense. I have just proven the contrary, since this misuse would not even be equivalent to destruction, and since destruction, far more serious than misuse, would not itself be criminal. Secondly, it is false that Nature intends this spermatic liquid to be employed only and entirely for reproduction; were this true, she would not permit its spillage under any circumstance save those appropriate to that end.

But experience shows that the contrary may happen, since we lose it both when and where we wish. Secondly, she would forbid the occurrence of those losses save in coitus, losses which, however, do take place, both when we dream and when we summon remembrances; were Nature miserly about this so precious sap, 'twould never but be into the vessel of reproduction she would tolerate its flow; assuredly, she would not wish this voluptuousness, wherewith at such moments she crowns us, to be felt by us when we divert our tribute; for it would not be reasonable to suppose she could consent to give us pleasures at the very moment we heaped insults upon her. Let us go further; were women not born save to produce—which most surely would be the case were this production so dear to Nature—, would it happen that, throughout the whole length of a woman's life, there are no more than seven years, all the arithmetic performed, during which she is in a state capable of conceiving and giving birth? What! Nature avidly seeks propagation, does she; and everything which does not tend to this end offends her, does it! and out of a hundred years of life the sex destined to produce cannot do so during more than seven years! Nature wishes for propagation only, and the semen she accords man to serve in these reproducings is lost, wasted, misused wherever and as often as it pleases man! He takes the same pleasures in this loss as in useful employment of his seed, and never the least inconvenience! . . .

Why, she would simply fail to notice it. Do you fancy races have not already become extinct? Buffon counts several of them perished, and Nature, struck dumb by a so precious loss, doesn't so much as murmur! The entire species might be wiped out and the air would not be the less pure for it, nor the Star less brilliant, nor the universe's march less exact. What idiocy it is to think that our kind is so useful to the world that he who might not labor to propagate it or he who might disturb this propagation would necessarily become a criminal! Let's bring this blindness to a stop and may the example of more reasonable peoples serve to persuade us of our errors. There is not one corner of the earth where the alleged crime of sodomy has not had shrines and votaries. The Greeks, who made of it, so to speak, a virtue, raised a statue unto Venus Callipygea; Rome sent to Athens for law, and returned with this divine taste. . . .

O my friends, can there be an extravagance to equal that of imagining that a man must be a monster deserving to lose his life because he has preferred enjoyment of the asshole to that of the cunt, because a young man with whom he finds two pleasures, those of being at once lover and mistress, has appeared to him preferable to a young girl, who promises him but half as much! He shall be a villain, a monster, for having wished to play the role of a sex not his own! Indeed! Why then has Nature created him susceptible of this pleasure?

Let us inspect his conformation; you will observe radical differences between it and that of other men who have not been blessed with this predilection for the behind; his buttocks will be fairer, plumper; never a hair will shade the altar of pleasure, whose interior, lined with a more delicate, more sensual, more sensitive membrane, will be found positively of the same variety as the interior of a woman's vagina; this man's character, once again unlike that of others, will be softer, more pliant, subtler; in him you will find almost all the vices and all the virtues native to women; you will recognize even their weaknesses there; all will have feminine manias and sometimes feminine habits and traits. Would it then be possible that Nature, having thuswise assimilated them into women, could be irritated by what they have of women's tastes? It is not evident that this is a category of men different from the other, a class Nature has created in order to diminish or minimize propagation, whose overgreat extent would infallibly be prejudicial to her? . . . Ah, dear Eugénie, did you but know how delicate is one's enjoyment when a heavy prick fills the behind, when, driven to the balls, it flutters there, palpitating; and then, withdrawn to the foreskin, it hesitates, and returns, plunges in again, up to the hair! No, no, in the wide world there is no pleasure to rival this one: 'tis the delight of philosophers, that of heroes, it would be that of the gods were not the parts used in his heavenly conjugation the only gods we on earth should reverence![1]

EUGENIE, *very much moved*—Oh, my friends, let me be buggered!. . . Here, my buttocks stand ready. . . . I present them to you!. . . Fuck me, for I discharge!. . . (*Upon pronouncing these words. she falls into the arms of Madame de Saint-Ange, who clasps her, embraces her, and offers the young lady's elevated flanks to Dolmancé.*)

MADAME DE SAINT-ANGE—Divine teacher, will you resist the proposal? Will you not be tempted by this sublime ass? See how it doth yawn, how it winks at thee!

DOLMANCE—I ask your forgiveness, beautiful Eugénie: it shall not be I, if indeed you wish it, who shall undertake to extinguish the fires I have lit. Dear child, in my eyes you possess the large fault of being a woman. I was so considerate as to forget much in order to harvest your virginity; deign to think well of me for going no further: the Chevalier is going to take the task in hand. His sister, equipped with this artificial

prick, will bestow the most redoubtable buffets upon her brother's ass, all the while presenting her noble behind to Augustin, who shall bugger her and whom I'll fuck meantime; for, I make no attempt to conceal it, this fine lad's ass has been signaling to me for an hour, and I wish absolutely to repay him for what he has done to me.

EUGENIE—I accept the revision; but, in truth, Dolmancé, the frankness of your avowal little offsets its impoliteness.

DOLMANCE—A thousand pardons, Mademoiselle; but we other buggers are very nice on the question of candor and the exactitude of our principles.

MADAME DE SAINT-ANGE—However, a reputation for candor is not the one we commonly grant those whom, like yourself, are accustomed only to taking people from behind.

DOLMANCE—We do have something of the treacherous, yes; a touch of the false, you may believe it. But after all, Madame, I have demonstrated to you that this character is indispensable to man in society. Condemned to live amidst people who have the greatest interest in hiding themselves from our gaze, in disguising the vices they have in order to exhibit nothing but virtues they never respect, there should be the greatest danger in the thing were we to show them frankness only; for then, 'tis evident, we would give them all the advantages over us they on their part refuse us, and the dupery would be manifest. The needs for dissimulation and hypocrisy are bequeathed us by society; let us yield to the fact. Allow me for an instant to offer my own example to you, Madame: there is surely no being more corrupt anywhere in the world; well, my contemporaries are deceived in me; ask them what they think of Dolmancé, and they all will tell you I am an honest man,

---

[1] A later part of this work promising us a much more extensive dissertation upon this subject, we have, here, limited ourselves to an analysis but roughly sketched and but boldly outlined.

whereas there is not a single crime whereof I have not gleaned the most exquisite delights.

MADAME DE SAINT-ANGE—Oh, you do not convince me that you have committed atrocities.

DOLMANCE—Atrocities . . . indeed, Madame, I have wrought horrors.

MADAME DE SAINT-ANGE—Fie, you are like the man who said to his confessor: "Needless to go into details, Sir; murder and theft excepted, you can be sure I've done everything."

DOLMANCE—Yes, Madame, I should say the same thing, omitting those exceptions.

MADAME DE SAINT-ANGE—What! libertine, you have permitted yourself . . .

DOLMANCE—Everything, Madame, everything; with a temperament and principles like mine, does one deny oneself anything?

MADAME DE SAINT-ANGE—Oh, let's fuck! fuck! . . .

DOLMANCE—One moment . . . one moment; I am the one who shall introduce it; but, by way of preliminary, and I ask the lovely Eugénie's pardon for it, she must allow me to flog her in order she be put in the proper humor. . . . (*He beats her.*) . . .

whipping merrily away—. . . Come, come, little bitch, you'll be lashed!

EUGENIE—My God, how he does wax hot! And my buttocks too, they are all afire! . . . But, indeed, you're hurting me! . . .

DOLMANCE—With all my heart; I ask but one favor of Eugénie: that she consent to be flogged as vigorously as I myself desire to be; you notice how well within natural law I am; but wait, let's arrange it: let Eugénie mount your flanks, Madame, she will clutch your neck, like those children whose mothers carry them on their backs; that way, I'll have two asses under my hand; I'll drub them together; the Chevalier and Augustin, both will work upon me, striking my buttocks. . . . Yes, 'tis thus . . . Well, there we are! . . . what ecstasy!

MADAME DE SAINT-ANGE—Do not spare this little rascal, I beseech you, and as I ask no quarter, I want you to grant it to no one.

EUGENIE—Aïe! aïe! aïe! I believe my blood is flowing!

MADAME DE SAINT-ANGE—'Twill embellish our buttocks by lending color to them. . . . Courage, my angel, courage; bear in mind that it is always by way of pain one arrives at pleasure.

EUGENIE—I can no more!

DOLMANCE, *halts a minute to contemplate his work; then, starting in again*—Another fifty, Eugénie; yes, precisely, fifty more on either cheek will do it. O bitches! how great shall now be your pleasure in fucking! (*The posture is dissolved.*)

MADAME DE SAINT-ANGE, *examining Eugénie's buttocks*—Oh, the poor little thing, her behind is all bloodied over! Beast, how much pleasure you take thus in kissing cruelty's vestiges!

DOLMANCE, *polluting himself*—Yes, I mask nothing, and my pleasures would be more ardent were the wounds more cruel. . . .

MADAME DE SAINT-ANGE—Cast an eye on this little tramp! How she quivers and wriggles!

EUGENIE—Is it my fault? I am dying from pleasure! That whipping . . . this immense prick . . .! My darling, my darling, I can no more! . . .

No more, enough. . . . My friends, tell me now if a woman must always accept the proposal, when 'tis made to her, thus to be fucked?

MADAME DE SAINT-ANGE—Always, dear heart, unfailingly. More, as this mode of fucking is delightful, she ought to require it of those of whom she makes use; but if she is dependent upon the person with whom she amuses herself, if she hopes to obtain favors from him, gifts or thanks, let her restrain her eagerness and not surrender her ass for nothing; cede it after being urged, besought, wheedled; there is not a man of all those who possess the taste who would not ruin himself for a woman clever enough to refuse him nothing save with the design of inflaming him further; she will extract from him all she wants if she well has the art of yielding only when pressed.

DOLMANCE—Well, little angel, are you converted? have you given over believing sodomy a crime?

EUGENIE—And were it one, what care I? Have you not demonstrated the nonexistence of crime? There are now very few actions which appear criminal in my view.

DOLMANCE—There is crime in nothing, dear girl, regardless of what it be: the most monstrous of deeds has, does it not, an auspicious aspect?

EUGENIE—Who's to gainsay it?

DOLMANCE—Well, as of this moment, it loses every aspect of crime; for, in order that what serves one by harming another be a crime, one should first have to demonstrate that the injured person is more important, more precious to Nature than the person who performs the injury and serves her; now, all individuals being of uniform importance in her eyes, 'tis impossible that she have a predilection for some one among them; hence, the deed that serves one person by causing suffering to another is of perfect indifference to Nature.

EUGENIE—But if the action were harmful to a very great quantity of individuals . . . and if it rewarded us with only a very small quantity of pleasure, would it not then be a frightful thing to execute it?

DOLMANCE—No more so, because there is no possible comparison between what others experience and what we sense; the heaviest dose of agony in others ought, assuredly, to be as naught to us, and the faintest quickening of pleasure, registered in us, does touch us; therefore, we should, at whatever the price, prefer this most minor excitation which enchants us, to the immense sum of others' miseries, which cannot affect us; but, on the contrary, should it happen that the singularity of our organs, some bizarre feature in our construction, renders agreeable to us the sufferings of our fellows, as sometimes occurs, who can doubt, then, that we should incontestably prefer anguish in others, which entertains us, to that anguish's absence, which would represent, for us, a kind of privation? The source of all our moral errors lies in the ridiculous acknowledgment of that tie of brotherhood the Christians invented in the age of their ill-fortune and sore distress. Constrained to beg pity from others, 'twas not unclever to claim that all men are brothers; how is one to refuse aid if this hypothesis be accepted? But its rational acceptance is impossible; are we not all born solitary, isolated? I say more: are we not come into the world all enemies, the one of the other, all in a state of perpetual and reciprocal warfare? Now, I ask whether such would be the situation if they did truly exist, this supposed tie of brotherhood and the virtues it enjoins? Are they really natural? Were they inspired in man by Nature's voice, men would be aware of them at birth. From that time onward, pity, good works, generosity, would be native virtues against which 'twould be impossible to defend oneself, and would render the primitive state of savage man totally contrary to what we observe it to be.

EUGENIE—Yet if, as you say, Nature caused man to be born alone, all independent of other men, you will at least grant me that his needs, bringing him together with other men, must necessarily have established some ties between them;

whence blood relationships, ties of love too, of friendship, of gratitude: you will, I hope, respect those at least.

DOLMANCE—No more than the others, I am afraid; but let us analyze them, I should like to: a swift glance, Eugénie, at each one in particular. Would you say, for example, that the need to marry or to prolong my race or to arrange my fortune or insure my future must establish indissoluble or sacred ties with the object I ally myself to? Would it not, I ask you, be an absurdity to argue thus? So long as the act of coition lasts, I may, to be sure, continue in need of that object, in order to participate in the act; but once it is over and I am satisfied, what, I wonder, will attach the results of this commerce to me? These latter relationships were the results of the terror of parents who dreaded lest they be abandoned in old age, and the politic attentions they show us when we are in our infancy have no object but to make them deserving of the same consideration when they are become old. Let us no longer be the dupes of this rubbish: we owe nothing to our parents . . . not the least thing, Eugénie, and since it is far less for our sake than for their own they have labored, we may rightfully test them, even rid ourselves of them if their behavior annoys us; we ought to love them only if they comport themselves well with us, and then our tenderness toward them ought not to be one degree greater than what we might feel for other friends, because the rights of birth establish nothing, are basis to nothing, and, once they have been wisely scrutinized and with deliberation, we will surely find nothing there but reasons to hate those who, exclusively thoughtful of their own pleasure, have often given us nothing but an unhappy and unhealthy existence.

You mention, Eugénie, ties of love; may you never know them! Ah! for the happiness I wish you, may such a sentiment never approach your breast! What is love? One can only consider it, so it seems to me, as the effect upon us of a beautiful object's qualities; these effects distract us; they inflame us; were we to possess this object, all would be well with us; if 'tis impossible to have it, we are in despair. But what is the foundation of this sentiment? desire. What are this sentiment's consequences? madness. Let us confine ourselves to the cause and guarantee ourselves against the effects. The cause is to possess the object: spendid! let's strive to succeed, but using our head, not losing our wits; let's enjoy it when we've got it; let's console ourselves if we fail: a thousand other identical and often much superior objects exist to soothe our regrets and our pride: all men, all women resemble each other: no love resists the effects of sane reflection. O 'tis a very great cheat and a dupery, this intoxication which puts us in such a state that we see no more, exist no more save through this object insanely adored! Is this really to live? Is it not rather voluntarily to deprive oneself of all life's sweetness? Is it not to wish to linger in a burning fever which devours, consumes us, without affording us other than metaphysical joys, which bear such a likeness to the effects of madness? Were we always to love this adorable object, were it certain we should never have to quit it, 'twould still be an extravagance without doubt, but at least an excusable one. Does this happen, however? Has one many examples of these deathless liaisons, unions which are never dissolved or repudiated? A few months of doting and dalliance soon restores the object to its proper size and shape, and we blush to think of the incense we have squanderingly burned upon that altar, and often we come to wonder that it ever could have seduced us at all. . . .

Women are not made for one single man; 'tis for men at large Nature created them. Listening only to this sacred voice, let them surrender themselves, indifferently, to all who want them: always whores, never mistresses, eschewing love, worshiping pleasure; it will be roses only they will discover in life's career; it will no longer be but flowers they proffer us! Ask, Eugénie, ask the charming woman who has so kindly consented to undertake your education, ask her what is to be done with a man after one has enjoyed him. (*In a lower voice, so as not to be heard by Augustin.*) Ask her if she would lift a finger to save this Augustin who, today, is the cause of her delights. Should it fall out that someone wished to steal him from her, she would take another, would think no more on this one and, soon weary of the new, would herself sacrifice him within two months' time, were new pleasures to be born of this maneuver. . . .

The final part of my analysis treats the bonds of friendship and those of gratitude. We shall respect the former, very well, provided they remain useful to us; let us keep our friends as long as they serve us; forget them immediately we have nothing further from them; 'tis never but selfishly one should love people; to love them for themselves is nothing but dupery; Nature never inspires other movements in mankind's soul, other sentiments than those which ought to prove useful in some sort, good for something; nothing is more an egoist than Nature; then let us be egoists too, if we wish to live in harmony with her dictates. As for gratitude, Eugénie, 'tis doubtless the most feeble of all the bonds. Is it then for ourselves men are obliging to us? Not a bit of it, my dear; 'tis through ostentation, for the sake of pride. Is it not humiliating thus to become the toy of others' pride? Is it not yet more so to fall into indebtedness to them? Nothing is more burdensome than a kindness one has received. No middle way, no compromise: you have got to repay it or ready yourself for abuse.

Upon proud spirits a good deed sits very heavily: it weighs upon them with such violence that the one feeling they exhale is hatred for their benefactors. . . .

EUGENIE—But if all the errors you speak of are in Nature, why do our laws oppose them?

DOLMANCE—Those laws, being forged for universal application, are in perpetual conflict with personal interest, just as personal interest is always in contradiction with the general interest. Good for society, our laws are very bad for the individuals whereof it is composed; for, if they one time protect the individual, they hinder, trouble, fetter him for three quarters of his life; and so the wise man, the man full of contempt for them, will be wary of them, as he is of reptiles and vipers which, although they wound or kill, are nevertheless sometimes useful to medicine; he will safeguard himself against the laws as he would against noxious beasts; he will shelter himself behind precautions, behind mysteries, the which, for prudence, is easily done. Should the fancy to execute a few crimes inflame your spirit, Eugénie, be very certain you may commit them peacefully in the company of your friend and me.

EUGENIE—Ah, the fancy is already in my heart! . . . *wild-eyed*—I want a victim. . . .

Oh, my friend, there is my ass! . . . do with it what you will! . . .

DOLMANCE—One moment, while I arrange this pleasure bout in a sufficiently lustful manner. (*As Dolmancé gives his orders, each person executes them, taking his post.*) Augustin, lie down on the bed; Eugénie, do you recline in his arms; while I sodomize her, I'll frig her clitoris with the head of Augustin's superb prick, and Augustin who must be sparing of his fuck will take good care not to discharge; the gentle Chevalier—who, without saying a word, softly frigs himself while listening to us—will have the kindness to arrange himself upon Eugénie's shoulders so as to expose his fine buttocks to my kisses: I'll frig him amain; so shall I have my engine in an ass and a prick in each hand, to pollute; and you, Madame, after having been your master, I want you to become mine: buckle on the most gigantic of your dildos. (*Madame de Saint-Ange opens a chest filled with a store of them, and our hero selects the most massive.*) Splendid! This, according to the label, is fourteen by ten; fit it about your loins, Madame, and spare me not.

MADAME DE SAINT-ANGE—Indeed, Dolmancé, you had best reconsider. I will cripple you with this device.

DOLMANCE—Fear not; push, my angel, penetrate: I'll not enter your dear Engénie's ass until your enormous member is well advanced into mine . . . and it is! it is! oh, little Jesus ! . . . You propel me heavenward! . . . No pity, my lovely one . . . I tell you I am going to fuck your ass without preparations . . . oh, sweet God! magnificent ass! . . .

EUGENIE—Oh, my friend, you are tearing me. . . . at least prepare the way.

DOLMANCE—I'll do nothing of the sort, by God: half the pleasure's lost by these stupid attentions. Put yourself in mind of our principles, Eugénie: I labor in my behalf only: now victim for a moment, my lovely angel, soon you'll persecute in your turn. . . . Ah, holy God, it enters! . . .

EUGENIE—You are putting me to death!

DOLMANCE—Ah God! I touch bottom! . . .

EUGENIE—Ah, do what you will, 'tis arrived . . . I feel nothing but pleasure! . . .

DOLMANCE—'Twould be my opinion that, while the avenue is open, the little bitch might instantly be fucked by Augustin!

EUGENIE—By Augustin! . . . a prick of those dimensions! . . . ah, immediately! . . . While I am still bleeding! . . . Do you then wish to kill me?

MADAME DE SAINT-ANGE—Dear heart . . . kiss me, I sympathize with you . . . but sentence has been pronounced; there is no appeal, my dearest: you have got to submit to it.

AUGUSTIN—Ah, zounds! here I am, all ready: soon's it means sticking this bonny girl and I'd come, by God, all the way from Rome, on foot.

LE CHEVALIER, *grasping Augustin's mammoth device*— Look at it, Eugénie, look how it is erect . . . how worthy it is to replace me. . . .

EUGENIE—Oh merciful heaven, what a piece! . . . Oh, 'tis clear, you design my death! . . .

AUGUSTIN, *seizing Eugénie*—Oh no, Mam'selle, that's never killed anybody.

DOLMANCE—One instant, my fine boy, one instant: she must present her ass to me while you fuck her . . . yes, that's it, come hither, Madame; I promised to sodomize you, I'll keep my word; but situate yourself in such a way that as I fuck you, I can be within reach of Eugénie's fucker. And let the Chevalier flog me in the meantime. (*All is arranged.*)

EUGENIE—Oh fuck! he cracks me! . . . Go gently, great lout! . . . Ah, the bugger! he digs in! . . . there 'tis, the fucking-john! . . . he's at the very bottom! . . . I'm dying! . . . Oh, Dolmancé, how you strike! . . . 'tis to ignite me before and behind; you're setting my buttocks afire!

DOLMANCE, *swinging his whip with all his strength*— You'll be afire . . . you'll burn, little bitch! . . . and you'll only discharge the more deliciously. How you frig her, Saint-Ange . . . let your deft fingers soothe the hurt that Augustin and I cause her! . . . But your anus contracts . . . I see it, Madame, I see it! we're going to come together. . . . Oh, 'tis I know not how divine thus to be, 'twixt brother and sister!

MADAME DE SAINT-ANGE, *to Dolmancé*—Fuck, my star, fuck! . . . Never do I believe I have had so much pleasure!

LE CHEVALIER—Dolmancé, let's change hands; be nimble: pass from my sister's ass to Eugénie's, so as to acquaint her with the intermediary's pleasures, and I will embugger my sister who meanwhile will shower upon your ass the very whip strokes wherewith you've just brought Eugénie's behind to blood.

DOLMANCE, *executing the proposal*—Agreed . . . there, my friend, hast ever seen a shift more cunningly effected?

EUGENIE—What! both of them on top of me, good heavens! . . . what will come next? I've really had enough of this oaf! . . . Ah, how much fuck this double pleasure is going to cost me! . . . it flows already. Without that sensual ejaculation, I believe I would be already dead. . . . Why, my dearest, you imitate me. . . . Oh, hear the bitch swear! . . . Discharge, Dolmancé, . . . discharge, my love . . . this fat peasant inundates me: he shoots to the depths of my entrails. . . . Oh, my good fuckers, what is this? Two at a time? Good Christ! . . . receive my fuck, dear companions, it conjoins itself with your own. . . . I am annihilated. . . . (*The attitudes are dissolved.*) Well, my dear, what think you of your scholar? . . . Am I enough of a whore now? . . . But what a state you do put me in . . . what an agitation! . . . Oh, yes, I swear, in my drunkenness, I swear I would have gone if necessary and got myself fucked in the middle of the street! . . .

Let's sit down and chat a little; I'm exhausted. Continue my instruction, Dolmancé, and say something that will console me for the excesses to which I have given myself over; stifle my remorse; encourage me. . . .

I should like to know whether manners are truly necessary in a governed society, whether their influence has any weight with the national genius.

DOLMANCE—Why, by God, I have something here with me. As I left home this morning I bought, outside the Palace of Equality, a little pamphlet, which if one can believe the title, ought surely to answer your question. . . . It's come straight from the press.

MADAME DE SAINT-ANGE—Let me see it. (*She reads:*) "Yet Another Effort, Frenchmen, If You Would Become Republicans." Upon my word, 'tis an unusual title: 'tis promising; Chevalier, you possess a fine organ, read it to us. . . .

LE CHEVALIER—Well, I'll begin.

YET ANOTHER EFFORT, FRENCHMEN, IF YOU WOULD BECOME REPUBLICANS

Religion

I am about to put forward some major ideas; they will be heard and pondered. If not all of them please, surely a few will; in some sort, then, I shall have contributed to the progress of our age, and shall be content. We near our goal, but haltingly: I confess that I am disturbed by the presentiment that we are on the eve of failing once again to arrive there. Is it thought that goal will be attained when at last we have been given laws? Abandon the notion; for what should we, who have no religion, do with laws? We must have a creed, a creed befitting the republican character, something far removed from ever being able to resume the worship of Rome. In this age, when we are convinced that morals must be the basis of religion, and not religion of morals, we need a body of beliefs in keeping with our customs and habits, something that would be their necessary consequence, and that could, by lifting up the spirit, maintain it perpetually at the high level of this precious liberty, which today the spirit has made its unique idol.

Well, I ask, is it thinkable that the doctrine of one of Titus' slaves, of a clumsy histrionic from Judaea, be fitting to a free and warlike nation that has just regenerated itself? No, my fellow countrymen, no; you think nothing of the sort. If, to his misfortune, the Frenchman were to entomb himself in the grave of Christianity, then on one side the priests' pride, their tyranny, their despotism, vices forever cropping up in that impure horde, on the other side the baseness, the narrowness, the platitudes of dogma and mystery of this infamous and fabulous religion, would, by blunting the fine edge of the republican spirit, rapidly put about the Frenchman's neck the yoke which his vitality but yesterday shattered.

Let us not lose sight of the fact this puerile religion was among our tyrants' best weapons: one of its key dogmas was to *render unto Caesar that which is Caesar's*. However, we have dethroned Caesar, we are no longer disposed to render him anything. Frenchmen, it would be in vain were you to suppose that your oath-taking clergy today is in any essential manner different from yesterday's non-juring clergy: there are inherent vices beyond all possibility of correction. Before ten years are out—utilizing the Christian religion, its superstitions, its prejudices—your priests, their pledges notwithstanding and though despoiled of their riches, are sure to reassert their empire over the souls they shall have undermined and captured; they shall restore the monarchy, because the power of kings has always reinforced that of the church; and your republican edifice, its foundations eaten away, shall collapse.

O you who have axes ready to hand, deal the final blow to the tree of superstition; be not content to prune its branches: uproot entirely a plant whose effects are so contagious. Well understand that your system of liberty and equality too rudely affronts the ministers of Christ's altars for there ever to be one of them who will either adopt it in good faith or give over seeking to topple it, if he is able to recover any dominion over consciences. What priest, comparing the condition to which he has been reduced with the one he formerly enjoyed, will not do his utmost to win back both the confidence and the authority he has lost? And how many feeble and pusillanimous creatures will not speedily become again the thralls of this cunning shavepate! Why is it imagined that the nuisances which existed before cannot be revived to plague us anew? In the Christian church's infancy, were priests less ambitious than they are today? You observe how far they advanced; to what do you suppose they owed their success if not to the means religion furnished them? Well, if you do not absolutely prohibit this religion, those who preach it, having yet the same means, will soon achieve the same ends. . . .

To convince ourselves, we have but to cast our eyes upon the handful of individuals who remain attached to our father's insensate worship: we will see whether they are not all irreconcilable enemies of the present system, we will see whether it is not amongst their numbers that all of that justly contemned caste of *royalists* and *aristocrats* is included. Let the slave of a crowned brigand grovel, if he pleases, at the feet of a plaster image; such an object is ready-made for his soul of mud. He who can serve kings must adore gods; but we, Frenchmen, but we, my fellow countrymen, we rather than once more crawl beneath such contemptible traces, we would die a thousand times over rather than abase ourselves anew! Since we believe a cult necessary, let us imitate the Romans: actions, passions, heroes—those were the objects of their respect. Idols of this sort elevated the soul, electrified it, and more; they communicated to the spirit the virtues of the respected being. Minerva's devotee coveted wisdom. Courage found its abode in his heart who worshiped Mars. Not a single one of that great people's gods was deprived of energy; all

of them infused into the spirit of him who venerated them the fire with which they were themselves
ablaze; and each Roman hoped someday to be
himself worshiped, each aspired to become as great
at least as the deity he took for a model. But what,
on the contrary, do we find in Christianity's futile
gods? What, I want to know, what does this idiot's
religion offer you?[2] Does the grubby Nazarene
fraud inspire any great thoughts in you? His foul,
nay repellent mother, the shameless Mary—does
she excite any virtues? And do you discover in the
saints who garnish the Christian Elysium, any example of greatness, of either heroism or virtue? So
alien to lofty conceptions is this miserable belief,
that no artist can employ its attributes in the monuments he raises; even in Rome itself, most of the
embellishments of the papal palaces have their origins in paganism, and as long as this world shall
continue, paganism alone will arouse the verve of
great men.

Shall we find more motifs of grandeur in pure
theism? Will acceptance of a chimera infuse into
men's minds the high degree of energy essential to
republican virtues, and move men to cherish and
practice them? Let us imagine nothing of the kind;
we have bid farewell to that phantom and, at the
present time, atheism is the one doctrine of all
those prone to reason. As we gradually proceeded
to our enlightenment, we came more and more to
feel that, motion being inherent in matter, the
prime mover existed only as an illusion, and that
all that exists essentially having to be in motion,
the motor was useless; we sensed that this chimerical divinity, prudently invented by the earliest leg-

islators, was, in their hands, simply one more
means to enthrall us, and that, reserving unto
themselves the right to make the phantom speak,
they knew very well how to get him to say nothing
but what would shore up the preposterous laws
whereby they declared they served us. Lycurgus,
Numa, Moses, Jesus Christ, Mohammed, all these
great rogues, all these great thought-tyrants, knew
how to associate the divinities they fabricated with
their own boundless ambition; and, certain of captivating the people with the sanction of those gods,
they were always studious, as everyone knows, either to consult them exclusively about, or to make
them exclusively respond to, what they thought
likely to serve their own interests. . . .

Frenchmen, only strike the initial blows; your
State education will then see to the rest. Get
promptly to the task of training the youth, it must
be amongst your most important concerns; above
all, build their education upon a sound ethical
basis, the ethical basis that was so neglected in your
religious education. Rather than fatigue your children's young organs with deific stupidities, replace
them with excellent social principles; instead of
teaching them futile prayers which, by the time
they are sixteen, they will glory in having forgotten, let them be instructed in their duties toward
society; train them to cherish the virtues you
scarcely ever mentioned in former times and
which, without your religious fables, are sufficient
for their individual happiness; make them sense
that this happiness consists in rendering others as
fortunate as we desire to be ourselves. If you repose
these truths upon Christian chimeras, as you so
foolishly used to do, scarcely will your pupils have
detected the absurd futility of its foundations than
they will overthrow the entire edifice, and they will
become bandits for the simple reason they believe
the religion they have toppled forbids them to be
bandits. On the other hand, if you make them
sense the necessity of virtue, uniquely because their

---

[2]A careful inspection of this religion will reveal to anyone that
the impieties with which it is filled come in part from the
Jews' ferocity and innocence, and in part from the indifference
and confusion of the Gentiles; instead of appropriating what
was good in what the ancient peoples had to offer, the Christians seem only to have formed their doctrine from a mixture
of the vices they found everywhere.

happiness depends upon it, egoism will turn them into honest people, and this law which dictates their behavior to men will always be the surest, the soundest of all. Let there then be the most scrupulous care taken to avoid mixing religious fantasies into this State education. Never lose sight of the fact it is free men we wish to form, not the wretched worshipers of a god. Let a simple philosopher introduce these new pupils to the inscrutable but wonderful sublimities of Nature; let him prove to them that awareness of a god, often highly dangerous to men, never contributed to their happiness, and that they will not be happier for acknowledging as a cause of what they do not understand, something they well understand even less; that it is far less essential to inquire into the workings of Nature than to enjoy her and obey her laws; that these laws are as wise as they are simple; that they are written in the hearts of all men; and that it is but necessary to interrogate that heart to discern its impulse. If they wish absolutely that you speak to them of a creator, answer that things always having been what now they are, never having had a beginning and never going to have an end, it thus becomes as useless as impossible for man to be able to trace things back to an imaginary origin which would explain nothing and do not a jot of good. Tell them that men are incapable of obtaining true notions of a being who does not make his influence felt on one of our senses.

All our ideas are representations of objects that strike us: what is to represent to us the idea of a god, who is plainly an idea without object? Is not such an idea, you will add when talking to them, quite as impossible as effects without causes? Is an idea without prototype anything other than an hallucination? Some scholars, you will continue, assure us that the idea of a god is innate, and that mortals already have this idea when in their mothers' bellies. But, you will remark, that is false; every principle is a judgment, every judgment the out-

come of experience, and experience is only acquired by the exercise of the senses; whence it follows that religious principles bear upon nothing whatever and are not in the slightest innate. How, you will go on, how have they been able to convince rational beings that the thing most difficult to understand is the most vital to them? It is that mankind has been terrorized; it is that when one is afraid one ceases to reason; it is, above all, that we have been advised to mistrust reason and defy it; and that, when the brain is disturbed, one believes anything and examines nothing. Ignorance and fear, you will repeat to them, ignorance and fear—those are the twin bases of every religion.

Man's uncertainty with respect to his god is, precisely, the cause for his attachment to his religion. Man's fear in dark places is as much physical as moral; fear becomes habitual in him, and is changed into need: he would believe he were lacking something even were he to have nothing more to hope for or dread. Next, return to the utilitarian value of morals: apropos of this vast subject, give them many more examples than lessons, many more demonstrations than books, and you will make good citizens of them: you will turn them into fine warriors, fine fathers, fine husbands: you will fashion men that much more devoted to their country's liberty, whose minds will be forever immune to servility, forever hostile to servitude, whose genius will never be troubled by any religious terror. And then true patriotism will shine in every spirit, and will reign there in all its force and purity, because it will become the sovereign sentiment there, and no alien notion will dilute or cool its energy; then your second generation will be sure, reliable, and your own work, consolidated by it, will go on to become the law of the universe. But if, through fear or faintheartedness, these counsels are ignored, if the foundations of the edifice we thought we destroyed are left intact, what then will happen? They will rebuild upon these foundations, and will set thereupon the same colossi, with this difference, and it will be a cruel one: the new structures will be cemented with such strength that neither your generation nor ensuing ones will avail against them. . . .

Manners

After having made it clear that theism is in no wise suitable to a republican government, it seems to me necessary to prove that French manners are equally unsuitable to it. This article is the more crucial, for the laws to be promulgated will issue from manners, and will mirror them.

Frenchmen, you are too intelligent to fail to sense that new government will require new manners. That the citizens of a free State conduct themselves like a despotic king's slaves is unthinkable: the differences of their interests, of their duties, of their relations amongst one another essentially determine an entirely different manner of behaving in the world; a crowd of minor faults and of little social indelicacies, thought of as very fundamental indeed under the rule of kings whose expectations rose in keeping with the need they felt to impose curbs in order to appear respectable and unapproachable to their subjects, are due to become as nothing with us; other crimes with which we are acquainted under the names of regicide and sacrilege, in a system where kings and religion will be unknown, in the same way must be annihilated in a republican State. In according freedom of conscience and of the press, consider, citizens—for it is practically the same thing—whether freedom of action must not be granted too: excepting direct clashes with the underlying principles of government, there remain to you it is impossible to say how many fewer crimes to punish, because in fact there are very few criminal actions in a society whose foundations are liberty and equality. Matters well weighed and things closely inspected, only that is really criminal which rejects

the law; for Nature, equally dictating vices and virtues to us, in reason of our constitution, yet more philosophically, in reason of the need Nature has of the one and the other, what she inspires in us would become a very reliable gauge by which to adjust exactly what is good and bad. But, the better to develop my thoughts upon so important a question, we will classify the different acts in man's life that until the present it has pleased us to call criminal, and we will next square them to the true obligations of a republican.

In every age, the duties of man have been considered under the following three categories:

1. Those his conscience and his credulity impose upon him, with what regards a supreme being;
2. Those he is obliged to fulfill toward his brethren;
3. Finally, those that relate only to himself. . . .

I trust I have said enough to make plain that no laws ought to be decreed against religious crimes, for that which offends an illusion offends nothing, and it would be the height of inconsistency to punish those who outrage or who despise a creed or a cult whose priority to all others is established by no evidence whatsoever. No, that would necessarily be to exhibit a partiality and, consequently, to influence the scales of equality, that foremost law of your new government.

We move on to the second class of man's duties, those which bind him to his fellows; this is of all the classes the most extensive.

Excessively vague upon man's relations with his brothers, Christian morals propose bases so filled with sophistries that we are completely unable to accept them, since, if one is pleased to erect principles, one ought scrupulously to guard against founding them upon sophistries. This absurd morality tells us to love our neighbor as ourselves.

Assuredly, nothing would be more sublime were it ever possible for what is false to be beautiful. The point is not at all to love one's brethren as oneself, since that is in defiance of all the laws of Nature, and since hers is the sole voice which must direct all the actions in our life; it is only a question of loving others as brothers, as friends given us by Nature, and with whom we should be able to live much better in a republican State, wherein the disappearance of distances must necessarily tighten the bonds.

May humanity, fraternity, benevolence prescribe our reciprocal obligations, and let us individually fulfill them with the simple degree of energy Nature has given us to this end; let us do so without blaming, and above all without punishing, those who, of chillier temper or more acrimonious humor, do not notice in these yet very touching social ties all the sweetness and gentleness others discover therein; for, it will be agreed, to seek to impose universal laws would be a palpable absurdity: such a proceeding would be as ridiculous as that of the general who would have all his soldiers dressed in a uniform of the same size; it is a terrible injustice to require that men of unlike character all be ruled by the same law: what is good for one is not at all good for another.

That we cannot devise as many laws as there are men must be admitted; but the laws can be lenient, and so few in number, that all men, of whatever character, can easily observe them. Furthermore, I would demand that this small number of laws be of such a sort as to be adaptable to all the various characters; they who formulate the code should follow the principle of applying more or less, according to the person in question. It has been pointed out that there are certain virtues whose practice is impossible for certain men, just as there are certain remedies which do not agree with certain constitutions. Now, would it not be to carry your injustice beyond all limits were you to send the law to strike the man incapable of bowing to the law? Would your iniquity be any less here than in a case where you sought to force the blind to distinguish amongst colors?

From these first principles there follows, one feels, the necessity to make flexible, mild laws and especially to get rid forever of the atrocity of capital punishment, because the law which attempts a man's life is impractical, unjust, inadmissible. Not, and it will be clarified in the sequel, that we lack an infinite number of cases where, without offense to Nature (and this I shall demonstrate), men have freely taken one another's lives, simply exercising a prerogative received from their common mother; but it is impossible for the law to obtain the same privileges, since the law, cold and impersonal, is a total stranger to the passions which are able to justify in man the cruel act of murder. Man receives his impressions from Nature, who is able to forgive him this act; the law, on the contrary, always opposed as it is to Nature and receiving nothing from her, cannot be authorized to permit itself the same extravagances: not having the same motives, the law cannot have the same rights. Those are wise and delicate distinctions which escape many people, because very few of them reflect; but they will be grasped and retained by the instructed to whom I recommend them, and will, I hope, exert some influence upon the new code being readied for us. . . .

The injuries we can work against our brothers may be reduced to four types: *calumny; theft*; the crimes which, caused by *impurity*, may in a disagreeable sense affect others; and *murder*. . . .

Lay partiality aside, and answer me: is theft, whose effect is to distribute wealth more evenly, to be branded as a wrong in our day, under our government which aims at equality? Plainly, the answer is no: it furthers equality and, what is more, renders more difficult the conservation of property. . . .

If, by your pledge, you perform an act of equity in protecting the property of the rich, do you not commit one of unfairness in requiring this pledge of the owner who owns nothing? What advantage does the latter derive from your pledge? and how can you expect him to swear to something exclusively beneficial to someone who, through his wealth, differs so greatly from him? Certainly, nothing is more unjust: an oath must have an equal effect upon all the individuals who pronounce it; that it bind him who has no interest in its maintenance is impossible, because it would no longer be a pact amongst free men; it would be the weapon of the strong against the weak, against whom the latter would have to be in incessant revolt. Well, such, exactly, is the situation created by the pledge to respect property the Nation has just required all the citizens to subscribe to under oath. . . .

Thus convinced, as you must be, of this barbarous inequality, do not proceed to worsen your injustice by punishing the man who has nothing for having dared to filch something from the man who has everything: your inequitable pledge gives him a greater right to it than ever. In driving him to perjury by forcing him to make a promise which, for him, is absurd, you justify all the crimes to which this perjury will impel him; it is not for you to punish something for which you have been the cause. I have no need to say more to make you sense the terrible cruelty of chastising thieves. . . .

The transgressions we are considering in this second class of man's duties toward his fellows include actions for whose undertaking libertinage may be the cause; among those which are pointed to as particularly incompatible with approved behavior are *prostitution, incest, rape,* and *sodomy.* We surely must not for one moment doubt that all those known as moral crimes, that is to say, all acts of the sort to which those we have just cited belong, are of total inconsequence under a government whose sole duty consists in preserving, by

whatever may be the means, the form essential to its continuance: there you have a republican government's unique morality. Well, the republic being permanently menaced from the outside by the despots surrounding it, the means to its preservation cannot be imagined as *moral means*, for the republic will preserve itself only by war, and nothing is less moral than war. I ask how one will be able to demonstrate that in a state rendered *immoral* by its obligations, it is essential that the individual be *moral?* . . .

Hence it would be no less absurd than dangerous to require that those who are to insure the perpetual *immoral* subversion of the established order themselves be *moral* beings: for the state of a moral man is one of tranquillity and peace, the state of an *immoral* man is one of perpetual unrest that pushes him to, and identifies him with, the necessary insurrection in which the republican must always keep the government of which he is a member. . . .

If you would avoid that danger, permit a free flight and rein to those tyrannical desires which, despite himself, torment man ceaselessly: content with having been able to exercise his small dominion in the middle of the harem of sultanas and youths whose submission your good offices and his money procure for him, he will go away appeased and with nothing but fond feelings for a government which so obligingly affords him every means of satisfying his concupiscence; proceed, on the other hand, after a different fashion, between the citizen and those objects of public lust raise the ridiculous obstacles in olden times invented by ministerial tyranny and by the lubricity of our Sardanapaluses[3]—, do that, and the citizen, soon em-

---

[3]It is well known that the infamous and criminal Sartine devised, in the interests of the king's lewdness, the plan of having Dubarry read to Louis XV, thrice each week, the private details, enriched by Sartine, of all that transpired in the evil corners of Paris. This department of the French Nero's libertinage cost the the State three millions.

bittered against your regime, soon jealous of the despotism he sees you exercise all by yourself, will shake off the yoke you lay upon him, and, weary of your manner of ruling, will, as he has just done, substitute another for it. . . .

I am going to try to convince you that the prostitution of women who bear the name of honest is no more dangerous than the prostitution of men, and that not only must we associate women with the lecheries practiced in the houses I have set up, but we must even build some for them, where their whims and the requirements of their temper, ardent like ours but in a quite different way, may too find satisfaction with every sex. . . .

Never may an act of possession be exercised upon a free being; the exclusive possession of a woman is no less unjust than the possession of slaves; all men are born free, all have equal rights: never should we lose sight of those principles; according to which never may there be granted to one sex the legitimate right to lay monopolizing hands upon the other, and never may one of these sexes, or classes, arbitrarily possess the other. Similarly, a woman existing in the purity of Nature's laws cannot allege, as justification for refusing herself to someone who desires her, the love she bears another, because such a response is based upon exclusion, and no man may be excluded from the having of a woman as of the moment it is clear she definitely belongs to all men. The act of possession can only be exercised upon a chattel or an animal, never upon an individual who resembles us, and all the ties which can bind a woman to a man are quite as unjust as illusory.

If then it becomes incontestable that we have received from Nature the right indiscriminately to express our wishes to all women, it likewise becomes incontestable that we have the right to compel their submission, not exclusively, for I should

then be contradicting myself, but temporarily.[4] It cannot be denied that we have the right to decree laws that compel woman to yield to the flames of him who would have her; violence itself being one of that right's effects, we can employ it lawfully. Indeed! has Nature not proven that we have that right, by bestowing upon us the strength needed to bend women to our will? . . .

If we admit, as we have just done, that all women ought to be subjugated to our desires, we may certainly allow then ample satisfaction of theirs. Our laws must be favorable to their fiery temperament. It is absurd to locate both their honor and their virtue in the antinatural strength they employ to resist the penchants with which they have been far more profusely endowed than we; this injustice of manners is rendered more flagrant still since we contrive at once to weaken them by seduction, and then to punish them for yielding to all the efforts we have made to provoke their fall. All the absurdity of our manners, it seems to me, is graven in this shocking paradox, and this brief outline alone ought to awaken us to the urgency of exchanging them for manners more pure. . . .

Is incest more dangerous? Hardly. It loosens family ties and the citizen has that much more love to lavish on his country; the primary laws of Nature dictate it to us, our feelings vouch for the fact; and nothing is so enjoyable as an object we have

---

[4]Let it not be said that I contradict myself here, and that after having established, at some point further above, that we have no right to bind a woman to ourselves, I destroy those principles when I declare now we have the right to constrain her; I repeat, it is a question of enjoyment only, not of property: I have no right of possession upon that fountain I find by the road, but I have certain rights to its use; I have the right to avail myself of the limpid water it offers my thirst; similarly, I have no real right of possession over such-and-such a woman, but I have incontestable rights to the enjoyment of her; I have the right to force from her this enjoyment, if she refuses me it for whatever the cause may be.

coveted over the years. . . . I would venture, in a word, that incest ought to be every government's law—every government whose basis is fraternity. How is it that reasonable men were able to carry absurdity to the point of believing that the enjoyment of one's mother, sister, or daughter could ever be criminal? Is it not, I ask, an abominable view wherein it is made to appear a crime for a man to place higher value upon the enjoyment of an object to which natural feeling draws him close? One might just as well say that we are forbidden to love too much the individuals Nature enjoins us to love best, and that the more she gives us a hunger for some object, the more she orders us away from it. . . . We shall turn our attention to rape, which at first glance seems to be, of all libertinage's excesses, the one which is most dearly established as being wrong, by reason of the outrage it appears to cause. It is certain, however, that rape, an act so very rare and so very difficult to prove, wrongs one's neighbor less than theft, since the latter is destructive to property, the former merely damaging to it. Beyond that, what objections have you to the ravisher? What will you say, when he replies to you that, as a matter of fact, the injury he has committed is trifling indeed, since he has done no more than place a little sooner the object he has abused in the very state in which she would soon have been put by marriage and love.

But sodomy, that alleged crime which will draw the fire of heaven upon cities addicted to it. . . .

What single crime can exist here? For no one will wish to maintain that all the parts of the body do not resemble each other, that there are some which are pure, and others defiled; but, as it is unthinkable such nonsense be advanced seriously, the only possible crime would consist in the waste of semen. . . .

In the second category of man's crimes against his brethren, there is left to us only murder to examine, and then we will move on to man's duties toward himself. Of all the offenses man may commit against his fellows, murder is without question the cruelest, since it deprives man of the single asset he has received from Nature, and its loss is irreparable. Nevertheless, at this stage several questions arise, leaving aside the wrong murder does him who becomes its victim.

1. As regards the laws of Nature only, is this act really criminal?
2. Is it criminal with what regards the laws of politics?
3. Is it harmful to society?
4. What must be a republican government's attitude toward it?
5. Finally, must murder be repressed by murder? . . .

What is man? and what difference is there between him and other plants, between him and all the other animals of the world? None, obviously. Fortuitously placed, like them, upon this globe, he is born like them; like them, he reproduces, rises, and falls; like them he arrives at old age and sinks like them into nothingness at the close of the life span Nature assigns each species of animal, in accordance with its organic construction. Since the parallels are so exact that the inquiring eye of philosophy is absolutely unable to perceive any grounds for discrimination, there is then just as much evil in killing animals as men, or just as little, and whatever be the distinctions we make, they will be found to stem from our pride's prejudices, than which, unhappily, nothing is more absurd. . . .

If Nature denies eternity to beings, it follows that their destruction is one of her laws. Now, once we observe that destruction is so useful to her that she absolutely cannot dispense with it, and that she cannot achieve her creations without drawing from the store of destruction which death prepares for her, from this moment onward the idea of annihilation which we attach to death ceases to be real; there is no more veritable annihilation; what we call the end of the living animal is no longer a true finis, but a simple transformation, a transmutation of matter, what every modern philosopher acknowledges as one of Nature's fundamental laws. According to these irrefutable principles, death is hence no more than a change of form, an imperceptible passage from one existence into another, and that is what Pythagoras called metempsychosis. . . .

Led still further in our series of inferences proceeding one from the other, we affirm that the act you commit in juggling the forms of Nature's different productions is of advantage to her, since thereby you supply her the primary material for her reconstructions, tasks which would be compromised were you to desist from destroying.

Well, let *her* do the destroying, they tell you; one ought to let her do it, of course, but they are Nature's impulses man follows when he indulges in homicide; it is Nature who advises him, and the man who destroys his fellow is to Nature what are the plague and famine, like them sent by her hand which employs every possible means more speedily to obtain of destruction this primary matter, itself absolutely essential to her works. . . .

Is murder then a crime against society? But how could that reasonably be imagined? What difference does it make to this murderous society, whether it have one member more, or less? Will its laws, its manners, its customs be vitiated? Has an individual's death ever had any influence upon the general mass? . . .

We have now but to speak of man's duties toward himself. As the philosopher only adopts such duties in the measure they conduce to his pleasure or to his preservation, it is futile to recommend their practice to him, still more futile to threaten him with penalties if he fails to adopt them.

The only offense of this order man can commit is suicide. I will not bother demonstrating here the imbecility of the people who make of this act a crime; those who might have any doubts upon the matter are referred to Rousseau's famous letter. Nearly all early governments, through policy or religion, authorized suicide. . . .

EUGENIE, *to Dolmancé*—Now, it strikes me as a very solidly composed document, that one, and it seems to me in such close agreement with your principles, at least with many of them, that I should be tempted to believe you its author.

DOLMANCE—Indeed my thinking does correspond with some part of these reflections, and my discourses—they've proven it to you—even lend to what has just been read to us the appearance of a repetition—

EUGENIE—That I did not notice; wise and good words cannot be too often uttered; however, I find several amongst these principles a trifle dangerous.

DOLMANCE—In this world there is nothing dangerous but pity and beneficence; goodness is never but a weakness of which the ingratitude and impertinence of the feeble always force honest folk to repent. Let a keen observer calculate all of pity's dangers, and let him compare them with those of a staunch, resolute severity, and he will see whether the former are not the greater. But we are straying, Eugénie; in the interests of your education, let's compress all that has just been said into this single word of advice: Never listen to your heart, my child; it is the most untrustworthy guide we have received from Nature; with greatest care close it up to misfortune's fallacious accents; far better for you to refuse a person whose wretchedness is genuine than to run the great risk of giving to a bandit, to an intriguer, or to a caballer: the one is of a very slight importance, the other may be of the highest disadvantage. . . .

LE CHEVALIER—Barbaric one, are these not at all human beings like you? and if they are of your kind, why should you enjoy yourself when they lie dying? Eugénie, Eugénie, never slay the sacred voice of Nature in your breast: it is to benevolence it will direct you despite yourself when you extricate from out of the fire of passions that absorb it the clear tenor of Nature. Leave religious principles far behind you—very well, I approve it; but abandon not the virtues sensibility inspires in us; 'twill never be but by practicing them we will taste the sweetest, the most exquisite of the soul's delights. A good deed will buy pardon for all your mind's depravities, it will soothe the remorse your misconduct will bring to birth. . . .

Oh, my friend, how you do speak to me of remorse! Can remorse exist in the soul of him who recognizes crime in nothing? . . . When you no longer believe evil anywhere exists, of what evil will you be able to repent?

It is not from the mind remorse comes; rather, 'tis the heart's issue, and never will the intellect's sophistries blot out the soul's impulsions.

DOLMANCE—However, the heart deceives, because it is never anything but the expression of the mind's miscalculations; allow the latter to mature and the former will yield in good time; we are constantly led astray by false definitions when we wish to reason logically: I don't know what the heart is, not I: I only use the word to denote the mind's frailties. . . .

Ah, Eugénie, believe me when I tell you that the delights born of apathy are worth much more than those you get of your sensibility; the latter can only touch the heart in one sense, the other titillates and overwhelms all of one's being. In a word, is it possible to compare permissible pleasures with pleasures which, to far more piquant delights, join those inestimable joys that come of bursting socially imposed restraints and of the violation of every law? . . .

EUGENIE—Why, it is even preferable to have the object experience pain, is it not?

DOLMANCE—To be sure, 'tis by much to be preferred. . . .

What is it one desires when taking one's pleasure? that everything around us be occupied with nothing but ourselves, think of naught but of us, care for us only. If the objects we employ know pleasure too, you can be very sure they are less concerned for us than they are for themselves, and lo! our own pleasure consequently disturbed. There is not a living man who does not wish to play the despot when he is stiff: it seems to him his joy is less when others appear to have as much as he; by an impulse of pride, very natural at this juncture, he would like to be the only one in the world capable of experiencing what he feels: the idea of seeing another enjoy as he enjoys reduces him to a kind of equality with that other, which impairs the unspeakable charm *despotism* causes him to feel.[5] 'Tis false as well to say there is pleasure in affording pleasure to others; that is to serve them, and the man who is erect is far from desiring to be useful to anyone. On the contrary, by causing them hurt he experiences all the charms a nervous personality relishes in putting its strength to use; 'tis then he dominates, is a *tyrant*; and what a difference is there for the *amourpropre*! Think not that it is silent during such episodes.

The act of enjoyment is a passion which, I confess, subordinates all others to it, but which simul-

---

[5]The poverty of the French language compels us to employ words which, today, our happy government, with so much good sense, disfavors; we hope our enlightened readers will understand us well and will not at all confound absurd political despotism with the very delightful despotism of libertinage's passions.

taneously unites them. This desire to dominate at this moment is so powerful in Nature that one notices it even in animals. See whether those in captivity procreate as do those others that are free and wild; the camel carries the matter further still: he will engender no more if he does not suppose himself alone: surprise him and, consequently, show him a master, and he will fly, will instantly separate himself from his companion. Had it not been Nature's intent that man possess this feeling of superiority, she would not have created him stronger than the beings she destines to belong to him at those moments. The debility to which Nature condemned woman incontestably proves that her design is for man, who then more than ever enjoys his strength, to exercise it in all the violent forms that suit him best, by means of tortures, if he be so inclined, or worse. Would pleasure's climax be a kind of fury were it not the intention of this mother of humankind that behavior during copulation be the same as behavior in anger? What well-made man, in a word, what man endowed with vigorous organs does not desire, in one fashion or in another, to molest his partner during his enjoyment of her? I know perfectly well that whole armies of idiots, who are never conscious of their sensations, will have much trouble understanding the systems I am establishing; but what do I care for these fools? 'Tis not to them I am speaking; soft-headed women-worshipers, I leave them prostrate at their insolent Dulcineas' feet, there let them wait for the sighs that will make them happy and, basely the slaves of the sex they ought to dominate, I abandon them to the vile delights of wearing the chains wherewith Nature has given them the right to overwhelm others! Let these beasts vegetate in the abjection which defiles them—twould be in vain to preach to them—, but let them not denigrate what they are incapable of understanding, and let them be persuaded that those who wish to establish their principles pertinent to this subject only upon the free outbursts of a vigorous and untrammeled imagination, as do we, you, Madame, and I, those like ourselves, I say, will always be the only ones who merit to be listened to, the only ones proper to prescribe laws unto them and to give lessons! . . .

chapter twenty-two

Georg Wilhelm Friedrich Hegel

Georg Wilhelm Friedrich Hegel (1770–1831) is widely regarded as the most influential philosopher of the nineteenth century. His work had a profound impact upon the philosophical systems of Søren Kierkegaard, Karl Marx, the Existentialists, the Pragmatists, and many others. Hegel's life work was the articulation of an expansive philosophical system that aimed to integrate all the great ideas of philosophy that preceded him, from the ancient Greeks to Kant, by chronicling the pattern of their historical development. Believing the history of philosophy to be the history of the evolution of consciousness, Hegel was certain that if he could demonstrate its logical and necessary pattern of development there would be no need for further philosophy—his system would complete all philosophy. While Hegel's system clearly did not succeed in this aim, it nevertheless served as the progenitor of some of the most important philosophical ideas of the nineteenth and twentieth centuries.

Hegel is classed among the German Idealists, those theorists, beginning with Kant, who assert that ultimate reality is spiritual, not material. Generally speaking, philosophical idealism holds that there is no reality or "thing-in-itself" that exists independently of a perceiving mind or consciousness; an object is real to us only when we perceive it. Idealists therefore emphasize the *relations between* perceiving subjects and perceived objects, since it is these relations that constitute reality. These theorists are called *idealists* because the relation between a perceiving subject and perceived object is understood to be the *idea* of the object. Hegel used the term Spirit (*Geist*) to refer to a consciousness that is aware of, and expresses the truth of, the interrelations between subjects and objects.

Although Hegel was an idealist, his absolute idealism is to be distinguished from other forms, such as Friedrich Schelling's aesthetic idealism, Johann Gottlieb Fichte's moral idealism, and, especially, Immanuel Kant's transcendental idealism. Hegel, in fact, published his first major work, the *Phenomenology of Spirit* (from which the passage included here is excerpted), to "correct" what he thought were significant problems in transcendental idealism. He rejected Kant's assertion that we can never know "things in themselves" as being itself unintelligible. Hegel set out to demonstrate that reality can be known and, in fact, is revealed *in* the relations between subjects and objects, the relations being what idealists have already determined to be the ultimately real.

Here it will be helpful to note Hegel's conception of the universe as fundamentally *one*—a unified whole—even though there appears to be a multitude of various and independent phenomena in the world. Hegel's conviction is that Absolute Spirit is expressing itself in the natural world so that through concrete existence it may come to know itself (achieve Absolute Knowing). The natural world is therefore at the same time natural and "divine"; the natural and divine are in an intimate relation.[1]

As Hegel believed that everything in the natural world is an expression of Absolute Spirit, he asserted that history can be understood as the process through which the Absolute comes to know itself. The Absolute, being manifest partly in conscious humans, achieves its self-knowledge through the experience of human consciousness, which is progressing toward greater understanding of the interrelations between entities in the world. These interrelations are the *content* of the unifying force of all things; the relations *are* the manifestation of Absolute Spirit from whence all things have come.

Hegel's endeavor to integrate all philosophy that preceded him can now be understood more clearly: By charting the historical development of theories of existence, Hegel believed he was chronicling the actual experience of Absolute Spirit as it progresses toward more complete knowledge of itself. In calling this investigation a phenomenology of spirit, Hegel meant that he was describing the appearances and actions of spirit as it proceeds along its educational journey. Accordingly, in the introduction to the *Phenomenology* Hegel writes,

> This exposition . . . can be regarded as the path of the natural consciousness which presses forward to true knowledge; or as the way of the Soul which journeys through the series of its own configurations, as though they were stations appointed for it by its own nature, so that it may purify itself for the life of the Spirit, and achieve finally, through a completed experience of itself, the awareness of what it really is in itself.[2]

The *Phenomenology* purports to demonstrate a necessary and logical movement through which human consciousness is evolving into self-knowing Absolute Spirit. Hegel focuses intently upon a great series of isolated moments in the evolution of consciousness, from its most "primitive" sense awareness to its ultimate achievement of Absolute Knowing. He intends to bring to scientific order what appear to most of us to be random moments of a chaotic human experience. Hegel wants to show not only that the development of consciousness is following a logical progression, but also that the various moments of this development *necessarily* evolve into higher ones.

Consciousness progresses through its stages of development via a long series of dialectical movements. In the first moment of a dialectical movement, consciousness studies an "object" (e.g., a thing, a person, a concept) in order to know it. Close examination reveals that the object is much more complex than it first appears to be—it is, for instance, a whole, yet it is at the same time multifaceted. As consciousness ponders the object's seeming contradiction, it is driven to the second moment of the dialectic, namely, examination of its own perceptive faculty. Realizing that it is necessarily in a relation with the object, by its very act of perceiving the object, consciousness is driven to the third moment of the dialectic: examination of this relation. When consciousness comprehends the nature of the relation, it achieves a new level of understanding. It also becomes aware of new kinds of "objects" and so must repeat the dialectic time and again until finally it resolves all contradictions, recognizes the inherent unity of all things, and thereby realizes itself *as* Absolute Spirit.

In the passage of the *Phenomenology* excerpted here, "Mastery and Slavery," consciousness has progressed through the knowledge of natural objects and has become self-conscious through the phenomenon of desire—specifically, its desire to *consume* (negate) natural objects. "Self-consciousness is *Desire*," Hegel writes (§167). Consciousness has two fundamental ways of relating to objects in the world. In a given moment, consciousness may not be concerned with any object, in which case we can say that it is simply immersed in its life. Alternatively, consciousness may desire an object, in which case it is in this moment both conscious of the object and self-conscious. In "Mastery and Slavery," Hegel describes the intricate dialectical development that occurs when two conscious beings suddenly are aware of each other. In this moment, neither consciousness is simply immersed in life; rather, each sees the other gazing at it and wonders, "Does this being desire me? Does this being recognize my desire?" A conflict ensues that, of course, constitutes a dialectical movement through which consciousness learns about its relation to other conscious beings.

The saga of consciousness does not end with the resolution of "Mastery and Slavery," however. Equipped with an understanding of one kind of relation with other conscious beings, consciousness continues its journey, pursuing a more satisfying experience of the world. It is a long and tortuous journey—Hegel called it "the way of despair"—but consciousness acquires abundant knowledge as a result of its trials and ultimately succeeds in realizing Absolute Spirit that knows itself.

The *Phenomenology of Spirit* was Hegel's first major published work (1807). His second work, the *Science of Logic* (1812–1816), is a systematic analysis of concepts, such as the notion of identity-within-difference that characterizes spirit. Hegel envisioned the *Science of Logic* as the first part of his *Encyclopedia of the Philosophical Sciences* (1817), the full articulation of his philosophical system. The *Philosophy of Right* (1821) was Hegel's last published work. Within a few years of his death, Hegel's students published his lectures on the philosophy of history, history of philosophy, philosophy of art, and philosophy of religion. Other works, only recently translated into English, include *Early Theological Writings* and *Philosophy of Nature*.

SC

QUESTIONS

1. Why does Hegel assert that self-consciousness exists "only in being acknowledged" (§178)? Do you agree or disagree?

2. Why does Hegel insist that a life-and-death struggle is necessary in the dialectic of self-consciousness? Do you agree that it is necessary, or can you envision other viable alternatives?

3. Explain why the life-and-death struggle necessarily ends with the enslavement of one consciousness.

4. Explain why it is the slave, and not the master, who achieves true self-consciousness.

5. How might Hegel explain the process of initial attraction in a love relationship?

6. Compare or contrast Hegel's conception of attraction to that offered by another philosopher you have studied since Descartes.

ENDNOTES

1. This is of course, in contrast to Kant's positing of two separate realms, one phenomenal and the other noumenal. Whereas Kant held that human minds perceive the real through a transcendental unity of apperception, Hegel dropped the term transcendental, calling our organizing mental apparatus simply a unity of apperception.

2. Hegel, *Phenomenology of Spirit*, trans. A.V. Miller, p. 77.

SELECTED BIBLIOGRAPHY

Hegel, G.W.F. *Phenomenology of Spirit*, trans. A.V. Miller. New York: Oxford University Press, 1977.

Hegel, G.W.F. "Mastery and Slavery," [original translation by Andrea Tschemplik and James H. Stam, 2003].

Hyppolite, Jean. *Genesis and Structure of Hegel's "Phenomenology of Spirit,"* trans. Samuel Cherniak and John Heckman. Evanston, Ill.: Northwestern University Press, 1974.

Kaufmann, Walter. *Discovering the Mind: Goethe, Kant, and Hegel.* New York: McGraw-Hill, 1980.

Pinkard, Terry. *Hegel: A Biography.* New York: Cambridge University Press, 2000.

Stace, W.T. *The Philosophy of Hegel: A Systematic Exposition.* New York: Dover Publications, 1955.

Taylor, Charles. *Hegel.* New York: Cambridge University Press, 1975.

from *Phenomenology of Spirit*

G. W. F. Hegel

MASTERY AND SLAVERY

B. SELF-CONSCIOUSNESS

IV. The Truth of Self-Certainty*

166. In the modes of certainty (examined in the previous sections) the true, for consciousness, is something other than itself.[1] The *concept* of this truth vanishes, however, in the experiencing of it:

as *the object* was immediate *in itself*—the mere *being* of sense-certainty; the concrete *thing* of perception, the *force* of understanding—proves to be not such in truth, but rather this *in itself* turns out to be a mode in which the object exists only for another.[2] The concept of the Object is superseded[3] in the actual object: or, the first immediate presentation is superseded in experience: Certainty got lost in Truth. But now there has arisen that which did not take place in the earlier relationships, namely a certainty which is the same as its truth; for this certainty is now an Object[4] to itself, and Consciousness is Truth *to itself*. In this, to be sure, there is "otherness": Consciousness in fact makes a distinction, but one which at the same time, for Consciousness, is *not* a distinction. If we use the

---

*Note on capitalization, italics, etc. In German all nouns are ordinarily capitalized; and in Hegel's printed editions extra spacing between letters is used as the equivalent of italics. Hegel uses such emphases more than his contemporaries and far more than would be stylistically acceptable in English translation. The present translation attempts to follow Hegel's principal emphases without repeating all of them, but it will also sometimes use capitalization or italics to alert the reader to Hegel's special or technical usage of a term or to the fact that the phrasing is not following colloquial English usage. There is no attempt at consistency in this: Thus *"the other,"* "Other," or "other" will be used mainly according the degree to which the meaning seems "natural" or "unusual" in ordinary English.

[1] Hegel refers to the first section and three subsections of the *Phenomenology* after the "Preface" and "Introduction": A. CONSCIOUSNESS. I. Sense Certainty and the "This" and "Opinion"; II. Perception, or the Thing and Deception; III. Force and Understanding, Appearance and the Supersensible World. In each section what appears to be an initial certainty or truth—what is "true for consciousness"—dissolves into its opposite. Thus the certainty about the immediate, the "here and now," in the first stage turns out to be but a passing moment in the flux of time and space; in the second stage, Perception, the apparently steadfast independent "thing" that is assumed to be the object of perception, is upon analysis part of a set of different factors and forces; and as the human understanding penetrates these factors, this "play of forces," Force itself is seen to have, so to speak, both an "inside" and an "outside," initiation and outcome, and the (mere) appearance of things (illusion) is also their appearing to our consciousness. "Truth" for the three modes of consciousness changes dialectically, leading to the present section on *self*-consciousness.

[2] In colloquial German the phrases *an sich* ("in itself") and *an und für sich* ("in and for itself") are both roughly equivalent to "as such" or "per se." Building on Kant's general contrast between "the inner" and the "outer" and his distinction between *things-in-themselves* as the *noumenal* (or that which can be thought but cannot be experienced) and *things-for-us* as the *phenomenal* (or that which can be experienced and appears to consciousness), Hegel loads these everyday phrases a bit more to contrast the *in-itself*, the *for-itself* (which is, as it were, in front of itself and thus *for us*) and the *in-and-for-itself* (which is both).

[3] "Supersede" is a less than adequate translation of Hegel's famous *aufheben, aufgehoben*—a triple pun, meaning in ordinary German all three of the following: (1) to cancel or rescind; (2) to preserve; and, literally, to lift up. Thus the dialectical process is simultaneously negative, positive, and "progressive."

[4] The German for "Object" is *Gegenstand*, literally, "that which stands against." (English "object" is from Latin *ob* + *iacere*, "to throw at, or in front of.") Hegel trades on the etymology, taking the object to be that which (seems to) stand—and thus persists—against us and thus independently of us, and in a negative dialectical relation to us.

term "Concept"[5] to refer to the movement of Consciousness, and use "Object" for knowledge (considered) as a stable unity—that is to say, as *the I* or *the Ego*—we then see that the Object corresponds to the Concept not only for us, but for knowledge itself. Or, in another way, if we call that which the Object is in itself "Concept," but call "Object" that which it is *as* an Object, or *for an Other*, then it is clear that *being-in-itself* and *being-for-another* are the same; for the *in-itself* is consciousness; but it is likewise that *for which* an Other (the *in-itself*) *is*; and it is for it that the *in-itself* of the Object and its Being are the same for another. *The I* is the content of the relation and it is the relation itself. Over against an Other, *the I* is its own self; and at the same time it grasps out beyond this Other, which for *the I* is likewise only *the I* itself.

167. With Self-consciousness, then, we have entered into the native realm of truth, where truth is at home. It remains to be seen how the shape of self-consciousness first makes its appearance. If we observe this new shape of knowledge, knowledge of itself, in relation to the foregoing, knowledge of something other, then this latter has in fact disappeared; but its moments have at the same time been preserved; and the loss consists in the fact that they are present here as they are *in themselves*. The Being of Opinion, the particularity of perception and the universality contrasted with and in opposition to it, just like the empty "inner" of the Understanding, no longer exist as essences, but now as moments of self-consciousness, i.e. as abstractions or differences, which are at the same time as nothing *for* consciousness, that is, non-differences and pure disappearing essences. It seems then that it is only the principal moment it-self that has been lost, namely the simple self-sufficient endurance for consciousness. But in actuality self-consciousness is a reflection from the being of the sensed and perceived world, and it is essentially the return from otherness. As self-consciousness, it is movement; but inasmuch as it only differentiates itself from itself *as* itself, the difference, as something which is other, is immediately superseded for it. Thus it is not (really) a difference, and it is only the motionless tautology of "*I am I*":[6] Inasmuch as, for self-consciousness, the difference does not have the shape of Being, it is not self-consciousness. Therewith, for it, it is *being-other*, something else, as a being or as a differentiated moment; but, for self-consciousness, it is also the unity of its self with this difference, as a second differentiated moment. With that first moment self-consciousness is *quâ consciousness*, and the entire expanse of the sensuous world is preserved for it—but at the same time only with respect to the second moment, the unity of self-consciousness with itself; and therewith that endures which is only appearance or difference, which has no Being in itself. This opposition between its appearance and its truth, however, has truth alone for its essence, namely the unity of self-consciousness with itself: this unity must become essential to self-consciousness, i.e. self-consciousness is *Desire* in general. Consciousness now, as self-consciousness, has a double object—the first immediate one, the object of sense certainty and of perception, which is marked for it, however, with the *Character of the Negative*; and the second, namely consciousness itself, which is the true essence and initially it is only present in opposition to the former. In this, self-consciousness

---

[5]German *Begriff* has the same root as English/Latin *con* + *cipio*, to grasp together. For Hegel the Concept is that which grasps together the many parts and aspects of phenomena.

[6]There is a particular reference here to Fichte's departure from Kant's "transcendental idealism" and to the question whether Descartes' "I think, therefore I am" can ever get us beyond the tautology of the subject's own subjectivity.

presents itself as the movement in which this op- position is superseded and the identity of itself with itself comes about for it.

168. The object—which, for self-consciousness, is the Negative, whether it is so *for us* or *in itself*— has, from its side, returned to itself, just as con- sciousness did. Through this reflection into itself, the object has become *Life*. What self- consciousness distinguishes from itself as (having) *being*, has, to the extent that it is posited as being, not merely the mode of sense certainty and percep- tion, but rather it is Being reflected into itself and the object of immediate Desire is something living. For the *in itself*, or the *universal* result of the rela- tion of the Understanding to the "inner" of things, is the differentiation of that which is not to be dif- ferentiated,—or, the unity of the differences. This unity, however, as we have seen, is just as much its repulsion from itself, and this Concept divides it- self into the opposition of self-consciousness and life; the former is the unity *for* which the unity of differences exists; but the latter is only this unity itself, so that it is not simultaneously *for itself*. To the extent that consciousness is independent, therefore, to that extent its Object is independent *in itself*. Self-consciousness, which is simply *for it- self* and immediately marks its object with the Character of the Negative, which is thus primarily Desire, will thus become acquainted with its inde- pendence.

169. The determination of Life as it proceeds from the Concept, the universal result with which we enter upon this sphere, is enough to character- ize it, without further developing its Nature there- from: Its sphere is entirely demarcated within the following moments: The *Essence* is infinity as the supersession of all distinctions, the genuine axial motion, its self-repose as absolutely restless infin- ity, independence itself, in which the differentia- tions of motion are dissolved: the simple essence of

Time, which in its self-identity has the solid shape of Space. The differences, are just as much present as *differences* in this simple universal medium; for universal flux has a negative nature only to the ex- tent that it is their supersession; but it cannot su- persede the differences if they have no endurance. Precisely this flux, as the self-identical indepen- dence itself is the endurance or substance of (such differences), in which therefore they exist as differ- entiated members and parts *being-for-themselves*. *Being* no longer has the meaning of an *Abstraction from Being*,[7] nor has their pure essentiality the meaning of an abstraction of universality; but its Being is precisely that simple flowing substance of pure motion in itself. The difference of these mem- bers in opposition to one another, but still *quâ* dif- ference, consists overall in no other determination than the determination of the moments of infin- ity—that is, of pure motion itself.

170. The independent members are *for them- selves*; but this *being-for-itself* is rather, just as im- mediately, their reflection into unity as that unity is the splitting up into independent shapes. The unity is split up because it is absolutely negative or infinite unity; and because it is endurance, there- fore the difference too has independence only with respect to it. This independence of the shape ap- pears as something determined, *for another*, be- cause it is split up; and the supersession of the splitting up occurs through an Other. But it is just as much *in itself*; for precisely that flux is the sub- stance of the independent shapes. But this sub- stance is infinite: the shape therefore is a splitting

---

[7]In the *Science of Logic* and elsewhere, Hegel analyzes "Pure Being" as a concept abstracted from all content and particular- ity and thus "Nothing." The dialectical tension between "Being" and "Nothing" is then resolved in "Becoming—thus Time, Motion, Flux.

up in its very endurance—that is, the supersession of its *being-for-itself*.

171. If we differentiate more closely the moments contained in this, we see that we have as the first moment the endurance of the independent shapes, or the stifling of that which is in itself *(the)* differentiation, namely for (something) not to be *in-itself* and not to have endurance. The *second* moment, however, is the subjection of that endurance to the infinity of the difference. In the first moment there is the enduring shape: as *being-for-itself* or in its determination as infinite substance, it appears in contrast with universal substance, betrays this flux and therewith also continuity, and insists that it is not dissolved in this universal, but rather maintains itself through its separation from this its inorganic nature by devouring the same. Life in the universal fluid medium, a peaceful separating out of the shapes, becomes, precisely thereby, their own motion—that is, life as process. The simple universal flux is the *in-itself*, and the difference of the shapes is the *Other*. But this flux itself becomes *the Other* through this difference: for (the flux) is now *for the difference*, which is *in-and-for-itself*, and is therefore infinite motion, from which that motionless moment is consumed—life (itself) as *a living thing*.

This inversion, however, is for that reason in turn an invertedness *in-its-very-self*.[8] What is consumed is the essence: the individuality which maintains itself at the cost of the universal, and which gives itself the feeling of unity with itself, precisely therewith supersedes its opposition to the Other, through which such individuality is *for itself*; the unity which it gives itself is precisely the flux of differences, or universal dissolution. Conversely, however, the supersession of individual endurance likewise produces it. Since the *essence* of the individual shape—universal Life—and *being-for-itself* is as such simple substance, this substance thus supersedes this its *simplicity* or its essence, when it posits the Other within itself—that is, it divides it and this division of the undifferentiated flux is precisely the positing of individuality. The simple substance of Life is, therefore, the division of itself into shapes, and simultaneously the dissolution of these enduring differences; and the dissolution of the division is just as much a division as an articulation (of the members). Therewith the two sides of the entire movement which were distinguished before—the quietly separated shapes in the general medium of independence, and the process of Life—collapse into one another. The latter is just as much a shaping as it is the supersession of shape; and the first, the shaping, is just as much a supersession as it is articulation. The fluid element is itself only the *Abstraction* of essence; or it is only *real* as shape; and its articulation involves once again a division of itself or a dissolution of the same. Life consists of this entire cycle—neither that which is expressed at first, the immediate continuity and solidity of its Essence; nor the enduring shape and discrete (thing as) *being-for-itself*; nor their pure process, nor even the simple putting-together of these moments; but the self-developing whole, dissolving its development and maintaining itself simply in this motion.

172. To the extent that we proceed from the first immediate unity through the moments of shaping and process all the way to the unity of both these moments, and therewith return again to the first simple substance, this reflected unity is different from the first. In contrast with that immediate unity, expressed as a *being*, this second one

---

[8]The previous section on "Force and Understanding" included a lengthy passage on the "Inverted World" or "Topsy-turvy World," in which everything is presumed to be the inverse of the familiar world, but in which the role of Force would be the same.

is universal, and it has all of these moments in it as superseded. It is the simple *genus*, which, in the motion of life itself does not exist *for itself as this simple thing*; but rather, in this *result*, Life points to something other than itself, namely to consciousness, for which it is this unity or genus.[9]

173. This other Life, however, self-consciousness, for which the genus is as such and which is the genus *for itself,* is *for itself* above all only as this simple essence, and has for itself the pure *I* as its object; in its experience, which must now be observed, this abstract object will enrich itself for the *I* and will undergo the unfolding which we have seen in the case of Life.

174. The simple *I* is this genus, or the simple universal, for which the differences are not such only to the extent that it is the negative essence of the formed independent moments. Self-consciousness is therewith certain of itself only through the supersession of this Other, which presents independent life for it: it is *Desire*. Certain of the nullity of this Other, it posits *for itself* the same as its truth, nullifies the independent object and grants itself thereby the certainty of itself as *true* certainty, which, as such, has become such for it in an objective manner.

175. In this satisfaction, however, it experiences the independence of its object. Desire, and the self-certainty gained through its satisfaction, is conditioned through the object, for Desire comes through the supersession of this other; in order for this supersession to exist, this other must exist. Self-consciousness, therefore, through its negative relation (to the object) is unable to supersede it; on the contrary, because of that it engenders the object yet again, and it engenders Desire also. The essence of Desire is in fact something other than self-consciousness, and through this experience this has become truth for self-consciousness itself. Simultaneously, however, it is likewise absolutely *for-itself* and it is such only through the supersession of the Object; and that must turn out to be its satisfaction, for that is the truth. For the sake of the independence of the object, therefore, it can only attain satisfaction, to the extent that this (object) itself accomplishes the negation for it, and must be what it is for the other. Since the object is its own negation, and is thereby at the same time independent, it is consciousness. In (the realm of) Life, which is the Object of Desire, negation is either in terms of an other, to wit in (terms of) Desire, or as a determination with respect to some other indifferent shape, or as Life's universal inorganic nature. This universal independent nature, however, in which negation is present as an absolute, it is genus itself or self-consciousness. Self-consciousness attains this satisfaction only in another self-consciousness.

176. It is in these three moments that the *Concept of Self-consciousness* is first completed: a) pure undifferentiated *I* is its first immediate object; b) This immediacy is itself, however, absolute mediation: it (exists) only as the supersession of the independent object, or it is Desire. The satisfaction of Desire is in fact the reflection of self-consciousness into itself, or certainty which has become truth; c) But its truth is rather the double reflexion, the doubling of self-consciousness. It is for consciousness an Object which in itself posits its Otherness or difference as a nullity, and therein it is independent. The differentiated, living shape supersedes its independence, even in the process of life; but with its difference, it stops being what it is; the object of self-consciousness is equally independent in this its negativity; and therewith it itself is *genus for itself,* universal flux in the peculiarity of its separation; it is living self-consciousness.

---

[9] *Gattung* can be translated as "genus," "species," "kind," or "sort." "Category" would work in English except that it is used more technically later in the *Phenomenology*.

177. It is a self-consciousness *for* a self-consciousness. Only through this is it in fact (self-consciousness); for it is in this that there first develops for it a unity of its self with its otherness; *the I* which is the object of its concept, is in fact not an object; the object of desire, however, is only independent, for it is the universal inextinguishable substance, the fluid self-identical *Essence*. Inasmuch as a self-consciousness is the object, it is just as much *I* as it is object.—Therewith we already have at hand the Concept of *Spirit*.[10] That which is still to come for consciousness is the experience of what Spirit is, this absolute Substance, which is the unity of self-consciousnesses *being-for-themselves*, different in the perfect freedom and independence of their oppositions: *the I* is *the We*, and *the We* is *the I*. It is first in Self-Consciousness, as the Concept of Spirit, that consciousness has its turning point, at which it leaves behind the colorful appearance of sensuous this-worldliness; and steps out of the empty night of the supersensuous otherworldly beyond into the spiritual daylight of the present.

A. INDEPENDENCE AND NON-INDEPENDENCE OF SELF-CONSCIOUSNESS: MASTERY AND SLAVERY

178. Self-consciousness is, *in-and-for-itself*, thereby and to the extent that it is *in-and-for-itself for an Other*, that is, it exists only as something recog-

nized.[11] The concept of this its unity in its duplication, of the infinity which realizes itself in self-consciousness, has many sides and many meanings, so that its moments must be kept precisely separate on the one hand, but must in this differentiation simultaneously be kept as undifferentiated on the other hand—or they must always be understood and recognized in their opposed meanings. The double meaning of the differentiated lies in the essence of self-consciousness as being infinite, or as immediately the opposite of the determinateness in which it is posited. The exposition of the Concept by taking apart[12] the spiritual unity in its duplication presents us with the motion of recognition.

179. There is another self-consciousness *for* self-consciousness; it has come out of itself. This has a double meaning: first of all, it has lost itself, since it discovers itself to be *another* essence; second, it has thereby superseded the other, for it does not see the other as an essence, but it sees itself in the other.

180. It must therefore supersede this its otherness: this is the supersession of the first double meaning, and therefore it is itself a second double meaning. First, it must be concerned with superseding the other independent essence, in order thereby to be certain of its own independent essence; secondly, this is a matter of superseding its (own) self, because this other is its self.

181. This double-sensed supersession of its double-sensed otherness is likewise a double-

---

[10]The German term *Geist* is broader in scope than English "spirit," including religious connotations, but not limited to those. It can refer generally to the human mind or to something broadly like "culture," but it is also cognate with "ghost."

[11]"Recognition": The relation between *Erkennen* and *Anerkennen* is roughly parallel to English "cognition" and "recognition" or "knowledge" and "acknowledge." Hegel's use here emphasizes the social and political sense of "recognition" as "acknowledging the status" of someone or something, as in "recognizing the government of *x*" or current discussions among multiculturalists of "the politics of recognition."

[12]"Exposition by taking apart": A double translation of *Auseinanderlegung*: This captures some of the literal meaning of the Greek term for "dialectic."

sensed return into itself; for, first, it gets itself back through this supersession, since it again becomes equal to itself by superseding this otherness. Secondly, however, the other self-consciousness gives back equally in turn, for it was for itself in the other, it supersedes this *its* being in the other, and thus also lets the other (go) free.

182. This movement of self-consciousness in relation to an other self-consciousness is represented, however, as the activity of the one; but this activity of the one has itself the double meaning of being *his* activity just as much as the activity of the other; for the other is equally independent and self-contained, and there is nothing in it which has not come about through it itself. The first does not have the object before it merely as it was for Desire, but as an (object) which exists for itself independently, concerning which it is therefore unable to do anything unless it does the same in itself which the other does to it. The movement, therefore, is simply the double movement of both self-consciousnesses. Each sees *the other* do what *he* does; and each does himself what the other demands; and he therefore does that which he does only to the extent that the other does the same: (for) one-sided activity would be pointless, since that which is supposed to happen can only come about through both of them.

183. This activity therefore is not only double-sensed to the degree that it is activity equally *toward itself* and *toward the other*, but also to the degree that it is inseparably as much *the activity of the one* as of *the other*.

184. In this movement we see the process repeating itself which was earlier exhibited as the "play of forces,"[13] but now in consciousness. That which was *for us* in the former is here true for the

extremes themselves. The middle term[14] is self-consciousness, which diffuses itself into the extremes, and each extreme is this exchange of its own determinateness and an absolute transition into its opposite. As consciousness, however, it surely comes *outside itself*, and nevertheless is simultaneously held back *for itself*, in its *being-outside-itself*, and its *outside-itself* is *for it* It is for it that it *is* and *is not* immediately another consciousness; and likewise this other is only for itself, inasmuch as it supersedes itself as *being-for-itself*, and is *for itself* only in the *being-for-itself* of the other. Each is the middle for the other, through which each mediates itself with itself and merges with itself, and each is to itself and to the other an immediate Essence *being-for-itself*, which simultaneously is only *for itself* by virtue of this mediation. They recognize one another as mutually recognizing one another.

185. This pure concept of recognition, of the duplication of self-consciousness in its unity, is now to be observed in the way its process appears for self-consciousness. It will first exhibit the side of the inequality of both, the emergence of the middle into the extremes, which, as extremes, are opposed to one another, so that the one is only the recognized and the other only the recognizing.

186. Self-consciousness is, first of all, simple *being-for-itself*, self-identical through the exclusion *from itself* of everything *other*; its essence and absolute object is, for it, *the I*; and it is an individual in this immediacy, that is in this *being* of its *being-for-itself*. What(ever) is *Other* for it is an object

---

[13]Cf. footnote 1 above.

[14]These terms—"middle" and "extremes" (major and minor)—are taken from Aristotelian logic, even though Hegel's dialectical logic rejects basic Aristotelian axioms. In the syllogism "All humans are rational, all slaves are human, therefore all slaves are rational," "human" is the middle term, connecting the minor (slaves) to the major (rational beings).

characterized as unessential, with the character of the negative. But *the Other* is also self-consciousness; it emerges as an individual over against an individual. Emerging in such immediacy, they *are* for one another in the manner of ordinary objects; independent shapes, individual consciousnesses immersed in the *Being* of *Life*—for the being Object determines itself as life. They have not yet completed *for-(one)-another* the movement of absolute abstraction, destroying all immediate Being, being only the pure negative Being of self-identical consciousness—that is, they have not yet represented themselves to one another as pure *being-for-itself*, i.e. as *self*-consciousness. Each is no doubt sure of itself, but not of the other, and therefore its own self-certainty does not yet have any truth; for its truth would only consist in its having its own *being-for-itself* as an independent object, or—what amounts to the same thing—as if the object had presented itself as this pure certainty of its own self. But this, according to the Concept of Recognition, is not possible unless each is for the other what the other is for him, and each is itself as such through its own activity, and through the activity of the other, in turn, it accomplishes this pure abstraction of *being-for-itself*.

187. The presentation of itself as the pure abstraction of self-consciousness, however, consists in showing itself as the pure negation of its objective mode—or in showing that it is not tied to any determinate *existence*, nor to the universal particularity of existence in general, i.e., that it is not tied to Life. This presentation is a double activity—activity of the other and activity through itself. To the extent that it is activity of the other, each aims at the death of the other. But therein the second activity is also present, activity on its own: for the former includes risking its own life. The relationship of both self-consciousnesses, therefore, is determined in such a way that they test themselves and each other through a life-and-death struggle. They must enter into this struggle because they must elevate their certainty of themselves, of *being-for-themselves*, into a truth with regard to the other and with regard to themselves. And it is only the risking of life whereby there is freedom, whereby it is proved that, for self-consciousness, it is not *Being*, not the immediate mode in which it appears, not its submergence in the expanse of Life—the Essence, but rather there is nothing present in it which would not be for it a vanishing moment, that it is only pure *being-for-itself*. Any individual that has not yet risked its life, can be recognized as a *person* to be sure; but it has not attained to the truth of this being recognized as an independent self-consciousness. Likewise, each must aim at the other's death, inasmuch as it risks its life; for the other no longer counts for him as itself; its essence presents itself to him as an Other, it is outside itself; it must supersede its *being-outside-itself*; the Other is multiply ensnared, and *being consciousness*; it must view its *being other* as pure *being-for-itself* or absolute negation.

188. This test by death, however, also supersedes the truth which was supposed to proceed from it, and so too with the certainty of itself in general; for just as life is the *natural* position of consciousness, independence without absolute negativity, just so (death) is its *natural* negation, negation without independence, which therefore remains even without the required significance of recognition. It is through death in fact that the certainty has come about that both risked their lives, and each disdained life, both his own and that of the other; but not for those who survived this struggle. They supersede their consciousness, posited in this alien essentiality which is natural existence; or they supersede themselves and are superseded as extremes wanting to be *for themselves*. But therewith disappears from the play of change

the essential moment, that of diffusing into the extremes of opposed determinations. And the middle collapses into a dead unity, which is broken up into dead, merely existing, non-contrary extremes; and neither of them gives or receives the other reciprocally through consciousness, but rather they leave each other free, but indifferently so, like things. Their activity is abstract negation, not the negation of consciousness, which supersedes in such a way that it preserves and upholds the superseded, and in this way survives its becoming superseded.

189. In this experience it becomes clear to self-consciousness that life is as essential to it as pure self-consciousness. In immediate self-consciousness the simple *I* is the absolute object, which, however, *for us* or *in itself*, is absolute mediation, and has enduring independence as its essential moment. The dissolution of that simple unity is the result of the first experience: There is posited through it a pure self-consciousness, and also a consciousness which is not purely *for itself*, but *for another*—that is, as *existing* consciousness or consciousness in the form of *thinghood*. Both moments are essential: since they are, to begin with, unequal and opposite, and their reflection into unity has not yet been achieved, they exist as two opposed shapes of consciousness—the one independent, for which the essence is *being-for-itself*, the other non-independent, for which the essence is *life* or *being-for-another*. The former is the master, the latter the slave.

190. The master is consciousness being *for itself*, but no longer only as the Concept thereof; but rather consciousness *being* for-itself, is mediated with itself through an *other* consciousness, namely through one whose essence entails that it is synthesized with independent Being or with thinghood in general. The master is related to both these moments: to a thing, as such, the object of desire; and to consciousness, for which thinghood is the essence. And to the extent that he, the Master, (a) is immediate relation of *being-for-itself* as the Concept of self-consciousness, but (b) now he is at the same time mediation, or *being-for-itself*, which is for itself only by virtue of an other; therefore he is related (a) immediately to both, and (b) mediately to each by virtue of the other. The master is related mediately to the slave through (an) *independent being*; for precisely therein the slave is bound: it is his chain, from which he could not "abstract" himself in the struggle, and therefore showed himself to be non-independent, to have his independence in thinghood. The master, however, is the power over this Being, because he proved in the struggle, that, for him, that only counts as something negative. Inasmuch as he, the master, has the power over this, but this being has the power over the Other, in this conclusion he holds the other subject to him. In precisely this way the master is related mediately to the thing through the slave; whereas the slave is also related to the thing as self-consciousness generally, and supersedes it; but it is simultaneously independent for him, the slave, and he can therefore not negate it to the point of annihilating and being rid of it: in other words he only works on it. For the master, in contrast, this *immediate* relation becomes, through such mediation, the pure negation of the thing, or enjoyment: What did not succeed for Desire, he thus succeeds in being rid of, and contents himself with enjoyment. Desire failed to accomplish this because of the independence of the thing; but the master, who has now interposed the slave between himself and the thing, is only connected to the non-independence of the thing and enjoys it purely. The aspect of its independence he leaves to the slave, who works on it.

191. In both of these moments, for the master recognition comes about through another consciousness; for in (the masters) this consciousness is posited as something unessential—in the first in-

stance because of its working on the thing, and in the second instance because of its dependence on a determinate existence. In neither case can it be master over its being and achieve its absolute negation. Thus is at hand this moment of recognition, namely that the other consciousness supersedes its *being-for-itself*, and therewith itself does that which the first does to it. Likewise, here is the other moment, that this action of the second is the first one's own action as well: for what the slave does is really the action of the master. For the latter there is only *being-for-himself*, essence: he is the pure negative power, for which the thing is nothing, and therefore the pure essential action in this relationship is his: whereas the slave's is not pure, but rather a non-essential action. But the moment is lacking for the actual recognition that what the master does against the other, he also does against himself, and what the slave does against himself he also does against the other. There has therefore emerged a recognition which is one-sided and unequal.

192. In this (recognition), the unessential consciousness is the object for the master, which amounts to the *truth* of his certainty. It becomes clear, however, that this object does not correspond to its own Concept, but that which the master has achieved has become for him something entirely other than an independent consciousness. It is not such for him at all, but rather something non-independent; and he is therefore not certain of the *being-for-itself* as his own truth, but rather his truth is instead an unessential consciousness and the unessential activity of the same.

193. The *truth* of the independent consciousness is therefore slavish consciousness. This appears indeed, at first, *outside* itself, not as the truth of self-consciousness. But just as mastery showed that its essence was the inverse of what it wanted to be, so too slavery will become in its completion the opposite of what it is immediately: it will return into itself as consciousness forced back into itself, and will be turned around into true independence.

194. We have only seen what slavery is in comparison with mastery. But it too is a self-consciousness and we must now observe what it accordingly is *in-and-for-itself*. At first, for slavery, the master is the essence; and thus the independent consciousness *being-for-itself* is the truth for it, which nonetheless is *for it* but not yet *in it*. Still, it has in fact in itself this truth of pure negativity and of *being-for-itself*, for it has experienced this essence therein. To be precise, this consciousness did not have fear of this or that (thing), nor of this or that moment, but of its entire essence, for it has experienced the fear of death, of the absolute master. In that it has been inwardly dissolved, and has thoroughly trembled inside itself, and everything fixed in it has quaked. This pure universal motion, the absolute fluidity of all endurance, is, however, the simple essence of self-consciousness—absolute negativity, pure *being-for-itself*, that is herewith present in this consciousness. This moment of pure *being-for-itself* is also *for it*, for the slave, since it exists for him in the master *as his object*. Furthermore, this is not only this universal dissolution *in general*, but in serving it actually accomplishes it. In all the *individual* moments (of his service) he supersedes his dependence on natural existence and works it away.

195. The feeling of absolute power, however, in general and in the particulars of service, is only the dissolution *in itself*; and although indeed "the fear of the Lord is the beginning of wisdom,"[15] consciousness is therein *for its own self*, not *being-for-*

---

[15]Psalm 111:10 (also Proverbs 9:10). Throughout *Herr/Herrschaft* can be translated either as "lord/lordship" or "master/mastery." In passages such as this one the religious connotations of the former version are clear—and ironic. Similarly, *Knecht/Knechtschaft* can be translated as "slave/slavery," "servant/servitude," or "bondsman/bondage" with distinct connotations.

itself. Through work, however, the slave "comes to" himself. In the moment which corresponds to desire in the consciousness of the master, it appeared indeed that the aspect of the unessential relation to the thing fell to the slave consciousness, since in that relation the thing maintained its independence. Desire kept to itself the pure negation of the object and thereby its unmixed self-feeling. This satisfaction, however, is for that reason itself only something vanishing, for it is lacking the objective side, permanence. Work, in contrast, is Desire *held in check,* the vanishing halted: work is formative. The negative relation to the object becomes its *Form* and becomes something permanent; and it is precisely for the worker that the Object has independence. This negative middle (term), or the formative activity, is simultaneously the particularity or the pure *being-for-itself* of consciousness, which now, in the work outside it, comes upon the element of permanence: the working consciousness thus comes through this to the view of independent being as its own independence.

196. The formative activity, however, does not only have this positive meaning that the slave consciousness, as pure *being-for-itself,* thereby becomes *the being thing;* but also the negative meaning, counter to its first moment, fear. For in the making of the thing its own negativity, its *being-for-itself,* becomes an Object by virtue of the fact that it supersedes the existing form opposed to it. But this opposed and objective negative is precisely the alien essence before which it had trembled. Now, however, it destroys this alien, sets itself up as such, (the negative), in the element of permanence; and thereby becomes for itself a *being-for-itself.* For the slave the *being-for-itself* in the master is an Other, but only *for it;* in fear, *being-for-itself* is present for the slave himself; in formative activity *being-for-itself* becomes its very own for it, and it "comes to" consciousness that it itself is *in-and-for-itself.* The

form does not become something other than itself by the fact that it is posited outside itself; for that very form is its pure *being-for-itself,* which thereby becomes its truth. And therefore through this rediscovery of himself through himself comes about his own sense, precisely in work, which had only seemed to have an alien meaning.—Both moments, fear and servitude in general, are necessary for this reflexion, as is formative activity, and simultaneously both of them in a universal manner. Without the discipline of service and obedience, fear remains stuck at something formal and does not spread out to the conscious actuality of existence. Without formative activity fear remains inward and mute, and consciousness does not become *for itself.* If consciousness forms the thing without absolute fear, it is only a vain stubbornness, having only its own sense, for its form or negativity is not negative *in itself;* and its formative activity therefore cannot give it the consciousness of itself as its essence. If he has not endured absolute fear, but only some anxiety, then the negative essence would have remained something external for him, its substance has not been thoroughly infected by it. To the extent that not all fulfillments of its natural consciousness have remained shaky, it belongs *in itself* to determinate being; its own sense is just self-will,[16] a freedom which remains within the bonds of slavery. Just as little as pure form can become essence for him, just so little is that form, considered as extended over the particular, a universal formation or an absolute Concept; rather it is a skill which is only powerful over some things, but not the universal power and the whole objective essence.

---

[16] *"Sein eigner Sinn ist Eigensinn"*—a clever pun, on the one hand, but also an indication that slave revolt, in order to succeed—which, according to Hegel, it inevitably will—must not just be "subjective" protest.

chapter twenty-three

Karl Marx

Karl Heinrich Marx (1818–1883), whose theories and interpretations of philosophy and history would create global uproar, was born into a family that had traditions of scholarly work and interpretation. Marx's mother's family had a century-long line of rabbis, and both his paternal grandfather and uncle served as rabbis in Trier, a city in the west of Germany near Luxemburg and France. In contrast to these religious traditions in the family, Marx's father was a successful lawyer. At least partially to retain the upper-middle class lifestyle in which his family was accustomed to living, he had the entire Marx household convert to Christianity in 1824. Marx excelled in school. Although his teachers cautioned that his writings routinely displayed "exaggerated searchings after unusual and picturesque expressions,"[1] he was highly commended for his ability to interpret the most difficult and subtle passages of the classics.

In 1835, Marx entered the University of Bonn to begin his study of law, though he appears to have done more drinking and frolicking than studying in his first year away from home. At the end of the year, Marx proposed to Jenny von Westphalen and (at the urging of his father) transferred to the University of Berlin to continue his studies in law and political economy. While in Berlin, Marx appears to have preferred to study independently rather than attend courses; he registered for only twelve courses in four and a half years. In addition to his prescribed studies, Marx also read quite a bit of history and philosophy. He quickly became a member of a group called the Young Hegelians, who wished to develop the spirit of Hegel's philosophy further, even if the development necessitated contradicting what Hegel himself had believed. During this time in Berlin, Marx first became acquainted with fellow student Friedrich Engels, who would become his lifelong collaborator.

After his father died in 1838, Marx officially deserted his law studies and began working toward a doctorate in philosophy. Since the philosophy departments of

From Karl Marx, *Economic and Philosophic Manuscripts of 1844*, translated by Martin Milligan and edited by Dirk J. Struik. Copyright © 1964 by International Publishers. Reprinted with permission.

From Karl Marx, *Capital: A Critique of Political Economy*, Vol. 3, translated by Samuel Moore and Edward Aveling, edited by Friedrich Engels. Copyright © 1967 by International Publishers. Reprinted with permission.

German universities disapproved of those who questioned Hegel's thought, Marx believed that if he received his degree from a smaller school and published his dissertation he would be able to teach at the University of Bonn as Doctor of a "foreign university" (which is to say, foreign to the Rhineland region of Germany). To this end, he arranged to have his dissertation on classical Greek philosophy accepted at the University of Jena. Unfortunately, the political climate in Bonn would not allow for the appointment of such a radical thinker to the faculty, so Marx never published his dissertation and turned instead to journalism as a way to advance his theories. After a newspaper he edited was officially banned in 1843, Marx decided to leave Germany. He married Jenny that summer, and they moved to Paris in October.

In Paris, Marx met up again with Engels; their personal and professional friendship would last until Marx's death. While in Paris, Marx published one issue of a newspaper and began to distance himself from the Young Hegelians. Also during this time he wrote the unfinished manuscript generally titled *The Economic and Philosophic Manuscript of 1844* (also known as *The Paris Manuscripts*). This work is in many ways the most philosophical of Marx's work, and while it was not published in his lifetime, it is possible through it to see ideas that would culminate in *Capital* (also known in English by its German title *Das Kapital*). Selections from both works are included here.

After a year in Paris, Marx was exiled at the request of the German government, which was troubled by the radical nature of Marx's work. He moved his family to Brussels. While there, Marx and Engels jointly wrote three works: *The Holy Family* (1845), *The German Ideology* (1845–1846), and *The Communist Manifesto* (1848). In 1848, Marx briefly returned to Germany only to be forced to leave, first to Paris and eventually to London in 1849. With the exception of short trips and travels, Marx and his family lived the rest of his life in Great Britain (both in London and Manchester), surviving largely on the kindness of Engels and other friends. He continued to publish sections of his work in various newspapers and small presses. Even though he was very sick in the last decade of his life, Marx was able largely to complete *Capital*, the first volume of which was published in 1867. The final two volumes were edited by Engels and published posthumously in 1885 and 1894, respectively. Karl and Jenny Marx had seven children, four of whom died as infants or adolescents. Jenny Marx died in 1881; Karl was survived by three daughters, all of whom became romantically involved with leaders of the labor movement in England and France.

Central to an understanding of Marx's project is his interpretation of Hegel's Master/Slave dialectic.[2] Where Hegel finds in the relationship between the lord (master) and the bondsman (slave) a desire for recognition of the other as individual, Marx focuses on the manner of continued alienation—including the failure of recognition—that can occur in political economies. Hegel begins by explaining that the lord understands the bondsman as an other only in a mediated sense;[3] that is, the lord never recognizes the bondsman simply as being a person, but always, first and foremost, as a slave. This is to say that the slave is understood not as a person, with all of the accompanying needs and complexities, but simply as a useful tool. Similarly, for Marx the laborer is not recognized as a full-fledged person, but only as a person to the extent that she must be human in order to be a worker. Hegel continues his analysis of recognition by examining the relationship between the slave and the product of his labor; Marx in turn examines the alienated relationship of the worker in a capitalist economy to the products of her labor. To that end, Marx looked at the historical and philosophical roots of capitalism and found that there were certain consistencies between variants of capitalism.

In every capitalist system, there is a group of people (the "capitalists") who own the raw product, land, and factories that are necessary for the production of goods. These capitalists rent land from one another, acquire the necessary tools for manufacturing, and assemble a workforce—that is, a group of laborers. The workforce sells labor as a commodity to the capitalist. The term "labor" in Marx's system is understood both as a social class (i.e., the working class) and as something exchanged.[4] After the finished product that the laborer makes is sold, the cost of doing business (rent, labor, raw materials) is deducted from the sales price. The remaining money is understood to be the profit from the sale of the product. Since the capitalist is seeking as much profit for himself as possible, he compensates the worker the minimum amount necessary for the worker to survive. In doing so, the capitalist appropriates the worker's labor, including the worker's "surplus value" or profit that the worker actually generates which is over and above what the worker needs to survive. This can best be understood by thinking about, for example, the number of chairs that a worker would need to make in order to purchase food, clothing, and housing. On his own the worker may need to produce two chairs a day in order to satisfy his needs, but when he works for the capitalist he would produce as many additional chairs a day as possible—not for his own good or benefit, but for the profit of the capitalist. The value of these additional chairs does not go to the worker, but to the factory owner. Thus, while the capitalist has paid for the worker's labor he is said to have appropriated the surplus value created by the worker.

Because capitalistic economies consider the workers' labor to be just another cost of doing business, the owners of capital will continue to exploit the labor force as much as they are able to without hindering the production of goods, refusing to recognize the full human value of the working class. For Marx, capitalism results in work environments and wages that minimize the recognition of the laborer as an individual. Further, since the individual worker can be replaced with another, the labor force is understood not as a collection of autonomous, unique individuals but rather as a type of raw material. Just as one would not worry which exact nail is used to fasten two pieces of wood, the capitalist does not care which individual is working at any given task. Any nail, and any worker, is as good as any other. This interchangeable approach to labor further alienates the worker from recognition because, like Hegel's slave who is understood not as a person but only as a tool, the worker is understood as a person only through her relationship to her work.

An additional alienation can occur between the worker and the product of his or her labor. Echoing Hegel's idea of self-recognition through work, Marx believed that in working with raw materials the laborer comes to understand himself or herself as a unique sort of entity. In an artisan economy, laborers sell their chairs directly; thus their labor is valued both as a separate good (the chair) and as a means to the end (the craftsmanship displayed in the chair). These two forms of valuation result in an authentic recognition by others. In the capitalist economy, since the result of the worker's labor is not his to do with as he wishes, the product of his work is alienated from him; he is paid for working hours, not for the product itself. Even though the worker produces the commodity that is sold, the owner of the factory owns the product. As many workers labor on any given product, the workers cannot discern which portion of the value of a product was due to their individual labor. Thus, the workers' labor is not rewarded by recognition of quality craftsmanship resulting in respect. Instead, workers are driven to expend their labor with the only recognition coming through wages. Marx's critique of the capitalist economy can be understood as the observation of two desires. The capitalist exploits the worker out of the desire for as much profit as possible; the worker desires recognition of herself as an individual instead of as a commodity. The worker is generally paid the minimum amount to provide a "means of subsistence which is absolutely requisite to keep the laborer in bare existence as a laborer."[5] However, her wages are spent in the same economic system that alienates her from her own labor. Thus, by purchasing the goods needed to survive, the worker reinforces the same economic conditions that cause worker alienation while multiplying the profits of the capitalist elite. Even the relatively well-paid worker still does not own the product of her work, and her spent wages are used to perpetuate an economic system of alienation. Since the continued success of capitalist systems depends on the continued acceptance by the labor class of their role, Marx believed that real change was possible only if a global working class united and brought about change. Thus he and Engels famously end the *Communist Manifesto* with the call, "working men of all countries, unite!"[6]

For Marx, the economic system is also social and political. Everything about society, from religious doctrine to acceptable family structure, reinforces the alienation of workers from their work. Religion, originally a means to escape human degradation, evolved to the point where it blinded people to both their own potential and the defects of the world around them.[7] Individuals are robbed in this process of the desire to bring about change. For this reason, Marx wrote, "Religion is the sigh of the oppressed creature, the sentiment of the heartless world, and the soul of soulless conditions. It is the opium of the people."[8] Religion, by blinding the worker to her potential to be more than she is, thus reinforces the economic system of capitalism. Similarly, traditional family structure parallels the structure of the state with a ruler (the father) and a group who obey (the mother and children). The father potentially redistributes the entire income of the family, just as the ruler can redistribute the wealth of the nation via taxation and government spending.[9]

While most of Marx's writings aim to provide the intellectual foundation of a society that is socialist in nature, his own work actually has very little to say about what an appropriately socialist system would be. Marx's writings have been reinterpreted in any number of ways, and have been influential in the political and economic systems of the former USSR (termed Marxist-Leninism after the leader of the Russian Revolution, Vladimir Illich Lenin, who lived from 1870 to 1924) and of the People's Republic of China (as interpreted by Mao Zedong, who lived from 1893–1976).

REK

QUESTIONS

1. Why does Marx believe that it is better to start out looking at "the economic fact *of the present*" instead of hypothetical bases for economic theory as the "political economist does"?

2. In what ways are workers alienated in capitalist economies? Marx's focus in the reading from *Capital* focuses more completely on the concept of surplus-value in contrast to the focus on general working conditions in the *Economic and Philosophical Manuscripts*. How does this emphasis change the nature of the understanding of alienation?

3. Societal and working conditions have changed since 1844, yet many still believe that Marx correctly pointed out a problem with capitalistic economies. In what ways do you think that Marx's criticisms still stand today? In what ways do you think that they have been overcome?

4. Marx believed that working life is a struggle for economic and social recognition. What are the desires of the owner in a capitalistic system? How are these desires in conflict with the worker's desire to be recognized as an individual?

5. Marx's examination of the capitalist-worker struggle draws from Hegel's examination of the lord-bondsman. How does the worker's struggle for recognition through work differ from the bondsman's recognition through work? What is the difference between the labor-derived recognitions?

ENDNOTES

1. Mehring, *Karl Marx,* p. 5.
2. See chapter 22 of this volume.
3. Hegel, *Phenomenology of Spirit,* p. 115.
4. Cf. Marx, *The German Ideology,* p. 21; and Marx, *Capital,* Vol. 1, p. 49.
5. Marx and Engels, *The Communist Manifesto,* p. 22.
6. *Ibid.*, p. 82.
7. Cf. Feuerbach, *The Essence of Christianity.* Marx responded to Feuerbach (a fellow Young Hegelian) in his "Theses on Feuerbach."
8. Marx, "Toward a Critique of Hegel's *Philosophy of Right,*" p. 28.
9. Cf. Engels. *The Origins of the Family, Private Property, and the State.*

SELECTED BIBLIOGRAPHY

Cohen, G.A. *Karl Marx's Theory of History: A Defence*. Princeton, N.J.: Princeton University Press, 2000.

Engels, Friedrich. *The Origins of the Family, Private Property, and the State*, trans. Evelyn Reed. New York: Pathfinder Press, 1972.

Feuerbach, Ludwig. *The Essence of Christianity*, trans. George Eliot. Amherst, N.Y.: Prometheus Books, 1989.

Hegel, Georg Wilhelm Friedrich. *Phenomenology of Spirit*, trans. A.V. Miller. Oxford: Oxford University Press, 1977.

Marx, Karl. *Capital: A Critique of Political Economy*, Vols. 1–3, trans. Samuel Moore and Edward Aveling, ed. Frederick Engels. New York: International Publishers, 1967.

Marx, Karl. *Economic and Philosophic Manuscripts of 1844*, trans. Martin Milligan, ed. Dirk J. Struik. New York: International Publishers, 1964.

Marx, Karl. *The German Ideology*, trans. and ed. R. Pascal. New York: International Publishers, 1947.

Marx, Karl. "Theses on Feuerbach," from *The Marx-Engels Reader*, ed. Robert C. Tucker. New York: W.W. Norton Company, 1978.

Marx, Karl. "Toward a Critique of Hegel's *Philosophy of Right*," from *Karl Marx: Selected Writings*, ed. Lawrence H. Simon. Indianapolis, Ind.: Hackett Publishing, 1994.

Marx, Karl and Friedrich Engels. *The Communist Manifesto*, trans. Samuel Moore. Garden City, N.Y.: Anchor Books, 1959.

Mehring, Franz. *Karl Marx*, trans. Edward Fitzgerald. Ann Arbor: University of Michigan Press, 1962.

Rosen, Michael. "Karl Marx," from *Routledge Encyclopedia of Philosophy*, Vol. 6, ed. Edward Craig. London: Routledge Press, 1998, pp. 118–33.

from *Economic and Philosophical Manuscripts of 1844*

Karl Marx

ESTRANGED LABOR

We have to grasp the essential connection between private property, greed, and the separation of labor, capital and landed property; between exchange and competition, value and the devaluation of men, monopoly and competition, etc.—the connection between this whole estrangement and the *money* system.

Do not let us go back to a fictitious primordial condition as the political economist does, when he tries to explain. Such a primordial condition explains nothing; it merely pushes the question away into a gray nebulous distance. It assumes in the form of a fact, of an event, what the economist is supposed to deduce—namely, the necessary relationship between two things—between, for example, division of labor and exchange. . . .

We proceed from an economic fact *of the present.*

The worker becomes all the poorer the more wealth he produces, the more his production increases in power and size. The worker becomes an ever cheaper commodity the more commodities he creates. With the *increasing value* of the world of things proceeds in direct proportion the *devaluation* of the world of men. Labor produces not only commodities: it produces itself and the worker as a *commodity*—and this in the same general proportion in which it produces commodities.

This fact expresses merely that the object which labor produces—labor's product—confronts it as *something alien*, as a *power independent* of the producer. The product of labor is labor which has been embodied in an object, which has become material: it is the *objectification* of labor. Labor's realization is its objectification. In the sphere of political economy this realization of labor appears as *loss of realization* for the workers; objectification as *loss of the object* and *bondage to it*; appropriation as *estrangement*, as *alienation*.

So much does labor's realization appear as loss of realization that the worker loses realization to the point of starving to death. So much does objectification appear as loss of the object that the worker is robbed of the objects most necessary not only for his life but for his work. Indeed, labor itself becomes an object which he can obtain only with the greatest effort and with the most irregular interruptions. So much does the appropriation of the object appear as estrangement that the more objects the worker produces the less he can possess and the more he falls under the sway of his product, capital.

All these consequences result from the fact that the worker is related to the *product of his labor* as to an *alien* object. For on this premise it is clear that the more the worker spends himself, the more powerful becomes the alien world of objects which he creates over and against himself, the poorer he himself—his inner world—becomes, the less belongs to him as his own. . . . The worker puts his life into the object; but now his life no longer belongs to him but to the object. Hence, the greater this activity, the greater is the worker's lack of objects. Whatever the product of his labor is, he is not. Therefore the greater this product, the less is he himself. The *alienation* of the worker in his product means not only that his labor becomes an object, an *external* existence, but that it exists *outside him*, independently, as something alien to him, and that it becomes a power on its own confronting him. It means that the life which he has conferred on the object confronts him as something hostile and alien.

Let us now look more closely at the *objectification*, at the production of the worker; and in it at the *estrangement*, the *loss* of the object, of his product.

The worker can create nothing without *nature*, without the *sensuous external world*. It is the material on which his labor is realized, in which it is active, from which and by means of which it produces.

But just as nature provides labor with the *means of life* in the sense that labor cannot *live* without objects on which to operate, on the other hand, it also provides the *means of life* in the more restricted sense, i.e., the means for the physical subsistence of the *worker* himself.

Thus the more the worker by his labor *appropriates* the external world, hence sensuous nature, the more he deprives himself of *means of life* in a double manner: first, in that the sensuous external world more and more ceases to be an object belonging to his labor—to be his labor's *means of life*; and secondly, in that it more and more ceases to be *means of life* in the immediate sense, means for the physical subsistence of the worker.

In both respects, therefore, the worker becomes a slave of his object, first, in that he receives an *object of labor*, i.e., in that he receives *work*; and secondly, in that he receives *means of subsistence*. Therefore, it enables him to exist, first, as a *worker*; and, second as a *physical subject*. The height of this bondage is that it is only as a *worker* that he continues to maintain himself as a *physical subject*, and that it is only as a *physical subject* that he is a *worker*. . . .

Political economy conceals the estrangement inherent in the nature of labor by not considering the direct relationship between the worker (labor) *and production.* It is true that labor produces for the rich wonderful things—but for the worker it produces privation. It produces palaces—but for the worker, hovels. It produces beauty—but for the worker, deformity. It replaces labor by machines, but it throws a section of the workers back to a barbarous type of labor, and it turns the other workers into machines. It produces intelligence—but for the worker stupidity, cretinism.

The direct relationship of labor to its products is the relationship of the worker to the objects of his production. The relationship of the man of means to the objects of production and to production itself is only a *consequence* of this first relationship—and confirms it. We shall consider this other aspect later.

When we ask, then, what is the essential relationship of labor we are asking about the relationship of the *worker* to production.

Till now we have been considering the estrangement, the alienation of the worker only in one of its aspects, i.e., the worker's *relationship to the products of his labor*. But the estrangement is manifested not only in the result but in the *act of production*, within the *producing activity*, itself. How could the worker come to face the product of his activity as a stranger, were it not that in the very act of production he was estranging himself from himself? The product is after all but the summary of the activity, of production. If then the product of labor is alienation, production itself must be active alienation, the alienation of activity, the activity of alienation. In the estrangement of the object

of labor is merely summarized the estrangement, the alienation, in the activity of labor itself.

What, then, constitutes the alienation of labor?

First, the fact that labor is *external* to the worker, i.e., it does not belong to his essential being; that in his work, therefore, he does not affirm himself but denies himself, does not feel content but unhappy, does not develop freely his physical and mental energy but mortifies his body and ruins his mind. The worker therefore only feels himself outside his work, and in his work feels outside himself. He is at home when he is not working, and when he is working he is not at home. His labor is therefore not voluntary, but coerced; it is *forced labor*. It is therefore not the satisfaction of a need; it is merely a *means* to satisfy needs external to it. Its alien character emerges clearly in the fact that as soon as no physical or other compulsion exists, labor is shunned like the plague. External labor, labor in which man alienates himself, is a labor of self-sacrifice, of mortification. Lastly, the external character of labor for the worker appears in the fact that it is not his own, but someone else's, that it does not belong to him, that in it he belongs, not to himself, but to another. . . .

As a result, therefore, man (the worker) only feels himself freely active in his animal functions—eating, drinking, procreating, or at most in his dwelling and in dressing-up, etc.; and in his human functions he no longer feels himself to be anything but an animal. What is animal becomes human and what is human becomes animal.

Certainly eating, drinking, procreating, etc., are also genuinely human functions. But abstractly taken, separated from the sphere of all other human activity and turned into sole and ultimate ends, they are animal functions.

We have considered the act of estranging practical human activity, labor, in two of its aspects. (1) The relation of the worker to the *product of labor* as an alien object exercising power over him. This relation is at the same time the relation to the sensuous external world, to the objects of nature, as an alien world inimically opposed to him. (2) The relation of labor to the *act of production* within the *labor* process. This relation is the relation of the worker to his own activity as an alien activity not belonging to him; it is activity as suffering, strength as weakness, begetting as emasculating, the worker's *own* physical and mental energy, his personal life indeed, what is life but activity?—as an activity which is turned against him, independent of him and not belonging to him. Here we have *self-estrangement*, as previously we had the estrangement of the *thing*. . . .

In estranging from man (1) nature, and (2) himself, his own active functions, his life activity, estranged labor estranges the *species* from man. It changes for him the *life of the species* into a means of individual life. . . .

In creating a *world of objects* by his practical activity, in *his work upon* inorganic nature, man proves himself a conscious species being, i.e., as a being that treats the species as its own essential being, or that treats itself as a species being. Admittedly animals also produce. They build themselves nests, dwellings, like the bees, beavers, ants, etc. But an animal only produces what it immediately needs for itself or its young. It produces one-sidedly, whilst man produces universally. It produces only under the dominion of immediate physical need, whilst man produces even when he is free from physical need and only truly produces in freedom therefrom. An animal produces only itself, whilst man reproduces the whole of nature. An animal's product belongs immediately to its physical body, whilst man freely confronts his product. An animal forms things in accordance with the standard and the need of the species to which it belongs, whilst man knows how to produce in accordance with the standard of every species, and knows how to apply everywhere the inherent standard to the object. Man therefore also forms things in accordance with the laws of beauty.

It is just in his work upon the objective world, therefore, that man first really proves himself to be a *species being*. This production is his active species life. Through and because of this production, nature appears as *his* work and his reality. The object of labor is, therefore, the *objectification of man's species life*: for he duplicates himself not only, as in consciousness, intellectually, but also actively, in reality, and therefore he contemplates himself in a world that he has created. In tearing away from man the object of his production, therefore, estranged labor tears from him his *species life*, his real objectivity as a member of the species and transforms his advantage over animals into the disadvantage that his inorganic body, nature, is taken away from him. . . .

If the product of labor is alien to me, if it confronts me as an alien power, to whom, then, does it belong?

If my own activity does not belong to me, if it is an alien, a coerced activity, to whom, then, does it belong?

To a being *other* than myself.

Who is this being?

The *gods*? To be sure, in the earliest times the principal production (for example, the building of temples, etc., in Egypt, India and Mexico) appears to be in the service of the gods, and the product belongs to the gods. However, the gods on their own were never the lords of labor. No more was *nature*. And what a contradiction it would be if, the more man subjugated nature by his labor and the more the miracles of the gods were rendered superfluous by the miracles of industry, the more man were to renounce the joy of production and the enjoyment of the product in favor of these powers.

The *alien* being, to whom labor and the product of labor belongs, in whose service labor is done and for whose benefit the product of labor is provided, can only be *man* himself.

If the product of labor does not belong to the worker, if it confronts him as an alien power, then this can only be because it belongs to some *other man than the worker*. If the worker's activity is a torment to him, to another it must be *delight* and his life's joy. Not the gods, not nature, but only man himself can be this alien power over man.

We must bear in mind the previous proposition that man's relation to himself only becomes for him *objective* and *actual*[8] through his relation to the other man. Thus, if the product of his labor, his labor *objectified*, is for him an *alien*, hostile, powerful object independent of him, then his position towards it is such that someone else is master of this object, someone who is alien, hostile, powerful, and independent of him. If his own activity is to him related as an unfree activity, then he is related to it as an activity performed in the service, under the dominion, the coercion, and the yoke of another man.

Every self-estrangement of man, from himself and from nature, appears in the relation in which he places himself and nature to men other than and differentiated from himself. . . . In the real practical world self-estrangement can only become manifest through the real practical relationship to other men. The medium through which estrangement takes place is itself *practical*. Thus through estranged labor man not only creates his relationship to the object and to the act of production as to men that are alien and hostile to him; he also creates the relationship in which other men stand to his production and to his product, and the relationship in which he stands to these other men. Just as he creates his own production as the loss of his reality, as his punishment; his own product as a loss, as a product not belonging to him; so he creates the domination of the person who does not produce over production and over the product. Just as he estranges his own activity from himself, so he confers to the stranger an activity which is not his own. . . .

Through *estranged, alienated labor*, then, the worker produces the relationship to this labor of a man alien to labor and standing outside it. The relationship of the worker to labor creates the relation to it of the capitalist (or whatever one chooses to call the master of labor). *Private property* is thus the product, the result, the necessary consequence, of *alienated labor*, of the external relation of the worker to nature and to himself.

Private property thus results by analysis from the concept of *alienated labor*, i.e., of *alienated man*, of estranged labor, of estranged life, of *estranged* man.

True, it is as a result of the *movement of private property* that we have obtained the concept of *alienated labor (of alienated life)* from political economy. But on analysis of this concept it becomes clear that though private property appears to be the source, the cause of alienated labor, it is rather its consequence. . . .

Only at the last culmination of the development of private property does this, its secret, appear again, namely, that on the one hand it is the *product* of alienated labor, and that on the other it is the *means* by which labor alienates itself, the *realization of this alienation*.

from *Capital*

Karl Marx

Like all its predecessors, the capitalist process of production proceeds under definite material conditions, which are, however, simultaneously the bearers of definite social relations entered into by individuals in the process of reproducing their life. Those conditions, like these relations, are on the one hand prerequisites, on the other hand results and creations of the capitalist process of production; they are produced and reproduced by it. We saw also that capital—and the capitalist is merely capital personified and functions in the process of production solely as the agent of capital—in its corresponding social process of production, pumps a definite quantity of surplus-labour out of the direct producers, or labourers; capital obtains this surplus-labour without an equivalent, and in essence it always remains forced labour—no matter how much it may seem to result from free contractual agreement. This surplus-labour appears as surplus-value, and this surplus-value exists as a surplus-product. Surplus-labour in general, as labour performed over and above the given requirements, must always remain. In the capitalist as well as in the slave system, etc., it merely assumes an antagonistic form and is supplemented by complete idleness of a stratum of society. A definite quantity of surplus-labour is required as insurance against accidents, and by the necessary and progressive expansion of the process of reproduction in keeping with the development of the needs and the growth of population, which is called accumulation from the viewpoint of the capitalist. It is one of the civilising aspects of capital that it enforces this surplus-labour in a manner and under conditions which are more advantageous to the development of the productive forces, social relations, and the creation of the elements for a new and higher form than under the preceding forms of slavery, serfdom, etc. Thus it gives rise to a stage, on the one hand, in which coercion and monopolisation of social development (including its material and intellectual advantages) by one portion of society at the expense of the other are eliminated; on the other hand, it creates the material means and embryonic conditions, making it possible in a higher form of society to combine this surplus-labour with a greater reduction of time devoted to material labour in general. For, depending on the development of labour productivity, sur-

plus-labour may be large in a small total working-day, and relatively small in a large total working-day. . . . The actual wealth of society, and the possibility of constantly expanding its reproduction process, therefore, do not depend upon the duration of surplus-labour, but upon its productivity and the more or less copious conditions of production under which it is performed. In fact, the realm of freedom actually begins only where labour which is determined by necessity and mundane considerations ceases; thus in the very nature of things it lies beyond the sphere of actual material production. Just as the savage must wrestle with Nature to satisfy his wants, to maintain and reproduce life, so must civilised man, and he must do so in all social formations and under all possible modes of production. With his development this realm of physical necessity expands as a result of his wants; but, at the same time, the forces of production which satisfy these wants also increase. Freedom in this field can only consist in socialised man, the associated producers, rationally regulating their interchange with Nature, bringing it under their common control, instead of being ruled by it as by the blind forces of Nature; and achieving this with the least expenditure of energy and under conditions most favourable to, and worthy of, their human nature. But it nonetheless still remains a realm of necessity. Beyond it begins that development of human energy which is an end in itself, the true realm of freedom, which, however, can blossom forth only with this realm of necessity as its basis. The shortening of the working-day is its basic prerequisite.

In a capitalist society, this surplus-value, or this surplus-product (leaving aside chance fluctuations in its distribution and considering only its regulating law, its standardising limits), is divided among capitalists as dividends proportionate to the share of the social capital each holds. In this form surplus-value appears as average profit which falls to the share of capital, an average profit which in turn divides into profit of enterprise and interest, and which under these two categories may fall into the laps of different kinds of capitalists. This appropriation and distribution of surplus-value, or surplus-product, on the part of capital, however, has its barrier in landed property. Just as the operating capitalist pumps surplus-labour, and thereby surplus-value and surplus-product in the form of profit, out of the labourer, so the landlord in turn pumps a portion of this surplus-value, or surplus-product, out of the capitalist in the form of rent in accordance with the laws already elaborated.

Hence, when speaking here of profit as that portion of surplus-value falling to the share of capital, we mean average profit (equal to profit of enterprise plus interest) which is already limited by the deduction of rent from the aggregate profit (identical in mass with aggregate surplus-value); the deduction of rent is assumed. Profit of capital (profit of enterprise plus interest) and ground-rent are thus no more than particular components of surplus-value, categories by which surplus-value is differentiated depending on whether it falls to the share of capital or landed property, headings which in no whit however alter its nature. Added together, these form the sum of social surplus-value. Capital pumps the surplus-labour, which is represented by surplus-value and surplus-product, directly out of the labourers. Thus, in this sense, it may be regarded as the producer of surplus-value. Landed property has nothing to do with the actual process of production. Its role is confined to transferring a portion of the produced surplus-value from the pockets of capital of its own. However, the landlord plays a role in the capitalist process of production not merely through the pressure he exerts upon capital, nor merely because large landed property is a prerequisite and condition of capitalist production since it is a prerequisite and condition of the expropriation of the labourer from the means of production, but particularly because he appears as the personification of one of the most essential conditions of production.

Finally, the labourer in the capacity of owner and seller of his individual labour-power receives a portion of the product under the label of wages, in which that portion of his labour appears which we call necessary labour, i.e., that required for the maintenance and reproduction of this labour-power, be the conditions of this maintenance and reproduction scanty or bountiful, favourable or unfavourable.

Whatever may be the disparity of these relations in other respects, they all have this in common: Capital yields a profit year after year to the capitalist, land a ground-rent to the land-lord, and labour-power, under normal conditions and so long as it remains useful labour-power, a wage to the labourer. These three portions of total value annually produced, and the corresponding portions of the annually created total product (leaving aside for the present any consideration of accumulation), may be annually consumed by their respective owners, without exhausting the source of their reproduction. They are like the annually consumable fruits of a perennial tree, or rather three trees; they form the annual incomes of three classes, capitalist, landowner and labourer, revenues distributed by the functioning capitalist in his capacity as direct extorter of surplus-labour and employer of labour in general. Thus, capital appears to the capitalist, land to the landlord, and labour-power, or rather labour itself, to the labourer (since he actually sells labour-power only as it is manifested, and since the price of labour-power, as previously shown, inevitably appears as the price of labour under the capitalist mode of production), as three different sources of their specific revenues, namely, profit, ground-rent and wages. They are really so in the sense that capital is a perennial pumping-machine of surplus-labour for the capitalist, land a perennial magnet for the landlord, attracting a portion of the surplus-value pumped out by capital, and finally, labour the constantly self-renewing condition and ever self-renewing means of acquiring under the title of wages a portion of the value created by the labourer and thus a part of the social product measured by this portion of value, i.e., the necessities of life. They are so, furthermore, in the sense that capital fixes a portion of the value and thereby of the product of the annual labour in the form of profit; landed property fixes another portion in the form of rent; and wage-labour fixes a third portion in the form of wages, and precisely by this transformation converts them into revenues of the capitalist, landowner, and labourer, without, however, creating the substance itself which is transformed into these various categories. The distribution rather presupposes the existence of this substance, namely, the total value of the annual product, which is nothing but materialised social labour. . . . Capital, landed property and labour appear to those agents of production as three different, independent sources, from which as such there arise three different components of the annually produced value—and thereby the product in which it exists; thus, from which there arise not merely the different forms of this value as revenues falling to the share of particular factors in the social process of production, but from which this value itself arises, and thereby the substance of these forms of revenue.

chapter twenty-four

Søren Kierkegaard

Søren Aabye Kierkegaard (1813–1855), Danish theologian and philosopher, is probably best remembered for his influence on existentialism. Writing in various personae, Kierkegaard produced a body of work intended to appeal to the reader as an individual, distinct from the public whole, and to lead this individual to Christian faith. In his writings, Kierkegaard was constantly aware of the reader and philosopher as existing human beings with natural limitations. Believing that the search for truth and faith must be a wholly subjective endeavor, Kierkegaard emulated Socrates' position of midwife to the truth.[1] Rather than attempting to communicate directly with his reader, Kierkegaard's goal was to induce and guide the reader's self-reflection so that it would lead to faith. In the end it was not Kierkegaard's religious aim but his existential approach that was his greatest contribution to philosophy; his emphasis on the subjectivity and developing state of existing beings influenced such twentieth-century philosophers as Heidegger, Sartre, and Beauvoir.

Kierkegaard was born in 1813 in Copenhagen, where he remained for the rest of his life, never venturing farther than Berlin. His childhood was dominated by the imposing figure of his strict, devout, and controlling father, a talented debater who awed his youngest son. Kierkegaard's journal preserves his youthful memories of conversations where he felt "as if his father were God and he God's favorite."[2] Kierkegaard watched his mother and five of his six siblings die before he entered the university. These sad losses experienced in his youth probably account for his renowned melancholy; in fact, fully expecting to follow his siblings to an early death, Kierkegaard believed his elderly father would outlive him. It is often speculated that Kierkegaard's odd, and at times estranged, relationship with this dominating patriarch influenced his religious ideas, especially his interpretation of Abraham's sacrifice of Isaac.

Although he never married, Kierkegaard's philosophy reflects a preoccupation with marriage. The happiest characters and personae Kierkegaard created were all married men, including his spiritual ideal, the knight of faith. Under the assumed identity of Judge William, he undertook a lengthy defense of marriage as a form of love superior to erotic emotion and as a resolution regarded "as the highest *telos* (goal) of individual life."[3] Kierkegaard spent much of his life regretting his own awkwardly broken engagement to Regine Olsen in 1841. He returned her ring almost a year after his proposal, believing such a melancholy man as he could never make a young woman happy. Years later Kierkegaard tried to renew communication with her and expressed his regret, describing his choice to leave Olsen as choosing death.[4] Upon his death he named her the sole beneficiary of his will.[5]

Kierkegaard was trained primarily as a theologian, but he also studied philosophy at the University of Copenhagen. Although he did not make an in depth study of any particular philosopher or system, Kierkegaard did take an interest, albeit an antagonistic one, in the popular Hegelian thinkers of the time. His tutor of German philosophy, Hans Lassen Martensen, became an adversary of sorts.[6] Kierkegaard's dissertation, *The Concept of Irony*, playfully manipulates Hegelian concepts and mocks the complicated language of serious Hegelians like Martensen. Despite this tongue-in-cheek treatment of the German philosopher's system, Kierkegaard was clearly influenced by Hegel's dialectics. In his pseudonymous works, Kierkegaard often set up arguments between various characters or narrators; *Either/Or*, for example, is presented as the published papers of two men, referred to as A and B. These characters represent two of the three stages or spheres of life that Kierkegaard identified, namely, the esthetic and ethical spheres. B's papers include his letters to A in which he points out the error of his correspondent's beliefs. Accordingly, in Kierkegaard's system the ethical stage involves a choice to reject the indifference of the esthetic stage, while the highest sphere, faith, embraces the absurdity recognized in the esthetic sphere but rejected in the ethical. Thus faith is something unique, but at the same time related to and developed out of the prior stages of life. These spheres of life represent a dialectical movement based on Hegel's philosophy, but for Kierkegaard dialectics are not just thought, but lived.

Kierkegaard believed that one's theory and way of life ought to be closely connected, and so there should be a coherent "life-view" behind an individual's body of writing. It is apparent that he held the belief in the necessity of a life-view even before he had worked out his own, for as early as 1838 Kierkegaard harshly criticized Hans Christian Andersen's work for lacking any such integrity. Developing a life-view involves more than accepting a philosophical system, "for a life view is more than a gathering-up of a sum of propositions, maintained in some sort of abstract neutrality, and it is more than mere experience, which as such is merely a collection of atoms. No, it is the very transubstantiation of experience, it is an unshakeable confidence in oneself which has been won in the teeth of the merely empirical."[7] Kierkegaard's philosophy draws from his life; his descriptions of the spheres of life are based on his own experiences, his melancholic and indifferent youth, the promise of marital bliss he passed up, and the despair he suffered through and the faith he regained. Having extrapolated a path to faith from his experiences and reflections, he writes as personae in every stage of life in order to coax his reader toward religion. In 1851 Kierkegaard published *On My Work as an Author* to clarify his own beliefs and goals in writing, so that after his death his indirect method of communication could not be misconstrued as a lack of adherence to a life-view.

As he believed that truth, which is identical to faith, can only be attained subjectively by the individual, Kierkegaard chose to publish pseudonymous memoirs, letters, and articles propounding views other than his own in order to prompt self-reflection in the individual reader. Because it was impossible for him to communicate truth directly to the reader, Kierkegaard sought "to *deceive into the truth*."[8] Deception was a necessary tool for Kierkegaard to achieve his goal, essentially to convert truly to Christian faith his readers who were under the illusion that they were already Christians. This illusion could only be dispelled through the deceit and gentle trickery of one pretending to share the reader's beliefs. Kierkegaard assumed a sympathetic persona to court the reader's interest, and then published subsequent articles under different, dissenting personae in order to counter the original argument, demonstrating the flaws in the beliefs shared by the first persona and his hapless reader. It was only his later, religious writings, including *Works of Love* (from which the following selection is taken), that he published under his own name, intending these works for the reader who had already been converted by his pseudonymous publications and was now prepared for religious inquiry. A criticism of the Danish state church lies implicit in Kierkegaard's missionary aims, and toward the end of his life, he went on to attack church officials directly as the usurpers of authority that belonged to God alone. On his deathbed Kierkegaard requested last rites from a layman and refused the sacrament completely rather than allow a clergyman to perform it.[9] Kierkegaard's theology, directed toward the individual who would experience a personal relationship with the divine, was inherently hostile to the organized church and its ministry of the public as a whole.

Kierkegaard noted in his journal that *Works of Love*, published in September 1847, was "written to 'arouse and vex', not to 'assuage and comfort.'"[10] He specifically identifies *Works of Love* as a deliberation to distinguish it clearly from the *Edifying Discourses* he published in March of that same year. "An edifying discourse on love presupposes that people really know what love is and then seeks to win them for it, to move them. But that, indeed, is not the case. So the 'deliberation' must first fetch them up the narrow cellar stairs, call on them and with truth's dialectic turn their convenient ways of thought upside down."[11] This reversal of convenient ways of thinking begins with the title itself, the conception of love as a work rather than as an emotion or inclination. *Works of Love*, like all of Kierkegaard's writings, was intended not merely as a mental exercise, or an exhortation to behave in certain manner, but to lead its readers through the subjective reflection necessary to lead a life of faith for themselves.

As a revolutionary thinker focused on the meaning of philosophy for a real, existing individual, Kierkegaard struggled to reconcile abstract thought with life. "Philosophy is perfectly right in saying that life must be understood backward. But then one forgets the other clause—that it must be lived forward."[12] It is for trying to unravel this paradox that Kierkegaard is remembered as the father of existentialism.

LM

QUESTIONS

1. What does Kierkegaard identify as the flaw of spontaneous love? How is it corrected?

2. According to Kierkegaard, under what circumstances is love free?

3. Explain the process by which "love is always reduplicated in itself." How does Kierkegaard relate this to forgiveness?

4. Why does the lover not discover any sins? How does Kierkegaard describe the nature of this lover?

5. Describe the two ways listed in which love can perform an even greater task than the concealment of sins.

ENDNOTES

1. Socrates believed that the search for truth is actually a process of recollection of the truth that lies forgotten within each individual's immortal soul. The teacher cannot give the truth directly to the student but only guide or stimulate her memory, aiding the birth of truth from and within her own soul. Kierkegaard also chose to adopt a *maieutic* role, but for a slightly different reason. While he did believe that the individual must subjectively seek truth for and within herself, he saw this search as a transformative religious awakening rather than as a process of recollection. Kierkegaard identified truth with faith, found in the subjective experience of the divine as the ground of one's being.

2. Kierkegaard, from Thompson, p. 31.

3. Kierkegaard, *Stages on Life's Way*, p. 101.

4. Thompson, p. 116.

5. Hannay, p. 419.

6. *Ibid.*, pp. 80–81.

7. Kierkegaard, from Poole, p. 29.

8. Kierkegaard, "On My Work as an Author," from *The Essential Kierkegaard*, p. 451.

9. Hannay, p. 416.

10. *Ibid.*, p. 358.

11. Kierkegaard, from Hannay, p. 358.

12. Kierkegaard, *Journals*, from *The Essential Kierkegaard*, p. 12.

SELECTED BIBLIOGRAPHY

Climacus, Johannes (pseud)/Søren Kierkegaard. *Philosophical Fragments or Fragments of Philosophy*, trans. Howard V. Hong. Princeton, N.J.: Princeton University Press, 1962.

Hannay, Alastair. *Kierkegaard, A Biography*. New York: Cambridge University Press, 2001.

Kierkegaard, Søren. *The Essential Kierkegaard*, ed. Howard V. Hong and Edna H. Hong. Princeton, N.J.: Princeton University Press, 1995.

Kierkegaard, Søren. *Stages on Life's Way*, trans. Howard V. Hong and Edna H. Hong. Princeton, N.J.: Princeton University Press, 1988.

Poole, Roger. *Kierkegaard, The Indirect Communication*. Charlottesville: University Press of Virginia, 1993.

Thompson, Josiah. *Kierkegaard*. New York: Alfred A. Knopf, 1973.

from *Works of Love*

Søren Kierkegaard

YOU SHALL LOVE

"You shall love." *Only when it is a duty to love, only then is love eternally secured against every change, eternally made free in blessed independence, eternally and happily secured against despair.*

However joyous, however happy, however indescribably confident instinctive and inclinational love, spontaneous love, can be in itself, it still feels precisely in its most beautiful moment the need to establish itself, if possible, more securely. Therefore the two pledge; they pledge fidelity or friendship to one another. And when we talk most solemnly we do not say of the two: "They love one another"; we say "They pledged fidelity" or "They pledged friendship to one another." By what, then, do they swear this love? We shall not confuse the issue and be distracted by calling to mind the great variety of invocations used by the poets, the spokesmen of this love—for in relation to erotic love it is the poet who makes the two promise, the poet who joins the two, the poet who prophesies an Eden for the two and lets them swear—in short, the poet is the priest. Does this love swear, then, by something which is higher than itself? No, this it does not do. Precisely this is the beautiful, touching, enigmatic, poetic misunderstanding—that the two do not themselves discover it, and for this very rea-

son the poet is their sole beloved confidant, because he does not discover it either. When erotic love swears fidelity, it really gives to itself the significance by which it swears; it is love itself which casts the lustre over that by which it swears. Therefore it not only does not swear by something higher but really swears by something which is less than itself. This love is indescribably rich in its own loving misunderstanding; just because it is itself an infinite richness, an unlimited certainty, when it wishes to swear it swears by something poor but does not itself realise this. The result is that this swearing, which should be and honestly thinks itself to be the highest seriousness, is nevertheless a most beguiling jest. And this mysterious friend, the poet, who as the closest-confidant has the best understanding of this love, does not understand it either. Yet it is easy to understand that if one is really to swear, he must swear by something higher; then God in heaven is the only one who is truly in a position to swear by himself. But the poet cannot understand this—that is, the individual who is a poet can well understand it, but insofar as he is a poet he cannot understand it, inasmuch as the *poet* cannot understand it; for the poet understands everything, in riddles, and marvellously explains everything, in riddles, but he cannot understand himself, or understand that he himself is a riddle. If he were compelled to understand this, he would, if he did not become indignant and embittered, sadly say: would that this understanding had not been forced on me—it disturbs what is most beautiful to me, it disturbs my life, and yet I can make no use of it. Thus far the poet is right in the matter, for true understanding means the decisive settlement of the life-problems of his existence. There are, then, two riddles: the first is the love of the two persons, and the second is the poet's explanation of it, or that the poet's explanation is also a riddle.

In such a way erotic love swears, and then the two add an Eden—they will love each other "for ever." If this is not added, the poet will not join the two; he turns away, indifferent, from such time-bound love, or mocking he turns against it, since he belongs eternally to this eternal love. There are, then, really two unions, first of the two who will love each other for ever, and then of the poet, who wants to belong to the two for ever. And the poet is right in this that when two persons will not love one another for ever, their love is not worth talking about, even less worthy of artistic celebration. But the poet does not detect the misunderstanding: that the two swear *by their love* to love each other for ever instead of swearing *by the eternal* their love to one another. The eternal is the higher. If one is to swear, then one must swear by the higher; but if one swears by the eternal, then one swears by duty—that "one *shall* love." Alas, but this favourite of the lovers, the poet, he who is even rarer than the real lovers whom his longing seeks, he who himself is love's marvel, he is also like the delicate child—he cannot endure this *shall* and as soon as it is mentioned he either becomes impatient or he begins to weep.

Therefore this spontaneous love has, according to the beautiful understanding of the imagination, the eternal in itself, but it is not consciously grounded upon the eternal and consequently can be *changed*. Even if it does not change, it still can be changed, for it is indeed happiness or good fortune, but what is true of fortune is true of happiness, which, if one thinks of the eternal, cannot be thought of without sadness, just as it is said with a shudder: "Happiness is when it has been." That is to say, as long as it lasted or was in existence change was possible; only after it is gone can one say that it lasted. "Count no man happy while he is living." As long as he is living his happiness can change; only when he is dead and happiness had not left him while he lived, only then is it certain that he was happy. That which merely exists, having undergone no change is continually confronted by the possibility of change; change may occur at any time; even in the last moment it can happen, and only when life has come to an end can one say: change did not take place—or perhaps it did. Whatever has undergone no change certainly has *continuance*, but it does not have *continuity*; insofar as it has continuance, it exists, but insofar as it has not won enduring continuity amid change, it cannot become contemporaneous with itself and is either happily unconscious of this misalignment or is disposed to sorrow. Only the eternal can be and become and remain contemporaneous with every age; temporality, on the other hand, divides within itself, and the present cannot become contemporary with the future, or the future with the past, or the past with the present. Of that which has won continuity in undergoing change, one can not only say when it has existed, "It existed," but one can say, "It had continuity throughout its existence." Just this is the safeguard, and the relationship is entirely different from that of happiness or good fortune. When love has undergone the transformation of the eternal by being made duty, it has won continuity, and then it follows of itself that it survives. It is not self-evident that what exists in this moment will exist in the next moment, but it is self-evident that the continuous survives. We say that something survives the test, and we praise it when it has survived the test; but this is said about the imperfect, for the survival of the continuous will not and cannot reveal itself by surviving a test—it is indeed the continuous—and only the transient can give itself the appearance of continuity by surviving a test. No one would think of saying that sterling silver [Prøve Sølv] must survive the test [Prøve] of time, for it is, after all, sterling silver. Thus it is also with regard to love. The love which simply exists, however fortunate, however blissful, however satisfying, however poetic it is, still must survive the test of the years. But the love which has undergone the transformation of the eternal by becoming duty has won continuity; it is sterling silver. Is such enduring love perhaps less useful, less applicable in life? Is, then, sterling silver less useful? Indeed not. Speech, involuntarily, and thought, consciously, honour sterling silver in a characteristic way merely by saying, "One uses it." There is no talk at all about testing; one does not insult it by wishing to test it; one knows in advance that sterling silver endures. Therefore when one uses a less reliable alloy, one is compelled to be more scrupulous and to speak less simply; one is compelled almost ambiguously to use double-talk and say, "One uses it, and while one uses it he also tests it," for it is always possible that it may undergo a change.

Consequently, *only when it is a duty to love, only then is love eternally secure.* This security of the eternal casts out all anxiety and makes the love perfect, perfectly secure. For in that love which has only existence, however confident it may be, there is still an anxiety, anxiety over the possibility of change. Such love does not itself understand any more than the poet that this is anxiety, for the anxiety is hidden; the only expression is a burning passion, whereby is merely hinted that anxiety is hidden at the bottom. Otherwise why is it that spontaneous love is so inclined to—yes, so in love with—making a test of the love? This is just because love has not, by becoming a duty, in the deepest sense undergone *the test*. From this comes what the poet would call sweet unrest, which more and more foolhardily wants to make the test. The lover wants to test the beloved. The friend wants to test the friend. Testing certainly has its basis in love, but this violently flaming desire to test and this hankering desire to be put to the test explain that the love itself is unconsciously uncertain. Here again is an enigmatic misunderstanding in this spontaneous love and in the poet's explanation. The lovers and the poet think that this urge to test love is precisely an expression of how certain it is. But is this really so? It is quite right that one does not care to test what is unimportant to him; but from this it certainly does not follow that wanting to test the beloved is an expression of certainty. The two love one another; they love one another for all eternity; they are so certain—that they put it to a test. Is this the highest certainty? Is not this relationship just like that of love's swearing and swearing again by what is lower than love? In this way the lovers' highest expression for the constancy of their love is an expression of its merely existing; and one tests that which merely has existence, one puts it to the test. But when it is a duty to love, neither is a test needed nor the insulting foolhardiness of wanting to test, because if love is higher than every test it has already more than passed the test in the same sense that faith "more than conquers." Testing is always related to possibility; there is always the possibility that what is being tested will not pass the test. Therefore if one would test whether he has faith or would try to get faith, it really means he will prevent himself from getting faith; he will bring himself into the unrest of covetousness where faith is never won, for "You *shall* believe." If a believer were to ask God to put his faith to a test, this would not be an expression of the believer's having faith in an extraordinarily high degree (to think this is a poetic misunderstanding, as it is also a misunderstanding to have faith in an *extraordinary* degree, since the ordinary degree is the highest), but it would be an expression of his having no faith at all, for "You *shall* believe." Never has any greater security been found and never shall the peace of the eternal be found in anything other than in this "You shall." The idea of testing, however congenial it may be, is an unquiet thought, and it is the disquietude which makes one fancy that this is a higher proof. For testing is in itself inventive and is not to be exhausted any more than human knowledge has ever been able to calculate all the contingencies; on the other hand, as the earnest one says so well, "Faith has encompassed all contingencies." When one *shall*, it is for ever decided; and when you will understand that you *shall* love, your love is for ever secure.

By this "You shall" love is also for ever secured *against every change.* For that love which has only existence can be changed; it can be changed *within itself*, and it can be changed *into something else.*

Spontaneous love can be changed within itself; it can be changed to its opposite, to *hate.* Hate is a love which has become its opposite, a ruined love. Deep down love is continually aflame, but it is the flame of hate. When love is first burned out, the flame of hate is also put out for the first time. Just as we say of the tongue, that "It is the same tongue with which we bless and curse," so may one also say that it is the same love which loves and hates. But just because it is the same love, just for that reason it is not in the eternal sense the true love which *unchanged remains the same*; rather, this spontaneous love is fundamentally *the same* even when *changed.* True love, which has undergone the transformation of the eternal by becoming duty, is never changed, it has integrity; it loves—and never hates; it never hates the beloved. It might seem as if this spontaneous love were the stronger because it can do both, because it can *both* love and hate; it might seem as if it had an entirely different power over its object when it says, "If you will not love

me, I will hate you"—but this is only an illusion. Even if changeableness is indeed a stronger power than unchangeableness, then who is stronger, he who says, "If you do not love me, I will hate you," or he who says, "If you hate me, I will still continue to love you?" Certainly it is terrifying and terrible when love is changed into hate, but for whom is it really terrible? I wonder if it is not most terrible for the one concerned, the one within whom love has turned to hate!

Spontaneous love can be changed within itself; by spontaneous combustion it can become *jealousy*; from the greatest happiness it can become the greatest torment. The heat of spontaneous love is so dangerous—no matter how great its passion is—so dangerous that this heat can easily become a fever. Spontaneity is, as it were, the fermenting element, so called because it has not yet undergone a change and therefore has not separated from itself the poison which engenders the heat in the fermenting element. If love kindles itself with this poison instead of expelling it, jealousy appears—alas, as the word itself [*Iversyge*] says, it is a zealousness for becoming sick, a sickness from zealousness. The jealous man does not hate the object of love, far from it; but he tortures himself with the flame of requited love which with purifying power should cleanse his love. The jealous man picks up—almost like a beggar—every beam of love in the beloved, but through the burning glass of jealousy he focuses all these beams of love upon his own love, and he is slowly consumed. On the other hand, the love which has undergone the change of the eternal by becoming duty does not know jealousy; it does not merely love as it is loved—but it loves. Jealousy loves as it is loved. Anxiously tortured by thoughts as to whether it is being loved, it is just as jealous about its own love, about the possibility of its being disproportionate in relation to the other's indifference, as it is jealous of the manifestation of the other's love. Anxiously tortured by preoccupation with itself, it dares neither absolutely trust the beloved nor wholeheartedly surrender itself, lest it give too much and thereby continually burn itself as one burns himself on that which is not burning—except in the contact of anxiety. Spontaneous combustion is comparable. It would seem as if spontaneous love were an entirely different kind of fire since it can become jealousy. Alas, but this fire is a dreadful thing. It would seem as if jealousy might hold its object far more securely since it watches with a hundred eyes, and simple love can have only one eye, as it were, for its love. But I wonder if multiplicity is stronger than unity. I wonder if a heart torn asunder is stronger than a whole, undivided heart. I wonder if a continually anxious grasp holds its object more securely than the unified power of simplicity? How, then, is this simple love secured against jealousy? I wonder if it is not by avoiding comparisons in loving? It does not begin by spontaneously loving according to preference—it just loves. Therefore it can never reach the point of morbidly loving in accordance with comparisons—it just loves.

Spontaneous love can be changed *into something else*. It can be changed through the years—something seen often enough. Thus love loses its ardour, its joy, its desire, its originative power, its living freshness. As the river which sprang out of rocks disperses farther down in the sluggishness of the dead-waters, so is love exhausted in the lukewarmness and indifference of habit. Alas, of all the enemies habit is perhaps the most cunning, and it is cunning enough never to let itself be seen, for he who sees the habit is saved from the habit. Habit is not like other enemies which one sees and against which one strives and defends himself. The struggle is really with oneself in order that one sees it. There is a preying creature, known for its cunning, which slyly falls upon the sleeping. While it sucks blood from the sleeping prey, it fans and cools him and makes his sleeping still more pleasant. Such is

habit—or it is even worse; for the vampire seeks its prey among the sleeping, but it has no means to lull to sleep those who are awake. Habit, however, can do this. It slinks, sleep-lulling, upon a man, and then drains the blood of the sleeper while it coolingly fans him and makes sleep still more pleasant to him.—In this way spontaneous love can be changed into something else and made unrecognisable—for love is still recognisable in hate and jealousy. Just as when a forgotten dream flashes by again, one himself becomes aware that habit has changed him; he wants to make up for it, but he does not know where he can go to buy new oil to rekindle his love. Then he becomes despondent, annoyed, weary of himself, weary of his love, weary of its being as paltry as it is, weary of not being able to get it transformed—alas, for he had not heeded the transformation of the eternal in time, and now he has lost the capacity to endure the cure. At times one sorrowfully sees a poverty-stricken man who had once lived prosperously, and still, how much more sorrowful than this is the change which one sees in a love changed almost to loathsomeness!—If, on the other hand, love undergoes the transformation of the eternal by becoming duty, it does not become characterised by habit; habit can never get power over it. To what is said of eternal life, that there is no sighing and no tears, one can add: there is no habit; certainly this is not saying anything less glorious. If you will save your soul or your love from habit's cunning—yes, men believe there are many ways of keeping oneself awake and secure, but there is really only one: the eternal's "You shall." Let the thunder of a hundred cannon remind you three times daily to resist the force of habit. Like that powerful Eastern emperor, keep a slave who reminds you daily—keep hundreds. Have a friend who reminds you every time he sees you. Have a wife who, in love, reminds you early and late—but be careful that all this also does not become a habit! For you can become accustomed to hearing the thunder of a hundred cannon so that you can sit at the table and hear the most trivial, insignificant things far more clearly than the thunder of the hundred cannon—which you have become accustomed to hearing. And you can become so accustomed to having a hundred slaves remind you every day that you no longer hear, because through habit you have acquired the ear which hears and still does not hear. No, only the eternal's "You shall" and the hearing ear which will hear this "shall" can save you from habit. Habit is the most miserable transformation, but on the other hand one can accustom himself to every change; only the eternal, and consequently that which has undergone the transformation of the eternal by becoming duty, is the unchangeable, but the unchangeable simply cannot become habit. However fast a habit fixes itself, it never becomes the unchangeable, even if the person becomes incorrigible. Habit is always that which *ought to be changed*; the unchangeable, on the contrary, is that which neither *can* nor *ought* to be changed! But the eternal never becomes old and never becomes habit.

Only when it is a duty to love, only then is love made eternally free in blessed independence. Is, then, spontaneous love not free? Has the lover no freedom at all in his love? But, on the other hand, should it be the purpose of the discourse to eulogise the miserable independence of self-love, which remains independent because it did not have the courage to bind itself and therefore remains independent through its cowardliness? Should it praise this miserable independence which swings suspended because it finds no foothold and is like him "who strolls here and there, an armed highwayman who turns in wherever twilight finds him?" Should it praise the miserable independence which independently submits to no bonds—at least not visibly? Far from it. On the contrary, in the foregoing portion we have pointed out that the

manifestation of the highest riches is to have a need; therefore to have a need in freedom is the true expression of freedom. He in whom love is a need certainly feels himself free in his love, and the very one who feels himself entirely dependent, so that he would lose everything by losing the beloved, that very one is independent. Yet there is one condition—that he does not confuse love with possession of the beloved. If one were to say, "Either love or die" and thereby signify that life without loving is not worth living, we should say he is absolutely right. But if he understood it to mean possession of the beloved and consequently to mean either to possess the beloved or die, either win this friend or die, then we must say that such a misconceived love is dependent. As soon as love, in its relation to its object, does not in that relationship relate just as much to itself, although it still is entirely dependent, then it is dependent in a false sense, then the law of its existence is outside itself, and therefore it is in a contemptible sense, in an earthly, in a temporal sense, dependent. But the love which has undergone the transformation of the eternal by becoming duty and which loves because it *shall* love—this love is independent; it has the law of its existence in the relationship of love itself to the eternal. This love can never become dependent in a false sense, for the only thing it is dependent upon is duty, and duty alone makes for genuine freedom. Spontaneous love makes a man free and in the next moment dependent. It is as with a man's existence. By coming into existence, by becoming a *self*, he becomes free, but in the next moment he is dependent on this self. Duty, however, makes a man dependent and at the same moment eternally independent. "Only law can give freedom." Alas, we often think that freedom exists and that it is law which binds freedom. Yet it is just the opposite; without law freedom does not exist at all, and it is law which gives freedom. We also think that it is law which makes distinctions, because where there is no law there is no distinction. Yet it is just the opposite—when it is law which makes distinctions, it is in fact the law which makes everyone equal before the law.

In this way the "You shall" makes love free in blessed independence; such a love stands and does not fall with variations in the object of love; it stands and falls with eternity's law, but therefore it never falls. Such a love is not dependent on this or on that. It is dependent on the one thing—that alone which makes for freedom—and therefore it is eternally independent. But nothing can be compared with this independence. Sometimes the world praises a proud independence which thinks it has no need of being loved, if at the same time it "needs other men—not in order to be loved by them, but in order to love them, in order nevertheless to have someone to love." How false is this independence! It feels no *need* of being loved, and yet *needs*, someone to love; consequently it stands in need of another person—in order to gratify its proud self-esteem. Is this not like the vanity which thinks it can dispense with the world and still needs the world, that is, needs the world to become conscious of the fact that vanity does not need the world! But the love which has undergone the transformation of the eternal by becoming duty feels unambiguously a need to be loved, and this need is therefore in eternally harmonising accord with the "You shall." But it can do without it if it *ought* to, while it still continues to love: is not this independence? This independence is dependent only on love itself through the *ought* of the eternal; it is not dependent on anything else, and therefore it is not dependent on the object of love as soon as it appears to be something else. Yet such a situation does not mean that this independent love has then ceased, has changed into proud self-approval—this is dependence. No, love abides; it is independent. Unchangeableness is true independence; every change—be it the swoon of weakness

or the strut of pride, be it sighing or self-satisfied—is dependence. If when another says, "I cannot love you any longer" one proudly answers, "Then I can also get along without loving you."—Is this independence? Alas, it is dependence, for whether he shall continue to love or not is dependent on whether the other will love. But he who answers, "Then I *will* still continue to love you nevertheless"—his love is made eternally free in blessed independence. He does not say it proudly—dependent on his pride—no, he says it humbly, humbling himself under the eternal's "You shall"; for that very reason he is independent.

Only when it is a duty to love, only then is love eternally and happily secured against despair. Spontaneous love can become unhappy, can reach the point of despair. Again this might seem to be an expression of the strength of this love, that it has the power of despair, but this is mere appearance. Despair's power, however highly it is regarded, is nevertheless impotence; its utmost is nothing more nor less than its defeat. Yet this—that spontaneous love can reach the point of despair—proves that it is in despair, that even when it is happy it loves with the power of despair—loves another person "more than himself, more than God." Of despair it must be said: only he can despair who is in despair. When spontaneous love despairs over misfortune, it only reveals that it was in despair, that in happiness it had also been in despair. The despair lies in relating oneself with infinite passion to a single individual, for with infinite passion one can relate oneself—if one is not in despair—only to the eternal. Spontaneous love is in despair in this way; but when it becomes happy, as it is called, its state of desperation is hidden; when it becomes unhappy it is revealed—that it was in despair. On the other hand, the love which has undergone the transformation of the eternal by becoming duty can never despair, simply because it *is* not in despair. Despair is not something which can happen to a man, an event such as fortune or misfortune. Despair is a disrelationship in one's inmost being; no fate or event can penetrate so far and so deep; events can only make manifest—that the disrelationship was there. For this reason there is only one assurance against despair: to undergo the transformation of the eternal through duty's "You shall"; everyone who has not undergone this transformation is in despair. Good fortune and prosperity can hide it; misfortune and difficulties, on the other hand, do not make him despair, as he thinks, but make manifest—that he was in despair. If one speaks otherwise, it is because one carelessly confuses the highest concepts. That which makes a man despair is not misfortune, but it is this: that he lacks the eternal. Despair is to lack the eternal; despair consists in not having undergone the transformation of the eternal through duty's "You shall." Despair is not, therefore, the loss of the beloved—that is misfortune, pain, and suffering; but despair is the lack of the eternal.

How, then, can this love which is commanded be secured against despair? Very simply—by the command—by this "You shall love." It consists first and foremost in this that you must not love in such a manner that the loss of the beloved would make manifest that you were in despair—that is, you absolutely must not love despairingly. Is loving thereby forbidden? By no means. It would be strange, indeed, if the command which says, "You shall love," were by its own order to forbid loving. Therefore the command only forbids loving in a manner which is not bidden. Essentially the command is not negative, but positive—it commands that you shall love. Therefore love's command does not secure itself against despair by means of feeble, lukewarm grounds of comfort; that one must not take things too seriously, *etc.* Indeed, is such wretched prudence which "has ceased to sorrow" any less despair than the lover's despair? Is it not rather a worse kind of despair! No, love's command forbids despair—by commanding one to love. Who would have this courage without the eternal; who is prepared to say this "You shall" without the eternal, which, in the very moment when love wants to despair over its unhappiness, commands one to love. Where can this command have its base except in the eternal? For when it is made impossible to possess the beloved in time, the eternal says, "You shall love"; that is, the eternal then rescues love precisely by making it eternal. Let it be death which separates the two—then when the bereaved one sinks in despair, what can be of help? Temporal help is a still more doleful kind of despair; then it is the eternal which helps. When it says "You shall love," it says, "Your love has an eternal worth." But it does not say this comfortingly, for that would not help; it says this commandingly, precisely because there is danger afoot. And when the eternal says, "You shall love," it becomes the eternal's responsibility to make sure that it can be done. What is all other consolation compared with that of the eternal! What is all other soul-care compared to that of the eternal! If it were to speak more mildly and say, "Console yourself," the sorrowing one would certainly have objections ready, but—yes, it is not because the eternal will proudly tolerate no objection—out of concern for the sorrowing one it commands, "You shall love." Marvellous words of comfort, marvellous compassion—because humanly speaking it is very odd, almost a mockery, to say to the despairing one that he *ought* to do that which is his only desire, but whose impossibility[32] brings him to despair. Is any other proof needed that the love-command is of divine origin? If you have tried it, or if you would try it, go to such a sorrowing person in the moment when the loss of the beloved is about to overpower him, and discover then what you can find to say. Confess that you want to bring consolation. The one thing you will not think of saying is, "You shall love." And on the other hand, see if it does not almost provoke the sorrowing one the very moment it is said, because it seems the most unsuitable thing to say on such an occasion. But you who have had this earnest experience, you who in the dark moment found emptiness and loathsomeness in the human grounds of consolation—but no consolation—you who discovered in a dreadful way that not even the exhortation of the eternal could keep you from sinking—you learned to love this "You shall" which saves from despair. What you perhaps often verified in lesser relationships, that true up-building consists in rigorous speaking, this you now learned in the deepest sense—that only the "You shall" eternally and happily rescues from despair. Eternally happy—yes, for only he is saved from despair who is eternally saved from despair. The love which has undergone the transformation of the eternal by becoming duty is not exempted from misfortune, but it is saved from despair, in fortune and misfortune equally saved from despair.

Behold, passion inflames, worldly sagacity cools, but neither this heat nor this cold nor the blending of this heat and this cold is the pure air of the eternal. There is something fiery in this heat and something sharp in this cold and in the blending something nondescript or an unconscious deceitfulness, as in the dangerous part of Spring. But this "You shall love" takes all the unsoundness away and preserves for eternity what is sound. So it is everywhere—this "You shall" of the eternal is the saving element, purifying, elevating. Sit with one who deeply mourns. There is relief for a moment if you have the ability to give to passion the expression of despair—something not even the mourner can do—but it is still false. It can be refreshingly tempting for a moment if at the same time you have the knowledge and experience to hold out a prospect where the mourner sees none—but it is still false. But this "You shall sorrow" is both true and beautiful. I do not have the right to harden

myself against the pains of life, for I *ought* to sorrow; but neither have I the right to despair, for I *ought* to sorrow; furthermore, neither do I have the right to stop sorrowing, for I *ought* to sorrow. So it is also with love. You have no right to harden yourself against this emotion, for you *ought* to love; but neither do you have the right to love despairingly, for you *ought* to love; just as little do you have the right to misuse this emotion in you, for you *ought* to love. You ought to preserve the love and you ought to preserve yourself and in and by preserving yourself to preserve the love. There where the merely human wants to storm forth, the command still holds; there where the merely human would lose courage, the command strengthens; there where the merely human would become tired and clever, the command flames up and gives wisdom. The command consumes and burns out what is unsound in your love, but through the command you shall be able to kindle it again when humanly considered it would cease. When you think you can easily give counsel, take the command as your counsel; but when you do not know how to counsel, the command shall prevail so that everything nevertheless comes out well.

LOVE HIDES THE MULTIPLICITY OF SINS

The temporal has three times and therefore essentially never *is* completely nor is completely in any one of the periods; the eternal *is*. A temporal object can have a multiplicity of varied characteristics; in a certain sense it can be said to have them simultaneously, insofar as in these definite characteristics it is that which it is. But reduplication in itself never has a temporal object; as the temporal disappears in time, so also it exists only in its characteristics. If, on the other hand, the eternal is in a man, the eternal reduplicates itself in him in such a way that every moment it is in him it is in him in a double mode: in an outward direction and in an inward direction back into itself, but in such a way that it is one and the same, for otherwise it is not reduplication. The eternal is not merely by virtue of its characteristics but in itself is in its characteristics; it does not merely have characteristics but exists in itself in having the characteristics.

So it is with love. What love does, it is; what it is, it does—at one and the same moment; simultaneously as it goes beyond itself (in an outward direction) it is in itself (in an inward direction), and simultaneously as it is in itself, it thereby goes beyond itself in such a way that this going beyond and this inward turning, this inward turning and this going beyond, are simultaneously one and the same.—When we say, "Love makes for confidence," we thereby say that the lover by his own makes others confident; wherever love is, confidence is propagated; people readily approach the lover, for he casts out fear. Whereas the mistrustful person scares everyone away; whereas the sly and cunning disseminate anxiety and painful unrest around them; whereas the presence of the domineering oppresses like the heavy pressure of sultry air—love makes for confidence. But when we say "Love makes for confidence," we also say something else: that the lover has confidence, as in "Love gives confidence on the day of judgment." That is, it makes the lover confident under judgment.—When we say, "Love saves from death," there is straightway a reduplication in thought: the lover saves another human being from death, and in entirely the same or yet in a different sense he saves himself from death. This he does at the same time; it is one and the same; he does not save the other at one moment and at another save himself, but in the moment he saves the other he saves himself from death. Only love never thinks about the latter, about saving oneself, about acquiring confidence itself; the lover in love thinks only about giving confidence and saving another from

death. But the lover is not thereby forgotten. No, he who in love forgets himself, forgets his sufferings in order to think of another's, forgets all his wretchedness in order to think of another's, forgets what he himself loses in order lovingly to consider another's loss, forgets his advantage in order lovingly to look after another's advantage: truly, such a person is not forgotten. There is one who thinks of him, God in heaven; or love thinks of him. God is love, and when a human being because of love forgets himself, how then should God forget him! No, while the lover forgets himself and thinks of the other person, God thinks of the lover. The self-lover is busy; he shouts and complains and insists on his rights in order to make sure he is not forgotten—and yet he is forgotten. But the lover, who forgets himself, is remembered by love. There is One who thinks of him, and in this way it comes about that the lover gets what he gives.

Note the reduplication here: what the lover does, he is or he becomes; what he gives, he is or, more accurately, this he acquires—which is as remarkable as "Out of the eater came forth meat." Yet someone may say, "It is not so remarkable that the lover has what he gives; it is always the case that what one does not have he certainly cannot give." Well, yes, but is it always the case that one retains what he gives or that one himself acquires what he gives to another, that one acquires precisely by giving and acquires the very same which he gives, so that the given and the received are one and the same? Ordinarily this is not the case at all, but, contrariwise, what I give, another receives, and I myself do not acquire what I give to another.

In this way love is always reduplicated in itself. This also holds when it is stated that love hides the multiplicity of sins.

In Scriptures we read, and these are *love's* own words, that many sins are forgiven one who loved much—because his love hides the multiplicity of sins. Yet of this we shall not speak at this time. In this little book we are continually concerned with the works of love; therefore we consider love in its outgoing movement. In this sense we shall now consider

That Love Hides the Multiplicity of Sins

Love hides the multiplicity of sins. For it does not discover the sins; but not to discover what nevertheless must be there, insofar as it can be discovered, means to hide.

The concept *multiplicity* is in itself ambiguous. Thus we speak of the multiplicity of creation; yet the same expression has considerably different meanings, depending on who uses it. A man who has lived out his whole life in a remote place and, in addition, has little taste for studying nature—how little he knows, even though he speaks of the multiplicity of creation! A natural scientist, on the other hand, who has travelled around the world, who has been all over, both over and under the surface of the earth, sees the abundance of what he has seen and, in addition, with instruments discovers at a distance otherwise invisible stars or discovers at very close range otherwise invisible living things—how astonishingly much he knows—and he, too, uses the phrase, "the multiplicity of creation." And further, although the natural scientist rejoices over what he has succeeded in observing, he readily admits that there is no limit to discovery, since there is indeed no limit to discovery with respect to the instruments used for discovery; consequently the multiplicity becomes greater according to the discoveries or according to the discovery of new instruments of discovery and therefore can become even greater, that is, its even greater multiplicity becomes apparent—and yet, everything considered, it is all comprehended in the phrase "the multiplicity of creation." The same holds true of the multiplicity of sins. The phrase has quite different meanings, depending on who is speaking.

Therefore one *discovers* the multiplicity of sins to be continually greater and greater; that is, through discovery it continually reveals itself to be greater and greater, and also by means of one's appropriate discoveries it quite naturally becomes apparent how cunningly and sceptically one must conduct himself in order to make the discoveries. Consequently he who *does not discover* the multiplicity hides it, because for him the multiplicity is less.

But to discover is something praiseworthy, something admirable, even though this admiration is at times constrained in a strange way to bring heterogeneity together. One admires the natural scientist who discovers a bird, and one also admires the dog that discovered purple. But we shall let this stand for what it is worth; nevertheless it is certain that discovery is praised and admired in the world. And on the other hand, he who does not discover something or who discovers nothing is rated rather low. In order to identify someone as eccentric, one who is preoccupied by his own thoughts, one readily says of him, "He doesn't really discover anything." And if one wishes to point out someone especially limited and stupid, he says, "He certainly didn't invent gunpowder"—which hardly needs doing in our time since it already has been invented; therefore it would be even more questionable if someone in our time were to think that he was the one who had invented gunpowder. But to discover something is so admired in the world that we cannot forget this enviable good fortune: to have invented gunpowder!

Thus far it is easy to see that the lover, who discovers nothing, makes a very poor showing in the eyes of the world. For to make discoveries even in the realms of evil, sin, and the multiplicity of sin, and to be a shrewd, cunning, penetrating, and perhaps half-corrupt observer who makes accurate discoveries—this is highly regarded in the world. Even the youth, in that first moment when he ventures out into life, will readily divulge that he knows and how he has discovered evil (for he does not like the world to call him a simpleton). Even a woman in her earliest youth will betray her vain desire to be a connoisseur of mankind, naturally in the direction of evil (for she does not like the world to call her a silly goose or a small-town beauty). Yes, it is incredible how the world has changed compared with ancient times—then there were but a few who knew themselves and now everybody is a connoisseur of mankind. And this is the remarkable thing—if one has discovered how basically good-natured almost everyone is, he nevertheless hardly dares make this discovery known; he fears to be laughed at, perhaps even fears that humanity might be offended thereby. However, when one discloses that he has discovered how basically shabby every human being is, how envious, how selfish, how unreliable, and what abominations can reside hidden in the purest people, that is, those regarded as the purest by simpletons, silly geese, and small-town beauties, then he conceitedly knows that he is welcome, that a premium is placed on his observation, his knowledge, and his discourse, which the world longs to hear. In this way sin and evil have greater power over men than one generally thinks: it is so silly to be good, so narrow-minded to believe in the good, so small-townish to betray ignorance or that one is uninitiated—uninitiated into the inmost secrets of sin. Here one sees quite clearly how evil and sin lie mainly on a conceited comparison-relationship to the world and to other men. For one can be quite sure that the same people who out of conceited fear of the world's judgment seek to be well-liked and entertaining in a crowd by revealing special acquaintance with evil, one can be quite sure that these same people, when they are alone in their heart of hearts where they do not need to be ashamed of the good, have an entirely different view. But in society, in daily associations, when

many or even more are together, and consequently comparison, the comparison-relationship, is along in the company, something which vanity cannot possibly remain ignorant of—each one tempts the other to reveal what he has discovered.

Nevertheless, even a completely worldly-minded person at times makes an exception and passes a little milder judgment on not discovering anything. Suppose two sly fellows had something to decide together and for which they wanted no witnesses, and yet they were in such a position that they had to make their decision in a room with a third person present—and this third person was, as they knew, very much in love, head-over-heels in the first throes of falling in love—is it not true that one sly fellow would say to the other: "He can just as well stay; he will discover nothing"? They will say it with a smile and with this smile honour their own cleverness; and yet they would have a certain respect for the one in love who discovers nothing.—And now the lover! If one laughs at him, if one ridicules him, if one pities him, and whatever the world says of him, it is certain that with respect to the multiplicity of sins he *discovers* nothing, not even this laughter, this ridicule, this pity—he *discovers* nothing—and he sees only very little. He discovers nothing; of course we make a distinction between the discovering which is conscious, the planned attempt to find out, and the seeing and hearing which can happen involuntarily. He discovers nothing. And yet, whether one laughs at him or does not laugh at him, whether one ridicules him or does not ridicule him, deep down inside one has a respect for him because, resting and deepened in his love, he discovers nothing.

The lover discovers nothing; consequently he hides the multiplicity of sins which could have been found by discovery. The life of the lover expresses the apostolic injunction to be a babe in evil. What the world admires as shrewdness is really an understanding of evil—wisdom is an

understanding of the good. The lover has no understanding of evil and does not wish it; he is and
he remains, he wishes to be and wishes to remain a
child in this respect. Put a child in a den of thieves
(but the child must not remain so long that he is
corrupted; therefore let it be only for a short time);
then let it come home and tell everything it has experienced: you will note that the child, who (like
every child) nevertheless is a good observer and has
excellent memory, will tell everything in the most
circumstantial way, yet in such a fashion that in a
certain sense the most important is left out, so that
on the strength of the child's narrative anyone not
previously informed will most likely not know that
the child had been among thieves. What has the
child left out; what has the child not discovered? It
is the evil. Yet the child's narrative of what he has
seen and heard is entirely factual. What, then, does
the child lack? What is it which very often makes a
child's narrative the most profound mockery of his
elders? It is an understanding of evil and that the
child lacks an understanding of evil, that the child
does not even desire to understand evil. In this the
lover is like the child. But at the basis of all *understanding* lies first of all an *understanding* between
him who is to understand and that which is to be
understood. Therefore an understanding of evil
(however much one tries to make himself and
others think that one can keep himself entirely
pure, that there is a pure understanding of evil)
nevertheless *involves* an *understanding with* evil. If
there were no such understanding, the under-
stander would not desire to understand it; he
would flee from understanding it and would rather
not understand it. If this understanding signifies
nothing else, it is still a dangerous curiosity about
evil, or it is cunning's way of spying out excuses for
its own flaws by means of knowledge of the prevalence of evil, or it is falsity's scheme to peg up its
own value by means of knowledge of others' corruption. But let one guard himself, for if out of cu-

riosity one gives evil a finger, it will soon take the
whole hand, and excuses are the most dangerous of
all to have in stock; to become better or seem to be
better by the help of comparisons with the badness
of others is indeed a bad way of becoming better.
Yet if this understanding has already discovered the
multiplicity of sins, what discoveries could not be
made by an even more intimate understanding
which is really in league with evil! As the miser sees
everything in terms of gold, likewise such a man,
after he sinks himself deeper and deeper, discovers
the multiplicity of sins to be greater and greater
round about him His eyes are sharpened and
equipped, alas, not in the understanding of truth,
rather of untruth, consequently his vision is nar-
rowed more and more so that infected he sees evil
in everything, in the impure and even in the
purest—and this sight (terrible thought!) is nevertheless to him a kind of consolation, for to him it
is important to discover as limitless a multiplicity
as possible. Finally, there is no limit for his discovery, for now he discovers sin even where he himself
knows it does not exist; he discovers it with the
help of slander, backbiting, and the manufacture
of lies, in which he has such long practice that finally he believes them himself. Such a one has discovered the multiplicity of sins!

But the lover discovers nothing. There is something so infinitely solemn and yet also so child-
like, something reminiscent of a child's game,
when the lover in this way, by discovering nothing,
hides the multiplicity of sins—something reminiscent of a child's game, for this is the way we play
with children; we play that we cannot see the child
or the child plays that it cannot see us, and this is
indescribably amusing to the child. The child-
likeness, then, is that the lover, as in a game, cannot see with open eyes what takes place right in
front of him; the solemnity consists in its being
evil which he cannot see. It is well known that the
orientals honour a deranged person; but this lover,

who is worthy of honour, is, as it were, deranged. It is well known that in ancient times, for good reason, a significant distinction was made between two kinds of madness; the one was a tragic sickness and men lamented such a misfortune, and the other was called divine madness. If for the moment one were to employ the pagan word *divine*, it is a divine kind of madness lovingly not to see the evil which takes place right in front of one. In truth, in these clever times which have so great a knowledge of evil, there is great need to do something to teach the honouring of this madness, because, I regret, in these times enough is done so that the love which has great understanding of the good and wants to have none of evil is taken to be a kind of derangement.

To use the highest example, consider Christ in that moment when he was brought before the San-hedrin; consider the raging mob; consider the circle of important people—and consider then, how many a glance was directed towards him, aimed at him, only with the expectation of catching his eye so that the glance might convey its ridicule, its contempt, its pity, its scorn to the accused! But he discovered nothing; out of love he hid the multiplicity of sins. Consider, how much abuse, how much contempt, how much taunting mockery had been shouted—and to the shouter it was a matter of great importance that his voice should be heard, in order that above all it should not seem as if he had missed the opportunity, which would be inde-scribably stupid, as if he had not been actively par-ticipating here where the main thing was to be united all together, and thereby as an instrument of the public and consequently of the true mind, as if he had missed the opportunity of scorning, mortifying, and misusing an innocent man! But he understood nothing; out of love he hid the multi-plicity of sins—by discovering nothing.

And he is the pattern. Of him the lover learns when he discovers nothing and thereby hides the multiplicity of sins, when as a worthy disciple, "de-spised, rejected, and carrying his cross," he walks between ridicule and pity, between scorn and lamentation, and yet out of love discovers noth-ing—truly something more marvellous than the episode of the three men walking unscathed in the fiery furnace. Yet ridicule and contempt really do no harm when the one scorned is not injured by *discovering*, that is, by becoming embittered; for if he becomes embittered, he discovers the multiplic-ity of sins. If you want to illustrate clearly how the lover hides the multiplicity of sins by discovering nothing, consider love again. Suppose that this lover had a wife who loved him. See, just because she loved him she would discover the multiplicity of sins against him; offended, with bitterness in her soul she would discover every mocking glance; with knotted heart she would hear the contempt—while he, the lover, discovered nothing. And when the lover, insofar as he could not escape seeing or hearing something, nevertheless had excuse in readiness for the attackers, that he himself was at fault—then the wife would be able to discover no wrong in him, but only all the more the multiplic-ity of sins against him. As you consider this, do you now see what the wife, and certainly with truth, discovered? Do you see how true it is that the lover, who discovers nothing, hides the multi-plicity of sins? Think of this in connection with all of life's relationships, and you will admit that the lover really hides the multiplicity!

Love hides the multiplicity of sins, for what it can-not avoid seeing or hearing, it hides in silence, in a mitigating explanation, in forgiveness.

It hides the multiplicity *in silence*.

It is sometimes the case that two lovers wish to keep their relationship secret. Suppose that in the moment they confessed their love to each other and promised each other silence a third person was quite accidentally present, but this uninvolved third was an upright and loving person to be depended upon, and he promised them to be silent: would not the love of the two nevertheless be and remain hidden? In the same way the lover conducts himself when unawares, quite accidentally, never because he has sought for it, he comes to know of a man's sin, of his fault, of some criminal act, or of how he was overcome by a weakness: the lover keeps this in silence and hides the multiplicity of sins.

Do not say "The multiplicity of sins remains just as great whether they are told or kept in silence, since silence simply cannot diminish anything and because one can be silent only about what actually is." Rather answer the question: does not the one who tells about his neighbour's sins and faults increase the multiplicity of sins? Even though the multiplicity remains just as great, whether I am silent about it or not, when I am silent about it, I nevertheless do my part by concealing. And further, do we not say that rumour tends to grow? We mean thereby that rumour tends to make the blame greater than it really is. But this is not our concern here. It is in quite another sense that one may say that rumour which reports the neighbour's faults increases the multiplicity of sins. One does not judge lightly of this witnessing to one's neighbour's faults, as if everything were all right if only the factuality of what was told had been determined. Truly, not every witness to what is true concerning his neighbour's faults is thereby innocent, and simply by becoming a witness one can himself easily become guilty. In this way rumour or one who reports his neighbour's faults augments the multiplicity of sins. That men through rumour and gossip inquisitively, frivolously, enviously, perhaps maliciously get into the habit of knowing about their neighbour's faults—this corrupts men. Certainly it is desirable that men should again learn to be silent. But if there must be gossip and consequently inquisitive and frivolous gossip, then let it be about

nonsense and trides—one's neighbour's faults are and ought to be too serious a matter; to talk about them inquisitively, frivolously, enviously is therefore a sign of corruption. But he who by reporting his neighbour's faults helps to corrupt men certainly increases the multiplicity of sins.

It is only too clear that every man, unfortunately, has a great inclination to see his neighbour's faults and perhaps an even greater inclination to want to tell about them. If it is nothing else, it is, alas, to use the mildest expression, a kind of nervousness which makes men so weak in this temptation, in this dizziness of being able to tell something evil about their neighbours, of being able for a moment to create for themselves an attentive audience with the aid of such entertaining reports. But what is already corrupting enough as a nervous urge which cannot keep quiet is sometimes a raging, demonic passion in a man, developed on the most terrifying scale. I wonder whether any robber, any thief, any man of violence, in short, any criminal is in the deepest sense as depraved as such a man who has taken upon himself as his contemptible means of livelihood the task of proclaiming on the greatest possible scale, loudly as no word of truth is heard, widely over the whole land in a way seldom achieved by something worthy, penetrating into every nook where God's word hardly penetrates, his neighbour's faults, his neighbour's weaknesses, his neighbour's sins and to press upon everyone, even upon unformed youth, this polluting knowledge—I really wonder whether any criminal is in the deepest sense so depraved as such a man, even if the evil he told were factual! Even if it were factual—but it is inconceivable that one with the earnestness of the eternal could be rigorous in taking care that the evil he told was unconditionally factual and then be able to use his life in this nauseous service of factuality: the reporting of evil. We pray in the Lord's Prayer that God will not lead into temptation. But if this should happen, if it should happen that I fell into temptation—may it please merciful God that my sin and my guilt nevertheless be such that the world regards it as detestable and revolting! But the most terrible of all must be to have guilt, heinous guilt, and to add guilt and more guilt and new guilt day in and day out—and not to become conscious of it, because one's whole environment, because existence itself had become transformed into an illusion which strengthened one in his view that it was nothing, not only that there was no guilt but that it was something almost meritorious. O, there are criminals whom the world does not call criminals, whom it rewards and almost honours—and yet, yet I would rather, God forbid, but I nevertheless would rather enter eternity with three repented murders on my conscience than as a retired scandalmonger with this horrible, incalculable load of criminality which was heaped up year after year, which was able to spread on an almost inconceivable scale, to put men in their graves, embitter the most intimate relationships, injure the most innocent sympathisers, besmirch the young, mislead and corrupt both young and old, in short, to spread itself on a scale which even the most vivid power of phantasy cannot imagine—this horrible load of criminality which I nevertheless never got time to begin repenting of, because the time had to be used for new offences, and because these innumerable offences had secured money for me, influence, prestige almost, and above all a pleasurable life! In connection with arson a distinction is made between setting fire to a house in the full knowledge of its being inhabited by many or being uninhabited. But scandalmongering is like setting fire to a whole community and it is not even regarded as a crime! We quarantine for diseases—but this disease which is worse than the bubonic plague, scandalmongering, which corrupts the mind and soul, we invite into all the houses; we pay money to become infected; we greet as a welcome guest one who brings the infection!

Now, then, is it not true that the lover hides the multiplicity of sins by keeping silent about his neighbour's faults, when you consider how one increases them in the telling.

The lover hides the multiplicity of sins *in a mitigating explanation.*

It is always the explanation which defines something that is. The fact or the facts are basic, but the explanation is decisive. Every event, every word, every act, in short, everything, can be explained in numerous ways. As we say, clothes make the man. Likewise one can truly say that the explanation makes the object of explanation what it is. With regard to another man's words, acts, and ways of thought there is no certainty, and to suppose it means to choose. Conceptions and explanations therefore exist, simply because a variation in explanation is possible—a choice. But if it is a choice, it is continually in my power, if I am a lover, to choose the most mitigating explanation. When, therefore, this milder or mitigating explanation explains what others frivolously, hastily, rigorously, hard-heartedly, enviously, maliciously, in short, unlovingly, declare straightway to be guilt, when the mitigating explanation explains this in another way, it takes now one and then another guilt away and thereby makes the multiplicity of sins less or hides it. O, if men would rightly understand what splendid use they could make of their imaginative powers, their acuteness, their inventiveness, and their ability to relate by using them to find if possible a mitigating explanation—then they would gain more and more a taste for one of the most beautiful joys of life; it would become for them a passionate desire and need which could lead them to forget everything else. Do we not observe this in other ways, how, for example, the hunter year by year becomes more and more passionately given to hunting? We do not admire his choice, but shall say nothing about this; we speak only of how year by year he devotes himself more and more passionately to this activity. And why does he do this? Because with each year he acquires experience, becomes more and more inventive, overcomes more and more difficulties, so that he, the old experienced hunter, now knows alternatives when others know none, knows how to track game where others do not, discerns signs which no one else understands, and has discovered a better way of setting traps, so that he is always rather sure of always having good hunting even when all others fail. We regard it as a burdensome task, yet in another respect satisfying and engaging, to be a detective, one who discovers guilt and crime. We are amazed at such a person's knowledge of the human heart, of all its evasions and devices, even the most subtle, how he can remember from year to year the most insignificant things just to establish, if possible, a clue, how by merely glancing at the circumstances he can, as it were, exorcise out of them an explanation detrimental to the guilty one, how nothing is too trivial for his attention insofar as it could contribute to illuminate his grasp of the crime. We admire such an official servant when by keeping after what he calls a thoroughly hardened hypocrite he succeeds in tearing the cloak away from him and making the guilt apparent. Should it not be just as satisfying and just as engaging, through perseverance with what would be called exceptionally base conduct, to discover that it was something quite different, something well-intentioned! Let the judges appointed by the state, let the detectives labour to discover guilt and crime; the rest of us are enjoined to be neither judges nor detectives—God has rather called us to love, consequently, to the hiding of the multiplicity of sins with the help of a mitigating explanation. Imagine this kind of lover, endowed by nature with such magnificent capacities that every judge must envy him, but all these capacities are employed with a zeal and rigour such as a judge would have to admire in the service of love, for the purpose of getting practice in the art and practising the art, the art of interpretation, which, with the help of mitigating explanation, hides the multiplicity of sins! Imagine his rich experience, blessed in the noblest sense: what knowledge he possesses of the human heart, how many remarkable and moving instances he knows about, in which he nevertheless succeeded, however complicated the matter may have seemed, in discovering the good or even the better, because for a long, long time he had kept his judgment suspended, until at just the right time a little circumstance came to light which helped him on the track, and then by quickly and boldly concentrating all his attention upon a completely different conception of the matter he had the fortune of discovering what he sought, by losing himself in a man's life-relationships, and by securing the most accurate information about his circumstances he was finally victorious in his explanation! Consequently "He found the clue." He had the good fortune of finding what he sought." "He conquered with his explanation."—Alas, is it not strange that when these words are read out of context almost every man will involuntarily think they concern the discovery of a crime—most of us are far more inclined to think of discovering evil than of discovering the good. The state appoints judges and detectives to discover and punish evil. Moreover, men unite for obviously praise-worthy causes to alleviate poverty, to bring up orphan children, to rescue the fallen— but for this splendid venture, with the aid of a mitigating explanation to secure, were it ever so little, yet a little power over the multiplicity of sins—for this no association has yet been organised.

But we shall not develop further here how the lover hides the multiplicity of sins with a mitigating explanation, inasmuch as in two foregoing portions we have considered that love believes all things and love hopes all things. But to believe all things in love and in love to hope all things are the two chief means which love, this mild interpreter, uses for a mitigating explanation, which hides the multiplicity of sins.

Love hides the multiplicity of sins by *forgiveness*. Silence really takes nothing away from the known multiplicity of sins; the mitigating interpretation removes something from the multiplicity by showing that this or that was nevertheless not sin. Forgiveness takes away what nevertheless cannot be denied to be sin. Thus love strives in every way to hide the multiplicity of sins, but forgiveness is the most significant way.

We alluded earlier to the expression "the multiplicity of creation"; let us now use this illustration once again. We say that the researcher *discovers* multiplicity; whereas the untutored person, who, to be sure, also speaks of the multiplicity of creation, knows very little comparatively. Consequently the untutored person does not know that this or that exists, but nevertheless it does exist; it is not removed from nature by his ignorance; it simply does not exist for him in his ignorance. It is quite different in the relationship of forgiveness to the multitude of sins: forgiveness takes the forgiven sin away.

This is a remarkable thought, as it is the thought of faith; for faith always relates itself to what is not seen. I *believe* that the seen came into being on the basis of that which cannot be seen. I see the world, but the unseen I do not see—this I believe. Thus it is also with *forgiveness—and sin*, a relationship of faith, which, however, men are rarely aware of. What, then, is the unseen here? The unseen is in this that forgiveness takes away that which nevertheless is; the unseen is in this that what is seen nevertheless is not seen, for when it is seen, its not being seen is manifestly unseen. The lover sees the sin which he forgives, but he believes that forgiveness takes it away. This, of course, cannot be seen, although the sin can be seen; and on

the other hand, if the sin did not exist to be seen, neither could it be forgiven. Just as one by faith *believes the unseen* in the seen, so the lover by forgiveness *believes* the seen away. Both are faith. Blessed is the man of faith; he believes what he cannot see. Blessed is the lover; he believes away what he nevertheless can see!

Who can believe this? The lover can. But why, I wonder, is forgiveness so rare? Is it not, I wonder, because faith in the power of forgiveness is so small and so rare? Even the better person, who is not at all inclined to carry malice and rancour and is far from being irreconcilable, is not infrequently heard to say: "I should like to forgive him, but I don't see how it could be of help." Alas, it is not seen! Yet, if you yourself have ever needed forgiveness, then you know what forgiveness accomplishes—why then do you speak so naively and so unlovingly about forgiveness? For there is something essentially unloving in saying: I don't see what help my forgiveness can give him. We do not say this as if a person were to become self-important by having in his power the ability to forgive another person—far from it—this is also lack of love; in truth there is a mode of forgiving which discernibly and conspicuously augments the guilt rather than diminishes it. Only love is—yes, it seems playful, but let us put it this way—only love is handy enough to take the sin away by forgiving it. When I hang weights on forgiveness (that is, when I am laggard in forgiving or make myself important by being able to forgive), no miracle occurs. But when love forgives, the miracle of faith occurs (every miracle is a miracle of faith; what wonder, then, that along with faith the miracles also are abolished!): that which is seen nevertheless by being forgiven is not seen.

It is blotted out; it is forgiven and forgotten, or, as Scriptures say of what God forgives, it is hidden behind his back. But one is not unaware of that which is forgotten, for one is unaware of that which he does not know or never knew. What one has forgotten he has known. To forget in the highest sense is therefore the opposite—not of remembering but of hoping—because to hope means to give being by thinking and to forget is by thinking to take being away from that which nevertheless is, to blot it out. Scriptures teach that faith is related to the unseen, but it also says that faith is the substance of what is hoped for. This is how the object of hope, like the unseen, does not have existence but is nevertheless given existence by *hope* thinking. When God forgets sin, forgetting is the opposite of creating, for to create means to bring forth out of nothing and to forget is to return it into nothing. What is hidden from my eyes I have never seen, but what is hidden behind my back I have seen. And this is the very way in which the lover forgives: he forgives, he forgets, he blots out sin; in love he turns to the one he forgives, but when he turns toward him he simply cannot see what lies behind his back. That it is impossible to see what is behind one's back is easy to understand, also therefore that this expression is rightly the invention of love. But, on the other hand, it is perhaps very difficult to become the lover, who with the help of forgiveness puts another's guilt behind his back. Generally people find it easy, in the case of a murder, to place the guilt upon another person's conscience; but with the help of forgiveness to put his guilt behind one's back comes very hard. But not for the lover, for he hides the multiplicity of sins.

Do not say "The multiplicity of sins remains just as great whether they are forgiven or not, since forgiveness neither adds nor subtracts." Rather answer the question: does not one who unlovingly withholds forgiveness increase the multiplicity of sins—not only because his irreconcilability becomes one sin more, which is certainly the case, and to that extent ought to be brought into the

reckoning? Yet we shall not emphasise this now. But is there not a secret relationship between sin and forgiveness? When a sin is not forgiven, it requires punishment, it cries to God or men for punishment; but when a sin cries for punishment, it appears quite different, far greater than when this same sin is forgiven. Is it not an optical illusion? No, it is really so. To employ an imperfect figure, it is no optical illusion that the wound which looked so frightful appears far less frightful when the physician has washed and cared for it, even though it is still the same wound. Therefore what does he do who withholds forgiveness? He increases the sin; he acts so that it appears greater. And further, forgiveness takes vitality away from sin; but to withhold forgiveness nourishes sin. Therefore even though no new sin arose, and if the one and the same sin merely continued, a new sin really comes into being, for sin grows on sin; the continuation of a sin is a new sin. And you could have prevented this new sin by forgiving in love and taking the old sin away, as does the lover who hides the multiplicity of sins.

Love hides the multiplicity of sins; for love prevents sin from coming into being, smothers it at birth.

Even though with respect to some undertaking or other, a task one wants to complete, one has everything prepared: one thing must still be waited for, the occasion. So it is also with sin. When it is in a man, it still waits for an occasion.

Occasions can vary greatly. Scriptures say that sin finds an opportunity in the commandment or in the prohibition. The simple fact of something being commanded or forbidden becomes the occasion or opportunity. It is not as though the occasion caused sin, for an occasion never causes anything. The opportunity is like a middle-man, an intermediary, helpful only in making the exchange, merely expediting into existence that which in another sense already was, namely, as possibility. The commandment and the prohibition tempt simply because they seek to constrain evil, and now sin takes the opportunity, *takes* it, for the prohibition *is* the opportunity. Thus the opportunity is like a nothing, a fleeting nothing, which intervenes between the sin and the prohibition and in a certain sense belongs to both, although in another sense it is as if it did not exist, and yet again nothing which really has come into being has become without an occasion.

The commandment, the prohibition, is the occasion. In a sorrier sense sin in others is the occasion which evokes sin in those who come in touch with them. How often has a thoughtlessly, frivolously spoken word been enough to give occasion to sin! How often has a frivolous glance occasioned an increase in the multiplicity of sins! Just note how often one sees and hears sin and ungodliness in ordinary daily life: what rich opportunity for sin in him, what an easy shifting between giving the opportunity and taking the opportunity! When sin in a man is encompassed by sin, it is in its element. Nourished by the omnipresence of occasions it thrives and grows (if one can rightly speak of thriving in connection with evil): it becomes more and more ill-natured; it achieves more and more form (if in connection with evil one can speak of achieving form, since evil is lies and deception and thus without form); it establishes itself more and more, even though its life hovers over the abyss and therefore has no foothold.

Nevertheless, everything which is an occasion contributes insofar as the opportunity to sin is taken—to increase the multiplicity of sins.

But there is one condition which unconditionally does not give and is not an occasion for sin: that is love. When sin in a man is encompassed by love, it is then out of its element; it is like a besieged city with all communications cut off; it is like a man addicted to drink, wasting away on meagre fare and vainly awaiting the opportunity to be stimulated by intoxicants. Certainly it is possible for sin to use love as an occasion (for what cannot a corrupt man use for corruption!); it can become embittered about it, rage against it. Yet in the long run sin cannot hold out against love; usually only at the beginning is there such an advantage, just as when the drunkard in the first days, before the medical treatment has had sufficient time to take effect, has the strength of weakness to rage. And further, if there were such a man whom even love had to give up—no, love never does that—but who continually took love as an occasion to sin because he was an incorrigible, it still does not follow that there are not many who are healed. Therefore, it remains just as completely true that love hides the multiplicity of sins.

The authorities must often devise many shrewd ways to imprison a criminal and the physicians often employ great inventiveness in order to develop restraints to hold the insane: with respect to sin, however, there are no conditions so coercive, but there are also no constraining conditions so rehabilitating as love. How frequently anger, smouldering within, only waiting for an occasion, how frequently it has been smothered because love gave no occasion! How frequently evil desire, watching and waiting for an occasion in the sensual anxiety of curiosity, how often it has perished in birth because love gave no occasion at all and lovingly watched lest any occasion at all be given! How often resentment in the soul has been stilled, resentment which was so assured and so prepared, yes, so poised to find yet a new occasion to be wronged by the world, by men, by God, by everything, how often it has been stilled into a quieter mood because love gave no occasion to be wronged at all. How frequently this conceited and defiant attitude passed away, this attitude of one who considered himself misjudged and misunderstood and thereby took occasion to become even more conceited while merely cultivating new occasions to prove that it was right; how frequently it passed away because love, so alleviating, so mildly dispersive, gave no occasion at all to the sick imagination! How often what was contemplated receded into itself, that which sought only to find a justifying occasion; how often it receded because love gave no occasion at all to find excuse—for evil!

chapter twenty-five

Friedrich Nietzsche

Friedrich Wilhelm Nietzsche (1844–1900) is one of the most interesting and provocative figures in philosophy. Nietzsche breaks with almost every convention of philosophy and expresses his thoughts in a manner that is guaranteed to elicit a response. For example, as part of his critique of religious thinking, Nietzsche called himself the Anti-Christ, and his analysis of power was used—certainly against his own intentions—to reinforce the views of Nazism.

When Nietzsche was five his father died, leaving Nietzsche to be raised by his mother and his older sister. He began his university education as a theologian at the University of Bonn, but later transferred to Leipzig and switched to philology.[1] His work at Leipzig was impressive enough that the University of Basel, acting upon the recommendation of one of Nietzsche's professors, appointed him to a chair in classical philology at the age of twenty-four. After his appointment, Nietzsche received his doctorate from Leipzig without a dissertation. Other than a brief interruption to serve as a medical orderly during the Franco-Prussian War, Nietzsche taught at Basel from 1869 to 1879. During his years in Basel, he entered into and then broke off from a famous friendship with Richard Wagner, the composer of such operas as *Tristan, Parsifal,* and the *Ring* cycle.[2]

Nietzsche was widely criticized in the philological community when he published his first book in 1872, *The Birth of Tragedy or Hellenism and Pessimism.* An unproven, unknown professor, Nietzsche had published a radical reinterpretation of Greek culture utilizing no footnotes, no quotations, and no citations to classical works. During his years at Basel, he published four essays, now known collectively as *Thoughts Out of Season* or *Unfashionable Observations* (1873–1876), and the first volume of *Human, All too*

Human (1878). In 1879, weary from battling his colleagues for respect for his work and increasingly sick (most likely from an illness he contracted during the Franco-Prussian War), Nietzsche accepted a pension of two-thirds his normal salary from Basel and never taught again.

The next ten years of his life were his most productive. From 1879 to 1889, Nietzsche traveled throughout Italy and Switzerland, writing ten books before he collapsed in a street in Turin. When he awoke he was declared insane. He lived out the rest of his life in institutions and under the care of his mother and sister. Unfortunately, Nietzsche's work was not recognized or popular until after his collapse. He never knew the extent to which his ideas would have a profound impact on the way that intellectuals understand morality, religion, and history, as well as drama and music. Following his death, Nietzsche's sister, Elizabeth Förster-Nietzsche, edited Nietzsche's works (and published fragments from his notebooks). She made many changes to his work—among them, the removal of Nietzsche's criticism of anti-Semitism. Her editing recast Nietzsche's critique of religion as a condemnation of the Jews (rather than of all religious thinking). Förster-Nietzsche's dissemination of this edited work was so successful that Nazi Germany built a museum to honor Nietzsche's contributions to German society—this despite Nietzsche's own adamant denouncement of the beliefs that became the core elements of national socialism.[3]

Understanding Nietzsche can be difficult, since his mature writing style is not linear. While his early works are more or less direct in their approach, his later works mark a significant change in writing style. Rather than following traditional philosophical approaches, Nietzsche makes use of aphorisms—pithy claims or statements—in his later writings. Thus, as Walter Kaufmann notes, "In Nietzsche's books the individual sentences seem clear enough and it is the total design that puzzles us."[4] It is not enough to read his aphorisms; one has to study them in depth. He admits that this sort of ruminating on a text is not easy and indeed is "something for which one has almost to be a cow and in any case *not* a 'modern man.'"[5] Nietzsche's image of a cow chewing its cud can be helpful when one reads his works; the reader is challenged to read the text repeatedly, as surface reading often misses Nietzsche's ironic intent with any given aphorism. While it is possible to deal in depth with various threads of thought that run throughout his writing, individual statements or aphorisms often distract many people.

Nietzsche argues that moral systems may seen as noble ("masterful") or slavish. Noble morality may include the domination of the weak by the strong, but it is based, he says, in self-affirmation and the constant striving to overcome one's own limits; in other words, it is first a matter of self-mastery which may extend, sometimes heedlessly, to the mastery of others. Slave morality he sees as based in resentment and an identification of everything but itself as evil; this becomes a herdlike attempt to destroy everything that is too strong or too weak. Another way of seeing this distinction is to note that noble morality is based in self-love and slavish morality in hate for what is different.

Nietzsche saw what he called the "will to power"—the will to grow and overcome constantly—as fundamental to being truly alive. That is, to live is to push further, not simply to survive. The full embrace of this will might result in harm to others or even to oneself, but this harm is incidental to one's true acceptance of power in and over her own life.

What's more, Nietzsche did not believe that there was an end to this reevaluation; to think that we have attained perfection is to let ourselves be static, the very opposite of embracing the will to power. Nietzsche asks us to imagine an eternal return of exactly the same life, the possibility of living this life infinitely many times. He suggests that we live with such joy that we can say yes to this often-terrifying possibility.[6]

Many people have criticized Nietzsche's embrace of a concept that could result in harm to others; however, he also believed that not everyone could or should undertake this reevaluation. Only the *Übermenschen* (roughly translated as overpeople or super-people, though dominance or extraordinary strength are not implied by the term) are capable of leaping over the day-to-day life of humanity and creating something new and better. The will to overcome is not merely "individual"; in fact, if we must overcome ourselves, the very idea of a clearly defined self becomes problematic. This will extends to the species level as well; humanity must overcome itself, become something more and better; the best of us strive to the condition of "overpeople."

Each individual should attempt to break out of his or her own perspective and see how another perspective would perceive the same events. At the same time, we need to remember that every view is the result of a single perspective, and thus truth is more or less relative to that perspective.[7] This perspectivalism is less an endorsement of a relativistic understanding of truth where "anything goes" than it is a criticism of the nature of Truth itself. We cannot understand what Truth is since we react to the knowledge we have from our limited perspective;[8] indeed, Nietzsche argues that there are no facts, no capital-T Truth, only interpretations more or less carefully and intelligently conceived. Because Nietzsche emphasizes the value of attaining multiple perspectives, overcoming the limits of one's own current perception along with limits of other sorts, his cannot be seen as a self-centered philosophy; and the desire to see from other perspectives must act as a constraint on our willingness to do harm.

In the readings that follow, it is helpful to remember that Nietzsche believed that everything needs to be reevaluated—including how we understand and experience love. Thus, the readings from *The Gay Science* find Nietzsche examining how we speak of love, and attempting to perceive through an examination of types of love what we mean when we say that we love another. At first glance the selections from *Beyond Good and Evil* may appear to be entirely unrelated to those from *The Gay Science*. However, when one ruminates on the aphorisms and on the links Nietzsche draws between kinds of love and types of persons, the connections between love, desire, morality, and observation of society become clearer. If the goal of love is simply sex, then there is nothing dangerous in the emancipation of women. But, if we recall Nietzsche's contrast between love and friendship in *The Gay Science* § 14, it becomes clear that what many people desire out of a relationship is not love itself, but friendship and a "*shared* thirst for an ideal above them."[9] If we understand emancipation not as a desire for equality but for dominance, then the friendship that is truly desired by those who seek love is in danger because the "lovers" will not begin on equal footing. The love we understand as friendship thus differs dramatically from the possessiveness often found in "romantic" love. A key point to remember when reading Nietzsche is that he sought a reevaluation of values—including the values of love and friendship—and a consideration of multiple perspectives. While most philosophical texts are open to multiple interpretations, Nietzsche's writing is particularly, and often deliberately, so open. In the act of reading his work, you are engaging in just the reevaluation that he intended.

REK

QUESTIONS

1. When Nietzsche considers love in these aphorisms, he appears to understand love and desire in terms different from those of ordinary meanings. In what ways does his concept of love differ from the conventional understanding? What elements of this common conception remain? How does Nietzsche criticize this view while retaining elements of it?

2. How is love for another (or even oneself) different from the love that people express when they say that they love a particular piece of music? How is it the same? In what ways might the examination of "musical love" be helpful in understanding "romantic love"?

3. In what ways is desire an important feature in the development of moralities?

4. Why is it that those who understand the pain in love do not all seek out death?

5. How does Nietzsche's claim in *Ecce Homo* that man is incapable of loving unless one stands "bravely on one's own two legs" relate to his dismissal of women's search for equality? What is the emancipated woman seeking if she is not seeking to stand on her "own two legs"?

ENDNOTES

1. Philology is approximately the equivalent of the study of the Ancient Greek and Roman literature and culture.

2. Nietzsche's evolving relationship with Wagner can be somewhat followed by reading Nietzsche's works in the order he wrote them. The key texts for this analysis are *Birth of Tragedy, Richard Wagner in Bayreuth, The Case of Wagner,* and *Nietzsche Contra Wagner.* There are additional comments on Wagner in *Ecce Homo,* but they largely duplicate the reactions to Wagner in the last two works.

3. For more on this perception and the history of Elizabeth's influence on the understanding of Nietzsche, see the appendix of Kaufmann's *Nietzsche,* as well as the final chapter in Hollingdale's *Nietzsche: The Man and His Philosophy.*

4. Kaufmann, p. 72.

5. Nietzsche, *Genealogy of Morals,* Preface §8.

6. Nietzsche, *Gay Science,* §341.

7. Nietzsche, *Birth of Tragedy,* §5.

8. A common philosophical distinction is between Truth and truth. Truth is thought of as an absolute, unchanging, objective set of facts that can be appealed to for evaluation. In contrast to this notion, truth is also verifiable, but could change given more information. For example, prior to the discovery of the planet Pluto it was "true" that Neptune was the last planet in our solar system; however, we now know that this "fact" was not "True."

9. Nietzsche, *Gay Science,* §14, italics in original.

SELECTED BIBLIOGRAPHY

Hollingdale, R.J. *Nietzsche: The Man and His Philosophy.* Revised Edition. Cambridge: Cambridge University Press, 1999.

Kaufmann, Walter. *Nietzsche: Philosopher, Psychologist, Antichrist,* 3d ed. Princeton, N.J.: Princeton University Press, 1968.

Nietzsche, Friedrich. *The Birth of Tragedy,* trans. Walter Kaufmann. In *The Birth of Tragedy and The Case of Wagner.* New York: Vintage Books, 1967, pp. 3–144.

Nietzsche, Friedrich. *The Gay Science,* trans. Walter Kaufmann. New York: Vintage Books, 1974.

Nietzsche, Friedrich. *On the Genealogy of Morals,* trans. Walter Kaufmann and R.J. Hollingdale. *On the Genealogy of Morals and Ecce Homo,* ed. Walter Kaufmann. New York: Vintage Books, 1967.

from *The Gay Science*

Friedrich Nietzsche

14

The Good Man

Better a whole-hearted feud
Than a friendship that is glued.

334

One must learn to love.—This is what happens to us in music: First one has to *learn to hear* a figure and melody at all, to detect and distinguish it, to isolate it and delimit it as a separate life. Then it requires some exertion and good will to *tolerate* it in spite of its strangeness, to be patient with its appearance and expression, and kindhearted about its oddity. Finally there comes a moment when we are *used* to it, when we wait for it, when we sense that we should miss it if it were missing; and now it continues to compel and enchant us relentlessly until we have become its humble and enraptured lovers who desire nothing better from the world than it and only it.

But that is what happens to us not only in music. That is how we have *learned to love* all things that we now love. In the end we are always rewarded for our good will, our patience, fairmindedness, and gentleness with what is strange; gradually, it sheds its veil and turns out to be a new and indescribable beauty. That is its *thanks* for our hospitality. Even those who love themselves will have learned it in this way; for there is no other way. Love, too, has to be learned.

from *Beyond Good and Evil*

Friedrich Nietzsche

260

Wandering through the many subtler and coarser moralities which have so far been prevalent on earth, or still are prevalent, I found that certain features recurred regularly together and were closely associated—until I finally discovered two basic types and one basic difference.

There are *master morality* and *slave morality*[1]—I add immediately that in all the higher and more mixed cultures there also appear attempts at mediation between these two moralities, and yet more often the interpenetration and mutual misunderstanding of both, and at times they occur directly alongside each other—even in the same human being, within a *single* soul.[2] The moral discrimination of values has originated either among a ruling group whose consciousness of its difference from the ruled group was accompanied by delight—or among the ruled, the slaves and dependents of every degree.

In the first case, when the ruling group determines what is "good," the exalted, proud states of the soul are experienced as conferring distinction and determining the order of rank. The noble human being separates from himself those in whom the opposite of such exalted, proud states finds expression: he despises them. It should be noted immediately that in this first type of morality the opposition of "good" and "*bad*" means approximately the same as "noble" and "contemptible." (The opposition of "good" and "*evil*" has a different origin.) One feels contempt for the cowardly, the anxious, the petty, those intent on narrow utility; also for the suspicious with their unfree glances, those who humble themselves, the doglike people who allow themselves to be maltreated, the begging flatterers, above all the liars: it is part of the fundamental faith of all aristocrats that the common people lie. "We truthful ones"— thus the nobility of ancient Greece referred to itself.

It is obvious that moral designations were everywhere first applied to *human beings* and only later, derivatively, to actions. Therefore it is a gross mistake when historians of morality start from such questions as: why was the compassionate act praised? The noble type of man experiences *itself* as determining values; it does not need approval; it judges, "what is harmful to me is harmful in itself"; it knows itself to be that which first accords honor to things; it is *value-creating*. Everything it

---

[1]While the ideas developed here, and explicated at greater length a year later in the first part of the *Genealogy of Morals,* had been expressed by Nietzsche in 1878 in section 45 of *Human, All-Too-Human,* this is the passage in which his famous terms "master morality" and "slave morality" are introduced.

[2]These crucial qualifications, though added immediately, have often been overlooked. "Modern" moralities are clearly mixtures; hence their manifold tensions, hypocrisies, and contradictions.

knows as part of itself it honors: such a morality is self-glorification. In the foreground there is the feeling of fullness, of power that seeks to overflow, the happiness of high tension, the consciousness of wealth that would give and bestow: the noble human being, too, helps the unfortunate, but not, or almost not, from pity, but prompted more by an urge begotten by excess of power. The noble human being honors himself as one who is powerful, also as one who has power over himself, who knows how to speak and be silent, who delights in being severe and hard with himself and respects all severity and hardness. "A hard heart Wotan put into my breast," says an old Scandinavian saga: a fitting poetic expression, seeing that it comes from the soul of a proud Viking. Such a type of man is actually proud of the fact that he is *not* made for pity, and the hero of the saga therefore adds as a warning: "If the heart is not hard in youth it will never harden." Noble and courageous human beings who think that way are furthest removed from that morality which finds the distinction of morality precisely in pity, or in acting for others, or in *désintéressement;* faith in oneself, pride in oneself, a fundamental hostility and irony against "selflessness" belong just as definitely to noble morality as does a slight disdain and caution regarding compassionate feelings and a "warm heart."

It is the powerful who *understand* how to honor; this is their art, their realm of invention. The profound reverence for age and tradition—all law rests on this double reverence—the faith and prejudice in favor of ancestors and disfavor of those yet to come are typical of the morality of the powerful; and when the men of "modern ideas," conversely, believe almost instinctively in "progress" and "the future" and more lack respect for age, this in itself would sufficiently betray the ignoble origin of these "ideas."

A morality of the ruling group, however, is most alien and embarrassing to the present taste in the severity of its principle that one has duties only to one's peers; that against beings of a lower rank, against everything alien, one may behave as one pleases or "as the heart desires," and in any case "beyond good and evil"—here pity and like feelings may find their place.[3] The capacity for, and the juty of, long gratitude and long revenge—both only among one's peers—refinement in repaying, the sophisticated concept of friendship, a certain necessity for having enemies (as it were, as drainage ditches for the affects of envy, quarrelsomeness, exuberance—at bottom, in order to be capable of being good *friends*): all these are typical characteristics of noble morality which, as suggested, is not the morality of "modern ideas" and therefore is hard to empathize with today, also hard to dig up and uncover.[4]

It is different with the second type of morality, *slave morality.* Suppose the violated, oppressed, suffering, unfree, who are uncertain of themselves and

---

[3]The final clause that follows the dash, omitted in the Cowan translation, is crucial and qualifies the first part of the sentence: a noble person has no *duties* to animals but treats them in accordance with his feelings, which means, if he is noble, with pity.

The ruling masters, of course, are not always noble in this sense, and this is recognized by Nietzsche in *Twilight of the Idols,* in the chapter "The 'Improvers' of Mankind," in which he gives strong expression to his distaste for Manu's laws concerning outcastes (*Portable Nietzsche,* pp. 503–05); also in *The Will to Power* (ed. W. Kaufmann, New York, Random House, 1967), section 142. Indeed, in *The Antichrist,* section 57, Nietzsche contradicts outright his formulation above: "When the exceptional human being treats the mediocre more tenderly than himself and his peers, this is not mere courtesy of the heart—it is simply his *duty.*"

More important: Nietzsche's obvious distaste for slave morality and the fact that he makes a point of liking master morality better does not imply that he endorses master morality. Cf. the text for note 5 above.

[4]Clearly, master morality cannot be discovered by introspection nor by the observation of individuals who are "masters" rather than "slaves." Both of these misunderstandings are widespread. What is called for is rather a rereading of, say, the *Iliad* and, to illustrate "slave morality," the New Testament.

weary, moralize: what will their moral valuations have in common? Probably, a pessimistic suspicion about the whole condition of man will find expression, perhaps a condemnation of man along with his condition. The slave's eye is not favorable to the virtues of the powerful: he is skeptical and suspicious, *subtly* suspicious, of all the "good" that is honored there—he would like to persuade himself that even their happiness is not genuine. Conversely, those qualities are brought out and flooded with light which serve to ease existence for those who suffer: here pity, the complaisant and obliging hand, the warm heart, patience, industry, humility, and friendliness are honored—for here these are the most useful qualities and almost the only means for enduring the pressure of existence. Slave morality is essentially a morality of utility.

Here is the place for the origin of that famous opposition of "good" and "evil": into evil one's feelings project power and dangerousness, a certain terribleness, subtlety, and strength that does not permit contempt to develop. According to slave morality, those who are "evil" thus inspire fear; according to master morality it is precisely those who are "good" that inspire, and wish to inspire, fear, while the "bad" are felt to be contemptible.

The opposition reaches its climax when, as a logical consequence of slave morality, a touch of disdain is associated also with the "good" of this morality—this may be slight and benevolent—because the good human being has to be *undangerous* in the slaves way of thinking: he is good-natured, easy to deceive, a little stupid perhaps, *un bonhomme.*[5] Wherever slave morality becomes preponderant, language tends to bring the words "good" and "stupid" closer together.

One last fundamental difference: the longing for *freedom,* the instinct for happiness and the subtleties of the feeling of freedom belong just as necessarily to slave morality and morals as artful and enthusiastic reverence and devotion are the regular symptom of an aristocratic way of thinking and evaluating.

This makes plain why love *as passion*—which is our European specialty—simply must be of noble origin: as is well known, its invention must be credited to the Provençal knight-poets, those magnificent and inventive human beings of the "*gai saber*"[6] to whom Europe owes so many things and almost owes itself.—

269

The more a psychologist—a born and inevitable psychologist and unriddler of souls—applies himself to the more exquisite cases and human beings, the greater becomes the danger that he might suffocate from pity.[7] He *needs* hardness and cheerfulness more than anyone else. For the corruption, the ruination of the higher men, of the souls of a stranger type, is the rule: it is terrible to have such a rule always before one's eyes. The manifold torture of the psychologist who has discovered this ruination, who discovers this whole inner hopelessness of the higher man, this eternal "too late" in every sense, first in one case and then *almost* always

---

[5]Literally "a good human being," the term is used for precisely the type described here.

[6]"Gay science": in the early fourteenth century the term was used to designate the art of the troubadours, codified in *Leys d'amors.* Nietzsche subtitled his own *Fröhliche Wissenschaft* (1882). "*la gaya scienza,*" placed a quatrain on the title page, began the book with a fifteen-page "Prelude in German Rhymes," and in the second edition (1887) added, besides a Preface and Book V, an "Appendix" of further verses.
[7]Cf. *Zarathustra,* Part IV.

through the whole of history—may perhaps lead him one day to turn against his own lot, embittered, and to make an attempt at self-destruction—may lead to his own "corruption."

In almost every psychologist one will perceive a telltale preference for and delight in association with everyday, well-ordered people: this reveals that he always requires a cure, that he needs a kind of escape and forgetting, away from all that with which his insights, his incisions, his "craft" have burdened his conscience. He is characterized by fear of his memory. He is easily silenced by the judgments of others; he listens with an immobile face as they venerate, admire, love, and transfigure where he has *seen*—or he even conceals his silence by expressly agreeing with some foreground opinion. Perhaps the paradox of his situation is so gruesome that precisely where he has learned the greatest pity coupled with the greatest contempt, the crowd, the educated, the enthusiasts learn the greatest veneration—the veneration for "great men" and prodigies for whose sake one blesses and honors the fatherland, the earth, the dignity of humanity, and oneself, and to whom one refers the young, toward whom one educates them—

And who knows whether what happened in all great cases so far was not always the same: that the crowd adored a god—and that the "god" was merely a poor sacrificial animal. Success has always been the greatest liar—and the "work" itself is a success; the great statesman, the conqueror, the discoverer is disguised by his creations, often beyond recognition; the "work," whether of the artist or the philosopher, invents the man who has created it, who is supposed to have created it; "great men," as they are venerated, are subsequent pieces of wretched minor fiction; in the world of historical values, counterfeit *rules*.

Those great poets, for example—men like Byron, Musset, Poe, Leopardi, Kleist, Gogol (I do not dare mention greater names, but I mean them)[8]—are and perhaps must be men of fleeting moments, enthusiastic, sensual, childish, frivolous and sudden in mistrust and trust; with souls in which they usually try to conceal some fracture; often taking revenge with their works for some inner contamination, often seeking with their high flights to escape into forgetfulness from an all-too-faithful memory; often lost in the mud and almost in love with it, until they become like the will-o'-the-wisps around swamps and *pose* as stars—the people may then call them idealists—often fighting against a long nausea, with a recurring specter of unbelief that chills and forces them to languish for *gloria* and to gobble their "belief in themselves" from the hands of intoxicated flatterers—what *torture* are these great artists and all the so-called higher men for anyone who has once guessed their true nature![9]

It is easy to understand that *these* men should so readily receive from woman—clairvoyant in the world of suffering and, unfortunately, also desirous far beyond her strength to help and save—those eruptions of boundless and most devoted *pity* which the multitude, above all the venerating mul-

---

[8]The parenthesis is not found in the first two editions of 1886 and 1891, but it appears in all standard editions, including Schlechta's, although he purports to follow the original edition. When Nietzsche included this passage in *Nietzsche contra Wagner* in slightly revised form, the remark was set off by dashes instead of parentheses and read. "I do not mention far greater names, but I mean them" (*Portable Nietzsche*, p. 678). The third edition of *Beyond Good and Evil* (1894) has "far greater names."

According to the table comparing the page numbers of the different editions of *Beyond Good and Evil* in Vol. VII (1903) of the Grossoktav edition of the *Werke,* the third edition of *Beyond* was dated 1893, the fourth 1894, and the page numbers of both are the same; but the Princeton University Library has a copy of the *Dritte Auflage* (third edition) dated 1894.

[9]Another leitmotif of *Zarathustra,* Part IV.

titude, does not understand and on which it lavishes inquisitive and self-satisfied interpretations. This pity deceives itself regularly about its powers; woman would like to believe that love can achieve *anything*—that is her characteristic *faith*. Alas, whoever knows the heart will guess how poor, stupid, helpless, arrogant, blundering, more apt to destroy than to save is even the best and profoundest love!

It is possible that underneath the holy fable and disguise of Jesus' life there lies concealed one of the most painful cases of the martyrdom of *knowledge about love:* the martyrdom of the most innocent and desirous heart, never sated by any human love; *demanding* love, to be loved and nothing else, with hardness, with insanity, with terrible eruptions against those who denied him love; the story of a poor fellow, unsated and insatiable in love, who had to invent hell in order to send to it those who did not *want* to love him—and who finally, having gained kowledge about human love, had to invent a god who is all love, all *ability* to love—who has mercy on human love because it is so utterly wretched and unknowing. Anyone who feels that way, who *knows* this about love—*seeks* death.

But why pursue such painful matters? Assuming one does not have to.—

from *Ecce Homo*

Friedrich Nietzsche

5

That a psychologist without equal speaks from my writings, is perhaps the first insight reached by a good reader—a reader as I deserve him, who reads me the way good old philologists read their Horace. Those propositions on which all the world is really agreed—not to speak of the world's common run of philosophers, the moralists and other hollow pots, cabbage heads[10]—appear in my books as naïve blunders: for example, the belief that "unegoistic" and "egoistic" are opposites, while the ego itself is really only a "higher swindle," an "ideal."—There are neither egoistic nor unegoistic acts: both concepts are psychological absurdities. Or the proposition: "man strives for happiness."— Or the proposition: "happiness is the reward of virtue."—Or the proposition: "pleasure and dis- pleasure are opposites."—The Circe of humanity, morality, has falsified all *psychologica* through and through—*moralizing* them—down to that gruesome nonsense that love is supposed to be something "unegoistic."—One has to sit firmly upon *oneself,* one must stand bravely on one's own two legs, otherwise one is simply *incapable* of loving. Ultimately, women know that only too well: they don't give a damn about selfless, merely objective men.

May I here venture the surmise that I *know* women? That is part of my Dionysian dowry. Who knows? Perhaps I am the first psychologist of the eternally feminine. They all love me—an old story—not counting *abortive* females, the "emancipated" who lack the stuff for children.—Fortunately, I am not willing to be torn to pieces: the perfect woman tears to pieces when she loves.—I know these charming maenads.—Ah, what a dangerous, creeping, subterranean little beast of prey she is! And yet so agreeable!—A little woman who

---

[10]Den Allerwelts-Philosophen, den Moralisten und andren Hohltöpfen, Kohlköpfen.

pursues her revenge would run over fate itself.—Woman is indescribably more evil than man; also cleverer: good nature is in a woman a form of degeneration.—In all so-called "beautiful souls" something is physiologically askew at bottom; I do not say everything, else I should become medicynical. The fight for equal rights is actually a symptom of a disease: every physician knows that.—Woman, the more she is a woman, resists rights in general hand and foot: after all, the state of nature, the eternal war between the sexes, gives her by far the first rank.

Has my definition of love been heard? It is the only one worthy of a philosopher. Love—in its means, war; at bottom, the deadly hatred of the sexes.

Has my answer been heard to the question how one *cures* a woman—"redeems" her? One gives her a child. Woman needs children, a man is for her always only a means: thus spoke *Zarathustra*.

"Emancipation of women"—that is the instinctive hatred of the abortive[11] woman, who is incapable of giving birth, against the woman who is turned out well[12]—the fight against the "man" is always a mere means, pretext, tactic. By raising themselves higher, as "woman in herself," as the "higher woman," as a female "idealist," they want to lower the level of the general rank of woman; and there is no surer means for that than higher education, slacks, and political voting-cattle rights. At bottom, the emancipated are anarchists in the world of the "eternally feminine," the underprivileged whose most fundamental instinct is revenge.

One whole species of the most malignant "idealism"—which, incidentally, is also encountered among men; for example, in Henrik Ibsen, this typical old virgin—aims to *poison* the good conscience, what is natural in sexual love.[13]

And lest I leave any doubt about my very decent and strict views in these matters, let me still cite a proposition against vice from my moral code: I use the word "vice" in my fight against every kind of antinature or, if you prefer pretty words, idealism. The proposition reads: "The preaching of chastity amounts to a public incitement to antinature. Every kind of contempt for sex, every impurification of it by means of the concept 'impure,' is the crime *par excellence* against life—is the real sin against the holy spirit of life."

---

[11] *Missraten.*
[12] *Wohlgeraten.*

[13] It seems plain that Nietzsche did not know most of Ibsen's plays. Cf. my edition of *The Will to Power* (New York, Random House, 1967), sections 86 (including my long note) and 747, and for some parallels between Ibsen and Nietzsche also my translation of *Beyond Good and Evil* (New York, Vintage Books, 1966)—the last section of my Preface to that volume as well as my note on section 213. Nietzsche would have loved *The Wild Duck.*

chapter twenty-six

Sigmund Freud

It is impossible to overestimate the importance of the theoretical achievements of Sigmund Freud (1856–1939) for virtually every subsequent intellectual development of the twentieth century. The insights of his psychoanalytic theory of psychosexual development continue to be absorbed, reformulated, and resisted, but rarely ignored, in contemporary debates in such disciplines as psychology, religion, aesthetics, economics, social theory, and philosophy. Of course the influence of psychoanalytic theory has not been confined to academic discussions. Basic Freudian categories (sublimation, repression, the unconscious, etc.) have become common notions on the level of popular culture as well. The global impact of psychoanalysis is hardly surprising given the provocative nature of its basic principles. Freud's revolutionary discovery that abnormal adult behaviors are reenactments of unresolved conflicts that occur in early childhood suggested that mental illness could not be adequately diagnosed in strictly physiological terms. His conviction that psychoanalytic reflection could discern empirical correlations between nervous disorders and the unconscious motives and ideas that produce them led Freud to develop a hermeneutics of the unconscious that allowed him to *interpret* those abnormal behaviors as *symptoms* of the *repression* of traumatic memories. As we will see, this implies that there is no firm distinction between normal and abnormal sexual behavior, but that its many forms of expression originate out of a universal developmental process.

"The Sexual Aberrations" is the first of Freud's *Three Essays on the Theory of Sexuality* (1905), which are generally regarded, along with *The Interpretation of Dreams* (1900), as Freud's most pioneering contributions to psychological theory. He continued to return to and revise these early essays on sexuality throughout his life.[1]

He concludes in "The Sexual Aberrations" that the "disposition to perversions is an original and universal disposition of the human sexual instinct and that normal sexual behaviour is developed out of it as a result of organic changes and psychical inhibitions occurring in the course of maturation."[2] The conventional beliefs that sexual instincts are absent or latent in children, that they become active only at the age of puberty, and that precocious or nonheterosexual behaviors are unnatural and should therefore be discouraged are, according to Freud, inconsistent with scientific evidence. He challenged the traditional notion[3] that normal sexual behavior serves (and *ought* to serve) the exclusive end of reproduction and should therefore be restricted within the confines of the conjugal family. In fact, an individual's sexual desire (who or what is desired and what form the satisfaction of desire assumes) is changing on a more or less continual basis until the age of puberty. Infants, for example, are *polymorphously perverse*, which means that they derive sexual pleasure not exclusively or even primarily from the excitation of the genitals (as is the case in "normal" adult sexual behavior) but equally from different *erotogenic zones* of the body, that is, those parts of the body whose biological function is also attended by sensations of pleasure (the consumption of food through the *mouth*, the expulsion of waste through the *anus*, etc.). As children mature, they pass through a series of stages the course of which will ultimately determine the sexual dispositions of their adult lives. "Normal" sexual behavior is therefore not a "natural" disposition at all, but is the result of a complex and highly contingent developmental process.[4] Because the object and the aim of the sexual instinct are reconstituted at each stage in accordance their respective conflicts, the eventual *accomplishment* of a "normal" organization of the sexual instinct in maturity presupposes their successful resolution.

At times, sexual desires and fantasies cannot be reconciled with the demands of social reality. Here the *pleasure principle* and the *reality principle* are intractably at odds with one another. The pleasure principle holds that all living beings seek pleasure (which Freud holds to be the release of tension) and avoid pain (increased tension). The often-conflicting reality principle belongs only to the ego, the part of the mind in contact with the outside world, and is the ego's insistence that real external and social conditions be taken into account. If, for example, I am hungry, the pleasure principle insists upon immediate consumption of food to reduce the tension of hunger, but the reality principle will have me wait for socially appropriate conditions before I consume food. In these conflicts, the *libido*[5] is either restructured through a progression to the next stage in the developmental process of maturation, or else gets redirected through alternative channels of expression. Thus perverse behavior in adult life is symptomatic of traumatic conflicts that have been repressed into the *unconscious*. In a therapeutic context, Freud experimented with a variety of techniques (dream interpretation, hypnosis, free association, etc.) that allowed patients suffering from *neurotic* disorders to "return" to the original scenes of conflict from childhood and reexperience them. (Unlike psychotic disorders, which fracture our ability to grasp external reality, neurotic symptoms occur in those who are nonetheless in touch with a shared outside world. Freud held only neuroses to be generally treatable by psychoanalysis.) Through a process that Freud called *transference*, patients "act out" their painful memories by projecting a certain role or identity onto the therapist who, in turn, "plays along" with the patient's fantasy. This provides the patient with the opportunity to successfully work through the repressed conflict in the expectation that the experience of *catharsis*[6] will result in the gradual dissolution of neurotic behaviors. From a psychoanalytic perspective, the unconscious is thus the key to understanding the hidden connection between traumatic experiences in childhood and the symptoms that issue from their repression. Freud writes in "The Sexual Aberrations" that "by systematically turning these symptoms back (with the help of a special technique) into emotionally cathected ideas—ideas that will now have become conscious—it is possible to obtain the most accurate knowledge of the nature and origin of these formerly unconscious psychical structures".[7]

Notice that for Freud, the interpretive procedure that provides insight into the forgotten origins of neurotic attachments must be "systematic" in nature. This means that causal relations between traumatic episodes from the past and pathological conditions in the present cannot be asserted arbitrarily, and insofar as Freud understood psychoanalysis to be a *science* of the mind, particular case studies must always refer back to a *general* theoretical framework that can lay claim to *universal* application. So while Freud rejected the idea that human sexuality does in fact or even typically resemble the traditional notion of heterosexual, reproductive sex, he nevertheless believed that the wide variety of sexual inclinations, behaviors, and practices could all be explained with reference to a single theory of development.

What, then, are the stages of psychosexual development? The initial state of polymorphous perversity is followed by the *oral* stage, during which time the mouth becomes the primary site of sexual excitation for the child. Freud claims that oral fixation is the manner by which we learn to manipulate our physical surroundings; think of the tendency of children to "explore" their environments by putting objects in their mouths. The stage concludes with the traumatic experience of *losing control* over the external environment when the mother weans the child. The oral stage is succeeded by the *anal* stage. The child now derives pleasure from the ability to control his bowel movements (which is related to the experience of *creativity*), for which he receives praise from his parents. At this stage, the child internalizes the principle of social order (i.e., he learns that his relationships with his external environment are mediated by social obligations that transcend his particular wishes). The third stage of development is the *phallic*. The child's creativity is now directed toward the act of masturbation.[8] Finally, around the age of six, the child enters the *Oedipal Complex* stage. A male child comes to *identify* with his father and, ultimately, to compete with him for his mother's love. In fear that his father will retaliate against him by castrating him, the child internalizes feelings of guilt and aggression toward his father. "Normal" sexual development depends on the successful negotiation of this final stage of psychosexual development.[9] The situation of girls is, of course, different (though notice that male and female children only part ways in their developmental trajectory at this point). Whereas boys experience *castration anxiety*, girls assume that they have already been castrated and so develop *penis envy*.[10]

Freud showed that sexuality does not emerge *ex nihilo* at the age of maturity and in accordance to some blueprint that is fixed by nature but is in fact the result of a hierarchically organized developmental process. This implies that the boundaries between diverse sexual phenomena are highly contingent and never absolute.

EH

QUESTIONS

1. Does Freud believe that object choice results from an innate disposition or from social experience? Do you agree or disagree?
2. Freud claims that "the pathological approach to the study of inversion has been displaced by the anthropological." How would you interpret this claim?
3. In what sense is Freud's account of the perversions a *scientific* one? In what senses is it not?

ENDNOTES

1. See Steven Marcus's excellent introduction to *Three Essays on the Theory of Sexuality*.
2. Freud, *Three Essays on the Theory of Sexuality*, p. 97.
3. In his famous study *The History of Sexuality: An Introduction*, Michel Foucault provides a genealogical analysis of the evolution of this traditional conception of normal sexuality: "Nothing that was not ordered in terms of generation or transfigured by it could expect sanction or protection. Nor did it merit a hearing. It would be driven out, denied, and reduced to silence. Not only did it not exist, it had no right to exist and would be made to disappear upon its least manifestation—whether in act or words. Everyone knew, for example, that children had no sex, which was why they were forbidden to talk about it, why one closed one's eyes and stopped one's ears whenever they came to show evidence to the contrary, and why a general and studied silence was imposed." See Michel Foucalt, *The History of Sexuality*, trans. Robert Hurley (New York: Vintage Books, 1990 [1976]).
4. Like many of his contemporaries, Freud was greatly influenced by the evolutionary theory of Charles Darwin. His relationship to philosophical theories of development, particularly those of Hegel and Nietzsche, has been comparatively neglected.
5. The Latin term *libido* means "desire."
6. The Greek term *catharsis* means "purification." It originally appears in Aristotle's *Poetics* and designates an audience's experience of emotional release during the climatic moments of "reversal" and "recognition" in Greek tragedy. Aristotle argued that catharsis contains three essential components: it is a mixture of fear, pity, and suffering. In our everyday lives we must repress the tragic truth of our existence (Aristotle had in mind primarily the fear of death and the experience of suffering that it provokes in beings who are tragically destined to die). Artistic representations of our tragic condition "make suffering beautiful" and so allow us to confront our repressed fears, as it were, from a safe distance. This aesthetic experience is cathartic because it allows us to release emotional energies (Freud called them the *affects*) that have become "dammed up" in the unconscious. This causes tension and, ultimately, neurotic symptoms that will persist until those blocked energies are allowed to express themselves.

7. Freud, p. 30. The greek term *cathexis* refers to the quantity of libidinal energies that attach to particular memories.

8. This applies equally for male and female children at this point.

9. Freud named the stage after the Greek hero Oedipus who unknowingly murdered his father and married his mother. He viewed the figure of Oedipus as an artistic representation of precisely the dynamic process of individuation that Freud described in scientific terms. Consider the the following line from Sophocles' *Oedipus Tyrannus*: "I say that with those you love best / you live in foulest shame unconsciously / and do not see where you are in calamity." See Sophocles. *Oedipus the King, Oedipus at Colonus, Antigone*, trans. David Grene (Chicago: University of Chicago Press, 1991).

10. Freudian theory has been especially criticized for its "phallocentrism" and the derivative status that is assigned to female sexuality. For a thorough discussion of the historical context of patriarchy in nineteenth-century Europe and biographical information about Freud's relationships with his mother other family members, see Samuel, Slipp M.D., *The Freudian Mystique: Freud, Women and Feminism*. New York: New York University Press, 1995. Also see Lisa Appignanesi, and John Forrester, *Freud's Women* (New York: Other Press, 2001).

SELECTED BIBLIOGRAPHY

Chamberlain, Leslie, *The Secret Artist: A Close Reading of Sigmund Freud*. New York: Seven Stories Press, 2001.

Freud, Sigmund. *Three Essays on the Theory of Sexuality*, trans. James Strachey. New York: Basic Books, 1962.

Gay, Peter. *Freud: A Life for Our Time*. New York: W. W. Norton, 1998.

Muchenhoupt, Margaret. *Sigmund Freud: Explorer of the Unconscious*. Oxford: Oxford University Press, 1999.

Wollheim, Richard. *Sigmund Freud*. Cambridge: Cambridge University Press, 1989.

from *Three Essays on the Theory of Sexuality*

Sigmund Freud

THE SEXUAL ABERRATIONS[1]

The fact of the existence of sexual needs in human beings and animals is expressed in biology by the assumption of a 'sexual instinct', on the analogy of the instinct of nutrition, that is of hunger. Everyday language possesses no counterpart to the word 'hunger', but science makes use of the word 'libido' for that purpose.[2]

Popular opinion has quite definite ideas about the nature and characteristics of this sexual instinct. It is generally understood to be absent in childhood, to set in at the time of puberty in connection with the process of coming to maturity and to be revealed in the manifestations of an irresistible attraction exercised by one sex upon the other; while its aim is presumed to be sexual union, or at all events actions leading in that direction. We have every reason to believe, however, that these views give a very false picture of the true situation. If we look into them more closely we shall find that they contain a number of errors, inaccuracies and hasty conclusions.

I shall at this point introduce two technical terms. Let us call the person from whom sexual attraction proceeds the *sexual object* and the act towards which the instinct tends the *sexual aim*. Scientifically sifted observation, then, shows that numerous deviations occur in respect of both of these—the sexual object and the sexual aim. The relation between these deviations and what is assumed to be normal requires thorough investigation.

(1) DEVIATIONS IN RESPECT OF THE SEXUAL OBJECT

The popular view of the sexual instinct is beautifully reflected in the poetic fable which tells how the original human beings were cut up into two halves—man and woman—and how these are always striving to unite again in love.[3] It comes as a great surprise therefore to learn that there are men whose sexual object is a man and not a woman, and women whose sexual object is a woman and not a man. People of this kind are described as having 'contrary sexual feelings', or better, as being 'inverts', and the fact is described as 'inversion'. The number of such people is very considerable, though there are difficulties in establishing it precisely.[4]

---

[1]The information contained in this first essay is derived from the well-known writings of Krafft-Ebing, Moll, Moebius, Havelock Ellis, Schrenck-Notzing, Löwenfeld, Eulenburg, Bloch and Hirschfeld, and from the *Jahrbuch für sexuelle Zwischenstufen*, published under the direction of the last-named author. Since full bibliographies of the remaining literature of the subject will be found in the works of these writers, I have been able to spare myself the necessity for giving detailed references. [*Added* 1910:] The data obtained from the psychoanalytic investigation of inverts are based upon material supplied to me by I. Sadger and upon my own findings.

[2][*Footnote added* 1910:] The only appropriate word in the German language, '*Lust*', is unfortunately ambiguous, and is used to denote the experience both of a need and of a gratification. [Unlike the English 'lust' it can mean either 'desire' or 'pleasure'.]

[3][This is no doubt an allusion to the theory expounded by Aristophanes in Plato's *Symposium*. Freud recurred to this much later, at the end of Chapter VI of *Beyond the Pleasure Principle* (1920*g*).]

[4]On these difficulties and on the attempts which have been made to arrive at the proportional number of inverts, see Hirschfeld (1904).

(A) Inversion

Behaviour of Inverts

Such people vary greatly in their behaviour in several respects.

(*a*) They may be *absolute* inverts. In that case their sexual objects are exclusively of their own sex. Persons of the opposite sex are never the object of their sexual desire, but leave them cold, or even arouse sexual aversion in them. As a consequence of this aversion, they are incapable, if they are men, of carrying out the sexual act, or else they derive no enjoyment from it.

(*b*) They may be *amphigenic* inverts, that is psychosexual hermaphrodites. In that case their sexual objects may equally well be of their own or of the opposite sex. This kind of inversion thus lacks the characteristic of exclusiveness.

(*c*) They may be *contingent* inverts. In that case, under certain external conditions—of which inaccessibility of any normal sexual object and imitation are the chief—they are capable of taking as their sexual object someone of their own sex and of deriving satisfaction from sexual intercourse with him.

Again, inverts vary in their views as to the peculiarity of their sexual instinct. Some of them accept their inversion as something in the natural course of things, just as a normal person accepts the direction of *his* libido, and insist energetically that inversion is as legitimate as the normal attitude; others rebel against their inversion and feel it as a pathological compulsion.[5]

Other variations occur which relate to questions of time. The trait of inversion may either date back to the very beginning, as far back as the subject's memory reaches, or it may not have become noticeable till some particular time before or after puberty.[6] It may either persist throughout life, or it may go into temporary abeyance, or again it may constitute an episode on the way to a normal development. It may even make its first appearance late in life after a long period of normal sexual activity. A periodic oscillation between a normal and an inverted sexual object has also sometimes been observed. Those cases are of particular interest in which the libido changes over to an inverted sexual object after a distressing experience with a normal one.

As a rule these different kinds of variations are found side by side independently of one another. It is, however, safe to assume that the most extreme form of inversion will have been present from a very early age and that the person concerned will feel at one with his peculiarity.

Many authorities would be unwilling to class together all the various cases which I have enumerated and would prefer to lay stress upon their differences rather than their resemblances, in accordance with their own preferred view of inversion. Nevertheless, though the distinctions cannot be disputed, it is impossible to overlook the existence of numerous intermediate examples of every type, so that we are driven to conclude that we are dealing with a connected series.

Nature of Inversion

The earliest assessments regarded inversion as an innate indication of nervous degeneracy. This corresponded to the fact that medical observers first

---

[5]The fact of a person struggling in this way against a compulsion towards inversion may perhaps determine the possibility of his being influenced by suggestion [*added* 1910:] or psycho-analysis.

[6]Many writers have insisted with justice that the dates assigned by inverts themselves for the appearance of their tendency to inversion are untrustworthy, since they may have repressed the evidence of their heterosexual feelings from their memory. [*Added* 1910:] These suspicions have been confirmed by psycho-analysis in those cases of inversion to which it has had access; it has produced decisive alterations in their anamnesis by filling in their infantile amnesia.—[In the first edition (1905) the place of this last sentence was taken by the following one: 'A decision on this point could be arrived at only by a psycho-analytic investigation of inverts.']

came across it in persons suffering, or appearing to suffer, from nervous diseases. This characterization of inversion involves two suppositions, which must be considered separately: that it is innate and that it is degenerate.

Degeneracy

The attribution of degeneracy in this connection is open to the objections which can be raised against the indiscriminate use of the word in general. It has become the fashion to regard any symptom which is not obviously due to trauma or infection as a sign of degeneracy. Magnan's classification of degenerates is indeed of such a kind as not to exclude the possibility of the concept of degeneracy being applied to a nervous system whose general functioning is excellent. This being so, it may well be asked whether an attribution of 'degeneracy' is of any value or adds anything to our knowledge. It seems wiser only to speak of it where

1. several serious deviations from the normal are found together, and

2. the capacity for efficient functioning and survival seem to be severely impaired.[7]

Several facts go to show that in this legitimate sense of the word inverts cannot be regarded as degenerate:

1. Inversion is found in people who exhibit no other serious deviations from the normal.

2. It is similarly found in people whose efficiency is unimpaired, and who are indeed

distinguished by specially high intellectual development and ethical culture.[8]

3. If we disregard the patients we come across in our medical practice, and cast our eyes round a wider horizon, we shall come in two directions upon facts which make it impossible to regard inversion as a sign of degeneracy:

a. Account must be taken of the fact that inversion was a frequent phenomenon—one might almost say an institution charged with important functions—among the peoples of antiquity at the height of their civilization.

b. It is remarkably widespread among many savage and primitive races, whereas the concept of degeneracy is usually restricted to states of high civilization (cf. Bloch); and, even amongst the civilized peoples of Europe, climate and race exercise the most powerful influence on the prevalence of inversion and upon the attitude adopted towards it.[9]

Innate Character

As may be supposed, innateness is only attributed to the first, most extreme, class of inverts, and the evidence for it rests upon assurances given by them that at no time in their lives has their sexual instinct shown any sign of taking another course. The very existence of the two other classes, and especially the third [the 'contingent' inverts], is difficult to reconcile with the hypothesis of the

---

[7]Moebius (1900) confirms the view that we should be chary in making a diagnosis of degeneracy and that it has very little practical value: 'If we survey the wide field of degeneracy upon which some glimpses of revealing light have been thrown in these pages, it will at once be clear that there is small value in ever making a diagnosis of degeneracy.'

[8]It must be allowed that the spokesmen of 'Uranism' are justified in asserting that some of the most prominent men in all recorded history were inverts and perhaps even absolute inverts.

[9]The pathological approach to the study of inversion has been displaced by the anthropological. The merit for bringing about this change is due to Bloch (1902–3), who has also laid stress on the occurrence of inversion among the civilizations of antiquity.

innateness of inversion. This explains why those who support this view tend to separate out the group of absolute inverts from all the rest, thus abandoning any attempt at giving an account of inversion which shall have universal application. In the view of these authorities inversion is innate in one group of cases, while in others it may have come about in other ways.

The reverse of this view is represented by the alternative one that inversion is an acquired character of the sexual instinct. This second view is based on the following considerations:

1. In the case of many inverts, even absolute ones, it is possible to show that very early in their lives a sexual impression occurred which left a permanent after-effect in the shape of a tendency to homosexuality.

2. In the case of many others, it is possible to point to external influences in their lives, whether of a favourable or inhibiting character, which have led sooner or later to a fixation of their inversion. (Such influences are exclusive relations with persons of their own sex, comradeship in war, detention in prison, the dangers of heterosexual intercourse, celibacy, sexual weakness, etc.)

3. Inversion can be removed by hypnotic suggestion, which would be astonishing in an innate characteristic.

In view of these considerations it is even possible to doubt the very existence of such a thing as innate inversion. It can be argued (cf. Havelock Ellis [1915]) that, if the cases of allegedly innate inversion were more closely examined, some experience of their early childhood would probably come to light which had a determining effect upon the direction taken by their libido. This experience would simply have passed out of the subject's conscious recollection, but could be recalled to his memory under appropriate influence. In the opin-

ion of these writers inversion can only be described as a frequent variation of the sexual instinct, which can be determined by a number of external circumstances in the subject's life.

The apparent certainty of this conclusion is, however, completely countered by the reflection that many people are subjected to the same sexual influences (e.g. to seduction or mutual masturbation, which may occur in early youth) without becoming inverted or without remaining so permanently. We are therefore forced to a suspicion that the choice between 'innate' and 'acquired' is not an exclusive one or that it does not cover all the issues involved in inversion.

Explanation of Inversion

The nature of inversion is explained neither by the hypothesis that it is innate nor by the alternative hypothesis that it is acquired. In the former case we must ask in what respect it is innate, unless we are to accept the crude explanation that everyone is born with his sexual instinct attached to a particular sexual object. In the latter case it may be questioned whether the various accidental influences would be sufficient to explain the acquisition of inversion without the co-operation of something in the subject himself. As we have already shown, the existence of this last factor is not to be denied.

Bisexuality

A fresh contradiction of popular views is involved in the considerations put forward by Lydston [1889], Kiernan [1888] and Chevalier [1893] in an endeavour to account for the possibility of sexual inversion. It is popularly believed that a human being is either a man or a woman. Science, however, knows of cases in which the sexual characters are obscured, and in which it is consequently difficult to determine the sex. This arises in the first instance in the field of anatomy. The genitals of the individuals concerned combine male and female characteristics. (This condition is known as hermaphroditism.) In rare cases both kinds of sexual apparatus are found side by side fully developed (true hermaphroditism); but far more frequently both sets of organs are found in an atrophied condition.[10]

The importance of these abnormalities lies in the unexpected fact that they facilitate our understanding of normal development. For it appears that a certain degree of anatomical hermaphroditism occurs normally. In every normal male or female individual, traces are found of the apparatus of the opposite sex. These either persist without function as rudimentary organs or become modified and take on other functions.

These long-familiar facts of anatomy lead us to suppose that an originally bisexual physical disposition has, in the course of evolution, become modified into a unisexual one, leaving behind only a few traces of the sex that has become atrophied.

It was tempting to extend this hypothesis to the mental sphere and to explain inversion in all its varieties as the expression of a psychical hermaphroditism. All that was required further in order to settle the question was that inversion should be regularly accompanied by the mental and somatic signs of hermaphroditism.

But this expectation was disappointed. It is impossible to demonstrate so close a connection between the hypothetical psychical hermaphroditism and the established anatomical one. A general lowering of the sexual instinct and a slight anatomical atrophy of the organs is found frequently in inverts (cf. Havelock Ellis, 1915). Frequently, but by no means regularly or even usually. The truth must therefore be recognized that inversion and somatic hermaphroditism are on the whole independent of each other.

A great deal of importance, too, has been attached to what are called the secondary and tertiary sexual characters and to the great frequency of the occurrence of those of the opposite sex in inverts (cf. Havelock Ellis, 1915). Much of this, again, is correct; but it should never be forgotten that in general the secondary and tertiary sexual characters of one sex occur very frequently in the opposite one. They are indications of hermaphroditism, but are not attended by any change of sexual object in the direction of inversion.

Psychical hermaphroditism would gain substance if the inversion of the sexual object were at least accompanied by a parallel change-over of the subject's other mental qualities, instincts and character traits into those marking the opposite sex. But it is only in inverted women that character-inversion of this kind can be looked for with any regularity. In men the most complete mental masculinity can be combined with inversion. If the belief in psychical hermaphroditism is to be persisted in, it will be necessary to add that its manifestations in various spheres show only slight signs of being mutually determined. Moreover the same is true of somatic hermaphroditism: according to Halban (1903),[11] occurrences of individual atrophied organs and of secondary sexual characters are to a considerable extent independent of one another.

The theory of bisexuality has been expressed in its crudest form by a spokesman of the male inverts: 'a feminine brain in a masculine body'. But we are ignorant of what characterizes a feminine brain. There is neither need nor justification for replacing the psychological problem by the anatomical one. Krafft-Ebing's attempted explanation seems to be more exactly framed than that of Ulrichs but does not differ from it in essentials. According to Krafft-Ebing (1895, 5), every individual's bisexual disposition endows him with masculine and feminine brain centres as well as

[10]For the most recent descriptions of somatic hermaphroditism, see Taruffi (1903), and numerous papers by Neugebauer in various volumes of the *Jahrbuch für sexuelle Zwischenstufen*.

[11]His paper includes a bibliography of the subject.

with somatic organs of sex; these centres develop only at puberty, for the most part under the influence of the sex-gland, which is independent of them in the original disposition. But what has just been said of masculine and feminine brains applies equally to masculine and feminine 'centres'; and incidentally we have not even any grounds for assuming that certain areas of the brain ('centres') are set aside for the functions of sex, as is the case, for instance, with those of speech.[12]

[12]It appears (from a bibliography given in the sixth volume of the *Fahrbuch für sexuelle Zwischenstufen*) that E. Gley was the first writer to suggest bisexuality as an explanation of inversion. As long ago as in January, 1884, he published a paper, 'Les aberrations de l'instinct sexuel', in the *Revue Philosophique*. It is, moreover, noteworthy that the majority of authors who derive inversion from bisexuality bring forward that factor not only in the case of inverts, but also for all those who have grown up to be normal, and that, as a logical consequence, they regard inversion as the result of a disturbance in development. Chevalier (1893) already writes in this sense. Krafft-Ebing (1895, 10) remarks that there are a great number of observations 'which prove at least the virtual persistence of this second centre (that of the subordinated sex)'. A Dr. Arduin (1900) asserts that 'there are masculine and feminine elements in every human being (cf. Hirschfeld, 1899); but one set of these—according to the sex of the person in question—is incomparably more strongly developed than the other, so far as heterosexual individuals are concerned. . . .' Herman (1903) is convinced that 'masculine elements and characteristics are present in every woman and feminine ones in every man', etc. [*Added* 1910:] Fliess (1906) subsequently claimed the idea of bisexuality (in the sense of *duality of sex*) as his own. [*Added* 1924:] In lay circles the hypothesis of human bisexuality is regarded as being due to O. Weininger, the philosopher, who died at an early age, and who made the idea the basis of a somewhat unbalanced book (1903). The particulars which I have enumerated above will be sufficient to show how little justification there is for the claim.

[Freud's own realization of the importance of bisexuality owed much to Fliess (cf. p. 86 *n*.), and his forgetfulness of this fact on one occasion provided him with an example in his *Psychopathology of Everyday Life*, 1901*b*, Chapter VII (11). He did not, however, accept Fliess's view that bisexuality provided the explanation of repression. See Freud's discussion of this in 'A Child is Being Beaten' (1919*e*, half-way through Section VI). The whole question is gone into in detail by Kris in Section IV of his introduction to the Fliess correspondence (Freud, 1950*a*).].

Nevertheless, two things emerge from these discussions. In the first place, a bisexual disposition is somehow concerned in inversion, though we do not know in what that disposition consists, beyond anatomical structure. And secondly, we have to deal with disturbances that affect the sexual instinct in the course of its development.

Sexual Object of Inverts

The theory of psychical hermaphroditism presupposes that the sexual object of an invert is the opposite of that of a normal person. An inverted man, it holds, is like a woman in being subject to the charm that proceeds from masculine attributes both physical and mental: he feels he is a woman in search of a man.

But however well this applies to quite a number of inverts, it is, nevertheless, far from revealing a universal characteristic of inversion. There can be no doubt that a large proportion of male inverts retain the mental quality of masculinity, that they possess relatively few of the secondary characters of the opposite sex and that what they look for in their sexual object are in fact feminine mental traits. If this were not so, how would it be possible to explain the fact that male prostitutes who offer themselves to inverts—to-day just as they did in ancient times—imitate women in all the externals of their clothing and behaviour? Such imitation would otherwise inevitably clash with the ideal of the inverts. It is clear that in Greece, where the most masculine men were numbered among the inverts, what excited a man's love was not the *masculine* character of a boy, but his physical resemblance to a woman as well as his feminine mental qualities—his shyness, his modesty and his need for instruction and assistance. As soon as the boy became a man he ceased to be a sexual object for men and himself, perhaps, became a lover of boys. In this instance, therefore, as in many others, the sexual object is not someone of the same sex but someone who combines the characters of both sexes; there is, as it were, a compromise between an impulse that seeks for a man and one that seeks for a woman, while it remains a paramount condition that the object's body (i.e. genitals) shall be masculine. Thus the sexual object is a kind of reflection of the subject's own bisexual nature.[13]

The position in the case of women is less ambiguous; for among them the active inverts exhibit masculine characteristics, both physical and mental, with peculiar frequency and look for femininity in their sexual objects—though here again a closer knowledge of the facts might reveal greater variety.

---

[13][This last sentence was added in 1915.—*Footnote added* 1910:] It is true that psycho-analysis has not yet produced a complete explanation of the origin of inversion; nevertheless, it has discovered the psychical mechanism of its development, and has made essential contributions to the statement of the problem involved. In all the cases we have examined we have established the fact that the future inverts, in the earliest years of their childhood, pass through a phase of very intense but short-lived fixation to a woman (usually their mother), and that, after leaving this behind, they identify themselves with a woman and take *themselves* as their sexual object. That is to say, they proceed from a narcissistic basis, and look for a young man who resembles themselves and whom *they* may love as their mother loved *them*. Moreover, we have frequently found that alleged inverts have been by no means insusceptible to the charms of women, but have continually transposed the excitation aroused by women on to a male object. They have thus repeated all through their lives the mechanism by which their inversion arose. Their compulsive longing for men has turned out to be determined by their ceaseless flight from women.

[At this point the footnote proceeded as follows in the 1910 edition only: 'It must, however, be borne in mind that hitherto only a single type of invert has been submitted to psycho-analysis—persons whose sexual activity is in general stunted and the residue of which is manifested as inversion. The problem of inversion is a highly complex one and includes very various types of sexual activity and development. A strict conceptual distinction should be drawn between different cases of inversion according to whether the sexual character of the *object* or that of the *subject* has been inverted.']

[*Added* 1915:] Psycho-analytic research is most decidedly opposed to any attempt at separating off homosexuals from the rest of mankind as a group of a special character. By studying sexual excitations other than those that are manifestly displayed, it has found that all human beings are capable of making a homosexual object-choice and have in fact made one in their unconscious. Indeed, libidinal attachments to persons of the same sex play no less a part as factors in normal mental life, and a greater part as a motive force for illness, than do similar attachments to the opposite sex. On the contrary, psycho-analysis considers that a choice of an object independently of its sex—freedom to range equally over male and female objects—as it is found in childhood, in primitive states of society and early periods of history, is the original basis from which, as a result of restriction in one direction or the other, both the normal and the inverted types develop. Thus from the point of view of psycho-analysis the exclusive sexual interest felt by men for women is also a problem that needs elucidating and is not a self-evident fact based upon an attraction that is ultimately of a chemical nature. A person's final sexual attitude is not decided until after puberty and is the result of a number of factors, not all of which are yet known; some are of a constitutional nature but others are accidental. No doubt a few of these factors may happen to carry so much weight that they influence the result in their sense. But in general the multiplicity of determining factors is reflected in the variety of manifest sexual attitudes in which they find their issue in mankind. In inverted types, a predominance of archaic constitutions and primitive psychical mechanisms is regularly to be found. Their most essential characteristics seem to be a coming into operation of narcissistic object-choice and a retention of the erotic significance of the anal zone. There is nothing to be gained, however, by separating the most extreme types of inversion from the rest on the basis of constitutional peculiarities of that kind. What we find as an apparently sufficient explanation of these types can be equally shown to be present, though less strongly, in the constitution of transitional types and of those whose manifest attitude is normal. The differences in the end-products may be of a qualitative nature, but analysis shows that the differences between their determinants are only quantitative. Among the accidental factors that influence object-choice we have found that frustration (in the form of an early deterrence, by fear, from sexual activity) deserves attention, and we have observed that the presence of both parents plays an important part. The absence of a strong father in childhood not infrequently favours the occurrence of inversion. Finally, it may be insisted that the concept of inversion in respect of the sexual object should be sharply distinguished from that of the occurrence in the subject of a mixture of sexual characters. In the relation between these two factors, too, a certain degree of reciprocal independence is unmistakably present.

[*Added* 1920:] Ferenczi (1914) has brought forward a number of interesting points on the subject of inversion. He

(cont.)

Sexual Aim of Inverts

The important fact to bear in mind is that no one single aim can be laid down as applying in cases of inversion. Among men, intercourse *per anum* by no means coincides with inversion; masturbation is quite as frequently their exclusive aim, and it is even true that restrictions of sexual aim—to the point of its being limited to simple outpourings of emotion—are commoner among them than among heterosexual lovers. Among women, too, the sexual aims of inverts are various: there seems to be a special preference for contact with the mucous membrane of the mouth.

Conclusion

It will be seen that we are not in a position to base a satisfactory explanation of the origin of inversion upon the material at present before us. Neverthe-less our investigation has put us in possession of a piece of knowledge which may turn out to be of greater importance to us than the solution of that problem. It has been brought to our notice that we have been in the habit of regarding the connection between the sexual instinct and the sexual object as more intimate than it in fact is. Experience of the cases that are considered abnormal has shown us that in them the sexual instinct and the sexual object are merely soldered together—a fact which we have been in danger of overlooking in consequence of the uniformity of the normal picture, where the object appears to form part and parcel of the instinct. We are thus warned to loosen the bond that exists in our thoughts between instinct and object. It seems probable that the sexual instinct is in the first instance independent of its object; nor is its origin likely to be due to its object's attractions.

---

rightly protests that, because they have in common the symptom of inversion, a large number of conditions, which are very different from one another and which are of unequal importance both in organic and psychical respects, have been thrown together under the name of 'homosexuality' (or, to follow him in giving it a better name, 'homo-erotism'). He insists that a sharp distinction should at least be made between two types: 'subject homo-erotics', who feel and behave like women, and 'object homo-erotics', who are completely masculine and who have merely exchanged a female for a male object. The first of these two types he recognizes as true 'sexual intermediates' in Hirschfeld's sense of the word; the second he describes, less happily, as obsessional neurotics. According to him, it is only in the case of object homo-erotics that there is any question of their struggling against their inclination to inversion or of the possibility of their being influenced psychologically. While granting the existence of these two types, we may add that there are many people in whom a certain quantity of subject homo-erotism is found in combination with a proportion of object homo-erotism.

During the last few years work carried out by biologists, notably by Steinach, has thrown a strong light on the organic determinants of homo-erotism and of sexual characters in general. By carrying out experimental castration and subsequently grafting the sex-glands of the opposite sex, it was possible in the case of various species of mammals to transform a male into a female and vice versa. The transformation affected more or less completely both the somatic sexual characters and the psychosexual attitude (that is, both subject and object erotism). It appeared that the vehicle of the force which thus acted as a sex-determinant was not the part of the sex-gland which forms the sex-cells but what is known as its interstitial tissue (the 'puberty-gland'). In one case this transformation of sex was actually effected in a man who had lost his tests owing to tuberculosis. In his sexual life he behaved in a feminine manner, as a passive homosexual, and exhibited very clearly-marked feminine sexual characters of a secondary kind (e.g. in regard to growth of hair and beard and deposits of fat on the breasts and hips). After an undescended testis from another male patient had been grafted into him, he began to behave in a masculine manner and to direct his libido towards women in a normal way. Simultaneously his somatic feminine characters disappeared. (Lipschütz, 1919, 356–7.)

It would be unjustifiable to assert that these interesting experiments put the theory of inversion on a new basis, and it would be hasty to expect them to offer a universal means of 'curing' homosexuality. Fliess has rightly insisted that these experimental findings do not invalidate the theory of the general bisexual disposition of the higher animals. On the contrary, it seems to me probable that further research of a similar kind will produce a direct confirmation of this presumption of bisexuality.

(B) Sexually Immature Persons and Animals as Sexual Objects

People whose sexual objects belong to the normally inappropriate sex—that is, inverts—strike the observer as a collection of individuals who may be quite sound in other respects. On the other hand, cases in which sexually immature persons (children) are chosen as sexual objects are instantly judged as sporadic aberrations. It is only exceptionally that children are the exclusive sexual objects in such a case. They usually come to play that part when someone who is cowardly or has become impotent adopts them as a substitute, or when an urgent instinct (one which will not allow of postponement) cannot at the moment get possession of any more appropriate object. Nevertheless, a light is thrown on the nature of the sexual instinct by the fact that it permits of so much variation in its objects and such a cheapening of them—which hunger, with its far more energetic retention of its objects, would only permit in the most extreme instances. A similar consideration applies to sexual intercourse with animals, which is by no means rare, especially among country people, and in which sexual attraction seems to override the barriers of species.

One would be glad on aesthetic grounds to be able to ascribe these and other severe aberrations of the sexual instinct to insanity; but that cannot be done. Experience shows that disturbances of the sexual instinct among the insane do not differ from those that occur among the healthy and in whole races or occupations. Thus the sexual abuse of children is found with uncanny frequency among school teachers and child attendants, simply because they have the best opportunity for it. The insane merely exhibit any such aberration to an intensified degree; or, what is particularly significant, it may become exclusive and replace normal sexual satisfaction entirely.

The very remarkable relation which thus holds between sexual variations and the descending scale from health to insanity gives us plenty of material for thought. I am inclined to believe that it may be explained by the fact that the impulses of sexual life are among those which, even normally, are the least controlled by the higher activities of the mind. In my experience anyone who is in any way, whether socially or ethically, abnormal mentally is invariably abnormal also in his sexual life. But many people are abnormal in their sexual life who in every other respect approximate to the average, and have, along with the rest, passed through the process of human cultural development, in which sexuality remains the weak spot.

The most general conclusion that follows from all these discussions seems, however, to be this. Under a great number of conditions and in surprisingly numerous individuals, the nature and importance of the sexual object recedes into the back-ground. What is essential and constant in the sexual instinct is something else.[14]

(2) Deviations in Respect of the Sexual Aim

The normal sexual aim is regarded as being the union of the genitals in the act known as copulation, which leads to a release of the sexual tension and a temporary extinction of the sexual instinct—a satisfaction analogous to the sating of hunger. But even in the most normal sexual process we may detect rudiments which, if they had devel-

---

[14][*Footnote added* 1910:] The most striking distinction between the erotic life of antiquity and our own no doubt lies in the fact that the ancients laid the stress upon the instinct itself, whereas we emphasize its object. The ancients glorified the instinct and were prepared on its account to honour even an inferior object; while we despise the instinctual activity in itself, and find excuses for it only in the merits of the object.

oped, would have led to the deviations described as 'perversions'. For there are certain intermediate relations to the sexual object, such as touching and looking at it, which lie on the road towards copulation and are recognized as being preliminary sexual aims. On the one hand these activities are themselves accompanied by pleasure, and on the other hand they intensify the excitation, which should persist until the final sexual aim is attained. Moreover, the kiss, one particular contact of this kind, between the mucous membrane of the lips of the two people concerned, is held in high sexual esteem among many nations (including the most highly civilized ones), in spite of the fact that the parts of the body involved do not form part of the sexual apparatus but constitute the entrance to the digestive tract. Here, then, are factors which provide a point of contact between the perversions and normal sexual life and which can also serve as a basis for their classification. Perversions are sexual activities which either (*a*) extend, in an anatomical sense, beyond the regions of the body that are designed for sexual union, or (*b*) linger over the intermediate relations to the sexual object which should normally be traversed rapidly on the path towards the final sexual aim.

(A) Anatomical Extensions

Overvaluation of the Sexual Object

It is only in the rarest instances that the psychical valuation that is set on the sexual object, as being the goal of the sexual instinct, stops short at its genitals. The appreciation extends to the whole body of the sexual object and tends to involve every sensation derived from it. The same over-valuation spreads over into the psychological sphere: the subject becomes, as it were, intellectually infatuated (that is, his powers of judgement are weakened) by the mental achievements and perfections of the sexual object and he submits to the latter's

judgements with credulity. Thus the credulity of love becomes an important, if not the most fundamental, source of *authority*.[15]

This sexual overvaluation is something that cannot be easily reconciled with a restriction of the sexual aim to union of the actual genitals and it helps to turn activities connected with other parts of the body into sexual aims.[16]

The significance of the factor of sexual overvaluation can be best studied in men, for their erotic life alone has become accessible to research. That of women—partly owing to the stunting effect of civilized conditions and partly owing to their con-

---

[15] In this connection I cannot help recalling the credulous submissiveness shown by a hypnotized subject towards his hypnotist. This leads me to suspect that the essence of hypnosis lies in an unconscious fixation of the subject's libido to the figure of the hypnotist, through the medium of the masochistic components of the sexual instinct. [*Added* 1910:] Ferenczi (1909) has brought this characteristic of suggestibility into relation with the 'parental complex'.—[The relation of the subject to the hypnotist was discussed by Freud much later, in Chapter VIII of his *Group Psychology* (1921c). See also 1905b, *S.E.*, 7, 294 ff.]

[16] [In the editions earlier than 1920 this paragraph ended with the further sentence: 'The emergence of these extremely various anatomical extensions clearly implies a need for variation, and this has been described by Hoche as "craving for stimulation".' The first two sentences of the footnote which follows were added in 1915, before which date it had begun with the sentence: 'Further consideration leads me to conclude that I. Bloch has over-estimated the theoretical importance of the factor of craving for stimulation.' The whole footnote and the paragraph in the text above were recast in their present form in 1920:] It must be pointed out, however, that sexual overvaluation is not developed in the case of *every* mechanism of object-choice. We shall become acquainted later on with another and more direct explanation of the sexual role assumed by the other parts of the body. The factor of 'craving for stimulation' has been put forward by Hoche and Bloch as an explanation of the extension of sexual interest to parts of the body other than the genitals; but it does not seem to me to deserve such an important place. The various channels along which the libido passes are related to each other from the very first like inter-communicating pipes, and we must take the phenomenon of collateral flow into account.

ventional secretiveness and insincerity—is still veiled in an impenetrable obscurity.[17]

Sexual Use of the Mucous Membrane of the Lips and Mouth

The use of the mouth as a sexual organ is regarded as a perversion if the lips (or tongue) of one person are brought into contact with the genitals of another, but not if the mucous membranes of the lips of both of them come together. This exception is the point of contact with what is normal. Those who condemn the other practices (which have no doubt been common among mankind from primaeval times) as being perversions, are giving way to an unmistakable feeling of *disgust*, which protects them from accepting sexual aims of the kind. The limits of such disgust are, however, often purely conventional: a man who will kiss a pretty girl's lips passionately, may perhaps be disgusted at the idea of using her tooth-brush, though there are no grounds for supposing that his own oral cavity, for which he feels no disgust, is any cleaner than the girl's. Here, then, our attention is drawn to the factor of disgust, which interferes with the libidinal over-valuation of the sexual object but can in turn be overridden by libido. Disgust seems to be one of the forces which have led to a restriction of the sexual aim. These forces do not as a rule extend to the genitals themselves. But there is no doubt that the genitals of the opposite sex can in themselves be an object of disgust and that such an attitude is one of the characteristics of all hysterics, and especially of hysterical women. The sexual instinct in its strength enjoys overriding this disgust.

Sexual Use of the Anal Orifice

Where the anus is concerned it becomes still clearer that it is disgust which stamps that sexual aim as a perversion. I hope, however, I shall not be accused of partisanship when I assert that people who try to account for this disgust by saying that the organ in question serves the function of excretion and comes in contact with excrement—a thing which is disgusting in itself—are not much more to the point than hysterical girls who account for their disgust at the male genital by saying that it serves to void urine.

The playing of a sexual part by the mucous membrane of the anus is by no means limited to intercourse between men: preference for it is in no way characteristic of inverted feeling. On the contrary, it seems that *paedicalio* with a male owes its origin to an analogy with a similar act performed with a woman; while mutual masturbation is the sexual aim most often found in intercourse between inverts.

Significance of Other Regions of the Body

The extension of sexual interest to other regions of the body, with all its variations, offers us nothing that is new in principle; it adds nothing to our knowledge of the sexual instinct, which merely proclaims its intention in this way of getting possession of the sexual object in every possible direction. But these anatomical extensions inform us that, besides sexual overvaluation, there is a second factor at work which is strange to popular knowledge. Certain regions of the body, such as the mucous membrane of the mouth and anus, which are constantly appearing in these practices, seem, as it were, to be claiming that they should themselves be regarded and treated as genitals. We shall learn later that this claim is justified by the history of the development of the sexual instinct and that it is fulfilled in the symptomatology of certain pathological states.

Unsuitable Substitutes for the Sexual Object—Fetishism

There are some cases which are quite specially remarkable—those in which the normal sexual

---

[17][*Footnote added* 1920:] In typical cases women fail to exhibit any sexual overvaluation towards men; but they scarcely ever fail to do so towards their own children.

object is replaced by another which bears some relation to it, but is entirely unsuited to serve the normal sexual aim. From the point of view of classification, we should no doubt have done better to have mentioned this highly interesting group of aberrations of the sexual instinct among the deviations in respect of the sexual *object*. But we have postponed their mention till we could become acquainted with the factor of sexual overvaluation, on which these phenomena, being connected with an abandonment of the sexual aim, are dependent.

What is substituted for the sexual object is some part of the body (such as the foot or hair) which is in general very inappropriate for sexual purposes, or some inanimate object which bears an assignable relation to the person whom it replaces and preferably to that person's sexuality (e.g. a piece of clothing or underlinen). Such substitutes are with some justice likened to the fetishes in which savages believe that their gods are embodied.

A transition to those cases of fetishism in which the sexual aim, whether normal or perverse, is entirely abandoned is afforded by other cases in which the sexual object is required to fulfil a fetishistic condition—such as the possession of some particular hair-colouring or clothing, or even some bodily defect—if the sexual aim is to be attained. No other variation of the sexual instinct that borders on the pathological can lay so much claim to our interest as this one, such is the peculiarity of the phenomena to which it gives rise. Some degree of diminution in the urge towards the normal sexual aim (an executive weakness of the sexual apparatus) seems to be a necessary precondition in every case.[18] The point of contact with the normal is provided by the psychologically essential overvaluation of the sexual object, which inevitably extends to everything that is associated with it. A certain degree of fetishism is thus habitually present in normal love, especially in those stages of it in which the normal sexual aim seems unattainable or its fulfilment prevented:

> Schaff' mir ein Halstuch von ihrer Brust,
> Ein Strumpf band meiner Liebeslust![19]

The situation only becomes pathological when the longing for the fetish passes beyond the point of being merely a necessary condition attached to the sexual object and actually *takes the place* of the normal aim, and, further, when the fetish becomes detached from a particular individual and becomes the *sole* sexual object. These are, indeed, the general conditions under which mere variations of the sexual instinct pass over into pathological aberrations.

Binet (1888) was the first to maintain (what has since been confirmed by a quantity of evidence) that the choice of a fetish is an after-effect of some sexual impression, received as a rule in early childhood. (This may be brought into line with the proverbial durability of first loves: *on revient toujours á ses premiers amours.*) This derivation is particularly obvious in cases where there is merely a fetishistic condition attached to the sexual object. We shall come across the importance of early sexual impressions again in another connection [p. 108].[20]

---

[18][*Footnote added* 1915:] This weakness would represent the *constitutional* precondition. Psycho-analysis has found that the phenomenon can also be *accidentally* determined, by the occurrence of an early deterrence from sexual activity owing to fear, which may divert the subject from the normal sexual aim and encourage him to seek a substitute for it.

[19][Get me a kerchief from her breast,

A garter that her knee has pressed.

Goethe, *Faust*, Part I, Scene 7. (*Trans.* Bayard Taylor.)]

[20][*Footnote added* 1920:] Deeper-going psycho-analytic research has raised a just criticism of Binet's assertion. All the observations dealing with this point have recorded a first meeting with the fetish at which it already aroused sexual interest without there being anything in the accompanying circumstances to explain the fact. Moreover, all of these 'early' sexual impressions relate to a time after the age of five or six, whereas psycho-analysis makes it doubtful whether fresh pathological fixations can occur so late as this. The true explanation is that behind the first recollection of the fetish's ap-

In other cases the replacement of the object by a fetish is determined by a symbolic connection of thought, of which the person concerned is usually not conscious. It is not always possible to trace the course of these connections with certainty. (The foot, for instance, is an age-old sexual symbol which occurs even in mythology;[21] no doubt the part played by fur as a fetish owes its origin to an association with the hair of the *mons Veneris*.) None the less even symbolism such as this is not always unrelated to sexual experiences in childhood.[22]

---

pearance there lies a submerged and forgotten phase of sexual development. The fetish, like a 'screen-memory', represents this phase and is thus a remnant and precipitate of it. The fact that this early infantile phase turns in the direction of fetishism, as well as the choice of the fetish itself, are constitutionally determined.

[21][*Footnote added* 1910:] The shoe or slipper is a corresponding symbol of the *female* genitals.

[22][*Footnote added* 1910:] Psycho-analysis has cleared up one of the remaining gaps in our understanding of fetishism. It has shown the importance, as regards the choice of a fetish, of a coprophilic pleasure in smelling which has disappeared owing to repression. Both the feet and the hair are objects with a strong smell which have been exalted into fetishes after the olfactory sensation has become unpleasurable and been abandoned. Accordingly, in the perversion that corresponds to foot-fetishism, it is only dirty and evil-smelling feet that become sexual objects. Another factor that helps towards explaining the fetishistic preference for the foot is to be found among the sexual theories of children (see below p. 61): the foot represents a woman's penis, the absence of which is deeply felt. [*Added* 1915:] In a number of cases of foot-fetishism it has been possible to show that the scopophilic instinct, seeking to reach its object (originally the genitals) from underneath, was brought to a halt in its pathway by prohibition and repression. For that reason it became attached to a fetish in the form of a foot or shoe, the female genitals (in accordance with the expectations of childhood) being imagined as male ones.—[The importance of the repression of pleasure in smell had been indicated by Freud in two letters to Fliess of January 11 and November 14, 1897 (Freud, 1950a, Letters 55 and 75). He returned to the subject at the end of his analysis of the 'Rat Man' (Freud, 1909d), and discussed it at considerable length in two long footnotes to Chapter IV of *Civilization and Its Discontents* (1930a). The topic of fetishism was further considered in Freud's paper on that subject

(B) Fixations of Preliminary Sexual Aims

Appearance of New Aims

Every external or internal factor that hinders or postpones the attainment of the normal sexual aim (such as impotence, the high price of the sexual object or the danger of the sexual act) will evidently lend support to the tendency to linger over the preparatory activities and to turn them into new sexual aims that can take the place of the normal one. Attentive examination always shows that even what seem to be the strangest of these new aims are already hinted at in the normal sexual process.

Touching and Looking

A certain amount of touching is indispensable (at all events among human beings) before the normal sexual aim can be attained. And everyone knows what a source of pleasure on the one hand and what an influx of fresh excitation on the other is afforded by tactile sensations of the skin of the sexual object. So that lingering over the stage of touching can scarcely be counted a perversion, provided that in the long run the sexual act is carried further.

The same holds true of seeing—an activity that is ultimately derived from touching. Visual impressions remain the most frequent pathway along which libidinal excitation is aroused; indeed, natural selection counts upon the accessibility of this pathway—if such a teleological form of statement is permissible[23]—when it encourages the development of beauty in the sexual object. The progressive concealment of the body which goes along with civilization keeps sexual curiosity awake. This

---

(1927e) and again still later in a posthumously published fragment on the splitting of the ego (1940e[1938]) and at the end of Chapter VIII of his *Outline of Psycho-Analysis* (1940a[1938]).]

[23][The words in this parenthesis were added in 1915. Cf. footnote 1, p. 54.]

curiosity seeks to complete the sexual object by revealing its hidden parts. It can, however, be diverted ('sublimated') in the direction of art, if its interest can be shifted away from the genitals on to the shape of the body as a whole.[24] It is usual for most normal people to linger to some extent over the intermediate sexual aim of a looking that has a sexual tinge to it; indeed, this offers them a possibility of directing some proportion of their libido on to higher artistic aims. On the other hand, this pleasure in looking [scopophilia] becomes a perversion (a) if it is restricted exclusively to the genitals, or (b) if it is connected with the overriding of disgust (as in the case of *voyeurs* or people who look on at excretory functions), or (c) if, instead of being *preparatory* to the normal sexual aim, it supplants it. This last is markedly true of exhibitionists, who, if I may trust the findings of several analyses,[25] exhibit their own genitals in order to obtain a reciprocal view of the genitals of the other person.[26]

In the perversions which are directed towards looking and being looked at, we come across a very remarkable characteristic with which we shall be still more intensely concerned in the aberration that we shall consider next: in these perversions the sexual aim occurs in two forms, an *active* and a *passive* one.

The force which opposes scopophilia, but which may be overridden by it (in a manner parallel to what we have previously seen in the case of disgust), is *shame*.

Sadism and Masochism

The most common and the most significant of all the perversions—the desire to inflict pain upon the sexual object, and its reverse—received from Krafft-Ebing the names of 'sadism' and 'masochism' for its active and passive forms respectively. Other writers [e.g. Schrenck-Notzing (1899)] have preferred the narrower term 'algolagnia'. This emphasizes the pleasure in *pain*, the cruelty; whereas the names chosen by Krafft-Ebing bring into prominence the pleasure in any form of humiliation or subjection.

As regards active algolagnia, sadism, the roots are easy to detect in the normal. The sexuality of most male human beings contains an element of *aggressiveness*—a desire to subjugate; the biological significance of it seems to lie in the need for overcoming the resistance of the sexual object by means other than the process of wooing. Thus sadism would correspond to an aggressive component of the sexual instinct which has become independent and exaggerated and, by displacement, has usurped the leading position.[27]

In ordinary speech the connotation of sadism oscillates between, on the one hand, cases merely

---

[24][This seems to be Freud's first published use of the term 'sublimate', though it occurs as early as May 2, 1897, in the Fliess correspondence (Freud, 1950a, Letter 61). It also appears in the 'Dora' case history, 1905e, actually published later than the present work (*S.E.*, 7, pp. 50 and 116) though drafted in 1901. The concept is further discussed below on p. 44.—*Footnote added* 1915:] There is to my mind no doubt that the concept of 'beautiful' has its roots in sexual excitation and that its original meaning was 'sexually stimulating'. [There is an allusion in the original to the fact that the German word '*Reiz*' is commonly used both as the technical term for 'stimulus' and, in ordinary language, as an equivalent to the English 'charm' or 'attraction'.] This is related to the fact that we never regard the genitals themselves, which produce the strongest sexual excitation, as really 'beautiful'.

[25][In the editions before 1924 this read 'of a single analysis']

[26][*Footnote added* 1920:] Under analysis, these perversions—and indeed most others—reveal a surprising variety of motives and determinants. The compulsion to exhibit, for instance, is also closely dependent on the castration complex: it is a means of constantly insisting upon the integrity of the subject's own (male) genitals and it reiterates his infantile satisfaction at the absence of a penis in those of women. [Cf. p. 61.]

[27][In the editions of 1905 and 1910 the following two sentences appeared in the text at this point: 'One at least of the roots of masochism can be inferred with equal certainty. It arises from sexual overvaluation as a necessary psychical consequence of the choice of a sexual object.' From 1915 onwards these sentences were omitted and the next two paragraphs were inserted in their place.]

characterized by an active or violent attitude to the sexual object, and, on the other hand, cases in which satisfaction is entirely conditional on the humiliation and maltreatment of the object. Strictly speaking, it is only this last extreme instance which deserves to be described as a perversion.

Similarly, the term masochism comprises any passive attitude towards sexual life and the sexual object, the extreme instance of which appears to be that in which satisfaction is conditional upon suffering physical or mental pain at the hands of the sexual object. Masochism, in the form of a perversion, seems to be further removed from the normal sexual aim than its counterpart; it may be doubted at first whether it can ever occur as a primary phenomenon or whether, on the contrary, it may not invariably arise from a transformation of sadism.[28] It can often be shown that masochism is nothing more than an extension of sadism turned round upon the subject's own self, which thus, to begin with, takes the place of the sexual object. Clinical analysis of extreme cases of masochistic perversion show that a great number of factors (such as the castration complex and the sense of guilt) have combined to exaggerate and fixate the original passive sexual attitude.

Pain, which is overridden in such cases, thus falls into line with disgust and shame as a force that stands in opposition and resistance to the libido.[29]

Sadism and masochism occupy a special position among the perversions, since the contrast between activity and passivity which lies behind them is among the universal characteristics of sexual life.

The history of human civilization shows beyond any doubt that there is an intimate connection between cruelty and the sexual instinct; but nothing has been done towards explaining the connection, apart from laying emphasis on the aggressive factor in the libido. According to some authorities this aggressive element of the sexual instinct is in reality a relic of cannibalistic desires—that is, it is a contribution derived from the apparatus for obtaining mastery, which is concerned with the satisfaction of the other and, ontogenetically, the older of the great instinctual needs.[30] It has also been maintained that every pain contains in itself the possibility of a feeling of pleasure. All that need be said is that no satisfactory explanation of this perversion has been put forward and that it seems possible that a number of mental impulses are combined in it to produce a single resultant.[31]

But the most remarkable feature of this perversion is that its active and passive forms are habitually found to occur together in the same individual. A person who feels pleasure in producing pain in someone else in a sexual relationship is also capable of enjoying as pleasure any pain which he may himself derive from sexual relations. A sadist is always at the same time a masochist, although the active or the passive aspect of the perversion may be the more strongly developed in

---

[28][*Footnote added* 1924:] My opinion of masochism has been to a large extent altered by later reflection, based upon certain hypotheses as to the structure of the apparatus of the mind and the classes of instincts operating in it. I have been led to distinguish a primary or *erotogenic* masochism, out of which two later forms, *feminine* and *moral* masochism, have developed. Sadism which cannot find employment in actual life is turned round upon the subject's own self and so produces a *secondary* masochism, which is superadded to the primary kind. (Cf. Freud, 1924c.)

[29][This short paragraph was in the first edition (1905), but the last two, as well as the next one, were only added in 1915.]

[30][*Footnote added* 1915:] Cf. my remarks below [p.64] on the pregenital phases of sexual development, which confirm this view.

[31][*Footnote added* 1924:] The enquiry mentioned above [in footnote 2] has led me to assign a peculiar position, based upon the origin of the instincts, to the pair of opposites constituted by sadism and masochism, and to place them outside the class of the remaining 'perversions'.

him and may represent his predominant sexual activity.[32]

We find, then, that certain among the impulses to perversion occur regularly as pairs of opposites; and this, taken in conjunction with material which will be brought forward later, has a high theoretical significance.[33] It is, moreover, a suggestive fact that the existence of the pair of opposites formed by sadism and masochism cannot be attributed merely to the element of aggressiveness. We should rather be inclined to connect the simultaneous presence of these opposites with the opposing masculinity and femininity which are combined in bisexuality—a contrast which often has to be replaced in psycho-analysis by that between activity and passivity.[34]

(3) The Perversions in General

Variation and Disease

It is natural that medical men, who first studied perversions in outstanding examples and under special conditions, should have been inclined to regard them, like inversion, as indications of degeneracy or disease. Nevertheless, it is even easier to dispose of that view in this case than in that of inversion. Everyday experience has shown that most of these extensions, or at any rate the less severe of them, are constituents which are rarely absent from the sexual life of healthy people, and are

---

[32]Instead of multiplying the evidence for this statement, I will quote a passage from Havelock Ellis (1913, 119): 'The investigation of histories of sadism and masochism, even those given by Krafft-Ebing (as indeed Colin Scott and Féré have already pointed out), constantly reveals traces of both groups of phenomena in the same individual.'

[33][*Footnote added* 1915:] Cf. my discussion of 'ambivalence' below [p. 65].

[34][The last clause did not occur in the 1905 or 1910 editions. In 1915 the following clause was added: 'a contrast whose significance is reduced in psycho-analysis to that between activity and passivity.' This was replaced in 1924 by the words now appearing in the text.]

judged by them no differently from other intimate events. If circumstances favour such an occurrence, normal people too can substitute a perversion of this kind for the normal sexual aim for quite a time, or can find place for the one alongside the other. No healthy person, it appears, can fail to make some addition that might be called perverse to the normal sexual aim; and the universality of this finding is in itself enough to show how inappropriate it is to use the word perversion as a term of reproach. In the sphere of sexual life we are brought up against peculiar and, indeed, insoluble difficulties as soon as we try to draw a sharp line to distinguish mere variations within the range of what is physiological from pathological symptoms.

Nevertheless, in some of these perversions the quality of the new sexual aim is of a kind to demand special examination. Certain of them are so far removed from the normal in their content that we cannot avoid pronouncing them 'pathological'. This is especially so where (as, for instance, in cases of licking excrement or of intercourse with dead bodies) the sexual instinct goes to astonishing lengths in successfully overriding the resistances of shame, disgust, horror or pain. But even in such cases we should not be too ready to assume that people who act in this way will necessarily turn out to be insane or subject to grave abnormalities of other kinds. Here again we cannot escape from the fact that people whose behaviour is in other respects normal can, under the domination of the most unruly of all the instincts, put themselves in the category of sick persons in the single sphere of sexual life. On the other hand, manifest abnormality in the other relations of life can invariably be shown to have a background of abnormal sexual conduct.

In the majority of instances the pathological character in a perversion is found to lie not in the *content* of the new sexual aim but in its relation to the normal. If a perversion, instead of appearing merely *alongside* the normal sexual aim and object, and only when circumstances are unfavourable to *them* and favourable to *it*—if, instead of this, it ousts them completely and takes their place in *all* circumstances—if, in short, a perversion has the characteristics of exclusiveness and fixation—then we shall usually be justified in regarding it as a pathological symptom.

The Mental Factor in the Perversions

It is perhaps in connection precisely with the most repulsive perversions that the mental factor must be regarded as playing its largest part in the transformation of the sexual instinct. It is impossible to deny that in their case a piece of mental work has been performed which, in spite of its horrifying result, is the equivalent of an idealization of the instinct. The omnipotence of love is perhaps never more strongly proved than in such of its aberrations as these. The highest and the lowest are always closest to each other in the sphere of sexuality: 'vom Himmel durch die Welt zur Hölle.'[35]

Two Conclusions

Our study of the perversions has shown us that the sexual instinct has to struggle against certain mental forces which act as resistances, and of which shame and disgust are the most prominent. It is

permissible to suppose that these forces play a part in restraining that instinct within the limits that are regarded as normal; and if they develop in the individual before the sexual instinct has reached its full strength, it is no doubt they that will determine the course of its development.[36]

In the second place we have found that some of the perversions which we have examined are only made intelligible if we assume the convergence of several motive forces. If such perversions admit of analysis, that is, if they can be taken to pieces, then they must be of a composite nature. This gives us a hint that perhaps the sexual instinct itself may be no simple thing, but put together from components which have come apart again in the perversions. If this is so, the clinical observation of these abnormalities will have drawn our attention to amalgamations which have been lost to view in the uniform behaviour of normal people.[37]

---

[35] ['From Heaven, across the world, to Hell.'
  Goethe, *Faust*, Prelude in the Theatre. (*Trans.* Bayard Taylor.) In a letter to Fliess of January 3, 1897 (Freud 1950*a*, Letter 54), Freud suggests the use of this same quotation as the motto for a chapter on 'Sexuality' in a projected volume. This letter was written at a time when he was beginning to turn his attention to the perversions. His first reference to them in the Fliess correspondence dates from January 1, 1896 (Draft K).]

[36] [*Footnote added* 1915:] On the other hand, these forces which act like dams upon sexual development—disgust, shame and morality—must also be regarded as historical precipitates of the external inhibitions to which the sexual instinct has been subjected during the psychogenesis of the human race. We can observe the way in which, in the development of individuals, they arise at the appropriate moment, as though spontaneously, when upbringing and external influence give the signal.

[37] [*Footnote added* 1920:] As regards the origin of the perversions, I will add a word in anticipation of what is to come. There is reason to suppose that, just as in the case of fetishism, abortive beginnings of normal sexual development occur before the perversions become fixated. Analytic investigation has already been able to show in a few cases that perversions are a residue of development towards the Oedipus complex and that after the repression of that complex the components of the sexual instinct which are strongest in the disposition of the individual concerned emerge once more.

chapter twenty-seven

Alexandra Kollontai

Alexandra Kollontai (1872–1952), Russian revolutionary, feminist, and philosopher, was a central figure in bridging the gap between socialist politics and the women's struggle in the early twentieth century. Adopting her own unique Marxist perspective, Kollontai created a vast and diverse body of work, ranging from fiction to revolutionary strategy. There is a persistent adherence throughout her writings to a radical vision of both female and human emancipation. As a revolutionary, Kollontai played an important, yet often controversial, role in the early stages of the creation of the Soviet Union.

Born into a family of aristocratic heritage, Kollontai grew up in a rather turbulent period of tsarist Russian history. At age sixteen, she rebelled against her parents' wishes by refusing to consider an arranged marriage and instead, in 1893, married a man of considerably lower social status. After having a child the following year, Kollontai began teaching workers and became involved in the underground opposition movement. Later in life, Kollontai claimed that her visit to a large textile factory in 1896 decided her fate as a revolutionary, and thereafter she remained a consistent supporter of the workers' movement. In 1898, Kollontai left her family to study Marxist economics in Switzerland, ultimately severing ties with her husband for the rest of her life. Some years later, Kollontai remarked, "The happy existence of housewife and consort were like a 'cage' to me. . . . My sympathies, my interests turned more and more to the Russian workers' revolutionary movement."[1]

Prior to officially joining the Bolsheviks in 1914, Kollontai spent most of her time as an agitator and organizer for various Marxist movements in Russia and Eastern Europe. During this period Kollontai wrote, among much else, the *Social Basis on the Women's Question*, a four hundred-page polemic attacking bourgeois feminism and outlining a socialist approach to the women's movement. In 1917, Kollontai was elected to the Bolshevik Party's Central Committee, and after the October Revolution, she became the only woman in Lenin's government when she was elected Commissioner of Social Welfare. In 1920, Kollontai was appointed director of the *Zhenotdel* (women's department), a post that allowed her to focus her energies on writing and speaking in support of

From *Selected Writings of Alexandra Kollontai*, Lawrence Hill Books, 1977. Reprinted with permission.

working women. After becoming frustrated with the increasingly authoritarian and bureaucratic direction of the Bolshevik Party, Kollontai joined the Workers' Opposition in 1920 and campaigned for democratization and against Lenin's New Economic Policy.

From 1922 to 1923, in the midst of her opposition to the official direction of the party, Kollontai penned a series of articles in the *Molodaya gvardiya*, or "Young Guard," aimed at the working youth of country. "Make Way for Winged Eros: A Letter to Working Youth," the fourth article in the series, began with a challenge: "You ask me, my young friend, what place proletarian ideology gives to love?"[2] This was a question of priorities: the working youth of Soviet Russia were becoming more preoccupied with love than with communal duty. Kollontai's "Letter" was thus constructed around the seeming conflict between duty to one's personal life on the one hand and duty to the demands of the community on the other. The conflict between duty to oneself and one's community is a familiar theme in the history of social philosophy, yet it took on particular immediacy in the early days of the Soviet Republic.

Kollontai saw this conflict as one of opposing ideologies: bourgeois and proletarian. By bourgeois ideology, Kollontai had in mind liberalism. Liberal ideology, perhaps best exemplified in works of John Locke and John Stuart Mill, is primarily concerned, at least rhetorically, with the expansion of individual liberty. Bourgeois liberalism defends a theory of limited government and laissez-faire economics, placing great emphasis on constitutional rights and the protection of private property. In opposition to bourgeois liberalism, proletarian ideology has its roots in the communist and anarchist working people's movements of the nineteenth century. Kollontai saw a fundamental incompatibility between bourgeois liberalism and proletarian communism not only in the political and economic realm, but also in the emotional realm. It is with the conflicting emotional and moral realms that Kollontai was most interested in the "Letter."

Conflicts in the emotional and moral realms, Kollontai argued, were manifest in the "great shift in the way men and women" thought in the early stages of the Russian revolution.[3] During the revolution the "riddle of love," or in other words the "question of the relationships between the sexes," took a backseat to the more immediate political and economic concerns. "Wingless Eros," Kollontai's term for relations based solely on physical satisfaction, reigned over relations based on the fusion of physical and emotional satisfaction characteristic of "winged Eros." Yet, as the title of the "Letter" indicates, "tender-winged Eros has emerged from the shadows and begun to demand his rightful place."[4] Kollontai maintained that as the revolution progresses the "ideology of the working class must pay even greater attention to the significance of love as a factor which can . . . be channeled to the advantage of the collective."[5] It is this innovative contention—that love is not only private but also a social matter—that Kollontai endeavored to demonstrate through historical analysis in the second section of the "Letter."

Kollontai's understanding of historical change had its roots in Karl Marx's historical materialist method. Marx adopted a materialist perspective—the philosophical stance that all reality is essentially material—and combined it with elements of German idealist philosophy, French socialism, and English classical economics in constructing a historical materialist method of examining social change. Kollontai's contention that "[a]s the cultural and economic base of humanity changes, so will love be transformed,"[6] echoed Marx's claim that "[t]he mode of production of material life conditions the social, political and intellectual life process in general."[7] It is through the historical materialist method that Kollontai established love as a historically constituted social force. Elsewhere, Kollontai further emphasized that, contrary to popular belief, all aspects of the social world are subject to change:

> It is only our ignorance that leads us to think that the things we are used to can never change. Nothing could be less true than people saying "as it was, so it shall be." We have only to read how people lived in the past to see that everything is subject to change and that no customs, political organizations or moral principles are fixed and inviolable. . . . That which is in line with the new life should be maintained, while all that is old and outdated . . . should be swept aside.[8]

It was this Marxist understanding of history and related faith in change that provided hope and inspiration for Kollontai's vision of life after the revolution.

Kollontai's beliefs about love and the family were greatly influenced by nineteenth- and early twentieth-century socialist feminism. During this period, feminism was divided generally along two divergent lines of thought: bourgeois and socialist. Bourgeois feminism, popularized mainly in Great Britain and the United States, was directed toward obtaining equal rights and opportunities for women through the removal of political, educational, and professional barriers. Socialist feminism grew out of Marxist and anarchist social thought. Socialist feminism held that the liberation of women from oppression and exploitation could only be achieved as part of the broader human liberation realized through a socialist revolution.

In the creation of her socialist feminism, Kollontai drew heavily from Friedrich Engels and August Bebel. Both Engels and Bebel addressed the origins of female oppression in their analysis of the development of the family. Drawing from their work, Kollontai maintained that marriage relations were marked by three main characteristics: the property basis of marriage created a sense of "spouse as possession"; female inequality promoted the objectification of women; and the individualism of bourgeois society produced a sense of isolation.[9]

Many of Kollontai's contemporaries, most notably the Russian American anarchist feminist Emma Goldman, were also critical of the role of marriage in bourgeois society. In her essay, "Marriage and Love," Goldman claimed, "The popular notion about marriage and love is that they are synonymous, that they spring from the same motives, and cover the same human needs. Like most popular notions this also rests not on actual facts, but on superstition."[10] Kollontai similarly saw marriage as an institution often devoid of love and reflective of broader socioeconomic inequality and oppression: "The bourgeoisie made love and marriage inseparable. In practice, of course, this class has always retreated from its ideal."[11] Kollontai also shared with her anarchist comrade, much to the chagrin of most other Bolsheviks, the belief that human nature was basically "good" and, if freed from institutional and ideological constraints, human beings could live harmoniously and organize social life spontaneously.

Kollontai's ideal vision of love and marriage, developed in the final section of the "Letter," was as a social force that corresponds to the interest of the proletariat. Kollontai adopted a more communal sense of "winged Eros," embracing the complex physical, personal, and social components of love. Just as Marx's vision of communism was to overcome the alienation of labor under capitalism, Kollontai's ideal of love-comradeship was to overcome the alienation of love under bourgeois morality: "Modern love always sins, because it absorbs the thoughts and feelings of 'loving hearts' and isolates the loving pair from the collective. In the future society, such a separation will . . . become superfluous."[12]

Because of her involvement in the Workers' Opposition and libertarian views on love and marriage, Kollontai was essentially banished to a minor diplomatic post in Oslo in 1922. Thereafter, she escaped the Stalinist purges of the more leftist elements of the party and became the Soviet ambassador to Sweden, a post she held to the end of her life. In 1945, Kollontai was nominated for the Nobel Peace Prize in recognition of her lifelong antiwar activism and her part in negotiating peace between Finland and Russia in 1940.

Kollontai died in 1952 in Russia of a heart attack. Although she was largely ignored in her own country, Kollontai remained a source of inspiration to socialist feminists in the West. Her major works include *Finland and Socialism* (1906), *The Social Basis of the Women Question* (1909), *Who Needs War?* (1916), *Communism and the Family* (1919), *Love of the Worker Bees* (1923), and *Autobiography of a Sexually Emancipated Communist Woman* (1926).

MS

QUESTIONS

1. What is the "riddle of love" that Kollontai is interested in?

2. Why has "wingless Eros" characterized relations between the sexes during the revolutionary period?

3. Explain Kollontai's claim: "From the early stages of its social being, humanity has sought to regulate not only sexual relations but love itself."

4. Why does Kollontai claim that love is not only a private force, but a social force as well?

5. Explain Kollontai's contention: "Proletarian ideology cannot accept exclusiveness and 'all embracing love.'"

6. How would you characterize Kollontai's ideal of "love-comradeship?"

ENDNOTES

1. Kollontai is quoted in Clements, p. 324.
2. Kollontai, "Make Way for Winged Eros," p. 276.
3. Ibid.
4. Ibid., p. 278.
5. Ibid., p. 279.
6. Ibid., p. 291.
7. Marx, p. 4.
8. Kollontai, "Communism and the Family," from *Selected Writings of Alexandra Kollontai*, pp. 250–51.
9. Clements, p. 27.
10. Goldman, p. 227.
11. Kollontai, "Make Way for Winged Eros," p. 283.
12. Ibid., p. 290.

SELECTED BIBLIOGRAPHY

Clements, Barbara. "Emancipation through Communism: The Ideology of A. M. Kollontai," *Slavic Review* 32 (June 1973).

Farnsworth, Beatrice. *Aleksandra Kollontai: Socialism, Feminism, and the Bolshevik Revolution.* Stanford, CA: Stanford University Press, 1980.

Farnsworth, Beatrice. "Bolshevism, the Women Question, and Aleksandra Kollontai." *American Historical Review* 81 (April 1976); 292–316.

Goldman, Emma. *Anarchism and Other Essays.* New York: Dover, 1969 (1917).

Kollontai, Alexandra. *Autobiography of a Sexually Emancipated Communist Woman*, trans. Salvator Attanasio, ed. Irving Fetscher. New York: Herder and Herder, 1971.

Kollontai, Alexandra. *Selected Writings of Alexandra Kollontai*, trans., comm., and intro. Alix Holt. New York: W. W. Norton, 1977.

Marx, Karl. "Preface to *A Contribution to the Critique of Political Economy*," from *The Marx-Engels Reader*, trans. and ed. Robert Tucker. New York: W. W. Norton, 1978 (1859).

Porter, Cathy. *Alexandra Kollontai: The Lonely Struggle of the Woman Who Defied Lenin.* New York: Dial Press, 1980.

Make Way for Winged Eros: A Letter to Working Youth

Alexandra Kollontai

LOVE AS A SOCIO-PSYCHOLOGICAL FACTOR

You ask me, my young friend, what place proletarian ideology gives to love? You are concerned by the fact that at the present time young workers are occupied more with love and related questions than with the tremendous tasks of construction which face the workers' republic. It is difficult for me to judge events from a distance, but let us try to find an explanation for this situation, and then it will be easier to answer the first question about the place of love in proletarian ideology.

There can be no doubt that Soviet Russia has entered a new phase of the civil war. The main theatre of struggle is now the front where the two ideologies, the two cultures—the bourgeois and the proletarian—do battle. The incompatibility of these two ideologies is becoming increasingly obvious, and the contradictions between these two fundamentally different cultures are growing more acute. Alongside the victory of communist principles and ideals in the sphere of politics and economics, a revolution in the outlook, emotions and the inner world of working people is inevitably taking place. A new attitude to life, society, work, art and to the rules of living (i.e. morality) can already be observed. The arrangement of sexual relationships is one aspect of these rules of living. Over the five years of the existence of our labour republic, the revolution on this non-military front has been accomplishing a great shift in the way men and women think. The fiercer the battle between the two ideologies, the greater the significance it assumes and the more inevitably it raises new "riddles of life" and new problems to which only the ideology of the working class can give a satisfactory answer.

The "riddle of love" that interests us here is one such problem. This question of the relationships between the sexes is a mystery as old as human society itself. At different levels of historical development mankind has approached the solution of this problem in different ways. The problem remains the same; the keys to its solution change. The keys are fashioned by the different epochs, by the classes in power and by the "spirit" of a particular age (in other words by its culture).

In Russia over the recent years of intense civil war and general dislocation there has been little interest in the nature of the riddle. The men and women of the working classes were in the grip of other emotions, passions and experiences. In those years everyone walked in the shadow of death, and it was being decided whether victory would belong to the revolution and progress or to counter-revolution and reaction. In face of the revolutionary threat, tender-winged Eros fled from the surface of life. There was neither time nor a surplus of inner strength for love's "joys and pains." Such is the law of the preservation of humanity's social and psychological energy. As a whole, this energy is always directed to the most urgent aims of the historical moment. And in Russia, for a time, the biological instinct of reproduction, the natural voice of nature dominated the situation. Men and women came together and men and women parted much more easily and much more simply than before. They came together without great commitment and parted without tears or regret. . . .

The unadorned sexual drive is easily aroused but is soon spent; thus "wingless Eros" consumes less inner strength than "winged Eros", whose love is woven of delicate strands of every kind of emotion. "Wingless Eros" does not make one suffer from sleepless nights, does not sap one's will, and does not entangle the rational workings of the mind. The fighting class could not have fallen under the power of "winged Eros" at a time when the clarion call of revolution was sounding. It would not have been expedient at such a time to waste the inner strength of the members of the collective on experiences that did not directly serve the revolution. Individual sex love, which lies at the heart of the pair marriage, demands a great expenditure of inner energy. The working class was interested not only in economising in terms of material wealth but also in preserving the intellectual and emotional energy of each person. For this reason, at a time of heightened revolutionary struggle, the undemanding instinct of reproduction spontaneously replaced the all-embracing "winged Eros."

But now the picture changes. The Soviet republic and the whole of toiling humanity are entering a period of temporary and comparative calm. The complex task of understanding and assimilating the achievements and gains that have been made is beginning. The proletariat, the creator of new forms of life, must be able to learn from all social and psychological phenomena, grasp the significance of these phenomena and fashion weapons from them for the self-defence of the class. Only when the proletariat has appropriated the laws not only of the creation of material wealth but also of inner, psychological life is it able to advance fully armed to fight the decaying bourgeois world. Only then will toiling humanity prove itself to be the victor, not only on the military and labour front but also on the psychological-cultural front.

Now that the revolution has proved victorious and is in a stronger position, and now that the atmosphere of revolutionary élan has ceased to absorb men and women completely, tender-winged Eros has emerged from the shadows and begun to demand his rightful place. "Wingless Eros" has ceased to satisfy psychological needs. Emotional energy has accumulated and men and women, even of the working class, have not yet learned to use it for the inner life of the collective. This extra energy seeks an outlet in the love-experience. The many-stringed lyre of the god of love drowns the monotonous voice of "wingless Eros." Men and women are now not only united by the momentary satisfaction of the sex instinct but are beginning to experience "love affairs" again, and to know all the sufferings and all the exaltations of love's happiness. . . .

What does this mean? Is this a reactionary step? A symptom of the beginning of the decline of revolutionary creativity? Nothing of the sort! It is time we separated ourselves from the hypocrisy of bourgeois thought. It is time to recognise openly that love is not only a powerful natural factor, a biological force, but also a social factor. Essentially love is a profoundly social emotion. At all stages of human development love has (in different forms, it is true) been an integral part of culture. Even the bourgeoisie, who saw love as a "private matter," was able to channel the expression of love in its class interests. The ideology of the working class must pay even greater attention to the significance of love as a factor which can, like any other psychological or social phenomenon, be channelled to the advantage of the collective. Love is not in the least a "private" matter concerning only the two loving persons: love possesses a uniting element which is valuable to the collective. This is clear from the fact that at all stages of historical development society has established norms defining when and under what conditions love is "legal" (i.e. corresponds to the interests of the given social collective), and when and under what conditions love is sinful and criminal (i.e. contradicts the tasks of the given society).

HISTORICAL NOTES

From the very early stages of its social being, humanity has sought to regulate not only sexual relations but love itself.

In the kinship community, love for one's blood relations was considered the highest virtue. The kinship group would not have approved of a woman sacrificing herself for the sake of a beloved husband; fraternal or sisterly attachment were the most highly regarded feelings. Antigone, who according to the Greek legend risked her life to bury the body of her dead brother, was a heroine in the eyes of her contemporaries. Modern bourgeois society would consider such an action on the part of a sister as highly curious. In the times of tribal rule, when the state was still in its embryonic stage, the love held in greatest respect was the love between two members of the same tribe. In an era when the social collective had only just evolved from the stage of kinship community and was still not firmly established in its new form, it was vitally important that its members were linked by mental and emotional ties. Love-friendship was the most suitable type of tie, since at that time the interests of the collective required the growth and accumulation of contacts not between the marriage pair but between fellow-members of the tribe, between the organisers and defenders of the tribe and state (that is to say, between the men of the tribe, of course; women at that time had no role to play in social life, and there was no talk of friendship among women). "Friendship" was praised and considered far more important than love between man and wife. . . .

The ancient world considered friendship and "loyalty until the grave" to be civic virtues. Love in the modern sense of the word had no place, and hardly attracted the attention either of poets or of writers. The dominant ideology of that time relegated love to the sphere of narrow, personal experiences with which society was not concerned; marriage was based on convenience, not on love. Love was just one among other amusements; it was a luxury which only the citizen who had fulfilled all his obligations to the state could afford. While bourgeois ideology values the "ability to love" provided it confines itself to the limits set down by bourgeois morality, the ancient world did not consider such emotions in its categories of virtues and positive human qualities. The person who accomplished great deeds and risked his life for his friend was considered a hero and his action "most virtuous," while a man risking himself for the sake of a woman he loved would have been reproached or even despised.

The morality of the ancient world, then, did not even recognise the love that inspired men to great deeds—the love so highly regarded in the feudal period—as worthy of consideration. The ancient world recognised only those emotions which drew its fellow-members close together and rendered the emerging social organism more stable. In subsequent stages of cultural development, however, friendship ceases to be considered a moral virtue. Bourgeois society was built on the principles of individualism and competition, and has no place for friendship as a moral factor. Friendship does not help in any way, and may hinder the achievement of class aims; it is viewed as an unnecessary manifestation of "sentimentality" and weakness. Friendship becomes an object of derision. . . .

The feudal system defended the interests of the noble family. Virtues were defined with reference not so much to relations between the members of that society as to the obligations of the individual to his or her family and its traditions. Marriage was contracted according to the interests of the family, and any young man (the girl had no rights whatever) who chose himself a wife against these interests was severely criticised. In the feudal era the individual was not supposed to place personal feelings and inclinations above the interests of family, and he who did so "sinned." Morality did not demand that love and marriage go hand in hand.

Nevertheless, love between the sexes was not neglected; in fact, for the first time in the history of humanity it received a certain recognition. It may seem strange that love was first accepted in this age of strict asceticism, of crude and cruel morals, an age of violence and rule by violence; but the reasons for acceptance become clear when we take a closer look. In certain situations and in certain circumstances, love can act as a lever propelling the man to perform actions of which he would otherwise have been incapable. The knighthood demanded of each member fearlessness, bravery, endurance and great feats of individual valour on the battlefield. Victory in war was in those days decided not so much by the organisation of troops as by the individual qualities of the participants. The knight in love with the inaccessible "lady of his heart" found it easier to perform miracles of bravery, easier to win tournaments, easier to sacrifice his life. The knight in love was motivated by the desire to "shine" and thus to win the attention of his beloved.

The ideology of chivalry recognised love as a psychological state that could be used to the advantage of the feudal class, but nevertheless it sought to organise emotions in a definite framework. Love between man and wife was not valued, for the family that lived in the knightly castle and in the Russian boyar's *terem* was not held together by emotional ties. The social factor of chivalrous love operated where the knight loved a woman outside the family and was inspired to military and other heroic feats by this emotion. The more inaccessible the woman, the greater the knight's determination to win her favour and the greater his need to develop in himself the virtues and qualities which were valued by his social class. . . .

Hence feudal morality combined recognition of the ideal of asceticism (sexual restraint) with recognition of love as a moral virtue. In his desire to free love from all that was carnal and sinful and to transform it into an abstract emotion completely divorced from its biological base the knight was prepared to go to great lengths, choosing as his lady a woman he had never seen or joining the ranks of the lovers of the Virgin Mary. Further he could not go. . . .

But while placing so much emphasis on spiritual love, feudal morality in no way demanded that love should determine legal marriage relationships. Love and marriage were kept separate by feudal ideology, and were only united by the bourgeois class that emerged in the fourteenth and fifteenth centuries. The exalted sophistication of feudal love existed, therefore, alongside indescribably crude norms of relations between the sexes. Sexual intercourse both within and outside marriage lacked the softening and inspiring element of love and remained an undisguisedly physiological act.

The church pretended to wage war on depravity, but by encouraging "spiritual love" it encouraged crude animal relations between the sexes. The knight who would not be parted from the emblem of the lady of his heart, who composed poetry in her honour and risked his life to win her smile, would rape a girl of the urban classes without a second thought or order his steward to bring him a beautiful peasant for his pleasure. The wives of the knights, for their part, did not let slip the opportunity to enjoy the delights of the flesh with the troubadours and pages of the feudal household.

With the weakening of feudalism and the growth of new conditions of life dictated by the interests of the rising bourgeoisie, a new moral ideal of relations between the sexes developed. Rejecting platonic love, the bourgeoisie defended the violated rights of the body and injected the combination of the spiritual and physical into the very conception of love. Bourgeois morality did not separate love and marriage; marriage was the expression of the mutual attraction of the couple. In practice of course the bourgeoisie itself, in the name of convenience, continually sinned against this moral teaching, but the recognition of love as the pillar of marriage had a profound class basis. . . .

At the end of the fourteenth and the beginning of the fifteenth centuries, the new economic way of life gave rise to a new ideology. The conceptions of love and marriage gradually changed. The religious reformer, Luther, and the other thinkers and public figures of the Renaissance and the Reformation, understood the social force of love perfectly. Aware that the stability of the family—the economic unit on which the bourgeois system rests—required that its members be linked by more than economic ties alone, the revolutionary ideologists of the rising bourgeoisie propagated the new moral ideal of a love that embraced both the flesh and the soul. The reformers of the period challenged the celibacy of the clergy and made merciless fun of the "spiritual love" of chivalry that kept the knight in a continual state of aspiration but denied him the hope of satisfying his sensual needs. The ideologists of the bourgeoisie and the reformation recognised the legitimacy of the body's needs. Thus, while the feudal world had divided love into the sexual act (relations within marriage or with concubines) on the one hand, and spiritual, platonic love (the relations between the knight and the lady of his heart) on the other, the bourgeois class included both the physical attraction between the sexes and emotional attachments in its concept of love. The feudal ideal had separated love from marriage; the bourgeoisie linked the two. The bourgeoisie made love and marriage inseparable. In practice, of course, this class has always retreated from its ideal; but while the question of mutual inclination was never raised under feudalism, bourgeois morality requires that even in marriages of convenience, the partners should practise hypocrisy and pretend affection. . . .

But though bourgeois morality defended the rights of two "loving hearts" to conclude a union even in defiance of tradition, and though it criticised "spiritual love" and asceticism, proclaiming love as the basis of marriage, it nevertheless defined love in a very narrow way. Love is permissible only when it is within marriage. Love outside legal marriage is considered immoral. Such ideas were often dictated, of course, by economic considerations, by the desire to prevent the distribution of capital among illegitimate children. The entire morality of the bourgeoisie was directed towards the concentration of capital. The ideal was the married couple, working together to improve their welfare and to increase the wealth of their particular family unit, divorced as it was from society. Where the interests of the family and society were in conflict, bourgeois morality decided in the interests of the family (cf. the sympathetic attitude of bourgeois morality—though not the law—to deserters and to those who, for the sake of their families, cause the bankruptcy of their fellow shareholders). This morality, with a utilitarianism typical of the bourgeoisie, tried to use love to its advantage, making it the main ingredient of marriage, and thereby strengthening the family.

Love, of course, could not be contained within the limits set down by bourgeois ideologists. Emotional conflicts grew and multiplied, and found their expression in the new form of literature—the novel—which the bourgeois class developed. Love constantly escaped from the narrow framework of legal marriage relations set for it, into free relationships and adultery, which were condemned but which were practised. The bourgeois ideal of love does not correspond to the needs of the largest section of the population—the working class. Nor is it relevant to the life-style of the working intelligentsia. This is why in highly developed capitalist countries one finds such an interest in the problems of sex and love and in the search for the key to its mysteries. How, it is asked, can relations between the sexes be developed in order to increase the sum of both individual and social happiness?

The working youth of Soviet Russia is confronting this question at this very moment. This brief survey of the evolution of the ideal of love-marriage relationships will help you, my young friend, to realise and understand that love is not the private matter it might seem to be at a first glance. Love is an important psychological and social factor, which society has always instinctively organised in its interests. Working men and women, armed with the science of marxism and using the experience of the past, must seek to discover the place love ought to occupy in the new social order and determine the ideal of love that corresponds to their class interests.

LOVE-COMRADESHIP

The new, communist society is being built on the principle of comradeship and solidarity. Solidarity is not only an awareness of common interests; it depends also on the intellectual and emotional ties linking the members of the collective. For a social system to be built on solidarity and co-operation it is essential that people should be capable of love and warm emotions. The proletarian ideology, therefore, attempts to educate and encourage every member of the working class to be capable of responding to the distress and needs of other members of the class, of a sensitive understanding of others and a penetrating consciousness of the individual's relationship to the collective. All these "warm emotions"—sensitivity, compassion, sympathy and responsiveness—derive from one source: they are aspects of love, not in the narrow, sexual sense but in the broad meaning of the word. Love

is an emotion that unites and is consequently of an organising character. The bourgeoisie was well aware of this, and in the attempt to create a stable family bourgeois ideology erected "married love" as a moral virtue; to be a "good family man" was, in the eyes of the bourgeoisie, an important and valuable quality. The proletariat should also take into account the psychological and social role that love, both in the broad sense and in the sense of relationships between the sexes, can and must play, not in strengthening family-marriage ties, but in the development of collective solidarity.

What is the proletariat's ideal of love? We have already seen that each epoch has its ideal; each class strives to fill the conception of love with a moral content that suits its own interests. Each stage of cultural development, with its richer intellectual and emotional experiences, redefines the image of Eros. With the successive stages in the development of the economy and social life, ideas of love have changed; shades of emotion have assumed greater significance or, on the other hand, have ceased to exist.

In the course of the thousand-year history of human society, love has developed from the simple biological instinct—the urge to reproduce which is inherent in all creatures from the highest to the lowest—into a most complex emotion that is constantly acquiring new intellectual and emotional aspects. Love has become a psychological and social factor. Under the impact of economic and social forces, the biological instinct for reproduction has been transformed in two diametrically opposed directions. On the one hand the healthy sexual instinct has been turned by monstrous social and economic relations, particularly those of capitalism, into unhealthy carnality. The sexual act has become an aim in itself—just another way of obtaining pleasure, through lust sharpened with excesses and through distorted, harmful titillations of the flesh. A man does not have sex in response to healthy instincts which have drawn him to a particular woman; a man approaches any woman, though he feels no sexual need for her in particular, with the aim of gaining his sexual satisfaction and pleasure through her. Prostitution is the organised expression of this distortion of the sex drive. If intercourse with a woman does not prompt the expected excitement, the man will turn to every kind of perversion.

This deviation towards unhealthy carnality takes relationships far from their source in the biological instinct. On the other hand, over the centuries and with the changes in human social life and culture, a web of emotional and intellectual experiences has come to surround the physical attraction of the sexes. Love in its present form is a complex state of mind and body; it has long been separated from its primary source, the biological instinct for reproduction, and in fact it is frequently in sharp contradiction with it. Love is intricately woven from friendship, passion, maternal tenderness, infatuation, mutual compatibility, sympathy, admiration, familiarity and many other shades of emotion. With such a range of emotions involved, it becomes increasingly difficult to distinguish direct connection between the natural drive of "wingless Eros" and "winged Eros," where physical attraction and emotional warmth are fused. The existence of love-friendship where the element of physical attraction is absent, of love for one's work or for a cause, and of love for the collective, testify to the extent to which love has become "spiritualised" and separated from its biological base.

In modern society, sharp contradictions frequently arise and battles are waged between the various manifestations of emotion. A deep intellectual and emotional involvement in one's work may not be compatible with love for a particular man or woman, love for the collective might conflict with love for husband, wife or children. It may be difficult for love-friendship in one person to coexist with passion in another; in the one case love is predominantly based on intellectual compatibility, and in the other case on physical harmony. "Love" has many faces and aspects. The various shades of feeling that have developed over the ages and which are experienced by contemporary men and women cannot be covered by such a general and inexact term.

Under the rule of bourgeois ideology and the capitalist way of life, the complexity of love creates a series of complex and insoluble problems. . . . And at this present moment many "small" people are weighed down by the difficulties of love and vainly seek for solutions within the framework of bourgeois thought. But the key to the solution is in the hands of the proletariat. Only the ideology and the life-style of the new, labouring humanity can unravel this complex problem of emotion.

We are talking here of the duality of love, of the complexities of "winged Eros"; this should not be confused with sexual relations "without Eros," where one man goes with many women or one woman with a number of men. Relations where no personal feelings are involved can have unfortunate and harmful consequences (the early exhaustion of the organism, venereal diseases etc.), but however entangled they are, they do not give rise to "emotional dramas". These "dramas" and conflicts begin only where the various shades and manifestations of love are present. A woman feels close to a man whose ideas, hopes and aspirations match her own; she is attracted physically to another. For one woman a man might feel sympathy and a protective tenderness, and in another he might find support and understanding for the strivings of his intellect. To which of the two must he give his love? And why must he tear himself apart and cripple his inner self, if only the possession of both types of inner bond affords the fullness of living?

Under the bourgeois system such a division of the inner emotional world involves inevitable suffering. For thousands of years human culture, which is based on the institution of property, has been teaching people that love is linked with the principles of property. Bourgeois ideology has insisted that love, mutual love, gives the right to the absolute and indivisible possession of the beloved person. Such exclusiveness was the natural consequence of the established form of pair marriage and of the ideal of "all-embracing love" between husband and wife. But can such an ideal correspond to the interests of the working class? Surely it is important and desirable from the proletariat's point of view that people's emotions should develop a wider and richer range? And surely the complexity of the human psyche and the many-sidedness of emotional experience should assist in the growth of the emotional and intellectual bonds between people which make the collective stronger? The more numerous these inner threads drawing people together, the firmer the sense of solidarity and the simpler the realisation of the working-class ideal of comradeship and unity.

Proletarian ideology cannot accept exclusiveness and "all-embracing love." The proletariat is not filled with horror and moral indignation at the many forms and facets of "winged Eros" in the way that the hypocritical bourgeoisie is; on the contrary, it tries to direct these emotions, which it sees as the result of complex social circumstances, into channels which are advantageous to the class during the struggle for and the construction of communist society. The complexity of love is not in conflict with the interests of the proletariat. On the contrary, it facilitates the triumph of the ideal of love-comradeship which is already developing.

At the tribal stage love was seen as a kinship attachment (love between sisters and brothers, love for parents). The ancient culture of the pre-christian period placed love-friendship above all else.

The feudal world idealised platonic courtly love between members of the opposite sex outside marriage. The bourgeoisie took monogamous marital love as its ideal. The working class derives its ideal from the labour co-operation and inner solidarity that binds the men and women of the proletariat together; the form and content of this ideal naturally differs from the conception of love that existed in other cultural epochs. The advocacy of love-comradeship in no way implies that in the militant atmosphere of its struggle for the dictatorship of the proletariat the working class has adopted a strait-jacket ideology and is mercilessly trying to remove all traces of tender emotion from relations between the sexes. The ideology of the working class does not seek to destroy "winged Eros" but, on the contrary, to clear the way for the recognition of the value of love as a psychological and social force.

The hypocritical morality of bourgeois culture resolutely restricted the freedom of Eros, obliging him to visit only the "legally married couple." Outside marriage there was room only for the "wingless Eros" of momentary and joyless sexual relations which were bought (in the case of prostitution) or stolen (in the case of adultery). The morality of the working class, on the other hand, in so far as it has already been formulated, definitely rejects the external forms of sexual relations. The social aims of the working class are not affected one bit by whether love takes the form of a long and official union or is expressed in a temporary relationship. The ideology of the working class does not place any formal limits on love. But at the same time the ideology of the working class is already beginning to take a thoughtful attitude to the content of love and shades of emotional experience. In this sense the proletarian ideology will persecute "wingless Eros" in a much more strict and severe way than bourgeois morality. "Wingless Eros" contradicts the interests of the working class.

In the first place it inevitably involves excesses and therefore physical exhaustion, which lower the resources of labour energy available to society. In the second place it impoverishes the soul, hindering the development and strengthening of inner bonds and positive emotions. And in the third place it usually rests on an inequality of rights in relationships between the sexes, on the dependence of the woman on the man and on male complacency and insensitivity, which undoubtedly hinder the development of comradely feelings. "Winged Eros" is quite different.

Obviously sexual attraction lies at the base of "winged Eros" too, but the difference is that the person experiencing love acquires the inner qualities necessary to the builders of a new culture—sensitivity, responsiveness and the desire to help others. Bourgeois ideology demanded that a person should only display such qualities in their relationship with one partner. The aim of proletarian ideology is that men and women should develop these qualities not only in relation to the chosen one but in relation to all the members of the collective. The proletarian class is not concerned as to which shades and nuances of feeling predominate in winged Eros. The only stipulation is that these emotions facilitate the development and strengthening of comradeship. The ideal of love-comradeship, which is being forged by proletarian ideology to replace the all-embracing and exclusive marital love of bourgeois culture, involves the recognition of the rights and integrity of the other's personality, a steadfast mutual support and sensitive sympathy, and responsiveness to the other's needs.

The ideal of love-comradeship is necessary to the proletariat in the important and difficult period of the struggle for and the consolidation of the dictatorship. But there is no doubt that with the realisation of communist society love will acquire a transformed and unprecedented aspect. By that time the "sympathetic ties" between all the members of the new society will have grown and strengthened. Love potential will have increased, and love-solidarity will become the lever that competition and self-love were in the bourgeois system. Collectivism of spirit can then defeat individualist self-sufficiency, and the "cold of inner loneliness," from which people in bourgeois culture have attempted to escape through love and marriage, will disappear. The many threads bringing men and women into close emotional and intellectual contact will develop, and feelings will emerge from the private into the public sphere. Inequality between the sexes and the dependence of women on men will disappear without trace, leaving only a fading memory of past ages.

In the new and collective society, where interpersonal relations develop against a background of joyful unity and comradeship, Eros will occupy an honourable place as an emotional experience multiplying human happiness. What will be the nature of this transformed Eros? Not even the boldest fantasy is capable of providing the answer to this question. But one thing is clear: the stronger the intellectual and emotional bonds of the new humanity, the less the room for love in the present sense of the word. Modern love always sins, because it absorbs the thoughts and feelings of "loving hearts" and isolates the loving pair from the collective. In the future society, such a separation will not only become superfluous but also psychologically inconceivable. In the new world the accepted norm of sexual relations will probably be based on free, healthy and natural attraction (without distortions and excesses) and on "transformed Eros."

But at the present moment we stand between two cultures. And at this turning-point, with the attendant struggles of the two worlds on all fronts, including the ideological one, the proletariat's interest is to do its best to ensure the quickest possible accumulation of "sympathetic feelings." In this period the moral ideal defining relationships is not the unadorned sexual instinct but the many-faceted love experience of love-comradeship. In order to answer the demands formulated by the new proletarian morality, these experiences must conform to three basic principles: 1. Equality in relationships (an end to masculine egoism and the slavish suppression of the female personality). 2. Mutual recognition of the rights of the other, of the fact that one does not own the heart and soul of the other (the sense of property, encouraged by bourgeois culture). 3. Comradely sensitivity, the ability to listen and understand the inner workings of the loved person (bourgeois culture demanded this only from the woman). But in proclaiming the rights of "winged Eros," the ideal of the working class at the same time subordinates this love to the more powerful emotion of love-duty to the collective. However great the love between two members of the collective, the ties binding the two persons to the collective will always take precedence, will be firmer, more complex and organic. Bourgeois morality demanded all for the loved one. The morality of the proletariat demands all for the collective.

But I can hear you objecting, my young friend, that though it may be true that love-comradeship will become the ideal of the working class, will this new "moral measurement" of emotions not place new constraints on sexual relationships? Are we not liberating love from the fetters of bourgeois morality only to enslave it again? Yes, my young friend, you are right. The ideology of the proletariat rejects bourgeois "morality" in the sphere of love-marriage relations. Nevertheless, it inevitably develops its own class morality, its own rules of behaviour, which correspond more closely to the tasks of the working class and educate the emotions in a certain direction. In this way it could be said that feelings are again in chains. The proletariat will undoubtedly clip the wings of bourgeois culture. But it would be short-sighted to regret this process, since the new class is capable of developing new facets of emotion which possess unprecedented beauty, strength and radiance. As the cultural and economic base of humanity changes, so will love be transformed.

The blind, all-embracing, demanding passions will weaken; the sense of property, the egoistical desire to bind the partner to one "forever", the complacency of the man and the self-renunciation of the woman will disappear. At the same time, the valuable aspects and elements of love will develop. Respect for the right of the other's personality will increase, and a mutual sensitivity will be learned; men and women will strive to express their love not only in kisses and embraces but in joint creativity and activity. The task of proletarian ideology is not to drive Eros from social life but to rearm him according to the new social formation, and to educate sexual relationships in the spirit of the great new psychological force of comradely solidarity.

I hope it is now clear to you that the interest among young workers in the question of love is not a symptom of "decline." I hope that you can now grasp the place love must occupy in the relationships between young workers.

chapter twenty-eight

Alexandre Kojève

The lectures of Alexandre Kojève (1902–1968) on G.W.F. Hegel's *Phenomenology of Spirit* were to have a profound impact on the direction of Hegelian thought in twentieth-century French philosophy. Born Aleksandr Vladimirovich Kozhevnikov, in Russia, Kojève studied under Karl Jaspers at Heidelberg, in Germany, where he completed a thesis on Vladimir Solovyov, a Russian religious philosopher who was deeply influenced by Hegel. Kojève turned to Hegel in an attempt both to gain a deeper understanding of the philosophical sources of Karl Marx's teachings and to go beyond what he viewed as the thinness of the human and metaphysical grounds of Marxian thought. Following his studies, Kojève moved to Paris, where, taking over from Alexandre Koyré, he began to teach a seminar on Hegel at the *École Pratique des Hautes Études*.

The collection of notes taken from 1933 to 1939 during Kojève's lectures on Hegel at the *École Pratique des Hautes Études* comprise the core of his *Introduction to the Reading of Hegel*, published for the first time in 1947. These lectures, which were attended by such thinkers as Raymond Aron, Maurice Merleau-Ponty, and Simone de Beauvoir, were to play a seminal role in the revival of Hegelian thought in France during the 1930s and 1940s. As late as 1931, Alexandre Koyré, at the time a prominent French philosopher, reported in the *Revue d'histoire de la philosophie* that Hegel studies in France were practically nonexistent.[1] In an interview with his biographer, John Gerassi, Jean-Paul Sartre would later echo the sentiment expressed by Koyré. Describing the state of philosophy in France during the 1920s and early 1930s, Sartre recalls that the professors of philosophy at the time "were just plain retrogrades. There had been one guy, dead by then, who had set the tone for philosophical studies in France at the beginning of the century, who had stated categorically that if any student even just mentioned the name Hegel, he would never let him get his *agrégation*."[2] Indeed, there is no greater indication of how thoroughly Hegel had fallen out of favor in France at the beginning of the twentieth century than the fact that Jean Hyppolite's translation of the

Phenomenology of Spirit—the first French translation of Hegel's seminal work—was not published until 1941.

By the 1940s, however, Hegel had come to occupy a central place in the development of French thought. In 1946, for instance, Merleau-Ponty would claim in *Sense and Non-Sense* that "all the great philosophical ideas of the past century—the philosophies of Marx and Nietzsche, phenomenology, German existentialism, and psychoanalysis—had their beginnings in Hegel."[3] Many of the works that emerged out of the 1940s and 1950s, such as Sartre's *Being and Nothingness* (1942), Beauvoir's *Second Sex* (1949), and Fanon's *Black Skin, White Masks* (1952), would make reference to Hegel's thought, and specifically to the *Phenomenology of Spirit*. Hegel's influence on French philosophy would endure well into the second half of the twentieth century. In 1961, Koyré, in a postscript to a reprinted edition of his 1931 essay on French Hegelian studies, remarked that Hegel's presence in philosophical studies had "changed beyond recognition."[4] Later, Michel Foucault, in his 1970 inaugural address to the Collège de France, would both support and instantiate this assertion, stating that "our entire era, whether through logic or through epistemology, whether through Marx or through Nietzsche, is attempting to get away from Hegel."[5] Over the span of a decade, Hegel's influence on French thought had gone from being nonexistent to being unavoidable. Today, it is found not only in the works of postwar thinkers like Sartre, Merleau-Ponty, and Beauvoir, but also in those of later thinkers like Foucault, Gilles Deleuze, and Jacques Lacan.

The importance of the role Kojève's lectures played in the emergence of this phenomenon, in the introduction—or reintroduction—of Hegelian thought into French philosophy, cannot be overstated. For many French students and intellectuals, the lectures on the *Phenomenology of Spirit* were the first contact they had had with Hegel over the course of their studies. For this reason, and because Kojève's lectures on Hegel are both commentaries and original works of philosophy, any inquiry into the influence of Hegel on the thought of French philosophers such as Sartre, Merleau-Ponty, and Beauvoir must first begin with an inquiry into Kojève's own reading of Hegel's *Phenomenology*.

Indeed, one should always keep in mind when reading the *Introduction to the Reading of Hegel* that Kojève is presenting one of several possible interpretations of the *Phenomenology of Spirit*, an interpretation that is informed by his own philosophical views and is in itself an exposition of those views. In this sense, Kojève is engaging in a dialogue with the *Phenomenology of Spirit*, alternately rejecting and emphasizing aspects of Hegel's work in accordance with his own philosophical priorities. Thus, Kojève's reading of the *Phenomenology* not only introduced an entire generation of French philosophers to Hegel's thought, but also in turn served to shape their own readings of Hegel. That is to say, if most references to Hegel found in mid-twentieth-century French philosophy concern the notion of desire, and in particular the dialectic of master and slave, it is because Kojève himself took this notion, and the chapter of the *Phenomenology* in which it is articulated, to be central to both Hegel's and his own thought.

Kojève's emphasis on the notion of desire is reflected in the structure of his *Introduction*. Its first chapter, which is presented here and was first published in 1939, is Kojève's translation, with commentary, of section A of chapter IV of the *Phenomenology of Spirit*, "Independence and Dependence of Self-Consciousness: Lordship and Bondage." In what is arguably the most famous passage of the *Phenomenology of Spirit*, Hegel describes the experience of consciousness once it has gone through the stages of sense-certainty, perception, and understanding.[6] According to Kojève's interpretation, the passage presents an historical account of relations between subjects that focuses on the subject's desire for recognition and the role of the other in attaining it: the encounter of one consciousness with another consciousness results in a struggle for recognition, at the end of which one consciousness will become lord, or master, and the other bondsman, or slave. The story of the master/slave dialectic told in this excerpt is Kojève's reading of Hegel's description of the genesis and eventual—if unsatisfactory—resolution of this struggle.

After World War II, Kojève went to work for the French Ministry of Economic Affairs, where he exerted a profound influence on French economic policy until his death in 1968, playing a crucial role in the genesis of both the European Economic Community (EEC) and the General Agreement on Tariffs and Trade (GATT). He continued to write philosophy during this time, including works on the pre-Socratics, Immanuel Kant, religion, and the development of capitalism.

DG

QUESTIONS

1. What is the role of desire in the dialectic of master and slave?
2. Why is the fight to the death bound to fail?
3. Why does Kojève say that "the relation between Master and Slave . . . is not recognition properly so-called"?
4. What does Kojève mean when he states that "the *truth* of autonomous Consciousness is *slavish Consciousness*"?
5. What is the role of work in the dialectic of master and slave?

ENDNOTES

1. Butler, p. 61.
2. Sartre, quoted in Gerassi, p. 74.
3. Merleau-Ponty, pp. 109-110.
4. Koyré, p. 34.

5. Foucault, p. 74.

6. See chapter 22 for a more thorough discussion of G.W.F. Hegel.

SELECTED BIBLIOGRAPHY

Butler, Judith. *Subjects of Desire: Hegelian Reflections in Twentieth-Century France.* New York: Columbia University Press, 1987.

Foucault, Michel. *L'ordre du discours.* Paris: Gallimard, 1971.

Gerassi, John. *Jean-Paul Sartre: Hated Conscience of His Century.* Vol. 1. Chicago: University of Chicago Press, 1989.

Hegel, G.W.F. *Phenomenology of Spirit*, trans. A.V. Miller. New York: Oxford University Press, 1977.

Kojève, Alexandre. *Introduction to the Reading of Hegel*, trans. James H. Nichols Jr. Ithaca: Cornell University Press, 1980.

Koyré, Alexandre. *Etudes d'histoire de la pensée philosophique.* Paris: Armand Colin, 1961.

Merleau-Ponty, Maurice. *Sense and Non-Sense*, trans. Herbert L. Dreyfus. Evanston, Illinois: Northwestern University Press, 1990.

from *Introduction to the Reading of Hegel*

Alexandre Kojève

IN PLACE OF AN INTRODUCTION*

Hegel . . . erfasst die *Arbeit* als das *Wesen*, als das sich bewährende Wesen des Menschen.

Karl Marx

[Man is Self-Consciousness. He is conscious of himself, conscious of his human reality and dignity; and it is in this that he is essentially different from animals, which do not go beyond the level of

---

*A translation with commentary of Section A of Chapter IV of the *Phenomenology of Spirit*, entitled: "Autonomy and Dependence of Self-Consciousness: Mastery and Slavery."

The commentary is in brackets. Words joined by hyphens correspond to a single German word.

simple Sentiment of self. Man becomes conscious of himself at the moment when—for the "first" time—he says "I." To understand man by understanding his "origin" is, therefore, to understand the origin of the I revealed by speech.

[Now, the analysis of "thought," "reason," "understanding," and so on—in general, of the cognitive, contemplative, passive behavior of a being or a "knowing subject"—never reveals the why or the how of the birth of the word "I," and consequently of self-consciousness—that is, of the human reality. The man who contemplates is "absorbed" by what he contemplates; the "knowing subject" "loses" himself in the object that is known. Contemplation reveals the object, not the subject. The object, and not the subject, is what shows itself to him in and by—or better, as—the act of knowing. The man who is "absorbed" by the object that he is contemplating can be "brought back to himself" only by a Desire; by the desire to eat, for example. The (conscious) Desire of a being is what constitutes that being as I and reveals it as such by moving it to say "I. . . ." Desire is what transforms Being, revealed to itself by itself in (true) knowledge, into an "object" revealed to a "subject" by a subject different from the object and "opposed" to it. It is in and by—or better still, as—"his" Desire that man is formed and is revealed—to himself and to others—as an I, as the I that is essentially different from, and radically opposed to, the non-I. The (human) I is the I of a Desire or of Desire.

[The very being of man, the self-conscious being, therefore, implies and presupposes Desire. Consequently, the human reality can be formed and maintained only within a biological reality, an animal life. But, if animal Desire is the necessary condition of Self-Consciousness, it is not the sufficient condition. By itself, this Desire constitutes only the Sentiment of self.

[In contrast to the knowledge that keeps man in a passive quietude, Desire dis-quiets him and moves him to action. Born of Desire, action tends to satisfy it, and can do so only by the "negation," the destruction, or at least the transformation, of the desired object: to satisfy hunger, for example, the food must be destroyed or, in any case, transformed. Thus, all action is "negating." Far from leaving the given as it is, action destroys it; if not in its being, at least in its given form. And all "negating-negativity" with respect to the given is necessarily active. But negating action is not purely destructive, for if action destroys an objective reality, for the sake of satisfying the Desire from which it is born, it creates in its place, in and by that very destruction, a subjective reality. The being that eats, for example, creates and preserves its own re-

ality by the overcoming of a reality other than its own, by the "transformation" of an alien reality into its own reality, by the "assimilation," the "internalization" of a "foreign," "external" reality. Generally speaking, the I of Desire is an emptiness that receives a real positive content only by negating action that satisfies Desire in destroying, transforming, and "assimilating" the desired non-I. And the positive content of the I, constituted by negation, is a function of the positive content of the negated non-I. If, then, the Desire is directed toward a "natural" non-I, the I, too, will be "natural." The I created by the active satisfaction of such a Desire will have the same nature as the things toward which that Desire is directed: it will be a "thingish" I, a merely living I, an animal I. And this natural I, a function of the natural object, can be revealed to itself and to others only as Sentiment of self. It will never attain Self-Consciousness.

[For there to be Self-Consciousness, Desire must therefore be directed toward a non-natural object, toward something that goes beyond the given reality. Now, the only thing that goes beyond the given reality is Desire itself. For Desire taken as Desire—i.e., before its satisfaction—is but a revealed nothingness, an unreal emptiness. Desire, being the revelation of an emptiness, the presence of the absence of a reality, is something essentially different from the desired thing, something other than a thing, than a static and given real being that stays eternally identical to itself. Therefore, Desire directed toward another Desire, taken as Desire, will create, by the negating and assimilating action that satisfies it, an I essentially different from the animal "I." This I, which "feeds" on Desires, will itself be Desire in its very being, created in and by the satisfaction of its Desire. And since Desire is realized as action negating the given, the very being of this I will be action. This I will not, like the animal "I," be "identity" or equality to itself, but "negating-negativity." In other words, the very being of this I will be becoming, and the universal form of this being will not be space, but time. Therefore, its continuation in existence will signify for this I: "not to be what it is (as static and given being, as natural being, as 'innate character') and to be (that is, to become) what it is not." Thus, this I will be its own product: it will be (in the future) what it has become by negation (in the present) of what it was (in the past), this negation being accomplished with a view to what it will become. In its very being this I is intentional becoming, deliberate evolution, conscious and voluntary progress; it is the act of transcending the given that is given to it and that it itself is. This I is a (human) individual, free (with respect to the given real) and historical (in relation to itself). And it is this I, and only this I, that reveals itself to itself and to others as Self-Consciousness.

[Human Desire must be directed toward another Desire. For there to be human Desire, then, there must first be a multiplicity of (animal) Desires. In other words, in order that Self-Consciousness be born from the Sentiment of self, in order that the human reality come into being within the animal reality, this reality must be essentially manifold. Therefore, man can appear on earth only within a herd. That is why the human reality can only be social. But for the herd to become a society, multiplicity of Desires is not sufficient by itself; in addition, the Desires of each member of the herd must be directed—or potentially directed—toward the Desires of the other members. If the human reality is a social reality, society is human only as a set of Desires mutually desiring one another as Desires. Human Desire, or better still, anthropogenetic Desire, produces a free and historical individual, conscious of his individuality, his freedom, his history, and finally, his historicity. Hence, anthropogenetic Desire is different from

animal Desire (which produces a natural being, merely living and having only a sentiment of its life) in that it is directed, not toward a real, "positive," given object, but toward another Desire. Thus, in the relationship between man and woman, for example, Desire is human only if the one desires, not the body, but the Desire of the other; if he wants "to possess" or "to assimilate" the Desire taken as Desire—that is to say, if he wants to be "desired" or "loved," or, rather, "recognized" in his human value, in his reality as a human individual. Likewise, Desire directed toward a natural object is human only to the extent that it is "mediated" by the Desire of another directed toward the same object: it is human to desire what others desire, because they desire it. Thus, an object perfectly useless from the biological point of view (such as a medal, or the enemy's flag) can be desired because it is the object of other desires. Such a Desire can only be a human Desire, and human reality, as distinguished from animal reality, is created only by action that satisfies such Desires: human history is the history of desired Desires.

[But, apart from this difference—which is essential—human Desire is analogous to animal Desire. Human Desire, too, tends to satisfy itself by a negating—or better, a transforming and assimilating—action. Man "feeds" on Desires as an animal feeds on real things. And the human I, realized by the active satisfaction of its human Desires, is as much a function of its "food" as the body of an animal is of its food.

[For man to be truly human, for him to be essentially and really different from an animal, his human Desire must actually win out over his animal Desire. Now, all Desire is desire for a value. The supreme value for an animal is its animal life. All the Desires of an animal are in the final analysis a function of its desire to preserve its life. Human Desire, therefore, must win out over this desire for preservation. In other words, man's humanity "comes to light" only if he risks his (animal) life for the sake of his human Desire. It is in and by this risk that the human reality is created and revealed as reality; it is in and by this risk that it "comes to light," i.e., is shown, demonstrated, verified, and gives proofs of being essentially different from the animal, natural reality. And that is why to speak of the "origin" of Self-Consciousness is necessarily to speak of the risk of life (for an essentially nonvital end).

[Man's humanity "comes to light" only in risking his life to satisfy his human Desire—that is, his Desire directed toward another Desire. Now, to desire a Desire is to want to substitute oneself for the value desired by this Desire. For without this substitution, one would desire the value, the desired object, and not the Desire itself. Therefore, to desire the Desire of another is in the final analysis to desire that the value that I am or that I "represent" be the value desired by the other: I want him to "recognize" my value as his value. I want him to "recognize" me as an autonomous value. In other words, all human, anthropogenetic Desire—the Desire that generates Self-Consciousness, the human reality—is, finally, a function of the desire for "recognition." And the risk of life by which the human reality "comes to light" is a risk for the sake of such a Desire. Therefore, to speak of the "origin" of Self-Consciousness is necessarily to speak of a fight to the death for "recognition."

[Without this fight to the death for pure prestige, there would never have been human beings on earth. Indeed, the human being is formed only in terms of a Desire directed toward another Desire, that is—finally—in terms of a desire for recognition. Therefore, the human being can be formed only if at least two of these Desires confront one another. Each of the two beings endowed with such a Desire is ready to go all the way

in pursuit of its satisfaction; that is, is ready to risk its life—and, consequently, to put the life of the other in danger—in order to be "recognized" by the other, to impose itself on the other as the supreme value; accordingly, their meeting can only be a fight to the death. And it is only in and by such a fight that the human reality is begotten, formed, realized, and revealed to itself and to others. Therefore, it is realized and revealed only as "recognized" reality.

[However, if all men—or, more exactly, all beings in the process of becoming human beings—behaved in the same manner, the fight would necessarily end in the death of one of the adversaries, or of both. It would not be possible for one to give way to the other, to give up the fight before the death of the other, to "recognize" the other instead of being "recognized" by him. But if this were the case, the realization and the revelation of the human being would be impossible. This is obvious in the case of the death of both adversaries, since the human reality—being essentially Desire and action in terms of Desire—can be born and maintained only within an animal life. But it is equally impossible when only one of the adversaries is killed. For with him disappears that other Desire toward which Desire must be directed in order to be a human Desire. The survivor, unable to be "recognized" by the dead adversary, cannot realize and reveal his humanity. In order that the human being be realized and revealed as Self-Consciousness, therefore, it is not sufficient that the nascent human reality be manifold. This multiplicity, this "society," must in addition imply two essentially different human or anthropogenetic behaviors.

[In order that the human reality come into being as "recognized" reality, both adversaries must remain alive after the fight. Now, this is possible only on the condition that they behave differently in this fight. By irreducible, or better, by unforeseeable or "undeducible" acts of liberty, they must constitute themselves as unequals in and by this very fight. Without being predestined to it in any way, the one must fear the other, must give in to the other, must refuse to risk his life for the satisfaction of his desire for "recognition." He must give up his desire and satisfy the desire of the other: he must "recognize" the other without being "recognized" by him. Now, "to recognize" him thus is "to recognize" him as his Master and to recognize himself and to be recognized as the Master's Slave.

[In other words, in his nascent state, man is never simply man. He is always, necessarily, and essentially, either Master or Slave. If the human reality can come into being only as a social reality, society is human—at least in its origin—only on the basis of its implying an element of Mastery and an element of Slavery, of "autonomous" existences and "dependent" existences. And that is why to speak of the origin of Self-Consciousness is necessarily to speak of "the autonomy and dependence of Self-Consciousness, of Mastery and Slavery."

[If the human being is begotten only in and by the fight that ends in the relation between Master and Slave, the progressive realization and revelation of this being can themselves be effected only in terms of this fundamental social relation. If man is nothing but his becoming, if his human existence in space is his existence in time or as time, if the revealed human reality is nothing but universal history, that history must be the history of the interaction between Mastery and Slavery: the historical "dialectic" is the "dialectic" of Master and Slave. But if the opposition of "thesis" and "antithesis" is meaningful only in the context of their reconciliation by "synthesis," if history (in the full sense of the word) necessarily has a final term, if man who becomes must culminate in man who has become, if Desire must end in satisfaction, if

the science of man must possess the quality of a definitively and universally valid truth—the interaction of Master and Slave must finally end in the "dialectical overcoming" of both of them.

[However that may be, the human reality can be begotten and preserved only as "recognized" reality. It is only by being "recognized" by another, by many others, or—in the extreme—by all others, that a human being is really human, for himself as well as for others. And only in speaking of a "recognized" human reality can the term *human* be used to state a truth in the strict and full sense of the term. For only in this case can one reveal a reality in speech. That is why it is necessary to say this of Self-Consciousness, of self-conscious man:] Self-Consciousness exists *in* and *for itself* in and by the fact that it exists (in and for itself) for another Self-Consciousness; i.e., it exists only as an entity that is recognized.

This pure concept of recognition, of the doubling of Self-Consciousness within its unity, must now be considered as its evolution appears to Self-Consciousness [i.e., not to the philosopher who speaks of it, but to the self-conscious man who recognizes another man or is recognized by him.]

In the first place, this evolution will make manifest the aspect of the inequality between the two Self-Consciousnesses [i.e., between the two men who confront one another for the sake of recognition], or the expansion of the middle-term [which is the mutual and reciprocal recognition] into the two extremes [which are the two who confront one another]; these are opposed to one another as extremes, the one only recognized, the other only recognizing. [To begin with, the man who wants to be recognized by another in no sense wants to recognize him in turn. If he succeeds, then, the recognition will not be mutual and reciprocal: he will be recognized but will not recognize the one who recognizes him.]

To begin with, Self-Consciousness is simple-or-undivided Being-for-itself; it is identical-to-itself by excluding from *itself* everything *other* [than itself]. Its essential-reality and its absolute object are, for it, *I* [I isolated from everything and opposed to everything that is not I]. And, in this *immediacy*, in this *given-being* [i.e., being that is not produced by an active, creative process] of its Being-for-itself, Self-Consciousness is *particular-and-isolated*. What is other for it exists as an object without essential-reality, as an object marked with the character of a negative-entity.

But [in the case we are studying] the other-entity, too, is a Self-Consciousness; a human-individual comes face to face with a human-individual. Meeting thus *immediately*, these individuals exist for one another as common objects. They are *autonomous* concrete-forms, Consciousnesses submerged in the *given-being* of *animal-life*. For it is as animal-life that the merely existing object has here presented itself. They are Consciousnesses that have not yet accomplished *for one another* the [dialectical] movement of absolute abstraction, which consists in the uprooting of all immediate given-being and in being nothing but the purely negative-or-negating given-being of the consciousness that is identical-to-itself.

Or in other words, these are entities that have not yet manifested themselves to one another as pure *Being-for-itself*—i.e., as *Self*-Consciousness. [When the "first" two men confront one another for the first time, the one sees in the other only an animal (and a dangerous and hostile one at that) that is to be destroyed, and not a self-conscious being representing an autonomous value.] Each of these two human-individuals is, to be sure, subjectively-certain of himself; but he is not certain of the other. And that is why his own subjective-certainty of himself does not yet possess truth [i.e., it does not yet reveal a reality—or, in other words, an entity that is objectively, intersubjectively, i.e., uni-

versally, recognized, and hence existing and valid]. For the truth of his subjective-certainty [of the idea that he has of himself, of the value that he attributes to himself] could have been nothing but the fact that his own Being-for-itself was manifested to him as an autonomous object; or again, to say the same thing: the fact that the object was manifested to him as this pure subjective-certainty of himself; [therefore, he must find the private idea that he has of himself in the external, objective reality.] But according to the concept of recognition, this is possible only if he accomplishes for the other (just as the other does for him) the pure abstraction of Being-for-itself; each accomplishing it in himself both by his own activity and also by the other's activity.

[The "first" man who meets another man for the first time already attributes an autonomous, absolute reality and an autonomous, absolute value to himself: we can say that he believes himself to be a man, that he has the "subjective certainty" of being a man. But his certainty is not yet knowledge. The value that he attributes to himself could be illusory; the idea that he has of himself could be false or mad. For that idea to be a truth, it must reveal an objective reality—i.e., an entity that is valid and exists not only for itself, but also for realities other than itself. In the case in question, man, to be really, truly "man," and to know that he is such, must, therefore, impose the idea that he has of himself on beings other than himself: he must be recognized by the others (in the ideal, extreme case, by all the others). Or again, he must transform the (natural and human) world in which he is not recognized into a world in which this recognition takes place. This transformation of the world that is hostile to a human project into a world in harmony with this project is called "action," "activity." This action—essentially human, because humanizing and anthropogenetic—will begin with the act of imposing oneself on the "first" other man one meets. And since this other, if he is (or more exactly, if he wants to be, and believes himself to be) a human being, must himself do the same thing, the "first" anthropogenetic action necessarily takes the form of a fight: a fight to the death between two beings that claim to be men, a fight for pure prestige carried on for the sake of "recognition" by the adversary. Indeed:]

The *manifestation* of the human-individual taken as pure abstraction of Being-for-itself consists in showing itself as being the pure negation of its objective-or-thingish mode-of-being—or, in other words, in showing that to be for oneself, or to be a man, is not to be bound to any determined *existence,* not to be bound to the universal isolated-particularity of existence as such, not to be bound to life. This manifestation is a *double* activity: activity of the other and activity by oneself. To the extent that this activity is activity *of the other,* each of the two men seeks the death of the other. But in that activity of the other is also found the second aspect, namely, the *activity by oneself:* for the activity in question implies in it the risk of the life of him who acts. The relation of the two Self-Consciousnesses, therefore, is determined in such a way that they come to light—each for itself and one for the other—through the fight for life and death.

[They "come to light"—that is, they prove themselves, they transform the purely subjective certainty that each has of his own value into objective, or universally valid and recognized, truth. Truth is the revelation of a reality. Now, the human reality is created, is constituted, only in the fight for recognition and by the risk of life that it implies. The truth of man, or the revelation of his reality, therefore, presupposes the fight to the death. And that is why] human-individuals are obliged to start this fight. For each must raise his subjective-certainty of *existing for self* to the level of truth, both in the other and in himself. And it is only through the risk of life that freedom comes to

light, that it becomes clear that the essential-reality of Self-Consciousness is not *given-being* [being that is not created by conscious, voluntary action], nor the *immediate* [natural, not mediated by action (that negates the given)] mode in which it first comes to sight [in the given world], nor submersion in the extension of animal-life; but that there is, on the contrary, nothing given in Self-Consciousness that is anything but a passing constituent-element for it. In other words, only by the risk of life does it come to light that Self-Consciousness is nothing but pure *Being-for-itself.* The human-individual that *has* not dared-to-risk his life can, to be sure, be recognized as a *human-person;* but he has not attained the truth of this fact of being recognized as an autonomous Self-Consciousness. Hence, each of the two human-individuals must have the death of the other as his goal, just as he risks his own life. For the other-entity is worth no more to him than himself. His essential-reality [which is his recognized, human reality and dignity] manifests itself to him as an other-entity [or another man, who does not recognize him and is therefore independent of him]. He is outside of himself [insofar as the other has not "given him back" to himself by recognizing him, by revealing that he has recognized him, and by showing him that he (the other) depends on him and is not absolutely other than he]. He must overcome his being-outside-of-himself. The other-entity [than he] is here a Self-Consciousness existing as a given-being and involved [in the natural world] in a manifold and diverse way. Now, he must look upon his other-being as pure Being-for-itself, i.e., as absolute negating-negativity. [This means that man is human only to the extent that he wants to impose himself on another man, to be recognized by him. In the beginning, as long as he is not yet actually recognized by the other, it is the other that is the end of his action; it is on this other, it is on recognition by this other, that his human value and reality depend; it is in this other that the meaning of his life is condensed. Therefore, he is "outside of himself." But his own value and his own reality are what are important to him, and he wants to have them in himself. Hence, he must overcome his "other-being." This is to say that he must make himself recognized by the other, he must have in himself the certainty of being recognized by another. But for that recognition to satisfy him, he has to know that the other is a human being. Now, in the beginning, he sees in the other only the aspect of an animal. To know that this aspect reveals a human reality, he must see that the other also wants to be recognized, and that he, too, is ready to risk, "to deny," his animal life in a fight for the recognition of his human being-for-itself. He must, therefore, "provoke" the other, force him to start a fight to the death for pure prestige. And having done this, he is obliged to kill the other in order not to be killed himself. In these circumstances, then, the fight for recognition can end only in the death of one of the adversaries—or of both together.] But this proving oneself by death does away with the truth [or revealed objective reality] that was supposed to come from it; and, for that very reason, it also does away with the subjective-certainty of oneself as such. For just as animal-life is the *natural* position of Consciousness, i.e., autonomy without absolute negating-negativity, so is death the *natural* negation of Consciousness, i.e., negation without autonomy, which negation, therefore, continues to lack the significance required by recognition. [That is to say: if both adversaries perish in the fight, "consciousness" is completely done away with, for man is nothing more than an inanimate body after his death. And if one of the adversaries remains alive but kills the other, he can no longer be recognized by the other; the man who has been defeated and killed does not recognize the victory of the conqueror. Therefore, the victor's certainty of his being and of his value

remains subjective, and thus has no "truth."] Through death, it is true, the subjective-certainty of the fact that both risked their lives and that each despised his own and the other's life has been established. But this certainty has not been established for those who underwent this struggle. Through death, they do away with their consciousness, which resides in that foreign entity, natural existence. That is to say, they do away with themselves. [For man is real only to the extent that he lives in a natural world. This world is, to be sure, "foreign" to him; he must "deny" it, transform it, fight it, in order to realize himself in it. But without this world, outside of this world, man is nothing.] And they are done away with as *extremes* that want to exist for self [i.e., consciously, and independently of the rest of the universe]. But, thereby, the essential constituent-element—i.e., the splitting up into extremes of opposed determinate things—disappears from the play of change. And the middle-term collapses in a dead unity, broken up into dead extremes, which merely exist as given-beings and are not opposed [to one another in, by, and for an action in which one tries "to do away with" the other by "establishing" himself and to establish himself by doing away with the other.] And the two do not give themselves reciprocally to one another, nor do they get themselves back in return from one another through consciousness. On the contrary, they merely leave one another free, indifferently, as things. [For the dead man is no longer anything more than an unconscious thing, from which the living man turns away in indifference, since he can no longer expect anything from it for himself.] Their murderous action is abstract negation. It is not negation [carried out] by consciousness, which overcomes in such a way that it *keeps* and *preserves* the overcome-entity and, for that very reason, survives the fact of being overcome. [This "overcoming" is "dialectical." "To overcome dialectically" means to overcome while preserving what is overcome; it is sublimated in and by that overcoming which preserves or that preservation which overcomes. The dialectically overcome-entity is annulled in its contingent (stripped of sense, "senseless") aspect of natural, given ("immediate") entity, but it is preserved in its essential (and meaningful, significant) aspect; thus mediated by negation, it is sublimated or raised up to a more "comprehensive" and comprehensible mode of being than that of its immediate reality of pure and simple, positive and static given, which is not the result of creative action (i.e., of action that negates the given).

[Therefore, it does the man of the Fight no good to kill his adversary. He must overcome him "dialectically." That is, he must leave him life and consciousness, and destroy only his autonomy. He must overcome the adversary only insofar as the adversary is opposed to him and acts against him. In other words, he must enslave him.]

In that experience [of the murderous fight] it becomes clear to Self-Consciousness that animal-life is just as important to it as pure self-conscious-ness. In the immediate Self-Consciousness [i.e., in the "first" man, who is not yet "mediated" by this contact with the other that the fight creates], the simple-or-undivided I [of isolated man] is the absolute object. But for us or in itself [i.e., for the author and the reader of this passage, who see man as he has been definitively formed at the end of history by the accomplished social inter-action] this object, i.e., the I, is absolute mediation, and its essential constituent-element is abiding autonomy. [That is to say, real and true man is the result of his inter-action with others; his I and the idea he has of himself are "mediated" by recognition obtained as a result of his action. And his true autonomy is the autonomy that he *maintains* in the social reality by the effort of that action.] The dissolution of that simple-or-undivided unity [which is the isolated I] is the result of the first experience [which

man has at the time of his "first" (murderous) fight]. By this experience are established: a pure Self-Consciousness [or an "abstract" one, since it has made the "abstraction" of its animal life by the risk of the fight—the victor], and a Consciousness that [being in fact a living corpse—the man who has been defeated and spared] does not exist purely for itself, but rather for another Consciousness [namely, for that of the victor]: i.e., a Conscious-ness that exists as a *given-being*, or in other words, a Consciousness that exists in the concrete-form of *thingness*. Both constituent-elements are essen-tial—since in the beginning they are unequal and opposed to one another and their reflection into unity has not yet resulted [from their action], they exist as two opposed concrete-forms of Conscious-ness. The one is autonomous Consciousness, for which the essential-reality is Being-for-itself. The other is dependent Consciousness, for which the essential-reality is animal-life, i.e., given-being for an other-entity. The former is the *Master*, the lat-ter—the *Slave*. [This Slave is the defeated adver-sary, who has not gone all the way in risking his life, who has not adopted the principle of the Mas-ters: to conquer or to die. He has accepted life granted him by another. Hence, he depends on that other. He has preferred slavery to death, and that is why, by remaining alive, he lives as a Slave.]

The Master is Consciousness existing *for itself*. And he is no longer merely the [abstract] concept of Consciousness, but a [real] Consciousness exist-ing for itself, which is mediated with itself by *another* Consciousness, namely, by a Conscious-ness to whose essential-reality it belongs to be syn-thesized with *given-being*, i.e., with thingness as such. [This "Consciousness" is the Slave who, in binding himself completely to his animal-life, is merely one with the natural world of things. By re-fusing to risk his life in a fight for pure prestige, he does not rise above the level of animals. Hence he considers himself as such, and as such is he considered by the Master. But the Slave, for his part, recognizes the Master in his human dignity and reality, and the Slave behaves accordingly. The Master's "certainty" is therefore not purely subjective and "immediate," but objectivized and "mediated" by another's, the Slave's, recognition. While the Slave still remains an "immediate," natural, "bestial" being, the Master—as a result of his fight—is already human, "mediated." And consequently, his behavior is also "mediated" or human, both with regard to things and with regard to other men; moreover, these other men, for him, are only slaves.] The Master is related to the following two constituent-elements: on the one hand, to a *thing* taken as such, i.e., the object of Desire; and, on the other hand, to the Consciousness for which thingness is the essential-entity [i.e., to the Slave, who, by refusing the risk, binds himself completely to the things on which he depends. The Master, on the other hand, sees in these things only a simple means of satisfying his desire; and, in satisfying it, he destroys them]. Given that: (1) the Master, taken as concept of self-consciousness, is the immediate relation of *Being-for-itself*, and that (2) he now [i.e., after his victory over the Slave] exists at the same time as mediation, i.e., as a Being-for-itself that exists for itself only through an other-entity [since the Master is Master only by the fact of having a Slave who recognizes him as Master]; the Master is related (1) immediately to both [i.e., to the thing and to the Slave], and (2) in a mediated way to each of the two through the other. The Master is related *in a mediated way to the Slave*, viz., by *autonomous given-being*; for it is precisely to this given-being that the Slave is tied. This given-being is his chain, from which he could not abstract in the fight, in which fight he was revealed—because of that fact—as dependent, as having his autonomy in thingness. The Master, on the other hand, is the power that rules over this given-being; for he revealed in the fight that this

given-being is worth nothing to him except as a negative-entity. Given that the Master is the power that rules over this given-being and that this given-being is the power that rules over the Other [i.e., over the Slave], the Master holds—in this [real or active] syllogism—that Other under his domination. Likewise, the Master is related *in a mediated way to the thing*, viz., *by the Slave*. Taken as Self-Consciousness as such, the Slave, too, is related to the thing in a negative or negating way, and he overcomes it [dialectically]. But—for him—the thing is autonomous at the same time. For that reason, he cannot, by his act-of-negating, finish it off to the point of the [complete] annihilation [of the thing, as does the Master who "consumes" it]. That is, he merely *transforms it by work* [i.e., he prepares it for consumption, but does not consume it himself]. For the Master, on the other hand, the *immediate* relation [to the thing] comes into being, through that mediation [i.e., through the work of the Slave who transforms the natural thing, the "raw material," with a view to its consumption (by the Master)], as pure negation of the object, that is, as *Enjoyment*. [Since all the effort is made by the Slave, the Master has only to enjoy the thing that the Slave has prepared for him, and to enjoy "negating" it, destroying it, by "consuming" it. (For example, he eats food that is completely prepared)]. What Desire [i.e., isolated man "before" the Fight, who was alone with Nature and whose desires were directed without detour toward that Nature] did not achieve, the Master [whose desires are directed toward things that have been transformed by the Slave] does achieve. The Master can finish off the thing completely and satisfy himself in Enjoyment. [Therefore, it is solely thanks to the work of another (his Slave) that the Master is free with respect to Nature, and consequently, satisfied with himself. But, he is Master of the Slave only because he previously freed himself from Nature (and from his own nature) by risking his life in a fight for pure prestige, which—as such—is not at all "natural."] Desire cannot achieve this because of the autonomy of the thing. The Master, on the other hand, who introduced the Slave between the thing and himself, is consequently joined only to the aspect of the thing's dependence, and has pure enjoyment from it. As for the aspect of the thing's autonomy, he leaves it to the Slave, who transforms the thing by work.

In these two constituent-elements the Master gets his recognition through another Consciousness; for in them the latter affirms itself as unessential, both by the act of working on the thing and by the fact of being dependent on a determinate existence. In neither case can this [slavish] Consciousness become master of the given-being and achieve absolute negation. Hence it is given in this constituent-element of recognition that the other Consciousness overcomes itself as Being-for-itself and thereby does itself what the other Consciousness does to it. [That is to say, the Master is not the only one to regard the Other as his Slave; this Other also considers himself as such.] The other constituent-element of recognition is equally implied in the relation under consideration; this other constituent-element is the fact that this activity of the second Consciousness [the slavish Consciousness] is the activity proper of the first Consciousness [i.e., the Master's]. For everything that the Slave does is, properly speaking, an activity of the Master. [Since the Slave works only for the Master, only to satisfy the Master's desire and not his own, it is the Master's desire that acts in and through the Slave.] For the Master, only Being-for-itself is the essential-reality. He is pure negative-or-negating power, for which the thing is nothing; and consequently, in this relation of Master and Slave, he is the pure essential activity. The Slave, on the other hand, is not pure activity, but nonessential activity. Now, for there to be an authentic recognition, there must also be the third

constituent-element, which consists in the Master's doing with respect to himself what he does with respect to the other, and in the Slave's doing with respect to the Other what he [the Slave] does with respect to himself. It is, therefore, an unequal and one-sided recognition that has been born from this relation of Master and Slave. [For although the Master treats the Other as Slave, he does not behave as Slave himself; and although the Slave treats the Other as Master, he does not behave as Master himself. The Slave does not risk his life, and the Master is idle.

[The relation between Master and Slave, therefore, is not recognition properly so-called. To see this, let us analyze the relation from the Master's point of view. The Master is not the only one to consider himself Master. The Slave, also, considers him as such. Hence, he is recognized in his human reality and dignity. But this recognition is one-sided, for he does not recognize in turn the Slave's human reality and dignity. Hence, he is recognized by someone whom he does not recognize. And this is what is insufficient—what is tragic—in his situation. The Master has fought and risked his life for a recognition without value for him. For he can be satisfied only by recognition from one whom he recognizes as worthy of recognizing him. The Master's attitude, therefore, is an existential impasse. On the one hand, the Master is Master only because his Desire was directed not toward a thing, but toward another desire—thus, it was a desire for recognition. On the other, when he has consequently become Master, it is as Master that he must desire to be recognized; and he can be recognized as such only by making the Other his Slave. But the Slave is for him an animal or a thing. He is, therefore, "recognized" by a thing. Thus, finally, his Desire is directed toward a thing, and not—as it seemed at first—toward a (human) Desire. The Master, therefore, was on the wrong track. After the fight that made him a Master, he is not what he wanted to be in starting that fight: a man recognized by another man. Therefore: if man can be satisfied only by recognition, the man who behaves as a Master will never be satisfied. And since—in the beginning—man is either Master or Slave, the satisfied man will necessarily be a Slave; or more exactly, the man who has been a Slave, who has passed through Slavery, who has "dialectically overcome" his slavery. Indeed:]

Thus the nonessential [or slavish] Consciousness is—for the Master—the object that forms the *truth* [or revealed reality] of the subjective-certainty he has of himself [since he can "know" he is Master only by being recognized as such by the Slave]. But it is obvious that this object does not correspond to its concept. For in the Master's fulfilling himself, something entirely different from an autonomous Consciousness has come into being [since he is faced with a Slave]. It is not such an autonomous Consciousness, but all to the contrary, a dependent Consciousness, that exists for him. Therefore, he is not subjectively certain of his *Being-for-itself* as of a truth [or of a revealed objective reality]. His truth, all to the contrary, is nonessential Consciousness, and the nonessential activity of that Consciousness. [That is to say, the Master's "truth" is the Slave and the Slave's Work. Actually, others recognize the Master as Master only because he has a Slave; and the Master's life consists in consuming the products of slavish Work, and in living on and by this Work.]

Consequently, the *truth* of autonomous Consciousness is *slavish Consciousness*. This latter first appears, it is true, as existing *outside* of itself and not as the truth of Self-Consciousness [since the Slave recognizes human dignity not in himself, but in the Master, on whom his very existence depends]. But, just as Mastery showed that its essential-reality is the reverse or perversion of what it wants to be, so much the more will Slavery, in its fulfillment, probably become the opposite of what

it is immediately; as *repressed* Consciousness it will go within itself and reverse and transform itself into true autonomy.

[The complete, absolutely free man, definitively and completely satisfied by what he is, the man who is perfected and completed in and by this satisfaction, will be the Slave who has "overcome" his Slavery. If idle Mastery is an impasse, laborious Slavery, in contrast, is the source of all human, social, historical progress. History is the history of the working Slave. To see this, one need only consider the relationship between Master and Slave (that is, the first result of the "first" human, social, historical contact), no longer from the Master's point of view, but from the Slave's.]

We have seen only what Slavery is in its relation to Mastery. But Slavery is also Self-Consciousness. What it is as such, in and for itself, must now be considered. In the first place, it is the Master that is the essential-reality for Slavery. *The autonomous Consciousness existing for itself* is hence, for it, *the truth* [or a revealed reality], which, however, *for it*, does not yet exist *in it*. [The Slave is subordinated to the Master. Hence the Slave esteems, recognizes, the value and the reality of "autonomy," of human freedom. However, he does not find it realized in himself; he finds it only in the Other. And this is his advantage. The Master, unable to recognize the Other who recognizes him, finds himself in an impasse. The Slave, on the other hand, recognizes the Other (the Master) from the beginning. In order that mutual and reciprocal recognition, which alone can fully and definitively realize and satisfy man, be established, it suffices for the Slave to impose himself on the Master and be recognized by him. To be sure, for this to take place, the Slave must cease to be Slave: he must transcend himself, "overcome" himself, as Slave. But if the Master has no desire to "overcome"—and hence no possibility of "overcoming"—himself as Master (since this would mean, for him, to become a Slave), the

Slave has every reason to cease to be a Slave. Moreover, the experience of the fight that made him a Slave predisposes him to that act of self-overcoming, of negation of himself (negation of his given I, which is a slavish I). To be sure, in the beginning, the Slave who binds himself to his given (slavish) I does not have this "negativity" in himself. He sees it only in the Master, who realized pure "negating-negativity" by risking his life in the fight for recognition.] However, Slavery *in fact* has *in itself* this truth [or revealed reality] of pure negating-negativity and of *Being-for-itself*. For it has *experienced* this essential-reality within itself. This slavish Consciousness was afraid not for this or that, not for this moment or that, but for its [own] entire essential-reality: it underwent the fear of death, the fear of the absolute Master. By this fear, the slavish Consciousness melted internally; it shuddered deeply and everything fixed-or-stable trembled in it. Now, this pure universal [dialectical] movement, this absolute liquefaction of every stable-support, is the simple-or-undivided essential-reality of Self-Consciousness, absolute negating-negativity, *pure Being-for-itself*. Thus, this Being-for-itself exists *in* the slavish Consciousness. [The Master is fixed in his Mastery. He cannot go beyond himself, change, progress. He must conquer—and become Master or preserve himself as such—or die. He can be killed; he cannot be transformed, educated. He has risked his life to be Master. Therefore, Mastery is the supreme given value for him, beyond which he cannot go. The Slave, on the other hand, did not want to be a Slave. He became a Slave because he did not want to risk his life to become a Master. In his mortal terror he understood (without noticing it) that a given, fixed, and stable condition, even though it be the Master's, cannot exhaust the possibilities of human existence. He "understood" the "vanity" of the given conditions of existence. He did not want to bind himself to the Master's condition, nor does he bind himself to his condition

as a Slave. There is nothing fixed in him. He is ready for change; in his very being, he is change, transcendence, transformation, "education"; he is historical becoming at his origin, in his essence, in his very existence. On the one hand, he does not bind himself to what he is; he wants to transcend himself by negation of his given state. On the other hand, he has a positive ideal to attain; the ideal of autonomy, of Being-for-itself, of which he finds the incarnation, at the very origin of his Slavery, in the Master.] This onstituent-element of Being-for-itself also exists *for slavish Consciousness*. For in the Master, Being-for-itself is, for it [the slavish Consciousness], its object. [An object that it knows to be external, opposed, to it, and that it tends to appropriate for itself. The Slave knows what it is to be free. He also knows that he is not free, and that he wants to become free. And if the experience of the Fight and its result predispose the Slave to transcendence, to progress, to History, his life as a Slave working in the Master's service realizes this predisposition.] In addition, slavish Consciousness is not only this universal dissolution [of everything fixed, stable, and given], taken *as such*; in the Master's service, it accomplishes this dissolution *in an objectively real way* [i.e., concretely]. In service [in the forced work done in the service of another (the Master)], slavish Consciousness [dialectically] overcomes its attachment to natural existence in all the *particular-and-isolated* constituent-elements, and it eliminates this existence by work. [The Master forces the Slave to work. And by working, the Slave becomes master of Nature. Now he became the Master's Slave only because—in the beginning—he was a slave of Nature, joining with it and subordinating himself to its laws by accepting the instinct of preservation. In becoming master of Nature by work, then, the Slave frees himself from his own nature, from his own instinct that tied him to Nature and made him the Master's Slave. Therefore, by freeing the

Slave from Nature, work frees him from himself as well, from his Slave's nature: it frees him from the Master. In the raw, natural, given World, the Slave is slave of the Master. In the technical world transformed by his work, he rules—or, at least, will one day rule—as absolute Master. And this Mastery that arises from work, from the progressive transformation of the given World and of man given in this World, will be an entirely different thing from the "immediate" Mastery of the Master. The future and History hence belong not to the warlike Master, who either dies or preserves himself indefinitely in identity to himself, but to the working Slave. The Slave, in transforming the given World by his work, transcends the given and what is given by that given in himself; hence, he goes beyond himself, and also goes beyond the Master who is tied to the given which, not working, he leaves intact. If the fear of death, incarnated for the Slave in the person of the warlike Master, is the *sine qua non* of historical progress, it is solely the Slave's work that realizes and perfects it.]

However, the feeling of absolute power that the Slave experienced as such in the fight and also experiences in the particularities of service [for the Master whom he fears] is as yet only dissolution effected *in itself*. [Without this sense of power—i.e., without the terror and dread inspired by the Master—man would never be Slave and consequently could not attain the final perfection. But this condition "in itself"—i.e., this objectively real and necessary condition—is not sufficient. Perfection (which is always conscious of itself) can be attained only in and by work. For only in and by work does man finally become aware of the significance, the value, and the necessity of his experience of fearing absolute power, incarnated for him in the Master. Only after having worked for the Master does he understand the necessity of the fight between Master and Slave and the value of the risk and terror that it implies.] Thus, although

the terror inspired by the Master is the beginning of wisdom, it can only be said that in this terror Consciousness exists *for itself*, but is not yet *Being-for-itself*. [In mortal terror man becomes aware of his reality, of the value that the simple fact of living has for him; only thus does he take account of the "seriousness" of existence. But he is not yet aware of his autonomy, of the value and the "seriousness" of his liberty, of his human dignity.] But through work Consciousness comes to itself. [In work, i.e.] in the constituent-element that corresponds to Desire in the Master's consciousness, it seemed, it is true, that the nonessential relation to the thing was what fell to the lot of the slavish Consciousness; this is because the thing preserves its autonomy. [It seemed that, in and by work, the Slave is enslaved to Nature, to the thing, to "raw material"; while the Master, who is content to consume the thing prepared by the Slave and to enjoy it, is perfectly free with respect to it. But this is not the case. To be sure] the [Master's] Desire has reserved for itself the pure act-of-negating the object [by consuming it] and has thereby reserved for itself the unmixed sentiment-of-self-and-of-one's-dignity [experienced in enjoyment]. But for the same reason this satisfaction itself is but a passing phase, for it lacks the *objective* aspect—i.e., the *stable support*. [The Master, who does not work, produces nothing stable outside of himself. He merely destroys the products of the Slave's work. Thus his enjoyment and his satisfaction remain purely subjective: they are of interest only to him and therefore can be recognized only by him; they have no "truth," no objective reality revealed to all. Accordingly, this "consumption," this idle enjoyment of the Master's, which results from the "immediate" satisfaction of desire, can at the most procure some pleasure for man; it can never give him complete and definitive satisfaction.] Work, on the other hand, is *repressed* Desire, an *arrested* passing phase; or, in other words, it forms-and-educates. [Work transforms the World and civilizes, educates, Man. The man who wants to work—or who must work—must repress the instinct that drives him "to consume" "immediately" the "raw" object. And the Slave can work for the Master—that is, for another than himself—only by repressing his own desires. Hence, he transcends himself by working—or, perhaps better, he educates himself, he "cultivates" and "sublimates" his instincts by repressing them. On the other hand, he does not destroy the thing as it is given. He postpones the destruction of the thing by first trans-forming it through work; he prepares it for consumption—that is to say, he "forms" it. In his work, he transforms things and trans-forms himself at the same time: he forms things and the World by transforming himself, by educating himself; and he educates himself, he forms himself, by transforming things and the World. Thus,] the negative-or-negating relation to the object becomes a *form* of this object and gains *permanence*, precisely because, for the worker, the object has autonomy. At the same time, the *negative-or-negating* middle-term—i.e., the forming *activity* [of work]—is the *isolated-particularity* or the pure Being-for-itself of the Consciousness. And this Being-for-itself, through work, now passes into what is outside of the Consciousness, into the element of permanence. The working Consciousness thereby attains a contemplation of autonomous given-being such that it contemplates *itself* in it. [The product of work is the worker's production. It is the realization of his project, of his idea; hence, it is he that is realized in and by this product, and consequently he contemplates himself when he contemplates it. Now, this artificial product is at the same time just as "autonomous," just as objective, just as independent of man, as is the natural thing. Therefore, it is by work, and only by work, that man *realizes* himself *objectively* as man. Only after producing an artificial object is man himself really and objectively

more than and different from a natural being; and only in this real and objective product does he become truly conscious of his subjective human reality. Therefore, it is only by work that man is a supernatural being that is conscious of its reality; by working, he is "incarnated" Spirit, he is historical "World," he is "objectivized" History.

[Work, then, is what "forms-or-educates" man beyond the animal. The "formed-or-educated" man, the completed man who is satisfied by his completion, is hence necessarily not Master, but Slave; or, at least, he who has passed through Slavery. Now, there is no Slave without a Master. The Master, then, is the catalyst of the historical, anthropogenetic process. He himself does not participate actively in this process; but without him, without his presence, this process would not be possible. For, if the history of man is the history of his work, and if this work is historical, social, human, only on the condition that it is carried out against the worker's instinct or "immediate interest," the work must be carried out in the service of another, and must be a forced work, stimulated by fear of death. It is this work, and only this work, that frees—i.e., humanizes—man (the Slave). On the one hand, this work creates a real objective World, which is a non-natural World, a cultural, historical, human World. And it is only in this World that man lives an essentially different life from that of animals (and "primitive" man) in the bosom of Nature. On the other hand, this work liberates the Slave from the terror that tied him to given Nature and to his own innate animal nature. It is by work in the Master's service performed in terror that the Slave frees himself from the terror that enslaved him to the Master.]

Now, the forming [of the thing by work] contains not only the positive significance that the slavish Consciousness, taken as pure *Being-for-itself*, becomes an *entity that exists as a given-being* [that is to say, work is something more than the action by which man creates an essentially human technical World that is just as real as the natural World inhabited by animals]. The forming [of the thing by work] has a further negative-or-negating significance that is directed against the first constituent-element of the slavish Consciousness; namely, against fear. For in the act of forming the thing, the negating-negativity proper of Consciousness—i.e., its Being-for-itself—comes to be an Object [i.e., a World] for Consciousness only by the fact that Consciousness [dialectically] overcomes the opposed *form* that exists as a [natural] given-being. Now, this objective *negative-entity* is precisely the foreign essential-reality before which slavish Consciousness trembled. Now, on the contrary, this Consciousness destroys that foreign negative-entity [in and by work]. Consciousness establishes *itself* as a negative-entity in the element of permanency; and thereby it becomes a thing *for itself*, an *entity-existing-for-itself*. In the Master, *Being-for-itself* is, for the slavish Consciousness, *an other* Being-for-itself; or again, Being-for-itself exists there only *for the slavish Consciousness*. In fear, Being-for-itself [already] exists *in the slavish Consciousness itself*. But in the act of forming [by work], Being-for-itself is constituted for slavish Consciousness as *its own*, and slavish Consciousness becomes aware of the fact that it itself exists in and for itself. The form [the idea or project conceived by the Consciousness], by being *established outside* [of the Consciousness, by being introduced—through work—into the objective reality of the World], does not become, for the [working] Consciousness, an other-entity than it. For it is precisely that form that is its pure Being-for-itself; and, in that form, this Being-for-itself is constituted for it [the Consciousness] as truth [or as revealed, conscious, objective reality. The man who works recognizes his own product in the World that has actually been transformed by his work: he recognizes himself in it, he sees in it his own

human reality, in it he discovers and reveals to others the objective reality of his humanity, of the originally abstract and purely subjective idea he has of himself.] By this act of finding itself by itself, then, the [working] Consciousness becomes *its own meaning-or-will*; and this happens precisely in work, in which it seemed to be *alien meaning-or-will*.

[Man achieves his true autonomy, his authentic freedom, only after passing through Slavery, after surmounting fear of death by work performed in the service of another (who, for him, is the incarnation of that fear). Work that frees man is hence necessarily, in the beginning, the forced work of a Slave who serves an all-powerful Master, the holder of all real power.]

For that reflection [of Consciousness into itself], the [following] two constituent-elements [first, that] of terror, and [second, that] of service as such, as well as the educative-forming [by work], are equally necessary. And, at the same time, the two elements are necessary in a universal way. [On the one hand,] without the discipline of service and obedience, terror remains in the formal domain and is not propagated in the conscious objective-reality of existence. [It is not sufficient to be afraid, nor even to be afraid while realizing that one fears death. It is necessary to live in terms of terror. Now, to live in such a way is to serve someone whom one fears, someone who inspires or incarnates terror; it is to serve a Master (a real, that is, a human Master, or the "sublimated" Master—God). And to serve a Master is to obey his laws. Without this service, terror could not transform existence, and existence, therefore, could never go beyond its initial state of terror. It is by serving another, by externalizing oneself, by binding oneself to others, that one is liberated from the enslaving dread that the idea of death inspires. On the other hand,] without the educative-forming [by work], terror remains internal-or-private and mute, and

Consciousness does not come into being for itself. [Without work that transforms the real objective World, man cannot really transform himself. If he changes, his change remains "private," purely subjective, revealed to himself alone, "mute," not communicated to others. And this "internal" change puts him at variance with the World, which has not changed, and with the others, who are bound to the unchanged World. This change, then, transforms man into a madman or a criminal, who is sooner or later annihilated by the natural and social objective reality. Only work, by finally putting the objective World into harmony with the subjective idea that at first goes beyond it, annuls the element of madness and crime that marks the attitude of every man who—driven by terror—tries to go beyond the given World of which he is afraid, in which he feels terrified, and in which, consequently, he could not be satisfied.] But, if the Consciousness forms [the thing by work] without having experienced absolute primordial terror, it is merely its vain intention or self-will; for the form or the negating-negativity of that Consciousness is not negating-negativity *in itself*; and consequently its act-of-forming cannot give it consciousness of itself as the essential-reality. If the Consciousness has not endured absolute terror, but merely some fear or other, the negative-or-negating essential-reality remains an external-entity for it, and its [own] substance is not entirely infected by this essential-reality. Since all the fulfillments-or-accomplishments of its natural consciousness have not vacillated, that Consciousness still belongs—*in itself*—to determined given-being. Its intention or self-will [*der eigene Sinn*] is then stubborn-capriciousness [*Eigensinn*]: a freedom that still remains within the bounds of Slavery. The pure form [imposed on the given by this work] cannot come into being for that Consciousness, as essential-reality. Likewise, considered as extension over particular-and-isolated entities, this form is not [a] universal educative-forming; it is not absolute Concept. This form, on the contrary, is a skillfulness that dominates only certain things, but does not dominate universal power and the totality of objective essential-reality.

[The man who has not experienced the fear of death does not know that the given natural World is hostile to him, that it tends to kill him, to destroy him, and that it is essentially unsuited to satisfy him really. This man, therefore, remains fundamentally bound to the given World. At the most, he will want to "reform" it—that is, to change its details, to make particular transformations without modifying its essential characteristics. This man will act as a "skillful" reformer, or better, a conformer, but never as a true revolutionary. Now, the given World in which he lives belongs to the (human or divine) Master, and in this World he is necessarily Slave. Therefore, it is not reform, but the "dialectical," or better, revolutionary, overcoming of the World that can free him, and—consequently—satisfy him. Now, this revolutionary transformation of the World presupposes the "negation," the non-accepting of the given World *in its totality*. And the origin of this absolute negation can only be the absolute dread inspired by the given World, or more precisely, by that which, or by him who, dominates this World, by the Master of this World. Now, the Master who (involuntarily) engenders the desire of revolutionary negation is the Master of the Slave. Therefore, man can free himself from the given World that does not satisfy him only if this World, in its totality, belongs properly to a (real or "sub-limated") Master. Now, as long as the Master lives, he himself is always enslaved by the World of which he is the Master. Since the Master transcends the given World only in and by the risk of his life, it is only his death that "realizes" his freedom. As long as he lives, therefore, he never attains the freedom that would raise him above the given World. The Master can never detach himself from the World in which he lives, and if this World perishes, he perishes with it. Only the Slave can transcend the given World (which is subjugated by the Master) and not perish. Only the Slave can transform the World that forms him and fixes him in slavery and create a World that he has formed in which he will be free. And the Slave achieves this only through forced and terrified work carried out in the Master's service. To be sure, this work by itself does not free him. But in transforming the World by this work, the Slave transforms himself, too, and thus creates the new objective conditions that permit him to take up once more the liberating Fight for recognition that he refused in the beginning for fear of death. And thus in the long run, all slavish work realizes not the Master's will but the will—at first unconscious—of the Slave, who—finally—succeeds where the Master—necessarily—fails. Therefore, it is indeed the originally dependent, serving, and slavish Consciousness that in the end realizes and reveals the ideal of autonomous Self-Consciousness and is thus its "truth."]

chapter twenty-nine

Jean-Paul Sartre

Jean-Paul Sartre (1905–1980), philosopher, novelist, playwright, and political activist, remains the figure most closely associated with the existentialist philosophy that emerged from France during the 1940s and 1950s. Born in Paris, into what was at the time considered a bourgeois family, Sartre became from an early age aware of the class struggles that characterized early twentieth-century French society. He was to spend the first half of his life developing an uninvolved, apolitical, and individualistic philosophical system, and the second half to reconciling that system with the fundamental tenets of Marxian thought.

By the time Sartre was born, his father, an engineer and naval officer, was dying of an illness he had contracted during his service in Coindochina. He would pass away shortly after Sartre's birth. In his autobiography, *The Words*, Sartre describes the death of his father as "the big event of my life. . . . it gave me freedom. . . . Had he lived, my father would have leaned on me at full length and would have crushed me. As luck had it, he died at a young age."[1] Widowed at the age of twenty, Sartre's mother, Anne-Marie Schweitzer, turned for support to her parents and particularly to her father, Charles, an atheist and schoolteacher who was to have a profound influence on the course of Sartre's life.

Taught by his grandfather, Sartre did not attend his first school until he was ten years old. He first attended the Lycée Henri IV, where he fared rather poorly but met his long-time friend, writer and political activist Paul Nizan. He then transferred to La Rochelle's Lycée for boys upon his mother's second marriage in 1917. Sartre read voraciously and began to take writing more seriously: "I understood that the writer, whatever he claims, no matter how unconscious, wants to change the world by giving it meaning. And since such an endeavor pits the writer against the most powerful creature ever invented, namely God, his method must be violent by definition."[2]

In the fall of 1920, Sartre's mother sent him back to Paris where he returned to the Lycée Henri IV as a boarder. There, he renewed ties with his close friend, Paul Nizan;

the two would eventually decide to prepare for and take the national entrance exam to the prestigious *Ecole Normale Supérieure* (ENS), where France's elite professors are trained. In 1922, both Sartre and Nizan enrolled in *hypokhâgne* and *khâgne*, the programs that prepare students for the entrance exam, and both passed the exam in August of 1924, with Sartre placing seventh out of thousands of examinees.[3]

It was philosophy that interested Sartre the most at the ENS:

> I got hooked on philosophy through [Henri] Bergson while still in lycée. . . . He showed that knowledge begins with intuition, that we must seize the world. Philosophy explains these intuitions. To communicate them, one had to resort to some other discipline—literature. So I decided to study philosophy and teach philosophy, but not to be a philosopher . . . I was going to be a writer in order to communicate the realities that the study of philosophy made me grasp.[4]

Sartre did in fact write several short stories during his time at the ENS, but also a three-hundred-page essay on the image that would later serve as an outline for his early philosophical works, *Imagination* (1936), *Psychology of the Imagination* (1940), and *Being and Nothingness* (1943). In 1929, Sartre passed the *agrégation* in philosophy (roughly equivalent to a doctorate in the United States), placing first on the exam, and in the process met the person who was to have the greatest impact on his life, his long-time friend and lover Simone de Beauvoir, who placed second on the exam and would go on to attain prominence in her own right.[5] Two years later, having completed his mandatory military service, Sartre was appointed to a teaching position in Le Havre, where he began writing what would become his most celebrated literary work, the novel *Nausea* (1938). In 1933 he discovered the radical idealism of G. W. F. Hegel and the phenomenology of Edmund Husserl, both of which would have a profound impact on the direction of his philosophical thought.

Sartre spent the next year in Berlin, and it was there that he "first took a position, that [he] committed [him]self in print for the first time."[6] Influenced by Husserl, Sartre wrote *The Transcendence of the Ego* (1937), in which he attacked Husserl. Indeed, Husserl had shown that consciousness is always consciousness *of* an object, that it has no content in itself, and that it is intentional, that is, always directed toward an object. But because Husserl had wanted to study that object separately from the "I" that was seeing or knowing it, he had then gone on to posit the existence of a transcendental "ego," or "I," that "stands behind" consciousness and can "separate" itself from the object it is perceiving. In *The Transcendence of the Ego*, his first philosophical essay, Sartre set out to purge consciousness of Husserl's transcendental ego, claiming instead that the ego is in-the-world, outside of consciousness, and that consciousness is therefore empty, having "nothing" for its content; consciousness is, in fact, an *act* rather than an entity. Having thus emptied consciousness of the transcendental ego, Sartre proposed that phenomenology could now concern itself with human activity in concrete situations, that is, with existence.

The principles set out by Sartre in *The Transcendence of the Ego* would later serve as the foundation of the philosophical essay excerpted here, *Being and Nothingness* (1943). Sartre wrote *Being and Nothingness* during World War II, while a prisoner of war in Germany, and, after his 1941 escape, while a member of the "intellectual" resistance group he and Simone de Beauvoir founded along with Maurice Merleau-Ponty. The text is a work of phenomenological ontology, which is to say that it sets out to grasp, in its totality, the relation of human beings to being (ontology) through a description of the way in which being reveals itself or appears to us (phenomenology). In it, Sartre describes three distinct modes of being: being-in-itself, being-for-itself, and being-for-others. The first ontological category, being-in-itself, is the existence of mere things: "Being is. Being is in-itself. Being is what it is."[7] In other words, the existence of things is a kind of all-encompassing, undifferentiated, never-changing stuff. Being-for-itself, the second ontological category, is the term Sartre uses to refer to human consciousness. Because consciousness is nothingness, an activity without content, it is *negating* activity, and through it negation is introduced into the world. We are free to imagine a world different than it is, as well as to imagine ourselves other than what we are, and are then responsible for acting toward these future possibilities.

Finally, the third ontological category, being-for-others, refers to a mode of being that is on par with the other two and not derivative of them. Sartre proposes that we encounter modes of consciousness that, even as they themselves remain within the structure of the for-itself, reveal the existence of a radically different ontological structure. Strictly speaking, this structure remains mine. It is for-itself in the sense that it concerns my being, my consciousness. But these modes of consciousness reveal to me a being that is mine without being for-me.[8] What does this mean?

Shame, for instance, is a mode of consciousness that reveals to me a being that is mine but not for-me. I am ashamed *of* myself, but I am also ashamed *before* somebody. Thus, I am ashamed of myself *as I appear to the other*, for the simple reason that the other acts as mediator between me and myself. Shame, by definition, is recognition: I recognize that I am as the other sees me. In this way, the other not only reveals to me what I am, namely, a shameful object, but fixes me in an entirely new and distinct mode of being: being-for-others.[9] This he accomplishes through his *look*.

Sartre begins from the premise that one's fundamental relation with the other is characterized by the constant possibility of being seen by the other. If "the other-as-object is defined in connection with the world as the object which sees what I see," he writes, then "my fundamental connection with the other-as-subject must be able to be referred back to my permanent possibility of *being seen* by the other."[10] This relation, Sartre proposes, is a fact that cannot be deduced either from the essence of the other-as-object or from my being-as-subject. It is "a concrete, daily relation which at each instant I experience."[11] Thus, if the other is by principle the being who looks at me, then we should be able to explain the meaning, and consequences, of the other's look.

Now, the look of the other "is first an intermediary that refers me to myself."[12] To understand what this means, we need only refer to our previous discussion of shame: I see myself as the other sees me; I recognize that I am as I appear to the other. To see the way in which this relation manifests itself concretely, Sartre proposes the famous example of a man who, believing himself to be alone, looks through the keyhole of a door.

At this point in the example, the man is pure consciousness, or being-for-itself. He is aware only of that which is on the other side of the door, and that which is on the other side of the door exists only to be seen, to be heard, by him. In a sense, the man *is* his acts, which means that the acts are free of his judgment and value. This is not, then, a reflective situation, which is to say that the man is not conscious of himself as *being* anything.[13]

The situation changes drastically, however, when the man hears footsteps and realizes that someone is looking at him. First, the look of the other brings about in him an awareness of himself that to this point had been absent. To put it another way, the look of the other results in an irruption of self that can be described in terms of the man's seeing himself because somebody sees him. A consciousness that was unreflective now becomes reflective, with the consequence that the man becomes conscious not only of himself, but also of his world and of himself as an object *in* that world. Where he had once been the foundation of his own being, the man now finds this foundation outside of himself—he is for himself only to the extent that he is pure reference to the other.[14]

It is important to note here that the other does not appear to the man as an object. Instead of being an object, the other, as we saw in Sartre's discussion of shame, appears to me as that being who fixes me in a mode of being of which I was not aware; it is, Sartre says, "shame or pride which reveals to me the other's look and myself at the end of that look.[15] To be looked-at is, in a sense, to be imprisoned in a mode of being of which I am not the foundation. My relation to this being—my being—is one of ambiguity. On one hand, I am this being, not in the sense of "having-to-be" or "was," but in-itself. I do not found it in its being, nor can I produce it directly. On the other hand, my being retains for me "a certain indetermination" which is the consequence not of the fact that I cannot know the other, but of the fact that the other is free. Or, to reverse the terms, the other's freedom is revealed to me through the indetermination of the being which I am for him. Thus, this being which the other confers to me is not *my* possibility, but rather "the limit of my freedom."[16] In this way, Sartre sets up a system in which my relation with the other is from the very beginning one of confrontation: I am either the one whose being is conferred to him by the other, or the one who confers to the other her being. The other represents for me nothing other than the limit of my freedom, or I the limit of hers.

For this reason, my concrete relations with the other will consist almost entirely in an attempt on my part to regain my freedom and to become once more the foundation of my being, to escape, that is, from the look of the other. In order to do so, Sartre proposes that I will adopt any one of six attitudes[17] toward the other, two of which, love and masochism, are described in the passage excerpted here.

In his later works, most notably in his *Critique of Dialectical Reason* (1958–1959), Sartre increasingly turned to politics, which he had for the most part spurned during the first half of his life, and in particular to the reconciliation of existentialist principles with those set out in traditional Marxian thought. This required that he overcome the insular and "bourgeois" consciousness described in *Being and Nothingness* and integrate his philosophy of freedom and action into the group-centered principles of Marxian thought, a process that, Sartre proposed, could be achieved through revolutionary engagement. True to his philosophy, Sartre became a vocal adversary of France's involvement in Algeria's war of independence and of U.S. involvement in Vietnam.

Weakened and blinded by a series of strokes, Jean-Paul Sartre died in Paris on the April 15, 1980. Over the course of his life, Sartre was awarded the 1964 Nobel Prize for literature and the Legion of Honor (France's highest award). He also was offered a prestigious teaching position at the Collège de France as well as one of the twenty-four seats on the French Academy. Refusing to be turned into what he termed a "bourgeois institution," Sartre turned them all down.

DG

QUESTIONS

1. What does Sartre mean he states that "we must recognize that we experience our inapprehensible being-for-others in the form of a *possession*"?

2. Explain what the "ideal of love" is for Sartre.

3. For Sartre, what is the lover's project? Why is love a conflict?

4. Why, according to Sartre, is the lover's project bound to fail?

5. What enterprise, according to Sartre, is "expressed concretely by the *masochistic* attitude"? Why is the masochist's project bound to fail?

ENDNOTES

1. Jean-Paul Sartre, *Les mots* (Paris: Gallimard, 1964), p. 18.

2. Sartre, quoted in Gerassi, p. 63.

3. Sartre's class at the ENS included Paul Nizan, who would go on to become a prominent writer and political activist, as well as Raymond Aron, who would become one of Sartre's most vocal adversaries, both philosophically and politically. The next year's class included Jean Hyppolite, the first to translate Hegel's *Phenomenology of Spirit* into French, and the class after that, Maurice Merleau-Ponty.

4. Gerassi, p. 75.

5. See chapter 30 for a more thorough discussion of Simone de Beauvoir.

6. Gerassi, p. 115.

7. Sartre, *Being and Nothingness*, p. 29.

8. Ibid., p. 301.

9. Ibid.

10. Ibid., p. 344.

11. Ibid., p. 345.

12. Ibid., p. 347.

13. Ibid., p. 348.

14. Ibid., p. 349.

15. Ibid.

16. Ibid., p. 351.

17. Thus, one's concrete relations with the other, though inherently confrontational, are not essentially sadomasochistic. In actuality, there are three fundamental attitudes toward the other (love, desire, and indifference) and their three perversions (respectively, masochism, sadism, and hate).

SELECTED BIBLIOGRAPHY

Gerassi, John. *Jean-Paul Sartre: Hated Conscience of His Century*. Chicago: University of Chicago Press, 1989.

Sartre, Jean-Paul. *Being and Nothingness: A Phenomenological Essay on Ontology*, trans. Hazel E. Barnes. New York: Washington Square Press, 1956.

from *Being and Nothingness*

Jean-Paul Sartre

CONCRETE RELATIONS WITH OTHERS

Up to this point we have described only our fundamental relation with the Other. This relation has enabled us to make explicit our body's three dimensions of being. And since the original bond with the Other first arises in connection with the relation between my body and the Other's body, it seemed clear to us that the knowledge of the nature of the body was indispensable to any study of the particular relations of my being with that of the Other. These particular relations, in fact, on both sides presuppose facticity; that is, our existence as body in the midst of the world. Not that the body is the instrument and the cause of my relations with others. But the body constitutes their meaning and marks their limits. It is as body-in-situation that I apprehend the Other's transcendence-transcended, and it is as body-in-situation that I experience myself in my alienation for the

Other's benefit. Now we can examine these concrete relations since we are cognizant of what the body is. They are not simple specifications of the fundamental relation. Although each one of them includes within it the original relation with the Other as its essential structure and its foundation, they are entirely new modes of being on the part of the for-itself. In fact they represent the various attitudes of the for-itself in a world where there are Others. Therefore each relation in its own way presents the bilateral relation: for-itself-for-others, in-itself. If then we succeed in making explicit the structures of our most primitive relations with the Other-in-the-world, we shall have completed our task. At the beginning of this work, we asked, "What are the relations of the for-itself with the in-itself?" We have learned now that our task is more complex. There is a relation of the for-itself with the in-itself *in the presence of the Other*. When we have described this concrete fact, we shall be in a position to form conclusions concerning the fundamental relations of the three modes of being, and we shall perhaps be able to attempt a metaphysical theory of being in general.

The for-itself as the nihilation of the in-itself temporalizes itself as a *flight toward*. Actually it surpasses its facticity (*i.e.*, to be either *given* or past or body) toward the in-itself which it would be if it were able to be its own foundation. This may be translated into terms already psychological—and hence inaccurate although perhaps clearer—by saying that the for-itself attempts to escape its factual existence (*i.e.*, its being there, as an in-itself for which it is in no way the foundation) and that this flight takes place toward an impossible future always pursued where the for-itself would be an in-itself-for-itself—*i.e.*, an in-itself which would be to itself its own foundation. Thus the for-itself is both a flight and a pursuit; it flees the in-itself and at the same time pursues it. The for-itself is a pursued-pursuing. But in order to lessen the danger of

a psychological interpretation of the preceding remarks, let us note that the for-itself is not *first* in order to attempt *later* to attain being; in short we must not conceive of it as an existent which would be provided with tendencies as this glass is provided with certain particular qualities. This pursuing flight is not a given which is added on to the being of the for-itself. The for-itself *is* this very flight. The flight is not to be distinguished from the original nihilation. To say that the for-itself is a pursued-pursuing, or that it is in the mode of having to be its being, or that it is not what it is and is what it is not—each of these statements is saying the same thing. The for-itself is not the in-itself and can not be it. But it is a relation to the in-itself. It is even the sole relation possible to the in-itself. Cut off on every side by the in-itself, the for-itself can not escape it because the for-itself is *nothing* and it is separated from the in-itself by *nothing*. The for-itself is the foundation of all negativity and of all relation. *The for-itself is relation.*

Such being the case, the upsurge of the Other touches the for-itself in its very heart. By the Other and for the Other the pursuing flight is fixed in in-itself. Already the in-itself was progressively recapturing it; already it was at once a radical negation of fact, an absolute positing of value and yet wholly paralyzed with facticity. But at least it was escaping by temporalization; at least its character as a totality detotalized conferred on it a perpetual "elsewhere." Now it is this very totality which the Other makes appear before him and which he transcends toward his own "elsewhere." It is this totality which is totalized. For the Other I am irremediably what I am, and my very freedom is a given characteristic of my being. Thus the in-itself recaptures me at the threshold of the future and fixes me wholly in my very flight, which becomes a flight foreseen and contemplated, a *given* flight. But this fixed flight is never the flight which I am for myself; it is fixed *outside*. The objectivity of my flight I experience as an alienation which I can neither transcend nor know. Yet by the sole fact that I experience it and that it confers on my flight that in-itself which it flees, I must turn back toward it and assume *attitudes* with respect to it.

Such is the origin of my concrete relations with the Other; they are wholly governed by my attitudes with respect to the object which I am for the Other. And as the Other's existence reveals to me the being which I am without my being able either to appropriate that being or even to conceive it, this existence will motivate two opposed attitudes: First—The Other *looks* at me and as such he holds the secret of my being, he knows what I *am*. Thus the profound meaning of my being is outside of me, imprisoned in an absence. The Other has the advantage over me. Therefore in so far as I am fleeing the in-itself which I am without founding it, I can attempt to deny that being which is conferred on me from outside; that is, I can turn back upon the Other so as to make an object out of him in turn since the Other's object-ness destroys my object-ness for him. But on the other hand, in so far as the Other as freedom is the foundation of my being-in-itself, I can seek to recover that freedom and to possess it without removing from it its character as freedom. In fact if I could identify myself with that freedom which is the foundation of my being-in-itself, I should be to myself my own foundation. To transcend the Other's transcendence, or, on the contrary, to incorporate that transcendence within me without removing from it its character as transcendence—such are the two primitive attitudes which I assume confronting the Other. Here again we must understand the words exactly. It is not true that I first am and then later "seek" to make an object of the Other or to assimilate him; but to the extent that the upsurge of my being is an upsurge in the presence of the Other, to the extent that I am a pursuing flight and a pursued-pursuing, I am—at the very root of my being—the

project of assimilating and making an object of the Other. I am the proof of the Other. That is the original fact. But this proof of the Other is in itself an attitude toward the Other; that is, I can not *be in the presence of the Other* without being that "in-the-presence" in the form of having to be it. Thus again we are describing the for-itself's structures of being although the Other's presence in the world is an absolute and self-evident fact, but a contingent fact—that is, a fact impossible to deduce from the ontological structures of the for-itself.

These two attempts which I am are opposed to one another. Each attempt is the death of the other; that is, the failure of the one motivates the adoption of the other. Thus there is no dialectic for my relations toward the Other but rather a circle—although each attempt is enriched by the failure of the other. Thus we shall study each one in turn. But it should be noted that at the very core of the one the other remains always present, precisely because neither of the two can be held without contradiction. Better yet, each of them is in the other and endangers the death of the other. Thus we can never get outside the circle. We must not forget these facts as we approach the study of these fundamental attitudes toward the Other. Since these attitudes are produced and destroyed in a circle, it is as arbitrary to begin with the one as with the other. Nevertheless since it is necessary to choose, we shall consider first the conduct in which the for-itself tries to assimilate the Other's freedom.

I. FIRST ATTITUDE TOWARD OTHERS: LOVE, LANGUAGE, MASOCHISM

EVERYTHING which may be said of me in my relations with the Other applies to him as well. While I attempt to free myself from the hold of the Other, the Other is trying to free himself from mine; while I seek to enslave the Other, the Other seeks to enslave me. We are by no means dealing with unilateral relations with an object-in-itself, but with reciprocal and moving relations. The following descriptions of concrete behavior must therefore be envisaged within the perspective of *conflict*. Conflict is the original meaning of being-for-others.

If we start with the first revelation of the Other as a *look*, we must recognize that we experience our inapprehensible being-for-others in the form of a *possession*. I am possessed by the Other; the Other's look fashions my body in its nakedness, causes it to be born, sculptures it, produces it as it *is*, sees it as I shall never see it. The Other holds a secret—the secret of what I am. He makes me be and thereby he possesses me, and this possession is nothing other than the consciousness of possessing me. I in the recognition of my object-state have proof that he has this consciousness. By virtue of consciousness the Other is for me simultaneously the one who has stolen my being from me and the one who causes "there to be" a being which is my being. Thus I have a comprehension of this ontological structure: I am responsible for my being-for-others, but I am not the foundation of it. It appears to me therefore in the form of a contingent given for which I am nevertheless responsible; the Other founds my being in so far as this being is in the form of the "there is." But he is not responsible for my being although he founds it in complete freedom—in and by means of his free transcendence. Thus to the extent that I am revealed to myself as responsible for my being, I *lay claim to* this being which I am; that is, I wish to recover it, or, more exactly, I am the project of the recovery of my being. I want to stretch out my hand and grab hold of this being which is presented to me as *my being* but at a distance—like the dinner of Tantalus; I want to found it by my very freedom. For if in one sense my being-as-object is an unbearable contingency and the pure

"possession" of myself by another, still in another sense this being stands as the indication of what I should be obliged to recover and found in order to be the foundation of myself. But this is conceivable only if I assimilate the Other's freedom. Thus my project of recovering myself is fundamentally a project of absorbing the Other.

Nevertheless this project must leave the Other's nature intact. Two consequences result: (1) I do not thereby cease to assert the Other—that is, to deny concerning myself that I am the Other. Since the Other is the foundation of my being, he could not be dissolved in me without my being-for-others disappearing. Therefore if I project the realization of unity for the Other, this means that I project my assimilation of the Other's Otherness as my own possibility. In fact the problem for me is to make myself be by acquiring the possibility of taking the Other's point of view on myself. It is not a matter of acquiring a pure, abstract faculty of knowledge. It is not the pure *category* of the Other which I project appropriating to myself. This category is not conceived nor even conceivable. But on the occasion of concrete experience with the Other, an experience suffered and realized, it is this concrete Other as an absolute reality whom in his otherness I wish to incorporate into myself. (2) The Other whom I wish to assimilate is by no means the Other-as-object. Or, if you prefer, my project of incorporating the Other in no way corresponds to a recapturing of my for-itself as myself and to a surpassing of the Other's transcendence toward my own possibilities. For me it is not a question of obliterating my object-state by making an object of the Other, which would amount to *releasing* myself from my being-for-others. Quite the contrary, I want to assimilate the Other as the Other-looking-at-me, and this project of assimilation includes an augmented recognition of my being-looked-at. In short, in order to maintain before me the Other's freedom which is looking at me, I identify myself totally with my being-looked-at. And since my being-as-object is the only possible relation between me and the Other, it is this being-as-object which alone can serve me as an instrument to effect my assimilation of the *other freedom.*

Thus as a reaction to the failure of the third ekstasis, the for-itself wishes to be identified with the Other's freedom as founding its own being-in-itself. To be other to oneself—the ideal always aimed at concretely in the form of being *this Other* to oneself—is the primary value of my relations with the Other. This means that my being-for-others is haunted by the indication of an absolute-being which would be itself as other and other as itself and which, by freely giving to itself its being-itself as other and its being-other as itself, would be the very being of the ontological proof—that is, God. This ideal can not be realized without my surmounting the original contingency of my relations to the Other; that is, by overcoming the fact that there is no relation of internal negativity between the negation by which the Other is made other than I and the negation by which I am made other than the Other. We have seen that this contingency is insurmountable; it is the *fact* of my relations with the Other, just as my body is the *fact* of my being-in-the-world. Unity with the Other is therefore *in fact* unrealizable. It is also unrealizable *in theory,* for the assimilation of the for-itself and the Other in a single transcendence would necessarily involve the disappearance of the characteristic of otherness in the Other. Thus the condition on which I project the identification of myself with the Other is that I persist in denying that I am the Other. Finally this project of unification is the source of *conflict* since while I experience myself as an object for the Other and while I project assimilating him in and by means of this experience, the Other apprehends me as an object in the midst of the world and does not project identifying me with himself. It would therefore be necessary—since being-for-others includes a double internal negation—to act upon the internal negation by which the Other transcends my transcendence and makes me exist for the Other; that is, *to act upon the Other's freedom.*

This unrealizable ideal which haunts my project of myself in the presence of the Other is not to be identified with love in so far as love is an enterprise; *i.e.,* an organic ensemble of projects toward my own possibilities. But it is the ideal of love, its motivation and its end, its unique value. Love as the primitive relation to the Other is the ensemble of the projects by which I aim at realizing this value.

These projects put me in direct connection with the Other's freedom. It is in this sense that love is a conflict. We have observed that the Other's freedom is the foundation of my being. But precisely because I exist by means of the Other's freedom, I have no security; I am in danger in this freedom. It moulds my being and *makes me be,* it confers values upon me and removes them from me; and my being receives from it a perpetual passive escape from self. Irresponsible and beyond reach, this protean freedom in which I have engaged myself can in turn engage me in a thousand different ways of being. My project of recovering my being can be realized only if I get hold of this freedom and reduce it to being a freedom subject to my freedom. At the same time it is the only way in which I can act on the free negation of interiority by which the Other constitutes me as an Other; that is the only way in which I can prepare the way for a future identification of the Other with me. This will be clearer perhaps if we study the problem from a purely psychological aspect. Why does the lover want to be *loved?* If Love were in fact a pure desire for physical possession, it could in many cases be easily satisfied. Proust's hero, for example, who installs his mistress in his home, who can see her and possess her at any hour of the day, who has been able to make her completely dependent on him economically, ought to be free from worry. Yet we know that he is, on the contrary, continually gnawed by anxiety. Through her consciousness Albertine escapes Marcel even when he is at her side, and that is why he knows relief only when he gazes on her while she sleeps. It is certain then that the lover wishes to capture a "consciousness," But why does he wish it? And how?

The notion of "ownership," by which love is so often explained, is not actually primary. Why should I want to appropriate the Other if it were not precisely that the Other makes me be? But this implies precisely a certain mode of appropriation; it is the Other's freedom as such that we want to get hold of. Not because of a desire for power. The tyrant scorns love, he is content with fear. If he seeks to win the love of his subjects, it is for political reasons; and if he finds a more economical way to enslave them, he adopts it immediately. On the other hand, the man who wants to be loved does not desire the enslavement of the beloved. He is not bent on becoming the object of passion which flows forth mechanically. He does not want to possess an automaton, and if we want to humiliate him, we need only try to persuade him that the beloved's passion is the result of a psychological determinism. The lover will then feel that both his love and his being are cheapened. If Tristan and Isolde fall madly in love because of a love potion, they are less interesting. The total enslavement of the beloved kills the love of the lover. The end is surpassed; if the beloved is transformed into an automaton, the lover finds himself alone. Thus the lover does not desire to possess the beloved as one possesses a thing; he demands a special type of appropriation. He wants to possess a freedom as freedom.

On the other hand, the lover can not be satisfied with that superior form of freedom which is a free and voluntary engagement. Who would be content with a love given as pure loyalty to a sworn oath? Who would be satisfied with the words, "I love you because I have freely engaged myself to love you and because I do not wish to go back on my word." Thus the lover demands a pledge, yet is irritated by a pledge. He wants to be loved by a freedom but demands that this freedom as freedom should no longer be free. He wishes that the Other's freedom should determine itself to become love—and this not only at the beginning of the affair but at each instant—and at the same time he wants this freedom to be captured *by itself*, to turn back upon itself, as in madness, as in a dream, so as to will its own captivity. This captivity must be a resignation that is both free and yet chained in our hands. In love it is not a determinism of the passions which we desire in the Other nor a freedom beyond reach; it is a freedom which *plays the role of* a determinism of the passions and which is caught in its own role. For himself the lover does not demand that he be the *cause* of this radical modification of freedom but that he be the unique and privileged occasion of it. In fact he could not want to be the cause of it without immediately submerging the beloved in the midst of the world as a tool which can be transcended. That is not the essence of love. On the contrary, in Love the Lover wants to be "the whole World" for the beloved. This means that he puts himself on the side of the world; he is the one who assumes and symbolizes the world; he is a *this* which includes all other *thises*. He is and consents to be an *object*. But on the other hand, he wants to be the object in which the Other's freedom consents to lose itself, the object in which the Other consents to find his being and his *raison d'être* as his second facticity—the object-limit of transcendence, that toward which the Other's transcendence transcends all other objects but which it can in no way transcend. And everywhere he desires the circle of the Other's freedom; that is, at each instant as the Other's freedom accepts this limit to his transcendence, this acceptance is *already* present as the motivation of the acceptance considered. It is in the capacity of an end already chosen that the lover wishes to be chosen as an end. This allows us to grasp what basically the lover demands of the beloved; he does not want to *act* on the Other's freedom but to exist a *priori* as the objective limit of this freedom; that is, to be given at one stroke along with it and in its very upsurge as the limit which the freedom must accept in order to be free. By this very fact, what he demands is a limiting, a gluing down of the Other's freedom by itself; this limit of structure is in fact a *given*, and the very appearance of the given as the limit of freedom means that the freedom *makes itself exist* within the given by being its own prohibition against surpassing it. This prohibition is envisaged by the lover *simultaneously* as something lived—that is, something suffered (in a word, as a facticity) and as something freely consented to. It must be freely consented to since it must be effected only with the upsurge of a freedom which chooses itself as freedom. But it must be only what is lived since it must be an impossibility always present, a facticity which surges back to the heart of the Other's freedom. This is expressed psychologically by the demand that the free decision to love me, which the beloved formerly has taken, must slip in as a magically determining motivation *within* his present free engagement.

Now we can grasp the meaning of this demand: the facticity which is to be a factual limit for the Other in my demand to be loved and which is to result in being *his own* facticity—this is *my* facticity. It is in so far as I am the object which the Other makes come into being that I must be the inherent limit to his very transcendence. Thus the Other by his upsurge into being makes me be as unsurpassable and absolute, not as a nihilating

For-itself but as a being-for-others-in-the-midst-of-the-world. Thus to want to be loved is to invest the Other with one's own facticity; it is to wish to compel him to re-create you perpetually as the condition of a freedom which submits itself and which is engaged; it is to wish both that freedom found fact and that fact have pre-eminence over freedom. If this end could be attained, it would result in the first place in my being *secure* within the Other's consciousness. First because the motive of my uneasiness and my shame is the fact that I apprehend and experience myself in my being-for-others as that which can always be surpassed toward something else, that which is the pure object of a value judgment, a pure means, a pure tool. My uneasiness stems from the fact that I assume necessarily and freely that being which another makes me be in an absolute freedom. "God knows what I am for him! God knows what he thinks of me!" This means "God knows what he makes me be." I am haunted by this being which I fear to encounter someday at the turn of a path, this being which is so strange to me and which is yet *my being* and which I know that I shall never encounter in spite of all my efforts to do so. But if the Other loves me then I become the *unsurpassable*, which means that I must be the absolute end. In this sense I am saved from *instrumentality*. My existence in the midst of the world becomes the exact correlate of my transcendence-for-myself since my independence is absolutely safeguarded. The object which the Other must make me be is an object-transcendence, an absolute center of reference around which all the instrumental-things of the world are ordered as pure *means*. At the same time, as the absolute limit of freedom—*i.e.*, of the absolute source of all values—I am protected against any eventual devalorization. I am the absolute value. To the extent that I assume my being-for-others, I assume myself as value. Thus to want to be loved is to want to be placed beyond the whole system of values posited by the Other and to be the condition of all valorization and the objective foundation of all values. This demand is the usual theme of lovers' conversations, whether as in *La Porte Etroite*, the woman who wants to be loved identifies herself with an ascetic morality of self-surpassing and wishes to embody the ideal limit of this surpassing—or as more usually happens, the woman in love demands that the beloved in his acts should sacrifice traditional morality for her and is anxious to know whether the beloved would betray his friends for her, "would steal for her," "would kill for her," *etc.*

From this point of view, my being must escape the *look* of the beloved, or rather it must be the object of a look with another structure. I must no longer be seen on the ground of the world as a "this" among other "thises," but the world must be revealed in terms of me. In fact to the extent that the upsurge of freedom makes a world exist, I must be, as the limiting-condition of this upsurge, the very condition of the upsurge of a world. I must be the one whose function is to makes trees and water exist, to make cities and fields and other men exist, in order to give them later to the Other who arranges them into a world, just as the mother in matrilineal communities receives titles and the family name not to keep them herself but to transfer them immediately to her children. In one sense if I am to be loved, I am the object by whose agency the world will exist for the Other; in another sense I am the world. Instead of being a "this" detaching itself on the ground of the world, I am the ground-as-object on which the world detaches itself. Thus I am reassured; the Other's look no longer paralyzes me with finitude. It no longer fixes my being in *what I am*. I can no longer be *looked at* as ugly, as small, as cowardly, since these characteristics necessarily represent a factual limitation of my being and an apprehension of my fini-

tude as finitude. To be sure, my possibles remain transcended possibilities, dead-possibilities; but I possess all possibles. I am all the dead-possibilities in the world; hence I cease to be the being who is understood from the standpoint of other beings or of its acts. In the loving intuition which I demand, I am to be given as an absolute totality in terms of which all its peculiar acts and all beings are to be understood. One could say, slightly modifying a famous pronouncement of the Stoics, that "the beloved can fail in three ways."[1] The ideal of the sage and the ideal of the man who wants to be loved actually coincide in this that both want to be an object-as-totality accessible to a global intuition which will apprehend the beloved's or the sage's actions in the world as partial structures which are interpreted in terms of the totality. Just as wisdom is proposed as a state to be attained by an absolute metamorphosis, so the Other's freedom must be absolutely metamorphosed in order to allow me to attain the state of being loved.

Up to this point our description would fall into line with Hegel's famous description of the Master and Slave relation. What the Hegelian Master is for the Slave, the lover wants to be for the beloved. But the analogy stops here, for with Hegel the Master demands the Slave's freedom only laterally and, so to speak, implicitly, while the lover wants the beloved's freedom *first and foremost*. In this sense if I am to be loved by the Other, this means that I am to be freely chosen as beloved. As we know, in the current terminology of love, the beloved is often called *the chosen one*. But this choice must not be relative and contingent. The lover is irritated and feels himself cheapened when he thinks that the beloved has chosen him *from among others*. "Then if I had not come into a certain city, if I had not visited the home of so and so, you would never have known me, you wouldn't

---

[1]Tr. Literally, "can tumble three times."

have loved me?" This thought grieves the lover; his love becomes one love among others and is limited by the beloved's facticity and by his own facticity as well as by the contingency of encounters. It becomes *love in the world*, an object which presupposes the world and which in turn can exist for others. What he is demanding he expresses by the awkward and vitiated phrases of "fatalism." He says, "We were made for each other," or again he uses the expression "soul mate." But we must translate all this. The lover knows very well that "being made for each other" refers to an original choice. This choice can be God's, since he is the being who is absolute choice, but God here represents only the farthest possible limit of the demand for an absolute. Actually what the lover demands is that the beloved should make of him an absolute choice. This means that the beloved's being-in-the-world must be a being-as-loving. The upsurge of the beloved must be the beloved's free choice of the lover. And since the Other is the foundation of my being-as-object, I demand of him that the free upsurge of his being should have his choice of *me* as his unique and absolute end; that is, that he should choose to be for the sake of founding my object-state and my facticity.

Thus my facticity is *saved*. It is no longer this unthinkable and insurmountable given which I am fleeing; it is that for which the Other freely makes himself exist; it is as an end which he has given to himself. I have infected him with my facticity, but as it is in the form of freedom that he has been infected with it, he refers it back to me as a facticity taken up and consented to. He is the foundation of it in order that it may be his end. By means of this love I then have a different apprehension of my alienation and of my own facticity. My facticity—as for-others—is no longer a fact but a right. My existence *is* because it is *given a name*. I am because I give myself away. These beloved veins on my hands exist—beneficently. How good I am to

have eyes, hair, eyebrows and to lavish them away tirelessly in an overflow of generosity to this tireless desire which the Other freely makes himself be. Whereas before being loved we were uneasy about that unjustified, unjustifiable protuberance which was our existence, whereas we felt ourselves "*de trop*," we now feel that our existence is taken up and willed even in its tiniest details by an absolute freedom which at the same time our existence conditions and which we ourselves will with our freedom. This is the basis for the joy of love when there is joy; we feel that our existence is justified.

By the same token if the beloved can love us, he is wholly ready to be assimilated by our freedom; for this being-loved which we desire is already the ontological proof applied to our being-for-others. Our objective essence implies the existence of the Other, and conversely it is the Other's freedom which founds our essence. If we could manage to interiorize the whole system, we should be our own foundation.

Such then is the real goal of the lover in so far as his love is an enterprise—*i.e.*, a project of himself. This project is going to provoke a conflict. The beloved in fact apprehends the lover as one Other-as-object among others; that is, he perceives the lover on the ground of the world, transcends him, and utilizes him. The beloved is a *look*. He can not therefore employ his transcendence to fix an ultimate limit to his surpassings, nor can he employ his freedom to captivate itself. The beloved can not will to love. Therefore the lover must seduce the beloved, and his love can in no way be distinguished from the enterprise of seduction. In seduction I do not try to reveal my subjectivity to the Other. Moreover I could do so only by *looking at* the other; but by this look I should cause the Other's subjectivity to disappear, and it is exactly this which I want to assimilate. To seduce is to risk assuming my object-state completely for the Other; it is to put myself beneath his look and to make him look at me; it is to risk the danger of *being-seen* in order to effect a new departure and to appropriate the Other in and by means of my object-ness. I refuse to leave the level on which I make proof of my object-ness; it is on this level that I wish to engage in battle by making myself a *fascinating object*. In Part Two we defined fascination as a *state*. It is, we said, the non-thetic consciousness of being *nothing* in the presence of being. Seduction aims at producing in the Other the consciousness of his state of nothingness as he confronts the seductive object. By seduction I aim at constituting myself as a fullness of being and at making myself *recognized as such*. To accomplish this I constitute myself as a meaningful object. My acts must *point* in two directions: On the one hand, toward that which is wrongly called subjectivity and which is rather a depth of objective and hidden being; the act is not performed for itself only, but it points to an infinite, undifferentiated series of other real and possible acts which I give as constituting my objective, unperceived being. Thus I try to guide the transcendence which transcends me and to refer it to the infinity of my dead-possibilities precisely in order to be the unsurpassable and to the exact extent to which the only unsurpassable is the infinite. On the other hand, each of my acts tries to point to the great density of possible-world and must present me as bound to the vastest regions of the world. At the same time I *present* the world to the beloved, and I try to constitute myself as the necessary intermediary between her and the world; I manifest by my acts infinitely varied examples of my power over the world (money, position, "connections," *etc.*). In the first case I try to constitute myself as an infinity of depth, in the second case to identify myself with the world. Through these different procedures I propose myself as unsurpassable. This proposal could not be sufficient in itself; it is only a besieging of the Other. It can not take on value

as fact without the consent of the Other's freedom, which I must capture by making it recognize itself as nothingness in the face of my plenitude of absolute being. . . .

Fascination, however, even if it were to produce a state of being-fascinated in the Other could not by itself succeed in producing love. We can be fascinated by an orator, by an actor, by a tightrope-walker, but this does not mean that we love him. To be sure we can not take our eyes off him, but he is still raised on the ground of the world, and fascination does not posit the fascinating object as the ultimate term of the transcendence. Quite the contrary, fascination *is* transcendence. When then will the beloved become in turn the lover?

The answer is easy: when the beloved projects being loved. By himself the Other-as-object never has enough strength to produce love. If love has for its ideal the appropriation of the Other qua Other (i.e., as a subjectivity which is looking at an object) this ideal can be projected only in terms of my encounter with the Other-as-subject, not with the Other-as-object. If the Other tries to seduce me by means of his object-state, then seduction can bestow upon the Other only the character of a *precious* object "to be possessed." Seduction will perhaps determine me to risk much to conquer the Other-as-object, but this desire to appropriate an object in the midst of the world should not be confused with love. Love therefore can be born in the beloved only from the proof which he makes of his alienation and his flight toward the Other. Still the beloved, if such is the case, will be transformed into a love only if he projects being loved; that is, if what he wishes to overcome is not a body but the Other's subjectivity as such. In fact the only way that he could conceive to realize this appropriation is to make himself be loved. Thus it seems that to love is in essence the project of making oneself be loved. Hence this new contradiction and this new conflict: each of the lovers is entirely the captive of the Other inasmuch as each wishes to make himself loved by the Other to the exclusion of anyone else; but at the same time each one demands from the other a love which is not reducible to the "project of being-loved." What he demands in fact is that the Other without originally seeking to make himself be loved should have at once a contemplative and affective intuition of his beloved as the objective limit of his freedom, as the ineluctable and chosen foundation of his transcendence, as the totality of being and the supreme value. Love thus exacted from the other could not *ask for* anything; it is a pure engagement without reciprocity. Yet this love can not exist except in the form of a demand on the part of the lover.

The lover is held captive in a wholly different way. He is the captive of his very demand since love is the demand to be loved; he is a freedom which wills itself a body and which demands an outside, hence a freedom which imitates the flight toward the Other, a freedom which qua freedom lays claim to its alienation. The lover's freedom, in his very effort to make himself be loved as an object by the Other, is alienated by slipping into the body-for-others; that is, it is brought into existence with a dimension of flight toward the Other. It is the perpetual refusal to posit itself as pure selfness, for this affirmation of self as itself would involve the collapse of the Other as a look and the upsurge of the Other-as-object—hence a state of affairs in which the very possibility of being loved disappears since the Other is reduced to the dimension of objectivity. This refusal therefore constitutes freedom as dependent on the Other; and the Other as subjectivity becomes indeed an unsurpassable limit of the freedom of the for-itself, the goal and supreme end of the for-itself since the Other holds the key to its being. Here in fact we encounter the true ideal of love's enterprise: alienated freedom. But it is the one who wants to be loved who by the mere fact of wanting someone to love him alienates his freedom.

My freedom is alienated in the presence of the Other's pure subjectivity which founds my objectivity. It can never be alienated before the Other-as-object. In this form in fact the beloved's alienation, of which the lover dreams, would be contradictory since the beloved can found the being of the lover only by transcending it on principle toward other objects of the world; therefore this transcendence can constitute the object which it surpasses both as a transcended object and as an object limit of all transcendence. Thus each one of the lovers wants to be the object for which the Other's freedom is alienated in an original intuition; but this intuition which would be love in the true sense is only a contradictory ideal of the for-itself. Each one is alienated only to the exact extent to which he demands the alienation of the other. Each one wants the other to love him but does not take into account the fact that to love is to want to be loved and that thus by wanting the other to love him, he only wants the other to want to be loved in turn. Thus love relations are a system of indefinite reference—analogous to the pure "reflection-reflected" of consciousness—under the ideal standard of the *value* "love"; that is, in a fusion of consciousnesses in which each of them would preserve his otherness in order to found the other. This state of affairs is due to the fact that consciousnesses are separated by an insurmountable nothingness, a nothingness which is both the internal negation of the one by the other and a factual nothingness between the two internal negations. Love is a contradictory effort to surmount the factual negation while preserving the internal negation. I demand that the Other love me and I do everything possible to realize my project; but if the Other loves me, he radically deceives me by his very love. I demanded of him that he should found my being as a privileged object by maintaining himself as pure subjectivity confronting me; and as soon as he loves me he experiences me as subject and is swallowed up in his objectivity confronting my subjectivity.

The problem of my being-for-others remains therefore without solution. The lovers remain each one for himself in a total subjectivity; nothing comes to relieve them of their duty to make themselves exist each one for himself; nothing comes to relieve their contingency nor to save them from facticity. At least each one has succeeded in escaping danger from the Other's freedom—but altogether differently than he expected. He escapes not because the Other makes him be as the object-limit of his transcendence but because the Other experiences him as subjectivity and wishes to experience him only as such. Again the gain is perpetually compromised. At the start, each of the consciousnesses can at any moment free itself from its chains and suddenly contemplate the other as an *object*. Then the spell is broken; the Other becomes one mean among means. He is indeed an object for others as the lover desires but an object-as-tool, a perpetually transcended object. The illusion, the game of mirrors which makes the concrete reality of love, suddenly ceases. Later in the experience of love each consciousness seeks to shelter its being-for-others in the Other's freedom. This supposes that the Other is beyond the world as pure subjectivity, as the absolute by which the world comes into being. But it suffices that the lovers should be *looked at* together by a third person in order for each one to experience not only his own objectivation but that of the other as well. Immediately the Other is no longer for me the absolute transcendence which founds me in my being; he is a transcendence-transcended, not by me but by another. My original relation to him—*i.e.*, my relation of being the beloved for my lover, is fixed as a dead-possibility. It is no longer the experienced relation between a limiting object of all

transcendence and the freedom which founds it; it is a love-as-object which is wholly alienated toward the third. Such is the true reason why lovers seek solitude. It is because the appearance of a third person, whoever he may be, is the destruction of their love. But factual solitude (*e.g.*, we are alone in my room) is by no means a theoretical solitude. Even if nobody sees us, we exist for all consciousnesses and we are conscious of existing for all. The result is that love as a fundamental mode of being-for-others holds in its being-for-others the seed of its own destruction.

We have just defined the triple destructibility of love: in the first place it is, in essence, a deception and a reference to infinity since to love is to wish to be loved, hence to wish that the Other wish that I love him. A pre-ontological comprehension of this deception is given in the very impulse of love—hence the lover's perpetual dissatisfaction. It does not come, as is so often said, from the unworthiness of being loved but from an implicit comprehension of the fact that the amorous intuition is, as a fundamental-intuition, an ideal out of reach. The more I am loved, the more I lose my *being,* the more I am thrown back on my own responsibilities, on my own power to be. In the second place the Other's awakening is always possible; at any moment he can make me appear as an object—hence the lover's perpetual insecurity. In the third place love is an absolute which is perpetually *made relative* by others. One would have to be alone in the world with the beloved in order for love to preserve its character as an absolute axis of reference—hence the lover's perpetual shame (or pride—which here amounts to the same thing).

Thus it is useless for me to have tried to lose myself in objectivity; my passion will have availed me nothing. The Other has referred me to my own unjustifiable subjectivity—either by himself or through others. This result can provoke a total despair and a new attempt to realize the identification of the Other and myself. Its ideal will then be the opposite of that which we have just described; instead of projecting the absorbing of the Other while preserving in him his otherness, I shall project causing myself to be absorbed by the Other and losing myself in his subjectivity in order to get rid of my own. This enterprise will be expressed concretely by the *masochistic* attitude. Since the Other is the foundation of my being-for-others, if I relied on the Other to make me exist, I should no longer be anything more than a being-in-itself founded in its being by a freedom. Here it is my own subjectivity which is considered as an obstacle to the primordial act by which the Other would found me in my being. It is my own subjectivity which above all must be denied by *my own freedom*. I attempt therefore to engage myself wholly in my being-as-object. I refuse to be anything more than an object. I rest upon the Other, and as I experience this being-as-object in shame, I will and I love my shame as the profound sign of my objectivity. As the Other apprehends me as object by means of *actual desire*, I wish to be desired, I make myself in shame an object of desire.

This attitude would resemble that of love if instead of seeking to exist for the Other as the object-limit of his transcendence, I did not rather insist on making myself be treated as one object among others, as an instrument to be used. Now it is *my* transcendence which is to be denied, not his. This time I do not have to project capturing his freedom; on the contrary I hope that this freedom may *be* and *will* itself to be radically free. Thus the more I shall feel myself surpassed toward other ends, the more I shall enjoy the abdication of my transcendence. Finally I project being nothing more than an *object*; that is, radically an *in-itself*. But inasmuch as a freedom which will have absorbed mine will be the foundation of this in-itself, my being will become again the foundation of itself. Masochism, like sadism, is the assumption of

guilt. I am guilty due to the very fact that I am an object, I am guilty toward myself since I consent to my absolute alienation. I am guilty toward the Other, for I furnish him with the occasion of being guilty—that is, of radically missing my freedom as such. Masochism is an attempt not to fascinate the Other by means of my objectivity but to cause myself to be fascinated by my objectivity-for-others; that is, to cause myself to be constituted as an object by the Other in such a way that I nonthetically apprehend my subjectivity as a *nothing* in the presence of the in-itself which I represent to the Other's eyes. Masochism is characterized as a species of vertigo, vertigo not before a precipice of rock and earth but before the abyss of the Other's subjectivity.

But masochism is and must be itself a failure. In order to cause myself to be fascinated by my self-as-object, I should necessarily have to be able to realize the intuitive apprehension of this object such as it is *for the Other*, a thing which is on principle impossible. Thus I am far from being able to be fascinated by this alienated Me, which remains on principle inapprehensible. It is useless for the masochist to get down on his knees, to show himself in ridiculous positions, to cause himself to be used as a simple lifeless instrument. It is *for the Other* that he will be obscene or simply passive, for the Other that he will *undergo* these postures; for himself he is forever condemned to *give them to himself*. It is in and through his transcendence that he disposes of himself as a being to be transcended. The more he tries to taste his objectivity, the more he will be submerged by the consciousness of his subjectivity—hence his anguish. Even the masochist who pays a woman to whip him is treating her as an instrument and by this very fact posits himself in transcendence in relation to her.

Thus the masochist ultimately treats the Other as an object and transcends him toward his own objectivity. Recall, for example, the tribulations of

Sacher Masoch, who in order to make himself scorned, insulted, reduced to a humiliating position, was obliged to make use of the great love which women bore toward him; that is, to act upon them just in so far as they experienced themselves as an object for him. Thus in every way the masochist's objectivity escapes him, and it can even happen—in fact usually does happen—that in seeking to apprehend his own objectivity he finds the Other's objectivity, which in spite of himself frees his own subjectivity. Masochism therefore is on principle a failure. This should not surprise us if we realize that masochism is a "vice" and that vice is, on principle, the love of failure. But this is not the place to describe the structures peculiar to vice. It is sufficient here to point out that masochism is a perpetual effort to *annihilate* the subject's subjectivity by causing it to be assimilated by the Other; this effort is accompanied by the exhausting and delicious consciousness of failure so that finally it is the failure itself which the subject ultimately seeks as his principal goal.[2]

---

[2]Consistent with this description, there is at least one form of exhibitionism which ought to be classed among masochistic attitudes. For example, when Rousseau exhibits to the washerwomen "not the obscene object but the ridiculous object." *Cf. Confessions,* Chapter III.

chapter thirty

Simone de Beauvoir

Simone de Beauvoir (1908–1986), French writer, philosopher, and feminist, was a singular figure among the circle of French intellectuals who gave literary as well as philosophical expression to existentialism in the mid-twentieth century. Fully committed to existentialist tenets of freedom and individual responsibility, Beauvoir authored an impressive corpus of essays, novels, plays, and autobiographies expounding an ethics founded upon the recognition of human freedom. She considered the freedom to realize one's unique possibilities to be the most important function of human existence and therefore emphasized human *becoming* (transcendence and possibility) over *being* (immanence and stasis). Accordingly, she vehemently opposed all forms of oppression, the major impediment to the individual's freedom to become, and scrutinized its underlying principle—the distinction between self and Other. Beauvoir discovered that the distinction of self and Other not only drives obviously oppressive relationships—as in racism and classism—but also shapes our most intimate relationships (although not always with negative results). This calls attention to the problem of gender, and Beauvoir's seminal work, her two-volume essay *The Second Sex* (1949), explores this problem by seeking an answer to the deceptively simple question, "What is a woman?" Simultaneously a rigorous investigation into traditional conceptions of femininity and a passionate plea for their renunciation, *The Second Sex* has become a classic of feminist literature.

Scholars frequently treat Beauvoir's philosophy only in the context of her association with her contemporaries in French-Existentialism, most notably, Albert Camus, Maurice Merleau-Ponty, and her closest intellectual partner, Jean-Paul Sartre. Although she shared their fundamental concern with freedom and individual responsibility, Beauvoir distinguished herself from her male contemporaries in a number of important ways. For example, while Sartre also treated the relation between self and Other,[1] he described the relationship as fundamentally oppositional and sadomasochistic, while Beauvoir stressed its intersubjectivity, which may yield benefits (such as genuine recognition and comfort)

---

as well as liabilities. A second distinction lies in Beauvoir's use of a descriptive rather than speculative philosophical method, which was to explore experience as it is actually lived rather than as it *might* be. Her descriptive methodology also facilitated her consideration of historicity, which she considered philosophically important in the analysis of human interaction; hence she valued autobiography as well as the biographies of the individuals about whom she wrote. Finally, Beauvoir is noted for having elucidated, more than her contemporaries, the ethical implications of existentialism through her emphasis upon, depiction of, and probing analysis of numerous forms of complex human interactions.

Beauvoir's writings stand out as intimate reflections upon her life experiences and what she perceived to be moral dilemmas of her time. Understanding key factors that shaped her life and thought will therefore contribute to an understanding of her work. Beauvoir enjoyed a very happy, typically bourgeois Parisian childhood in which she received special attention from her parents because of her exceptionally keen intellect. Her father, a lawyer, was well versed in the arts and cultivated the same passion in her—tutoring her, honing her skills, and shaping her artistic tastes. Beauvoir's mother, a devoted Catholic, attended to both her daughter's intellectual and spiritual development, carefully scrutinizing Beauvoir's reading material (ruling out texts that might "corrupt" her) and escorting her twice weekly to church and confession.

Beauvoir once noted, "Papa used to say with pride: Simone has a man's brain; she thinks like a man: she is a man."[2] She cherished her father's praise and emulated him, seeing in him the embodiment of the kind of intellectual she hoped to become. At the same time, both knew that her intellectual pursuits would eventually come into conflict with her identity as a female. In adolescence Beauvoir became increasingly committed to establishing her own identity rather than accepting the roles prescribed for her by her social class and gender. She continued to emulate her father but never relinquished her feminine identity. She *would* pursue her intellectual life to its fullest *as a woman*. Moreover, while Beauvoir embraced her femininity, she had no desire to imitate her mother: "I learnt from Mama to efface myself, to censor my desires, to say and do exactly what ought to be said and done."[3] Beauvoir thus completely rejected, for herself, the roles of wife and mother.

In time, Beauvoir's skepticism concerning the roles prescribed for her as a woman expanded into a more general criticism of bourgeois culture. Witnessing the often pernicious effects of bourgeois standards—most poignantly the premature death of her dearest friend, Zaza, from what Beauvoir was certain was mental anguish—she became committed to speaking out against all forms of oppression, social and political. "I was against any kind of oppression: the oppression of class, of individuals, of peoples—the oppression of individuals particularly. What was quite fundamental was the idea of freedom being the highest value for man, making man what he is. He must make the most of his freedom, and I knew one had to work to develop personal freedom and freedom for all."[4]

After completing secondary school and earning a number of other diplomas, Beauvoir entered the Sorbonne to study philosophy and literature. She also took courses at the prestigious École Normale Supérieure, which trained the elite professoriate of France. Beauvoir's diaries reveal a wide range of philosophical influences upon her own emerging thought. Most notable are the phenomenology of Edmund Husserl, the descriptive methodology of Henri Bergson and William James, Leibniz's metaphysics, Kant's critique of reason, Marx's analysis of history, and Kojève's reading of Hegel's *Phenomenology of Spirit*. Beauvoir consistently earned high praise for her mastery of these and other systems of thought. However, what she desired far more than praise for her mastery of other philosophers was to succeed in drawing her own existentialism to its logical conclusion: to give authentic expression to the issues that mattered most to her. She grew increasingly interested in the problems of her own existence, particularly as they concerned relations with others. In 1929, at age twenty-one, Beauvoir became the youngest woman in France to pass the *agrégation* in philosophy. She earned further distinction by placing second on the exam, the first place award going to her friend and lover Jean-Paul Sartre.

The famous intellectual partnership and love affair between Beauvoir and Sartre was, in her own words, "the model relationship, based on love and liberty."[5] Both were committed to confronting the moral dilemmas of their time as activists; in fact, Beauvoir noted, "We thought one must act by writing,"[6] and they did, each inspiring the other. Because Beauvoir and Sartre were also committed to the idea that freedom is the individual's highest value, the two never married, although they shared a profound love and pledged an undying commitment to one another. Theirs they called a "necessary love," which they distinguished from the "contingent loves" they were free to share with other partners. Although Beauvoir and Sartre never shared a permanent dwelling, children, or common property, they remained a devoted to each other until his death in 1980.

In the 1940s Beauvoir published a number of novels, essays, and memoirs, including *She Came to Stay* (1943), a novel that chronicles the slow destruction of a couple's relationship when a young girl comes to live with them, thus exploring the dialectic of self and Other in the context of fundamentally predatory relationships. The novel's publication was followed by what Beauvoir called her "ethical period" when the Nazi occupation of France compelled her to think even more deeply about political and historical realities. She studied Hegel's *Phenomenology*, cofounded in 1945 with Sartre a monthly journal called *Les Temps Modernes*, and penned her own ethical works, *The Blood of Others* (1945), *All Men Are Mortal* (1946), and *The Ethics of Ambiguity* (1947).

It was not until the 1949 publication of *The Second Sex*, however, that Beauvoir gained her due recognition as an intellectual to be reckoned with in her own right, acquiring for the first time a public identity separate from Sartre. Interestingly, Beauvoir determined to write the essay partly in answer to growing public criticism of Sartre's leftist philosophy and their unconventional relationship. She saw an opportunity to expound Sartre's philosophy and their way of life by explaining *herself*, "defin[ing] herself personally as a woman and philosophically as an existentialist."[7] She would *show* how her life fit successfully within an existentialist framework.

Beauvoir began to frame her essay by considering herself in relation to Sartre. She came to "the very profound and astonishing realization" that the most fundamental difference between them was that "he was a man and I was only a woman."[8] She would later write of this realization, "Somehow, I was beginning to formulate the thesis that women had not been given equality in our society, and I must tell you that this was an extremely troubling discovery for me. This is really how I began to be serious about writing about women—when I fully realized the disparity in our lives as compared to men."[9]

Despite the political implications of *The Second Sex*, Beauvoir insisted that it was not intended as a political work. Rather, the essay was to be an inquiry into the lived experience of women that would serve to enlighten Beauvoir as well as increase the understanding of others. She explains:

> I didn't think of it at all as a political book. I considered it to be an essay—a search to obtain a deeper knowledge of woman. It helped me personally to learn more about woman's condition because I'd had a fairly protected life: a rather exceptional one. . . . When I began to write the book, I didn't even suspect how heavily woman's condition weighs on her, and I found this out—discovered it—by reading, by talking to my friends, by getting housewives to speak to me, so my views on women developed and changed radically. I really came to see and feel that society allotted two very unequal shares to men and women. I hadn't really realized that before; it hadn't hit me in the face before. So writing my book was a revelation for me—an apprenticeship rather than a political act.[10]

The result of Beauvoir's "apprenticeship" was a two-volume work, widely considered to be the most important book on woman written in the twentieth century.[11] Volume One, titled "Facts and Myths," chronicles the evolutionary and cultural history of western civilization to locate the *sources* of the modern conception of woman. The volume is organized into three sections, "Destiny," "History," and "Myths," that examine how woman's identity has been presumed to be determined by biology but nonetheless invented by culture and reinforced by the creation of myths such as that of the mysterious "eternal feminine." Volume Two, "Woman's Life Today," considers the actual experience of contemporary woman. Its first three sections explore "The Formative Years" of woman, her "Situation," and "Justifications" of her self-conception—whether she be young or old, married or single, lesbian or heterosexual, promiscuous or celibate. The fourth section of Volume Two, "Toward Liberation," portrays the independent woman and prescribes an optimistic plan of action by which women can secure their own liberation.

Few people have succeeded in integrating their convictions, lifestyles, and work with as much courage and to such powerful effect as Simone de Beauvoir. In 1954, she was awarded the celebrated Prix Goncourt for her novel, *The Mandarins*, an account of the committed efforts of post–World War II intellectuals to political activism. In 1974 she received the Jerusalem Prize, awarded to leaders who advance the cause of individual freedom.

Other major works of Simone de Beauvoir include *America Day by Day* (1948), *Memoirs of a Dutiful Daughter* (1958), and *A Very Easy Death* (1964). In 1981 she wrote *Adieux: A Farewell to Sartre*, an account of Sartre's final years.

SC

QUESTIONS

1. What does Beauvoir mean when she says that men represent both the positive and the neutral?
2. What does Beauvoir mean by "the One" and "the Other"? How do these categories relate to women and men?
3. Do you agree or disagree with Beauvoir's assertion, "The category of the *Other* is as primordial as consciousness itself"?
4. What reasons does Beauvoir give to explain women's acceptance of their status as the Other?
5. Beauvoir writes that "[I]t is the difference in their situation that is reflected in the difference men and women show in their conceptions of love." What is the "difference in their situation" and what is the difference between men's and women's conceptions of love, according to Beauvoir?

ENDNOTES

1. It is often assumed that Beauvoir borrowed the concept of self and Other from Sartre, who formally introduced the concept in his *Being and Nothingness*. However, Beauvoir's diary of 1927 reveals that she had begun to address this issue two years before she met Sartre.
2. Judith Okely, *Simone de Beauvoir: A Re-Reading* (London: Virago, 1986), p. 2.
3. Mary Evans, *Simone de Beauvoir* (London: Sage, 1996), p. 39.
4. Simone de Beauvoir, Interview by Melvyn Bragg, January 9, 1983, from *South Bank Show*: "Simone de Beauvoir," ed. Michael Akester. Princeton, NJ,: Films for the Humanities and Sciences, 1999.
5. Beauvoir, *Memoirs of a Dutiful Daughter* (Paris: Penguin, 1963), p. 167.
6. Beauvoir, Interview with Melvyn Bragg.
7. Deirdre Bair, p. ix.
8. Ibid., p. x.
9. Ibid.

10. Beauvoir, Interview with Melvyn Bragg.

11. The abridged English translation is one volume with Books One and Two corresponding to the two French volumes.

SELECTED BIBLIOGRAPHY

Bair, Deirdre. *Simone de Beauvoir: A Biography*. New York: Summit Books, 1990.

Beauvoir, Simone de. *The Second Sex*, trans. and ed. H.M. Parshley. New York: Vintage Books, 1989.

Fallaize, Elizabeth, ed.*Simone de Beauvoir: A Critical Reader*. New York: Routledge, 1998.

Fullbrook, Kate, and Edward Fullbrook. *Simone de Beauvoir and Jean-Paul Sartre*. New York: Basic Books, 1994.

Simons, Margaret A. *Beauvoir and "The Second Sex": Feminism, Race, and the Origins of Existentialism*. Lanham, MD.: Rowman & Littlefield, 1999.

from *The Second Sex*

Simone de Beauvoir

INTRODUCTION

For a long time I have hesitated to write a book on woman. The subject is irritating, especially to women; and it is not new. Enough ink has been spilled in the quarreling over feminism, now practically over, and perhaps we should say no more about it. It is still talked about, however, for the voluminous nonsense uttered during the last century seems to have done little to illuminate the problem. After all, is there a problem? And if so, what is it? Are there women, really? Most assuredly the theory of the eternal feminine still has its adherents who will whisper in your ear: "Even in Russia women still are *women*"; and other erudite persons—sometimes the very same—say with a sigh: "Woman is losing her way, woman is lost." One wonders if women still exist, if they will always exist, whether or not it is desirable that they should, what place they occupy in this world, what their place should be. "What has become of women?" was asked recently in an ephemeral magazine.[1]

But first we must ask: what is a woman? "*Tota mulier in utero*," says one, "woman is a womb." But in speaking of certain women, connoisseurs declare that they are not women, although they are equipped with a uterus like the rest. All agree in recognizing the fact that females exist in the human species; today as always they make up about one half of humanity. And yet we are told that femininity is in danger; we are exhorted to be women, remain women, become women. It would appear, then, that every female human being is not necessarily a woman; to be so considered she must share in that mysterious and threatened reality known as femininity. Is this attribute something secreted by the ovaries? Or is it a Platonic essence, a product of the philosophic imagination? Is a

---

[1] *Franchise*, dead today.

rustling petticoat enough to bring it down to earth? Although some women try zealously to incarnate this essence, it is hardly patentable. It is frequently described in vague and dazzling terms that seem to have been borrowed from the vocabulary of the seers, and indeed in the times of St. Thomas it was considered an essence as certainly defined as the somniferous virtue of the poppy.

But conceptualism has lost ground. The biological and social sciences no longer admit the existence of unchangeably fixed entities that determine given characteristics, such as those ascribed to woman, the Jew, or the Negro. Science regards any characteristic as a reaction dependent in part upon a *situation*. If today femininity no longer exists, then it never existed. But does the word *woman*, then, have no specific content? This is stoutly affirmed by those who hold to the philosophy of the enlightenment, of rationalism, of nominalism; women, to them, are merely the human beings arbitrarily designated by the word *woman*. Many American women particularly are prepared to think that there is no longer any place for woman as such; if a backward individual still takes herself for a woman, her friends advise her to be psychoanalyzed and thus get rid of this obsession. In regard to a work, *Modern Woman: The Lost Sex*, which in other respects has its irritating features, Dorothy Parker has written: "I cannot be just to books which treat of woman as woman. . . . My idea is that all of us, men as well as women, should be regarded as human beings." But nominalism is a rather inadequate doctrine, and the antifeminists have had no trouble in showing that women simply *are not* men. Surely woman is, like man, a human being; but such a declaration is abstract. The fact is that every concrete human being is always a singular, separate individual. To decline to accept such notions as the eternal feminine, the black soul, the Jewish character, is not to deny that Jews, Negroes, women exist today—this denial does not represent a liberation for those concerned, but rather a flight from reality. Some years ago a well-known woman writer refused to permit her portrait to appear in a series of photographs especially devoted to women writers; she wished to be counted among the men. But in order to gain this privilege she made use of her husband's influence! Women who assert that they are men lay claim none the less to masculine consideration and respect. I recall also a young Trotskyite standing on a platform at a boisterous meeting and getting ready to use her fists, in spite of her evident fragility. She was denying her feminine weakness; but it was for love of a militant male whose equal she wished to be. The attitude of defiance of many American women proves that they are haunted by a sense of their femininity. In truth, to go for a walk with one's eyes open is enough to demonstrate that humanity is divided into two classes of individuals whose clothes, faces, bodies, smiles, gaits, interests, and occupations are manifestly different. Perhaps these differences are superficial, perhaps they are destined to disappear. What is certain is that right now they do most obviously exist.

If her functioning as a female is not enough to define woman, if we decline also to explain her through "the eternal feminine," and if nevertheless we admit, provisionally, that women do exist, then we must face the question: what is a woman?

To state the question is, to me, to suggest, at once, a preliminary answer. The fact that I ask it is in itself significant. A man would never get the notion of writing a book on the peculiar situation of the human male.[2] But if I wish to define myself, I must first of all say: "I am a woman"; on this truth

---

[2]The Kinsey Report [Alfred C. Kinsey and others: *Sexual Behavior in the Human Male* (W. B. Saunders Co., 1948)] is no exception, for it is limited to describing the sexual characteristics of American men, which is quite a different matter.

must be based all further discussion. A man never begins by presenting himself as an individual of a certain sex; it goes without saying that he is a man. The terms *masculine* and *feminine* are used symmetrically only as a matter of form, as on legal papers. In actuality the relation of the two sexes is not quite like that of two electrical poles, for man represents both the positive and the neutral, as is indicated by the common use of *man* to designate human beings in general; whereas woman represents only the negative, defined by limiting criteria, without reciprocity. In the midst of an abstract discussion it is vexing to hear a man say: "You think thus and so because you are a woman"; but I know that my only defense is to reply: "I think thus and so because it is true," thereby removing my subjective self from the argument. It would be out of the question to reply: "And you think the contrary because you are a man," for it is understood that the fact of being a man is no peculiarity. A man is in the right in being a man; it is the woman who is in the wrong. It amounts to this: just as for the ancients there was an absolute vertical with reference to which the oblique was defined, so there is an absolute human type, the masculine. Woman has ovaries, a uterus; these peculiarities imprison her in her subjectivity, circumscribe her within the limits of her own nature. It is often said that she thinks with her glands. Man superbly ignores the fact that his anatomy also includes glands, such as the testicles, and that they secrete hormones. He thinks of his body as a direct and normal connection with the world, which he believes he apprehends objectively, whereas he regards the body of woman as a hindrance, a prison, weighed down by everything peculiar to it. "The female is a female by virtue of a certain *lack* of qualities," said Aristotle; "we should regard the female nature as afflicted with a natural defectiveness." And St. Thomas for his part pronounced woman to be an "imperfect man," an "incidental"

being. This is symbolized in Genesis where Eve is depicted as made from what Bossuet called "a supernumerary bone" of Adam.

Thus humanity is male and man defines woman not in herself but as relative to him; she is not regarded as an autonomous being. Michelet writes: "Woman, the relative being. . . ." And Benda is most positive in his *Rapport d'Uriel*: "The body of man makes sense in itself quite apart from that of woman, whereas the latter seems wanting in significance by itself. . . . Man can think of himself without woman. She cannot think of herself without man." And she is simply what man decrees; thus she is called "the sex," by which is meant that she appears essentially to the male as a sexual being. For him she is sex—absolute sex, no less. She is defined and differentiated with reference to man and not he with reference to her; she is the incidental, the inessential as opposed to the essential. He is the Subject, he is the Absolute—she is the Other.[3]

The category of the *Other* is as primordial as consciousness itself. In the most primitive societies, in the most ancient mythologies, one finds

---

[3]E. Lévinas expresses this idea most explicitly in his essay *Temps et l'Autre*. "Is there not a case in which otherness, alterity [*altérité*], unquestionably marks the nature of a being, as its essence, an instance of otherness not consisting purely and simply in the opposition of two species of the same genus? I think that the feminine represents the contrary in its absolute sense, this contrariness being in no wise affected by any relation between it and its correlative and thus remaining absolutely other. Sex is not a certain specific difference . . . no more is the sexual difference a mere contradiction. . . . Nor does this difference lie in the duality of two complementary terms, for two complementary terms imply a pre-existing whole. . . . Otherness reaches its full flowering in the feminine, a term of the same rank as consciousness but of opposite meaning."

I suppose that Lévinas does not forget that woman, too, is aware of her own consciousness, or ego. But it is striking that he deliberately takes a man's point of view, disregarding the reciprocity of subject and object. When he writes that woman is mystery, he implies that she is mystery for man. Thus his description, which is intended to be objective, is in fact an assertion of masculine privilege.

the expression of a duality—that of the Self and the Other. This duality was not originally attached to the division of the sexes; it was not dependent upon any empirical facts. It is revealed in such works as that of Granet on Chinese thought and those of Dumézil on the East Indies and Rome. The feminine element was at first no more involved in such pairs as Varuna-Mitra, Uranus-Zeus, Sun-Moon, and Day-Night than it was in the contrasts between Good and Evil, lucky and unlucky auspices, right and left, God and Lucifer. Otherness is a fundamental category of human thought.

Thus it is that no group ever sets itself up as the One without at once setting up the Other over against itself. If three travelers chance to occupy the same compartment, that is enough to make vaguely hostile "others" out of all the rest of the passengers on the train. In small-town eyes all persons not belonging to the village are "strangers" and suspect; to the native of a country all who inhabit other countries are "foreigners"; Jews are "different" for the anti-Semite, Negroes are "inferior" for American racists, aborigines are "natives" for colonists, proletarians are the "lower class" for the privileged.

Lévi-Strauss, at the end of a profound work on the various forms of primitive societies, reaches the following conclusion: "Passage from the state of Nature to the state of Culture is marked by man's ability to view biological relations as a series of contrasts; duality, alternation, opposition, and symmetry, whether under definite or vague forms, constitute not so much phenomena to be explained as fundamental and immediately given data of social reality."[4] These phenomena would be

---

[4]See C. Lévi-Strauss: *Les Structures élémentaires de la parenté.* My thanks are due to C. Lévi-Strauss for his kindness in furnishing me with the proofs of his work, which, among others, I have used liberally in Part II.

incomprehensible if in fact human society were simply a *Mitsein* or fellowship based on solidarity and friendliness. Things become clear, on the contrary, if, following Hegel, we find in consciousness itself a fundamental hostility toward every other consciousness; the subject can be posed only in being opposed—he sets himself up as the essential, as opposed to the other, the inessential, the object.

But the other consciousness, the other ego, sets up a reciprocal claim. The native traveling abroad is shocked to find himself in turn regarded as a "stranger" by the natives of neighboring countries. As a matter of fact, wars, festivals, trading, treaties, and contests among tribes, nations, and classes tend to deprive the concept *Other* of its absolute sense and to make manifest its relativity; willy-nilly, individuals and groups are forced to realize the reciprocity of their relations. How is it, then, that this reciprocity has not been recognized between the sexes, that one of the contrasting terms is set up as the sole essential, denying any relativity in regard to its correlative and defining the latter as pure otherness? Why is it that women do not dispute male sovereignty? No subject will readily volunteer to become the object, the inessential; it is not the Other who, in defining himself as the Other, establishes the One. The Other is posed as such by the One in defining himself as the One. But if the Other is not to regain the status of being the One, he must be submissive enough to accept this alien point of view. Whence comes this submission in the case of woman?

There are, to be sure, other cases in which a certain category has been able to dominate another completely for a time. Very often this privilege depends upon inequality of numbers—the majority imposes its rule upon the minority or persecutes it. But women are not a minority, like the American Negroes or the Jews; there are as many women as men on earth. Again, the two groups concerned have often been originally independent; they may have been formerly unaware of each other's existence, or perhaps they recognized each other's autonomy. But a historical event has resulted in the subjugation of the weaker by the stronger. The scattering of the Jews, the introduction of slavery into America, the conquests of imperialism are examples in point. In these cases the oppressed retained at least the memory of former days; they possessed in common a past, a tradition, sometimes a religion or a culture.

The parallel drawn by Bebel between women and the proletariat is valid in that neither ever formed a minority or a separate collective unit of mankind. And instead of a single historical event it is in both cases a historical development that explains their status as a class and accounts for the membership of *particular individuals* in that class. But proletarians have not always existed, whereas there have always been women. They are women in virtue of their anatomy and physiology. Throughout history they have always been subordinated to men,[5] and hence their dependency is not the result of a historical event or a social change—it was not something that *occurred*. The reason why otherness in this case seems to be an absolute is in part that it lacks the contingent or incidental nature of historical facts. A condition brought about at a certain time can be abolished at some other time, as the Negroes of Haiti and others have proved; but it might seem that a natural condition is beyond the possibility of change. In truth, however, the nature of things is no more immutably given, once for all, than is historical reality. If woman seems to be the inessential which never becomes the essential, it is because she herself fails to bring about this change. Proletarians say "We"; Negroes also. Regarding themselves as subjects, they transform the bourgeois, the whites, into "others." But women do not say "We," except at some congress of feminists or similar formal demonstration; men say "women," and women use the same word in referring to themselves. They do not authentically assume a subjective attitude. The proletarians have accomplished the revolution in Russia, the Negroes in Haiti, the Indo-Chinese are battling for it in Indo-China; but the women's effort has never been anything more than a symbolic agitation. They have gained only what men have been willing to grant; they have taken nothing, they have only received.[6]

The reason for this is that women lack concrete means for organizing themselves into a unit which can stand face to face with the correlative unit. They have no past, no history, no religion of their own; and they have no such solidarity of work and interest as that of the proletariat. They are not even promiscuously herded together in the way that creates community feeling among the American Negroes, the ghetto Jews, the workers of Saint-Denis, or the factory hands of Renault. They live dispersed among the males, attached through residence, housework, economic condition, and social standing to certain men—fathers or husbands—more firmly than they are to other women. If they belong to the bourgeoisie, they feel solidarity with men of that class, not with proletarian women; if they are white, their allegiance is to white men, not to Negro women. The proletariat can propose to massacre the ruling class, and a sufficiently fanatical Jew or Negro might dream of getting sole possession of the atomic bomb and making humanity wholly Jewish or black; but woman cannot even dream of exterminating the males. The bond that unites her to her oppressors is not comparable to any other. The division of the sexes is a biological fact, not an event in human history. Male and female stand opposed within a primordial *Mitsein*,

---

[5]With rare exceptions, perhaps, like certain matriarchal rulers, queens, and the like.—Tr.

[6]See Part II [of *The Second Sex*], ch. viii.

and woman has not broken it. The couple is a fundamental unity with its two halves riveted together, and the cleavage of society along the line of sex is impossible. Here is to be found the basic trait of woman: she is the Other in a totality of which the two components are necessary to one another.

One could suppose that this reciprocity might have facilitated the liberation of woman. When Hercules sat at the feet of Omphale and helped with her spinning, his desire for her held him captive; but why did she fail to gain a lasting power? To revenge herself on Jason, Medea killed their children; and this grim legend would seem to suggest that she might have obtained a formidable influence over him through his love for his offspring. In *Lysistrata* Aristophanes gaily depicts a band of women who joined forces to gain social ends through the sexual needs of their men; but this is only a play. In the legend of the Sabine women, the latter soon abandoned their plan of remaining sterile to punish their ravishers. In truth woman has not been socially emancipated through man's need—sexual desire and the desire for offspring—which makes the male dependent for satisfaction upon the female.

Master and slave, also, are united by a reciprocal need, in this case economic, which does not liberate the slave. In the relation of master to slave the master does not make a point of the need that he has for the other; he has in his grasp the power of satisfying this need through his own action; whereas the slave, in his dependent condition, his hope and fear, is quite conscious of the need he has for his master. Even if the need is at bottom equally urgent for both, it always works in favor of the oppressor and against the oppressed. That is why the liberation of the working class, for example, has been slow.

Now, woman has always been man's dependent, if not his slave; the two sexes have never shared the world in equality. And even today woman is heavily handicapped, though her situation is beginning to change. Almost nowhere is her legal status the same as man's,[7] and frequently it is much to her disadvantage. Even when her rights are legally recognized in the abstract, long-standing custom prevents their full expression in the mores. In the economic sphere men and women can almost be said to make up two castes; other things being equal, the former hold the better jobs, get higher wages, and have more opportunity for success than their new competitors. In industry and politics men have a great many more positions and they monopolize the most important posts. In addition to all this, they enjoy a traditional prestige that the education of children tends in every way to support, for the present enshrines the past—and in the past all history has been made by men. At the present time, when women are beginning to take part in the affairs of the world, it is still a world that belongs to men—they have no doubt of it at all and women have scarcely any. To decline to be the Other, to refuse to be a party to the deal—this would be for women to renounce all the advantages conferred upon them by their alliance with the superior caste. Man-the-sovereign will provide woman-the-liege with material protection and will undertake the moral justification of her existence; thus she can evade at once both economic risk and the metaphysical risk of a liberty in which ends and aims must be contrived without assistance. Indeed, along with the ethical urge of each individual to affirm his subjective existence, there is also the temptation to forgo liberty and become a thing. This is an inauspicious road, for he who takes it—passive, lost, ruined—becomes henceforth the creature of another's will, frustrated in his transcendence and deprived of every value. But it is an

---

[7]At the moment an "equal rights" amendment to the Constitution of the United States is before Congress.—TR.

easy road; on it one avoids the strain involved in undertaking an authentic existence. When man makes of woman the *Other*, he may, then, expect her to manifest deep-seated tendencies toward complicity. Thus, woman may fail to lay claim to the status of subject because she lacks definite resources, because she feels the necessary bond that ties her to man regardless of reciprocity, and because she is often very well pleased with her role as the *Other*.

But it will be asked at once: how did all this begin? It is easy to see that the duality of the sexes, like any duality, gives rise to conflict. And doubtless the winner will assume the status of absolute. But why should man have won from the start? It seems possible that women could have won the victory; or that the outcome of the conflict might never have been decided. How is it that this world has always belonged to the men and that things have begun to change only recently? Is this change a good thing? Will it bring about an equal sharing of the world between men and women?

These questions are not new, and they have often been answered. But the very fact that woman *is the Other* tends to cast suspicion upon all the justifications that men have ever been able to provide for it. These have all too evidently been dictated by men's interest. A little-known feminist of the seventeenth century, Poulain de la Barre, put it this way: "All that has been written about women by men should be suspect, for the men are at once judge and party to the lawsuit." Everywhere, at all times, the males have displayed their satisfaction in feeling that they are the lords of creation. "Blessed be God . . . that He did not make me a woman," say the Jews in their morning prayers, while their wives pray on a note of resignation: "Blessed be the Lord, who created me according to His will." The first among the blessings for which Plato thanked the gods was that he had been created free, not enslaved; the second, a man, not a woman. But the

males could not enjoy this privilege fully unless they believed it to be founded on the absolute and the eternal; they sought to make the fact of their supremacy into a right. "Being men, those who have made and compiled the laws have favored their own sex, and jurists have elevated these laws into principles," to quote Poulain de la Barre once more.

Legislators, priests, philosophers, writers, and scientists have striven to show that the subordinate position of woman is willed in heaven and advantageous on earth. The religions invented by men reflect this wish for domination. In the legends of Eve and Pandora men have taken up arms against women. They have made use of philosophy and theology, as the quotations from Aristotle and St. Thomas have shown. Since ancient times satirists and moralists have delighted in showing up the weaknesses of women. We are familiar with the savage indictments hurled against women throughout French literature. Montherlant, for example, follows the tradition of Jean de Meung, though with less gusto. This hostility may at times be well founded, often it is gratuitous; but in truth it more or less successfully conceals a desire for self-justification. As Montaigne says, "It is easier to accuse one sex than to excuse the other." Sometimes what is going on is clear enough. For instance, the Roman law limiting the rights of woman cited "the imbecility, the instability of the sex" just when the weakening of family ties seemed to threaten the interests of male heirs. And in the effort to keep the married woman under guardianship, appeal was made in the sixteenth century to the authority of St. Augustine, who declared that "woman is a creature neither decisive nor constant," at a time when the single woman was thought capable of managing her property. Montaigne understood clearly how arbitrary and unjust was woman's appointed lot: "Women are not in the wrong when they decline to accept the rules laid down for them, since the men make these rules without consulting them. No wonder intrigue and strife abound." But he did not go so far as to champion their cause.

It was only later, in the eighteenth century, that genuinely democratic men began to view the matter objectively. Diderot, among others, strove to show that woman is, like man, a human being. Later John Stuart Mill came fervently to her defense. But these philosophers displayed unusual impartiality. In the nineteenth century the feminist quarrel became again a quarrel of partisans. One of the consequences of the industrial revolution was the entrance of women into productive labor, and it was just here that the claims of the feminists emerged from the realm of theory and acquired an economic basis, while their opponents became the more aggressive. Although landed property lost power to some extent, the bourgeoisie clung to the old morality that found the guarantee of private property in the solidity of the family. Woman was ordered back into the home the more harshly as her emancipation became a real menace. Even within the working class the men endeavored to restrain woman's liberation, because they began to see the women as dangerous competitors—the more so because they were accustomed to work for lower wages.[8]

In proving woman's inferiority, the antifeminists then began to draw not only upon religion, philosophy, and theology, as before, but also upon science—biology, experimental psychology, etc. At most they were willing to grant "equality in difference" to the *other* sex. That profitable formula is most significant; it is precisely like the "equal but separate" formula of the Jim Crow laws aimed at the North American Negroes. As is well known, this so-called equalitarian segregation has resulted only in the most extreme discrimination. The similarity just noted is in no way due to chance, for

whether it is a race, a caste, a class, or a sex that is reduced to a position of inferiority, the methods of justification are the same. "The eternal feminine" corresponds to "the black soul" and to "the Jewish character." True, the Jewish problem is on the whole very different from the other two—to the anti-Semite the Jew is not so much an inferior as he is an enemy for whom there is to be granted no place on earth, for whom annihilation is the fate desired. But there are deep similarities between the situation of woman and that of the Negro. Both are being emancipated today from a like paternalism, and the former master class wishes to "keep them in their place"—that is, the place chosen for them. In both cases the former masters lavish more or less sincere eulogies, either on the virtues of "the good Negro" with his dormant, childish, merry soul—the submissive Negro—or on the merits of the woman who is "truly feminine"—that is, frivolous, infantile, irresponsible—the submissive woman. In both cases the dominant class bases its argument on a state of affairs that it has itself created. As George Bernard Shaw puts it, in substance, "The American white relegates the black to the rank of shoeshine boy; and he concludes from this that the black is good for nothing but shining shoes." This vicious circle is met with in all analogous circumstances; when an individual (or a group of individuals) is kept in a situation of inferiority, the fact is that he *is* inferior. But the significance of the verb *to be* must be rightly understood here; it is in bad faith to give it a static value when it really has the dynamic Hegelian sense of "to have become." Yes, women on the whole *are* today inferior to men; that is, their situation affords them fewer possibilities. The question is: should that state of affairs continue?

Many men hope that it will continue; not all have given up the battle. The conservative bourgeoisie still see in the emancipation of women a menace to their morality and their interests. Some

---

[8]See Part II [of *The Second Sex*], pp. 115–17.

men dread feminine competition. Recently a male student wrote in the *Hebdo-Latin:* "Every woman student who goes into medicine or law robs us of a job." He never questioned his rights in this world. And economic interests are not the only ones concerned. One of the benefits that oppression confers upon the oppressors is that the most humble among them is made to *feel* superior; thus, a "poor white" in the South can console himself with the thought that he is not a "dirty nigger"—and the more prosperous whites cleverly exploit this pride.

Similarly, the most mediocre of males feels himself a demigod as compared with women. It was much easier for M. de Montherlant to think himself a hero when he faced women (and women chosen for his purpose) than when he was obliged to act the man among men—something many women have done better than he, for that matter. And in September 1948, in one of his articles in the *Figaro littéraire*, Claude Mauriac—whose great originality is admired by all—could[9] write regarding woman: "*We* listen on a tone [*sic!*] of polite indifference ... to the most brilliant among them, well knowing that her wit reflects more or less luminously ideas that come from *us.*" Evidently the speaker referred to is not reflecting the ideas of Mauriac himself, for no one knows of his having any. It may be that she reflects ideas originating with men, but then, even among men there are those who have been known to appropriate ideas not their own; and one can well ask whether Claude Mauriac might not find more interesting a conversation reflecting Descartes, Marx, or Gide rather than himself. What is really remarkable is that by using the questionable *we* he identifies himself with St. Paul, Hegel, Lenin, and Nietzsche, and from the lofty eminence of their grandeur looks down disdainfully upon the bevy of women who make bold to converse with him on a footing

of equality. In truth, I know of more than one woman who would refuse to suffer with patience Mauriac's "tone of polite indifference."

I have lingered on this example because the masculine attitude is here displayed with disarming ingenuousness. But men profit in many more subtle ways from the otherness, the alterity of woman. Here is miraculous balm for those afflicted with an inferiority complex, and indeed no one is more arrogant toward women, more aggressive or scornful, than the man who is anxious about his virility. Those who are not fear-ridden in the presence of their fellow men are much more disposed to recognize a fellow creature in woman; but even to these the myth of Woman, the Other, is precious for many reasons[10] They cannot be blamed for not cheerfully relinquishing all the benefits they derive from the myth, for they realize what they would lose in relinquishing woman as they fancy her to be, while they fail to realize what they have to gain from the woman of tomorrow. Refusal to pose oneself as the Subject, unique and absolute, requires great self-denial. Furthermore, the vast majority of men make no such claim explicitly. They do not *postulate* woman as inferior, for today they are too thoroughly imbued with the ideal of democracy not to recognize all human beings as equals.

In the bosom of the family, woman seems in the eyes of childhood and youth to be clothed in the same social dignity as the adult males. Later on,

---

[9]Or at least he thought he could.

[10]A significant article on this theme by Michel Carrouges appeared in No. 292 of the *Cahiers du Sud*. He writes indignantly: "Would that there were no woman-myth at all but only a cohort of cooks, matrons, prostitutes, and bluestockings serving functions of pleasure or usefulness!" That is to say, in his view woman has no existence in and for herself; he thinks only of her *function* in the male world. Her reason for existence lies in man. But then, in fact, her poetic "function" as a myth might be more valued than any other. The real problem is precisely to find out why woman should be defined with relation to man.

the young man, desiring and loving, experiences the resistance, the independence of the woman desired and loved; in marriage, he respects woman as wife and mother, and in the concrete events of conjugal life she stands there before him as a free being. He can therefore feel that social subordination as between the sexes no longer exists and that on the whole, in spite of differences, woman is an equal. As, however, he observes some points of inferiority—the most important being unfitness for the professions—he attributes these to natural causes. When he is in a co-operative and benevolent relation with woman, his theme is the principle of abstract equality, and he does not base his attitude upon such inequality as may exist. But when he is in conflict with her, the situation is reversed: his theme will be the existing inequality, and he will even take it as justification for denying abstract equality.[11]

So it is that many men will affirm as if in good faith that women *are* the equals of man and that they have nothing to clamor for, while *at the same time* they will say that women can never be the equals of man and that their demands are in vain. It is, in point of fact, a difficult matter for man to realize the extreme importance of social discriminations which seem outwardly insignificant but which produce in woman moral and intellectual effects so profound that they appear to spring from her original nature.[12] The most sympathetic of men never fully comprehend woman's concrete situation. And there is no reason to put much trust in the men when they rush to the defense of privileges whose full extent they can hardly measure.

We shall not, then, permit ourselves to be intimidated by the number and violence of the attacks launched against women, nor to be entrapped by the self-seeing eulogies bestowed on the "true woman," nor to profit by the enthusiasm for woman's destiny manifested by men who would not for the world have any part of it.

We should consider the arguments of the feminists with no less suspicion, however, for very often their controversial aim deprives them of all real value. If the "woman question" seems trivial, it is because masculine arrogance has made of it a "quarrel"; and when quarreling one no longer reasons well. People have tirelessly sought to prove that woman is superior, inferior, or equal to man. Some say that, having been created after Adam, she is evidently a secondary being; others say on the contrary that Adam was only a rough draft and that God succeeded in producing the human being in perfection when He created Eve. Woman's brain is smaller; yes, but it is relatively larger. Christ was made a man; yes, but perhaps for his greater humility. Each argument at once suggests its opposite, and both are often fallacious. If we are to gain understanding, we must get out of these ruts; we must discard the vague notions of superiority, inferiority, equality which have hitherto corrupted every discussion of the subject and start afresh.

Very well, but just how shall we pose the question? And, to begin with, who are we to propound it at all? Man is at once judge and party to the case; but so is woman. What we need is an angel—neither man nor woman—but where shall we find one? Still, the angel would be poorly qualified to speak, for an angel is ignorant of all the basic facts involved in the problem. With a hermaphrodite we should be no better off, for here the situation is most peculiar; the hermaphrodite is not really the combination of a whole man and a whole woman, but consists of parts of each and thus is neither. It looks to me as if there are, after all, certain women

---

[11]For example, a man will say that he considers his wife in no wise degraded because she has no gainful occupation. The profession of housewife is just as lofty, and so on. But when the first quarrel comes, he will exclaim: "Why, you couldn't make your living without me!"

[12]The specific purpose of Book II of this study is to describe this process.

who are best qualified to elucidate the situation of woman. Let us not be misled by the sophism that because Epimenides was a Cretan he was necessarily a liar; it is not a mysterious essence that compels men and women to act in good or in bad faith, it is their situation that inclines them more or less toward the search for truth. Many of today's women, fortunate in the restoration of all the privileges pertaining to the estate of the human being, can afford the luxury of impartiality—we even recognize its necessity. We are no longer like our partisan elders; by and large we have won the game. In recent debates on the status of women the United Nations has persistently maintained that the equality of the sexes is now becoming a reality, and already some of us have never had to sense in our femininity an inconvenience or an obstacle. Many problems appear to us to be more pressing than those which concern us in particular, and this detachment even allows us to hope that our attitude will be objective. Still, we know the feminine world more intimately than do the men because we have our roots in it, we grasp more immediately than do men what it means to a human being to be feminine; and we are more concerned with such knowledge. I have said that there are more pressing problems, but this does not prevent us from seeing some importance in asking how the fact of being women will affect our lives. What opportunities precisely have been given us and what withheld? What fate awaits our younger sisters, and what directions should they take? It is significant that books by women on women are in general animated in our day less by a wish to demand our rights than by an effort toward clarity and understanding. As we emerge from an era of excessive controversy, this book is offered as one attempt among others to confirm that statement.

But it is doubtless impossible to approach any human problem with a mind free from bias. The way in which questions are put, the points of view assumed, presuppose a relativity of interest; all characteristics imply values, and every objective description, so called, implies an ethical background. Rather than attempt to conceal principles more or less definitely implied, it is better to state them openly at the beginning. This will make it unnecessary to specify on every page in just what sense one uses such words as *superior, inferior, better, worse, progress, reaction*, and the like. If we survey some of the works on woman, we note that one of the points of view most frequently adopted is that of the public good, the general interest; and one always means by this the benefit of society as one wishes it to be maintained or established. For our part, we hold that the only public good is that which assures the private good of the citizens; we shall pass judgment on institutions according to their effectiveness in giving concrete opportunities to individuals. But we do not confuse the idea of private interest with that of happiness, although that is another common point of view. Are not women of the harem more happy than women voters? Is not the housekeeper happier than the working-woman? It is not too clear just what the world *happy* really means and still less what true values it may mask. There is no possibility of measuring the happiness of others, and it is always easy to describe as happy the situation in which one wishes to place them.

In particular those who are condemned to stagnation are often pronounced happy on the pretext that happiness consists in being at rest. This notion we reject, for our perspective is that of existentialist ethics. Every subject plays his part as such specifically through exploits or projects that serve as a mode of transcendence; he achieves liberty only through a continual reaching out toward other liberties. There is no justification for present existence other than its expansion into an indefinitely open future. Every time transcendence falls back into immanence, stagnation, there is a degradation of existence into the *"en-soi"*—the brutish life of subjection to given conditions—and of liberty into constraint and contingence. This downfall represents a moral fault if the subject consents to it; if it is inflicted upon him, it spells frustration and oppression. In both cases it is an absolute evil. Every individual concerned to justify his existence feels that his existence involves an undefined need to transcend himself, to engage in freely chosen projects.

Now, what peculiarly signalizes the situation of woman is that she—a free and autonomous being like all human creatures—nevertheless finds herself living in a world where men compel her to assume the status of the Other. They propose to stabilize her as object and to doom her to immanence since her transcendence is to be overshadowed and forever transcended by another ego (*conscience*) which is essential and sovereign. The drama of woman lies in this conflict between the fundamental aspirations of every subject (ego)—who always regards the self as the essential—and the compulsions of a situation in which she is the inessential. How can a human being in woman's situation attain fulfillment? What roads are open to her? Which are blocked? How can independence be recovered in a state of dependency? What circumstances limit woman's liberty and how can they be overcome? These are the fundamental questions on which I would fain throw some light. This means that I am interested in the fortunes of the individual as defined not in terms of happiness but in terms of liberty.

Quite evidently this problem would be without significance if we were to believe that woman's destiny is inevitably determined by physiological, psychological, or economic forces. Hence I shall discuss first of all the light in which woman is viewed by biology, psychoanalysis, and historical materialism. Next I shall try to show exactly how the concept of the "truly feminine" has been fashioned—why woman has been defined as the Other—and what have been the consequences from man's point of view. Then from woman's point of view I shall describe the world in which women must live; and thus we shall be able to envisage the difficulties in their way as, endeavoring to make their escape from the sphere hitherto assigned them, they aspire to full membership in the human race.

THE WOMAN IN LOVE

The word *love* has by no means the same sense for both sexes, and this is one cause of the serious misunderstandings that divide them. Byron well said: "Man's love is of man's life a thing apart; 'Tis woman's whole existence." Nietzsche expresses the same idea in *The Gay Science*:

> The single word love in fact signifies two different things for man and woman. What woman understands by love is clear enough: it is not only devotion, it is a total gift of body and soul, without reservation, without regard for anything whatever. This unconditional nature of her love is what makes it a *faith*,[13] the only one she has. As for man, if he loves a woman, what he *wants*[13] is that love from her; he is in consequence far from postulating the same sentiment for himself as for woman; if there should be men who also felt that desire for complete abandonment, upon my word, they would not be men.

Men have found it possible to be passionate lovers at certain times in their lives, but there is not one of them who could be called "a great lover";[14] in their most violent transports, they never abdicate completely; even on their knees before a mistress, what they still want is to take possession of her; at the very heart of their lives they remain sovereign subjects; the beloved woman is only one

---

[13]Nietzsche's italics.
[14]In the sense that a woman may sometimes be called *"une grande amoureuse."*—TR.

value among others; they wish to integrate her into their existence and not to squander it entirely on her. For woman, on the contrary, to love is to relinquish everything for the benefit of a master. As Cécile Sauvage puts it: "Woman must forget her own personality when she is in love. It is a law of nature. A woman is nonexistent without a master. Without a master, she is a scattered bouquet."

The fact is that we have nothing to do here with laws of nature. It is the difference in their situations that is reflected in the difference men and women show in their conceptions of love. The individual who is a subject, who is himself, if he has the courageous inclination toward transcendence, endeavors to extend his grasp on the world: he is ambitious, he acts. But an inessential creature is incapable of sensing the absolute at the heart of her subjectivity; a being doomed to immanence cannot find self-realization in acts. Shut up in the sphere of the relative, destined to the male from childhood, habituated to seeing in him a superb being whom she cannot possibly equal, the woman who has not repressed her claim to humanity will dream of transcending her being toward one of these superior beings, of amalgamating herself with the sovereign subject. There is no other way out for her than to lose herself, body and soul, in him who is represented to her as the absolute, as the essential. Since she is anyway doomed to dependence, she will prefer to serve a god rather than obey tyrants—parents, husband, or protector. She chooses to desire her enslavement so ardently that it will seem to her the expression of her liberty; she will try to rise above her situation as inessential object by fully accepting it; through her flesh, her feelings, her behavior, she will enthrone him as supreme value and reality: she will humble herself to nothingness before him. Love becomes for her a religion. . . .

[T]he adolescent girl wishes at first to identify herself with males; when she gives that up, she then seeks to share in their masculinity by having one of them in love with her; it is not the individuality of this one or that one which attracts her; she is in love with man in general.[15]. . . Of course the male is to belong to the same class and race as hers, for sexual privilege is in play only within this frame. If man is to be a demigod, he must first of all be a human being, and to the colonial officer's daughter the native is not a man. If the young girl gives herself to an "inferior," it is for the reason that she wishes to degrade herself because she believes she is unworthy of love; but normally she is looking for a man who represents male superiority. She is soon to ascertain that many individuals of the favored sex are sadly contingent and earthbound, but at first her presumption is favorable to them; they are called on less to prove their worth than to avoid too gross a disproof of it—which accounts for many mistakes, some of them serious. A naïve young girl is caught by the gleam of virility, and in her eyes male worth is shown, according to circumstances, by physical strength, distinction of manner, wealth, cultivation, intelligence, authority, social status, a military uniform; but what she always wants is for her lover to represent the essence of manhood.

Familiarity is often sufficient to destroy his prestige; it may collapse at the first kiss, or in daily association, or during the wedding night. Love at a distance, however, is only a fantasy, not a real experience. The desire for love becomes a passionate love only when it is carnally realized. Inversely, love can arise as a result of physical intercourse; in this case the sexually dominated woman acquires an exalted view of a man who at first seemed to her quite insignificant.

But it often happens that a woman succeeds in deifying none of the men she knows. Love has a

---

[15]Haenigsen's newspaper comic strip "Penny" gives never flagging popular expression to this truth.—Tr.

smaller place in woman's life than has often been supposed. Husband, children, home, amusements, social duties, vanity, sexuality, career, are much more important. Most women dream of a *grand amour*, a soul-searing love. They have known substitutes, they have been close to it; it has come to them in partial, bruised, ridiculous, imperfect, mendacious forms; but very few have truly dedicated their lives to it. The *grandes amoureuses* are most often women who have not frittered themselves away in juvenile affairs; they have first accepted the traditional feminine destiny: husband, home, children; or they have known pitiless solitude; or they have banked on some enterprise that has been more or less of a failure. And when they glimpse the opportunity to salvage a disappointing life by dedicating it to some superior person, they desperately give themselves up to this hope. . . .

Even if they can choose independence, this road seems the most attractive to a majority of women: it is agonizing for a woman to assume responsibility for her life. Even the male, when adolescent, is quite willing to turn to older women for guidance, education, mothering; but customary attitudes, the boy's training, and his own inner imperatives forbid him to content himself in the end with the easy solution of abdication; to him such affairs with older women are only a stage through which he passes. It is man's good fortune—in adulthood as in early childhood—to be obliged to take the most arduous roads, but the surest; it is woman's misfortune to be surrounded by almost irresistible temptations; everything incites her to follow the easy slopes; instead of being invited to fight her own way up, she is told that she has only to let herself slide and she will attain paradises of enchantment. When she perceives that she has been duped by a mirage, it is too late; her strength has been exhausted in a losing venture.

The psychoanalysts are wont to assert that woman seeks the father image in her lover; but it is because he is a man, not because he is a father, that he dazzles the girl child, and every man shares in this magical power. Woman does not long to reincarnate one individual in another, but to reconstruct a situation: that which she experienced as a little girl, under adult protection. She was deeply integrated with home and family, she knew the peace of quasi-passivity. Love will give her back her mother as well as her father, it will give her back her childhood. What she wants to recover is a roof over her head, walls that prevent her from feeling her abandonment in the wide world, authority that protects her against her liberty. This childish drama haunts the love of many women; they are happy to be called "my little girl, my dear child"; men know that the words: "you're just like a little girl," are among those that most surely touch a woman's heart. We have seen that many women suffer in becoming adults; and so a great number remain obstinately "babyish," prolonging their childhood indefinitely in manner and dress. To become like a child again in a man's arms fills their cup with joy. The hackneyed theme: "To feel so little in your arms, my love," recurs again and again in amorous dialogue and in love letters. "Baby mine," croons the lover, the woman calls herself "your little one," and so on. A young woman will write: "When will he come, he who can dominate me?" And when he comes, she will love to sense his manly superiority.

Only in love can woman harmoniously reconcile her eroticism and her narcissism; we have seen that these sentiments are opposed in such a manner that it is very difficult for a woman to adapt herself to her sexual destiny. To make herself a carnal object, the prey of another, is in contradiction to her self-worship: it seems to her that embraces blight and sully her body or degrade her soul. Thus it is that some women take refuge in frigidity, thinking that in this way they can preserve the integrity of the ego. . . .

But for other women, on the contrary, only the esteem, affection, and admiration of the man can eliminate the sense of abasement. They will not yield to a man unless they believe they are deeply loved. A woman must have a considerable amount of cynicism, indifference, or pride to regard physical relations as an exchange of pleasure by which each partner benefits equally. As much as woman—and perhaps more—man revolts against anyone who attempts to exploit him sexually;[16] but it is woman who generally feels that her partner is using her as an instrument. Nothing but high admiration can compensate for the humiliation of an act that she considers a defeat.

We have seen that the act of love requires of woman profound self-abandonment; she bathes in a passive languor; with closed eyes, anonymous, lost, she feels as if borne by waves, swept away in a storm, shrouded in darkness: darkness of the flesh, of the womb, of the grave. Annihilated, she becomes one with the Whole, her ego is abolished. But when the man moves from her, she finds herself back on earth, on a bed, in the light; she again has a name, a face: she is one vanquished, prey, object.

This is the moment when love becomes a necessity. As when the child, after weaning, seeks the reassuring gaze of its parents, so must a woman feel, through the man's loving contemplation, that she is, after all, still at one with the Whole from which her flesh is now painfully detached. She is seldom wholly satisfied even if she has felt the orgasm, she is not set completely free from the spell of her flesh; her desire continues in the form of affection. In giving her pleasure, the man increases her attachment, he does not liberate her. As for him, he no longer desires her; but she will not pardon this momentary indifference unless he has dedicated to her a timeless and absolute emotion. Then the immanence of the moment is transcended; hot memories are not regret, but a treasured delight; ebbing pleasure becomes hope and promise; enjoyment is justified; woman can gloriously accept her sexuality because she transcends it; excitement, pleasure, desire are no longer a state, but a benefaction; her body is no longer an object: it is a hymn, a flame.

Then she can yield with passion to the magic of eroticism; darkness becomes light; the loving woman can open her eyes, can look upon the man who loves her and whose gaze glorifies her; through him nothingness becomes fullness of being, and being is transmuted into worth; she no longer sinks in a sea of shadows, but is borne up on wings, exalted to the skies. Abandon becomes sacred ecstasy. When she *receives* her beloved, woman is dwelt in, visited, as was the Virgin by the Holy Ghost, as is the believer by the Host. This is what explains the obscene resemblance between pious hymns and erotic songs; it is not that mystical love always has a sexual character, but that the sexuality of the woman in love is tinged with mysticism. "'My God, my adored one, my lord and master'—the same words fall from the lips of the saint on her knees and the loving woman on her bed; the one offers her flesh to the thunderbolt of Christ, she stretches out her hands to receive the stigmata of the Cross, she calls for the burning presence of divine Love; the other, also, offers and awaits: thunderbolt, dart, arrow, are incarnated in the male sex organ. In both women there is the same dream, the childhood dream, the mystic dream, the dream of love: to attain supreme existence through losing oneself in the other.

It has sometimes been maintained that this desire for annihilation leads to masochism.[17] But as I have noted in connection with eroticism, it can be

---

[16]Lawrence, for example, in *Lady Chatterley's Lover*, expresses through Mellors his aversion for women who make a man an instrument of pleasure.

[17]As by Helene Deutsch in her *Psychology of Women*.

called masochism only when I essay "to be fascinated by my own status as object, through the agency of others";[18] that is to say, when the consciousness of the subject is directed back toward the ego to see it in a humiliating position. Now, the woman in love is not simply and solely a narcissist identified with her ego; she feels, more than this, a passionate desire to transcend the limitations of self and become infinite, thanks to the intervention of another who has access to infinite reality. She abandons herself to love first of all to *save herself*; but the paradox of idolatrous love is that in trying to save herself she *denies herself* utterly in the end. Her feeling gains a mystical dimension; she requires her God no longer to admire her and approve of her; she wants to merge with him, to forget herself in his arms. "I would wish to be a saint of love," writes Mme d'Agoult.[19] "I would long for martyrdom in such moments of exaltation and ascetic frenzy." What comes to light in these words is a desire for a complete destruction of the self, abolishing the boundaries that separate her from the beloved. There is no question here of masochism, but of a dream of ecstatic union.

In order to realize this dream, what woman wants in the first place is to serve; for in responding to her lover's demands, a woman will feel that she is necessary; she will be integrated with his existence, she will share his worth, she will be justified. Even mystics like to believe, according to Angelus Silesius, that God needs man; otherwise they would be giving themselves in vain. The more demands the man makes, the more gratified the woman feels. Although the seclusion imposed by Victor Hugo on Juliette Drouet weighed heavily on the young woman, one feels that she is happy in obeying him: to stay by the fireside is to do something for the master's pleasure. She tries also to be useful to him in a positive way. She cooks choice dishes for him and arranges a little nest where he can be at home; she looks after his clothes. "I want you to tear your clothes as much as possible," she writes to him, "and I want to mend and clean them all myself." She reads the papers, clips out articles, classifies letters and notes, copies manuscripts, for him. She is grieved when the poet entrusts a part of the work to his daughter Léopoldine.

Such traits are found in every woman in love. If need be, she herself tyrannizes over herself in her lover's name; all she is, all she has, every moment of her life, must be devoted to him and thus gain their *raison d'être*; she wishes to possess nothing save in him; what makes her unhappy is for him to require nothing of her, so much so that a sensitive lover will invent demands. She at first sought in love a confirmation of what she was, of her past, of her personality; but she also involves her future in it, and to justify her future she puts it in the hands of one who possesses all values. Thus she gives up her transcendence, subordinating it to that of the essential other, to whom she makes herself vassal and slave. It was to find herself, to save herself, that she lost herself in him in the first place; and the fact is that little by little she does lose herself in him wholly; for her the whole of reality is in the other. . . .

The woman who finds pleasure in submitting to male caprices also admires the evident action of a sovereign free being in the tyranny practiced on her. It must be noted that if for some reason the lover's prestige is destroyed, his blows and demands become odious; they are precious only if they manifest the divinity of the loved one. But if they do, it is intoxicating joy to feel herself the prey of another's free action. An existent finds it a most amazing adventure to be justified through the

---

[18]Sartre in *L'Être et le néant*.
[19]She eloped with Franz Liszt and became the mother of Cosima Wagner. Under the name of Daniel Stern she wrote historical and philosophical books.—TR.

varying and imperious will of another; one wearies of living always in the same skin, and blind obedience is the only chance for radical transformation known to a human being. Woman is thus slave, queen, flower, hind, stained-glass window, wanton, servant, courtesan, muse, companion, mother, sister, child, according to the fugitive dreams, the imperious commands, of her lover. She lends herself to these metamorphoses with ravishment as long as she does not realize that all the time her lips have retained the unvarying savor of submission. On the level of love, as on that of eroticism, it seems evident that masochism is one of the bypaths taken by the unsatisfied woman, disappointed in both the other and herself; but it is not the natural tendency of a happy resignation. Masochism perpetuates the presence of the ego in a bruised and degraded condition; love brings forgetfulness of self in favor of the essential subject.

The supreme goal of human love, as of mystical love, is identification with the loved one.[20] The measure of values, the truth of the world, are in his consciousness; hence it is not enough to serve him. The woman in love tries to see with his eyes; she reads the books he reads, prefers the pictures and the music he prefers; she is interested only in the landscapes she sees with him, in the ideas that come from him; she adopts his friendships, his enmities, his opinions; when she questions herself, it is his reply she tries to hear; she wants to have in her lungs the air he has already breathed; the fruits and flowers that do not come from his hands have no taste and no fragrance. Her idea of location in space, even, is upset: the center of the world is no longer the place where she is, but that occupied by her lover; all roads lead to his home, and from it. She uses his words, mimics his gestures, acquires

his eccentricities and his tics. "I am Heathcliffe," says Catherine in *Wuthering Heights*; that is the cry of every woman in love; she is another incarnation of her loved one, his reflection, his double: she is *he*. She lets her own world collapse in contingence, for she really lives in his.

The supreme happiness of the woman in love is to be recognized by the loved man as a part of himself; when he says "we," she is associated and identified with him, she shares his prestige and reigns with him over the rest of the world; she never tires of repeating—even to excess—this delectable "we." As one necessary to a being who is absolute necessity, who stands forth in the world seeking necessary goals and who gives her back the world in necessary form, the woman in love acquires in her submission that magnificent possession, the absolute. It is this certitude that gives her lofty joys; she feels exalted to a place at the right hand of God. Small matter to her to have only second place if she has *her* place, forever, in a most wonderfully ordered world. So long as she is in love and is loved by and necessary to her loved one, she feels herself wholly justified: she knows peace and happiness. . . .

But this glorious felicity rarely lasts. No man really is God. The relations sustained by the mystic with the divine Absence depend on her fervor alone; but the deified man, who is not God, is present. And from this fact are to come the torments of the woman in love. Her most common fate is summed up in the famous words of Julie de Lespinasse:[21] "Always, my dear friend, I love you, I suffer and I await you." To be sure, suffering is linked with love for men also; but their pangs are either of short duration or not overly severe. . . . Whereas woman, in assuming her role as the

---

[20]See T. Reik's *Psychology of Sex Relations* (Farrar, Straus & Co., 1945).—TR.

[21]Famous intellectual woman of the eighteenth century, noted for her salon and her fervid correspondence with the rather undistinguished military officer and writer Count Guibert, mentioned below.—TR.

inessential, accepting a total dependence, creates a hell for herself. Every woman in love recognizes herself in Hans Andersen's little mermaid who exchanged her fishtail for feminine legs through love and then found herself walking on needles and live coals. It is not true that the loved man is absolutely necessary, above chance and circumstance, and the woman is not necessary to him; he is not really in a position to justify the feminine being who is consecrated to his worship, and he does not permit himself to be possessed by her.

An authentic love should assume the contingence of the other; that is to say, his lacks, his limitations, and his basic gratuitousness. It would not pretend to be a mode of salvation, but a human interrelation. Idolatrous love attributes an absolute value to the loved one, a first falsity that is brilliantly apparent to all outsiders. "*He* isn't worth all that love," is whispered around the woman in love, and posterity wears a pitying smile at the thought of certain pallid heroes, like Count Guibert. It is a searing disappointment to the woman to discover the faults, the mediocrity of her idol. Novelists, like Colette, have often depicted this bitter anguish. The disillusion is still more cruel than that of the child who sees the father's prestige crumble, because the woman has herself selected the one to whom she has given over her entire being.

Even if the chosen one is worthy of the profoundest affection, his truth is of the earth, earthy, and it is no longer this mere man whom the woman loves as she kneels before a supreme being; she is duped by that spirit of seriousness which declines to take values as incidental—that is to say, declines to recognize that they have their source in human existence. Her bad faith[22] raises barriers be-

tween her and the man she adores. She offers him incense, she bows down, but she is not a friend to him since she does not realize that he is in danger in the world, that his projects and his aims are as fragile as he is; regarding him as the Faith, the Truth, she misunderstands his freedom—his hesitancy and anguish of spirit. This refusal to apply a human measuring scale to the lover explains many feminine paradoxes. The woman asks a favor from her lover. Is it granted? Then he is generous, rich, magnificent; he is kingly, he is divine. Is it refused? Then he is avaricious, mean, cruel; he is a devilish or a bestial creature. One might be tempted to object: if a "yes" is such an astounding and superb extravagance, should one be surprised at a "no"? If the "no" discloses such abject selfishness, why wonder so much at the "yes"? Between the superhuman and the inhuman is there no place for the human?

A fallen god is not a man: he is a fraud; the lover has no other alternative than to prove that he really is this king accepting adulation—or to confess himself a usurper. If he is no longer adored, he must be trampled on. In virtue of that glory with which she has haloed the brow of her beloved, the woman in love forbids him any weakness; she is disappointed and vexed if he does not live up to the image she has put in his place. If he gets tired or careless, if he gets hungry or thirsty at the wrong time, if he makes a mistake or contradicts himself, she asserts that he is "not himself" and she makes a grievance of it. In this indirect way she will go so far as to take him to task for any of his ventures that she disapproves; she judges her judge, and she denies him his liberty so that he may deserve to remain her master. Her worship sometimes finds better satisfaction in his absence than in his presence; as we have seen, there are women who devote themselves to dead or otherwise inaccessible heroes, so that they may never have to face them in person, for beings of flesh and blood would be fatally contrary to their dreams. . . .

---

[22]In Sartre's existentialist terminology, "bad faith" means abdication of the human self with its hard duty of choice, the wish therefore to become a thing, the flight from the anguish of liberty.—TR.

Even in mutual love there is fundamental difference in the feelings of the lovers, which the woman tries to hide. The man must certainly be capable of justifying himself without her, since she hopes to be justified through him. If he is necessary to her, it means that she is evading her liberty; but if he accepts his liberty, without which he would be neither a hero nor even a man, no person or thing can be necessary to him. The dependence accepted by woman comes from her weakness; how, therefore, could she find a reciprocal dependence in the man she loves in his strength?

A passionately demanding soul cannot find repose in love, because the end she has in view is inherently contradictory. Torn and tortured, she risks becoming a burden to the man instead of his slave, as she had dreamed; unable to feel indispensable, she becomes importunate, a nuisance. This is, indeed, a common tragedy. If she is wiser and less intransigent, the woman in love becomes resigned. She is not all, she is not necessary: it is enough to be useful; another might easily fill her place: she is content to be the one who is there. She accepts her servitude without demanding the same in return. Thus she can enjoy a modest happiness; but even within these limits it will not be unclouded.

The woman in love, much more grievously than the wife, is one who waits. If the wife is herself exclusively of the amorous type, maternity and housewifely duties, occupations, and pleasures will have no value for her: only the presence of her husband lifts her from the limbo of ennui. "After you're gone it seems hardly worth while to look out the window; then all that happens to me is dead, I am no more than a little dress flung on a chair," writes Cécile Sauvage in the early days of her marriage. . . .[23]

Waiting can be a joy; to the woman who watches for her beloved in the knowledge that he is hastening toward her, that he loves her, the wait is a dazzling promise. But with the fading of the confident exaltation that can change absence itself into presence, tormenting uneasiness begins to accompany the absence: he may never come back. I knew a woman who received her lover each time with astonishment: "I thought you wouldn't come back any more," she would say. And if he asked why: "You might not return; when I wait for you I always get the feeling that I shall never see you again."

Worst of all, he may cease to love her: he may love another woman. For the intensity of a woman's effort to create her illusion—saying to herself: "He loves me madly, he can love me alone"—does not exclude the tortures of jealousy. It is characteristic of bad faith to permit passionate and contradictory affirmations. Thus the madman who obstinately insists he is Napoleon is not embarrassed in admitting that he is also a barber. Woman rarely consents to ask herself the question: does he really love me? but she asks herself a hundred times: does he love someone else? She does not admit that the fervor of her lover can have died down little by little, nor that he values love less than she does: she immediately invents rivals.

She regards love as a free sentiment and at the same time a magic spell; and she supposes that "her" male continues, of course, to love her as a free agent while he is being "bewitched," "ensnared," by a clever schemer. A man thinks of a woman as united with him, in her immanence; that is why he readily plays the Boubouroche;[24] it is difficult for him to imagine that she is also another person who may be getting away from him.

---

[23]It is a different matter if the woman has found her independence in marriage; then love between husband and wife can be a free exchange by two beings who are each self-sufficient.

[24]A naïve, easygoing character in a novel and a play by Courteline, deceived by his mistress and exploited by his friends.—TR.

Jealousy with him is ordinarily no more than a passing crisis, like love itself; the crisis may be violent and even murderous, but it is rare for him to acquire a lasting uneasiness. His jealousy is usually derivative: when his business is going badly, when he feels that life is hurting him, then he feels his woman is flouting him.[25]

Woman, on the other hand, loving her man in his alterity and in his transcendence, feels in danger at every moment. There is no great distance between the treason of absence and infidelity. From the moment when she feels less than perfectly loved, she becomes jealous, and in view of her demands, this is always pretty much her case; her reproaches and complaints, whatever the pretexts, come to the surface in jealous scenes; she will express in this way the impatience and ennui of waiting, the bitter taste of her dependence, her regret at having only a mutilated existence. Her entire destiny is involved in each glance her lover casts at another woman, since she has identified her whole being with him. Thus she is annoyed if his eyes are turned for an instant toward a stranger; but if he reminds her that she has just been contemplating some stranger, she firmly replies: "That is not the same thing at all." She is right. A man who is looked at by a woman receives nothing; no gift is given until the feminine flesh becomes prey. Whereas the coveted woman is at once metamorphosed into a desirable and desired object; and the woman in love, thus slighted, is reduced to the status of ordinary clay. And so she is always on the watch. What is he doing? At whom is he looking? With whom is he talking? What a desire has given her, a smile can take away from her; it needs only an instant to cast her down from "the pearly light of immortality" to the dim light of the everyday. She has received all from love, she can lose all in

losing it. Vague or definite, ill-founded or justified, jealousy is maddening torture for the woman, because it is radically at variance with love: if the treason is unquestionable, she must either give up making love a religion or give up loving. This is a radical catastrophe and no wonder the woman in love, suspicious and mistaken in turn, is obsessed by the desire to discover the fatal truth and the fear that she will. . . .

In a state of uncertainty, every woman is a rival, a danger. Love destroys the possibility of friendship with other women because the woman in love is shut off in her lover's universe; jealousy increases her isolation and thereby narrows her dependence. It relieves her ennui, however; keeping a husband is work, but keeping a lover is a kind of sacred ministry. . . .

The man may be annoyed and abandon her, now that she is indifferent to him; he wants her free, yes; but he wants her devoted. She understands this risk, and it paralyzes her flirtatiousness. It is almost impossible for a woman in love to play this game well; she is too afraid of being caught in her own trap. And to the extent that she still has regard for her lover, she will feel it repugnant to dupe him: how could he remain a god in her eyes? If she wins the game, she destroys her idol; if she loses it, she loses herself. There is no salvation. . . .

Genuine love ought to be founded on the mutual recognition of two liberties; the lovers would then experience themselves both as self and as other: neither would give up transcendence, neither would be mutilated; together they would manifest values and aims in the world. For the one and the other, love would be revelation of self by the gift of self and enrichment of the world. . . .

But most often woman knows herself only as different, relative; her *pour-autrui*, relation to others, is confused with her very being; for her, love is not an intermediary "between herself and herself" because she does not attain her subjective

---

[25]This is brought out, for example, in Lagache's work: *Nature et formes de la jalousie.*

existence; she remains engulfed in this loving woman whom man has not only revealed, but created. Her salvation depends on this despotic free being that has made her and can instantly destroy her. She lives in fear and trembling before this man who holds her destiny in his hands without quite knowing it, without quite wishing to. She is in danger through an other, an anguished and powerless onlooker at her own fate. Involuntary tyrant, involuntary executioner, this other wears a hostile visage in spite of her and of himself. And so, instead of the union sought for, the woman in love knows the most bitter solitude there is; instead of co-operation, she knows struggle and not seldom hate. For woman, love is a supreme effort to survive by accepting the dependence to which she is condemned; but even with consent a life of dependency can be lived only in fear and servility.

Men have vied with one another in proclaiming that love is woman's supreme accomplishment. "A woman who loves as a woman becomes only the more feminine," says Nietzsche; and Balzac: "Among the first-rate, man's life is fame, woman's life is love. Woman is man's equal only when she makes her life a perpetual offering, as that of man is perpetual action." But therein, again, is a cruel deception, since what she offers, men are in no wise anxious to accept. Man has no need of the unconditional devotion he claims, nor of the idolatrous love that flatters his vanity; he accepts them only on condition that he need not satisfy the reciprocal demands these attitudes imply. He preaches to woman that she should give—and her gifts bore him to distraction; she is left in embarrassment with her useless offerings, her empty life. On the day when it will be possible for woman to love not in her weakness but in her strength, not to escape herself but to find herself, not to abase herself but to assert herself—on that day love will become for her, as for man, a source of life and not of mortal danger. In the meantime, love represents in its most touching form the curse that lies heavily upon woman confined in the feminine universe, woman mutilated, insufficient unto herself. The innumerable martyrs to love bear witness against the injustice of a fate that offers a sterile hell as ultimate salvation.

chapter thirty-one

Frantz Fanon

Frantz Fanon (1925–1961), psychiatrist, philosopher, and political activist, remains a controversial figure whose writings had a profound influence on the political movements of the 1960s, in both Europe and the United States. Born in Martinique, an island in the West Indies that remains to this day an overseas *département* of France, Fanon devoted much of his work to the analysis of colonialism's effects on the colonized and much of his life to its eradication.

Fanon's first experiences with colonialism occurred during his childhood in Martinique, where the French colonial ideology maintained that its subjects, regardless of race, could, if they tried hard enough, be accepted as completely French. In school, Fanon was taught that the French language had "brought Martinicans out of the darkness of obscurity and into the light of a universal culture.[1] He was, like all other Martinicans, dissuaded from using his native Creole and told instead to speak French at all times. For many, this was the first step in a process that would eventually allow them to become true subjects of France. In the French West Indies, Fanon himself explains, "the young black man, who in school never ceases to recite 'our fathers, the Gauls,' identifies with the explorer, the civilizer, the white man who brought truth to the savages, a truth that is completely white. There is an identification, which is to say that the young black man subjectively adopts the attitude of a white man."[2] Thus, Fanon was, as a young man in Martinique, raised to think of himself not as a "Negro"—for the Martinican, the Negro lives in Africa—but as a West Indian, a Frenchman.

Like other middle-class Martinicans, Fanon was immersed in French culture and thought himself to be equal to any other citizen of France. Accordingly, he decided in 1944 to leave Martinique and fight for the Free French Forces in France. It was upon setting foot in France for the first time that he discovered, with a shock, that he was in French eyes nothing more than a "black man," a "Negro."[3] This was, psychologically, a traumatic experience for Fanon. Disillusioned, he returned to Martinique in 1945 in order to complete his studies. By 1946, Fanon was a decorated war veteran who had passed his *baccalauréat,* the exam all French high school students must take upon the completion of their studies. He was free to attend the university of his choice, and he decided that same year to return to France, where he would study dentistry. Fanon spent three weeks in Paris before changing his mind and deciding to move to Lyon in order to study medicine; he would later study psychiatry. Though respected by his peers, Fanon continued to be the object of their racism. He recalls, for instance, giving a lecture in which he traced a parallel between black poetry and European poetry. After it, a white friend attempted to congratulate Fanon by telling him: "Basically, you're white."[4] Incidents such as these were a common occurrence during the period of time in which Fanon wrote his first book, *Black Skin, White Masks,* and they were to have a profound influence on the theoretical direction of his work.

Shortly before he completed his studies in psychiatry, Fanon published *Black Skin, White Masks* (1952), an account of the "lived experience" of the colonized black man. Drawing from his own experiences with colonialism and racism as an adolescent in Martinique, as a soldier during the Second World War, and as a medical student in France, Fanon's project is to address, through an analysis of the black man's "being-in-the-world," the inferiority complex that is widely ascribed to colonized peoples. The text is challenging, in part because it is grounded in a broad assortment of theoretical influences and perspectives. Accordingly, it should first be approached as a work of *bricolage,* a term French anthropologist Claude Lévi-Strauss used to describe the way in which myths are created from available materials.[5] The literal meaning of the word is "do-it-yourself," but there is another sense in which *bricolage* denotes the process whereby disparate materials are "thrown together" to create a complete whole. This process is clearly at work in *Black Skin, White Masks:* Fanon borrows not only from the phenomenology of Jean-Paul Sartre and Maurice Merleau-Ponty, but also from the psychiatry in which he had just been trained, the fragments of psychoanalytic theory he had encountered in books, and from the various works of literature and poetry he felt could illustrate the points he was attempting to make. The result is a narrative whose constant changes of register, from psychiatry to philosophy to literature and back again, can at times be difficult to follow.

This variety of influences becomes easier to understand if we return to Fanon's overall project: "I believe that there is," he writes in the introduction to *Black Skin, White Masks,* "due to the presence of the black race and the white race to one another, the mass adoption of a psycho-existential complex [on the part of the colonized]. By analyzing it, I aim to destroy it."[6] From the beginning, Fanon approaches his project as a psychiatrist would a patient: "the analysis that I undertake is psychological," he states, a "clinical case study."[7] Thus, the theories of psychologists such as Alfred Adler and Anna Freud provide Fanon with the language necessary to address the "illness" he sees as resulting from the colonization of the black man, namely, the black man's inferiority complex. But in order to articulate the framework in which his case study occurs, the inauthentic lived experience of the black man, Fanon turns to the existentialist phenomenology of such philosophers as Sartre and Merleau-Ponty.

Fanon's extensive use of philosophy in *Black Skin, White Masks* can be attributed to the fact that he began to read voraciously upon his arrival in Lyon. He had moved from a culture that was poor in books—that of Fort-de-France and its small Bibliothèque Schoelcher—to one that was rich in them, and he began right away to take advantage of the libraries and bookshops Lyon had to offer. His interests, moreover, were not limited to works of medicine and psychiatry. He read journals like *Esprit* and Sartre's *Les Temps Modernes.* He read quite extensively in philosophy and developed a particular interest in the line of thought that had begun with Hegel and had recently developed into the existentialism that was so prevalent in the immediate postwar years.[8] Fanon was looking for the theoretical tools—a vocabulary—with which to articulate his experiences as a black man. And while works of fiction, poetry, and drama allowed him to illustrate his experiences, psychology and philosophy allowed him to analyze them within a coherent framework.

Of all the philosophical theories available to Fanon, phenomenology, a branch of philosophy that concerns itself with the description of one's experience of the world, of one's "being-in-the-world," was the most useful.[9] In *Black Skin, White Masks,* he sought "to identify the various positions that the Negro adopts in the face of white civilization."[10] Phenomenology—specifically, the concept of "lived experience," which first appears in the thought of early twentieth-century German philosophers like Edmund Husserl and Martin Heidegger and is subsequently taken up by Merleau-Ponty in his *Phenomenology of Perception*—provided Fanon with the language he needed to do so. A translation of the German word, *Erlebnis,* "lived experience" is not simply synonymous with experience in the everyday sense. Rather, lived experience refers to an experience that is deeply felt, that is perceived as having a profound effect on one's being-in-the-world. Merleau-Ponty describes lived experiences as "acts of consciousness."[11] In this sense, they are not the passive experiences of a subject who stands outside of the world, but form instead a mode of being, or existence, through which the subject encounters the world and attempts to mold it to a project.[12]

For the colonized black man, whose encounter with the white man has resulted in an inferiority complex, the project is that of "whitening" himself; it is a fact, Fanon proposes, that "some black men want at all costs to prove to the white man the richness of their thought, the equal power of their spirit."[13] In order to ensure his separation from the black race and his integration into the white race—the project to which the black man's lived experience leads—Fanon says that the Martinican will do a number of things, such as abandoning his native Creole in favor of the French language, moving to France, and adopting an attitude of disdain toward his fellow black men.

These attitudes and behaviors, according to Fanon, are not restricted to the black man. For instance, the first of the two chapters excerpted here, "The Woman of Color and the White Man," provides an account of the relations between the black woman and the white man. In it, Fanon gives an analysis of Mayotte Capécia's *Je suis Martiniquaise,* in which Capécia expresses a desire—and describes her attempts—to gain acceptance into the white society of Fort-de-France, the capital of Martinique. As is the case for the rest of *Black Skin, White Masks,* Fanon's analysis in this chapter occurs on two levels, the psychological and the philosophical. To begin with, *Je suis Martiniquaise,* he argues, is "a cut-rate work, an endorsement of disordered behavior."[14] Like the black men of Martinique, Mayotte Capécia suffers from an inferiority complex that compels her to seek integration into the white race. Hers is a "feeling of lessening," and her behavior is akin to that of one who suffers from a phobia, in this case a phobia of one's own "blackness."[15] But Fanon's indictment of Capécia's behavior—and that of the colonized in general—also takes into account the notions of bad faith and inauthenticity developed by Sartre in *Being and Nothingness.*[16]

From a philosophical standpoint, *Black Skin, White Masks* can be described not only as an analysis of the lived experience of the colonized, but also as a bid for black authenticity in the face of the white man. Fanon takes up Sartre's proposal that human beings have the capacity to reflect on their being, to stand apart from their own existence. For this reason, the existence of human beings is characterized by freedom: They are free to separate themselves from that which they both have been and will be. Accordingly, there is an "existential ethic" whereby human beings, because they alone can be responsible for who and what they are, have an obligation to develop "future possibilities," that is, potential versions of themselves, and act toward them. This freedom, according to Sartre, induces anguish in some people, and they refuse to accept the responsibility of being the foundation of their own existence. Those who do so are said to be in bad faith, insofar as they either refuse to define themselves or allow others to do so for them; their existence is said to be inauthentic. In this light, much of *Black Skin, White Masks* can be read as an exercise in which Fanon first presents and then analyzes a number of instances of inauthenticity on the part of the colonized, taken either from his own experiences or from the fictional or autobiographical works of others.[17]

If the Martinican's inferiority complex is the psychological consequence of colonization, then inauthenticity is for Fanon its existential equivalent. In the two chapters excerpted here, Fanon considers the Martinican's "psycho-existential complex" in terms of its role in love and sexual relationships. Is authentic love between the colonizer and the colonized possible? This is the question Fanon seeks to answer in "The Woman of Color and the White Man" and "The Man of Color and the White Woman."

Black Skin, White Masks was Fanon's first published work. In 1953, Fanon was appointed to the Blida-Joinville psychiatric hospital in Algeria, which was at the time still a French colony. Fanon's arrival at Blida occurred shortly before the eruption in 1954 of Algeria's war for independence and the emergence of the Algerian *Front de Libération National* (FLN). His experience in Algeria, treating patients whose mental disorders had been brought about by violence and torture, only served to reinforce the view of colonialism he had developed in *Black Skin, White Masks,* and he would soon adopt Algeria's movement for independence as his own. During this time, Fanon's concerted efforts to modernize Blida's psychiatric hospital—as well as his involvement in the war—became the object of increasing suspicion; he was expelled from Algeria in 1957. He moved to Tunis, where he became a roving ambassador for the FLN, dedicating his efforts to the Algerian nationalist cause, as well as to the liberation of colonized peoples in general. In 1959, Fanon published his second work, *Studies in a Dying Colonialism,* in which he described how the Algerian people had liberated themselves of the inferiority complex he had diagnosed in *Black Skin, White Masks.* His last work, *The Wretched of the Earth,* was published in 1961, the year of his death. In it, Fanon outlined what he believed to be the necessary steps toward the complete liberation of all colonized and oppressed peoples.

Frantz Fanon died of leukemia in Bethesda, Maryland, a suburb of Washington, D.C. By October 1961, his illness had become so severe that neither Algerian nor Soviet doctors were able to treat him. Because using a hospital in France was out of the question, he reluctantly agreed to fly to the United States for treatment. When he reached Washington on October 3, he was first placed in a hotel room, where his wife and son soon joined him. Under the supervision of an agent of the Central Intelligence Agency, he was admitted to the Clinical Center of the National Institutes of Health on October 10 and expired on December 6.[18] He is buried in Algeria, which gained its independence from France in July 1962.

DG

QUESTIONS

1. According to Fanon, what is Mayotte Capécia seeking in her relationship with her white lover? Why does Fanon claim that "love is forbidden for the Mayotte Capécias of all countries?"

2. What is the significance of Fanon's assertion that "it is customary in Martinique to dream of a form of salvation that consists of magically whitening oneself?"

3. Explain why Capécia's book is, for Fanon, an example of inauthenticity.

4. How does Jean Vaneuse's inferiority complex manifest itself? Compare this to the case of Mayotte Capécia.

5. Explain what Fanon means when he says that the love of the white woman for the black man opens for him "the illustrious corridor that leads to complete meaningfulness."

6. What are the similarities and differences that exist between the behavior of the black woman and that of the black man? Are their desires the same or different? Their goals?

ENDNOTES

1. Sablé, Victor, from Macey, p. 62.
2. Fanon, p. 120.
3. Macey, p. 114.
4. Fanon, p. 30.
5. Macey, p. 162.
6. Fanon, p. 9.
7. Ibid., pp. 8, 10.
8. Macey, p. 127.
9. Macey, p. 163
10. Fanon, p. 9.
11. Merleau-Ponty, p. 466. See chapter 33 of this volume for a more thorough discussion of Maurice Merleau-Ponty.
12. Macey, p. 164.
13. Fanon, p. 7.
14. Ibid., p. 34.
15. Ibid., p. 40.
16. See chapter 29 for a more thorough discussion of Jean-Paul Sartre.
17. Macey, p. 168.
18. Ibid., p. 163.

SELECTED BIBLIOGRAPHY

Fanon, Frantz. *Peau noire, masques blancs.* Paris: Editions de seuil, 1952.

Macey, David. *Frantz Fanon: A Biography.* New York: Picador, 2000.

Merleau-Ponty, Maurice. *Phénoménologie de la perception.* Paris: Gallimard, 1945.

The Woman of Color and the White Man

Frantz Fanon

BLACK SKIN, WHITE MASKS

Man is motion toward the world and toward his like. A movement of aggression, which brings about enslavement or conquest; a movement of love, a gift of self, the final stage of what is conventionally called the ethical orientation. Every consciousness seems to have the capacity to demonstrate, simultaneously or alternatively, these two attitudes. The person whom I love will energetically reinforce my assumption of virility, while my preoccupation with earning the admiration or love of the other will erect a value-conferring superstructure across the entirety of my vision of the world.

In the attempt to reach an understanding of phenomena of this sort, the task of the analyst and the phenomenologist reveals itself to be an arduous one. And if there appeared a Sartre to formulate a description of love as failure, *Being and Nothingness* consisting in nothing more than an analysis of bad faith and inauthenticity, the fact remains that true, authentic love—wishing for others that which one demands for oneself, when this demand brings together the permanent values of human reality—requires the mobilization of psychic processes fundamentally freed of unconscious conflicts.

Far, far behind us, the last aftereffects of a titanic struggle with the other have dissipated. Today, we believe in the possibility of love, which is why we endeavor to identify its imperfections, its perversions.

We must, in this chapter devoted to the relations between the woman of color and the European man, ascertain to what extent authentic love will remain unattainable so long as one has not rid oneself of that feeling of inferiority or that Adlerian[1] exaltation, that overcompensation, which seem to be the indicator of the black *Weltanschauung*.[2]

For after all, we have a right to be worried when we read, in *Je suis Martiniquaise:* "I would have liked to be married, but to a white man. Only, a woman of color is never completely respectable in the eyes of a white man. Even if he loves her. I knew that."[3] This passage, which in a sense serves as the conclusion to a vast delusion, gives one pause. One day, a woman by the name of Mayotte Capécia, obeying a motivation whose elements are difficult to identify, wrote 202 pages—her life—in which the most absurd propositions proliferated at random. The enthusiastic reception that greeted this work in certain circles compels us to analyze it. For us, there can be no equivocation: *Je suis Martiniquaise* is a cut-rate work, an endorsement of disordered behavior.

Mayotte loves a white man to whom she submits in everything. He is her lord. She makes no claims, demands nothing, except a bit of whiteness in her life. And as she tries to determine in her own mind whether the man with whom she is in love is handsome or ugly, she tells us, "All I know is that he had blue eyes, blond hair, light skin, and that I loved him." Now, it is not difficult to see that when we put the terms in their proper place, we obtain more or less the following: "I loved him because he had blue eyes, blond hair, and light skin." And we who come from the Antilles know one thing only too well: the Negro, it is said there, fears blue eyes.

When we observed in our introduction that inferiority has historically been felt economically, we were hardly mistaken.

Unfortunately, there were evenings when he had to leave me alone in order to fulfill his social obligations. He would go to Didier, the fashionable part of Fort-de-France inhabited by the "Martinique *békés*," who are perhaps not too pure racially but who are often very rich (it is understood that one is white above a certain level of wealth), and the "France *békés*," who are for the most part government workers and military officers.[4]

Among André's colleagues, who, like him, found themselves stranded in the Antilles by the war, some had managed to have their wives come over. I understood that André could not always keep himself apart from them. I also accepted that I was barred from this circle because I was a woman of color; but I could not help being jealous. And though he explained to me that his private life was something that belonged to him alone and that his social and military life was something else, over which he had no control, I insisted so much that one day he took me to Didier. We spent the evening with two officers and their wives, in one of those little villas I had admired since my childhood. The women looked at me with a condescension I found unbearable. I felt that I had dolled myself up too much, that I was not dressed properly, that I was not doing André credit, perhaps simply because of the color of my skin—in short, I spent so unpleasant an evening that I decided never again to ask André to take me with him.[5]

It is Didier, haven of the richest people in Martinique that magnetizes all of the woman's desires. And she herself tells us: one is white above a certain level of wealth. The villas of the neighborhood have long fascinated her. We get the impression, however, that Mayotte Capécia is misleading us: she tells us that she did not go to Fort-de-France until she was older, at about the age of eighteen, and yet the villas of Didier had beguiled her childhood. There is an inconstancy here that becomes understandable once we consider the context in which it occurs. Indeed, it is customary in Martinique to dream of a form of salvation that consists of magically whitening[6] oneself. A villa in Didier, her integration into that high society (Didier is on a hill that dominates the city), and here is Hegel's subjective certainty made flesh. And it is easy for us to see, incidentally, the place that would occupy the dialectic of being and having[7] in the description of this behavior. However, this is not yet the case with Mayotte. She is looked at with hostility. Things begin their usual course. . . . It is because she is a woman of color that she is not tolerated in these circles. It is from her facticity that resentment of her will grow. We will see why love is forbidden for the Mayotte Capécias of all countries. For the other should not allow me to turn my infantile fantasies into reality: on the contrary, he must help me to overcome them. We encounter in Mayotte Capécia's childhood a certain number of characteristics that illustrate the line of orientation she follows as an adult. And each time there is a movement, a shock, it will be in direct relation to this goal. Indeed, it would seem that black and white represent for her the two poles of a world, two poles in perpetual conflict: a genuinely Manichean conception of the world; the word has been spoken, it must be remembered—white or black, that is the question.

I am white; that is to say, I possess beauty and virtue, which have never been black. I am the color of daylight.

I am black; I embody a total fusion with the world, a sympathetic understanding of the earth, an abandonment of my self in the heart of the cosmos, and no white man, no matter how intelligent he may be, could ever understand [Louis] Armstrong and the chants of the Congo. If I am black, it is not the result of a curse, but it is because, having stretched my skin, I was able to harness all of the cosmic discharges. I am truly a drop of sunlight under the earth.

And one enters a hand-to-hand struggle with one's blackness or one's whiteness, in full narcissistic drama, each sealed within his own particularity—with, it is true, now and then a few glimmers, but these are threatened at their source.

From the start, this is how the problem appears to Mayotte—at the age of five and on the third page of her book: "She would take her inkwell out of her desk and empty it over his head." This was her own way of turning whites into blacks. But she soon recognized the futility of her efforts; and then there were Loulouze and her mother, who told her that life was difficult for a woman of color. Thus, unable to blacken, to negrify the world, she would try, in her own body and in her own mind, to whiten it.

Instead of discovering for herself her own blackness absolutely, she proceeds to turn it into an accident. She learns that her grandmother was white.

I was proud of it. Certainly, I was not the only one who had white blood, but a white grandmother was not as ordinary as a white grandfather.[8] And my mother, then, was of mixed race? I should have guessed it when I saw her light color. I found her prettier than ever, and more refined, and more distinguished. If she had married a white man, perhaps would I have been completely white? And life might not have been so difficult for me? I would daydream about this grandmother whom I'd never known and who had died because she had loved a colored man of Martinique. . . . How could a Canadian woman have loved a man of Martinique? I could not stop thinking of our priest, and I decided that I could only ever love a white man, a blonde with blue eyes, a Frenchman.[9]

We are thus informed that what Mayotte wants is a kind of lactification. For the race must be whitened; every woman in Martinique knows this, says it, repeats it. Whiten the race, save the race, but not in the sense that one might think: the issue is not to "preserve the uniqueness of that part of the world in which they grew up," but to guarantee its whiteness. Every time we have sought to analyze certain behaviors, we have been unable to avoid the appearance of certain nauseating phenomena. The number of sayings, of proverbs, of petty rules of conduct that govern the choice of a lover in the Antilles is astounding. It is a matter of not sinking once more into the mass of blackness, and every woman of the Antilles will strive, whether in casual flirtation or in serious affairs, to select the least black of the men. Sometimes, in order to justify a poor investment, she is compelled to resort to such arguments as: "X is black, but misery is blacker than he." I know many girls from Martinique, students in France, who admit to me with complete candor—completely white candor—that they would find it impossible to marry a black man. (Escape from that and then willingly return to it? No, thank you.) Besides, they add, it

is not that we deny black men any value whatsoever; but you know, it is better to be white.

All of these frantic women of color in search of a white man are waiting. And one of these days, surely, they will be surprised to find themselves not wanting to turn around, they will dream of "a wonderful night, of a wonderful lover, of a white man." One day, perhaps, they too will realize that "white men do not marry black women." But they have accepted to run this risk; what they need is whiteness at any price. For what reason? Nothing could be simpler. Here is a tale that satisfies the mind:

> One day, St. Peter sees three men arrive at the gate of heaven: a white man, a mulatto, a Negro.
> "What do you desire," he asks the white man.
> "Money."
> "And you?" he asks the mulatto.
> "Fame."
> And as he turns to the Negro, the latter tells him with a wide smile:[10] "I'm here to carry these gentlemen's bags."

Quite recently, Etiemble, speaking of one of his disappointments: "I was stupefied, as an adolescent, when a friend who knew me well jumped up, offended because I had said to her, in a situation where the word was not only appropriate but the only one that suited the occasion: 'You who are a Negress.' 'Me? a Negress? Can't you see that I'm practically white? I hate Negroes. Negroes stink. They're dirty, lazy. Never mention Negroes to me.'"[11]

I know another black girl who had a list of Parisian dance halls "where-one-does-not-run-the-risk-of-running-into-Negroes."

At issue is whether it is possible for the black man to overcome his feeling of lessening, to rid his life of the compulsive trait that makes it so like the behavior of the phobic. There is in the Negro an affective exacerbation, anger at feeling small, an incapacity for any human communication, all of which confine him within an unbearable insularity.

For him, there is only one exit, and it leads to the white world. Hence this constant preoccupation with attracting the attention of the white man, this concern with being powerful like the white man, this determined wish to acquire the properties of a [white] sheath, that is, the part of being or having that constitutes the ego. As I said earlier, it is from within that the black man will attempt to join the white sanctuary.

In the thralls of a mystical euphoria, intoning a beautiful canticle, Mayotte Capécia feels as though she were an angel taking flight, "all pink and white." And yet there is this film, *Green Pastures,* in which angels and God are black, but it has shocked our author terribly: "How can one imagine God as having the traits of a Negro? This is not how I imagine Heaven to be. But, after all, it was only an American film."[12]

Really, no, the good and merciful God cannot be black; it is the white man who has cheeks that are nice and pink. From black to white, such is the course of mutation. One is white in the same way that one is rich, that one is handsome, that one is intelligent.

Meanwhile, André has left for parts unknown to bring the *white Message* to other Mayottes: delightful little blue-eyed genes, pedaling down the chromosomal corridors. But like a good white man, he left instructions. He spoke of their child: "You will raise him; you will tell him about me; you will tell him: he was a great man. You must make every effort to be worthy of him."[13]

And dignity? He no longer had to acquire it; it was now woven into the labyrinth of his arteries, deeply set in his little pink nails, nice and wedged, nice and white.

And the father? Here is what Etiemble has to say about him: "A fine example of his type; he would talk about the family, about work, about the homeland, about our good Pétain and our good God, which allowed him to knock her up according to the rules.[14] God used us, the bastard would say, the beautiful white man, the handsome officer. After which, he ditches her according to those same Pétainist and godly rules."

Before we're through with the one whose white Lord is "as good as dead" and who is escorted by the dead in a book full of dismally dead things, I would like to ask Africa to send us a messenger.

She does not make us wait; Abdoulaye Sadji, in "Nini,"[15] gives us a description of what the behavior of blacks can be like when they are faced with Europeans. As I have said, there exist Negrophobes. It is not their hatred of the black man, however, that drives them; they do not have the courage for it, or no longer do. Hatred is not a given: it has to conquer itself at all times, to lift itself up to being, in conflict with guilt complexes more or less avowed. Hatred demands to exist and the one who hates must reveal this hatred through his actions, through a suitable behavior; in a sense, he must make himself *hatred.* This is why the Americans have substituted segregation for lynching. Each to his own side. Thus, we are not surprised that there is, in the cities of black (French?) Africa, a European quarter. Mounier's work, *The Awakening of Black Africa,* had already drawn my attention, but I was impatiently awaiting an African voice. Thanks to Alioune Diop's magazine, I have been able to organize the psychological motivations that drive men of color.

By analyzing a few passages from Mr. Abdoulaye Sadji's novel, I will try to capture unmediated the reactions of the woman of color to the European man. To begin with, there are the Negress and the mulatto woman. The former has only one possibility and one concern: to whiten. The latter not only wants to whiten, but to avoid a regression. Indeed, what could be more illogical than a mulatto woman who marries a black man?

For it must be understood once and for all that it is a question of saving the race.

Hence Nini's extreme indecision: has a Negro not plucked up his courage to the point of asking for her hand in marriage? Has a Negro not gone so far as to write:

> The love that I offer you is pure and strong, it has nothing of an inopportune tenderness intended to lull you with lies and illusions. . . . I would like to see you happy, completely happy, in an environment that is consistent with your charms, which I believe I know how to appreciate. . . . I would consider it the highest honor and the greatest happiness to have you in my house and to dedicate myself to you, body and soul. Your graces would radiate in my home and would illuminate the darkest corners. Besides, I believe you are too civilized and refined to decline brutally the offer of a devoted love concerned only with assuring your happiness.[16]

This last sentence should not surprise us. Normally, the mulatto woman must mercilessly reject the pretentious black man. But since she is civilized, she will turn a blind eye to her lover's color and attach importance only to his devotion. Describing Mactar, Abdoulaye Sadji writes: "Idealistic and a firm believer in progress to the point of excess, he still believes in the genuineness of men, in their honesty, and he readily thinks that in all matters, merit alone must triumph."[17]

Who is Mactar? He has passed his baccalaureate, he is an accountant for the Company of rivers, and he is addressing himself to a plain little stenographer who nevertheless possesses the least disputable of qualities: she is almost white. One will apologize, then, for taking the liberty of writing her a letter: "the great impudence, perhaps the first a Negro has dared to perpetrate."[18]

One will apologize for daring to offer a black love to a white soul. We will encounter this again

in René Maran: the fear, the timidity, the humility of the black man in his relations with the white woman, or in any event with a woman whiter than he. Just as Mayotte Capécia tolerates anything from her lord André, Mactar makes himself the slave of Nini, the mulatto. Prepared to sell his soul. But what awaits this impudent man is an objection. The mulatto considers his letter to be an insult, an affront to her honor as a "white lady," This Negro is a fool, a crook, a lout who needs to be given a lesson. She will give him that lesson; she will teach him to be more courteous and less bold; she will make him understand that "white skins" are not for "bougnouls."[19]

Such a breach of principle should be punished by castration. And it is the police, when all is said and done, that will be asked to admonish Mactar. For "if he returns to his unhealthy ravings, we will have him brought before Mr. Dru, a police inspector whose colleagues have nick-named the-really-vicious-white-man."[20]

We have just seen how a girl of color reacts to a declaration of love made by one of her peers. We now inquire as to what happens in the case of a white man. We turn once again to Sadji. The long passage he devotes to the reactions prompted by the marriage of a white man to a mulatto will serve as our vehicle.[21]

> For some time now, a rumor has been spreading all over the city of Saint-Louis. . . . It is at first a little whisper that travels from ear to ear, that fills the wrinkled faces of the old "signaras" with joy, that brings new light to their dull eyes; then the young women, their white eyes open wide and their thick lips formed into circles, noisily pass on the news, which evokes cries of: "Oh, it can't be! . . . How do you know? . . . Is it possible? . . . That's delightful. . . . What a riot."[22] The news that has been running through Saint-Louis for a month is pleasant, more pleasant than all the promises in the world. It crowns a certain dream

of greatness, of refinement, that makes all the mulatto women, the Ninis, the Nanas, and the Ninettes, live outside of the natural conditions of their country. The great dream that haunts them is to be the bride of a white man from Europe. One could say that all of their efforts are directed toward this end, which is almost never attained.

Very pleasant news . . . Mr. Darrivey, a completely white European and an assistant in the civil service, has requested the hand of Dédée, a half-toned mulatto. It can't be.[23]

On the day that the white man declared his love to the mulatto, something extraordinary must have happened. There occurred recognition, integration into a community that had seemed impenetrable. This psychological depreciation, this feeling of lessening and its corollary, the impossibility of attaining lucidity, disappeared completely. Overnight, the mulatto had passed from the ranks of the slaves to those of the master.

She was recognized through her overcompensating behavior. She was no longer the one who had wanted to be white; she was white. She was joining the white world.

Every story, however, has two sides; whole families were ridiculed. Three or four mulatto women were given mulatto escorts, while all of their friends had white men. "This was particularly seen as an insult to the family as a whole; an insult, moreover, that demanded redress."[24] For these families had been humiliated in their most legitimate aspirations; the mutilation to which they were subjected affected the very movement of their lives, the course of their existence. . . .

Referring back to a profound desire, they wanted to change, to "evolve." This right was denied to them. In any event, it was challenged.

What is there to say, after these expositions?

Whether in the case of Mayotte Capécia of Martinique or that of Nini of Saint-Louis, the same process was encountered. A bilateral process, an attempt to recover—through their internalization—assets that were originally prohibited. It is because the Negress feels inferior that she aspires to gain admittance to the white world. In this attempt, she will make use of a phenomenon that we shall call *affective erethism*.[25]

Nini, Mayotte Capécia: two instances of a behavior that moves us to thought.

Are there no other possibilities?

But these are pseudo-questions that we will not consider. I will say, however, that any criticism of the existing implies a solution, provided that one can propose a solution to one's kind, that is, to a free being.

What I assert is that the abnormality must be expelled once and for all.

ENDNOTES

1. Tr. Adlerian: refers to the theory of psychologist Alfred Adler (1870–1937), who posited the crux of human existence to be the struggle against feelings of inferiority, whether conscious or unconscious, physical, psychological, or social.

2. Tr. *Weltanschauung:* one's worldview.

3. Mayotte Capécia, *Je suis Martiniquaise.* Paris: Corréa, 1948, p. 202.

4. Tr. *Békés:* Creole word used to describe Creoles from Martinique or Guadeloupe who are descendants of white immigrants.

5. *Je suis Martiniquaise,* p. 150.

6. Tr. The literal definition of the verb used in the original text, *blanchir,* is to make white, or to whiten. However, there is also a secondary sense in which *blanchir* means to launder or clean. And there is yet another sense in which it means to exonerate, or to clear of charges.

7. Marcel, Gabriel. *Etre et avoir.* Paris: Aubier, 1935.

8. The white man, as master and more simply as male, can allow himself the luxury of sleeping with many women. This is true in every country and es-

pecially in colonies. But when a white woman accepts a black man, there is automatically a romantic aspect. It is a gift, not a rape. Indeed, in the colonies, where there is neither marriage nor cohabitation between whites and blacks, the number of persons of mixed race is extraordinary. This is because the white men sleep with their black servants. Mayotte Capécia is correct: it is an honor to be the daughter of a white woman. This proves that she was not "made in the bushes." (This expression is reserved exclusively for the illegitimate children of the *békés* in Martinique; we know that they are extremely numerous: Aubery, for instance, is reputed to have fathered almost fifty.)

9. *Je suis Martiniquaise,* p. 59.

10. The black man's smile, the *grin* (in English in the original text), seems to have captured the attention of numerous writers. Here is what Bernard Wolfe says about it: "We like to think of the black man as showing us all of his teeth in a smile addressed to us. And his smile, as we see it—as we create it—always signifies a *gift*."

   A gift without end, in every advertisement, on every screen, on every food-product label. . . . The black man gives Madame the new "dark Creole colors" for her pure nylons, courtesy of the Vigny company; her "grotesque," "coiled," bottles of Golliwogg cologne and perfume. Shoe-shines, linens white as snow, comfortable lower bunks, quick baggage-handling; jazz, jitterbug, jive, comedies, and the wonderful tales of Br'er Rabbit to amuse the little ones. Service with a smile, always. . . .

11. "Sur le *Martinique* de Michel Cournot," *Les Temps Modernes,* February, 1950.

12. *Je suis Martiniquaise,* p. 65.

13. *Ibid.,* p. 185.

14. Tr. Pétain: a hero during the First World War, Marshal Henri Phillipe Pétain became prime minister of France in 1940. He recommended that France sue for an armistice with Germany and soon thereafter took office as head of state at Vichy, in unoccupied France.

15. *Présence Africaine,* p. 1–3.

16. "Nini." *Présence Africaine,* p. 286.

17. *Ibid.,* pp. 281–282.

18. *Ibid.,* p. 281.

19. *Ibid.,* p. 287. Tr. *Bougnouls:* racist term used to refer to natives of North Africa. It is also used to refer to any member of a race thought to be inferior to that of the person using the word.

20. "Nini." *Présence Africaine,* p. 289.

21. Tr. Vehicle: the original word, *excipient,* refers to an inert substance used as a diluent, or vehicle, for a drug.

22. Tr. *Signaras:* refers to the black women or mulattos whom European men would marry for the duration of their stay in Sénégal. They made up the high society of Saint-Louis—the capital of Sénégal at that time—until the middle of the 19th century, when advances in medicine and the modernization of living conditions allowed European wives to accompany their husbands.

23. "Nini." *Présence Africaine,* p. 489.

24. *Ibid.,* p. 498.

25. Tr. Affective erethism: an abnormally high sensitivity to emotional stimulation.

THE MAN OF COLOR AND THE WHITE WOMAN

From the blackest part of my soul, through the area that is hatched in black and white, arises this desire to be suddenly *white*.

I want to be recognized not as *black,* but as *white*.

Now—and this is a form of recognition Hegel has not described—who can do this for me, if not a white woman? By loving me, she proves to me that I am worthy of a white love. I am loved as a white man.

I am a white man.

Her love opens for me the illustrious corridor that leads to complete meaningfulness. . . .

I embrace white culture, white beauty, white whiteness.

In these white breasts that my restless hands caress, it is white civilization and white dignity that I appropriate for myself.

In the analysis of *Je suis Martiniquaise* and *Nini,* we have seen how the Negress behaves in the face of the white man. Through a novel by René Maran—the author's autobiography, it would seem—let us try to understand what happens in the case of the black man.

The problem is superbly set out, for Jean Veneuse will allow us to delve further into the attitude of the black man. What is the matter at hand? Jean Veneuse is a Negro. Born in the Antilles, he has lived in Bordeaux for a long time; he is therefore a European. But he is black; he is therefore a Negro. Therein lies the problem. He does not understand his own race, and the whites do not understand him. And, he observes, "Europeans in general, the French in particular, not satisfied with ignoring the Negro of the colonies, fail to acknowledge the one whom they have shaped in their own image."[1]

The author's personality does not reveal itself as easily as one might wish. Orphan, boarder at a provincial secondary school, he is sentenced during his vacations to stay at the boarding school. His friends and schoolmates, on the slightest pretext, scatter across France, while the little Negro gets into the habit of rumination, so that his best friends will be his books. In the extreme, I would say that there is a certain protest, a certain resentment, a barely-restrained aggressiveness, in the long—too long—list of "traveling companions" the author gives us: I say in the extreme, but it is precisely there that we must go.

Unable to assimilate himself, unable to pass unnoticed, he is going to converse with the dead, or at least with the absent. And this conversation, contrary to his life, will [fly over] the centuries and the oceans. Marcus Aurelius, Joinville, Pascal, Perez Galdos, Rabindranath Tagore. . . . If we were compelled to give Jean Veneuse an attribute, we would make him an introvert, others would say a sensitive man, but a sensitive man who reserves for himself the possibility of winning on the level of ideas and knowledge. The fact is, his schoolmates and friends think highly of him: "What an incorrigible dreamer! He's a character, you know, my pal Veneuse! He only ever takes his nose out of his books to scribble all over his notebook."[2]

But a sensitive man who sings Spanish songs and translates into English, one after the other. A shy man, but also a worrier: "As I walk away, I hear Divrande tell him: 'A good guy, that Veneuse—he tends to be sad and quiet, but he's very helpful. You can rely on him. You'll see. He's the kind of Negro we'd want to see a lot of whites be like.'"[3]

Yes, definitely a worrier. A worrier stuck to his own body. (But) There is the fact that Veneuse is black. He is a bear who loves solitude. He is a thinker. And when a woman tries to flirt with him: "You have come to find a bear! Be careful, my dear.

Courage is a fine thing, but you're going to jeopardize your reputation if you continue to be seen like this! A Negro. You should be ashamed! You demean yourself by associating with anybody of that race."[4]

First and foremost, he wants to prove to others that he is a man, that he is of their kind. But let there be no misunderstanding, Jean Veneuse is the man who needs to be convinced. It is at the heart of his soul, as complicated as that of any European, that his uncertainty lies. The expression will be forgiven: Jean Veneuse is the man whom we have to bring [pin] down. We will endeavor to do so.

Having cited Stendhal and the phenomenon of "crystallization," he observes that he loves

> Andrée emotionally in Madame Coulanges and physically with Clarisse. It is insane. But that is how it is: I love Clarisse, I love Madame Coulanges, despite the fact that I really think of neither one nor the other. They are for me nothing more than an alibi that allows me to deceive myself. I observe Andrée in both of them and learn to know her inside and out. . . . I don't know. I don't know anymore. I don't want to know anything, or, rather, I know only one thing, which is that the Negro is a man similar to all others, a man like all others, and that his heart, which appears simple only to the ignorant, is as complicated as that of the most complicated European.[5]

For the Negro's simplicity is a myth fabricated by shallow observers. "I love Clarisse, I love Madame Coulanges, and it is Andrée Marielle whom I love. Her alone, and no other."[6]

Who is Andrée Marielle? You know, the daughter of the poet, Louis Marielle! But this Negro, "who has raised himself through his own intelligence and hard work to the thought and culture of Europe,"[7] is incapable of escaping his race.

Andrée Marielle is white; no solution seems possible. Even so, reading Payot, Gide, Moréas and Voltaire had seemed to have wiped out all of that. In good faith, Jean Veneuse "believed in that culture and set [him]self to love this new world [he] had discovered and conquered for [his] own use. What a mistake [he] made! [He] had only to mature and go off to serve [his] adoptive homeland in the land of [his] ancestors to wonder whether [he] was not being betrayed by everything around [him], for the white race would not acknowledge [him] as one of its own and the black race practically repudiated [him]."[8]

Jean Veneuse, who feels incapable of existing without love, is going to dream it. He is going to dream it and it will take the form of poems:

> When one loves, nothing must be said;
> It is better to hide [from] it from oneself.

Andrée Marielle has written to him that she loves him, but Jean Veneuse needs permission. A white man has to tell him: take my sister. Veneuse has asked his friend Coulanges a certain number of questions. Here is, nearly *in extenso*, what Coulanges answers:

> Old boy,[9]
> Once again, you ask for my advice concerning your situation, and I will give you my opinion, once again and once and for all. Let us take things in order. Your situation as you have explained it to me is quite clear. Nevertheless, allow me to clear the ground in front of me. It can only be to your benefit.
> How old were you when you left your country for France? Three or four, I think. You have never seen your native island since, and you do not have the slightest interest in seeing it again. You have lived in Bordeaux ever since. It is in Bordeaux, ever since you became a colonial official, that you spend the majority of your administrative leaves. In short, you are really one of us. Perhaps you are not altogether aware of that fact. In that case, know that you are a Frenchman from Bordeaux.

Get that into your thick head. You know nothing of your compatriots from the Antilles. In fact, I would be amazed if you could even manage to get along with them. What's more, the ones I know are nothing like you.

In reality, you are like us, you are "us." Your thoughts are ours. You behave as we behave, as we would behave. You think of yourself—and others think of you—as a Negro? Mistake! You merely look like one. Where everything else is concerned, you think as a European. It is therefore natural that you love as a European. Since the European man loves only the European woman, you can hardly marry anyone but a woman of the country where you have always lived, a girl of our good old France, your real, your only country. Having said that, let us move on to the subject of your last letter. On the one hand, we have one Jean Veneuse, who resembles you like a brother; on the other hand, we have Mademoiselle Andrée Marielle. Andrée Marielle, whose skin is white, loves Jean Veneuse, who is exceedingly brown and who adores Andrée Marielle. But that does not stop you from asking me what should done. You delightful moron! . . .

As soon as you are back in France, rush to the father of the one who already belongs to you in spirit and shout at him as you strike your own heart with a savage sound [thud]: "I love her. She loves me. We love each other. She must become my wife. Otherwise, I will kill myself here and now."[10]

Approached by Jean Veneuse, then, the white man agrees to give his sister [daughter] to him—but on one condition: you have nothing in common with real Negroes. You are not black, you are "exceedingly brown."

This process is well known to students of color in France. People refuse to consider them genuine Negroes. The Negro is the savage, whereas the student is civilized [advanced]. You are "us," Coulanges tells him, and if anyone thinks you are a Negro it is by mistake, because you only look like one. But Jean Veneuse does not want this. He cannot, because he knows.

He knows that "enraged by this humiliating ostracism, common mulattoes and Negroes have only one thought upon their arrival in Europe: to assuage their appetite for the white woman."

There, the majority of them, and including those who, of lighter skin, often go so far as to renounce both their countries and their mothers, enter marriages not so much out of inclination as marriages in which the satisfaction of dominating the European woman is seasoned with a certain sense of proud revenge.

And so I wonder whether I am not like all the rest; and whether, by marrying you, who are a European, I won't appear to be proclaiming not only that I despise the women of my own race, but also that, drawn by the desire for white flesh, which has been forbidden to us Negroes as long as white men have ruled the world, I am vaguely endeavoring to revenge myself on a European woman for everything her ancestors have inflicted on mine throughout the centuries."[11]

So much effort to rid oneself of a purely subjective emergency. I am a white man, I was born in Europe, all of my friends are white. There were not eight Negroes in the city where I lived. I think in French, France is my religion. I am a European, do you hear me? I am not a Negro, and in order to prove it to you, I am going, in my capacity as civil servant, to show the genuine Negroes the difference that exists between them and me.

Monsieur Veneuse has baggage porters. He has a young Negress in his hut. And to the Negroes who seem to be upset by his departure, he feels that the only thing to say is: "Go away, go away! You see . . . it makes me unhappy to leave you. Go away! I will not forget you. I am going away only because this is not my country and I feel too alone here, too empty, too deprived of the comfort that I need and that you do not yet require, fortunately for you."[12]

When we read such remarks, we cannot help thinking of Felix Eboué, who is undeniably black, and who under the same conditions saw his duty quite differently. Jean Veneuse is not a Negro and does not wish to be a Negro. And yet, unbeknownst to him [without his knowledge], there appeared a gap. There is something indefinable, irreversible, truly the *that within* of Harold Rosenberg.[13]

Louis-T. Achille, in his statement to the Interracial Conferences of 1949, said:

Where a truly interracial marriage is concerned, one can legitimately wonder to what extent it is sometimes not for the colored spouse a kind of subjective consecration of the extermination, within himself and in his own eyes, of the prejudice of color from which he has suffered so long. Indeed, some men or some women marry from another race persons of a rank or a culture inferior to their own whom they would not have wanted as spouses in their own race and whose chief asset seems to be the assurance of a change of scenery and of "deracialization" (that dreadful word) for the former. In certain people of color, the fact that they are marrying a person of the white race seems to have taken precedence over any other consideration. In that fact, they find accession to complete equality with this illustrious race, master of the world, ruler of the peoples of color.[14] . . .

Historically, we know that the Negro who is guilty of having slept with a white woman is castrated. The Negro who has had a white woman makes himself taboo to his peers. It is easy for the mind to see this drama as stemming from a sexual preoccupation. And it is precisely to this that the archetype of *Uncle Remus* aspires: Br'er Rabbit, who represents the black man. Will he or will he not succeed in sleeping with the two daughters of Mrs. Meadows? There are ups and downs, all of it told by a laughing, good-natured, jovial Negro; a Negro who gives [serves] with a smile.

But what is important here is to examine Jean Veneuse.

We had made of Jean Veneuse an introvert. We know characterologically—or, better, phenomenologically—that autistic thinking can be seen as depending on a primary introversion.[15]

In a subject of the negative-aggressive type, an obsession with the past, with its frustrations, its gaps, its failures, paralyses his enthusiasm for life. Generally more introverted than the negative-loving type, he has a tendency to dwell on his past and present disappointments, creating within himself a more or less secret area of bitter and disillusioned thoughts and resentments, which often represents a kind of autism. What's more, the absence of self-esteem, and therefore of affective security, is in his case virtually complete; hence an overwhelming feeling of impotence in the face of life and of people, and the utter rejection of the feeling of responsibility. Others have betrayed and thwarted him, and yet it is solely from others that he expects any improvement of his lot.[16]

A marvelous description, into which the character of Jean Veneuse fits perfectly. For, he tells us, "I had only to mature and go off to serve my adoptive homeland in the land of my ancestors to wonder whether *I was not being betrayed*[17] by everything around me, for the white race would not acknowledge me as one of its own and the black race practically repudiated me. That is my exact situation."[18]

An attitude of recrimination toward the past, a devaluation of self, the inability to be understood as he would like to be. Listen to Jean Veneuse:

I was one of these occasional orphans and will suffer for it for the rest of my life. At the age of seven, my academic childhood was entrusted to a large, bleak school located far out in the country. . . . But the thousand games of adolescence were never able to make me forget how painful mine was. It is to it that my character owes its profound melancholy and this fear of social situations that today stifles even my slightest impulses.[19]. . .

And yet he would have liked to be surrounded, sheathed [enclosed, protected]. He would have liked not be to be *abandoned.* During school vacations, everyone would leave, and alone, note that word, alone in the big white school.. . .

> Oh, these tears of a child who has no one to comfort him. . . . He will never forget that he was from an early age apprenticed to loneliness. . . . A cloistered existence, a withdrawn and secluded existence in which I learned too soon to meditate and to reflect. A solitary life that eventually is profoundly affected by the slightest trifle—because of you, sensitive on the inside, incapable of expressing my joy or my pain, I push away everything that I love and turn my back in spite of myself on everything that attracts me.[20]

What is this about? Two processes: I do not want to be loved. Why not? Because one day, a long time ago, I sketched out an object relation and I was *abandoned.* I have never forgiven my mother. Having been abandoned, I will make the other suffer, and abandoning the other will be the direct expression of my need for revenge. I am going to Africa; I do not want to be loved and I flee from the object. I do not want to be loved, I adopt a defensive position. And if the object persists, I will announce: "I do not want to be loved."

A devaluation? Surely, yes.

Jean Veneuse would like to be a man like all others, but he knows that this position is a false one. He is a beggar. He seeks peace of mind, permission in the white man's eyes. For he is the "Other."

> The "Other" is an expression that I have encountered on numerous occasions in the language of

the abandonic. To be the "Other" is to feel that one is always in an unstable position, to remain on guard, ready to be rejected and . . . unconsciously doing everything that is needed for the anticipated catastrophe to occur.[21]

The abandonic demands proof. He is no longer satisfied with isolated affirmations. He does not trust. Before he enters into an objective relationship, he requires repeated proof from his partner. The direction [meaning] of his attitude is "not to love in order to avoid being abandoned." The abandonic is a demanding person. He feels entitled to every possible amend. He wants to be loved completely, absolutely and forever. Listen:

> My beloved Jean,
>
>   It is only today that I received your letter of last July. It is completely irrational. Why do you torment me in this way? You are—are you aware of this?—you are of a cruelty to which nothing comes close. You give me happiness mixed with anxiety. You make it so that I am at the same time the happiest and the unhappiest of creatures [women]. How many times will I have to tell you that I love you, that I belong to you, that I am waiting for you. Come.[22]

At last, the abandonic has abandoned. He is called for. He is needed. He is loved. And yet what fantasies! Does she really love me? Does she see me objectively?

"One day, a man came, a great friend of daddy Ned who had never seen Pontaponte. He came from Bordeaux. But God, he was dirty! God, he was ugly, this man who was such a great friend of daddy Ned! He had a hideous black face, completely black, proof that he must not wash often."[23]

Jean Veneuse, preoccupied with finding external reasons for his Cinderella complex, projects onto a child of three or four years his arsenal of racist stereotypes. And to Andrée, he will say: "Tell me,

Andrée darling . . ., in spite of my color, would you agree to marry me, if I asked you?"[24]

He is terribly full of doubt.

And yet Jean Veneuse does not lead a life devoid of compensations. He dabbles in poetry. His reading list is impressive, his analysis of Suarès is quite perceptive.

What is the aim of this analysis? Nothing less than to prove to Jean Veneuse that he is actually not like the rest. To make people ashamed of their existence, Jean-Paul Sartre said. Yes: to make them aware of the possibilities they denied themselves, of the passivity they showed in precisely those situations in which what was needed was to hold on tightly, like a splinter, to the heart of the world, to go against, if necessary, the rhythm of the heart of the world, to upset, if necessary, the chain of command, but in any case—but certainly—*to face up to the world.*

Jean Veneuse is the crusader of the inner life. When he sees Andrée again, faced with this woman whom he has desired for months, he takes refuge in silence . . . the eloquent silence of those who "know the artificiality of words and acts."

Jean Veneuse is a neurotic and his color is nothing but an attempt to explain a mental structure. Had this objective difference not existed, he would have fabricated it out of nothing.

Jean Veneuse is one of those intellectuals who try to consider things solely on the level of ideas. Incapable of realizing any concrete contact with his fellow man. Is he treated benevolently, kindly, humanely? It is because he has stumbled upon some blabbermouth's secrets. He "knows these people" and he is on guard.

He accepts the drinks, but buys others in return. He does not want to be obligated to anyone. For if he does not buy them, he is a Negro, ungrateful like all the others.

Is he treated badly? It is precisely because he is a Negro. For it is impossible not to loathe him.

Now, I contend that Jean Veneuse, a.k.a. [alias] Maran, René. is neither more nor less than a black abandonic. And he is put back in his place, in his proper place. He is a neurotic who needs to be freed of his infantile fantasies. And I contend that Jean Veneuse represents not an example of black-white relations, but a certain mode of behavior in a neurotic who happens to be black.

Jean Veneuse is ugly. He is black. What more is needed? If one reads again the few observations of Germaine Guex, one will be accept the obvious: *Un homme pareil aux autres* [*A Man Like the Others*] is a fraud, an attempt to make the contact between two races dependent on a constitutional morbidity. It must be admitted: on the level of psychoanalysis as on that of philosophy, one's [organic] constitution is a myth only for the one who overcomes it. If, from a heuristic[25] point of view, one must totally deny the existence of the [organic] constitution, the fact remains, and we can do nothing about it, that some individuals endeavor to fit into pre-established frameworks. Or, rather, yes, we can do something about it.

For the notion of constitution as it was understood by the French school, I am substituting that of structure,—"encompassing the unconscious mental life such as it is possible for us to know it in part, in particular in the form of repression and inhibition, insofar as these elements take an active part in the proper organization of each mental individuality."[26]

The neurotic structure of an individual will precisely be the elaboration, the formation, the eruption within the self of conflictual nodes arising in part out of the environment and in part out of the purely personal in which that individual reacts to these influences.

In the same way that there was an attempt at deception in wanting to infer from the behavior of Nini or Mayotte Capécia a general law for the behavior of the black woman in relation to the white man, there would be, I assert, a lack of objectivity in extending Veneuse's attitude to the black man as such. And I hope to have discouraged any attempt aimed at reducing the failures of a Jean Veneuse to the greater or lesser concentration of melanin in his epidermis.

This sexual myth—the quest for white flesh—perpetuated by alienated minds must no longer hinder active understanding.

In no way should I regard my color as a flaw. From the moment the Negro accepts the separation imposed by the European, he has no further respite, and "from then on, is it not understandable that he try to elevate himself to the white man's level? To elevate himself in the range of colors to which he attributes a kind of hierarchy?"[27]

We will see that another solution is possible. It entails a restructuring of the world.

ENDNOTES

1. Maran, René. *Un homme pareil aux autres.* Paris: Editions Arc-en-ciel, 1947, p. 11.
2. *Ibid.,* p. 87.
3. *Ibid.,* pp. 18–19.
4. *Ibid.,* pp. 45–46.
5. *Ibid.,* p. 83.
6. *Ibid.,* p. 83.
7. *Ibid.,* p. 36.
8. *Ibid.,* p. 36.
9. Tr. In English in the original text.
10. Maran. *Un homme pareil aux autres,* pp. 152–154.
11. *Ibid.,* p. 185.
12. *Ibid.,* p. 162.
13. "Du Jeu au Je, Esquisse d'une géographie de l'action." from *Les Temps Modernes,* April, 1948, p. 1732.
14. *Rythmes du monde,* 1949, p. 113.
15. Minkowski, E. *La Schizophrénie.* Paris: Fayot, 1927.
16. Germaine Guex. *La Névrose d'abandon.* Paris: Presses Universitaires de France, 1950, pp. 27–28.
17. My italics—F.F.
18. Maran. *Un homme pareil aux autres,* p. 36. Tr. In the original text, this citation is incorrectly attributed to Germaine Guex.
19. *Ibid.,* p. 227.
20. *Ibid.,* p. 228.
21. Guex, Germaine. *La Névrose d'abandon,* pp. 35–36.
22. Maran, René. *Un homme pareil aux autres,* pp. 203–204.
23. *Ibid.,* pp. 84–85.
24. *Ibid.,* pp. 247–248.
25. Tr. Heuristic: term used to denote a sophisticated, directed method for discovery, a procedure for solving a problem.
26. Guex, Germaine. *La Névrose d'abandon,* p. 54.
27. Nordey, Claude. *L'homme de couleur.* Paris: Collection "Présences," Plon, 1939.

chapter thirty-two

Octavio Paz

Octavio Paz (1914–1998), poet, essayist, and thinker, is a renowned figure in twentieth-century Hispanic letters. Extremely proficient at explaining features of national culture, Paz was a particularly astute observer of the ways in which Mexican culture interacts or collides with North American and northern European cultures. His philosophical concerns are centered in post-World War II philosophy, and he deals primarily with the challenges of the irrational, pursuing expression focused on wants, needs, and desires. Rather than being logical mathematically or scientifically philosophical, Paz is literarily philosophical, not unlike his friend Albert Camus or Jean-Paul Sartre.

Born during the Mexican Revolution in Mixcoac, near Mexico City, Paz was of Spanish and Indian descent. His father worked as a journalist and served as a secretary for Emiliano Zapata, leader of the Mexican campesinos. Paz did not get along well with his father, who turned to alcohol after Zapata was killed in 1919 and died when Octavio was twenty-two. An only child, Paz was closer to his mother and his grandfather, in whose library he spent considerable time. Paz also spent part of his childhood in southern California where he felt he experienced first-hand the discrimination directed toward Mexicans in the United States.

Paz developed an abiding interest in poetry at the age of fourteen. At sixteen, he published his first poem. He took classes at the Universidad Nacional Autónoma de México, though he did not complete a degree. As a young man, Paz worked as a journalist and magazine editor. Extremely disciplined and essentially self-taught, Paz famously demonstrates a vast knowledge of language, literature, and art; Eastern and Western philosophy; and cultural anthropology.

Paz's travels took him to civil war Spain, where he met many important Hispanic writers, and to surrealist Paris, where he met Andre Breton and Albert Camus. A Guggenheim fellowship enabled him to travel to San Francisco, New York, Vermont, Washington, D.C., and many U.S. universities, including Harvard, where he eventually taught periodically. In 1946, Paz entered his country's foreign service and held various diplomatic posts in France, Japan, the United States, Switzerland, and India.

It would be difficult to overstate the importance of Paz's groundbreaking essay, *The Labyrinth of Solitude* (1950, with a revised and expanded edition published in 1959), excerpted here. Paz wrote *The Labyrinth of Solitude* over a two-year period during which he resided in France. In Mexico during this same period, the late 1940s and early 1950s, the Hyperion Group, an intellectual group led by philosopher Leopoldo Zea, was studying Mexican identity issues such as the Mexican inferiority complex. Mexican philosophers in that era were turning their attention to Mexican reality and determining whether they had any unique philosophical contributions of their own to make. They were attempting to adapt classic Western philosophies to their own concerns and contexts, rather than merely to adopt them as relevant and necessary. Against this backdrop, Paz's *Labyrinth* was a radical study of Mexican character, an exposé of sorts. While Mexicans had traditionally blamed, for example, U.S. imperialism and the historic intervention of the Catholic Church in Mexican politics for many of Mexico's ills, Paz instead turned his gaze inward. He focused on what he viewed as the tormented self-identification of Mexicans as products of a raped woman. He portrayed Mexicans as the progeny of Spanish conquistador Hernan Cortés and his Indian mistress, Marina, known among Mexicans as *La Malinche* (The Traitor). Paz argued that the ambiguity of that symbolic relationship exemplified deep insecurities in Mexicans, who were uncertain how to balance their European and indigenous roots. The book was deeply provocative and controversial in Latin America for several years after its publication. Today it is a revered classic, though it remains controversial today primarily for its essentialist portrayals of woman.[1]

In *The Labyrinth of Solitude,* Paz seeks to analyze many Mexican identity issues. When he lived in Los Angeles (today the second-largest "Mexican" city in the world), he observed that Mexicans act like persons who are wearing disguises, who are afraid of a stranger's look because it could strip them and leave them stark naked. Paz analyzed the rebellious, contradictory psychology of the *pachucos,* youths of Mexican origin (today called *cholos*) who formed gangs in southern California. Paz extended his analysis of *pachucos* to Mexicans in general. Other chapters in *Labyrinth,* such as "Mexican Masks," allege that Mexicans hide their conflictive inner selves behind masks they wear to protect themselves from being discovered. He claims that the worst fear of the Mexican *macho* is that he might "crack" or "open up" in front of another, destroying his tough façade. At one point in his analysis of "The Day of the Dead," the Feast of All Souls celebrated on November 2 when Mexicans go to cemeteries to visit their ancestors, sing, and share the favorite foods of the deceased, Paz claims that the best way for a Mexican to die is at a party surrounded by others. He claims that Mexicans, though afraid of solitude, are not afraid of death and view it as part of a natural process whereas North Americans fear death and view it as finality.

Readers of the excerpt below, about solitude and love, may benefit from knowing some additional details about Paz's life. In 1937 he married Mexican writer Elena Garro. They had a daughter, Helena, and ultimately divorced in 1959. In 1966, Paz married Marie-José Tramini and remained married to her until he died of cancer in 1998 at the age of eighty-four. They had no children. Paz served as ambassador to India from 1962 to 1968 when he resigned his post in protest over the Mexican government's massacre, during the 1968 Olympic games, of hundreds of protesting students in the downtown Mexico City Plaza of Tlatelolco. At this time, he severed his relationship with the official government party, the *Partido Revolucionario Institucional*. In 1976 Paz founded and edited the influential journal *Vuelta* (Return; 1976–1998).

Octavio Paz produced more than forty books of poetry and essays, and his works have been translated into more than thirty languages. His perhaps most highly acclaimed poem is "Piedra del sol" ("Sunstone") in which Aztec myths and time are melded together with Western myths in search of personal identity and the meaning of life. In celebration of his work, Paz was awarded several of the major literary prizes in the Hispanic World—the Prince of Asturias, Cervantes, and Alexis de Tocqueville—and numerous honorary doctorates from U.S. universities. In 1990, he was awarded the Nobel Prize for Literature.

When *The Labyrinth of Solitude* was published in 1950, José Vasconcelos, an eminent Mexican philosopher, praised Paz as "the most brilliant poet of his generation." He proclaimed, moreover, that while "Octavio Paz started out as a poet, an enviable way to begin, pity the poet who does not branch out into prose! The prose of poets tends to be excellent. Such is the case with the prose of Octavio Paz."

AAO

QUESTIONS

1. What obstacles stand in the way of love for men? For women?
2. Why, according to Paz, must love violate the conventions of our world to realize itself?
3. What is the "dialectic of solitude," and how does it make love possible?

ENDNOTE

1. Interestingly, Paz is also well known for *Sor Juana, or the Traps of Faith,* his landmark study of the life and legacy of seventeenth-century Mexican poet, dramatist, and essayist, Sor Juana Inés de la Cruz, who is usually considered the first feminist in the Americas. A nun, Sor Juana chose the convent primarily because it was preferable to marriage, toward which she expressed a total disinclination. Paz probably identified with Sor Juana as a poet and a tortured intellectual with a passion for knowledge and writing.

SELECTED BIBLIOGRAPHY

Paz, Octavio. *The Collected Poems of Octavio Paz,* 1957–1987. New York: New Directions, 1991.

Paz, Octavio. *The Double Flame: Love and Eroticism.* New York: Harcourt Brace, 1995.

Paz, Octavio. *The Labyrinth of Solitude.* New York: Penguin, 1997.

from *The Labyrinth of Solitude*

Octavio Paz

THE DIALECTIC OF SOLITUDE

Solitude—the feeling and knowledge that one is alone, alienated from the world and oneself—is not an exclusively Mexican characteristic. All men, at some moment in their lives, feel themselves to be alone. And they are. To live is to be separated from what we were in order to approach what we are going to be in the mysterious future. Solitude is the profoundest fact of the human condition. Man is the only being who knows he is alone, and the only one who seeks out another. His nature—if that word can be used in reference to man, who has "invented" himself by saying "No" to nature—consists in his longing to realize himself in another. Man is nostalgia and a search for communion. Therefore, when he is aware of himself he is aware of his lack of another, that is, of his solitude.

The foetus is at one with the world around it; it is pure brute life, unconscious of itself. When we are born we break the ties that joined us to the blind life we lived in the maternal womb, where there is no gap between desire and satisfaction. We sense the change as separation and loss, as abandonment, as a fall into a strange or hostile atmosphere. Later this primitive sense of loss becomes a feeling of solitude, and still later it becomes awareness: we are condemned to live alone, but also to transcend our solitude, to re-establish the bonds that united us with life in a paradisiac past. All our forces strive to abolish our solitude. Hence the feeling that we are alone has a double significance: on the one hand it is self-awareness, and on the other it is a longing to escape from ourselves. Solitude—the very condition of our lives—appears to us as a test and a purgation, at the conclusion of which our anguish and instability will vanish. At the exit from the labyrinth of solitude we will find reunion (which is repose and happiness), and plenitude, and harmony with the world.

Popular language reflects this dualism by identifying solitude with suffering. The pangs of love are pangs of solitude. Communion and solitude are opposite and complementary. The redemptive power of solitude clarifies our obscure but vivid sense of guilt: the solitary man is "forsaken by the hand of God." Solitude is both a sentence and an expiation. It is a punishment but it is also a promise that our exile will end. All human life is pervaded by this dialectic.

Death and birth are solitary experiences. We are born alone and we die alone. When we are expelled from the maternal womb, we begin the painful struggle that finally ends in death. Does death mean a return to the life that precedes life? Does it mean to relive that prenatal life in which rest and motion, day and night, time and eternity are not opposites? Does dying mean to cease existing as a being and finally, definitively, to be? Is death the truest kind of life? Is birth death, and is death birth? We do not know. But although we do not know, our whole being strives to escape the opposites that torment us. Everything—self-awareness, time, reason, customs, habits—tends to make us exiles from life, but at the same time everything impels us to return, to descend to the creative womb from which we were cast out. What we ask of love (which, being desire, is a hunger for communion, a will to fall and to die as well as to be reborn) is that it give us a bit of true life, of true death. We do not ask it for happiness or repose, but simply for an instant of that full life in which opposites vanish, in which life and death, time and eternity are united. In some obscure way we realize that life and death are but two phases—antagonistic but complementary—of a single reality. Creation and destruction become one in the act of love, and during a fraction of a second man has a glimpse of a more perfect state of being.

In our world, love is an almost inaccessible experience. Everything is against it: morals, classes, laws, races and the very lovers themselves. Woman has always been for man the "other," his opposite and complement. If one part of our being longs to unite itself with her, another part—equally imperious—rejects and excludes her. Woman is an object, sometimes precious, sometimes harmful, but always different. By converting her into an object and by subjecting her to the deformations which his interests, his vanity, his anguish and his very love dictate, man changes her into an instrument, a means of obtaining understanding and pleasure, a way of achieving survival. Woman is an idol, a goddess, a mother, a witch or a muse, as Simone de Beauvoir has said, but she can never be her own self. Thus our erotic relationships are vitiated at

the outset, are poisoned at the root. A phantasm comes between us, and this phantasm is her image, the image we have made of her and in which she clothes herself. When we reach out to touch her, we cannot even touch unthinking flesh, because this docile, servile vision of a surrendering body always intrudes. And the same thing happens to her: she can only conceive of herself as an object, as something "other." She is never her own mistress. Her being is divided between what she really is and what she imagines she is, and this image has been dictated to her by her family, class, school, friends, religion and lover. She never expresses her femininity because it always manifests itself in forms men have invented for her. Love is not a "natural" thing. It is something human, the most human trait of all. Something that we have made ourselves and that is not found in nature. Something that we create—and destroy—every day.

These are not the only obstacles standing between love and ourselves. Love is a choice . . . perhaps a free choosing of our destiny, a sudden discovery of the most secret and fateful part of our being. But the choosing of love is impossible in our society. In one of his finest books—*Mad Love*—Breton has said that two prohibitions restrict it from the very outset: social disapproval and the Christian idea of sin. To realize itself, love must violate the laws of our world. It is scandalous and disorderly, a transgression committed by two stars that break out of their predestined orbits and rush together in the midst of space. The romantic conception of love, which implies a breaking away and a catastrophe, is the only one we know today because everything in our society prevents love from being a free choice.

Women are imprisoned in the image masculine society has imposed on them; therefore, if they attempt a free choice it must be a kind of jail break. Lovers say that "love has transformed her, it has made her a different person." And they are right.

Love changes a woman completely. If she dares to love, if she dares to be herself, she has to destroy the image in which the world has imprisoned her.

A man is also prevented from choosing. His range of possibilities is very limited. He discovers femininity as a child, in his mother or sisters, and from then on he identifies love with taboos. Our eroticism is conditioned by the horror and attraction of incest. Also, modern life stimulates our desires excessively, while it also frustrates them with all sorts of prohibitions: social, moral, even hygienic. Guilt is both the spur and rein of desire. Everything restricts our choice. We have to adjust our profoundest affections to the image of what our social group approves of in a woman. It is difficult to love persons of other races, cultures or classes, even though it is perfectly possible for a light-skinned man to love a dark-skinned woman, for her to love a Chinese, for a "gentleman" to love his maid. And vice versa. But these possibilities make us blush, and since we are prevented from choosing freely, we select a wife from among the women who are "suitable." We never confess that we have married a woman we do not love, a woman who may love us, perhaps, but who is incapable of being her true self. Swann says: "And to think that I have wasted the best years of my life with a woman who was not my type." The majority of modern men could repeat that sentence on their deathbeds. And with the change of one word, so could the majority of modern women.

Society denies the nature of love by conceiving of it as a stable union whose purpose is to beget and raise children. It identifies it, that is, with marriage. Every transgression against this rule is punished, the severity of the punishment depending on the time and place. (In Mexico the punishment is often fatal if the transgressor is a woman, because—like all Hispanic peoples—we have two sets of morals: one for the "señor," another for

women, children and the poor.) The protection given to marriage would be justifiable if society permitted free choice. Since it does not, it should accept the fact that marriage is not the supreme realization of love, but rather a legal, social and economic form whose purposes are different from love's. The stability of the family depends upon marriage, which becomes a mere protection for society with no other object but the reproducing of that same society. Hence marriage is by nature profoundly conservative. To attack it is to attack the very bases of society. And love, for the same reason, is an antisocial act, though not deliberately so. Whenever it succeeds in realizing itself, it breaks up a marriage and transforms it into what society does not want it to be: a revelation of two solitary beings who create their own world, a world that rejects society's lies, abolishes time and work, and declares itself to be self-sufficient. It is hardly strange, then, that society should punish love and its testimony—poetry—with equal malevolence, condemning them to the confused, clandestine world of the forbidden, the absurd, the abnormal. Nor it is strange that both love and poetry explode in strange, pure forms: a scandal, a crime, a poem.

As a result of this protection afforded to marriage, love is persecuted and prostitution is either tolerated or given official blessing. Our ambiguous attitude toward prostitution is quite revealing. Some peoples consider the institution to be sacred, but among us it is alternately contemptible and desirable. The prostitute is a caricature of love, a victim of love, a symbol of the powers that are debasing our world. But even this travesty of love is not enough: in some circles the bonds of marriage are loosened so much that promiscuity is the general rule. The person who goes from bed to bed is no longer considered a libertine. The seducer—the man who cannot transcend himself because women are always instruments of his vanity or anxiety—is a figure as outmoded as the knight errant. There is no longer anyone to seduce, just as there are no maidens to rescue or ogres to destroy. Modern eroticism has a different meaning from that of Sade, for example. Sade was a tragic character, a man who was completely possessed, and his work is an explosive revelation of the human condition. There are no heroes as desperate as his. Modern eroticism, on the other hand, is almost always rhetorical, a complacent literary exercise. It is not a revelation of man; it is simply one more document describing a society that encourages crime and condemns love. Freedom of passion? Divorce has ceased to be a conquest. It is not so much a way of casting off established ties as it is of permitting men and women to choose more freely. In an ideal society, the only basis for divorce would be the disappearance of love or the appearance of a new love. In a society in which everyone could choose, divorce would become an anachronism or a rarity, like prostitution and promiscuity and adultery.

Society pretends to be an organic whole that lives by and for itself. But while it conceives of itself as an indivisible unit, it is inwardly divided by a dualism which perhaps originated when man ceased to be an animal, when he invented his self, his conscience and his ethics. Society is an organism that suffers the strange necessity of justifying its ends and appetites. Sometimes its ends—disguised as moral precepts—coincide with the desires and needs of those who comprise it. But sometimes they deny the aspirations of important minorities or classes, and too often they even deny man's profoundest instincts. When this last occurs, society lives through a period of crisis: it either explodes or stagnates. Its components cease to be human beings and are converted into mere soulless instruments.

The dualism inherent in every society, and which every society tries to resolve by transforming itself into a community, expresses itself today in many ways: good and evil, permission and taboo, the ideal and the real, the rational and the irrational, beauty and ugliness, dreams and vigils, poverty and wealth, bourgeoisie and proletariat, innocence and knowledge, imagination and reason. By an irresistible movement of its own being, society attempts to overcome this dualism and to convert its hostile, solitary components into a harmonious whole. But modern society attempts to do this by suppressing the dialectic of solitude, which alone can make love possible. Industrial societies, regardless of their differing "ideologies," politics and economics, strive to change qualitative—that is, human—differences into quantitative uniformity. The methods of mass production are also applied to morality, art and the emotions. Contradictions and exceptions are eliminated, and this results in the closing off of our access to the profoundest experience life can offer us, that of discovering reality as a oneness in which opposites agree. The new powers prohibit solitude by fiat . . . and thus they also prohibit love, a clandestine and heroic form of communion. Defending love has always been a dangerous, antisocial activity. Now it is even beginning to be revolutionary. The problem of love in our world reveals how the dialectic of solitude, in its deepest manifestation, is frustrated by society. Our social life prevents almost every possibility of achieving true erotic communion.

Love is one of the clearest examples of that double instinct which causes us to dig deeper into our own selves and, at the same time, to emerge from ourselves and to realize ourselves in another: death and re-creation, solitude and communion. But it is not the only one. In the life of every man there are periods that are both departures and reunions, separations and reconciliations. Each of these phases is an attempt to transcend our solitude, and is followed by an immersion in strange environments.

The child must face an irreducible reality, and at first he responds to its stimuli with tears or silence. The cord that united him with life has been broken, and he tries to restore it by means of play and affection. This is the beginning of a dialogue that ends only when he recites the monologue of his death. But his relations with the external world are not passive now, as they were in his prenatal life, because the world demands a response. Reality has to be peopled by his acts. Thanks to games and fantasies, the inert natural world of adults—a chair, a book, anything—suddenly acquires a life of its own. The child uses the magic power of language or gesture, symbol or act, to create a living world in which objects are capable of replying to his questions. Language, freed of intellectual meanings, ceases to be a collection of signs and again becomes a delicate and magnetic organism. Verbal representation equals reproduction of the object itself, in the same way that a carving, for the primitive man, is not a representation but a double of the object represented. Speech again becomes a creative activity dealing with realities, that is, a poetic activity. Through magic the child creates a world in his own image and thus resolves his solitude. Self-awareness begins when we doubt the magical efficacy of our instruments.

Adolescence is a break with the world of childhood and a pause on the threshold of the adult world. Spranger points out that solitude is a distinctive characteristic of adolescence. Narcissus, the solitary, is the very image of the adolescent. It is during this period that we become aware of our singularity for the first time. But the dialectic of the emotions intervenes once more: since adolescence is extreme self-consciousness, it can only be transcended by self-forgetfulness, by self-surrender. Therefore solitude is not only a time of solitude

but also of great romances, of heroism and sacrifice. The people have good reason to picture the hero and the lover as adolescents. The vision of the adolescent as a solitary figure, closed up within himself and consumed by desire or timidity, almost always resolves into a crowd of young people dancing, singing or marching as a group, or into a young couple strolling under the arched green branches in a park. The adolescent opens himself up to the world: to love, action, friendship, sports, heroic adventures. The literature of modern nations—except Spain, where they never appear except as rogues or orphans—is filled with adolescents, with solitaries in search of communion: of the ring, the sword, the Vision. Adolescence is an armed watch, at the end of which one enters the world of facts.

Solitude is not characteristic of maturity. When a man struggles with other men or with things, he forgets himself in his work, in creation or in the construction of objects, ideas and institutions. His personal consciousness unites with that of others: time takes on meaning and purpose and thus becomes history, a vivid, significant account with both a past and a future. Our singularity—deriving from the fact that we are situated in time, in a particular time which is made up of our own selves and which devours us while it feeds us—is not actually abolished, but it is attenuated and, in a certain sense, "redeemed." Our personal existence takes part in history, which becomes, in Eliot's phrase, "a pattern of timeless moments." During vital and productive epochs, therefore, a mature man suffering from the illness of solitude is always an anomaly. This type of solitary figure is very frequent today, and indicates the gravity of our ills. In an epoch of group work, group songs, group pleasures, man is more alone than ever. Modern man never surrenders himself to what he is doing. A part of him—the profoundest part—always remain detached and alert. Man spies on himself.

Work, the only modern god, is no longer creative. It is endless, infinite work, corresponding to the inconclusive life of modern society. And the solitude it engenders—the random solitude of hotels, offices, shops and movie theaters—is not a test that strengthens the soul, a necessary purgatory. It is utter damnation, mirroring a world without exit.

The dual significance of solitude—a break with one world and an attempt to create another—can be seen in our conception of heroes, saints and redeemers. Myth, biography, history and poetry describe a period of withdrawal and solitude—almost always during early youth—preceding a return to the world and to action. These are years of preparation and study, but above all they are years of sacrifice and penitence, of self-examination, of expiation and purification. Arnold Toynbee gives many illustrations of this idea: the myth of Plato's cave, the lives of St. Paul, Buddha, Mahomet, Machiavelli, Dante. And all of us in our own lives, and within our limitations, have lived in solitude and retirement, in order to purify ourselves and then return to the world.

The dialectic of solitude—"the twofold motion of withdrawal-and-return," to use Toynbee's words—is clearly revealed in the history of every people. Perhaps the ancient societies, less complex than ours, are better illustrations of this double motion.

It is not difficult to imagine the extent to which solitude is a dangerous and terrifying condition for the persons we refer to—complacently and inaccurately—as "primitives." In archaic societies, a complex and rigid systems of prohibitions, rules and rituals protects the individual from solitude. The group is the only source of health. The solitary man is an invalid, a dead branch that must be lopped off and burned, for society as a whole is endangered if one of its components becomes ill. Repetition of secular beliefs and formulas assures not only the permanence of the group but also its unity and cohesion; while religious ritual, and the constant presence of the dead, create a center of relationships which restrict independent action, thus protecting the individual from solitude and the group from dissolution.

To the primitive man, health and society are synonymous terms, and so are death and dispersion. Lévy-Bruhl says that anyone who leaves his native region "ceases to belong to the group. He dies, and receives the customary funeral rites."[1] Permanent exile, then, is the same as a death sentence. The social group's identification with the spirits of its ancestors, and its identification of these with the land, is expressed in this symbolic African ritual: "When a native brings back a wife from Kimberley, they carry with them a little dirt from his home place. Every day she has to eat a bit of this dirt. . . . to accustom herself to this change of residence." The social solidarity of these people has "a vital, organic character. The individual is literally part of a body." Therefore individual conversions are rare. "No one is either saved or damned on his own account," and each person's actions affect the entire group.

Despite all these safeguards, the group is not immune to dispersion. Anything can break it up: wars, religious schisms, changes in the systems of production, conquests. . . . As soon as the group is divided, each of its fragments is faced with a drastic new situation. When the source of health—the old, closed society—is destroyed, solitude is no longer merely a threat or an accident: it is a condition, the basic and ultimate condition. And it leads to a sense of sin—not a sin resulting from the violation of some rule, but rather one that forms a part of their nature. Or, to be more precise, one that now *is* their nature. Solitude and original sin

---

[1] Lucien Lévy-Bruhl: *La mentalité primitive* (Paris: 1922).

become one and the same. Also, health and communion again become synonymous, but are located in a remote past. They constitute the golden age, an era which preceded history and to which we could perhaps return if we broke out of time's prison. When we acquire a sense of sin, we also grow aware of our need for redemption and a redeemer.

A new mythology and a new religion are then created. The new society—unlike the old—is open and fluid, since it is made up of exiles. The fact of having been born within the group no longer assures a man that he belongs: he has to be worthy of belonging. Prayer begins to take the place of magic formulas, and initiation rites put more and more emphasis on purification. The idea of redemption fosters religious speculation, theology, asceticism and mysticism. Sacrifice and communion cease to be totem feasts (if that is what they actually were) and become means of entering the new society. A god—almost always a god who is also a son, a descendant of ancient creation-gods—dies and is resurrected at fixed periods. He is a fertility god but he is also a redeemer, and his sacrifice is a pledge that the group is an earthly prefiguration of the perfect society awaiting us on the other side of death. These hopes concerning the next life are in part a nostalgic longing for the old society. A return to the golden age is implicit in the promise of salvation.

Of course it is difficult to discover all these factors in the history of any one society. Nevertheless, there are various societies that fit the scheme in almost every detail. Consider, for instance, the birth of Orphism. The Orphic cult arose after the destruction of Achaean civilization, which caused a general dispersion of the Greek world and a vast reaccommodation of its peoples and cultures. The necessity of reforging the ancient links, both social and sacred, created a number of secret cults in which the only participants were "uprooted, transplanted beings . . . who dreamed of fashioning an organization from which they could not be separated. Their only collective name was that of 'orphans.'"[2] (I should mention that *orphanos* means both "orphan" and "empty." Solitude and orphanhood are similar forms of emptiness.)

The Orphic and Dionysiac religions, like the proletarian religions that flourished during the collapse of the ancient world, show very clearly how a closed society becomes an open one. The sense of guilt, of solitude and expiation, plays the same dual role as it does in the life of an individual.

The feeling of solitude, which is a nostalgic longing for the body from which we were cast out, is a longing for a place. According to an ancient belief, held by virtually all peoples, that place[3] is the center of the world, the navel of the universe. Sometimes it is identified with paradise, and both of these with the group's real or mythical place of origin. Among the Aztecs, the dead returned to Mictlán, a place situated in the north, from which they had emigrated. Almost all the rites connected with the founding of cities or houses allude to a search for that holy center from which we were driven out. The great sanctuaries—Rome, Jerusalem, Mecca—are at the center of the world, or symbolize and prefigure it. Pilgrimages to these sanctuaries are ritual repetitions of what each group did in the mythical past before establishing itself in the promised land. The custom of circling a house or city before entering it has the same origin.

The myth of the labyrinth pertains to this set of beliefs. Several related ideas make the labyrinth

---

[2]Amable Audin: *Les Fêtes Solaires* (Paris, 1945).
[3]On the idea of "sacred place," see Mircia Eliade: *Histoire des Religions* (Paris, 1949).

one of the most fertile and meaningful mythical symbols: the talisman or other object, capable of restoring health or freedom to the people, at the center of a sacred area; the hero or saint who, after doing penance and performing the rites of expiation, enters the labyrinth or enchanted palace; and the hero's return either to save or redeem his city or to found a new one. In the Perseus myth the mystical elements are almost invisible, but in that of the Holy Grail asceticism and mysticism are closely related: sin, which causes sterility in the lands and subjects of the Fisher King; purification rites; spiritual combat; and, finally, grace—that is, communion.

We have been expelled from the center of the world and are condemned to search for it through jungles and deserts or in the underground mazes of the labyrinth. Also, there was a time when time was not succession and transition, but rather the perpetual source of a fixed present in which all times, past and future, were contained. When man was exiled from that eternity in which all times were one, he entered chronometric time and became a prisoner of the clock and the calendar. As soon as time was divided up into yesterday, today and tomorrow, into hours, minutes and seconds, man ceased to be one with time, ceased to coincide with the flow of reality. When one says, "at this moment," the moment has already passed. These spatial measurements of time separate man from reality—which is a continuous present—and turn all the presences in which reality manifests itself, as Bergson said, into phantasms.

If we consider the nature of these two opposing ideas, it becomes clear that chronometric time is a homogeneous succession lacking all particularity. It is always the same, always indifferent to pleasure or pain. Mythological time, on the other hand, is impregnated with all the particulars of our lives: it is as long as eternity or as short as a breath, ominous or propitious, fecund or sterile. This idea allows for the existence of a number of varying times. Life and time coalesce to form a single whole, an indivisible unity. To the Aztecs, time was associated with space, and each day with one of the cardinal points. The same can be said of any religious calendar. A fiesta is more than a date or anniversary. It does not celebrate an event: it *reproduces* it. Chronometric time is destroyed and the eternal present—for a brief but immeasurable period—is reinstated. The fiesta becomes the creator of time; repetition becomes conception. The golden age returns. Whenever the priest officiates in the Mystery of the Holy Mass, Christ descends to the here and now, giving himself to man and saving the world. The true believers, as Kierkegaard wished, are "contemporaries of Jesus." And myths and religious fiestas are not the only ways in which the present can interrupt succession. Love and poetry also offer us a brief revelation of this original time. Juan Ramón Jiménez wrote: "More time is not more eternity," referring to the eternity of the poetic instant. Unquestionably the conception of time as a fixed present and as pure actuality is more ancient than that of chronometric time, which is not an immediate apprehension of the flow of reality but is instead a rationalization of its passing.

This dichotomy is expressed in the opposition between history and myth or between history and poetry. In myth—as in religious fiestas or children's stories—time has no dates: "Once upon a time . . ." "In the days when animals could talk . . ." "In the beginning . . ." And that beginning, which is not such-and-such a year or day, contains all beginnings and ushers us into living time where everything truly begins every instant. Through ritual, which realizes and reproduces a mythical account, and also through poetry and fairy tales, man gains access to a world in which opposites are reconciled and united. As Van der Leeuw said, "all rituals have the property of taking place in the now, at this very instant."[4] Every poem we read is a re-creation, that is, a ceremonial ritual, a fiesta.

The theater and the epic are also fiestas. In theatrical performances and in the reciting of poetry, ordinary time ceases to operate and is replaced by original time. Thanks to participation, this mythical time—father of all the times that mask reality—coincides with our inner, subjective time. Man, the prisoner of succession, breaks out of his invisible jail and enters living time: his subjective life becomes identical with exterior time, because this has ceased to be a spatial measurement and has changed into a source, a spring, in the absolute present, endlessly re-creating itself. Myths and fiestas, whether secular or religious, permit man to emerge from his solitude and become one with creation. Therefore myth—disguised, obscure, hidden—reappears in almost all our acts and intervenes decisively in our history: it opens the doors of communion.

Contemporary man has rationalized the myths, but he has not been able to destroy them. Many of our scientific truths, like the majority of our moral, political and philosophical conceptions, are only new ways of expressing tendencies that were embodied earlier in mythical forms. The rational language of our day can barely hide the ancient myths behind it. Utopias—especially modern political utopias (despite their rationalistic disguises)—are violently concentrated expressions of the tendency that causes every society to imagine a golden age from which the social group was exiled and to which man will return on the Day of Days. Modern fiestas—political meetings, parades, demonstrations and other ritual acts—prefigure the advent of that day of redemption. Everyone hopes society will return to its original freedom, and man to his primitive purity. Then time will cease to torment us with doubts, with the necessity of choosing between good and evil, the just and the unjust, the real and the imaginary. The kingdom of the fixed present, of perpetual communion, will be re-established. Reality will tear off its masks, and at last we will be able to know both it and our fellow men.

Every moribund or sterile society attempts to save itself by creating a redemption myth which is also a fertility myth, a creation myth. Solitude and sin are resolved in communion and fertility. The society we live in today has also created its myth. The sterility of the bourgeois world will end in suicide or a new form of creative participation. This is the "theme of our times," in Ortega y Gasset's phrase; it is the substance of our dreams and the meaning of our acts.

Modern man likes to pretend that his thinking is wide-awake. But this wide-awake thinking has led us into the mazes of a nightmare in which the torture chambers are endlessly repeated in the mirrors of reason. When we emerge, perhaps we will realize that we have been dreaming with our eyes open, and that the dreams of reason are intolerable. And then, perhaps, we will begin to dream once more with our eyes closed.

---

[4]Van der Leeuw: *L'homme primitif et la Religion* (Paris, 1940).

chapter thirty-three

Maurice Merleau-Ponty

Maurice Merleau-Ponty (1908-1961) ranks as one of the most important French philosophers of the twentieth century. His untimely death at the age of fifty-three cut short a work whose importance has only in recent years begun to be fully appreciated. He and Jean-Paul Sartre are often credited with introducing phenomenology to France in the 1940s and 1950s. In its contemporary form, this approach to philosophical inquiry was developed by Edmund Husserl, whose early work attempted to integrate mathematical formalism with the study of "pure consciousness." Born on the west coast of France, Merleau-Ponty often reported that his childhood had been one of "incomparable happiness," and this sense of joy is often evident in his writings.

From his earliest essays, Merleau-Ponty evinced a deep regard for the crucial role embodied experience plays in philosophical inquiry, and this adroit revisioning of the nature of embodied human experience radically challenged one of the major tenets of Western philosophy, namely, that of "dualism."[1] He does this in a variety of ways by calling into question the mind-body dualism usually associated with the work of René Descartes. Although the actual extent to which Descartes' philosophy is grounded in dualism is fertile ground for inquiry (see *The Passions of the Soul* in this volume), the association of Descartes with dualism persists in the Western tradition through the twentieth century. In his major work, *The Phenomenology of Perception* (1945), Merleau-Ponty notes that vision is ambiguous: anyone or anything that can *see* must have a body, and this body may *be seen.* Thus, we are both visible and seeing creatures, not simply subjects who see or objects who are seen. Instead, Merleau-Ponty argues that the body is the place where humans enter into relationship with the world. Over the next fifteen years, Merleau-Ponty expanded and deepened these reflections on the fundamentally embodied nature of human existence in a series of essays whose collective impact would not only change the character of phenomenology, but also profoundly influence all of French philosophy in the second half of the twentieth century.

In Merleau-Ponty's thought, the body, which had long been regarded in Western philosophy as a hindrance to discovering the "truth" of the world, is transformed into the crucial means by which any such investigations are even possible. This emphasis on the complex relationship of body and world, seer and seen, represents an attempt to understand what ought to be obvious: everything we do, we do with and through our bodies. That is, every perception is a bodily perception, which can easily be demonstrated when we reflect on the simple fact that up and down, in and out, near and far are consequences of embodied perspectives relative to the location of our bodies in space. For example, Merleau-Ponty notes that the anchoring of the body in space, or "the laying down of first co-ordinates" is an essential part of human existence. Our understanding of space, he argues, originates from our embodied experience. Indeed, our actions take place in the world (that is, in space), and it is through human movement that we discover our spatiality, both bodily and worldly. Our bodies belong to space, and space belongs to our bodies.[2] This insight leads to one of Merleau-Ponty's most important discoveries: that the necessarily ambiguous nature of embodied experience is even more evident when we recognize that humans can only know the world from partial and specifically situated perspectives (i.e., since we know the world through our bodies, we cannot know all of it from everywhere at once). While it may seem as though embodied, and therefore partial, perspectives of the world would limit what we can know, Merleau-Ponty proposes another perspective. Each human subject, because her or his perspective is always partial, must necessarily sort through a constant stream of information regarding the state of the world at any given moment. This is what he means when he claims that the world is "pregnant" with meaning: We know the world through an ongoing series of embodied experiences. There is, therefore, no necessary limit to how body and world will interact; hence, there is no necessary limit to what we can know of the world.

An important consequence, for Merleau-Ponty, of our embodied knowledge of the world is the realization that human consciousness is not a phenomenon confined to isolated, individual human subjects, but is, rather, deeply entangled with other subjectivities, that is, with the consciousness of others. We are not as a dualist perspective would have it—merely minds and bodies in the world, disconnected and alienated from other entities. Instead, Merleau-Ponty shows that the *inter*subjective character of conscious experiences produces the provisional (yet nonetheless concrete) nature of embodied human being by announcing a world in which we are already deeply entangled with other, bodily subjects. This, in turn, suggests that consciousness itself, because it is entangled, situated, and embodied, can be understood as bearing a deeply erotic potential—a potential for union and interaction at the very basis of our awareness. Furthermore, since Merleau-Ponty consistently rejects any sort of Cartesian split between mind and body, it must be the case that bodies are also marked by the possibilities of the erotic.

These points concerning the erotic potential borne by human bodies become clearer when we consider the simple experience of touching and being touched. We are, says

Merleau-Ponty, the always provisional product of the "intertwining of vision and movement."[3] He names the intertwining of world and body the "flesh." This difficult but central term in his later philosophy directs us back to his early research in the *Phenomenology of Perception* and the emphasis on vision as our primary sensory encounter with the world (although he realizes that the other senses play vital roles in our embodied relationships with the world). The flesh, for Merleau-Ponty, is both surface and, to some extent, container. It is a "chiasm," a crisscrossing web of relationships that interweave individual bodies (actual flesh) with the "body of the world." The chiasm represents a constant back-and-forth movement between human being and the world that manifests itself as a unitary experience—not unlike the single visual image that is formed by the "optic chiasm" between the right and left eyes. Most importantly, it should be noted, again, that the relationship between human bodies and world is reciprocal. Merleau-Ponty conceives of the chiasm, the intertwined reciprocity of world and bodies, as perception itself. Thus the primacy of the body and the erotic, sensual nature of human experience represent a fundamental point of departure in his philosophy from the overly objectified and disembodied tendencies in mainstream Western analytic traditions.

The idea of "Flesh" as an expression of our erotic, embodied nature constitutes a problem of utmost importance for philosophical inquiry. The difficulty and the richness of the problem are suggested by the November, 1960 entry to his "Working Notes," where Merleau-Ponty writes:

> The things touch me as I touch them and touch myself: flesh of the world—distinct from my flesh: the double inscription of outside and inside. The inside receives without flesh: not a 'psychic state,' but intra-corporeal, reverse of the outside that my body shows to things.[4]

Rejecting in his later philosophy, as he had in the earlier writings, the disembodied metaphysical assumptions that he believed undermined Western thought, Merleau-Ponty's explication of "flesh" seems to articulate eloquently the embodied character of human being in the world. His early death leaves unfinished the task of mapping out the intricate character of our fleshy entanglement with the world. This will not be a simple task since the world constantly imposes itself on us through the senses. The crisscrossing, the chiasm of body and world is always a fact that we cannot eliminate from our experiences. Desire, for instance, may be something we choose to engage consciously or actively to ignore. What we may not do, however, is choose to disengage from the erotic, desire-laden, and embodied character of human being in the world. This is where Merleau-Ponty's work prematurely ends, just as it is beginning to map the deepest relationships of human being and world.

WDC

QUESTIONS

1. How would you explain Merleau-Ponty's concept of "flesh?"
2. Why does Merleau-Ponty say that "our vision forms in the heart of the visible?"
3. Why does Merleau-Ponty believe that there is a "fundamental narcissism of all vision"?
4. Explain how acts such as one hand touching the other are "movements that incorporate themselves into the universe."
5. Flesh is not an empirical idea. Why?

ENDNOTES

1. The idea of dualism can be traced back to the origins of Greek philosophy in pre-Socratic thought, as well as that of Plato (see the "Allegory of the Cave" in Plato's *Republic* for an example of how education is, in part, at least, a matter of leaving behind the delusions of the flesh for the rarified heights of intellectual knowledge). In modern philosophical treatments, dualism often arises as a problem growing out of the work of René Descartes (see *Meditations* and *Discourse on Method*).
2. Merleau-Ponty, *Phenomenology of Perception,* p. 100.
3. Merleau-Ponty, *Primacy of Perception,* p. 162.
4. Merleau-Ponty, "Working Notes," from *The Visible and the Invisible,* p. 261.

SELECTED BIBLIOGRAPHY

Bennan, J.F. *The Philosophy of Merleau-Ponty.* New York: Harcourt Brace and World, 1967.

Dillon, M.C. *Merleau-Ponty's Ontology,* 2d ed. Evanston, Ill.: Northwestern University Press, 1988.

Merleau-Ponty, Maurice. *Phenomenology of Perception,* trans. C. Smith. London: Routledge & Kegan Paul, 1962.

Merleau-Ponty, Maurice. *Primacy of Perception,* ed. and intro. James M. Edie. Evanston, Ill.: Northwestern University Press, 1964.

Merleau-Ponty, Maurice. *Sense and Non-Sense,* trans. H. Dreyfus. Evanston, Ill.: Northwestern University Press, 1964.

Merleau-Ponty, Maurice. *The Visible and the Invisible,* trans. Alphonso Lingis, ed. Claude Lefort. Evanston, Ill.: Northwestern University Press, 1968.

from *The Visible and the Invisible*

Maurice Merleau-Ponty

THE INTERTWINING—THE CHIASM

If it is true that as soon as philosophy declares itself to be reflection or coincidence it prejudges what it will find, then once again it must recommence everything, reject the instruments reflection and intuition had provided themselves, and install itself in a locus where they have not yet been distinguished, in experiences that have not yet been "worked over," that offer us all at once, pell-mell, both "subject" and "object," both existence and essence, and hence give philosophy resources to redefine them. Seeing, speaking, even thinking (with certain reservations, for as soon as we distinguish thought from speaking absolutely we are already in the order of reflection), are experiences of this kind, both irrecusable and enigmatic. They have a name in all languages, but a name which in all of them also conveys significations in tufts, thickets of proper meanings and figurative meanings, so that, unlike those of science, not one of these names clarifies by attributing to what is named a circumscribed signification. Rather, they are the repeated index, the insistent reminder of a mystery as familiar as it is unexplained, of a light which, illuminating the rest, remains at its source in obscurity. If we could rediscover within the exercise of seeing and speaking some of the living references that assign them such a destiny in a language, perhaps they would teach us how to form our new instruments, and first of all to understand our research, our interrogation, themselves.

The visible about us seems to rest in itself. It is as though our vision were formed in the heart of the visible, or as though there were between it and us an intimacy as close as between the sea and the strand. And yet it is not possible that we blend into it, nor that it passes into us, for then the vision would vanish at the moment of formation, by disappearance of the seer or of the visible. What there is then are not things first identical with themselves, which would then offer themselves to the seer, nor is there a seer who is first empty and who, afterward, would open himself to them—but something to which we could not be closer than by palpating it with our look, things we could not dream of seeing "all naked" because the gaze itself envelops them, clothes them with its own flesh. Whence does it happen that in so doing it leaves them in their place, that the vision we acquire of them seems to us to come from them, and that to be seen is for them but a degradation of their eminent being? What is this talisman of color, this singular virtue of the visible that makes it, held at the end of the gaze, nonetheless much more than a correlative of my vision, such that it imposes my vision upon me as a continuation of its own sovereign existence? How does it happen that my look, enveloping them, does not hide them, and, finally, that, veiling them, it unveils them?[1]

---

[1]EDITOR: Here in the course of the text itself, these lines are inserted: "it is that the look is itself incorporation of the seer into the visible, quest for itself, which *is of it,* within the visible—it is that the visible of the world is not an envelope of *quale,* but what is between the qualia, a connective tissue of exterior and interior horizons—it is as flesh offered to flesh that the visible has its aseity, and that it is mine—The flesh as *Sichtigkeit* and generality. → whence vision is question and response. . . . The openness through flesh: the two leaves of my body and the leaves of the visible world. . . . It is between these intercalated leaves that there is visibility. . . . My body model of the things and the things model of my body: the body bound to the world through all its parts, up against it → all this means: the world, the flesh not as fact or sum of facts, but as the locus of an inscription of truth: the false crossed out, not nullified."

We must first understand that this red under my eyes is not, as is always said, a *quale,* a pellicle of being without thickness, a message at the same time indecipherable and evident, which one has or has not received, but of which, if one has received it, one knows all there is to know, and of which in the end there is nothing to say. It requires a focusing, however brief; it emerges from a less precise, more general redness, in which my gaze was caught, into which it sank, before—as we put it so aptly—*fixing* it. And, now that I have fixed it, if my eyes penetrate into it, into its fixed structure, or if they start to wander round about again, the *quale* resumes its atmospheric existence. Its precise form is bound up with a certain wooly, metallic, or porous [?] configuration or texture, and the *quale* itself counts for very little compared with these participations. Claudel has a phrase saying that a certain blue of the sea is so blue that only blood would be more red. The color is yet a variant in another dimension of variation, that of its relations with the surroundings: this red is what it is only by connecting up from its place with other reds about it, with which it forms a constellation, or with other colors it dominates or that dominate it, that it attracts or that attract it, that it repels or that repel it. In short, it is a certain node in the woof of the simultaneous and the successive. It is a concretion of visibility, it is not an atom. The red dress a fortiori holds with all its fibers onto the fabric of the visible, and thereby onto a fabric of invisible being. A punctuation in the field of red things, which includes the tiles of roof tops, the flags of gatekeepers and of the Revolution, certain terrains near Aix or in Madagascar, it is also a punctuation in the field of red garments, which includes, along with the dresses of women, robes of professors, bishops, and advocate generals, and also in the field of adornments and that of uniforms. And its red literally is not the same as it appears in one constellation or in the other, as the pure essence of the Revolution of 1917 precipitates in it, or that of the eternal feminine, or that of the public prosecutor, or that of the gypsies dressed like hussars who reigned twenty-five years ago over an inn on the Champs-Elysées. A certain red is also a fossil drawn up from the depths of imaginary worlds. If we took all these participations into account, we would recognize that a naked color, and in general a visible, is not a chunk of absolutely hard, indivisible being, offered all naked to a vision which could be only total or null, but is rather a sort of straits between exterior horizons and interior horizons ever gaping open, something that comes to touch lightly and makes diverse regions of the colored or visible world resound at the distances, a certain differentiation, an ephemeral modulation of this world—less a color or a thing, therefore, than a difference between things and colors, a momentary crystallization of colored being or of visibility. Between the alleged colors and visibles, we would find anew the tissue that lines them, sustains them, nourishes them, and which for its part is not a thing, but a possibility, a latency, and a *flesh* of things.

If we turn now to the seer, we will find that this is no analogy or vague comparison and must be taken literally. The look, we said, envelops, palpates, espouses the visible things. As though it were in a relation of pre-established harmony with them, as though it knew them before knowing them, it moves in its own way with its abrupt and imperious style, and yet the views taken are not desultory—I do not look at a chaos, but at things—so that finally one cannot say if it is the look or if it is the things that command. What is this prepossession of the visible, this art of interrogating it according to its own wishes, this inspired exegesis? We would perhaps find the answer in the tactile palpation where the questioner and the questioned are closer, and of which, after all, the palpation of the eye is a remarkable variant. How does it happen that I give to my hands, in particular, that degree, that rate, and that direction of movement that are capable of making me feel the textures of the sleek and the rough? Between the exploration and what it will teach me, between my movements and what I touch, there must exist some relationship by principle, some kinship, according to which they are not only, like the pseudopods of the amoeba, vague and ephemeral deformations of the corporeal space, but the initiation to and the opening upon a tactile world. This can happen only if my hand, while it is felt from within, is also accessible from without, itself tangible, for my other hand, for example, if it takes its place among the things it touches, is in a sense one of them, opens finally upon a tangible being of which it is also a part. Through this crisscrossing within it of the touching and the tangible, its own movements incorporate themselves into the universe they interrogate, are recorded on the same map as it; the two systems are applied upon one another, as the two halves of an orange. It is no different for the vision—except, it is said, that here the exploration and the information it gathers do not belong "to the same sense." But this delimitation of the senses is crude. Already in the "touch" we have just found three distinct experiences which subtend one another, three dimensions which overlap but are distinct: a touching of the sleek and of the rough, a touching of the things—a passive sentiment of the body and of its space—and finally a veritable touching of the touch, when my right hand touches my left hand while it is palpating the things, where the "touching subject" passes over to the rank of the touched, descends into the things, such that the touch is formed in the midst of the world and as it were in the things. Between the massive sentiment I have of the sack in which I am enclosed, and the control from without that my hand exercises over my hand, there is as much difference as between the movements of my eyes and the changes they produce in the visible. And as, conversely, every experience of the visible has always been given to me within the context of the movements of the look, the visible spectacle belongs to the touch neither more nor less than do the "tactile qualities." We must habituate ourselves to think that every visible is cut out in the tangible, every tactile being in some manner promised to visibility, and that there is encroachment, infringement, not only between the touched and the touching, but also between the tangible and the visible, which is encrusted in it, as, conversely, the tangible itself is not a nothingness of visibility, is not without visual existence. Since the same body sees and touches, visible and tangible belong to the same world. It is a marvel too little noticed that every movement of my eyes—even more, every displacement of my body—has its place in the same visible universe that I itemize and explore with them, as, conversely, every vision takes place somewhere in the tactile space. There is double and crossed situating of the visible in the tangible and of the tangible in the visible; the two maps are complete, and yet they do not merge into one. The two parts are total parts and yet are not superposable.

Hence, without even entering into the implications proper to the seer and the visible, we know that, since vision is a palpation with the look, it must also be inscribed in the order of being that it discloses to us; he who looks must not himself be foreign to the world that he looks at. As soon as I see, it is necessary that the vision (as is so well indicated by the double meaning of the word) be doubled with a complementary vision or with another vision: myself seen from without, such as another would see me, installed in the midst of the visible, occupied in considering it from a certain spot. For the moment we shall not examine how far this identity of the seer and the visible goes, if we have a complete experience of it, or if there is something missing, and what it is. It suffices for us for the moment to note that he who sees cannot possess the visible unless he is possessed by it, unless he *is of it,** unless, by principle, according to what is required by the articulation of the look with the things, he is one of the visibles, capable, by a singular reversal, of seeing them—he who is one of them.†

We understand then why we see the things themselves, in their places, where they are, according to their being which is indeed more than their being-perceived—and why at the same time we are separated from them by all the thickness of the look and of the body; it is that this distance is not the contrary of this proximity, it is deeply consonant with it, it is synonymous with it. It is that the thickness of flesh between the seer and the thing is constitutive for the thing of its visibility as for the seer of his corporeity; it is not an obstacle between them, it is their means of communication. It is for the same reason that I am at the heart of the visible and that I am far from it: because it has thickness and is thereby naturally destined to be seen by a body. What is indefinable in the *quale,* in the color, is nothing else than a brief, peremptory manner of giving in one sole something, in one sole tone of being, visions past, visions to come, by whole clusters. I who see have my own depth also, being backed up by this same visible which I see and which, I know very well, closes in behind me. The thickness of the body, far from rivaling that of the world, is on the contrary the sole means I have to go unto the heart of the things, by making myself a world and by making them flesh.

The body interposed is not itself a thing, an interstitial matter, a connective tissue, but a *sensible for itself,* which means, not that absurdity: color

that sees itself, surface that touches itself—but this paradox [?]: a set of colors and surfaces inhabited by a touch, a vision, hence an *exemplar sensible,* which offers to him who inhabits it and senses it the wherewithal to sense everything that resembles himself on the outside, such that, caught up in the tissue of the things, it draws it entirely to itself, incorporates it, and, with the same movement, communicates to the things upon which it closes over that identity without superposition, that difference without contradiction, that divergence between the within and the without that constitutes its natal secret.[2] The body unites us directly with the things through its own ontogenesis, by welding to one another the two outlines of which it is made, its two laps: the sensible mass it is and the mass of the sensible wherein it is born by segregation and upon which, as seer, it remains open. It is the body and it alone, because it is a two-dimensional being, that can bring us to the things themselves, which are themselves not flat beings but beings in depth, inaccessible to a subject that would survey them from above, open to him alone that, if it be possible, would coexist with them in the same world. When we speak of the flesh of the visible, we do not mean to do anthropology, to describe a world covered over with all our own projections, leaving aside what it can be under the human mask. Rather, we mean that carnal being, as a being of depths, of several leaves or several faces, a being in latency, and a presentation of a certain absence, is a prototype of Being, of which our body, the sensible sentient, is a very remarkable variant, but

---

*The *Uerpräsentierbarkeit* is the flesh.
†The visible is not a tangible zero, the tangible is not a zero of visibility (relation of encroachment).

[2]EDITOR: Here, in the course of the text itself, between brackets, these lines are inserted: "One can say that we perceive the things themselves, that we are the world that thinks itself—or that the world is at the heart of our flesh. In any case, once a body-world relationship is recognized, there is a ramification of my body and a ramification of the world and a correspondence between its inside and my outside, between my inside and its outside."

whose constitutive paradox already lies in every visible. For already the cube assembles within itself incompossible *visibilia,* as my body is at once phenomenal body and objective body, and if finally it is, it, like my body, is by a tour de force. What we call a visible is, we said, a quality pregnant with a texture, the surface of a depth, a cross section upon a massive being, a grain or corpuscle borne by a wave of Being. Since the total visible is always behind, or after, or between the aspects we see of it, there is access to it only through an experience which, like it, is wholly outside of itself. It is thus, and not as the bearer of a knowing subject, that our body commands the visible for us, but it does not explain it, does not clarify it, it only concentrates the mystery of its scattered visibility; and it is indeed a paradox of Being, not a paradox of man, that we are dealing with here. To be sure, one can reply that, between the two "sides" of our body, the body as sensible and the body as sentient (what in the past we called objective body and phenomenal body), rather than a spread, there is the abyss that separates the In Itself from the For Itself. It is a problem—and we will not avoid it—to determine how the sensible sentient can also be thought. But here, seeking to form our first concepts in such a way as to avoid the classical impasses, we do not have to honor the difficulties that they may present when confronted with a *cogito,* which itself has to be re-examined. Yes or no: do we have a body— that is, not a permanent object of thought, but a flesh that suffers when it is wounded, hands that touch? We know: hands do not suffice for touch— but to decide for this reason alone that our hands do not touch, and to relegate them to the world of objects or of instruments, would be, in acquiescing to the bifurcation of subject and object, to forego in advance the understanding of the sensible and to deprive ourselves of its lights. We propose on the contrary to take it literally to begin with. We say therefore that our body is a being of two leaves,

from one side a thing among things and otherwise what sees them and touches them; we say, because it is evident, that it unites these two properties within itself, and its double belongingness to the order of the "object" and to the order of the "subject" reveals to us quite unexpected relations between the two orders. It cannot be by incomprehensible accident that the body has this double reference; it teaches us that each calls for the other. For if the body is a thing among things, it is so in a stronger and deeper sense than they: in the sense that, we said, it *is of them,* and this means that it detaches itself upon them, and, accordingly, detaches itself from them. It is not simply a thing *seen* in fact (I do not see my back), it is visible by right, it falls under a vision that is both ineluctable and deferred. Conversely, if it touches and sees, this is not because it would have the visibles before itself as objects: they are about it, they even enter into its enclosure, they are within it, they line its looks and its hands inside and outside. If it touches them and sees them, this is only because, being of their family, itself visible and tangible, it uses its own being as a means to participate in theirs, because each of the two beings is an archetype for the other, because the body belongs to the order of the things as the world is universal flesh. One should not even say, as we did a moment ago, that the body is made up of two leaves, of which the one, that of the "sensible," is bound up with the rest of the world. There are not in it two leaves or two layers; fundamentally it is neither thing seen only nor seer only, it is Visibility sometimes wandering and sometimes reassembled. And as such it is not in the world, it does not detain its view of the world as within a private garden: it sees the world itself, the world of everybody, and without having to leave "itself," because it is wholly—because its hands, its eyes, are nothing else than—this reference of a visible, a tangible-standard to all those whose resemblance it bears and whose evidence it gathers, by a magic that is the vision, the touch themselves. To speak of leaves or of layers is still to flatten and to juxtapose, under the reflective gaze, what coexists in the living and upright body. If one wants metaphors, it would be better to say that the body sensed and the body sentient are as the obverse and the reverse, or again, as two segments of one sole circular course which goes above from left to right and below from right to left, but which is but one sole movement in its two phases. And everything said about the sensed body pertains to the whole of the sensible of which it is a part, and to the world. If the body is one sole body in its two phases, it incorporates into itself the whole of the sensible and with the same movement incorporates itself into a "Sensible in itself." We have to reject the age-old assumptions that put the body in the world and the seer in the body, or, conversely, the world and the body in the seer as in a box. Where are we to put the limit between the body and the world, since the world is flesh? Where in the body are we to put the seer, since evidently there is in the body only "shadows stuffed with organs," that is, more of the visible? The world seen is not "in" my body, and my body is not "in" the visible world ultimately: as flesh applied to a flesh, the world neither surrounds it nor is surrounded by it. A participation in and kinship with the visible, the vision neither envelops it nor is enveloped by it definitively. The superficial pellicle of the visible is only for my vision and for my body. But the depth beneath this surface contains my body and hence contains my vision. My body as a visible thing is contained within the full spectacle. But my seeing body subtends this visible body, and all the visibles with it. There is reciprocal insertion and intertwining of one in the other. Or rather, if, as once again we must, we eschew the thinking by planes and perspectives, there are two circles, or two vortexes, or two spheres, concentric when I live naïvely, and

as soon as I question myself, the one slightly decentered with respect to the other. . . .

We have to ask ourselves what exactly we have found with this strange adhesion of the seer and the visible. There is vision, touch, when a certain visible, a certain tangible, turns back upon the whole of the visible, the whole of the tangible, of which it is a part, or when suddenly it finds itself *surrounded* by them, or when between it and them, and through their commerce, is formed a Visibility, a Tangible in itself, which belong properly neither to the body qua fact nor to the world qua fact—as upon two mirrors facing one another where two indefinite series of images set in one another arise which belong really to neither of the two surfaces, since each is only the rejoinder of the other, and which therefore form a couple, a couple more real than either of them. Thus since the seer is caught up in what he sees, it is still himself he sees: there is a fundamental narcissism of all vision. And thus, for the same reason, the vision he exercises, he also undergoes from the things, such that, as many painters have said, I feel myself looked at by the things, my activity is equally passivity—which is the second and more profound sense of the narcissim: not to see in the outside, as the others see it, the contour of a body one inhabits, but especially to be seen by the outside, to exist within it, to emigrate into it, to be seduced, captivated, alienated by the phantom, so that the seer and the visible reciprocate one another and we no longer know which sees and which is seen. It is this Visibility, this generality of the Sensible in itself, this anonymity innate to Myself that we have previously called flesh, and one knows there is no name in traditional philosophy to designate it. The flesh is not matter, in the sense of corpuscles of being which would add up or continue on one another to form beings. Nor is the visible (the things as well as my own body) some "psychic" material that would be—God knows how—brought into being by the things factually existing and acting on my factual body. In general, it is not a fact or a sum of facts "material" or "spiritual." Nor is it a representation for a mind: a mind could not be captured by its own representations; it would rebel against this insertion into the visible which is essential to the seer. The flesh is not matter, is not mind, is not substance. To designate it, we should need the old term "element," in the sense it was used to speak of water, air, earth, and fire, that is, in the sense of a *general thing*, midway between the spatio-temporal individual and the idea, a sort of incarnate principle that brings a style of being wherever there is a fragment of being. The flesh is in this sense an "element" of Being. Not a fact or a sum of facts, and yet adherent to *location* and to the *now*. Much more: the inauguration of the *where* and the *when*, the possibility and exigency for the fact; in a word: facticity, what makes the fact be a fact. And, at the same time, what makes the facts have meaning, makes the fragmentary facts dispose themselves about "something." For if there is flesh, that is, if the hidden face of the cube radiates forth somewhere as well as does the face I have under my eyes, and coexists with it, and if I who see the cube also belong to the visible, I am visible from elsewhere, and if I and the cube are together caught up in one same "element" (should we say of the seer, or of the visible?), this cohesion, this visibility by principle, prevails over every momentary discordance. In advance every vision or very partial visible that would here definitively come to naught is not nullified (which would leave a gap in its place), but, what is better, it is replaced by a more exact vision and a more exact visible, according to the principle of visibility, which, as though through a sort of abhorrence of a vacuum, already invokes the true vision and the true visible, not only as substitutes for their errors, but also as their expla-

nation, their relative justification, so that they are, as Husserl says so aptly, not erased, but "crossed out." . . . such are the extravagant consequences to which we are led when we take seriously, when we question, vision. And it is, to be sure, possible to refrain from doing so and to move on, but we would simply find again, confused, indistinct, non-clarified, scraps of this ontology of the visible mixed up with all our theories of knowledge, and in particular with those that serve, desultorily, as vehicles of science. We are, to be sure, not finished ruminating over them. Our concern in this preliminary outline was only to catch sight of this strange domain to which interrogation, properly so-called, gives access. . . .

But this domain, one rapidly realizes, is unlimited. If we can show that the flesh is an ultimate notion, that it is not the union or compound of two substances, but thinkable by itself, if there is a relation of the visible with itself that traverses me and constitutes me as a seer, this circle which I do not form, which forms me, this coiling over of the visible upon the visible, can traverse, animate other bodies as well as my own. And if I was able to understand how this wave arises within me, how the visible which is yonder is simultaneously my landscape, I can understand a fortiori that elsewhere it also closes over upon itself and that there are other landscapes besides my own. If it lets itself be captivated by one of its fragments, the principle of captation is established, the field open for other Narcissus, for an "intercorporeity." If my left hand can touch my right hand while it palpates the tangibles, can touch it touching, can turn its palpation back upon it, why, when touching the hand of another, would I not touch in it the same power to espouse the things that I have touched in my own? It is true that "the things" in question are my own, that the whole operation takes place (as we say) "in me," within my landscape, whereas the problem is to institute another landscape. When one of my hands touches the other, the world of each opens upon that of the other because the operation is reversible at will, because they both belong (as we say) to one sole space of consciousness, because one sole man touches one sole thing through both hands. But for my two hands to open upon one sole world, it does not suffice that they be given to one sole *consciousness*—or if that were the case the difficulty before us would disappear: since other bodies would be known by me in the same way as would be my own, they and I would still be dealing with the same world. No, my two hands touch the same things because they are the hands of one same body. And yet each of them has its own tactile experience. If nonetheless they have to do with one sole tangible, it is because there exists a very peculiar relation from one to the other, across the corporeal space—like that holding between my two eyes—making of my hands one sole organ of experience, as it makes of my two eyes the channels of one sole Cyclopean vision. A difficult relation to conceive—since one eye, one hand, are capable of vision, of touch, and since what has to be comprehended is that these visions, these touches, these little subjectivities, these "consciousnesses of . . . ," could be assembled like flowers into a bouquet, when each being "consciousness of," being For Itself, reduces the others into objects. We will get out of the difficulty only by renouncing the bifurcation of the "consciousness of" and the object, by admitting that my synergic body is not an object, that it assembles into a cluster the "consciousnesses" adherent to its hands, to its eyes, by an operation that is in relation to them lateral, transversal; that "my consciousness" is not the synthetic, uncreated, centrifugal unity of a multitude of "consciousnesses of . . ." which would be centrifugal like it is, that it is sustained, subtended, by the prereflective and preobjective unity of my body. This means that while each monocu-lar vision, each touching with one sole hand has its own visible, its tactile, each is bound to every other vision, to every other touch; it is bound in such a way as to make up with them the experience of one sole body before one sole world, through a possibility for reversion, reconversion of its language into theirs, transfer, and reversal, according to which the little private world of each is not juxtaposed to the world of all the others, but surrounded by it, levied off from it, and all together are a Sentient in general before a Sensible in general. Now why would this generality, which constitutes the unity of my body, not open it to other bodies? The handshake too is reversible; I can feel myself touched as well and at the same time as touching, and surely there does not exist some huge animal whose organs our bodies would be, as, for each of our bodies, our hands, our eyes are the organs. Why would not the synergy exist among different organisms, if it is possible within each? Their landscapes interweave, their actions and their passions fit together exactly: this is possible as soon as we no longer make belongingness to one same "consciousness" the primordial definition of sensibility, and as soon as we rather understand it as the return of the visible upon itself, a carnal adherence of the sentient to the sensed and of the sensed to the sentient. For, as overlapping and fission, identity and difference, it brings to birth a ray of natural light that illuminates all flesh and not only my own. It is said that the colors, the tactile reliefs given to the other, are for me an absolute mystery, forever inaccessible. This is not completely true; for me to have not an idea, an image, nor a representation, but as it were the imminent experience of them, it suffices that I look at a landscape, that I speak of it with someone. Then, through the concordant operation of his body and my own, what I see passes into him, this individual green of the meadow under my eyes invades his vision without quitting my own, I recognize in my green his green, as the customs officer recognizes suddenly in a traveler the man whose description he had been given. There is here no problem of the *alter ego* because it is not *I* who sees, not *he* who sees, because an anonymous visibility inhabits both of us, a vision in general, in virtue of that primordial property that belongs to the flesh, being here and now, of radiating everywhere and forever, being an individual, of being also a dimension and a universal.

What is open to us, therefore, with the reversibility of the visible and the tangible, is—if not yet the incorporeal—at least an intercorporeal being, a presumptive domain of the visible and the tangible, which extends further than the things I touch and see at present.

There is a circle of the touched and the touching, the touched takes hold of the touching; there is a circle of the visible and the seeing, the seeing is not without visible existence;[3] there is even an inscription of the touching in the visible, of the seeing in the tangible—and the converse; there is finally a propagation of these exchanges to all the bodies of the same type and of the same style which I see and touch—and this by virtue of the fundamental fission or segregation of the sentient and the sensible which, laterally, makes the organs of my body communicate and founds transitivity from one body to another.

As soon as we see other seers, we no longer have before us only the look without a pupil, the plate glass of the things with that feeble reflection, that phantom of ourselves they evoke by designating a place among themselves whence we see them: henceforth, through other eyes we are for ourselves fully visible; that lacuna where our eyes, our back, lie is filled, filled still by the visible, of which we are not the titulars. To believe that, to bring a vision that is not our own into account, it is to be sure inevitably, it is always from the unique treasury of our own vision that we draw, and experience therefore can teach us nothing that would not be outlined in our own vision. But what is proper to the visible is, we said, to be the surface of an inexhaustible depth: this is what makes it able to be open to visions other than our own. In being realized, they therefore bring out the limits of our factual vision, they betray the solipsist illusion that consists in thinking that every going beyond is a surpassing accomplished by oneself. For the first time, the seeing that I am is for me really visible; for the first time I appear to myself completely turned inside out under my own eyes. For the first time also, my movements no longer proceed unto the things to be seen, to be touched, or unto my own body occupied in seeing and touching them, but they address themselves to the body in general and for itself (whether it be my own or that of another), because for the first time, through the other body, I see that, in its coupling with the flesh of the world, the body contributes more than it receives, adding to the world that I see the treasure necessary for what the other body sees. For the first time, the body no longer couples itself up with the world, it clasps another body, applying [itself to it][4] carefully with its whole extension, forming tirelessly with its hands the strange statue which in its turn gives everything it receives; the body is lost outside of the world and its goals, fascinated by the unique occupation of floating in Being with another life, of making itself the outside of its inside and the inside of its outside. And henceforth movement, touch, vision, applying themselves to the other and to themselves, return toward their source and, in the patient and silent labor of desire, begin the paradox of expression.

---

[3]EDITOR: Here is inserted between brackets, in the course of the text itself, the note: "what are these adhesions compared with those of the voice and the hearing?"

[4]EDITOR: These words, which we reintroduce into the text, had been erased apparently by error.

Yet this flesh that one sees and touches is not all there is to flesh, nor this massive corporeity all there is to the body. The reversibility that defines the flesh exists in other fields; it is even incomparably more agile there and capable of weaving relations between bodies that this time will not only enlarge, but will pass definitively beyond the circle of the visible. Among my movements, there are some that go nowhere—that do not even go find in the other body their resemblance or their archetype: these are the facial movements, many gestures, and especially those strange movements of the throat and mouth that form the cry and the voice. Those movements end in sounds and I hear them. Like crystal, like metal and many other substances, I am a sonorous being, but I hear my own vibration from within; as Malraux said, I hear myself with my throat. In this, as he also has said, I am incomparable; my voice is bound to the mass of my own life as is the voice of no one else. But if I am close enough to the other who speaks to hear his breath and feel his effervescence and his fatigue, I almost witness, in him as in myself, the awesome birth of vociferation. As there is a reflexivity of the touch, of sight, and of the touch-vision system, there is a reflexivity of the movements of phonation and of hearing; they have their sonorous inscription, the vociferations have in me their motor echo. This new reversibility and the emergence of the flesh as expression are the point of insertion of speaking and thinking in the world of silence.[5]

At the frontier of the mute or solipsist world where, in the presence of other seers, my visible is confirmed as an exemplar of a universal visibility, we reach a second or figurative meaning of vision, which will be the *intuitus mentis* or idea, a sublimation of the flesh, which will be mind or thought. But the factual presence of other bodies could not produce thought or the idea if its seed were not in my own body. Thought is a relationship with oneself and with the world as well as a relationship with the other; hence it is established in the three dimensions at the same time. And it must be brought to appear directly in the infrastructure of vision. Brought to appear, we say, and not brought to birth: for we are leaving in suspense for the moment the question whether it would not be already implicated there. Manifest as it is that feeling is dispersed in my body, that for example my hand touches, and that consequently we may not in advance ascribe feeling to a thought of which it would be but a mode—it yet would be absurd to conceive the touch as a colony of assembled tactile experiences. We are not here proposing any empiricist genesis of thought: we are asking precisely what is that central vision that joins the scattered visions, that unique touch that governs the whole tactile life of my body as a unit, that *I think* that must be able to accompany all our experiences. We are proceeding toward the center, we are seeking to comprehend how there is a center, what the unity consists of, we are not saying that it is a sum or a result; and if we make the thought appear upon an infrastructure of vision, this is only

---

[5]EDITOR: Inserted here between brackets: "in what sense we have not yet introduced thinking: to be sure, we are not in the in itself. From the moment we said *seeing, visible,* and described the dehiscence of the sensible, we were, if one likes, in the order of thought. We were not in it in the sense that the thinking we have introduced was *there is,* and not it *appears to me that . . .* (appearing that would make up the whole of being, self-appearing). Our thesis is that this *there is* by inherence is necessary, and our problem to show that thought, in the restrictive sense (pure signification, thought of seeing and

of feeling), is comprehensible only as the accomplishment by other means of the will of the *there is,* by sublimation of the *there is* and realization of an invisible that is exactly the reverse of the visible, the power of the visible. Thus between sound and meaning, speech and what it means to say, there is still the relation of reversibility, and no question of priority, since the exchange of words is exactly the differentiation of which the thought is the integral."

in virtue of the uncontested evidence that one must see or feel in some way in order to think, that every thought known to us occurs to a flesh.

Once again, the flesh we are speaking of is not matter. It is the coiling over of the visible upon the seeing body, of the tangible upon the touching body, which is attested in particular when the body sees itself, touches itself seeing and touching the things, such that, simultaneously, *as* tangible it descends among them, *as* touching it dominates them all and draws this relationship and even this double relationship from itself, by dehiscence or fission of its own mass. This concentration of the visibles about one of them, or this bursting forth of the mass of the body toward the things, which makes a vibration of my skin become the sleek and the rough, makes me *follow with my eyes* the movements and the contours of the things themselves, this magical relation, this pact between them and me according to which I lend them my body in order that they inscribe upon it and give me their resemblance, this fold, this central cavity of the visible which is my vision, these two mirror arrangements of the seeing and the visible, the touching and the touched, form a close-bound system that I count on, define a vision in general and a constant style of visibility from which I cannot detach myself, even when a particular vision turns out to be illusory, for I remain certain in that case that in looking closer I would have had the true vision, and that in any case, whether it be this one or another, *there is a true vision.* The flesh (of the world or my own) is not contingency, chaos, but a texture that returns to itself and conforms to itself. I will never see my own retinas, but if one thing is certain for me it is that *one* would find at the bottom of my eyeballs those dull and secret membranes. And finally, I believe it—I believe that I have a man's senses, a human body—because the spectacle of the world that is my own, and which, to judge by our confrontations, does not notably differ from that of the others, with me as with them refers with evidence to typical dimensions of visibility, and finally to a virtual focus of vision, to a detector also typical, so that at the joints of the opaque body and the opaque world there is a ray of generality and of light. Conversely, when, starting from the body, I ask how it makes itself a seer, when I examine the critical region of the aesthesiological body, everything comes to pass (as we have shown in an earlier work[6]) as though the visible body remained incomplete, gaping open; as though the physiology of vision did not succeed in closing the nervous functioning in upon itself, since the movements of fixation, of convergence, are suspended upon the advent to the body of a visible world for which they were supposed to furnish the explanation; as though, therefore, the vision came suddenly to give to the material means and instruments left here and there in the working area a convergence which they were waiting for; as though, through all these channels, all these prepared but unemployed circuits, the current that will traverse them was rendered probable, in the long run inevitable: the current making of an embryo a newborn infant, of a visible a seer, and of a body a mind, or at least a flesh. In spite of all our substantialist ideas, the seer is being premeditated in counterpoint in the embryonic development; through a labor upon itself the visible body provides for the hollow whence a vision will come, inaugurates the long maturation at whose term suddenly it will see, that is, will be visible for itself, will institute the interminable gravitation, the indefatigable metamorphosis of the seeing and the visible whose principle is posed and which gets underway with the first vision. What we are calling flesh, this interiorly worked-over mass, has no name in any philosophy. As the formative medium

---

[6] *The Structure of Behavior* [trans. Alden L. Fisher (Boston, 1963)].

of the object and the subject, it is not the atom of being, the hard in itself that resides in a unique place and moment: one can indeed say of my body that it is not *elsewhere,* but one cannot say that it is *here* or *now* in the sense that objects are; and yet my vision does not soar over them, it is not the being that is wholly knowing, for it has its own inertia, its ties. We must not think the flesh starting from substances, from body and spirit—for then it would be the union of contradictories—but we must think it, as we said, as an element, as the concrete emblem of a general manner of being. To begin with, we spoke summarily of a reversibility of the seeing and the visible, of the touching and the touched. It is time to emphasize that it is a reversibility always imminent and never realized in fact. My left hand is always on the verge of touching my right hand touching the things, but I never reach coincidence; the coincidence eclipses at the moment of realization, and one of two things always occurs: either my right hand really passes over to the rank of touched, but then its hold on the world is interrupted; or it retains its hold on the world, but then I do not really touch *it*—my right hand touching, I palpate with my left hand only its outer covering. Likewise, I do not hear myself as I hear the others, the sonorous existence of my voice is for me as it were poorly exhibited; I have rather an echo of its articulated existence, it vibrates through my head rather than outside. I am always on the same side of my body; it presents itself to me in one invariable perspective. But this incessant escaping, this impotency to superpose exactly upon one another the touching of the things by my right hand and the touching of this same right hand by my left hand, or to superpose, in the exploratory movements of the hand, the tactile experience of a point and that of the "same" point a moment later, or the auditory experience of my own voice and that of other voices—this is not a failure. For if these experiences never exactly overlap, if they slip away at the very moment they are about to rejoin, if there is always a "shift," a "spread," between them, this is precisely because my two hands are part of the same body, because it moves itself in the world, because I hear myself both from within and from without. I experience—and as often as I wish—the transition and the metamorphosis of the one experience into the other, and it is only as though the hinge between them, solid, unshakeable, remained irremediably hidden from me. But this hiatus between my right hand touched and my right hand touching, between my voice heard and my voice uttered, between one moment of my tactile life and the following one, is not an ontological void, a non-being: it is spanned by the total being of my body, and by that of the world; it is the zero of pressure between two solids that makes them adhere to one another. My flesh and that of the world therefore involve clear zones, clearings, about which pivot their opaque zones, and the primary visibility, that of the *quale* and of the things, does not come without a second visibility, that of the lines of force and dimensions, the massive flesh without a rarefied flesh, the momentary body without a glorified body. When Husserl spoke of the horizon of the things—of their exterior horizon, which everybody knows, and of their "interior horizon," that darkness stuffed with visibility of which their surface is but the limit—it is necessary to take the term seriously. No more than are the sky or the earth is the horizon a collection of things held together, or a class name, or a logical possibility of conception, or a system of "potentiality of consciousness": it is a new type of being, a being by porosity, pregnancy, or generality, and he before whom the horizon opens is caught up, included within it. His body and the distances participate in one same corporeity or visibility in general, which reigns between them and it, and even beyond the horizon, beneath his skin, unto the depths of being.

We touch here the most difficult point, that is, the bond between the flesh and the idea, between the visible and the interior armature which it manifests and which it conceals. No one has gone further than Proust in fixing the relations between the visible and the invisible, in describing an idea that is not the contrary of the sensible, that is its lining and its depth. For what he says of musical ideas he says of all cultural beings, such as *The Princess of Clèves* and *René,* and also of the essence of love which "the little phrase" not only makes present to Swann, but communicable to all who hear it, even though it is unbeknown to themselves, and even though later they do not know how to recognize it in the loves they only witness. He says it in general of many other notions which are, like music itself "without equivalents," "the notions of light, of sound, of relief, of physical voluptuousness, which are the rich possessions with which our inward domain is diversified and adorned."[7] Literature, music, the passions, but also the experience of the visible world are—no less than is the science of Lavoisier and Ampère—the exploration of an invisible and the disclosure of a universe of ideas.[8] The difference is simply that this invisible, these ideas, unlike those of that science, cannot be detached from the sensible appearances and be erected into a second positivity. The musical idea, the literary idea, the dialectic of love, and also the articulations of the light, the modes of exhibition of sound and of touch speak to us, have their logic, their coherence, their points of intersection, their concordances, and here also the appearances are the disguise of unknown "forces" and "laws." But it is as though the secrecy wherein they lie and whence the literary expression draws them were

their proper mode of existence. For these truths are not only hidden like a physical reality which we have not been able to discover, invisible in fact but which we will one day be able to see facing us, which others, better situated, could already see, provided that the screen that masks it is lifted. Here, on the contrary, there is no vision without the screen: the ideas we are speaking of would not be better known to us if we had no body and no sensibility; it is then that they would be inaccessible to us. The "little phrase," the notion of the light, are not exhausted by their manifestations, any more than is an "idea of the intelligence"; they could not be given to us *as ideas* except in a carnal experience. It is not only that we would find in that carnal experience the *occasion* to think them; it is that they owe their authority, their fascinating, indestructible power, precisely to the fact that they are in transparency behind the sensible, or in its heart. Each time we want to get at it[9] immediately, or lay hands on it, or circumscribe it, or see it unveiled, we do in fact feel that the attempt is misconceived, that it retreats in the measure that we approach. The explicitation does not give us the idea itself; it is but a second version of it, a more manageable derivative. Swann can of course close in the "little phrase" between the marks of musical notation, ascribe the "withdrawn and chilly tenderness" that makes up its essence or its sense to the narrow range of the five notes that compose it and to the constant recurrence of two of them: while he is thinking of these signs and this sense, he no longer has the "little phrase" itself, he has only "bare values substituted for the mysterious entity he had perceived, for the convenience of his understanding."[10] Thus it is essential to this sort of ideas that they be "veiled with shadows," appear "under a disguise." They give us the assurance that

---

[7] *Du côté de chez Swann,* II (Paris, 1926), 190. [English translation by C. K. Scott Moncrieff, *Swann's Way* (New York, 1928), p. 503.]

[8] *Ibid.,* p. 192. [Eng. trans., p. 505.]

[9] EDITOR: It: that is, the idea.

[10] *Du côté de chez Swann,* II, 189. [Eng. trans., p. 503.]

the "great unpenetrated and discouraging night of our soul" is not empty, is not "nothingness"; but these entities, these domains, these worlds that line it, people it, and whose presence it feels like the presence of someone in the dark, have been acquired only through its commerce with the visible, to which they remain attached. As the secret blackness of milk, of which Valéry spoke, is accessible only through its whiteness, the idea of light or the musical idea doubles up the lights and sounds from beneath, is their other side or their depth. Their carnal texture presents to us what is absent from all flesh; it is a furrow that traces itself out magically under our eyes without a tracer, a certain hollow, a certain interior, a certain absence, a negativity that is not nothing, being limited very precisely to *these* five notes between which it is instituted, to that family of sensibles we call lights. We do not see, do not hear the ideas, and not even with the mind's eye or with the third ear: and yet they are there, behind the sounds or between them, behind the lights or between them, recognizable through their always special, always unique manner of entrenching themselves behind them, "perfectly distinct from one another, unequal among themselves in value and in significance."[11]

With the first vision, the first contact, the first pleasure, there is initiation, that is, not the positing of a content, but the opening of a dimension that can never again be closed, the establishment of a level in terms of which every other experience will henceforth be situated. The idea is this level, this dimension. It is therefore not a *de facto* invisible, like an object hidden behind another, and not an absolute invisible, which would have nothing to do with the visible. Rather it is the invisible *of* this world, that which inhabits this world, sustains it, and renders it visible, its own and interior possibility, the Being of this being. At the moment one

says "light," at the moment that the musicians reach the "little phrase," there is no lacuna in me; what I live is as "substantial," as "explicit," as a positive thought could be—even more so: a positive thought is what it is, but, precisely, is only what it is and accordingly cannot hold us. Already the mind's volubility takes it elsewhere. We do not possess the musical or sensible ideas, precisely because they are negativity or absence circumscribed; they possess us. The performer is no longer producing or reproducing the sonata: he feels himself, and the others feel him to be at the service of the sonata; the sonata sings through him or cries out so suddenly that he must "dash on his bow" to follow it. And these open vortexes in the sonorous world finally from one sole vortex in which the ideas fit in with one another. "Never was the spoken language so inflexibly necessitated, never did it know to such an extent the pertinence of the questions, the evidence of the responses."[12] The invisible and, as it were, weak being is alone capable of having this close texture. There is a strict ideality in experiences that are experiences of the flesh: the moments of the sonata, the fragments of the luminous field, adhere to one another with a cohesion without concept, which is of the same type as the cohesion of the parts of my body, or the cohesion of my body with the world. Is my body a thing, is it an idea? It is neither, being the measurant of the things. We will therefore have to recognize an ideality that is not alien to the flesh, that gives it its axes, its depth, its dimensions.

But once we have entered into this strange domain, one does not see how there could be any question of *leaving* it. If there is an animation *of* the body; if the vision and the body are tangled up in one another; if, correlatively, the thin pellicle of the *quale,* the surface of the visible, is doubled up over its whole extension with an invisible reserve;

---

[11] *Ibid.*

[12] *Ibid.*, p. 192. [Eng. trans., p. 505.]

and if finally, in our flesh as in the flesh of things, the actual, empirical, ontic visible, by a sort of folding back, invagination, or padding, exhibits a visibility, a possibility that is not the shadow of the actual but is its principle, that is not the proper contribution of a "thought" but is its condition, a style, allusive and elliptical like every style, but like every style inimitable, inalienable, an interior horizon and an exterior horizon between which the actual visible is a provisional partitioning and which, nonetheless, open indefinitely only upon other visibles—then (the immediate and dualist distinction between the visible and the invisible, between extension and thought, being impugned, not that extension be thought or thought extension, but because they are the obverse and the reverse of one another, and the one forever behind the other) there is to be sure a question as to how the "ideas of the intelligence" are initiated over and beyond, how from the ideality of the horizon one passes to the "pure" ideality, and in particular by what miracle a created generality, a culture, a knowledge come to add to and recapture and rectify the natural generality of my body and of the world. But, however we finally have to understand it, the "pure" ideality already streams forth along the articulations of the aesthesiological body, along the contours of the sensible things, and, however new it is, it slips through ways it has not traced, transfigures horizons it did not open, it derives from the fundamental mystery of those notions "without equivalent," as Proust calls them, that lead their shadowy life in the night of the mind only because they have been divined at the junctures of the visible world. It is too soon now to clarify this type of surpassing that does not leave its field of origin. Let us only say that the pure ideality is itself not without flesh nor freed from horizon structures: it lives of them, though they be another flesh and other horizons. It is as though the visibility that animates the sensible world were to emigrate, not

outside of every body, but into another less heavy, more transparent body, as though it were to change flesh, abandoning the flesh of the body for that of language, and thereby would be emancipated but not freed from every condition. Why not admit—what Proust knew very well and said in another place—that language as well as music can sustain a sense by virtue of its own arrangement, catch a meaning in its own mesh, that it does so without exception each time it is conquering, active, creative language, each time something is, in the strong sense, said? Why not admit that, just as the musical notation is a *facsimile* made after the event, an abstract portrait of the musical entity, language as a system of explicit relations between signs and signified, sounds and meaning, is a result and a product of the operative language in which sense and sound are in the same relationship as the "little phrase" and the five notes found in it afterwards? This does not mean that musical notation and grammar and linguistics and the "ideas of the intelligence"—which are acquired, available, honorary ideas—are useless, or that, as Leibniz said, the donkey that goes straight to the fodder knows as much about the properties of the straight line as we do; it means that the system of objective relations, the acquired ideas, are themselves caught up in something like a second life and perception, which make the mathematician go straight to entities no one has yet seen, make the *operative* language and algorithm make use of a second visibility, and make ideas be the other side of language and calculus. When I think they animate my interior speech, they haunt it as the "little phrase" possesses the violinist, and they remain beyond the words as it remains beyond the notes—not in the sense that under the light of another sun hidden from us they would shine forth but because they are that certain divergence, that never-finished differentiation, that openness ever to be reopened between the sign and the sign, as the flesh is, we said, the dehiscence of the seeing into the visible and of the visible into the seeing. And just as my body sees only because it is a part of the visible in which it opens forth, the sense upon which the arrangement of the sounds opens reflects back upon that arrangement. For the linguist language is an ideal system, a fragment of the intelligible world. But, just as for me to see it is not enough that my look be visible for X, it is necessary that it be visible for itself, through a sort of torsion, reversal, or specular phenomenon, which is given from the sole fact that I am born; so also, if my words have a meaning, it is not *because* they present the systematic organization the linguist will disclose, it is because that organization, like the look, refers back to itself: the operative Word is the obscure region whence comes the instituted light, as the muted reflection of the body upon itself is what we call natural light. As there is a reversibility of the seeing and the visible, and as at the point where the two metamorphoses cross what we call perception is born, so also there is a reversibility of the speech and what it signifies; the signification is what comes to seal, to close, to gather up the multiplicity of the physical, physiological, linguistic means of elocution, to contract them into one sole act, as the vision comes to complete the aesthesiological body. And, as the visible takes hold of the look which has unveiled it and which forms a part of it, the signification rebounds upon its own means. it annexes to itself the speech that becomes an object of science, it antedates itself by a retrograde movement which is never completely belied—because already, in opening the horizon of the nameable and of the sayable, the speech acknowledged that it has its place in that horizon; because no locutor speaks without making himself in advance allocutary, *be it only for himself;* because with one sole gesture he closes the circuit of his relation to himself and that of his relation to the others and, with the same stroke, also sets himself up as *delocutary,*

speech of which one speaks: he offers himself and offers every word to a universal Word. We shall have to follow more closely this transition from the mute world to the speaking world. For the moment we want only to suggest that one can speak neither of a destruction nor of a conservation of silence (and still less of a destruction that conserves or of a realization that destroys—which is not to solve but to pose the problem). When the silent vision falls into speech, and when the speech in turn, opening up a field of the nameable and the sayable, inscribes itself in that field, in its place, according to its truth—in short, when it metamorphoses the structures of the visible world and makes itself a gaze of the mind, *intuitus mentis*—this is always in virtue of the same fundamental phenomenon of reversibility which sustains both the mute perception and the speech and which manifests itself by an almost carnal existence of the idea, as well as by a sublimation of the flesh. In a sense, if we were to make completely explicit the architectonics of the human body, its ontological framework, and how it sees itself and hears itself, we would see that the structure of its mute world is such that all the possibilities of language are already given in it. Already our existence as seers (that is, we said, as beings who turn the world back upon itself and who pass over to the other side, and who catch sight of one another, who see one another with eyes) and especially our existence as sonorous beings for others and for ourselves contain everything required for there to be speech from the one to the other, speech about the world. And, in a sense, to understand a phrase is nothing else than to fully welcome it in its sonorous being, or, as we put it so well, to *hear what it says (l'entendre).* The meaning is not on the phrase like the butter on the bread, like a second layer of "psychic reality" spread over the sound: it is the totality of what is said, the integral of all the differentiations of the verbal chain; it is given with the words for those who have ears to hear. And conversely the whole landscape is overrun with words as with an invasion, it is henceforth but a variant of speech before our eyes, and to speak of its "style" is in our view to form a metaphor. In a sense the whole of philosophy, as Husserl says, consists in restoring a power to signify, a birth of meaning, or a wild meaning, an expression of experience by experience, which in particular clarifies the special domain of language. And in a sense, as Valéry said, language is everything, since it is the voice of no one, since it is the very voice of the things, the waves, and the forests. And what we have to understand is that there is no dialectical reversal from one of these views to the other; we do not have to reassemble them into a synthesis: they are two aspects of the reversibility which is the ultimate truth.

chapter thirty-four

Herbert Marcuse

Herbert Marcuse (1898–1979) was a German-American social theorist sometimes called "the philosopher of the New Left." His *Eros and Civilization: A Philosophical Inquiry into Freud* was an attempt to synthesize and go beyond Hegel, Marx, and Freud.

Marcuse was born in Berlin, the son of a prosperous assimilated Jew. He received a classical *Gymnasium* (high school) education and was drafted during the First World War, serving on zeppelin maintenance. Toward the end of the war, for the first and only time, Marcuse joined a political party, the antiwar wing of the Social Democrats, led by Rosa Luxemburg and Karl Liebknecht. He attended the Universities of Berlin and Freiburg, studying philosophy, German literature, and economics, and completing a dissertation on the German "artist-novel." Edmund Husserl, founder of the phenomenological movement in philosophy, was on his dissertation committee and remained a lifelong friend. In many European systems, those planning for a university career write a kind of "second dissertation"—"*Habilitationsschrift*" in Germany—and Marcuse undertook this work with Martin Heidegger.[1] That was published as *Hegel's Ontology and the Foundation of the Theory of Historicity* (1932). By this time Marcuse had also become associated with the Institute for Social Research in Frankfurt.

As events transpired, it would be decades before Marcuse held a university position. The Frankfurt Institute had a branch in Geneva, to which Marcuse moved after Hitler's accession to power, and then on to Paris and New York, where the Institute resided "in exile" at Columbia University. During the war and until 1951, Marcuse held various positions with the Office of Strategic Services and the U.S. State Department. It fell to him to interview Heidegger in the postwar program of "de-Nazification." With the rise of McCarthyism in the United States, the attacks on State Department "leftists," and the death of his first wife, Marcuse left Washington for work with Russian Studies Centers at Columbia and Harvard. In 1958 he was appointed professor of philosophy and politics at Brandeis University. There he was a very popular teacher and chair of the history of ideas program until 1965. He then taught at the University of California in San

Diego until his final retirement in 1976. Marcuse died of a stroke on a visit to Germany in 1979.

Marcuse was often referred to as the "philosopher of the New Left," a loosely organized movement during the height of the civil rights movement and opposition to the Vietnam War, which was critical of Soviet and Eastern European Marxism, as well as Cold War American policies. Marcuse's critique of postwar Western capitalism is elaborated in *One-Dimensional Man: Studies in the Ideology of Advanced Industrial Society* (1964). In the *Essay on Liberation* (1969) he supported the resistance movements of the 1960s. Marcuse was influential in Europe, particularly Germany and France, as well as in the United States.

Many view *Eros and Civilization: A Philosophical Inquiry into Freud* (1955) as Marcuse's most important work. Although there is only a brief discussion of Hegel's *Phenomenology*, and Karl Marx is not once mentioned, the work is often seen as an attempt to synthesize Hegel, Marx, and Freud, moving beyond the main historical developments of Marxism during the twentieth century, and attempting to use Freudian categories of psychological and social analysis to move beyond some of Freud's own conclusions. Throughout Marcuse's writings probably the strongest and most continuous influence is the dialectical method of Hegelian philosophizing. For Marcuse, as for Hegel, concrete states of affairs and specific processes of thought can only be understood through their opposites; those opposites, however, are not mere empty negations, but determinate negations: *Non-x* is not only *non-*, but the specific *non-* of *this particular x*. In the case at hand, Freud's analysis of civilization, the repression of the libido is, according to Marcuse, not just repression in general, but the repression of this particular individual in this particular culture. In this sense too Marcuse's critique of Freud will itself turn out to be Freudian, the "non-Freud" of a Freudian dialectic.

In *Civilization and Its Discontents* (1930), Freud developed what is widely seen as a very pessimistic view of civilization. All civilization, according to Freud's thesis there, is repressive of instincts and therefore of human freedom. As instinctive animals, human beings act on Eros (love, desire) or libido, sexual drive, but civilization organizes effective barriers against the possibility that all people should simply act so as to get whatever they want and thus fulfill their desires. The course of Eros runs up against the strictures of Ananke (Necessity).[2] Humans act not only on the basis of Eros, but also on instinctive aggression, Thanatos, or the death principle. The irrepressibility of this violent Thanatos instinct is in part a result of the evolution of civilization itself. People enter into family structures, particularly patriarchal families, in order to reduce the insecurity of uninhibited genital sexuality; and they enter upon civilized societies in order to gain some safety, predictability, and order—once again to reduce the dangerous arbitrariness of ordinary human existence. To accomplish this, they establish one or another system of ordered "justice," so that members of a society cannot simply do whatever their sexual or other urges tell them that they want. Thus the suppression of the libido and its desires is a fundamental feature of civilization from the outset and in its very foundation. Since Eros cannot simply be eliminated or suppressed outright, however, it must be redirected in one manner or another: It may be deflected in the less obviously erotic desires for scientific or professional achievement; it may be sublimated in artistic and creative activities; or there may be a substitution of some other kind of love for Eros in philanthropy, humanitarianism, charity, the love of God. Many of these deflections—in particular artistic sublimation for Freud—can lead to the output of the valued products of civilization—but as substitutes they are not entirely fulfilling. In addition, the political entities that evolve out of the basic process of civilization—cities, empires, nation-states—lead to the substitute Eros of patriotism and the violent warfare it can inspire. Thus the civilizing of Eros leads to further aggression and the possibility that society in general will become organized primarily around Thanatos.

Eros and Civilization does not so much argue that Freud's analysis of repression in culture is incorrect as that it is incomplete. The unresolved conflict between instinct and civilization is historically accurate; but it is not inevitable. Specific forms of social repression derive from specific economic and historical conditions which themselves are not irreversible. Marcuse takes exception to Freud's treatment of Ananke (Necessity). For Freud, Necessity refers not only to the sheer physical restrictions of a material world but to the needs and "neediness" of people's lives in a hostile environment, hunger, and poverty in an economy of scarcity. For Marcuse this economy of scarcity is not fate, but a sociohistorical condition. Technological economy could produce enough food and other material goods to ameliorate or even eliminate hunger and poverty. It is the inequality of social class, especially the superconsumption of the superrich, which sustains the dynamics of Ananke as an economics of scarcity. But this is a condition with a particular historical background, specific social, economic, and political determinations. By the same token, the historical future could change it. Necessity and determinations are involved indeed, but it is not an ultimate necessity grounded intractably in human nature.

Two features of twentieth-century society are particularly important for Marcuse's rethinking of Freud. First Thanatos, the death instinct, has taken on a particularly acute social and geopolitical form in the nuclear age, when the death of civilization itself has become a realistic fear. The arms race fostered a common narcissistic pride in the paraphernalia of death. In order to rationalize—in both senses of that term—this investment in death and aggression, the culture had to compensate in many ways. Second, Marx's analysis of "alienated labor" in the context of nineteenth-century capitalism was accurate enough, but the alienation of labor became more severe with the invention of the assembly line, the dominance of large corporations, and the co-optation of the labor movement. Those hoping for social change could no longer look to labor as a revolutionary vanguard. And sex itself has come to be understood on the model of labor: rather than serving pleasure, sex fulfils the goals of production. At the same time, recent technology has led to greater leisure, convenience, and even health. As with applications of early agricultural and commercial technology in antiquity, however, it has only led to an increase of leisure, convenience, and health for some, not for all. Such inequities indicate the prevalence of repression in society, but they also suggest that mitigation of repression is possible.

For the analysis of the specific forms of social repression and their historical and economic background, Marcuse introduces the new principles of "surplus repression" and the "performance principle." If there is some process of psychic repression inherent in all civilization and in individuals' reactions to and interactions with their culture, some cultures carry this further than others: "surplus repression" is, so to speak, repression beyond the call of cultural duty, processes of generalized repression in the name of political or religious principles. Guilt, abstinence, and control become ends in themselves. The general discontent of civilization, however, involves not only repression, but also deflections of repression in sublimation, art, philanthropy, whereas "surplus repression" deflects repression back into such sublimation itself, so that art or even sexuality become part of the repression rather than a partial release from them.

In addition to the pleasure principle and the reality principle, Marcuse maintains, we must acknowledge a *performance principle,* "the prevailing historical form of the *reality principle,*"[3] which dictates the way that the reality principle concretely operates in a specific society:

> [T]he institutions and relations that constitute the social "body" of the reality principle . . . do not just represent the changing external manifestations of one and the same reality principle but actually change the reality principle itself. Consequently, in our attempt to elucidate the scope and the limits of the prevalent repressiveness in contemporary civilization, we shall have to describe it in terms of the specific reality principle that has governed the origins and the growth of this civilization. We designate it as performance principle in order to emphasize that under its rule society is stratified according to the competitive economic performance of its members.[4]

Marcuse's choice of the term "performance principle" emphasizes that the reality principle dictates different sorts of performance in different societies, but also that modern Western capitalist society dictates competitive performance, even if inequities, advantages, and disadvantages may be built into the starting points and even into the ground rules of many of the competitors.

"The Transformation of Sexuality into Eros," the tenth chapter of *Eros and Civilization,* analyzes ways in which repression and its deflections in civilization can be redirected onto more positive and humane paths. The chapter is preceded by an analysis of play and the "aesthetic dimension." Not all work is alienated, and creative activities can cross the line between work and play. The more leisure and freedom there is in a society, the more possible is a general transformation of work into play. Whereas repressive civilization makes sex into a mode of productive work and then limits sexual activities to those which further the labor of reproduction, a free society would foster sex as play. This point leads Marcuse into a discussion of homosexuality and some disagreements both with Freud and with revisionist Freudianism. The transformation of sexuality into eros is a form of nonrepressive or free sublimation, a model for free social relations and the transformation of work into play. Ultimately the same model leads to a new view of reason that is not pitted against pleasure, but harmonizes with it.

Marcuse has been counted among utopian thinkers of the twentieth century. It is not that he denies the fact of repression in civilization. It is not that he thinks there is some clear historical law of progress—that despite the swings of the dialectic and the twists of temporary setbacks man's condition inevitably improves. Although he was sympathetic to the position of Hegel, Marx, and others, that freedom and reason must ultimately triumph, he was not sanguine about imminent prospects. He had no use for loose talk of revolution: The labor movement, he thought, the engine of old-time socialist revolution, was "co-opted." But he did think that it was possible for societies to be more free than they are now. And he thought there were hopeful signs in the late twentieth century, particularly in the years after he wrote *Eros and Civilization.* He supported the emerging feminist movement, but worried that it might simply try to gain an equal place for women in the general "rat race," giving women the right to an equality of repression, rather than learning from women and women's lives that social relations might be different and more free. He championed the international student movement, but regularly warned against excess. The problem, he said, is not overestimating the youth movement, but overestimating the results that can come from the youth movement. The utopian strain is balanced by a caution and realism about immediate change. When someone suggested that Marcuse was a pessimist; he replied, "All right, so I'm a cheerful pessimist."[5]

JHS

QUESTIONS

1. For Freud the conflict between the pleasure principle and reality principle is ultimately unresolvable. Do you think that Marcuse is successful in trying to resolve it?

2. Marcuse tries to take the category of Eros or Desire through sexuality and beyond—and beyond reproductive sexuality too. What are specific ways that he does this? Do you think that he succeeds?

3. Many commentators see Marcuse as a "utopian" and others see him as pessimistic. He himself said jokingly that he was a "cheerful pessimist." Which do you think most accurately describes Marcuse's thought?

ENDNOTES

1. After the publication of his *Being and Time* (1927) Heidegger became the most influential philosopher in Germany. Referred to as a "phenomenological existentialist," he himself would not use the latter term. Although many of his closest students were Jewish and all insisted that he never showed signs of anti-Semitism, as Rector of the University of Freiburg in 1933, Heidegger joined the Nazi party and implemented early Nazi policies.

2. Although some commentators take the pairing of Eros and Ananke to be based on Plato's *Timaeus* 47e-48c, the pairing there is of Mind (*Nous*) and Necessity and the mixture of the two is used to explain the generation of the four physical elements. It is more likely that Freud is here thinking of pre-Socratic philosophers: Anaximander, Empedocles, or Parmenides.

3. Marcuse, *Eros and Civilization,* p. 35.

4. Marcuse, *Eros and Civilization,* p. 44.

5. Katz, p. 165.

SELECTED BIBLIOGRAPHY

Bokina, John, and Timothy J. Lukes, eds. *Marcuse: From the New Left to the Next Left.* Lawrence: University Press of Kansas, 1994.

Jay, Martin. *The Dialectical Imagination: A History of the Frankfurt School and the Institute of Social Research, 1923–1950.* Boston, Mass.: Little, Brown, 1973.

Katz, Barry. *Herbert Marcuse: Art of Liberation: An Intellectual Biography.* London: Verso Editions, 1982.

Marcuse, Herbert. *Eros and Civilization: A Philosophical Inquiry into Freud.* Boston, Mass.: Beacon Press, 1966.

Marcuse, Herbert. *One-Dimensional Man: Studies in the Ideology of Advanced Industrial Society.* Boston, Mass.: Beacon Press, 1964.

from *Eros and Civilization*

Herbert Marcuse

THE TRANSFORMATION OF SEXUALITY INTO EROS

The vision of a non-repressive culture, which we have lifted from a marginal trend in mythology and philosophy, aims at a new relation between instincts and reason. The civilized morality is reversed by harmonizing instinctual freedom and order: liberated from the tyranny of repressive reason, the instincts tend toward free and lasting existential relations—they generate a *new* reality principle. In Schiller's idea of an "aesthetic state," the vision of a non-repressive culture is concretized at the level of mature civilization. At this level, the organization of the instincts becomes a social problem (in Schiller's terminology, *political*), as it does in Freud's pyschology. The processes that create the ego and superego also shape and perpetuate specific societal institutions and relations. Such psychoanalytical concepts as sublimation, identification, and introjection have not only a psychical but also a social content: they terminate in a system of institutions, laws, agencies, things, and customs that confront the individual as objective entities. Within this antagonistic system, the mental conflict between ego and superego, between ego and id, is at one and the same time a conflict between the individual and his society. The latter embodies the rationality of the whole, and the individual's struggle against the repressive forces is a struggle against objective reason. Therefore, the emergence of a non-repressive reality principle involving instinctual liberation would *regress* behind the attained level of civilized rationality. This regression would be psychical as well as social: it would reactivate early stages of the libido which were surpassed in the development of the reality ego, and it would dissolve the institutions of society in which the reality ego exists. In terms of these institutions, instinctual liberation is relapse into barbarism. However, occurring at the height of civilization, as a consequence not of defeat but of victory in the struggle for existence, and supported by a free society, such liberation might have very different results. It would still be a reversal of the process of civilization, a subversion of culture—but *after* culture had done its work and created the mankind and the world that could be free. It would still be "regression"—but in the light of mature consciousness and guided by a new rationality. Under these conditions, the possibility of a non-repressive civilization is predicated not upon the arrest, but upon the liberation, of progress—so that man would order his life in accordance with his fully developed knowledge, so that he would ask again what is good and what is evil. If the guilt accumulated in the civilized domination of man by man can ever be redeemed by freedom, then the "original sin" must be committed again: "We must again eat from the tree of knowledge in order to fall back into the state of innocence."[1]

---

[1] "Wir müssen wieder vom Baum der Erkenntnis essen, um in den Stand der Unschuld zurückzufallen." Heinrich von Kleist, "Ueber das Marionettentheater," conclusion.

The notion of a non-repressive instinctual order must first be tested on the most "disorderly" of all instincts—namely, sexuality. Non-repressive order is possible only if the sex instincts can, by virtue of their own dynamic and under changed existential and societal conditions, generate lasting erotic relations among mature individuals. We have to ask whether the sex instincts, after the elimination of all surplus-repression, can develop a "libidinal rationality" which is not only compatible with but even promotes progress toward higher forms of civilized freedom. This possibility will be examined here in Freud's own terms.

We have reiterated Freud's conclusion that any genuine decrease in the societal controls over the sex instincts would, even under optimum conditions, reverse the organization of sexuality toward precivilized stages. Such regression would break through the central fortifications of the performance principle: it would undo the channeling of sexuality into monogamic reproduction and the taboo on perversions. Under the rule of the performance principle, the libidinal cathexis of the individual body and libidinal relations with others are normally confined to leisure time and directed to the preparation and execution of genital intercourse; only in exceptional cases, and with a high degree of sublimation, are libidinal relations allowed to enter into the sphere of work. These constraints, enforced by the need for sustaining a large quantum of energy and time for non-gratifying labor, perpetuate the desexualization of the body in order to make the organism into a subject-object of socially useful performances. Conversely, if the work day and energy are reduced to a minimum, without a corresponding manipulation of the free time, the ground for these constraints would be undermined. Libido would be released and would overflow the institutionalized limits within which it is kept by the reality principle.

Freud repeatedly emphasized that the lasting interpersonal relations on which civilization depends presuppose that the sex instinct is inhibited in its aim.[2] Love, and the enduring and responsible relations which it demands, are founded on a union of sexuality with "affection," and this union is the historical result of a long and cruel process of domestication, in which the instinct's legitimate manifestation is made supreme and its component parts are arrested in their development.[3] This cultural refinement of sexuality, its sublimation to love, took place within a civilization which established possessive private relations apart from, and in a decisive aspect conflicting with, the possessive societal relations. While, outside the privacy of the family, men's existence was chiefly determined by the exchange value of their products and performances, their life in home and bed was to be permeated with the spirit of divine and moral law. Mankind was supposed to be an end in itself and never a mere means; but this ideology was effective in the private rather than in the societal functions of the individuals, in the sphere of libidinal satisfaction rather than in that of labor. The full force of civilized morality was mobilized against the use of the body as mere object, means, instrument of pleasure; such reification was tabooed and remained the ill-reputed privilege of whores, degenerates, and perverts. Precisely in his gratification, and especially in his sexual gratification, man was to be a higher being, committed to higher values; sexuality was to be dignified by love. With the emergence of a non-repressive reality principle, with the abolition of the surplus-repression necessitated by the performance principle, this process

would be reversed. In the societal relations, reification would be reduced as the division of labor became reoriented on the gratification of freely developing individual needs; whereas, in the libidinal relations, the taboo on the reification of the body would be lessened. No longer used as a full-time instrument of labor, the body would be resexualized. The regression involved in this spread of the libido would first manifest itself in a reactivation of all erotogenic zones and, consequently, in a resurgence of pregenital polymorphous sexuality and in a decline of genital supremacy. The body in its entirety would become an object of cathexis, a thing to be enjoyed—an instrument of pleasure. This change in the value and scope of libidinal relations would lead to a disintegration of the institutions in which the private interpersonal relations have been organized, particularly the monogamic and patriarchal family.

These prospects seem to confirm the expectation that instinctual liberation can lead only to a society of sex maniacs—that is, to no society. However, the process just outlined involves not simply a release but a *transformation* of the libido: from sexuality constrained under genital supremacy to erotization of the entire personality. It is a spread rather than explosion of libido—a spread over private and societal relations which bridges the gap maintained between them by a repressive reality principle. This transformation of the libido would be the result of a societal transformation that released the free play of individual needs and faculties. By virtue of these conditions, the free development of transformed libido *beyond* the institutions of the performance principle differs essentially from the release of constrained sexuality *within* the dominion of these institutions. The latter process explodes *suppressed* sexuality; the libido continues to bear the mark of suppression and manifests itself in the hideous forms so well

---

[2] *Collected Papers* (London: Hogarth Press, 1950), IV, 203ff; *Group Psychology and the Analysis of the Ego* (New York: Liveright Publishing Corp., 1949), pp. 72, 78.
[3] *Collected Papers,* IV, 215.

known in the history of civilization; in the sadistic and masochistic orgies of desperate masses, of "society elites," of starved bands of mercenaries, of prison and concentration-camp guards. Such release of sexuality provides a periodically necessary outlet for unbearable frustration; it strengthens rather than weakens the roots of instinctual constraint; consequently, it has been used time and again as a prop for suppressive regimes. In contrast, the free development of transformed libido within transformed institutions, while eroticizing previously tabooed zones, time, and relations, would *minimize* the manifestations of *mere* sexuality by integrating them into a far larger order, including the order of work. In this context, sexuality tends to its own sublimation: the libido would not simply reactivate precivilized and infantile stages, but would also transform the perverted content of these stages.

The term *perversions* covers sexual phenomena of essentially different origin. The same taboo is placed on instinctual manifestations incompatible with civilization and on those incompatible with repressive civilization, especially with monogamic genital supremacy. However, within the historical dynamic of the instinct, for example, coprophilia and homosexuality have a very different place and function. A similar difference prevails within one and the same perversion: the function of sadism is not the same in a free libidinal relation and in the activities of SS Troops. The inhuman, compulsive, coercive, and destructive forms of these perversions seem to be linked with the general perversion of the human existence in a repressive culture, but the perversions have an instinctual substance distinct from these forms; and this substance may well express itself in other forms compatible with normality in high civilization. Not all component parts and stages of the instinct that have been suppressed have suffered this fate because they pre-

vented the evolution of man and mankind. The purity, regularity, cleanliness, and reproduction required by the performance principle are not naturally those of any mature civilization. And the reactivation of prehistoric and childhood wishes and attitudes is not necessarily regression; it may well be the opposite—proximity to a happiness that has always been the repressed promise of a better future. In one of his most advanced formulations, Freud once defined happiness as the "subsequent fulfillment of a prehistoric wish. That is why wealth brings so little happiness: money was not a wish in childhood."[4]

But if human happiness depends on the fulfillment of childhood wishes, civilization, according to Freud, depends on the suppression of the strongest of all childhood wishes: the Oedipus wish. Does the realization of happiness in a free civilization still necessitate this suppression? Or would the transformation of the libido also engulf the Oedipus situation? In the context of our hypothesis, such speculations are insignificant; the Oedipus complex, although the primary source and model of neurotic conflicts, is certainly not the central cause of the discontents in civilization, and not the central obstacle for their removal. The Oedipus complex "passes" even under the rule of a repressive reality principle. Freud advances two general interpretations of the "passing of the Oedipus complex": it "becomes extinguished by its lack of success"; or it "must come to an end because the time has come for its dissolution, just as the milk-teeth fall out when the permanent ones begin to press forward."[5] The passing of the complex appears as a "natural" event in both cases.

---

[4] Ernest Jones, *The Life and Work of Sigmund Freud*, Vol. I (New York: Basic Books, 1953), p. 330.
[5] *Collected Papers*, II, 269.

We have spoken of the *self-sublimation of sexuality.* The term implies that sexuality can, under specific conditions, create highly civilized human relations without being subjected to the repressive organization which the established civilization has imposed upon the instinct. Such self-sublimation presupposes historical progress beyond the institutions of the performance principle, which in turn would release instinctual regression. For the development of the instinct, this means regression from sexuality in the service of reproduction to sexuality in the "function of obtaining pleasure from zones of the body."[6] With this restoration of the primary structure of sexuality, the primacy of the genital function is broken—as is the desexualization of the body which has accompanied this primacy. The organism in its entirety becomes the substratum of sexuality, while at the same time the instinct's objective is no longer absorbed by a specialized function—namely, that of bringing "one's own genitals into contact with those of someone of the opposite sex."[7] Thus enlarged, the field and objective of the instinct becomes the life of the organism itself. This process almost naturally, by its inner logic, suggests the conceptual transformation of sexuality into Eros.

The introduction of the term Eros in Freud's later writings was certainly motivated by different reasons: Eros, as life instinct, denotes a larger biological instinct rather than a larger scope of sexuality.[8] However, it may not be accidental that Freud does not rigidly distinguish between Eros and sexuality, and his usage of the term *Eros* (especially in *The Ego and the Id, Civilization and Its Discontents,* and in *An Outline of Psychoanalysis*) implies an enlargement of the meaning of sexuality itself. Even without Freud's explicit reference to Plato the change in emphasis is clear: Eros signifies a quantitative and qualitative aggrandizement of sexuality. And the aggrandized concept seems to demand a correspondingly modified concept of sublimation. The modifications of sexuality are not the same as the modifications of Eros. Freud's concept of sublimation refers to the fate of sexuality under a repressive reality principle. Thus, sublimation means a change in the aim and object of the instinct "with regard to which our social values come into the picture."[9] The term is applied to a group of unconscious processes which have in common that

> . . . as the result of inner or outer deprivation, the aim of object-libido undergoes a more or less complete deflection, modification, or inhibition. In the great majority of instances, the new aim is one distinct or remote from sexual satisfaction, i.e., is an asexual or non-sexual aim.[10]

This mode of sublimation is to a high degree dictated by specific societal requirements and cannot be automatically extended to other and less repressive forms of civilization with different "social values." Under the performance principle, the diversion of libido into useful cultural activities takes place after the period of early childhood. Sublimation then operates on a preconditioned instinctual structure, which includes the functional and temporal restraints of sexuality, its channeling into monogamic reproduction, and the desexualization

---

[6]*An Outline of Psychoanalysis* (New York: W. W. Norton, 1949), p. 26.
[7]*Ibid.,* p. 25.
[8]See the papers of Siegfried Bernfeld and Edward Bibring in *Imago,* Vols. XXI, XXII (1935, 1936).

[9]Freud, *New Introductory Lectures on Psychoanalysis* (New York: W. W. Norton, 1933), p. 133.
[10]Edward Glover, "Sublimation, Substitution, and Social Anxiety," in *International Journal of Psychoanalysis,* Vol. XII, No. 3 (1931), p. 264.

of most of the body. Sublimation works with the thus preconditioned libido and its possessive, exploitative, aggressive force. The repressive "modification" of the pleasure principle precedes the actual sublimation, and the latter carries the repressive elements over into the socially useful activities.

However, there are other modes of sublimation. Freud speaks of aim-inhibited sexual impulses which need not be described as sublimated although they are "closely related" to sublimated impulses. "They have not abandoned their directly sexual aims, but they are held back by internal resistances from attaining them; they rest content with certain approximations to satisfaction."[11] Freud calls them "social instincts" and mentions as examples "the affectionate relations between parents and children, feelings of friendship, and the emotional ties in marriage which had their origin in sexual attraction." Moreover, in *Group Psychology and the Analysis of the Ego*, Freud has emphasized the extent to which societal relations ("community" in civilization) are founded on *un*sublimated as well as sublimated libidinous ties: "sexual love for women" as well as "desexualized, sublimated, homosexual love for other men" here appear as instinctual sources of an enduring and expanding culture.[12] This conception suggests, in Freud's own work, an idea of civilization very different from that derived from repressive sublimation, namely, civilization evolving from and sustained by free libidinal relations. Géza Róheim used Ferenczi's notion of a "genitofugal libido"[13] to support his theory of the libidinous origin of culture. With the relief of extreme tension, libido flows back from the object to the body, and this "recathecting of the whole organism with libido results in a feeling of happiness in which the organs find their reward for work and stimulation to further activity."[14] The concept assumes a genitofugal "libido trend to the development of culture" —in other words, an inherent trend in the libido itself toward "cultural" expression, *without* external repressive modification. And this "cultural" trend in the libido seems to be *genitofugal,* that is to say, *away* from genital supremacy toward the erotization of the entire organism.

These concepts come close to recognizing the possibility of non-repressive sublimation. The rest is left to speculation. And indeed, under the established reality principle, non-repressive sublimation can appear only in marginal and incomplete aspects; its fully developed form would be sublimation without desexualization. The instinct is not "deflected" from its aim; it is gratified in activities and relations that are not sexual in the sense of "organized" genital sexuality and yet are libidinal and erotic. Where repressive sublimation prevails and determines the culture, non-repressive sublimation must manifest itself in contradiction to the entire sphere of social usefulness; viewed from this sphere, it is the negation of all accepted productivity and performance. The Orphic and Narcissistic

---

[11]Encyclopaedia article "The Libido Theory," reprinted in *Collected Papers,* V, 134.

[12]Page 57.

[13]*Versuch einer Genitaltheorie* (Leipzig: Internationaler Psychoanalytischer Verlag, 1924), pp. 51–52. This book has appeared in English as *Thalassa,* transl. H. A. Bunker (Albany: Psychoanalytic Quarterly, Inc., 1938).

[14]Róheim, *The Origin and Function of Culture,* (New York: Nervous and Mental Disease Monograph No. 69, 1943), p. 74. In his article "Sublimation" in the *Yearbook of Psychoanalysis,* Vol. I (1945), Róheim stresses that in sublimation "id strivings reconquer the ground in a disguised form." Thus, "in contrast to the prevailing view, . . . in sublimation we have no ground wrested from the id by the super-ego, but quite to the contrary, what we have is super-ego territory inundated by the id" (p. 117). Here, too, the emphasis is on the *ascendancy* of libido in sublimation.

images are recalled: Plato blames Orpheus for his "softness" (he was only a harp-player), which was duly punished by the gods[15]—as was Narcissus' refusal to "participate." Before the reality as it is, they stand condemned: they rejected the required sublimation. However,

> . . . La sublimation n'est pas toujours la négation d'un désir; elle ne se présente pas toujours comme une sublimation *contre* des instincts. Elle peut être une sublimation *pour* un idéal. Alors Narcisse ne dit plus: "Je m'aime tel que je suis," il dit: "Je suis tel que je m'aime."[16]

The Orphic and Narcissistic Eros engulfs the reality in libidinal relations which transform the individual and his environment; but this transformation is the isolated deed of unique individuals, and, as such, it generates death. Even if sublimation does not proceed *against* the instincts but as their affirmation, it must be a supra-individual process on common ground. As an isolated individual phenomenon, the reactivation of narcissistic libido is not culture-building but neurotic:

> The difference between a neurosis and a sublimation is evidently the social aspect of the phenomenon. A neurosis isolates; a sublimation unites. In a sublimation something new is created—a house, or a community, or a tool—and it is created in a group or for the use of a group.[17]

Libido can take the road of self-sublimation only as a *social* phenomenon: as an unrepressed force, it can promote the formation of culture only under conditions which relate associated individuals to each other in the cultivation of the environment for their developing needs and faculties. Reactivation of polymorphous and narcissistic sexuality ceases to be a threat to culture and can itself lead to culture-building if the organism exists not as an instrument of alienated labor but as a subject of self-realization—in other words, if socially useful work is at the same time the transparent satisfaction of an individual need. In primitive society, this organization of work may be immediate and "natural"; in mature civilization, it can be envisaged only as the result of liberation. Under such conditions, the impulse to "obtain pleasure from the zones of the body" may extend to seek its objective in lasting and expanding libidinal relations because this expansion increases and intensifies the instinct's gratification. Moreover, nothing in the nature of Eros justifies the notion that the "extension" of the impulse is confined to the corporeal sphere. If the antagonistic separation of the physical from the spiritual part of the organism is itself the historical result of repression, the overcoming of this antagonism would open the spiritual sphere to the impulse. The aesthetic idea of a sensuous reason suggests such a tendency. It is essentially different from sublimation in so far as the spiritual sphere becomes the "direct" object of Eros and remains a libidinal object: there is a change neither in energy nor in aim.

The notion that Eros and Agape may after all be one and the same—not that Eros is Agape but that Agape is Eros—may sound strange after almost two thousand years of theology. Nor does it seem justifiable to refer to Plato as a defender of this identification—Plato who himself introduced the repressive definition of Eros into the household of

---

[15]*Symposium* 179 D.

[16]"Sublimation is not always the negation of a desire; it does not always take the form of sublimation *against* the instincts. It could be sublimation *for* an ideal. Thus Narcissus no longer says: 'I love myself such as I am.' He says: 'I am such that I love myself.'" Gaston Bachelard, *L'Eau et les Rêves* (Paris: José Corti, 1942), pp. 34–35.

[17]Róheim, *The Origin and Function of Culture*, p. 74.

Western culture. Still, the *Symposium* contains the clearest celebration of the sexual origin and substance of the spiritual relations. According to Dictima, Eros drives the desire for one beautiful body to another and finally to all beautiful bodies, for "the beauty of one body is akin to the beauty of another," and it would be foolish "not to recognize that the beauty in every body is one and the same."[18] Out of this truly polymorphous sexuality arises the desire for that which animates the desired body: the psyche and its various manifestations. There is an unbroken ascent in erotic fulfillment from the corporeal love of one to that of the others, to the love of beautiful work and play (ἐπιϑηϑεεύματα), and ultimately to the love of beautiful knowledge (καλὰ μαϑήματα). The road to "higher culture" leads through the true love of boys (ὀρϑῶς παιδεραστειν).[19] Spiritual "procreation" is just as much the work of Eros as is corporeal procreation, and the right and true order of the Polis is just as much an erotic one as is the right and true order of love. The culture-building power of Eros is non-repressive sublimation: sexuality is neither deflected from nor blocked in its objective; rather, in attaining its objective, it transcends it to others, searching for fuller gratification.

In the light of the idea of non-repressive sublimation, Freud's definition of Eros as striving to "form living substance into ever greater unities, so that life may be prolonged and brought to higher development"[20] takes on added significance. The biological drive becomes a cultural drive. The pleasure principle reveals its own dialectic. The erotic aim of sustaining the entire body as subject-object of pleasure calls for the continual refinement of the organism, the intensification of its receptivity, the growth of its sensuousness. The aim generates its own projects of realization: the abolition of toil, the amelioration of the environment, the conquest of disease and decay, the creation of luxury. All these activities flow directly from the pleasure principle, and, at the same time, they constitute *work* which associates individuals to "greater unities"; no longer confined within the mutilating dominion of the performance principle, they modify the impulse without deflecting it from its aim. There is sublimation and, consequently, culture; but this sublimation proceeds in a system of expanding and enduring libidinal relations, which are in themselves work relations.

The idea of an erotic tendency toward work is not foreign to psychoanalysis. Freud himself remarked that work provides an opportunity for a "very considerable discharge of libidinal component impulses, narcissistic, aggressive and even erotic."[21] We have questioned this statement because it makes no distinction between alienated and non-alienated labor (between labor and work): the former is by its very nature repressive of human potentialities and therefore also repressive of the "libidinal component impulses" which may enter into work. But the statement assumes a different significance if it is seen in the context of the social psychology which Freud proposes in *Group Psychology and the Analysis of the Ego.* He suggests that "the libido props itself upon the satisfaction of the great vital needs, and chooses as its first objects the people who have a share in that process."[22] This proposition, if unfolded in its implications, comes close to vitiating Freud's basic assumption that the "struggle for existence" (that is, for the "satisfaction of the great vital needs") is *per se*

---

[18]210 B. Jowett translates, not "body," but "form."
[19]211 B. Jowett translates: ". . . under the influence of true love."
[20]Freud, *Collected Papers,* V, 135.

[21]*Civilization and Its Discontents* (London: Hogarth Press, 1949), p. 34 note.
[22]Page 57.

anti-libidinous in so far as it necessitates the regimentation of the instinct by a constraining reality principle. It must be noted that Freud links the libido not merely to the *satisfaction* of the great vital needs but to the joint human efforts to *obtain* satisfaction, i.e., to the work process:

> . . . experience has shown that in cases of collaboration libidinal ties are regularly formed between the fellow-workers which prolong and solidify the relations between them to a point beyond what is merely profitable.[23]

If this is true, then Ananke is not a sufficient cause for the instinctual constraints of civilization—and not a sufficient reason for denying the possibility of a non-repressive libidinous culture. Freud's suggestions in *Group Psychology and the Analysis of the Ego* do more than reformulate his thesis of Eros as the builder of culture; culture here rather appears as the builder of Eros—that is to say, as the "natural" fulfillment of the innermost trend of Eros. Freud's psychology of civilization was based on the inexorable conflict between Ananke and free instinctual development. But if Ananke itself becomes the primary field of libidinal development, the contradiction evaporates. Not only would the struggle for existence not necessarily cancel the possibility of instinctual freedom (as we suggested in Chapter 6); but it would even constitute a "prop" for instinctual gratification. The work relations which form the base of civilization, and thus civilization itself, would be "propped" by non-desexualized instinctual energy. The whole concept of sublimation is at stake.

The problem of work, of socially useful activity, without (repressive) sublimation can now be restated. It emerged as the problem of a change in the character of work by virtue of which the latter would be assimilated to play—the free play of human faculties. What are the instinctual preconditions for such a transformation? The most far-reaching attempt to answer this question is made by Barbara Lantos in her article "Work and the Instincts."[24] She defines work and play in terms of the instinctual stages involved in these activities. Play is entirely subject to the pleasure principle: pleasure is in the movement itself in so far as it activates erotogenic zones. "The fundamental feature of play is, that it is gratifying in itself, without serving any other purpose than that of instinctual gratification." The impulses that determine play are the pregenital ones: play expresses objectless autoeroticism and gratifies those component instincts which are already directed toward the objective world. Work, on the other hand, serves ends outside itself—namely, the ends of self-preservation. "To work is the active effort of the ego . . . to get from the outside world whatever is needed for self-preservation." This contrast establishes a parallelism between the organization of the instincts and that of human activity:

> Play is an aim in itself, work is the agent of self-preservation. Component instincts and autoerotic activities seek pleasure with no ulterior consequences; genital activity is the agent of procreation. The genital organization of the sexual instincts has a parallel in the work-organization of the ego-instincts.[25]

Thus it is the purpose and not the content which marks an activity as play or work.[26] A transformation in the instinctual structure (such as that from the pregenital to the genital stage) would entail a change in the instinctual value of the human activity *regardless of its content*. For example, if work were accompanied by a reactivation of

---

[23]*Ibid.*

[24]In *International Journal of Psychoanalysis,* Vol. XXIV (1943), Parts 3 and 4, pp. 114ff.
[25]*Ibid.,* p. 117.
[26]*Ibid.,* p. 118.

pregenital polymorphous eroticism, it would tend to become gratifying in itself without losing its *work* content. Now it is precisely such a reactivation of polymorphous eroticism which appeared as the consequence of the conquest of scarcity and alienation. The altered societal conditions would therefore create an instinctual basis for the transformation of work into play. In Freud's terms, the less the efforts to obtain satisfaction are impeded and directed by the interest in domination, the more freely the libido could prop itself upon the satisfaction of the great vital needs. Sublimation and domination hang together. And the dissolution of the former would, with the transformation of the instinctual structure, also transform the basic attitude toward man and nature which has been characteristic of Western civilization.

In psychoanalytic literature, the development of libidinal work relations is usually attributed to a "general maternal attitude as the dominant trend of a culture."[27] Consequently, it is considered as a feature of primitive societies rather than as a possibility of mature civilization. Margaret Mead's interpretation of Arapesh culture is entirely focused on this attitude:

> To the Arapesh, the world is a garden that must be tilled, not for one's self, not in pride and boasting, not for hoarding and usury, but that the yams and the dogs and the pigs and most of all the children may grow. From this whole attitude flow many of the other Arapesh traits, the lack of conflict between the old and young, the lack of any expectation of jealousy or envy, the emphasis upon co-operation.[28]

Foremost in this description appears the fundamentally different experience of the world: nature is taken, not as an object of domination and exploitation, but as a "garden" which can grow while making human beings grow. It is the attitude that experiences man and nature as joined in a non-repressive and still functioning order. We have seen how the otherwise most divergent traditions of thought converged on this idea: the philosophical opposition against the performance principle; the Orphic and Narcissistic archetypes; the aesthetic conception. But while the psychoanalytical and anthropological concepts of such an order have been oriented on the prehistorical and precivilized *past,* our discussion of the concept is oriented on the *future,* on the conditions of fully mature civilization. The transformation of sexuality into Eros, and its extension to lasting libidinal work relations, here presuppose the rational reorganization of a huge industrial apparatus, a highly specialized societal division of labor, the use of fantastically destructive energies, and the co-operation of vast masses.

The idea of libidinal work relations in a developed industrial society finds little support in the tradition of thought, and where such support is forthcoming it seems of a dangerous nature. The transformation of labor into pleasure is the central idea in Fourier's giant socialist utopia. If

> . . . l'industrie est la destination qui nous est assignée par le créateur, comment penser qu'il veuille nous y amener par la violence, et qu'il n'ait pas su mettre en jeu quelque ressort plus noble, quelqu'amorce capable de transformer les travaux en plaisirs.[29]

---

[27]Róheim, *The Origin and Function of Culture,* p. 75.
[28]*Sex and Temperament in Three Primitive Societies* (New York: New American Library, 1952), p. 100.

[29]If "industry is the fate assigned to us by the Creator, how can one believe that he wishes to force us into it—that he does not know how to bring to bear some nobler means, some enticement capable of transforming work into pleasure." F. Armand and R. Maublanc, *Fourier: Textes Choisis* (Paris: Editions Sociales Internationales, 1937), III, 154.

Fourier insists that this transformation requires a complete change in the social institutions: distribution of the social product according to need, assignment of functions according to individual faculties and inclinations, constant mutation of functions, short work periods, and so on. But the possibility of "attractive labor" (*travail attrayant*) derives above all from the release of libidinal forces. Fourier assumes the existence of an *attraction industrielle* which makes for pleasurable co-operation. It is based on the *attraction passionnée* in the nature of man, which persists despite the opposition of reason, duty, prejudice. This *attraction passionnée* tends toward three principal objectives: the creation of "luxury, or the pleasure of the five senses"; the formation of libidinal groups (of friendship and love); and the establishment of a harmonious order, organizing these groups for work in accordance with the development of the individual "passions" (internal and external "play" of faculties).[30] Fourier comes closer than any other utopian socialist to elucidating the dependence of freedom on non-repressive sublimation. However, in his detailed blueprint for the realization of this idea, he hands it over to a giant organization and administration and thus retains the repressive elements. The working communities of the *phalanstère* anticipate "strength through joy" rather than freedom, the beautification of mass culture rather than its abolition. Work as free play cannot be subject to administration; only alienated labor can be organized and administered by rational routine. It is beyond this sphere, but on its basis, that non-repressive sublimation creates its own cultural order.

Once more, we emphasize that non-repressive sublimation is utterly incompatible with the institutions of the performance principle and implies the negation of this principle. This contradiction is the more important since post-Freudian psychoanalytic theory itself shows a marked tendency to obliterate it and to glorify repressive productivity as human self-realization. A striking example is provided by Ives Hendrick in his paper "Work and the Pleasure Principle."[31] He suggests that the "energy and the need to exercise the physiological organs available for work" are not provided by the libido but rather by a special instinct, the "mastery instinct." Its aim is "to control, or alter a piece of the environment . . . by the skillful use of perceptual, intellectual, and motor techniques." This drive for "integration and skillful performance" is "mentally and emotionally experienced as the need to perform work efficiently."[32] Since work is thus supposed to be itself the gratification of an instinct rather than the "temporary negation" of an instinct, work "yields pleasure" in efficient performance. Work pleasure results from the satisfaction of the mastery instinct, but "work pleasure" and libidinal pleasure usually coincide, since the ego organizations which function as work are "generally, and perhaps always, utilized concurrently for the discharge of surplus libidinal tension."[33]

As usual, the revision of Freudian theory means a retrogression. The assumption of any special instinct begs the question, but the assumption of a special "mastery instinct" does even more: it destroys the entire structure and dynamic of the "mental apparatus" which Freud has built. Moreover, it obliterates the most repressive features of the performance principle by interpreting them as gratification of an instinctual need. Work pure and simple is the chief social manifestation of the reality principle. In so far as work is conditional upon delay and diversion of instinctual gratification (and

---

[30] *Ibid.,* II, 240ff.

[31] *Psychoanalytic Quarterly,* Vol. XII, No. 3 (1943).
[32] *Ibid.,* p. 314.
[33] *Ibid.,* p. 317.

according to Freud it is), it contradicts the pleasure principle. If work pleasure and libidinal pleasure "usually coincide," then the very concept of the reality principle becomes meaningless and superfluous, and the vicissitudes of the instincts as described by Freud would at best be an abnormal development. Nor can the reality principle be saved by stipulating (as Hendrick does) a work principle different from the reality principle; for if the latter does not govern work it has practically nothing to govern in the reality.

To be sure, there is work that yields pleasure in skillful performance of the bodily organs "available for work." But what kind of work, and what kind of pleasure? If pleasure is indeed in the act of working and not extraneous to it, such pleasure must be derived from the acting organs of the body and the body itself, activating the erotogenic zones or eroticizing the body as a whole; in other words, it must be libidinal pleasure. In a reality governed by the performance principle, such "libidinal" work is a rare exception and can occur only outside or at the margin of the work world— as "hobby," play, or in a directly erotic situation. The normal kind of work (socially useful occupational activity) in the prevailing division of labor is such that the individual, in working, does *not* satisfy *his* own impulses, needs, and faculties but performs a pre-established function. Hendrick, however, takes no notice of the fact of *alienated* labor, which is the predominant mode of work under the given reality principle. Certainly there can be "pleasure" in alienated labor too. The typist who hands in a perfect transcript, the tailor who delivers a perfectly fitting suit, the beauty-parlor attendant who fixes the perfect hairdo, the laborer who fulfills his quota—all may feel pleasure in a "job well done." However, either this pleasure is extraneous (anticipation of reward), or it is the satisfaction (itself a token of repression) of being well occupied, in the right place, of contributing one's part to the functioning of the apparatus. In either case, such pleasure has nothing to do with primary instinctual gratification. To link performances on assembly lines, in offices and shops with instinctual needs is to glorify dehumanization as pleasure. It is no wonder that Hendrick considers as the "sublime test of men's will to perform their work effectively" the efficient functioning of an army which has no longer any "fantasies of victory and a pleasant future," which keeps on fighting for no other reason than because it is the soldier's job to fight, and "to do the job was the only motivation that was still meaningful."[34] To say that the job must be done because it is a "job" is truly the apex of alienation, the total loss of instinctual and intellectual freedom—repression which has become, not the second, but the first nature of man.

In contrast to such aberrations, the true spirit of psychoanalytic theory lives in the uncompromising efforts to reveal the anti-humanistic forces behind the philosophy of productiveness:

> Of all things, hard work has become a virtue instead of the curse it was always advertised to be by our remote ancestors. . . . Our children should be prepared to bring their children up so they won't have to work as a neurotic necessity. The necessity to work is a neurotic symptom. It is a crutch. It is an attempt to make oneself feel valuable even though there is no particular need for one's working.[35]

---

[34] *Ibid.*, p. 324.
[35] C. B. Chisholm in the panel discussion "The Psychiatry of Enduring Peace and Social Progress," in *Psychiatry*, Vol. IX, No. 1 (1946), p. 31.

chapter thirty-five
Emmanuel Levinas

Emmanuel Levinas (1906–1995), philosopher and Talmudic[1] commentator, made ethical responsibility for "the Other" the centerpiece of his philosophical system. Levinas challenged what he believed was the Western philosophical tradition's erroneous privileging of ontology (the study of being) as first philosophy. Ethics, not ontology, is fundamental, Levinas argued, for long before human beings are ever concerned with knowing what *is*, we are already "passively" immersed in, and responding to, a world of others; we are ethical *before* we are concerned with consciousness. The starting point of Levinas's philosophical analysis is therefore not the conscious ego, epitomized by Descartes' *cogito*, but rather the ethical subject as she experiences the world "on the hither side of consciousness."[2] Levinas's system is therefore devoted to analyzing the nature and implications of this primordial ethical experience. He concludes that the self is only possible in the context of recognition of "the Other"—before the subject is "for-itself" it is already "for-the-Other"—and that what this preconscious recognition reveals is that the self is always *responsible for* the Other. This conclusion, which Levinas believed both held the answer to the social and political problems of modernity and was the source of peace, influenced several generations of French philosophers endeavoring to develop a genuinely postmodern philosophy, among them Jacques Derrida, Paul Ricoeur, and Jean-Luc Nancy.

Levinas was born in Kaunas, Lithuania, to a family prominent within Kaunas's large Jewish community. The Levinas family prized learning (Emmanuel's father owned a bookshop) and spoke both Russian and Yiddish in their home; Emmanuel was also taught to read the Bible in Hebrew. When the family moved to Kharkov, Ukraine, during World War I, Emmanuel attended the Jewish Russian-language lyceum there. The Levinases returned to Lithuania after the Russian Revolution.

In 1923 Levinas entered Strasbourg University to study philosophy, and there he met Charles Blondel, Maurice Blanchot (with whom he shared a lifelong friendship), and other influential figures. In 1928 Levinas went to Freiburg University to study phenomenology under Edmund Husserl. There he also met Martin Heidegger, whose *Being and*

From Emmanuel Levinas, *Time and the Other*, translated by Richard A. Cohen. Copyright © 1987 by Duquesne University Press. Reprinted with permission.

Time (1927) had a lasting influence on his thought. Levinas introduced the ideas of Husserl and Heidegger in France—first by way of his doctoral dissertation, *The Theory of Intuition in Husserl's Phenomenology* (1930), and subsequently by translating Husserl's *Cartesian Meditations* into French and writing an essay on Heidegger in 1932.[3] Levinas's reputation in France as an authority on Husserl earned him a distinguished audience, Jean-Paul Sartre being among his readers. After completing his doctorate, Levinas taught at the Ecole Normale Israelite Orientale in Paris.

Levinas's own philosophical system began to emerge after World War II; it was a philosophy that grew out of, and reflected, his own harrowing experience of the war, and it elaborated his diagnosis of the crisis of modernity. Levinas, at that time a French citizen and soldier, was imprisoned in a camp in Germany. Meanwhile, his wife and daughter were forced to hide in a French monastery, and his family in Lithuania was killed in the Holocaust. Against the background of these horrifying events, Levinas came to reject philosophy's traditional preoccupation with the ethically neutral subdisciplines of metaphysics and epistemology. Emphasizing ethics instead, Levinas began to conceive a philosophical system specifically to reach *beyond* ontology.

In leaving ontology to explore the ethical "hither" side of consciousness, Levinas opened a completely new horizon for exploring the ego's primordial relationships to its own being and to other beings. He found in Descartes' Third Meditation the idea to guide his analysis of these primordial phenomena: the idea of infinity, which Descartes had portrayed as being both innate in the thinking human subject and also transcending the subject. This idea of infinity suggested a valuable counterpoint to philosophical idealism's assertion that the world is constituted solely by mind, for, as one Levinas scholar explains, "When the I contemplates the idea of infinity, it thinks more than it thinks in the sense that there is an *excess* in this idea for which the I which contemplates is unable to account. The I is forced to acknowledge that it is not the source or origin of what it thinks; rather, it is *overflowed* by what it thinks."[4] In other words, the mind can never fully grasp infinity, and so, contrary to the claim of the philosophical idealist, there is more to reality than what the minds perceives or grasps. Vetlesen continues, "Having transcended the I's idea of it, infinity is assumed by the I as the absolute other. Not of our making, nor an object of recollection for a soul already familiar with it, the idea of infinity can only have been given to us by a reality outside of us."[5]

Levinas believed that the Infinite, the Absolute Other, is revealed concretely in the face of the other person. When I confront the face of another person, I confront it as having already existed prior to this meeting; it is an absolute otherness that is prior to my life, beyond my life, and incomprehensible to me. As such, the face of the other person is experienced by the ego in the same way that the ego experiences the Infinite. Whereas in consciousness the ego may, as Hegel claimed, conceive of its relation to the Other as intersubjective and hence comprehensible, on the hither side of consciousness the face of the Other has already confronted the ego from a beyond, is *prior* to the ego, and therefore can never be grasped by the ego. Levinas writes, "Here . . . the face is meaning all by itself. . . . It is what cannot become a content, which your thoughts would embrace; it is uncontainable, it leads you beyond."[6]

Furthermore, Levinas claims that when the face of the Other confronts me, it commands me; *I am responsible for the Other*. However, even as Levinas emphasizes the command of the face upon the vulnerable ego, he acknowledges at the same time a vulnerability, even a poverty, in the face of the Other. Thus the face appears to me in two ways: it commands me as a master and, at the same time, as a completely defenseless being. The Other's command is that I *choose not to kill him*.[7]

Levinas emphasizes the human being's primordial responsibility for the Other because he sees in it the solution to the larger problem of human existence: the ego's desire for *excendence*, escape from being. *Excendence* is related to, but distinguished from, transcendence. Levinas traces both to the problem of the ego's enchainment to bodily existence, but whereas the desire for transcendence is asserted in traditional philosophy as the wish to exceed human finitude, the desire for *excendence*, identified by Levinas, expresses the human longing, not merely to transcend finitude, the limits of one's existence, but to *escape* existence altogether. Levinas writes in an early essay, "Escape is the need to get out of oneself, that is, *to break that most radical and unalterably binding of chains, the fact that the ego is oneself*." My only chance for escape, according to Levinas, lies in a situation in which I am "somewhere else than myself." I achieve *excendence* when I encounter absolute otherness, "the most radical breakup of the very categories of the ego." In *excendence*, I encounter mystery in the Other and hold up that mystery rather than seeking to sublate it, for "it is not possible," Levinas reminds us, "to grasp the alterity of the other."[8]

In *Time and the Other*, Levinas points to the erotic relationship as a concrete example of the human subject's encounter with ungraspable absolute otherness: "It is in eros that transcendence can be conceived as something radical, which brings the ego caught up in being, ineluctably returning to itself, something else than this return, can free it of its shadow."[9] Thus the specific feature of eros that makes transcendence possible is the confrontation with ungraspable alterity, the mystery of the Other, which the subject must embrace but can never possess. Levinas observes, "The pathos of love . . . consists in an insurmountable duality of beings. It is a relationship with what always slips away."[10]

For Levinas, the Other *par excellence* is the feminine, which he describes as "essentially other."[11] He identifies woman as other not because he is himself a man, nor does he mean by her mystery "any romantic notions of the mysterious, unknown, or misunderstood woman." Rather, woman's essential alterity lies in the fact of her modesty—a woman withdraws, retreats in modesty, and therein lies her mystery:

> Hiding is the way of the feminine, and this fact of hiding is precisely her modesty. So this feminine alterity does not consist in the object's simple exteriority. Neither is it made up of an opposition of wills. The Other is not a being we encounter that menaces us or wants to lay hold of us. The feat of being refractory to our power is not a power greater than ours. Alterity makes for all its power. Its mystery constitutes its alterity.[12]

Thus the very phenomenon of eros itself is mysterious, something beyond our power: "Love is not a possibility, is not due to our initiative, is without reason; it invades and wounds us, and nevertheless the *I* survives in it."[13] In the erotic relationship the ego confronts what it cannot grasp and possess—the mystery of the Other and of eros itself, which overtake the ego—such the ego gets out of itself without losing itself entirely. In embracing the "ungraspable" Other and entering into the mystery of eros, the ego stumbles upon the means of escape.

For Levinas, the first step to resolving the crisis of modernity lies in our ability to recognize that "responsibility or saying, prior to being and entities, is not said in ontological categories."[14] Ethical responsibility for the Other—not metaphysics—is first philosophy. The erotic relationship is one such ethical relationship, but, as Levinas claims in later texts, in the encounter with the Other I meet *all* others. This is the origin of justice. In light of this it is important to observe, says Levinas, that the Other "does not limit but promotes my freedom, by arousing my goodness."[15] "Philosophy here," Levinas writes, "is like the wisdom of love."[16]

Levinas served as director of the Ecole until 1961, when he was appointed professor of philosophy at the University of Poitiers. That year he published his first major work, *Totality and Infinity* (1961), which extends his treatment of the "face-to-face" relation with the Other through further analyses of such phenomena as desire, language, and justice. In 1967, Levinas accepted a position at University of Paris-Nanterre; he moved to the Sorbonne in 1973. Levinas's second major work, *Otherwise than Being or Beyond Essence* (1974), is a further elaboration of his system, widely considered to be his most important contribution to the contemporary debate concerning the end of metaphysical discourse. Subsequently, Levinas produced a number of "confessional writings," including the Talmudic commentaries *Quatre lectures Talmudiques* (*Four Talmudic Lectures,* 1968), *Du sacré au saint* (*The Sacred to the Saint,* 1977), and *L'au-delà du verset* (*Beyond the Verse,* 1982).

Levinas retired in 1979 and devoted his last years to writing books that sometimes sold as many as 200,000 copies. He died in Paris on December 25, 1995.

SC

QUESTIONS

1. Explain Levinas's claim that the face of another person is *absolutely other.*

2. Why does Levinas say, "I am responsible for the Other"?

3. Explain and evaluate Levinas's claims that the feminine is "the absolutely contrary contrary" and "[h]iding is the way of existing of the feminine." Can a female person be "I" according to Levinas's account? Can a male person be the Other in an erotic relationship? Defend your answer.

4. Why does Levinas say that the "relationship with the other through Eros" can be "characterized as a failure," but there is nothing of the features that characterize failure in eros?

5. Compare Levinas's conception of eros to that offered by another philosopher you have studied so far.

ENDNOTES

1. The Talmud is the body of Jewish religious and civil law, with related commentaries and discussion.

2. Levinas, "Substitution," from *Basic Philosophical Writings*, p. 83.

3. Levinas later regretted his enthusiasm for Heidegger, who joined the Nazi Party in 1933. Commenting on a Talmudic discussion of forgiveness Levinas wrote, "One can forgive many Germans, but there are some Germans it is difficult to forgive. It is difficult to forgive Heidegger"; quoted in Steinfels, "Emmanuel Levinas."

4. Vetlesen, p. 368.

5. Ibid.

6. Levinas, *Ethics and Infinity*, pp. 86–87.

7. Compare Levinas's analysis here of the original encounter of two consciousnesses with Hegel's analysis in "Mastery and Slavery" (see pages 429–434).

8. Levinas, *Time and the Other*, pp. 85–86.

9. Ibid., pp. 99–100.

10. Ibid., p. 86.

11. This claim would be the subject of Simone de Beauvoir's critique in *The Second Sex* (1949). See note 3 of her introduction, p. 568.

12. Levinas, *Time and the Other*, pp. 86–87.

13. Ibid., pp. 88–89.

14. Levinas, "Humanism and An-Archy," from *Collected Philosophical Papers*, p. 139.

15. Levinas, *Totality and Infinity*, p. 200.

16. Levinas, "Peace and Proximity," from *Basic Philosophical Writings*, p. 169.

SELECTED BIBLIOGRAPHY

Levinas, Emmanuel. *Basic Philosophical Writings*, ed. Adriaan T. Peperzak, Simon Critchley, and Robert Bernasconi. Indianapolis: Indiana University Press, 1996.

Levinas, Emmanuel. *Collected Philosophical Papers*, trans. Alphonso Lingis. Pittsburgh, Penn.: Duquesne University Press, 1998.

Levinas, Emmanuel. *Ethics and Infinity: Conversations with Philippe Nemo*, trans. Richard A. Cohen. Pittsburgh, Penn.: Duquesne University Press, 1985.

Levinas, Emmanuel. *Existence and Existents*, trans. Alphonso Lingis. Pittsburgh, Penn.: Duquesne University Press, 1988.

Levinas, Emmanuel. *Otherwise than Being or Beyond Essence*, trans. Alphonso Lingis. Pittsburgh, Penn.: Duquesne University Press, 1998.

Levinas, Emmanuel. *Totality and Infinity: An Essay on Exteriority*, trans. Alphonso Lingis. Pittsburgh, Penn.: Duquesne University Press, 1969.

Steinfels, Peter. "Emmanuel Levinas." *New York Times*, December 27, 1995.

Vetlesen, Arne Johan. "Relations with Others in Sartre and Levinas: Assessing Some Implications for an Ethics of Proximity," from *Constellations* 1995, AK 1:3.

from *Time and the Other*

Emmanuel Levinas

[PART IV]

Part III began with suffering as the event whereby the existent manages to accomplish all its solitude—that is, all the intensity of its tie with itself, all the finality of its identity—and at the same time it is that whereby the subject finds itself in relationship with the event that it does not assume, which is absolutely other, and in regard to which it is a pure passivity and no longer able to be able. This future of death determines the future for us, the future insofar as it is not present. It determines what in the future contrasts strongly with all anticipation, projection, and élan. Starting from such a notion of the future to understand time, one never again meets with time as a "moving image of eternity."[1] . . .

Power and Relationship With The Other

The strangeness of the future of death does not leave the subject any initiative. There is an abyss between the present and death, between the ego and the alterity of mystery. It is not the fact that death cuts existence short, that it is end and nothingness, but the fact that the ego is absolutely without initiative in the face of it. Vanquishing death is not a problem of eternal life. Vanquishing death is to maintain, with the alterity of the event, a relationship that must still be personal.

What, then, is this personal relationship other than the subject's power over the world, meanwhile protecting its personality? How can the subject be given a definition that somehow lies in its passivity? Is there another mastery in the human other than the virility of grasping the possible, the *power to be able* ["*pouvoir de pouvoir*"]? If we find it, it is in it, in this relation that very place of time will consist. I already said in Part III that this relation is the relationship with the Other.

But a solution does not consist in repeating the terms of the problem. It is a matter of specifying what this relationship with the Other can be. Someone has objected to me that in my relationship with the Other it is not only the Other's future that I encounter, that the other as existent already has a past for me and, consequently, does not have a privilege over the future. This objection will allow me to approach the main part of my exposition here. . . .

If the relationship with the other involves more than relationships with mystery, it is because one has accosted the other in everyday life where the solitude and fundamental alterity of the other are already veiled by decency. One is for the other what the other is for oneself; there is no exceptional place

---

[1] Plato, *Timaeus*, 37.

for the subject. The other is known through sympathy, as another (my)self, as the alter ego.[2] In Blanchot's novel *Aminadab*, this situation is pushed to the absurd. Between the persons circulating in the strange house where the action takes place, where there is no work to pursue, where they only abide—that is, exist—this social relationship becomes total reciprocity. These beings are not interchangeable but reciprocal, or rather they are interchangeable because they are reciprocal. And then the relationship with the other becomes impossible.

But already, in the very heart of the relationship with the other that characterizes our social life, alterity appears as a nonreciprocal relationship—that is, as contrasting strongly with contemporaneousness. The Other as Other is not only an alter ego: the Other is what I myself am not.[3] The Other is this, not because of the Other's character, or physiognomy, or psychology, but because of the Other's very alterity. The Other is, for example, the weak, the poor, "the widow and the orphan,"[4] whereas I am the rich or the powerful. It can be said that intersubjective space is not symmetrical.[5] The exteriority of the other is not simply due to the space that separates what remains identical through the concept, nor is it due to any difference the concept would manifest through spatial exteriority. The relationship with alterity is neither spatial nor conceptual. Durkheim has misunderstood the specificity of the other when he asks in what Other rather than myself is the object of a virtuous action.[6] Does not the essential difference between charity and justice come from the preference of charity for the other, even when, from the point of view of justice, no preference is any longer possible?[7]

Eros[8]

In civilized life there are traces of this relationship with the other that one must investigate in its original form. Does a situation exist where the alterity of

---

[2]It is at the level of the "decency" of "everyday life" then, that Levinas finds a place for the sympathy and pairing that he has rejected as ultimately constitutive of the inter-subjective relationship.

[3]For Levinas this formulation does not necessarily lead to the conclusion of the German Idealists—namely, that alterity is only encountered through *negation*. Philosophers can perhaps hardly be reminded too often of this difference. For Levinas the alterity encountered through negativity is merely a relative, not an absolute, alterity. To grasp alterity *outside* even negativity, and thus in a truly positive "sense," is perhaps the essence of Levinas' entire effort.

[4]The Hebrew Bible contains many references to the orphan and the widow jointly: Exodus 22:21; Deuteronomy 10:18, 24:17, 24:19, 24:20, 24:21, 26:12, 27:19; Isaiah 1:17, 9:16, 10:2; Jeremiah 7:6, 22:3; Ezekiel 22:7; Zechariah 7:10; Malachi 3:5; Psalms 68:6, 109:9, 146:9; Lamentations 5:3. Relevant to Levinas' emphasis on the alterity of the other, in all these instances (except Isaiah, and at 68:6 in Psalms where the "solitary" is mentioned; and, one should add, in James 1:27, where the orphan and the widow are mentioned together), the *stranger* is always also mentioned in conjunction with the orphan and the widow.

[5]See the section entitled "The Asymmetry of the Interpersonal" in *Totality and Infinity*, pp. 215–16, also p. 251 and passim.

[6]According to Durkheim, "morality is the product of the collective" and not the result of the face-to-face encounter. See "The Determination of Moral Facts" and "Replies to Objections" in Emile Durkheim, *Sociology and Philosophy*, translated by D. Pocock (New York: MacMillan Publishing Co., 1974), pp. 35–79.

[7]Although, inasmuch as our culture is predominately Christian, one might see here an allusion only to the alleged opposition between "Christian mercy" and "Jewish justice," in addition to being an internal Christian opposition (often enough, it is true, expressed in terms of a Christian vision of Judaism), the allusion here is certainly also to an ancient and properly internal Jewish opposition—namely, that between God's *chesed*, kindness, and God's *gevurah*, justice. To be sure, this opposition is equally a secular, moral opposition.

[8]For a fuller development of the analysis of eros and fecundity (the topic of the next section), see section 4, "Beyond the Face," of *Totality and Infinity*, pp. 254–85. Also see "Phenomenology of the Face and Carnal Intimacy" by A. Lingis in his book, *Libido: The French Existential Theories* (Bloomington: Indiana University Press, 1985), pp. 58–73; and "The Fecundity of the Caress" by L. Irigaray, in *Face to Face with Levinas*, edited by R. Cohen (Albany: State University of New York Press, 1986), pp. 231–56.

the other appears in its purity? Does a situation exist where the other would not have alterity only as the reverse side of its identity, would not comply only with the Platonic law of participation where every term contains a sameness and through this sameness contains the Other? Is there not a situation where alterity would be borne by a being in a positive sense, as essence? What is the alterity that does not purely and simply enter into the opposition of two species of the same genus? I think the absolutely contrary contrary [*le contraire absolutement contraire*], whose contrariety is in no way affected by the relationship that can be established between it and its correlative, the contrariety that permits its terms to remain absolutely other, is the *feminine*.[9]

Sex is not some specific difference. It is situated beside the logical division into genera and species. This division certainly never manages to reunite an empirical content. But it is not in this sense that it does not permit one to account for the difference between the sexes. The difference between the sexes is a formal structure, but one that carves up reality in another sense and conditions the very possibility of reality as multiple, against the unity of being proclaimed by Parmenides.

Neither is the difference between the sexes a contradiction. The contradiction of being and nothingness leads from one to the other, leaving no room for distance. Nothingness converts into being, which has led us to the notion of the "there is." The negation of being occurs at the level of the anonymous existing of being in general.

Neither is the difference between the sexes the duality of two complementary terms, for two complementary terms presuppose a preexisting whole. To say that sexual duality presuppose a whole is to posit love beforehand as fusion.[10] The pathos of love, however, consists in an insurmountable duality of beings. It is a relationship with what always slips away. The relationship does not *ipso facto* neutralize alterity but preserves it. The pathos of voluptuousness lies in the fact of being two. The other as other is not here an object that becomes ours or becomes us; to the contrary, it withdraws into its mystery. Neither does this mystery of the feminine—the feminine: essentially other—refer to any romantic notions of the mysterious, unknown, or misunderstood woman. Let it be understood that if, in order to uphold the thesis of the exceptional position of the feminine in the economy of being, I willingly refer to the great themes of Goethe or Dante, to Beatrice and the *ewig Weibliches*, to the cult of the *Woman* in chivalry and in modern society (which is certainly not explained solely by the necessity of lending a strong arm to the weaker sex)—if, more precisely, I think of the admirably bold pages of Léon Bloy in his *Letters to his Fiancée*,[11] I do not want to ignore the legitimate claims of the feminism that presupposes all the acquired attainments of civilization. I simply want to say that this mystery must not be understood in the ethereal sense of a certain literature; that in the

---

[9]This sentence and some of those that follow were cited by Simone de Beauvoir in 1949 in *The Second Sex* (translated by H. Parshley [New York: Bantam Books, Inc., 1970], p. xvi, n. 3) to condemn Levinas for sexism.

De Beauvoir takes Levinas to task for allegedly assigning a secondary, derivative status to women: subject (he) as absolute, woman as other. The issue is important but certainly not as simple as de Beauvoir, in this instance, makes it out to be, because for Levinas the other has a priority over the subject. For a more sympathetic treatment of Levinas' thought on this issue, see C. Chalier, *Figures du féminin* (Paris: La nuit surveillée, 1982).

For Levinas' most recent thoughts on this issue, with regard to *Time and the Other*, see "Love and Filiation" in Levinas, *Ethics and Infinity*, translated by R. Cohen (Pittsburgh: Duquesne University Press, 1985), pp. 65–72.

[10]This is Aristophanes' position in Plato's *Symposium*.

[11]*Lettres à sa Fiancée* (Paris: Stock, 1922); English translation (New York: Sheed and Ward, 1937). Léon Bloy (1846–1917) was a prolific French Catholic writer with a strong Jansenist bent.

most brutal materiality, in the most shameless or the most prosaic appearance of the feminine, neither her mystery nor her modesty are abolished. Profanation is not a negation of mystery, but one of the possible relationships with it.

What matters to me in this notion of the feminine is not merely the unknowable, but a mode of being that consists in slipping away from the light. The feminine in existence is an event different from that of spatial transcendence or of expression that go toward light. It is a flight before light. Hiding is the way of existing of the feminine, and this fact of hiding is precisely modesty. So this feminine alterity does not consist in the object's simple exteriority. Neither is it made up of an opposition of wills. The Other is not a being we encounter that menaces us or wants to lay hold of us. The feat of being refractory to our power is not a power greater than ours. Alterity makes for all its power. Its mystery constitutes its alterity. A fundamental comment: I do not initially posit the Other as freedom, a characteristic in which the failure of communication is inscribed in advance. For with a freedom there can be no other relationship than that of submission or enslavement. In both cases, one of the two freedoms is annihilated. The relationship between master and slave can be grasped at the level of struggle, but then it becomes reciprocal. Hegel has shown precisely how the master becomes slave of the slave and the slave becomes master of the master.[12]

---

[12]Surely, in addition to Hegel, Levinas has Sartre's philosophy of freedom in mind. *Being and Nothingness* was published only five years earlier than *Time and the Other* (although Levinas, a German captive for the duration of W.W. II, had not yet read it in 1946, by his own admission [see Jean Wahl, *A Short History of Existentialism*, translated by F. Williams and S. Maron (New York: Philosophical Library, 1949)], p. 51).

For some recent critical remarks by Levinas on the early Sartre, see Richard Kearney's "Dialogue with Emmanuel Levinas," in *Face to Face with Levinas*, edited by R. Cohen (Albany: State University of New York Press, 1986), pp. 16–17.

In positing the Other's alterity as mystery, itself defined by modesty, I do not posit it as a freedom identical to and at grips with mine; I do not posit another existent in front of me, I posit alterity. Just as with death, I am not concerned with an existent, but with the event of alterity, with alienation. The other is not initially characterized as freedom, from which alterity would then be deduced; the other bears alterity as an essence. And this is why I have sought this alterity in the absolutely original relationship of eros, a relationship that is impossible to translate into powers and must not be so translated, if one does not want to distort the meaning of the situation.

I am thus describing a category that falls neither into the being-nothingness opposition, nor into the notion of the existent. It is an event in existing different from the hypostasis by which an existent arises. The existent is accomplished in the "subjective" and in "consciousness"; alterity is accomplished in the feminine. This term is on the same level as, but in meaning opposed to, consciousness. The feminine is not accomplished as a *being [étant]* in a transcendence toward light, but in modesty.

The movement here is thus inverse. The transcendence of the feminine consists in withdrawing elsewhere, which is a movement opposed to the movement of consciousness. But this does not make it unconscious or subconscious, and I see no other possibility than to call it mystery.

Even when by positing the Other as freedom, by thinking of the Other in terms of light, I am obliged to admit the failure of communication, I have merely admitted the failure of the movement that tends to grasp or to possess a freedom. It is only by showing in what way eros differs from possession and power that I can acknowledge a communication in eros. It is neither a struggle, nor a fusion, nor a knowledge. One must recognize its exceptional place among relationships. It is a relationship with alterity, with mystery—that is to say, with the future, with what (in a world where there is everything) is never there, with what cannot be there when everything is there—not with a being that is not there, but with the very dimension of alterity. There where all possibles are impossible, where one can no longer be able, the subject is still a subject through eros. Love is not a possibility, is not due to our initiative, is without reason; it invades and wounds us, and nevertheless the *I* survives in it.

A phenomenology of voluptuousness, which I am only going to touch upon here—voluptuousness is not a pleasure like others, because it is not solitary like eating or drinking—seems to confirm my views on the exceptional role and place of the feminine, and on the absence of any fusion in the erotic.

The caress is a mode of the subject's being, where the subject who is in contact with another goes beyond this contact. Contact as sensation is part of the world of light. But what is caressed is not touched, properly speaking. It is not the softness or warmth of the hand given in contact that the caress seeks. The seeking of the caress constitutes its essence by the fact that the caress does not know what it seeks. This "not knowing," this fundamental disorder, is the essential. It is like a game with something slipping away, a game absolutely without project or plan, not with what can become ours or us, but with something other, always other, always inaccessible, and always still to come [*à venir*]. The caress is the anticipation of this pure future [*avenir*],[13] without content. It is made up of

this increase of hunger, of ever richer promises, opening new perspectives onto the ungraspable. It feeds on countless hungers.

This intentionality of the voluptuous—the sole intentionality of the future itself, and not an expectation of some future fact—has always been misunderstood by philosophical analysis. Freud himself says little more about the libido than that it searches for pleasure, taking pleasure as a simple content, starting with which one begins an analysis but which itself one does not analyze. Freud does not search for the significance of this pleasure in the general economy of being. My thesis, which consists in affirming voluptuousness as the very event of the future, the future purified of all content, the very mystery of the future, seeks to account for its exceptional place.

Can this relationship with the other through Eros be characterized as a failure? Once again, the answer is yes, if one adopts the terminology of current descriptions, if one wants to characterize the erotic by "grasping," "possessing," or "knowing." But there is nothing of all this, or the failure of all this, in eros. If one could possess, grasp, and know the other, it would not be other. Possessing, knowing, and grasping are synonyms of power.

Furthermore, the relationship with the other is generally sought out as a fusion. I have precisely wanted to contest the idea that the relationship with the other is fusion. The relationship with the Other is the absence of the other; not absence pure and simple, not the absence of pure nothingness, but absence in a horizon of the future, an absence that is time. This is the horizon where a personal life can be constituted in the heart of the transcendent event, what I called above the "victory over death." I must say a few words about it in concluding. . . .

---

[13] *Venir* is a verb meaning "to come" or—especially in the construction *à venir*—"about to come"; *avenir* is a noun meaning "future." These latter two terms sound exactly the same in French. Levinas is emphasizing the essential connection between their meanings: the future is what is always about to come—that is, what is always about to come into the present but has not yet done so and never will (lest it be present rather than future).

chapter thirty-six

Michel Foucault

Michel Foucault (1926–1984), philosopher, psychologist, and historian of thought, was, along with contemporaries like Jacques Derrida, Gilles Deleuze, and Louis Althusser, one of the most influential thinkers in post-1950s French philosophy. Born in Poitiers, into what was at the time a prominent bourgeois family, Foucault devoted his entire philosophical system, first implicitly and then explicitly, to the concept of "power" and to its effects on the institutional structures and arrangements of knowledge encountered in various distinct historical epochs, or periods.

On the rare occasions Foucault spoke of his childhood, it was usually in very negative terms. He complained of provincial Poitiers's narrow-mindedness, as well as of having to participate in his parents' active social lives. His father, a doctor, organized numerous dinner parties, and Foucault would later recall how his father's social functions imposed on his son "the obligation of speaking, of making conversation with strangers." Foucault's few recollections of his childhood hint at a strained relationship with his father, due, on the one hand, to the obligations imposed on Michel by his father's medical practice and, on the other, by Michel's difficulties in school and his eventual refusal to follow the plan his father had set out for him. Though Foucault had from the beginning been a good, if not exemplary, student, he underwent in 1940 a crisis that would lead to his failing his end-of-year examinations. Foucault never explained exactly what had led to the deterioration of his academic performance, but whatever the reason, his mother took immediate action. In the autumn of 1940, he transferred to a new school, the Collège Saint-Stanislas, a compromise between the secular *lycée* he had been attending and a devout Jesuit school that would have imposed a far more rigorous discipline on him.[1] The change in school had the desired effect on Foucault. His academic performance recovered quickly and he would gain excellent marks over the next three years, regularly winning prizes in French, history, Greek, and English.

In 1943, Foucault passed his *baccalauréat,* the exam all French students must take upon the completion of their secondary studies, with better than average results. The plan, as formulated by Foucault's father, now called for Michel to study medicine and eventually take over his father's practice. Foucault's reluctance to follow his father's plan was to be a cause of great tension between father and son, until Foucault's mother finally convinced her husband that their son should not be forced into doing anything he did not want to do. Disappointed, Foucault's father reluctantly agreed; Michel was now free to do as he chose.

Foucault's vision of the future was one in which he became a student at the *Ecole Normale Supérieure,* France's most prestigious university. Unable to study in Paris due to both the Nazi occupation and monetary restrictions, Foucault was forced to enter *hypokhâgne,* the program through which students must go in order to prepare the rigorous entrance examination, in Poitiers. This greatly reduced his chances of being admitted to the ENS, whose students almost exclusively came from the most prestigious Parisian *lycées.* In October of 1945, however, the end of World War II allowed Foucault to move to Paris, where he enrolled in the prestigious Lycée Henri-IV and once more set about preparing for the ENS's entrance examination. It is at Henri-IV that Foucault first met Jean Hyppolite, who had become France's most prominent Hegel scholar. Hyppolite would soon leave Henri-IV to teach at the University of Strasbourg, but their paths would cross again, first at the Sorbonne and then at the ENS. In the meantime, Foucault continued his studies, making rapid progress in philosophy, as well as in history, Greek, and Latin. In 1946, Foucault sat the entrance examination for the second time, finishing fourth overall. It was during the oral component of the examination that Foucault was to meet Georges Canguilhem, a medically qualified historian of science who later was to have a profound impact on the direction of Foucault's philosophical thought.

Foucault began his studies at the ENS in 1946 and soon decided on pursuing the *aggrégation* in philosophy (though he developed a parallel interest in psychology), in which he would earn a degree in 1949.[2] The intellectual landscape of postwar France was dominated not so much by Jean-Paul Sartre, who had published *Being and Nothingness* only three years earlier, but by Hegel's *Phenomenology of Spirit,* on which Alexandre Kojève had lectured for several years and which Hyppolite had only recently translated into French. Thus, many of the theses that emerged from the ENS at the time, including both Louis Althusser's and Foucault's, directly addressed the *Phenomenology* but ignored Sartre's phenomenological existentialism. Also prominent was Maurice Merleau-Ponty, whose lectures at the Sorbonne Foucault regularly attended and whose thought he deemed to be more rigorous than Sartre's.[3] It was during this time that Foucault also developed an interest in Nietzsche, Heidegger, and the literature of Maurice Blanchot and Georges Bataille. Foucault was also reading texts on the history of science, and by the time he sat, and passed, the *aggrégation* in 1951, he had already demarcated the line of study with which he would later become associated: the point at which the history of the sciences, a Heideggerian and Nietzschean philosophical line of thought, and literature intersect.

The logical step for those students who passed the *aggrégation* was to teach at a *lycée*. Foucault, however, who was at best ambivalent about teaching and had in the summer of 1952 completed a diploma course on psychopathology, chose instead to obtain admission to the Fondation Thiers in order to prepare a doctoral thesis on the history of psychiatry. Foucault spent only one year at the Fondation, moving to Lille in 1953 to teach at the university. Commuting from Paris to Lille and back again until his move to Sweden in 1955, Foucault continued work on the doctoral thesis that would become, in a circuitous way, his first great work, *Madness and Civilization.* He would also spend time in Poland and Germany before returning to Paris in 1960. There, he set about publishing his first book in view of earning his doctorate.

In *Madness and Civilization,* which was finally published in 1961, Foucault sought to determine what could be known about mental illness in a given epoch, or historical period. As he would later recall, "an object took shape for me: the knowledge invested in complex systems of institutions."[4] It is in this work that Foucault first puts to use the method of "archaeology," wherein arrangements of knowledge, that is, systems of thought, are treated as discursive formations independent of the beliefs and intentions of individuals. Focusing on discourse, or language, archaeology analyzes the way in which discursive formations, such as the discourse of medicine or of psychology, are created within a certain arrangement of knowledge that does not progress through history, but rather is peculiar to the material conditions of a given historical period. Thus, archaeology reveals that history does not flow toward a logical end in a progressive straight line, but rather is discontinuous, broken up into distinct epochs and therefore into distinct arrangements of knowledge.

In *Madness and Civilization,* Foucault identifies three such epochs, and they will serve as the background for most of his subsequent inquiries: the late Middle Ages and Renaissance, the classical era, and the modern period, which begins for Foucault in the late eighteenth century. The result of this archaeological approach to history is the realization that the modern concepts we think of as having always existed, such as that of mental illness or that of medicine (or, in later works, that of sexuality), are in fact recent inventions that could only come about within the arrangement of knowledge peculiar to the modern epoch. Thus, *Madness and Civilization* is an analysis of the way in which the concept of "madness" became, in the modern period, that of "mental illness." The book recounts the way in which the invention of the discourse of clinical psychology provided society with the means to establish a line between reason and unreason and silence those whom it deemed to be unreasonable.

Foucault further refined his archaeological approach to history in *The Order of Things* (1966). In this book, he provides an archaeology of three modern fields of study—philology (the study of language), economics, and biology—that culminates with an account of the way in which the human sciences (psychology, sociology, and the study of literature) came to be—and could only have come to be—in the modern period. Delving once more into how contemporary thought is both made possible and shaped by social institutions and practices, which are in turn made possible and shaped by an implicit arrangement of knowledge, Foucault proposes that it was only in the modern period that our concept of "man," as both a *subject* who engages in scientific study *and* as the very *object* of that scientific study, could have emerged.

In *The Archaeology of Knowledge* (1969), his sole methodological text, Foucault sought to define more clearly his archaeological method, describing the object of archaeology as the archive, that is, the collection of discourses that taken together reflect the arrangement of knowledge for any given historical epoch. It is around this time that the concept of power makes its explicit entrance into Foucault's thought: where his previous works had focused on implicit arrangements of knowledge as the conditions for the possibility of social institutions and practices and, ultimately, systems of thought, Foucault's work would now inquire into power as an assembling of forces underlying the production of these arrangements. It is also around this time that Foucault began to use a genealogical method to complement the method of archaeology he had used up to that point. While the difference between the two methods remains a point of contention both among scholars and within Foucault's work itself, genealogy seems to be concerned with nondiscursive practices, that is, the social practices that accompanied the emergence of new discourses and systems of thought.

Thus, in *Discipline and Punish* (1975), Foucault provides a genealogical account of punishment, describing three mechanisms of punishment (the *supplice,* or public torture, during the late Middle Ages and Renaissance, the "corrective city" during the classical period, and the prison during the modern period) as "modalities according to which the power to punish is exercised: three technologies of power."[5] He recounts the way in which a change in the way was exercised produced a corresponding change in the arrangement of knowledge concerning criminality and thus a change in the discourses and the social institutions and practices concerned with its punishment.

It should be noted that the concept of power as Foucault understands it is not that of a power that is *possessed* by any one person or group of persons, but rather one in which power is *exercised.* For Foucault, power is the underlying condition for the possibility of any given arrangement of knowledge: It invests institutions and relations between persons, it produces knowledge, and it is to be found in all aspects of society, rather than merely in those who are traditionally thought to be its possessors. In this sense, power is not solely oppressive, but is also a productive assembling of forces: power produces not only a given arrangement of knowledge and the discourses and institutions that accompany it, but also a certain conception of the human subject.

It is this last aspect of power that Foucault sought to investigate in his unfinished *History of Sexuality,* of which he published three volumes: an *Introduction* (1976), *Care of the Self* (1984), and *The Use of Pleasure* (1984). Specifically, Foucault attempts to provide a genealogy of the desiring subject as a product of the relation between power and knowledge that he had for the first time explicitly, if sketchily, formulated in *Discipline and Punish,* and he investigates the ways in which social institutions and practices serve to circumscribe and control the subjective human experience of sexuality. Sexuality itself is understood here not as a given force of nature but as a historical human construct. Throughout the three volumes of *The History of Sexuality,* Foucault gradually ceases to focus on contemporary conceptions of sexual subjectivity, inquiring instead into the sexual subject as conceived during the period of Antiquity. Thus, there is an effort on Foucault's part, in the words of Maurice Blanchot, "to move from the torments of sexuality to the simplicity of pleasures and to illuminate with a new light the problems they nevertheless pose, even though they occupy the attention of free men much less and escape the felicity and scandal of prohibitions."[6] In distancing himself from modernity and delving into the epoch of antiquity, Foucault encountered in its *êthos* the notion of the care of the self as a basis for practices of freedom. Genuine freedom, Foucault concludes, can only be achieved through detachment from what is expected of us as "normal," that is, through the transgression of norms, sexual or otherwise, specified within society through the operation of power.

The question of the subject and its relation to truth, power, and freedom is once more taken up in the interview presented here. Foucault's thought is distinctive in that much of it was presented in "minor" texts, that is, interviews and articles in which he constantly revisited and refined the positions he had set out in his longer works. Indeed, the minor texts in themselves constitute an entire body of work: the French two-volume edition in which they are collected, *Dits et écrits,* amounts to more than two thousand pages. In this interview, conducted several months before Foucault's death in 1984, Foucault expounds on the views at which he had arrived in the first three volumes of *The History of Sexuality* and reformulates certain aspects of his thought that had been present, in one form or another, since *Madness and Civilization.*

During his life, Foucault occupied teaching positions at various French universities before accepting a position at the prestigious Collège de France in 1970. He also spent time at the University of California at Berkeley and the University of Vermont. He became increasingly engaged in social and political matters, most notably on the question of the state of prisons in France and through his involvement with the Polish Solidarity movement. In January 1969, Foucault participated in the occupation of the University of Vincennes, an aftereffect of the events of May 1968.[7] He was also vocal in his condemnation of American policy in Vietnam and of French policy toward immigration and racial matters. Michel Foucault died on June 25, 1984, of AIDS-related complications.

DG

QUESTIONS

1. Explain the distinction Foucault makes between liberation and freedom.
2. How does Foucault define his concept of domination? What is its role in his discussion of the practice of freedom?

3. What does Foucault mean when he proposes that ethics is the practice of freedom? In what way is ethics linked to "the game of truth"?

4. What is the "subject" for Foucault? How does the subject relate to truth? To Foucault's concept of power?

ENDNOTES

1. Macey, p. 10.

2. The equivalent of a doctorate, the *aggrégation* is the exam all French students must pass in order to teach at the high school and university level.

3. Macey, p. 33.

4. Foucault, from Macey, p. 94.

5. Foucault, *Discipline and Punish,* p. 131.

6. Blanchot, p. 107.

7. Macey, pp. 226–27, 206–8. The culmination of growing discontent on the part of students and workers with the state of social and economic affairs in France, May 1968 consisted of a series of protests, university occupations, and strikes that nearly brought down the government of Charles De Gaulle. The movement began in student unrest and grew to include not only professors but also most of the workers in France. Although the student movement eventually failed to effect the cultural revolution it had envisioned, the events of May 1968 had a profound effect on the country as a whole, and particularly on France's intellectual community, many of whose members participated in, and led, the student demonstrations.

SELECTED BIBLIOGRAPHY

Blanchot, Maurice. "Foucault as I Imagine Him," from *Foucault/Blanchot,* trans. Jeffrey Mehlman. New York: Zone Books, 1987.

Dreyfus, Hubert L., and Paul Rabinow. *Michel Foucault: Beyond Structuralism and Hermeneutics.* Chicago: University of Chicago Press, 1983.

Foucault, Michel. *Discipline and Punish,* trans. Alan Sheridan. New York: Vintage Books, 1977.

Foucault, Michel. *Essential Works of Foucault,* ed. Paul Rabinow. New York: New Press, 1997.

Macey, David. *The Lives of Michel Foucault.* New York: Vintage Books, 1993.

The Ethics of the Concern for Self as a Practice of Freedom*

Michel Foucault

Q. First of all, I would like to ask what is the focus of your current thinking. Having followed the latest developments in your thought, particularly your lectures at the Collège de France in 1981–82 on the hermeneutics of the subject, I would like to know if your current philosophical approach is still determined by the poles of subjectivity and truth.

M.F. In actual fact, I have always been interested in this problem, even if I framed it somewhat differently. I have tried to find out how the human subject fits into certain games of truth, whether they were truth games that take the form of a science or refer to a scientific model, or truth games such as those one may encounter in institutions or practices of control. This is the theme of my book *The Order of Things,* in which I attempted to see how, in scientific discourses, the human subject defines itself as a speaking, living, working individual. In my courses at the Collège de France, I brought out this problematic in its generality.

Q. Isn't there a "break" between your former problematic and that of subjectivity/truth, particularly starting with the concept of the "care of the self"?

M.F. Up to that point I had conceived the problem of the relationship between the subject and

games of truth in terms either of coercive practices—such as those of psychiatry and the prison system—or of theoretical or scientific games—such as the analysis of wealth, of language, and of living beings. In my lectures at the Collège de France, I tried to grasp it in terms of what may be called a practice of the self; although this phenomenon has not been studied very much, I believe it has been fairly important in our societies ever since the Greco-Roman period. In the Greek and Roman civilizations, such practices of the self were much more important and especially more autonomous than they were later, after they were taken over to a certain extent by religious, pedagogical, medical, or psychiatric institutions.

Q. Thus there has been a sort of shift: these games of truth no longer involve a coercive practice, but a practice of self-formation of the subject.

M.F. That's right. It is what one could call an ascetic practice, taking asceticism in a very general sense—in other words, not in the sense of a morality of renunciation but as an exercise of the self on the self by which one attempts to develop and transform oneself, and to attain to a certain mode of being. Here I am taking asceticism in a more general sense than that attributed to it by Max Weber, for example, but along the same lines.

Q. A work of the self on the self that may be understood as a certain liberation, as a process of liberation?

M.F. I would be more careful on that score. I have always been somewhat suspicious of the notion of liberation, because if it is not treated with

*This interview was conducted by H. Becker, R. Fornet-Betancourt, and A. Gomez-Müller on January 20, 1984. It appeared in *Concordia: Revista internacional de filosophia* 6 (July-December 1984), pp. 96–116. The translation, by P. Aranov and D. McGrawth, has been amended and the footnotes of the French text added.

excellent Point!

precautions and within certain limits, one runs the risk of falling back on the idea that there exists a human nature or base that, as a consequence of certain historical, economic, and social processes, has been concealed, alienated, or imprisoned in and by mechanisms of repression. According to this hypothesis, all that is required is to break these repressive deadlocks and man will be reconciled with himself, rediscover his nature or regain contact with his origin, and reestablish a full and positive relationship with himself. I think this idea should not be accepted without scrutiny. I am not trying to say that liberation as such, or this or that form of liberation, does not exist: when a colonized people attempts to liberate itself from its colonizers, this is indeed a practice of liberation in the strict sense. But we know very well, and moreover in this specific case, that this practice of liberation is not in itself sufficient to define the practices of freedom that will still be needed if this people, this society, and these individuals are to be able to define admissible and acceptable forms of existence or political society. This is why I emphasize practices of freedom over processes of liberation; again, the latter indeed have their place, but they do not seem to me to be capable by themselves of defining all the practical forms of freedom. This is precisely the problem I encountered with regard to sexuality: does it make any sense to say, "Let's liberate our sexuality"? Isn't the problem rather that of defining the practices of freedom by which one could define what is sexual pleasure and erotic, amorous and passionate relationships with others? This ethical problem of the definition of practices of freedom, it seems to me, is much more important than the rather repetitive affirmation that sexuality or desire must be liberated.

Q. But doesn't the exercise of practices of freedom require a certain degree of liberation?

M.F. Yes, absolutely. And this is where we must introduce the concept of domination. The analyses I am trying to make bear essentially on relations of power. By this I mean something different from states of domination. Power relations are extremely widespread in human relationships. Now, this means not that political power is everywhere, but that there is in human relationships a whole range of power relations that may come into play among individuals, within families, in pedagogical relationships, political life, and so on. The analysis of power relations is an extremely complex area; one sometimes encounters what may be called situations or states of domination in which the power relations, instead of being mobile, allowing the various participants to adopt strategies modifying them, remain blocked, frozen. When an individual or social group succeeds in blocking a field of power relations, immobilizing them and preventing any reversibility of movement by economic, political, or military means, one is faced with what may be called a state of domination. In such a state, it is certain that practices of freedom do not exist or exist only unilaterally or are extremely constrained and limited. Thus, I agree with you that liberation is sometimes the political or historical condition for a practice of freedom. Taking sexuality as an example, it is clear that a number of liberations were required vis-à-vis male power, that liberation was necessary from an oppressive morality concerning heterosexuality as well as homosexuality. But this liberation does not give rise to the happy human being imbued with a sexuality to which the subject could achieve a complete and satisfying relationship. Liberation paves the way for new power relationships, which must be controlled by practices of freedom.

Q. Can't liberation itself be a mode or form of practice of the freedom?

M.F. Yes, in some cases. You have situations where liberation and the struggle for liberation are indispensable for the practice of freedom. With respect to sexuality, for example—and I am not indulging in polemics, because I don't like polemics, I think they are usually futile—there is a Reichian model derived from a certain reading of Freud. Now, in Reich's view the problem was entirely one of liberation. To put it somewhat schematically, according to him there is desire, drive, prohibition, repression, internalization, and it is by getting rid of these prohibitions, in other words, by liberating oneself, that the problem gets resolved. I think—and I know I am vastly oversimplifying much more interesting and refined positions of many authors—this completely misses the ethical problem of the practice of freedom: How can one practice freedom? With regard to sexuality, it is obvious that it is by liberating our desire that we will learn to conduct ourselves ethically in pleasure relationships with others.

Q. You say that freedom must be practiced ethically . . . .

M.F. Yes, for what is ethics, if not the practice of freedom, the conscious [réfléchie] practice of freedom?

Q. In other words, you understand freedom as a reality that is already ethical in itself.

M.F. Freedom is the ontological condition of ethics. But ethics is the considered form that freedom takes when it is informed by reflection.

Q. Ethics is what is achieved in the search for or the care of the self?

M.F. In the Greco-Roman world, the care of the self was the mode in which individual freedom—or civic liberty, up to a point—was reflected [se réfléchie] as an ethics. If you take a whole series of texts going from the first Platonic dialogues up to the major texts of late Stoicism—Epictetus, Marcus Aurelius, and so on—you will see that the theme of the care of the self thoroughly permeated moral reflection. It is interesting to see that, in our societies on the other hand, at a time that is very difficult to pinpoint, the care of the self became somewhat suspect. Starting at a certain point, being concerned with oneself was readily denounced as a form of self-love, a form of selfishness or self-interest in contradiction with the interest to be shown in others or the self-sacrifice required. All this happened during Christianity; however, I am not simply saying that Christianity is responsible for it. The question is much more complex, for, with Christianity, achieving one's salvation is also a way of caring for oneself. But in Christianity, salvation is attained through the renunciation of self. There is a paradox in the care of the self in Christianity—but that is another problem. To come back to the question you were talking about, I believe that among the Greeks and Romans—especially the Greeks—concern with the self and care of the self were required for right conduct and the proper practice of freedom, in order to know oneself [se connaître]—the familiar aspect of the gnōthi seauton—as well as to form oneself, to surpass oneself, to master the appetites that threaten to overwhelm one. Individual freedom was very important for the Greeks—contrary to the commonplace derived more or less from Hegel that sees it as being of no importance when placed against the imposing totality of the city. Not to be a slave (of another city, of the people around you, of those governing you, of your own passions) was an absolutely fundamental theme. The concern with freedom was an essential and permanent problem for eight full centuries of ancient culture. What we have here is an entire ethics revolving around the care of the self; this is what gives ancient ethics its particular form. I am not saying that ethics is synonymous with the care of the self, but that, in antiquity, ethics as the conscious practice of freedom has revolved around this fundamental imperative: "Take care of yourself" [*soucie-toi de toi-même*].

Q. An imperative that implies the assimilation of the *logoi*, truths.

M.F. Certainly. Taking care of oneself requires knowing [*connaître*] oneself. Care of the self is, of course, knowledge [*connaissance*] of the self—this is the Socratic-Platonic aspect—but also knowledge of a number of rules of acceptable conduct or of principles that are both truths and prescriptions. To take care of the self is to equip oneself with these truths: this is where ethics is linked to the game of truth.

Q. You are saying that it involves making this truth that is learned, memorized, and progressively applied into a quasi subject that reigns supreme in yourself. What is the status of this quasi subject?

M.F. In the Platonic current of thought, at least at the end of the *Alcibiades,* the problem for the subject or the individual soul is to turn its gaze upon itself, to recognize itself in what it is and, recognizing itself in what it is, to recall the truths that issue from it and that it has been able to contemplate;[1] on the other hand, in the current of thinking we can broadly call Stoicism, the problem is to learn through the teaching of a number of truths and doctrines, some of which are fundamental principles while others are rules of conduct. You must proceed in such a way that these principles tell you in each situation and, as it were, spontaneously, how to conduct yourself. It is here that one encounters a metaphor that comes not from the Stoics but from Plutarch: "You must learn the principles in such a constant way that whenever

your desires, appetites, and fears awake like barking dogs, the *logos* will speak like the voice of the master who silences his dogs with a single cry."[2] Here we have the idea of a *logos* functioning, as it were, without any intervention on your part; you have become the *logos,* or the *logos* has become you.

Q. I would like to come back to the question of the relationship between freedom and ethics. When you say that ethics is the reflective part [*la partie réfléchie*] of freedom, does that mean that freedom can become aware of itself as ethical practice? Is it first and always a freedom that is, so to speak, "moralized," or must one work on oneself to discover the ethical dimension of freedom?

M.F. The Greeks problematized their freedom, and the freedom of the individual, as an ethical problem. But ethical in the sense in which the Greeks understood it: *ēthos* was a way of being and of behavior. It was a mode of being for the subject, along with a certain way of acting, a way visible to others. A person's *ēthos* was evident in his clothing, appearance, gait, in the calm with which he responded to every event, and so on. For the Greeks, this was the concrete form of freedom; this was the way they problematized their freedom. A man possessed of a splendid *ēthos,* who could be admired and put forward as an example, was someone who practiced freedom in a certain way. I don't think that a shift is needed for freedom to be conceived as *ēthos*; it is immediately problematized as *ēthos.* But extensive work by the self on the self is required for this practice of freedom to take shape in an *ēthos* that is good, beautiful, honorable, estimable, memorable, and exemplary.

Q. Is this where you situate the analysis of power?

M.F. I think that insofar as freedom for the Greeks signifies non-slavery—which is quite a different definition of freedom from our own—the problem is already entirely political. It is political in that nonslavery to others is a condition: a slave has no ethics. Freedom is thus inherently political. And it also has a political model insofar as being free means not being a slave to oneself and one's appetites, which means that with respect to oneself one establishes a certain relationship of domination, of mastery, which was called *arkhē,* or power, command.

Q. As you have stated, care of the self is in a certain sense care for others. In this sense, the care of the self is also always ethical, and ethical in itself.

M.F. What makes it ethical for the Greeks is not that it is care for others. The care of the self is ethical in itself; but it implies complex relationships with others insofar as this *ēthos* of freedom is also a way of caring for others. This is why it is important for a free man who conducts himself as he should to be able to govern his wife, his children, his household; it is also the art of governing. *Ethos* also implies a relationship with others, insofar as the care of the self enables one to occupy his rightful position in the city, the community, or interpersonal relationships, whether as a magistrate or a friend. And the care of the self also implies a relationship with the other insofar as proper care of the self requires listening to the lessons of a master. One needs a guide, a counselor, a friend, someone who will be truthful with you. Thus, the problem of relationships with others is present throughout the development of the care of the self.

Q. The care of the self always aims for the well-being of others; it aims to manage the space of power that exists in all relationships, but to manage it in a nonauthoritarian manner. What role could a philosopher play in this context,

as a person who is concerned with care for others?

M.F. Let's take Socrates as an example. He would greet people in the street or adolescents in the gymnasium with the question: Are you caring for yourself? For he has been entrusted with this mission by a god and he will not abandon it even when threatened with death. He is the man who cares about the care of others; this is the particular position of the philosopher. But let me simply say that in the case of the free man, I think the postulate of this whole morality was that a person who took proper care of himself would, by the same token, be able to conduct himself properly in relation to others and for others. A city in which everybody took proper care of himself would be a city that functioned well and found in this the ethical principle of its permanence. But I don't think we can say that the Greek who cares for himself must first care for others. To my mind, this view only came later. Care for others should not be put before the care of oneself. The care of the self is ethically prior in that the relationship with oneself is ontologically prior.

Q. Can this care of the self, which possesses a positive ethical meaning, be understood as a sort of conversion of power?

M.F. A conversion, yes. In fact, it is a way of limiting and controlling power. For if it is true that slavery is the great risk that Greek freedom resists, there is also another danger that initially appears to be the opposite of slavery: the abuse of power. In the abuse of power, one exceeds the legitimate exercise of one's power and imposes one's fantasies, appetites, and desires on others. Here we have the image of the tyrant, or simply of the rich and powerful man who uses his wealth and power to abuse others, to impose an unwarranted power on them. But one can see—in any case, this is what the Greek philosophers say—that such a man is the slave of his appetites. And the good ruler is precisely the one who exercises his power as it ought to be exercised, that is, simultaneously exercising his power over himself. And it is the power over oneself that thus regulates one's power over others.

Q. Doesn't the care of the self, when separated from care for others, run the risk of becoming an absolute? And couldn't this "absolutization" of the care of the self become a way of exercising power over others, in the sense of dominating others?

M.F. No, because the risk of dominating others and exercising a tyrannical power over them arises precisely only when one has not taken care of the self and has become the slave of one's desires. But if you take proper care of yourself, that is, if you know ontologically what you are, if you know what you are capable of, if you know what it means for you to be a citizen of a city, to be the master of a household in an *oikos,* if you know what things you should and should not fear, if you know what you can reasonably hope for and, on the other hand, what things should not matter to you, if you know, finally, that you should not be afraid of death—if you know all this, you cannot abuse your power over others. Thus, there is no danger. That idea will appear much later, when love of self becomes suspect and comes to be perceived as one of the roots of various moral offenses. In this new context, renunciation of self will be the prime form of care of the self. All this is evident in Gregory of Nyssa's *Treatise on Virginity,* which defines the care of the self, the *epimeleia heautou,* as the renunciation of all earthly attachments. It is the renunciation of all that may be love of self, of attachment to an earthly self.[3] But I think that in Greek and Roman thought the care of the self cannot in itself tend toward

so exaggerated a form of self-love as to neglect others or, worse still, to abuse one's power over them.

Q. Thus it is a care of the self that, in thinking of itself, thinks of others?

M.F. Yes, absolutely. He who takes care of himself to the point of knowing exactly what duties he has as master of a household and as a husband and father will find that he enjoys a proper relationship with his wife and children.

Q. But doesn't the human condition, in terms of its finitude, play a very important role here? You have talked about death: if you are not afraid of death, then you cannot abuse your power over others. It seems to me that this problem of finitude is very important; the fear of death, of finitude, of being hurt, is at the heart of the care of the self.

M.F. Of course. And this is where Christianity, by presenting salvation as occurring beyond life, in a way upsets or at least disturbs the balance of the care of the self. Although, let me say it again, to seek one's salvation definitely means to take care of oneself. But the condition required for attaining salvation is precisely renunciation. Among the Greeks and Romans, however, given that one takes care of oneself in one's own life, and that the reputation one leaves behind is the only afterlife one can expect, the care of the self can be centered entirely on oneself, on what one does, on the place one occupies among others. It can be centered totally on the acceptance of death—this will become quite evident in late Stoicism—and can even, up to a point, become almost a desire for death. At the same time, it can be, if not a care for others, at least a care of the self which will be beneficial to others. In Seneca, for example, it is interesting to note the importance of the theme, let us hurry and get old, let us hasten toward the end, so that we may thereby come back to ourselves. This type of moment before death, when nothing more can happen, is different from the desire for death one finds among the Christians, who expect salvation through death. It is like a movement to rush through life to the point where there is no longer anything ahead but the possibility of death.

Q. I would now like to turn to another topic. In your lectures at the Collège de France you spoke about the relationship between power and knowledge [*savoir*]. Now you are talking about the relationship between subject and truth. Are these pairs of concepts—power-knowledge and subject-truth—complementary in some way?

M.F. As I said when we started, I have always been interested in the problem of the relationship between subject and truth. I mean, how does the subject fit into a certain game of truth? The first problem I examined was why madness was problematized, starting at a certain time and following certain processes, as an illness falling under a certain model of medicine. How was the mad subject placed in this game of truth defined by a medical model or a knowledge? And it was while working on this analysis that I realized that, contrary to what was rather common practice at that time (around the early sixties), this phenomenon could not be properly accounted for simply by talking about ideology. In fact, there were practices—essentially the widespread use of incarceration which had been developed starting at the beginning of the seventeenth century, and had been the condition for the insertion of the mad subject in this type of truth game—that sent me back to the problem of institutions of power much more than to the problem of ideology. This is what led me to pose the problem of knowledge and power, which for me is not the fundamental problem but an instrument that makes it possible to analyze the problem of the relationship between subject and truth in what seems to me the most precise way.

Q. But you have always "forbidden" people to talk to you about the subject in general?

M.F. No, I have not "forbidden" them. Perhaps I did not explain myself adequately. What I rejected was the idea of starting out with a theory of the subject—as is done, for example, in phenomenology or existentialism—and, on the basis of this theory, asking how a given form of knowledge [*connaissance*] was possible. What I wanted to try to show was how the subject constituted itself, in one specific form or another, as a mad or a healthy subject, as a delinquent or nondelinquent subject, through certain practices that were also games of truth, practices of power, and so on. I had to reject a priori theories of the subject in order to analyze the relationships that may exist between the constitution of the subject or different forms of the subject and games of truth, practices of power, and so on.

Q. That means that the subject is not a substance.

M.F. It is not a substance. It is a form, and this form is not primarily or always identical to itself. You do not have the same type of relationship to yourself when you constitute yourself as a political subject who goes to vote or speaks at a meeting and when you are seeking to fulfill your desires in a sexual relationship. Undoubtedly there are relationships and interferences between these different forms of the subject; but we are not dealing with the same type of subject. In each case, one plays, one establishes a different type of relationship to oneself. And it is precisely the historical constitution of these various forms of the subject in relation to the games of truth which interests me.

Q. But the mad, the ill, the delinquent subject—and perhaps even the sexual subject—was a subject that was the object of a theoretical dis-course, let us say a "passive" subject, while the subject you have been speaking about over the past two years in your lectures at the Collège de France is an "active," a politically active subject. The care of the self concerns all the problems of political practice and government, and so on. It would seem, then, that there has been a change for you, a change not of perspective but of problematic.

M.F. If it is indeed true that the constitution of the mad subject may be considered the consequence of a system of coercion—this is the passive sub-ject—you know very well that the mad subject is not an unfree subject, and that the mentally ill person is constituted as a mad subject pre-cisely in relation to and over against the one who declares him mad. Hysteria, which was so important in the history of psychiatry and in the asylums of the nineteenth century, seems to me to be the very picture of how the subject is constituted as a mad subject. And it is certainly no accident that the major phenomena of hyste-ria were observed precisely in those situations where there was a maximum of coercion to force individuals to constitute themselves as mad. On the other hand, I would say that if I am now interested in how the subject consti-tutes itself in an active fashion through practices of the self, these practices are nevertheless not something invented by the individual himself. They are models that he finds in his culture and are proposed, suggested, imposed upon him by his culture, his society, and his social group.

Q. It would seem that there is something of a defi-ciency in your problematic, namely, in the no-tion of resistance against power. Which presupposes a very active subject, very con-cerned with the care of itself and of others and, therefore, competent politically and philosophi-cally.

M.F. This brings us back to the problem of what I mean by power. I scarcely use the word *power,* and if I use it on occasion it is simply as short-hand for the expression I generally use: *relations of power.* But there are readymade models: when one speaks of *power,* people immediately think of a political structure, a government, a domi-nant social class, the master and the slave, and so on. I am not thinking of this at all when I speak of *relations of power.* I mean that in human relationships, whether they involve ver-bal communication such as we are engaged in at this moment, or amorous, institutional, or eco-nomic relationships, power is always present: I mean a relationship in which one person tries to control the conduct of the other. So I am speak-ing of relations that exist at different levels, in different forms; these power relations are mo-bile, they can be modified, they are not fixed once and for all. For example, the fact that I may be older than you, and that you may ini-tially have been intimidated, may be turned around during the course of our conversation, and I may end up being intimidated before someone precisely because he is younger than I am. These power relations are thus mobile, re-versible, and unstable. It should also be noted that power relations are possible only insofar as the subjects are free. If one of them were com-pletely at the other's disposal and became his thing, an object on which he could wreak boundless and limitless violence, there wouldn't be any relations of power. Thus, in order for power relations to come into play, there must be at least a certain degree of freedom on both sides. Even when the power relation is com-pletely out of balance, when it can truly be claimed that one side has "total power" over the other, a power can be exercised over the other only insofar as the other still has the option of killing himself, of leaping out the window, or of killing the other person. This means that in power relations there is necessarily the possibility of resistance because if there were no possibility of resistance (of violent resistance, flight, deception, strategies capable of reversing the situation), there would be no power relations at all. This being the general form, I refuse to reply to the question I am sometimes asked: "But if power is everywhere, there is no freedom." I answer that if there are relations of power in every social field, this is because there is freedom everywhere. Of course, states of domination do indeed exist. In a great many cases, power relations are fixed in such a way that they are perpetually asymmetrical and allow an extremely limited margin of freedom. To take what is undoubtedly a very simplified example, one cannot say that it was only men who wielded power in the conventional marital structure of the eighteenth and nineteenth centuries; women had quite a few options: they could deceive their husbands, pilfer money from them, refuse them sex. Yet they were still in a state of domination insofar as these options were ultimately only stratagems that never succeeded in reversing the situation. In such cases of domination, be they economic, social, institutional, or sexual, the problem is knowing where resistance will develop. For example, in a working class that will resist domination, will this be in unions or political parties; and what form will it take—a strike, a general strike, revolution, or parliamentary opposition? In such a situation of domination, all of these questions demand specific answers that take account of the kind and precise form of domination in question. But the claim that "you see power everywhere, thus there is no room for freedom" seems to me absolutely inadequate. The idea that power is a system of domination that controls everything and leaves no room for freedom cannot be attributed to me.

Q. You were talking before about the free man and the philosopher as two different modes of the care of the self. The care of the self of the philosopher would have a specificity that cannot be confused with that of the free man.

M.F. I would say that these figures represent two different places in the care of the self, rather than two forms of care of the self. I believe that the form of such care remains the same, but in terms of intensity, in the degree of zeal for the self, and, consequently, also for others, the place of the philosopher is not that of just any free man.

Q. Is there a fundamental link we can make at this point between philosophy and politics?

M.F. Yes, certainly. I believe that the relationship between philosophy and politics is permanent and fundamental. It is certain that if one takes the history of the care of the self in Greek philosophy, the relationship with politics is obvious. And it takes a very complex form: on the one hand, you have, for example, Socrates as well as Plato in the *Alcibiades*[4] and Xenophon in the *Memorabilia*[5]—greeting young men, saying to them: "You want to become a politician, to govern a city, to care for others, and you haven't even taken care of yourself. If you do not care for yourself you will make a poor ruler." From this perspective, the care of the self appears a pedagogical, ethical, and also ontological condition for the development of a good ruler. To constitute oneself as a governing subject implies that one has constituted oneself as a subject who cares for oneself. Yet, on the other hand, we have Socrates saying in the *Apology* that he approaches everyone because everyone has to take care of himself;[6] but he also adds, "In doing so, I am performing the highest service for the city, and instead of punishing me, you should reward me even more than you reward a winner in the Olympic Games."[7] Thus we see a very strong connection between philosophy and politics, which was to develop further when the philosopher would care not only for the soul of the citizen but for that of the prince. The philosopher becomes the prince's counselor, teacher, and spiritual adviser.

Q. Could the problematic of the care of the self be at the heart of a new way of thinking about politics, of a form of politics different from what we know today?

M.F. I admit that I have not got very far in this direction, and I would very much like to come back to more contemporary questions to try to see what can be made of all this in the context of the current political problematic. But I have the impression that in the political thought of the nineteenth century—and perhaps one should go back even farther, to Rousseau and Hobbes—the political subject was conceived of essentially as a subject of law, whether natural or positive. On the other hand, it seems to me that contemporary political thought allows very little room for the question of the ethical subject. I don't like to reply to questions I haven't studied. However, I would very much like to come back to the questions I examined through ancient culture.

Q. What is the relationship between the path of philosophy, which leads to knowledge of the self, and the path of spirituality?

M.F. By spirituality I mean—but I'm not sure this definition can hold for very long—the subject's attainment of a certain mode of being and the transformations that the subject must carry out on itself to attain this mode of being. I believe that spirituality and philosophy were identical or nearly identical in ancient spirituality. In any case, philosophy's most important preoccupation centered around the self, with knowledge [connaissance] of the world coming after and serving, most often, to support the care of the self. Reading Descartes, it is remarkable to find in the *Meditations* this same spiritual concern with the attainment of a mode being where doubt was no longer possible, and where one could finally know [connaît].[8] But by thus defining the mode of being to which philosophy gives access, one realizes that this mode of being is defined entirely in terms of knowledge, and that philosophy in turn is defined in terms of the development of the knowing [connaissant] subject, or of what qualifies the subject as such. From this perspective, it seems to me that philosophy superimposes the functions of spirituality upon the ideal of a grounding for scientificity.

Q. Should the concept of the care of the self in the classical sense be updated to confront this modern thought?

M.F. Absolutely, but I would certainly not do so just to say, "We have unfortunately forgotten about the care of the self; so here, here it is, the key to everything." Nothing is more foreign to me than the idea that, at a certain moment, philosophy went astray and forgot something, that somewhere in its history there is a principle, a foundation that must be rediscovered. I feel that all such forms of analysis, whether they take a radical form and claim that philosophy has from the outset been a forgetting, or whether they take a much more historical view-point and say, "Such and such a philosopher forgot something"— neither of these approaches is particularly interesting or useful. Which does not mean that contact with such and such a philosopher may not produce something, but it must be emphasized that it would be something new.

Q. This leads me to ask: Why should one have access to the truth today, to *truth* in the political sense, in other words, in the sense of a political strategy directed against the various "blockages" of power in the system of relations?

M.F. This is indeed a problem. After all, why truth? Why are we concerned with truth, and more so than with the care of the self? And why must the care of the self occur only through the concern for truth? I think we are touching on a fundamental question here, what I would call *the* question for the West: How did it come about that all of Western culture began to revolve around this obligation of truth which has taken a lot of different forms? Things being as they are, nothing so far has shown that it is possible to define a strategy outside of this concern. It is within the field of the obligation to truth that it is possible to move about in one way or another, sometimes against effects of domination which may be linked to structures of truth or institutions entrusted with truth. To greatly simplify matters, there are numerous examples: there has been a whole so-called ecological movement—a very ancient one, by the way, that did not just start in the twentieth century—that was often in opposition, as it were, to a science or, at least, to a technology underwritten by claims to truth. But this same ecology articulated its own discourse of truth: criticism was authorized in the name of a knowledge [*connaissance*] of nature, the balance of life processes, and so on. Thus, one escaped from a domination of truth not by playing a game that was totally different from the game of truth but by playing the same game differently, or playing another game, another hand, with other trump cards. I believe that the same holds true in the order of politics; here one can criticize on the basis, for example, of the consequences of the state of domination caused by an unjustified political situation, but one can only do so by playing a certain game of truth, by showing its consequences, by pointing out that there are other reasonable options, by teaching people what they don't know about their own situation, their working conditions, and their exploitation.

Q. With regard to the question of games of truth and games of power, don't you think that there can be found in history evidence of a particular kind of these games of truth, one that has a particular status in relation to all other possible games of truth and power, and is marked by its essential openness, its opposition to all blockages of power—power here meaning domination/subjugation?

M.F. Yes, absolutely. But when I talk about power relations and games of truth, I am absolutely not saying that games of truth are just concealed power relations—that would be a horrible exaggeration. My problem, as I have already said, is in understanding how truth games are set up and how they are connected with power relations. One can show, for example, that the medicalization of madness, in other words, the organization of medical knowledge [*savoir*] around individuals designated as mad, was connected with a whole series of social and economic processes at a given time, but also with institutions and practices of power. This fact in no way impugns the scientific validity or the therapeutic effectiveness of psychiatry: it does not endorse psychiatry, but neither does it invalidate it. It is also true that mathematics, for example, is linked, albeit in a completely different manner than psychiatry, to power structures, if only in the way it is taught, the way in which consensus among mathematicians is organized, functions in a closed circuit, has its values, determines what is good (true) or bad (false) in mathematics. This is no way means that mathematics is only a game of power, but that the game of truth of mathematics is linked in a certain way—without thereby being invalidated in any way—to games and institutions of power. It is clear that in some cases these connections are such that one could write the entire history of mathematics without taking them into account, although this problematic is always interesting and even historians of mathematics are now beginning to study the history of their institutions. Finally, it is clear that the connection that may exist between power relations and games of truth in mathematics is totally different from what it is in psychiatry; in any case, one simply cannot say that games of truth are nothing but games of power.

Q. This question takes us back to the problem of the subject because, with games of truth, it is a question of knowing *who* is speaking the truth, how he speaks it, and why he speaks it. For, in games of truth, one can play at speaking the truth: there is a game, one plays at truth or truth is a game.

M.F. The word "game" can lead you astray: when I say "game," I mean a set of rules by which truth is produced. It is not a game in the sense of an amusement; it is a set of procedures that lead to a certain result, which, on the basis of its principles and rules of procedure, may be considered valid or invalid, winning or losing.

Q. There remains the problem of "who": Is it a group, a body?

M.F. It may be a group or an individual. Indeed, there is a problem here. With regard to these multiple games of truth, one can see that ever since the age of the Greeks our society has been marked by the lack of a precise and imperative definition of the games of truth which are permitted to the exclusion of all others. In a given game of truth, it is always possible to discover something different and to more or less modify this or that rule, and sometimes even the entire game of truth. This has undoubtedly given the

West possibilities for development not found in other societies. Who speaks the truth? Free individuals who establish a certain consensus, and who find themselves within a certain network of practices of power and constraining institutions.

Q. So truth is not a construction?

M.F. That depends. There are games of truth in which truth is a construction and others in which it is not. One can have, for example, a game of truth that consists of describing things in such and such a way: a person giving an anthropological description of a society supplies not a construction but a description, which itself has a certain number of historically changing rules, so that one can say that it is to a certain extent a construction with respect to another description. This does not mean that there's just a void, that everything is a figment of the imagination. On the basis of what can be said, for example, about this transformation of games of truth, some people conclude that I have said that nothing exists—I have been seen as saying that madness does not exist, whereas the problem is absolutely the converse: it was a question of knowing how madness, under the various definitions that have been given, was at a particular time integrated into an institutional field that constituted it as a mental illness occupying a specific place alongside other illnesses.

Q. At the heart of the problem of truth there is ultimately a problem of communication, of the transparency of the words of a discourse. The person who has the capacity to formulate truths also has a power, the power of being able to speak the truth and to express it in the way he wants.

M.F. Yes, and yet this does not mean that what the person says is not true, which is what most people believe. When you tell people that there may be a relationship between truth and power, they say: "So it isn't truth after all!"

Q. This is tied up with the problem of communication because, in a society where communication has reached a high level of transparency, games of truth are perhaps more independent of structures of power.

M.F. This is indeed an important problem; I imagine you are thinking a little about Habermas when you say that. I am quite interested in his work, although I know he completely disagrees with my views. While I, for my part, tend to be a little more in agreement with what he says, I have always had a problem insofar as he gives communicative relations this place which is so important and, above all, a function that I would call "utopian." The idea that there could exist a state of communication that would allow games of truth to circulate freely, without any constraints or coercive effects, seems utopian to me. This is precisely a failure, to see that power relations are not something that is bad in itself, that we have to break free of. I do not think that a society can exist without power relations, if by that one means the strategies by which individuals try to direct and control the conduct of others. The problem, then, is not to try to dissolve them in the utopia of completely transparent communication but to acquire the rules of law, the management techniques, and also the morality, the *ēthos*, the practice of the self, that will allow us to play these games of power with as little domination as possible.

Q. You are very far from Sartre, who told us power is evil.

M.F. Yes, and that idea, which is very far from my way of thinking, has often been attributed to me. Power is not evil. Power is games of strategy. We all know that power is not evil! For example, let us take sexual or amorous relationships: to wield power over the other in a sort of open-ended strategic game where the situation may be reversed is not evil; it's a part of love, of passion and sexual pleasure. And let us take, as another example, something that has often been rightly criticized—the pedagogical institution. I see nothing wrong in the practice of a person who, knowing more than others in a specific game of truth, tells those others what to do, teaches them, and transmits knowledge and techniques to them. The problem in such practices where power—which is not in itself a bad thing—must inevitably come into play is knowing how to avoid the kind of domination effects where a kid is subjected to the arbitrary and unnecessary authority of a teacher, or a student put under the thumb of a professor who abuses his authority. I believe that this problem must be framed in terms of rules of law, rational techniques of government and ēthos, practices of the self and of freedom.

Q. Are we to take what you have just said as the fundamental criteria of what you have called a new ethics? It is a question of playing with as little domination as possible. . . .

M.F. I believe that this is, in fact, the hinge point of ethical concerns and the political struggle for respect of rights, of critical thought against abusive techniques of government and research in ethics that seeks to ground individual freedom.

Q. When Sartre speaks of power as the supreme evil, he seems to be alluding to the reality of power as domination. On this point you are probably in agreement with Sartre.

M.F. Yes, I believe that all these concepts have been ill defined, so that one hardly knows what one is talking about. I am not even sure if I made myself clear, or used the right words, when I first became interested in the problem of power. Now I have a clearer sense of the problem. It seems to me that we must distinguish between power relations understood as strategic games between liberties—in which some try to control the conduct of others, who in turn try to avoid allowing their conduct to be controlled or try to control the conduct of the others—and the states of domination that people ordinarily call "power." And between the two, between games of power and states of domination, you have technologies of government—understood, of course, in a very broad sense that includes not only the way institutions are governed but also the way one governs one's wife and children. The analysis of these techniques is necessary because it is very often through such techniques that states of domination are established and maintained. There are three levels to my analysis of power: strategic relations, techniques of government, and states of domination.

Q. In your lectures on the hermeneutics of the subject there is a passage in which you say that the first and only useful point of resistance to political power is in the relationship of the self to the self.

M.F. I do not believe that the only possible point of resistance to political power—understood, of course, as a state of domination—lies in the relationship of the self to the self. I am saying that "governmentality" implies the relationship of the self to itself, and I intend this concept of "governmentality" to cover the whole range of practices that constitute, define, organize, and instrumentalize the strategies that individuals in their freedom can use in dealing with each other. Those who try to control, determine, and limit the freedom of others are themselves free individuals who have at their disposal certain instruments they can use to govern others. Thus, the basis for all this is freedom, the relationship of the self to itself and the relationship to the other. (Whereas,) if you try to analyze power not on the basis of freedom, strategies, and governmentality, but on the basis of the po-

litical institution, you can only conceive of the subject as a subject of law. One then has a subject who has or does not have rights, who has had these rights either granted or removed by the institution of political society; and all this brings us back to a legal concept of the subject. On the other hand, I believe that the concept of governmentality makes it possible, to bring out the freedom of the subject and its relationship to others—which constitutes the very stuff [matière] of ethics.

Q. Do you think that philosophy has anything to say about why there is this tendency to try to control the conduct of others?

M.F. The way the conduct of others is controlled takes very different forms and arouses desires and appetites that vary greatly in intensity depending on the society. I don't know anything about anthropology, but I can well imagine societies in which the control of the conduct of others is so well regulated in advance that, in a sense, the game is already over. On the other hand, in a society like our own, games can be very numerous, and the desire to control the conduct of others is all the greater—as we see in family relationships, for example, or emotional or sexual relationships. However, the freer people are with respect to each other, the more they want to control each other's conduct. The more open the game, the more appealing and fascinating it becomes.

Q. Do you think the role of philosophy is to warn of the dangers of power?

M.F. This has always been an important function of philosophy. In its critical aspect—and I mean critical in a broad sense—philosophy is that which calls into question domination at every level and in every form in which it exists, whether political, economic, sexual, institutional, or what have you. To a certain extent, this critical function of philosophy derives from the Socratic injunction "Take care of yourself," in other words, "Make freedom your foundation, through the mastery of yourself."

NOTES

1. Plato, *Alcibiade,* trans. M. Croiset (Paris: Belles Lettres, 1925), pp. 109–110 [*Alcibiades,* trans. W. R. M. Lamb, in *Plato* (Cambridge, Mass.: Harvard University, 1967), vol. 12, pp. 210–13].

2. Plutarch, *De la tranquillité de l'âme,* trans. J. Dumortier and J. Defradas, in *Oeuvres Morales* (Paris: Belles Lettres, 1975), vol. 3, pt. 1, 465c, p. 99 [*Tranquility of Mind,* in *The Complete Works of Plutarch: Essays and Miscellanies,* ed. W. L. Bevan (New York: Thomas Y. Crowell, 1909), vol. 2, pp. 283–84]. The citation is an inexact paraphrase.

3. Gregory of Nyssa, *Traité de la virginité,* trans. M. Aubineau (Paris: Cerf, 1966), ch. 13, 303c–305c, pp. 411–17 [*Treatise on Virginity,* in *Saint Gregory of Nyssa: Ascetical Works,* trans. V. W. Callahan (Washington, D.C.: Catholic Universities of America Press, 1966), pp. 46–48].

4. Plato, *Alcibiade,* 124b, p. 92; 127d–e, p. 99 [*Alcibiades,* pp. 173–75; p. 189].

5. Xenophon, *Mémorables,* trans. E. Chambry (Paris: Garnier, 1935), bk. 3, ch. 7, §9, p. 412 [*Memorabilia,* trans. A. L. Bonnette (Ithaca: Cornell University, 1994), bk. 3, ch. 7, §9, p. 91].

6. Plato, *Apologie de Socrate,* trans. M. Croiset (Paris: Belles Lettres, 1925), 30b, p. 157 [*Socrates' Defense (Apology),* trans. H. Tredennick, in *Plato: The Collected Dialogues,* eds. E. Hamilton and H. Cairns (Princeton: Princeton University Press, 1961), 30b, p. 16].

7. Plato, *Apologie de Socrate,* 36c–d, p. 166 [*Socrates' Defense (Apology),* 36c–d, pp. 21–22].

8. R. Descartes, *Méditations sur la philosophie première,* in *Oeuvres* (Paris: Gallimard, 1952), pp. 253–334 [*Meditations on First Philosophy,* trans. and ed. J. Cottingham (Cambridge: Cambridge University Press, 1996)].

chapter thirty-seven

Judith Butler

Judith Butler (b. 1956) is one of the most influential figures in contemporary philosophy. Her work deals with power structures, gender, sexuality, and identity. But Butler radically alters the meaning of the underlying questions at the very heart of these issues, especially the questions about being a gendered person in a system that allows for exactly two genders.

Although some critics of Butler's work find it to be somewhat esoteric and arcane, Butler maintains the political and practical importance of her project. In the piece presented here, Butler both interprets the governmental response to the AIDS epidemic and warns against identity politics as a strategy of liberation.

In a 1993 interview, Butler proclaimed that what philosophy needs "is a dynamic and more diffuse conception of power, one which is committed to the difficulty of cultural translation as well as the need to re-articulate 'universality' in non-imperialist directions."[1] That is, philosophy needs to understand power in new terms, beyond our old conceptions of power as centralized in static entities like kings or governments. In these new terms, we must be aware that power relations vary from culture to culture, and if we belong to one of the powerful and dominant cultures, we have to be careful not to impose our own sense of human and ethical truth on others. This reconceptualization has both theoretical and practical implications; Butler argues that contemporary feminism needs a new understanding of gender and the kinds of power related to it. That is, feminism needs to focus not simply on "the question of woman" but on the question of the gender system within which our ideas of "woman" and "man" are formed.

"Sexual Inversions," the essay presented here, extends the questions of power and the construction of gender with which Butler is most famously concerned, taking up the complex relations among sex, sexuality, and death. The ways in which male and female, masculine and feminine, are constructed and regulated extend into ways in which "proper" and "improper" sexualities change our understandings of sex and gender, as well as of the workings of power.

Judith Butler, "Sexual Inversions," from *Discourses of Sexuality: From Aristotle to AIDS,* edited by Domna Stanton. Ann Arbor: University of Michigan Press, 1992, pp. 344–61. Reprinted by permission of author.

Butler's call for a reconfiguration of our notion of power is both influenced by and critical of the work of Michel Foucault. For Foucault, power is not a *thing* possessed by individuals or organizations, but a set of *relations* on every scale from the global to the intrapersonal (that is, within one person). It is not the case that one person or group simply "has" power over another; rather, power is something that always exists between—between persons, social groups, nations, et cetera. For example, in a patriarchal society men don't simply possess power which they wield over women; rather, power exists in the relationships between men and women. This is not to say that these relationships are equal ones, however; Foucault's insight is that power exists only as a part of relationships and not above or beyond them.

In his *History of Sexuality,* Foucault makes the controversial claim that the concept of sex as our real biological and even psychological nature or essence is not an innocent scientific discovery but in fact a production of power. Foucault argues that in eighteenth-century Europe, as famine and death became less constant concerns, sex (normalized as heterosexual) emerged as the site of the production and securing of the life of humankind. The reigning view was that so long as one is a healthy member of the species, one's natural drive is heterosexual, thus reflective of one's reproductive function. Desire was construed as natural, even healthy, only insofar as it was heterosexual and thereby aimed towards the reproduction of human life.

In making this argument, Foucault distinguishes two kinds of power relations. *Juridical* power is concerned with control and regulation, while *productive* power actually generates or creates concepts and the objects to be controlled by them. Although juridical power is concerned with the preservation of life over and against the immediate threats by disease and harsh living conditions, eighteenth-century Europe is marked by a transfiguration of power into *productive* power. The new notion that we *have* a sex is a result of *productive* power; at this point in history, sex becomes an object which can be studied, controlled, regulated, and (most significantly) even *generated* by this power. Power exerts itself not so much in the control and regulation of nature, but in the *production* of so-called natural tendencies, traits, and functions that can thereby be understood and managed by the very power which generated these concepts in the first place.

Butler amends Foucault's claims somewhat: Rather than saying that we didn't always *have* a sex, she maintains that "we *were* not always our sex." In other words, sex did not always have the capacity to construct and identify us in the way it does now. A whole range of sciences and social practices are predicated on the notion that we are so determined by our sex that we cannot construct a self-narrative without delving into this originary characteristic. In the article presented here, Butler argues that the emergence of the AIDS epidemic challenges Foucault's account of the production of sex.

Since AIDS entered public consciousness, our concept of certain sexual identities, notably that of homosexual male, includes the idea that they are essentially, necessarily linked to death. As Butler notes, "within the medico-juridical discourse that has emerged to manage and reproduce the epidemic of AIDS, the juridical and productive forms of power *converge* to effect a production of the homosexual subject as a bearer of death." Since Foucault's notion of sex emerges out of a conquering of epic disease, it cannot account for a notion of sex understood *both* in terms of reproduction *and* in terms of death. The concept of sex does not emerge in the transition from one form of power to another; instead, it has always made the distinction between restrictive and productive power an unstable one. The power shift to which Foucault refers is thus not between two modes of power (juridical and productive) but within power itself, as a production of sex which is at the same time a regulation of it.

A secondary problem concerns the manner in which the production of a concept of sex amounts to a "leveling out" of sexual difference—that is, we have one concept of sex which is supposed to serve for all of us, despite vast differences in sexes and sexualities. Butler wonders if "sex" itself does not have the singular conceptual coherence that Foucault attributes to its production, and that furthermore "sex" as an historical category always already amounts to a leveling out of sexual difference, whereby masculine and feminine (male and female) are disparately subjected to a totalizing concept of sex. Following the French philosopher Luce Irigaray, Butler suggests that the only sex which counts—the sex which we assume as normal and which forms our secondary concepts about the sexes—is a masculine one. Butler concludes that power not only regulates and shapes desires and identities but necessarily excludes and erases sexual difference.

The limits of Foucault's notion of power and sex become especially evident in a time racked by AIDS-related deaths. According to Butler, what Foucault (perhaps over-optimistically) failed to recognize is that sex is not an overcoming of death; rather, the discourse on sex can itself produce, maintain, and characterize death. While Foucault rightly points out that one must not confuse the affirmation of sex with the overcoming of power (as if power were only repressive instead of creative), he himself died before he could see that death might not be the limit of power but its very aim. Under the guise of preserving and enhancing life, power (made manifest not only in politics but in the scientific community at large) takes on a form whereby the political and medical aim to preserve life tacitly condones the death of those whose sex has taken on the "valence of death," namely, homosexual males. The depth of this claim is that it is not simply the government and/or science that have failed us in the face of the AIDS epidemic but rather the very notion of sex that was to have slowed the procession of death and disease in the first place.

Butler attended Bennington College and then Yale University, where she received her B.A. and Ph.D. in philosophy. She taught at Wesleyan, George Washington, and Johns Hopkins universities before becoming Maxine Elliot Professor of Rhetoric and Comparative Literature at the University of California at Berkeley. She is also Hannah Arendt Professor of Philosophy at the European Graduate School. Her books include *Subjects of Desire: Hegelian Reflections in Twentieth-Century France* (1987); *Gender Trouble: Feminism and the Subversion of Identity* (1990); *Bodies that Matter: The Discursive*

Limits of "Sex" (1993); *Excitable Speech: A Politics of the Performative* (1997); and *The Psychic Life of Power: Theories of Subjection* (1997).

JGJ

QUESTIONS

1. Consider Foucault's claim that we did not always have a sex. What is Butler's critique of this notion?
2. Explain the relationship Butler delineates between sex and power. How is it that the AIDS epidemic undermines Foucault's history of sex and power?
3. What does it mean to say that sex has become a site of power? Does one's sex give or inhibit one's potency, or is sex rather produced by power as a means of maintaining itself?
4. What does Butler mean by the "discursive regulation of sex"? What are some examples of regulatory modes and practices?
5. How might the very concept of sexuality be understood to establish heterosexuality as the norm?

ENDNOTE

1. Osborn and Segal p. 39.

SELECTED BIBLIOGRAPHY

Butler, Judith. *Bodies That Matter: On the Discursive Limits of "Sex."* New York: Routledge, 1993.

Butler, Judith. *Excitable Speech: A Politics of the Performative.* New York: Routledge, 1997.

Butler, Judith. *Gender Trouble: Feminism and the Suvbersion of Identity.* New York: Routledge, 1990.

Butler, Judith. *The Psychic Life of Power: Theories of Subjection.* Stanford, Calif: Stanford University Press, 1997.

Butler, Judith. *Subjects of Desire: Hegelian Reflections in Twentieth-Century France.* New York: Columbia University Press, 1987.

Foucault, Michel, *The History of Sexuality,* Volume I: *An Introduction,* trans. Robert Hurley. New York: Vintage, 1990.

Osborn, Peter, and Lynne Segal. "Performance: An Interview with Judith Butler." *Radical Philosophy* 67:32–39 (summer 1994).

Sexual Inversions

Judith Butler

In honor and memory of Linda Singer

Some might say that the scandal of the first volume of Foucault's *History of Sexuality* consists in the claim that we did not always have a sex. What can such a notion mean? Foucault proposes that there was a decisive historical break between a socio-political regime in which sex existed as an attribute, an activity, a dimension of human life, and a more recent regime in which sex became established as an identity. This particularly modern scandal suggests that for the first time sex is not a contingent or arbitrary feature of identity but, rather, that there can be no identity without sex and that it is precisely through being sexed that we become intelligible as humans. So it is not exactly right to claim we did not always *have* a sex. Perhaps the historical scandal is that we *were* not always our sex, that sex did not always have the power to characterize and constitute identity with such thoroughgoing power (later, there will be occasion to ask after the exclusions that condition and sustain the Foucaultian "we," but for now we will try on this "we," if only to see where it does not fit). As Foucault points out, sex has come to characterize and unify not only biological functions and anatomical traits but sexual activities as well as a kind of psychic core that gives clues to an essential, or final meaning to, identity. Not only is one one's sex, but one has sex, and in the having, is supposed to show the sex one "is" even as the sex one "is" is psychically deeper and more unfathomable than the "I" who lives it can ever know. Hence, this "sex" requires and secures a set of sciences that can meditate endlessly on that pervasive indecipherability.

What conditioned the introduction into history of this notion of sex that totalizes identity? Fou-cault argues that during the course of the eighteenth century in Europe, famines and epidemics start to disappear and that power, which had previously been governed by the need to ward off death, now becomes occupied with the production, maintenance, and regulation of *life*. It is in the course of this regulatory cultivation of life that the category of sex is established. Naturalized as heterosexual, it is designed to regulate and secure the reproduction of life. Having a true sex with a biological destiny and natural heterosexuality thus becomes essential to the aim of power, now understood as the disciplinary reproduction of life. Foucault characterizes early modern Europe as governed by *juridical* power. As juridical, power operates negatively to impose limits, restrictions, and prohibitions; power reacts defensively, as it were, to preserve life and social harmony over and against the threat of violence or natural death. Once the threat of death is ameliorated, as he claims it is in the eighteenth century, those juridical laws are transformed into instances of *productive* power, in which power effectively *generates* objects to control, in which power elaborates all sorts of objects and identities that guarantee the augmentation of regulatory scientific regimes.[1] The category of "sex" is constructed as an "object" of study and control, which assists in the elaboration and justification of productive power regimes. It is as if once the threat of death is overcome, power turns its idle attention to the construction of objects to control. Or, rather, power

---

[1] See Michel Foucault, *The History of Sexuality, Volume 1: An Introduction,* trans. Robert Hurley (New York: Pantheon, 1978) 85–91. This text was originally published as *La Volonté de savoir* (Paris: Editions Gallimard, 1976).

exerts and articulates its control through the formation and proliferation of objects that concern the continuation of life. (Later I will briefly examine the way in which the term "power" operates in Foucault's text, its susceptibility to personification and the interrelations of the juridical and productive modalities.

I want to raise two kinds of questions in this essay, one concerning the problematic history Foucault tries to tell, and why it cannot work in light of the challenge of the recent emergence of the epidemic of AIDS, and a second, subordinate here, concerning the category of sex and its suppression of sexual difference. To be sure, Foucault could not have known in 1976 when he published the first volume of *The History of Sexuality* that an epidemic would emerge within the very terms of late modern power that would call the terms of his analysis into question. "Sex" is not only constructed in the service of life or reproduction but, what might turn out to be a logical corollary, in the service of the regulation and apportionment of death. In some recent medico-juridical discursive efforts to produce sex, death is installed as a formative and essential feature of that sex. In some recent discourse, the male homosexual is figured time and again as one whose desire is somehow structured by death, either as the desire to die or as one whose desire is inherently punishable by death (Mapplethorpe); paradoxically and painfully, this has also been the case in the postmortem figuration of Foucault himself. Within the medico-juridical discourse that has emerged to manage and reproduce the epidemic of AIDS, the juridical and productive forms of power *converge* to effect a production of the homosexual subject as a bearer of death. This is a matrix of discursive and institutional power that adjudicates matters of life and death through the construction of homosexuality as a category of sex. Within this matrix, homosexual sex is "inverted" into death, and a death-bound

desire becomes the figure for the sexual invert. One might ask here whether lesbian sexuality even qualifies as *sex* within hegemonic public discourse. "What is it that they do" might be read as "Can we be sure they do anything at all?"

For the most part, I will concentrate on the question of how Foucault's historical account of the shift in power calls now to be rewritten in light of the power/discourse regime that regulates AIDS. For Foucault, the category of "sex" emerges only on the condition that epidemics are over. So how are we now, via Foucault, to understand the elaboration of the category of sex within the very matrix of this epidemic?

Along the way, I will ask about the adequacy of this notion of "sex" in the singular. Is it true that "sex" as an historical category can be understood apart from the sexes or a notion of sexual difference? Are notions of "male" and "female" similarly subjected to a monolithic notion of sex, or is there here an erasure of difference that precludes a Foucaultian understanding of "the sex which is not one."[2]

LIFE, DEATH, AND POWER

In the final section of the first volume, the "Right of Death and Power over Life," Foucault describes a cataclysmic "event" which he attributes to the eighteenth century: "nothing less than the entry of life into history" (1:141). What he means, it seems, is that the study and regulation of life becomes an object of historical concern, that is, that life becomes the site for the elaboration of power. Before this unprecedented "entry" of life into history, it seems that history and, more important,

---

[2]See Luce Irigaray, *The Sex Which is Not One,* trans. Catherine Porter with Carolyn Burke (Ithaca: Cornell University Press, 1985).

power were concerned with combatting death. Foucault writes:

> the pressure exerted by the biological on the historical had remained very strong for thousands of years; epidemics and famine were the two great dramatic forms of this relationship that was always dominated by the menace of death. *But through a circular process,* the economic—and primarily agricultural—development of the 18th century, and an increase in productivity and resources even more rapid than the demographic growth it encouraged, allowed a measure of relief from those profound threats: despite some renewed outbreaks, the period of great ravages from starvation and plague had come to a close before the *French Revolution;* death was ceasing to torment life so directly. But at the same time, the development of the different fields of knowledge concerned with life in general, the improvement of agricultural techniques, and the observations and measures relative to man's life and survival contributed to this relaxation: a relative control over life averted some of the imminent risks of death. (1:142)

There are of course several reasons to be suspicious of this kind of epoch-making narrativizing. It appears that Foucault wants to mark an historical shift from a notion of politics and history that is always threatened by death, and guided by the aim of negotiating that threat, to a politics that can to some extent *presume* the continuation of life and, hence, direct its attention to the regulation, control, and cultivation of life. Foucault notes the Eurocentrism in his account, but it alters nothing. He writes,

> it is not that life has been totally integrated into techniques that govern and administer it; it constantly escapes them. Outside the Western world, famine exists, on a greater scale than ever; and the biological risks confronting the species are perhaps greater, and certainly more serious, than before the birth of microbiology. (1:143)

Foucault's historical account can perhaps be read only as a wishful construction: death is effectively expelled from Western modernity, cast *behind* it as an historical possibility, surpassed or cast *outside* it as a non-Western phenomenon. Can these exclusions hold? To what extent does his characterization of later modernity require and institute an exclusion of the threat of death? It seems clear that Foucault must tell a phantasmatic history in order to keep modernity and productive power free of death and full of sex. Insofar as the category of sex is elaborated within the context of productive power, a story is being told in which sex, it seems, surpasses and displaces death.

If we accept the historically problematic character of this narration, can we accept it on logical grounds? Can one even defend against death without also promoting a certain version of life? Does juridical power in this way entail productive power as its logical correlate? "Death," whether figured as *prior* to modernity as that which is warded off and left behind or as a threat *within* premodern nations *elsewhere,* must always be the death, the end of a specific way of life; and the life to be safe-guarded is always already a normatively construed *way* of life, not life and death pure and simple. Does it make sense, then, to reject the notion that life entered into history as death took its exit from history? On the one hand, neither one ever entered or departed, since the one can only appear as the immanent possibility of the other; on the other hand, life and death might be construed as the incessant entering and departing that characterizes any field of power. Perhaps we are referring neither to an historical shift nor to a logical shift in the formation of power. For even when power is in the business of warding off death, that can only be in the name of some specific form of life and through the insistence on the right to produce and reproduce that way of life. At this point, the distinction between juridical and productive power appears to collapse.

And yet this shift must make sense for Foucault to argue convincingly that "sex" enters history in later modernity and becomes an object that productive power formulates, regulates, and produces. When sex becomes a site of power, it becomes an object of legal and regulatory discourses; it becomes that which power in its various discourses and institutions *cultivates* in the image of its own normative construction. There is no "sex" to which a supervening law attends; in attending to sex, in monitoring sex, sex itself is constructed, produced as that which calls to be monitored and *is* inherently regulatable. There is a normative development to sex, laws that inhere in sex itself, and the inquiry that attends to that lawlike development postures as if it merely discovers in sex the very laws that it has itself installed at the site of sex. In this sense, the regulation of "sex" finds no sex there, external to its own regulation; regulation produces the object it comes to regulate; regulation has regulated in advance what it will only disingenuously attend to as the object of regulation. In order to exercise and elaborate its own power, a regulatory regime will generate the very object it seeks to control.

And here is the crucial point: it is not as if a regulatory regime first controls its object and then produces it or first produces it in order then to control it; there is no temporary lag between the production and the regulation of sex; they occur at once, for regulation is always generative, producing the object it claims merely to discover or to find in the social field in which it operates. Concretely, this means that we are not, as it were, (merely) discriminated against on the basis of our sex; power is more *insidious* than that: either discrimination is built into the very formulation of our sex, or enfranchisement is precisely the formative and generative principle of some one else's sex. And this is why, for Foucault, sex can never be liberated *from power:* the formation of sex is an enacted of power. In a sense, power works on sex more deeply than we can know, not only as an external constraint or repression but as the formative principle of its intelligibility.

Here we can locate a shift or inversion at the center of power, in the very structure of power, for what appears at first to be a law that imposes itself upon "sex" as a ready-made object, a juridical view of power as constraint or *external* control, turns out to be—all along—performing a fully different ruse of power; silently, it is *already productive* power, forming the very object that will be suitable for control and then, in an act that effectively disavows that production, claiming to discover that "sex" outside of power. Hence, the category of "sex" will be precisely what power produces in order to have an object of control.

What this suggests, of course, is that there is no historical shift from juridical to productive power but that juridical power is a kind of dissimulated or concealed productive power from the start and that the shift, the inversion, is within power, not between two historically or logically distinct forms of power.

The category of "sex," which Foucault claims is understandable only as the result of an historical shift, is actually, as it were, produced in the midst of this shift, this very shiftiness of power that produces in advance that which it will come to subordinate. This is not a shift from a version of power as constraint or restriction to a version of power as productive but a production that is *at the same time* constraint, a constraining in advance of what will and will not qualify as a properly sexed being. This constraining production works through linking the category of sex with that of identity; there will be two sexes, discrete and uniform, and they will be expressed and evidenced in gender and sexuality, so that any social displays of nonidentity, discontinuity, or sexual incoherence will be punished, controlled, ostracized, reformed. Hence, by producing sex as a category of identity, that is, by defining sex as one sex or another, the discursive regulation of sex begins to take place. It is only after this procedure of definition and production has taken place that power comes to posture as that which is external to the object—"sex"—that it finds. In effect, it has already installed control in the object by defining the object as a self-identical object; its self-identity, presumed to be immanent to sex itself, is precisely the trace of this installation of power, a trace that is simultaneously erased, covered over, by the posturing of power as that which is external to its object.

What propels power? It cannot be human subjects, precisely because they are one of the occasions, enactments, and effects of power. It seems, for Foucault, that power seeks to augment itself within modernity just as life sought to augment itself prior to modernity. Power acts as life's proxy, as it were, taking over its function, reproducing itself always in excess of any need, luxuriating in a kind of self-elaboration that is no longer hindered by the immanent threat of death. Power thus becomes the locus of a certain displaced vitalism in Foucault; power, conceived as productive, is the form life takes when it no longer needs to guard itself against death.

SEX AND SEXUALITY

How does this inversion from early to late modern power affect Foucault's discussion of yet another inversion, that between *sex and sexuality*? Within ordinary language we sometimes speak, for instance, of being a given sex, and having a certain sexuality, and we even presume for the most part that our sexuality in some way *issues* from that sex, is perhaps an *expression* of that sex, or is even partially or fully *caused* by that sex. Sexuality is understood to come from sex, which is to say that the biological locus of "sex" in and on the body is somehow conjured as the originating source of a sexuality that, as it were, flows out from that locus, remains inhibited within that locus, or somehow takes its bearings with respect to that locus. In any case, "sex" is understood logically and temporally to *precede* sexuality and to function, if not as its primary cause, then at least as its necessary precondition.

However, Foucault performs an *inversion* of this relation and claims that this inversion is correlated with the shift from early to late modern power. For Foucault, "it is apparent that the deployment of sexuality, with its different strategies, was what established this notion of 'sex'" (1:154). Sexuality is here viewed as a discursively constructed and highly regulated network of pleasures and bodily exchanges, produced through prohibitions and sanctions that quite literally give form and directionality to pleasure and sensation. As such a network or regime, sexuality does not emerge from bodies as their prior causes; sexuality takes bodies as its instrument and its object, the site at which it consolidates, networks, and extends its power. As a regulatory regime sexuality operates primarily by *investing bodies with the category of sex,* that is, making bodies into the *bearers of a principle of identity*. To claim that bodies are one sex or the other appears at first to be a purely *descriptive* claim. For Foucault, however, this claim is itself a *legislation* and a *production* of bodies, a discursive demand, as it were, that bodies become produced according to principles of heterosexualizing coherence and integrity, unproblematically as either female or male. Where sex is taken as a principle of identity, it is always positioned within a field of two mutually exclusive and fully exhaustive identities; one is either male or female, never both at once, and never neither one of them.

the notion of sex brought about a fundamental reversal; it made it possible to invert the representation of the relationships of power to sexuality, causing the latter to appear, not in its essential and positive relation to power, but as being rooted in a specific and irreducible urgency which power tries as best it can to dominate; thus the idea of "sex" makes it possible to evade what gives "power" its power; it enables one to conceive power solely as law and taboo. (1:155)

For Foucault, sex, whether male or female, operates as a principle of identity that imposes a fiction of coherence and unity on an otherwise random or unrelated set of biological functions, sensations, pleasures. Under the regime of sex, every pleasure becomes symptomatic of "sex," and "sex" itself functions not merely as the biological ground or cause of pleasure but as that which determines its directionality, a principle of teleology or destiny, and as that repressed, psychical core which furnishes clues to the interpretation of its ultimate meaning. As a fictional imposition of uniformity, sex is "an imaginary point" and an "artificial unity," but as fictional and as artificial, the category wields enormous power.[3] Although Foucault does not quite claim it, the science of reproduction produces intelligible "sex" by imposing a compulsory heterosexuality on the description of bodies. One might claim that sex is here produced according to a heterosexual morphology.

The category of "sex" thus establishes a principle of intelligibility for human beings, which is to say that no human being can be taken to be human, can be recognized *as* human unless that human being is fully and coherently marked by sex. And yet it would not capture Foucault's meaning merely to claim that there are humans who are marked by sex and thereby become intelligible; the point is stronger: to qualify as legitimately human, one must be coherently sexed. The incoherence of sex is precisely what marks off the abject and the dehumanized from the recognizably human.

Luce Irigaray would clearly take this point further and turn it against Foucault. She would, I think, argue that the only sex that qualifies as a sex is a masculine one, which is not marked as masculine but parades as the universal and thereby silently extends its dominion. To refer to a sex which is not one is to refer to a sex which cannot be designated univocally as sex but is outside identity from the start. Are we not right to ask, which sex is it that renders the figure of the human intelligible, and within such an economy, is it not the case that the feminine functions as a figure for unintelligibility? When one speaks of the "one" in language—as I do now—one makes reference to a neuter term, a purely human term. And whereas Foucault and Irigaray would agree that sex is a necessary precondition for human intelligibility, Foucault appears to think that any sanctioned sex will do, but Irigaray would argue that the only sanctioned sex is the masculine one; that is, the masculine that is reworked as a "one," a neuter, a universal. If the coherent subject is always sexed as masculine, then it is constructed through the abjection and erasure of the feminine. For Irigaray, masculine and feminine sexes are not similarly constructed as sexes or as principles of intelligible identity; in fact, she argues that the masculine sex is constructed as the only "one," and that it figures the feminine other as a reflection only of itself; within that model, then, both masculine and feminine reduce to the masculine, and the feminine,

---

[3]"It is through sex," Foucault writes, "—in fact an imaginary point determined by the deployment of sexuality—that each individual has to pass in order to have access to his own intelligibility, (seeing that it is both the hidden aspect and the generative principle of meaning), to the whole of his body (since it is a real and threatened part of it, while symbolically constituting the whole), to his identity (since it joins the force of a drive to the singularity of a history)" (1:155–56).

left outside this male autoerotic economy, is not even designatable within its terms or is, rather, designatable as a radically disfigured masculine projection, which is yet a different kind of erasure.[4]

This hypothetical critique from an Irigarayan perspective suggests something problematic about Foucault's constructivism. Within the terms of productive power, regulation and control work through the discursive articulation of identities. But those discursive articulations effect certain exclusions and erasures; oppression works not merely through the mechanism of regulation and production but by foreclosing the very possibility of articulation. If Foucault claims that regulation and control operate as the formative principles of identity, Irigaray in a somewhat more Derridean vein would argue that oppression works through other means as well, through the *exclusion* and *erasure* effected by any discursive formation, and that here the feminine is precisely what is erased and excluded in order for intelligible identities to be produced.[5]

---

[4]In this sense, the category of sex constitutes and regulates what will and will not be an intelligible and recognizable human existence, what will and will not be a citizen capable of rights or speech, an individual protected by law against violence or injury.

The political question for Foucault, and for those of us who read him now is *not* whether "improperly sexed" beings should or should not be treated fairly or with justice or with tolerance. The question is whether, if improperly sexed, such a being can even be a being, a human being, a subject, one whom the law can condone or condemn. For Foucault has outlined a region that is, as it were, outside of the purview of the law, one that excludes certain kinds of improperly sexed beings from the very category of the human subject. The journals of Herculine Barbin, the hermaphrodite (ed: Michel Foucault, *Herculine Barbin, Being the Recently Discovered Memoirs of a Nineteenth Century Hermaphrodite,* trans. Richard Mac-Dougall (New York: Colophon, 1980), demonstrate the violence of the law that would legislate identity on a body that resists it. But Herculine is to some extent a *figure* for a sexual ambiguity or inconsistency that emerges at the site of bodies and that contests the category of subject and its univocal or self-identical "sex."

CONTEMPORARY IDENTITY IN THE AGE OF EPIDEMIC

This is a limitation of Foucault's analysis. And yet he offers a counterwarning, I think, to those who might be tempted to treat femaleness or the feminine as an identity to be liberated. To attempt that would be to repeat the gesture of the regulatory regime, taking some aspect of "sex" and making it stand synecdochally for the entirety of the body and its psychic manifestations. Similarly, Foucault did not embrace an identity politics that might in the name of homosexuality combat the regulatory effort to produce the symptomatic homosexual or to erase the homosexual from the domain of intelligible subjects. To take identity as a rallying point for liberation would be to subject one-self at the very moment that one calls for a release from subjection. For the point is not to claim, "yes, I am fully totalized by the category of homosexuality, just as you say, but only that the meaning of that totalization will be different from the one that you attribute to me." If identity imposes a fictive coherence and consistency on the body or, better, if identity is a regulatory principle that produces bodies in conformity with that principle, then it is no more liberatory to embrace an unproblematized gay identity than it is to embrace the diagnostic category of homosexuality devised by juridico-medical regimes. The political challenge Foucault poses here is whether a resistance to the diagnostic category can be effected that does not reduplicate the very mechanism of that subjection, this time—painfully, paradoxically—under the sign of liberation. The task for Foucault is to refuse the totalizing category under either guise, which is why Foucault will not confess or "come out" in the *History of Sexuality* as a homosexual or privilege

---

[5]This gives some clues to what a deconstructive critique of Foucault might look like.

homosexuality as a site of heightened regulation. But perhaps Foucault remains significantly and politically linked to this problematic of homosexuality all the same.

Is Foucault's strategic *inversion* of identity perhaps a redeployment of the medicalized category of the invert? The diagnostic category "invert" presumes that someone with a given sex somehow acquired a set of sexual dispositions and desires that do not travel in the appropriate directions; sexual desire is "inverted" when it misses its aim and object and travels wrong-headedly to its opposite or when it takes itself as the object of its desire and then projects and recovers that "self" in a homosexual object. Clearly, Foucault gives us a way to laugh at this construction of the proper relation between "sex" and "sexuality," to appreciate its contingency, and to question the causal and expressive lines that are said to run from sex to sexuality. Ironically, or perhaps tactically, Foucault engages a certain activity of "inversion" here but reworks that term from a noun to a verb. His theoretical practice is, in a sense, marked by a series of inversions: in the shift to modern power, an inversion is performed; in the relation of sex and sexuality, another inversion is performed. And with respect to the category of the "invert," yet another inversion is performed, one that might be understood to stand as a strategy of refiguration according to which the various other inversions of the text can be read.[6]

The traditional invert gets its name because the *aim* of its desire has run off the rails of heterosexuality. According to the construction of homosexuality as narcissism, the aim has turned back against itself or exchanged its position of identification for the position of the object desired, an exchange that constitutes a kind of psychic mistake. But to locate inversion as an exchange between psychic disposition and aim, or between an identification and an object, or as a return of an aim upon itself is still to operate within the heterosexualizing norm and its teleological explanations. Foucault calls this kind of explanation into question, however, through an explanatory inversion which establishes sexuality as a regulatory regime that dissimulates itself by setting up the category of "sex" as a quasi-naturalistic

---

[6] If sexuality takes sex as its instrument and object, then sexuality is by definition more diffuse and less uniform than the category of sex; through the category of sex, sexuality performs a kind of self-reduction. Sexuality will always exceed sex, even as sex sets itself up as a category that accounts for sexuality *in toto* by posturing as its primary cause. In order to claim that one is a given sex, a certain radical reduction must take place, for "sex" functions to describe not only certain relatively stable biological or anatomical traits but also an activity, what one does, and a state of mind or psychic disposition. The ambiguities of the term are temporarily overcome when "sex" is understood as the biological basis for a psychic disposition, which then manifests itself in a set of acts. In this sense, the category of "sex" functions to establish a fictive causality among these dimensions of bodily existence, so that to be female is to be disposed sexually in a certain way, namely, heterosexually, and to be positioned within sexual exchange such that the biological and psychic dimensions of "sex" are consummated, integrated, and demonstrated. On the one hand, the category of sex works to blur the distinctions among biology, psychic reality, and sexual practice, for sex is all of these things, even as it proceeds through a certain force of teleology to relate each of these terms. But once the teleology is disrupted, shown to be disruptible, then the very discreteness of terms like biology and psyche becomes contestable. For if sex proves no longer to be as encompassing as it seems, then what in biology is "sex," and what contests the univocity of that term, and where, if at all, is sex to be found in the psyche, if sex can no longer be placed within that heterosexualizing teleology? These terms become disjoined and internally destabilized when a biological female is perhaps psychically disposed in nonheterosexual ways or is positioned in sexual exchanges in ways that the categories of heterosexuality cannot quite describe. Then what Foucault has called "the fictive unity of sex" is no longer secure. This disunity or disaggregation of "sex" suggests that the category only works to the extent that it describes a hyperbolic heterosexuality, a normative heterosexuality, one that, in its idealized coherence, is uninhabitable by practicing heterosexuals and as such is bound to oppress in its status as an impossible idealization. This is an idealization before which everyone is bound to fail and which of course is a failure, for clear political reasons, to be savored and safeguarded.

fictive unity. Exposed as a fiction, the body becomes a site for unregulated pleasures, sensations, practices, convergences and refigurations of masculine and feminine such that the naturalizing status of those terms is called radically into question.

Hence, the task for Foucault is not to claim the category of invert or of homosexual and to rework that term to signify something less pathological, mistaken, or deviant. The task is to call into question the explanatory gesture that requires a true identity and, hence, a mistaken one as well. If diagnostic discourse would make of Foucault an "invert," then he will invert the very logic that makes something like "inversion" possible. And he will do this by inverting the relation between sex and sexuality. This is an intensification and redoubling of inversion, one that is perhaps mobilized by the diagnosis but that has as its effect the disruption of the very vocabulary of diagnosis and cure, true and mistaken identity. This is as if to say: "Yes, an invert, but I will show you what inversion can do; I can invert and subvert the categories of identity such that you will no longer be able to call me that and know what it is you mean."

The pathologization of homosexuality was to have a future that Foucault could not have foreseen in 1976. For if homosexuality is pathological from the start, then any disease that homosexuals may sometimes contract will be uneasily conflated with the disease that they already are. Foucault's effort to delineate a modern epoch and to claim a break between the era of epidemics and that of recent modernity must now become subject to an inversion, which he himself did not perform but which in a sense he taught us how to perform. For Foucault claims that the epidemic is over, and yet he may well have been one of its hosts at the time he made that claim, a silent carrier who could not know the historical future that arrived to defeat his claim. Death is the limit to power, he argued, but there is something that he missed here, namely,

that in the maintenance of death and of the dying, power is still at work and that death is and has its own discursive industry.

When Foucault gives his grand narrative of epidemiology, he can only be mistaken, for to believe that technological advance forecloses the possibility of an age of epidemic, as Linda Singer has called the contemporary sexual regime,[7] is finally evidence of a phantasmatic projection and a vainly utopian faith. For it not only presumes that technology will ward off death, or already has, but that it will preserve life (a highly questionable presumption). And it fails to account for the way in which technology is differentially deployed to save some lives and to condemn others. When we consider which technology receives federal funding, and we note that recent AIDS appropriations bills have been drastically cut, it becomes clear that inasmuch as AIDS is understood to afflict marginalized communities and is itself taken as a further token of their marginalization, technology can be precisely what is withheld from a life-preserving deployment.

On the Senate floor one hears quite specific references to AIDS as that which is somehow caused by gay sexual practices. Here homosexuality is itself made into a death-bearing practice, but this is hardly new. Jeff Nunokawa argues that a long-standing discursive tradition figures the male homosexual as always already dying, as one whose desire is a kind of incipient and protracted dying.[8] The discourse that attributes AIDS to homosexuality is an intensification and reconsolidation of that same tradition.

---

[7]See Linda Singer, "Bodies—Powers—Pleasures," *differences* 1 (1989): 45–66; see also her forthcoming manuscript, *Erotic Welfare: Sexual Theory and Politics in the Age of Epidemic* (Routledge).

[8]Jeff Nunokawa, "*In Memoriam* and the Extinction of the Homosexual," *English Literary History,* forthcoming.

On Sunday, October 21, 1990, the *New York Times*[9] ran a memorial story on Leonard Bernstein who had recently died from lung disease. Although this appears not to be a death from AIDS or from AIDS-related complications, a journalistic effort is nevertheless made to link his death with his homosexuality and to figure his homosexuality as a death drive. The essay tacitly constructs the scene of his death as the logical consequence of a life which, even in the romantic music he liked, seemed to know that "death was always standing in the wings." It is usually friends, admirers, lovers who stand in the wings when a conductor performs, but here it is somehow death who is uneasily collapsed into the homosexual phantasm. Immediately following this statement comes another: "his compulsive smoking and other personal excesses certainly could be interpreted in classic death-wish terms. In the Romantically committed mind, for every plus there must be a minus, for every blessing of love, a compensating curse." Here death is

understood as a necessary compensation for homosexual desire, as the *telos* of male homosexuality, its genesis and its demise, the principle of its intelligibility.

In 1976, Foucault sought to disjoin the category of sex from the struggle against death; in this way, he sought, it seems, to make of sex a life-affirming and perpetuating activity. Even as an effect of power, "sex" is precisely that which is said to reproduce itself, augment and intensify itself, and pervade mundane life. Foucault sought to separate sex from death by announcing the end of the era in which death reigns; but what kind of radical hopefulness would consign the constitutive power of death to an irrecoverable historical past? What promise did Foucault see in sex, and in sexuality, to overcome death, such that sex is precisely what marks the overcoming of death, the end to the struggle against it? He did not consider that the regulatory discourse on sex could itself produce death, pronounce death, even proliferate it. And that, insofar as "sex" as a category was supposed to secure reproduction and life, those instances of "sex" that are not directly reproductive might then take on the valence of death.

He warned us, wisely, that "we must not think that by saying yes to sex, one says no to power; on the contrary, one tracks along the course laid out by the general deployment of sexuality. It is the agency of sex that we must break away from" (?). And that is right, for sex does not cause AIDS. There are discursive and institutional regimes that regulate and punish sexuality, laying down tracks that will not save us, indeed, that may lead rather quickly to our demise.

One ought not to think that by saying yes to power, one says no to death, for death can be not the limit of power but its very aim.

Foucault clearly saw that death could become an aim of politics, for he argued that war itself had become sublimated into politics: "the force

---

[9]Donal Henahan (H:1, 25). Later Henahan remarks that "It struck some who knew him as contradictory that the conductor who struggled to reveal himself in every performance, faithful to the great romantic tradition, nevertheless kept his private life out of the public eye. His homosexuality, never a secret in musical circles, became more overt after the death of his wife, but, perhaps, out of his concern for his carefully cultivated image, he was not eager to disillusion the straight-arrow public that had adopted him as the all-American boy of music." Here the romantic tradition of self-disclosure would appear to demand that he disclose his homosexuality, which suggests that his homosexuality is at the heart of his romanticism and, hence, his commitment to being cursed by love. The use of "straight-arrow" for straight imports the sense of "straight as an arrow," a phrase used to connote honesty. The association here suggests that to be straight is to be honest, and to be gay is to be dishonest. This links back to the question of disclosure suggesting that the author takes Bernstein's insistence on privacy as an act of deceit, and at the same time, that homosexuality itself, that is, the content of what is concealed, is a kind of necessary deceitfulness. This culminates the moralistic circle of the story, which now constructs the homosexual as one who, by virtue of his essential deceitfulness, is cursed by his own love to death.

relationships that for a long time had found expression in war, in every form of warfare, gradually became invested in the order of political power" (1:102). He wrote in the *History of Sexuality* "One might say that the ancient right to *take* life or *let* live was replaced by a power to *foster* life or *disallow* it to the point of death" (1:138).

When he claims that "sex is worth dying for," he means that preserving the regime of "sex" is worth dying for and that political wars are waged so that populations and their reproduction can be secured. "Wars are no longer waged in the name of a sovereign who must be defended; they are waged on behalf of the existence of everyone; entire populations are mobilized for the purpose of wholesale slaughter in the name of life necessity: massacres," he writes, "have become vital" (1:137). He then adds,

> the principle underlying the tactics of battle—that one has to be capable of killing in order to go on living—has become the principle that defines the strategy of the states. But the existence in question is no longer the juridical existence of sovereignty; at stake is the biological existence of a population. If genocide is indeed the dream of modern powers, this is not because of a recent return of the ancient right to kill; it is because power is situated and exercised at the level of life, the species, the race, and the large-scale phenomena of population. (1:137)

It is not only that modern states have the capacity to destroy one another through nuclear arsenals but that "populations" have become the objects of war, and it is in the name of whole "populations" that ostensibly defensive wars are waged.

In a sense, Foucault knew full well that death had not ceased to be the goal of "modern" states but only that the aim of annihilation is achieved through more subtle means. In the political decisions that administer the scientific, technological, and social resources to respond to the epidemic of AIDS, the parameters of that crisis are insidiously circumscribed; the lives to be saved are insidiously demarcated from those who will be left to die; "innocent" victims are separated from those who "deserve it." But this demarcation is, of course, largely implicit, for modern power "administers" life in part through the silent withdrawal of its resources. In this way, politics can achieve the goal of death, can target its own population, under the very sign of the administration of life. This "inversion" of power performs the work of death under the signs of life, scientific progress, technological advance, that is, under the signs that ostensibly promise the preservation of life. And because this kind of dissimulated killing takes place through the public, discursive production of a scientific community in competition to find a cure, working under difficult conditions, victims of economic scarcity, the question of how little is allocated and how poorly it is directed can hardly be heard. The technological aim to preserve life, then, becomes the silent sanction by which this dissimulated killing silently proceeds. We must not think that by saying yes to technology, we say no to death, for there is always the question of how and for what aim that technology is produced. The deeper offense is surely to be found in the claim that it is neither the failure of government nor of science but "sex" itself that continues this unfathomable procession of death.

chapter thirty-eight

bell hooks

bell hooks (the *nom de plume* of Gloria Watkins, b. 1952) often refers to herself as an insurgent black intellectual. Situating herself in this way, hooks makes clear her commitment both to the political project of black liberation and to a "critical engagement with ideas."[1] This perspective on intellectual work is informed by the notion of praxis—"action and reflection upon the world in order to change it."[2] In describing her own intellectual development, hooks states that she was very influenced by political thinkers who worked in liberation struggles in different parts of the globe—Malcolm X, Paulo Freire, Frantz Fanon, and Amical Cabral. She notes that the writers Lorraine Hansberry and James Baldwin were equally important influences on her, and she values each of them for "exuding radical openness."[3] hooks also praises African American female writers such as Toni Morrison, Toni Cade Bambara, and Audre Lorde, suggesting that they have crafted a critical body of literature that speaks about African American psychologies, epistemologies, and ethics. In looking to literature and political struggles to inform her philosophical inquiries, hooks embraces what academia often dismisses—the body, the soul, and the emotions. This is a crucial strategy for hooks, as she often states that love and passion are necessary components of revolutionary praxis.

Born and raised in the segregated (what she calls *apartheid*) American South, hooks has been critically conscious of many forms of oppression from an early age. She writes about the legacies of slavery and the continuing existence of white supremacy from the perspective of someone who began her education in segregated schools and who then experienced the turmoil and broken promises of the era of racial integration. She writes about feminism from the perspective of a woman who has been called a traitor to her race for her criticism of patriarchal thought in the black community and who has been criticized for introducing questions of race into discussions of feminism. hooks also takes great care to address the impact of capitalism and economic inequality on racial and gender issues. Her own critical engagement with ideas does not allow her to privilege a single lens, and, indeed, she seeks to investigate the complex relations between race, gender, and class.

Part of hooks's motivation for her work is her belief that "Black people are wounded in our hearts, minds, bodies and spirits."[4] Committed to praxis, hooks sees her goal as healing those wounds. Since beginning her intellectual career, hooks's attempts at healing have taken place in a variety of disciplines. She has written books on feminism (*Ain't I a Woman*), on race (*Black Looks: Race and Representation*), on cultural criticism (*Reel to Real: Race, Class and Sex at the Movies*), and on self-help (*Sisters of the Yam: Black Women and Self-recovery*). While many intellectuals might feel some unease at writing a book that is labeled "self-help," hooks embraces the self-help movement. Believing that one can't be revolutionary without being self-actualized, hooks's concern is to posit ways for that self-actualization (and the revolution) to take place. She writes that "[b]lack female self-recovery, like all black self-recovery, is an expression of liberatory political practice."[5]

The process of self-actualization and decolonization is by nature a difficult one, as it entails confronting both institutionalized racism and the white supremacist ideology that supports it. Dealing with the latter is proving to be the more vexing problem. hooks suggests that while overt racist discrimination and oppression may have lessened to some extent, black people are wounded in their hearts, minds, bodies, and spirits because they have been assaulted with a pervasive devaluing of blackness. This means that in addition to attacking unjust social structures, black radicals and their allies must challenge the internalized results of white supremacist thinking. As an example, she points to the politics of skin tone in the African American community, where lighter skinned women are thought by some to be more beautiful and desirable. This can take place without the physical presence of whites, because white supremacist values (e.g., white skin is better than black skin) have been internalized. In this way, hooks suggests that black people "can exercise 'white supremacist control' over other black people."[6] Thus, decolonization is not simply about chasing the colonizer out of the country, but also about chasing colonial ideologies out of the minds and souls of the formerly colonized.

Looking at the impact of white supremacy from another angle, hooks writes that "one mark of oppression was that black folks were compelled to assume the mantle of invisibility, to erase all traces of their subjectivity during slavery and the long years of racial apartheid, so that they could be better, less threatening servants."[7] For this reason, hooks sees the decolonization process as moving the formerly colonized from "manipulatable objects to self-empowered subjects."[8] Indeed, she cites Freire's comment that "We cannot enter the struggle as objects in order later to become subjects."[9] Decolonization begins with the reclaiming of subjectivity. hooks writes that "Following in the path of Sojourner Truth and other wise black women elders, black females must constantly assert our full humanity to counter the impact of dehumanizing forces."[10]

This movement from object status to subjectivity can be supported by the practice of "expressing our full range of emotions," and in fact doing so "is healing to the spirit and engages us in the practice of self-acceptance, which is so essential to self-love."[11] This concern with self-acceptance and self-love (part of what hooks calls "home-psychoanalysis") has led to hooks being dismissed as less than rigorous, or as not academic enough. hooks counters these accusations by criticizing (black) academics who speak and write in a jargon that limits the size of their audience and reduces the potential impact of their work on the daily lives of African Americans. As an intellectual she embraces the vernacular and feels that words such as *love* and *passion* have great explanatory power. Indeed, over the course of her career the concept of love has played a key role in her explorations of society.

Even though hooks has approached love from many perspectives, one definition she provides is that love is "a combination of care, knowledge, responsibility, respect, trust and commitment."[12] Viewing love in those terms, hooks suggests that American society is profoundly loveless and that turning to love in such a context is a radical act. hooks writes that "[m]aking the choice to love can heal our wounded spirits and our body politic. It is the deepest revolution, the turning away from the world as we know it, toward the world we must make if we are to be one with the planet—one healing heart giving and sustaining life. Love is our hope and our salvation."[13] Yet love cannot be seen as effortless or as painless. hooks uses a quote from James Baldwin's *The Fire Next Time* as an epigraph for her book, *Salvation: Black People and Love*. Baldwin writes, "Love takes off the masks that we fear we cannot live without and know we cannot live within. I use the word love here not merely in the personal sense but as a state of being, or a state of grace—not in the infantile American sense of being made happy but in the tough and universal sense of quest and growth."[14] Again, the process of self-love and decolonization is not an easy one.

Love, as quest and growth, is also not an individualized experience. hooks cites Sam Keen's work *The Passionate Life* as an influence, especially in its "vision of life that links our sense of self with communion and community."[15] Through her work, hooks hopes to create beloved communities, in which "loving ties of care and knowing bind us together in our differences."[16] In this way, the goal is not to transcend differences (such as race) but to affirm them, so that each of us can express our full humanity and recognize the full humanity of others. Keen refers to this vision as an "erotic metaphysic," which is "based on the assumption that we become more fully who we are in the act of loving."[17] As hooks explains in the chapter that follows, while the erotic metaphysic includes sexuality, it is not limited to that. It is a stance of radical openness, a questing energy that supports the expression of a full range of emotions.[18]

The article presented in this volume, "Eros, Eroticism, and the Pedagogical Process" comes from hooks's *Teaching to Transgress: Education as the Practice of Freedom*. This book is a collection of essays that attempts to translate the concept of healing love and the erotic metaphysic into a classroom setting. By looking at education as the practice of freedom, hooks echoes Freire's concern with liberatory praxis. She recounts that when she was a child in a segregated school, all of her teachers were supportive black females. They were inspiring examples of true intellectuals who were committed to supporting students' engagement with ideas. She remembers that "school was a place of ecstasy—pleasure and danger. To be changed by ideas was pure pleasure. But to learn ideas that ran counter to values and beliefs learned at home was to place oneself at risk, to enter the danger zone."[19] This ecstasy is not what one encounters in most classrooms, where students are seen as empty receptacles to be filled with knowledge doled out by teachers (what Freire calls the "banking model" cf education). In these classes, there is no concern about the fact that students are stupefied and bored to tears. In sharp contrast to that, hooks, like Freire, looks to create educational practice that is participatory and empowering. This is an educational model where teachers and students work to build a beloved community in the classroom, where they take off their masks and grow together. While *Teaching to Transgress* is the first book by hooks that treats pedagogy as its central concern, the pedagogical possibilities of an "erotic metaphysic" are a consistent aspect of hooks's work.

EJ

QUESTIONS

1. How does hooks use the concept of "the body" as a critical tool and pedagogic device?
2. What are the multiple meanings of "erotic" that hooks presents?
3. What role does the erotic have in hocks' approach to education for critical consciousness? What role does love play?
4. How comfortable are you with the idea of a "passionate teacher/student relationship"? What does that term bring to mind? Why?
5. How would a pedagogy that embraces the erotic make use of an emotion such as rage? Is rage erotic?

ENDNOTES

1. hooks, *Killing Rage*, p. 228.
2. hooks, *Teaching to Transgress*, p. 14.
3. hooks, *Killing Rage*, p. 229.
4. hooks, *Sisters of the Yam*, p. 11.
5. Ibid.
6. hooks, *Killing Rage*, p. 14.
7. Ibid., p. 35.

8. hooks, *Sisters of the Yam*, p. 2.

9. hooks, *Teaching to Transgress*, p. 46.

10. hooks, *Salvation*, p. 112.

11. Ibid.

12. Ibid., p. xviii.

13. Ibid., p. 225.

14. Ibid., p. 1.

15. hooks, *Sisters of the Yam*, p. 115.

16. hooks, *Killing Rage*, p. 264.

17. hooks, *Sisters of the Yam*, p. 115.

18. For example, hooks points to the importance of emotions such as rage. Specifically with regard to the experience of racism and white supremacy, hooks wants to "see black rage as something other than sickness, to see it as a potentially healthy, potentially healing response to oppression and exploitation." She recounts reading Malcolm X and how profound an impact it made on her that he "dared black folks to claim our emotional subjectivity and that we could do this only by claiming our rage." She concludes, "Progressive black activists must show how we can take that rage and move it beyond fruitless scapegoating of any group, linking it instead to a passion for freedom and justice that illuminates, heals and makes redemptive struggle possible." Harnessing erotic power in all its guises, as hooks suggests, can heal the body politic.

19. hooks, *Teaching to Transgress*, p. 3.

SELECTED BIBLIOGRAPHY

hooks, bell. *Ain't I a Woman: Black Women and Feminism*. Boston, Mass.: South End Press, 1981.

hooks, bell. *All About Love: New Visions*. New York: Harper Perennial, 2001.

hooks, bell. *Black Looks: Race and Representation*. Boston, Mass.: South End Press, 1992.

hooks, bell. *Killing Rage: Ending Racism*. New York: Henry Holt and Company, 1995.

hooks, bell. *Reel to Real: Race, Class and Sex at the Movies*. New York: Routledge, 1996.

hooks, bell. *Salvation: Black People and Love*. New York: HarperCollins, 2001.

hooks, bell. *Sisters of the Yam: Black Women and Self-Recovery*. Boston, Mass.: South End Press, 1993.

hooks, bell. *Teaching to Transgress: Education as the Practice of Freedom*. New York: Routledge, 1994.

hooks, bell. *Wounds of Passion: A Writing Life*. New York: Henry Holt, 1997.

Keen, Sam. *The Passionate Life: Stages of Learning*. New York: Harper and Row, 1983.

Eros, Eroticism, and the Pedagogical Process

bell hooks

Professors rarely speak of the place of eros or the erotic in our classrooms. Trained in the philosophical context of Western metaphysical dualism, many of us have accepted the notion that there is a split between the body and the mind. Believing this, individuals enter the classroom to teach as though only the mind is present, and not the body. To call attention to the body is to betray the legacy of repression and denial that has been handed down to us by our professorial elders, who have been usually white and male. But our nonwhite elders were just as eager to deny the body. The predominantly black college has always been a bastion of repression. The public world of institutional learning was a site where the body had to be erased, go unnoticed. When I first became a teacher and needed to use the restroom in the middle of class, I had no clue as to what my elders did in such situations. No one talked about the body in relation to teaching. What did one do with the body in the classroom? Trying to remember the bodies of my professors, I find myself unable to recall them. I hear voices, remember fragmented details, but very few whole bodies.

Entering the classroom determined to erase the body and give ourselves over more fully to the mind, we show by our beings how deeply we have accepted the assumption that passion has no place in the classroom. Repression and denial make it possible for us to forget and then desperately seek to recover ourselves, our feelings, our passions in some private place—after class. I remember reading an article in *Psychology Today* years ago when I was still an undergraduate, reporting a study which revealed that every so many seconds while giving lectures many male professors were thinking about sexuality—were even having lustful thoughts about students. I was amazed. After reading this article, which as I recall was shared and talked about endlessly in the dormitory, I watched male professors differently, trying to connect the fantasies I imagined them having in their minds with lectures, with their bodies that I had so faithfully learned to pretend I did not see. During my first semester of college teaching, there was a male student in my class whom I always seemed to see and not see at the same time. At one point in the middle of the semester, I received a call from a school therapist who wanted to speak with me about the way I treated this student in the class. The therapist told me that the students had said I was unusually gruff, rude, and downright mean when I related to him. I did not know exactly who the student was, could not put a face or body with his name, but later when he identified himself in class, I realized that I was erotically drawn to this student. And that my naive way of coping with feelings in the classroom that I had been taught never to have was to deflect (hence my harsh treatment of him), repress, and deny. Overly conscious then about ways such repression and denial could lead to the "wounding" of students, I was determined to face whatever passions were aroused in the classroom setting and deal with them.

Writing about Adrienne Rich's work, connecting it to the work of men who thought critically about the body, in her introduction to *Thinking Through the Body*, Jane Gallop comments:

Men who do find themselves in some way thinking through the body are more likely to be recognized as serious thinkers and heard. Women have first to prove that we are thinkers, which is easier when we conform to the protocol that deems serious thought separate from an embodied subject in history. Rich is asking women to enter the realms of critical thought and knowledge without becoming disembodied spirit, universal man.

Beyond the realm of critical thought, it is equally crucial that we learn to enter the classroom "whole" and not as "disembodied spirit." In the heady early days of Women's Studies classes at Stanford University, I learned by the example of daring, courageous woman professors (particularly Diane Middlebrook) that there was a place for passion in the classroom, that eros and the erotic did not need to be denied for learning to take place. One of the central tenets of feminist critical pedagogy has been the insistence on not engaging the mind/body split. This is one of the underlying beliefs that has made Women's Studies a subversive location in the academy. While women's studies over the years has had to fight to be taken seriously by academics in traditional disciplines, those of us who have been intimately engaged as students or teachers with feminist thinking have always recognized the legitimacy of a pedagogy that dares to subvert the mind/body split and allow us to be whole in the classroom, and as a consequence wholehearted.

Recently, Susan B., a colleague and friend, whom I taught in a Women's Studies class when she was an undergraduate, stated in conversation that she felt she was having so much trouble with her graduate courses because she has to come to expect a quality of passionate teaching that is not present where she is studying. Her comments made me think anew about the place of passion, of erotic recognition in the classroom setting because I believe that the energy she felt in our Women's Studies classes was there because of the extent to which women professors teaching those courses dared to give fully of ourselves, going beyond the mere transmission of information in lectures. Feminist education for critical consciousness is rooted

in the assumption that knowledge and critical thought done in the classroom should inform our habits of being and ways of living outside the classroom. Since so many of our early classes were taken almost exclusively by female students, it was easier for us to not be disembodied spirits in the classroom. Concurrently, it was expected that we would bring a quality of care and even "love" to our students. Eros was present in our classrooms, as a motivating force. As critical pedagogues we were teaching students ways to think differently about gender, understanding fully that this knowledge would also lead them to live differently.

To understand the place of eros and eroticism in the classroom, we must move beyond thinking of those forces solely in terms of the sexual, though that dimension need not be denied. Sam Keen, in his book *The Passionate Life*, urges readers to remember that in its earliest conception "erotic potency was not confined to sexual power but included the moving force that propelled every life-form from a state of mere potentiality to actuality." Given that critical pedagogy seeks to transform consciousness, to provide students with ways of knowing that enable them to know themselves better and live in the world more fully, to some extent it must rely on the presence of the erotic in the classroom to aid the learning process. Keen continues:

> When we limit "erotic" to its sexual meaning, we betray our alienation from the rest of nature. We confess that we are not motivated by anything like the mysterious force that moves birds to migrate or dandelions to spring. Furthermore, we imply that the fulfillment or potential toward which we strive is sexual—the romantic-genital connection between two persons.

Understanding that eros is a force that enhances our overall effort to be self-actualizing, that it can provide an epistemological grounding informing how we know what we know, enables both professors and students to use such energy in a classroom setting in ways that invigorate discussion and excite the critical imagination.

Suggesting that this culture lacks a "vision or science of hygeology" (health and well-being) Keen asks: "What forms of passion might make us whole? To what passions may we surrender with the assurance that we will expand rather than diminish the promise of our lives?" The quest for knowledge that enables us to unite theory and practice is one such passion. To the extent that professors bring this passion, which has to be fundamentally rooted in a love for ideas we are able to inspire, the classroom becomes a dynamic place where transformations in social relations are concretely actualized and the false dichotomy between the world outside and the inside world of the academy disappears. In many ways this is frightening. Nothing about the way I was trained as a teacher really prepared me to witness my students transforming themselves.

It was during the years that I taught in the African American Studies department at Yale (a course on black women writers) that I witnessed the way education for critical consciousness can fundamentally alter our perceptions of reality and our actions. During one course we collectively explored in fiction the power of internalized racism, seeing how it was described in the literature as well as critically interrogating our experiences. However, one of the black female students who had always straightened her hair because she felt deep down that she would not look good if it were not processed—were worn "natural"—changed. She came to class after a break and told everyone that this class had deeply affected her, so much so that when she went to get her usual "perm" some force within said no. I still remember the fear I felt when she testified that the class had changed her. Though I believed deeply in the philosophy of ed-

ucation for critical consciousness that empowers, I had not yet comfortably united theory with practice. Some small part of me still wanted us to remain disembodied spirits. And her body, her presence, her changed look was a direct challenge that I had to face and affirm. She was teaching me. Now, years later, I read again her final words to the class and recognize the passion and beauty of her will to know and to act:

> I am a black woman. I grew up in Shaker Heights, Ohio. I cannot go back and change years of believing that I could never be quite as pretty or intelligent as many of my white friends—but I can go forward learning pride in who I am. . . . I cannot go back and change years of believing that the most wonderful thing in the world would be to be Martin Luther King, Jr.'s wife—but I can go on and find the strength I need to be the revolutionary for myself rather than the companion and help for someone else. So no, I don't believe that we change what has already been done but we can change the future and so I am reclaiming and learning more of who I am so that I can be whole.

Attempting to gather my thoughts on eroticism and pedagogy, I have reread student journals covering a span of ten years. Again and again, I read notes that could easily be considered "romantic" as students express their love for me, our class. Here an Asian student offers her thoughts about a class:

> White people have never understood the beauty of silence, of connection and reflection. You teach us to speak, and to listen for the signs of the wind. Like a guide, you walk silently through the forest ahead of us. In the forest everything has sound, speaks. . . . You too teach us to talk, where all life speaks in the forest, not just the white man's. Isn't that part of feeling whole—the ability to be able to talk, to not have to be silent or performing all the time, to be able to be critical and honest—openly? This is the truth you have taught us: all people deserve to speak.

Or a black male student writing that he will "love me now and always" because our class has been a dance, and he loves to dance:

I love to dance. When I was a child, I danced everywhere. Why walk there when you can shuffle-ball-change all the way. When I danced my soul ran free. I was poetry. On my Saturday grocery excursions with my mother, I would flap, flap, flap, ball change the shopping cart through the aisles. Mama would turn to me and say, "Boy, stop that dancing. White people think that's all we can do anyway." I would stop but when she wasn't looking I would do a quick high bell kick or tow. I didn't care what white people thought, I just loved to dance-dance-dance. I still dance and I still don't care what people think white or black. When I dance my soul is free. It is sad to read about men who stop dancing, who stop being foolish, who stop letting their souls fly free. . . . I guess for me, surviving whole means never to stop dancing.

These words were written by O'Neal LaRon Clark in 1987. We had a passionate teacher/student relationship. He was taller than six feet; I remember the day he came to class late and came right up to the front, picked me up and whirled me around. The class laughed. I called him "fool" and laughed. It was by way of apologizing for being late, for missing any moment of classroom passion. And so he brought his own moment. I, too, love to dance. And so we danced our way into the future as comrades and friends bound by all we had learned in class together. Those who knew him remember the times he came to class early to do funny imitations of the teacher. He died unexpectedly last year—still dancing, still loving me now and always.

When eros is present in the classroom setting, then love is bound to flourish. Well-learned distinctions between public and private make us believe that love has no place in the classroom. Even though many viewers could applaud a movie like *The Dead Poets Society*, possibly identifying with the passion of the professor and his students, rarely is such passion institutionally affirmed. Professors are expected to publish, but no one really expects or demands of us that we really care about teaching in uniquely passionate and different ways. Teachers who love students and are loved by them are still "suspect" in the academy. Some of the suspicion is that the presence of feelings, of passions, may not allow for objective consideration of each student's merit. But this very notion is based on the false assumption that education is neutral, that there is some "even" emotional ground we stand on that enables us to treat everyone equally, dispassionately. In reality, special bonds between professors and students have always existed, but traditionally they have been exclusive rather than inclusive. To allow one's feeling of care and will to nurture particular individuals in the classroom—to expand and embrace everyone—goes against the notion of privatized passion. In student journals from various classes I have taught there have always been complaints about the perceived special bonding between myself and particular students. Realizing that my students were uncertain about expressions of care and love in the classroom, I found it necessary to teach on the subject. I asked students once: "Why do you feel that the regard I extend to a particular student cannot also be extended to each of you? Why do you think there is not enough love or care to go around?" To answer these questions they had to think deeply about the society we live in, how we are taught to compete with one another. They had to think about capitalism and how it informs the way we think about love and care, the way we live in our bodies, the way we try to separate mind from body.

There is not much passionate teaching or learning taking place in higher education today. Even when students are desperately yearning to be touched by knowledge, professors still fear the challenge, allow their worries about losing control to override their desires to teach. Concurrently, those of us who teach the same old subjects in the same old ways are often inwardly bored—unable to rekindle passions we may have once felt. If, as Thomas Merton suggests in his essay on pedagogy "Learning to Live," the purpose of education is to show students how to define themselves "authentically and spontaneously in relation" to the world, then professors can best teach if we are self-actualized. Merton reminds us that "the original and authentic 'paradise' idea, both in the monastery and in the university, implied not sim-

ply a celestial store of theoretic ideas to which the Magistri and Doctores held the key, but the inner self of the student" who would discover the ground of their being in relation to themselves, to higher powers, to community. That the "fruit of education . . . was in the activation of that utmost center." To restore passion to the classroom or to excite it in classrooms where it has never been, professors must find again the place of eros within ourselves and together allow the mind and body to feel and know desire.

chapter thirty-nine

Martha C. Nussbaum

Martha Craven Nussbaum (b. 1947), contemporary philosopher and classicist, is a prolific writer whose work centers around such themes as the relationship between emotions and philosophy, the relationship between philosophy and literature, human mortality and vulnerability, liberal feminism and the equality of women in developing countries, and education. Nussbaum's philosophies manifest her belief that there is an intimate relation between philosophy and human life. The combination of the questions that her work takes up and her active participation in the wider community and across disciplines embodies a vision of philosophy that is both practical and compassionate. She describes this vision in *The Therapy of Desire: Theory and Practice in Hellenistic Ethics* (1994) as "a philosophy that exists for the sake of human beings, in order to address their deepest needs, confront their most urgent perplexities, and bring them from misery to some greater measure of flourishing."[1] In other words, for Nussbaum, ideally philosophy should be therapeutic in that it seeks to remedy what afflicts human life in both its social and individual spheres.

Nussbaum's commitment to address the deepest concerns of human life fosters the recurrent juxtapositions of philosophy and literature, ancient philosophy and contemporary problems, international feminism and liberal theory, and theory and practice that are so characteristic of her work. *The Fragility of Goodness: Luck and Ethics in Greek Tragedy and Philosophy* (2001) explicates, through the medium of Greek tragedy, one of her signature philosophical claims, namely, that human vulnerability and the good life are deeply intertwined. Nussbaum not only feels that philosophy should speak to the most distinctive features of the human condition, namely mortality, emotions, vulnerability, and mutability, but she also considers philosophy to be a tool with which to address concrete contemporary social problems. *Sex and Social Justice* (1999), from which "Constructing Love, Desire, and Care" is drawn, and *Women and Human Development: The Capabilities Approach* (2000) are theoretical proposals that ground themselves in the actions that women are already taking to change their situations and that emphasize the experiences of impoverished women in developing nations.

Nussbaum's thought reflects her embeddedness in the contemporary period, for her unique pluralistic philosophy not only combines at least three historically prominent strains of philosophical thought—Aristotelianism, liberalism, and feminism—but is also attentive to the international and cross-cultural concerns that are constitutive of the contemporary world. Nussbaum owes to Aristotle her "sympathetic perception of complex particulars" and her philosophical focus that is directed not to "anchor . . . conclusions to extrahistorical first principles, but to seek the best comprehensive fit among principles and concrete judgements."[2] She highlights the liberal notion that human beings have equal worth based on "basic human capacities for choice and reasoning."[3] Finally, Nussbaum is a feminist who believes that human beings have equal worth regardless of their sex, gender, or sexuality. Her work at the World Institute for Development Economic Research provided the foundation for her theory that promoting improvement in the social conditions within which women live can come in part from adopting theoretical models that recognize "central human capabilities" that include life, bodily health, bodily integrity, practical reason, and emotions.[4] Nussbaum's feminism is also characteristically contemporary in that it is concerned with the lives of women regardless of their nationalities, races, classes, and sexualities. Whether Nussbaum is drawing from the resources of liberal thinkers such as Kant and Mill, or from the Stoics or Aristotle, she always does so with a critical eye. She directs her thinking toward the improvement of contemporary human life, and as such is an Aristotelian or a proponent of liberalism only in so far as those theories are mediated by her own agency, rationality, and the emotions that make up her person.

The present excerpt from *Sex and Social Justice* begins to describe Nussbaum's detailed theory of the emotions, which she deems "a cognitive-evaluative view," and which she later describes in detail in *Upheavals of Thought*.[5] Emotions are "cognitive" because they "are not blind animal forces but intelligent and discriminating parts of the personality, closely related to beliefs of a certain sort, and therefore responsive to cognitive modification."[6] In addition, Nussbaum thinks that emotions are about particular objects in the world: people never feel for no reason at all. Emotions are "evaluative" not only because they are judgments about the world but also because they are one's judgments about how the world relates to oneself. According to Nussbaum, emotions have "intentionality"; they are dependent on the way the one who is having the emotion sees the object of one's emotion. Furthermore, emotions are "*eudaimonistic*"; the way one sees the object of one's emotion involves one's complex beliefs about that object, which include beliefs about how the object fits into one's own life and personal projects.[7] In *Upheavals of Thought* Nussbaum writes, "Emotions involve judgments about important things, judgments in which, appraising an external object as salient for our own well-being, we acknowledge our own neediness and incompleteness before parts of the world that we do not fully control."[8] Throughout the work, following the example of Seneca who uses personal stories to explicate his ideas, Nussbaum uses an example of her own grief, namely, her grief over the death of her mother, to explain her "cognitive-evaluative" view. *Upheavals of Thought* exemplifies Nussbaum's characteristic interdisciplinary breadth in that it draws upon recent research in psychology and anthropology and uses discussions of philosophy (Plato, Spinoza, Augustine), literature (Proust, Dante, Emily Brontë, Whitman, Joyce), and music (Mahler) to illustrate her theory. Not surprisingly, Nussbaum theorizes about emotions not for the sake of theory alone, but because she sees emotions as integral to the moralities of individuals and societies. She writes, "in an ethical and social/political creature, emotions themselves are ethical and social/political, parts of and answers to the questions, 'What is worth caring about?' 'How should I live?'"[9]

In the essay from *Sex and Social Justice*, Nussbaum's arguments that love, sexual desire, and family life are the products of a dynamic "social construction" rather than functions of a static "human nature" rests upon her cognitive-evaluative view of the emotions. Emotions vary across cultures and between different groups of individuals from the same culture (e.g., men and women) because they are not merely bodily forces that influence an individual; they vary because one's beliefs and judgments about an object and about how an object fits into one's conception of the good life are embedded within a social and cultural context. Nussbaum claims not only that the beliefs and judgments that constitute emotions vary across cultures, but also that the experience of the individual who possesses an emotion varies as well. Her arguments for the role of social construction in love, sexual desire, and family life are consistent with the liberal feminist theories that are central to *Sex and Social Justice*. A theory of justice that speaks to the equal worth of individual members of the global community must address the fact that women are situated differently in relation to central human capabilities than are men. Nussbaum accounts for commonalities across cultures, not by appealing to common human biology, but by pointing to the common problems that human life entails: mortality, vulnerability, embeddedness in relationships, and change.

Nussbaum received her B.A. in classics from New York University in 1969, her M.A. from Harvard University in 1971, and her Ph.D. in classical philology from Harvard University in 1975. Presently, she is the Ernst Freund Distinguished Service Professor of Law and Ethics at the University of Chicago, where she holds appointments in the Philosophy department, the Law School, and the Divinity School. She has also taught at Harvard, Brown, and Oxford Universities and has served as a research advisor at the World Institute for Development Economics Research, a division of the United Nations University, in Helsinki, Finland (1986–1993). In addition to authoring ten books from *Aristotle's "De Motu Animalium"* (1978) to *Upheavals of Thought: The Intelligence of Emotions* (2001) and being the editor of ten more, Nussbaum served as president of the Central Division of the American Philosophical Association in 1999–2000, has chaired the Committee on the Status of Women and the Committee on International Cooperation for that organization, and has received eighteen honorary degrees.

JM

QUESTIONS

1. What does Nussbaum's cognitive view of the emotions entail? How is it different from what she terms the "adversary's view"?

2. According to Nussbaum, how are love and sexual desire different, if at all, in terms of being socially constructed? Do you think that different social groups experience emotions differently (e.g., men and women)?

3. Reflect upon an emotional experience of your own. Does Nussbaum's view of the emotions cohere with that experience? Why or why not?

4. What does Nussbaum's example of Glaukon illustrate? Do you agree with her argument? What is the relationship, if any, between advocating equal worth for lesbians and gays and advocating equal worth for women?

5. How do Nussbaum's discussions of social construction in terms of sexual desire and emotions speak to the injustices that women face around the globe?

ENDNOTES

1. Nussbaum, *The Therapy of Desire*, p. 3.
2. Nussbaum, *Sex and Social Justice*, p. 23.
3. Ibid., p. 24.
4. Nussbaum, *Women and Human Development*, pp. 78–80.
5. Nussbaum, *Upheavals of Thought*, p. 23.
6. Nussbaum, *The Therapy of Desire*, p. 78.
7. Nussbaum, *Upheavals of Thought*, p. 31. Nussbaum is referring to the Greek concept of *eudaimonia*, which she translates as "human flourishing."
8. Nussbaum, *Upheavals of Thought*, p 19.
9. Ibid., p. 149.

SELECTED BIBLIOGRAPHY

Hall, Ronald L. *The Human Embrace: The Love of Philosophy and the Philosophy of Love: Kierkegaard, Cavell, Nussbaum*. University Park, Pennsylvania: Pennsylvania State University Press, 2000, pp. 173–256.

Nussbaum, Martha Craven. *Aristotle's "De Motu Animalium."* Princeton, N.J.: Princeton University Press, 1978.

Nussbaum, Martha Craven. *The Fragility of Goodness: Luck and Ethics in Greek Tragedy*. New York: Cambridge University Press, 1986.

Nussbaum, Martha Craven. *Love's Knowledge: Contemporary Essays in Philosophy and Literature*. New York: Oxford University Press, 1990.

Nussbaum, Martha Craven. *The Therapy of Desire: Theory and Practice in Helenistic Ethics*. Princeton, N.J.: Princeton University Press, 1994.

Nussbaum, Martha Craven. *Upheavals of Thought: The Intelligence of the Emotions*. New York: Cambridge University Press, 2001.

Nussbaum, Martha C., *Women and Human Development: The Capabilities Approach*. New York: Cambridge University Press, 2000.

Pyle, Andrew, ed. "Martha Nussbaum," from *Key Philosophers in Conversation: The "Cogito" Interviews*. New York: Routledge, 1999.

from Constructing Love, Desire, and Care

Martha C. Nussbaum

NATURE AND CULTURE

Like most of us, the ancient Greeks tended to think that where sex is concerned some things are natural and other things are not, some up for grabs as expressions of personal preference and others ruled out (or in) by our universal animal nature itself. Like most civilizations, they had strong views about what "nature" was in this domain, and they were prepared to argue for these views using examples from the animal kingdom. Consider the following passage from Philo's *On Animals*, written in the first century A.D., in which Philo "proves" the naturalness of having heterosexual sex relations only for reproductive purposes, and "proves," too, the naturalness of male self-restraint, which subdues female greediness:

> Not only among animals domesticated and reared by us but also among the other species there are those which appear to have self-restraint. When the Egyptian crocodile . . . is inclined to copulate, he diverts the female to the bank and turns her over, it being natural to approach her (when she is) lying on her back. After copulating, he turns her over with his forearms. But when she senses the copulation and the impregnation, she becomes malicious in purpose and pretends to desire copulation once more, displaying a harlot-like affection and assuming the usual position for copulation. So he immediately comes to ascertain, either by scent or by other means, whether the invitation is genuine or merely pretense. By nature he is alert to hidden things. When the intent of the action is truly established by their looking into each other's eyes, he claws her guts and consumes them, for they are tender. And unhindered by armored skin or hard and pointed spines, he tears her flesh apart. But enough about self-restraint.[1]

The very biological implausibility of this story is suggestive: for it shows us how much the picture of "nature" has been shaped by assumptions deriving from culture. Philo appeals to the animal kingdom to demonstrate that male control over female sexual greed is grounded in nature. When we look at the crocodile world, we are supposed to discover that there is one natural position for intercourse (did the crocodiles get it from the missionaries, or the missionaries from the crocodiles?[2]); that it is natural for males to initiate and control sexual activity; that reproduction is the single legitimate purpose for heterosexual intercourse; that females are rapacious and that males need to keep them in line, by bloody means if necessary. But of course the modern reader (to whom such assumptions are not as customary as they were in Philo's time) finds in the very concocted character of Philo's account of the crocodile world reasons to call the whole set of "nature" claims into question. He has clearly been none too neutral a student of animals, projecting onto that prepolitical domain customs and laws of his own Jewish-Greek milieu. Because we stand at a distance from Philo, we can easily see this dynamic operating, when we might be inclined to miss it in the work of biologists of our own era. "Nature" is the name Philo gives to the firmest of the cultural assumptions, those he does not intend to question. We are prompted to ask whether the same is true of our own practices of distinguishing between the "natural" and the "unnatural."

Consider now a passage from Xenophon's *Hieron*, in which the poet Simonides and the ruler Hieron are conversing about erotic passion. Both have been introduced by Xenophon as high-minded, morally sensitive figures. The two men discuss nature and its compulsions:

> "How do you mean, Hieron? Are you telling me that erotic passion for young men does not grow by nature in a ruler, as it does in other people? How is it then that you are in love with Dailochos?" "My erotic passion for Dailochos is for what human nature perhaps compels us to want from the beautiful, but I have a very strong desire to attain the object of my passion only with his love and consent."[3]

Hieron insists that his strong premoral desire for the beautiful young man is suitably constrained by social morality: Though he is extremely passionate about him, he will hold off until he has consent and (friendly) love. But consider Hieron's view about what lies in the realm of the "natural," behind social convention, a view that both his interlocutor and the author seem to find unremarkable. The view is that "nature" compels a normal adult man to want sex with beautiful young men. But this desire and its expression are considered "unnatural" by many societies, including a large segment of our own. This striking divergence in ideas of what lies in "nature," behind the social and customary realm, does not show us that there is no such realm or that it too is shaped by social forces. But it prompts us to raise those questions. If what Hieron and Xenophon think paradigmatically natural is what we frequently think paradigmatically unnatural in sex, maybe the whole idea of the "natural" deserves our critical scrutiny. Maybe there is more custom and law in nature than we usually think.

We use the term "nature" in multiple and slippery ways.[4] When we say that a certain way of doing things exists "by nature," we sometimes mean that this is the way things are given in our innate equipment, without the transformative influence of human choice and effort. Sometimes we simply mean that this is a deeply habitual way for things to be, that anything else seems weird. Sometimes we mean that things cannot be otherwise. Sometimes, finally, we mean that it is fitting and proper that they should be this way. ("Unnatural" here means "to be shunned.") All four meanings are logically independent: The fact that something is customary does not imply that it is given in our innate equipment, nor does an innate basis always imply customariness. (We are born with many tendencies that we alter or remove as we mature.) Neither of these implies that the way of proceeding is necessary and immutable. And, finally, none of the other three implies that the way of proceeding is right and proper. Innate tendencies can be defective or bad: We seek to correct myopia and other bodily defects; we teach children not to put their own concerns at the center of the universe. So too with customs: We criticize them if they do not seem to promote well-being or justice. The necessary character of bodily weakness and death is not usually thought to make them good things. And the fact that something is fitting and proper does not by itself show that it is innate, customary, or necessary.

And yet we often argue badly, sliding from one sense of "nature" to another: inferring from the habitual character of something that it has its roots in innate biology, inferring from the biological rootedness of something that it is fitting and proper, inferring from the fact that many people think a custom fitting and proper that it is unchangeable and must remain as it is. Philo imputes to our biological nature certain behavioral tendencies that he evidently prizes and wishes to validate; to show crocodiles behave this way is supposed to show us that people who do not act like this are shameful and bad. (To such an argument, citing roosters instead of crocodiles, the father in Aristophanes' *Clouds* replied, "If you imitate roosters in everything, why don't you eat shit and sleep on a perch?" (1430–31) Hieron imputes to biology a desire customary among males of his class but whose full description could probably not be given in neutral transcultural language, so thoroughly is it shaped by the institutions and categories of Greek homosexuality. Unlike Philo, he seems to think the desire itself neither good nor bad, because he holds that the appropriateness of the action depends on precisely how the desire is expressed.[5] The two cases are similar, however, in that the elements of human life that are traced to biology seem to be in part artifacts of custom and social norms.

In this chapter I shall investigate the philosophical basis for the thesis that human love, desire, and sexuality are "socially constructed." We need to look clearly at the philosophical arguments involved and at the bearing of historical and cross-cultural data on such arguments. I shall begin with the case of love and other related emotions, because here the issues seem to me somewhat clearer than in the case of sexual desire, where biological arguments begin to complicate the issue. I shall then turn to sexual desire itself and the related issues of sexual preference and gender structure, assessing the strength of the case that these phenomena too are "socially constructed." This will involve looking at the status of the sexual body and the sexual organs, asking whether even these are in some significant sense social and historical artifacts. I shall then draw on all this material to make some concluding remarks about the social construction of the family.

My general thesis will be that in many central respects, the sexual domain of human life, and its close relative, the domain of the family, are domains of symbolic cultural interpretation, shaped by historical and institutional forces, though within constraints imposed by biology; that cultural formations affect not just the theoretical explanation of desire but the very experience of desire, and of oneself as a desiring agent; that such considerable overlap as one does encounter among cultures in these areas can best be explained by the considerable overlap in the problems with which different human societies must grapple as they try to get on in the world[6], that the feeling most human beings have that certain ways of doing things sexually are "natural" and necessary is often best explained not by biology but by the depth of social conditioning in the life of every human being, in giving a sense of what is possible and impossible, what is an available role, and what is not.

Finally, I shall argue that recognizing the depth of interpretation in sexuality does not remove rational debate or force us into a rootless relativism; instead, it opens up a space for normative argument, political criticism, and reasoned change.

These claims will sound peculiar to some and excessively familiar to others. To those who find them overly familiar, from the large "cultural studies" literature that has investigated them for some time, I can only say that I believe this literature has not set out the philosophical arguments surrounding the issue as clearly as might be done, and that I shall try in that way to take the investigation further; nor has it connected questions about the constructedness of desire and sexuality to a study of the cultural construction of emotion, a comparison I believe to be very illuminating.

When we speak of "social construction" or "cultural construction," we should be careful not to suggest that cultures are monoliths. The account presented here will be one that makes a great deal of room for plurality, contestation, and individual variety within cultures, and for overlap and borrowing among cultures. This very fact makes it likely that we will find less impenetrable foreignness in the emotions and desires of other societies than some anthropological accounts at times suggest; as I shall argue, the fact that all human beings face similar problems as they try to get around in the world makes for even less foreignness and more convergence.

EMOTIONS AND THEIR SOCIAL FORM

The thesis that emotions are to some extent socially constructed, in the form in which I shall defend it, rests on a cognitive view of emotion—a view, that is, that holds that perceptions and beliefs

of a certain sort play a central role in emotional experience.[7] We shall see that a cognitive view, although necessary for the social-construction thesis in the form in which I shall defend it, is not sufficient for that thesis. I shall add further arguments to get to that thesis, holding that human cognition in the relevant area is socially shaped. But we can best begin by articulating and defending the cognitive view itself. This view, in turn, can best be understood by beginning with its theoretical adversary—which is also the thesis most commonly held by opponents of social construction.[8]

The adversary claims that emotions such as grief, anger, fear, and love do not involve any form of cognitive interpretation of the world: They are just unthinking energies that push a person around. Like gusts of wind or the currents of the sea, they move, and move the person, but obtusely, without a vision of an object or beliefs about it. The view is frequently linked with the idea that emotions are "natural," "innate," or "bodily," rather than learned—for this seems to be the adversary's characteristic way of explaining how these unthinking forces got there and why most people seem to have them. The adversary's view has had a certain influence in behaviorist experimental psychology and also in popular talk and thought about the emotions.[9] But it never fared well in philosophy, where most major writers, in the Western tradition, and in what is known to me of non-Western traditions,[10] have endorsed some form of cognitive analysis. And by now it has been thoroughly repudiated in anthropology, in psychoanalysis, and even in cognitive psychology—where, as one major theorist[11] ironically observes, the field has just managed to fight its way back to the position defended in Aristotle's *Rhetoric*. What are the reasons for this shift? For if we see what has led to the current consensus about a cognitive analysis for emotion—which, as I have said, is a necessary, if not a sufficient, condition for a social-constructionist project of the sort I shall describe[12]—we will be in a better position to understand the arguments in favor of that project. We need an example: I shall take one from Euripides' tragedy, *The Trojan Women*.

Hecuba kneels in front of the shield of her dead son Hector.[13] On the shield is the dead body of her little grandson Astyanax. The victorious Greek commanders, fearing that this royal child might later cause them political trouble, have arranged for him to be thrown from the walls of the Trojan city. Hecuba pours out her grief in a speech of intense passion and lyrical beauty, as she remembers how each bodily part that now lies dead used to be full of hope, and brightness, and humor, and love, as she sees how the face that once smiled at her is now just a mass of splintered bones and blood. She angrily denounces the Greeks for their cruelty and their cowardice. She observes that human life is in general ferociously unstable, and all the most important things are beyond our control, without any firm foundation. What makes Hecuba's emotions here so different from the mindless currents hypothesized by the adversary?

First of all, Hecuba's emotions have an object: Her grief is for the death of her grandson, and her anger is at his killers. They are *about* these objects, in a way that a wind is not *about* the tree against which it strikes. Internal to the emotion itself is a focusing on the object, and the emotion contains a representation of the object, seeing it in the way in which the person interprets and sees it. Hecuba's grief sees Astyanax as both enormously important and as irrevocably cut off from her; her anger sees the Greeks as culpable wrongdoers,[14] and their wrongdoing as bad and serious. This aboutness comes from her active ways of seeing and interpreting: It is not like being given a snapshot of the object but requires looking at the object, so to

speak, through her own interpretive window. This perception might contain an accurate vision of the object or it might not. It is what she thinks that matters: If it were not the Greeks but a suddenly invading Scythian army who had killed the boy, she would still be angry at the Greeks until she knew this—for in her view they are the agents of wrong.

This brings out a further point about these emotions: that they embody not just ways of seeing but also beliefs; and, as Aristotle already stressed, they are highly responsive to a change in beliefs.[15] If Hecuba comes to believe that Scythian invaders, not Greeks, killed her grandson, her anger will change its object. If she finds out that Astyanax was not killed but fell from the walls by accident, she will not be angry at anyone, and she will grieve very differently. If she finds out that the body at her feet is not her grandson after all but a dummy dressed in her child's clothes,[16] she will stop grieving altogether.

And this brings me to one last point, in some ways the most important of all. Hecuba's emotions involve various beliefs, including beliefs about what events have and have not taken place and who caused them. But very prominent in the emotions are beliefs of a very particular sort, namely, beliefs about value, worth, and salience. It is because Hecuba has invested her grandson's life with tremendous importance that his death crushes her as it does, and in the way that the death of a stranger would not do. Again, it is because his death is so salient in her life that her anger is so intense; the destruction of a drinking cup would not affect her in the same way. And these beliefs too may alter. The Greek Stoics, teaching the importance of self-sufficiency, claimed that they ought to alter, so that nothing outside one's own virtue would seem to have real importance. A good Stoic father, reports Cicero, responded to the news of his son's death with the words, "I was already aware that I had begotten a mortal."[17]

To show all this about how perceptions and beliefs figure in emotions does not by itself show that there is much social variation in emotional life, or that emotions are in any meaningful sense "socially constructed." It does establish that an emotional repertory is not innate but learned,[18] and that it is in principle possible to alter emotions through altering the beliefs on which they rest.[19] But there might be some beliefs that would almost inevitably be formed by a living creature interacting with an uncertain world, beliefs so central to the creature's whole way of life that the idea of removing them or significantly changing them makes little sense. And this is to a large extent the way things seem to be with the emotions of nonhuman animals.[20] According to the best recent studies, the fear and anger and grief of animals cannot be explained without invoking the animal's own cognitive interpretation of the world, and this interpretation must contain patterns of salience or importance. As psychologists Richard Lazarus and Keith Oatley have put it in the two most acute recent studies of the topic, the emotions are the animal's way of taking in news of how things are going in the world, with respect to its most cherished or most urgent projects and needs. These ways of responding must be learned, because no creature comes into the world knowing what parts of the world are helpful and harmful to it in important ways. On the other hand, the emotional repertory is highly functional and crucial in guiding the animal's actions; it is therefore likely to be pretty uniform, given a type of creature and a general form of life. It would not be plausible, for example, that we should find a "higher animal"[21] who never experienced fear: The belief that one's important projects are threatened is not only true for every mortal living creature at some times but highly useful in prompting evasive behavior.[22]

To some extent, much the same seems to be true of human beings. Fear of death and bodily injury is ubiquitous in some form, because the belief that these are important bad things is ubiquitous,[23] so too with grief at the deaths of loved ones, joy at their presence and safety, anger at the agents of willful damages to them or to oneself. Furthermore, the human body, whose states of pain, hunger, need for warmth and cold, and so on, are so prominent within the emotional life as occasions for fear, anger, joy, relief, and also love and gratitude, is itself ubiquitous. Although infants are from the beginning handled in accordance with cultural rules, there is much about them—their hungry neediness, the way their cognitive capacities develop over time, the shape of their bodies,[24] and the ways in which the body metabolizes nutrients—that is not itself a cultural construct, and that gives emotional experience a common terrain and geography. On the other hand, within this generally shared framework, there is a great deal of room, in the human case, for social shaping and variation. This variation takes four different forms.

(1) *Rules for emotional expression and behavior vary.* Each society teaches rules for the proper expression of emotions such as grief, love, and anger. The public wailing and tearing of clothing and hair that seemed normal to ancient Greeks mourning the death of a loved one would cause a social scandal in contemporary England. The public displays of love and affection that are acceptable among Brown undergraduates would have been regarded as morally hideous in nineteenth-century India. And, of course, most societies also have different rules internally for different types of social actors, dividing them along lines of age, gender, and social class.

(2) *Normative judgments about an emotion vary.* Judgments about the entire emotion type—I have said that most societies contain some species of anger and grief and fear and love because it is hard

to find a society whose members do not ascribe to objects outside themselves a salience or importance that leads to these emotions in certain circumstances. But not all societies take the same view about the value of these attachments to objects or the concomitant emotions. Let me focus here on anger. In a remarkable study of an Eskimo tribe, the Utku, anthropologist Jean Briggs[25] carefully showed that these people strongly disapprove of anger, viewing it as all right in children, who feel weak and dependent and therefore ascribe to slights and damages a considerable significance, but as totally defective in an adult, who ought to have a kind of proud self-mastery that would make all such damages seem trivial. (In effect, this society seems to realize quite a lot of what the ancient Greek and Roman Stoics taught and tried to practice.) The Utku admit that it is hard to get rid of attachments that give rise to anger; they therefore expect anger to occur. But they describe it always in pejorative language, as a socially pernicious force. Contrast the attitude to anger in ancient Rome. It seems that being a truly manly man in the Rome of Seneca's time actually required getting extremely angry at all sorts of slights and damages, to oneself, one's property, one's family, and one's honor and reputation. If one did not get angry, one was being soft. Here I want to say not only that the behavior of angry people in these two cultures will be very different—the Utku trying to cover things up and looking shamefaced, the Roman proudly proclaiming his rage and his vindictive intentions—but also that the experience of anger will differ. For an Utku, being angry will be hooked up to the experience of shame and a sense of diminished adulthood; one will feel infantilized by anger. The Roman, by contrast, will feel his anger accompanied by a feeling of manly self-assertion and full adulthood, and by a quasi-erotic excitement,[26] as he prepares to smash the adversary. In much the same way—to jump ahead to sexual-

ity itself for a minute—one can expect the experience of sexual desire, in a society that has deeply internalized the idea of original sin, to be different from the experience of desire in a society that has no such teaching. The Augustinian Christian will feel desire itself tainted with shame and possibly even revulsion[27]; the ancient Greek has no such general shame to contend with.

Judgments internal to the emotion type—every society teaches norms about the proper objects and occasions for anger, fear, grief, and so forth. Once again, these norms exhibit considerable variation—both across societies and over time in a single society. In the United States, for example, the distinction between first-degree murder and voluntary manslaughter is defined in accordance with normative judgments about the anger of a "reasonable man." The events that are taken to supply this person with "adequate provocation" evolve and change. In the nineteenth century, the paradigm triggering event was a woman's adultery, seen as an invasion of a man's property. Today, the "reasonable man" may be a woman, and her anger may be about domestic violence.[28]

(3) *The taxonomy of emotions recognized varies.* This grows directly out of the observation about variation in norms: We can say that the anger experienced by the Utku is not precisely the same emotion as the anger experienced by the Roman, given its different links to shame and childishness. And, in general, we find that the precise description of the emotion-taxonomy of any society yields subtle variations from that of any other. The fact that Roman taxonomies recognize numerous varieties and subspecies of retributive anger, subtly differentiated according to the type of revenge sought, the length of time one spends planning one's revenge, and the type of slight that occasioned the anger, is not separable from the fact that the Romans are enthusiastic cultivators of this emotional plant and love to observe its every

nuance. One assumes that as a result of this cultivation, Romans felt their anger differently, just as a
cultivated wine taster tastes wine differently.[29] One
can even find categories of emotion that are important for one culture or group but do not occur
at all in another, given the differences in forms of
life and in metaphysical beliefs. The precise species
of guilt and shame about the body that many
Christian cultures experience and cultivate has no
one-one equivalent in ancient Greece and Rome.
Seneca describes a type of joy that he claims one
can only experience when one has become detached from external worldly events and is no
longer dependent upon their vicissitudes. (Notice
that this Stoic emotion is not likely to be felt by
the entirety of a culture and is quite likely to be experienced by individuals in many different cultures
who have deeply internalized Stoic teachings.
When we speak of "social construction," once
again, we must not ignore the fact that cultures are
plural, overlapping, and complex.)

Often, a taxonomical difference will be constituted by the different ways in which societies relate
elements that are apparently similar, when examined in isolation from one another. Thus, the connections made by Japanese society among apology,
exculpation, forgiveness, and guilt seem to be subtly different from similar connections in America.
Americans, for example, insist on sincerity and internal emotional consistency in context of apology;
Japanese society is more tolerant of the ambivalent
and the unexpressed. Americans, again, typically
insist on accompanying apology by narratives that
at least mitigate blame, if they do not altogether
exculpate; in Japanese society such an attempt to
mitigate will be a sign that the apology is insin-
cere.[30] These cultural connections express subtle
differences in evaluation of what is desirable for
persons and society; these differences shape what
apology *is* in the two societies, what guilt is, what

the desire for restored harmony and acceptance is.
These experiences will still be closely related in the
two cultures but not precisely the same.

Sometimes, as in the previous cases, such taxonomical variations show differences in evaluation;
sometimes they seem attributable, instead, to differences in geography and form of life. I spend
part of every summer in Finland and have had described to me an emotion that is connected with
the experience of being alone in the forest; it combines awe, the sense of one's own insignificance, a
terror of death. It is said to be expressed by certain
passages in Sibelius's music. I had never had precisely that emotion, though by now, taking on the
form of life (and being anyway a devotee of long
solitary walks in the forest) I am beginning to see
what it is all about.

(4) *Individual histories vary, and emotions bear
traces of their history.* Human emotions are unlike
most other animal emotions in that the present
object is often not alone: It bears the trace of loved
or feared or hated objects from one's past, and the
past lends the present some of its wonder or terror.
This history is all along culturally mediated; even
infants are handled from the beginning in accordance with cultural scenarios. But there is much
variation within the general cultural pattern.

Let me now put all this together, focusing on the
case of erotic love. It is not surprising to find that
more or less all known societies have some emotion or other that might roughly be called erotic
love—a kind of intense attachment to an object
connected with sexual feeling. But it is obvious to
any devotee of love poetry and love stories that this
allegedly single emotion turns up in remarkably
different forms in different times and places, forms
that do not all share a common core or essence, although they may exhibit many complicated inter-
relationships. In fact, we find here all four of the

types of variation I have identified. First, and most obvious, norms of expression and behavior for lovers vary enormously across cultures and within a culture in connection with differences in age, gender, and social status. A vivid example of this is given in Vikram Seth's novel *A Suitable Boy*, in which the young female university student in Delhi in the 1950s encounters severe conflict with her family when she accepts the role of Olivia in *Twelfth Night* in an English Department production. Her mother is convinced that even to go through the motions of that role is highly improper for a young woman of her class, who should exhibit no erotic behavior until betrothed.

Normative judgments on the emotion also vary: The ancient Greeks seem, on the whole, to have considered *erôs* a fearful and terrible sort of bondage and constraint; medieval courtly lovers think of it as a tender and lofty sentiment issuing from a "gentle heart"; modern Americans tend to think of it as connected with deep projects of self-expression and self-transcendence.[31] Here as with anger, the normative judgment can be expected to enter into the experience itself: The ancient Greek feels bound and made passive by *erôs*; the medieval courtly lover describes his heart as a *cor gentil*, both sensitive and bound by pleasing rules of reverence and courtesy. By contrast, a modern American romantic will be likely to feel love as awesome, something that sweeps one away against one's will.[32] It is also clear that normative judgments internal to the type vary: Ideas about what characteristics make someone an appropriate object of love, and what is an appropriate occasion for love, vary greatly among my three cases. An adult man in ancient Greece will learn from his culture's scenarios and narratives that the paradigm love object is a younger man who exhibits both physical beauty and educability; the same man, born in thirteenth-century Italy, would learn to love a remote ideal lady, seen as chaste and pure; in America, his sources for cultural norms will derive from Hollywood movies, advertisements, and other sources of cultural eroticism. There has been so much recent discussion of these images of ideal desirability that it is unnecessary to comment on them further except to say that they usually do not include the medieval idea of the woman as inaccessible and pure, although they do include a highly ambivalent set of reactions to the absence of those characteristics.

Third, the emotional taxonomy itself exhibits cultural variation. Plato perceptively defined his culture's erotic emotion as a longing for possession of an object one views as good.[33] In that sense it has nothing about mutuality or reciprocity built into its definition; and we can also see that it is closely bound up with jealous wishes to immobilize the object.[34] It is also important that *erôs* is explicitly contrasted in Greek society with *philia*, a type of love defined as involving reciprocity and mutual benefit—and, at least in later texts, with *agapé*, a selfless and usually nonsexual[35] benevolent love. Although a language without a plurality of love words could articulate these distinctions (and authors in the Latin language, using only the term *amor*, try to do so, when they replicate the arguments of Greek philosophers[36]), this highly developed conceptual contrast both represents and shapes, it would seem, real differences in experience: A Greek will not expect erotic love, as such, to pursue mutuality. Contemporary American conceptions of erotic love, by contrast, place a heavy stress on reciprocity. This means that we really are dealing with subtly different emotions: Plato and John Updike are not describing the same passion. Again, medieval courtly love has some distinctive features that could not be present in contemporary America, such as the idealization of the female object seen as chaste and unapproachable, and the paradigm of selfless devotion to and risk in the service of such a perfect being. Given the changes in cosmology and in women's role in our society, we cannot possibly recover that world (although we should not ignore its continuing influence on our own, shaping men's views, especially, of what women ought to be and are not). What we have to get rid of here is the idea that there is bound to be some one *thing* beneath the surface that is simply being described in different language. For the language itself reproduces (even as it represents) the structure of a form of life; these forms, and the experiences of the agents who inhabit them, have obvious similarities, but also some very important differences.[37]

Finally, of course, all this variation is made vastly more complicated by each person's early history, as intense attachments to parents—themselves impregnated with cultural information—are worked out in individual ways, and color the perception of future objects. . . .

To return, now, to my thesis and to the example of erotic love: What I have said shows that there is considerable relativity in erotic emotion, as in emotion generally. It does not make a case for cultural relativism in the normative sense, that is, for the view that there are no criteria of adjudication by which we can assess these different patterns, asking which are conducive to human flourishing and which are not. Cultural variation, here as elsewhere, means that it will be difficult to ask and answer normative questions, for no language we use will be free of particularity, and there will be many consequent dangers of false translation, of blindness, and of either excessive romanticization of the strange or excessive chauvinism toward the familiar.[38] But there is no reason why these dangers should be taken to defeat the project of normative analysis.[39] We will, of course, have to rule out, as unavailable, any cultural variant that is built on metaphysical beliefs we can no longer accept, or

forms of life we can never replicate: In that sense, medieval courtly love is not a live option. But among the many live options, we may still make ethical arguments as we do with anything else in life. We may judge, as the Stoics did, that the value judgments on which the Romans based their conceptions of anger are wrong, that they ascribe too much importance to honor and reputation; we may judge that the negative attitude to sexuality embodied in the Augustinian conception of original sin is without a sound foundation and is an impediment to human flourishing. We must ask these questions holistically, as we attempt to make the best overall coherent sense of our theories and our concrete judgments. (Aristotle and John Rawls have given us good models to follow as we do so.) We may ask ourselves what forms of erotic love are and are not compatible with our other commitments, to justice, to equality, to productive work, to other loves and friendships.

In all these cases, judgment does not lead directly to change. To change beliefs in matters of this depth and importance cannot be a matter of a one-shot argument, but, if at all, of a life's patient effort. As Seneca said of anger, "Slow is the resistance to evils that are continuous and prolific."[40] But this does not mean that change is impossible, that an ironic distance is our only option. First, no cultural scheme is as monolithic and as universally constraining as the social-constructionist story sometimes suggests. In every society there is room to maneuver, room for individuals to wink knowingly at the rules, to play games with the rules, even to improvise mutual love in a situation of distance and hierarchy. (This aspect of the issue has been beautifully treated in some fundamental work on women and men in Greece by the late John J. Winkler.[41]) Second, individuals within societies, and societies themselves, do change, however slowly. One might consider the related case of racist beliefs: One does not change these views overnight in oneself or in another simply as a result of becoming convinced by an ethical argument. On the other hand, once one is convinced, one can go to work on oneself and, I believe, to a significant extent transform oneself—first conduct, then, gradually, the inner world. And at the same time, of course, if one is involved in educating the next generation, one goes to work on them—and, at the same time, on the political and social institutions that shape their experience—with greater optimism. This sort of patient effort is at the core of what morality is.[42] And the payoff of the position that emotions are not given in nature but are socially constructed is that emotions become a part of the domain of moral effort, so construed.[43] . . .

Let me illustrate my general claim about sexuality . . . by taking one complex example, involving both male-female and male-male relations, so as to investigate, in the process, the related claim that homosexuality is itself a cultural construct.[44]

Let us consider, then, the life of a young male in Athens of the fifth century B.C. Let us call this young man Glaukon, after the young Athenian gentleman who is one of the participants in Plato's *Republic*.[45] Glaukon will not be one of Winkler's resourceful real-life actors but, rather, a collection of prevalent social norms, but we can assume that these norms impinge to at least a large degree upon behavior and experience. Glaukon grows up in a culture in which being a real adult man is defined largely in terms of honor and status in the community. Assuming the status of an adult citizen entails a certain attitude toward the needs of the body. Glaukon learns as he grows up that a real man has strong bodily desires, including sexual desire and the desires for food and drink; he exercises them but is not mastered by them. Sexual desire is not specially problematic or an occasion of shame[46]; it is problematic in just the way other strong appetites are. (Already here we see a big difference in experience from the experience of bodily desire in a Christian culture.) What is crucial about sexual desire is, first, that Glaukon should not pursue it in a way that distracts him from his other pursuits or wastes his fortune and, second, that it should be exercised solely in the act of penetration, by entering a suitably receptive body. The crucial opposition Glaukon learns is that of activity and passivity, and he knows that it is a good thing—indeed an exciting and a desirable thing—to be the active penetrator, a shameful and terrible thing to be the passive penetratee.[47] One sphere in which he will exercise his active dominance will be marriage, in order to produce children for the city. But he will not expect much from marriage, either in the way of companionship or in the way of sexual artistry and know-how: An uneducated sixteen-year-old girl who is never permitted to go out of the house[48] may well not completely occupy his imagination. On the other hand, trips to both male and female prostitutes are considered a good thing, as long as he does not spend too much money, and it does not make too much difference which sort he goes to, as long as it is clear that he goes there to penetrate.[49] Finally, given that he is urban and well off, his most intense erotic relationships are likely to be with young males, the *eromenoi*, "beloveds," for whom he is the *erastes*, lover. These young males are future citizens, so he is not to dishonor them by anal penetration; on the other hand, intercrural intercourse (intercourse in which he achieves orgasm by thrusting between the boy's tightly clenched thighs[50]) is all right. And if he is seen to be an intense lover of males, his friends will not judge that he has a "homosexual preference" and dislikes sex with women: On the contrary, they will infer that he is a sexually greedy fellow, and they will run to guard their wives.[51]

Glaukon's world, compared to our own, exhibits with respect to sexual desire all the four types of difference I identified when I talked about emotion. He learns different norms of sexual behavior.

He internalizes different normative judgments about sexual activity as such (unaffected by the Christian conception of original sin), and different norms about appropriate sexual acts and desirable sexual objects. He has an individual history of a distinctive sort. And, especially important, the very taxonomy of types of sexual desire exhibits variation from our own: For Glaukon does not conceive of, and therefore in a significant sense does not feel the desire for, males qua males, for females qua females—any more than most modern Americans feel a generalized desire to penetrate, regardless of the gender of the object.

Is Glaukon a homosexual? This is a peculiar question. For unless we suppose that there is buried inside him somewhere a thing called a preference, rather like an extra bodily organ, we have no reason at all, in his behavior or in his statements, for saying that he has a stable disposition toward partners of one gender rather than another. He sees partners as receptive bodies of various sorts: In a sense, women are a species of a class to which anally penetrable male prostitutes also belong, and the citizen boy escapes belonging only by his conventionally ordained anal chastity.[52] On the one hand, he certainly does not have a steady inclination toward males rather than toward females— he likes young men for the conversation they afford, but he likes sex with women also. On the other hand, he is also not simply an "opportunistic homosexual," as Richard Posner has used that term to describe a basically heterosexual man who has intercourse with males in special conditions when females are not available.[53] Glaukon has ready access to women of various educational levels and sexual abilities and does not opt for boys simply out of frustration.[54] The way his desire sees the world, it is a scene for the enactment of various strategies of possession and penetration: That is his role, and it is the possibility of that that excites him.

Ancient Greece, in short, does not divide its sexual actors according to the concept of a stable inner "preference" for objects of a particular gender. In that sense, it lacks the very experience of homosexuality in its modern sense.[55] And this affects the way we cast our normative political arguments. The libertarian ideal articulated in Richard Posner's *Sex and Reason* is that our society contains various sexual kinds, some of them "normal" and some of them not so "normal," but that no moral or legal judgment should be passed on the less normal. We should protect liberty of sexual activity, except where compelling arguments show grave harm to others. But the social-constructionist holds that this way of seeing things does not drive the criticism deep enough: It does not problematize the so-called normal, does not recognize the extent to which the contemporary heterosexual male, like the homosexual male, is the inhabitant of a social role that might have been otherwise.[56] Both are in that sense "unnatural actors."[57] And the heterosexual may well have the more morally problematic role in this social drama, because his role includes the domination of women.[58] Seeing things this way is likely to move one from the combination of complacence about self and slightly condescending tolerance of the other so frequently encountered in liberal rhetoric to a more radical critical scrutiny of society's sexual drama as a whole.

THE SOCIAL MEANING OF THE BODY

But isn't this all given in the body? And don't bodies come by nature in different kinds? Even if we grant that nobody has shown that "homosexual" bodies are in any biological way different from "straight" bodies, surely we at least have a naturally given division between men and women. Surely this counts for something and provides a "natural" basis for social role divisions.

Yes and no. The body is not simply a cultural sign—as some culture theorists tend to suggest it is.[59] Questions of life and death, of good and bad nutritional status, of fitness and strength, of good and ill health, are not simply matters of cultural advertising, though of course experiences that are culturally shaped may influence them in many ways. And in the domain of sexuality the same is also true: There is much that is independent of cultural representation. The fact that individuals begin to feel sexual desire at a certain age, for example, or that sexual desire fluctuates with fatigue or changing health status—all these things appear to be rooted in the body independently of culture, though at every point they interact with culturally shaped factors in highly complex ways.

On the other hand, culture does enter in, even here. It used to be common to distinguish "sex"—the biological category—from "gender," a socially constructed category, to think of one's sex as "given," one's gender as a socially learned role. But matters are actually not quite so simple. Bodily parts are not self-interpreting. As any woman knows who grew up during the change from the 1950s to the 1960s in the United States, and from Marilyn Monroe and Jayne Mansfield to Twiggy as norms of the woman, the meaning of breasts and legs is not given in nature: What is made of it by social advertising makes all the difference.[60] It is not so different with the so-called sexual organs. They have to some extent a form and a biological function independently of culture's interpretation of them, but much of their role in people's lives depends on what parents and other social actors make of them, what uses they ascribe to them, what metaphors they use about them, what roles and experiences they attach to them. No less a biologist than Charles Darwin, at the conclusion of a lengthy study of sexual dimorphism in plants and animals, expressed the limits of strictly biological knowledge on this topic when he wrote that we

"do not even in the least know" what the significance of dimorphic reproduction is, as opposed to a process of parthenogenesis: "The whole subject is as yet hidden in darkness."[61] Nor does today's knowledge seem to have illuminated this mysterious issue in a decisive way.

What we do know a lot about, by contrast, is the insistent way in which parents classify children on the basis of their external genitalia, forcing a binary choice even when the genitalia themselves do not clearly announce their affiliation.[62] What we do know a lot about is the way in which this genital identification leads to pervasive differences in the shaping and interpretation of behavior. Anne Fausto-Sterling has shown, for example, that the same emotional behavior on the part of infants is differently labeled in accordance with the sex announced to the observer: so-called boys are called angry, so-called girls frightened, though the cries they utter are the same.[63] Other "cross-labeling" experiments show that infants are handled and played with differently depending on the perceived sex: Boys are bounced and tossed in the air; girls carefully cradled. These are ways in which societies create men and women.

Genital organs, in short, do not interpret themselves; they do not announce to their bearers what they are and what is salient about them. On the other hand, they are the objects of cultural interpretation and representation from the time an infant is born; they figure in human experience only as mediated through many representations, and these representations interact in many ways with other representations of gender. Historical inquiry has shown that there is, here again, tremendous latitude for differences of reading, even in the apparently neutral domain of science.[64] Historian Thomas Laqueur concludes that the whole question whether there are in a morphologically salient sense two sexes, to be contrasted with one another, or a single sex, whose members vary by degree, is a question to which Western science has given sharply varying answers, even over a rather short period of history.[65] It seems to me that Laqueur pushes the evidence too far: For the Greeks, like all known societies, made a very sharp binary division of humans into two categories in connection with the shape of their genitalia. It would be surprising if any society in which reproduction took its (until now[66]) usual form of insemination and pregnancy did not so divide animals, humans among them. And yet, Laqueur seems right to stress that exactly how we conceptualize these distinctions, and what social significance we attach to them, can vary greatly over time. As sex becomes increasingly divorced from reproduction, this is likely to prove even more evident.

Biological research points both ways on the question of social construction. There have been countless studies of the biology of male-female difference—but, as Fausto-Sterling has painstakingly argued, these studies are riddled with conceptual and empirical problems. Moreover, given the mounting evidence of differential treatment of infants by gender, it seems clear that separating biology from culture, though in principle possible, is practically next to impossible at this time. Some modern biological research, moreover, lends support to at least some social-constructionist claims by stressing the extent to which human (unlike most animal) sexuality is plastic, not subject to rigid genetic or hormonal patterning but determined by the learning and symbolic areas of the brain.[67]

But this hardly means that there is no biological basis for differences in sexual desire and attraction. The thesis of social construction is good at explaining how societies come to have the sexual categories they do. It is also good at showing how deeply such social patterning enters into the experience of each and every member of society from early infancy on, informing not just reflection but also the very experience of desire and of oneself as desiring. It is far less adequate as an account of how particular social actors come to inhabit the categories they do inhabit. With the male and the female, we can see how parental recognition of differences in external genitalia leads from the start to differences in experience that end up producing a "man" or a "woman." Even in this case, however, it is very likely that biological factors play a significant role in influencing behavioral tendencies, even if we cannot say now what that role is, or how sharply it is divided between the sexes. In the end we are likely to discover a great deal of variation within each sex and consequently much overlap between them.

In the case of sexual orientation, social explanation has even more evident shortcomings. The fact that of two infants whose external genital appearance does not differ in any way, one turns out a "homosexual" and the other a "heterosexual" still seems inadequately explained by social construction all by itself: For the two may be in exactly the same stratum of society and may have had very similar experiences. The feeling of determination and constraint that is such a common feature of self-reports concerning homosexuality in our society suggests that either biological factors or very early individual experiences, or both, need to be invoked to complete the picture. . . .

Biological accounts should still be pursued energetically because there are questions, it seems, that only such an account could answer. But social construction will lead us to ask the right skeptical questions about premature claims in these areas as research evolves and will also show the researcher how complicated the conceptual terrain of her explanandum actually is—that the experiential category one is led to inhabit, by whatever combination of causal factors, is not, in many crucial respects, a transcultural and transhistorical category. . . .

The role of society goes very deep, in shaping matters that our tradition has tended to define as outside society, as "private" and "natural." This can feel like a source of constraint, as we come to see to what extent we are artifacts, even in our apparently most internal and intimate lives. On the other hand, and this is what I want to emphasize, it can also feel like a source of freedom, because we can see that many ways of experiencing the body, the emotions, and the care of children that might have seemed given and inevitable are actually made by us and can therefore be otherwise. This freedom, as I have said, is not limitless. For social construction does not deny that biology imposes constraints on the lives both of groups and of individuals, though it encourages a healthy skepticism about research that too quickly discovers a root in "nature" for the social status quo. Even when a social origin for a distinction is agreed, freedom to change does not follow unproblematically: It is difficult to change anything that is as deeply rooted in many people's very ways of seeing the world as is, for example, the perception that sexual relations between men and women are a way of exerting domination over women. With sex as with race, the only changes are likely to be hard-won, slow, and incremental, occurring in individual minds and in the possibilities that these create for the education of the next generation. Such changes are unlikely to take place without broader institutional and legal changes. Nor is it easy even to get agreement on the proper direction for change, for what we are saying is that there is no Archimedean point on which we can unquestioningly rely, that the constraints come not from immutable necessity but from our own ethical convictions and choices, our commitments to justice and equality, our sense of what human flourishing is and should be. Belief in immutable "nature" may be confining, but at least it gets us off the hook without having to make a respectable argument, without having to evaluate the values with which tradition has presented us. The freedom of social construction is a freedom to follow good human arguments, which may lead to the conclusion that tradition is in many ways stupid, oppressive, and bad. And that freedom imposes responsibilities that are all too easy to evade.

In Plato's *Republic*, Socrates, having discussed the radical changes he proposes in the structure of the family and the role of women, remarks to the young Glaukon that people usually do not pursue such discussions very far because they stop with the agreements people have made over the ages and think that these agreements are sufficient. "They do this," answers Glaukon, "out of laziness." "Laziness, however," replies Socrates, "is a quality that the guardians of a city and of laws can afford to do without." "That's likely to be true," answers Glaukon.[68]

ENDNOTES

1. Philo, *De Animalibus*, ed. and trans. A. Terian (*Studies in Hellenistic Judaism* 1 Chico, CA: 1981), discussed in John J. Winkler, *The Constraints of Desire: The Anthropology of Sex and Gender in Ancient Greece* (New York: Routledge, 1990), 23. Philo is a Jewish Platonist living in Alexandria whose views are in some key ways different from those held by both philosophers and nonphilosophers in classical Athenian culture; he does, however, reflect views rather broadly shared in his own later time.

2. See Winkler, 23.

3. See the discussion of this passage in Kenneth J. Dover, *Greek Homosexuality* 2nd ed. (Cambridge, MA: Harvard University Press, 1989), 61. The younger man's love is *philia*, not *erôs*.

4. See John Stuart Mill, *The Subjection of Women* (1869), ed. Susan M. Okin (Indianapolis, IN: Hackett, 1988). Similar points are made in Mill's essay "On Nature."

5. Strictly speaking, he says only that this is what he wants, but the context suggests that he means that this is what he has decided to pursue, and that (by both character and author) an ethical point is being made.

6. These problems include having a body of a certain type that demands a certain sort and quantity of nutrition; in that way biological commonality does shape the experience of emotion and desire. See the discussion to follow.

7. The material in this section is presented much more fully, and with more complete references to relevant philosophical and anthropological studies, in Martha C. Nussbaum, *Upheavals of Thought: A Theory of the Emotions* (The Gifford Lectures, University of Edinburgh, 1993) (Cambridge: Cambridge University Press, forthcoming).

8. The argument in what follows is closely related to the argument of Gifford Lecture 1, a version of which is published as "Emotions as Judgments of Value and Importance," in *Relativism, Suffering and Beyond: Essays in Memory of Bimal K. Matilal,* ed. P. Bilimoria and J. N. Mohanty (Delhi: Oxford University Press, 1997), 231–51. See also the related account of ancient Greek Stoic views in *The Therapy of Desire: Theory and Practice in Hellenistic Ethics* (Princeton: Princeton University Press, 1994) chap. 10.

9. There is much confusion here between two importantly distinct claims: (1) the claim that emotions are "irrational" in the sense of "noncognitive," and (2) the claim that they are "irrational" in a normative sense, meaning "ill-suited to guide us when we wish to think well." One might, of course hold (2) without (1); and indeed most of the major philosophical holders of (2)—such as Plato, the ancient Greek and Roman Stoics, Spinoza, and Kant—were all defenders of some type of cognitive view of emotion. They just though that the cognitions in question were inaccurate because they ascribed too much importance to aspects of the world outside ourselves that we do not control.

10. In the Gifford Lectures, I discuss related views from Chinese and Indian traditions.

11. Richard Lazarus, *Emotion and Adaptation* (New York: Oxford University Press, 1991).

12. There might be a very different type of social-construction project that would accept the adversary's view and still think of emotions as material to be formed by a noncognitive process of behavioral conditioning. See D. Kahan and M. Nussbaum, "Two Conceptions of Emotion in Criminal Law," *Columbia Law Review* 96 (1996), 270–374.

13. Euripides, *Trojan Women*, 1158–207.

14. Hecuba's criticism focuses on the gratuitous exercise of overwhelming power to crush a helpless small child who could have been rendered politically ineffectual by less brutal means—in particular, by sending him off into exile with his mother. Hecuba sees in the Greek action a sign of cowardice and weakness, not of political good sense.

15. This does not mean that a person who has a certain emotion—and therefore the beliefs that go with that—could not also have contradictory beliefs about the same matter. For example, if I am trying to become a good Stoic, I may find myself grieving at the death of a loved one (and having the beliefs about the badness of that event and the importance of the person that this grief entails) while also believing that the Stoics are correct—that these things have no real importance. What my view says about these cases is that they are instances of internal conflict in which the conflict has the form of a debate about what is really true, not the form of a noncognitive struggle between forces.

16. An intermediate case would be one in which she discovered that it was a real child but not her grandchild. Here she would presumably have some emotion, but not of this intensity. I discuss this problematic unevenness in the emotions in several of the Gifford Lectures.

17. Cicero, *Tusculan Disputations* III. 30.

18. I am assuming here that the relevant beliefs and other cognitive activities are not innate, but learned. This has in fact been experimentally confirmed in some very interesting work by Martin Seligman on animal learning. See Martin Seligman, *Helplessness* (New York: W. H. Freeman, 1975).

19. Here I have only argued that beliefs are necessary for emotions—and necessary as constituent parts of what a given emotion is. (One cannot say what grief *is* without mentioning the typical beliefs that differentiate grief from anger and fear and pity.) I do not argue here for the thesis that cognitions of a certain type are sufficient conditions for the emotion. But in fact I am prepared to argue for that thesis, and I do argue for it in Gifford Lecture 1. Indeed, I argue (though with some qualification) that the emotion is identical with a cognition of this sort.

20. I discuss this in Gifford Lecture 2. The works on which I most prominently rely in constructing my account are Seligman, *Helplessness*; Lazarus, *Emotion and Adaptation*; Keith Oatley, *Best-Laid Schemes* (Cambridge: Cambridge University Press, 1992). See also Nico Frijda, *The Emotions* (Cambridge: Cambridge University Press, 1986). Of particular importance for my purposes here is the work of James Averill, which combines cognitive-psychological analysis with an analysis of socially constructed role playing. See "Grief: Its Nature and Significance," *Psychological Bulletin* 70 (1968), 721–48; and *Anger and Aggression: An Essay on Emotion* (New York: Springer, 1982). Within philosophy, an excellent and rigorous account of the cognitive dimensions of emotion, with an analysis of their adaptive significance in the lives of animals generally, is in Ronald de Sousa, *The Rationality of Emotion* (Cambridge, MA: MIT Press, 1987).

It should be noted that a good deal of the psychological literature implicitly commits itself to mental "representationalism"—that is, to the view that the way in which the world impinges upon animals is through mental representations that they produce and that then have causal properties. Because the psychologists who use this language do not offer arguments in favor of representationalism or against other ways of understanding the animal/world relation, and because I myself have grave doubts about the adequacy of representationalism as a view of mind, I shall simply speak here of the animal's "interpretation" of the world, remaining neutral concerning the mental mode of the interpreting. The psychologists' basic argument is untouched by this change, and one may note that more philosophically trained psychologists such as Lazarus and Oatley do not use representationalist language.

21. How far "down" do emotions go? Experimental evidence suggests that it is not possible to give adequate explanations of the behavior even of rats without positing cognitive representations of the sort involved in fear. See Seligman, *Helplessness*. And Darwin long ago discovered remarkable cognitive complexity in the activities of worms. See James Rachels, *Created From Animals* (New York: Oxford University Press, 1990). But Darwin also argued convincingly that evasive behavior in some insects could be explained without invoking cognitive interpretations, and the issue clearly needs to be resolved by prolonged inspection of the behavior of each species.

22. My cognitive position is perfectly compatible with the thesis that emotions have evolved as they have *because* of their adaptive value. (I stress this thesis in Gifford Lecture 2.) Evolutionary biologists who offer functional accounts of emotion do not presently hold that such accounts require us to believe that emotions are "hard-wired" rather than learned in interaction with other animals. The best philosophical investigation of this issue is in de Sousa, *The Rationality of Emotion*. And see also Oatley, Lazarus, and Seligman, op. cit. Because emotions can be shown to require cognitive interpretations that must be learned, and that can—as Seligman shows with painstaking experimental work—be disrupted by a disruption of ordinary learning processes, they occupy a different status from that of reflex activities such as sneezes.

23. This does not mean that individuals could not be taught to lose that fear—either through religious belief or through becoming so hardened to risk that it no longer seems terrible, or through losing the love of life. But no known society is, as a whole, totally without that fear.

24. Although, as we shall shortly see, cultural manipulation of bodily shape begins very early in life.

25. Jean Briggs, *Never in Anger* (Cambridge, MA: Harvard University Press, 1970); for a related anthropological study, see Catherine Lutz, *Unnatural Emotions* (Chicago: University of Chicago Press, 1988).

26. On the close connection between erotic excitement and anger in Roman life, see *The Therapy of Desire*, chaps. 11 and 13. A full study of this phenomenon would include a study of Roman erotic language—very different from Greek erotic language in the role played by invective, enemy smashing, and humiliation, and a study of the sexual activities reported in Roman biography—in which assertions of power over one's male enemies are very frequently linked with sexual arousal. Here one may note that the *Penthouse* magazine film of Suetonius' life of Caligula, which looked obscene to many American eyes, looked evasive and prettified to a student of ancient Rome, because consensual sexual activity between adults was again and again substituted for the exercise of vindictive sexual humiliation and mutilation against powerless inferiors (usually male). At the trial of the film, historian Glen Bowersock, pressed by the district attorney to describe the divergences between film and "book" (in the expectation that we would find that the film had introduced gratuitous obscenity), repeatedly demonstrated how the sensibility of *Penthouse* lacked the connection between arousal and revenge that is intrinsic to Suetonius' narrative. There is not a really good account of Roman sexuality corresponding to Dover's work on Greece, but for a start, see J. Adams, *The Latin Sexual Vocabulary* (Baltimore: Johns Hopkins University Press, 1982). For related observations about the role of cruelty in the "social construction" of Roman parenthood, see Richard Saller's excellent studies of child-beating and related phenomena, including "Pietas, Obligation and Authority in the Roman Ramily," *Festschrift Karl Christ* (Darmstadt: Wissenscheftliche Buchgesellschaft, 1988), 393–410.

27. For a wonderful literary embodiment of this idea, see Samuel Beckett's *Molloy* trilogy; I discuss its emotion taxonomy in Martha C. Nussbaum, "Narrative Emotions," in *Love's Knowledge* (New York: Oxford University Press, 1990). Consider, for example, the following passage:

> The idea of punishment came to his mind, addicted it is true to that chimera and probably impressed by the posture of the body and the fingers clenched as though in torment. And without knowing exactly what his sin was he felt full well that living was not a sufficient atonement for it or that this atonement was in itself a sin, calling for more atonement, and so on, as if there could be anything but life, for the living. And no doubt he would have wondered it if was really necessary to be guilty in order to be punished but for the memory, more and more galling, of his having consented to live in his mother, then to leave her. And this again he could not see as his true sin, but as yet another atonement which had miscarried and, far from cleansing him of his sin, plunged him in it deeper than before. And truth to tell the ideas of guilt and punishment were confused together in his mind, as those of cause and effect so often are in the minds of those who continue to think. And it was often in fear and trembling that he suffered, saying, This, will cost me dear. . . . (Beckett, *Molloy* [New York: Grove Press, 1955], 239–40)

Here we see a specifically Irish-Christian taxonomy of emotions in which desire, guilt, fear, disgust, self-hatred, and the desire for atonement are all interwoven in a characteristic way.

28. See Kahan and Nussbaum, "Two Conceptions."

29. It is not simply that they give names to emotions that we experience but do not bother to name. A longer study of the example would show, I think, that the zealous interest in and pride concerning anger that emerges in this taxonomic activity also enters into the experience of the emotion, tinging it with a manly pride and a self-conscious classificatory zeal that would be no part of the Utku experience.

30. See Hiroshi Wagatsuma and Arthur Rossett, "The Implications of Apology: Law and Culture in Japan and the United States," *Law and Society Review* 20 (1986), 461–98. Unfortunately, the authors do not distinguish between mitigation and exculpation, and present American explanations as "exculpatory." This is unlikely to be the case, given the long tradition of linking explanation with mercy as opposed to acquittal. See chapter 12 (in this volume).

31. See Winkler, "The Constraints of Desire: Erotic Magic Spells," *The Constraints of Desire* (New York: Routledge, 1990), 71–98.

32. I am not claiming that this is universally true. Our culture, where *erôs* is concerned, stands at the confluence of quite a few different traditions, prominently including the Christian and the Romantic, both of which have darker understandings of *erôs*.

33. Plato, *Symposium*, 199E. On the close relationship of this definition to popular understandings, see Winkler, *The Constraints of Desire*; and David M. Halperin, *One Hundred Years of Homosexuality and Other Essays on Greek Love* (New York: Routledge, 1990). Plato's primary departure from tradition is in holding that *erôs* is all along really directed toward an object—the form of the *kalon*—that is immortal and unchanging; popular accounts take it for granted that the object is a human being, and that the goal of *erôs* is intercourse with that human being.

34. Lucretius describes a closely related cultural pattern in which fusion with a divine or quasi-divine object is the goal. See Nussbaum, *Therapy of Desire*, chaps. 5 and 7.

35. But we should not forget the topless *hetaira* called Agape on an early red-figure vase, R20 in Dover's list (in *Greek Homosexuality*).

36. Cicero complains that he has only one term to use to capture these varied experiences; and yet he still thinks his audience knows well what the experiences are: see *Tusculan Disputations* IV. Japanese, more like Greek than like Latin and English, contains a plurality of words for love: *ai*, used to translate *agapê* in the Bible, is strictly nonsexual and is

appropriate for parental love; *koi* is strictly sexual; *suki* is connected with liking. (I owe these observations to Mark Ramseyer.)

37. All this could be pursued further by discussing Wittgenstein's ideas of "family resemblance" and his views about the connections between meanings and forms of life.

38. See the excellent discussion of these pitfalls in Lee Yearley, *Mencius and Aquinas: Comparing Virtues and Theories of Courage* (Albany: SUNY Press, 1990).

39. See Nussbaum, "Non-Relative Virtues," in *The Quality of Life*, ed. M. C. Nussbaum and Amartya Sen (Oxford: Clarendon Press, 1993), 242–69.

40. Seneca, *On Anger*, II.10.

41. See Winkler, *The Constraints of Desire*, esp. "Penelope's Cunning and Homer's," and "The Laughter of the Oppressed."

42. See Iris Murdoch, *The Sovereignty of Good* (London: Routledge, 1970).

43. See Seneca, *On Anger*, esp. I.5. It is important to qualify this optimistic claim, in three ways, for constraints of two different sorts may make the success (or the complete success) of such a project impossible: (1) It may turn out that the experience in question does indeed have a biological component that cannot itself be changed by change of thought; I shall discuss this further below. (2) It may turn out that the structure of human life makes it impossible not to have experiences that engender the emotion—unless one withdraws one's cares from the world in such a radical way as to lose all motives for action. This is, I think, Seneca's final position about anger. (3) The roots of the emotion may lie so deep in infancy, and may so permeate the personality, that change will not know where to locate its target, or, if it does, may find the costs of alteration too high.

44. This claim is associated above all with the work of Michel Foucault: especially *The Use of Pleasure* Vol. 2: *The History of Sexuality*, trans. Robert Hurley (New York: Pantheon, 1984); for ancient Greece, it has also been well discussed by Halperin, *One*

Hundred Years. The best historical account of Greek sexual customs is Dover, *Greek Homosexuality.*

45. Glaukon is also Plato's own half-brother.

46. Although the other bodily appetites are contrasted with the desire *to be penetrated* in respect of shamefulness. See Ps.-Aristotle, *Problemata* IV.27.

47. See Winkler, "Laying Down the Law: The Oversight of Men's Sexual Behavior in Classical Athens," in *The Constraints of Desire*, 45–70: "The concept of a *kinaidos* was of a man socially deviant in his entire being, principally observable in behavior that flagrantly violated or contravened the dominant social definition of masculinity" (45–6). For a fascinating attempt to explain how such a creature could ever be produced, see Ps.-Aristotle, *Problemata* IV.27, brilliantly analyzed by Winkler, 67–9. After a lengthy appeal to innate biological difference supported by a theory that the ducts that in most men run to the penis run, in some, to the anus by mistake, the author throws up his hands and says, "Besides, in some people habit is a second nature."

48. There are occasional exceptions for religious festivals, and possibly the theater, a religious institution. But on the whole even the complex operations of a woman who manages her husband's estate—like the young wife described in Xenophon's *Oeconomicus*—are carried on indoors. Xenophon's advice to her is to get some exercise dusting the pots and pans so that her complexion will glow without makeup.

49. See Halperin, "The Democratic Body," in *One Hundred Years.* The evidence makes it clear that prostitutes were available at a price within any man's means. A comic fragment (Philemon fr. 3 K.-A.) opines that the existence of low-price public brothels was the idea of Solon the lawgiver himself, in order to reinforce the idea of democratic equality by guaranteeing to all citizens regardless of means a way of exercising manly domination in matters of pleasure.

50. For the visual evidence on this point, with many reproductions, see Dover, *Greek Homosexuality* and chapter 12 (in this volume). It is worthy of note that the apparently obvious alternative of oral sex is disdained in Greek culture in both male-female and male-male relationships. The activity is considered "unclean," and the performer of either fellatio or cunnilingus is thought to be humiliated by the act. Artemidoros, the second-century A.D. dream interpreter, explains at length that dreams of oral sex are always ill-omened—unless the dreamer is a person who "makes his living by his mouth," such as "trumpet players, rhetoricians, sophists, and the like." In that case, the dream is a happy sign of the profitable exercise of one's chosen profession. Ancient India also had a strong taboo against oral sex: The permissive *Kama Sutra* is sternly negative.

51. On this, see the evidence in the title essay of Halperin, *One Hundred Years.*

52. On the boy's lack of sexual arousal, see Dover on the artistic evidence, which displays cultural norms if not invariable cultural practices.

53. Richard Posner, *Sex and Reason* (Cambridge, MA: Harvard University Press, 1992); see chapter 14 (in this volume).

54. The most recent version of Posner's thesis about Greek homosexuality is "The Economics of Homosexuality," in *Sex, Preference, and Family: Essays on Law and Nature,* ed. David Estlund and Martha Nussbaum (New York: Oxford University Press, 1997); and also (under the title "Economics and the Social Construction of Homosexuality") in Posner, *Overcoming Law* (Cambridge, MA: Harvard University Press, 1996), 552–80. Here Posner makes a more complicated and, I think, much more plausible argument. Given, Posner says, that relationships with women could rarely involve companionship and friendship, the male formed relations of that sort with other males and then felt in some cases the desire to "cement" that companionship with sex. I think that this represents a marked departure from the book's analysis of opportunistic homosexuality, because it represents the desire for sex with the young male as arising not from frustrated desire for (unavailable) women but

from the boy's own attractiveness in other respects, and thus it recognizes the intentional and interpretive character of sexual desire to a far greater degree than Posner's book usually does. On the other hand, it seems to me still to recognize the role of culture too little. The Greek male did not just find himself desiring to make love with a male friend: In fact, the entire culture saturated his experience with images proclaiming the beauty of young males, as well as their suitability for friendship. And the relationship thus constructed was different in all sorts of ways from Posner's image of "companionate marriage" (in its asymmetry and nonmutuality, for example, and its intense focus on a particular sort of bodily beauty), whereas Posner's analysis tends to assimilate the two.

55. Compare to both the Greek and the modern cases the case of the Navajo "berdache," discussed in Harriet Whitehead, "The Bow and the Burden Strap: A New Look at Institutionalized Homosexuality in Native North America," in Ortner and Whitehead, 80–115; and also in Walter Williams, *The Spirit and the Flesh: Sexual Diversity in American Indian Culture* (Boston: Beacon Press, 1988). This male who shows a preference for female work (especially basket weaving) gets classified as socially female *on that account*, and for this reason is steered into wearing female dress. "She" will become the wife of some male, usually one too poor to pay the usual bride-price. Whereas Christian missionaries who encountered this custom recoiled in horror, seeing "sodomy" and "unnatural activity" before their eyes, the Navajo clearly regard the intercourse of such a couple as male-female intercourse, albeit of a peculiar sort, since the berdache has been previously classified as female. And occupational classification is the central *definiens*, on which sexual role follows; there is no reason to see the berdache as having an antecedent preference for sex with males. To read the evidence this way is to impose our sexual categories a priori.

56. This does not mean that there is no biological element involved in explaining how, given the society one is in, one gets assigned to this sexual category rather than that. See section IV to follow.

57. See the excellent article by William Eskridge, "A Social Constructionist Critique of Posner's *Sex and Reason*: Steps Toward a Gaylegal Agenda," *Yale Law Journal* 102 (1992), 333–86. It should be noted that although Posner's libertarianism traces its origins to Mill, Posner on the whole does not follow Mill in his radical criticism of the current erotic preferences of men and women, which Mill holds to be distorted and highly irrational. See chapter 5 (in this volume).

58. See Cass R. Sunstein, in Estlund and Nussbaum, chap. 10.

59. This is the main defect of Bordo's imaginative analysis. For example, she criticizes those who call extremely obese people self-destructive, saying that such people are in the grip of cultural images of thinness, although of course extreme obesity is linked to various causes of death, in a causal chain that does not run through cultural perceptions—although, of course, the cultural discrimination experienced by obese people may make their health worse in a variety of ways. Again, she treats exercise as simply a matter of sculpting one's bodily "signifier," without recognizing that a person who is fitter and stronger can actually do certain things that she could not do before, say, lift a heavy object without damaging herself. The fact that lifting weight has a certain effect on the muscles and on their ability to perform certain tasks appears to be independent of the muscles' cultural symbolism.

60. For much more along these lines, see Hollander, *Seeing Through Clothes*. It is instructive to note that the first Miss America (in the 1920s) had a bust measurement of 28 inches. To take another case in point, the most cursory reading of classical Indian poetry reveals an eroticization of fleshy thighs (so fleshy that they make it hard to walk) that strikes contemporary American readers as peculiar and even a bit disgusting, rather like a praise of decaying food. Again, see Bordo, *Unbearable Weight*, for the current American norm.

61. Charles Darwin, "On the Two Forms, or Dimorphic Condition, in the Species of *Primula*, and on Their Remarkable Sexual Relations," in *The Collected Papers of Charles Darwin: Volume Two* (Chicago: University of Chicago Press, 1977), 61.

62. See Judith Butler, *Gender Trouble: Feminism and the Subversion of Identity* (New York: Routledge, 1990); M. Foucault, *Herculine Barbin, Being the Recently Discovered Memoirs of a Nineteenth Century Hermaphrodite*, trans. Richard McDongall (New York: Pantheon, 1980).

63. Anne Fausto-Sterling, *Myths of Gender* (New York: Basic Books, 1985; 2nd ed., 1992).

64. Here my argument connects with a broader set of issues in contemporary metaphysics, concerning the "interest relativity" of all categorization, in science and elsewhere. I cannot defend a general position in this complex debate here, but the position I would wish to defend is close to that of Hilary Putnam, who argues that all distinctions are in a significant sense made by human beings and relative to human interests—but that there are many constraints on the ways in which this can be done, and some categorizations are therefore superior to others. In the area of emotion and sexuality, however, I think we see considerably more variation of schematization than we do in many of the areas investigated by Putnam, given the intensity of the political interests in the outcome. This does not mean that we cannot still argue cogently that some categorizations are better than others; it does mean that it will be a long and difficult process.

65. Thomas Laqueur, *Making Sex: Body and Gender from the Greeks to Freud* (Cambridge, MA: Harvard University Press, 1990). Laqueur's treatment of the ancient Greek evidence does not seem to me very satisfactory, but the later chapters, which deal with his real period of expertise, appear convincing.

66. On February 24, 1995, the successful cloning of an adult sheep was first announced to the world.

67. This research also stresses that insofar as hormones govern sexual arousal, the operative hormone, androgen, is the same for "men" and for "women." For a good summary of recent research, see Salvatore Cucchiari, "The Origins of Gender Hierarchy," in Ortner and Whitehead, 31–79. Among the studies whose results are discussed are: John Money, "Psychosexual Differentiation," in *Sex Research: New Developments*, ed. John Money (New York: Holt, Rinehart, and Winston, 1965) 3–23; Money and Patricia Tucker, *Sexual Signatures: On Being a Man or a Woman* (Boston: Little, Brown, 1975); Frank A. Beach, "Evolutionary Changes in the Physiological Control of Mating Behavior in Mammals," *The Psychological Review* 54 (1947), 346–55; Saul Rosenzweig, "Human Sexual Autonomy as an Evolutionary Attainment, Anticipating Proceptive Sex Choice and Idiodynamic Bisexuality," in *Contemporary Sexual Behavior: Critical Issues for the 70's*, ed. J. Zubin and J. Money (Baltimore: Johns Hopkins University Press, 1973), 189–229. And for a brilliant and persistent account of the misreading of biological evidence on the question of sex difference, see Fausto-Sterling, *Myths of Gender*.

68. *Republic*, 504 A–D.

chapter forty

Alan Soble
Eva Feder Kittay

Antioch College is a small school outside of Dayton, Ohio, with approximately seven-hundred students and a policy of community governance. Any group can propose college policy, and faculty, administrators, and elected students consider proposed changes or additions to the campus code at a weekly meeting of Antioch's Community Government. In the fall of 1990, "Womyn of Antioch," a student group, proposed a college policy on sexual assault after a series of date rapes occurred on campus. This initial policy was seen by some to be overly rigid and draconian: the only punishment was expulsion, and some expressed concern about procedural limitations to the accused individual's right to prove his or her innocence. When the lone case brought forth under the initial policy found that no offense had occurred because the facts were unclear, a second round of community hearings was initiated to clarify the code and its purpose within the community. The result of these meetings was the Sexual Offense Policy that is the central topic of the following exchange between two contemporary American philosophers: Alan Soble and Eva Feder Kittay.

In the wake of national discussion following indiscretions former President Clinton committed in the White House, it might seem natural to engage in discussions concerning what acts may count as "sexual." We should remember that the deliberation and debate that resulted in Antioch's Sexual Offense Policy was groundbreaking at the time; it occurred long before President Clinton's denial that oral sex is a sexual act. At the same time that Antioch was revising its code, the United States was confronting the problem of sexual harassment in the workplace, the central issue in Clarence Thomas's Supreme Court confirmation hearings that took place in the fall of 1991. Thomas had been accused by a former employee, Anita Hill, of creating and fostering a hostile workplace by making inappropriate sexual remarks and describing scenes from pornographic videos.

Alan Soble, "Antioch's 'Sexual Offense Policy': A Philosophical Exploration"; Eva Feder Kittay, "AH! My Foolish Heart: A Reply to Alan Soble's 'Antioch's "Sexual Offense Policy": A Philosophical Examination,' *Journal of Social Philosophy,* Vol. 28 No. 1, Spring 1997, 22–36; 153–159. © 1997 *Journal of Social Philosophy.*

These allegations were examined in detail in the Senate hearings on Thomas' confirmation to the court; the wide media exposure that followed prompted public discussion about actions that had previously been taken to be private matters. At a time when the whole country was becoming accustomed to talking about "private" actions in a public way, Antioch College stepped forward and asked its community members to be sure that any sexual activity was consensual by obtaining consent "verbally before there is any sexual contact or conduct."

   This new policy (which since the writings of Soble and Kittay has been revised once again) drew national attention because it calls for explicit consent between participants engaging in sexual activity. Since the "request for consent must be specific to each act," and "consent is an on-going process," the code ensures that every sexual act is freely consented to by all parties. Thus, an encounter would likely begin with the question "May I kiss you?" and could culminate with consent to intercourse, or might stop at some earlier stage either through mutual agreement or when one party states that they wish to go no further. Consent could be withdrawn at any point, and prior consent to any activity would not imply that consent to the same act had been granted for future encounters. The policy was not embraced by all of Antioch's students. When the *New York Times* reported on the first freshman orientation that covered the code, an incoming student was quoted as saying, "If I have to ask those questions I won't get what I want." Of course, that seems to be exactly the point of the policy: sex should not be what one person wants, but instead a mutually agreed upon activity.

   In his essay, Alan Soble examines the nature of consent, specifically sexual consent. While he situates the discussion in the context of a larger discussion of understanding verbal consent, and when "yes" can mean less than consent, Soble focuses here on the emphasis the policy places on verbal consent. The reasons for this emphasis are clear when the policy is understood as the outgrowth of efforts to safeguard against occurrences of "date rape," in which initial mutual consent to sexual activity, or even the suggestion of such consent, may be willfully misunderstood by one party to imply consent to further activity. Soble is interested in exploring the possibility of nonverbal consent such as that communicated in "body language." The Antioch policy allows for refusal of consent to occur through "physical resistance," but does not seem to allow for escalation of sexual activity without explicit verbal consent to the activity. Soble is concerned that this restriction robs sexual engagement of genuine pleasure and, ultimately, of the individual autonomy it is intended to protect.

   In her response to Soble, Eva Kittay presents a reading of the policy that sees it as not a limitation to sexuality so much as a reconceptualization of the nature of consent. Picking up on Soble's hints toward mutual initiation, Kittay finds that consent would not have to be verbal if, for example, actions taken were matched by both parties, such as the simultaneous disrobing of each partner. As for Soble's concerns about the nature of body talk and consent itself, Kittay proposes that we take Antioch's policy as a statement of community expectations. The policy attempts to ensure that everyone understands what is meant by consent and seems to point towards a less passive role in sexuality for women in that the policy is neutral both on gender roles and sexual orientation.

Soble began his education in the sciences and received his Ph.D. in philosophy in 1976 from the State University of New York (SUNY) at Buffalo. He founded the Society for the Philosophy of Sex and Love in 1977 and served as its director until 1992. He is Research Professor and Professor of Philosophy at the University of New Orleans where he has taught since 1986. He has written extensively on aspects of sex and love in philosophy and has published several books, most notably *Philosophy of Sex* and *Sexual Investigations*.

Kittay received her Ph.D. in philosophy from the City University of New York (CUNY) in 1978 and is a leading figure in feminist ethics. Her earliest work focused on the nature of metaphor, an interest that continues to influence her work. Much of her recent writing has revolved around questioning the role of caring and the care giver in society. She has taught since 1979 at SUNY Stony Brook where she is a full professor. Her most recent book is *Love's Labor*.

These two pieces were first presented in a slightly different form at a meeting of the American Philosophical Association in 1995. Soble first read his paper, and Kittay (who had previously been provided with a copy of the text) read her response. A brief response from Soble and questions from the audience for both authors followed.

REK

QUESTIONS

1. Soble uses Antioch's policy as an example of a particular approach to sexuality. What does Soble think that approach is, and is the Antioch policy a good example of it?

2. Kittay starts her essay by commenting that she was initially conflicted about Antioch's policy. What are the two positions she is torn between?

3. What conception of "mutual aggression" does Soble have? Is it the same as Kittay's?

4. How is St. Paul's idea of a marital contract important for Soble? Is Kittay's dismissal of their importance correct?

5. What sort of "Sexual Offense Policy" would you propose be adopted at your school?

SELECTED BIBLIOGRAPHY

Antioch College. "The Antioch College Sexual Offense Prevention Policy." http://www.antioch-college.edu/survival/html/sopp.html.

Associated Press. "Sex Consent Policy Set At Antioch." *Columbus Dispatch*, September 9, 1993, p. 4d.

Francis, Leslie, ed. *Date Rape: Feminism, Philosophy, and the Law.* University Park: Pennsylvania State University Press, 1996.

Gross, Jane. "Combating Rape on Campus in a Class on Sexual Consent." *New York Times*, September 25, 1993, Section 1, p. 1.

Stan, Adele, ed. *Debating Sexual Correctness: Pornography, Sexual Harrasment, Date Rape, and the Politics of Sexual Equality.* New York: Delta Trade Paperbacks, 1995.

Antioch's "Sexual Offense Policy": A Philosophical Exploration

Alan Soble

She: For the last time, do you love me or don't you?

He: I DON'T!

She: Quit stalling, I want a *direct* answer.

—*Jane Russell and Fred Astaire*[1]

1. "WHEN IN DOUBT, ASK"

Consider this seemingly innocuous moral judgment issued by philosopher Raymond Belliotti:

> "teasing" without the intention to fulfill that which the other can reasonably be expected to think was offered is immoral since it involves the nonfulfillment of that which the other could reasonably be expected as having been agreed upon.[2]

This might be right in the abstract; provocative and lingering flirtatious glances sometimes can reasonably be taken as an invitation to engage in sex; hence brazenly flirting and not fulfilling its meaning, or never intending to fulfill its meaning, is, like failing to honor other promises or invitations, *ceteris paribus* a moral defect—even if not a moral sin.[3] Abstractions aside, however, how are we to

grasp "can *reasonably* be taken as"? A woman's innocent, inquisitive glance might be taken as a sexual invitation by an awfully optimistic fellow, and he and his peers might judge his perception "reasonable." This is the reason Catharine MacKinnon says that to use "reasonable belief as a standard without asking on a substantive social basis, to whom the belief is reasonable and why—meaning, what conditions make it reasonable—is one-sided: male-sided."[4] Similarly, a man's innocent, inquisitive glance might be taken as a sexual leer by an anxiously sensitive woman, and she and her peers might judge this perception "reasonable." Belliotti writes as if all were well with "reasonable":

> Although sexual contracts are not as formal or explicit as corporation agreements the rule of thumb should be the concept of reasonable expectation. If a woman smiles at me and agrees to have a drink I cannot reasonably assume . . . that she has agreed to spend the weekend with me.[5]

I suppose not. But why not? We do not now have in our culture a convention, a practice like the display of colored hankies, in which a smile before an accepted drink has that meaning. But nothing intrinsic to the action prevents its having, in the proper circumstances, that very meaning. And an optimistic fellow might say that the *special* sort of smile she, or another he, gave him constituted a sexual invitation. Belliotti continues his example:

> On the other hand if she did agree to share a room and bed with me for the weekend I could reasonably assume that she had agreed to have sexual intercourse.

Not true for many American couples as they travel through foreign lands together. Or maybe in accepting the invitation to share a room or sleeping car she agreed only to snuggle. Cues indicating the presence and kind of sexual interest are fluid; at one time in the recent past, a woman's inviting a man to her apartment or room carried more sexual meaning than it does now—even if that meaning still lingers on college campuses and elsewhere.[6] To forestall such objections, Belliotti offers these instructions:

> If there is any doubt concerning whether or not someone has agreed to perform a certain sexual act with another, I would suggest that the doubting party simply ask the other and make the contract more explicit. . . . [W]hen in doubt assume nothing until a more explicit overture has been made.[7]

What could be more commonsensically true than this? But it is wrong. The man who thinks it reasonable in a given situation to assume that the woman has agreed to have sex will not have any doubt and so will have no motive to ask more explicitly what she wants. His failure to doubt, or his failure to imagine the bare possibility of doubting, whether the other has consented to engage in sex is brought about by the same factors that determine, for him, the reasonableness of his belief in her consent. It is silly to suggest "*when* in doubt, ask," because the problem is that not enough doubt arises in the first place, i.e., the brief look is taken too readily as reasonable or conclusive evidence of a sexual invitation. A man touches the arm of a woman who briefly glanced at him; she pulls away abruptly; but he is not caused to have doubts about her interest. Even if he does not take her resistance as further evidence of her desire, the reasonableness, for him, of his belief that her earlier glance was intentionally sexual is enough to prevent doubt from taking root when it should—immediately.

2. "'NO' MEANS 'NO'"

According to Susan Estrich, a man who engages in sex with a woman on the basis of an unreasonable belief in her consent should be charged with rape; only a genuinely reasonable belief in her consent should exculpate an accused rapist. Estrich wants it to be legally impossible for a man accused of rape to plead that he believed that the woman consented, when that belief was unreasonable, even though *he* thought it was reasonable. Estrich realizes that "reasonable belief" is a difficult notion. Still, she heroically proposes that "the reasonable man in the 1980s should be the one who understands that a woman's word is deserving of respect, whether she is a perfect stranger or his own wife." The reasonable man "is the one who . . . understands that 'no means no'."[8] The man pawing the arm of the woman who pulls abruptly away—the physical equivalent of "no"—had better immediately doubt the quality of his belief in her sexual interest. At the psychological level, this man might not doubt that she is sexually interested in him; Estrich's normative proposal is that he is to be held liable anyway, because he *should* be doubtful. Beyond this crude sort of case, I think Estrich means that, for the reasonable man, a woman's qualified locution ("Please, not tonight, I think I'd rather not"; "I don't know, I just don't feel like it") is not an invitation to continue trying, but "no." Her wish is expressed softly because she is tactful or frightened or because this is the women's language she has learned to speak. For the reasonable man, her "I'm not sure I want to" is either a tactful "no" or a request to back off while she autonomously makes up her own mind.

As congenial as Estrich's proposal is, she muddies the water with a tantalizing piece of logic:

> Many feminists would argue that so long as women are powerless relative to men, viewing a "yes" as a sign of true consent is misguided. . . . [M]any women who say yes to men they know, whether on dates or on the job, would say no if they could. I have no doubt that women's silence sometimes is the product not of passion and desire but of pressure and fear. Yet if yes may often mean no, at least from a woman's perspective, it does not seem so much to ask men, and the law, to respect the courage of the woman who does say no and to take her at her word.[9]

Estrich's reasoning seems to be: if something as antithetical to "no" as "yes" can mean "no," then surely something as consistent with "no," "no" itself, means "no." This argument has a curious consequence. If "yes" can mean "no," at least from a woman's *own* perspective (the woman who consents for financial reasons but whose heart and desire are not wrapped up in the act; a woman who agrees, but only after a barrage of pleading),[10] then it will be difficult to deny that "no" spoken by some women can mean "maybe" or even "yes." From the perspective of some women, "no" can mean "try harder to convince me" or "show me how manly you are." Charlene Muehlenhard and Lisa Hollabaugh reported in 1988 that some women occasionally say "no" but do not mean it; 39.3 percent of the 610 college women they surveyed at Texas A&M University indicated that they had offered "token resistance" to sex "even though [they] had every intention to and [were] willing to engage in sexual intercourse."[11] Susan Rae Peterson partially explains these findings: "typical sexual involvement includes some resistance on the part of women . . . because they have been taught to do so, or they do not want to appear 'easy' or 'cheap'."[12]

Men cannot always tell when a woman's resistance is real or token, serious or playful; men are, moreover, often insensitive, even callous, as to what a woman does intend to communicate; and, after all, Muehlenhard and Hollabaugh's figure is only 39 percent and not 99 percent. For these reasons, as well as her own, Estrich's proposal is a wise suggestion. Men, and the courts, should always assume, in order to be cognitively, morally, and legally safe, that a woman's "no" means "no"—*even in those cases when it does or might not.* A man who takes "no" as "no" even when he suspects that a woman is testing his masculinity with token resistance is advised by Estrich to risk suffering a loss of sexual pleasure and a possible blow to his ego, in order to secure the greater good, for both him and her, of avoiding rape.

But if men are always to assume that "no" means "no," even though there is a nontrivial chance that it means "keep trying" or "yes," then Estrich, to be consistent, should permit men to assume that a woman's "yes" always means "yes"— even though, on her view, a woman's "yes" sometimes means "no."[13] If, instead, Estrich wants men to sort out when a woman's "yes" really means "yes" and when it does not, in order that he be able to decide whether to take the "yes" at its face value and proceed with sex, she should propose some workable procedure for men to follow. Yet her description of the reasonable man mentions only what his response to "no" should be, and not what his response to "yes" should be. Encouraging women to abandon the token resistance maneuver, to give up saying "no" when they mean "maybe" or "yes," is helpful. But it will not take theorists of sex, or men in the presence of an apparently consenting woman, very far in deciphering when "yes" means "no."[14]

3. THE ANTIOCH POLICY

I propose that we understand Antioch University's "Sexual Offense Policy" as addressing the issues raised in our discussion of Belliotti and Estrich. The Policy's central provisions are these.[15]

A1. "Consent must be obtained verbally before there is any sexual contact or conduct."

A2. "[O]btaining consent is an on-going process in any sexual interaction."

A3. "If the level of sexual intimacy increases during an interaction . . . the people involved need to express their clear verbal consent before moving to that new level."

A4. "The request for consent must be specific to each act."

A5. "If you have had a particular level of sexual intimacy before with someone, you must still ask each and every time."

A6. "If someone has initially consented but then stops consenting during a sexual interaction, she/he should communicate withdrawal verbally and/or through physical resistance. The other individual(s) must stop immediately."

A7. "Don't ever make any assumptions about consent."

In an ethnically, religiously, economically, socially, and sexually diverse population, there might be no common and comprehensive understanding of what various bits of behavior mean in terms of expressing interest in or consenting to sex. In the absence of rigid conventions or a homogeneous community, a glance, either brief or prolonged, is too indefinite to be relied on to transmit information; an invitation to come to one's room, or sharing a room, or a bed, on a trip might or might not

have some settled meaning; clothing and cosmetics in a pluralistic culture are equivocal. (Young men, more so than young women, take tight jeans and the absence of a bra under a top to signal an interest in sex.)[16] Because physical movements and cues of various kinds can be interpreted in widely different ways, sexual activity entered into or carried out on the basis of this sort of (mis)information is liable to violate someone's rights or otherwise be indecent or offensive. Antioch insists that consent to sexual activity be verbal (A1) instead of behavioral.[17] Following this rule will minimize miscommunication and the harms it causes and encourage persons to treat each other with respect as autonomous agents.

Further, bodily movements or behaviors of a sexual sort that occur in the early stages of a possible sexual encounter can also be ambiguous and do not necessarily indicate a willingness to increase the intensity of, or to prolong, the encounter (hence A2, A3). Verbal communication is supposed to prevent misunderstandings rooted in indefinite body language; we should not assume consent on the basis of expressions of desire (lubrication, groans) or failures to resist an embrace (A1). Neither of these bodily phenomena—reacting with sexual arousal to a touch; not moving away when intimately touched—necessarily mean that the touched person welcomes the touch or wants it to continue. There are times when one's body responds with pleasure to a touch but one's mind disagrees with the body's judgment; Antioch's insistence on verbal consent after discussion and deliberation is meant to give the mind the decisive and autonomous say. Similarly, the verbal request for, and the verbal consent to, sexual contact must be not only explicit, but also specific for any sexual act that might occur (A4). Consenting to and then sharing a kiss does not imply consent to any other sexual act; the bodily movements that accompany the sexual arousal created by the kiss do not signal permission to proceed to some other sexual activity not yet discussed.

One provision (A7) is a rebuttal of Belliotti's advice, "when in doubt, ask." Antioch demands, more strictly than this, that the sexual partners entertain *universal* doubt and therefore *always* ask. Doubt about the other's consent must be categorical rather than hypothetical: not Belliotti's "when in doubt, assume nothing," but a Cartesian "doubt!" and "assume nothing!" To be on the cognitive, moral, and legal safe side, to avoid mistakes about desire or intention, always assume "no" unless a clear, verbal, explicit "yes" is forthcoming (A1, A3, A4). Men no longer have to worry about distinguishing a woman's mildly seductive behavior from her "incomplete rejection strategy,"[18] about which men and boys are often confused; in the absence of an explicit "yes" on her part, he is, as demanded by Estrich, to assume a respectful "no." There's still the question of how a man is to know, when obvious consent-negating factors are lacking (e.g., she's had too much alcohol), whether a woman's "yes" truly means "yes." Antioch's solution is to rely on explicit, probing verbal communication that must occur not only before but also during a sexual encounter (A3, A5). The constant dialogue, the "on-going process" (A2) of getting consent in what Lois Pineau calls "communicative sexuality,"[19] is meant to provide the man with an opportunity to assess whether the woman's "yes" means "yes," to give her the opportunity to say a definite even if tactful "no," and to clear up confusions created by her silence or passive acquiescence. At the same time, there is to be no constant badgering—especially not under the rubric of "communicative sexuality"—of a woman by a man in response to her "no." A man's querying whether a woman's "no" really means "no" is to disrespect her "no" and fails to acknowledge her autonomy. It is also to embark on a course that might constitute verbal coercion.[20]

It is illuminating to look at the Antioch policy from the perspective of the sadomasochistic subculture, in particular its use of "safe words." A set of safe words is a language, a common understanding, a convention jointly created (hence a Cartesian foundation) in advance of sex by the partners, to be used during a sexual encounter as a way to say "yes," "more," "no," to convey details about wants and dislikes, without spoiling the erotic mood. Thus the use of safe words attempts to achieve some of the goals of Antioch's policy without the cumbersome apparatus of explicit verbal consent at each level of sexual interaction (A3, A4). And a tactful safe word can gently accomplish an Antiochian withdrawal of consent to sex (A6). But there is a major difference between sadomasochism and Antiochian sex: a sadomasochistic pair want the activities to proceed smoothly, spontaneously, realistically, so one party grants to the other the right to carry on as she wishes, subject to the veto or modifications of safe words, which are to be used sparingly, only when necessary, as a last resort; the couple therefore eschew Antiochian constant dialogue. In dispensing with the incessant chatter of on-going consent to higher levels of sexual interaction (A2, A3), the sadomasochistic pair violate another provision (A7): consent is assumed throughout the encounter in virtue of the early granting of rights. No such prior consent to sex into an indefinite future is admissible by Antioch (A2, A3, A4).[21]

4. PLEASURE

Does Antioch's policy make sex less exciting? Does it force a couple to slow down, to savor each finger and tooth, when they would rather be overwhelmed by passion? Sarah Crichton criticizes the Antioch policy on the grounds that "it criminalizes the delicious unexpectedness of sex—a hand suddenly moves to here, a mouth to there."[22] But this consideration is not decisive. One goal of the Policy is to decrease the possibility that a person will unexpectedly experience (i.e., without being warned by being asked) something unpleasant that he or she does not want to experience: a mouth sucking on the wrong toe, a finger too rudely rammed in the rectum. The risk of undergoing unwanted acts or sensations is especially great with strangers, and it is in such a context that the requirement that consent be obtained specifically for each act makes the most sense. Sometimes we do not want the unexpected but only the expected, the particular sensations we know, trust, and yearn for. So there is in the Antioch policy a trade off: we lose the pleasure, if any, of the unexpected, but we also avoid the unpleasantness of the unexpected. This is why Crichton's point is not decisive. Perhaps for young people, or for those more generally who do not yet know what they like, verbal consent to specifically described touches or acts might make less sense. But in this case, too, reason exists to insist, for the sake of caution, on such consent.

Julia Reidhead also attempts to rebut the objection that Antioch's policy begets dull sex.[23] She claims that the Policy gives the partners a chance to be creative with language, to play linguistically with a request to touch the breast or "kiss the hollow of your neck" and to "reinvent [sex] privately." But Antioch thinks that sexual language needs to be less, rather than more, private; more specific, not less.[24] Hence Reidhead's praise for Antioch's policy misses its point: common linguistic understandings cannot be assumed in a heterogenous population. To encourage the creative, poetic use of language in framing sexual requests to proceed to a new level of sex is to provoke the misunderstandings the Policy was designed to prevent. Thus, when Reidhead queries, "What woman or man on Antioch's campus, or elsewhere, wouldn't

welcome . . . 'May I kiss the hollow of your neck'," her homogenizing "or elsewhere" betrays the insensitivity to cultural and social differences and their linguistic concomitants that Antioch is trying to overcome.

Reidhead defends Antioch also by arguing that vocalizing creatively about sex before we do it is a fine way to mix the pleasures of language with the pleasures of the body. Indeed, the pleasures of talk are themselves sensual. "Antioch's subtle and imaginative mandate is an erotic windfall: an opportunity for undergraduates to discover that wordplay and foreplay can be happily entwined." Reidhead is right that talking about sex can be sexy and arousing, but wrong that this fact is consistent with the Antioch policy and one of its advantages. This cute reading of communication as itself sex almost throws Antioch's procedure into a vicious regress: if no sexual activity is permissible without prior consent (A1), and consent must be spoken, then if a request for sexual activity is constructed to be a sexually arousing locution, it would amount to a sexual act and hence would be impermissible unless it, in turn, had already received specific consent (A1, A4). So Y's consent to nonverbal sexual activity must be preceded by X's request for that activity *and* by X's request to utter that request. Further, to try to get consent for the sexual act of kissing the neck by talking sensually about kissing the neck is to employ the pleasure elicited by one sexual act to bring about the occurrence of another sexual act. But obtaining consent for a sexual act by causing even mild sexual pleasure with a seductive request is to interfere with calm and rational deliberation—as much as a shot or two of whiskey would. This is why Antioch insists (A3) that between any two sexual levels there must be a pause, a sexual gap, that makes space for three things: (1) a thoughtful, verbal act of request, (2) deliberations about whether or not to proceed, and then (3) either consent or denial. A well-timed hiatus respected by both parties provides an obstacle to misreadings; Augustinian bodily perturbations are to be checked while the mind reconsiders.

5. BODY TALK

The body should not be dismissed. When two people in love embrace tightly, eyes glued to the other's eyes, bodies pulsating with pleasure, they often do know (*how*, is the mystery) without explicit verbalization, from the way they touch each other and respond to these touches, that each wants and consents to the sex that is about to occur. Other cases of successful communication—in and out of sexual contexts—are explicit and specific without being verbal. So even if the truth of the particular claim that the mouth can say "no" while the body exclaims an overriding "yes" is debatable, the general idea, that the body sometimes does speak a clear language, seems fine. Maybe this is why Antioch, even though it requires a verbal "yes" for proceeding with sex (A1), allows a nonverbal "no" to be sufficient for *withdrawing* consent (A6); nonverbal behavior can have a clear meaning. Certain voluntary actions, even some impulsive, reflex-like, bodily movements, do mean "no," and about these there should be no mistake, in the same Estrichian way that about the meaning of the simple verbal "no" there should be no mistake. But if such motions can be assumed or demanded to be understood in a pluralistic community—*pulling away when touched means "no"*—then some voluntary behaviors and involuntary bodily movements must reliably signal "yes."

According to the Policy, a verbal "yes" replaces any possible bodily movement or behavior as the one and only reliable sign that proceeding with sexual activity is permissible. If I ask, "may I kiss you?" I may not proceed on the basis of your bodily reply, e.g., you push your mouth out at mine, or groan and open your mouth invitingly, because even though it seems obvious what these behaviors mean ("yes"), I might be making an interpretive mistake: I see your open mouth as presented "invitingly" because I have with undue optimism deceived myself into thinking that's what you mean. So I must wait for the words, "yes, you may kiss me,"[25] about which interpretive unclarity is not supposed to arise, else the problem Antioch set for itself is unsolvable. The verbal "yes," *after* communicative probing, is Antioch's Cartesian foundation. But can the ambiguities of the verbal be cleared up by language itself? How much communicative probing is *enough*? This question opens up a hermeneutic circle that traps Antioch's policy. Her "yes," repeated several times under the third-degree of communicative sex, can always be probed more for genuineness, if I wanted to *really* make sure. But, losing patience, she shows her "yes" to be genuine when she grabs me. The body reasserts itself.

My continuing to probe her "yes" over and over again, to make sure that her heart and desire are wrapped up in the act to which she is apparently consenting (must I ask her whether her agreement has been engineered for my benefit by "compulsory heterosexuality"?), is a kind of paternalism. Because the robust respect that Antioch's policy fosters for a woman's "no" is offset by the weaker respect it fosters for her "yes," conceiving of the Antioch policy not as attempting to foster respect for the autonomy of the other, but as attempting to prevent acquaintance rape, i.e., harmful behaviors, is more accurate. At best, the relationship between Antioch's policy and autonomy is unclear. One Antioch student, Suzy Martin, defends the Policy by saying that "It made me aware I *have* a voice. I didn't know that before."[26] Coming in the mid-90s from a college-age woman, the kind of person we expect to know better, this remark is astonishing. In effect, she admits that what Antioch is doing for her, at such an advanced age, is what her parents and earlier schooling should have done long ago, to teach her that she has a voice. Thus Antioch is employing an, anti-autonomy principle in its treatment of young adults—*in loco parentis*—that my college generation had fought to eliminate.

6. CONSENT

The Policy lays it down that previous sexual encounters between two people do not relax or change the rules to be followed during their later encounters (A5); the casual sex of one-night stands and that of on-going relationships are governed by the same standards. Nor does a person's sexual biography (reputation) count for anything. No historical facts allow "assumptions about consent" (A7). Indeed, in requiring consent at each different level of a single sexual encounter, Antioch applies the same principle of the irrelevance of history to each sub-act within that encounter. Earlier consent to one sub-act within a single encounter creates no presumption that one may proceed, without repeating the procedure of obtaining explicit and specific consent, to later sub-acts in the same encounter, in the same way that one sexual encounter does not mean that consent can be assumed for later encounters. The history of the relationship, let alone the history of the evening, counts for nothing.[27] The Antioch policy, then, implies that one cannot consent in advance to a whole night of sex, but only to a single atomistic act, one small part of an encounter. Similarly, in denying the relevance of the historical, Antioch makes a Pauline marriage contract impossible.[28] In such a marriage, one consents at the very beginning, in advance, to a whole series of sexual acts that might comprise the rest of one's sexual life; consent to sex is presumed after the exchange of vows and rings; each spouse owns the body and sexual powers of the

other; and so marital rape is conceptually impossible, replaced by a notion of fulfilling the "marriage debt." In rejecting the possibility of such an arrangement, even if voluntarily contracted, Antioch cuts back on a traditional power of consent, its ability to apply to an indefinite, open future. For Antioch, consent is short-lived; it dies an easy death, and must always be replaced by a new generation of consents.

Antioch also cuts back on the power of consent by making it not binding: one can withdraw consent at any time during any act or sub-act (A6). Nothing in the Policy indicates that the right to withdraw is limited by the sexual satisfaction or other expectations of one's partner. Any such qualification would also run counter to the Policy's spirit. This is a difference between Antioch's policy and Belliotti's libertarianism, according to which breaking a sexual promise is at least a *prima facie* moral fault. It is also contrary to the indissolubility of Pauline marriage. But that Antioch would be indulgent about withdrawing consent makes sense, given Antioch's distrust of the historical. Consenting is an act that occupies a discrete location in place and time; it is a historical event, and that it has occurred is a historical fact; thus consent is itself precisely the kind of thing whose weight Antioch discounts. Consenting to a sexual act does not entail, for Antioch, that one ought to perform the act, and not even that one has a *prima facie* duty to do so; the act need not take place because the only justification for it to occur is the act of consenting that has already receded into the past and has become a mere piece of impotent history. When consent into the future, given today for tomorrow, is ruled out, so too is consent into the future, now for ten seconds from now. How could consent have the power to legitimize any subsequent sexual act? An air of paradox surrounds the Policy: it makes consent the centerpiece of valid sexual conduct, yet its concept of consent is emaciated. Of course, "unless refusal of consent or withdrawal of consent are real possibilities, we can no longer speak of 'consent' in any genuine sense."[29] But that withdrawing consent must be possible does not entail that we have carte blanche permission to do so. My guess is that Belliotti is right, that withdrawing consent to an act to which one has consented is *prima facie* wrong. The logical possibility that consent is binding in this way is necessary for taking consent seriously as a legitimizer of sexual activity.

Still, if *X* has promised a sexual act to *Y*, but withdraws consent and so reneges, it does *not* follow from libertarianism that *Y* has a right to compel *X* into compliance.[30] Nor does it follow from the terms of Pauline marriage, in which the spouses consent to a lifetime of sexual acts. Neither the fact that each person has a duty, the marriage debt, to provide sexual pleasure for the other whenever the other wants it, nor the fact that in such a marriage the one initial act of consent makes rape conceptually impossible, imply that a spurned spouse may rightfully force himself upon the other. Pauline marriage is egalitarian; the wife owns the husband and his ability to perform sexually as much as he owns her capacity to provide pleasure. In patriarchal practice, the man expects sexual access to his wife in exchange for economic support, and even if rape is conceptually impossible he might extract the marriage debt: "if she shows unwillingness or lack of inclination to engage with him in sexual intercourse, he may wish to remind her of the nature of the bargain they struck. The act of rape may serve conveniently as a communicative vehicle for reminding her."[31] Neither violence nor abuse are legitimated by the principles of Pauline marriage; perhaps their possibility explains why Paul admonishes spouses to show "benevolence" to each other (1 Cor. 7:3).[32]

Finally, Antioch's policy also does not permit "metaconsent," or consent about (the necessity of) consent. Consent, in principle, should be able to alter the background presumption, in the relationship between two people, *from* "assume 'no' unless you hear an explicit 'yes'" to "assume 'yes' unless you hear an explicit 'no'," or *from* "don't you dare try without an explicit go-ahead" *to* "feel free to try but be prepared for a 'no'." This power of consent is abolished by Antioch's making history irrelevant; consent to prior acts creates no presumption in favor of "yes" tonight (A5). Further, to give consent into the future allows one's partner to make a prohibited assumption (A7). There is no provision in the Policy that empowers a couple to jettison the Policy by free and mutual consent; here is another way Antioch's policy is not designed to foster autonomy. In Pauline marriage, by contrast, one act of consent, the marriage vow, has the power to change presumptions from "no" to an ongoing "yes." Such is the power of consent for Paul, that it both applies to the future and is binding: we make our bed and then lie in it. Antioch's notion of consent has freed us from such stodgy concerns.

Assistance was provided by the University of New Orleans and its College of Liberal Arts, through the release time of a research professor appointment, and by the Research Support Scheme of the Open Society Institute. The earliest version of this paper was presented as a seminar at the philosophy department of the Budapest Technical University, May 1994. (Travel to Budapest was made possible by grants from the International Research and Exchanges Board and the Hungarian Ministry of Culture and Education.) A later version was given in February 1995 as a "Current Research in Philosophy" colloquium at Tulane University; and one more version was read at the Eastern Division meetings of the American Philosophical Association in December 1995 (Eva Kittay provided comments). This version has been cannibalized from my Sexual Investigations *(New York: New York University Press, 1996), but also goes beyond it.*

ENDNOTES

1. The epigraph to chapter 9 of Susan Haack's *Evidence and Inquiry* (Oxford: Blackwell, 1993), 182. Professor Haack thanks David Stove for supplying it.

2. "A Philosophical Analysis of Sexual Ethics," *Journal of Social Philosophy* 10, no. 3 (1979): 8–11, at 11.

3. According to John Sabini and Maury Silver ("Flirtation and Ambiguity," ch. 6 of *Moralities of Everyday Life* [New York: Oxford University Press, 1982], 107–123, at 116 n.11), "Flirtation . . . offers no commitment and gives no right to claim abuse. To claim you were teased is to claim [the other] went beyond flirting to committing. Of course, the disappointed one may be inclined to see a tease in a flirt." That is indeed the problem.

4. *Toward a Feminist Theory of the State* (Cambridge: Harvard University Press, 1989), 183; see 181.

5. "A Philosophical Analysis of Sexual Ethics," 9.

6. See T. Perper and D. Weis, "Proceptive and Rejective Strategies of U.S. and Canadian College Women," *Journal of Sex Research* 23, no. 4 (1987): 455–90, at 462.

7. Belliotti repeats the "when in doubt, ask" advice in his essay "Sex" (in Peter Singer, ed., *A Companion to Ethics* [Oxford: Blackwell, 1991], 315–26, at 325) and in his treatise *Good Sex: Perspectives on Sexual Ethics* (Lawrence, Kan.: University Press of Kansas, 1993), 106–107. See my "book note" in *Ethics* 105, no. 2 (1995): 447–48.

8. *Real Rape* (Cambridge: Harvard University Press, 1987), 97–98.

9. Ibid., 102.

10. These examples are Robin West's, "The Harms of Consensual Sex," *American Philosophical Association Newsletters* 92, no. 2 (1995): 52–55, at 53 (who might not approve of my use of them). I am not sure that the examples capture what Estrich's brief remark, that some women who say "yes" would say "no" *if they could*, means. She makes the point, elsewhere, this way: "many women who say 'yes' are not in fact choosing freely but are submitting because they feel a lack of power to say 'no'" ("Rape," in Patricia Smith, ed., *Feminist Jurisprudence* [New York: Oxford University Press, 1993], 158–87, at 177).

11. "Do Women Sometimes Say No When They Mean Yes? The Prevalence and Correlates of Token Resistance to Sex," *Journal of Personality and Social Psychology* 54, no. 5 (1988): 872–79.

12. "Coercion and Rape: The State as a Male Protection Racket," in Mary Vetterling-Braggin, Frederick A. Elliston, and Jane English, eds., *Feminism and Philosophy* (Totowa, N.J.: Littlefield, Adams, 1977), 360–71, at 365. See also Muehlenhard and Hollabaugh on the wide variety of reasons women have for carrying out this sometimes "rational" strategy (875, 878).

Rae Langton suggests that men's failure to take a woman's "no" as "no" is an effect of pornography ("Speech Acts and Unspeakable Acts," *Philosophy and Public Affairs* 22, no. 4 [1993]: 293–330, at 324–25). This thesis is surprising, because in most pornography women are portrayed as active seekers of sexual activity, as eschewing the traditional games, and not as reluctant participants. Consistent with men's fantasies, women's favorite word, it seems, is "yes." Still, Langton supposes that because women as portrayed in pornography rarely say "no," men who learn "the rules of the [sexual] game" from pornography do not learn to recognize refusals for what they are. But do men learn about sex (only, mostly, or at all) from pornography? Do men really (and stupidly) take the fact that women rarely say "no" in pornography to mean that women do not mean "no" when they do say it? Beatrice Faust proposes a way, more plausible than Langton's, in which pornography might have an effect:

> Many nonviolent rapes are simply results of scrambled signals between the sexes. Pornography is relevant to this category of rape, since it reinforces the belief that women respond to sex exactly as men do. (*Women, Sex, and Pornography* [New York: Macmillan, 1980], 132.)

Women in pornography energetically seek sexual encounters and respond to the sexual advances of others without hesitation; they are portrayed as being as much interested in sex for its own sake, as eager to consent, and as easily aroused as men are (or as men think they are). Men who believe that women are as quick-triggered as they are might have difficulty comprehending a woman's unwillingness to proceed directly from a long kiss to more intimate sexual touches; a man, being already aroused and wanting to proceed, might assume that she is just as aroused and hence also wants to proceed—despite her pauses or silence. But men, especially when young, likely assimilate the sexuality of women to their own not in virtue of pornographic portrayals of sexually assertive women, but out of simple sexual inexperience.

Indeed, boys discover that "no" does not always mean "no" when they are young (i.e., pre-pornographically). Boys detect the maneuver in girls who say "no" but soon show they do not mean it; these girls say "no" only because they have been pushed by their mothers to say "no," even though pushed by their mothers, without complete success, to mean it. Muehlenhard and Hollabaugh's research shows that the phenomenon extends beyond grade school into college and strongly suggests that mechanisms other than pornography are at work. If we are worried, as we should be, about where college-age men get the idea, or have it reinforced, that a woman's "no" does not always mean "no," we might want to consider the effects of Muehlenhard's publication itself, which let a popular cat out of the scholarly bag. Men can read "39.3 percent" in print in a refereed, respected journal, which must be a more persuasive documentation of women's artifice than the fantasy world of pornography. Robin Warshaw and Andrea Parrot ("The Contribution of Sex-Role Socialization to Acquaintance Rape," in Andrea Parrot and Laurie Bechhofer, eds., *Acquaintance Rape: The Hidden Crime* [New York: John Wiley, 1991], 73–82) claim that "men's social training tells them . . . that women who say 'no' don't really mean it" (75) and "men are socialized to believe . . . that women do not mean 'no' when they say 'no'" (80). But if men discover that "no" does not always mean "no" *first*

hand, from women who say "no" but do not mean it, it is a conceptual disaster to point the causal finger at "socialization" or "social training."

13. Carole Pateman turns this around: "if 'no,' when uttered by a woman, is to be reinterpreted as 'yes,' then . . . why should a woman's 'yes' be more privileged, be any the less open to invalidation" ("Women and Consent," *Political Theory* 8, no. 2 [1980]: 149–68, at 162)—that is, if men do not take "no" as "no," they have no right to take "yes" as "yes."

14. Stephen Schulhofer ("The Gender Question in Criminal Law," in Jeffrie G. Murphy, ed., *Punishment and Rehabilitation*, 3rd ed. [Belmont, Cal.: Wadsworth, 1995], 274–311, at 308-309) discusses some cases in which "yes" does not mean "yes": the man obtains a woman's consent through fraud or deception. Estrich does not seem to have this sort of case in mind. Maybe she agrees with MacKinnon's point about the indistinguishability in patriarchy of rape and consensual sex, or with her rhetorical skepticism: "What is it reasonable for a man to believe concerning a woman's desire for sex when heterosexuality is compulsory?" (*Toward a Feminist Theory of the State*, 183). "Nothing" is the implied answer; he may never assume that "yes" means "yes."

15. I quote from a copy of the Policy and its introduction sent to me in 1994 by the Office of the President, Antioch University. The numbering of the provisions is my own. The Policy was intended to be gender- and sexual orientation-neutral, allowing the possibility of gay or lesbian acquaintance rape and the rape of a man by a woman.

16. Jacqueline D. Goodchilds and Gail L. Zellman, "Sexual Signaling and Sexual Aggression in Adolescent Relationships," in Neil M. Malamuth and Edward Donnerstein, eds., *Pornography and Sexual Aggression* (Orlando, Fla.: Academic Press, 1984), 233–43, at 236. In any event, "males have a more sexualized view of the world than females, attributing more sexual meaning to a wide range of behaviors" (239).

17. At least seven times in the Policy and its introduction, it is stated that consent to sexual activity must

be verbal. Only once does the Policy depart from this formula: "the person with whom sexual contact/conduct is initiated is responsible to express verbally and/or physically her/his willingness or lack of willingness when reasonably possible." Because the bulk of the Policy insists that consent be verbal, I discount this one awk-ward and *possibly* contradictory sentence. Further, "reasonably" here nearly destroys the power of the Policy to resolve issues *about* reasonableness.

The Policy also says, "If sexual contact . . . is *not* mutually and simultaneously initiated, then the person who initiates sexual contact . . . is responsible for getting the verbal consent of the other individuals(s) involved" (italics added). From the statement that when mutual and simultaneous initiation is absent, verbal consent is required, it does not follow (nor does the Policy ever assert) that when mutual and simultaneous initiation is present, verbal consent can be dispensed with. To claim otherwise—to deny that the Antioch policy always requires verbal consent—is to commit an elementary logical fallacy. (This mistake was made by my commentator at the APA session.) Anyway, if we are to construe the Antioch policy as an interesting and novel approach to the problems we are discussing, we should not read it as asserting that "mutual and simultaneous initiation" cancels the need for verbal consent. The aroused and optimistic person who subjectively has no doubt that the other person is consenting, but is mistaken about that, is a version of the aroused and optimistic person who assumes that his initiation is reciprocated mutually and simultaneously by the other, but is similarly mistaken. Thus the good intentions of the Antioch policy would fall prey to the same psychological and moral delusions that undermined Belliotti's principle, "when in doubt, ask."

18. Perper and Weis, "Proceptive," 476.

19. A man "cannot know, except through the practice of communicative sexuality, whether his partner has any sexual reason for continuing the encounter"—or any other reason for doing so ("Date Rape: A Feminist Analysis," *Law and Philosophy* 8 [1989]: 217-43, at 239). The essays in Leslie Francis's anthology *Date Rape* (University Park: Penn State University Press, 1996) explore both the Antioch policy and Pineau's essay.

20. Is a man's badgering a woman for sex "coercion"? Charlene Muehlenhard and Jennifer Schrag think so: "We define verbal sexual coercion as a woman's consenting to unwanted sexual activity because of a man's verbal arguments, not including verbal threats of physical force" ("Nonviolent Sexual Coercion," in Parrot and Bechhofer, *Acquaintance Rape*, 115–28, at 122). Muehlenhard and Schrag describe ways in which they think "women are coerced into having unwanted sexual intercourse," ways that are "more subtle" than being violently raped (115). Among the things listed that *coerce* women into unwanted sexual intercourse are "compulsory heterosexuality" (116–17), "status coercion" (119), "verbal sexual coercion" (122–23), and "discrimination against lesbians" (121). In agreement with Muehlenhard, Mary Koss uses the expression "sexually coercive men" to refer to those who obtain sex "after continual discussions and arguments" or by false avowals of love (Mary P. Koss and Kenneth E. Leonard, "Sexually Aggressive Men: Empirical Findings and Theoretical Implications," in Malamuth and Donnerstein, *Pornography and Sexual Aggression*, 213–32, at 216). For discussion, see Neil Gilbert, "Realities and Mythologies of Rape," *Society*, May/June, 1992, 4–10, at 7.

21. Pineau proposes that consensual sadomasochism be admissible by law, if "the court has a right to require that there be a system of signals whereby each partner can convey to the other whether she has had enough" ("Date Rape," 242). The safe words of consensual sadomasochism apparently fulfill the requirements of communicative sexuality (see her note 23).

22. "Sexual Correctness. Has It Gone Too Far?" in Susan J. Bunting, ed., *Human Sexuality 95/96* (Guilford, Conn.: Dushkin, 1995), 208–211, at 209.

23. "Good Sex" [letter], *The New Yorker* (Jan. 10, 1994), 8.

24. Antioch, however, does very little to make specific the "specific" of A4. Thus the Policy is vulnerable to wisecracks:

    [*X* and *Y* sit on a couch, face-to-face.]

    X: May I kiss you?

    Y: Of course. Go ahead.

    [*Y* makes *Y*'s mouth available; *X* slides *X*'s tongue deeply into *Y*'s oral cavity. *Y* pulls sharply away.]

    Y: I didn't say you could *French* kiss me!

25. According to the Policy, "Consent must be clear and verbal (i.e., saying: yes, I want to kiss you also)."

26. Jennifer Wolf, "Sex By the Rules," *Glamour* (May 1994), 256–59, 290, at 258.

27. According to the Model Anti-Pornography Law drafted by Catharine MacKinnon and Andrea Dworkin (see "Symposium on Pornography. Appendix," *New England Law Review* 20, no. 4 [1984–85]: 759–77; section 3.1, 760), that a woman is or has been a prostitute outside of the making of an item of pornography means nothing in deciding whether she has been coerced into making this particular item. The historical fact of earlier or concurrent prostitution cannot be used as evidence by the defendant to show that her acts of prostitution in the making of this item of pornography were entered into by her free consent. So the Model Law resembles the Antioch policy, which

makes history irrelevant. Several other clauses in the Model Law have similar rationales. That a woman is connected by blood or marriage to, or has had sexual relations with, anyone involved in the making of the pornography, or that she has made pornography before, does not negate a legal finding that she has been coerced into the making of this particular item of pornography.

28. See 1 Cor. 7: [4]The wife hath not power of her own body, but the husband: and likewise also the husband hath not power of his own body, but the wife. [5]Defraud ye not one the other, except it be with consent for a time, that ye may give yourselves to fasting and prayer; and come together again, that Satan tempt you not for your incontinency.

29. Pateman, "Women and Consent," 150.

30. Some teenagers (of both sexes) think that male anger and even assault are justified by a girl's apparently reneging on a sexual deal. See Goodchilds and Zellman, "Sexual Signaling," 237, 241–42.

31. Carolyn Shafer and Marilyn Frye, "Rape and Respect," in Mary Vetterling-Braggin et al., *Feminism and Philosophy*, 333–46, at 342.

32. "It is in fact justly observed that a conjugal act imposed upon one's partner without regard for his or her condition and lawful desires is not a true act of love, and therefore denies an exigency of right moral order in the relationships between husband and wife" (Paul VI, "Humanae Vitae," in Robert Baker and Frederick Elliston, eds., *Philosophy and Sex*, 2nd ed. [Buffalo, N.Y.: Prometheus, 1984], 167–83, at 173).

AH! My Foolish Heart: A Reply to Alan Soble's "Antioch's 'Sexual Offense Policy': A Philosophical Exploration"[1]

Eva Feder Kittay

A sexual code occupies an uneasy position at the intersection of the public and private, the communal and intimate, the codifiable and spontaneous, the articulate and ineffable. And sexual conduct is located at the troubling interface of pleasure and offense; passion and power; freedom and submission; desire as an individual drive and desire as the epiphany of mutuality—the desiring of the other's desire. How do we regulate sexual conduct? How can any code legislate sexual desire or successfully thwart abusive sexuality? Here the wise say that only fools do tread. Since Antioch announced its *Sexual Offense Policy*, Antioch has, in the eyes of the media and some retro (and not so retro) feminists and academics, worn a dunce cap. Is it well-deserved?

After a clear, and seemingly sympathetic, discussion of the code that includes much of the motivation for the policy, Alan Soble weighs in with the wise. On three grounds: pleasure, body talk, and consent.[2]

Upon first learning of the *Sexual Offense Policy*, my romantic heart declared this was a silly, foolish code—though my feminist mind urged a more cautious judgment. To have to verbally consent to each level (and just what is a level anyway?) of sexual intimacy? each time? even with a partner with whom one had been intimate many times before? Many of us lose the capacity of articulate speech at these moments. Are we to be deprived of our hearts' desire since, unlike Molly Bloom, we don't utter an ecstatic "Yes! yes! yes!" at the appropriate moment?

Reading the harrowing accounts of date rapes recounted by Robin Warshaw,[3] I kept wondering if a code such as Antioch's would help in any of these cases. And if it would not, what *was* the point? Being on sabbatical, I was unable to canvas my classes for the student point of view. Fortunately, I had some private college-aged informants, my twenty-year-old son, his girlfriend (whom I questioned separately), and their friends. I also queried colleagues who had discussed the code with their students. There seemed to be a rather interesting response that came up again and again: "The code is silly, but I wouldn't mind it being there. It would be a way of opening up discussion on these issues." Only one young man I spoke to said it would encourage him to only have sex with himself—he always would know that the answer was "yes."

Taking a closer look at the code, I noticed some interesting phrases that are omitted in Alan Soble's summary. In the seven-point discussion of consent, the first point justifies Soble's claim that "verbal' 'yes' . . . is Antioch's "Cartesian foundation":[4]

> 1. For the purpose of this policy, "consent" shall be defined as follows: "the act of willingly and verbally agreeing to engage in a specific sexual contact or conduct."[5]

And yet the next point has an antecedent clause that implies that verbal consent is not *always* demanded:

> 2. If sexual contact and/or conduct is not mutually and simultaneously initiated, then the person who initiates sexual contact/conduct is responsible for

getting the verbal consent of the other individual(s) involved.[6]

"*If* sexual contact and/or conduct is *not mutually* and *simultaneously* initiated. . . ." So, if my partner and I simultaneously are seized with the desire to kiss, we don't need to say a thing as our mouths spontaneously move toward each other. And if I am as passionately unbuttoning my partner and my partner unbuttons me, we can both remain undisturbed in our inarticulate bliss.

Therefore, contrary to Soble's reading, we are not always obliged to obtain verbal consent, not forced to "mix the pleasures of language with the pleasures of the body"[7] *if* the sex is mutually initiated.

Now consider the fourth point:

4. The person with whom sexual contact/conduct is initiated is responsible to express verbally and/or *physically* his/her willingness or lack of willingness when *reasonably* possible (emphasis mine).[8]

To express verbally *or physically* willingness or unwillingness, when *reasonably* possible. Aha! If the initiator asks, I can respond physically, I don't have to utter "yes" or even moan. And if the noninitiator is in a swoon of delight and tongue-tiedness, the whole sexual encounter can go on with a minimal amount of question and answer. But, if there is any ambiguity at all, the code protects both the noninitiator and the initiator alike by defining responsibilities for each.

Now this begins to sound less absurd. Under the heading of "Body Talk" Soble writes:" According to the policy, a verbal 'yes' replaces all bodily movements as the only reliable sign that proceeding with sex is permissible. If I ask, "may I kiss you?" I may not proceed on the basis of your bodily reply, e.g., you push your mouth out at mine and open it invitingly . . .".[9] A verbal yes may be

the only fully *reliable* sign, but it's not at all clear from the passages cited above that the code *proscribes* sex based on such "body talk," or that it construes heeding (affirmative) body talk—in limited and unambiguous circumstances—as sexual offense.

Soble furthermore insists that the verbal "yes" is only a yes after sufficient probing. The probing requirement isn't explicit in the code, but arises from the possibility that women, because of their socialization to be cooperative and nonconfrontational, may say "yes" when they mean "no." Rather than explicitly calling for the sort of probing Soble envisions, the code sets out a clear set of responsibilities for both initiator and noninitiator: The initiator is responsible for obtaining verbal consent; the noninitiator is responsible for responding verbally or physically whenever possible. As Soble points out, this privileges the physical withdrawal over the physical assent since consent is, both by definition and by explicit statement, verbal. But it also opens the window, when there is no ambiguity in the situation, for the sexual activity to respond to body talk.

Two things are learned from considering the passages omitted in Soble's summary.

First: there are allowances for the body language so often more in tune with the heightened sexual state than articulate speech. Perhaps this is a contradiction in the policy. Or perhaps the policy only starts to make sense in a context where there is a great deal of discussion that helps to clarify its intent and purpose.

Second: The noninitiator has a responsibility in this interaction, along with the initiator. A young woman socialized in a stereotypical feminine way has a responsibility to work her way out of such constricting socializing influences. If the policy is more educative and preventative than proscriptive and punitive, as it declares itself to be, "The educational aspects of this policy are intended to prevent sexual offenses and ultimately to heighten community awareness,"[10] then this code serves to encourage previously unassertive partners to be more assertive and to encourage overly assertive partners to reign in their overbearing behavior. Rather than undermining autonomy and acting paternalistically *in loco parentis*, Antioch encourages autonomy in the form of more responsible and responsive sexuality.

These considerations mark a considerable change in my first reaction to the Antioch code. The clincher came when I located Antioch College on a websurfing night and read the home page addressed to prospective students: "Antioch believes it should be a single cohesive community based on principles of democracy and citizenship. . . . Because Antioch students are considered equal members of the community, they participate in major decision-making committees at the College and have responsibility for student organizations and activities on campus." Although many student handbooks read like this, Antioch has always had a very strong tradition of taking such words seriously. As Alan Guskin, President of Antioch at the time the policy was first formulated, writes,[11] and as discussions with Antioch alumnae confirmed,[12] the policy was arrived at through intensive campus discussion among students and faculty. Even more significant, the code is reviewed each year and each year students elect whether to retain it, modify it, or discard it.

This contextualization of the code is, I believe, crucial to evaluating it. If this policy were handed down from on high by the administration to a reluctant student body that had to puzzle its way through the sorts of unclarities and paradoxes Soble highlights, then I would continue to share his skepticism. Likewise, if this policy were to be adopted outside of a specific and close community in which the code serves as a prod to discussing consensual sex, then again, we should be swayed by Soble's arguments. Although there is a sense in which the policy is, as Matthew Silliman declares in the title of an article, "a community experiment in communicative sexuality,"[13] the policy is also a product of an understanding of a *particular* community. How does contextualizing the policy to the Antioch community help?

Consider first the question of pleasure. Those who mutually initiate sex, at all levels, can have pleasure non-interruptus. But when one initiates sex, then a verbal consent is necessary. Can the verbal question and the consent be less intrusive to the romance than it seems at first? Soble says no, because sexy speech (as MacKinnon likes to remind us) is already sex. So either we have a non-sexy way of asking or we have an infinite regress. When I raised this point with the president of the Alum Association, he responded that the permissibility of making the request a part of the sexual encounter is part of the social contract which established the code in the first place. That is to say, in the numerous workshops and discussions around the policy, the permissibility of this initiatory level of sexual contact is established. It forms part of the background condition and is not explicitly stated in the code.[14] Take the Antioch out of "Antioch's Sexual Offense Policy" and you have a different policy. Of course, this understanding of the policy leaves the door open to a lascivious and unwanted sexual invitation of, say, a faculty member to a student. Such a sexual invitation/question has all the power imbalances in place that can, at worst, make refusal difficult, and, at best, be shocking and highly offensive to the more vulnerable party. Such a possibility exposes a limitation of the policy and the need for more than a code to insure fully consensual sex. But it doesn't vitiate the usefulness of the code.[15]

Second, consider the question of "body talk." We have already seen that in the situation in which all partners are mutually initiating at all points in the encounter, they can speak, moan, groan or remain silent—as long as everything is completely clear to both. For the rest of the cases, Soble argues that not only do we have to ask and reply, but the initiator has to probe for a sincere "yes." This, he suggests, is because the Antioch policy does not sufficiently respect the ways in which the body talks, not only in sexual affairs, but in all matters. This argument is premised on a sexual scenario of a "yes" meaning a "no," one common enough. Soble directs us to a Texas A&M study in which 39 percent of college women polled indicated that they have offered token "resistance" when they *intended* to engage in sex.[16] However, within a community that affirms the sexual offense policy in question each year anew, where the policy becomes the prod to open discussion of matters sexual, and where the responsibility for learning to say no when you mean no is understood as part of the educative purpose of the code, the probing is *de trop*. The demand for verbal consent is not about a disregard for body talk (when affirmative) but about setting forth the conditions for a communication sufficiently *unambiguous* to minimize the dangers and harm of date rape. So contextualized, Soble's claim that "the robust respect that Antioch's policy fosters for a woman's 'no' is offset by the weaker respect it fosters for her 'yes'" is false.

Finally let us consider the question of consent. It is true that "Antioch cuts back on a traditional power of consent, its ability to apply to an indefinite, open future."[17] But perhaps that is just right, when it comes to matters of sexual desire. A Pauline marriage, after all, makes marital rape an oxymoron, and any woman who has been raped by her husband will tell you that there is nothing oxymoronic about her trauma. Antioch's policy, however, is not meant to govern long-term relationships or marriages, Pauline or otherwise. In the context of the Antioch College, the code applies to an undergraduate population that does not, in general, have many long-term relationships. Probably most sexual encounters are first-, second-, third-time contacts.[18] It is to these transient relations that the policy is directed. In this context it is inappropriate to think that consent applies to "an indefinite, open future." This is not to say that a marriage or long term relation in which one could not make a transition from "assume 'no' unless you get a 'yes'" to "assume 'yes' unless you get a no" would be a sad affair.

Soble, however, raises a more difficult issue with respect to consent. He points out that Antioch cuts back on the power of consent by making it not binding: I agree to have so much sex with you and while halfway through I change my mind and want you to stop. Am I immoral? Is the policy fostering the immorality of the tease in countering the immorality of the rapist? If I agree to a sexual act in bad faith, then I am a tease. But if I agree in good faith, and if in the midst of the experience I find it unpleasant or unexciting and so ask my partner to stop, I am not *teasing* but responding to something important to my own self-respect. To continue sex past the point of my own desiring is to experience myself as a mere object for another's use. "But," says my partner, "you consented and you are obliged to let me continue." Why doesn't that work? There is a feature of sexuality that is not amenable to a notion of consent. Consent within policies or codes are generally understood through the model of contract: I voluntarily agree to a specified such and such, and you forming your expectations based on the agreement hold me to the contractual terms.

The contractual model, however, is inappropriate in many intimate domains. Consent in these contexts is less an agreement binding into the future that will override itinerant desires than the expression of a willing, wanting, desiring self that seeks fulfillment with and through another. So-called "surrogate mothering" falls into this category. If a birth mother gives up the child she has born as a gift, that is one thing; if she gives it up for payment, that is quite another. A contractual relation demands the action of an agreed-to giving, whether or not the desire to give continues to be present at the moment, past the time the contract is signed. If I promise you a gift and don't deliver on the promise, I will disappoint you, but you will not have a claim on that gift. While you can accuse me of breaking my promise, you cannot make a claim to that gift. The strong sense that surrogacy ought not to be bound to contract in the same way other transactions are arises from the nature of the act as a gift, that is a giving to which we attach a desire to give another satisfaction through our own actions. Sexual contact has a similar nature. If the sexual contact is not desired at *that* moment, then one makes of oneself a sexual object and not a sexual agent. One makes oneself into a thing, and the other who insists on the sexual act makes of the partner a means only, a means to one's own pleasure regardless of the desire of the partner.

Barbara Herman in a fascinating article argues that Kant's view of sexuality is remarkably akin to that of some radical feminists, in particular, Andrea Dworkin and MacKinnon. Kant's resolution to the problem of sexual love, which makes of the other an object of one's own sexual desire without regard to human nature but to sex alone, is marriage:

> The sole condition on which we are free to make use of our sexual desire depends upon the right to dispose over the person as a whole—over the welfare and happiness and generally over all the circumstances of that person. . . . [I obtain these rights over the whole person (and so have the right of sexual use of that person)] only by giving the person the same rights over myself.[19]

But why not say instead: A sexual encounter with another, which has the recognition of the other's desire (and so the other's sexual agency) as a *sine qua non*, is the sole way in which we can engage in sex without reducing the other to an object— whether in marriage or in a one-night stand. In that case, consent cannot be understood on the contractual model, but on a model of mutual desiring, a desiring which must be alive at each moment. This, I believe, stands behind the model of communicative sex as better sex that is advocated by Lois Pineau.[20] To the extent that the Antioch policy's demand for consent is understood contractually, it will be a limitation of the policy. But if the policy is used as an educative tool, accompanied by discussion about its meaning and intent, then it can serve to instruct and train young persons for sexual encounters that promote mutuality and respect. In so doing, it can foster both good sex and the autonomy of the one who initiates and the one who responds.

Now I have made a full 180-degree turnabout from my first reactions to the policy. Of course, it seems that some things might be lost: That surprise (not yet consented to) touch that thrills beyond measure; the awakening of ardor through a kiss by someone who never before moved you; and doubtless much else. Then again it would also be fun to drive without seatbelts and road signs, and with only a watchful eye. But even with the road signs there are too many car accidents. Best to keep the seatbelts on.

Maybe the policy seen in context is not so foolish after all. And perhaps it teaches me that I do well to listen to my feminist mind before allowing my foolish heart the last word.

NOTES

1. This paper was first delivered as a commentary to Alan Soble's "Antioch's 'Sexual Offense Policy': A Philosophical Exploration," Dec. 1995, at the Eastern Division APA Meetings.

2. Alan Soble, "Antioch's 'Sexual Offense Policy': A Philosophical Exploration," *Journal of Social Philosophy* 28, no. 1 (Spring 1997): 22–36.

3. Robin Warshaw, *I Never Called It Rape: The Ms. Report on Recognizing, Fighting and Surviving Date Rape* (New York: Harper & Row, 1988).

4. Soble, 27.

5. Antioch College, "The Antioch College Sexual Offense Policy," in *Date Rape: Feminism Philosophy, and the Law*, ed. Leslie Francis (University Park, PA: The Pennsylvania University Press, 1992), 140.

6. Antioch, 140.

7. Soble, 28.

8. Antioch, 140.

9. Soble, 29.

10. Antioch, 139.

11. Alan E. Guskin, "The Antioch Response: Sex, You Just Don't Talk About It," in *Date Rape: Feminism Philosophy, and the Law*, 155–66.

12. My discussions included one with Eric Bates, president of Antioch's Alumnae Association.

13. "The Antioch Policy, a Community Experiment in Communicative Sexuality" in *Date Rape: Feminism Philosophy, and the Law*, 167–76.

14. Personal Communication with Eric Bates.

15. There is, however, a clause in the "Consent" discussion which covers situations of intimidation and coercion used for obtaining the verbal consent:

7. If someone verbally agrees to engage in specific contact or conduct, but it is not of her/his own free will due to any of the circumstances stated in (a) through (d) below, then the person initiating shall be considered in violation of this policy if: . . .(d) the person initiating has forced, threatened, coerced, or intimidated the other individual(s) into engaging in sexual contact and/or sexual conduct.

Antioch College, "The Antioch College Sexual Offense Policy," in *Date Rape: Feminism Philosophy, and the Law*, 141.

16. This study is cited in Soble, 24.

17. Soble, 31.

18. This point is emphasized in Guskin, 1996.

19. Kant, *Lectures on Ethics*, p. 167, quoted in Barbara Herman, "Thinking about Kant on Sex and Marriage," in Anthony and Witt, eds., *A Mind of One's Own: Feminist Essays on Reason and Objectivity* (Boulder: Westview Press, 1993, p. 60.

20. Lois Pineau, "Date Rape: A Feminist Analysis," in *Date Rape: Feminism Philosophy, and the Law*, 1–26.

Index